Name and Type of Organization Used in Main Illustration of Each Chapter

Chapter Title	Organization Used in Main Illustration	Organization Logo	Type of Organization
11. Responsibility Accounting, Cost Allocation, and Income Reporting	Aloha Hotels and Resorts		Hotel chain
12. Investment Centers and Transfer Pricing	Suncoast Food Centers		Retail grocery chain
13. Decision Making: Relevant Costs and Benefits	Worldwide Airways		Airline company
14. Cost Analysis and Pricing Decisions	Sydney Sailing Supplies		Manufacturer of sailboats in Sydney, Australia
15. Capital Expenditure Decisions: An Introduction	City of Mountainview		City government
16. Further Aspects of Capital Expenditure Decisions	High Country Department Stores		Retail department store chain
17. Cost Allocation: A Closer Look	Riverside Clinic and International Chocolate Company		Health care institution and food products company, respectively
18. Analyzing Financial Statements	Contemporary Interiors		Retail furniture company
19. Preparing the Statement of Cash Flows	Alpine Trails Ski Resort		Ski resort

(See Index of Companies and Organizatons inside back cover)

MANAGERIAL
ACCOUNTING

MANAGERIAL ACCOUNTING

RONALD W. HILTON

Cornell University

McGRAW-HILL, INC.

New York St. Louis San Francisco Auckland Bogotá Caracas Hamburg
Lisbon London Madrid Mexico Milan Montreal New Delhi
Paris San Juan São Paulo Singapore Sydney Tokyo Toronto

MANAGERIAL ACCOUNTING

2   3   4   5   6   7   8   9   0   VNH VNH   9   5   4   3   2   1

ISBN 0-07-028963-8

This book was set in Times Roman by Progressive Typographers, Inc.
The editors were Kenneth MacLeod and Edwin Hanson;
the designer was Rafael Hernandez;
the production supervisor was Diane Renda.
Von Hoffmann Press, Inc., was printer and binder.

Library of Congress Cataloging-in-Publication Data

Hilton, Ronald W.
    Managerial accounting / Ronald W. Hilton.
      p.   cm.
    Includes index.
    ISBN 0-07-028963-8
    1. Managerial accounting.   I. Title.
HF5657.4.H55   1991
658.15′11—dc20   90-38852

About
the Author

Ronald W. Hilton is a Professor of Accounting at Cornell University. With bachelor's and master's degrees in accounting from The Pennsylvania State University, he received his Ph.D. from The Ohio State University.

A Cornell faculty member since 1977, Professor Hilton also has taught accounting at Ohio State and the University of Florida, where he held the position of Walter J. Matherly Professor of Accounting. Prior to pursuing his doctoral studies, Hilton worked for Peat, Marwick, Mitchell and Company and served as an officer in the United States Air Force.

Professor Hilton is a member of the National Association of Accountants and has been active in the American Accounting Association. He is currently associate editor of *The Accounting Review* and was formerly a member of its editorial board. Hilton has served on the resident faculties of both the Doctoral Consortium and the New Faculty Consortium sponsored by the American Accounting Association.

With wide-ranging research interests, Hilton has published articles in many journals, including the *Journal of Accounting Research, The Accounting Review,* and *Contemporary Accounting Research.* He also has published a monograph in the AAA *Studies in Accounting Research* series, is a co-author of *Budgeting: Profit Planning and Control,* and is a co-author of *Cost Accounting: Concepts and Managerial Applications.*

To my wife,
Meg,
and our sons,
Brad and Tim.

Contents
in Brief

ix

Contents

Preface

Managers in all types of organizations rely heavily on managerial-accounting information for decision making, planning, and control. The goal of this text is to acquaint students of management with the fundamentals of managerial accounting. The emphasis throughout the book is on *using* accounting information in managing an organization. *Managerial Accounting* is intended to be used by students after they have completed a basic course in financial accounting. The bulk of the material in the text can be covered in one semester or one and one-half quarters. The book includes enough material, however, to allow an instructor some choice of topics when designing the course.

Objectives of This Textbook

Seven major objectives were of paramount importance in the development of this textbook.

1. **To convey the importance of managerial accounting and stimulate students' interest in the topic.**

Each chapter is built around one major illustration, in which all aspects of the chapter's coverage are addressed. The illustration is used consistently throughout the chapter, allowing students to gain a deeper understanding of all dimensions of the topic. Each illustration has a management case flavor, with enough descriptive background to involve students in the scenario. These illustrations are built around realistic situations with plausible decisions and believable people. The types of illustrations vary widely across chapters.

The text includes frequent descriptions of the actual managerial-accounting practices of real-world organizations. These *illustrations from management accounting practice* are highlighted to catch the students' attention and are dispersed throughout the book. Among the many organizations represented in these real-world scenarios are Aetna Casualty and Life, American Can, American Express, B. F. Goodrich, Bristol-Myers, Chesebrough-Ponds, Chrysler, City of Charlotte, North Carolina, Cornell University, Corning Glass Works, Dow Chemical, Dutch Pantry, Federal Express, Firestone Tire & Rubber, General Electric, Hewlett-Packard, J. C. Penney, McDonald's, Pan Am, a public school district in suburban Rochester, New York, United Parcel Service, UNYSIS, USAir, and Wal-Mart.

2. To provide balanced coverage of managerial accounting topics in manufacturing, retail, nonprofit, and service-industry settings.

A large percentage of the students pursuing studies in management will choose careers in nonmanufacturing environments. It is important that students realize the applicability of managerial accounting to a variety of organizations. Some managerial accounting topics are integrally related to the manufacturing sector; others are just as applicable in nonmanufacturing settings. The major illustrations, around which the chapters in this text are built, are drawn from a wide variety of enterprises. As the chapter outline on the endpaper shows, seven of the illustrations are set in the manufacturing sector, seven illustrations involve service-industry firms, four illustrations are built around retail companies, and three illustrations involve nonprofit or governmental settings.

3. To provide a flexible sequence of chapters written in modular style.

Since managerial accounting instructors often have differing views on the optimal chapter sequence, flexibility in usage was a paramount objective in writing the text. Each chapter is a module, which can be assigned out of sequence if the instructor desires. For example, some instructors might prefer to cover cost behavior and estimation (Chapter 6) and cost-volume-profit analysis (Chapter 7) before delving into cost-accumulation issues. Other instructors may wish to cover these two topics in the section of the course on decision making. In this text, Chapters 6 and 7 can be assigned as early as immediately after Chapter 2 or as late as just prior to Chapter 13. The decision-oriented chapters (13, 14, 15, and 16) can be moved up to an earlier point in the course if the instructor prefers. These four chapters could be assigned any time after the students have completed Chapters 1, 2, 6, and 7. Chapter 17 covers the details of cost allocation for service-departments and joint products. These two modules in Chapter 17 could be covered along with the cost accumulation chapters (3, 4, and 5) if the instructor prefers. Chapters 11 and 12, which cover a variety of issues pertaining to responsibility accounting and decentralization, can be assigned later in the course if desired. In short, the instructor has great flexibility in course design and topical sequence when using *Managerial Accounting.*

4. To provide a blend of traditional material and up-to-date coverage of emerging topics in managerial accounting.

There is no doubt that managerial accounting is undergoing a revolution in thought and practice. Much of this change is due to recent changes in manufacturing technology and philosophy. Such innovations as just-in-time inventory systems, flexible manufacturing, and computer integrated manufacturing systems are dramatically changing the manufacturing environment. As a result, managerial accounting systems are changing as well. New concepts and procedures have been devised, and many traditional approaches have been challenged.

Managerial Accounting provides thorough coverage of these contemporary issues. Chapter 5 is devoted entirely to cost management systems for the new manufacturing environment. Issues such as cost drivers, transactions-based costing systems, activity accounting, non-value-added costs, and costing systems for just-in-time production environments are covered in this chapter. In addition, several related issues are covered in Chapters 3 and 4, where they can be related meaningfully to traditional cost-accumulation procedures. Other emerging issues are woven throughout the remainder of the text, to continually reemphasize the extent of their influence on a range of managerial accounting topics. For example, the issue of justifying capital expenditures for flexible manufacturing systems is addressed in Chapter 15, which covers capital budgeting.

5. To provide a textbook with both breadth and depth in its coverage of managerial accounting.

This textbook is thoroughly comprehensive in that it includes all topics of relevance for an introductory managerial accounting course. Moreover, the book provides enough depth to give students an appreciation for the relationship of each topic to the management process. When appropriate, the behavioral implications of managerial accounting information and procedures are explored. For a thorough understanding of managerial accounting, students should not only be able to produce accounting information, but also understand how managers are likely to use and react to the information.

6. To provide a teaching tool with an array of pedagogical features designed to enhance the learning process.

To help students learn managerial accounting and gain an appreciation for its importance, *Managerial Accounting* includes a wide range of pedagogical features.

Learning Objectives Each chapter begins with a list of learning objectives to help students identify the most important issues in the chapter.

Comprehensive Illustrations with a Real-World Flavor As noted previously, each chapter is built around a major illustration that progresses throughout the chapter. These diverse illustrations include enough background to add realism to the presentation and stimulate the students' interest in the topic.

Photos A photograph at the beginning of each chapter and a logo for each organization add to the realism of the presentation.

Clarity and Step-by-Step Presentation Great care was taken to write this text in a clear, readable, and lively style. Extensive review by managerial accounting instructors coupled with classroom testing have helped in achieving this goal. The text contains numerous exhibits, graphs, tables, and step-by-step instructions to help students master the material.

Illustrations from Management Accounting Practice As noted previously, the managerial accounting practices of well-known, real-world organizations are highlighted in these numerous illustrations. They are intended to stimulate student interest and provide a springboard for classroom discussion.

Review Problems Most chapters include a review problem along with its solution to provide students with a vehicle for testing their understanding of the material.

Key Terms Each chapter includes a list of key terms with page references. A complete glossary is included at the end of the text.

Review Questions, Exercises, Problems, and Cases Each chapter includes a wide selection of assignment material. This end-of-chapter material, which has been classroom tested, is comprehensive in covering the points in the chapter. The assignment material exhibits a wide range of difficulty, and the Instructor's Guide provides guidance for the instructor on the difficulty level and time required for each problem. Numerous adapted CMA and CPA problems are included in the text. In many cases, these problems were very heavily adapted to preserve the essence of the problems while ensuring that they were pitched at a level appropriate for the text.

7. **To provide instructors with a first-rate and comprehensive supplements package to assist in course design, teaching, and student performance evaluation.**

For the Instructor

Solutions Manual (prepared by Ronald W. Hilton, Cornell University)   Contains complete solutions to all of the text's end-of-chapter review questions, exercises, and problems.

Instructor's Guide (prepared by Margaret Hubbert, Cornell University)   Contains learning objectives, chapter overviews, chapter outlines, lecture topics, assignment grids for the text's problems and cases, alternate assignment outlines and suggestions, and transparency masters.

Computerized Test Banks   Available for the IBM and Macintosh computers.

Test Bank (prepared by Charles Pineno, Clarion University)   Consists of 1200 test items including multiple choice and short problems. Each question is keyed to the text's learning objectives.

Solutions Manual for Print and Computerized Practice Sets

Overhead Transparencies   Solutions to all end-of-chapter exercises and problems in the text.

Teaching Transparencies   Text and non-text enrichment material for classroom use.

Electronic Transparencies   A complete set of computerized instructional materials that can be easily projected in class to highlight lectures and stimulate student involvement. Consists of animated illustrations, graphics, demonstration problems, definitions, charts, and more.

Videotapes   A series of 10 to 15 minute segments that highlight the manufacturing process and its relationship to the topics covered in managerial accounting.

For the Student

Study Guide (prepared by Roland Minch, SUNY at Albany)   Consists of learning objectives, overview of the text's main topics in outline form, key words and descriptions, and self-test questions for each chapter. The self-test questions consist of true/false, fill-ins, multiple choice, and short problems.

Working Papers   Forms for all the end-of-chapter problems.

Print Practice Set I (prepared by John Garlick, Ithaca College)   This application provides comprehensive coverage of all the managerial accounting topics developed in the text. It is structured in such a way to permit students to begin the practice case in the early chapters of the text and then move progressively throughout the remainder of the course.

Executive Woodcraft Co., Print Practice Set (prepared by Ronald W. Hilton, Cornell University)   A comprehensive application with an emphasis on product costing. Other topics covered include cost-volume-profit analysis, budgeting, standard costs, responsibility accounting, relevant information, and decision analysis.

The Phish Corporation   A Practice Case in Managerial Accounting (prepared by

Mark Zmijewski, University of Chicago; Sanford Gunn, SUNY at Buffalo; Ronald Huefner, SUNY at Buffalo; and Robert Derstine, Villanova University) This comprehensive application brings together all of the elements of managerial accounting in a realistic on-the-job environment. Thirteen modules cover such topics as cost classification, product costing, budgeting, standard costs, cost-volume-profit analysis, and special decisions. All assignments are drawn from a common data base for a manufacturing company.

The Anderton Instrument Co., Computerized Practice Set (prepared by Roland Minch, SUNY at Albany) This microcomputer-oriented case study, which uses LOTUS compatible spreadsheets, is intended to emphasize some of the key contemporary issues and emerging methods of modern cost management systems. The case is an adaptation of the ideas set forth in the ACMS (Advance Cost Management System) model developed by Price Waterhouse and Westinghouse. It is divided into four self-contained modules which can be studied in sequence or worked independently. (5 ¼″ and 3.5″ versions)

Computerized Practice Set II (prepared by John Garlick, Ithaca College) A comprehensive series of problems covering all of the major topics in the text (process costing, cost-volume-profit analysis, budgeting, variance analysis, statement analysis, etc.). Students are asked to supply needed headings and formulas in spreadsheet outlines to complete the required problems. Quattro and Lotus spreadsheet outlines are available on the disk provided with the package. (5 ¼″ and 3.5″ versions)

The Accounting/Lotus Connection (prepared by E. James Meddaugh, Ohio University) This software package contains approximately forty problems taken directly from the text and arranged in template format to be solved on the IBM or compatible computers using Lotus 1-2-3 or similar spreadsheet programs. (5 ¼″ and 3.5″ versions)

Acknowledgments

I would like to express my appreciation to several people who have provided assistance in the development of this textbook. First, my gratitude goes to the hundreds of managerial accounting students I have had the privilege to teach over many years. Their enthusiasm, comments, and questions have challenged me to clarify my thinking about many topics in managerial accounting. Second, I express my sincere thanks to the following professors who provided extensive reviews of the manuscript and, in some cases, provided classroom testing opportunities: Penne Ainsworth, Kansas State Univerisity; Wayne G. Bremser, Villanova University; Peter Chalos, University of Illinois; Philip C. Cheng, East Carolina University; Robert H. Colson, Case Western Reserve University; Joseph R. Curran, Northeastern University; Neil Dale, Mt. Hood Community College; Larry R. Davis, University of Notre Dame; Stephen J. Dempsey, University of Vermont; Joel S. Demski, Yale University; Kenneth E. Ernst, LeMoyne College; Werner G. Frank, University of Wisconsin, Madison; John Garlick, Ithaca College; Susan S. Hamlen, State University of New York, Buffalo; Jay S. Holmen, University of Wisconsin, Eau Claire; Frederic Jacobs, Michigan State University; Michael Kinney, Texas A & M University; Anne Kotheimer, Widener University; Donald L. Madden, University of Kentucky; Duane Moser, D. Moser Financial Services; Pradyot K. Sen, University of California, Berkeley; and Donald Stone, University of Massachusetts, Amherst. Third, I want to thank Corolyn E. Clark, St. Joseph's University; James M. Emig, Ph.D., Villanova University, Monica D. Frizzell, CMA, Western Connecticut State University; and John G.

Hamer, University of Lowell for their thorough checking of the text and solutions manual for accuracy and completeness. Fourth, I thank Monroe Bennett, Shelby Clark, Barbara Guile, Donna Phoenix, Tina Weyland, and Teresa Wong for their expert typing and clerical assistance. I acknowledge the National Association of Accountants for allowing the use of excerpts from *Management Accounting* and the Institute of Certified Management Accountants of the National Association of Accountants for permission to use problems from Certified Management Accountant (CMA) examinations. I also acknowledge the American Institute of Certified Public Accountants for permission to use problems from the Uniform CPA Examinations, Questions, and Unofficial Answers. Acknowledgment also is given to the President and Fellows of Harvard College, from whom permission was obtained to use several published Harvard Business School cases. I am indebted to Professors Roland Minch and David Solomons for allowing the use of their case materials in the text. Finally, I wish to express my gratitude to the many fine people of McGraw-Hill who so professionally guided this book through the publication process. Robert Lynch, Elisa Adams, and Allan Forsyth gave valuable assistance during the early stages of manuscript preparation. Kenneth MacLeod, Edwin Hanson, Diane Renda, Judy Motto, Rafael Hernandez, San Rao, and Safra Nimrod provided their expertise during the production phase.

RONALD W. HILTON

MANAGERIAL ACCOUNTING

PART 1 FUNDAMENTALS AND COST ACCUMULATION SYSTEMS

OLYMPIA
REGIONAL HOSPITAL

Chapter 1 Managerial Accounting: An Overview

After completing this chapter, you should be able to:

- Explain four fundamental management processes that help organizations attain their goals.

- List and describe four objectives of managerial accounting activity.

- Explain the major differences between managerial and financial accounting.

- Describe the roles of an organization's controller, treasurer, and internal auditor.

- Discuss the professional organizations, certification process, and ethical standards in the field of managerial accounting.

Many different kinds of organizations affect our daily lives. Manufacturers, retailers, service industry firms, agribusiness companies, nonprofit organizations, and government agencies provide us with a vast array of goods and services. All of these organizations have two things in common. First, every organization has a set of *goals* or objectives. An airline's goals might be profitability and customer service. A city police department's goals would include public safety and security coupled with cost minimization. Second, in pursuing an organization's goals, managers need *information*. The information needs of management range across financial, production, marketing, legal, and environmental issues. Generally, the larger the organization is, the greater is management's need for information.

Managerial accounting is part of an organization's management information system. Managers rely on managerial accounting information to plan and control an organization's operations. In this chapter, we will explore the role of managerial accounting within the overall management process. In the remaining chapters, we will expand our study by exploring the many concepts and tools used in managerial accounting.

ORGANIZATIONS AND THEIR GOALS

The goals of organizations vary widely. Some of the most frequently stated organizational goals are:

Profitability   Market diversification
Growth   Product quality
Financial self-sufficiency   Environmental responsibility
Cost minimization   Community service
Product leadership

Aetna Casualty and Life, a $72 billion insurance company, listed the following goals in a recent annual report to its stockholders:[1]

- To provide responsive, market-oriented products and services to customers
- To achieve superior performance in return on investment and growth in earnings per common share
- To maintain the highest ethical standards
- To play a significant role in the development of positions on regulatory, legislative, and environmental issues
- To recognize employees and agents as its greatest assets and most crucial factors in achieving success

THE MANAGEMENT PROCESS

The owners, directors, or trustees of an organization set the organization's goals, often with the help of management. For example, IBM's goals are set by its board of directors, who are elected by the company's stockholders. The goals of Cornell University are established by its board of trustees.

Whatever the goals of an organization are, the task of management is to see that they are achieved. In pursuing an organization's goals, managers engage in four basic activities:

- Decision making
- Planning
- Directing operations
- Controlling

Decision Making

Suppose Olympia Regional Hospital's board of trustees has chosen, as one of the hospital's goals, to establish comprehensive health care in a nearby, economically depressed neighborhood. What is the best way to accomplish that goal? Should an outpatient clinic be built in the neighborhood? Or would several mobile health units serve the purpose more effectively? Perhaps a community outreach program should be established, in which physicians speak in schools and civic organizations. How will each of these alternatives mesh with the hospital's other goals, which include financial self-sufficiency? The hospital's management must *make a decision* regarding the

---

[1] Aetna Casualty and Life annual report.

best way to bring health care into the neighborhood, which means *choosing among the available alternatives.*

Planning

Let's assume that Olympia Regional Hospital's administrator has decided to build an outpatient clinic. How will the clinic be organized and operated? How many physicians, nurses, medical technicians, and support personnel will be needed? How many examination and treatment rooms will be required, and how should they be equipped? How much will it cost to operate the clinic for a year, and how much money will be saved at the hospital? Finally, how should the clinic's services be priced, keeping in mind its economically depressed location? The hospital's management must *plan* for running the clinic, which means *developing a detailed financial and operational description of anticipated operations.*

Directing Operations

Now the clinic has been built, equipped, and staffed. How many physicians should be on duty on Saturday morning? How much penicillin should be kept on hand? Should sports physicals be done at the clinic or in the school? How much cash will be needed to meet the payroll, pay the utility bills, and buy medical supplies next month? All of these questions fall under the general heading of *directing operations,* which means *running the organization on a day-to-day basis.*

Controlling

Let's assume the clinic has operated for six months. Is the clinic's goal being accomplished? More specifically, have the clinic's operations adhered to the plans developed by management for achieving the goal? In seeking to answer these questions, management is engaged in *control,* which means *ensuring that the organization operates in the intended manner and achieves its goals.*

THE ROLE OF MANAGERIAL ACCOUNTING

For all of the managerial activities described in the preceding section, managers need information. That information comes from a variety of sources, including economists, financial experts, marketing and production personnel, and the organization's managerial accountants.

Objectives of Managerial Accounting Activity

The four major objectives of managerial accounting activity are:

- Providing managers with information for decision making and planning
- Assisting managers in directing and controlling operations
- Motivating managers toward the organization's goals
- Measuring the performance of managers and subunits within the organization

To illustrate these objectives of managerial accounting activity, let us continue with the example of Olympia Regional Hospital.

Providing Managers with Information for Decision Making and Planning For virtually all major decisions, the hospital's management would rely largely on managerial accounting information. For example, the *decision* to establish the new clinic would be influenced heavily by estimates of the costs of building the clinic and maintaining it throughout its life. The hospital's managers would also rely on managerial accounting data in formulating plans for the clinic's operations. Prominent in those *plans* would be a budget detailing the projected revenues and costs of providing health care.

Assisting Managers in Directing and Controlling Operations Directing and controlling day-to-day operations requires a variety of data about the process of providing health-care services. For example, in *directing* operations, management would need data about the cost of providing medical services in order to set service fees and seek reimbursement from insurance companies. Finally, in *controlling* operations, management would compare actual costs incurred with those specified in the budget.

Managerial accounting information often assists management through its **attention-directing function.** Managerial accounting reports rarely solve a decision problem. However, managerial accounting information often directs managers' attention to an issue that requires their skills. To illustrate, suppose Olympia Regional Hospital's clinic incurred electricity costs that significantly exceeded the budget. This fact does not explain why the budget was exceeded, nor does it tell management what action to take, but it does direct management's attention to the situation. Suppose that upon further investigation, the accounting records reveal that the local electric rates have increased substantially. This information will help management in framing the decision problem. Should steps be taken to conserve electricity? Should the clinic's hours be curtailed? Perhaps management should consider switching to natural gas for heating.

Motivating Managers toward the Organization's Goals Organizations have goals. However, organizations are comprised of people who have goals of their own. The goals of individuals are diverse, and they do not always match those of the organization. A key purpose of managerial accounting is to motivate managers to direct their efforts toward achieving the organization's goals. One means of achieving this purpose is through budgeting. In establishing a budget for Olympia Regional Hospital's outpatient clinic, top management indicates how resources are to be allocated and what activities are to be emphasized. When actual operations do not conform to the budget, the clinic's managers will be asked to explain the reasons for the deviation.

Measuring the Performance of Managers and Subunits within the Organization One means of motivating people toward the organization's goals is to measure their performance in achieving those goals. Such measurements then can be used as the basis for rewarding performance through positive feedback, promotions, and pay raises. For example, most large corporations compensate their executives, in part, on the basis of the profit achieved by the subunits they manage. For Olympia Regional Hospital's outpatient clinic, performance measures might focus on the success of the clinic in promoting prenatal care and other forms of preventive medicine in the neighborhood. Achieving such goals would also support the main hospital's goal of reducing crowding in its emergency room.

In addition to measuring the performance of people, managerial accountants measure the performance of an organization's subunits, such as divisions, product lines, geographical territories, and departments. These measurements help the sub-units' managers obtain the highest possible performance level in their units. Such measurements also help top management decide whether a particular subunit is a viable economic investment. For example, it may turn out that Olympia Regional Hospital's new clinic proves too costly an activity to continue, despite the efforts of a skilled management team.

Managerial versus Financial Accounting

Take another look at the four major objectives of managerial accounting activity. Notice that the focus in each of these objectives is on *managers*. Thus, the focus of **managerial accounting** is on the needs of managers *within* the organization, rather than interested parties outside the organization.

 Financial accounting is the use of accounting information for reporting to parties outside the organization. The annual report distributed by McDonald's Corporation to its stockholders is an example of the output from a financial accounting system. Users of financial accounting information include current and prospective stockholders, lenders, investment analysts, unions, consumer groups, and government agencies.

There are many similarities between managerial accounting information and financial accounting information, because they both draw upon data from an organization's basic *accounting system*. This is the system of procedures, personnel, and computers used to accumulate and store financial data in the organization. One part of the overall accounting system is the **cost accounting system,** which accumulates cost data for use in both managerial and financial accounting. For example, production cost data typically are used in helping managers set prices, which is a managerial accounting use. However, production cost data also are used to value inventory on a manufacturer's balance sheet, which is a financial accounting use.

Exhibit 1-1 depicts the relationships among an organization's basic accounting system, cost accounting system, managerial accounting, and financial accounting. Although similarities exist between managerial and financial accounting, the differences are even greater. Exhibit 1-2 lists the most important differences.

Managerial Accounting in Different Types of Organizations

All organizations need information, whether they are profit-seeking or nonprofit enterprises, and regardless of the activities they pursue. As a result, managerial accounting information is vital in all organizations. Chrysler, Sears, American Airlines, Marriott Hotels, Prudential Insurance, American Express, Cornell University, The United Way, Mayo Clinic, the City of Los Angeles, and the Department of Defense all have managerial accountants who provide information to management. Moreover, the four basic purposes of managerial accounting activity are relevant in each of these organizations.

ROLE OF THE MANAGERIAL ACCOUNTANT

To understand the managerial accountant's role in an organization, we must know how organizations are structured. To focus our discussion, we will rely on the organization chart for Olympia Regional Hospital presented in Exhibit 1-3. Olympia is a public hospital, partially supported by funds from the state and local governments.

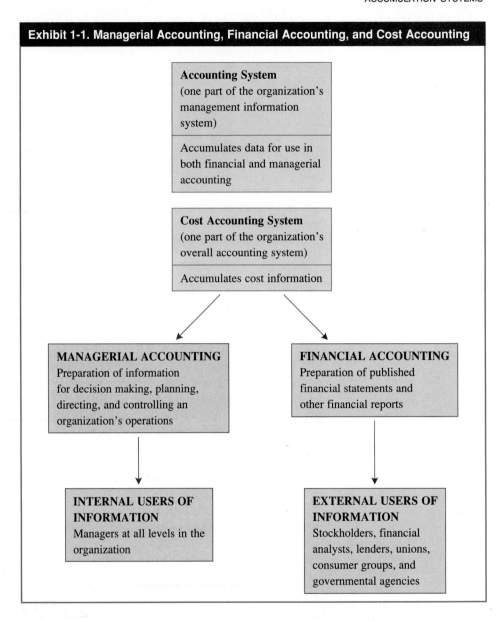

Exhibit 1-1. Managerial Accounting, Financial Accounting, and Cost Accounting

The hospital's governing body is the board of trustees, and its chief executive officer is the administrator. Also included in top management is the deputy administrator.

Line and Staff Positions

The other positions shown in the organization chart are of two types: line positions and staff positions. Managers in **line positions** are *directly* involved in the provision of medical care or in the operation of the facilities. Olympia Regional Hospital's line positions include the various chiefs of the hospital's professional medical personnel, the director of admissions and patient records, and the director of purchasing, house-keeping, and facilities. All of these people are involved directly in serving patients or in operating the physical facilities.

Managers in **staff positions** supervise activities that support the hospital's mis-

---

Exhibit 1-2. Differences between Managerial and Financial Accounting

Managerial Accounting	Financial Accounting
Users of Information	
Managers, within the organization	Interested parties, outside the organization.
Regulation	
Not required and unregulated, since it is intended only for management.	Required and must conform to generally accepted accounting principles. Regulated by the Financial Accounting Standards Board, and, to a lesser degree, the Securities and Exchange Commission.
Source of Data	
The organization's basic accounting system, plus various other sources, such as rates of defective products manufactured, physical quantities of material and labor used in production, occupancy rates in hotels and hospitals, and average take-off delays in airlines.	Almost exclusively drawn from the organization's basic accounting system, which accumulates financial information.
Nature of Reports and Procedures	
Reports often focus on subunits within the organization, such as departments, divisions, geographical regions, or product lines. Based on a combination of historical data, estimates, and projections of future events.	Reports focus on the enterprise in its entirety. Based almost exclusively on historical transaction data.

---

sion, but they are *indirectly* involved in the hospital's operation. The counsel is the hospital's lawyer, and the personnel director hires the hospital's employees and maintains all employment records. The controller and treasurer are Olympia Regional Hospital's chief accountants. The existence of two staff-level accounting positions reflects a division of responsibilities, as portrayed in Exhibit 1-4.

Controller   In most organizations, the **controller** (sometimes called the **comptroller**) is the chief managerial and financial accountant. The controller usually is responsible for supervising the personnel in the accounting department and for preparing the information and reports used in both managerial and financial accounting. As the organization's chief managerial accountant, the controller often interprets accounting information for line managers and serves as a consultant when decisions and plans are made. Most controllers are involved in planning and decision making at all levels and across all functional areas of the enterprise. This broad role has enabled many managerial accountants to rise to the top of their organizations. In recent years, former accountants have served as top executives in such companies as General Motors, Singer, General Electric, and Fruehauf.[2]

---

[2] "The Controller: Inflation Gives Him More Clout with Management," *Business Week,* August 15, 1977, pp. 86–95.

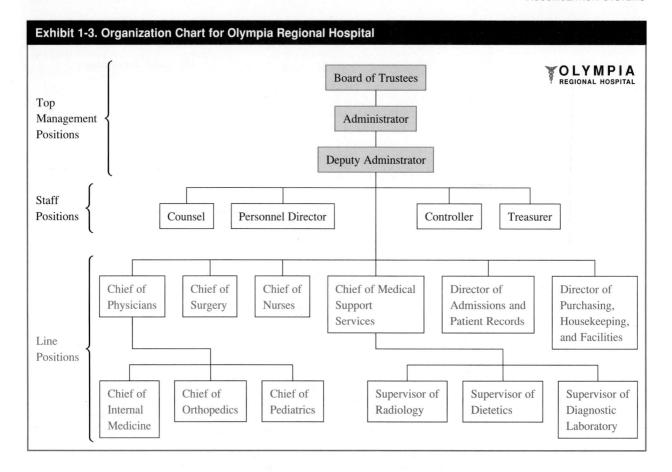

Exhibit 1-3. Organization Chart for Olympia Regional Hospital

Exhibit 1-4. Controller versus Treasurer at Olympia Regional Hospital

Controller	Treasurer
(1) Supervises the accounting department	(1) Manages relationships with donors, creditors, investors, and government agencies that provide financial support
(2) Prepares all reports for external parties (financial accounting)	(2) Maintains custody of cash and other assets
(3) Prepares all reports and information for internal users (managerial accounting)	(3) Manages investments
(4) Assists line managers throughout the hospital in interpreting and using managerial accounting information	(4) Responsible for credit policy and collection of accounts
(5) Prepares reports required for taxation and governmental reporting; advises management on tax-related issues	(5) Manages the hospital's insurance coverage

Treasurer The **treasurer** typically is responsible for raising capital and safeguarding the organization's assets. Olympia Regional Hospital's treasurer oversees the relationships between the hospital and its donors, lenders, investors, and the governmental agencies that supply partial funding. In addition, the treasurer is responsible for the hospital's assets, the management of its investments, its credit policy, and its insurance coverage.

Internal Auditor Olympia Regional Hospital does not have an internal auditor, but most large corporations and many governmental agencies do. An organization's **internal auditor** is responsible for reviewing the accounting procedures, records, and reports in both the controller's and the treasurer's areas of responsibility. The auditor then expresses an independent opinion to top management regarding the effectiveness of the organization's accounting system. In some organizations, the internal auditor also makes a broad performance evaluation of middle and lower management.

MAJOR THEMES IN MANAGERIAL ACCOUNTING

Several major themes influence virtually all aspects of managerial accounting. We will briefly introduce these themes now, and they will be apparent throughout the text.

Information and Incentives

 The need for information is the driving force behind managerial accounting. However, managerial accounting information often serves two functions: a *decision-facilitating* function and a *decision-influencing* function. Information usually is supplied to a decision maker to assist that manager in choosing an alternative. Often, that information is also intended to influence the manager's decision.

To illustrate, let us consider Olympia Regional Hospital's annual budget. Although the budget is prepared under the direction of the controller, it must be approved by the hospital's administrator and, ultimately, by the board of trustees. As part of the budget approval process, the administrator and the trustees will make important decisions that determine how the hospital's resources will be allocated. Throughout the year, the decisions of management will be facilitated by the information contained in the budget. Management decisions also will be influenced by the budget, since at year-end actual expenditures will be compared with the budgeted amounts. Explanations will then be requested for any significant deviations.

Behavioral Issues

The reactions of both individuals and groups to managerial accounting information will significantly affect the course of events in an organization. How will Olympia Regional Hospital's chief of surgery react to a budget? How will data regarding the cost of providing radiological services affect the way the supervisor of radiology prices those services? How much detail should be included in the quarterly accounting reports to the administrator? If too much detail is provided, will the administrator be overloaded with information and distracted from the main points?

All of these questions involve the behavioral tendencies of people and their cognitive limitations in using information. The better a managerial accountant's understanding of human behavior is, the more effective he or she will be as a provider of information.

Costs and Benefits

Information is a commodity, much like wheat or corn. Like other goods, information can be produced, purchased, and consumed. It can be of high or low quality, timely or late, appropriate for its intended use or utterly irrelevant. As is true of all goods and services, information entails both costs and benefits. The costs of providing managerial accounting information to the managers in Olympia Regional Hospital include the cost of compensation for the controller and Accounting Department personnel, the cost of purchasing and operating computers, and the cost of the time spent by the information users to read, understand, and utilize the information. The benefits include improved decisions, more effective planning, greater efficiency of operations at lower costs, and better direction and control of operations.

Thus, there are both costs and benefits associated with managerial accounting information. The desirability of any particular managerial accounting technique or information must be determined in light of its costs and benefits. We will reinforce this cost-benefit trade-off throughout the text by pointing out areas where managerial accounting information could be improved, but only at too great a cost.

Evolution and Adaptation in Managerial Accounting

Compared to financial accounting, managerial accounting is a young discipline. As a result, managerial accounting concepts and tools are still evolving as new ways are found to provide information that assists management. Moreover, the business environment is changing rapidly. For managerial accounting to be as useful a tool in the future as it has been in the recent past, managerial accounting information must be adapted to reflect those changes. Several changes in the business environment that are especially pertinent to managerial accounting are discussed briefly here. The effect of these changes on various topics in managerial accounting will be explored in subsequent chapters.[3]

Service versus Manufacturing Firms The service sector occupies a growing role in the United States economy. As more and more companies provide financial, medical, communication, transportation, consulting, and hospitality services, managerial accounting techniques must be adapted to meet the needs of managers in those industries. The key difference between service and manufacturing firms is that most services are consumed as they are produced. Services cannot be inventoried like manufactured goods. Service organizations also tend to be more labor intensive than manufacturing firms. Many of the techniques developed for measuring costs and performance in manufacturing companies have been adapted successfully to service industry firms. Throughout the text, you will notice that roughly two-thirds of the illustrations of managerial accounting techniques involve service industry firms and nonprofit organizations.

Emergence of New Industries Scientific discoveries are opening up whole new industries that were not even contemplated a short time ago. Such discoveries as genetic engineering, superconductivity, and artificial hearts have spawned business activities in which managers face new challenges. Managerial accountants face new

---

[3] Further discussion of the changing role of managerial accounting is available in Robert S. Kaplan, "The Evolution of Management Accounting," *The Accounting Review* (*59,* no. 3, July 1984), pp. 390–418.

challenges as they seek to provide relevant information in these new high-tech industries.

Just-in-Time Inventory Management Several manufacturers have recently adopted a new inventory strategy in their multistage production processes. In a *just-in-time* (or *JIT*) production environment, raw materials and components are purchased or produced just in time to be used at each stage in the production process. This approach to inventory management brings considerable cost savings from reduced inventory levels.

Product Quality and Productivity One implication of a just-in-time inventory philosophy is the need to emphasize product quality. If a component is to be produced just in time for the next production stage, it must be "just right" for its intended purpose. One flawed component can shut down the entire production line, entailing considerable cost. Therefore, managerial accountants have become involved increasingly in monitoring product quality and measuring the costs of maintaining quality.

As global competition increases in virtually all industries, businesses are forced to reach higher levels of productivity in order to price their products and services competitively. Once again, managerial accountants have been called upon to develop productivity measures to help management meet the challenges of international competition.

Computer-Integrated Manufacturing Over a long period of time, manufacturing processes have evolved from labor-intensive methods to more automated processes, in which most of the work is accomplished by machines. This trend continues today, as *computer-integrated-manufacturing* (or *CIM*) systems become more common. A CIM process is fully automated, with computers controlling the entire production process. In CIM systems, the types of costs incurred by the manufacturer are quite different from those in traditional manufacturing environments.

Cost Management Systems

The explosion in technology we are experiencing, coupled with increasing worldwide competition, is forcing managers to produce high-quality goods and services, provide outstanding customer service, and do so at the lowest possible cost. These demands are placing ever-greater requirements on the information provided by managerial accounting systems. Many companies are moving away from a historical cost-accounting perspective and toward a proactive *cost management* perspective. A **cost management system** is a management planning and control system with the following objectives.[4]

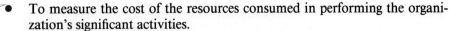

- To measure the cost of the resources consumed in performing the organization's significant activities.
- To identify and eliminate **non-value-added costs.** These are the costs of activities that can be eliminated with no deterioration of product quality, performance, or perceived value.
- To determine the efficiency and effectiveness of all major activities performed in the enterprise.

[4] This section draws upon Callie Berliner and James A. Brimson, eds., *Cost Management for Today's Advanced Manufacturing* (Boston: Harvard Business School Press), 1988, pp. 3, 10, 13–15.

- To identify and evaluate new activities that can improve the future performance of the organization.

Notice the emphasis of a cost management system on the organization's activities. This emphasis, sometimes called **activity accounting,** is crucial to the goal of producing quality goods and services at the lowest possible cost. We will have more to say about the role of a cost management system throughout the text.

A Systems Perspective

Managerial accounting constitutes one of several *systems* used by managers in running an organization. A **system is an integrated structure designed to accomplish a stated purpose.** A system consists of a set of inputs, a process, and a set of outputs, which are defined as follows:

Input: data entered into a system, which are intended to have a measurable effect on the system.
Process: a set of activities performed by the system in order to achieve the stated purpose.
Output: information generated by the system, which is available to the system's users for a variety of purposes.

Exhibit 1-5 shows the components of a system and illustrates them for Olympia Regional Hospital. As you study this text, you will see that the managerial accounting function incorporates elements of many systems, all of which are intended to help managers run an organization.

Accounting and Computers

Few innovations have affected our daily lives as greatly as the computer. Whether we are attempting to find a book in the library, make an airline reservation, or balance a

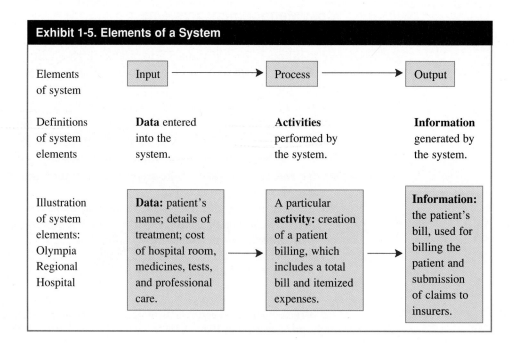

Exhibit 1-5. Elements of a System

	Input	→	Process	→	Output
Elements of system					
Definitions of system elements	**Data** entered into the system.		**Activities** performed by the system.		**Information** generated by the system.
Illustration of system elements: Olympia Regional Hospital	**Data:** patient's name; details of treatment; cost of hospital room, medicines, tests, and professional care.	→	A particular **activity:** creation of a patient billing, which includes a total bill and itemized expenses.	→	**Information:** the patient's bill, used for billing the patient and submission of claims to insurers.

checkbook, we cannot escape the influence of computers. Just as computers have dramatically affected our personal lives, they have revolutionized the way in which business operations are conducted. Most businesses rely on computers for virtually all functions that involve data. Accounting, personnel, and other administrative functions are computerized, as are significant aspects of production and marketing operations. As a major component of an enterprise's management information system, the accounting system is inextricably tied to the organization's computer system. Thus, any study of managerial accounting requires some understanding of its relationship to computer information systems.

Components of Computer Information Systems   The four major components of a **computer information system (CIS)** are as follows:[5]

Hardware component: the central processing unit, which does the actual computing; the input and output devices; and the storage devices, such as floppy disks.

Software component: the computer programs, which give the computer its instructions.

Data component: numbers and words entered into the computer to be stored or manipulated in a systematic way.

Human component: personnel who operate and maintain the computer hardware, select and develop software, and assist users of the CIS.

Database Management   Data stored in the CIS, either in the computer's memory or on secondary storage devices, is called a *database.* Usually a database will have several files, which are used for different purposes. To illustrate, one of the files included in Olympia Regional Hospital's CIS is a patient-records file. This file includes the name, address, social security number, insurance coverage, medical history, and hospital treatment for each of Olympia's current and former patients. Each of the files in a database typically will be relevant to the needs of several CIS users. For example, Olympia Regional Hospital's patient records file would be used by the Accounting Department for patient billing, by the medical staff in determining treatment methods, by the dieticians for selecting each patient's diet, and by the Admissions Department for scheduling the occupancy of hospital rooms.

A **database management system** is software designed to allow the CIS to make the most efficient use of its database. Olympia Regional Hospital's database management system allows for the interaction of its various files and allows access to each file by the relevant set of users. The hospital's database management system also provides data security by preventing access to specific data by unauthorized personnel. Managerial accountants often work together with CIS personnel in designing an organization's database and database management system. The managerial accountant knows how financial data are generated and is often in the best position to indicate which CIS users will need access to the data.

Decision Support Systems   Decision making is a crucial part of the management process, and decision makers require information. A **decision support system** is a computer-based system that is designed to assist managers in making certain types of decisions. A decision support system includes access to a database, decision methods

---

[5] This section draws on material from Mawdudur Rahman and Maurice Halladay, *Accounting Information Systems: Principles, Applications and Future Directions* (Englewood Cliffs, N.J.: Prentice Hall), 1988.

pertinent to the decisions facing the user, and various ways of displaying the results. Because managerial accountants are familiar with much of the relevant data as well as with the types of decisions managers face, they often help to design an organization's decision support system.[6]

MANAGERIAL ACCOUNTING AS A CAREER

Managerial accountants serve a crucial function in virtually any enterprise. As the providers of information, they are often in touch with the heartbeat of the organization. In most businesses, managerial accountants interact frequently with sales personnel, finance specialists, production people, and managers at all levels. To perform their duties effectively, managerial accountants must be knowledgeable not only in accounting but in the other major business disciplines as well.

Professional Organizations

To keep up with new developments in their field, managerial accountants often belong to one or more professional organizations. The largest of these is the National Association of Accountants (NAA). The NAA publishes a monthly journal entitled *Management Accounting,* and it also has published many research studies on managerial accounting topics. Other professional organizations in which managerial accountants hold membership include the Financial Executives Institute, the American Institute of Certified Public Accountants, the Institute of Internal Auditors, and the American Accounting Association.

The primary professional association for managerial accountants in Canada is the Society of Management Accountants of Canada (La Société des Comptables en Management du Canada). Great Britain's main professional organization is the Institute of Chartered Management Accountants, and Australia's organization is the Institute of Chartered Accountants in Australia. In all, over 75 countries have professional organizations for their practicing accountants.

Professional Certification

In keeping with the importance of their role and the specialized knowledge they must have, managerial accountants can earn a professional certification. In the United States, the NAA has established the Institute of Certified Management Accountants (ICMA), which administers the Certified Management Accountant (CMA) program. The requirements for becoming a **Certified Management Accountant** include meeting specified educational requirements and passing the CMA examination.[7] In Canada, a managerial accountant may be certified as a Registered Industrial Accountant (RIA) by the Society of Management Accountants of Canada. Great Britain and many other countries also have professional certification programs for their managerial accountants.

---

[6] For further discussion of decision support systems, see R. H. Bonczek, C. W. Holsapple, and A. B. Whinston, "Future Directions for Developing Decision Support Systems," *Decision Sciences, 11* (1980), pp. 616–631.

[7] For information about the CMA program, write to the Institute of Certified Management Accountants, 10 Paragon Drive, Montvale, N.J. 07645-0405.

Professional Ethics

As professionals, managerial accountants have an obligation to themselves, their colleagues, and their organizations to adhere to high standards of ethical conduct. In recognition of this obligation, the National Association of Accountants has developed the following ethical standards for managerial accountants.[8]

Competence Managerial accountants have a responsibility to:

- Maintain an appropriate level of professional competence by ongoing development of their knowledge and skills.
- Perform their professional duties in accordance with relevant laws, regulations, and technical standards.
- Prepare complete and clear reports and recommendations after appropriate analyses of relevant and reliable information.

Confidentiality Managerial accountants have a responsibility to:

- Refrain from disclosing confidential information acquired in the course of their work except when authorized, unless legally obligated to do so.
- Inform subordinates as appropriate regarding the confidentiality of information acquired in the course of their work and monitor their activities to assure the maintenance of that confidentiality.
- Refrain from using or appearing to use confidential information acquired in the course of their work for unethical or illegal advantage either personally or through third parties.

Integrity Managerial accountants have a responsibility to:

- Avoid actual or apparent conflicts of interest and advise all appropriate parties of any potential conflict.
- Refrain from engaging in any activity that would prejudice their ability to carry out their duties ethically.
- Refuse any gift, favor, or hospitality that would influence or appear to influence their actions.
- Refrain from either actively or passively subverting the attainment of the organization's legitimate and ethical objectives.
- Recognize and communicate professional limitations or other constraints that would preclude responsible judgment or successful performance of an activity.
- Communicate unfavorable as well as favorable information and professional judgments or opinions.
- Refrain from engaging in or supporting any activity that would discredit the profession.

Objectivity Managerial accountants have a responsibility to:

- Communicate information fairly and objectively.
- Disclose fully all relevant information that could reasonably be expected to

[8] This material appeared in *Management Accounting* (Montvale, N.J.: National Association of Accountants, January 1987), p. 38. The source is *Statement on Management Accounting, Standards of Ethical Conduct for Management Accountants* (Montvale, N.J., National Association of Accountants, 1983). See also the June 1990 issue of *Management Accounting,* entirely devoted to ethics in managerial accounting.

influence an intended user's understanding of the reports, comments, and recommendations presented.

In resolving an ethical problem, the managerial accountant should discuss the situation with his or her immediate supervisor, assuming that individual is not involved in the problem. If the supervisor is involved in the ethical problem, the accountant should discuss the matter with the next higher level of management.

IMPORTANCE OF MANAGERIAL ACCOUNTING

We conclude our overview of managerial accounting with two illustrations from real-world companies. These two examples emphasize the importance of managerial accounting information in the effective management of any enterprise, large or small.

ILLUSTRATION FROM MANAGEMENT ACCOUNTING PRACTICE

ITT

For 17 years Harold Geneen was the chief executive officer of International Telephone and Telegraph Company (ITT). During that period, ITT became one of the largest and most profitable industrial companies in the world. In a book entitled *Managing,* Mr. Geneen described his management style and methods. The following excerpts from the book show the importance Mr. Geneen placed on "the numbers," a catch phrase for the quantitative data upon which plans and decisions are made. Many of "the numbers" are the products of managerial accounting systems.[9]

"The efficacy of management is quantifiable. It can be measured by the profit and loss statement. In an established company, you can measure performance by the quarter. I used to tell my management team at ITT that making the first quarter's quotas was the most important challenge of the year. If you don't make your budget quota that first quarter, then you probably won't be able to catch up in subsequent quarters. Worrying about the quarterly numbers is not short-term management: careful study of them will alert you to potential long-term problems in time to take appropriate action.

"At ITT we used everything available to us to get results. We used everything we had learned at school, everything we had learned from our own experience in business, everything we could learn from one another. We used our intuition. We used our brains. And we always used the numbers.

"No business could run without them. Numbers serve as a thermometer that measures the health and well-being of the enterprise. They serve as the first line of communication to inform management what is going on. The more precise the numbers are, the more they are based upon unshakeable facts, the clearer the line of communication.

"The difference between well-managed companies and not-so-well-managed companies is the degree of attention they pay to numbers, the temperature chart of their business. How often are the numbers reported up the chain of command? How accurate are those numbers? How much variation is tolerated between budget forecasts and actual results? How deep does management dig for its answers?

[9] Harold Geneen with Alvin Moscow, *Managing* (Garden City, N.Y.: Doubleday & Company, Inc.), 1984.

"The truth is that the drudgery of the numbers will make you free. The confidence that you are in control, that you are aware of the significant variations from the expected, gives you the freedom to do things that you would have been unable to do otherwise. You can build a new plant, or finance risk-laden research, or go out and buy a company. You can do it with assurance because you are able to sit down and figure out what that new venture will do to the balance sheet. You will be able, in short, to manage."

ILLUSTRATION FROM MANAGEMENT ACCOUNTING PRACTICE

Need for Managerial Accounting in a Small Business

The following true story was reported in the *Wall Street Journal.* It describes the experience of a small company that almost went bankrupt because it had an inadequate managerial accounting system.[10]

The company owner was a skilled designer of cutting tools, with over 100 patents to his credit. He could create a cutting tool to meet any customer's particular needs. But he had no use for a precise accounting system to enable him to run the business by the numbers. He considered accountants to be "just more overhead."

The cost accounting system was inadequate to determine the cost of manufacturing various products. Jobs were priced on the basis of an estimate that certain manufacturing costs amounted to $25 per labor hour. Later, these costs were discovered to be almost $45 per hour. The result was that products were often underpriced, and the company lost thousands of dollars in profits that could have been earned.

Eventually, a financial crisis forced the company's owner to install new cost accounting and purchasing systems and to manage the business by the numbers. Now the revitalized manufacturing operation is much more profitable than in the past. The owner lamented that if he had used the new cost accounting and purchasing systems from the start, "I would have been a wealthy man."

CHAPTER SUMMARY

All organizations have goals, and their managers need information as they strive to attain those goals. Information is needed for the management functions of decision making, planning, directing operations, and controlling.

Managerial accounting is an important part of any organization's management information system. The four objectives of managerial accounting activity are: (1) providing information for decision making and planning, (2) assisting managers in directing and controlling operations, (3) motivating managers toward the organization's goals, and (4) measuring the performance of managers and subunits within the organization.

Managerial accounting differs from financial accounting in several ways. The users of managerial accounting information are managers inside the organization. Managerial accounting information is not mandatory, is unregulated, and draws on data from the basic accounting system as well as other data sources. The users of financial accounting information are interested parties outside the organization,

[10] "This Company Is Run Better Because It Nearly Went Under," *The Wall Street Journal,* September 30, 1985, p. 23.

such as investors and creditors. Financial accounting information is required for publicly held companies, is regulated by the Financial Accounting Standards Board, and is based almost entirely on historical transaction data.

Managerial accounting is a profession with a certification process and a code of ethical standards. Managerial accountants are highly trained professionals, who can contribute significantly to the success of any enterprise.

KEY TERMS For each term's definition refer to the indicated page, or turn to the glossary at the end of the text.

Activity accounting, p. 14; Attention-directing function, p. 6; Certified Management Accountant (CMA), p. 16; Computer information system (CIS), p. 15; Controller (or comptroller), p. 9, Controlling, p. 5; Cost accounting system, p. 7; Cost management system, p. 13; Database management system, p. 15; Decision making, p. 4; Decision support system, p. 15; Directing operations, p. 5; Financial accounting, p. 7; Internal auditor, p. 11; Line positions, p. 8; Managerial accounting, p. 3; Non-value-added costs, p. 13; Planning, p. 5; Staff positions, p. 8; System, p. 14; Treasurer, p. 11.

REVIEW QUESTIONS

1-1. List two plausible goals for each of these organizations: American Red Cross, General Motors, J. C. Penney, the City of Pittsburgh, and Hertz.

1-2. List and define the four basic management activities.

1-3. Give examples of each of the four primary management activities in the context of a national fast-food chain.

1-4. Give examples of how each of the objectives of managerial accounting activity would be important in an airline company.

1-5. List and describe four important differences between managerial and financial accounting.

1-6. Distinguish between cost accounting and managerial accounting.

1-7. Distinguish between line and staff positions. Give two examples of each in a university setting.

1-8. Distinguish between the following two accounting positions: controller and treasurer.

1-9. What is meant by the following statement? "Managerial accounting often serves an attention-directing role."

1-10. What is the chief difference between manufacturing and service industry firms?

1-11. Define the following terms: just-in-time, computer-integrated manufacturing, cost management system, non-value-added costs, system, computer information system, database management, and decision support system.

1-12. Define and explain the significance of the term *CMA*.

1-13. Briefly explain what is meant by each of the following ethical standards for managerial accountants: competence, confidentiality, integrity, and objectivity.

1-14. What did Harold Geneen mean when he referred to *managing by the numbers?*

1-15. Managerial accounting is an important part of any enterprise's management information system. Name two other information systems that supply information to management.

1-16. Can a managerial accountant play an important role in a nonprofit organization? Explain your answer.

1-17. A large manufacturer of electronic machinery stated the following as one of its goals: "The company should become the low-cost producer in its industry." How can managerial accounting help the company achieve this goal?

1-18. What do you think it means to be a professional? In your view, are managerial accountants professionals?

EXERCISES

Exercise 1-19 Objectives of Managerial Accounting Activity. For each of the following activities, explain which of the objectives of managerial accounting activity is involved. In some cases, several objectives may be involved.

1. Developing a bonus reward system for the managers of the various offices run by a large travel agency.
2. Comparing the actual and planned cost of a consulting engagement completed by an engineering firm.
3. Determining the cost of manufacturing a guitar.
4. Measuring the cost of the inventory of compact disk players on hand in a retail electronics store.
5. Estimating the annual operating cost of a newly proposed branch bank.
6. Measuring the following costs incurred during one month in a hotel owned by a national hospitality-industry firm.
   a. Wages of table-service personnel.
   b. Property taxes.

Exercise 1-20 Managerial Accounting and Decision Making. Give an example of managerial accounting information that could help a manager make each of the following decisions.

1. The president of a rental car agency is deciding whether or not to add luxury cars to the rental car fleet.
2. The production manager in an automobile plant is deciding whether to have routine maintenance performed on a machine weekly or biweekly.
3. The manager of a discount department store is deciding how many security personnel to employ for the purpose of reducing shoplifting.
4. The county board of representatives is deciding whether or not to build an addition on the county library.

PROBLEMS

Problem 1-21   Role of the Divisional Controller. A division manager is responsible for each of Coastal Products Corporation's divisions. Each division's controller, assigned by the corporate controller's office, manages the division's accounting system and provides analysis of financial information for the division manager. The division manager evaluates the performance of the division controller and makes recommendations for salary increases and promotions. However, the final responsibility for promotion evaluation and salary increases rests with the corporate controller.

Each of Coastal's divisions is responsible for product design, sales, pricing, operating expenses, and profit. However, corporate management exercises tight control over divisional financial operations. For example, all capital expenditures above a modest amount must be approved by corporate management. The method of financial reporting from the division to corporate headquarters provides further evidence of the degree of financial control. The division manager and the division controller submit to corporate headquarters separate and independent commentary on the financial results of the division. Corporate management states that the division controller is there to provide an independent view of the division's operations, not as a spy.

REQUIRED:

1. Discuss the arrangements for line and staff reporting in Coastal Products Corporation.
2. Coastal Products Corporation's dual reporting systems for divisions may create problems for the divisional controller.
   a. Identify and discuss the factors that make the division controller's role difficult in this type of situation.
   b. Discuss the effect of the dual reporting relationship on the motivation of the divisional controller.

(CMA, adapted)

Problem 1-22   Quality Control; Ethical Behavior. FulRange Company manufactures printed circuits for stereo amplifiers. A common product defect is a "drift" caused by failure to maintain precise heat levels during the production process. Rejects from the 100 percent testing program can be reworked to acceptable levels if the defect is drift. However, in a recent analysis of customer complaints, Marie Allen, the assistant controller, and the quality control engineer determined that normal rework does not bring the circuits up to standard. Sampling showed that about half of the reworked circuits will fail after extended amplifier operation. The incidence of failure in the reworked circuits is projected to be about 10 percent over five years.

Unfortunately, there is no way to determine which reworked circuits will fail, because testing will not detect the problem. The rework process could be changed to correct the problem, but the cost-benefit analysis for the suggested change indicates that it is not economically feasible. FulRange's marketing analyst has indicated that this problem will have a significant impact on the company's reputation and customer satisfaction. Consequently, the board of directors would interpret this problem as having serious negative implications for the company's profitability.

Allen included the circuit failure and rework problem in her report prepared for the upcoming quarterly meeting of the board of directors. Due to the potential adverse economic impact, Allen followed a long-standing practice of highlighting this information. After reviewing the reports to be presented, the plant manager and his staff complained to the controller that he should control his people better. "We can't upset the board with this kind of material. Tell Allen to tone that down. Maybe we can get it by the board in this meeting and have some time to work on it. People who buy those cheap systems and play them that loud shouldn't expect them to last forever."

The controller called Allen into his office and said, "Marie, you'll have to bury this one. The probable failure of reworks can be mentioned briefly in the oral presentation, but it should not be mentioned or highlighted in the advance material mailed to the board."

Allen feels strongly that the board will be misinformed on a potentially serious loss of income if she follows the controller's orders. Allen discussed the problem with the quality control engineer, who simply remarked, "That's your problem, Marie."

REQUIRED:

1. Discuss the ethical considerations that Marie Allen should recognize in deciding how to proceed.
2. Explain what ethical responsibilities should be accepted by: (a) the controller, (b) the quality control engineer, and (c) the plant manager.
3. What should Marie Allen do? Explain your answer.

(CMA, adapted)

Problem 1-23   Ethical Code for Managerial Accountants. Jay Leslie, corporate controller for Wuster Company, was concerned because there was no code of professional ethics for the company's managerial accountants. Leslie believed such a code should be developed. The steps he suggested following to develop such a code are:

- Review the role of the managerial accounting function within the company.
- Determine the objectives of such a code and what it would accomplish.
- Establish general ethical standards, classified according to the nature of the obligations of managerial accounting.
- Review specific situations in order to establish guidelines that would enable managerial accountants to interpret and apply ethical standards.

REQUIRED: Formulate a statement of objectives for a code of professional ethics, including an identification of expected company benefits from such a code, which Jay Leslie could present in order to justify the establishment of such a code for Wuster Company's managerial accountants.

(CMA, adapted)

Chapter 2 Basic Cost Terms and Concepts

After completing this chapter, you should be able to:

- Explain what is meant by "different costs for different purposes."

- Describe the behavior of variable and fixed costs, both in total and on a per-unit basis.

- Distinguish between direct and indirect costs and controllable and uncontrollable costs.

- Distinguish between product costs, period costs, and expenses.

- Give examples of merchandise costs, marketing costs, administrative costs, research and development costs, and three types of manufacturing costs.

- Describe the role of costs on the income statement and balance sheet of a merchandising company, a manufacturing company, and a service industry firm.

- Define and give examples of an opportunity cost, an out-of-pocket cost, a sunk cost, a differential cost, a marginal cost, and an average cost.

- Explain the behavioral tendencies many people show when dealing with opportunity costs and sunk costs.

The process of management involves planning, control, and decision making. Managers can perform each of these functions more effectively with information provided by managerial accountants. Much of this information focuses on the costs incurred in the organization. For example, in *planning* the routes and flight schedules of American Airlines, managers must consider aircraft fuel costs, salaries of flight crews, and airport landing fees. *Controlling* the costs of manufacturing personal computers requires that Hewlett Packard's accountants carefully measure and keep track of production costs. In *making decisions* about tuition and admission requirements, a university's board of trustees must have information about the costs of providing educational services.

Each of these examples focuses on costs of one type or another. An important first step in studying managerial accounting is to gain an understanding of the various types of costs incurred by organizations. In this chapter, we will study the cost terms, concepts, and classifications routinely used by managerial accountants.

COST CLASSIFICATIONS: DIFFERENT COSTS FOR DIFFERENT PURPOSES

The word *cost* can have different meanings depending on the context in which it is used. Cost data that are classified and recorded in a particular way for one purpose may be inappropriate for another use. For example, the costs incurred in producing gasoline last year are important in measuring Exxon's income for the year. However, those costs may not be useful in planning the company's refinery operations for the next year if the cost of oil has changed significantly or if the methods of producing gasoline have improved. The important point is that different cost concepts and classifications are used for different purposes. Understanding these concepts and classifications enables the managerial accountant to provide appropriate cost data to the managers who need it.

Fixed and Variable Costs

One of the most important cost classifications involves the way a cost changes in relation to changes in the activity of the organization. **Activity** refers to a measure of the organization's output of products or services. The number of automobiles manufactured by General Motors, the number of days of patient care provided by Massachusetts General Hospital, and the number of insurance claims settled by Allstate are all measures of activity. In some organizations, the activities that cause costs to be incurred are called **cost drivers**. This term is coming into more frequent usage, particularly in automated manufacturing environments.

Variable Costs A **variable cost** changes in total in direct proportion to a change in the level of activity (or cost driver). If activity increases by 20 percent, total variable cost increases by 20 percent also. For example, the cost of sheet metal used by Chrysler will increase by approximately 5 percent if automobile production increases by 5 percent. The cost of napkins and other paper products used at a Pizza Hut will increase by roughly 10 percent if the restaurant's patronage increases by 10 percent.

Panel A of Exhibit 2-1 displays a graph of variable cost. As this graph shows, *total* variable cost increases proportionately with activity. When activity doubles, from 10 to 20 units, total variable cost doubles, from $1,000 to $2,000. However, the variable cost *per unit* remains the same as activity changes. The variable cost associated with each unit of activity is $100, whether it is the first unit, the fourth, or the eighteenth. The table in panel B of Exhibit 2-1 illustrates this point.

To summarize, as activity changes, total variable cost increases or decreases proportionately with the activity change, but unit variable cost remains the same.

Fixed Costs A **fixed cost** remains unchanged in total as the level of activity (or cost driver) varies. If activity increases or decreases by 20 percent, total fixed cost remains the same. Examples of fixed costs include depreciation of plant and equip-

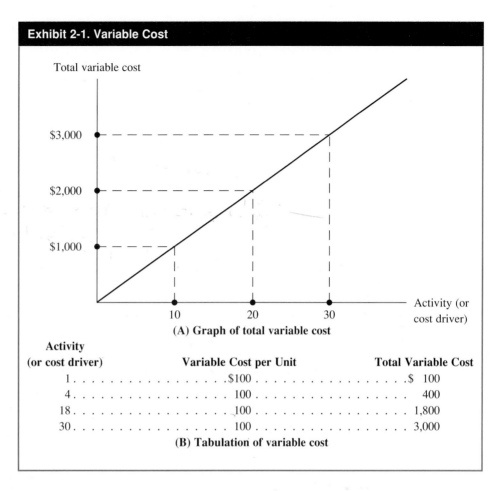

Exhibit 2-1. Variable Cost

Total variable cost

(A) Graph of total variable cost

Activity (or cost driver)	Variable Cost per Unit	Total Variable Cost
1	$100	$ 100
4	100	400
18	100	1,800
30	100	3,000

(B) Tabulation of variable cost

ment at a Texas Instruments factory, the cost of property taxes at a Ramada Inn, and the salary of a subway driver employed by the New York Transit Authority.

A fixed cost is graphed in panel A of Exhibit 2-2.

From the graph in Exhibit 2-2, it is apparent that *total* fixed cost remains unchanged as activity changes. When activity triples, from 10 to 30 units, total fixed cost remains constant at $1,500. However, the fixed cost *per unit* does change as activity changes. If the activity level is only 1 unit, then the fixed cost per unit is $1,500 per unit ($1,500 ÷ 1). If the activity level is 10 units, then the fixed cost per unit declines to $150 per unit ($1,500 ÷ 10). The behavior of total fixed cost and unit fixed cost is illustrated by the table in panel B of Exhibit 2-2.

Another way of viewing the change in unit fixed cost as activity changes is in a graph, as shown in panel C of Exhibit 2-2. Unit fixed cost declines steadily as activity increases. Notice that the decrease in unit fixed cost when activity changes from 1 to 2 units is much larger than the decrease in unit fixed cost when activity changes from 10 to 11 units or from 20 to 21 units. Thus, the amount of the change in unit fixed cost declines as the activity level increases.

To summarize, as the activity level increases, total fixed cost remains constant but unit fixed cost declines. As you will see in subsequent chapters, it is vital in

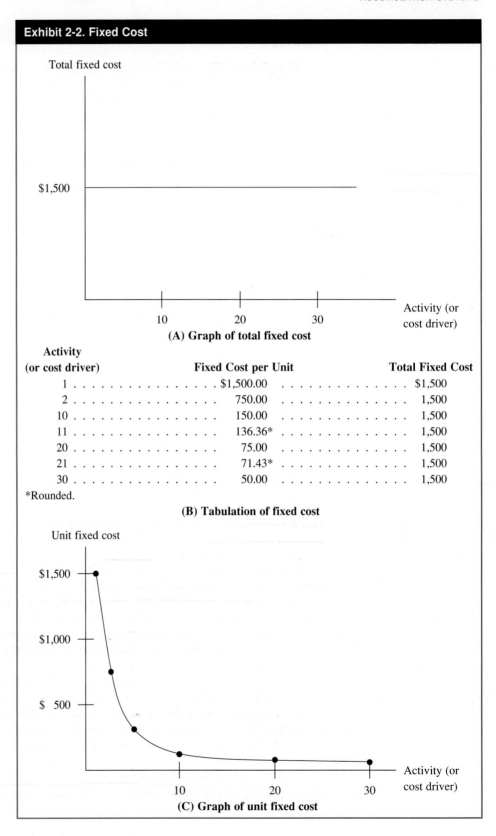

Exhibit 2-2. Fixed Cost

Total fixed cost

$1,500

Activity (or cost driver)

10   20   30

(A) Graph of total fixed cost

Activity (or cost driver)	Fixed Cost per Unit	Total Fixed Cost
1	$1,500.00	$1,500
2	750.00	1,500
10	150.00	1,500
11	136.36*	1,500
20	75.00	1,500
21	71.43*	1,500
30	50.00	1,500

*Rounded.

(B) Tabulation of fixed cost

Unit fixed cost

$1,500

$1,000

$ 500

Activity (or cost driver)

10   20   30

(C) Graph of unit fixed cost

managerial accounting to thoroughly understand the behavior of both total fixed costs and unit fixed costs.

Cost Drivers The activities or cost drivers upon which cost behavior depends vary widely among industries. We will discuss the various cost drivers used in manufacturing firms in subsequent chapters. The following description of cost drivers in U.S. airlines illustrates the concept in the service sector.

ILLUSTRATION FROM
MANAGEMENT
ACCOUNTING
PRACTICE

Cost Drivers in the Airline Industry

A recent study of the U.S. airline industry revealed that two distinct types of cost drivers have significant effects on an airline's costs.[1] *Volume-based cost drivers* include (1) aircraft capacity, including both passenger and cargo capacity, and (2) number of passengers. *Operations-based cost drivers* include the following characteristics of an airline's operations: (1) product-line diversity, as measured by route density — "by increasing the number of flights over its network, a carrier is offering a more diversified set of services"; (2) degree of hub concentration, which refers to the extent to which an airline structures its "route systems so that many flights arrive and depart hubs within a few hours of each other, with passengers and cargo exchanging planes in between"; and (3) hub domination, which is the extent to which an airline is able to monopolize, and thus control, the facilities and services at its hub airports.

Direct and Indirect Costs

An important objective of managerial accounting is to assist managers in controlling costs. Sometimes cost control is facilitated by tracing costs to the department or work center in which the cost was incurred. Such tracing of costs to departments is known as *responsibility accounting.* A cost that can be traced to a particular department is called a **direct cost** of the department. For example, the salary of an auto mechanic is a direct cost of the automotive service department in a Sears department store. The cost of paint used in the painting department of a Toyota plant is a direct cost of the painting department.

 A cost that is not directly traceable to a particular department is called an **indirect cost** of the department. The costs of national advertising for Walt Disney World are indirect costs of each of the departments or subunits of the recreational complex, such as the Magic Kingdom and Epcot Center. The salary of a General Electric Company plant manager is an indirect cost of each of the plant's production departments. The plant manager's duties are important to the smooth functioning of each of the plant's departments, but there is no way to trace a portion of the plant manager's salary cost to each department.

 Whether a cost is a direct cost or an indirect cost of a department often depends on which department is under consideration. A cost can be a direct cost of one department or subunit in the organization but an indirect cost of other departments. While the salary of the General Electric Company plant manager is an *indirect* cost of the plant's departments, the manager's salary is a *direct* cost of the plant.

---

[1] This illustration is from Rajiv D. Banker and Holly H. Johnston, "Cost Driver Analysis in the Service Sector: An Empirical Study of U.S. Airlines," unpublished working paper (University of Minnesota and Carnegie-Mellon University), 1989.

An important objective of a *cost management system* is to trace as many costs as possible directly to the activities that cause them to be incurred. Sometimes called *activity accounting,* this process is vital to management's objective of eliminating *non-value-added costs.* These are costs of activities that can be eliminated without deterioration of product quality, performance, or perceived value.

Controllable and Uncontrollable Costs

Another cost classification that can be helpful in cost control involves the controllability of a cost item by a particular manager. If a manager can control or heavily influence the level of a cost, then that cost is classified as a **controllable cost** of that manager. Costs that a manager cannot influence significantly are classified as *uncontrollable costs* of that manager. Many costs are not completely under the control of any individual. In classifying costs as controllable or uncontrollable, managerial accountants generally focus on a manager's ability to influence costs. The question is not, Who controls the cost? but, Who is in the best position to influence the level of a cost item? Exhibit 2-3 lists several cost items along with their typical classification as controllable or uncontrollable.

Some costs may be controllable in the long run but not in the short run. For example, the long-term costs associated with computing equipment leased by a hospital are controllable when the 10-year lease is negotiated. In the short run, however, after the lease is signed, the rental costs are uncontrollable until the lease period ends.

Manufacturing Costs

To assist managers in planning and cost control, managerial accountants classify costs by the functional area of the organization to which the costs relate. Some examples of functional areas are manufacturing, service production, merchandise, marketing, administration, and research and development.

Exhibit 2-3. Controllable and Uncontrollable Costs

Cost Item	Manager	Classification
Cost of raw material used to produce circuit boards in a Hewlett-Packard factory	Supervisor of the production department for circuit boards	Controllable (Quantity is controllable, but the price probably is not.)
Cost of food used in a McDonald's restaurant	Restaurant manager	Controllable (Quantity is controllable, but the price probably is not.)
Cost of national advertising for the Hertz car rental company	Manager of the Hertz rental agency at the Syracuse airport	Uncontrollable
Cost of national accounting and data processing operations for Penney's	Manager of a Penney's store in Gainesville, Florida	Uncontrollable

Manufacturing costs are further classified into the following three categories: direct material, direct labor, and manufacturing overhead.

Direct Material Raw material that is consumed in the manufacturing process, is physically incorporated in the finished product, and can be traced to products conveniently is called **direct material.** Examples include the sheet metal in a General Electric refrigerator and the paper in a *Sports Illustrated* magazine.

Direct Labor The cost of salaries, wages, and fringe benefits for personnel who work directly on the manufactured product is classified as **direct-labor cost.** Examples include the wages of personnel who assemble Compaq computers and who operate the equipment in a Standard Oil Company refinery.

The cost of fringe benefits for direct-labor personnel, such as employer-paid health-insurance premiums and the employer's pension contributions, should also be classified as direct-labor costs. Such costs are just as much a part of the employees' compensation as are their regular wages. Although conceptually correct, this treatment of fringe benefits is not always observed in practice. Many companies classify all fringe-benefit costs as overhead, which is defined next.

Manufacturing Overhead All other costs of manufacturing are classified as **manufacturing overhead,** which includes three types of costs: indirect material, indirect labor, and other manufacturing costs.

Indirect Material The cost of materials that are required for the production process but do not become an integral part of the finished product are classified as indirect-material costs. An example is the cost of drill bits used in a metal-fabrication shop. The drill bits wear out and are discarded, but they do not become part of the product. Materials that do become an integral part of the finished product but are insignificant in cost are also often classified as indirect material. Materials such as glue or paint may be so inexpensive that it is not worth tracing their costs to specific products as direct materials.

Indirect Labor The costs of personnel who do not work directly on the product, but whose services are necessary for the manufacturing process, are classified as indirect labor. Such personnel include production-department supervisors, custodial employees, and security guards.

Other Manufacturing Costs All other manufacturing costs that are neither material nor labor costs are classified as manufacturing overhead. These costs include depreciation of plant and equipment, property taxes, insurance, and utilities such as electricity, as well as the costs of operating service departments. **Service departments** are those that do not work directly on manufacturing products but are necessary for the manufacturing process to occur. Examples include equipment-maintenance departments and computer-aided-design (CAD) departments. In some manufacturing firms, departments are referred to as *work centers.*

Other manufacturing overhead costs include overtime premiums and the cost of idle time. An **overtime premium** is the extra compensation paid to an employee who works beyond the time normally scheduled. Suppose an electronics technician who assembles radios earns $16.00 per hour. The technician works 48 hours during a week instead of the scheduled time of 40 hours. The overtime pay scale is time and a half, or 150 percent of the regular wage. The technician's compensation for the week is classified as follows:

Direct-labor cost ($16 × 48) $768
Overhead (overtime premium: ½ × $16 × 8) 64
Total compensation paid.. $832

Only the *extra* compensation of $8 per hour is classified as overtime premium. The regular wage of $16 per hour is treated as direct labor, even for the eight hours worked on overtime.

Idle time is time that is not spent productively by an employee due to such events as equipment breakdowns or new setups of production runs. Such idle time is an unavoidable feature of most manufacturing processes. The cost of an employee's idle time is classified as overhead so that it may be spread across all production jobs, rather then being associated with a particular production job. Suppose that during one 40-hour shift, a machine breakdown resulted in idle time of 1½ hours and a power failure idled workers for an additional ½ hour. If an employee earns $14 per hour, the employee's wages for the week will be classified as follows:

Direct-labor cost ($14 × 38) $532
Overhead (idle time: $14 × 2).. 28
Total compensation paid.. $560

Both overtime premiums and the cost of idle time should be classified as manufacturing overhead, rather than associated with a particular production job, because the particular job on which idle time or overtime may occur tends to be selected at random. Suppose several production jobs are scheduled during an eight-hour shift, and the last job remains unfinished at the end of the shift. The overtime to finish the last job is necessitated by all of the jobs scheduled during the shift, not just the last one. Similarly, if a power failure occurs during one of several production jobs, the idle time that results is not due to the job that happens to be in process at the time. The power failure is a random event, and the resulting cost should be treated as a cost of all of the department's production.

To summarize, manufacturing costs include direct material, direct labor, and manufacturing overhead. Direct labor and overhead are often called **conversion costs,** since they are the costs of "converting" raw material into finished products. Direct material and direct labor are often referred to as **prime costs**.

Changing Cost Structures An organization's **cost structure** refers to the relative proportion of its variable and fixed costs. As manufacturing firms move toward *computer-integrated manufacturing systems,* their cost structures are shifting toward proportionately greater fixed costs. In such highly automated manufacturing environments, variable costs such as direct labor constitute a much lower proportion of total manufacturing cost than in the past. Fixed costs, such as depreciation of computer and robotic equipment, occupy a much larger proportion of production costs.

Production Costs in Service Industry Firms and Nonprofit Organizations

Service industry firms and many nonprofit organizations are also engaged in production. What distinguishes these organizations from manufacturers is that a service is consumed as it is produced, whereas a manufactured product can be stored in inventory. Such businesses as hotels, banks, airlines, professional sports franchises, and automotive repair shops are in the business of producing services. Similarly, nonprofit organizations such as the American Red Cross or the Greater Miami Opera Association also are engaged in service production. While less commonly observed in service firms, the same cost classifications used in manufacturing companies can be applied. For example, an airline produces air transportation services. Direct material includes such costs as jet fuel, aircraft parts, and food and beverages. Direct labor includes the salaries of the flight crew and the wages of aircraft-maintenance personnel. Overhead costs include depreciation of baggage-handling equipment, insurance, and airport landing fees.

The process of recording and classifying costs is important in service industry firms and nonprofit organizations for the same reasons as in manufacturing firms. Cost analysis is used in pricing banking and insurance services, locating travel and car-rental agencies, setting enrollment targets in universities, and determining cost reimbursements in hospitals. As such organizations occupy an ever-growing role in our economy, applying managerial accounting to their activities will take on ever-greater importance.

Nonmanufacturing Costs

Many other functional cost classifications are used besides manufacturing costs. Four of the most important ones are:

1. Merchandise costs
2. Marketing costs – selling & distribution
3. Administrative costs
4. Research and development costs

Merchandise costs are the costs incurred by retailers and wholesale firms to acquire merchandise for resale. Merchandise costs include the purchase cost of the goods plus transportation costs.

Marketing costs include the costs of selling goods or services and the costs of distribution. **Selling costs** (or order-getting costs) include salaries, commissions and travel costs of sales personnel, and the costs of advertising and promotion. **Distribution costs** (or order-filling costs) refer to the costs of storing, handling, and shipping finished products.

Administrative costs refer to all costs of running the organization as a whole. The salaries of top-management personnel and the costs of the accounting, legal, and public relations activities are examples of administrative costs.

Research and develement costs include all costs of developing new products and services. Such costs are becoming increasingly important as international competition increases and as high-technology firms make up a growing segment of the economy. The costs of running laboratories, building prototypes of new products, and testing new products are all classified as **research and development** (or **R&D**) **costs.**

Product Costs, Period Costs, and Expenses

An important issue in both managerial and financial accounting is the timing with which the costs of acquiring assets or services are recognized as expenses. An **expense** is defined as the cost incurred when an asset is used up or sold for the purpose of generating revenue. The terms *product cost* and *period cost* are used to describe the timing with which various expenses are recognized.

A **product cost** is a cost assigned to goods that were either purchased or manufactured for resale. The product cost is used to value the inventory of manufactured goods or merchandise until the goods are sold. During the time period of the sale, the product costs are recognized as an expense called **cost of goods sold.** The product cost of merchandise inventory acquired by a retailer or wholesaler for resale consists of the purchase cost of the inventory plus any shipping charges. The product cost of manufactured inventory consists of direct material, direct labor, and manufacturing overhead. For example, the labor cost of a production employee at Texas Instruments is included as a product cost of the calculators manufactured. Exhibit 2-4 illustrates the relationship between product costs and cost-of-goods-sold expense.

Another term for product cost is **inventoriable cost,** since a product cost is stored as the cost of inventory until the goods are sold. In addition to retailers, wholesalers, and manufacturers, the concept of product cost is relevant to other producers of **inventoriable goods.** Agricultural firms, lumber companies, and mining firms are examples of nonmanufacturers that produce inventoriable goods. Apples, timber,

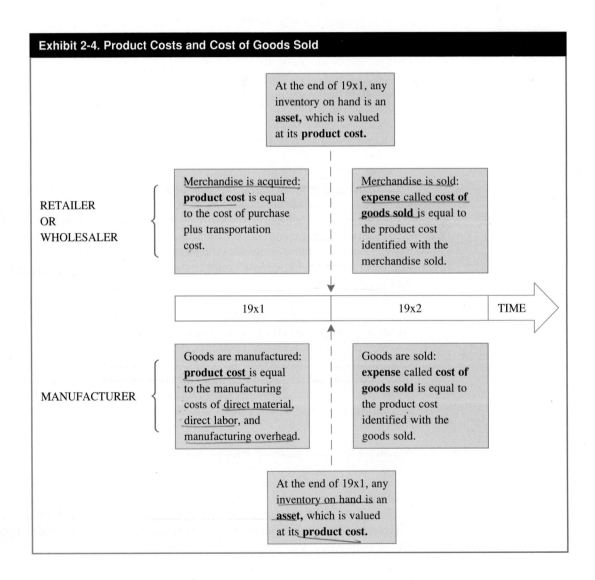

Exhibit 2-4. Product Costs and Cost of Goods Sold

At the end of 19x1, any inventory on hand is an **asset,** which is valued at its **product cost.**

RETAILER OR WHOLESALER — Merchandise is acquired: **product cost** is equal to the cost of purchase plus transportation cost.

Merchandise is sold: **expense** called **cost of goods sold** is equal to the product cost identified with the merchandise sold.

19x1 | 19x2 | TIME

MANUFACTURER — Goods are manufactured: **product cost** is equal to the manufacturing costs of direct material, direct labor, and manufacturing overhead.

Goods are sold: **expense** called **cost of goods sold** is equal to the product cost identified with the goods sold.

At the end of 19x1, any inventory on hand is an **asset,** which is valued at its **product cost.**

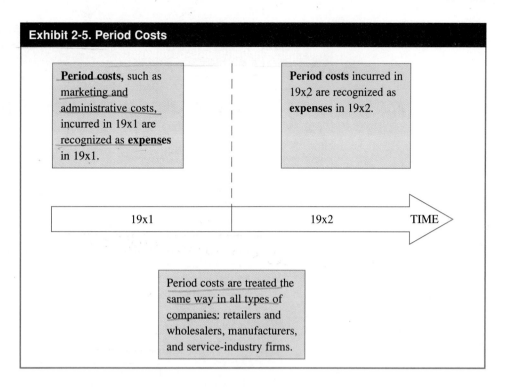

Exhibit 2-5. Period Costs

Period costs, such as marketing and administrative costs, incurred in 19x1 are recognized as **expenses** in 19x1.

Period costs incurred in 19x2 are recognized as **expenses** in 19x2.

| 19x1 | 19x2 | TIME |

Period costs are treated the same way in all types of companies: retailers and wholesalers, manufacturers, and service-industry firms.

coal, and other such goods are inventoried at their product cost until the time period during which they are sold.

All costs that are not product costs are called **period costs.** These costs are identified with the period of time in which they are incurred rather than with units of purchased or produced goods. Period costs are recognized as expenses during the time period in which they are incurred. All research and development, marketing, and administrative costs are treated as period costs. This is true in manufacturing, retail, and service industry firms. Examples of period costs are salaries of sales personnel, advertising expenditures, depreciation of office equipment, salaries of top management, and the costs of running product-research programs. Exhibit 2-5 illustrates the nature of period costs.

COSTS ON FINANCIAL STATEMENTS

The distinction between product costs and period costs is emphasized by examining financial statements from three different types of firms.

Income Statement

Exhibit 2-6 displays recent income statements, in highly summarized form, from Bristol-Myers Company, Wal-Mart Stores, Inc., and USAir Group, Inc. These companies are from three different industries. Bristol-Myers is a manufacturer of various household and medical products. Wal-Mart Stores is a large retail firm with merchandising operations throughout most of the nation. Representing the service industry is USAir, a major airline with operations across the United States.

Selling and administrative costs are period costs on all three income statements shown in Exhibit 2-6. For example, Bristol-Myers lists $1,104,300,000 of marketing,

**Exhibit 2-6. Income Statements from Three Different Industries
(all figures in thousands of dollars)**

Bristol-Myers Company
Statement of Earnings for a Recent Year

Value measured by product costs → Net sales	$4,189,400
Cost of goods sold	1,409,100
Gross margin	2,780,300
Less expenses:	
Marketing, selling, and administrative	1,104,300
Advertising and product promotion	743,800
Research and development, and other	151,700
Earnings before income taxes	780,500
Provision for income taxes	308,100
Net earnings	$ 472,400

Wal-Mart Stores, Inc.
Statement of Income for a Recent Year

Revenues:	
Net sales	$8,451,489
Rental revenue (from licensed departments)	13,011
Other revenue (net)	42,116
Total	$8,506,616
Value measured by product costs → Less expenses:	
Cost of sales	6,361,271
Operating, selling, and general and administrative expenses	1,485,210
Interest expense	56,543
Income before income taxes	603,592
Provision for federal and state income taxes	276,119
Net income	$ 327,473

selling, and administrative expenses. Travel agency commissions, a selling expense on USAir's income statement, amount to $105,567,000.

For Bristol-Myers, the costs of manufactured inventory are product costs. Direct-material, direct-labor, and manufacturing overhead costs are stored in inventory until the time period when the products are sold. Then the product costs of the inventory sold become cost of goods sold, an expense on the income statement. The following formula is used to determine cost of goods sold for a particular time period.

Exhibit 2-6. (continued)

USAir Group, Inc.
Statement of Operations for a Recent Year

Operating revenues:

Passenger	$1,520,682
Freight, express and mail	49,819
Other	59,195
	1,629,696

Less operating expenses:

Employee wages and benefits	584,579
Aviation fuel	310,921
Travel agency commissions	105,567
Rentals and landing fees	70,180
Aircraft maintenance	47,719
Depreciation and amortization	66,413
Other	252,449
Operating income	191,868
Add other income and expenses	12,275
Income before provision for income taxes	204,143
Provision for income taxes	82,500
Net income	$ 121,643

| **Beginning inventory of finished goods** | + | **cost of goods manufactured during period** | − | **ending inventory of finished goods** | = | **cost-of-goods-sold expense** |

In this formula, the **cost of goods manufactured** during a particular time period includes the following elements:

1. Cost of direct materials consumed in production during the period
2. Direct-labor costs incurred during the period
3. Manufacturing overhead costs incurred during the period

The accounting procedures used to accumulate these costs will be covered in detail in Chapters 3 and 4.

Product costs for Wal-Mart include all costs of acquiring merchandise inventory for resale. These product costs are stored in inventory until the time period during which the merchandise is sold. Then these costs become cost of goods sold. (Wal-Mart uses the term "cost of sales.")

There are no inventoried product costs at USAir. Although this firm does engage in the production of air transportation services, its service output is consumed as soon as it is produced. Service industry firms, such as USAir, Chase Manhattan Bank,

Sheraton Hotels, Nationwide Insurance, and McDonald's Corporation, generally refer to the costs of producing services as **operating expenses.** Operating expenses are treated as period costs and are expensed during the periods in which they are incurred. USAir includes costs such as employee wages, aviation fuel, and aircraft maintenance in operating expenses for the period.

Balance Sheet

Since retailers, wholesalers, and manufacturers sell inventoriable products, their balance sheets are also affected by product costs. Exhibit 2-7 displays the current-assets section from recent balance sheets of Bristol-Myers and Wal-Mart. Included in the current-assets section of each of these balance sheets is inventory. Manufacturers, such as Bristol-Myers, have three types of inventory. **Raw-materials** inventory includes all materials before they are placed into production. **Work-in-process** inventory refers to manufactured products that are only partially completed at the date when the balance sheet is prepared. **Finished-goods** inventory refers to manufactured goods that are complete and ready for sale. The values of the work-in-process and finished-goods inventories are measured by their product costs.

On the Wal-Mart balance sheet, the cost of acquiring merchandise is listed as the value of the merchandise inventories.

Exhibit 2-7. Partial Balance Sheets for a Manufacturer and a Retailer (all figures in thousands of dollars)

Bristol-Myers Company
Partial Balance Sheet for a Recent Year

Current assets:

	Cash and time deposits	$ 215,600
	Marketable securities	543,800
	Accounts receivable (net)	612,900
Value measured by product costs →	Other receivables	65,300
	Inventories	592,800
	Prepaid expenses	64,700
	Prepaid taxes	74,400
	Total current assets	$2,169,500

Wal-Mart Stores, Inc.
Partial Balance Sheet for a Recent Year

Current assets:

	Cash	$ 9,250
	Short-term money-market investments	165,168
Value measured by product costs →	Receivables	57,662
	Inventories	1,338,168
	Prepaid expenses	11,617
	Other	152,410
	Total current assets	$1,734,275

ECONOMIC CHARACTERISTICS OF COSTS

In addition to accounting cost classifications, such as product costs and period costs, managerial accountants also employ economic concepts in classifying costs. Such concepts are often useful in helping accountants decide what cost information is relevant to the decisions faced by the organization's managers. Several of the most important economic cost concepts are discussed next.

Opportunity Costs

An **opportunity cost** is defined as the benefit that is sacrificed when the choice of one action precludes taking an alternative course of action. If beef and fish are the available choices for dinner, the opportunity cost of eating beef is the foregone pleasure associated with eating fish.

Opportunity costs arise in many business decisions. For example, suppose a baseball manufacturer receives a special order for softballs from the city of Boston. If the firm accepts the softball order, it will not have enough productive capacity (labor and machine time) to produce its usual output of baseballs for sale to a large chain of sporting-goods stores. The opportunity cost of accepting the softball order is the foregone benefit from the baseball production that cannot be achieved. This foregone benefit is measured by the potential revenue from the baseball sales minus the cost of manufacturing the baseballs.

Opportunity costs also arise in personal decisions. The opportunity cost of a student's college education includes the salary that is foregone as a result of not taking a full-time job during the student's years in college.

From an economic perspective, a dollar of opportunity cost associated with an action should be treated as equivalent to a dollar of out-of-pocket cost. **Out-of-pocket costs** are those that require the payment of cash or other assets as a result of their incurrence. The out-of-pocket costs associated with the softball order consist of the manufacturing costs required to produce the softballs. In making the decision to accept or reject the softball order, the firm's management should consider *both* the out-of-pocket cost and the opportunity cost of the order.

Studies by behavioral scientists and economists have shown that many people have a tendency to ignore or downplay the importance of opportunity costs. For example, in one study people were asked if they would pay $500 for two 50-yard-line tickets to the Super Bowl. Most people responded that they would not. However, many of the same people said that they would not sell the Super Bowl tickets for $500 if they were given the tickets free of charge. These people refused to incur the $500 out-of-pocket cost of buying the Super Bowl tickets. However, they were willing to incur the $500 opportunity cost of going to the game rather than sell the tickets. In each case, a couple who attends the game ends up $500 poorer than a couple who does not attend the game. (Try surveying your friends with this scenario.)

Behavior such as that illustrated in the Super Bowl example is economically inconsistent. Ignoring or downplaying the importance of opportunity costs can result in inconsistent and faulty business decisions.

Sunk Costs

Sunk costs are costs that have been incurred in the past. Consequently, they do not affect future costs and cannot be changed by any current or future action. Examples of such costs include the acquisition cost of equipment previously purchased and the manufacturing cost of inventory on hand. Regardless of the current usefulness of the equipment or the inventory, the costs of acquiring them cannot be changed by any prospective action. Hence these costs are irrelevant to all future decisions.

Suppose, for example, that a university's traffic department purchased a minicomputer to assist in the vehicle registration process. A year has passed, the computer's warranty has expired, and the computer is not working well. An investigation reveals that this brand of computer is very sensitive to humidity and temperature changes. The traffic department is located in an old building with poor heating and no air-conditioning. As a result, the computer works only intermittently, repair bills have been high, and the office staff is fed up. The office manager requests that the department director junk the computer and instruct the staff to return to the old manual registration system. The director responds by insisting, "We can't afford to junk the computer! We paid $3,400 for it."

This illustration is a typical example of the inappropriate attention paid to sunk costs. The $3,400 paid for the minicomputer is sunk. No future decision about the computer or the office's procedures can affect that cost. Future decisions should be based on future costs, such as the computer repair bills or the costs of upgrading the building's heating and air-conditioning systems.

Although it is incorrect, from an economic perspective, to allow sunk costs to affect future decisions, people often do so. It is human nature to attempt to justify past decisions. When there is a perceived need to demonstrate competence, either to themselves or to others, managers may seek to justify their decisions. The response of the traffic department director that "We can't afford to junk the computer!" may represent the director's need to justify the past decision to purchase the computer. It is important for managerial accountants to be aware of such behavioral tendencies. Such an awareness enables the accountant to prepare the most relevant data for managers' decisions, and sometimes to train the managers in using the information.

Differential Costs

A **differential cost** is the amount by which the cost differs under two alternative actions. Suppose, for example, that a county government is considering two competing sites for a new landfill. If the northern site is chosen, the annual cost of transporting refuse to the site is projected at $85,000. If the southern site is selected, annual transportation charges are expected to be $70,000. The annual differential cost of transporting refuse is calculated as follows:

Annual cost of transporting refuse to northern site. $85,000
Annual cost of transporting refuse to southern site. 70,000
Annual differential cost $15,000

Differential costs are also known as **incremental costs.** In the landfill example, the annual incremental cost of refuse transportation is $15,000 if the site is moved from the southern location to the northern location. Differential or incremental costs are found in a variety of economic decisions. The additional cost incurred by Gulliver's Travels, a travel agency, in locating a new office in the suburbs is the incremental cost of the new business location. The difference in the total cost incurred by the travel agency with or without the suburban location is the differential cost of the decision whether to establish the new office. Decisions about establishing new airline

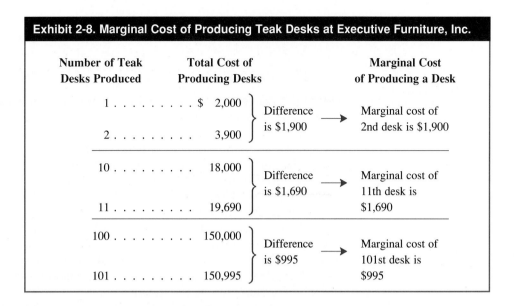

Exhibit 2-8. Marginal Cost of Producing Teak Desks at Executive Furniture, Inc.

Number of Teak Desks Produced	Total Cost of Producing Desks		Marginal Cost of Producing a Desk
1	$ 2,000	Difference is $1,900 →	Marginal cost of 2nd desk is $1,900
2	3,900		
10	18,000	Difference is $1,690 →	Marginal cost of 11th desk is $1,690
11	19,690		
100	150,000	Difference is $995 →	Marginal cost of 101st desk is $995
101	150,995		

routes, adding additional shifts in a manufacturing firm, or increasing the nursing staff in a hospital all involve differential costs.

Marginal Costs and Average Costs

 A special case of the differential cost concept is the **marginal cost,** which is the extra cost incurred when one additional unit is produced. The additional cost incurred by Executive Furniture, Inc., when one additional teak desk is made is the marginal cost of manufacturing the desk. The table in Exhibit 2-8 shows how marginal cost can change across different ranges of production quantities.

Marginal costs typically differ across different ranges of production quantities because the efficiency of the production process changes. At Executive Furniture, Inc. the marginal cost of producing a desk declines as output increases. It is much more efficient for the company to manufacture 101 desks than to make only one.

It is important to distinguish between *marginal costs* and *average costs.* In the Executive Furniture example, the marginal cost of the second desk is $1,900. However, the average cost per unit when two desks are manufactured is $3,900 divided by 2, or $1,950. Similarly, the marginal cost of the eleventh desk is $1,690, but the average cost per unit when 11 desks are produced is $1,790 (calculated by dividing $19,690 by 11). What is the marginal cost of the 101st desk? The average cost per unit when 101 desks are manufactured?[2]

 To summarize, the marginal cost of production is the extra cost incurred when one more unit is produced. The **average cost per unit** is the total cost, for whatever quantity is manufactured, divided by the number of units manufactured. Marginal costs and average costs arise in a variety of economic situations. A Harvard University administrator might be interested in the marginal cost of educating one additional student, and a Toyota executive might want to know the marginal cost of

[2] Marginal cost of 101st desk is $995 (from Exhibit 2-8). Average cost per unit when 101 desks are produced is $1,495 ($150,995 ÷ 101).

producing one more Toyota van. A bus tour company manager might be interested in the average cost per mile on the Pittsburgh to New York City route.

COSTS AND BENEFITS OF INFORMATION

Many different cost concepts have been explored in this chapter. An important task of the managerial accountant is to determine which of these cost concepts is most appropriate in each situation. The accountant attempts to structure the organization's accounting information system to record data that will be useful for a variety of purposes. The benefits of measuring and classifying costs in a particular way are realized through the improvements in planning, control, and decision making that the information facilitates.

Another important task of the managerial accountant is to weigh the benefits of providing information against the costs of generating, communicating, and using that information. Some accountants, eager to show that they have not overlooked anything, tend to provide too much information. But when managers receive more data than they can utilize effectively, **information overload** occurs. Struggling to process large amounts of information, managers may be unable to recognize the most important facts. In deciding how much and what type of information to provide, managerial accountants should consider these human limitations. The following example is a case in point.

ILLUSTRATION FROM MANAGEMENT ACCOUNTING PRACTICE

Dow Chemical Company

The controller for Dow Chemical Company suspected that too much internal accounting information was being provided for managers to use effectively. A complete set of monthly financial statements was provided to managers at all levels in the company. The controller realized that a lot of "time was being devoted to analysis of the data; but he questioned whether too much analysis was taking place. Were better decisions being made as a result of the faster information flow? Was the flow of information the most efficient?"

To follow up on his hunch, the controller and his staff interviewed managers throughout the company to determine what information was really needed. Managers were asked, "Who needs the information?" and "How is the information used?" The controller's survey revealed that too many reports were being provided, and managers were spending an excessive amount of time on analyzing the reports. As a result, the controller decided to switch to a quarterly internal-reporting cycle. Elimination of the monthly reports enabled the company to achieve large cost savings on information provision and managerial analysis. Yet the managers could do their jobs just as well with the quarterly reports.[3]

CHAPTER SUMMARY

The term *cost* is familiar to everyone. We all discuss the cost of a sweater, a movie ticket, or a semester's tuition. Yet, as we have seen in this chapter, the word *cost* can have a variety of meanings in different situations. Managerial accountants often find

[3] Dennis Dankoski, "Dow Opts for Less — and Gains," *Management Accounting,* June 1986, pp. 56, 57.

it useful to classify costs in different ways for different purposes. An understanding of cost terms, concepts, and classifications is fundamental in any study of managerial accounting.

Several cost classifications are defined and illustrated in the chapter. Fixed and variable costs are defined by the behavior of total cost as the organization's activity level changes. Direct and indirect costs refer to the ability of the accountant to trace costs to various departments in the organization. The terms *controllable* and *uncontrollable* are used to describe the extent to which a manager can influence a cost. Costs are classified into such functional categories as manufacturing costs, marketing costs, and administrative costs. Manufacturing costs are further subdivided into direct-material, direct-labor, and manufacturing overhead costs. The terms *product cost* and *period cost* refer to the timing with which costs become expenses.

Economic concepts are also important in describing costs. An opportunity cost is the benefit foregone because the choice of one action precludes another action. Sunk costs are costs incurred in the past that cannot be altered by a current or future decision. The term *differential cost* or *incremental cost* refers to the difference in the costs incurred under two alternative actions. Marginal cost is defined as the cost of producing one additional unit. Finally, the average cost per unit is the total cost for whatever quantity is produced, divided by the number of units produced.

These cost terms are an integral part of the specialized language of business administration.

REVIEW PROBLEMS ON COST CLASSIFICATIONS

Problem 1

Several costs incurred by Myrtle Beach Golf Equipment, Inc. are listed below. For each cost, indicate which of the following classifications best describe the cost. More than one classification may apply to the same cost item. For example, a cost may be both a variable cost *and* a product cost.

Cost Classifications

(a) Variable
(b) Fixed
(c) Period
(d) Product
(e) Administrative
(f) Marketing
(g) Manufacturing
(h) Research and development
(i) Direct material
(j) Direct labor
(k) Manufacturing overhead

Cost Items

1 Metal used in golf clubs.
2. Salary of plant manager.
3. Cost of natural gas used to heat factory.
4. Commissions paid to sales personnel.
5. Wages paid to employees who assemble golf bags.

C ,B ,H **6.** Salary of engineer who is working on a prototype of a new solar-powered golf cart.

B ,E ,C **7.** Depreciation on the word processing equipment used by the company president's secretary.

Problem 2

Listed below are several costs incurred in the loan department of Suwanee Bank and Trust Company. For each cost, indicate which of the following classifications best describe the cost. More than one classification may apply to the same cost item.

Cost Classifications

(a) Controllable by the loan department manager
(b) Uncontrollable by the loan department manager
(c) Direct cost of the loan department
(d) Indirect cost of the loan department
(e) Differential cost
(f) Marginal cost
(g) Opportunity cost
(h) Sunk cost
(i) Out-of-pocket cost

Cost Items

1. The salary of the loan department manager.
2. Cost of office supplies used in the loan department.
3. Cost of the department's personal computers purchased by the loan department manager last year.
4. Cost of general advertising by the bank, which is allocated to the loan department.
5. The revenue that the loan department would have generated for the bank if a branch loan office had been located downtown instead of in the next county.
6. The difference in the cost incurred by the bank when one additional loan application is processed.

Solution to Review Problems

Problem 1	Problem 2
1. a, d, g, i	**1.** b, c, i
2. b, d, g, k	**2.** a, c, i
3. a, d, g, k	**3.** a, c, h
4. a, c, f	**4.** b, d, i
5. a, d, g, j	**5.** g
6. b, c, h	**6.** e, f
7. b, c, e	

KEY TERMS Activity, p. 26; **Administrative costs,** p. 33; **Average cost per unit,** p. 41; **Controllable cost,** p. 30; **Conversion costs,** p. 32; **Cost drivers,** p. 26; **Cost of goods manufactured,** p. 37; **Cost of goods sold,** p. 34; **Cost structure,** p. 32; **Differential cost,** p. 40; **Direct cost,** p. 29; **Direct-labor**

cost, p. 31; **Direct material,** p. 31; **Distribution costs,** p. 33; **Expense,** p. 33; **Finished goods,** p. 38; **Fixed cost,** p. 26; **Idle time,** p. 32; **Incremental costs,** p. 40; **Indirect cost,** p. 29; **Indirect labor,** p. 31; **Indirect material,** p. 31; **Information overload,** p. 42; **Inventoriable cost,** p. 34; **Inventoriable goods,** p. 34; **Manufacturing costs,** p. 30; **Manufacturing overhead,** p. 31; **Marginal cost,** p. 41; **Marketing costs,** p. 33; **Merchandise costs,** p. 33; **Operating expenses,** p. 38; **Opportunity cost,** p. 39; **Out-of-pocket costs,** p. 39; **Overtime premium,** p. 31; **Period costs,** p. 35; **Prime costs,** p. 32; **Product cost,** p. 34; **Raw material,** p. 38; **Research and development (R & D) costs,** p. 33; **Selling costs,** p. 33; **Service departments,** p. 31; **Service firm,** p. 32; **Sunk costs,** p. 39; **Variable cost,** p. 26; **Work in process,** p. 38.

REVIEW QUESTIONS

2-1. What is meant by the phrase "different costs for different purposes"?

2-2. Give examples to illustrate how the city of Los Angeles could use cost information in planning, controlling costs, and making decisions.

2-3. Distinguish between fixed costs and variable costs.

2-4. How does the fixed cost per unit change as the level of activity (or cost driver) increases? Why?

2-5. How does the variable cost per unit change as the level of activity (or cost driver) increases? Why?

2-6. List three direct costs of the food and beverage department in a hotel. List three indirect costs of the department.

2-7. List three costs that are likely to be controllable by a city's airport manager. List three costs that are likely to be uncontrollable by the manager.

2-8. Why is the cost of idle time treated as manufacturing overhead?

2-9. Explain why overtime premium is included in manufacturing overhead.

2-10. Give two examples of each of the following costs, using well-known organizations: merchandise costs, selling costs, distribution costs, administrative costs, and research and development costs.

2-11. Distinguish between product and period costs.

2-12. What is the most important difference between a manufacturing firm and a service industry firm, with regard to the classification of costs as product costs or period costs?

2-13. Why are product costs also called inventoriable costs?

2-14. Distinguish between out-of-pocket costs and opportunity costs.

2-15. Define the terms *sunk cost, differential cost,* and *information overload.*

2-16. Distinguish between marginal and average costs.

2-17. Think about the process of registering for classes at your college or university. What additional information would you like to have before you register? How would it help you? What sort of information might create information overload for you?

2-18. Two years ago the manager of a large department store purchased new cash registers costing $50,000. A salesman recently tried to sell the manager a new automated checkout system for the store. The new system would save the store a substantial amount of money each year. The recently purchased cash registers could be sold in the secondhand market for $20,000. The store manager refused to listen to the salesman, saying, "I just bought those cash registers. I can't get rid of them until I get my money's worth out of them."

   What type of cost is the cost of purchasing the old cash registers? What common behavioral tendency is the manager exhibiting?

2-19. Indicate whether each of the following costs is a direct cost of the restaurant in a hotel.
   a. Cost of food served.
   b. Chef's salary and fringe benefits.

    c. Part of the cost of maintaining the grounds around the hotel, which is allocated to the restaurant.

    d. Part of the cost of advertising the hotel, which is allocated to the restaurant.

2-20. Which of the following costs are likely to be controllable by the chief of nursing in a hospital?

    a. Cost of medication administered.

    b. Cost of overtime paid to nurses due to scheduling errors.

    c. Cost of depreciation of hospital beds.

EXERCISES   *Exercise 2-21*   *Cost of Goods Manufactured and Sold.* For each case below, find the missing amount.

	Case I	Case II	Case III
Beginning inventory of finished goods..............	$10,000	?	$ 5,000
+ Cost of goods manufactured during period..........	95,000	$428,000	?
− Ending inventory of finished goods	8,000	98,000	21,000
Cost of goods sold.............................	?	405,000	304,000

Exercise 2-22   *Idle Time.* A foundry employee worked a normal 40-hour shift, but four hours were idle due to a small fire in the plant. The employee earns $17 per hour.

REQUIRED:

1. Calculate the employee's total compensation for the week.
2. How much of this compensation is a direct-labor cost? How much is overhead?

Exercise 2-23   *Overtime Cost.* A loom operator in a textile factory earns $14.00 per hour. The employee earns $20.00 for overtime hours. The operator worked 45 hours during the first week of May, instead of the usual 40 hours.

REQUIRED:

1. Compute the loom operator's compensation for the week.
2. Calculate the employee's total overtime premium for the week.
3. How much of the employee's total compensation for the week is direct-labor cost? How much is overhead?

Exercise 2-24   *Fixed and Variable Costs; Hotel.* A hotel pays the phone company $100 per month plus $.25 for each call made. During January 6,000 calls were made. In February 5,000 calls were made.

REQUIRED:

1. Calculate the hotel's phone bills for January and February.
2. Calculate the cost per phone call in January and in February.
3. Separate the January phone bill into its fixed and variable components.

Exercise 2-25   *Marginal versus Average Costs.* Refer to the preceding exercise.

REQUIRED:

1. What is the marginal cost of one additional phone call in January?
2. What was the average cost of a phone call in January?

Exercise 2-26 Computing Costs; Government Agency. The state Department of Education owns a computer system, which its employees use for word processing and keeping track of educational statistics. The governor's office recently began using this computer also. As a result of the increased usage, the demands on the computer soon exceeded its capacity. The director of the Department of Education was soon forced to lease several personal computers to meet the computing needs of her employees. The annual cost of leasing the equipment is $12,500.

REQUIRED:

1. What type of cost is this $12,500?
2. Should this cost be associated with the governor's office or the Department of Education? Why?

Exercise 2-27 Economic Characteristics of Costs. Suppose you paid $50 for a ticket to see your university's football team compete in a bowl game. Someone offered to buy your ticket for $75, but you decided to go to the game.

REQUIRED:

1. What did it really cost you to see the game?
2. What type of cost is this?

Exercise 2-28 Economic Characteristics of Costs. Martin Shrood purchased a vacant lot for $10,000, because he heard that a shopping mall was going to be built on the other side of the road. He figured that he could make a bundle by putting in a fast-food outlet on the site. As it turned out, the rumor was false. A sanitary landfill was located on the other side of the road, and Martin's land was worthless.

REQUIRED: What type of cost is the $10,000 that Martin paid for the vacant lot?

Exercise 2-29 Differential Cost. Satronics, Inc. manufactures communications satellites used in TV signal transmission. The firm currently purchases one component for its satellites from a European firm. A Satronics engineering team has found a way to use the company's own component, part number A200, instead of the European component. However, the Satronics component must be modified at a cost of $500 per part. The European component costs $8,500 per part. Satronics' part number A200 costs $4,900 before it is modified. Satronics currently uses 10 of the European components per year.

REQUIRED: Calculate the annual differential cost between Satronics' two production alternatives.

Exercise 2-30 Marginal Costs. List the costs that would likely be included in each of the following marginal-cost calculations.

1. The marginal cost of serving one additional customer in a restaurant.
2. The marginal cost of one additional passenger on a jet flight.
3. The marginal cost of adding a flight from Honolulu to Seattle.
4. The marginal cost of keeping a travel agency open one additional hour on Saturdays.
5. The marginal cost of manufacturing one additional pair of water skis.

Exercise 2-31 Fixed and Variable Costs; Automobile Service. Mighty Muffler, Inc. operates an automobile service facility, which specializes in replacing mufflers on compact cars. The following table shows the costs incurred during a month when 600 mufflers were replaced.

	Number of Muffler Replacements		
	500	600	700
Total costs:			
Fixed costs	a	$42,000	b
Variable costs	c	30,000	d
Total costs	e	$72,000	f
Cost per muffler replacement:			
Fixed cost	g	h	i
Variable cost	j	k	l
Total cost per muffler replacement	m	n	o

(handwritten annotations: "Constant" over the fixed costs row, "Constant" over the variable cost row)

REQUIRED: Fill in the missing amounts, labeled (a) through (o), in the table.

PROBLEMS *Problem 2-32 Cost Terminology.* The following cost data for 19x0 pertain to Heartstrings, Inc., a greeting card manufacturer:

Direct material used in production	$1,100,000
Advertising expense	120,000
Depreciation on factory building	115,000
Direct labor: wages	485,000
Cost of finished goods inventory at year-end	115,000
Indirect labor: wages	140,000
Production supervisor's salary	45,000
Service department costs*	100,000
Direct labor: fringe benefits	95,000
Indirect labor: fringe benefits	30,000
Fringe benefits for production supervisor	9,000
Total overtime premiums paid	55,000
Cost of idle time: production employees	40,000
Administrative costs	150,000
Rental of office space for sales personnel†	15,000
Sales commissions	5,000
Product promotion costs	10,000

(handwritten annotations: "Sunk" next to Depreciation on factory building and Cost of finished goods inventory; "Opp." next to Rental of office space for sales personnel)

* All services are provided to manufacturing departments.
† The rental of sales space was made necessary when the sales offices were converted to storage space for raw material.

REQUIRED:

1. Compute each of the following costs for 19x0: (a) total prime costs, (b) total manufacturing overhead costs, (c) total conversion costs, (d) total product costs, and (e) total period costs.
2. One of the costs listed above is an opportunity cost. Identify this cost, and exlain why it is an opportunity cost.
3. One of the costs listed above is a sunk cost. Identify this cost, and explain why it is a sunk cost.

Problem 2-33   Variable Costs; Graphical and Tabular Analyses. Wilcox Sheet Metal, Inc. incurs a variable cost of $40 per pound for raw material to produce a special alloy used in manufacturing aircraft.

REQUIRED:

1. Draw a graph of the firm's raw material cost, showing the total cost at the following production levels: 10,000 pounds, 20,000 pounds, and 30,000 pounds.
2. Prepare a table that shows the unit cost and total cost of raw material at the following production levels: 1 pound, 10 pounds, and 10,000 pounds.

Problem 2-34   Fixed Costs; Graphical and Tabular Analyses. Hightide Upholstery Company manufactures a special fabric used to upholster the seats in power boats. The company's annual fixed production cost is $100,000.

REQUIRED:

1. Draw a graph of the company's fixed production cost showing the total cost at the following production levels of upholstery fabric: 10,000 yards, 20,000 yards, and 30,000 yards.
2. Prepare a table that shows the unit cost and the total cost for the firm's fixed production costs at the following production levels: 1 yard, 10 yards, and 10,000 yards.
3. Prepare a graph that shows the unit cost for the company's fixed production cost at the following production levels: 10,000 yards, 20,000 yards, and 30,000 yards.

Problem 2-35   Direct, Indirect, Controllable, and Uncontrollable Costs. For each of the following costs, indicate whether the amount is a direct or indirect cost of the equipment maintenance department. Also indicate whether each cost is at least partially controllable by the department supervisor.

1. Depreciation on the building space occupied by the maintenance department.
2. Idle time of maintenance department employees.
3. Cost of plant manager's salary, which is allocated to the maintenance department.
4. Cost of property taxes allocated to the maintenance department.
5. Cost of electricity used in the maintenance department.

Problem 2-36   Product Costs and Period Costs. Indicate for each of the following costs whether it is a product cost or a period cost.

1. Cost incurred by a department store chain to transport merchandise to its stores.
2. Cost of grapes purchased by a winery.
3. Depreciation on pizza ovens in a pizza restaurant.
4. Wages of aircraft mechanics employed by an airline.
5. Wages of drill-press operators in a manufacturing plant.
6. Cost of food in a TV dinner.
7. Cost of plant manager in a computer production facility.
8. Wages of security personnel in a department store.
9. Cost of utilities in a manufacturing facility.

Problem 2-37   Direct and Indirect Labor. Calvin Cutlery manufactures kitchen knives. One of the employees, whose job is to cut out wooden knife handles, worked 46 hours during a week in January. The employee earns $12 per hour for a 40-hour week. For additional hours the employee is paid an overtime rate of $16 per hour. The employee's time was spent as follows:

Regular duties involving cutting out knife handles . . . . 36 hours
General shop cleanup duties . . . . 9 hours
Idle time due to power outage . . . . 1 hour

REQUIRED:

1. Calculate the total cost of the employee's wages during the week described above.
2. Determine the portion of this cost to be classified in each of the following categories:
   a. Direct labor
   b. Manufacturing overhead (idle time)
   c. Manufacturing overhead (overtime premium)
   d. Manufacturing overhead (indirect labor)

Problem 2-38 *Interpretation of Accounting Reports.* Refer to Exhibit 2-6, and answer the following questions.

REQUIRED:

1. List the major differences between the income statements shown for Bristol-Myers Company, Wal-Mart Stores, Inc., and USAir Group, Inc.
2. Explain how cost accounting data were used to prepare these income statements.
3. On the income statement for USAir Group, Inc., where would the ticket agents' salaries be shown? Where would the costs of the computer equipment used to keep track of reservations be included on the statement?
4. On the income statement for Wal-Mart Stores, Inc., where would the cost of newspaper advertising be shown? How about the cost of merchandise?
5. Refer to the income statement for Bristol-Myers Company. Where would the salary of a research chemist be shown? How about the salary of a production employee? Where would the cost of the ingredients in the company's products be included on the statement?

Problem 2-39 *Cost Classifications; Hotel.* Several costs incurred by Water's Edge Hotel and Restaurant are listed below. For each cost, indicate which of the following classifications best describe the cost. More than one classification may apply to the same cost item.

Cost Classifications

(a) Direct cost of the food and beverage department
(b) Indirect cost of the food and beverage department
(c) Controllable by the kitchen manager
(d) Uncontrollable by the kitchen manager
(e) Controllable by the hotel general manager
(f) Uncontrollable by the hotel general manager
(g) Differential cost
(h) Marginal cost
(i) Opportunity cost
(j) Sunk cost
(k) Out-of-pocket cost

Cost Items

1. The difference in the total cost incurred by the hotel when one additional guest is registered.
2. The cost of food used in the kitchen.
3. The cost of general advertising by the hotel, which is allocated to the food and beverage department.
4. The cost of space (depreciation) occupied by the kitchen.
5. The cost of space (depreciation) occupied by a sauna next to the pool. The space could otherwise have been used for a magazine and book shop.
6. The profit that would have been earned in a magazine and book shop, if the hotel had one.
7. The discount on room rates given as a special offer for a "Labor Day Getaway Special."
8. The wages earned by table-service personnel.
9. The salary of the kitchen manager.
10. The cost of the refrigerator purchased 13 months ago. The unit was covered by a warranty for 12 months, during which time it worked perfectly. It conked out after 13 months, despite an original estimate that it would last five years.
11. The hotel has two options for obtaining fresh pies, cakes, and pastries. The goodies can be purchased from a local bakery for approximately $1,600 per month, or they can be made in the hotel's kitchen. To make the pastries on the premises, the hotel will have to hire a part-time pastry chef. This will cost $600 per month. The cost of ingredients will amount to roughly $800 per month. Thus, the savings from making the goods in the hotel's kitchen amount to $200 per month.
12. The cost of dishes broken by kitchen employees.
13. The cost of leasing a computer used for reservations, payroll, and general hotel accounting.
14. The cost of a pool service that cleans and maintains the hotel's swimming pool.
15. The wages of the hotel's maintenance employees, who spent 12 hours (at $15 per hour) repairing the dishwasher in the kitchen.

Problem 2-40   Marginal Costs and Average Costs. Peter Marlas makes custom mooring covers for boats. Each mooring cover is hand sewn to fit a particular boat. If covers are made for two or more identical boats, each successive cover generally requires less time to make. Marlas has been approached by a local boat dealer to make mooring covers for all of the boats sold by the dealer. Marlas has developed the following cost schedule for mooring covers made to fit 17-foot outboard power boats.

Number of Mooring Covers Made	Total Cost of Covers
1	$ 450
2	850
3	1,210
4	1,540
5	1,850

REQUIRED: Compute the following:

1. Marginal cost of second mooring cover.
2. Marginal cost of fourth mooring cover.

3. Marginal cost of fifth mooring cover.
4. Average cost if two mooring covers are made.
5. Average cost if four mooring covers are made.
6. Average cost if five mooring covers are made.

Problem 2-41 Cost Classifications; Government Agency. The Department of Natural Resources is responsible for maintaining the state's parks and forest lands, stocking the lakes and rivers with fish, and generally overseeing the protection of the environment. Several costs incurred by the agency are listed below. For each cost, indicate which of the following classifications best describe the cost. More than one classification may apply to the same cost item.

Cost Classifications

(a) Variable
(b) Fixed
(c) Controllable by the department director
(d) Uncontrollable by the department director
(e) Differential cost
(f) Marginal cost
(g) Opportunity cost
(h) Sunk cost
(i) Out-of-pocket cost
(j) Direct cost of the agency
(k) Indirect cost of the agency
(l) Direct cost of providing a particular service
(m) Indirect cost of providing a particular service

Cost Items

1. Cost of live-trapping and moving beaver, which were creating a nuisance in recreational lakes.
2. Cost of the fish purchased from private hatcheries, which are used to stock the state's public waters.
3. The department director's salary.
4. Cost of containing naturally caused forest fires, which are threatening private property.
5. Cost of the automobiles used by the department's rangers. These cars were purchased by the state, and they would otherwise have been used by the state police.
6. The difference between (a) the cost of purchasing fish from private hatcheries and (b) the cost of running a state hatchery.
7. Cost of producing literature that describes the department's role in environmental protection. This literature is mailed free, upon request, to schools, county governments, libraries, and private citizens.
8. Cost of sending the department's hydroengineers to inspect one additional dam for stability and safety.
9. Cost of operating the state's computer services department, a portion of which is allocated to the Department of Natural Resources.
10. Cost of administrative supplies used in the agency's head office.
11. Cost of providing an 800 number for the state's residents to report environmental problems.

12. Cost of a ranger's wages, when the ranger is giving a talk about environmental protection to elementary school children.
13. Cost of direct-mailing to 1 million state residents a brochure explaining the benefits of voluntarily recycling cans and bottles.
14. The cost of producing a TV show to be aired on public television. The purpose of the show is to educate people on how to spot and properly dispose of hazardous waste.

Problem 2-42   Overtime Premiums and Fringe Benefit Costs; Airline. Great Plains Airways operates commuter flights in three midwestern states. Due to a political convention held in Topeka, the airline added several extra flights during a two-week period. Additional cabin crews were hired on a temporary basis. However, rather than hiring additional flight attendants, the airline used its current attendants on overtime. Monica Gaines worked the following schedule on August 10. All of Gaines's flights on that day were extra flights that the airline would not normally fly.

Regular time: 2 round-trip flights between Topeka and St. Louis (8 hours)
Overtime: 1 one-way flight from Topeka to Kansas City (3 hours)

Gaines earns $12 per hour plus time and a half for overtime. Fringe benefits cost the airline $3 per hour for any hour worked, regardless of whether it is a regular or overtime hour.

REQUIRED:

1. Compute the direct cost of compensating Gaines for her services on the flight from Topeka to Kansas City.
2. Compute the cost of Gaines's services that is an indirect cost.
3. How should the cost computed in requirement (2) be treated for cost accounting purposes?
4. Gaines ended her workday on August 10 in Kansas City. However, her next scheduled flight departed Topeka at 11:00 a.m. on August 11. This required Gaines to "dead-head" back to Topeka on an early-morning flight. This means she traveled from Kansas City to Topeka as a passenger, rather than as a working flight attendant. Since the morning flight from Kansas City to Topeka was full, Gaines displaced a paying customer. The revenue lost by the airline was $82. What type of cost is the $82? To what flight, if any, is it chargeable? Why?

Problem 2-43   Fixed and Variable Costs; Forecasting. Martin Electronics Corporation incurred the following costs during 19x0. The company sold all of its products manufactured during the year.

Direct materials	$1,000,000
Direct labor	1,200,000
Manufacturing overhead	
Utilities (primarily electricity)	140,000
Depreciation on plant and equipment	230,000
Insurance	160,000
Supervisory salaries	300,000
Property taxes	210,000
Selling costs	
Advertising	180,000
Sales commissions	90,000

Administrative costs

Salaries of top management and staff   350,000
Office supplies   40,000
Depreciation on building and equipment   80,000

During 19x0, the company operated at about half of its capacity, due to a slowdown in the economy. Prospects for 19x1 are slightly better, with the marketing manager forecasting a 20 percent growth in sales over the 19x0 level.

REQUIRED: Categorize each of the costs listed above as to whether it is most likely variable or fixed. Forecast the 19x1 cost amount for each of the cost items listed above.

Problem 2-44   Cost Classifications; Manufacturer. Outer Banks Shirt Shop manufactures T-shirts and decorates them with custom designs for retail sale on the premises. Several costs incurred by the company are listed below. For each cost, indicate which of the following classifications best describe the cost. More than one classification may apply to the same cost item.

Cost Classifications

(a) Variable
(b) Fixed
(c) Period
(d) Product
(e) Administrative
(f) Marketing
(g) Manufacturing
(h) Research and development
(i) Direct material
(j) Direct labor
(k) Manufacturing overhead

Cost Items

1. Cost of new sign in front of retail T-shirt shop.
2. Wages of the employee who repairs the firm's sewing machines.
3. Cost of fabric used in T-shirts.
4. Wages of shirtmakers.
5. Cost of electricity used in the sewing department.
6. Wages of T-shirt designers and painters.
7. Wages of sales personnel.
8. Depreciation on sewing machines.
9. Rent on the building. Part of the building's first floor is used to make and paint T-shirts. Part of it is used for a retail sales shop. The second floor is used for administrative offices and storage of raw material and finished goods.
10. Cost of daily advertisements in local media.
11. Wages of designers who experiment with new fabrics, paints, and T-shirts designs.
12. Cost of hiring a pilot to fly along the beach pulling a banner advertising the shop.
13. Salary of the owner's secretary.
14. Cost of repairing the gas furnace.
15. Cost of insurance for the production employees.

Problem 2-45   Economic Characteristics of Costs. The following terms are used to describe various economic characteristics of costs.

Opportunity cost   Differential cost
Out-of-pocket cost   Marginal cost
Sunk cost   Average cost

REQUIRED: Choose one of the terms listed above to characterize each of the amounts described below.

1. The cost of including one extra child in a day-care center.
2. The cost of merchandise inventory purchased two years ago, which is now obsolete.
3. The cost of feeding 500 children in a public school cafeteria is $750 per day, or $1.50 per child per day. What economic term describes this $1.50 cost?
4. The management of a high-rise office building uses 2,500 square feet of space in the building for its own management functions. This space could be rented for $250,000. What economic term describes this $250,000 in lost rental revenue?
5. The cost of building an automated assembly line in a factory is $800,000. The cost of building a manually operated assembly line is $350,000. What economic term is used to describe the difference between these two amounts?
6. Referring to the preceding question, what economic term is used to describe the $800,000 cost of building the automated assembly line?

Problem 2-46   Variable and Fixed Costs; Make or Buy a Component. Vermont Industries currently manufactures 30,000 units of part MR24 each month for use in production of several of its products. The facilities now used to produce part MR24 have a fixed monthly cost of $150,000 and a capacity to produce 84,000 units per month. If the company were to buy part MR24 from an outside supplier, the facilities would be idle, but its fixed costs would continue at 40 percent of their present amount. The variable production costs of part MR24 are $11 per unit.

REQUIRED:

1. If Vermont Industries continues to use 30,000 units of part MR24 each month, it would realize a net benefit by purchasing part MR24 from an outside supplier only if the supplier's unit price is less than what amount?
2. If Vermont Industries is able to obtain part MR24 from an outside supplier at a unit purchase price of $12.875, what is the monthly usage at which it will be indifferent between purchasing and making part MR24?

(CMA, adapted)

Problem 2-47   Unit Costs; Profit-Maximizing Output. The controller for Oneida Vineyards, Inc. has predicted the following costs at various levels of wine output.

	Wine Output (.75 Liter Bottles)		
	10,000 Bottles	**15,000 Bottles**	**20,000 Bottles**
Variable production costs.....................	$ 35,000	$ 52,500	$ 70,000
Fixed production costs	100,000	100,000	100,000
Variable selling and administrative costs...........	2,000	3,000	4,000
Fixed selling and administrative costs	40,000	40,000	40,000
Total	$177,000	$195,500	$214,000

The company's marketing manager has predicted the following prices for the firm's fine wines at various levels of sales.

	Wine Sales		
	10,000 Bottles	**15,000 Bottles**	**20,000 Bottles**
Sales price per .75-liter bottle	$18.00	$15.00	$12.00

REQUIRED:

1. Calculate the unit costs of wine production and sales at each level of output. At what level of output is the unit cost minimized?
2. Calculate the company's profit at each level of production. Assume that the company will sell all of its output. At what production level is profit maximized?
3. Which of the three output levels is best for the company?
4. Why does the unit cost of wine decrease as the output level increases? Why might the sales price per bottle decline as sales volume increases?

Problem 2-48 Economic Characteristics of Costs; Multiple Choice. Grady Corporation is considering dropping one of its products that requires special equipment. Unit data for the product are as follows:

Selling price.		$14.00
Costs:		
Direct materials	$2.40	
Direct labor.	3.60	
Manufacturing overhead:		
Variable.	2.75	
Fixed	2.25	
Depreciation of special equipment	.50	11.50
Net amount.		$ 2.50

The unit charge for the special equipment depreciation cost ($.50 per unit) was determined by dividing the annual depreciation charge on the equipment ($20,000) by the normal annual volume for the product (40,000 units).

If production of this product is discontinued, the special equipment can be sold for $15,000. If production continues, the equipment would be useless for further production at the end of the year and would have no salvage value. The equipment had an original cost of $100,000 four years ago and would be fully depreciated at the end of one more year. The fixed manufacturing overhead cost ($2.25 per unit) represents the fixed cost of the plant and would continue to be incurred whether or not production continues.

REQUIRED: Choose the correct answer.

1. The sum of the direct material, direct labor, and variable overhead costs ($8.75) are the total variable costs of the product. These costs will be avoided if production is discontinued.
   a. True
   b. False

2. The original cost of the equipment ($100,000) in this situation would be referred to as:
   a. a sunk cost
   b. an opportunity cost
   c. a fixed cost
   d. an incremental cost
   e. an avoidable cost
3. The sales price of the equipment, which would not be realized if the firm continues production, would be referred to as:
   a. a sunk cost
   b. an opportunity cost
   c. a fixed cost
   d. a differential cost
   e. a marginal cost

(CMA, adapted)

CASE   *Case 2-49   Economic Characteristics of Costs; Closing a Department.* Compucraft Company manufactures printers for use with home computing systems. The firm currently manufactures both the electronic components for its printers and the plastic cases in which the devices are enclosed. Jim Cassanitti, the production manager, recently received a proposal from Universal Plastics Corporation to manufacture the cases for Compucraft's printers. If the cases are purchased outside, Compucraft will be able to close down its Printer Case Department. To help decide whether to accept the bid from Universal Plastics Corporation, Cassanitti asked Compucraft's controller to prepare an analysis of the costs that would be saved if the Printer Case Department were closed. Included in the controller's list of annual cost savings were the following items.

Building rental (The Printer Case Department occupies $\frac{1}{6}$ of the factory building,
   which Compucraft rents for $150,000 per year.)........................ $25,000
Salary of the printer department supervisor 45,000

In a lunchtime conversation with the controller, Cassanitti learned that Compucraft was currently renting space in a warehouse for $40,000. The space is used to store completed printers. If the Printer Case Department were discontinued, the entire storage operation could be moved into the factory building and occupy the space vacated by the closed department. Cassanitti also learned that the supervisor of the Printer Case Department would be retained by Compucraft even if the department were closed. The supervisor would be assigned the job of managing the assembly department, whose supervisor recently gave notice of his retirement. All of Compucraft's department supervisors earn the same salary.

REQUIRED: You have been hired as a consultant by Jim Cassanitti to advise him in his decision. Write a memo to Cassanitti commenting on the costs of space and supervisory salaries included in the controller's cost analysis. Explain in your memo about the "real" costs of the space occupied by the Printer Case Department and the supervisor's salary. What types of costs are these?

Chapter Job-Order
3 Costing Systems

After completing
this chapter, you
should be able to:

- Discuss the role of product and service costing in manufacturing and nonmanufacturing firms.

- Diagram the flow of costs through the manufacturing accounts used in product costing.

- Distinguish between job-order costing and process costing.

- Compute a predetermined overhead rate and explain its use in job-order costing.

- Prepare journal entries to record the costs of direct labor, direct material, and manufacturing overhead in a job-order costing system.

- Prepare a schedule of cost of goods manufactured, a schedule of cost of goods sold, and an income statement for a manufacturer.

- Discuss the cost-benefit issue of accuracy versus timeliness of information in accounting for overhead.

- Describe the process of project costing used in service industry firms and nonprofit organizations.

PRODUCT AND SERVICE COSTING

A **product costing system** accumulates the costs incurred in a production process and assigns those costs to the organization's final products. As the following diagram shows, product costs are the *output* of the product costing *system*.

Input of the Product Costing System	Activities Performed by the System	Output of the Product Costing System
Costs incurred in the production process	→ Procedures used to accumulate and assign costs to final products	→ Product costs

Product costs are needed for a variety of purposes in both financial accounting and managerial accounting.

Use in Financial Accounting In financial accounting, product costs are needed to value inventory on the balance sheet and to compute cost-of-goods-sold expense on the income statement. Under generally accepted accounting principles, inventory is valued at its cost until it is sold. Then the cost of the inventory becomes an expense of the period in which it is sold.

Use in Managerial Accounting In managerial accounting, product costs are needed for planning, for cost control, and to provide managers with data for decision making. Decisions about product prices, the mix of products to be produced, and the quantity of output to be manufactured are among those for which product cost information is needed.

Use in Reporting to Interested Organizations In addition to financial statement preparation and internal decision making, there is an ever-growing need for product cost information in relationships between firms and various outside organizations. Public utilities, such as electric and gas companies, record product costs to justify rate increases that must be approved by state regulatory agencies. Hospitals keep track of the costs of medical procedures that are reimbursed by insurance companies or by the federal government under the Medicare program. Manufacturing firms often sign cost-plus contracts with the government, where the contract price depends on the cost of manufacturing the product.

Product Costing in Nonmanufacturing Firms

The need for product costs is not limited to manufacturing firms. Merchandising companies include the costs of buying and transporting merchandise in their product costs. Producers of inventoriable goods, such as mining products, petroleum, and agricultural products, also record the costs of producing their goods. The role of product costs in these companies is identical to that in manufacturing firms. For example, the pineapples grown and sold by Dole are inventoried at their product cost until they are sold. Then the product cost becomes cost-of-goods-sold expense.

Service Firms and Nonprofit Organizations The production output of service firms and nonprofit organizations consists of services that are consumed as they are produced. Since services cannot be stored and sold later like manufactured goods, there are no inventoriable costs in service industry firms and nonprofit organizations. However, such organizations need information about the costs of producing services. Banks, insurance companies, restaurants, airlines, law firms, hospitals, and city governments all record the costs of producing various services for the purposes of planning, cost control, and decision making. For example, in making a decision about adding a flight from Chicago to Los Angeles, United Airlines' management needs to know the cost of flying the proposed route. A manager can make a better decision as to whether a university or city government should begin a drug counseling program if the cost of providing similar, existing services is known.

FLOW OF COSTS IN MANUFACTURING FIRMS

Manufacturing costs consist of direct material, direct labor, and manufacturing overhead. The product costing systems used by manufacturing firms employ several manufacturing accounts. As production takes place, all manufacturing costs are added to the *Work-in-Process Inventory* account. Work in process is partially completed inventory. A debit to the account increases the cost-based valuation of the asset represented by the unfinished products. As soon as products are completed, their product costs are transferred from Work-in-Process Inventory to *Finished-Goods Inventory.* This is accomplished with a credit to Work in Process and a debit to Finished Goods. During the time period when products are sold, the product cost of the inventory sold is removed from Finished Goods and added to *Cost of Goods Sold,* which is an expense of the period during which the sale occurred. A credit to Finished Goods and a debit to Cost of Goods Sold completes this step. Cost of Goods Sold is closed into the Income Summary account at the end of the accounting period, along with all other expenses and revenues of the period. Exhibit 3-1 depicts the flow of costs through the manufacturing accounts.

Example of Manufacturing Cost Flows Suppose that the Bradley Paper Company incurred the following manufacturing costs during 19x1.

Direct material.	$30,000
Direct labor	20,000
Manufacturing overhead.	40,000

During 19x1, products costing $60,000 were finished and products costing $25,000 were sold for $32,000. Exhibit 3-2 shows the flow of costs through the Bradley Paper Company's manufacturing accounts and the effect of the firm's product costs on its balance sheet and income statement.

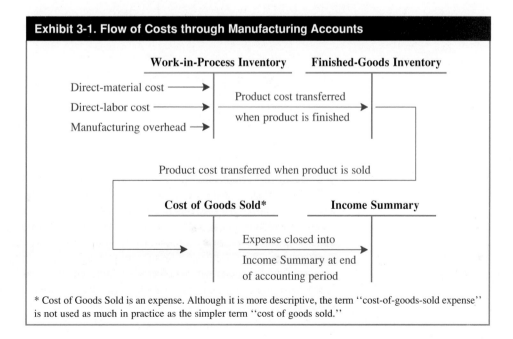

Exhibit 3-1. Flow of Costs through Manufacturing Accounts

Work-in-Process Inventory   **Finished-Goods Inventory**

Direct-material cost ⟶

Direct-labor cost ⟶   Product cost transferred

Manufacturing overhead ⟶   when product is finished

Product cost transferred when product is sold

Cost of Goods Sold*   **Income Summary**

Expense closed into

Income Summary at end

of accounting period

* Cost of Goods Sold is an expense. Although it is more descriptive, the term ''cost-of-goods-sold expense'' is not used as much in practice as the simpler term ''cost of goods sold.''

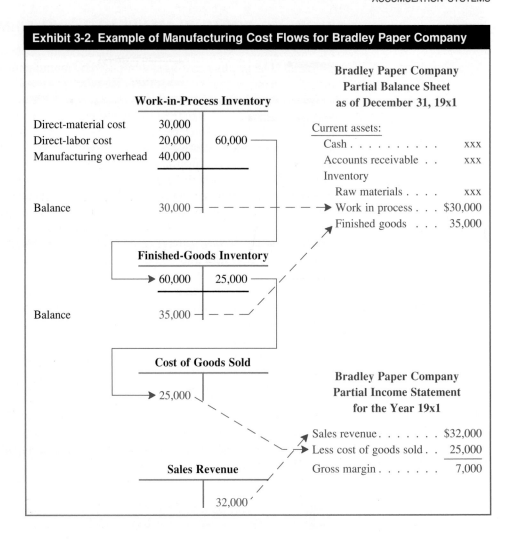

Exhibit 3-2. Example of Manufacturing Cost Flows for Bradley Paper Company

TYPES OF PRODUCT COSTING SYSTEMS

The detailed accounting procedures used in product costing systems depend on the type of industry involved. Two basic sets of procedures are used.

Job-Order Costing Systems

Job-order costing is used by companies where goods are produced in distinct batches, and there are significant differences among the batches. Examples of firms that use job-order costing are aircraft manufacturers, printers, furniture manufacturers, and custom machining firms. In job-order costing, each distinct batch of production is called a *job* or *job order*. The cost accounting procedures are designed to assign costs to each job. Then the costs assigned to each job are averaged over the units of production in the job to obtain an average cost per unit. For example, suppose that AccuPrint worked on two printing jobs during October, and the following costs were incurred.

	Job A27 (1,000 campaign posters)		Job B39 (100 wedding invitations)
Direct material.	$100	. . . .	$ 20
Direct labor	250	. . . .	50
Manufacturing over- head	150	. . . .	30
Total manufacturing cost.	$500	. . . .	$100

The cost per campaign poster is $.50 per poster ($500 divided by 1,000 posters), and the cost per wedding invitation is $1.00 ($100 divided by 100 invitations).

Procedures similar to those used in job-order costing are also used in many service industry firms, although these firms have no work-in-process or finished-goods inventories. In a public accounting firm, for example, costs are assigned to audit engagements in much the same way they are assigned to a batch of products by a furniture manufacturer. Similar procedures are used to assign costs to "cases" in health-care facilities, to "programs" in government agencies, to research "projects" in universities, and to "contracts" in consulting and architectural firms.

Process Costing Systems

Process costing is used by companies that produce large numbers of identical units. Firms that produce chemicals, microchips, gasoline, beer, fertilizer, textiles, processed food, and electricity are among those using process costing. In these kinds of firms, there is no need to trace costs to specific batches of production, because the products in the different batches are identical. A **process costing system** accumulates all of the production costs for a large number of units of output, and then these costs are averaged over all of the units. For example, suppose the Silicon Valley Company produced 40,000 microchips during November. The following manufacturing costs were incurred in November.

Direct material.	$1,000
Direct labor	2,000
Manufacturing overhead.	3,000
Total manufacturing cost	$6,000

The cost per microchip is $.15 (total manufacturing cost of $6,000 ÷ 40,000 units produced).

Summary of Alternative Product-Costing Systems

The distinction between job-order and process costing hinges on the type of production process involved. Job-order costing systems assign costs to distinct production jobs that are significantly different. Then an average cost is computed for each unit of product in each job. Process costing systems average costs over a large number of identical units of product.

The remainder of this chapter examines the details of job-order costing. The next chapter covers process costing.

ACCUMULATING COSTS IN A JOB-ORDER COSTING SYSTEM

In a job-order costing system, costs of direct material, direct labor, and manufacturing overhead are assigned to each production job. These costs comprise the *inputs* of the product costing *system*. As costs are incurred, they are added to the Work-in-Process Inventory account in the ledger. To keep track of the manufacturing costs

---

Exhibit 3-3. Job-Cost Sheet

Job-Cost Sheet

Job Number _____   Description _____

Date Started _____   Date Completed _____

Number of Units Completed _____

Direct Material				
Date	Requisition Number	Quantity	Unit Price	Cost

Direct Labor				
Date	Time Card Number	Hours	Rate	Cost

Manufacturing Overhead				
Date	Activity Base	Quantity	Application Rate	Cost

Cost Summary	
Cost Item	Amount
Total direct material Total direct labor Total manufacturing overhead	
Total cost	
Unit cost	

Shipping Summary		
Date	Number of Units Shipped	Cost Balance

assigned to *each job,* a subsidiary ledger is maintained. The subsidiary ledger account assigned to each job is a document called a **job-cost sheet.**

Job-Cost Sheet

An example of a job-cost sheet is displayed in Exhibit 3-3. Three sections on the job-cost sheet are used to accumulate the costs of direct material, direct labor, and manufacturing overhead assigned to the job. The other two sections are used to record the total cost and average unit cost for the job, and to keep track of units shipped to customers. A job-cost sheet may be a paper document upon which the entries for direct material, direct labor, and manufacturing overhead are written. Increasingly, it is a computer file on which entries are made using a computer terminal.

The procedures used to accumulate the costs of direct material, direct labor, and manufacturing overhead for a job constitute the *set of activities* performed by the job-order costing *system.* These procedures are discussed next.

Direct-Material Costs

As raw materials are needed for the production process, they are transferred from the warehouse to the production department. To authorize the release of materials, the production department supervisor completes a **material requisition form** and presents it to the warehouse supervisor. A copy of the material requisition form goes to the cost accounting department. There it is used as the basis for transferring the cost of the requisitioned material from the Raw Material Inventory account to the Work-in-Process Inventory account, and to enter the direct-material cost on the job-cost sheet for the production job in process. A document such as the material requisition form, which is used as the basis for an accounting entry, is called a **source document.** Exhibit 3-4 shows an example of a material requisition form.

In many factories, material requisitions are entered directly into a computer terminal by the production department supervisor. The requisition is automatically transmitted to terminals in the warehouse and in the cost accounting department. Such automation reduces the flow of paperwork, minimizes clerical errors, and speeds up the product costing process.

Material Requirements Planning For products and product components that are produced routinely, the required materials are known in advance. For these products and components, material requisitions are based on a **bill of materials** that lists all of the materials needed.

Exhibit 3-4. Material Requisition Form

Material Requisition Number __352__   Date __1/28/x9__
Job Number to Be Charged __J621__   Department __Painting__
Department Supervisor's Signature __Timothy Williams__

Item	Quantity	Unit Cost	Amount
White enamel paint	8 gallons	$14.00	$112
Clear lacquer	2 gallons	11.00	22

In complex manufacturing operations, in which production takes place in several stages, **material requirements planning** (or **MRP**) may be used. MRP is an operations management tool that assists managers in scheduling production in each stage of the manufacturing process. Such careful planning ensures that, at each stage in the production process, the required subassemblies, components, or partially processed materials will be ready for the next stage. MRP systems, which are generally computerized, include files that list of all of the component parts and materials in inventory and all of the parts and materials needed in each stage of the production process. The MRP concept is diagrammed in Exhibit 3-5. As the diagram indicates, the bill of materials for component A includes materials 1, 2, and 3. This bill of materials would be consulted by the supervisor of Production Department I when requisitioning materials.

Direct-Labor Costs

The assignment of direct-labor costs to jobs is based on time tickets filled out by employees. A **time ticket** is a form that records the amount of time an employee spends on each production job. The time ticket is the source document used in the cost accounting department as the basis for adding direct-labor costs to Work-in-Process Inventory and to the job-cost sheets for the various jobs in process. In some factories, a computerized time-clock system may be used. Employees enter the time they begin and stop work on each job into the time clock. The time clock is connected to a computer, which records the time spent on various jobs and transmits the information to the accounting department.

Exhibit 3-6 displays an example of a time ticket. As the example shows, most of the employee's time was spent working on two different production jobs. In the accounting department, the time spent on each job will be multiplied by the employee's wage rate and the cost will be recorded in Work-in-Process Inventory and on the appropriate job-cost sheets. The employee also spent one-half hour on shop

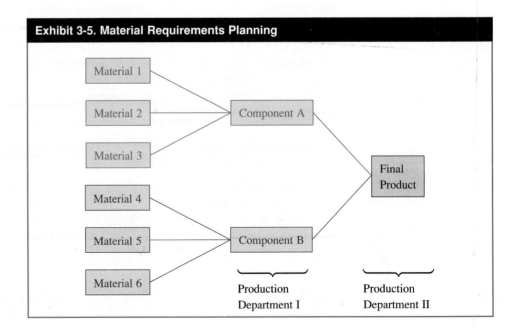

Exhibit 3-5. Material Requirements Planning

Material 1, Material 2, Material 3 → Component A → Final Product

Material 4, Material 5, Material 6 → Component B → Final Product

Production Department I   Production Department II

Exhibit 3-6. Time Ticket		

Employee Name ___Brian Williams___ Date ___1/22/x8___
Employee Number ___62___ Department ___Drilling___

Time Started	Time Stopped	Job Number
8:00	11:30	A267
11:30	12:00	Shop cleanup
1:00	5:00	J122

cleanup duties. This time will be classified by the accounting department as indirect labor, and its cost will be included in manufacturing overhead.

Manufacturing Overhead Costs

It is relatively simple to trace direct-material and direct-labor costs to production jobs, but manufacturing overhead is not easily traced to jobs. By definition, manufacturing overhead is a heterogeneous pool of indirect production costs, such as indirect material, indirect labor, utility costs, and depreciation. These costs often bear no obvious relationship to individual jobs or units of product, but they must be incurred for production to take place. Therefore, it is necessary to assign manufacturing overhead costs to jobs in order to have a complete picture of product costs.

Overhead Distribution, Allocation, and Application

The assignment of manufacturing overhead costs to jobs is accomplished in three steps. First, all manufacturing overhead costs are assigned to **departmental overhead centers**. This step is called **cost distribution** (or sometimes **cost allocation**). For example, the costs of heating a factory with natural gas would be distributed among all of the departments in the factory, possibly in proportion to the cubic feet of space in each department. In the cost distribution step, manufacturing overhead costs are assigned to both production departments and service departments. Service departments, such as equipment maintenance and material-handling departments, do not work directly on the firm's products, but they are necessary for production to take place.

Second, all service department costs are assigned to the production departments through a process called **service department cost allocation.** In this step, an attempt is made to allocate service department costs on the basis of the relative proportion of each service department's output that is used by the various production departments. For example, production departments with more equipment would be allocated a larger share of the maintenance department's costs.

Now all manufacturing overhead costs have been assigned to the production departments. The third step is to assign all manufacturing overhead costs accumulated in a production department to the jobs that the department has worked on. This step is called **overhead application** (or sometimes **overhead absorption**).

The processes of manufacturing overhead distribution, service department cost allocation, and overhead application are portrayed in Exhibit 3-7. The techniques of overhead distribution and service department cost allocation will be covered later in the text. Here we will focus on the process of overhead application.

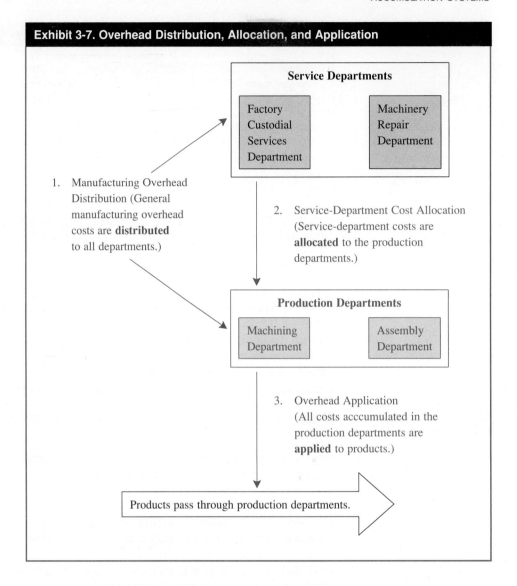

Exhibit 3-7. Overhead Distribution, Allocation, and Application

Service Departments

Factory Custodial Services Department

Machinery Repair Department

1. Manufacturing Overhead Distribution (General manufacturing overhead costs are **distributed** to all departments.)

2. Service-Department Cost Allocation (Service-department costs are **allocated** to the production departments.)

Production Departments

Machining Department

Assembly Department

3. Overhead Application (All costs acccumulated in the production departments are **applied** to products.)

Products pass through production departments.

Overhead Application For product costing information to be useful, it must be provided to managers on a timely basis. Suppose the cost accounting department waited until the end of an accounting period so that the *actual* costs of manufacturing overhead could be determined before applying overhead costs to the firm's products. The result would be very accurate overhead application. However, the information might be useless because it was not available to managers for planning, control, and decision making during the period.

Predetermined Overhead Rate The solution to this problem is to apply overhead to products on the basis of estimates made at the beginning of the accounting period. The accounting department chooses some measure of productive activity to use as the basis for overhead application. In traditional product-costing systems, this measure usually is some **volume-based cost driver** (or **activity base**), such as direct-labor hours, direct-labor cost, or machine hours. An estimate is made of (1) the amount of manufacturing overhead that will be incurred during a specified period of time and

(2) the amount of the cost driver (or activity base) that will be used or incurred during the same time period. Then a **predetermined overhead rate** is computed as follows:

$$\text{Predetermined overhead rate} = \frac{\text{estimated manufacturing overhead cost}}{\text{estimated amount of cost driver (or activity base)}}$$

For example, suppose that AccuPrint has chosen machine hours as its cost driver (or activity base). For the next year, the firm estimates that overhead cost will amount to $90,000 and that total machine hours used will be 10,000 hours. The predetermined overhead rate is computed as follows:

$$\text{Predetermined overhead rate} = \frac{\$90,000}{10,000 \text{ hours}} = \$9.00 \text{ per machine hour}$$

In our discussion of the predetermined overhead rate, we have emphasized the term *cost driver,* because increasingly this term is replacing the more traditional term *activity base.* Furthermore, we have emphasized that *traditional* product costing systems tend to rely on a *single, volume-based cost driver.* We will discuss more elaborate product costing systems based on multiple cost drivers in Chapter 5.

Applying Overhead Costs The predetermined overhead rate is used to apply manufacturing overhead costs to production jobs. The quantity of the cost driver (or activity base) required by a particular job is multiplied by the predetermined overhead rate to determine the amount of overhead cost applied to the job. For example, suppose AccuPrint's job number C22, consisting of 1,000 brochures, requires three machine hours. The overhead applied to the job is computed as follows:

Predetermined overhead rate...	$ 9
Machine hours required by job C22	× 3
Overhead applied to job C22...	$27

The $27 of applied overhead will be added to Work-in-Process Inventory and recorded on the job-cost sheet for job C22. The accounting entries made to add manufacturing overhead to Work-in-Process Inventory may be made daily, weekly, or monthly, depending on the time required to process production jobs. Before the end of an accounting period, entries should be made to record all manufacturing costs incurred to date in Work-in-Process Inventory. This is necessary to properly value Work in Process on the balance sheet.

Summary of Event Sequence in Job-Order Costing

The flowchart in Exhibit 3-8 summarizes the sequence of activities performed by the job-order costing system. The role of the various documents used in job-order costing is also emphasized in the flowchart.

ILLUSTRATION OF JOB-ORDER COSTING

To illustrate the procedures used in job-order costing, we will examine the accounting entries made by Adirondack Outfitters, Inc. during November of 19x3. The company worked on two production jobs:

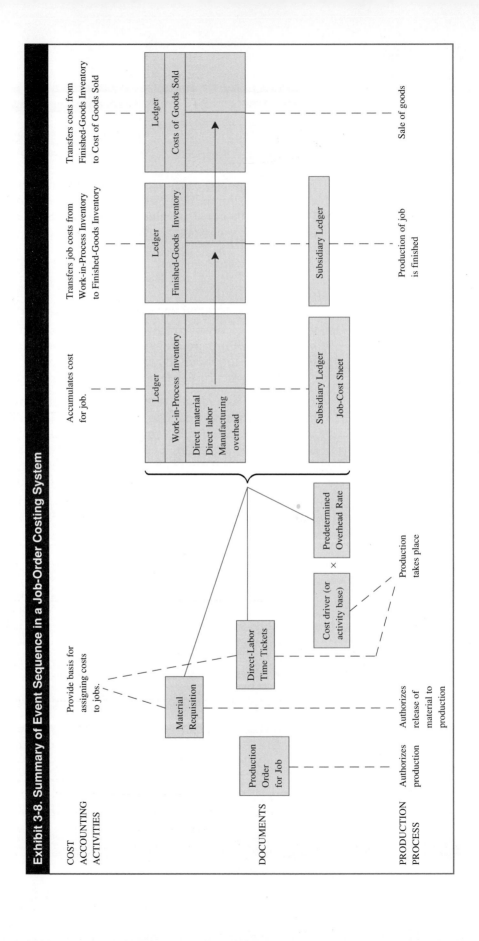

Exhibit 3-8. Summary of Event Sequence in a Job-Order Costing System

Job number C12, 80 deluxe wooden canoes
Job number F16, 80 deluxe aluminum fishing boats

The job numbers designate these as the twelfth canoe production job and the six-teenth fishing boat production job undertaken during the year. The events of November are described below along with the associated accounting entries.

Purchase of Material

Four thousand square feet of rolled aluminum sheet metal were purchased on account for $10,000. The purchase is recorded with the following journal entry.

(1) Raw Material Inventory 10,000
              Accounts Payable 10,000

The postings of this and all subsequent journal entries to the ledger are shown in Exhibit 3-14.

Use of Direct Material

On November 1, the following material requisitions were filed.

Requisition number 802:   8,000 board feet of lumber, at $2 per board
(for job number C12)   foot, for a total of $16,000

Requisition number 803:   7,200 square feet of aluminum sheet metal, at
(for job number F16) $2.50 per square foot, for a total of $18,000.

The following journal entry records the release of these raw materials to production.

(2) Work-in-Process Inventory 34,000
              Raw Material Inventory 34,000

The associated ledger posting is shown in Exhibit 3-14. These direct-material costs are also recorded on the job-cost sheet for each job. The job-cost sheet for job number F16 is displayed in Exhibit 3-9 (page 73). Since the job-cost sheet for job number C12 is similar, it is not shown.

Use of Indirect Material

On November 15, the following material requisition was filed.

Requisition number 804:   5 gallons of bonding glue, at $10 per gallon, for
                             a total cost of $50.

Small amounts of bonding glue are used in the production of all classes of boats manufactured by Adirondack Outfitters. Since the cost incurred is small, no attempt is made to trace the cost of glue to specific jobs. Instead, glue is considered an indirect material, and its cost is included in manufacturing overhead. The company accumulates all manufacturing overhead costs in the Manufacturing Overhead account. All actual overhead costs are recorded by debiting this account. The account is debited when indirect materials are requisitioned, when indirect labor costs are incurred, when utility bills are paid, when depreciation is recorded on manufacturing equipment, and so forth. The journal entry made to record the usage of glue is as follows:

(3) Manufacturing Overhead 50
            Manufacturing Supplies Inventory.......................... 50

The posting of this journal entry to the ledger is shown in Exhibit 3-14. No entry is made on any job-cost sheet for the usage of glue, since its cost is not traced to individual production jobs.

Use of Direct Labor

At the end of November, the cost accounting department uses the labor time tickets filed during the month to determine the following direct-labor costs of each job.

Direct labor: job number C12...... $ 9,000
Direct labor: job number F16...... 12,000
Total direct labor............... $21,000

The journal entry made to record these costs is shown below.

(4) Work-in-Process Inventory 21,000
            Wages Payable.................................... 21,000

The associated ledger posting is shown in Exhibit 3-14. These direct-labor costs are also recorded on the job-cost sheet for each job. The job-cost sheet for job number F16 is displayed in Exhibit 3-9. Only one direct-labor entry is shown on the job-cost sheet. In practice, there would be numerous entries made on different dates at a variety of wage rates for different employees.

Use of Indirect Labor

The analysis of labor time cards undertaken on November 30 also revealed the following use of indirect labor.

Indirect labor: not charged to any particular job, $14,000

This cost is comprised of the production supervisor's salary and the wages of various employees who spent some of their time on maintenance and general cleanup duties during November. The following journal entry is made to add indirect-labor costs to manufacturing overhead.

(5) Manufacturing Overhead 14,000
            Wages Payable.................................... 14,000

No entry is made on any job-cost sheet, since indirect-labor costs are not traceable to any particular job. In practice, journal entries (4) and (5) are usually combined into one compound entry as follows:

Work-in-Process Inventory 21,000
Manufacturing Overhead. 14,000
      Wages Payable   35,000

Exhibit 3-9. Job-Cost Sheet: Adirondack Outfitters, Inc.

Job-Cost Sheet

ADIRONDACK
Outfitters

Job Number ___F16___ Description ___80 deluxe aluminum fishing boats___
Date Started ___Nov. 1, 19x3___ Date Completed ___Nov. 22, 19x3___
      Number of Units Completed ___80___

Direct Material

Date	Requisition Number	Quantity	Unit Price	Cost
11/1	803	7,200 sq ft	$2.50	$18,000

Direct Labor

Date	Time Card Number	Hours	Rate	Cost
Various dates	Various time cards	600	$20	$12,000

Manufacturing Overhead

Date	Activity Base	Quantity	Application Rate	Cost
11/30	Machine hours	2,000	$9.00	$18,000

Cost Summary

Cost Item	Amount
Total direct material	$18,000
Total direct labor	12,000
Total manufacturing overhead	18,000
Total cost	$48,000
Unit cost	$ 600

Shipping Summary

Date	Units Shipped	Units Remaining in Inventory	Cost Balance
11/30	60	20	$12,000

Incurrence of Manufacturing Overhead Costs

The following manufacturing overhead costs were incurred during November.

Manufacturing overhead:	
Rent on factory building	$ 3,000
Depreciation on equipment	5,000
Utilities (electricity and natural gas)	4,000
Property taxes	2,000
Insurance	1,000
Total	$15,000

The following compound journal entry is made on November 30 to record these costs.

(6) Manufacturing Overhead	15,000	
Rent Payable		3,000
Accumulated Depreciation—Equipment		5,000
Accounts Payable (utilities and property taxes)		6,000
Prepaid Insurance		1,000

The entry is posted in Exhibit 3-14. No entry is made on any job-cost sheet, since manufacturing overhead costs are not traceable to any particular job.

Application of Manufacturing Overhead

Various manufacturing overhead costs were incurred during November, and these costs were accumulated by debiting the Manufacturing Overhead account. However, no manufacturing overhead costs have yet been added to Work-in-Process Inventory or recorded on the job-cost sheets. The application of overhead to the firm's products is based on a predetermined overhead rate. This rate was computed by the accounting department at the beginning of 19x3 as follows:

$$\text{Predetermined overhead rate} = \frac{\text{estimated total manufacturing overhead for 19x3}}{\text{estimated total machine hours for 19x3}}$$

$$= \frac{\$360,000}{40,000} = \$9.00 \text{ per machine hour}$$

Factory machine-usage records indicate the following usage of machine hours during November.

Machine hours used: job number C12	1,200 hours
Machine hours used: job number F16	2,000 hours
Total machine hours	3,200 hours

The total manufacturing overhead applied to Work-in-Process Inventory during November is calculated as follows:

	Machine Hours		Predetermined Overhead Rate		Manufacturing Overhead Applied
Job number C12:	1,200	×	$9.00	=	$10,800
Job number F16:	2,000	×	$9.00	=	18,000
Total manufacturing overhead applied					$28,800

The following journal entry is made to add **applied manufacturing overhead** to Work-in-Process Inventory.

(7) Work-in-Process Inventory 28,800
               Manufacturing Overhead 28,800

The entry is posted in Exhibit 3-14, and the manufacturing overhead applied to job number F16 is entered on the job-cost sheet in Exhibit 3-9.

Summary of Overhead Accounting

Exhibit 3-10 summarizes the accounting procedures used for manufacturing overhead. The left side of the Manufacturing Overhead account is used to accumulate **actual manufacturing overhead** costs as they are incurred throughout the accounting period. The actual costs incurred for indirect material, indirect labor, factory rental, equipment depreciation, utilities, property taxes, and insurance are recorded as debits to the account.

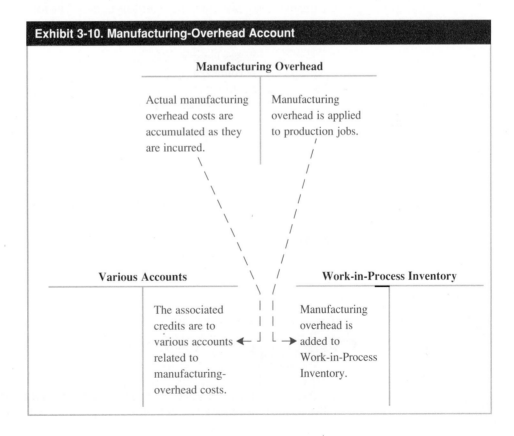

Exhibit 3-10. Manufacturing-Overhead Account

Manufacturing Overhead

Actual manufacturing overhead costs are accumulated as they are incurred.	Manufacturing overhead is applied to production jobs.

Various Accounts

Work-in-Process Inventory

The associated credits are to various accounts related to manufacturing-overhead costs.	Manufacturing overhead is added to Work-in-Process Inventory.

The right side of the Manufacturing Overhead account is used to record overhead *applied* to Work-in-Process Inventory.

While the left side of the Manufacturing Overhead account accumulates *actual* overhead costs, the right side applies overhead costs using the predetermined overhead rate, based on *estimated* overhead costs. The estimates used to calculate the predetermined overhead rate will generally prove to be incorrect to some degree. Consequently, there will usually be a nonzero balance left in the Manufacturing Overhead Account at the end of the year. This balance is usually relatively small, and its disposition is covered later in this illustration.

Selling and Administrative Costs

During November, Adirondack Outfitters incurred selling and administrative costs as follows:

Rental of sales and administrative offices.	$ 1,500
Salaries of sales personnel	4,000
Salaries of management	8,000
Advertising.	1,000
Office supplies used	300
Total.	$14,800

Since these are not manufacturing costs, they are not added to Work-in-Process Inventory. Selling and administrative costs are period costs, not product costs. They are treated as expenses of the accounting period. The following journal entry is made.

(8) Selling and Administrative Expenses	14,800	
Wages Payable.		12,000
Accounts Payable		1,000
Rent Payable.		1,500
Office Supplies Inventory		300

The entry is posted in Exhibit 3-14.

Completion of a Production Job

Job number F16 was completed during November, whereas job number C12 remained in process. As the job-cost sheet in Exhibit 3-9 indicates, the total cost of job number F16 was $48,000. The following journal entry records the transfer of these job costs from Work-in-Process Inventory to Finished-Goods Inventory.

(9) Finished-Goods Inventory.	48,000	
Work-in-Process Inventory.		48,000

The entry is posted in Exhibit 3-14.

Sale of Goods

Sixty deluxe aluminum fishing boats manufactured in job number F16 were sold for $900 each during November. The cost of each unit sold was $600 as shown on the job-cost sheet in Exhibit 3-9. The following journal entries are made.

(10)	Accounts Receivable	54,000	
	Sales Revenue		54,000
(11)	Cost of Goods Sold	36,000	
	Finished-Goods Inventory		36,000

These entries are posted in Exhibit 3-14.

The remainder of the manufacturing costs for job number F16 remain in Finished-Goods Inventory until some subsequent accounting period when the units are sold. Therefore, the cost balance for job number F16 remaining in inventory is $12,000 (20 units remaining times $600 per unit). This balance is shown on the job-cost sheet in Exhibit 3-9.

Underapplied and Overapplied Overhead

During November, Adirondack Outfitters incurred total *actual* manufacturing overhead costs of $29,050, but only $28,800 of overhead was *applied* to Work-in-Process Inventory. The amount by which actual overhead exceeds applied overhead, called **underapplied overhead,** is calculated below.

Actual manufacturing overhead*	$29,050
Applied manufacturing overhead†	28,800
Underapplied overhead	$ 250

* Sum of debit entries in the Manufacturing Overhead account: $50 + $14,000 + $15,000 = $29,050. See Exhibit 3-14.
† Applied overhead: $9.00 per machine hour × 3,200 machine hours.

If actual overhead had been less than applied overhead, the difference would have been called **overapplied overhead.** Underapplied or overapplied overhead is caused by errors in the estimates of overhead and activity used to compute the predetermined overhead rate. In this illustration, Adirondack Outfitters' predetermined overhead rate was underestimated by a small amount.

Disposition of Underapplied or Overapplied Overhead At the end of an accounting period, the managerial accountant has two alternatives for the disposition of underapplied or overapplied overhead. Under the most common alternative, the underapplied or overapplied overhead is closed into Cost of Goods Sold. This is the method used by Adirondack Outfitters, and the required journal entry is shown below.

| (12) | Cost of Goods Sold | 250 | |
| | Manufacturing Overhead | | 250 |

This entry, which is posted in Exhibit 3-14, brings the balance in the Manufacturing Overhead account to zero. The account is then clear to accumulate manufacturing overhead costs incurred in the next accounting period. Journal entry (12) has the effect of increasing cost-of-goods-sold expense. This reflects the fact that the cost of the units sold had been underestimated due to the slightly underestimated predetermined overhead rate. Most companies use this approach because it is simple, and the amount of underapplied or overapplied overhead is usually small.

Proration of Underapplied or Overapplied Overhead Some companies use a more accurate procedure to dispose of underapplied or overapplied overhead. This approach recognizes that underestimation or overestimation of the predetermined overhead rate affects not only Cost of Goods Sold, but also Work-in-Process Inventory and Finished-Goods Inventory. As shown below, applied overhead passes through all three of these accounts. Therefore, all three accounts are affected by any inaccuracy in the predetermined overhead rate.

Work-in-Process Inventory	Finished-Goods Inventory	Cost of Goods Sold
Applied overhead → → is added to work in process	Applied overhead is included in cost of goods completed →	Applied overhead → is included in cost of goods sold →

When underapplied or overapplied overhead is allocated among the three accounts shown above, the process is called **proration**. The amount of the current period's applied overhead remaining in each account is the basis for the proration procedure. In the Adirondack Outfitters illustration, the amounts of applied overhead remaining in the three accounts on November 30 are determined as follows:

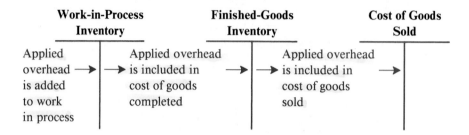

Work-in-Process Inventory	Finished-Goods Inventory	Cost of Goods Sold
Overhead applied to job C12 · 10,800		
Overhead applied to job F16 · 18,000 │ 18,000 →	Applied overhead transferred to Finished Goods when job F16 was completed · 18,000 │ 13,500 →	Applied overhead transferred to Cost of Goods Sold when 60 out of 80 units were sold. · 13,500 →

Applied Overhead Remaining in Each Account on November 30

Account	Explanation	Amount	Percentage	Calculation of Percentages
Work in Process	Job C12 only.......	$10,800...	37.5%	...10,800 ÷ 28,800
Finished Goods.....	¼ of units in job F16 .	4,500...	15.6%*	... 4,500 ÷ 28,800
Cost of Goods Sold..	¾ of units in job F16 .	13,500...	46.9%*	...13,500 ÷ 28,800
Total overhead applied in November.......		$28,800...	100.0%	

* Rounded.

Using the percentages calculated above, the proration of Adirondack Outfitters' underapplied overhead is determined as follows:

Account	Underapplied Overhead	×	Percentage	=	Amount Added to Account
Work in Process	$250	×	37.5%	=	$ 93.75
Finished Goods...........	250	×	15.6%	=	39.00
Cost of Goods Sold........	250	×	46.9%	=	117.25
Total Underapplied Overhead Prorated					$250.00

If Adirondack Outfitters had chosen to prorate underapplied overhead, the following journal entry would have been made.

Work-in-Process Inventory	93.75	
Finished-Goods Inventory	39.00	
Cost of Goods Sold...................................	117.25	
Manufacturing Overhead..........................		250.00

Since this is *not* the method used by Adirondack Outfitters in our continuing illustration, this entry is *not* posted to the ledger in Exhibit 3-14.

Proration of underapplied and overapplied overhead is used by a small number of firms that are required to do so under the rules specified by the **Cost Accounting Standards Board (CASB).** This federal agency was chartered by Congress in 1970 to develop cost accounting standards for large government contractors. The agency was discontinued by Congress in 1980, but it was recreated in 1990. The standards set forth by the agency apply to significant government contracts and have the force of federal law.

Schedule of Cost of Goods Manufactured

Many manufacturing companies periodically prepare a **schedule of cost of goods manufactured.** This schedule details the manufacturing costs incurred during an accounting period and shows the change in Work-in-Process Inventory. The statement is an internal report, for management's use only.

Exhibit 3-11 displays the November schedule of cost of goods manufactured for Adirondack Outfitters. The schedule shows the costs of direct material, direct labor, and manufacturing overhead *applied* to work in process during November. The **cost of goods manufactured,** shown in the last line of the schedule, is $48,000. This is the amount transferred from Work-in-Process Inventory to Finished-Goods Inventory during November, as recorded in journal entry number (9).

Schedule of Cost of Goods Sold

A **schedule of cost of goods sold** for Adirondack Outfitters is displayed in Exhibit 3-12. This schedule, prepared for management's use, shows the November cost of goods sold and details the changes in Finished-Goods Inventory during the month. Exhibit 3-13 displays the company's November income statement.

Exhibit 3-11. Schedule of Cost of Goods Manufactured

Adirondack Outfitters, Inc.
Schedule of Cost of Goods Manufactured
For the Month of November, 19x3

Direct Material:		
Raw material inventory, November 1	$30,000	
Add: November purchases of raw material	10,000	
Raw material available for use	40,000	
Deduct: Raw material inventory, November 30	6,000	
Raw material used		$34,000
Direct labor		21,000
Manufacturing overhead:		
Indirect material	50	
Indirect labor	14,000	
Rent on factory building	3,000	
Depreciation on equipment	5,000	
Utilities	4,000	
Property taxes	2,000	
Insurance	1,000	
Total actual manufacturing overhead	29,050	
Deduct: Underapplied overhead	250*	
Overhead applied to work in process		28,800
Total manufacturing costs		83,800
Add: Work-in-process inventory, November 1		4,000
Subtotal		87,800
Deduct: Work-in-process inventory, November 30		39,800
Cost of goods manufactured		$48,000

* The schedule of cost of goods manufactured lists the manufacturing costs *applied* to work in process. Therefore, the underapplied overhead, $250, must be deducted from total actual overhead to arrive at the amount of overhead *applied* to work in process during November. If there had been overapplied overhead, the balance would have been *added* to total actual manufacturing overhead.

Posting Journal Entries to the Ledger

All of the journal entries in the Adirondack Outfitters illustration are posted to the ledger in Exhibit 3-14. An examination of these T-accounts provides a summary of the cost flows discussed throughout the illustration.

FURTHER ASPECTS OF OVERHEAD APPLICATION

Accuracy versus Timeliness of Information: A Cost-Benefit Issue

One of the themes of managerial accounting mentioned in Chapter 1 is the theme of costs and benefits. The issue of overhead application illustrates the importance of the cost-benefit theme. A product costing system could be designed to use an *actual*

Exhibit 3-12. Schedule of Cost of Goods Sold

Adirondack Outfitters, Inc.
Schedule of Cost of Goods Sold
For the Month of November, 19x3

Finished-goods inventory, November 1	$12,000
Add: Cost of goods manufactured*	48,000
Cost of goods available for sale	60,000
Finished-goods inventory, November 30	24,000
Cost of goods sold	36,000
Add: Underapplied overhead†	250
Cost of goods sold (adjusted for underapplied overhead)	$36,250

 * The cost of goods manufactured is obtained from the schedule of cost of goods manufactured in Exhibit 3-11.
 † The company closes underapplied or overapplied overhead into cost of goods sold. Hence the $250 balance in underapplied overhead is added to cost of goods sold for the month.

overhead rate instead of a *predetermined overhead rate*. An actual overhead rate would be computed as follows:

$$\text{Actual overhead rate} = \frac{\text{actual overhead for the accounting period}}{\text{actual amount of cost driver (or activity base)}}$$

An actual overhead rate can only be computed at the end of the accounting period. The result is more accurate, but rather untimely, product costing information. A trade-off exists between accuracy and timeliness. Accurate information is useful when decisions are based on the information. Better pricing or cost-control decisions may result from more accurate product costs. However, late information entails a cost, in terms of missed opportunities and late responses to events. Therefore, manag-

Exhibit 3-13. Income Statement

Adirondack Outfitters, Inc.
Income Statement
For the Month of November, 19x3

Sales revenue	$54,000
Less: Cost of goods sold*	36,250
Gross margin	17,750
Selling and administrative expenses	14,800
Income before taxes	$ 2,950
Income tax expense	1,420
Net income	$ 1,530

 * The cost of goods sold is obtained from the schedule of cost of goods sold in Exhibit 3-12.

Exhibit 3-14. Ledger Accounts for Adirondack Outfitters Illustration*

ADIRONDACK Outfitters

Accounts Receivable				Accounts Payable	
Bal.	11,000			3,000	Bal.
(10)	54,000			10,000	(1)
				6,000	(6)
				1,000	(8)

Prepaid Insurance				Wages Payable	
Bal.	2,000	1,000	(6)	10,000	Bal.
				21,000	(4)
				14,000	(5)
				12,000	(8)

Office Supplies Inventory				Rent Payable	
Bal.	900	300	(8)	4,000	Bal.
				3,000	(6)
				1,500	(8)

Manufacturing Supplies Inventory				Accumulated Depreciation: Equipment	
Bal.	750	50	(3)	105,000	Bal.
				5,000	(6)

Raw-Material Inventory				Manufacturing Overhead			
Bal.	30,000	34,000	(2)	(3)	50	28,800	(7)
(1)	10,000			(5)	14,000	250	(12)
				(6)	15,000		

Work-in-Process Inventory				Cost of Goods Sold			
Bal.	4,000	48,000	(9)	(11)	36,000		
(2)	34,000			(12)	250		
(4)	21,000						
(7)	28,800						

Selling and Administrative Expenses			

Finished-Goods Inventory						
Bal.	12,000	36,000	(11)	(8)	14,800
(9)	48,000				

Sales Revenue		
	54,000	(10)

* The numbers in parentheses relate T-account entries to the associated journal entries. The numbers in blue are the November 1 account balances.

ers and managerial accountants must weigh the costs and benefits of the following choices.

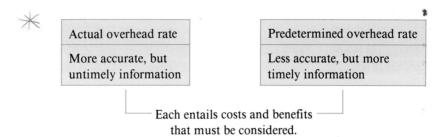

Actual overhead rate	Predetermined overhead rate
More accurate, but untimely information	Less accurate, but more timely information

Each entails costs and benefits
that must be considered.

When designing product costing systems, accountants generally recommend predetermined overhead rates.

It might be tempting to solve the overhead rate problem by using an actual rate and recomputing the rate frequently to provide more timely information. For example, the rate could be recomputed monthly. The problem with this approach is that some manufacturing overhead costs are seasonal. For example, heating costs are higher in the winter, and air-conditioning costs are higher in the summer. Since overhead costs are incurred unevenly throughout the year, the monthly overhead rate would fluctuate widely. Moreover, the level of a volume-based cost driver, used as the denominator of the overhead rate, also may vary from period to period. Fluctuations in the number of workdays in a month and seasonal fluctuations in production volume can cause such variations. These activity variations can add to the fluctuations in the overhead rate. The resulting inconsistency in product costs could give misleading signals for product pricing and other decisions that may depend on product cost information.

Accountants generally choose to smooth out fluctuations in the overhead rate by computing the rate over a long period of time. One-, two-, and three-year periods are common. An overhead rate computed in this fashion is called a **normalized overhead rate.** The use of a relatively long time period forces the accountant to face the trade-off between accuracy and timeliness that was discussed above. The effects of using different time periods to compute overhead rates are illustrated in the appendix at the end of the chapter.

Actual and Normal Costing Most firms use a predetermined overhead rate, based on overhead and activity estimates for a relatively long time period. When direct material and direct labor are added to Work-in-Process Inventory at their actual amounts, but overhead is applied to Work-in-Process Inventory using a *predetermined overhead rate,* the product costing system is referred to as **normal costing.** This approach, which takes its name from the use of an overhead rate that is *normalized* over a fairly long time period, is used in the Adirondack Outfitters illustration.

A few companies use an **actual costing** system, in which direct material and direct labor are added to work in process at their actual amounts, and actual overhead is allocated to work in process using an *actual overhead rate* computed at the *end* of each accounting period. Note that even though an actual overhead rate is used, the amount of overhead assigned to each production job is still an allocated amount. Overhead costs, which are by definition indirect costs, cannot be traced easily to individual production jobs. Actual and normal costing may be summarized as follows:

ACTUAL COSTING Work-in-Process Inventory		NORMAL COSTING Work-in-Process Inventory	
Actual direct-material costs		Actual direct-material costs	
Actual direct-labor costs		Actual direct-labor costs	
Overhead allocated:		Overhead applied:	
Actual overhead rate (computed at *end* of period)	Actual amount of cost driver × used (e.g., direct-labor hours)	*Predetermined* overhead rate (computed at *beginning* of period)	Actual amount of cost driver × used (e.g., direct-labor hours)

Choosing the Cost Driver for Overhead Application

Manufacturing overhead includes various indirect manufacturing costs that vary greatly in their relationship to the production process. If a single, volume-based cost driver (or activity base) is used in calculating the predetermined overhead rate, it should be some productive input that is common across all of the firm's products. If, for example, all of the firm's products require direct labor, but only some products require machine time, direct labor hours would be a preferable activity base. If machine time were used as the base, products not requiring machine time would not be assigned any overhead cost.

In selecting a volume-based cost driver (or activity base), the goal is to choose an input that varies in a pattern that is most similar to the pattern with which overhead costs vary. Products that indirectly cause large amounts of overhead costs should also require large amounts of the cost driver, and vice versa. During periods when the cost driver is at a low level, the overhead costs incurred should be low. Thus, there should be a correlation between the incurrence of overhead costs and use of the cost driver.

Limitation of Direct Labor as a Cost Driver In traditional product-costing systems, the most common volume-based cost drivers are direct-labor hours and direct-labor cost. However, there is a trend away from using direct labor as the overhead application base. Many production processes are becoming increasingly automated, through the use of robotics and computer-integrated manufacturing systems. Increased automation brings two results. First, manufacturing overhead costs represent a larger proportion of total production costs. Second, direct labor decreases in importance as a factor of production. As direct labor declines in importance as a productive input, it becomes less appropriate as a cost driver. For this reason, some firms have switched to machine hours, process time, or throughput time as cost drivers that better reflect the pattern of overhead cost incurrence. **Throughput time** (or **cycle time**) is the average amount of time required to convert raw materials into finished goods ready to be shipped to customers. Throughput time includes the time required for material handling, production processing, inspection, and packaging.

Multiple Overhead Rates

In some production processes, the relationship between overhead costs and various cost drivers differs substantially across production departments. For example, suppose HiTech Electronics Company has two production departments, which work sequentially on the firm's products. Department A is highly automated, requiring little direct labor. Department B is labor-intensive and uses machinery very little. Instead of a single, **plantwide overhead rate,** the firm uses multiple **departmental overhead rates.** The predetermined overhead rates are computed as follows:

Department A: Predetermined Overhead Rate

$$\frac{\text{Estimated overhead for department A}}{\text{Estimated machine hours in department A}} = \frac{\$10,000}{2,000 \text{ hours}} = \$5.00 \text{ per machine hour}$$

Department B: Predetermined Overhead Rate

$$\frac{\text{Estimated overhead for department B}}{\text{Estimated direct-labor-hours in department B}} = \frac{\$4,000}{4,000 \text{ hours}} = \$1.00 \text{ per direct-labor hour}$$

Separate Work-in-Process Inventory accounts are maintained for each department, and product costs are accumulated as follows:

Work-in-Process Inventory Department A		Work-in-Process Inventory Department B	
Direct material used in department A	Cost of units finished in department A and transferred to department B	Cost of units finished in department A and transferred to department B	Cost of units finished in department B and transferred to Finished-Goods Inventory
Direct-labor costs incurred in department A			
Applied overhead:		Direct material used in department B	
$\left(\begin{array}{c}\text{Machine} \\ \text{hours} \\ \text{used in} \\ \text{depart-} \\ \text{ment A}\end{array}\right) \times \left(\begin{array}{c}\$5.00 \\ \text{per} \\ \text{machine} \\ \text{hour}\end{array}\right)$		Direct-labor costs incurred in department B	
		Applied overhead:	
		$\left(\begin{array}{c}\text{Direct-} \\ \text{labor} \\ \text{hours} \\ \text{used in} \\ \text{depart-} \\ \text{ment B}\end{array}\right) \times \left(\begin{array}{c}\$1.00 \\ \text{per} \\ \text{direct-} \\ \text{labor} \\ \text{hour}\end{array}\right)$	

Costs and Benefits The theme of costs and benefits arises again with respect to using a single, plantwide overhead rate or multiple overhead rates. A product costing system using multiple cost drivers and overhead rates is more complicated and more costly to use. However, the product costing information that results is more accurate and more useful for decision making. Weighing these costs and benefits is part of the managerial accountant's job in designing a product costing system.

The trend in today's highly automated manufacturing environments is toward greater use of multiple cost drivers for overhead application. We will study these product costing systems in Chapter 5.

PROJECT COSTING: JOB-ORDER COSTING IN NONMANUFACTURING ORGANIZATIONS

Job-order costing is also used in nonmanufacturing organizations. However, rather than referring to production "jobs," such organizations use terminology that reflects their operations. Hospitals and law firms assign costs to "cases," consulting firms and advertising agencies have "contracts," and governmental agencies often refer to "programs" or "missions." The need for cost accumulation exists in these and similar organizations for the same reasons found in manufacturing firms. For example, a NASA mission to launch a commercial satellite is assigned a cost for the purposes of planning, cost control, and pricing of the launch service.

To illustrate the cost accumulation system used in a service industry firm, the following information is given for Midtown Advertising Agency, Inc.

Budgeted overhead for 19x4:

Indirect labor (secretarial and custodial)	$120,000
Indirect materials	15,000
Photocopying	4,000
Computer leasing	17,000
Supplies	14,000
Utilities	21,000
Building rental	90,000
Insurance	8,000
Postage	11,000
Total	$300,000
Budgeted direct professional labor (salaries of advertising account executives)	$120,000

Budgeted Overhead Rate:

$$\frac{\text{Budgeted overhead}}{\text{Budgeted direct professional labor}} = \frac{\$300,000}{\$120,000} = 250\%$$

Overhead is assigned to each contract at the rate of 250 percent of the contract's direct-labor cost. During June of 19x4, Midtown Advertising Agency completed a project for the Super Scoop Ice Cream Company. The contract required $800 in direct materials, to build an advertising display to use in trade shows, and $4,000 in direct professional labor. The cost of the contract is computed as follows:

Contract B628: Advertising Program for Super Scoop Ice Cream Company

Direct material.	$ 800
Direct professional labor	4,000
Overhead (250% × $4,000).	10,000
Total contract cost.	$14,800

The contract cost of $14,800 includes actual direct-material and direct-labor costs, and applied overhead based on the predetermined overhead rate of 250 percent of direct-labor cost. The contract cost can be used by the firm in controlling costs, for planning cash flows and operations, and as one informational input in its contract-pricing decisions. In addition to the contract cost, the firm should also consider the demand for its advertising services and the prices charged by its competitors.

The discussion above provides only a brief overview of cost accumulation procedures in service industry and nonprofit organizations. The main point is that job-order costing systems are used in a wide variety of organizations, and these systems provide important information to managers for planning, decision making, and control. The following case in point illustrates the role of cost accumulation in controlling costs.

ILLUSTRATION FROM MANAGEMENT ACCOUNTING PRACTICE

Controlling Costs in an Advertising Agency

The management of JKL, Inc., an advertising agency based in New York City, became aware that some of the firm's advertising accounts were unprofitable. As part of the firm's cost accumulation procedures, the amounts of various types of labor used in servicing each account were recorded. One account manager noticed that much of the creative work for one of her accounts was being done by supervisors in the creative department, rather than by the creative staff of the department. Since the cost of supervisory time is much higher than the cost of staff time, the labor costs incurred on the account were much higher than was necessary. The account manager pointed this out to her supervisors, and a staff creative team was appointed to her account. The result was considerable cost savings for the firm.[1]

CHAPTER SUMMARY

Product costing is the process of accumulating the costs of a production process and assigning them to the firm's products. Product costs are needed for three major purposes: (1) to value inventory and cost of goods sold in financial accounting, (2) to provide managerial accounting information to managers for planning, cost control, and decision making, and (3) to provide cost data to various organizations outside the firm, such as governmental agencies or insurance companies. Information about the costs of producing goods and services is needed in manufacturing companies, service industry firms, and nonprofit organizations.

Two types of product costing systems are used, depending on the type of product manufactured. Process costing is used by companies that produce large numbers of nearly identical products, such as canned dog food and motor oil. Job-order costing,

[1] W. B. Mills, "Drawing Up a Budgeting System for an Ad Agency," *Management Accounting,* December 1983, p. 59.

the topic of this chapter, is used by firms that produce relatively small numbers of dissimilar products, such as furniture and kitchen appliances.

In a job-order costing system, the costs of direct material, direct labor, and manufacturing overhead are first entered into the Work-in-Process Inventory account. When goods are completed, the accumulated manufacturing costs are transferred from Work-in-Process Inventory to Finished-Goods Inventory. Finally, these product costs are transferred from Finished-Goods Inventory to Cost of Goods Sold when sales occur. Direct material and direct labor are traced easily to specific batches of production, called job orders. In contrast, manufacturing overhead is an indirect cost with respect to job orders or units of product. Therefore, overhead is applied to production jobs using a predetermined overhead rate, which is based on estimates of manufacturing overhead and the level of some cost driver (or activity base). The most commonly used volume-based cost drivers are direct-labor hours, direct-labor cost, and machine hours. Since these estimates will seldom be completely accurate, the amount of overhead applied during an accounting period to Work-in-Process Inventory will usually differ from the actual costs incurred for overhead items. The difference between actual overhead and applied overhead, called overapplied or underapplied overhead, may be closed out into Cost of Goods Sold or prorated among Work-in-Process Inventory, Finished-Goods Inventory, and Cost of Goods Sold.

Job-order costing methods also are used in a variety of service industry firms and nonprofit organizations. Accumulating costs of projects, contracts, cases, programs, or missions provides important information to managers in such organizations as hospitals, law firms, and government agencies.

KEY TERMS   Activity base, p. 68; Actual costing, p. 83; Actual manufacturing overhead, p. 75; Actual overhead rate, p. 81; Applied manufacturing overhead, p. 75; Bill of materials, p. 65; Cost Accounting Standards Board (CASB), p. 79; Cost distribution (sometimes called cost allocation), p. 67; Cost of goods manufactured, p. 79; Cycle time, p. 84; Departmental overhead centers, p. 67; Departmental overhead rate, p. 85; Job-cost sheet, p. 65; Job-order costing, p. 62; Material requirements planning (MRP), p. 66; Material requisition form, p. 65; Normal costing, p. 83; Normalized overhead rate, p. 83; Overapplied overhead, p. 77; Overhead application (or absorption), p. 67; Plantwide overhead rate, p. 85; Predetermined overhead rate, p. 69; Process costing system, p. 63; Product costing system, p. 59; Proration, p. 78; Schedule of cost of goods manufactured, p. 79; Schedule of cost of goods sold, p. 79; Service department cost allocation, p. 67; Source document, p. 65; Time ticket, p. 66; Throughput time, p. 84; Underapplied overhead, p. 77; Volume-based cost driver, p. 68.

Computing the Predetermined Overhead Rate over Different Time Periods

Backyard Barbecue Company manufactures a variety of barbecue grills and related equipment. The firm uses a job-order costing system. Manufacturing overhead is applied using a predetermined rate based on direct-labor hours. Due to seasonal sales of its products, the company produces at a higher volume from January through June than from July through December. Seasonal and part-time labor is used to augment the labor force during peak production periods. The following estimates have been made for 19x6. Predetermined overhead rates, computed for each quarter, are also shown below.

	Estimated Manufacturing Overhead	Estimated Direct-Labor Hours	Quarterly Predetermined Overhead Rate (per direct-labor hour)
First quarter (January–March)	$ 70,000	20,000	$3.50
Second quarter (April–June).	50,000	10,000	5.00
Third quarter (July–September) . . .	35,000	10,000	3.50
Fourth quarter (October–December)	25,000	5,000	5.00
Total	$180,000	45,000	

If Backyard Barbecue Company were to compute an annual predetermined overhead rate, the rate would be $4.00 per direct-labor hour ($180,000 ÷ 45,000 hours). Two implications of the firm's use of a quarterly overhead rate instead of an annual rate are discussed below.

Pricing Based on Product Costs One of the company's products, a gas barbeque grill with preparation table and storage cabinet, requires the following material and labor inputs.

Direct material	$30 per unit
Direct labor (5 hours at $15.00 per hour).	75 per unit

Identical grills manufactured in January and June will be assigned the following product costs.

	January	June
Direct material	$ 30.00	$ 30.00
Direct labor	75.00	75.00
Applied overhead:		
5 hours at $3.50 per hour in January	17.50	
5 hours at $5.00 per hour in June		25.00
Total cost	$122.50	$130.00

The difference of $7.50 per unit may not seem to be very significant. However, if product prices are based, at least partially, on these product costs, the result may be an erratic and noncompetitive pricing policy.

Suppose that Backyard Barbecue Company were to use an annual overhead rate of $4.00 per direct labor hour. Then the two identical grills will be assigned the same product cost, as computed below.

	June or December
Direct material	$ 30.00
Direct labor	75.00
Applied overhead (5 hours at $4.00 per hour annual rate)	20.00
Total cost	125.00

If product prices are based in part on this product cost, the result will be a more stable pricing policy.

Income Measurement Assume that Backyard Barbecue Company uses quarterly predetermined overhead rates. To simplify matters, suppose the firm has only one product line, the gas barbecue grill. The following production and sales levels occurred during the first and second quarters of 19x6.

	First Quarter	Second Quarter
Sales	3,000 units	3,000 units
Production	4,000 units	2,000 units

We will assume that Backyard Barbecue Company has a stable pricing policy based on a competitive market price of $150 per unit. Selling and administrative costs during each quarter were $40,000. The following quarterly income statements were prepared.

	First Quarter	Second Quarter
Sales revenue (3,000 units at $150 per unit)	$450,000	$450,000
Cost of goods sold:		
3,000 units at $122.50* per unit in first quarter	367,500	
1,000 units at $122.50* per unit in first quarter†		122,500
2,000 units at $130.00* per unit in second quarter		260,000
Gross margin	82,500	67,500
Selling and administrative expenses	40,000	40,000
Net income	$42,500	$ 27,500

* Product prices for the first and second quarter were computed in the preceding section.
† Sales in the second quarter were as follows: 1,000 units left over from first-quarter production and 2,000 units produced in the second quarter.

Why is there such a large change in income between the first and second quarters when sales were the same? The reason behind the income change is the use of quarterly predetermined overhead rates coupled with different production volumes in the first and second quarters. In the first quarter, estimated overhead of $70,000 was spread over *20,000* estimated direct-labor hours (for 4,000 units of product). In the second quarter, estimated overhead of $50,000 was spread over only *10,000* estimated direct-labor hours (for 2,000 units of product). The result is that products produced in the second quarter appear to be more costly than those produced in the first quarter.

Most managers reject the notion that the first-quarter products were less costly to produce. With no changes in the production technology, relatively stable input prices, and no significant change in efficiency, the grills produced in January and June should cost about the same amount. Managers could be misled by the quarterly income statements shown above. For example, they might erroneously conclude that there were significant changes in production efficiency resulting in a large jump in profit in the second quarter.

The problem described above would not occur if Backyard Barbecue Company were to use an annual predetermined overhead rate. Then the income statements for the first two quarters of 19x6 would appear as follows:

	First Quarter	Second Quarter
Sales revenue (3,000 units at $150 per unit).	$450,000	$450,000
Cost of goods sold (3,000 units at $125 per unit)*.	375,000	375,000
Gross margin	75,000	75,000
Selling and administrative expenses	40,000	40,000
Net income.	$ 35,000	$ 35,000

* The product cost, using an annual overhead rate, was computed in the preceding section.

Use of an overhead rate that is normalized over a year or more smooths out fluctuations in the product cost that can cause large changes in income, even when sales remain constant. For this reason, most managers prefer to use information based on normalized overhead rates.

REVIEW QUESTIONS

3-1. List and explain three purposes of product costing.

3-2. How is the concept of product costing applied in service industry firms?

3-3. Explain the difference between job-order and process costing.

3-4. What are the purposes of the following documents: (a) job-cost sheet, (b) material requisition form, and (c) labor time ticket.

3-5. Define each of the following terms, and explain the relationship between them: (a) overhead cost distribution, (b) service department cost allocation, and (c) overhead application.

3-6. Why is manufacturing overhead applied to products when product costs are used in making pricing decisions?

3-7. Explain the benefits of using a predetermined overhead rate instead of an actual overhead rate.

3-8. Describe one advantage and one disadvantage of prorating overapplied or underapplied overhead.

3-9. Describe an important cost-benefit issue involving accuracy versus timeliness in accounting for overhead.

3-10. Explain the difference between actual and normal costing.

3-11. When a single, volume-based cost driver (or activity base) is used to apply manufacturing overhead, what is the managerial accountant's primary objective in selecting the cost driver?

3-12. Describe some costs and benefits of using multiple overhead rates instead of a plantwide overhead rate.

3-13. Describe how job-order costing concepts are used in professional service firms, such as law practices and consulting firms.

3-14. What is meant by *material requirements planning* or *MRP*?

3-15. What is meant by the term *cost driver?* What is a *volume-based cost driver?*

3-16. Describe the flow of costs through a product costing system. What special accounts are involved, and how are they used?

3-17. Give an example of how a hospital might use job-order costing concepts.

3-18. Why are some manufacturing firms switching from direct-labor hours to machine hours or throughput time as the basis for overhead application?

3-19. What is the cause of overapplied or underapplied overhead?

3-20. Briefly describe two ways of closing out overapplied or underapplied overhead at the end of an accounting period.

EXERCISES   *Exercise 3-21   Manufacturing Cost Flows.* Reimel's Furniture Company, Inc. incurred the following costs during 19x3.

Direct material.	$158,000
Direct labor	340,000
Manufacturing overhead.	180,000

During 19x3, products costing $120,000 were finished, and products costing $132,000 were sold for $190,000. The beginning balances in the firm's inventory accounts are shown below.

Raw materials	$211,000
Work in process.	18,000
Finished goods.	30,000

REQUIRED:

1. Prepare T-accounts to show the flow of costs through the company's manufacturing accounts during 19x3.
2. Prepare a partial balance sheet and a partial income statement to reflect the information given above. (Hint: See Exhibit 3-2.)

Exercise 3-22   Job-Cost Sheet. Garrett Toy Company incurred the following costs to produce job number M42, which consisted of 1,000 teddy bears that can walk, talk, and play cards.

Direct Material:

4/1/x0 Requisition number 101: 400 yards of fabric at $.75 per yard
4/5/x0 Requisition number 108: 500 cubic feet of stuffing at $.25 per cubic foot

Direct Labor:

4/15/x0 Time card number 72: 500 hours at $12 per hour

Manufacturing Overhead:

Applied on the basis of direct-labor hours at $2.00 per hour.

On April 30, 800 of the bears were shipped to a local toy store.

REQUIRED: Prepare a job-cost sheet and record the information given above. (Use Exhibit 3-3 as a guide.)

Exercise 3-23 **Schedule of Cost of Goods Manufactured.** Oakley Canning Company incurred the following actual costs during 19x7.

Direct material used	$270,000
Direct labor	120,000
Manufacturing overhead....................................	252,000

The firm's predetermined overhead rate is 210 percent of direct-labor cost. The January 1, 19x7 inventory balances were as follows:

Raw material	$ 25,000
Work in process..	39,000
Finished goods..	42,000

Each of these inventory balances was 10 percent higher at the end of the year.

REQUIRED:

1. Prepare a schedule of cost of goods manufactured for 19x7.
2. What was the cost of goods sold for the year?

Exercise 3-24 **Predetermined Overhead Rate; Various Cost Drivers.** The following data pertain to the Elk Lake Marine Supply Company for 19x8.

Budgeted machine hours.....................................	10,000
Budgeted direct-labor hours	20,000
Budgeted direct-labor rate...................................	$14
Budgeted manufacturing overhead............................	$364,000
Actual machine hours.......................................	11,000
Actual direct-labor hours	18,000
Actual direct-labor rate.....................................	$15
Actual manufacturing overhead..............................	$330,000

REQUIRED:

1. Compute the firm's 19x8 predetermined overhead rate using each of the following common cost drivers: (a) machine hours, (b) direct-labor hours, and (c) direct-labor dollars.
2. Calculate the overapplied or underapplied overhead for 19x8 using each of the cost drivers listed above.

Exercise 3-25 **Actual versus Normal Costing.** Refer to the data for the preceding exercise for Elk Lake Marine Supply Company. Prepare a journal entry to add to work-in-process inventory the total manufacturing overhead cost for 19x8, assuming:

1. The firm uses actual costing.
2. The firm uses normal costing, with a predetermined overhead rate based on machine hours.

Exercise 3-26 **Basic Journal Entries in Job-Order Costing.** Caroline Educational Products started and finished job number B67 during June. The job required $4,000 of direct material and 40 hours of direct labor at $17 per hour. The predetermined overhead rate is $5 per direct-labor hour.

REQUIRED: Prepare journal entries to record the incurrence of production costs and the completion of job number B67.

Exercise 3-27 **Overapplied or Underapplied Overhead.** The following information pertains to Johnson City Metal Works for 19x4.

Budgeted direct-labor cost: 75,000 hours at $14 per hour
Actual direct-labor cost: 80,000 hours at $15 per hour
Budgeted manufacturing overhead: $997,500
Actual manufacturing overhead:

Depreciation.	$240,000
Property taxes	12,000
Indirect labor	82,000
Supervisory salaries	200,000
Utilities.	59,000
Insurance	30,000
Rental of space.	300,000
Indirect material (see data below)	79,000
Indirect material:	
Beginning inventory, 12/31/x3	$ 42,000
Purchases during 19x4.	100,000
Ending inventory, 12/31/x4	63,000

REQUIRED:

1. Compute the firm's predetermined overhead rate, which is based on direct-labor hours.
2. Calculate the overapplied or underapplied overhead for 19x4.
3. Prepare a journal entry to close out the Manufacturing Overhead account into Cost of Goods Sold.

Exercise 3-28 **Fixed and Variable Costs; Overhead Rate; Agribusiness.** The controller for Turkey Hill Poultry, Inc. estimates that the company's fixed overhead is $100,000 per year. She also has determined that the variable overhead is approximately $.10 per chicken raised and sold. Since the firm has a single product, overhead is applied on the basis of output units, chickens raised and sold.

REQUIRED:

1. Calculate the predetermined overhead rate under each of the following output predictions: 200,000 chickens, 300,000 chickens, and 400,000 chickens.
2. Does the predetermined overhead rate change in proportion to the change in predicted production? Why?

Exercise 3-29   Project Costing; Interior Decorating. Design Arts Associates is an interior decorating firm in St. Louis. The following costs were incurred in the firm's contract to redecorate the mayor's offices.

Direct material. $2,800
Direct professional labor. 6,000

The firm's budget for the year included the following estimates:

Budgeted overhead $400,000
Budgeted direct professional labor 250,000

Overhead is applied to contracts using a predetermined overhead rate calculated annually. The rate is based on direct professional labor cost.

REQUIRED: Calculate the total cost of the firm's contract to redecorate the mayor's offices.

Exercise 3-30   Proration of Underapplied Overhead. Mount Pleasant Confectionary incurred $149,000 of manufacturing overhead costs during 19x1. However, only $141,000 of overhead was applied to production. At the conclusion of 19x1, the following amounts of the year's applied overhead remained in the various manufacturing accounts.

	19x1 Applied Overhead Remaining in Account on December 31, 19x1
Work-in-Process Inventory.	$35,250
Finished-Goods Inventory	49,350
Cost of Goods Sold	56,400

REQUIRED: Prepare a journal entry to close out the balance in the Manufacturing Overhead account and prorate the balance to the three manufacturing accounts.

Exercise 3-31   Cost Drivers; Different Production Methods. Hudson Bay Leatherworks, which manufactures saddles and other leather goods, has three departments. The Assembly Department manufactures various leather products, such as belts, purses, and saddlebags, using an automated production process. The Saddle Department produces handmade saddles and uses very little machinery. The Tanning Department produces leather. The tanning process requires little in the way of labor or machinery, but it does require space and process time. Due to the different production processes in the three departments, the company uses three different cost drivers for the application of manufacturing overhead. The cost drivers and overhead rates are as follows:

	Cost Driver	Predetermined Overhead Rate
Tanning Department	Square feet of leather	$2 per square foot
Assembly Department	Machine time	$8 per machine hour
Saddle Department	Direct-labor time	$5 per direct-labor hour

The company's deluxe saddle and accessory set consists of a handmade saddle, two saddlebags, a belt, and a vest, all coordinated to match. The entire set uses 100 square feet of leather from the Tanning Department, 3 machine hours in the Assembly Department, and 40 direct-labor hours in the Saddle Department.

REQUIRED: Job number DS-20 consisted of 20 deluxe saddle and accessory sets. Prepare journal entries to record applied manufacturing overhead in the Work-in-Process Inventory account for each department.

Exercise 3-32   Choice of a Cost Driver for Overhead Application. Suppose you are the controller for a company that produces handmade glassware. Choose a volume-based cost driver upon which to base the application of overhead. Write a memo to the company president explaining your choice.

Now you have changed jobs. You are the controller of a microchip manufacturer that uses a highly automated production process. Repeat the same requirements stated above.

PROBLEMS   *Problem 3-33   Basic Manufacturing Cost Flows.* Selected data concerning the past year's operations of the Televans Manufacturing Company are presented below.

	Inventories	
	Beginning	Ending
Raw materials	$75,000	$ 85,000
Work-in-process.	80,000	30,000
Finished goods.	90,000	110,000
Other data:		
Direct materials used.		$326,000
Total manufacturing costs charged to production during the year (includes direct material, direct labor, and manufacturing overhead applied at a rate of 60% of direct-labor cost)		686,000
Cost of goods available for sale.		826,000
Selling and administrative expenses		25,000

REQUIRED:

1. What was the cost of raw materials purchased during the year?
2. What was the direct-labor cost charged to production during the year?
3. What was the cost of goods manufactured during the year?
4. What was the cost of goods sold during the year?

(CMA, adapted)

Problem 3-34   Schedules of Cost of Goods Manufactured and Sold; Income Statement. The following data refers to Sprintco, Inc. for the year 19x8.

Raw material inventory, 12/31/x7	$ 80,000
Purchases of raw material in 19x8.	740,000
Raw material inventory, 12/31/x8	65,000
Direct-labor cost incurred	480,000
Selling and administrative expenses	270,000

Indirect labor cost incurred	150,000
Property taxes.	90,000
Depreciation on factory building.	125,000
Income tax expense	25,000
Indirect material used.	45,000
Depreciation on factory equipment.	60,000
Insurance on factory and equipment.	40,000
Utilities for factory.	70,000
Work-in-process inventory, 12/31/x7	-0-
Work-in-process inventory, 12/31/x8	40,000
Finished goods inventory, 12/31/x7	35,000
Finished goods inventory, 12/31/x8	40,000
Applied manufacturing overhead	577,500
Sales revenue	2,105,000

REQUIRED:

1. Prepare Sprintco's schedule of cost of goods manufactured for 19x8.
2. Prepare Sprintco's schedule of cost of goods sold for 19x8. The company closes overapplied or underapplied overhead into Cost of Goods Sold.
3. Prepare Sprintco's income statement for 19x8.

Problem 3-35 *Interpreting the Schedule of Cost of Goods Manufactured.* Refer to the schedule of cost of goods manufactured prepared in the preceding problem.

REQUIRED:

1. How much of the manufacturing costs incurred during 19x8 remained associated with work-in-process inventory on December 31, 19x8?
2. Suppose Sprintco had increased its production in 19x8 by 20 percent. Would the direct-material cost shown on the schedule have been larger or the same? Why?
3. Answer the same question as in requirement (2) for depreciation on the factory building.
4. Suppose only half of the $60,000 in depreciation on equipment had been related to factory machinery, and the other half was related to selling and administrative equipment. How would this have changed the schedule of cost of goods manufactured?

Problem 3-36 *Basic Job-Order Costing; Journal Entries.* Lancaster Clock Works manufactures fine, handcrafted clocks. The firm uses a job-order costing system, and manufacturing overhead is applied on the basis of direct-labor hours. Estimated manufacturing overhead for 19x9 is $240,000. The firm employs 10 master clockmakers, who constitute the direct-labor force. Each of these employees is expected to work 2,000 hours during the year. The following events occurred during October 19x9.

(a) The firm purchased 2,000 board feet of mahogany veneer at $10 per board foot.
(b) Twenty brass counterweights were requisitioned for production. Each weight cost $25.
(c) Five gallons of glue were requisitioned for production. The glue cost $20 per gallon. Glue is treated as an indirect material.
(d) Depreciation on the clockworks building for October was $8,000.
(e) A $400 utility bill was paid in cash.

(f) Time cards showed the following usage of labor:

Job number G60:   12 grandfather's clocks, 1,000 hours of direct labor
Job number C81:   20 cuckoo clocks, 700 hours of direct labor

The master clockmakers (direct-labor personnel) earn $20 per hour.

(g) The October property tax bill for $850 was received but not yet paid in cash.
(h) The firm employs laborers who perform various tasks such as material handling and shop cleanup. Their wages for October amounted to $2,500.
(i) Job number G60, which was started in July, was finished in October. The total cost of the job was $14,400.
(j) Nine of the grandfather's clocks from job number G60 were sold in October for $1,500 each.

REQUIRED:

1. Calculate the firm's predetermined overhead rate for 19x9.
2. Prepare journal entries to record the events described above.

Problem 3-37   Cost of Goods Manufactured; Prime and Conversion Costs. Matson Company's cost of goods sold for March 19x4 was $345,000. March 31 work-in-process inventory was 90 percent of March 1 work-in-process inventory. Manufacturing overhead applied was 50 percent of direct-labor cost. Other information pertaining to Matson Company's inventories and production for the month of March is as follows:

Beginning inventories, March 1:	
Direct material...	$ 20,000
Work in process...	40,000
Finished goods..	102,000
Purchases of direct material during March	110,000
Ending inventories, March 31:	
Direct material...	26,000
Work in process...	?
Finished goods..	105,000

REQUIRED:

1. Prepare a schedule of cost of goods manufactured for the month of March.
2. Prepare a schedule to compute the prime costs (direct material and direct labor) incurred during March.
3. Prepare a schedule to compute the conversion costs (direct labor and manufacturing overhead) charged to work in process during March.

(CPA, adapted)

Problem 3-38   Cost of Goods Manufactured; Overapplied or Underapplied Overhead. Haverford Company uses job-order costing. Manufacturing overhead is applied to production at a predetermined overhead rate of 150 percent of direct-labor cost. Any overapplied or underapplied manufacturing overhead is closed into cost of goods sold at the end of each month. Additional information follows.

● Job 101 was the only job in process on January 31, 19x2, with accumulated costs as follows:

Direct material...	$4,000
Direct labor	2,000
Applied manufacturing overhead	3,000
Total...	$9,000

- Jobs 102, 103, and 104 were started during February.
- Direct-materials requisitions during February totaled $26,000.
- Direct-labor cost of $20,000 was incurred during February.
- Actual manufacturing overhead was $32,000 in February.
- The only job still in process on February 28, 19x2, was job 104, with costs of $2,800 for direct material and $1,800 for direct labor.

REQUIRED:

1. Calculate the cost of goods manufactured during February 19x2.
2. Calculate the amount of overapplied or underapplied overhead to be closed into cost of goods sold on February 28, 19x2.
3. Prepare journal entries to record the events described in requirements (1) and (2).
(CPA, adapted)

Problem 3-39 *Journal Entries in Job-Order Costing.* Harbor Master Corporation manufactures outboard motors and an assortment of other marine equipment. The company uses a job-order costing system. Normal costing is used, and manufacturing overhead is applied on the basis of machine hours. Estimated manufacturing overhead for 19x0 is $1,480,000, and management expects that 74,000 machine hours will be used.

REQUIRED:

1. Calculate Harbor Master Corporation's predetermined overhead rate for 19x0.
2. Prepare journal entries to record the following events, which occurred during April 19x0.
   a. The firm purchased marine propellers from Seaway Corporation for $8,000 on account.
   b. A requisition was filed by the Gauge Department supervisor for 200 pounds of clear plastic. The material cost $.50 per pound when it was purchased.
   c. The Motor Testing Department supervisor requisitioned 300 feet of electrical wire, which is considered an indirect material. The wire cost $.10 per foot when it was purchased.
   d. An electric utility bill of $800 was paid in cash.
   e. Direct-labor costs incurred in April were $75,000.
   f. April's insurance cost was $1,800 for insurance on the cars driven by sales personnel. The policy had been prepaid in March.
   g. Metal tubing costing $3,000 was purchased on account.
   h. A cash payment of $1,700 was made on outstanding accounts payable.
   i. Indirect-labor costs of $21,000 were incurred during April.
   j. Depreciation on equipment for April amounted to $7,000.
   k. Job number G22, consisting of 50 tachometers, was finished during April. The total cost of the job was $1,100.
   l. During April, 7,000 machine hours were used.
   m. Sales on account for April amounted to $180,000. The cost of goods sold in April was $145,000.

Problem 3-40 Schedules of Cost of Goods Manufactured and Sold; Income Statement. The following data refer to Twisto Pretzel Company for the year 19x6.

Income tax expense...	$ 4,100
Work-in-process inventory, 12/31/x5............................	9,200
Selling and administrative salaries	14,000
Insurance on factory and equipment	3,600
Work-in-process inventory, 12/31/x6............................	9,400
Finished-goods inventory, 12/31/x5.............................	14,000
Indirect material used	4,900
Depreciation on factory equipment	2,100
Raw material inventory, 12/31x5...............................	10,100
Property taxes	2,400
Finished-goods inventory, 12/31x6	15,400
Purchases of raw material in 19x6	39,000
Utilities for factory	6,000
Utilities for sales and administrative offices.....................	2,000
Other selling and administrative expenses.......................	4,500
Indirect-labor cost incurred....................................	29,000
Depreciation on factory building	3,800
Depreciation on cars used by sales personnel	1,200
Direct-labor cost incurred......................................	79,000
Raw material inventory, 12/31/x6	11,000
Rental for warehouse space to store raw materials	3,100
Rental of space for company president's office	1,500
Applied manufacturing overhead...............................	58,000
Sales revenue	205,800

REQUIRED:

1. Prepare Twisto Pretzel Company's schedule of cost of goods manufactured for 19x6.
2. Prepare the company's schedule of cost of goods sold for 19x6. The company closes overapplied or underapplied overhead into Cost of Goods Sold.
3. Prepare the company's income statement for 19x6.

Problem 3-41 Predetermined Overhead Rate; Overhead Application. Bayline Company uses a job-order costing system for its production costs. A predetermined overhead rate based on direct-labor hours is used to apply overhead to jobs. A budget of manufacturing overhead costs was prepared for 19x7 as shown below.

Direct-labor hours	100,000	120,000	140,000
Variable manufacturing overhead costs	$325,000	$390,000	$455,000
Fixed manufacturing overhead costs	216,000	216,000	216,000
Total overhead.......................	$541,000	$606,000	$671,000

Although the plant could accommodate 150,000 direct-labor hours in a year, management has determined that the plant normally operates at 120,000 direct-labor hours. The information presented below is for November 19x7. Jobs 50 and 51 were completed during November.

Inventories, November 1:

Direct material and supplies	$ 10,500
Work-in-process (job 50)	54,000
Finished goods	112,500

Purchases of direct material and supplies:

Direct material	$135,000
Supplies (indirect material)	15,000

Direct material and supplies requisitioned for production:

Job 50	$ 45,000
Job 51	37,500
Job 52	25,500
Supplies (indirect material)	12,000
Total	$120,000

Factory direct-labor hours:

Job 50	3,500
Job 51	3,000
Job 52	2,000

Labor costs:

Direct-labor wages	$ 51,000
Indirect-labor wages (4,000 hours)	15,000
Supervisory salaries	6,000

Building occupancy costs (heat, light, depreciation, etc.):

Factory facilities	$ 6,500
Sales offices	1,500
Administrative offices	1,000
Total	$ 9,000

Factory equipment costs:

Power	$ 4,000
Repairs and maintenance	1,500
Depreciation	1,500
Other	1,000
Total	$ 8,000

REQUIRED:

1. Calculate the predetermined overhead rate for 19x7.
2. Calculate the total cost of job 50.
3. Compute the amount of manufacturing overhead applied to job 52 during November of 19x7.
4. What was the total amount of manufacturing overhead applied during November of 19x7?
5. Compute the actual manufacturing overhead incurred during November of 19x7.
6. Calculate the overapplied or underapplied overhead for November of 19x7.

(CMA, adapted)

Problem 3-42   *Project Costing; Research and Development; Cost Control..* Fargo Company has an extensive research program. Each research project is broken down into phases, with the completion times and the cost of each phase estimated. The project descriptions and related estimates serve as the basis for the development of the research department's annual budget.

The schedule below presents the costs for the approved research activities for a recent year. The actual costs incurred, by project or overhead category, are compared to the budgeted cost.

The director of research prepared a statement of research performance for the year to accompany the schedule. The director's statement follows the schedule.

Fargo Company
Comparison of Actual with Budgeted Research Costs
(in thousands)

	Budgeted Costs for the Year	Actual Costs for the Year	(Over) Under Budget
Projects in progress:			
74-1..............................	$ 23.2	$ 46.8	$(23.6)
75-3..............................	464.0*	514.8	(50.8)
New projects:			
78-1..............................	348.0	351.0	(3.0)
78-2..............................	232.0	257.4	(25.4)
78-3..............................	92.8	—	92.8
Total research costs	$1,160.0	$1,170.0	$(10.0)
General research:			
Overhead costs (allocated to projects in proportion to their direct costs)			
Administration......................	$ 50.0	$ 52.0	$ (2.0)
Laboratory facilities..................	110.0	118.0	(8.0)
Total............................	$ 160.0	$ 170.0	$(10.0)
Allocated to projects	(160.0)	(170.0)	(10.0)
Balance...........................	$ 0	$ 0	$ 0
Total research costs	$1,160.0	$1,170.0	$(10.0)

* Phases 3 and 4 only.

Director's Statement: "The year has been very successful. The two projects, 74-1 and 78-1, scheduled for completion in 19x8 were finished. Project 78-2 is progressing satisfactorily and should be completed in 19x9 as scheduled. The fourth phase of project 75-3, with estimated direct research costs of $100,000 and the first phase of project 78-3, both included in the budgeted costs for the year, could not be started because the principal researcher left our employment. These two projects were resubmitted for approval in next year's activity plan."

REQUIRED:

1. Prepare an alternative schedule that does not allocate indirect costs to projects. Which schedule do you believe is more useful to management? Why?
2. Should project 78-3 be included in the schedule? Justify your answer.

(CMA, adapted)

Problem 3-43 *Proration of Overapplied or Underapplied Overhead.* Noblette Electronics Company uses normal costing, and manufacturing overhead is applied to work-in-process on the basis of machine hours. On January 1, 19x2 there were no balances in work-in-process or finished-goods inventories. The following estimates were included in the 19x2 budget.

Total estimated manufacturing overhead. $200,000
Total estimated machine hours 40,000

During January, the firm began the following production jobs:

A79:   1,000 machine hours
N08:   2,500 machine hours
P82:   500 machine hours

During January, job numbers A79 and N08 were completed, and job number A79 was sold. The actual manufacturing overhead incurred during January was $24,000.

REQUIRED:

1. Compute the company's predetermined overhead rate for 19x2.
2. How much manufacturing overhead was applied to production during January 19x5?
3. Calculate the overapplied or underapplied overhead for January 19x5.
4. Prepare a journal entry to close the balance calculated in requirement (3) into Cost of Goods Sold.
5. Prepare a journal entry to prorate the balance calculated in requirement (3) among the Work-in-Process Inventory, Finished-Goods Inventory, and Cost of Goods Sold accounts.

Problem 3-44 *Plantwide versus Departmental Overhead Rates; Product Pricing.* Home Data Systems Corporation manufactures two popular personal computers for the household market. Cost estimates for the two computer models for the year 19x4 are shown below.

	Basic System	**Advanced System**
Direct material.	$ 400	$ 800
Direct labor (20 hours at $15 per hour)	300	300
Manufacturing overhead*	400	400
	$1,100	$1,500

* The predetermined overhead rate is $20 per direct-labor hour.

Each computer model requires 20 hours of direct labor. The basic system requires 5 hours in department A and 15 hours in department B. The advanced system requires 15 hours in department A and 5 hours in department B. The overhead costs incurred in these two production departments are as follows:

	Department A	**Department B**
Variable cost	$16 per direct-labor hour	$4 per direct-labor hour
Fixed cost.	$200,000	$200,000

The firm's management expects to operate at a level of 20,000 direct-labor hours in each production department during 19x4.

REQUIRED:

1. Show how the company's predetermined overhead rate was determined.
2. If the firm prices each computer model at 10 percent over its cost, what will be the price of each model?
3. Suppose the company were to use departmental predetermined overhead rates. Calculate the rate for each of the two production departments.
4. Compute the product cost of each model using the departmental overhead rates calculated in requirement (3).
5. Compute the price to be charged for each model, assuming the company continues to price each product at 10 percent above cost. Use the revised product costs calculated in requirement (4).
6. Write a memo to the president of Home Data Systems Corporation making a recommendation as to whether the firm should use a plantwide overhead rate or departmental rates. Consider the potential implications of the overhead rates and the firm's pricing policy. How might these considerations affect the firm's ability to compete in the marketplace?

Problem 3-45   Comprehensive Job-Order Costing Problem. Bandway Corporation manufactures brass musical instruments for use by high school students. The company uses a normal costing system, in which manufacturing overhead is applied on the basis of direct-labor hours. The company's budget for 19x5 included the following predictions.

Budgeted total manufacturing overhead $420,000
Budgeted total direct-labor hours   20,000

During March of 19x5, the firm worked on the following two production jobs:

Job number T81, consisting of 76 trombones
Job number C40, consisting of 110 cornets

The events of March are described below.

(a) One thousand square feet of rolled brass sheet metal was purchased for $5,000 on account.
(b) Four hundred pounds of brass tubing was purchased on account for $4,000.
(c) The following requisitions were filed on March 5.

Requisition number 112: (for job number T81)	250 square feet of brass sheet metal, at $5 per square foot
Requisition number 113: (for job number C40)	1,000 pounds of brass tubing, at $10 per pound
Requisition number 114:	10 gallons of valve lubricant, at $10 per gallon

All brass used in production is treated as direct material. Valve lubricant is an indirect material.

(d) An analysis of labor time cards revealed the following labor usage for March.

Direct labor: Job number T81, 800 hours at $20 per hour
Direct labor: Job number C40, 900 hours at $20 per hour
Indirect labor: General factory cleanup, $4,000
Indirect labor: Factory supervisory salaries, $9,000

(e) Depreciation of the factory building and equipment during March amounted to $12,000.

(f) Rent paid in cash for warehouse space used during March was $1,200.

(g) Utility costs incurred during March amounted to $2,100. The invoices for these costs were received, but the bills were not paid in March.

(h) March property taxes on the factory were paid in cash, $2,400.

(i) The insurance cost covering factory operations for the month of March was $3,100. The insurance policy had been prepaid.

(j) The costs of salaries and fringe benefits for sales and administrative personnel paid in cash during March amounted to $8,000.

(k) Depreciation on administrative office equipment and space amounted to $4,000.

(l) Other selling and administrative expenses paid in cash during March amounted to $1,000.

(m) Job number T81 was completed during March.

(n) Half of the trombones in job number T81 were sold on account during March for $700 each.

The March 1, 19x5 balances in selected accounts are shown below.

Cash	$ 10,000
Accounts Receivable	21,000
Prepaid Insurance	5,000
Raw Material Inventory	149,000
Manufacturing Supplies Inventory	500
Work-in-Process Inventory	91,000
Finished-Goods Inventory	220,000
Accumulated Depreciation: Buildings and Equipment	102,000
Accounts Payable	13,000
Wages Payable	8,000

REQUIRED:

1. Calculate the company's predetermined overhead rate for 19x5.
2. Prepare journal entries to record the events of March 19x5.
3. Set up T-accounts, and post the journal entries made in requirement (2).
4. Calculate the overapplied or underapplied overhead for March 19x5. Prepare a journal entry to close this balance into Cost of Goods Sold.
5. Prepare a schedule of cost of goods manufactured for March 19x5.
6. Prepare a schedule of cost of goods sold for March 19x5.
7. Prepare an income statement for March 19x5.

Problem 3-46 Job-Cost Sheet; Continuation of Preceding Problem. Refer to the preceding problem regarding Bandway Corporation. Complete the following job-cost sheet for job number T81.

Job-Cost Sheet

Job Number ____T81____   Description _____
                                     _____

Date Started _____   Date Completed _____
                                  Number of Units Completed _____

Direct Material

Date	Requisition Number	Quantity	Unit Price	Cost

Direct Labor

Dates	Time Card Numbers	Hours	Rate	Cost
3/8 to 3/12	308 to 312			

Manufacturing Overhead

Dates	Activity Base	Quantity	Application Rate	Cost
3/8 to 3/12				

Cost Summary

Cost Item	Amount
Total direct material Total direct labor Total manufacturing overhead	
Total cost	
Unit cost	

Shipping Summary

Date	Units Shipped	Units Remaining in Inventory	Cost Balance

Problem 3-47 *Predetermined Overhead Rate; Different Time Periods; Pricing; Appendix.*
Pittsburgh Foundry Company calculates its predetermined overhead rate on a quarterly basis.
The following estimates were made for 19x3.

	Estimated Manufacturing Overhead	Estimated Direct-Labor Hours	Quarterly Predetermined Overhead Rate (per direct-labor hour)
First quarter	$100,000	25,000	?
Second quarter	80,000	16,000	?
Third quarter	50,000	12,500	?
Fourth quarter	70,000	14,000	?
Total	$300,000	67,500	

The firm's main product, part number A200, requires $100 of direct material and 20 hours of direct labor per unit. The labor rate is $15 per hour.

REQUIRED:

1. Calculate the firm's quarterly predetermined overhead rate for each quarter of 19x3.
2. Determine the cost of one unit of part number A200 if it is manufactured in January or in April.
3. Suppose the company's pricing policy calls for a 10 percent markup over cost. Calculate the price to be charged for a unit of part number A200 if it is produced in January or in April.
4. Calculate the company's predetermined overhead rate for 19x3 if the rate is calculated annually.
5. Based on your answer to requirement (4), what is the cost of a unit of part number A200 if it is manufactured in January? In April?
6. What is the price of a unit of part number A200 if the predetermined overhead rate is calculated annually?

CASE   *Case 3-48   Cost Flows in a Job-Order Costing System.* GardenCo, Inc. which manufactures gardening equipment, uses a job-order costing system. The balances in selected accounts for the 11-month period ended November 30, 19x5, are as follows:

Raw-Material Inventory.....................................	$ 32,000
Work-in-Process Inventory	1,200,000
Finished-Goods Inventory...................................	2,785,000
Manufacturing Overhead....................................	2,260,000
Cost of Goods Sold.......................................	14,200,000

Work-in-process inventory consists of two jobs:

Job Number	Units	Items	Accumulated Cost
3005	...... 50,000	Estate sprinklers	$ 700,000
3006	...... 40,000	Economy sprinklers	500,000
Total			$1,200,000

The finished goods inventory consists of five items:

Items	Quantity and Unit Cost	Total Cost
Estate sprinklers	5,000 units at $22 each	$ 110,000
Deluxe sprinklers	115,000 units at $17 each	1,955,000
Brass nozzles	10,000 gross at $14 per gross	140,000
Rainmaker nozzles	5,000 gross at $16 per gross	80,000
Connectors	100,000 gross at $ 5 per gross	500,000
Total		$2,785,000

The manufacturing overhead budget prepared for 19x5 is presented below. The company applies manufacturing overhead on the basis of direct-labor hours.

The activities during the first 11 months of the year were quite close to the budget. A total of 367,000 direct-labor hours have been worked through November 30, 19x5. The budget for 19x5 contained the following data.

Budgeted direct material	$3,800,000
Budgeted purchased parts	6,000,000
Budgeted direct labor (at $10 per hour)	4,000,000

Manufacturing Overhead Budget
For the Year Ending December 31, 19x5

Indirect material...	$ 190,000
Indirect labor	700,000
Supervision..	250,000
Depreciation...	950,000
Utilities	200,000
Insurance	10,000
Property taxes...	40,000
Miscellaneous...	60,000
Total	$2,400,000

The December 19x5 transactions are summarized below.

1. All direct material, purchased parts, and indirect material are charged to Raw-Material Inventory. The December purchases were as follows:

Direct material..	$410,000
Purchased parts	285,000
Indirect material	13,000

2. The direct material, purchased parts, and indirect material were requisitioned from Raw-Material Inventory as shown below.

Job Number	Purchased Parts	Direct Material	Indirect Material	Total Requisitions
3005.....................	$110,000	$100,000	$ —	$210,000
3006.....................	—	6,000	—	6,000
4001 (30,000 gross rainmaker nozzles)	—	181,000	—	181,000
4002 (10,000 deluxe sprinklers).	—	92,000	—	92,000
4003 (50,000 ring sprinklers)...	163,000	—	—	163,000
Indirect material.............	—	—	20,000	20,000
Total	$273,000	$379,000	$20,000	$672,000

3. The payroll summary for December is as follows:

Job Number	Hours	Cost
3005...	6,000	$ 62,000
3006...	2,500	26,000
4001...	18,000	182,000
4002...	500	5,000
4003...	5,000	52,000
Indirect labor	8,000	60,000
Supervision	—	24,000
Sales and administration	—	120,000
		$531,000

4. Other manufacturing overhead costs incurred during December were as follows:

Depreciation	$62,500
Utilities...	15,000
Insurance..	1,000
Property taxes	3,500
Miscellaneous	5,000
Total..	$87,000

5. Jobs completed during December and the actual quantities were as follows:

Job Number	Quantity	Item
3005	48,000 units	Estate sprinklers
3006	39,000 units	Economy sprinklers
4001	29,500 gross	Rainmaker nozzles
4003	49,000 units	Ring sprinklers

6. The following finished products were shipped to customers during December.

Items	Quantity
Estate sprinklers	16,000 units
Deluxe sprinklers	32,000 units
Economy sprinklers	20,000 units
Ring sprinklers	22,000 units
Brass nozzles...	5,000 gross
Rainmaker nozzles.....................................	10,000 gross
Connectors	26,000 gross

REQUIRED:

1. Calculate the overapplied or underapplied overhead for the year ended December 31, 19x5. Be sure to indicate whether the overhead is overapplied or underapplied.
2. What is the appropriate accounting treatment for this overapplied or underapplied overhead balance? Explain your answer.
3. Calculate the balance in the Work-in-Process Inventory account as of December 31, 19x5.
4. Calculate the balance in Finished-Goods Inventory as of December 31, 19x5, for the estate sprinklers. Use a first-in, first-out (FIFO) inventory assumption, which assumes that the units sold came from the first job to be produced.

(CMA, adapted)

Chapter 4 Process Costing and Hybrid Product-Costing Systems

After completing this chapter, you should be able to:

- List and explain the similarities and important differences between job-order and process costing.

- Prepare journal entries to record the flow of costs in a process costing system with sequential production departments.

- Prepare a table of equivalent units under both weighted-average and FIFO process costing.

- Compute the cost per equivalent unit under the weighted-average and FIFO methods of process costing.

- Analyze the total production costs for a department under the weighted-average and FIFO methods.

- Describe how an operation costing system accumulates and assigns the costs of direct material and conversion activity in a batch manufacturing process.

We have seen that a product costing system performs two primary functions:

1. Accumulating production costs
2. Assigning those production costs to the firm's products

Product costs are needed for the purposes of planning, cost control, decision making, and reporting to various outside organizations, such as governmental regulatory agencies.

Job-order costing was described in Chapter 3. This type of product costing system is used when relatively small numbers of products are produced in distinct batches or job orders, and these products differ significantly from each other. This chapter covers **process costing systems.** Process costing is used in **repetitive production** environments, where large numbers of identical or very similar products are manufactured in a continuous flow. Industries using process costing include paper, petroleum, chemicals, textiles, food processing, lumber, and electronics.

COMPARISON OF JOB-ORDER COSTING AND PROCESS COSTING

In many ways, job-order costing and process costing are similar. Both product costing systems have the same ultimate purpose — assignment of production costs to units of output. Moreover, the flow of costs through the manufacturing accounts is the same in the two systems.

Flow of Costs   Exhibit 4-1 displays the flow of costs in two process costing situations: one with a single production department and one with two production departments used in sequence. The same accounts are used in this process costing illustration as were used in job-order costing in the preceding chapter. As the illustration shows, direct-material, direct-labor, and manufacturing overhead costs are

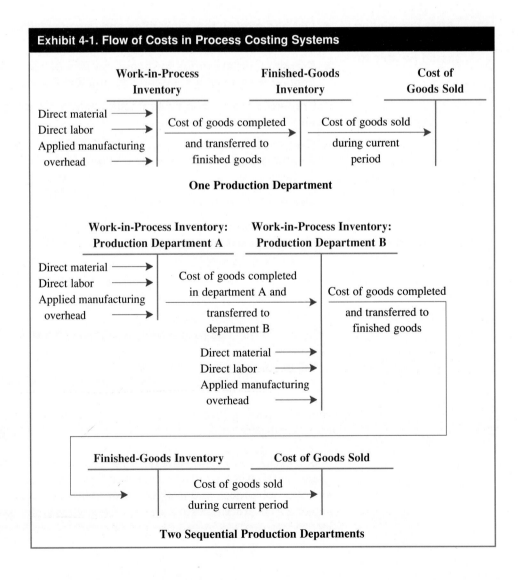

Exhibit 4-1. Flow of Costs in Process Costing Systems

added to a Work-in-Process Inventory account. As goods are finished, costs are transferred to Finished-Goods Inventory. During the period when goods are sold, the product costs are transferred to Cost of Goods Sold. In the two-department case, when goods are finished in the first production department, costs accumulated in the Work-in-Process Inventory account for production department A are transferred to the Work-in-Process Inventory account for production department B.

The journal entries for the case of two sequential production departments, as illustrated in Exhibit 4-1, are as follows:

1. As direct material and direct labor are used in production department A, these costs are added to the Work-in-Process Inventory account for department A. Overhead is applied using a predetermined overhead rate. The predetermined overhead rate is computed in the same way in job-order and process costing.

   Work-in-Process Inventory: Production Department A XXX
      Raw Material Inventory   XXX
      Wages Payable   XXX
      Manufacturing Overhead   XXX

2. When production department A completes its work on some units of product, these units are transferred to production department B. The costs assigned to these goods are transferred from the Work-in-Process Inventory account for department A to the Work-in-Process Inventory account for department B. In department B, the costs assigned to these partially completed products are called **transferred-in costs.**

   Work-in-Process Inventory: Production Department B XXX
      Work-in-Process Inventory: Production Department A   XXX

3. Direct material and direct labor are used in production department B, and manufacturing overhead is applied using a predetermined overhead rate.

   Work-in-Process Inventory: Production Department B XXX
      Raw Material Inventory   XXX
      Wages Payable   XXX
      Manufacturing Overhead   XXX

4. Goods are completed in production department B and transferred to the finished-goods warehouse.

   Finished-Goods Inventory XXX
      Work-in-Process Inventory: Production Department B   XXX

5. Goods are sold.

   Cost of Goods Sold XXX
      Finished-Goods Inventory   XXX

Differences between Job-Order and Process Costing

In job-order costing, *costs are accumulated by job order* and recorded on job-cost sheets. The cost of each unit in a particular job order is found by dividing the total cost of the job order by the number of units in the job.

In process costing, *costs are accumulated by department,* rather than by job order or batch. The cost per unit is found by averaging the total costs incurred over the units produced. Exhibit 4-2 summarizes this key difference between job-order and process costing.

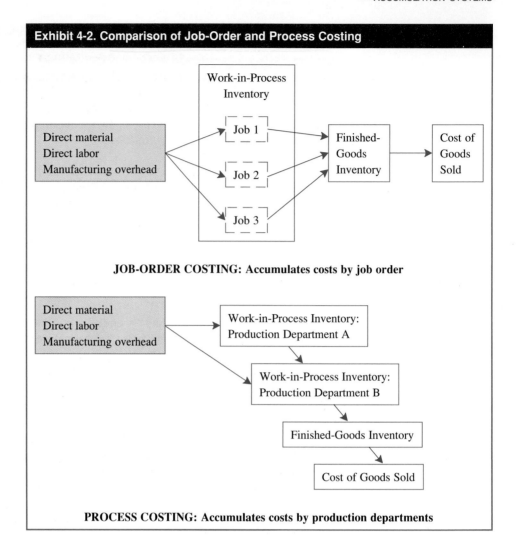

Exhibit 4-2. Comparison of Job-Order and Process Costing

JOB-ORDER COSTING: Accumulates costs by job order

PROCESS COSTING: Accumulates costs by production departments

EQUIVALENT UNITS: A KEY CONCEPT

Material, labor, and overhead costs often are incurred at different rates in a production process. Direct material is usually placed into production at one or more discrete points in the process. In contrast, direct labor and manufacturing overhead, called *conversion costs,* usually are incurred continuously throughout the process. When an accounting period ends, the partially completed goods that remain in process generally are at different stages of completion with respect to material and conversion activity. For example, the in-process units may be 75 percent complete with respect to conversion, but they may already include all of their direct materials. This situation is portrayed in Exhibit 4-3.

Equivalent Units In the graphical illustration in Exhibit 4-3, suppose there are 1,000 physical units in process at the end of an accounting period. Each of the physical units is 75 percent complete with respect to conversion (direct labor and manufacturing overhead). How much conversion activity has been applied to these partially completed units? Conversion activity occurs uniformly throughout the production process. Therefore, the amount of conversion activity required to do 75 percent of the conversion on 1,000 units is *equivalent* to the amount of conversion

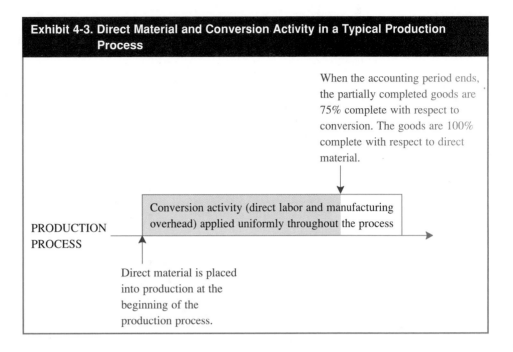

Exhibit 4-3. Direct Material and Conversion Activity in a Typical Production Process

When the accounting period ends, the partially completed goods are 75% complete with respect to conversion. The goods are 100% complete with respect to direct material.

Conversion activity (direct labor and manufacturing overhead) applied uniformly throughout the process

PRODUCTION PROCESS

Direct material is placed into production at the beginning of the production process.

activity required to do all of the conversion on 750 units. This number is computed as follows:

$$\text{1,000 partially completed physical units in process} \times \text{75\% complete with respect to conversion} = 750$$

The term **equivalent units** is used in process costing to refer to the amount of manufacturing activity that has been applied to a batch of physical units. The *1,000 physical units* in process represent *750 equivalent units* of conversion activity.

The term *equivalent units* is also used to measure the amount of direct materials represented by the partially completed goods. Since direct materials are incorporated at the beginning of the production process, the *1,000 physical units* represent *1,000 equivalent units of direct material* (1,000 physical units × 100% complete with respect to direct materials).

The most important feature of process costing is that the costs of direct material and conversion are assigned to equivalent units rather than to physical units. Refer again to Exhibit 4-3. For simplicity, suppose that the only production activity of the current accounting period was to start work on the 1,000 physical units and complete 75 percent of the required conversion activity. Assume that the costs incurred were $1,500 for conversion (direct labor and manufacturing overhead) and $5,000 for direct material. These costs would then be assigned as follows:

$$\frac{\$1,500 \text{ conversion cost}}{750 \text{ equivalent units of conversion}} = \$2.00 \text{ per equivalent unit for conversion}$$

$$\frac{\$5,000 \text{ direct-material cost}}{1,000 \text{ equivalent units of direct material}} = \$5.00 \text{ per equivalent unit for direct material}$$

This is a highly simplified example, because there is no work-in-process inventory at the beginning of the accounting period and no goods were completed during the period. Nevertheless, it illustrates the important concept that, under process costing, costs are assigned to equivalent units rather than physical units.

ILLUSTRATION OF PROCESS COSTING

The key document in a typical process-costing system is the **departmental production report,** prepared for each production department at the end of every accounting period. This report replaces the job-cost sheet, which is used to accumulate costs by job in a job-order costing system. The departmental production report summarizes the flow of production quantities through the department, and it shows the amount of production cost transferred out of the department's Work-in-Process Inventory account during the period. The following four steps are used in preparing a departmental production report.

1. Analysis of physical flow of units.
2. Calculation of equivalent units (for direct material and conversion activity).
3. Computation of unit costs (i.e., the cost per equivalent unit for direct material and conversion).
4. Analysis of total costs (determine the cost to be removed from work-in-process and transferred either to the next production department or to finished goods).

Either of two methods may be used to prepare the departmental production report: the **weighted-average** method or the **first-in, first-out (FIFO)** method. Each of these methods will be illustrated after we present the basic data used in the illustration.

Basic Data for Illustration

The New York Division of Milligan Sports Equipment Company manufactures baseball gloves. Two production departments are used in sequence: the Cutting Department and the Stitching Department. In the Cutting Department, direct material consisting of imitation leather is placed into production at the beginning of the process. Direct-labor and manufacturing overhead costs are incurred uniformly throughout the process. The material is rolled to make it softer, and it is then cut into the pieces needed to produce baseball gloves. The predetermined overhead rate used in the Cutting Department is 125 percent of direct-labor *cost.*

Exhibit 4-4 presents a summary of the activity and costs in the Cutting Department during March of 19x3. The direct-material and conversion costs listed in Exhibit 4-4 for the March 1 work in process consist of costs that were incurred during February. These costs were assigned to the units remaining in process at the end of February.

Based on the data in Exhibit 4-4, the Cutting Department's Work-in-Process Inventory account has the following balance on March 1:

Work-in-Process Inventory:
Cutting Department

3/1/x3 balance 57,200

The following journal entry is made during March to add the costs of direct material, direct labor, and manufacturing overhead to Work-in-Process Inventory.

Exhibit 4-4. Basic Data for Illustration—Cutting Department

Work in process, March 1: 20,000 units:

Direct material: 100% complete, cost of	$ 50,000*
Conversion: 10% complete, cost of	7,200*
Balance in work in process, March 1	$ 57,200*

Units started during March . . . .   30,000 units

Units completed during March and transferred
      out of the Cutting Department . . . .   40,000 units

Work in process, March 31 . . . .   10,000 units
      Direct material: 100% complete
      Conversion: 50% complete

Costs incurred during March:
      Direct material . . . . $ 90,000

Conversion costs:
      Direct labor . . . . $ 86,000
      Applied manufacturing overhead . . . .   107,500†
      Total conversion costs $193,500

*These costs were incurred during the prior month, February.

$^†\left(\begin{array}{c}\text{Predetermined}\\\text{overhead rate}\end{array}\right) \times \left(\begin{array}{c}\text{direct-}\\\text{labor cost}\end{array}\right) = 125\% \times \$86{,}000 = \$107{,}500$

Work-in-Process Inventory: Cutting Department 283,500		
Raw-Material Inventory.		90,000
Wages Payable		86,000
Manufacturing Overhead.		107,500

Weighted-Average Method

The weighted-average method of process costing is illustrated first, because it is the method most widely used in practice.

Step 1: Analysis of Physical Flow of Units The first step is to prepare a table summarizing the physical flow of production units during March. The table is shown in Exhibit 4-5. The table reflects the following inventory formula.

$$\left(\begin{array}{c}\textbf{Physical units}\\\textbf{in beginning}\\\textbf{work in process}\end{array}\right) + \left(\begin{array}{c}\textbf{physical}\\\textbf{units}\\\textbf{started}\end{array}\right) - \left(\begin{array}{c}\textbf{physical units}\\\textbf{completed and}\\\textbf{transferred out}\end{array}\right) = \left(\begin{array}{c}\textbf{physical units}\\\textbf{in ending}\\\textbf{work in process}\end{array}\right)$$

Step 2: Calculation of Equivalent Units The second step in the process-costing procedure is to calculate the equivalent units of direct material and conversion activity. A table of equivalent units, displayed in Exhibit 4-6, is based on the table of physical flows prepared in step 1 (Exhibit 4-5). The 40,000 physical units that were

---

Exhibit 4-5. Step 1: Analysis of Physical Flow of Units—Cutting Department

	Physical Units
Work in process, March 1	20,000
Units started during March	30,000
Total units to account for	50,000
Units completed and transferred out during March	40,000
Work in process, March 31	10,000
Total units accounted for	50,000

---

completed and transferred out of the Cutting Department were 100 percent complete. Thus, they represent 40,000 equivalent units for both direct material and conversion. The 10,000 units in the ending work-in-process inventory are complete with respect to direct material, and they represent 10,000 equivalent units of direct material. However, they are only 50 percent complete with respect to conversion. Therefore, the ending work-in-process inventory represents 5,000 equivalent units of conversion activity (10,000 physical units × 50 percent complete).

As Exhibit 4-6 indicates, the total number of equivalent units is calculated as follows:

Equivalent units of activity in units completed and transferred out
+ Equivalent units of activity in ending work in process

Total equivalent units of activity

Exhibit 4-6. Step 2: Calculation of Equivalent Units—Cutting Department (weighted-average method)

	Physical Units	Percentage of Completion with Respect to Conversion	Equivalent Units Direct Material	Equivalent Units Conversion
Work in process, March 1	20,000	10%		
Units started during March	30,000			
Total units to account for	50,000			
Units completed and transferred out during March	40,000	100%	40,000	40,000
Work in process, March 31	10,000	50%	10,000	5,000
Total units accounted for	50,000			
Total equivalent units			50,000	45,000

Note that the total equivalent units of activity, for both direct material and conversion, exceeds the activity accomplished in the current period alone. Since only 30,000 physical product units were started during March and direct material is added at the beginning of the process, only 30,000 equivalent units of direct material were actually placed into production during March. However, the total number of equivalent units of direct material used for weighted-average process costing is 50,000 (see Exhibit 4-6). The other 20,000 equivalent units of direct material were actually entered into production during the preceding month. *This is the key feature of the weighted-average method. The number of equivalent units of activity is calculated without making a distinction as to whether the activity occurred in the current accounting period or the preceding period.*

Step 3: Computation of Unit Costs The third step in the process costing procedure, calculating the cost per equivalent unit for both direct material and conversion activity, is presented in Exhibit 4-7. The cost per equivalent unit for direct material is computed by dividing the total direct-material cost, including the cost of the beginning work in process and the cost incurred during March, by the total equivalent units (from step 2, Exhibit 4-6). An analogous procedure is used for conversion costs.

Step 4: Analysis of Total Costs Now we can complete the process costing procedure by determining the total cost to be transferred out of the Cutting Department's Work-in-Process Inventory account and into the Stitching Department's Work-in-Process Inventory account. Exhibit 4-8 provides the required calculations. For convenience, the computations in step 3 are repeated in Exhibit 4-8. At the bottom of Exhibit 4-8, a check is made to be sure that the total costs of $340,700 have been fully accounted for in the cost of goods completed and transferred out and the balance remaining in work-in-process inventory.

The calculations in Exhibit 4-8 are used as the basis for the following journal entry to transfer the cost of goods completed and transferred out to the Stitching Department.

Exhibit 4-7. Step 3: Computation of Unit Costs—Cutting Department (weighted-average method)

	Direct Material	Conversion	Total
Work in process, March 1 (from Exhibit 4-4)	$ 50,000	$ 7,200	$ 57,200
Costs incurred during March (from Exhibit 4-4). . .	90,000	193,500	283,500
Total costs to account for	$140,000	$200,700	$340,700
Equivalent units (from step 2, Exhibit 4-6)	50,000	45,000	
Costs per equivalent unit	$ 2.80	$ 4.46	$ 7.26
	$\dfrac{\$140,000}{50,000}$	$\dfrac{\$200,700}{45,000}$	$2.80 + \$4.46

Exhibit 4-8. Step 4: Analysis of Total Costs—Cutting Department (weighted-average method)

	Direct Material	Conversion	Total
Work in process, March 1 (from Exhibit 4-4)	$ 50,000	$ 7,200	$ 57,200
Costs incurred during March (from Exhibit 4-4). . .	90,000	193,500	283,500
Total costs to account for	$140,000	$200,700	$340,700
Equivalent units (from step 2, Exhibit 4-6)	50,000	45,000	
Costs per equivalent unit	$ 2.80	$ 4.46	$ 7.26

$$\frac{\$140,000}{50,000} \quad \frac{\$200,700}{45,000} \quad \$2.80 + \$4.46$$

Cost of goods completed and transferred
 out of the Cutting Department during March

$$\binom{\text{number of units}}{\text{transferred out}} \times \binom{\text{total cost per}}{\text{equivalent unit}} \quad \text{. . . . .} \quad 40,000 \times \$7.26 \quad \underline{\$290,400}$$

Cost remaining in March 31 work-in-process
 inventory in the Cutting Department:

 Direct material:

$$\begin{pmatrix}\text{number of equivalent} \\ \text{units of direct} \\ \text{material}\end{pmatrix} \times \begin{pmatrix}\text{cost per} \\ \text{equivalent unit} \\ \text{of direct material}\end{pmatrix} \quad \text{. . . . . . .} \quad 10,000 \times \$2.80 \quad \$ 28,000$$

 Conversion:

$$\begin{pmatrix}\text{number of equivalent} \\ \text{units of conversion}\end{pmatrix} \times \begin{pmatrix}\text{cost per} \\ \text{equivalent unit} \\ \text{of conversion}\end{pmatrix} \quad \text{. . . . .} \quad 5,000 \times \$4.46 \quad \underline{22,300}$$

Total cost of March 31 work in process . . . . $ 50,300

Check:	Cost of goods completed and transferred out	$290,400
	Cost of March 31 work-in-process inventory	50,300
	Total costs accounted for	$340,700

Work-in-Process Inventory: Stitching Department 290,400
    Work-in-Process Inventory: Cutting Department.   290,400

On March 31, the Cutting Department's Work-in-Process Inventory account appears as follows:

**Work-in-Process Inventory:
Cutting Department**

3/2/x3 balance	57,200		
March cost of	283,500	290,400	Cost of goods
direct material,			completed and
direct labor, and			transferred out of
applied manufacturing			Cutting Department
overhead			
3/31/x3 balance	50,300		

The March 31 balance in the account agrees with that calculated in Exhibit 4-8.

Departmental Production Report We have now completed all four steps neces-sary to prepare a production report for the Cutting Department. The report, which is displayed in Exhibit 4-9, simply combines the tables presented in Exhibits 4-6 and 4-8. The report provides a convenient summary of all the process costing calculations made under the weighted-average method.

Why is this process costing method called the *weighted-average* method? Be-cause the cost per equivalent unit for March, for both direct material and conversion activity, is computed as a weighted average of the costs incurred during two different accounting periods, February and March. To demonstrate this fact, we will focus on direct material. Since direct material is placed into production at the beginning of the process, the 20,000 physical units in the March 1 work in process already have their direct material. The direct-material cost per equivalent unit in the March 1 work in process is $2.50 ($50,000 ÷ 20,000, from Exhibit 4-4). This cost was actually in-curred in *February.*

In March, 30,000 physical units were entered into work in process and received their direct material. The direct-material cost incurred in March was $90,000. Thus, the direct-material cost per equivalent unit experienced in *March* was $3.00 ($90,000 ÷ 30,000).

Under the weighted-average method of processing costing, the cost per equiva-lent unit for direct material was calculated in Exhibit 4-7 to be $2.80. *This $2.80 unit-cost figure is a weighted average,* as the following calculation shows.

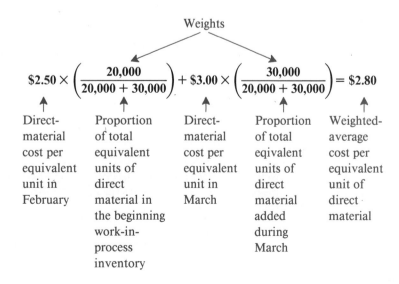

Exhibit 4-9. Production Report—Cutting Department (weighted-average method)

	Physical Units	Percentage of Completion with Respect to Conversion	Equivalent Units Direct Material	Conversion
Work in process, March 1	20,000	10%		
Units started during March	30,000			
Total units to account for	50,000			
Units completed and transferred out during March	40,000	100%	40,000	40,000
Work in process, March 31	10,000	50%	10,000	5,000
Total units accounted for	50,000			
Total equivalent units			50,000	45,000

	Direct Material	Conversion	Total
Work in process, March 1 (from Exhibit 4-4)	$ 50,000	$ 7,200	$ 57,200
Costs incurred during March (from Exhibit 4-4). . .	90,000	193,500	283,500
Total costs to account for	$140,000	$200,700	$340,700
Equivalent units (from step 2, Exhibit 4-6)	50,000	45,000	
Costs per equivalent unit	$ 2.80	$ 4.46	$ 7.26
	↑	↑	↑
	$140,000	$200,700	$2.80 + $4.46
	50,000	45,000	

The point of this demonstration is that under weighted-average process costing, unit-cost figures are weighted averages of costs incurred over two or more accounting periods.

FIFO Method

Skip

Now we will illustrate the first-in, first-out, or FIFO, method of process costing, using the data for Milligan Sports Equipment Company (Exhibit 4-4). Unlike the weighted-average method, the FIFO method does not commingle costs from two or more accounting periods. As the illustration will show, the costs from each period are treated separately.

Step 1: Analysis of Physical Flow of Units The *physical* flow of units is unaffected by the process costing method used. Therefore, step 1 is identical under the weighted-average and FIFO methods. See Exhibit 4-5.

**Exhibit 4-9 (continued). Production Report—Cutting Department
(weighted-average method)**

Cost of goods completed and transferred
  out of the Cutting Department during March

$$\begin{pmatrix} \text{number of units} \\ \text{transferred out} \end{pmatrix} \times \begin{pmatrix} \text{total cost per} \\ \text{equivalent unit} \end{pmatrix}$$ . . . . 40,000 × \$7.26   <u>\$290,400</u>

Cost remaining in March 31 work-in-process
  inventory in the Cutting Department:
    Direct material:

$$\begin{pmatrix} \text{number of equivalent} \\ \text{units of direct} \\ \text{material} \end{pmatrix} \times \begin{pmatrix} \text{cost per} \\ \text{equivalent unit} \\ \text{of direct material} \end{pmatrix}$$ . . . . . . 10,000 × \$2.80   \$ 28,000

    Conversion:

$$\begin{pmatrix} \text{number of equivalent} \\ \text{units of conversion} \end{pmatrix} \times \begin{pmatrix} \text{cost per} \\ \text{equivalent unit} \\ \text{of conversion} \end{pmatrix}$$ . . . . . . 5,000 × \$4.46   <u> 22,300</u>

Total cost of March 31 work in process . . . .   <u>\$ 50,300</u>

Check: Cost of goods completed and transferred out \$290,400
          Cost of March 31 work-in-process inventory   50,300
          Total costs accounted for . . . . <u>\$340,700</u>

Step 2: Calculation of Equivalent Units A table of equivalent units, under FIFO process costing, is presented in Exhibit 4-10. It is identical to the table prepared under the weighted-average method except for one important difference. Under the FIFO method, the equivalent units of direct material and conversion represented by the March 1 work-in-process inventory are subtracted in the last row of the table. By subtracting the equivalent units in the beginning work in process, we are able to determine the *new equivalent units of activity accomplished in March only*. The 20,000 physical units in the March 1 work in process have all of their materials, so they represent 20,000 equivalent units of direct material. However, these units are only 10 percent complete with respect to conversion, so they represent only 2,000 equivalent units of conversion activity (20,000 physical units × 10% complete).

Step 3: Computation of Unit Costs The calculation of unit costs is presented in Exhibit 4-11. The cost per equivalent unit for direct material is computed by dividing the direct-material cost incurred *during March only* by the new equivalent units of direct material added *during March only*. An analogous procedure is used for conversion costs. Note that the costs for direct material and conversion assigned to the beginning inventory are *not* added to the costs incurred during March for the purpose of calculating unit costs.

Exhibit 4-10. Step 2: Calculation of Equivalent Units—Cutting Department (FIFO method)

	Physical Units	Percentage of Completion with Respect to Conversion	Equivalent Units Direct Material	Equivalent Units Conversion
Work in process, March 1	20,000	10%		
Units started during March	30,000			
Total units to account for	50,000			
Units completed and transferred				
out during March	40,000	100%	40,000	40,000
Work in process, March 31	10,000	50%	10,000	5,000
Total units accounted for	50,000			
Total equivalent units			50,000	45,000
Less: equivalent units represented				
in March 1 work in process			20,000	2,000
New equivalent units accomplished				
in March only			30,000	43,000

Step 4: Analysis of Total Costs To complete the process costing procedure, we determine the total cost to be transferred out of the Cutting Department's Work-in-Process Inventory account and into the Stitching Department's Work-in-Process Inventory account. Exhibit 4-12 presents this analysis of total costs. The calculations from step 3 are repeated in Exhibit 4-12 for convenient reference.

Calculating the cost of goods completed and transferred out is more complicated under the FIFO method than under the weighted-average method. FIFO (first-in, first-out) implies that the units in the March 1 work-in-process inventory are completed and transferred out first. Under the FIFO method, the costs assigned to the March 1 work in process are not mingled with those incurred during March. Instead, these costs are kept separate and transferred out first. The units in the March 1 work in process need to be completed during March. Since 90 percent of the conversion remains to be done, 18,000 equivalent units of conversion is applied during March to the March 1 work in process. These equivalent units of conversion cost $4.50 per unit, since they are accomplished during March. The remainder of the 40,000 units completed and transferred out during March had to be *started and finished* during March. Thus, the remaining 20,000 units (40,000 units completed minus 20,000 units in the beginning work in process) cost $7.50 each during March.

The calculations in Exhibit 4-12 are used as the basis for the following journal entry to transfer the cost of goods completed and transferred out to the Stitching Department.

Exhibit 4-11. Step 3: Computation of Unit Costs—Cutting Department (FIFO method)

	Direct Material	Conversion	Total
Work in process, March 1 (from Exhibit 4-4)	These costs were incurred during February. They are not included in the unit-cost calculation for March.		$ 57,200
Costs incurred during March (from Exhibit 4-4).	$90,000	$193,500	283,500
Total costs to account for			$340,700
Equivalent units for March only (from step 2, Exhibit 4-10)	30,000	43,000	
Costs per equivalent unit	$ 3.00	$ 4.50	$ 7.50
	↑	↑	↑
	$90,000	$193,500	$3.00 + $4.50
	30,000	43,000	

Work-in-Process Inventory: Stitching Department 288,200
      Work-in-Process Inventory: Cutting Department.   288,200

On March 31, the Cutting Department's Work-in-Process Inventory account appears as follows:

Work-in-Process Inventory:
Cutting Department

3/1/x3 balance	57,200		
March cost of direct material, direct labor, and applied manufacturing overhead	283,500	288,200	Cost of goods completed and transferred out of Cutting Department
3/31/x3 balance	52,500		

The March 31 balance in the account agrees with that calculated in Exhibit 4-12. Note that the March 31 balance in the Cutting Department's Work-in-Process Inventory account differs under the FIFO and weighted-average methods of process costing.

**Exhibit 4-12. Step 4: Analysis of Total Costs—Cutting Department
(FIFO method)**

	Direct Material	Conversion	Total
Work in process, March 1 (from Exhibit 4-10)	These costs were incurred during February. They are not included in the unit-cost calculation for March.		$ 57,200
Costs incurred during March (from Exhibit 4-4).	$90,000	$193,500	283,500
Total costs to account for			$340,700
Equivalent units for March only (from step 2, Exhibit 4-10)	30,000	43,000	
Costs per equivalent unit	$ 3.00	$ 4.50	$ 7.50
	↑	↑	↑
	$90,000 / 30,000	$193,500 / 43,000	$3.00 + $4.50

Cost of goods completed and transferred
out of the Cutting Department during March:

Cost of March 1 work-in-process inventory,
which is transferred out first . . . . $ 57,200

Cost incurred to finish the March 1
work-in-process inventory

$$\left(\begin{array}{c}\text{number}\\\text{of units}\end{array}\right) \times \left(\begin{array}{c}\text{percentage}\\\text{of conversion}\\\text{remaining}\end{array}\right) \times \left(\begin{array}{c}\text{cost per}\\\text{equivalent unit}\\\text{of conversion}\end{array}\right) . . \ 20{,}000 \times .90 \times \$4.50 \qquad 81{,}000$$

Cost incurred to produce units that were
both started and completed during March

$$\left(\begin{array}{c}\text{number}\\\text{of units}\end{array}\right) \times \left(\begin{array}{c}\text{total cost}\\\text{per equivalent}\\\text{unit}\end{array}\right) . . . . \ 20{,}000^* \times \$7.50 \qquad 150{,}000$$

Total cost of goods completed and transferred out $288,200

* Units started and completed during March: 40,000 units completed and transferred out minus 20,000 units
in the March 1 work-in-process inventory.

**Exhibit 4-12 (continued) Step 4: Analysis of Total Costs—Cutting Department
FIFO method**

Cost remaining in March 31 work-in-process
  inventory in the Cutting Department:
    Direct material:

$$\left(\begin{array}{l}\text{number of equivalent}\\ \text{units of direct}\\ \text{material}\end{array}\right) \times \left(\begin{array}{l}\text{direct material}\\ \text{cost per}\\ \text{equivalent unit}\end{array}\right) \ldots \ldots \ldots \text{ 10,000} \times \$3.00 \quad \$ \ 30,000$$

    Conversion:

$$\left(\begin{array}{l}\text{number of equivalent}\\ \text{units of conversion}\end{array}\right) \times \left(\begin{array}{l}\text{conversion cost}\\ \text{per equivalent}\\ \text{unit}\end{array}\right) \ldots \ldots \ldots \text{ 5,000} \times \$4.50 \quad \underline{\quad 22,500}$$

Total cost of March 31 work-in-process inventory . . . . $\underline{\$ \ 52,500}$

Check: Cost of goods completed and transferred out $288,200
          Cost of March 31 work-in-process inventory   52,500
          Total costs accounted for . . . . $\underline{\underline{\$340,700}}$

Departmental Production Report   The tables presented in Exhibits 4-10 and 4-12 can now be combined to form a production report for the Cutting Department. This report, which is displayed in Exhibit 4-13, provides a convenient summary of the FIFO process costing method.

Comparison of Weighted-Average and FIFO Methods

The graph presented in Exhibit 4-14 highlights the differences between the weighted-average and FIFO methods of process costing. The graph is based on the same continuing illustration; the basic data are presented in Exhibit 4-4. The graph focuses on conversion activity, but an analogous graph could be prepared for direct materials. Groups of physical units are graphed on the horizontal axis, and the percentage of conversion activity accomplished during March is graphed on the vertical axis. Area I represents the equivalent units of conversion accomplished *during February* on the March 1 work-in-process inventory. Area II represents the equivalent units of conversion required during March to complete the conversion of the beginning work-in-process inventory. Area III represents the equivalent units of conversion activity accomplished during March on the units that were *both started and finished during March.* Area IV represents the equivalent units of conversion activity accomplished during March on the March 31 work-in-process inventory.

The key difference between the weighted-average and FIFO methods lies in the treatment of area I. Under the weighted-average method, the conversion costs associated with areas I, II, III, and IV are divided by the total equivalent units of conversion activity represented by areas I, II, III, and IV. The resulting conversion cost per equivalent unit is a weighted average of some of the conversion costs incurred in

Exhibit 4-13. Production Report—Cutting Department (FIFO method)

	Physical Units	Percentage of Completion with Respect to Conversion	Equivalent Units Direct Material	Equivalent Units Conversion
Work in process, March 1	20,000	10%		
Units started during March	30,000			
Total units to account for	50,000			
Units completed and transferred out during March	40,000	100%	40,000	40,000
Work in process, March 31	10,000	50%	10,000	5,000
Total units accounted for	50,000			
Total equivalent units			50,000	45,000
Less: equivalent units represented in March 1 work in process			20,000	2,000
New equivalent units accomplished in March only			30,000	43,000

	Direct Material	Conversion	Total
Work in process, March 1 (from Exhibit 4-4)	These cost were incurred during February. They are not included in the unit-cost calculation for March.		$ 57,200
Costs incurred during March (from Exhibit 4-4) . . .	$90,000	$193,500	$283,500
Total costs to account for			$340,700
Equivalent units for March only (from step 2, Exhibit 4-10)	30,000	43,000	
Costs per equivalent unit	$ 3.00	$ 4.50	$ 7.50
	↑	↑	↑
	$90,000 / 30,000	$193,500 / 43,000	$3.00 + $4.50

Exhibit 4-13 (continued). Production Report—Cutting Department (FIFO method)

Cost of goods completed and transferred
 out of the Cutting Department during March:

    Cost of March 1 work-in-process inventory,
     which is transferred out first . . . . $ 57,200

    Cost incurred to finish the March 1
     work-in-process inventory

$$\begin{pmatrix} \text{number} \\ \text{of units} \end{pmatrix} \times \begin{pmatrix} \text{percentage} \\ \text{of conversion} \\ \text{remaining} \end{pmatrix} \times \begin{pmatrix} \text{cost per} \\ \text{equivalent} \\ \text{unit of} \\ \text{conversion} \end{pmatrix} \ldots\ 20{,}000 \times .90 \times \$4.50 \quad 81{,}000$$

    Cost incurred to produce units that were
     both started and completed during March

$$\begin{pmatrix} \text{number} \\ \text{of units} \end{pmatrix} \times \begin{pmatrix} \text{total cost per} \\ \text{equivalent} \\ \text{unit} \end{pmatrix} \ldots\ldots\ldots\ 20{,}000^* \times \$7.50 \quad \underline{150{,}000}$$

Total cost of goods completed and transferred out . . . . $\underline{\underline{\$288{,}200}}$

Cost remaining in March 31 work-in-process
 inventory in the Cutting Department:

Direct material:

$$\begin{pmatrix} \text{number of equivalent} \\ \text{units of direct} \\ \text{material} \end{pmatrix} \times \begin{pmatrix} \text{direct material} \\ \text{cost per} \\ \text{equivalent unit} \end{pmatrix} \ldots\ldots\ 10{,}000 \times \$3.00 \quad \$\ 30{,}000$$

   Conversion:

$$\begin{pmatrix} \text{number of equivalent} \\ \text{units of conversion} \end{pmatrix} \times \begin{pmatrix} \text{conversion cost} \\ \text{per equivalent} \\ \text{unit} \end{pmatrix} \ldots\ldots\ 5{,}000 \times \$4.50 \quad \underline{22{,}500}$$

Total cost of March 31 work in process inventory . . . . $\underline{\underline{\$\ 52{,}500}}$

*Units started and completed during March: 40,000 units completed and transfered out minus 20,000 units
in the March 1 work-in-process inventory.

Check: Cost of goods completed and transferred out $288,200
           Cost of March 31 work-in-process inventory   52,500
              Total costs accounted for $340,700

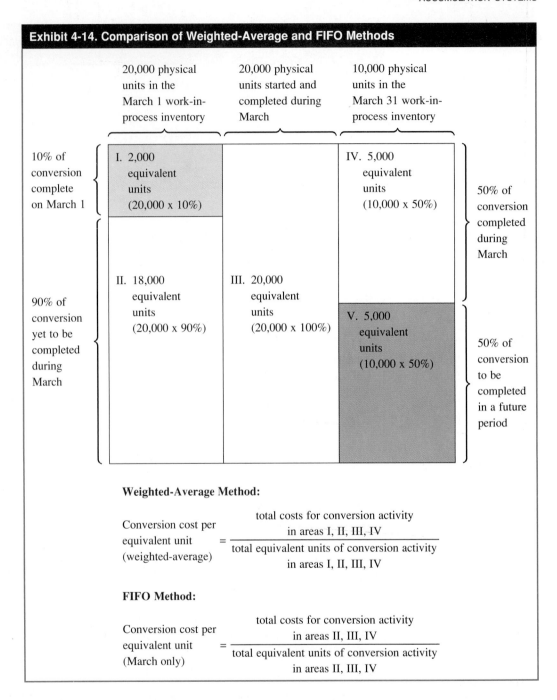

Exhibit 4-14. Comparison of Weighted-Average and FIFO Methods

February (area I) and the conversion costs incurred during March (areas II, III, and IV).

In contrast, under the FIFO method, the total conversion costs associated only with areas II, III, and IV are divided by the equivalent units of conversion activity represented by areas II, III, and IV. The resulting conversion cost per equivalent unit is a pure March unit cost, because areas II, III, and IV represent conversion costs and activity of March only.

A Systems Perspective The difference between weighted-average and FIFO process costing lies in the *activities* performed by the product costing *system.* As the following diagram shows, the inputs to the system are the same, but the output depends on the process costing method used.

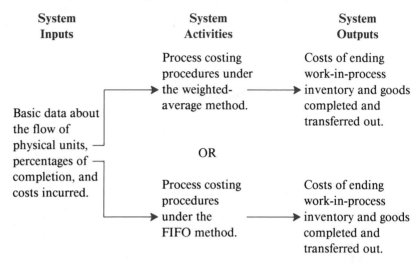

System Inputs	System Activities	System Outputs
Basic data about the flow of physical units, percentages of completion, and costs incurred.	Process costing procedures under the weighted-average method.	Costs of ending work-in-process inventory and goods completed and transferred out.
	OR	
	Process costing procedures under the FIFO method.	Costs of ending work-in-process inventory and goods completed and transferred out.

Evaluation of Weighted-Average and FIFO The weighted-average method of process costing is more widely used than the FIFO method, probably because it is somewhat simpler. Most product costing systems were designed before the wide use of computers, when the complexity of the system was an important consideration. Nowadays, most product costing systems are computerized; operating a process costing system is equally simple when using either the weighted-average method or the FIFO method.

Behavioral Implications For purposes of cost control and performance evaluation, FIFO process costing is superior to the weighted-average method. To provide incentives for departmental managers to control costs, it is important to evaluate their performance on the basis of current-period costs only. When current-period and prior-period costs are averaged, a departmental manager's *current* performance is less clear. Moreover, performance evaluation based partially on costs incurred in prior periods is less timely. Behavioral scientists generally agree that for performance evaluation to be more effective, it should be done on a timely basis.

OTHER ISSUES IN PROCESS COSTING

Several other issues related to process costing are worth discussion.

Actual versus Normal Costing Our illustration of process costing assumed that *normal costing* was used. As explained in Chapter 3, in a normal costing system, direct material and direct labor are applied to Work-in-Process Inventory at their *actual* amounts, but manufacturing overhead is applied to Work-in-Process Inventory using a predetermined overhead rate. In contrast, under an *actual costing* system, the actual costs of direct material, direct labor, *and manufacturing overhead* is entered into Work-in-Process Inventory.

Either actual or normal costing may be used in conjunction with a process costing system. Our illustration used normal costing, since a predetermined overhead rate was used to compute applied manufacturing overhead in Exhibit 4-4. This resulted in applied overhead for March of $107,500 (125% × $86,000). If actual costing had been used, the manufacturing overhead cost for March would have been the actual overhead cost incurred instead of the applied overhead amount given in Exhibit 4-4. In all other ways, the process costing procedures used under actual and normal costing are identical.

Other Cost Drivers for Overhead Application Our illustration used a predetermined overhead rate based on direct-labor cost. Since the application of manufacturing overhead was based on direct-labor cost, direct labor and manufacturing overhead were combined into the single cost element *conversion costs*. This procedure is quite common in practice. If some cost driver (or activity base) other than direct labor had been used to apply manufacturing overhead, then overhead costs would be accounted for separately from direct-labor costs in the process costing calculations.

Suppose, for example, that manufacturing overhead is applied on the basis of machine hours. A group of 100 physical units is 100 percent complete as to direct material, 60 percent complete as to direct labor, and 40 percent complete as to machine time. This situation could arise in a production process that is labor intensive in its early stages, but more automated in its later stages. In this case, the 100 physical units represent the following quantities of equivalent units:

Equivalent Units

Physical Units	Direct Material	Direct Labor	Manufacturing Overhead
100	100	60	40
	↑	↑	↑
	100 × 100%	100 × 60%	100 × 40%

Throughout the entire process costing procedure, there will now be three cost elements (direct material, direct labor, and manufacturing overhead) instead of only two (direct material and conversion). In all other respects, the process costing calculations will be identical to those illustrated earlier in the chapter.

Subsequent Production Departments In our illustration, production requires two sequential production operations: cutting and stitching. Although the process costing procedures for the second department are similar to those illustrated for the first, there is one additional complication. The cost of goods completed and transferred out of the Cutting Department must remain assigned to the partially completed product units as they undergo further processing in the Stitching Department. Process costing procedures for subsequent production departments are covered in the appendix at the end of this chapter.

HYBRID PRODUCT-COSTING SYSTEMS

Job-order and process costing represent the polar extremes of product costing systems. But some production processes exhibit characteristics of both job-order and process costing environments. Examples of such production processes include some clothing and food processing operations. In these production processes, the conversion activities may be very similar or identical across all of the firm's product lines, even though the direct materials may differ significantly. Different clothing lines require significantly different direct materials, such as cotton, wool, or polyester.

However, the conversion of these materials, involving direct labor and manufacturing overhead, may not differ much across product types. In the food industry, production of economy-grade or premium applesauce differs with regard to the quality and cost of the direct-material input, apples. However, the cooking, straining, and canning operations for these two product lines are similar.

Operation Costing for Batch Manufacturing Processes

The production processes described above often are referred to as **batch manufacturing processes**. Such processes are characterized by high-volume production of several product lines that differ in some important ways but are nearly identical in others. Since batch manufacturing operations have characteristics of both job-order costing and process costing environments, a **hybrid product-costing system** is required. One common approach is called **operation costing**. This product costing system is used when conversion activities are very similar across product lines, but the direct materials differ significantly. *Conversion costs* are accumulated by *department,* and process costing methods are used to assign these costs to products. In contrast, *direct-material costs* are accumulated by *job order or batch,* and job-order costing is used to assign material costs to products.

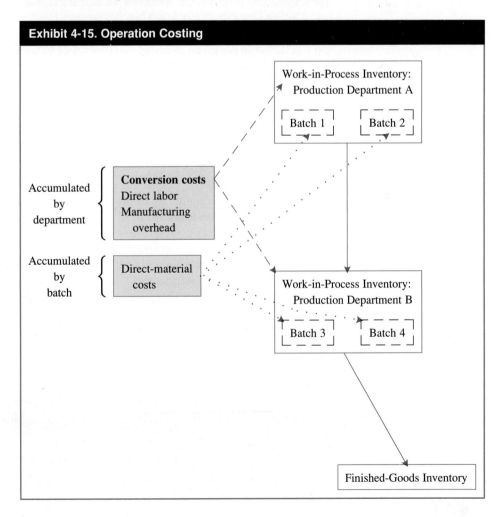

Exhibit 4-15. Operation Costing

The main features of operation costing are illustrated in Exhibit 4-15. Notice in the exhibit that products pass sequentially through production departments A and B. Direct material costs are traced directly to each batch of goods, but conversion costs are applied on a departmental basis. Direct labor and manufacturing overhead are combined in a single cost category called conversion costs, rather than separately identifying direct labor. Moreover, under operation costing, conversion costs are applied to products using a *predetermined application rate.* This predetermined rate is based on *budgeted conversion costs,* as follows:

$$\text{Predetermined application rate for conversion costs} = \frac{\text{budgeted conversion costs (direct labor and manufacturing overhead)}}{\text{budgeted cost driver (or activity base)}}$$

As an illustration of operation costing, we will focus on the Pennsylvania Division of Milligan Sports Equipment Company. This division manufactures two different grades of basketballs: professional balls, which have genuine leather exteriors; and scholastic balls, which use imitation leather. The cutting and stitching operations for the two different products are identical. Scholastic balls are sold without special packaging, but professional balls are packaged in an attractive cardboard box.

During October of 19x3 two batches were entered into production and finished. There was no beginning or ending inventory of work in process for October. Cost and production data are given in Exhibit 4-16. Notice in Exhibit 4-16 that the direct-material costs are identified by *batch.* The conversion costs, however, are associated with the two production departments and the Packaging Department.

The product cost for each of the basketballs is computed as follows:

	Professional	Scholastic
Direct material:		
Batch P19 ($20,000 ÷ 1,000)	$20.00	
Batch S28 ($30,000 ÷ 3,000)		$10.00
Conversion: Preparation Department (conversion costs of $30,000 ÷ 4,000 units produced)*	7.50	7.50
Conversion: Finishing Department (conversion costs of $24,000 ÷ 4,000 units produced)*	6.00	6.00
Conversion: Packaging Department (conversion costs of $500 ÷ 1,000 units packaged)*	.50	–0–
Total product cost	$34.00	$23.50

* The two production departments each worked on a total of 4,000 balls, but the Packaging Department handled only the 1,000 professional balls.

Notice in the preceding display that each ball receives the same conversion costs in the Preparation Department and the Finishing Department, since these operations are identical for the two products. Direct material costs and packaging costs, though, differ for the products. The total costs of $104,500 (Exhibit 4-16) are accounted for in the product costs, as shown below.

Professional balls: 1,000 × $34.00	$ 34,000
Scholastic balls: 3,000 × $23.50	70,500
Total	$104,500

Exhibit 4-16. Basic Data for Illustration of Operation Costing

Direct material costs:

Batch P19 (1,000 professional balls) . . . . $ 20,000 (includes $1,000
                                                                              for packaging
                                                                              material)

Batch S28 (3,000 scholastic balls)   30,000
Total direct material costs . . . . $ 50,000

Conversion costs (budgeted):
Preparation Department . . . . $ 30,000
Finishing Department   24,000
Packaging Department   500

Total costs:

Direct material . . . . $ 50,000
Conversion: Preparation $30,000
             Finishing   24,000
             Packaging   500
             Total conversion costs   54,500
Total $104,500

Predetermined application rates for conversion costs*:

Preparation Department

$$\frac{\text{Budgeted conversion costs}}{\text{Budgeted production}} = \frac{\$30,000}{4,000 \text{ units}} = \$7.50 \text{ per unit}$$

Finishing Department

$$\frac{\text{Budgeted conversion costs}}{\text{Budgeted production}} = \frac{\$24,000}{4,000 \text{ units}} = \$6.00 \text{ per unit}$$

Packaging Department

$$\frac{\text{Budgeted conversion costs}}{\text{Budgeted units packaged}} = \frac{\$500}{1,000 \text{ units}} = \$.50 \text{ per unit}$$

*The cost driver (or activity base) is the number of units processed.

The following journal entries are made to record the Pennsylvania Division's flow of costs. The first entry is made to record the requisition of raw material by the Preparation Department, when batch P19 is entered into production. (This amount excludes the $1,000 in packaging costs to be incurred subsequently for batch P19.)

Work-in-Process Inventory: Preparation Department	19,000	
Raw-Material Inventory		19,000

The following entry is made to record the requisition of raw material by the Preparation Department, when batch S28 is entered into production.

Work-in-Process Inventory: Preparation Department	30,000	
Raw-Material Inventory		30,000

Conversion costs are applied in the Preparation Department with the following journal entry.

Work-in-Process Inventory: Preparation Department	30,000	
Applied Conversion Costs		30,000

The following entry records the transfer of the partially completed professional and scholastic basketballs to the Finishing Department.

Work-in-Process Inventory: Finishing Department	79,000	
Work-in-Process Inventory: Preparation Department		79,000

The conversion costs applied in the Finishing Department are recorded as follows:

Work-in-Process Inventory: Finishing Department	24,000	
Applied Conversion Costs		24,000

Next, the professional balls are transferred to the Packaging Department, and the scholastic balls are transferred to finished goods.

Work-in-Process Inventory: Packaging Department	32,500	
Finished-Goods Inventory	70,500	
Work-in-Process Inventory: Finishing Department		103,000

Raw material (packaging) costs and conversion costs are recorded in the Packaging Department as follows:

Work-in-Process Inventory: Packaging Department	1,500	
Raw-Material Inventory		1,000
Applied Conversion Costs		500

Finally, the professional basketballs are transferred to finished goods.

Finished-Goods Inventory	34,000	
Work-in-Process Inventory: Packaging Department		34,000

Suppose that at the end of an accounting period, applied conversion costs differ from the actual conversion costs incurred. Then the difference, called overapplied or underapplied conversion costs, would be closed into Cost of Goods Sold. This accounting treatment is similar to that described in Chapter 3 for overapplied or underapplied overhead.

ADAPTING PRODUCT COSTING SYSTEMS TO TECHNOLOGICAL CHANGE

Managerial accountants should continually monitor the costs and benefits of the information they produce. In this age of rapidly changing production technologies and manufacturing practices, it is vital to reassess frequently the need for the data generated by traditional product costing systems. As manufacturing processes are automated through the use of robots and other computer-controlled machinery, direct-labor costs decline in importance and manufacturing overhead increases. As JIT (just-in-time) production and inventory-management systems are installed, the amount of work-in-process inventory declines substantially.[1] When these and other changes occur in the production environment, the product costing system should be adapted to fit the new situation. Such adaptation is illustrated by the following description of circuit-board production.

ILLUSTRATION FROM MANAGEMENT ACCOUNTING PRACTICE

Hewlett-Packard Company

The Disc Memory Division of Hewlett-Packard Company manufactures printed circuit boards for use in computers and other electronic equipment. After a JIT production management system was implemented, the quantities of work-in-process and finished-goods inventories declined to very low levels. Moreover, automation in the production process resulted in direct-labor costs comprising only 3 percent to 5 percent of the total product cost. As a result, the company simplified its product costing system. Direct labor was combined with manufacturing overhead in a single cost category. Much simpler methods were implemented to account for work-in-process inventories. As a result, an estimated 100,000 journal entries per month were eliminated.

By adapting its product costing system to its changing manufacturing environment, Hewlett-Packard realized considerable cost savings in information production while still providing the data needed by management.[2]

CHAPTER SUMMARY

Process costing is used in production processes where relatively large numbers of nearly identical products are manufactured. The purpose of a process costing system is the same as that of a job order costing system—to accumulate costs and assign these costs to units of product. Product costs are needed for planning, cost control, decision making, and reporting to various outside organizations.

The flow of costs in process costing systems and job-order costing systems is the same. Costs of direct material, direct labor, and manufacturing overhead are added to a Work-in-Process Inventory account. Direct labor and manufacturing overhead are often combined into a single cost category termed *conversion costs*. When products are completed, the costs assigned to them are transferred either to Finished-Goods Inventory or to the next production department's Work-in-Process Inventory ac-

---

[1] In a JIT production and inventory-management system, inventories are kept to the bare minimum at all stages of production. Materials and components are ordered or manufactured "just in time" for their use in the production process. JIT systems minimize the costs of holding inventory.

[2] R. Hunt, L. Garrett, and C. M. Merz, "Direct Labor Cost Not Always Relevant at H-P," *Management Accounting,* February 1985, pp. 58–62.

count. In sequential production processes, the cost of the goods transferred from one production department to another is called transferred-in cost.

There are some important differences between job-order and process costing systems. Chief among these is that job-order costing systems accumulate production costs by job or batch, whereas process costing systems accumulate costs by department. Another important difference is the focus on equivalent units in process costing. An equivalent unit is a measure of the amount of productive input that has been applied to a fully or partially completed unit of product. In process costing, production costs per equivalent unit are calculated for direct material and conversion costs.

The key document in a process costing system is the departmental production report, rather than the job-cost sheet used in job-order costing. There are four steps in preparing a departmental production report: (1) analyze the physical flow of units, (2) calculate the equivalent units, (3) compute the cost per equivalent unit, and (4) analyze the total costs of the department.

The two methods of process costing are the weighted-average method and the FIFO method. In the weighted-average method, the cost per equivalent unit, for each cost category, is a weighted average of (1) the costs assigned to the beginning work-in-process inventory and (2) the costs incurred during the current period. In the FIFO method, the cost assigned to the beginning work-in-process inventory is kept separate from the costs incurred during the current period. The beginning work-in process inventory is assumed to be completed and transferred out first, along with the costs assigned to those units.

The weighted-average method is somewhat simpler than the FIFO method, although neither is burdensome with a computerized accounting system. The FIFO method has the advantage that current-period costs are not commingled with prior-period costs. This results in more precise and timely cost-control information.

Job-order and process costing represent the polar extremes of product costing systems. Operation costing is a hybrid of these two methods. It is designed for production processes in which the direct material differs significantly among product lines, but the conversion activities are essentially the same. Direct-material costs are accumulated by batches of products using job-order costing methods. Conversion costs are accumulated by production departments and are assigned to product units by process costing methods.

KEY TERMS   Batch manufacturing, p. 133; **Departmental production report**, p. 116; **Equivalent units**, p. 115; **FIFO (first-in, first-out) method**, p. 116; **Hybrid product-costing system**, p. 133; **Operation costing**, p. 133; **Percentage of completion**, p. 122; **Physical unit**, p. 122; **Process costing system**, p. 111; **Repetitive production**, p. 111; **Sequential production process**, p. 112; **Transferred-in costs**, p. 113; **Weighted-average method**, p. 116.

Process Costing in Sequential Production Departments

In manufacturing operations with sequential production departments, the costs assigned to the units transferred out of one department remain assigned to those units as they enter the next department. In our illustration, the partially completed baseball gloves transferred out of the Cutting Department go next to the Stitching Department. There the cut-out pieces are stitched together. Since the cost of the thread used in the stitching is very small, it is treated as an indirect-material cost and included in manufacturing overhead. At the end of the process in the Stitching Department, rawhide lacing is woven through the fingers and along some edges of each baseball glove. The rawhide lacing is treated as a direct material.

The cost of goods completed and transferred out of the Cutting Department is transferred as shown below.

Work-in-Process Inventory: Cutting Department		Work-in-Process Inventory: Stitching Department	
Direct material	Cost of goods completed and transferred out	Transferred-in costs →	
Conversion: Direct labor Manufacturing overhead		Direct material	
		Conversion: Direct labor Manufacturing overhead	

As the T-accounts show, the Cutting Department has two cost elements: direct material and conversion costs. However, the Stitching Department has three cost elements: direct material, conversion, and *transferred-in costs*. Transferred-in costs are the costs assigned to the units transferred from the Cutting Department to the Stitching Department. Transferred-in costs are conceptually similar to direct-material costs. The only difference is that direct-material costs relate to raw materials, whereas transferred-in costs relate to partially completed products.

Exhibit 4-17 presents the basic data for our illustration of process costing in the Stitching Department. The March 1 work-in-process inventory in the department

Exhibit 4-17. Basic Data for Illustration—Stitching Department

Work in process, March 1—10,000 units:

Transferred-in: 100% complete, cost of	$ 61,000*
Direct material: none	—0—
Conversion: 20% complete, cost of	7,600*
Balance in work in process, March 1	$ 68,600*

Units transferred in from Cutting Department during March	40,000 units
Units completed during March and transferred out to finshed-goods inventory	30,000 units
Work in process, March 31	20,000 units

    Transferred in: 100% complete

    Direct material: none

    Conversion: 90% complete

Costs incurred during March:

    Transferred in from Cutting Department: depends on whether weighted-
average or FIFO method is
used for Cutting Department.

Direct material	$ 7,500
Conversion costs:	
Direct labor	$115,000
Applied manufacturing overhead	115,000†
Total conversion costs	$230,000

*These costs were incurred during the prior month, February.

† $\left(\begin{array}{c}\text{Predetermined} \\ \text{overhead rate}\end{array}\right) \times \left(\begin{array}{c}\text{Direct-} \\ \text{labor cost}\end{array}\right) = 100\% \times \$115{,}000 = \$115{,}000$

consists of 10,000 units that received some work in the Stitching Department during February, but were not completed. The $61,000 of transferred-in costs in the March 1 work-in-process inventory are costs that were transferred into the Stitching Department's Work-in-Process Inventory account during February. Note that any partially completed baseball glove in the Stitching Department must have received all of its transferred-in input, or it would not have been transferred from the Cutting Department. The March 1 work-in-process inventory has not yet received any direct material in the Stitching Department, because the direct material (rawhide lacing) is not added until the end of the process.

As Exhibit 4-17 shows, 40,000 units were transferred into the Stitching Department during March. This agrees with Exhibit 4-4, which shows that 40,000 units were completed and transferred out of the Cutting Department during March. The Stitching Department completed 30,000 units during March and transferred them to finished-goods inventory. This left 20,000 units in the Stitching Department's March 31 work-in-process inventory.

Exhibit 4-17 shows that the costs incurred in the Stitching Department during March were $7,500 for direct material, $115,000 for direct labor, and $115,000 for *applied* manufacturing overhead. The predetermined overhead rate in the Stitching Department is 100 percent of direct-labor cost. Note that the predetermined overhead rates are different in the two production departments. The March transferred-in cost in the Stitching Department is the cost of goods completed and transferred out of the Cutting Department. The amount of this cost depends on whether the weighted-average or FIFO process costing method is used in the Cutting Department. The two methods produce different results as follows:

	Cost of Goods Completed and Transferred Out of Cutting Department	Transferred-in Cost: Stitching Department
Weighted-average method used in Cutting Department	$290,400 ⟶ (Exhibit 4-8)	$290,400
FIFO method used in Cutting Department	$288,200 ⟶ (Exhibit 4-12)	$288,200

Weighted-Average Method

We will assume that the same method of process costing is used in both departments. Exhibit 4-18 presents a completed production report for the Stitching Department using weighted-average process costing. Steps 1 through 4 are identified in the exhibit. The process costing procedures used for the Stitching Department are identical to those used for the Cutting Department, except for one important difference. While there were only two cost elements (direct material and conversion) in the Cutting Department, there are three cost elements in the Stitching Department. In each of the four steps in Exhibit 4-18, transferred-in costs are listed along with direct material and conversion as a separate cost element.

The analysis of the physical flow of units (step 1 in Exhibit 4-18) is like the analysis for the Cutting Department. Now focus on step 2. In calculating equivalent units, we add a "transferred-in" column. Both the 30,000 units completed and transferred out of the Stitching Department and the March 31 work-in-process inventory are 100 percent complete as to transferred-in activity. Thus, the number of equivalent units is the same as the number of physical units. The calculation yields 50,000 total equivalent units of transferred-in activity for March. The equivalent units of direct material and conversion are determined as described earlier for the Cutting Department.

Costs per equivalent unit are computed in step 3. Since we are using the weighted-average method, the transferred-in costs in the March 1 work-in-process inventory are added to the March transferred-in costs before dividing by the equivalent units. Direct material and conversion costs are handled like those for the Cutting Department.

The analysis of total costs is done in step 4. The 30,000 units completed and transferred out of the Stitching Department are assigned a total weighted-average cost per unit of $12.228. This unit cost includes the transferred-in cost per equivalent unit of $7.028 calculated in step 3. The cost remaining in the work-in-process inventory

Exhibit 4-18. Production Report—Stitching Department (weighted-average method)

STEP 1 STEP 2

	Physical Units	Percentage of Completion with Respect to Conversion	Equivalent Units Transferred in	Direct Material	Conversion
Work in process, March 1	10,000	20%			
Units transferred in during March	40,000				
Total units to account for	50,000				
Units completed and transferred out during March	30,000		30,000	30,000	30,000
Work in process, March 31	20,000	90%	20,000	-0-	18,000
Total units accounted for	50,000				
Total equivalent units			50,000	30,000	48,000

STEP 3

	Transferred in	Direct Material	Conversion	Total
Work in process, March 1 (from Exhibit 4-17)	$ 61,000	-0-	$ 7,600	$ 68,600
Costs incurred during March (from Exhibit 4-17)	290,400*	$ 7,500	230,000	527,900
Total costs to account for	$351,400	$ 7,500	$237,600	$596,500
Equivalent units	50,000	30,000	48,000	
Costs per equivalent unit	$ 7.028	$ .25	$ 4.95	$ 12.228
	↑	↑	↑	↑
	$351,400	$ 7,500	$237,600	$7.028 +
	50,000	30,000	48,000	$.25 +
				$4.95

* Cost of goods completed and transferred out of Cutting Department during March, under the *weighted-average* method (calculated in Exhibit 4-8).

on March 31 consists of two cost elements: transferred-in costs (20,000 equivalent units × $7.028 per equivalent unit) and conversion costs (18,000 equivalent units × $4.95 per equivalent unit). The March 31 work-in-process inventory has not received any direct material in the Stitching Department.

The following journal entry is made to transfer the cost of the units completed to the Finished-Goods Inventory account.

Exhibit 4-18 (continued). Production Report—Stitching Department (weighted-average method)

STEP 4

Cost of goods completed and transferred
out of the Stitching Department during March:

$$\begin{pmatrix} \text{number of units} \\ \text{transferred out} \end{pmatrix} \times \begin{pmatrix} \text{total cost per} \\ \text{equivalent unit} \end{pmatrix} \quad \ldots \ldots \ldots \ldots \quad 30{,}000 \times \$12.228 \quad \underline{\$366{,}840}$$

Cost remaining in March 31 work-in-process
inventory in the Stitching Department:

Transferred-in costs:

$$\begin{pmatrix} \text{number of equivalent} \\ \text{units of transferred-} \\ \text{in costs} \end{pmatrix} \times \begin{pmatrix} \text{cost per} \\ \text{equivalent unit} \\ \text{of transferred-} \\ \text{in cost} \end{pmatrix} \quad \ldots \ldots \quad 20{,}000 \times \$7.028 \quad \$140{,}560$$

Direct material:

none   -0-

Conversion:

$$\begin{pmatrix} \text{number of equivalent} \\ \text{units of conversion} \end{pmatrix} \times \begin{pmatrix} \text{cost per} \\ \text{equivalent unit} \\ \text{of conversion} \end{pmatrix} \quad \ldots \ldots \quad 18{,}000 \times \$4.95 \quad \underline{\$\ 89{,}100}$$

Total $\underline{\$229{,}660}$

Check: Cost of goods completed and transferred out $366,840
        Cost of March 31 work-in-process inventory 229,660
        Total costs accounted for . . . . $\underline{\underline{\$596{,}500}}$

Finished-Goods Inventory. 366,840
    Work-in-Process Inventory: Stitching Department.   366,840
To transfer the cost of goods completed, as computed under the
weighted-average method.

FIFO Method

Exhibit 4-19 presents a production report for the Stitching Department using the
FIFO process costing method. Step 1, which details the physical flow of units, is the
same as in the previous exhibit. In step 2, the calculation of equivalent units, the
equivalent units in the March 1 work-in process inventory are subtracted to arrive at

Exhibit 4-19. Production Report—Stitching Department (FIFO method)

	STEP 1		STEP 2	

	Physical Units	Percentage of Completion with Respect to Conversion	Equivalent Units Transferred in	Direct Material	Conversion
Work in process, March 1	10,000	20%			
Units transferred in during March .	40,000				
Total units to account for	50,000				
Units completed and transferred out during March	30,000		30,000	30,000	30,000
Work in process, March 31	20,000	90%	20,000	–0–	18,000
Total units accounted for	50,000				
Total equivalent units			50,000	30,000	48,000
Less equivalent units represented in March 1 work in process . . .			10,000	–0–	2,000
New equivalent units accomplished in March only			40,000	30,000	46,000

	STEP 3			

	Transferred in	Direct Material	Conversion	Total
Work in process, March 1 (from Exhibit 4-17)	These costs were incurred during February. They are not included in the unit-cost calculation for March.			$ 68,600
Costs incurred during March (from Exhibit 4-17)	$288,200*	$ 7,500	$230,000	525,700
Total costs to account for				$594,300
Equivalent units for March only . .	40,000	30,000	46,000	
Costs per equivalent unit	$ 7.205	$ .25	$ 5.00	$ 12.455
	↑	↑	↑	↑
	$288,200	$ 7,500	$230,000	$7.205 +
	40,000	30,000	46,000	$.25 +
				$5.00

* Cost of goods completed and transferred out of Cutting Department during March, under the FIFO method (calculated in Exhibit 4-12).

Exhibit 4-19 (continued). Production Report—Stitching Department (FIFO method)

STEP 4

Cost of goods completed and transferred
 out of the Stitching Department during March:
  Cost of March 1 work-in-process inventory,
   which is transferred out first . . . . $ 68,600
  Cost incurred to finish the March 1
   work-in-process inventory

$$\begin{pmatrix} \text{number} \\ \text{of units} \end{pmatrix} \times \begin{pmatrix} \text{percentage of} \\ \text{direct material} \\ \text{remaining} \end{pmatrix} \times \begin{pmatrix} \text{cost per} \\ \text{equivalent unit} \\ \text{of material} \end{pmatrix} \; . \; . \; 10{,}000 \times 100\% \times \$.25 \qquad 2{,}500$$

$$\begin{pmatrix} \text{number} \\ \text{of units} \end{pmatrix} \times \begin{pmatrix} \text{percentage} \\ \text{of conversion} \\ \text{remaining} \end{pmatrix} \times \begin{pmatrix} \text{cost per} \\ \text{equivalent unit} \\ \text{of conversion} \end{pmatrix} \; . \; . \; 10{,}000 \times 80\% \times \$5.00 \qquad 40{,}000$$

  Cost incurred to produce units that were
   both started and completed during March:

$$\begin{pmatrix} \text{number} \\ \text{of units} \end{pmatrix} \times \begin{pmatrix} \text{total cost per} \\ \text{equivalent} \\ \text{unit} \end{pmatrix} \; . \; . \; . \; . \; . \; . \; . \; . \; . \; . \; . \; . \; 20{,}000\dagger \times \$12.455 \qquad \underline{249{,}100}$$

Total cost of goods completed and transferred out $\underline{\$360{,}200}$

Cost remaining in March 31 work-in-process
 inventory in the Stitching Department:
 Transferred-in costs:

$$\begin{pmatrix} \text{number of equivalent} \\ \text{units of transferred-} \\ \text{in costs} \end{pmatrix} \times \begin{pmatrix} \text{transferred-in} \\ \text{cost per} \\ \text{equivalent unit} \end{pmatrix} \; . \; . \; . \; . \; . \; 20{,}000 \times \$7.205 \qquad \$144{,}100$$

  Conversion:

$$\begin{pmatrix} \text{number of equivalent} \\ \text{units of conversion} \end{pmatrix} \times \begin{pmatrix} \text{conversion cost} \\ \text{per equivalent} \\ \text{unit} \end{pmatrix} \; . \; . \; . \; . \; 18{,}000 \times \$5.00 \qquad \underline{90{,}000}$$

Total cost of March 31 work-in-process inventory . . . . $\underline{\$234{,}100}$

†Units started and completed during March: 30,000 units completed and transferred out minus 10,000 units in the March 1 work-in-process inventory.

Check: Cost of goods completed and transferred out $360,200
      Cost of March 31 work-in-process inventory   234,100
       Total costs accounted for . . . . $\underline{\underline{\$594{,}300}}$

the new equivalent units of activity for March only. This is done for transferred-in activity, direct material, and conversion.

The costs per equivalent unit are computed in step 3. Under FIFO, the cost assigned to the March 1 work-in-process inventory is *not* added to the cost incurred during March. The March transferred-in cost is $288,200. This is the cost of goods completed and transferred out of the Cutting Department, computed using the FIFO method (Exhibit 4-12).

An analysis of the total costs in the Stitching Department is presented in step 4 of Exhibit 4-19. Under the FIFO method, the cost assigned to the March 1 work-in-process inventory, $68,600, is transferred out first. Note that the cost incurred to complete the March 1 work-in-process inventory includes the cost of direct material, since direct material is not added in the Stitching Department until the end of the process. The cost of the 20,000 units, started and completed in the Stitching Department during March, is found by multiplying 20,000 by the total cost per equivalent unit computed in step 3, $12.455. Finally, the cost remaining in the Stitching Department's Work-in-Process Inventory account on March 31 includes not only conversion costs but also transferred-in costs. The transferred-in cost per equivalent unit in March, under FIFO, is $7.205 (see step 3). The following journal entry is made to transfer the cost of the units completed to the Finished-Goods Inventory account.

Finished-Goods Inventory................................ 360,200
    Work-in-Process Inventory: Stitching Department...........   360,200
  To transfer the cost of goods completed, as computed under the
  FIFO method.

Summary of Transferred-in Costs

When manufacturing is done in sequential production departments, the cost assigned to the units completed in each department is transferred to the next department's Work-in-Process Inventory account. This cost is termed *transferred-in cost,* and it is handled as a distinct cost element in the process costing calculations. In this way, the final cost of the product is built up cumulatively as the product progresses through the production sequence.

REVIEW QUESTIONS

4-1. List five types of manufacturing in which process costing would be an appropriate product costing system. What is the key characteristic of these products that makes process costing a good choice?

4-2. List three nonmanufacturing businesses in which process costing could be used. For example, a public accounting firm could use process costing to accumulate the costs of processing clients' tax returns.

4-3. Explain the primary differences between job-order and process costing.

4-4. What are the purposes of a product costing system?

4-5. Define the term *equivalent unit,* and explain how the concept is used in process costing.

4-6. List and briefly describe the purpose of each of the four process costing steps.

4-7. Show how to prepare a journal entry to enter direct material costs into the Work-in-Process Inventory account for the first department in a sequential production process. Show how to prepare the journal entry recording the transfer of goods from the first to the second department in the sequence.

4-8. What are transferred-in costs?

4-9. A food processing company has two sequential production departments: mixing and cooking. The cost of the January 1, 19x4 work in process in the cooking department is shown below.

Direct material	$40,000
Conversion	10,000
Transferred-in costs	90,000

During what time period and in what department were the $90,000 of costs listed above incurred? Explain your answer.

4-10. Explain how the computation of equivalent units differs between the weighted-average and FIFO methods.

4-11. Explain the reasoning underlying the name of the weighted-average method.

4-12. How are the costs of the beginning work-in-process inventory treated differently under the weighted-average and FIFO methods?

4-13. How does process costing differ under normal or actual costing?

4-14. How would the process costing computations differ from those illustrated in the chapter if overhead were applied on some activity base other than direct labor?

4-15. Why might the FIFO method of process costing be more effective than the weighted-average method from a behavioral standpoint?

4-16. Explain the concept of *operation costing.* How does it differ from process or job-order costing? Why is operation costing well suited for batch manufacturing processes?

4-17. What is the purpose of a departmental production report prepared using process costing?

EXERCISES *Exercise 4-18 Physical Flow of Units.* In each case below, fill in the missing amount.

1. Work in process, January 1 .... 10,000 units
   Units started during January .... 2,000 units *3000*
   Units completed during January .... 9,000 units
   Work in process, January 31 .... ?
2. Work in process, September 1 .... 9,000 tons
   Units started during September .... ? *12,000*
   Units completed during September .... 19,000 tons
   Work in process, September 30 .... 2,000 tons
3. Work in process, January 1 .... 100,000 gallons
   Units started during the year .... 850,000 gallons
   Units completed during the year .... ? *750,000*
   Work in process, December 31 .... 200,000 gallons

Exercise 4-19 Equivalent Units; Weighted Average and FIFO. Higrade Chemical Company refines a variety of petrochemical products. The following data are from the firm's Cincinnati plant.

WIPB Work in process, August 1 .... 2,000,000 gallons
   Direct material.. 100% complete
   Conversion.. 25% complete
   + Units started in process during August .... 950,000 gallons
WIPE Work in process, August 31 .... 240,000 gallons
   Direct material.. 100% complete
   Conversion.. 80% complete

REQUIRED:

1. Compute the equivalent units of direct material and conversion for the month of August. Use the weighted-average method of processing costing.
2. Repeat requirement (1) using the FIFO method.

Exercise 4-20   Physical Flow and Equivalent Units. Country Life Corporation produces breakfast cereal. The following data pertain to 19x0.

		Percentage of Completion	
	Units	Direct Material	Conversion
Work in process, January 1	20,000 pounds	80%	60%
Work in process, December 31	15,000 pounds	70%	30%

During the year the company started 120,000 pounds of material in production.

REQUIRED:

1. Prepare a schedule analyzing the physical flow of units and computing the equivalent units of both direct material and conversion for 19x0. Use weighted-average process costing.
2. Repeat requirement (1) using the FIFO method.

Exercise 4-21   Equivalent Units; FIFO and Weighted Average. Glass Creations, Inc. manufactures decorative glass products. The firm employs a process costing system for its manufacturing operations. All direct materials are added at the beginning of the process, and conversion costs are incurred uniformly throughout the process. The company's production quantity schedule for November follows.

	Units
Work-in-process on November 1 (60% complete as to conversion).	1,000
Units started during November	5,000
Total units to account for.	6,000
Units from beginning work in process, which were completed and transferred out during November	1,000
Units started and completed during November	3,000
Work-in-process on November 30 (20% complete as to conversion).	2,000
Total units accounted for	6,000

REQUIRED: Calculate each of the following amounts.

1. Equivalent units of direct material during November. Use the FIFO method.
2. Equivalent units of conversion activity during November. Use the FIFO method.
3. Equivalent units of direct material during November. Use the weighted-average method.
4. Equivalent units of conversion activity during November. Use the weighted-average method.

(CMA, adapted)

Exercise 4-22   Cost Flows in Process Costing; Journal Entries. Montreal Glass Works manufactures window glass in two sequential departments. The following cost data pertain to the month of October.

	Department 1	Department 2
Direct material entered into production	$ 80,000	$ 20,000
Direct labor	340,000	280,000
Applied manufacturing overhead	680,000	420,000
Cost of goods completed and transferred out	900,000*	400,000†

* Cost of goods transferred to department 2.
† Cost of goods transferred to finished goods.

REQUIRED: Prepare journal entries to record the following events.

1. Incurrence of costs for direct material and direct labor and application of manufacturing overhead in department 1.
2. Transfer of goods from department 1 to department 2.
3. Incurrence of costs for direct material and direct labor and application of manufacturing overhead in department 2.
4. Transfer of goods from department 2 to finished-goods inventory.

Exercise 4-23   Cost per Equivalent Unit. Northern Michigan Lumber Company grows, harvests, and processes timber for use as building lumber. The following data pertain to the company's sawmill.

Work in process, June 1:
   Direct material . . . . $ 37,000
   Conversion 36,750
Costs incurred during June:
   Direct material $150,000
   Conversion 230,000

The equivalent units of activity for June were as follows:

	Weighted Average	FIFO
Direct material	17,000	15,000
Conversion.	48,500	46,000

REQUIRED:

1. Calculate the cost per equivalent unit, for both direct material and conversion, during June. Use weighted-average process costing.
2. Repeat requirement (1) using the FIFO method.

Exercise 4-24   Cost per Equivalent Unit. London Porcelain Company manufactures fine porcelain dishes. The following data pertain to the firm's Mixing Department during November.

Work in process, November 1:
Direct material .... $ 65,000
Conversion 180,000
Costs incurred during November:
Direct material $425,000
Conversion 690,000

The equivalent units of activity for November were as follows:

	Weighted Average	FIFO
Direct material	7,000	4,250
Conversion	1,740	1,000

REQUIRED:

1. Calculate the cost per equivalent unit, for both direct material and conversion, during the month of November. Use weighted-average process costing.
2. Repeat requirement (1) using the FIFO method.

Exercise 4-25 *Analysis of Total Costs.* Carolina Textiles Company manufactures a variety of natural fabrics for the clothing industry. The following data pertain to the Weaving Department for the month of September.

Work in process, September 1.................................... 20,000 units*
Direct material .... $ 94,000
Conversion 44,400
Costs incurred during September
Direct material $164,000
Conversion 272,800

* Complete as to direct material; 40% complete as to conversion.

The equivalent units of activity for September were as follows:

	Weighted Average	FIFO
Direct material	60,000	40,000
Conversion...	52,000	44,000
Units completed and transferred out during September..........	50,000	

REQUIRED:

1. Compute each of the following amounts using weighted-average process costing.
   a. Cost of goods completed and transferred out of the Weaving Department during September.
   b. Cost of the September 30 work-in-process inventory in the Weaving Department.
2. Repeat requirement (1) using the FIFO method.

Exercise 4-26   Analysis of Total Costs. The data below pertain to Philadelphia Paperboard Company, a manufacturer of cardboard boxes.

Work in process, February 1	10,000 units*
Direct material	$ 5,500
Conversion	17,000
Costs incurred during February	
Direct material	$110,000
Conversion	171,600

* Complete as to direct material; 40% complete as to conversion.

The equivalent units of activity for February were as follows:

	Weighted Average	FIFO
Direct material	110,000	100,000
Conversion	92,000	88,000

During February, 90,000 units were completed and transferred out.

REQUIRED:

1. Compute each of the following amounts using weighted-average process costing.
   a.   Cost of goods completed during February.
   b.   Cost of the February 28 work-in-process inventory.
2. Repeat requirement (1) using the FIFO method.

Exercise 4-27   Weighted-Average versus FIFO; Journal Entry. On January 1, 19x2 the Molding Department of Portland Plastic Company had no work-in-process inventory. On January 31, the following journal entry was made to record the cost of goods completed and transferred out of the Molding Department.

Finished-Goods Inventory	$115,000
Work-in-Process Inventory: Molding Department	$115,000

The company uses weighted-average process costing.

REQUIRED: What would the amount have been in the journal entry above if Portland Plastics Company had used the FIFO method of process costing? Why?

Exercise 4-28   Operation Costing. The Pennsylvania Division's November 19x4 production consisted of batch P25 (2,000 professional basketballs) and batch S33 (4,000 scholastic basketballs). Each batch was started and finished during November, and there was no beginning or ending work in process. Costs incurred were as follows:

Direct Material

Batch P25, $42,000, including $2,500 for packaging material; batch S33, $45,000.

Conversion Costs

Preparation Department, predetermined rate of $7.50 per unit; Finishing Department, predetermined rate of $6.00 per unit; Packaging Department, predetermined rate of $.50 per unit.

REQUIRED:

1. Draw a diagram depicting the division's batch manufacturing process. Refer to Exhibit 4-15 for guidance.
2. Compute the November product cost for each type of basketball.
3. Prepare journal entries to record the cost flows during November of 19x4.

PROBLEMS *Problem 4-29 Partial Production Report; Journal Entries; Weighted-Average Method.*
Xenia Company accumulates costs for its single product using weighted-average process costing. Direct material is added at the beginning of the production process, and conversion activity occurs uniformly throughout the process.

Production Report
For August 19x9
(Weighted-Average Method)

	Physical Units	Percentage of Completion with Respect to Conversion	Equivalent Units — Direct Material	Equivalent Units — Conversion
Work in process, August 1	40,000	80%		
Units started during August	80,000			
Total units to account for	120,000			
Units completed and transferred out during August	100,000		100,000	100,000
Work in process, August 31	20,000	30%	20,000	6,000
Total units accounted for	120,000			

	Direct Material	Conversion	Total
Work in process, August 1	$ 42,000	$ 305,280	$ 347,280
Costs incurred during August	96,000	784,400	880,400
Total costs to account for	$138,000	$1,089,680	$1,227,680
Costs per equivalent unit	$1.15	$10.28	$11.43

REQUIRED:

1. Prepare a schedule of equivalent units for Xenia Company.
2. Show how the costs per equivalent unit were determined in the production report.
3. Compute the cost of goods completed and transferred out during August.
4. Compute the cost remaining in the work-in-process inventory on August 31.
5. Prepare a journal entry to record the transfer of the cost of goods completed and transferred out during August.

6. How would the production report above be different if the company used FIFO
process costing?

Problem 4-30   Straightforward FIFO Process Costing; Journal Entries; Step-by-Step Approach. Refer to the data for Xenia Company given in the preceding problem.

REQUIRED:

1. Complete each of the following process costing steps using FIFO process costing.
   a. Calculation of equivalent units.
   b. Computation of unit costs.
   c. Analysis of total costs.
2. Prepare a journal entry to record the transfer of the cost of goods completed and
   transferred out during August.

Problem 4-31   Partial Production Report; Journal Entries; FIFO Method. Lake City Chemical Company accumulates costs for its single product using FIFO process costing. Direct material is added at the beginning of the production process, and conversion activity occurs uniformly throughout the process. Below is a partially completed production report for the month of May 19x1.

Production Report
For May 19x1
(FIFO Method)

	Physical Units	Percentage of Completion with Respect to Conversion	Equivalent Units Direct Material	Conversion
Work in process, May 1	25,000	40%		
Units started during May	30,000			
Total units to account for.........	55,000			
Units completed and transferred out				
during May	35,000		35,000	35,000
Work in process, May 31	20,000	80%	20,000	16,000
Total units accounted for	55,000			

	Direct Material	Conversion	Total
Work in process, May 1	$143,000	$ 474,700	$ 617,700
Costs incurred during May................	165,000	2,009,000	2,174,000
Total costs to account for.................	$308,000	$2,483,700	$2,791,700
Costs per equivalent unit	$5.50	$49.00	$54.50

REQUIRED:

1. Prepare a schedule of equivalent units for Lake City Chemical Company.
2. Show how the costs per equivalent unit were determined in the production report
   above.

3. Compute the cost of goods completed and transferred out during May.
4. Compute the cost remaining in the work-in-process inventory on May 31.
5. Prepare a journal entry to record the transfer of the cost of goods completed and transferred out during May.
6. How would the production report above be different if the company used weighted-average process costing?

Problem 4-32   *Straightforward Weighted-Average Process Costing; Journal Entries; Step-by-Step Approach.* Refer to the data for Lake City Chemical Company given in the preceding problem.

REQUIRED:

1. Complete each of the following process costing steps using weighted average process costing:
   a. Calculation of equivalent units.
   b. Computation of unit costs.
   c. Analysis of total costs.
2. Prepare a journal entry to record the transfer of the cost of goods completed and transferred out during August.

Problem 4-33   *Straightforward Weighted-Average Process Costing; Step-by-Step Approach.* The following data has been compiled for Gemini Company for the month of April. Conversion activity occurs uniformly throughout the production process.

Work in process, April 1 — 10,000 units:
　Direct material: 100% complete, cost of . . . . $ 22,000
　Conversion: 20% complete, cost of . . . . 　4,500
　　Balance in work in process, April 1 . . . . $ 26,500

Units started during April 100,000
Units completed during April and transferred out to finished-goods inventory.   80,000
Work in process, April 30
　Direct material: 100% complete
　Conversion: 33⅓% complete
Costs incurred during April:
　Direct material $198,000
　Conversion costs:
　　Direct labor . . . . $ 52,800
　　Applied manufacturing overhead . . . . 　105,600
　　Total conversion costs $158,400

REQUIRED: Prepare schedules to accomplish each of the following process costing steps for the month of April. Use the weighted-average method of process costing.

1. Analysis of physical flow of units.
2. Calculation of equivalent units.
3. Computation of unit costs.
4. Analysis of total costs.

Problem 4-34   Straightforward FIFO Process Costing; Step-by-Step Approach. Refer to the data for Gemini Company given in the preceding problem. Complete the same requirements, but use the FIFO method of process costing.

Problem 4-35   Comparison of Weighted-Average and FIFO Process Costing. This problem can be completed only if problems 4-33 and 4-34 have been solved. Referring to your solutions for those two problems, prepare a graph similar to Exhibit 4-14 to reconcile the weighted-average and FIFO process costing methods.

Problem 4-36   Step-by-Step Weighted-Average Process Costing. You are engaged in the audit of the December 31, 19x8 financial statements of Spirit Corporation, a manufacturer of digital watches. You are attempting to verify the costing of the ending inventories of work in process and finished goods. The inventory quantities on December 31, 19x8 are as follows:

	Units
Work in process (50% complete as to labor and overhead)	300,000
Finished goods	200,000

Materials are added to production at the beginning of the manufacturing process, and overhead is applied to each product at the rate of 60 percent of direct-labor costs. There was no finished-goods inventory on January 1, 19x8. A review of Spirit's inventory cost records disclosed the following information:

		Costs	
	Units	**Materials**	**Labor**
Work in process, January 1, 19x8 (80% complete as to conversion)	200,000	$ 200,000	$ 315,000
Units started in production	1,000,000		
Material costs		$1,300,000	
Labor costs			$1,995,000
Units completed	900,000		

REQUIRED: Prepare schedules as of December 31, 19x8 to compute the following:

1. Physical flow of units.
2. Equivalent units of production using the weighted-average method.
3. Costs per equivalent unit for material and conversion.
4. Cost of the December 31, 19x8 finished-goods inventory and work-in-process inventory.

(CPA, adapted)

Problem 4-37   Process Costing in a Public Accounting Firm. Mason and Company, a public accounting firm, is engaged in the preparation of income tax returns for individuals. The firm uses the weighted-average method of process costing for internal reporting. The following information pertains to the month of March.

Returns in process, March 1:	
(25% complete)	200
Returns started in March	825
Returns in process, March 31:	
(80% complete)	125
Returns in process, March 1:	
Labor	$ 6,000
Overhead	2,500
Labor, March 1 to March 31:	
(4,000 hours)	89,000
Overhead, March 1 to March 31	45,000

REQUIRED:

1. Compute the following amounts for labor and for overhead:
   a. Equivalent units of activity.
   b. Cost per equivalent unit.
2. Compute the cost of returns in process as of March 31.

(CMA, adapted)

Problem 4-38   *Weighted-Average Process Costing; Production Report; Journal Entries.* West
Corporation manufactures a product called aggregate in one department of its California
Division. Aggregate is transferred upon completion to the Utah division at a predetermined
price, where it is used in the manufacture of other products.

In the California Division, the raw material is added at the beginning of the process. Labor
and overhead are applied continuously throughout the process. All direct departmental overhead is charged to the departments, and divisional overhead is allocated to the departments on
the basis of direct-labor hours. The divisional overhead rate for 19x9 is $.40 per direct-labor
dollar.

The following information relates to production during November 19x9 in the Aggregate
Department.

(a) Work in process, November 1 (4,000 pounds, 75% complete as to conver-	
sion):	
Raw material.	$22,800
Direct labor at $5.00 per hour	24,650
Departmental overhead	12,000
Divisional overhead	9,860
(b) Raw material:	
Inventory, November 1, 2,000 pounds	10,000
Purchases, November 3, 10,000 pounds	51,000
Purchases, November 18, 10,000 pounds	51,500
Released to production during November, 16,000 pounds	
(c) Direct labor costs at $5.00 per hour, $103,350	
(d) Direct departmental overhead costs, $52,000	
(e) Transferred to Utah division, 15,000 pounds	
(f) Work in process, November 30, 5,000 pounds, $33\frac{1}{3}$% complete	

The company uses weighted-average process costing to accumulate product costs. However, for raw-material inventories the firm uses the FIFO inventory method.

REQUIRED:

1. Prepare a production report for the Aggregate Department for November 19x9. The report should show:
   a. Equivalent units of production by cost factor of aggregate (raw material and conversion).
   b. Cost per equivalent unit for each cost factor of aggregate. (Round your answers to the nearest cent.)
   c. Cost of aggregate transferred to the Utah Division.
   d. Cost of the work-in-process inventory on November 30, 19x9 in the California Division.

2. Prepare journal entries to record the following events:
   a. Release of direct material to production during November.
   b. Incurrence of direct-labor costs in November.
   c. Application of overhead costs for the Aggregate Department (direct departmental and allocated divisional costs).
   d. Transfer of finished aggregate out of the Aggregate Department.

(CMA, adapted)

Problem 4-39   Operation Costing. (Roland Minch) Wilkey Company manufactures a variety of glass windows in its Egalton plant. In department I clear glass sheets are produced, and some of these sheets are sold as finished goods. Other sheets made in department I have metallic oxides added in department II to form colored glass sheets. Some of these colored sheets are sold; others are moved to department III for etching, and then are sold. The company uses operation costing.

Wilkey Company's production costs applied to products in May are given in the following table. There was no beginning or ending inventory of work in process for May.

Cost Category	Dept. I	Dept. II	Dept. III
Direct materials	$450,000	$72,000	–0–
Direct labor	38,000	22,000	$35,000
Manufacturing overhead	230,000	68,000	74,000

Products	Units	Dept. I Dir. Mat.	Dept. II Dir. Mat.
Clear Glass, sold after dept. I	11,000	$247,500	–0–
Unetched colored glass, sold after dept. II	4,000	90,000	$32,000
Etched colored glass, sold after dept. III	5,000	112,500	40,000

Each sheet of glass requires the same steps within each operation.

REQUIRED: Compute each of the following amounts.

1. The conversion cost per unit in department I.
2. The conversion cost per unit in department II.
3. The cost of a clear glass sheet.
4. The cost of an unetched, colored glass sheet.
5. The cost of an etched, colored glass sheet.

Problem 4-40   Transferred-in Costs; Weighted-Average Method; Appendix. Jensen Company uses a process costing system. A unit of product passes through three departments—molding, assembly, and finishing—before it is completed.

The following activity took place in the Finishing Department during May.

	Units
Work-in-process inventory, May 1	1,400
Units transferred in from the Assembly Department	14,000
Units transferred out to finished-goods inventory	11,900

Raw material is added at the beginning of processing in the Finishing Department. The work-in-process inventory was 70 percent complete as to conversion on May 1 and 40 percent complete as to conversion on May 31.

Jensen Company uses the weighted-average method of process costing. The equivalent units and current costs per equivalent unit of production for each cost factor are as follows for the Finishing Department.

	Equivalent Units	Current Costs per Equivalent Unit
Transferred-in costs	15,400	$5.00
Raw materials	15,400	1.00
Conversion cost	13,300	3.00
Total		$9.00

REQUIRED:

1. Calculate the following amounts:
   a. Cost of units transferred to finished-goods inventory during May.
   b. Cost of the Finishing Department's work-in-process inventory on May 31.
2. If the total costs of prior departments included in the work-in-process inventory of the Finishing Department on May 1 amounted to $6,300, calculate the total cost transferred from the Assembly Department to the Finishing Department during May.

(CMA, adapted)

Problem 4-41   Sequential Manufacturing Process; Weighted-Average Method; Appendix.
Felix Manufacturing Company uses weighted-average process costing to account for the costs of its single product. Production begins in the Fabrication Department, where units of raw material are molded into various connecting parts. After fabrication is complete, the units are transferred to the Assembly Department. No material is added in the Assembly Department. After assembly is complete, the units are transferred to the Packaging Department, where the units are packaged for shipment. At the completion of this process the units are complete, and they are transferred to the Shipping Department.

On December 31, 19x7, the following inventory is on hand:

1. No unused raw material or packing material.
2. Fabrication Department: 6,000 units, 25% complete as a direct material and 40% complete as to direct labor.
3. Assembly Department: 10,000 units, 75% complete as to direct labor.

4. Packaging Department: 3,000 units, 60% complete as to packing material and 75% complete as to direct labor.
5. Shipping Department: 8,000 units.

REQUIRED: Prepare schedules showing the following on December 31, 19x7.

1. The number of equivalent units of direct material in all inventories.
2. The number of equivalent units of Fabrication Department direct labor in all inventories.
3. The number of equivalent units of Packaging Department direct material and direct labor in the Packaging Department inventory.

(CPA, adapted)

Problem 4-42 *Sequential Production Departments; FIFO Method; Appendix.* Home and Garden Products Company manufactures a plant nutrient known as Garden Pride. The manufacturing process begins in the Grading Department when raw materials are started in process. Upon completion of processing in the Grading Department, the output is transferred to the Saturating Department for the final phase of production. Here the product is saturated with water and then dried again. There is no weight gain in the process, and the water is virtually cost free.

The following information is available for the month of November.

| Work in Process Inventories | November 1 | | November 30 |
	Quantity (pounds)	Cost	Quantity (pounds)
Grading Department...................	None	—	None
Saturating Department..................	1,600	$17,600*	2,000

* Includes $3,750 in Saturating Department conversion costs.

The work-in-process inventory in the Saturating Department is estimated to be 50 percent complete both at the beginning and end of November. Costs of production for November are as follows:

Costs of Production	Materials Used	Conversion
Grading Department................................	$265,680	$86,400
Saturating Department	—	85,920

The material used in the Grading Department weighed 36,000 pounds. The firm uses the FIFO method of process costing.

REQUIRED: Prepare production reports for both the Grading and Saturating Departments for the month of November. Show supporting computations. The answer should include:

1. Equivalent units of production (in pounds)
2. Total manufacturing costs
3. Cost per equivalent unit (pounds)

4. Cost of ending work-in-process inventory
5. Cost of goods completed and transferred out
(CPA, adapted)

Problem 4-43   Sequential Production Departments; Weighted-Average Method; Appendix.
Refer to the data given in the preceding problem. Complete the same requirements assuming that Home and Garden Products Company uses weighted-average process costing. In calculating unit costs, round your answer to four decimal places. (Hint: What special feature does the problem have which simplifies your work for the Grading Department?)

CASE   *Case 4-44   Weighted-Average Process Costing.* Leather Products Company manufactures high-quality leather goods. The company's profits have declined during the past nine months. In an attempt to isolate the causes of poor profit performance, management is investigating the manufacturing operations of each of its products.

One of the company's main products is fine leather belts. The belts are produced in a single, continuous process in the Bluett Plant. During the process, leather strips are sewn, punched, and dyed. The belts then enter a final finishing stage to conclude the process. Labor and overhead are applied continuously during the manufacturing process. All materials, leather strips, and buckles, are introduced at the beginning of the process. The firm uses the weighted-average method to calculate its unit costs.

The leather belts produced at the Bluett Plant are sold wholesale for $9.95 each. Management wants to compare the current manufacturing costs per unit with the market prices for leather belts. Top management has asked the Bluett Plant controller to submit data on the cost of manufacturing the leather belts for the month of October. These cost data will be used to determine whether modifications in the production process should be initiated or whether an increase in the selling price of the belts is justified. The cost per belt used for planning and control is $5.35.

The work-in-process inventory consisted of 400 partially completed units on October 1. The belts were 25 percent complete as to conversion. The costs included in the inventory on October 1 were as follows:

Leather strips.	$1,000
Buckles	250
Conversion costs.	300
Total	$1,550

During October 7,600 leather strips were placed into production. A total of 7,000 leather belts were completed. The work-in-process inventory on October 31 consisted of 1,000 belts, which were 50 percent complete as to conversion.

The costs charged to production during October were as follows:

Leather strips.	$20,600
Buckles	4,550
Conversion costs.	20,700
Total	$45,850

REQUIRED: In order to provide cost data regarding the manufacture of leather belts in the Bluett Plant to the top management of Leather Products Company, compute the following amounts for the month of October.

1. The equivalent units for material and conversion.
2. The cost per equivalent unit for material and conversion.
3. The assignment of production costs to the October 31 work-in-process inventory and to goods transferred out.
4. The weighted-average unit cost of the leather belts completed and transferred to finished goods. Comment on the company's cost per belt used for planning and control.

(CMA, adapted)

AEROTECH CORPORATION

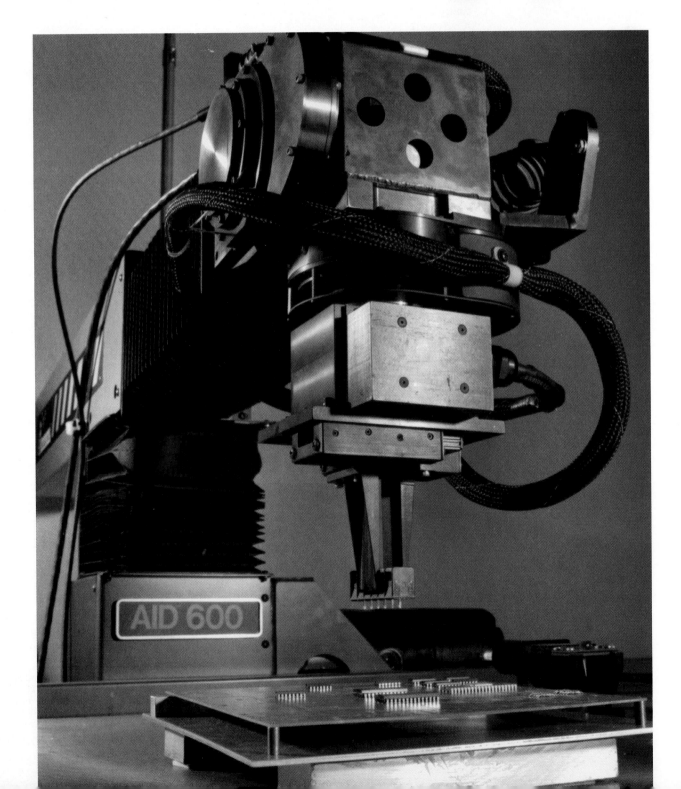

Chapter 5

Cost Management Systems for the New Manufacturing Environment

After completing this chapter, you should be able to:

- Explain the chief differences between a traditional manufacturing process and a highly automated, computer-assisted manufacturing environment.

- Compute product costs under a traditional, volume-based product-costing system and a transaction-based product-costing system.

- List and explain the key features of a transaction-based product-costing system.

- Describe the key features of a cost management system, including cost drivers, activity costing, and elimination of non-value-added costs.

- List and explain eight important features of just-in-time inventory and production management systems.

- Prepare journal entries to record the cost flows under a just-in-time product-costing system.

- Describe the performance measures appropriate for the new manufacturing environment.

- Briefly describe the concepts of product life-cycle costs and justification of capital expenditures for computer-integrated manufacturing systems.

A revolution is transforming the manufacturing industry. Not since the mid-nineteenth century have changes been as sweeping and dramatic as they are today. The growth of international competition, the breakneck pace of technological innovation, and startling advances in computerized systems have resulted in a new playing field for manufacturers around the globe. Some manufacturers have emerged as world-class producers, while others have fallen by the wayside.

What is behind these dramatic changes in the manufacturing industry? And what is the role of managerial accounting in this rapidly changing environment? These questions are the focus of this chapter. To explore the issues that arise in the new manufacturing environment, we will review recent events in the life of Aerotech Corporation, an electronics manufacturer in the southwest.

AEROTECH CORPORATION: A TALE OF TWO CITIES

Aerotech Corporation manufactures complex printed circuit boards used in aircraft radar and communications equipment. The company has operated its Phoenix plant for 20 years. Within the past year, Aerotech opened a new production facility in Bakersfield, California. While the Phoenix plant utilizes a traditional plant layout and production process, the Bakersfield plant employs the latest in advanced manufacturing technology. We will begin by describing the production process used in the Phoenix facility. Then we will describe the adaptations Aerotech's controller has made in the managerial accounting system used in the Phoenix plant. Finally, we will examine the production process and managerial accounting system used in the Bakersfield plant.

PHOENIX PLANT: TRADITIONAL PRODUCTION PROCESS AND PLANT LAYOUT

Three complex printed circuit boards are manufactured in Aerotech's Phoenix plant. These products are referred to as Mode I, Mode II and Mode III boards. Mode I is the simplest of the three circuit boards, and Aerotech sells 10,000 units of the product each year. The Mode II circuit board, which is only slightly more complex, has a high sales volume compared to the other two boards. Aerotech sells 20,000 Mode II boards each year. The Mode III circuit board, which is the most complicated, is a low-volume product with annual sales of 4,000 units.

Production Process

The production process for all three printed circuit boards involves the attachment of various electrical components to a raw circuit board. Aerotech purchases the raw boards and all of the electrical components from other electronics manufacturers. Most of the electrical devices are small axial-lead components, such as diodes and resistors. These components are attached to a circuit board by bending the two lead wires at 90-degree angles and inserting the leads into predrilled holes in the raw boards. A few of the electrical components are large or oddly shaped instruments that require special handling in the production process.

The sequence of production steps is the same for all three boards.[1]

1. *Sequencing* First, the small axial-lead components are placed in the proper sequence for insertion into the board. Each type of axial-lead component is purchased in taped reels. The individual components can be peeled off the reel one at a time, just as a piece of tape can be peeled off a roll. A

---

[1] The circuit-board production process is based on descriptions given in Richard J. Schonberger, *World Class Manufacturing Casebook* (New York: The Free Press, 1987), pp. 65–76; and James M. Patell, "Cost Accounting, Process Control, and Product Design: A Case Study of the Hewlett-Packard Personal Office Computer Division," *The Accounting Review, 62,* no. 4 (October 1987), pp. 808–839.

sequencing machine is programmed to select the components off the proper reels in the sequence required for each type of circuit board.

2. *Auto-insertion* The sequenced, axial-lead components are fed into an auto-inserter machine, which bends the leads and inserts them into the predrilled holes in the raw boards.

3. *Hand-insertion* Next, the large or oddly shaped components are manually attached to the boards.

4. *Wave soldering* The boards pass through a wave-solder machine. Here a wave of molten solder passes under each board, and the components' leads are secured to the board.

5. *Wash/dry* The wash/dry cycle is similar to the operation of a home dishwasher. The boards are washed to remove foreign particles; then they are dried with warm air.

6. *Hand insertion* The next step is to insert manually any components that could not withstand either the wave-solder or wash/dry operation.

7. *Bed of nails* Each completed circuit board then is placed on a bed-of-nails tester. This machine consists of a set of vertical probes that make contact with the lead wires from each component on the circuit board. Each individual component then is tested independently. The bed-of-nails tester can be programmed so that its probes make contact with the different patterns of lead wires on the Mode I, Mode II, and Mode III circuit boards.

8. *Burn-in* The final step is a burn-in test wherein electrical power is applied to each circuit board. This procedure takes three hours, and the entire board is tested for functionality. In other words, does the entire circuit board work properly? If problems are detected in a board, it is sent immediately to engineering for a full checkout procedure.

9. *Packaging* After the burn-in test, the printed circuit boards are packaged and sent to finished-goods storage.

Plant Layout

The layout of Aerotech's Phoenix plant is shown in Exhibit 5-1. Colored arrows depict the flow of production from one operation to the next. Notice that each production operation is performed in a separate department. A storage area for work-in-process inventory is located next to each department. Here, partially completed circuit boards are stored until the next production department is ready for them.

Traditional, Volume-Based Product-Costing System

Until recently, Aerotech's Phoenix plant used a job-order product-costing system similar to the one described in Chapter 3 for Adirondack Outfitters. The cost of each product was the sum of its actual direct-material cost, actual direct-labor cost, and applied manufacturing overhead. Overhead was applied using a predetermined overhead rate based on direct-labor hours. Exhibit 5-2 provides the basic data upon which the traditional costing system was based.

Exhibit 5-3 shows the calculation of the product cost for each of the three circuit boards. Overhead is applied to the products at the rate of $33 per direct-labor hour. Notice that all of the Phoenix plant's budgeted manufacturing overhead costs are lumped together in a single cost pool. This total budgeted overhead amount

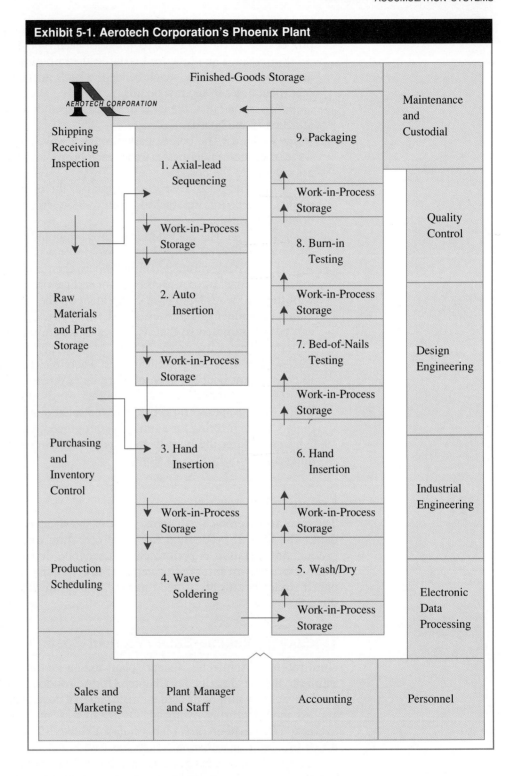

Exhibit 5-1. Aerotech Corporation's Phoenix Plant

($3,894,000) then is divided by the plant's total budgeted direct-labor hours (118,000 hours).

Aerotech's labor-hour-based product-costing system is typical of many manufacturing companies. Labor hours are related closely to the volume of activity in the factory, which sometimes is referred to as *throughput.* Consequently, these traditional product-costing systems often are said to be **volume-based** (or **throughput-based) costing systems.**[2]

Trouble in Phoenix

The profitability of Aerotech's Phoenix operation has been faltering in recent years. The company's pricing policy has been to set a target price for each circuit board equal to 125 percent of the full product cost. Thus, the target prices were determined as shown in Exhibit 5-4. Also shown are the actual prices that Aerotech has been obtaining for its products.

Mode I circuit boards were selling at their target price of $261.25. However, price competition from foreign companies had forced Aerotech to lower its price on Mode II boards to $320, well below the target price of $377.50. Even at this lower price, Aerotech was having difficulty getting orders for its planned volume of Mode II circuit board production. Fortunately, the lower profitability of the Mode II boards was offset partially by greater-than-expected profits on the Mode III circuit boards. Aerotech's sales personnel had discovered that the company was swamped with orders for the Mode III boards when the target price of $157.50 was charged. Consequently, Aerotech had raised the price on its Mode III boards several times, and eventually the product was selling at $250 per board. Even at this price, customers did not seem to hesitate to place orders. Moreover, Aerotech's competitors did not mount a challenge in the Mode III market. Aerotech's management was pleased to have a niche for the Mode III circuit boards, which appeared to be a highly profitable, low-volume specialty product. Nevertheless, concern continued to mount in Phoenix about the difficulty with the Mode II boards. After all, the Mode II board was the Phoenix plant's bread-and-butter product, with projected annual sales of 20,000 units.

Refined Product-Costing System

Aerotech Corporation's controller, Chuck Dickens, had been thinking for some time about a refinement in the Phoenix plant's product-costing system. He wondered if the traditional, volume-based system was providing management with accurate data about product costs. On an experimental basis, Dickens implemented a new, refined product-costing system in the Phoenix plant. In the refined system, Dickens abandoned the single overhead rate based on direct-labor hours. Instead, overhead was applied to products in three parts, as follows:

Setup time: separately identified and charged to each product.
Receiving/inspection and material handling: applied to products on the basis of their direct-material costs.
Other overhead: applied to products on the basis of machine hours.

[2] The illustration of alternative product-costing systems in Aerotech's Phoenix plant parallels an example given by John Shank and Vijay Govindarajan, "The Perils of Cost Allocations Based on Production Volumes," *Accounting Horizons,* December 1988, pp. 71–79.

**Exhibit 5-2. Basic Production and Cost Data: Aerotech Corporation's
Phoenix Plant**

AEROTECH CORPORATION		Mode I Boards	Mode II Boards	Mode III Boards
Production:				
Units	. . . .	10,000	20,000	4,000
Runs	. . . .	1 run of 10,000	4 runs of 5,000 each	10 runs of 400 each
Direct material (raw boards and components)	. . . .	$50.00	$90.00	$20.00
Direct labor* (not including setup time)	. . . .	3 hours per board	4 hours per board	2 hours per board
Setup time*	. . . .	10 hours per run	10 hours per run	10 hours per run
Machine time	. . . .	1 hour per board	1.25 hours per board	2 hours per board

*Direct labor and setup labor costs $20 per hour, including fringe benefits.

Dickens reasoned that receiving/inspection and material-handling costs were related more closely to each product's materials than to direct labor. In other words, Dickens felt that a product's direct material *drives* its material-related costs. The controller also felt that machine hours would constitute a better basis than direct-labor hours for the application of all other overhead costs. As the production process had become more automated, more work was being done by machines and less by manual labor. Finally, Dickens wanted to charge each product line for the setup costs of its production runs. The results of Dickens's refined costing system are shown in Exhibit 5-5. Examine this exhibit carefully, as it provides all of the details of the new costing system.

Notice that the product cost reported for each of the circuit boards is different from that computed under the traditional costing system. Both the Mode I and Mode II circuit boards exhibit lower product costs under the refined costing system. In Chuck Dickens's view, this partially explained the price competition that Aerotech was experiencing on its Mode II circuit boards. Perhaps Aerotech's competitors were selling the Mode II boards at a lower price because the managers of those firms realized that the cost of producing a Mode II board was lower than Aerotech's traditional costing system had indicated. However, as Chuck Dickens scanned the new product costs shown in Exhibit 5-5, he was alarmed by the substantial increase in the reported cost of a Mode III circuit board. Although Aerotech's actual selling price

---

**Exhibit 5-3. Product Costs from Traditional Volume-Based Product-Costing
System: Aerotech Corporation's Phoenix Plant**

	Mode I Boards		Mode II Boards		Mode III Boards	
Direct material (raw boards and components)	$ 50.00		$ 90.00		$ 20.00	
Direct labor (not including setup time)	60.00	(3 hr. at $20)	80.00	(4 hr. at $20)	40.00	(2 hr. at $20)
Manufacturing overhead*	99.00	(3 hr. at $33)	132.00	(4 hr. at $33)	66.00	(2 hr. at $33)
Total	$209.00		$302.00		$126.00	

*Calculation of predetermined-overhead rate:

Manufacturing-overhead budget:

Machinery costs (maintenance, depreciation, computer support, lubrication, electricity, calibration)	$1,720,000
Setup time	3,000
Engineering	700,000
Receiving and inspection of materials	200,000
Material handling (purchasing, storage, moving)	600,000
Quality assurance (bed-of-nails and burn-in testing)	421,000
Packaging and shipping	250,000
Total	$3,894,000

Direct labor, budgeted hours:

Mode I:	10,000 units × 3 hours	30,000
Mode II:	20,000 units × 4 hours	80,000
Mode III:	4,000 units × 2 hours	8,000
Total		118,000

Predetermined-overhead rate:

$$\frac{\text{Budgeted manufacturing overhead}}{\text{Budgeted direct-labor hours}} = \frac{\$3,894,000}{118,000} = \$33 \text{ per hour}$$

---

of $250 was still sufficient to cover the Mode III board's reported cost, the margin earned on the product was not nearly as great as management had thought.

Transaction-Based Product-Costing System

Before Chuck Dickens presented the results of his refined costing system to Aerotech's president, he discussed them with Anne Marlowe, the assistant controller.

Exhibit 5-4. Target and Actual Selling Prices: Aerotech Corporation's Phoenix Plant

AEROTECH CORPORATION	Mode I Boards	Mode II Boards	Mode III Boards
Production cost under traditional volume-based system (Exhibit 5-3)	$209.00	$302.00	$126.00
Target selling price (cost × 125%)	261.25	377.50	157.50
Actual selling price	261.25	320.00	250.00

Exhibit 5-5. Product Costs from Refined Product-Costing System: Aerotech Corporation's Phoenix Plant

AEROTECH CORPORATION	Mode I Boards	Mode II Boards	Mode III Boards
Direct material (raw boards and components)	$ 50.00	$ 90.00	$ 20.00
Direct labor (not including setup time)	60.00 (3 hr. at $20)	80.00 (4 hr. at $20)	40.00 (2 hr. at $20)
Setup time[a]	.02	.04	.50
Material-based overhead[b]	16.81	30.25	6.72
Machine-based overhead[c]	71.88 (1 mach. hr. at $71.88)	89.85 (1.25 mach. hr. at $71.88)	143.76 (2 mach. hr. at $71.88)
Total	$198.71	$290.14	$210.98

[a]Calculation of setup-time cost:

Mode I: $\dfrac{\text{(10 hr. per run) (\$20 per hr.) (1 run)}}{\text{10,000 units}}$ = \$.02 per unit

Mode II: $\dfrac{\text{(10 hr. per run) (\$20 per hr.) (4 runs)}}{\text{20,000 units}}$ = \$.04 per unit

Mode III: $\dfrac{\text{(10 hr. per run) (\$20 per hr.) (10 runs)}}{\text{4,000 units}}$ = \$.50 per unit

Exhibit 5-5 (continued). Product Costs from Refined Product-Costing System: Aerotech Corporation's Phoenix Plant

[h]Calculation of material-based overhead:

Overhead related to material, budgeted costs:

Receiving and inspection	$ 200,000
Material handling	600,000
Total	$ 800,000

Direct material, budgeted costs:

Mode I: 10,000 units × $50	$ 500,000
Mode II: 20,000 units × $90	1,800,000
Mode III: 4,000 units × $20	80,000
Total	$2,380,000

Material-based overhead rate:

$$\frac{\text{Budgeted material-related overhead}}{\text{Budgeted direct-material cost}} = \frac{\$800,000}{\$2,380,000} = 33.61\%$$

Material-based overhead costs per unit:

Mode I: $\dfrac{(\$500,000)\,(33.61\%)}{10,000 \text{ units}} = \dfrac{\$168,050}{10,000 \text{ units}} = \$16.81 \text{ per unit}$

Mode II: $\dfrac{(\$1,800,000)\,(33.61\%)}{20,000 \text{ units}} = \dfrac{\$604,980}{20,000 \text{ units}} = \$30.25 \text{ per unit}$

Mode III: $\dfrac{(\$80,000)\,(33.61\%)}{4,000 \text{ units}} = \dfrac{\$26,888}{4,000 \text{ units}} = \$6.72 \text{ per unit}$

[c]Calculation of machine-based overhead:

Other overhead, budgeted costs:

Machinery costs	$1,720,000
Engineering	700,000
Quality assurance	421,000
Packaging and shipping	250,000
Total	$3,091,000

Machine time, budgeted hours:

Mode I: 10,000 units × 1 hour	10,000 hours
Mode II: 20,000 units × 1.25 hours	25,000 hours
Mode III: 4,000 units × 2 hours	8,000 hours
Total	43,000 hours

Machine-based overhead rate:

$$\frac{\text{Budgeted overhead}}{\text{Budgeted machine hours}} = \frac{\$3,091,000}{43,000} = \$71.88 \text{ per machine hour}$$

Marlowe liked the idea of trying to identify the activities that drive production costs, as Dickens had attempted to do with the material-related overhead costs. However, Marlowe suggested that the costing system could be refined even further. She pointed out that many of the overhead costs incurred by Aerotech were *driven* by the number of transactions related to each overhead item. Engineering costs, for example, were driven by the number of engineering change orders and the complexity of the engineering design for a product. Receiving and inspection costs were driven by the number of different components involved in a product and the number of shipments received and inspected. Material-handling costs were driven by the number of times materials and partially completed units were moved, and the amount of time they remained in storage between production operations. Quality assurance costs were driven by the number of production lots to be tested and the complexity of the product being tested. Packaging and shipping costs were driven by the number of production runs to be packed and the number of shipments made, in addition to the total number of circuit boards being shipped.

As Dickens and Marlowe talked, they began to realize that a **transaction-based product-costing system** might provide management with the most accurate product-cost data possible. Under this costing approach, a *cost driver* is identified for each cost or pool of costs. Then each cost is applied to products on the basis of the number of transactions generated for the identified cost driver by the various products. For example, if Mode I circuit boards generate 25 percent of the engineering transactions, then 25 percent of the engineering costs would be applied to the Mode I product line. As they concluded their conversation, Dickens and Marlowe agreed to develop a transaction-based costing system for the Phoenix plant.

The first step in the process was to develop a data base showing the proportion of transactions for each overhead cost item that were related to each of the three circuit boards. A painstaking and lengthy analysis resulted in the data shown in Exhibit 5-6.

Exhibit 5-6. Data for Transaction-Based Product-Costing System: Aerotech Corporation's Phoenix Plant

	Mode I Boards	Mode II Boards	Mode III Boards
AEROTECH CORPORATION			
Breakdown of transactions generated by each product:			
Engineering (Total cost, $700,000)	25%	45%	30%
Receiving and inspection (Total cost, $200,000)	6%	24%	70%
Material handling (Total cost, $600,000)	7%	30%	63%
Quality assurance (Total cost, $421,000)	10%	25%	65%
Packaging and shipping (Total cost, $250,000)	4%	30%	66%
Machine time:			
Machine hours per board	1 hr.	1.25 hr.	2 hr.

This information was obtained from extensive interviews with key employees in each of Aerotech's support departments and a careful review of each department's records. In the engineering area, for example, Anne Marlowe interviewed each of the engineers to determine the breakdown of their time spent on each of the three products. Marlowe also examined every engineering change order completed in the past two years. She concluded that engineering costs were driven largely by change orders, and that the breakdown was 25 percent for Mode I, 45 percent for Mode II, and 30 percent for Mode III.

The product costs developed from the transaction-based costing system are displayed in Exhibit 5-7. Examine this exhibit carefully, as all of the details of the costing system are shown. Notice that the costs of direct material, direct labor, and setup time are the same as in Chuck Dickens's refined costing system (Exhibit 5-5). However, each of the remaining overhead cost items is applied to the three products much differently under the transaction-based system.

Chuck Dickens was amazed to see the product costs reported under the transaction-based system. The costs of both the Mode I boards and the Mode II boards were much lower than previously reported. However, the cost of a Mode III board had skyrocketed to over three times the company's original estimate. The complexity of the Mode III boards, and its impact on costs, were hidden completely by the traditional, volume-based costing system. Even Dickens's refined system had failed to capture fully the cost of the Mode III boards. To compare the results of the three alternative costing systems, Dickens prepared Exhibit 5-8.

The Mode I boards emerged as an extremely profitable product, selling for over 146 percent of their reported cost under the transaction-based costing system ($261.25 ÷ $178.13). The Mode II boards were selling at approximately 125 percent of their new reported product cost ($320.00 ÷ $256.20). "No wonder we couldn't sell the Mode II boards at $377.50," mused Chuck Dickens, as he looked over the data. "Our competitors probably knew the Mode II boards cost around $256, and they priced them accordingly." When he got to the Mode III column, Dickens was appalled. "We thought those Mode III's were a winner," lamented Dickens, "but we've been selling them at a loss of over $180 per board!" After looking over the data, Dickens almost ran to the president's office. "We've got to get this operation straightened out," he thought.

The Punch Line

What has happened at Aerotech's Phoenix plant? The essence of the problem is that the traditional, volume-based costing system was overcosting the high-volume product lines (Mode I and Mode II) and undercosting the complex, low-volume product line (Mode III). The high-volume products essentially were subsidizing the low-volume line. The refined costing system, developed by Aerotech's controller prior to the change to transaction costing, only partially resolved the cost-distortion problem.

Does this sort of product-cost distortion occur in other companies? As the following case in point shows, the answer is yes.

ILLUSTRATION FROM MANAGEMENT-ACCOUNTING PRACTICE

Cost Distortion at Rockwell International

When managers at Rockwell International noticed erratic sales in one of the company's lines of truck axles, they investigated. One of the company's best axle products was losing market share. A special cost study revealed that the firm's costing system, which applied costs to products in proportion to di-

**Exhibit 5-7. Product Costs from Transaction-Based Product-Costing System:
Aerotech Corporation's Phoenix Plant**

	Mode I Boards	Mode II Boards	Mode III Boards
Direct material (raw boards and components)	$ 50.00	$ 90.00	$ 20.00
Direct labor (not including setup time)	60.00 (3 hr. at $20)	80.00 (4 hr. at $20)	40.00 (2 hr. at $20)
Setup time (from Exhibit 5-5).	.02	.04	.50
Engineering[a]	17.50	15.75	52.50
Receiving and inspection[b]	1.20	2.40	35.00
Material handling[c]	4.20	9.00	94.50
Quality assurance[d]	4.21	5.26	68.41
Packaging and shipping[e]	1.00	3.75	41.25
Machine time[f]	40.00	50.00	80.00
Total	$178.13	$256.20	$432.16

rect-labor costs, had resulted in major distortions. The reported product costs for high-volume axles were approximately 20 percent too high, and the low-volume axles were being undercosted by roughly 40 percent. The firm's practice of basing prices on reported product costs resulted in the overpricing of the high-volume axles. As a consequence, Rockwell's competitors entered the market for the high-volume axle business.[3]

Transaction-Based Costing: The Key Features

Aerotech Corporation's movement toward transaction-based product costing is typical of changes currently under way in many companies. The pressure of foreign competition is forcing manufacturers to strive for a better understanding of their cost structures. Moreover, the cost structures of many manufacturers have changed significantly over the past decade. Years ago, a typical manufacturer produced a relatively small number of products, which did not differ much in the amount and types of manufacturing support they required. Labor was the dominant element in such a

[3] Ford S. Worthy, "Accounting Bores You? Wake Up," *Fortune, 116,* no. 8 (October 12, 1987), pp. 43–53.

Exhibit 5-7 (continued). Product Costs from Transaction-Based Product-Costing System: Aerotech Corporation's Phoenix Plant

Data in these
two columns
from Exhibit 5-6

Data in this
column from
Exhibit 5-2

[a] **Engineering:**

Mode I:	($700,000 × 25%) ÷ 10,000 units = $17.50
Mode II:	($700,000 × 45%) ÷ 20,000 units = $15.75
Mode III:	($700,000 × 30%) ÷ 4,000 units = $52.50

[b] **Receiving and inspection:**

Mode I:	($200,000 × 6%) ÷ 10,000 units = $ 1.20
Mode II:	($200,000 × 24%) ÷ 20,000 units = $ 2.40
Mode III:	($200,000 × 70%) ÷ 4,000 units = $35.00

[c] **Material handling:**

Mode I:	($600,000 × 7%) ÷ 10,000 units = $ 4.20
Mode II:	($600,000 × 30%) ÷ 20,000 units = $ 9.00
Mode III:	($600,000 × 63%) ÷ 4,000 units = $94.50

[d] **Quality assurance:**

Mode I:	($421,000 × 10%) ÷ 10,000 units = $ 4.21
Mode II:	($421,000 × 25%) ÷ 20,000 units = $ 5.26
Mode III:	($421,000 × 65%) ÷ 4,000 units = $68.41

[e] **Packaging and shipping:**

Mode I:	($250,000 × 4%) ÷ 10,000 units = $ 1.00
Mode II:	($250,000 × 30%) ÷ 20,000 units = $ 3.75
Mode III:	($250,000 × 66%) ÷ 4,000 units = $41.25

[f] **Machine time:**

Calculation of machine cost per hour:

From Exhibit 5-5: $\dfrac{\text{Total budgeted machine costs}}{\text{Total budgeted machine hours}} = \dfrac{\$1,720,000}{43,000 \text{ hr.}} = \$40 \text{ per hour}$

Machine costs for each product:

Mode I:	1 machine hr. × $40 =	$40 per unit
Mode II:	1.25 machine hr. × $40 =	$50 per unit
Mode III:	2 machine hr. × $40 =	$80 per unit

---

firm's cost structure. Nowadays, it's a different ball game. Products are more numerous, are more complicated, and vary more in their production requirements. Perhaps most importantly, labor is becoming an ever-smaller component of total production costs. All of these factors are forcing manufacturers to take a close look at their traditional, volume-based costing systems and consider a move toward transaction costing.

Another factor in the move toward transaction costing is related to the information requirements of such systems. The type of data required for transaction costing is becoming more readily available than in the past. Increasing automation, coupled

Exhibit 5-8. Comparison of Product Costs From Alternative Product-Costing Systems: Aerotech Corporation's Phoenix Plant

AEROTECH CORPORATION	Mode I Boards	Mode II Boards	Mode III Boards
Reported product costs:			
Traditional volume-based costing system (from Exhibit 5-3)	$209.00	$302.00	$126.00
Refined costing system (from Exhibit 5-5)	198.71	290.14	210.98
Transaction-based costing system (from Exhibit 5-7)	178.13	256.20	432.16
Sales price data:			
Original target price (based on traditional, volume-based costing system; Exhibit 5-4)	261.25	377.50	157.50
Actual selling price (Exhibit 5-4)	261.25	320.00	250.00

with sophisticated real-time information systems, provides the kind of data necessary to implement such product-costing systems. The key features of transaction-based costing systems are described in the following sections.[4]

Cost Drivers A **cost driver** is an event or activity that results in the incurrence of costs. In transaction-based costing systems, the most significant cost drivers are identified. Then a data base is created, which shows how these cost drivers are distributed across products. It is not necessary to identify every activity that drives costs in the factory. Only those drivers that are related to the bulk of costs need to be identified and tracked.

Activity Accounting Costs are incurred in organizations because of activities. A sales order triggers a series of activities, from the purchase of materials, through various production phases, and ending with shipping the product. A key feature of

[4] Many of the concepts in this and the remaining sections of the chapter are derived from the following sources: Callie Berliner and James A. Brimson, eds., *Cost Management for Today's Advanced Manufacturing* (Boston: Harvard Business School Press, 1988); Robin Cooper and R. Kaplan, "How Cost Accounting Systematically Distorts Product Costs," in *Accounting and Management: Field Study Perspectives,* edited by William J. Bruns, Jr. and Robert S. Kaplan (Boston: Harvard Business School Press, 1987, pp. 204–228); Robert D. McIlhattan, "How Cost Management Systems Can Support the JIT Philosophy," *Management Accounting,* September 1987, pp. 20–26; Robert A. Howell and Stephen R. Soucy, "Operating Controls in the New Manufacturing Environment," *Management Accounting,* October 1987, pp. 25–31; and H. Thomas Johnson and Robert S. Kaplan, *Relevance Lost: The Rise and Fall of Management Accounting* (Boston: Harvard Business School Press, 1987).

transaction-based costing systems is that the costs of significant activities are mea-sured and tracked over time. **Activity accounting** is the collection of financial or operational performance information about significant activities in the enterprise. The reasons for the emphasis on activity accounting are twofold. First, the costing system attempts to assign the costs of significant activities to the products that cause those costs to be incurred. Second, by identifying the cost of activities, managers can attempt the reduction or elimination of unnecessary costs. (We will say more about this goal of the *cost management system* later in the chapter.) Activity accounting tends to strike a familiar chord with a variety of managers and employees throughout an enterprise. Activities are expressed in terms of events that are familiar to such diverse people as sales personnel, engineers, purchasing managers, inspectors, mate-rial handlers, production employees, and shipping personnel.

Transaction Costing   The output of an organization's various departments con-sists of the activities performed by personnel or machines in those departments. Activities usually result in paperwork or the generation of computer documents. For example, engineering departments typically deal with documents such as specifica-tion sheets and engineering change orders. Purchasing departments handle requisi-tions and orders, which may be either hard-copy or computer documents. The point is that transactions provide a readily measurable gauge of the activity in a depart-ment. In a transaction-costing system, the costs of activities are assigned to product lines on the basis of the number of transactions generated by each product. In the Engineering Department of Aerotech's Phoenix plant, for example, we have the following relationships:

Cost: Salaries and fringe benefits of engineers, depreciation and mainte-nance of design equipment, and other departmental costs.
Activity: Product design, specification, and improvement.
Cost driver: Time spent by engineers on product design, specification, and improvement.
Transactions: Number of engineering change orders and design specs.
Transaction costing system: Assigns the costs of engineering to the Mode I, II, and III circuit boards on the basis of the number of engineering transac-tions generated by each product line.

ILLUSTRATION FROM MANAGEMENT-ACCOUNTING PRACTICE

Cost Drivers and Transactions

Some cost drivers used in practice, as measured in terms of transactions, are listed below.[5]

Number of labor transactions	**Number of accessories**
Number of material moves	**Number of vendors**
Number of part numbers	**Number of units scrapped**
Number of parts received per month	**Numbr of engineering change orders**
Average number of part numbers in a product	**Number of production process changes**
Number of products	**Number of units reworked**
Average number of customer options per product	**Number of new parts introduced**
	Amount of hazardous materials
Number of schedule changes	

[5] The source for most of these cost drivers and related transactions is Robert D. McIlhattan, loc. cit.

Direct versus Indirect Costs In traditional, volume-based costing systems, only direct material and direct labor are considered direct costs. All other production costs are lumped together in one (or a few) overhead cost pools and applied to products on the basis of a volume-related measure like direct labor. Thus, all of these costs are treated as indirect costs with respect to the firm's products. In contrast, under a transaction-based costing system, an effort is made to account for as many costs as possible as direct costs of production. Any cost that can possibly be traced to a particular product line is treated as a direct cost of that product. A good example is setup time in Aerotech's Phoenix plant. Under the traditional costing system, the cost of setup time was included in manufacturing overhead and applied to products on the basis of direct-labor hours. Under the transaction-based costing system, setup time was measured for each product line, and setup costs were assigned as *direct costs* to each type of circuit board.

COST MANAGEMENT SYSTEMS

When Aerotech Corporation moved to a transaction-based costing system in its Phoenix plant, the company was in a much better position to price its products competitively. The firm's management was able to see why Aerotech was being forced to lower the price on its high-volume Mode II circuit boards. Moreover, the high cost of the complex, low-volume Mode III boards became apparent. The type of analysis undertaken by Aerotech's controller in the Phoenix plant sometimes is called **strategic cost analysis.** This is a broad-based, managerial-accounting analysis that supports strategic management decisions, such as pricing and product-mix decisions.

A strategic cost analysis identifies the activities by which the organization creates a valuable product or service. Then the analysis identifies the cost drivers that determine the costs of these activities. Finally, the analysis examines possibilities for building a sustainable competitive advantage. Such an advantage could be achieved through a combination of strategic pricing, controlling cost drivers, and altering the organization's significant production activities.[6]

In addition to facilitating strategic pricing decisions, Aerotech's new product-costing system served as the catalyst for a new perspective on the role of managerial accounting in the company. Management no longer viewed the managerial-accounting system merely as a means of costing its products. Instead, management came to view the firm's managerial-accounting function as a **cost management system (CMS).** A cost management system is a management planning and control system with the following objectives.[7]

- To measure the cost of the resources consumed in performing the organization's significant *activities.*
- To identify and eliminate **non-value-added costs.** These are the costs of *activities* that can be eliminated with no deterioration of product quality, performance, or perceived value.
- To determine the efficiency and effectiveness of all major *activities* performed in the enterprise.

[6] Vijay Govindarajan and John K. Shank, "Strategic Cost Analysis: The Crown Cork and Seal Case," *Journal of Cost Management, 2,* no. 4, (Winter 1989), p. 6.

[7] Callie Berliner and James A. Brimson, op. cit., pp. 3, 10, 13–15.

- To identify and evaluate new *activities* that can improve the future performance of the organization.

A cost management system takes a more comprehensive role in an organization than a traditional cost-accounting system. "While cost accounting takes an historical perspective and focuses on reporting costs, cost management takes a proactive role in planning, managing and reducing costs."[8]

Non-Value-Added Costs

The emphasis of a cost management system on activities can help management to identify non-value-added costs and eliminate the activities that cause them. To see how this might occur, let's return to our illustration of Aerotech Corporation's Phoenix plant. How is the time spent in Aerotech's production process from the moment raw material arrives at the Phoenix plant until a finished circuit board is shipped to a customer? As in most manufacturing operations, the time is spent in the following five ways.[9]

- *Process time:* the time during which a product is undergoing conversion activity
- *Inspection time:* the amount of time spent assuring that the product is of high quality
- *Move time:* the time spent moving raw materials, work in process, or finished goods between operations
- *Waiting time:* the amount of time that raw materials or work in process spend waiting for the next operation
- *Storage time:* the time during which materials, partially completed products, or finished goods are held in stock before further processing or shipment to customers

Keep these five types of activities in mind as you reexamine the layout of Aerotech's Phoenix plant (Exhibit 5-1). **Process time** is the amount of time the circuit boards actually are being worked on in one of the production operations (departments 1 through 6) or the packaging operation (department 7). **Inspection time** is the time spent on the bed-of-nails or burn-in-testing procedures (departments 7 and 8). **Move time** includes the following activities: receiving raw materials and moving them into storage; moving raw materials and components to the axial-lead sequencing operation (department 1) or the two hand-insertion operations (departments 3 and 6); moving partially completed products from one department to the next; and moving packaged circuit boards to finished-goods storage. **Waiting time** includes the time that partially completed circuit boards spend in the holding areas located next to each department waiting for the next production operation. **Storage time** includes the time spent by raw materials and parts in storage, and the time spent by packaged circuit boards in finished-goods storage.

Identifying Non-Value-Added Costs in the Phoenix Plant

Can you identify any activities in Exhibit 5-1 that potentially could result in non-value-added costs? The identification of non-value-added activities will vary from

---

[8] *Ibid.,* p. 3.
[9] McIlhattan, loc. cit.

company to company, but each of the five types of activities mentioned above has at least some potential for causing non-value-added costs.

Storage Time Perhaps the most obvious is storage time. Manufacturers traditionally have stored large inventories of materials, parts, and finished goods in order to avoid running out. In recent years, however, that philosophy has been challenged. More and more manufacturers are adopting a *just-in-time philosophy,* in which nothing is purchased or produced until it is needed. In Aerotech's Phoenix operation, the large amounts of space devoted to storage activities are indicative of potentially large non-value-added costs of storage.

Waiting Time Refer again to Exhibit 5-1. Notice the large amount of space devoted in the factory to partially completed circuit boards waiting for the next operation. This is again indicative of potentially large non-value-added costs. The firm's working capital is tied up in work in process, and space is unnecessarily wasted on numerous production queues.

Move Time Think about the amount of time Aerotech's Phoenix employees must spend just moving materials and products around in the plant. Every product must be moved 17 times between the axial-lead sequencing operation (department 1) and finished-goods storage. In addition, raw materials and parts must be moved to three different production operations (departments 1, 3, and 6). Once again, we find the potential for significant non-value-added costs associated with the Phoenix plant's material-handling operations.

Inspection Time Aerotech employs three inspection operations. As Exhibit 5-1 indicates, raw materials and components are inspected upon arrival. Later, the circuit boards are tested in the bed-of-nails procedure (department 7) and the burn-in-test (department 8). It is difficult to say whether inspection procedures result in non-value-added costs without detailed knowledge of the production technology and inspection procedures. Certainly some type of inspection is necessary to assure product quality. However, many manufacturers are striving to reduce the costs of maintaining product quality, and to virtually eliminate the costs of reworking defective products.

Process Time The actual production process that transforms raw material into finished products is certainly a value-added activity *overall.* However, this does not preclude the possibility that some non-value-added activities exist within the overall production process. The goal of the cost management system is to evaluate the efficiency of every part of the production process. Is each step necessary? Is each operation being accomplished in the most efficient way?

Conclusion Aerotech's management concluded that substantial non-value-added costs were being incurred in the Phoenix operation. The following activities were identified in a memo from Aerotech's president to key management personnel.

1. *Storage* A considerable reduction in storage space and time is both possible and essential.
2. *Waiting* Circuit boards should be processed through each operation only as they are required in the subsequent operation. Thus, the amount of time products spend waiting for the next operation should be virtually eliminated.

3. *Moving* The time devoted to moving raw material and work in process is excessive. Ways must be found to reduce the costs of these material-handling activities.
4. *Inspection* The bed-of-nails and burn-in-tests appear to be necessary and efficiently conducted. Nevertheless, management should continually reassess the need for these inspection operations.
5. *Processing* The manual insertion of components in departments 3 and 6 can be performed by industrial robots. The desirability of this change should be explored.

AEROTECH'S BAKERSFIELD PLANT: ADVANCED MANUFACTURING TECHNOLOGY

After a careful study, Aerotech's board of directors decided to build a new production facility. The site chosen for the new plant was Bakersfield, California, which is much nearer to Aerotech's material suppliers and customers. Initially, the plants in Phoenix and Bakersfield both would manufacture Aerotech's three lines of circuit boards. Eventually, however, all of Aerotech's production would be moved to Bakersfield.

The Bakersfield plant was designed to employ state-of-the-art manufacturing technology. When the new plant was designed, Aerotech's management insisted on a plant layout and production process that would reduce or eliminate the non-value-added costs incurred in the Phoenix operation. The two key features of the Bakersfield operation were a *just-in-time (JIT) philosophy* of inventory and production management and a *flexible manufacturing system (FMS)*. These key features of the Bakersfield plant are discussed next.

Just-in-Time Inventory and Production Management

A **just-in-time (or JIT) inventory and production system** is a comprehensive inventory and manufacturing control system in which no materials are purchased and no products are manufactured until they are needed. Raw materials and parts are purchased only as they are needed in some phase of the production process. Component parts and subassemblies are not manufactured in any stage of production until they are required in the next stage. Finished goods are manufactured only as they are needed to fill customer orders. The goal of a JIT production system is to *reduce or eliminate inventories* at every stage of production, from raw materials to finished goods. The JIT philosophy, made famous by Toyota, has been credited with the success of many of the world's leading manufacturers. Tremendous cost savings have been realized by many companies that adopted the JIT philosophy.[10]

ILLUSTRATION FROM MANAGEMENT ACCOUNTING PRACTICE

JIT Cost Savings: Ingersoll-Rand and Honeywell

In a large-scale installation of JIT systems by Ingersoll-Rand, the company saved $3,500,000. The installation of a JIT production system in only one of 10 production lines at Honeywell's Process Control Division netted cost savings of $26,000.

---

[10] J. Swartley-Loush, "Just-in-Time: Is It Right For You?," *Production Engineering,* June 1985, pp. 61–64.

How does a JIT system achieve its vast reductions in inventory and associated cost savings? A production-systems expert lists the following key features of the JIT philosophy.[11]

1. *A smooth, uniform production rate* An important goal of a JIT system is to establish a smooth production flow, beginning with the arrival of materials from suppliers and ending with the delivery of goods to customers. Widely fluctuating production rates result in delays and excess work-in-process inventories. These non-value-added costs are to be eliminated.

2. *A pull method of coordinating steps in the production process* Most manufacturing processes occur in multiple stages. Under the **pull method,** goods are produced in each manufacturing stage only as they are needed at the next stage. This approach reduces or eliminates work-in-process inventory between production steps. The result is a reduction in waiting time and its associated non-value-added cost.

3. *Purchase of materials and manufacture of subassemblies and products in small lot sizes* This is an outgrowth of the pull method of production planning. Materials are purchased and goods are produced only as required, rather than for the sake of building up stocks. The result is a reduction in storage and waiting time, and the related non-value-added costs.

4. *Quick and inexpensive setups of production machinery* In order to produce in small lot sizes, a manufacturer must be able to set up production runs quickly. Advanced manufacturing technology aids in this process, as more and more machines are computer-controlled.

5. *High quality levels for raw material and finished products* If raw materials and parts are to arrive "just in time" for production, they must be "just right" for their intended purpose. Otherwise, the production line will be shut down and significant non-value-added costs of waiting will result. Moreover, if very small stocks of finished goods are to be maintained, then finished products must be of uniform high quality. For this reason, a **total quality control** (or **TQC**) program often accompanies a just-in-time production environment.

6. *Effective preventive maintenance of equipment* If goods are to be manufactured just in time to meet customer orders, a manufacturer cannot afford significant production delays. By strictly adhering to routine maintenance schedules, the firm can avoid costly down time from machine breakdowns.

7. *An atmosphere of teamwork to improve the production system* A company can maintain a competitive edge in today's worldwide market only if it is constantly seeking ways to improve its product or service, achieve more efficient operations, and eliminate non-value-added costs. My favorite football coach often says that a team must improve from one week to the next. Otherwise the team will get worse, because it rarely will stay at the same level. So it goes in business as well. If a company's employees are not constantly seeking ways to improve the firm's performance, before long the company will be bowled over by its competitors. Many organizations

[11] James B. Dilworth, *Production and Operations Management,* 3d ed. (New York: Random House, 1986), pp. 354–361.

encourage employees to make suggestions for improvement. Rewards are given when cost-saving suggestions are implemented.

8. *Multiskilled workers and flexible facilities* To facilitate just-in-time production, manufacturing equipment must be flexible enough to produce a variety of components and products. Otherwise, if a particular production line can produce only one item, bottlenecks may result. A bottleneck can hold up production in subsequent manufacturing stages and result in the non-value-added costs associated with waiting time. As high-tech production equipment becomes more versatile, production employees must be capable of handling a variety of machines and operations. By grouping machines into *cells* that produce a variety of items requiring similar production technology, multiskilled workers are able to operate several machines. This approach is called *group technology.* We will describe this form of organizing operations in the next section.

Flexible Manufacturing System

To achieve the eight objectives of a just-in-time production environment listed in the preceding section, many manufacturers are moving toward more highly automated manufacturing systems. As you may know if you have recently shopped for a VCR, compact disk system, or personal computer, electronic and computer technology is changing at a breathtaking pace. Even as manufacturing facilities are built, engineering breakthroughs make even more efficient operations possible. As a result, a range of automation can be observed even among the most recent production facilities. Before describing Aerotech's Bakersfield plant, let's go over some of the terminology used to describe today's new manufacturing environment.

Computer-Numerically-Controlled (CNC) Machines Stand-alone machines controlled by a computer via a numerical, machine-readable code. Each CNC machine is individually controlled by a single computer dedicated to that machine. An example of a CNC machine is the axial-lead sequencing machine used by Aerotech in its Phoenix plant. CNC machines represent one of the initial steps toward a computer-controlled manufacturing system.

Computer-Aided Manufacturing (CAM) System Any production process in which computers are used to help control production equipment. Aerotech's Phoenix plant has a CAM system, since it utilizes some CNC machines.

Computer-Aided Design (CAD) System Computer software used by engineers in the design of a product. *CAD* enables the engineer to visualize the contemplated design of a product on a video display terminal. Frequently, **CAD/CAM systems** are encountered, which combine the features of both CAD and CAM.

Automated Material-Handling System (AMHS) Computer-controlled equipment that automatically moves materials, parts, and products from one production stage to another.

Flexible Manufacturing System (FMS) An integrated system of computer-controlled machines and automated material-handling equipment, which is capable of producing a variety of technologically similar products.

FMS Cell A particular grouping of machines and personnel within a flexible manufacturing system.

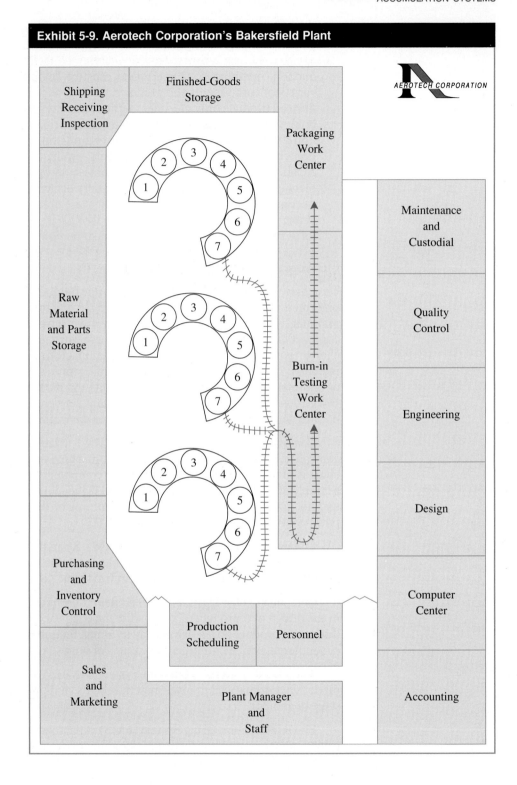

Exhibit 5-9. Aerotech Corporation's Bakersfield Plant

Computer-Integrated-Manufacturing (CIM) System The most advanced level of automated manufacturing. Virtually all parts of the production process are accomplished by computer-controlled machines and automated material-handling equipment. Moreover, the entire production system is an integrated network, centrally controlled via a computer.

Plant Layout at Aerotech's Bakersfield Facility

The layout of Aerotech's Bakersfield plant is shown in Exhibit 5-9. This facility is designed around the following advanced manufacturing features.

1. *Flexible manufacturing system* The Bakersfield plant has three FMS cells. Each cell includes seven computer-controlled machines that are capable

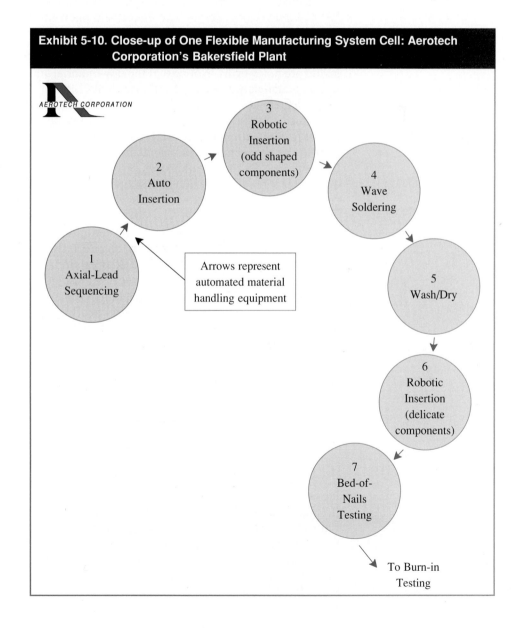

Exhibit 5-10. Close-up of One Flexible Manufacturing System Cell: Aerotech Corporation's Bakersfield Plant

of performing almost all of the manufacturing operations on *any* of Aerotech's three circuit boards. With a minor setup operation, each of these FMS cells can be readied for a new production run. A close-up of one FMS cell is shown in Exhibit 5-10. Notice that the two hand-insertion operations used in the Phoenix plant have been replaced by robots, which are programmed to insert odd-shaped or delicate electrical components.

2. *Automated material-handling system* The Bakersfield plant uses an AMHS for two purposes: to move circuit boards between operations in each FMS cell, and to move completed circuit boards from each cell to the burn-in testing work center. The AMHS includes a conveyor that carries the boards while the burn-in testing procedure is completed on their way to the packaging work center. Bakersfield's AMHS has resulted in substantial reductions in the non-value-added costs of move time.

3. *Computer-aided design* The Bakersfield plant utilizes a CAD system in its design department. Notice its location next to the computer department.

Observations on the Bakersfield Layout Several features of the new plant's layout are noteworthy. Notice that the raw-material and parts storage area is located so that materials are easily accessible to each FMS cell. The space devoted to storage of raw materials and finished goods is much smaller in the Bakersfield plant than in the Phoenix facility. This reflects the JIT philosophy of little or no inventory and results in elimination of non-value-added storage costs. Notice that the holding areas next to the production departments in the Phoenix plant have been eliminated in Bakersfield. Now the circuit boards flow continuously through each FMS cell. This eliminates the non-value-added cost of waiting time. Orders that required days to complete in Phoenix, due to delays between operations, are completed in a few hours in Bakersfield.

The amount of space devoted to the computer department is greater in Bakersfield than in Phoenix. This reflects the significantly greater role of computer aided manufacturing (CAM) in the Bakersfield operation. A large amount of space also is devoted in Bakersfield to design, engineering, and quality control. The JIT philosophy demands strict adherence to high quality standards. These three departments are located near each other to enhance the notion of **off-line quality control.** This refers to activities during the product design and engineering phases which will improve the manufacturability of the product, reduce production costs, and ensure high quality.

Cost Management System in Bakersfield

The cost management system developed for the Bakersfield operation is an integral part of Aerotech's effort to regain a competitive edge in the market for its products. Several features of the CMS are discussed in this section.

Elimination of Non-Value-Added Costs We have discussed the features of the Bakersfield production system that enabled Aerotech to reduce or eliminate non-value-added costs. Chief among these is the elimination of storage and waiting time and the significant reduction in move time. The AMHS has virtually eliminated material-handling costs. Added to these cost reductions is a significant decrease in indirect-labor costs. Many manufacturing support jobs that were considered indirect labor (and thus overhead) in the Phoenix plant are performed by direct-labor personnel in the Bakersfield facility. In the new plant, direct-labor employees now operate each FMS cell. These workers are trained in the setup, operation, and routine maintenance of several machines. When a machine broke down in Phoenix, an entire production department could be shut down while maintenance department personnel were called in to do repairs. In the meantime, the direct-labor personnel in the department were idled. In contrast, the FMS cell operators in Bakersfield are trained to perform routine maintenance and repairs and spot other, more serious machinery problems before they get out of hand. The result of this multiskilled labor force is the reduction of manufacturing support costs in Bakersfield.

A crucial step in bringing about the significant reduction in non-value-added costs in the *Bakersfield plant* was the institution of *activity accounting in the Phoenix plant.* It was this system of identifying costs with the key activities in the production process that first alerted Aerotech's management to the possibilities for cost reduction. Aerotech has continued its activity accounting system in the Bakersfield facility. Management's attitude is one of never being complacent about the existence of non-value-added costs. There is a continuing effort to identify and eliminate these barriers to maintaining the firm's competitive edge.

Cost Drivers and Transaction Costing   The transaction-based costing system developed for the Phoenix operation has been instituted in the Bakersfield plant. Cost drivers have been identified for each significant product cost.

Direct versus Indirect Costs   In the Bakersfield plant almost all production costs are traced directly to an FMS cell. Very few costs are considered to be general factory overhead as in more traditional cost-accounting systems. Direct-material costs are

---

Exhibit 5-11. Basic Production and Cost Data: Aerotech Corporation's Bakersfield Plant

AEROTECH CORPORATION

	Mode I Boards	Mode II Boards	Mode III Boards
Production:			
Units	10,000	20,000	4,000
Runs.	10	20	10
Direct material (raw boards and components)	$50.00	$90.00	$20.00
Machine time per board	1 hour per board	1.25 hours per board	2 hours per board

Conversion cost budget:

Labor	$ 598,400	(including setup time)
Machinery costs	3,397,000	
Engineering	600,000	
Receiving and inspection	50,000	
Material handling	100,000	
Quality assurance	350,000	
Packaging and shipping	250,000	
Total conversion costs	$5,345,400	

traced directly to products. Direct-labor costs have been reduced substantially, due to the advanced level of automation in the Bakersfield plant. In fact, direct labor has been reduced to the point where it is combined with other conversion costs traceable to each FMS cell. Depreciation on the computers and machinery in an FMS cell is traceable directly to the cell. The salaries of computer programmers and maintenance personnel also are traceable to each FMS cell. Conversion costs that have been traced directly to an FMS cell then are assigned to the products that are produced in the cell.

Shift in the Cost Structure Aerotech's Bakersfield plant is **capital-intensive,** which means that the production process is accomplished largely by machinery rather than by manual labor. In contrast, the Phoenix plant is only *semiautomated,*

Exhibit 5-12. Product Costs from Transaction-Based Product-Costing System: Aerotech Corporation's Bakersfield Plant

AEROTECH CORPORATION	Mode I Boards	Mode II Boards	Mode III Boards
Direct material (raw boards and components)	$ 50.00	$ 90.00	$ 20.00
Conversion costs:			
Labor (including setup time)	17.60	17.60	17.60
Engineering[a]	15.00	13.50	45.00
Receiving and inspection[b].	.30	.60	8.75
Material handling[c]	.07	1.50	15.75
Quality assurance[d]	3.50	4.38	56.88
Packaging and shipping[e]	1.00	3.75	41.25
Machine time[f]	79.00	98.75	158.00
Total product cost per unit	$166.47	$230.08	$363.23

with all the material handling and several significant production steps performed manually. Thus, the Phoenix plan is more **labor-intensive** than the Bakersfield facility.

A capital-intensive plant, such as the one in Bakersfield, generally has a *cost structure* with a much larger proportion of fixed costs than would be observed in a labor-intensive plant. Direct-labor costs, often a variable cost, are much lower. Depreciation on plant and equipment generally is much higher.

Reduced Product Costs in Bakersfield   The result of all Aerotech's efforts has been a significant reduction in the cost of producing its three circuit board lines. Exhibit 5-11 displays the budgeted costs for the production of 10,000 Mode I boards, 20,000 Mode II boards, and 4,000 Mode III boards in Bakersfield. Labor is included

---

Exhibit 5-12 (continued). Product Costs from Transaction-Based Product-Costing System: Aerotech Corporation's Bakersfield Plant

The percentages in this column are the same as those used in the Phoenix plant. See Exhibits 5-6 and 5-7.

AEROTECH CORPORATION

[a] **Engineering:**
Mode I:	($600,000 × 25%) ÷ 10,000 units = $15.00
Mode II:	($600,000 × 45%) ÷ 20,000 units = $13.50
Mode III:	($600,000 × 30%) ÷ 4,000 units = $45.00

[b] **Receiving and inspection:**
Mode I:	($50,000 × 6%) ÷ 10,000 units = $ .30
Mode II:	($50,000 × 24%) ÷ 20,000 units = $ .60
Mode III:	($50,000 × 70%) ÷ 4,000 units = $ 8.75

[c] **Material handling:**
Mode I:	($100,000 × 7%) ÷ 10,000 units = $ .07
Mode II:	($100,000 × 30%) ÷ 20,000 units = $ 1.50
Mode III:	($100,000 × 63%) ÷ 4,000 units = $15.75

[d] **Quality assurance:**
Mode I:	($350,000 × 10%) ÷ 10,000 units = $ 3.50
Mode II:	($350,000 × 25%) ÷ 20,000 units = $ 4.38
Mode III:	($350,000 × 65%) ÷ 4,000 units = $56.88

[e] **Packaging and shipping:**
Mode I:	($250,000 × 4%) ÷ 10,000 units = $ 1.00
Mode II:	($250,000 × 30%) ÷ 20,000 units = $ 3.75
Mode III:	($250,000 × 66%) ÷ 4,000 units = $41.25

[f] **Machine time:**

Calculation of machine cost per hour:

From Exhibit 5-11: $\dfrac{\text{Total budgeted machine costs}}{\text{Total budgeted machine hours}} = \dfrac{\$3,397,000}{43,000 \text{ hr.}} = \$79 \text{ per hour}$

Machine costs for each product:
Mode I:	1 machine hr. × $79 =	$79.00 per unit
Mode II:	1.25 machine hr. × $79 =	$98.75 per unit
Mode III:	2 machine hr. × $79 =	$158.00 per unit

along with other conversion costs in the budget. Notice that the costs of labor, receiving and inspection, and material handling are substantially lower in Bakersfield than in Phoenix (see Exhibit 5-3).

Exhibit 5-12 shows the calculation of product costs for the product lines using Bakersfield's transaction-based costing system. Direct-material costs are traced directly to each product line. Labor costs are assigned to products on a unit basis ($17.60 = budgeted labor cost of $598,400 ÷ 34,000 budgeted units of production). The other conversion costs are assigned to products using the transaction-based costing system. Since the Bakersfield plant opened only six months ago, the percentages used in the supporting calculations of Exhibit 5-12 are the same as those derived in the Phoenix plant. Eventually, as Aerotech gains more experience with the Bakersfield operation, these percentages are likely to change.

Exhibit 5-13 compares the product costs achieved in Bakersfield with those incurred in Phoenix. Each circuit board is produced at a significantly lower cost in the new plant.

Aerotech's Strategic Options Examination of Exhibit 5-13 reveals that Mode I and Mode II boards are currently selling at a price well above the target price necessary to achieve a 25 percent markup. Aerotech has two strategic options for these two products. The prices can be kept at their current levels, since they are not out of line with competitors' prices. This strategy would allow Aerotech to earn large profits on these two products. Alternatively, Aerotech could lower the prices on these products

---

Exhibit 5-13. Comparison of Product Costs in Phoenix and Bakersfield Plants

AEROTECH CORPORATION

	Mode I Boards	Mode II Boards	Mode III Boards
Phoenix product costs (transaction-based costing system)	$178.13	$256.20	$432.16
Bakersfield product costs (transaction-based costing system)	$166.47	$230.08	$363.23
Percentage by which Phoenix product costs have been reduced	6.5%	10.2%	16.0%
$\left(\dfrac{\text{Phoenix cost—Bakersfield cost}}{\text{Phoenix cost}}\right)$			
New target price for products manufactured in Bakersfield (125% of full product cost)	$208.09	$287.60	$454.04
Actual current selling price	$261.25	$320.00	$250.00

with the aim of gaining a larger market share. Either way, Aerotech's new manufacturing facility, coupled with a first-rate cost management system, have given the firm a potential advantage over its competitors.

What about the Mode III circuit boards? Even with the lower costs in Bakersfield, an accurate product-costing system shows that these circuit boards cost $363.23 to manufacture. The current actual selling price is only $250. Aerotech could raise the price of these highly complex boards or redesign the boards to reduce their cost. Under a strategy called **target costing,** the market price for a product is taken as a given. Then an attempt is made to design the product so that it can be sold at the market price. We will explore pricing decisions in more depth in Chapter 14. Yet another option may be to discontinue the product line, although this may not be feasible if Aerotech's Mode I and Mode II customers demand a supplier with a full product line. In any case, Aerotech's cost management system has directed management's attention to its strategic options.

Just-in-Time (JIT) Costing

Some firms that have adopted a JIT production system have simplified their system for tracking cost flows through the manufacturing accounting system. The simplified system is a *hybrid costing system,* since it does not match up precisely with the job-order or process-costing systems studied in Chapters 3 and 4.

Under **JIT costing** (sometimes called **backflush costing**), raw-material purchases are recorded directly in an account called **Raw and In-Process Inventory** (the **RIP account**). Thus, there is no distinction between Raw-Material Inventory and Work-in-Process Inventory, as in a more traditional cost-accounting system. When products are finished, the raw-material cost is transferred from Raw and In-process Inventory to Finished-Goods Inventory. When goods are sold, the raw-material costs flow from Finished-Goods Inventory to Cost of Goods Sold.

Conversion costs, including both labor and manufacturing overhead costs, are handled very simply under JIT costing. *Actual* conversion costs are accumulated by debiting a temporary account with a title such as Conversion Costs. Additional details may be recorded by first entering these amounts in various departmental labor and overhead accounts, and then closing these temporary accounts into the Conversion Costs account. When conversion costs are *applied,* the Conversion Costs account is credited, and these costs are added directly to Cost of Goods Sold. Periodically (say, at month's end), an adjustment is made to record the conversion costs that remain in finished goods or partially completed products.

Illustration of JIT Costing   Aerotech adopted a JIT costing system in its Bakersfield plant. During January the following events occurred.

1. Raw materials were purchased on account for $50,000.
2. Circuit boards containing $45,000 in raw materials were finished.
3. Circuit boards containing raw materials of $42,000 were sold.
4. Production employees earned $50,000, and bills for various overhead items totaling $54,000 were paid in cash.
5. Conversion costs totaling $110,000 were applied.
6. A production engineer estimated that the conversion costs represented in the partialy completed products and finished goods on January 31 were as follows:

Partially completed products	$5,000
Finished goods...	7,000

The following journal entries were made to record these events under Aerotech's JIT costing system.

1. Raw and In-process Inventory	50,000	
Accounts Payable		50,000
To record purchase of raw materials.		
2. Finished-Goods Inventory	45,000	
Raw and In-process Inventory		45,000
To record transfer of raw materials to finished goods.		
3. Cost of Goods Sold	42,000	
Finished-Goods Inventory		42,000
To record costs of raw materials in products sold.		
4. Conversion Costs	104,000	
Wages Payable		50,000
Cash		54,000
To record actual conversion costs incurred.		
5. Cost of Goods Sold	110,000	
Conversion Costs		110,000
To record total applied conversion costs for January.		
6. Raw and In-process Inventory	5,000	
Finished-Goods Inventory	7,000	
Cost of Goods Sold		12,000
To record conversion costs applicable to January's ending inventories.		

The main points are that under JIT costing, raw-material purchase costs are added directly to the RIP account instead of first being inventoried in Raw-Material Inventory, and conversion costs (including direct labor and manufacturing overhead) are added to Cost of Goods Sold, instead of first being entered in Work-in-Process Inventory.

Costs and Benefits JIT costing is a simpler and less expensive approach to product costing than the job-order and process-costing systems described in chapters 3 and 4. However, it also provides much less detailed information than a job-order costing system provides. There is a cost-benefit decision to be made as to whether the cost savings justify the loss in detailed information for management's use. Only in a JIT production environment, where all production-related inventories are kept low, is JIT costing likely to be used in product costing. Although the use of JIT costing is becoming more frequent, it is still used by a small minority of manufacturers. Most manufacturing firms use the more elaborate product-costing procedures discussed in earlier chapters.

OTHER COST MANAGEMENT ISSUES IN THE NEW MANUFACTURING ENVIRONMENT

The pressures of international competition, coupled with the advent of advanced manufacturing systems, are causing fundamental changes in the managerial-accounting systems used in manufacturing firms. We will explore several of these changes here and then return to them in subsequent chapters.

Performance Measurement

The appropriateness of using traditional criteria to measure manufacturing performance in the new manufacturing environment has been challenged. As a result, new
performance measures have been suggested and implemented. Moreover, managerial accountants have begun to measure performance in whole new areas of operations previously considered beyond the domain of the accounting system.[12]

Importance of Nonfinancial Measures Managerial accountants traditionally
have focused on financial measures of performance, such as deviations from budgeted costs. Financial measures are still very important, but to an ever-greater extent,
financial performance criteria are being augmented by nonfinancial measures. Physical measures, such as cycle time and defective product rates, are playing a greater role
than ever in helping managers keep their businesses competitive. For example, some
firms compute a measure of **manufacturing cycle efficiency (MCE),** defined as follows:

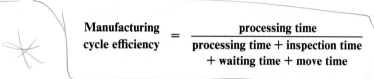

$$\text{Manufacturing cycle efficiency} = \frac{\text{processing time}}{\text{processing time} + \text{inspection time} + \text{waiting time} + \text{move time}}$$

In many manufacturing companies, MCE is less than 10 percent. In contrast, an
optimized production process would exhibit an MCE near 100 percent.[13]

Product Quality A JIT philosophy demands adherence to strict quality standards for raw materials, manufactured components, and finished products. Some
companies routinely prepare a quality-cost report, such as the report shown in Exhibit 5-14.[14]

In addition to quality costs, various nonfinancial data are vital for assessing a
manufacturer's effectiveness in maintaining product quality. **Customer-acceptance
measures** focus on the extent to which a firm's customers perceive its product to be of
high quality. Typical performance measures include the number of customer complaints, the number of warranty claims, the number of products returned, and the
cost of repairing returned products. **In-process quality controls** refer to procedures
designed to assess product quality before production is completed. For example, in a
quality audit program, partially completed products are randomly inspected at
various stages of production. Defect rates are measured, and corrective actions are
suggested. A third area of quality measurement relates to *raw-material quality.* Suppliers are rated on the basis of the quality of their materials as well as customer service.

Productivity Global competitiveness has forced virtually all manufacturers to
strive for greater productivity. One productivity measure is **aggregate** (or **total**)
productivity, defined as total output divided by total input.

A firm's total output is measured as the sum, across all of the goods and services
produced, of those products and services times their sales prices. Total input is the
sum of the direct-material, direct-labor and overhead costs incurred in production.

---

[12] This section draws upon Robert A. Howell and Stephen R. Soucy, loc. cit.

[13] Berliner and Brimson, p. 4.

[14] Harold P. Roth and Wayne J. Morse, "Let's Help Measure and Report Quality Costs," *Management Accounting,* August 1983, p. 50.

Exhibit 5-14. Typical Quality-Cost Report

	Current Month's Cost	Percent of Total
Prevention costs (costs of preventing defects):		
Quality training	$ 2,000	1.3
Reliability engineering	10,000	6.5
Pilot studies	5,000	3.3
Systems development	8,000	5.2
Total prevention costs	$ 25,000	16.3
Appraisal costs (costs of determining whether defects exist):		
Materials inspection	$ 6,000	3.9
Supplies inspection	3,000	2.0
Reliability testing	5,000	3.3
Laboratory	25,000	16.3
Total appraisal costs	39,000	25.5
Internal failure costs (costs of repairing defects found prior to product sale):		
Scrap	$ 15,000	9.8
Repair	18,000	11.8
Rework.	12,000	7.8
Downtime	6,000	3.9
Total internal failure costs	51,000	33.3
External failure costs (costs incurred when defective products have been sold):		
Warranty costs	$ 14,000	9.2
Out-of-warranty repairs and replacement	6,000	3.9
Customer complaints	3,000	2.0
Product liability	10,000	6.5
Transportation losses	5,000	3.3
Total external failure costs	38,000	24.9
Total quality costs	$153,000	100.00

A preferable approach to productivity measurement is to record multiple physical measures that capture the most important determinants of a company's productivity. For example, a large automobile manufacturer routinely records the following data for one of its plants: the number of engines produced per day per employee, and the number of square feet of floor space required per engine produced in a day. A large chemical company keeps track of the amount of energy (in British thermal units, BTUs) required to convert a kilogram of raw chemicals into a kilogram of finished product. Data such as these convey more information to management than a summary financial measure such as aggregate productivity.

Delivery Performance A company will achieve little success if it manufactures a great product but delivers it to the customer a week late. World-class manufacturers are striving toward a goal of filling 100 percent of their orders on time. Common measures of product delivery performance include the percentage of on-time deliveries and the percentage of orders filled. Another measure is the average time between the receipt of a customer order and delivery of the goods.

Raw-Material Cost and Scrap Raw material continues to be a significant cost element in any manufacturing process, whether labor-intensive or highly automated. Worldwide material sourcing and international competition have resulted in the purchasing function's taking on greater importance in many firms. As a result, purchasing performance has become an important area of measurement; criteria include total raw-material cost, deviations between actual and budgeted material prices, the quality of raw materials, and the delivery performance of vendors.

Inventory The essence of the just-in-time production environment is low inventories at every stage of production. Thus, inventory control is of paramount importance in achieving the benefits of the JIT philosophy. Inventory control measures include the average value of inventory, the average amount of time various inventory items are held, and other inventory turnover measures, such as the ratio of inventory value to sales revenue.

Machine Maintenance If inventories are to be kept low, as the JIT philosophy demands, then the production process must be capable of producing goods quickly. This goal requires that production machinery must work when it is needed, which means that routine maintenance schedules must be adhered to scrupulously. Performance controls in this area include measures of machine down time and machine availability, and detailed maintenance records. Some manufacturers make a distinction between *bottleneck machinery* and nonbottleneck machinery. A bottleneck operation is one that limits the production capacity of the entire facility. It is vital that the machinery in bottleneck operations be available 100 percent of the time, excluding time for routine required maintenance. In an advanced manufacturing environment, based on JIT and FMS, the investment in machinery is extremely large. To obtain the anticipated return from this investment, through the benefits of JIT and FMS, the machinery has to be kept running.

ILLUSTRATION FROM MANAGEMENT ACCOUNTING PRACTICE

Harley Davidson

Harley Davidson, the well-known manufacturer of motorcycles, uses the following 10 criteria to measure its manufacturing effectiveness.[15]

1. **Attainment of production schedules**
2. **Personnel requirements**
3. **Conversion costs**
4. **Overtime requirements**
5. **Inventory levels**

[15] McIlhattan, p. 25.

6. Material-cost variance (difference between actual and budgeted cost)
7. Scrap and rework costs
8. Manufacturing cycle time
9. Product quality
10. Productivity improvement.

Product Life-Cycle Costs

A new area of reporting in cost management systems is **product life-cycle costing,** which is the accumulation of costs for activities that occur over the entire life cycle of a product.[16] A product's life cycle begins with its inception, and continues through the following five stages: (1) product planning, (2) preliminary design, (3) detailed design, (4) production, and (5) product logistics support. Traditional cost-accounting systems tend to focus almost exclusively on accumulating production costs. However, as product life cycles become shorter, due to rapid technological change, the other costs in a product's life cycle are taking on greater significance. The decision to launch a product involves many costs besides production costs. Moreover, a company makes a commitment to the lion's share of these costs early in the product's life cycle. If the managerial-accounting system ignores these other costs, management is not in a position to make an informed decision about launching a new product, discontinuing a mature product, or changing a product's design. A cost management system should accumulate the costs in each phase of a product's life and associate them with the product via special cost analyses and reports.

Justifying Capital Expenditures for Advanced Manufacturing Systems

How do the managers of a company like Aerotech make a decision to invest in a new manufacturing system? Flexible manufacturing systems can cost $50 million or more. Such a huge investment must be given very special analysis and thought. In Chapters 15 and 16 we will explore techniques used by managers to make decisions involving large outlays of money and cash flows that occur over many years. We will leave the details of these techniques until them. It should be noted, however, that any analysis of investment in advanced manufacturing systems must consider the costs and benefits of the equipment over its entire life. This is a tall order, since the complexity of the equipment coupled with the rapid pace of technological change make the costs and benefits difficult to predict. Some costs and benefits may be rather obvious, but others may be overlooked. Some examples of costs and benefits that should be considered when evaluating a JIT production system, an FMS, or a CIM system are listed in Exhibit 5-15.

CHAPTER SUMMARY

Sweeping changes are revolutionizing the manufacturing industry. Global competition coupled with rapid technological innovation are changing manufacturing in a dramatic way. To reduce non-value-added costs and gain a competitive edge, companies are moving toward a just-in-time inventory and production management philosophy. Under this production system no raw materials are purchased and no products

---

[16] This section draws upon Berliner and Brimson, pp. 22, 32–33, 88, and 140–141.

Exhibit 5-15. Justifying Capital Expenditures for Advanced Manufacturing Systems

Initial Costs to Be Capitalized	Benefits[17]
Acquisition cost of the advanced equipment (FS, CIM, AMHS, etc.)	Reduced inventory levels (including savings on working capital investment, storage space, and reduced obsolescence)
Installation costs	
Plant redesign or construction	
Personnel training	Lower floor-space requirements (less space required by a FMS that can do the same job as many stand-alone machines)
Engineering systems design	
Software development	
Hardware and software upgrades	
	Higher and more constant product quality
Recurring Operating Costs	Greater flexibility in production
	Shorter cycle times and greater throughput
Equipment maintenance	
Electricity	
Security	
Compensation of equipment operators, computer maintenance personnel, and software specialists	

are manufactured until they are needed. Along with JIT production systems, many companies are modernizing their production processes with computer-assisted manufacturing systems. Although these systems are extremely expensive, the cost savings and strategic benefits they facilitate often justify their acquisition.

Along with manufacturing systems, the role of managerial accounting is changing also. Many firms are moving from a traditional cost-accounting approach toward a more proactive cost-management-system perspective. A cost management system (CMS) measures the cost of significant activities, identifies non-value-added costs, and identifies activities that will improve organizational performance. The CMS emphasis on activities helps a company gain a competitive edge by facilitating production of a high-quality product at the lowest cost possible.

As the manufacturing environment has changed, many managers have come to believe that traditional, volume-based product-costing systems do not accurately reflect product costs. Product-costing systems structured on single, volume-based cost drivers, such as direct labor or machine hours, often tend to overcost high-volume products and undercost low-volume or complex products. These cost distortions can have serious effects on pricing and other decisions. To alleviate these problems, more and more firms are adopting a transaction-based costing system, based on multiple cost drivers. Such costing systems provide better information for strategic management decisions, and help in the identification of non-value-added costs.

Other important areas in which managerial accounting systems are changing

---

[17] Robert S. Kaplan, "Must CIM Be Justified by Faith Alone?" *Harvard Business Review,* March–April 1986, pp. 87–95.

involve manufacturing performance measurement, reporting product life-cycle
costs, and the justification of capital expenditures on advanced manufacturing systems.

REVIEW PROBLEM ON COST DRIVERS AND PRODUCT-COST DISTORTION

Edgeworth Box Corporation manufactures a variety of special packaging boxes used
in the pharmaceutical industry. The company's Dallas plant is semiautomated, but
the special nature of the boxes requires some manual labor. The controller has chosen
the following cost drivers and overhead rates for the Dallas plant's product-costing
system.

Overhead Cost Pool	Overhead Cost	Cost Driver	Budgeted Level for Cost Driver	Predetermined Overhead Rate
Purchasing, stor-age, and mate-rial handling	$200,000	Raw-material costs	$1,000,000	20% of mate-rial cost
Engineering and product design	100,000	Hours in design department	5,000 hours	$20 per hour
Machine setup costs	70,000	Production runs	1,000 runs	$70 per run
Machine depre-ciation and maintenance	300,000	Machine hours	100,000 hours	$3 per hour
Factory depre-ciation, taxes, insurance, and utilities	200,000	Machine hours	100,000 hours	$2 per hour
Other manufac-turing overhead costs	150,000	Machine hours	100,000 hours	$1.50 per hour
Total	$1,020,000			

Two recent production orders had the following requirements.

	20,000 Units of Box C52	10,000 Units of Box W29
Direct-labor hours	42 hours	21 hours
Raw-material cost	$40,000	$35,000
Hours in design department	10	25
Production runs	2	4
Machine hours	24	20

REQUIRED:

1. Compute the total overhead that should be assigned to each of the two
   production orders, C52 and W29.

2. Compute the overhead cost per box in each order.
3. Suppose the Dallas plant were to use a single predetermined overhead rate based on direct-labor hours. The direct-labor budget calls for 4,000 hours.
   a. Compute the predetermined overhead rate per direct-labor hour.
   b. Compute the total overhead cost that would be assigned to the order for box C52 and the order for box W29.
   c. Compute the overhead cost per box in each order.
4. Why do the two product-costing systems yield such widely differing overhead costs per box?

Solution to Review Problem

1.

	Box C52	Box W29
Purchasing, storage, and material handling.......	$8,000 (20% $\times$ $40,000)	$7,000 (20% $\times$ $35,000)
Engineering and product design	200 (10 $\times$ $20/hr.)	500 (25 $\times$ $20/hr.)
Machine setup costs......	140 (2 $\times$ $70/run)	280 (4 $\times$ $70/run)
Machine depreciation and maintenance...........	72 (24 $\times$ $3/hr.)	60 (20 $\times$ $3/hr.)
Factory depreciation, taxes, insurance, and utilities	48 (24 $\times$ $2/hr.)	40 (20 $\times$ $2/hr.)
Other manufacturing costs	36 (24 $\times$ $1.50/hr.)	30 (20 $\times$ $1.50/hr.)
Total overhead assigned to production order	$8,496	$7,910

2. Overhead cost per box $.4248 per box $\left(\dfrac{\$8,496}{20,000}\right)$ $.791 per box $\left(\dfrac{\$7,910}{10,000}\right)$

3. Computations based on single predetermined overhead rate based on direct-labor hours:

   a. $\dfrac{\text{Total budgeted overhead}}{\text{Total budgeted direct-labor hours}} = \dfrac{\$1,020,000}{4,000} = \$255/\text{hr.}$

   b. Total overhead assigned to each order:

   Box C52 order: 42 direct-labor hours $\times$ $255/hr. = $10,710
   Box W29 order: 21 direct-labor hours $\times$ $255/hr. = $ 5,355

   c. Overhead cost per box:

   Box C52: $10,710 $\div$ 20,000 = $.5355 per box
   Box W29: $ 5,355 $\div$ 10,000 = $.5355 per box

4. The widely differing overhead costs are assigned as a result of the inherent inaccuracy of the single volume-based overhead rate. The relative usage of direct labor by the two production orders does not reflect their relative usage of other manufacturing support services.

KEY TERMS   Activity accounting, p. 177; **Aggregate (or total) productivity**, p. 193; **Appraisal costs**, p. 194; **Automated material-handling system (AMHS)**, p. 183; **CAD/CAM system**, p. 183; **Capital-intensive**, p. 188; **Computer-aided design (CAD) system**, p. 183; **Computer-aided manufacturing (CAM) system**, p. 183; **Computer-integrated manufacturing (CIM) system**, p. 185; **Computer-numerically-controlled (CNC) machines**, p. 183; **Cost driver**, p. 176; **Cost management**

system (CMS), p. 178; **Customer-acceptance measures,** p. 193; **External failure costs,** p. 194; **Flexible manufacturing systems (FMS),** p. 183; **FMS cell,** p. 183; **In-process quality controls,** p. 193; **Inspection time,** p. 179; **Internal failure costs,** p. 194; **Just-in-time (JIT) inventory and production-management system,** p. 181; **Just-in-time (JIT) costing (or backflush costing),** p. 191; **Labor-intensive,** p. 189; **Manufacturing cycle efficiency (MCE),** p. 193; **Move time,** p. 179; **Non-value-added costs,** p. 178; **Off-line quality control,** p. 186; **Prevention costs,** p. 194; **Process time,** p. 179; **Product life-cycle costing,** p. 196; **Pull method,** p. 182; **Raw and in-process inventory (RIP account),** p. 191; **Storage time,** p. 179; **Strategic cost analysis,** p. 178; **Target costing,** p. 191; **Total quality control (TQC),** p. 182; **Transaction-based product-costing system,** p. 172; **Volume-based (or throughput-based) costing system,** p. 167; **Waiting time,** p. 179.

REVIEW QUESTIONS

5-1. Briefly explain how a traditional, volume-based product-costing system operates.

5-2. What improvements over the traditional product-costing system did Aerotech's controller make in the refined system?

5-3. Why was Aerotech Corporation's management being misled by the traditional product-costing system? What mistakes were being made?

5-4. Explain how a transaction-based product-costing system operates?

5-5. What are cost drivers? What is their role in a transaction-based product-costing system?

5-6. How can a transaction-based costing system alleviate the problems Aerotech was having under its traditional, volume-based product-costing system?

5-7. Why do product-costing systems based on a single, volume-based cost driver tend to overcost high-volume products? What undesirable strategic effects can such distortion of product costs have?

5-8. How is the distinction between direct and indirect costs handled differently under volume-based versus transaction-based product-costing systems?

5-9. List four objectives of a cost management system.

5-10. What is meant by the term *non-value-added costs?* Give four examples.

5-11. What is meant by the term *activity accounting?*

5-12. List and define the five ways that time is spent in a manufacturing process. Which of these types of activities are likely candidates for non-value-added activities? Why?

5-13. Briefly describe the JIT philosophy.

5-14. List eight key features of a just-in-time inventory and production management system.

5-15. Define the following acronyms: CMS, JIT, CNC, CAM, CAD, AMHS, FMS, CIM, RIP, and MCE.

5-16. Briefly describe the key differences in plant layout between Aerotech's Phoenix and Bakersfield facilities.

5-17. How is a firm's cost structure likely to change if an FMS is installed?

5-18. Briefly explain how JIT costing operates. What is the role of the RIP account?

5-19. Define the term *manufacturing cycle efficiency.*

5-20. List and define four types of product quality costs.

5-21. List four examples of customer-acceptance measures.

5-22. What is meant by an aggregate productivity measure, and what are its limitations?

5-23. What are product life-cycle costs? List the five stages in a product's life cycle.

5-24. List several costs and benefits that should be considered in justifying a capital investment in a CIM system.

5-25. What behavioral problems can you think of that a company such as Aerotech might encounter in modifying its managerial-accounting system to fit the new manufacturing environment?

EXERCISES   *Exercise 5-26   Non-Value-Added Costs.* These costs occur in nonmanufacturing firms also.

REQUIRED: Identify four potential non-value-added costs in (1) an airline, (2) a bank, and (3) a hotel.

Exercise 5-27   Cost Drivers. Cosmic Systems Corporation manufactures VCRs in its Memphis plant. The factory utilizes a JIT production philosophy. The production process takes place in three FMS cells. The following costs are budgeted for January.

Raw materials and components	$320,000
Engineering design.	45,000
Depreciation, plant	70,000
Depreciation, machinery.	140,000
Insurance, plant.	60,000
Electricity, machinery	12,000
Electricity, light	6,000
Custodial wages, plant.	4,000
Equipment maintenance, wages	15,000
Equipment maintenance, parts.	3,000
Computer programming, FMS.	16,000
Setup wages	4,000
Inspection	3,000
Property taxes	12,000
Natural gas, heating.	3,000

REQUIRED: Divide these costs into cost pools, and identify a cost driver for assigning each pool of costs to products.

Exercise 5-28   Distortion of Product Costs. Wheelco, Inc. manufactures automobile and truck wheels. The company produces four basic, high-volume wheels used by each of the large automobile and pickup truck manufacturers. Wheelco also has two specialty wheel lines. These are fancy, complicated wheels used in expensive sports cars.

Lately, Wheelco's profits have been declining. Foreign competitors have been undercutting Wheelco's prices in three of its bread-and-butter product lines, and Wheelco's sales volume and market share have declined. In contrast, Wheelco's specialty wheels have been selling steadily, although in relatively small numbers, in spite of three recent price increases. At a recent staff meeting, Wheelco's president made the following remarks: "Our profits are going down the tubes, folks. It costs us 29 dollars to manufacture our A22 wheel. That's our best seller, with a volume last year of 17,000 units. But our chief competitor is selling basically the same wheel for 27 bucks. I don't see how they can do it. I think it's just one more example of foreign dumping. I'm going to write my senator about it! Thank goodness for our specialty wheels. I think we've got to get our sales people to push those wheels more and more. Take the D52 model, for example. It's a complicated thing to make and we don't sell many. But look at the profit margin. Those wheels cost us 49 dollars to make, and we're selling them for 105 bucks each."

REQUIRED: What do you think is behind the problems faced by Wheelco? Comment on the president's remarks. Do you think his strategy is a good one? What do you recommend, and why?

Exercise 5-29   Key Features of Transaction Costing. Refer to the description given for Wheelco, Inc. in the preceding exercise. Suppose the firm's president has decided to implement a transaction-based product-costing system.

REQUIRED:

1. List and describe five key features that Wheelco's new accounting system should have.
2. What impact will the new system be likely to have on the company's situation?
3. What strategic options would you expect to be suggested by the product-costing results from the new system?

Exercise 5-30   Basic Elements of a Production Process; Non-Value-Added Costs. Better Bagels, Inc. manufactures a variety of bagels, which are frozen and sold in grocery stores. The production process consists of the following steps.

1. Ingredients, such as flour and raisins, are received and inspected. Then they are stored until needed.
2. Ingredients are carried on hand carts to the mixing room.
3. Dough is mixed in 40-pound batches in four heavy-duty mixers.
4. Dough is stored on large boards in the mixing room, until a bagel machine is free.
5. A board of dough is carried into the bagel room. The board is tipped and the dough slides into the hopper of a bagel machine. This machine pulls off a small piece of dough, rolls it into a cylindrical shape, and then squeezes it into a doughnut shape. The bagel machines can be adjusted in a setup procedure to accommodate different sizes and styles of bagels. Workers remove the uncooked bagels and place them on a tray, where they are kept until a boiling vat is free.
6. Next the trays of uncooked bagels are carried into an adjoining room, which houses three 50-gallon vats of boiling water. The bagels are boiled for approximately one minute.
7. Bagels are removed from the vats with a long-handled strainer and placed on a wooden board. The boards full of bagels are carried to the oven room, where they are kept until an oven rack is free. The two ovens contain eight racks which rotate but remain upright, much like the seats on a Ferris wheel. A rack full of bagels is finished baking after one complete revolution in the oven. When a rack full of bagels is removed from the oven, a fresh rack replaces it. The oven door is opened and closed as each rack completes a revolution in the oven.
8. After the bagels are removed from the oven, they are placed in baskets for cooling.
9. While the bagels are cooling, they are inspected. Misshapen bagels are removed and set aside. (Most are eaten by the staff.)
10. After the bagels are cool, the wire baskets are carried to the packaging department. Here the bagels are dumped into the hopper on a bagging machine. This machine packages a half dozen bagels in each bag and seals the bag with a twist tie.
11. Then the packaged bagels are placed in cardboard boxes, each holding 24 bags. The boxes are placed on a forklift and are driven to the freezer, where the bagels are frozen and stored for shipment.

REQUIRED:

1. Identify the steps in the bagel-production process that fall into each of the following categories: process time, inspection time, move time, waiting time, storage time.
2. List the steps in the production process that could be candidates for non-value-added activities.

Exercise 5-31   Key Features of JIT Production Systems. Refer to the information given in the preceding exercise for Better Bagels, Inc.

REQUIRED: Redesign the bagel production process so that it adheres to the JIT philosophy. Explain how the eight key features of JIT systems would be present in the new production process. What new equipment would the company need to purchase in order to implement the JIT approach fully?

Exercise 5-32   Direct and Indirect Costs; Traditional versus JIT Manufacturing Environment. The following costs were incurred in each of two automobile-parts factories in June.

Raw materials	Supervisory salaries
Electricity, machines	Property taxes
Electricity, lighting and air-conditioning	Depreciation, plant
Engineering salaries	Depreciation, equipment
Custodial wages	Insurance
Machine repair, wages	Factory supplies
Machine repair, parts	Inspection
Direct labor	

REQUIRED: For every cost listed above, indicate whether it is more likely to be treated as a direct cost or an indirect cost in each of the following.

1. A traditional factory, with a traditional cost-accounting system.
2. A JIT/FMS factory, with a transaction-based product-costing system.

Explain your choices for each cost item in each manufacturing environment.

Exercise 5-33   Just-in-Time (JIT) Costing. The following events pertain to Detroit Pipe and Fitting, Inc. during February 19x4.

1. Raw material costing $190,000 is purchased on account.
2. Finished goods with raw-material costs of $68,000 are completed.
3. Goods with raw-material costs of $32,000 are sold for $75,000 on account.
4. Conversion costs of $120,000 are applied.
5. On February 28, an engineer estimates that the conversion costs remaining in inventory are as follows: $80,000 in work in process, $22,000 in finished goods.

REQUIRED: Prepare journal entries to record the events listed above. The company uses just-in-time costing.

Exercise 5-34   Just-in-Time (JIT) Costing. Albany Lighting Corporation manufactures a wide range of lighting fixtures for the housing industry. The company recently adopted a JIT costing system. The following events occurred in August.

1. Purchased $275,000 of raw materials on account.
2. Applied conversion costs of $150,000.
3. Finished products with raw material costs of $200,000.
4. Sold products with raw material costs of $190,000 for $450,000 on account.
5. The production manager made the following estimates on August 31.
   a. Conversion costs that pertain to August 31 work in process, $30,000.
   b. Conversion costs that pertain to August 31 finished goods, $15,000.

REQUIRED: Prepare journal entries to record these events under the firm's new JIT costing system.

Exercise 5-35   Quality Costs. The following costs were incurred by Geneva Metals Company to maintain the quality of its products.

1. Operating an X-ray machine to detect faulty welds
2. Repairs of products sold last year
3. Cost of rewelding faulty joints
4. Cost of sending machine operators to a three-week training program so they could learn to use new production equipment with a lower defect rate.

REQUIRED: Classify each of these costs as a prevention, appraisal, internal failure, or external failure cost.

Exercise 5-36   Productivity Measurement. Managerial-accounting procedures developed for the manufacturing industry often are applied in nonmanufacturing settings also. Ontario Bank and Trust Company's total output of financial services in 19x3 was valued at $10 million. The total cost of the firm's inputs, primarily direct labor and overhead, was $8 million.

REQUIRED:

1. Compute Ontario's aggregate (or total) productivity for 19x3.
2. Do you believe this is a useful measure? Why? Suggest an alternative approach that Ontario Bank and Trust might use to measure productivity.

Exercise 5-37   Cost Drivers and Departmental Overhead Rates. Zodiac Metals Company has two production departments with the following characteristics.

	Production Department A	Production Department B
Direct-labor hours per month............	10,000	10,000
Machine hours......................	—	10,000
Machinery and equipment, monthly depreciation	None	$50,000
Floor space........................	1,000 sq. ft.	29,000 sq. ft.
Power cost per month.................	$100 (lighting only)	$5,000

Some of Zodiac's products are produced exclusively in department A; others require activity only in department B.

The following costs are budgeted for the month and are the basis for computing the predetermined overhead rate.

Depreciation of machinery and equipment.......................	$50,000
Building costs...	30,000
Power costs	5,100
Total..	$85,100

REQUIRED:

1. Compute a single predetermined overhead rate for Zodiac Metals based on direct-labor hours.

2. Suppose product I requires one direct-labor hour in department A and product II requires one direct-labor hour in department B. How much overhead will each product be assigned, assuming Zodiac uses a single predetermined overhead rate?

3. Compute an overhead rate for each production department, based on two different cost drivers: direct-labor hours in department A and machine hours in department B.

4. Based on the rates computed in requirement (3), how much overhead will be assigned to product I and product II? Each unit of Product II requires one machine hour in department B.

5. Suppose Zodiac implements the departmental overhead rates computed in requirement (3). Has the company gone as far as it can go in terms of improving its product-costing system? If not, what do you recommend? Why?

PROBLEMS　　*Problem 5-38　Design Your Own Production Process Using Advanced Manufacturing Systems; Non-Value-Added Costs.* Since you always wanted to be an industrial baron, invent your own product and describe at least five steps used in its production.

REQUIRED: Design a plant layout using the latest in advanced manufacturing technology to manufacture your product. Explain how your plant will eliminate non-value-added costs.

Problem 5-39　Plant Layouts; Traditional and Flexible Manufacturing System. Skybolt Corporation manufactures special heavy bolts used in spacecraft. The production process consists of the following operations: (1) metal rods are cut to the proper length in a cutting machine; (2) a heading machine flattens the end of the cut rod to form a head; (3) a slotting machine cuts a slot in the bolt's head; (4) the bolt is run through a threading machine, which cuts the bolt's threads; (5) the bolt is washed to remove metal shavings and other foreign particles; (6) the bolt is heat-treated for hardness in a salt-bath; (7) the bolt is inspected; (8) the bolt is wrapped and packaged.

The salt bath is a very expensive operation because of the electricity requirements. Another expensive operation is the central oil-filtration system, which is used to provide oil to all of the cutting and threading machines. The oil acts as a lubricant and coolant. After passing through a cutting machine, the oil is pumped back to a central oil filtration station, which filters foreign particles from the oil.

REQUIRED:

1. Draw a factory-layout diagram showing how a traditional layout of Skybolt's production process might appear. (Refer to Exhibit 5-1 for guidance.)

2. Repeat requirement (1), assuming that Skybolt has adopted a JIT production system and purchased an FMS and an AMHS. Assume that only one central salt bath will be used, and that the company will keep its centralized oil-filtration system.

Problem 5-40　Non-Value-Added Costs. Refer to the information given in the preceding problem for Skybolt Corporation.

REQUIRED: Identify the non-value-added costs that might be present in Skybolt's traditional plant layout and production process. Write a memo to the company president pointing these costs out and advocating an FMS.

Problem 5-41　Overhead Cost Drivers. The controller for Liverpool Photographic Supply Company has established the following overhead cost pools and cost drivers.

Overhead Cost Pool	Budgeted Overhead Cost	Cost Driver	Budgeted Level for Cost Driver	Overhead Rate
Machine setups	$200,000	Number of setups	100	$2,000 per setup
Material handling	100,000	Weight of raw material	50,000 pounds	$2 per pound
Hazardous waste control	50,000	Weight of hazardous chemicals used	10,000 pounds	$5 per pound
Quality control	75,000	Number of inspections	1,000	$75 per inspection
Other overhead costs	200,000	Machine hours	20,000	$10 per machine hour
Total	$625,000			

An order for 1,000 boxes of film development chemicals has the following production requirements.

Machine setups	4 setups
Raw material	10,000 pounds
Hazardous materials	2,000 pounds
Inspections	10 inspections
Machine hours	500 machine hours

REQUIRED:

1. Compute the total overhead that should be assigned to the development-chemical order.
2. What is the overhead cost per box of chemicals?
3. Suppose Liverpool Photographic Supply Company were to use a single predetermined overhead rate based on machine hours. Compute the rate per hour.
4. Under the approach in requirement (3), how much overhead would be assigned to the development-chemical order?
   a. In total.
   b. Per box of chemicals.
5. Explain why these two product-costing systems result in such widely differing costs. Which system do you recommend? Why?

Problem 5-42   Overhead Cost Drivers. Refer to the original data given in the preceding problem for Liverpool Photographic Supply Company.

REQUIRED: Calculate the unit cost of a production order for 100 specially coated plates used in film development. In addition to direct material costing $120 per plate and direct labor costing $40 per plate, the order requires:

Machine setups	2
Raw materials	800 pounds
Hazardous materials	300 pounds
Inspections	3
Machine hours	50

Problem 5-43   Use of Multiple Cost Drivers by Hewlett-Packard Company. Hewlett-Packard Company's Personal Office Computer Division uses two overhead application rates based on two different cost drivers. One rate is based on direct labor and assigns overhead costs associated with production. The second rate is based on material cost and assigns overhead costs associated with procurement. Overhead costs are initially categorized into three cost categories, called "buckets" in the company's terminology. Then the overhead costs associated with overall manufacturing support functions are allocated between the production cost bucket and the procurement cost bucket. This allocation is based on the number of employees and the estimated percentage of time spent on these two types of activities. The following diagram illustrates the system.[18]

SUPPORT MANUFACTURING OVERHEAD:

Includes costs that support the entire manufacturing process but cannot be associated directly with either production or procurement (e.g., production engineering, quality assurance, and central electronic data processing.

PRODUCTION MANUFACTURING OVERHEAD

Includes such costs as production supervision, indirect labor, depreciation, and operating costs associated with production, assembly, testing and shipping.

PROCUREMENT MANUFACTURING OVERHEAD

Includes such costs as purchasing, receiving, inspection of raw materials, material handling, production planning and control and subcontracting.

Applied on the basis of DIRECT LABOR

Applied on the basis of DIRECT MATERIAL

REQUIRED:

1. Explain why Hewlett-Packard Company uses two cost drivers to assign overhead costs instead of a single predetermined overhead rate.
2. What benefits does such an approach provide to management?
3. What costs would such a system entail?

Problem 5-44   Traditional versus Transaction-Based Product-Costing System. Gigobyte, Inc. manufactures three products for the computer industry:

Gismos (product G): annual sales, 8,000 units
Thingamajigs (product T): annual sales, 15,000 units
Whatchamacallits (product W): annual sales, 4,000 units

---

[18] This description was provided by James M. Patell, "Cost Accounting, Process Control, and Product Design: A Case Study of the Hewlett-Packard Personal Office Computer Division," *The Accounting Review, 62,* no. 4 (October 1987), pp. 808–839.

The company uses a traditional, volume-based product-costing system with manufacturing overhead applied on the basis of direct-labor dollars. The product costs have been computed as follows:

	Product G	Product T	Product W
Raw material..............	$ 35.00	$ 52.50	$17.50
Direct labor..............	16.00 (.8 hr. at $20)	12.00 (.6 hr. at $20)	8.00 (.4 hr. at $20)
Manufacturing overhead* ...	140.00	105.00	70.00
Total product cost	$191.00	$169.50	$95.50

* Calculation of predetermined overhead rate:
  Manufacturing overhead budget:

Machine setup	$5,250
Machinery	1,225,000
Inspection	525,000
Material handling	875,000
Engineering	344,750
Total	$2,975,000

  Direct-labor budget (based on budgeted annual sales):

Product G:	8,000 × $16.00 =	$128,000
Product T:	15,000 × $12.00 =	180,000
Product W:	4,000 × $8.00 =	32,000
Total		$340,000

$$\text{Predetermined overhead rate} = \frac{\text{budgeted overhead}}{\text{budget direct labor}} = 875\%$$

Gigobyte's pricing method has been to set a target price equal to 150 percent of full product cost. However, only the thingamajigs have been selling at their target price. The target and actual current prices for all three products are the following:

	Product G ↓	Product T	Product W ↑
Product cost......................	$191.00	$169.50	$ 95.50
Target price	286.50	254.25	143.25
Actual current selling price.......	213.00	254.25	200.00

Gigobyte has been forced to lower the price of gismos in order to get orders. In contrast, Gigobyte has raised the price of whatchamacallits several times, but there has been no apparent loss of sales. Gigobyte, Inc. has been under increasing pressure to reduce the price even further on gismos. In contrast, Gigobyte's competitors do not seem to be interested in the market for whatchamacallits. Gigobyte apparently has this market to itself.

REQUIRED:

1. Is product G the company's least profitable product?
2. Is product W a profitable product for Gigobyte, Inc.?
3. Comment on the reactions of Gigobyte's competitors to the firm's pricing strategy. What dangers does Gigobyte, Inc. face?
4. Gigobyte's controller, Nan O'Second, recently attended a conference at which transaction-based costing systems were discussed. She is convinced that such a

system would help Gigobyte's management to understand its product costs better. As a first step, she identified cost drivers for Gigobyte's overhead costs. Then she launched a special study, which determined that Gigobyte's three products are responsible for the following proportions of each cost driver.

Overhead Item	Cost Driver	Product G	Product T	Product W
Machine setup	Number of setups	20%	30%	50%
Machinery	Machine hours	25%	50%	25%
Inspection	Number of inspections	15%	45%	40%
Material handling	Raw-material costs	25%	69%	6%
Engineering	Number of change orders	35%	10%	55%

Show how the controller determined the percentages given above for raw-material costs. (Round to the nearest whole percent.)

5. Develop product costs for the three products on the basis of a transaction-based costing system. (Round to the nearest cent.)

6. Calculate a target price for each product, using Gigobyte's pricing formula. Compare the new target prices with the current actual selling prices and previously reported product costs.

Problem 5-45 *Strategic Cost Analysis: Continuation of Preceding Problem.* Refer to the new target prices for Gigobyte's three products, based on the new transaction-based costing system.

REQUIRED: Write a memo to the company president commenting on the situation Gigobyte, Inc. has been facing regarding the market for its products and the actions of its competitors. Discuss the strategic options available to management. What do you recommend, and why?

Problem 5-46 *Traditional versus Transaction-Based Costing Systems.* Minneapolis Industries, Inc. manufactures electric fans for household and commercial use. The company produces three models, designated as standard, deluxe, and heavy-duty. The company uses a job-order cost-accounting system with manufacturing overhead applied on the basis of direct-labor hours. The system has been in place with little change for 25 years. Product costs and annual sales data are given in Table I on the next page.

For the past 10 years Minneapolis Industries' pricing formula has been to set each product's target price at 110 percent of its full product cost. Recently, however, the standard-model fan has come under increasing price pressure from offshore competitors. The result was that the price on the standard model has been lowered to $110.

The company president recently asked the controller, "Erin, why can't we compete with these other companies? They're selling fans just like our standard model for 106 dollars. That's only a buck more than our production cost. Are we really that inefficient? What gives?"

The controller responded by saying, "I think this is due to an outmoded product-costing system. As you may remember, I raised a red flag about our system when I came on board last year. But the decision was to keep our current system in place. In my judgment, our product-costing system is distorting our product costs. Let me run a few numbers to demonstrate what I mean."

Getting the president's go-ahead, the controller determined that factory space and manufacturing-support activities were used by the firm's three product lines in the proportions shown in Table II on the next page.

Table I	Standard Model	Deluxe Model	Heavy-Duty Model
Annual sales (units) ..	20,000	1,000	10,000
Product costs:			
Raw material	$10	$25	$42
Direct labor.......	10 (.5 hr. at $20)	20 (1 hr. at $20)	20 (1 hr. at $20)
Manufacturing overhead*	85	170	170
Total product cost ...	$105	$215	$232

* Calculation of predetermined overhead rate:

Manufacturing-overhead budget:

Depreciation, machinery	$1,480,000
Maintenance, machinery	120,000
Depreciation, taxes and insurance for factory............................	300,000
Engineering	350,000
Purchasing, receiving and shipping	250,000
Inspection and repair of defects	375,000
Material handling	400,000
Miscellaneous manufacturing overhead costs.............................	295,000
Total..	$3,570,000

Direct-labor budget:

Standard model:	10,000 hours
Deluxe model:	1,000
Heavy-duty model:	10,000
Total	21,000 hours

Predetermined overhead rate:

$$\frac{\text{Budgeted overhead}}{\text{Budgeted direct-labor hours}} = \frac{\$3,570,000}{21,000 \text{ hours}} = \$170 \text{ per hour}$$

Table II	Standard Model	Deluxe Model	Heavy-Duty Model
Machine time	40%	13%	47%
Engineering, inspection, and repair of defects. . .	47%	6%	47%
Purchasing, receiving, shipping, and material handling.....................................	47%	8%	45%
Factory space	42%	15%	43%

Based on these percentages, the controller developed new product costs with overhead costs assigned on the basis of the relevant cost drivers. Factory depreciation, taxes, insurance, and miscellaneous overhead costs were assigned to products on the basis of factory space usage.

REQUIRED:

1. Compute the target prices for the three fan models, based on the traditional, volume-based product-costing system.
2. Compute new product costs for the three products, based on the new data collected by the controller.
3. Calculate a new target price for the three fans, based on a transaction-based product-costing system. Compare the new target price with the current actual selling price for the standard-model fan.

4. Write a memo to the company president explaining what has been happening as a result of the firm's traditional, volume-based product-costing system.
5. What strategic options does Minneapolis Industries have? What do you recommend, and why?

Problem 5-47   Non-Value-Added Costs; Changeover to a JIT Production System. Pickwick Paper Company's Charlotte plant manufactures paperboard. Its production process involves the following operations.

1. Harvested trees arrive by rail in the wood yard and are stored outside.
2. Logs are moved by a flume into the plant where they pass through a debarker and are cut up into chips.
3. The chips are stored in large bins near the chipping machines.
4. The chips then are transported by small trucks to another building and are placed in a digester, a large pressure cooker where heat, steam, and chemicals convert the chips into moist fibers.
5. The fibers are stored near the digester.
6. In the next step, the fibers are loaded by workers onto a conveyor belt, which carries the fibers to a lepressurized blow tank. This operation separates the fibers.
7. The separated fibers are placed on wooden pallets and stored next to the blow tank.
8. Forklifts are used to carry the separated fibers to the refining area, where the fibers are washed, refined, and treated with chemicals and caustic substances until they become pulp.
9. The wood pulp then enters the paper machines through a headbox, which distributes pulp evenly across a porous belt of forming fabric.
10. Water is removed from the pulp by passing it over a wire screen.
11. Additional water is removed from the pulp in a series of presses.
12. Dryers then remove any remaining water from the pulp.
13. The thin, dry sheets of pulp are then smoothed and polished by large rollers called calenders.
14. Then the paperboard is wound into large rolls, and workers place the rolls on wooden pallets.
15. Forklifts are used to move the rolls of paperboard to the labeling building.
16. There the rolls are labeled and stored for shipment.
17. The rolls of paperboard are shipped to customers from the loading dock in the labeling building.

The partially processed product sometimes is stored between production operations for two to three days. This delay can be caused either by a faster production rate in the earlier processes than in the later processes or by breakdowns in the production machinery. The Charlotte plant's average cycle time is about 15 days.

REQUIRED: Your consulting firm has been hired to advise Pickwick Paper's management on how to improve its production process.

1. Diagram the current production process.
2. Point out areas that you believe to be candidates for non-value-added activities.
3. Prepare a plan for Pickwick to change its production process to a JIT process. Include a diagram of your suggested process. The company is not in a position to buy new production machinery but management will consider purchasing an AMHS. The plant currently operates in three buildings, which are not far apart. Management is willing to consider minor construction to connect the buildings.

Problem 5-48   JIT Costing. Tuscon Tileworks uses JIT costing to record the flow of production costs. The following events occurred in May.

1. Purchased raw material for $178,000 on account.
2. Salaries of $21,000 were earned by the production manager and production supervisors.
3. Production workers earned wages of $108,000, which were paid in cash.
4. Other employees who work in the tile plant earned wages of $25,000, which were paid in cash. Included in this amount are the wages of machine-repair personnel, custodians, security guards, etc.
5. Bills of $170,000 were paid for plant utilities, property taxes, and insurance.
6. Depreciation on the factory building and machinery amounted to $95,000.
7. Engineering salaries amounted to $18,000.
8. Material handlers earned wages of $11,000.
9. A truck was purchased for $52,000.
10. The tile finished in May included raw material costing $160,000.
11. Tile with raw material costs of $140,000 was sold for $700,000 on account.
12. Conversion costs of $450,000 were applied in May.
13. The production manager made the following estimates on May 31:
    (a) The conversion costs pertaining to the May 31 work in process amount to $40,000; (b) The conversion costs pertaining to the May 31 finished goods amount to $51,000.

REQUIRED:

1. Prepare journal entries to record the events of May.
2. Explain the role of the Raw and In-process Inventory account. How does it differ from a Raw-Material Inventory account?

Problem 5-49   JIT Costing. VideoFun Corporation manufactures video games. The firm has been using an actual-costing system, in which the actual cost of direct material, direct labor, and manufacturing overhead are entered into work in process. On January 1, the company switched to JIT costing.

The following events occurred during January.

1. Electronic components were purchased on account for $245,000.
2. Production-line employees earned wages of $110,000.
3. Production supervisory salaries amounted to $15,000.
4. Machine-repair personnel earned wages of $8,000.
5. Utility bills amounting to $29,000 were paid.
6. Depreciation on the factory building and equipment amounted to $90,000.
7. Other overhead costs of $60,000 were incurred and paid for in cash.
8. The products that were finished in January included raw materials costing $200,000.
9. The products sold in January included raw materials costing $150,000. These products were sold for $500,000 on account.
10. Conversion costs of $300,000 were applied in January.
11. The production manager made the following estimates on January 31: (a) The conversion costs pertaining to January 31 work in process amounted to $47,000; (b) The conversion costs pertaining to January 31 finished goods were $67,000.

REQUIRED:

1. Prepare journal entries to record January's events under JIT costing.
2. Post these journal entries to T-accounts.

3. Explain how VideoFun Corporation's current product-costing system differs from its previous system.
4. Which product-costing system would you expect to be less expensive to operate? Why?

*Problem 5-50   **Production Efficiency Report; Nonfinancial Data.*** Pittsburgh Plastics Corporation manufactures a range of molded plastic products, such as kitchen utensils and desk accessories. The production process in the North Hills plant is a JIT system, which operates in four FMS cells. An AMHS is used to transport products between production operations. Each month the controller prepares a production efficiency report, which is sent to corporate headquarters. The data compiled in these reports, for the first six months of 19x0, follow:

PRODUCTION EFFICIENCY REPORT
Pittsburgh Plastics Corporation
North Hills Plant
January, 19x0 through June, 19x0

	Jan.	Feb.	Mar.	Apr.	May	June	Average
Overtime hours	60	70	75	80	85	105	79.2
Total setup time	70	70	65	64	62	62	65.5
Cycle time (average in hours)	20	20	19	18	19	17	18.8
Manufacturing-cycle efficiency	95%	94%	96%	90%	89%	90%	92.3%
Percentage of orders filled	100%	100%	100%	100%	100%	100%	100%
Percentage of on-time deliveries	99%	98%	99%	100%	96%	94%	97.7%
Inventory value/sales revenue	5%	5%	5%	4%	5%	5%	4.8%
Number of defective units, finished goods	80	82	75	40	25	22	54
Number of defective units, in process	10	30	35	40	60	60	39.2
Number of raw-material shipments with defective materials	3	3	2	0	0	0	1.3
Number of products returned	0	0	0	0	0	0	0
Aggregate productivity	1.3	1.3	1.2	1.25	1.2	1.15	1.23
Power consumption (thousands of kilowatt-hours)	800	795	802	801	800	800	800
Machine downtime (hours)	30	25	25	20	20	10	21.7
Bottleneck machine downtime	0	0	2	0	15	2	3.2
Number of unscheduled machine maintenance calls	0	0	1	0	2	3	1

REQUIRED:

1. Write a memo to the company president evaluating the North Hills plant's performance. Structure your report by dividing it into the following parts: (1) production processing and productivity, (2) product quality and customer acceptance, (3) delivery performance, (4) raw material, scrap, and inventory, and (5) machine maintenance.
2. If you identify any areas of concern in your memo, indicate an appropriate action for management.

Problem 5-51 Measuring Productivity. Productivity, often defined as output divided by input, has been the center of attention recently because of the general below-average perform-ance of U.S. industries in the past decade. Improved productivity is necessary if companies wish to remain competitive and improve their profitability.

Many companies have developed measures of productivity. For example, one manufac-turing firm employs the rather simplistic measure: productivity = total revenue ÷ total labor costs. A company in a regulated industry developed the following productivity evaluation from its work-measurement system: productivity = total applicable budgeted labor hours ÷ total actual reported labor hours. An equipment manufacturer uses the following productivity measure: productivity = sales billed ÷ direct cost incurred to produce and sell the product.

REQUIRED:

1. Comment on the validity of this statement: "Productivity is just another ratio and, when considered by itself, suffers from the same shortcomings as any other simplistic analysis."
2. What criteria should the management accountant consider in the initial implementation of a productivity measurement and analysis program?
3. Discuss the pros and cons of the three productivity measures presented above.
(CMA adapted)

Problem 5-52 Quality-Cost Report. Universal Circuitry manufactures electrical instru-ments for a variety of purposes. The following costs related to maintaining product quality were incurred in May of 19x1.

Inspection of electrical components purchased from outside suppliers ..	$12,000
Costs of rework on faulty instruments	9,000
Replacement of instruments already sold, which were still covered by warranty...	16,500
Costs of defective parts that cannot be salvaged	6,100
Training of quality-control inspectors	21,000
Tests of instruments before sale	30,000

REQUIRED: Prepare a quality-cost report similar to the report shown in Exhibit 5-14.

Problem 5-53 Manufacturing Performance Measurement. Medical Systems Corporation manufactures diagnostic testing equipment used in hospitals. The company practices JIT production management and has a state-of-the-art manufacturing system, including an FMS and an AMHS. The following nonfinancial data were collected biweekly in the Harrisburg plant during the first quarter of 19x1.

	Biweekly Measurement Period					
	1	**2**	**3**	**4**	**5**	**6**
Cycle time (days)	1.5	1.3	1.3	1.2	1.2	1.1
Number of defective finished products	4	4	3	4	3	3
Manufacturing-cycle efficiency	94%	94%	96%	96%	97%	96%
Customer complaints	6	7	6	5	7	8
Unresolved complaints	2	1	0	0	0	0
Products returned	3	3	2	2	1	1
Warranty claims	2	2	2	0	1	0
In-process products rejected	5	5	7	9	10	10
Aggregate productivity	1.5	1.5	1.5	1.5	1.4	1.5
Number of units produced per day per employee	410	405	412	415	415	420
Percentage of on-time deliveries	94%	95%	95%	97%	100%	100%
Percentage of orders filled	100%	100%	100%	98%	100%	100%
Inventory value/sales revenue	2%	2%	2%	1.5%	2%	1.5%
Machine downtime (minutes)	80	80	120	80	70	75
Bottleneck machine downtime (minutes)	25	20	15	0	60	10
Overtime (minutes) per employee	20	0	0	10	20	10
Average setup time (minutes)	120	120	115	112	108	101

REQUIRED:

1. For each nonfinancial performance measure, indicate which of the following areas of manufacturing performance is involved: (1) production processing, (2) product quality, (3) customer acceptance, (4) in-process quality control, (5) productivity, (6) delivery performance, (7) raw material and scrap, (8) inventory, (9) machine maintenance. Some measures may relate to more than one area.
2. Write a memo to management commenting on the performance data collected for the Harrisburg plant. Be sure to note any trends or other important results you see in the data. Evaluate the Harrisburg plant in each of the areas listed in requirement (1).

Problem 5-54   Cost Drivers; Direct and Indirect Costs; Non-Value-Added Costs; JIT and FMS. Kiefer Autoworks Company manufactures a variety of small parts for the automotive industry. The company's manufacturing overhead cost budget for 19x5 is as follows:

Supervision	$ 200,000
Machine maintenance — labor.	70,000
Machine maintenance — materials	20,000
Electrical power	50,000
Natural gas (for heating).	30,000
Factory supplies	40,000
Setup labor	30,000
Lubricants.	10,000
Property taxes.	25,000
Insurance	35,000
Depreciation on manufacturing equipment	105,000
Depreciation of trucks and forklifts.	70,000

Depreciation on material conveyors	15,000
Building depreciation	160,000
Grinding wheels	5,000
Drill bits	2,000
Purchasing	80,000
Waste collection	4,000
Custodial labor	40,000
Telephone service	5,000
Engineering design	70,000
Inspection of raw materials	20,000
Receiving	20,000
Inspection of finished goods	30,000
Packaging	60,000
Shipping	30,000
Wages of parts clerks (find parts for production departments)	60,000
Wages of material handlers	70,000
Fuel for trucks and forklifts	30,000
Depreciation on raw-materials warehouse	50,000
Depreciation on finished-goods warehouse	60,000
Total budgeted manufacturing overhead	$1,496,000

The budgeted amount of direct-labor in 19x5 is 20,000 hours.

REQUIRED:

1. Compute the predetermined overhead rate based on direct-labor hours.
2. Kiefer's management has decided to implement a transaction-based costing system based on multiple cost drivers. The cost drivers under consideration are the following:

   Production (in units)
   Raw-material cost
   Factory space
   Machine hours
   Number of production runs
   Number of shipments of finished goods
   Number of shipments of raw materials
   Number of different raw materials and parts used in a product
   Engineering specifications and change orders

   Divide Kiefer Autoworks' manufacturing-overhead costs into separate cost pools, and identify a cost driver for each cost pool.
3. For each overhead cost, indicate which of the five types of production activity (time) is involved.
4. Which of the overhead costs are candidates for elimination as non-value-added costs?
5. How would activity accounting help management reduce or eliminate some of Kiefer's overhead costs? Be specific.
6. Suppose that Kiefer Autoworks adopted a JIT production approach and purchased an FMS. Which of Kiefer's overhead costs are likely to be treated as direct costs of an FMS cell?
7. For those costs that are not likely to be traceable to an FMS cell, how would you assign them to Kiefer Autoworks' products?

CASE   *Case 5-55   Overhead Cost Drivers; Product Lines.* Chefway Company manufactures custom-designed restaurant and kitchen furniture. The firm uses a job-order costing system.
Actual manufacturing-overhead costs incurred during the month are applied to products on
the basis of actual direct-labor hours. Overhead consists primarily of supervision, utilities,
maintenance costs, property taxes, and depreciation.

Chefway recently won a contract to manufacture the furniture for a new fast-food chain.
This furniture is durable but of a lower quality than Chefway normally manufactures. To
produce this new line, Chefway must purchase more molded plastic parts for the furniture
than for its current line. Through innovative industrial engineering, an efficient manufacturing process for this new furniture has been developed, which requires only a small capital
investment. Management is optimistic about the profit improvement the new product line will
bring.

At the end of October, the start-up month for the new line, the controller prepared a
separate income statement for the new product line. On a consolidated basis, the company's
gross profit was normal; however, the profitability of the new line was lower than expected. By
the end of November, the results were somewhat improved. Company profits were acceptable,
but the reported profitability for the new product line still was less than expected. The president of the corporation is concerned that the stockholders will criticize the decision to add this
lower-quality product line when profitability appeared to be increasing with the standard
product line. The results, as published for the first nine months, for October, and for November are as follows:

Chefway Corporation
(in thousands)

	Fast-Food Furniture	Custom Furniture	Combined
Nine months year-to-date, 19x8:			
Gross sales............................	—	$8,100	$8,100
Direct material	—	$2,025	$2,025
Direct labor:			
Forming............................	—	758	758
Finishing	—	1,314	1,314
Assembly...........................	—	558	558
Manufacturing overhead	—	1,779	1,779
Cost of goods sold....................	—	$6,434	$6,434
Gross profit	—	$1,666	$1,666
Gross profit percentage*................	—	20.6%	20.6%
October, 19x8:			
Gross sales............................	$ 400	$ 900	$1,300
Direct material	$ 200	$ 225	$ 425
Direct labor:			
Forming............................	17	82	99
Finishing	40	142	182
Assembly...........................	33	60	93
Manufacturing overhead	60	180	240
Cost of goods sold....................	$ 350	$ 689	$1,039
Gross profit	$ 50	$ 211	$ 261
Gross profit percentage*................	12.5%	23.4%	20.1%

	Fast-Food Furniture	Custom Furniture	Combined
November, 19x8:			
Gross sales..........................	$ 800	$ 800	$1,600
Direct material	$ 400	$ 200	$ 600
Direct labor:			
Forming............................	31	72	103
Finishing	70	125	195
Assembly..........................	58	53	111
Manufacturing overhead	98	147	245
Cost of goods sold....................	$ 657	$ 597	$1,254
Gross profit	$ 143	$ 203	$ 346
Gross profit percentage*...............	17.9%	25.4%	21.6%

* Gross profit ÷ gross sales

Marcea Jameson, controller, says that the overhead application based only on direct-labor hours is no longer appropriate. On the basis of a recently completed study of the overhead accounts, she feels that only the supervision and utilities should be applied on the basis of direct-labor hours, and the balance of the overhead should be applied on a machine-hour basis. In her judgment, the increase in the profitability of the custom-design furniture is due to inaccurate application of overhead in the present system.

The actual direct-labor hours and machine hours for the past two months are as follows:

	Fast-Food Furniture	Custom Furniture
Machine hours:		
October:		
Forming......................................	660	10,700
Finishing	660	7,780
Assembly	—	—
Total..	1,320	18,480
November:		
Forming......................................	1,280	9,640
Finishing	1,280	7,400
Assembly	—	—
Total..	2,560	17,040
Direct-labor hours:		
October:		
Forming......................................	1,900	9,300
Finishing	3,350	12,000
Assembly	4,750	8,700
Total..	10,000	30,000
November:		
Forming......................................	3,400	8,250
Finishing	5,800	10,400
Assembly	8,300	7,600
Total..	17,500	26,250

The actual overhead costs for the past two months were as follows:

	October	November
Supervision	$ 13,000	$ 13,000
Utilities	95,000	109,500
Maintenance	50,000	48,000
Depreciation	42,000	42,000
Property taxes	8,000	8,000
All other	32,000	24,500
Total	$240,000	$245,000

REQUIRED:

1. Based on Marcea Jameson's recommendation, apply the overhead for October and November using direct-labor hours as the cost driver for supervision and utilities. Use machine hours as the cost driver for the remaining overhead costs.

2. Support or criticize Marcea Jameson's conclusion that the increase in custom-design profitability is due to inaccurate application of overhead. Use the data developed in requirement (1) as the basis for your analysis.

3. Marcea Jameson also has recommended that consideration be given to using predetermined overhead rates calculated on an annual basis rather than applying actual cost using actual activity each month. Discuss the advantages of predetermined overhead rates.

4. How could Marcea Jameson go even further in revising Chefway's product-costing system? What steps would be involved?

(CMA, adapted)

PART 2 PLANNING AND CONTROL SYSTEMS

Chapter 6 Cost Behavior and Estimation

After completing this chapter, you should be able to:

- Explain the relationships between cost estimation, cost behavior, and cost prediction.

- Define and describe the behavior of the following types of costs: variable, step-variable, fixed, step-fixed, semivariable (or mixed), and curvilinear.

- Explain the importance of the relevant range in using a cost behavior pattern for cost prediction.

- Define and give examples of engineered costs, committed costs, and discretionary costs.

- Describe and use the following cost-estimation methods: account classification, visual fit, high-low, and least-squares regression.

- Describe the multiple regression, engineering, and work-measurement approaches to cost estimation.

- Describe some problems often encountered in collecting data for cost estimation.

Managers in almost any organization want to know how costs will be affected by changes in the organization's activity. The relationship between cost and activity, called **cost behavior,** is relevant to the management functions of planning, control, and decision making. In order to *plan* operations and prepare a budget, managers at Nabisco need to predict the costs that will be incurred at different levels of production and sales. To *control* the costs of providing commercial-loan services at Chase Manhattan Bank, executives need to have a feel for the costs that the bank should incur at various levels of commercial-loan activity. In *deciding* whether to add a new intensive care unit, a hospital's administrators need to predict the cost of operating the new unit at various levels of patient demand. In each of these situations, knowledge of *cost behavior* will help the manager to make the desired cost prediction. A **cost prediction** is a forecast of cost at a particular level of activity. In the first half of this chapter, we will study cost behavior patterns and their use in making cost predictions.

How does a managerial accountant determine the cost behavior pattern for a particular cost item? The determination of cost behavior, which is often called **cost estimation,** can be accomplished in a number of ways. One way is to analyze historical data concerning costs and activity levels. Cost estimation is covered in the second half of this chapter.

The following diagram summarizes the key points in the preceding discussion.

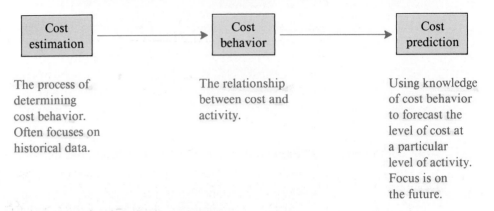

| Cost estimation | → | Cost behavior | → | Cost prediction |

The process of determining cost behavior. Often focuses on historical data.

The relationship between cost and activity.

Using knowledge of cost behavior to forecast the level of cost at a particular level of activity. Focus is on the future.

COST BEHAVIOR PATTERNS

Our discussion of cost behavior patterns, also called *cost functions,* will be set in the context of a restaurant business. Tasty Donuts, Inc. operates a chain of 10 donut shops in the city of Toronto, Canada. Each shop sells a variety of donuts, muffins, and sweet rolls as well as various beverages. Beverages, such as coffee and fruit juices, are prepared in each donut shop, but all of the company's donuts and baked products are made in a centrally located bakery. The company leases several small delivery trucks to transport the bakery items to its restaurants. Use of a central bakery is more cost-efficient. Moreover, this approach allows the firm to smooth out fluctuations in demand for each type of product. For example, the demand for glazed donuts may change from day to day in each donut shop, but these fluctuations tend to cancel each other out when the total demand is aggregated across all 10 shops.

The corporate controller for Tasty Donuts has recently completed a study of the company's cost behavior to use in preparing the firm's budget for the coming year. The controller studied the following costs.

Direct material: ingredients for donuts, muffins and sweet rolls; beverages; paper products, such as napkins and disposable cups
Direct labor: wages and fringe benefits of bakers, restaurant sales personnel and delivery truck drivers
Overhead:
    Facilities costs: property taxes; depreciation on bakery building, donut shops, and equipment; salaries and fringe benefits of maintenance personnel
    Indirect labor: salaries and fringe benefits of managers and assistant managers for bakery and restaurants
    Delivery trucks: rental payments under lease contract; costs of gasoline, oil, tires, and maintenance
    Utilities: electricity, telephone, and trash collection

In studying the behavior of each of these costs, the controller measured company *activity* in terms of *dozens of bakery items sold.* Thus, dozens of bakery items sold is the *cost driver* for each of the costs studied. A bakery item is one donut, muffin, or sweet roll. The costs to make each of these products are nearly identical. The number of bakery items sold each day is roughly the same as the number produced, since bakery goods are produced to keep pace with demand as reported by the company's restaurant managers.

Variable Costs

Variable costs were discussed briefly in Chapter 2. We will summarize that discussion here in the context of the Tasty Donuts illustration. A **variable cost** changes *in total* in direct proportion to a change in the activity level (or cost driver). Tasty Donuts' direct-material cost is a variable cost. As the company sells more donuts, muffins, and sweet rolls, the total cost of the ingredients for these goods increases in direct proportion to the number of items sold. Moreover, the quantities of beverages sold and paper products used by customers also increase in direct proportion to the

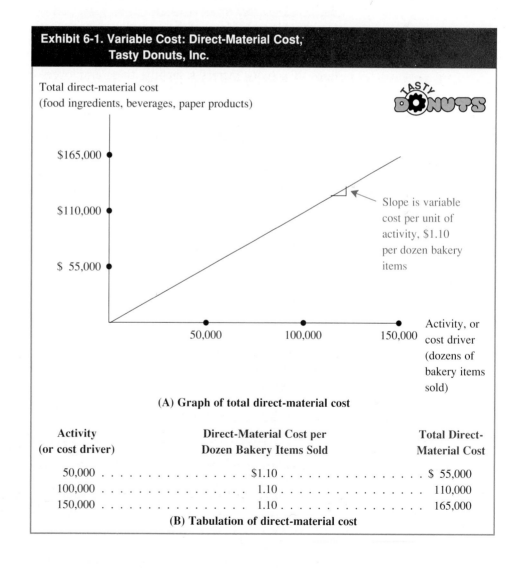

Exhibit 6-1. Variable Cost: Direct-Material Cost, Tasty Donuts, Inc.

Total direct-material cost
(food ingredients, beverages, paper products)

Slope is variable cost per unit of activity, $1.10 per dozen bakery items

Activity, or cost driver (dozens of bakery items sold)

(A) Graph of total direct-material cost

Activity (or cost driver)	Direct-Material Cost per Dozen Bakery Items Sold	Total Direct-Material Cost
50,000	$1.10	$ 55,000
100,000	1.10	110,000
150,000	1.10	165,000

(B) Tabulation of direct-material cost

number of bakery items sold. As a result, the costs of beverages and paper products are also variable costs.

Panel A of Exhibit 6-1 displays a graph of Tasty Donuts' direct-material cost. As the graph shows, *total* variable cost increases in proportion to the activity level (or cost driver). When activity triples, for example, from 50,000 dozen items to 150,000 dozen items, total direct-material costs triple, from $55,000 to $165,000. However, the variable cost *per unit* remains the same as activity changes. The total direct-material cost incurred *per dozen* items sold is constant at $1.10 per dozen. The table in panel B of Exhibit 6-1 illustrates this point. The variable cost per unit is also represented in the graph in panel A of Exhibit 6-1 as the slope of the cost line.

To summarize, as activity changes, total variable cost increases in direct proportion to the change in activity level, but the variable cost per unit remains constant.

Step-Variable Costs

Some costs are nearly variable, but they increase in small steps instead of continuously. Such costs, called **step-variable costs,** usually include inputs that are purchased and used in relatively small increments. At Tasty Donuts, Inc. the direct-labor cost of bakers, restaurant counter-service personnel, and delivery-truck drivers is a step-variable cost. Many of these employees are part-time workers, called upon for relatively small increments of time, such as a few hours. On a typical day, for example, Tasty Donuts may have 35 employees at work in the bakery and the donut shops. If activity increases slightly, these employees can handle the extra work.

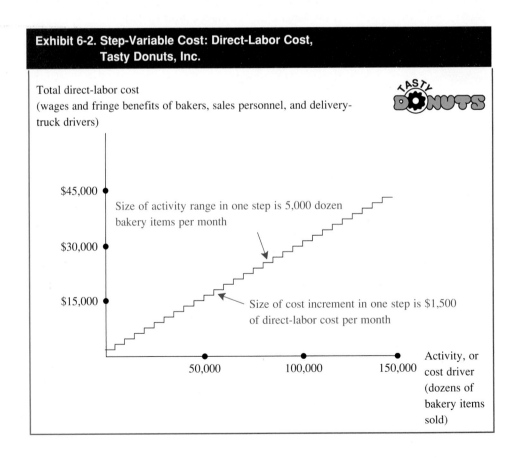

Exhibit 6-2. Step-Variable Cost: Direct-Labor Cost, Tasty Donuts, Inc.

However, if activity increases substantially, the bakery manager or various restaurant managers may call on additional help. Exhibit 6-2, a graph of Tasty Donuts' monthly direct-labor cost, shows that this cost remains constant within an activity range of about 5,000 dozen bakery items per month. When monthly activity increases beyond this narrow range, direct-labor costs increase.

Approximating a Step-Variable Cost   If the steps in a step-variable cost behavior pattern are small, the step-variable cost function may be approximated by a variable cost function without much loss in accuracy. Exhibit 6-3 shows such an approximation for Tasty Donuts' direct-labor cost.

Fixed Costs

Fixed costs were covered briefly in Chapter 2. We will summarize that discussion here, using the Tasty Donuts illustration. A **fixed cost** remains unchanged *in total* as the activity level (or cost driver) varies. Facilities costs, which include property taxes, depreciation on buildings and equipment, and the salaries of maintenance personnel, are fixed costs for Tasty Donuts, Inc. These fixed costs are graphed in panel A of Exhibit 6-4. This graph shows that the *total* monthly cost of property taxes, depreciation, and maintenance personnel is $200,000 regardless of how many dozen bakery items are produced and sold during the month.

   The fixed cost *per unit* does change as activity varies. Exhibit 6-4 (panel B) shows that the company's facilities cost per dozen bakery items is $4.00 when 50,000 dozen items are produced and sold. However, this unit cost declines to $2.00 when 100,000

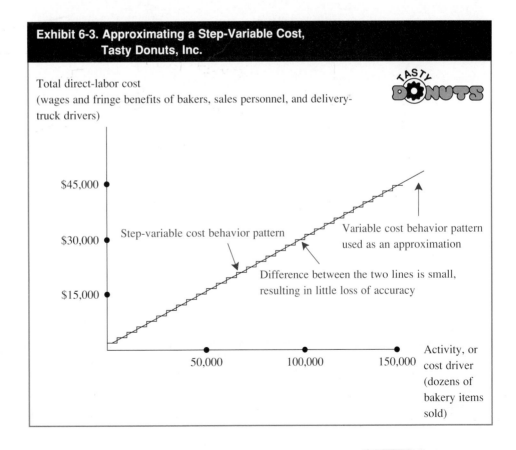

Exhibit 6-3. Approximating a Step-Variable Cost, Tasty Donuts, Inc.

Total direct-labor cost
(wages and fringe benefits of bakers, sales personnel, and delivery-truck drivers)

Step-variable cost behavior pattern

Variable cost behavior pattern used as an approximation

Difference between the two lines is small, resulting in little loss of accuracy

Activity, or cost driver (dozens of bakery items sold)

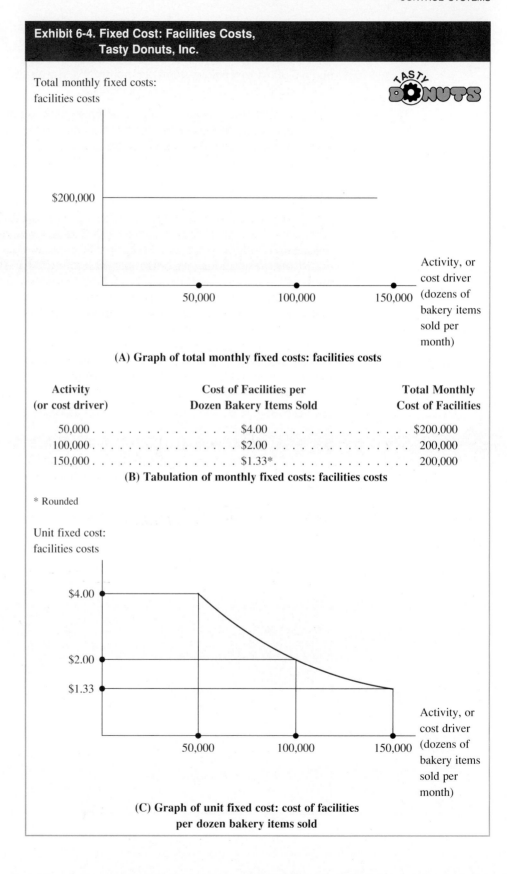

**Exhibit 6-4. Fixed Cost: Facilities Costs,
Tasty Donuts, Inc.**

Total monthly fixed costs:
facilities costs

(A) Graph of total monthly fixed costs: facilities costs

Activity (or cost driver)	Cost of Facilities per Dozen Bakery Items Sold	Total Monthly Cost of Facilities
50,000	$4.00	$200,000
100,000	$2.00	200,000
150,000	$1.33*	200,000

(B) Tabulation of monthly fixed costs: facilities costs

* Rounded

Unit fixed cost:
facilities costs

(C) Graph of unit fixed cost: cost of facilities
per dozen bakery items sold

dozen items are produced and sold. If activity increases to 150,000 dozen items, unit fixed cost will decline further, to about $1.33.

A graph provides another way of viewing the change in unit fixed cost as activity changes. Panel C of Exhibit 6-4 displays a graph of Tasty Donuts' cost of property taxes, depreciation, and maintenance personnel *per dozen bakery items.* As the graph shows, the fixed cost per dozen bakery items declines steadily as activity increases.

To summarize, as the activity level increases, total fixed cost does not change, but unit fixed cost declines. For this reason, it is preferable in any cost analysis to work with total fixed cost rather than fixed cost per unit.

Step-Fixed Costs

Some costs remain fixed over a wide range of activity, but jump to a different amount for activity levels outside that range. Such costs are called **step-fixed costs.** Tasty Donuts' cost of indirect labor is a step-fixed cost. Indirect-labor cost consists of the salaries and fringe benefits for the managers and assistant managers of the company's bakery and restaurants. Tasty Donuts' monthly indirect-labor cost is graphed in Exhibit 6-5.

As Exhibit 6-5 shows, for activity in the range of 50,000 to 100,000 dozen bakery items per month, Tasty Donuts' monthly indirect-labor cost is $35,000. For this range of activity, the company employs a full-time manager and a full-time assistant manager in the bakery and in each restaurant. When monthly activity exceeds this range during the summer tourist season, the company employs additional part-time assistant managers in the bakery and in its busiest donut shops. The company hires college students who are majoring in restaurant administration for these summer

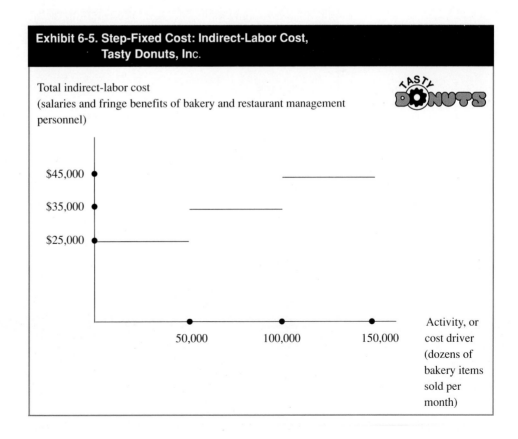

Exhibit 6-5. Step-Fixed Cost: Indirect-Labor Cost, Tasty Donuts, Inc.

Total indirect-labor cost
(salaries and fringe benefits of bakery and restaurant management personnel)

positions. Their salaries boost the monthly indirect-labor cost to $45,000. Tasty Donuts has not experienced demand of less than 50,000 dozen bakery items per month. However, the controller anticipates that if such a decrease in demand were to occur, the company would reduce the daily operating hours for its donut shops. This would allow the firm to operate each restaurant with only a full-time manager and no assistant manager. As the graph in Exhibit 6-5 indicates, such a decrease in managerial personnel would reduce monthly indirect-labor cost to $25,000.

Semivariable Cost

A **semivariable (or mixed) cost** has both a fixed and a variable component. The cost of operating delivery trucks is a semivariable cost for Tasty Donuts, Inc. These costs are graphed in Exhibit 6-6. As the graph shows, the company's delivery-truck costs have two components. The fixed-cost component is $3,000 per month, which is the monthly rental payment paid under the lease contract for the delivery trucks. The monthly rental payment is constant, regardless of the level of activity (or cost driver). The variable-cost component consists of the costs of gasoline, oil, routine maintenance, and tires. These costs vary with activity, since greater activity levels result in more deliveries. The distance between the fixed-cost line (dashed line) and the total-cost line in Exhibit 6-6 is the amount of variable cost. For example, at an activity level of 100,000 dozen bakery items, the total variable cost component is $10,000.

The slope of the total-cost line is the variable cost per unit of activity. For Tasty Donuts, the variable cost of operating its delivery trucks is $.10 per dozen bakery items sold.

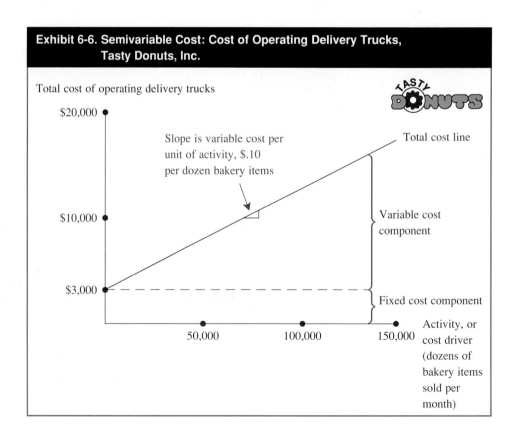

Exhibit 6-6. Semivariable Cost: Cost of Operating Delivery Trucks, Tasty Donuts, Inc.

Curvilinear Cost

The graphs of all of the cost behavior patterns examined so far consist of either
straight lines or several straight-line sections. A **curvilinear cost** behavior pattern has a
curved graph. Tasty Donuts' utilities cost, depicted as the *solid curve* in Exhibit 6-7, is
a curvilinear cost. For low levels of activity, this cost exhibits *decreasing marginal
costs.* As the discussion in Chapter 2 indicated, a marginal cost is the cost of producing the next unit, in this case the next dozen bakery items. As the graph in Exhibit 6-7
shows, the marginal utilities cost of producing the next dozen bakery items declines as
activity increases in the range zero to 100,000 dozen items per month. For activity
greater than 100,000 dozen bakery items per month, the graph in Exhibit 6-7 exhibits
increasing marginal costs.

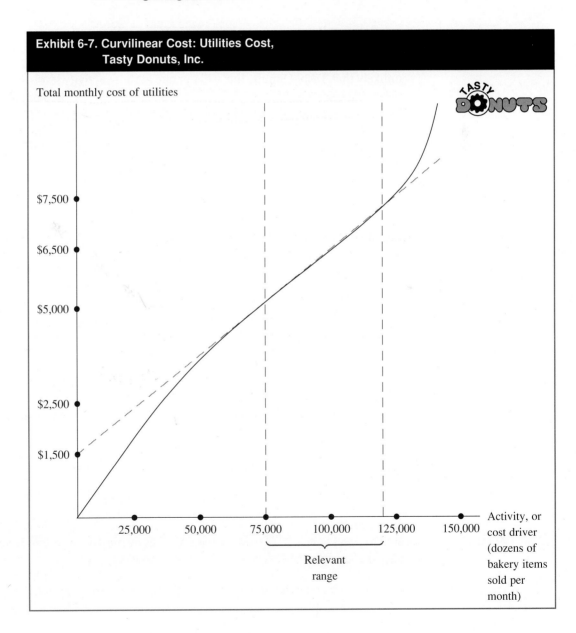

**Exhibit 6-7. Curvilinear Cost: Utilities Cost,
          Tasty Donuts, Inc.**

Tasty Donuts' utilities cost includes electricity, telephone, and trash-collection costs. The utilities cost is curvilinear as a result of the company's pattern of electricity usage in the bakery. If the demand in a particular month is less than 100,000 dozen bakery items, the goods can be produced entirely in the modernized section of the bakery. This section uses recently purchased deep-fat fryers and ovens, which are very energy-efficient. As long as the bakery operates only the modernized section, the utilities cost per dozen items declines as production increases.

During the summer tourist months, when Tasty Donuts' sales exceed 100,000 dozen items per month, the older section of the bakery also must be used. This section uses much older cooking equipment, which is less energy-efficient. As a result, the marginal utilities cost per dozen bakery items rises as monthly activity increases in the range above 100,000 dozen items per month.

Relevant Range The cost behavior graphed in Exhibit 6-7 is very different at low activity levels (below 50,000) than it is at high activity levels (above 125,000). However, management need not concern itself with these extreme levels of activity if it is unlikely that Tasty Donuts, Inc. will operate at those activity levels. Management is interested in cost behavior within the company's **relevant range,** the range of activity within which management expects the company to operate. Tasty Donuts' management believes the firm's relevant range to be 75,000 to 120,000 dozen bakery items per month. Based on past experience and sales projections, management does not expect the firm to operate outside of that range of monthly activity. Tasty Donuts' relevant range is shown in Exhibit 6-7 as the section of the graph between the dashed lines.

Approximating a Curvilinear Cost within the Relevant Range The straight, dashed line in Exhibit 6-7 may be used to approximate Tasty Donuts' utilities cost. Notice that the approximation is quite accurate for activity levels within the relevant range. However, as the activity level gets further away from the boundary of the relevant range, the approximation declines in accuracy. For monthly activity levels of 25,000 or 150,000, for example, the approximation is very poor.

The straight, dashed line used to approximate Tasty Donuts' utilities cost *within the relevant range* represents a semivariable cost behavior pattern. This straight-line graph has a slope of $.05, which represents a unit variable-cost component of $.05 per dozen bakery items. The line intersects the vertical axis of the graph at $1,500, which represents a fixed-cost component of $1,500 per month. Managerial accountants often use a semivariable cost behavior pattern to approximate a curvilinear cost. However, it is important to limit this approximation to the range of activity in which its accuracy is acceptable.

Using Cost Behavior Patterns to Predict Costs

How can Tasty Donuts' corporate controller use the cost behavior patterns identified in the cost study to help in the budgeting process? First, a sales forecast is made for each month during the budget year. Suppose management expects Tasty Donuts' activity level to be 110,000 dozen bakery items during the month of June. Second, a *cost prediction* is made for each of the firm's cost items. The following cost predictions are based on the cost behavior patterns discussed earlier. (Try to verify these cost predictions by referring to the graphs in Exhibits 6-1 through 6-7.)

Cost Item	Cost Prediction for June (110,000 dozen bakery items per month)
Direct material.	$121,000
Direct labor	33,000
Overhead:	
Facilities costs.	200,000
Indirect labor	45,000
Delivery trucks.	14,000
Utilities.	7,000

The preparation of a complete budget involves much more analysis and detailed planning than is shown here.[1] The point is that cost prediction is an important part of the planning process. The cost behavior patterns discussed in this chapter make those cost predictions possible.

Engineered, Committed, and Discretionary Costs

In the process of budgeting costs, it is often useful for management to make a distinction between engineered, committed, and discretionary costs. An **engineered cost** bears a definitive physical relationship to the activity measure. Tasty Donuts' direct-material cost is an engineered cost. It is impossible to produce more donuts without incurring greater material cost for food ingredients.

A **committed cost** results from an organization's ownership or use of facilities and its basic organization structure. Property taxes, depreciation on buildings and equipment, costs of renting facilities or equipment, and the salaries of management personnel are examples of committed fixed costs. Tasty Donuts' facilities cost is a committed fixed cost.

A **discretionary cost** arises as a result of a *management decision* to spend a particular amount of money for some purpose. Examples of discretionary costs include amounts spent on research and development, advertising and promotion, management development programs, and contributions to charitable organizations. For example, suppose Tasty Donuts' management has decided to spend $12,400 each month on promotion and advertising.

The distinction between committed and discretionary costs is an important one. Management can change committed costs only through relatively major decisions that have long-term implications. Decisions to build a new production facility, lease a fleet of vehicles, or add more management personnel to oversee a new division are examples of such decisions. These decisions will generally influence costs incurred over a long period of time. In contrast, discretionary costs can be changed in the short run much more easily. Management can be flexible about expenditures for advertising, promotion, employee training, or research and development. This does not imply that such programs are unimportant, but simply that management can alter them over time. For example, the management of a manufacturing firm may decide to spend $100,000 on research and development in 19x1, but cut back to $60,000 in 19x2 because of an anticipated economic downturn.

[1] The budgeting process is covered in Chapter 8.

Cost Behavior in Other Industries

We have illustrated a variety of cost behavior patterns for Tasty Donuts' restaurant business. The same cost behavior patterns are used in other industries. The cost behavior pattern appropriate for a particular cost item depends on the organization and the activity base (or cost driver). In manufacturing firms, production quantity, direct-labor hours, and machine hours are common cost drivers. Direct-material and direct-labor costs are usually considered variable costs. Other variable costs include some manufacturing-overhead costs, such as indirect material and indirect labor. Fixed manufacturing costs are generally the costs of creating production capacity. Examples include depreciation on plant and equipment, property taxes, and the plant manager's salary. Such overhead costs as utilities and equipment maintenance are usually semivariable or curvilinear costs. A semivariable cost behavior pattern is generally used to approximate a curvilinear cost within the relevant range. Supervisory salaries are usually step-fixed costs, since one person can supervise production over a range of activity. When activity increases beyond that range, such as when a new shift is added, an additional supervisor is added.

In merchandising firms, the activity base (or cost driver) is usually sales revenue. The cost of merchandise sold is a variable cost. Most labor costs are fixed or step-fixed costs, since a particular number of sales and stock personnel can generally handle sales activity over a fairly wide range of sales. Store facility costs, such as rent, depreciation on buildings and furnishings, and property taxes, are fixed costs.

In some industries, the choice of the cost driver is not obvious, and the cost behavior pattern can depend on the cost driver selected. In an airline, for instance, the cost driver could be air miles flown, passengers flown, or passenger miles flown. A passenger mile is the transportation of one passenger for one mile. Fuel costs are variable with respect to air miles traveled, but are not necessarily variable with respect to passenger miles flown. An airplane uses more fuel in flying from New York to San Francisco than from New York to Chicago. However, a plane does not require significantly more fuel to fly 200 people from one city to another than to fly 190 people the same distance. In contrast, an airport landing fee is a fixed cost for a particular number of aircraft arrivals, regardless of how far the planes have flown or how many people were transported. The point of this discussion is that both the organization and the cost driver are crucial determinants of the cost behavior for each cost item. Conclusions drawn about cost behavior in one industry are not necessarily transferrable to another industry.

ILLUSTRATION FROM MANAGEMENT-ACCOUNTING PRACTICE

Cost Behavior in a Hospital

The Leonard Morse Hospital in Massachusetts has found that a variety of cost behavior patterns are represented in its labor costs. For example, the cost of compensating anesthesiologists is a step-fixed cost. One anesthesiologist is sufficient for up to 10 operations per day. For 11 or more daily operations, another anesthesiologist is required. In contrast, labor costs in the dietary department are fixed. The hospital has contracted with an outside firm to supply the services of dieticians for a fixed fee.[2]

---

[2] S. A. Larracey, "Hospital Planning for Cost Effectiveness," *Management Accounting,* July 1982, p. 47.

Shifting Cost Structures Fixed costs are becoming more prevalent in many industries. This is due to two factors. First, automation is replacing labor to an increasing extent. Second, labor unions have been increasingly successful in negotiating agreements that result in a relatively stable work force. This makes management less flexible in adjusting a firm's work force to the desired level of production.

COST ESTIMATION

As the preceding discussion indicates, different costs exhibit a variety of cost behavior patterns. **Cost estimation** is the process of determining how a particular cost behaves. Several methods are commonly used to estimate the relationship between cost and activity. Some of these methods are simple, while some are quite sophisticated. In some firms, managers use more than one method of cost estimation. The results of the different methods are then combined by the cost analyst on the basis of experience and judgment. We will examine five methods of cost estimation in the context of the Tasty Donuts illustration.

Account-Classification Method

The **account-classification method** of cost estimation, also called **account analysis,** involves a careful examination of the organization's ledger accounts. The cost analyst classifies each cost item in the ledger as a variable, fixed, or semivariable cost. The classification is based on the analyst's knowledge of the organization's activities and experience with the organization's costs. For example, it may be obvious to the analyst going through the ledger that direct-material cost is variable, building depreciation is fixed, and utility costs are semivariable.

Once the costs have been classified, the cost analyst estimates cost amounts by examining job-cost sheets, paid bills, labor time cards, or other source documents. A property-tax bill, for example, will provide the cost analyst with the information needed to estimate this fixed cost. This examination of historical source documents is combined with other knowledge that may affect costs in the future. For example, the municipal government may have recently enacted a 10 percent property-tax increase, which takes effect the following year.

For some costs, particularly those classified as semivariable, the cost analyst may use one of several more systematic methods of incorporating historical data in the cost estimate. These methods are discussed next.

Visual-Fit Method

When a cost has been classified as semivariable, or when the analyst has no clear idea about the behavior of a cost item, it is helpful to plot recent observations of the cost at various activity levels. The resulting **scatter diagram** helps the analyst to visualize the relationship between cost and the level of activity (or cost driver). To illustrate, suppose Tasty Donuts' controller has compiled the following historical data for the company's utility costs.

Month	Utility Cost for Month		Activity or Cost Driver (dozens of bakery items sold per month)
January	$5,100	....	75,000
February	5,300	....	78,000
March	5,650	....	80,000
April................	6,300	....	92,000
May	6,400	....	98,000
June	6,700	....	108,000
July.................	7,035	....	118,000
August	7,000	....	112,000
September	6,200	....	95,000
October	6,100	....	90,000
November	5,600	....	85,000
December	5,900	....	90,000

The scatter diagram of these data is shown in Exhibit 6-8. The cost analyst can *visually fit a line* to these data by laying a ruler on the plotted points. The line is positioned so that a roughly equal number of plotted points lie above and below the line. Using this method, Tasty Donuts' controller visually fit the line shown in Exhibit 6-8.

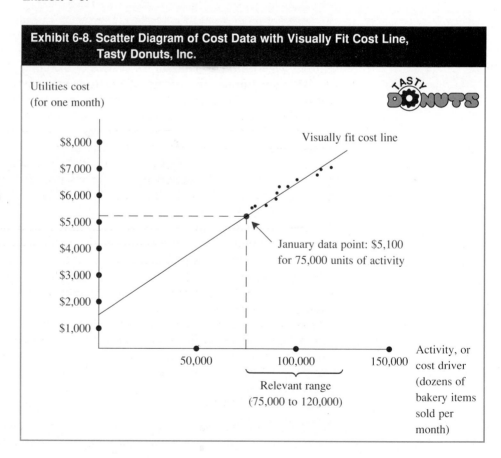

Exhibit 6-8. Scatter Diagram of Cost Data with Visually Fit Cost Line, Tasty Donuts, Inc.

Just a glance at the visually-fit cost line reveals that Tasty Donuts' utilities cost is a semivariable cost *within the relevant range*. The scatter diagram provides little or no information about the cost relationship outside the relevant range. Recall from the discussion of Tasty Donuts' utilities cost (see Exhibit 6-7) that the controller believes the cost behavior pattern to be curvilinear over the *entire range* of activity. This judgment is based on the controller's knowledge of the firm's facilities and an understanding of electricity usage by the modern bakery equipment and the older bakery equipment. As Exhibit 6-7 shows, however, the curvilinear utilities cost can be approximated closely by a semivariable cost *within the relevant range*. The data plotted in the scatter diagram lie within the relevant range. Consequently, the data provide a sound basis for the semivariable approximation that the controller has chosen to use.

The visually-fit cost line in Exhibit 6-8 intercepts the vertical axis at $1,500. Thus, $1,500 is the estimate of the fixed-cost component in the semivariable-cost approximation. To determine the variable cost per unit, subtract the fixed cost from the total cost at any activity level. The remainder is the total variable cost for that activity level. For example, the total variable cost for an activity level of 50,000 dozen items is $2,500 (total cost of $4,000 minus fixed cost of $1,500). This yields a variable cost of $.05 per dozen bakery items ($.05 = $2,500 ÷ 50,000).

These variable and fixed cost estimates were used for the semivariable cost approximation discussed earlier in the chapter (Exhibit 6-7). These estimates are only valid *within the relevant range.*

Evaluation of Visual-Fit Method The scatter diagram and visually-fit cost line provide a valuable first step in the analysis of any cost item suspected to be semivariable or curvilinear. The method is easy to use and to explain to others, and it provides a useful view of the overall cost behavior pattern.

The visual-fit method also enables an experienced cost analyst to spot **outliers** in the data. An outlier is a data point that falls far away from the other points in the scatter diagram and is not representative of the data. Suppose, for example, that the data point for January had been $6,000 for 75,000 units of activity. Exhibit 6-8 reveals that such a data point would be way out of line with the rest of the data. The cost analyst would follow up on such a cost observation to discover the reasons behind it. It could be that the data point is in error. Perhaps a utility bill was misread when the data were compiled, or possibly the billing itself was in error. Another possibility is that the cost observation is correct but due to unusual circumstances. Perhaps Toronto experienced a record cold wave during January that required the company's donut shops to use unusually high amounts of electric heat. Perhaps an oven in the bakery had a broken thermostat during January that caused the oven to overheat consistently until discovered and repaired. An outlier can result from many causes. If the outlier is due to an error or very unusual circumstances, the data point should be ignored in the cost analysis.

The primary drawback of the visual-fit method is its lack of objectivity. Two cost analysts may draw two different visually-fit cost lines. This is not usually a serious problem, however, particularly if the visual-fit method is combined with other, more objective methods.

High-Low Method

In the **high-low method** the semivariable cost approximation is computed using exactly two data points. The high and low *activity levels* are chosen from the available data set. These activity levels, together with their associated cost levels, are used to compute the variable and fixed cost components as follows:

$$\begin{array}{c}\textbf{Variable cost per} \\ \textbf{dozen bakery items}\end{array} = \frac{\textbf{difference in cost levels}}{\textbf{difference in activity levels}}$$

$$= \frac{\$7,035 - \$5,100}{118,000 - 75,000} = \frac{\$1,935}{43,000}$$

$$= \$.045 \text{ per dozen items}$$

Now we can compute the total variable cost at either the high or low activity level. At the low activity of 75,000 dozen items, the total variable cost is $3,375 ($.045 × 75,000). Subtracting the total variable cost from the total cost at the 75,000 dozen activity level, we obtain the fixed-cost estimate of $1,725 ($5,100 − $3,375).

Exhibit 6-9 presents a graph of Tasty Donuts' utilities cost, which is based on the high-low method of cost estimation. As in any cost-estimation method, this estimate of the cost behavior pattern should be *restricted to the relevant range.*

Evaluation of High-Low Method The high-low method is more objective than the visual-fit method, since it leaves no room for the cost analyst's judgment. However, the high-low method suffers from a major weakness. Only two data points are used to estimate the cost behavior pattern; the remainder of the data points are

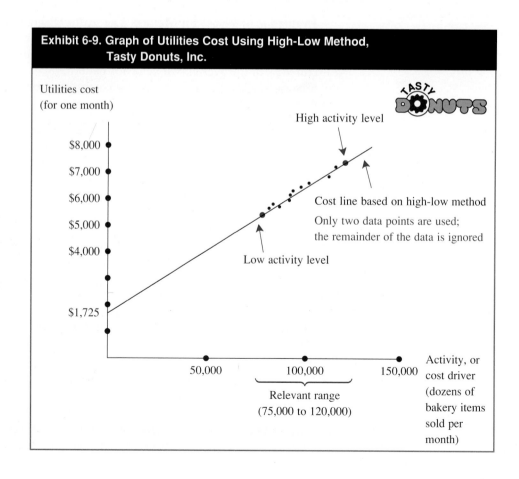

Exhibit 6-9. Graph of Utilities Cost Using High-Low Method, Tasty Donuts, Inc.

ignored. In this regard, the visual-fit method is superior to the high-low method, since the former approach uses all of the available data.

Least-Squares Regression Method

Statistical techniques may be used to estimate objectively a cost behavior pattern using all of the available data. The most common of these methods is called *least-squares regression.* To understand this method, examine Exhibit 6-10, which repeats the scatter diagram of Tasty Donuts' utilities cost data. The exhibit also includes a cost line that has been drawn through the plotted data points. Since the data points do not lie along a perfectly straight line, any cost line drawn through this scatter diagram will miss some or most of the data points. The objective is to draw the cost line so as to make the deviations between the cost line and the data points as small as possible.

In the **least-squares regression method,** the cost line is positioned so as to *minimize* the sum of the *squared deviations* between the cost line and the data points. The inset to Exhibit 6-10 depicts this technique graphically. Note that the deviations between the cost line and the data points are measured vertically on the graph rather than perpendicular to the line. The cost line fit to the data using least-squares regression is called a *least-squares regression line* (or simply a **regression line**).

Why is the regression method based on minimizing the *squares* of the deviations between the cost line and the data points? A complete answer to this question lies in the theory of statistics. In short, statistical theorists have proven that a least-squares regression line possesses some very desirable properties for making cost predictions and drawing inferences about the estimated relationship between cost and activity. As always, the least-squares regression estimate of the cost behavior pattern should be restricted to the relevant range.

Equation Form of Least-Squares Regression Line The least-squares regression line shown in Exhibit 6-10 may be represented by the equation of a straight line. In the equation shown below, X denotes Tasty Donuts' activity level for a month, and Y denotes the estimated utilities cost for that level of activity. The intercept of the line on the vertical axis is denoted by a, and the slope of the line is denoted by b. *Within the relevant range, a* is interpreted as an estimate of the fixed-cost component, and b is interpreted as an estimate of the variable cost per unit of activity.

$$Y = a + bX \tag{1}$$

In regression analysis, X is referred to as the **independent variable,** since it is the variable upon which the estimate is based. Y is called the **dependent variable,** since its estimate depends on the independent variable.

The least-squares regression line for Tasty Donuts' utilities cost is shown below in equation form.

$$Y \;=\; 1{,}920 \;+\; .0448\,X$$

Estimated utilities cost for one month   Activity level for one month

Within the relevant range of activity, the regression estimate of the fixed-cost component is $1,920 per month, and the regression estimate of the variable-cost component

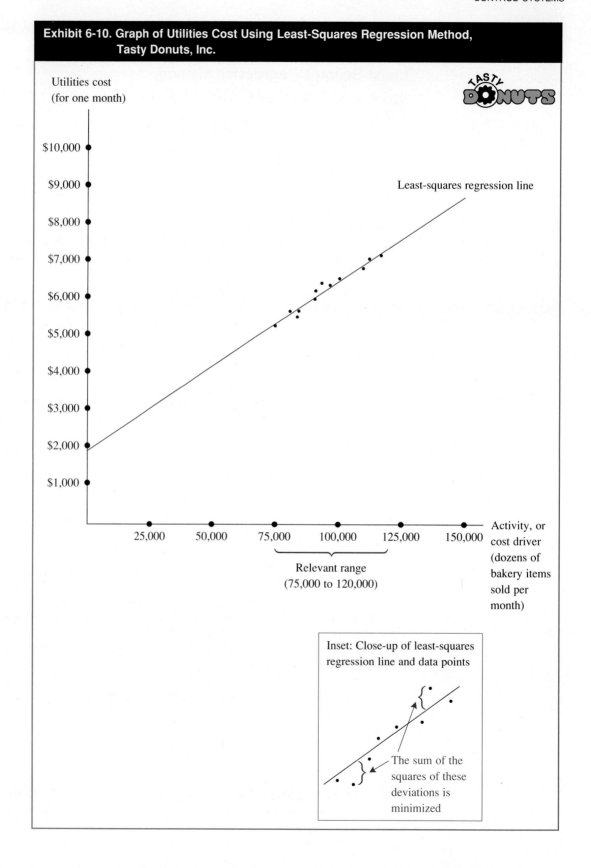

Exhibit 6-10. Graph of Utilities Cost Using Least-Squares Regression Method,
Tasty Donuts, Inc.

is $.0448 per dozen bakery items. These estimates are derived in the appendix at the end of this chapter, which you may want to read now.

Evaluation of Least-Squares Regression Method We have seen that least-squares regression is an objective method of cost estimation that makes use of all available data. Moreover, the regression line has desirable statistical properties for making cost predictions and drawing inferences about the relationship between cost and activity. The method does require considerably more computation than either the visual-fit or high-low method. However, computer programs are readily available to perform least-squares regression, even on small desktop computers.

Evaluating a Particular Least-Squares Regression Line We have seen the benefits of least-squares regression *in general.* How does a cost analyst evaluate a *particular* regression line based on a specific set of data? A number of criteria may be used, including *economic plausibility* and *goodness of fit.*

The cost analyst should always evaluate a regression line from the perspective of *economic plausibility.* Does the regression line make economic sense? Is it inuitively plausible to the cost analyst? If not, the analyst should reconsider using the regression line to make cost predictions. It may be that the chosen independent variable is not a good predictor of the cost behavior being analyzed. Perhaps another independent variable should be considered. Alternatively, there may be errors in the data upon which the regression is based. Rechecking the data will resolve this issue. It could be that fundamental assumptions that underlie the regression method have been violated. In this case, the analyst may have to resort to some other method of cost estimation.

Another criterion commonly used to evaluate a particular regression line is to assess its **goodness of fit.** Statistical methods can be used to determine objectively how well a regression line fits the data upon which it is based. If a regression line fits the data well, a large proportion of the variation in the dependent variable will be explained by the variation in the independent variable. One frequently used measure of goodness of fit is described in the appendix at the end of this chapter.[3]

Multiple Regression

In each of the cost-estimation methods discussed so far, we have based the estimate on a single independent variable. Moreover, all of Tasty Donuts' cost behavior patterns were specified with respect to a single activity (or cost driver), dozens of bakery items produced and sold. However, there may be two or more independent variables that are important predictors of cost behavior.

To illustrate, we will continue our analysis of Tasty Donuts' utilities costs. The company uses electricity for two primary purposes: operating cooking equipment, such as deep-fat fryers and ovens, and heating the bakery and donut shops. The cost of electricity for food production is a function of the firm's activity, as measured in dozens of bakery items produced and sold. However, the cost of electricity for restaurant heating is related more closely to the number of customers than to the number of bakery items sold. A restaurant's heating costs go up each time the restaurant door is opened, resulting in loss of heat. Two customers purchasing half a dozen donuts each result in greater heating costs than one customer buying a dozen donuts.

---

[3] We have only scratched the surface of regression analysis as a tool for cost estimation. For an expanded discussion of the least-squares regression method, see any statistics text.

Suppose Tasty Donuts' controller wants to estimate a cost behavior pattern for utilities cost that is based on both units of sales and number of customers. The method of **multiple regression** may be used for this purpose. Multiple regression is a statistical method that estimates a linear (straight-line) relationship between one dependent variable and two or more independent variables. In Tasty Donuts' case, the following regression equation would be estimated.

$$Y = a + b_1 X_1 + b_2 X_2 \tag{2}$$

where Y denotes the dependent variable, utilities cost
  X_1 denotes the first independent variable, dozens of bakery items sold
  X_2 denotes the second independent variable, number of customers served

In regression equation (2), a denotes the regression estimate of the fixed-cost component. b_1 denotes the regression estimate of the variable utilities cost per dozen bakery items, and b_2 denotes the regression estimate of the variable utilities cost per customer served. The multiple-regression equation will likely enable Tasty Donuts' controller to make more accurate cost predictions than could be made with the **simple regression** discussed previously. A simple regression is based on a single independent variable. Multiple regression is covered more extensively in cost-accounting and statistics texts.

Data Collection Problems

Regardless of the method used, the resulting cost estimation will be only as good as the data upon which it is based. The collection of data appropriate for cost estimation requires a skilled and experienced cost analyst. Six problems frequently complicate the process of data collection:

1. *Missing data* Misplaced source documents or failure to record a transaction can result in missing data.
2. *Outliers* We have discussed these extreme observations of cost-activity relationships. If outliers are determined to represent errors or highly unusual circumstances, they should be eliminated from the data set.
3. *Mismatched time periods* The units of time for which the dependent and independent variables are measured may not match. For example, production activity may be recorded daily but costs may be recorded monthly. A common solution is to aggregate the production data to get monthly totals.
4. *Trade-offs in choosing the time period* In choosing the length of the time period for which data are collected, there are conflicting objectives. One objective is to obtain as many data points as possible, which implies a short time period. Another objective is to choose a long enough time period to ensure that the accounting system has accurately associated costs with time periods. If, for example, a cost that resulted from production activity in one period is recorded in a later period, the cost and activity data will not be matched properly. Longer time periods result in fewer recording lags in the data.
5. *Allocated and discretionary costs* Fixed costs are often *allocated* on a per-unit-of-activity basis. For example, fixed manufacturing-overhead costs such as depreciation are allocated to units of production. As a result, such

costs may appear to be variable in the cost records. *Discretionary* costs often are budgeted in a manner that makes them appear variable. A cost such as advertising, for example, may be fixed once management decides on the level of advertising. If management's policy is to budget advertising on the basis of sales dollars, however, the cost will appear to be variable to the cost analyst. An experienced analyst will be wary of such costs and take steps to learn how their amounts are determined.

6. *Inflation* During periods of inflation, historical cost data may not reflect future cost behavior. One solution is to choose historical data from a period of low inflation and then factor in the current inflation rate. Other, more sophisticated approaches are also available, and they are covered in cost-accounting texts.

Engineering Method of Cost Estimation

All of the methods of cost estimation examined so far are based on historical data. Each method estimates the relationship between cost and activity by studying the relationship observed in the past. A completely different method of cost estimation is to study the process that results in cost incurrence. This approach is called the **engineering method** of cost estimation. In a manufacturing firm, for example, a detailed study is made of the production technology, materials, and labor used in the manufacturing process. Rather than asking the question, What was the cost of material last period?, the engineering approach is to ask, How much material should be needed and how much should it cost? Industrial engineers often perform *time and motion studies,* which determine the steps required for people to perform the manual tasks that are part of the production process. Cost behavior patterns for various types of costs are then estimated on the basis of the engineering analysis. Engineering cost studies are time-consuming and expensive, but they often provide highly accurate estimates of cost behavior. Moreover, in rapidly evolving, high-technology industries, there may not be any historical data on which to base cost estimates. Such industries as genetic engineering, superconductivity, and electronics are evolving so rapidly that historical data are often irrelevant in estimating costs.

Effect of Learning on Cost Behavior

In many production processes, production efficiency increases with experience. As cumulative production output increases, the average labor time required per unit declines. A graphical expression of this phenomenon is called a **learning curve.** An example is shown in panel A of Exhibit 6-11. In this learning curve, when cumulative output doubles, the average labor time per unit declines by 20 percent. Panel B of Exhibit 6-11 displays the total labor time and average labor time per unit for various levels of cumulative output. As cumulative output doubles from 5 to 10 units, for example, the average labor time per unit declines by 20 percent, from 100 hours per unit to 80 hours per unit.

Learning curves have been used extensively in such industries as aircraft production, shipbuilding, and electronics to assist cost analysts in predicting labor costs. These cost predictions are then used in scheduling production, budgeting, setting product prices, and other managerial decisions. The following illustration demonstrates the importance of the learning-curve phenomenon.

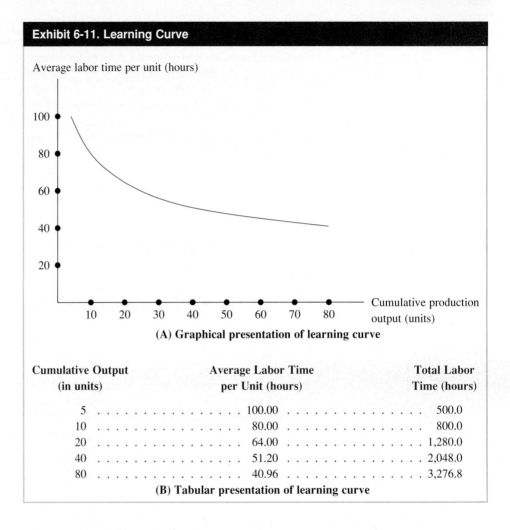

Exhibit 6-11. Learning Curve

Average labor time per unit (hours)

(A) Graphical presentation of learning curve

Cumulative Output (in units)	Average Labor Time per Unit (hours)	Total Labor Time (hours)
5	100.00	500.0
10	80.00	800.0
20	64.00	1,280.0
40	51.20	2,048.0
80	40.96	3,276.8

(B) Tabular presentation of learning curve

ILLUSTRATION FROM MANAGEMENT-ACCOUNTING PRACTICE

B. F. Goodrich Company

Fortune magazine reported that the learning curve for tire manufacturing helped B. F. Goodrich Company in formulating its business strategy. The learning curve showed the firm's management that it was not necessary to sell tires to automobile manufacturers at a minimal markup in order to obtain enough experience with a tire model to drive down costs. It was possible to move far enough out on the curve for efficient production simply by selling tires in the more lucrative market for replacements.[4]

Costs and Benefits of Information

We have discussed a variety of cost-estimation methods ranging from the simple visual-fit approach to sophisticated techniques involving regression or learning curves. Which of these methods is best? In general, the more sophisticated methods will yield more accurate cost estimates than the simpler methods. However, even a

---

[4] "The Decline of the Experience Curve," *Fortune,* October 5, 1981.

sophisticated method still yields only an imperfect estimate of an unknown cost-behavior pattern.

All cost-estimation methods are based on simplifying assumptions. The two most important assumptions are as follows:

1. Except for the multiple-regression technique, all of the methods assume that cost behavior depends on *one activity variable*. Even multiple regression uses only a small number of independent variables. In reality, however, costs are affected by a host of factors including the weather, the mood of the employees, and the quality of the raw materials used.
2. Another simplifying assumption usually made in cost estimation is that cost behavior patterns are linear (straight lines) within the relevant range.

The cost analyst must consider on a case-by-case basis whether these assumptions are reasonable. The analyst also must decide when it is important to use a more sophisticated, and more costly, cost-estimation method and when it is acceptable to use a simpler approach. As in any choice among managerial-accounting methods, the costs and benefits of the various cost-estimation techniques must be weighed.

WORK MEASUREMENT

Cost-estimation methods are used to determine the behavior of all kinds of costs in a wide variety of organizations. In organizations such as banks, insurance companies, and many government agencies, cost estimation is facilitated by a technique called **work measurement.** Work measurement is the systematic analysis of a task for the purpose of determining the inputs needed to perform the task. The analysis focuses on such factors as the steps required to perform the task, the time needed to complete each step, the number and type of employees required, and the materials or other inputs needed. Some examples of work-measurement applications are listed below.

Industry	Activity	Work Measure
Banking	Processing loan applications	Applications processed
U.S. Postal Service	Sorting mail	Pieces of mail sorted
Manufacturing	Billing customers	Invoices processed
Internal Revenue Service	Processing tax returns	Returns processed
Insurance	Settling claims	Claims settled
Airlines	Ticketing passengers	Passengers ticketed

The measure of work or activity is often called a **control factor unit.** In the loan department of a bank, for example, the control factor unit is loan applications processed. To apply work measurement to the loan department, experts would first determine the steps required to process a loan application, the most efficient order for those steps, and the average amount of time that should be needed for each step. The first steps in processing a car-loan application, for example, would be to (1) verify that the application is complete and filled out properly, and (2) verify the applicant's credit references, through phone calls or computer checks.

After the task has been analyzed in terms of its steps, time needed, and other inputs required, the cost of each of these steps is computed. For example, suppose it takes an average of 15 minutes to verify that a loan application is completed properly,

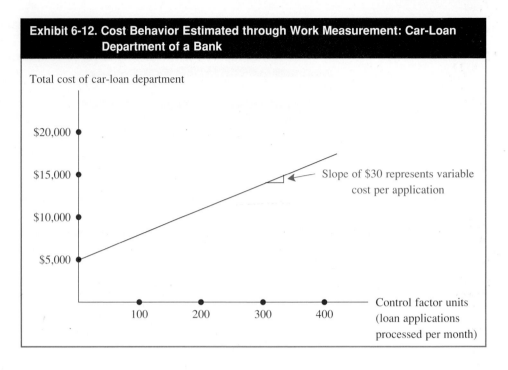

Exhibit 6-12. Cost Behavior Estimated through Work Measurement: Car-Loan Department of a Bank

and the loan-department employee's time costs $10.00 per hour (including fringe benefits). The cost of this loan-processing step is computed as follows:

$$\begin{pmatrix}\text{Time required to verify} \\ \text{application is complete}\end{pmatrix} \times \begin{pmatrix}\text{cost of compensating employee} \\ \text{for one hour, including fringe} \\ \text{benefits}\end{pmatrix}$$

$$(1/4 \text{ hour}) \times (\$10.00 \text{ per hour}) = \$2.50$$

The cost of each step in processing the loan application is determined in a similar manner. Other inputs, such as computer time and long-distance telephone calls, are also included in the cost of processing the loan application. When the average cost of processing a loan application has been determined, the cost behavior for this activity can be specified. Suppose that the variable cost of processing each car-loan application is determined to be $30. In addition, the car-loan department has fixed costs of $5,000 per month, which includes the department manager's salary and depreciation on office space and equipment. Then the cost behavior of the car-loan-processing activity may be represented by the graph in Exhibit 6-12.

Work measurement has been successfully employed in a wide variety of organizations. The following case in point illustrates its use in the financial-services industry.

ILLUSTRATION FROM MANAGEMENT-ACCOUNTING PRACTICE

American Express Company

American Express Company initiated a productivity-improvement program for its customer service department. Traditional industrial engineering methods were used to analyze various customer service tasks, such as replacing a lost American Express card. Each task was broken down into the steps required to perform the task, and the time required to complete each step was determined. *Business Week* reported that American Express executives feel the program has improved both department performance and customer satisfaction.[5]

CHAPTER SUMMARY

Understanding an organization's cost behavior enables managers to anticipate changes in cost when the organization's level of activity (or cost driver) changes. Cost predictions, which are based on cost behavior patterns, facilitate planning, control, and decision making throughout the organization. These cost predictions should be confined to the relevant range, which is the range of activity expected for the organization.

A variety of cost behavior patterns exist, ranging from simple variable and fixed costs to more complicated semivariable and curvilinear costs. Several cost-estimation methods are used to determine which cost behavior pattern is appropriate for a particular cost. The account-classification, visual-fit, high-low, and regression methods are all based on an analysis of historical cost data observed at a variety of activity levels. The engineering and work-measurement methods are based on a detailed analysis of the process in which the costs are incurred. These methods are frequently used in combination to provide a more accurate cost estimate.

As in selecting any managerial-accounting technique, the choice of a cost-estimation method involves a trade-off of costs and benefits. More accurate estimation methods provide the benefits of better information, but they are often more costly to apply.

REVIEW PROBLEMS ON COST BEHAVIOR AND ESTIMATION

Problem 1

Erie Hardware, Inc. operates a chain of four retail stores. Data on the company's maintenance costs for its store buildings and furnishings are presented below.

Month	Maintenance Cost	Sales
January	$53,000	$600,000
February	55,000	700,000
March	47,000	550,000
April	51,000	650,000
May	45,000	500,000
June	49,000	610,000

Using the high-low method, estimate and graph the cost behavior for the firm's maintenance costs.

Problem 2

The *Keystone Sentinel* is a weekly newspaper sold throughout Pennsylvania. The following costs were incurred by its publisher during a week when circulation was

[5] "Boosting Productivity at American Express," *Business Week,* October 5, 1981, pp. 66–68.

100,000 newspapers: total variable costs, $40,000; total fixed costs, $66,000. Fill in your predictions for the cost amounts listed below.

	Circulation	
	110,000 Newspapers	**120,000 Newspapers**
Total variable cost	———————	———————
Variable cost per unit	———————	———————
Total fixed cost.	———————	———————
Fixed cost per unit.	———————	———————

Solution to Review Problems

Problem 1

	Sales	**Cost**
At high activity.	$700,000	$55,000
At low activity	500,000	45,000
Difference.	$200,000	$10,000

$$\text{Variable cost per sales dollar} = \frac{\$10,000}{200,000} = \$.05 \text{ per sales dollar}$$

Total cost at $700,000 of sales	$55,000
Total variable cost at $700,000 of sales (700,000 × $.05).	35,000
Difference is total fixed cost	$20,000

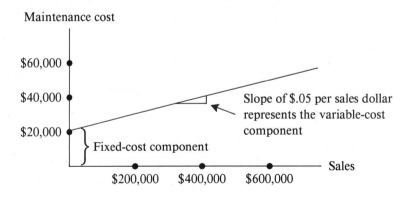

Problem 2

	Circulation	
	110,000 Newspapers	**120,000 Newspapers**
Total variable cost.	$40,000 × $\left(\frac{110,000}{100,000}\right)$ = $44,000	$40,000 × $\left(\frac{120,000}{100,000}\right)$ = $48,000
Variable cost per unit	$40,000 ÷ 100,000 = $.40	$40,000 ÷ 100,000 = $.40
Total fixed cost .	$66,000	$66,000
Fixed cost per unit	$66,000 ÷ 110,000 = $.60	$66,000 ÷ 120,000 = $.55

KEY TERMS   **Account-classification method (also called account analysis),** p. 235; **Committed cost,** p. 233; **Control factor unit,** p. 245; **Cost behavior,** p. 223; **Cost estimation,** p. 235; **Cost prediction,** p. 223; **Curvilinear cost,** p. 231; **Dependent variable,** p. 239; **Discretionary cost,** p. 233; **Engineered cost,** p. 233; **Engineering method,** p. 243; **Fixed cost,** p. 227; **Goodness of fit,** p. 241; **High-low method,** p. 237; **Independent variable,** p. 239; **Learning curve,** p. 243; **Least-squares regression method,** p. 239; **Multiple regression,** p. 242; **Outlier,** p. 237; **Regression line,** p. 239; **Relevant range,** p. 232; **Scatter diagram,** p. 235; **Semivariable (or mixed) cost,** p. 230; **Simple regression,** p. 242; **Step-fixed costs,** p. 229; **Step-variable costs,** p. 226; **Variable cost,** p. 225; **Visual-fit method,** p. 235; **Work measurement,** p. 245.

Finding the Least-Squares Regression Estimates

The least-squares regression line, which is shown below in equation form, includes two estimates. These estimates, which are called *parameters,* are denoted by a and b in the equation.

$$Y = a + bX \tag{3}$$

where   **X denotes the independent variable (activity level for one month)**
               Y denotes the dependent variable (cost for one month)

Statistical theorists have shown that these parameters are defined by the following two equations, which are called **normal equations.**[6]

$$\Sigma XY = a\Sigma X + b\Sigma X^2 \tag{4}$$
$$\Sigma Y = na + b\Sigma X \tag{5}$$

where   **n denotes the number of data points**
            Σ denotes summation; for example, ΣY denotes the sum of the Y (cost) values in the data

Equations (4) and (5) may be rearranged algebraically to solve for a and b, as shown below.

$$a = \frac{(\Sigma Y)(\Sigma X^2) - (\Sigma X)(\Sigma XY)}{n(\Sigma X^2) - (\Sigma X)(\Sigma X)} \tag{6}$$

$$b = \frac{n(\Sigma XY) - (\Sigma X)(\Sigma Y)}{n(\Sigma X^2) - (\Sigma X)(\Sigma X)} \tag{7}$$

Panel A of Exhibit 6-13 shows the numbers used to compute the regression parameters, a and b, for Tasty Donuts' utilities cost. Notice that the X values (activity levels) are expressed in thousands to make the numbers more convenient to handle.

---

[6] The derivation of these equations, which requires calculus, is covered in any introductory statistics text.

Exhibit 6-13. Computation of Least-Squares Regression Estimates

Tasty Donuts, Inc.

Month of Preceding Year	Utility Cost for Month Y	Activity during Month (in thousands) X	X^2	XY	Predicted Cost Based on Regression Line* Y'	$(Y-Y')^2$	$(Y-\bar{Y})^2$
January	5,100	75	5,625	382,500	5,282	33,124	1,014,216
February	5,300	78	6,084	413,400	5,416	13,456	651,384
March	5,650	80	6,400	452,000	5,506	20,736	208,925
April	6,300	92	8,464	579,600	6,043	66,049	37,217
May	6,400	98	9,604	627,200	6,312	7,744	85,800
June	6,700	108	11,664	723,600	6,761	3,721	351,550
July	7,035	118	13,924	830,130	7,209	30,276	861,029
August	7,000	112	12,544	784,000	6,940	3,600	797,300
September	6,200	95	9,025	589,000	6,178	484	8,634
October	6,100	90	8,100	549,000	5,954	21,316	50
November	5,600	85	7,225	476,000	5,730	16,900	257,134
December	5,900	90	8,100	531,000	5,954	2,916	42,884
Total	73,285	1,121	106,759	6,937,430	73,285	220,322	4,316,123

(A) For computation of regression estimates, a and b   **(B) For computation of R^2**

*For example, at 75,000 units of activity, Y' is computed as follows:
  $Y' = 1,920 + (44.82)(75) = 5,282$

Substituting these numbers into equations (6) and (7) yields the following estimates for a and b.

$$a = \frac{(73,285)(106,759) - (1,121)(6,937,430)}{(12)(106,759) - (1,121)(1,121)} = 1,920* \qquad (8)$$

$$b = \frac{(12)(6,937,430) - (1,121)(73,285)}{(12)(106,759) - (1,121)(1,121)} = 44.82* \qquad (9)$$

* Rounded.

The intercept of the regression line on the vertical axis is $1,920. The slope of the line, as solved in equation (9) above, is $44.82. However, the X (activity) values were rescaled in Exhibit 6-13 to be expressed in thousands. Thus, the b value computed above represents a variable cost of $44.82 *per thousand* dozen bakery items. Dividing this number by 1,000 yields the variable cost per dozen bakery items, $.0448 (rounded to the nearest hundredth of a cent). This is the regression estimate of the variable cost per dozen bakery items reported earlier in the chapter.

Goodness of Fit The goodness of fit for Tasty Donuts' regression line may be measured by the **coefficient of determination,** commonly denoted by R^2. This measure is defined as the percentage of the variability of the dependent variable about its mean that is explained by the variability of the independent variable about its mean. The higher the R^2, the better the regression line fits the data. The interpretation for a high R^2 is that the independent variable is a good predictor of the behavior of the dependent variable. In cost estimation, a high R^2 means that the cost analyst can be relatively confident in the cost predictions based on the estimated cost behavior pattern.

Statistical theorists have shown that R^2 can be computed using the following formula:

$$R^2 = 1 - \frac{\Sigma(Y - Y')^2}{\Sigma(Y - \overline{Y})^2} \qquad (10)$$

where
- Y **denotes the observed value of the dependent variable (cost) at a particular activity level**
- Y' **denotes the predicted value of the dependent variable (cost), based on the regression line, at a particular activity level**
- $\overline{Y}$ **denotes the mean (average) observation of the dependent variable (cost)**

The numbers needed for the R^2 formula are displayed in panel B of Exhibit 6-13 for the Tasty Donuts illustration. Substituting these numbers in equation (10) yields the following value for R^2:

$$R^2 = 1 - \frac{220{,}322}{4{,}316{,}123} = .949 \qquad (11)$$

This is a high value for R^2, and Tasty Donuts' controller may be quite confident in the resulting cost predictions. As always, these predictions should be confined to the relevant range.

KEY TERMS: APPENDIX   Coefficient of determination, p. 252; **Normal equations,** p. 250.

REVIEW QUESTIONS

6-1. Define the following terms, and explain the relationship between them: (a) cost estimation, (b) cost behavior, and (c) cost prediction.

6-2. Describe the importance of cost behavior patterns in planning, control, and decision making.

6-3. Draw a simple graph of each of the following types of cost behavior patterns: (a) variable, (b) step-variable, (c) fixed, (d) step-fixed, (e) semivariable, and (f) curvilinear.

6-4. Explain the impact of an increase in the level of activity (or cost driver) on (a) total fixed cost and (b) fixed cost per unit of activity.

6-5. Suggest an appropriate activity base (or cost driver) for each of the following organizations: (a) hotel, (b) hospital, (c) computer manufacturer, (d) computer sales store, (e) computer repair service, and (f) public accounting firm.

6-6. Explain why a manufacturer's cost of supervising production might be a step-fixed cost.

6-7. Explain the impact of an increase in the level of activity (or cost driver) on (a) total variable cost and (b) variable cost per unit.

6-8. Using graphs, show how a semivariable (or mixed) cost behavior pattern can be used to approximate (a) a step-variable cost and (b) a curvilinear cost.

6-9. Indicate which of the following descriptions is most likely to describe each cost listed below.

Descriptions	Costs
Engineered cost	Annual cost of maintaining an interstate highway
Committed cost	Cost of ingredients in a breakfast cereal
Discretionary cost	Cost of advertising for a credit card company
	Depreciation on an insurance company's computer
	Cost of charitable donations that are budgeted as 1 percent of sales revenue
	Research and development costs, which have been budgeted at $50,000 per year

6-10. A cost analyst showed the company president a graph that portrayed the firm's utility cost as semivariable. The president criticized the graph by saying, "This fixed-cost component doesn't look right to me. If we shut down the plant for six months, we wouldn't incur half of those costs." How should the cost analyst respond?

6-11. What is meant by a learning curve? Explain its role in cost estimation.

6-12. How is work measurement used in cost estimation? Suggest an appropriate control factor unit for the following tasks.

    a. Handling materials at a loading dock.

    b. Registering vehicles at a county motor vehicle office.

    c. Picking apples.

    d. Inspecting computer components in an electronics firm.

6-13. What is an outlier? List some possible causes of outliers. How should outliers be handled in cost estimation?

6-14. Explain the cost-estimation problem caused by allocated and discretionary costs.

6-15. Describe the visual-fit method of cost estimation. What are the main strengths and weaknesses of this method?

6-16. What is the chief drawback of the high-low method of cost estimation? What problem could an outlier cause if the high-low method were used?

6-17. Explain the meaning of the term *least squares* in the least-squares regression method of cost estimation.

6-18. Use an equation to express a least-squares regression line. Interpret each term in the equation.

6-19. Distinguish between simple regression and multiple regression.

6-20. Briefly describe two methods that can be used to evaluate a particular least-squares regression line.

EXERCISES *Exercise 6-21 Behavior of Fixed and Variable Costs; Television Station.* WMEJ is an independent television station run by a major state university. The station's broadcast hours vary during the year depending on whether the university is in session. The station's production-crew and supervisory costs are as follows for July and September.

Cost Item	Cost Behavior	Cost Amount	Broadcast Hours during Month
Production crew.......................	Variable		
July		$5,000	400
September..........................		8,000	640
Supervisory employees.................	Fixed		
July		5,000	400
September..........................		5,000	640

REQUIRED:

1. Compute the cost per broadcast hour during July and September for each of these cost items.
2. What will be the total amount incurred for each of these costs during December, when the station's activity will be 420 broadcast hours?
3. What will be the cost per broadcast hour in December for each of the cost items?

Exercise 6-22   Graphing Cost Behavior Patterns; Hospital. Draw a graph of the cost behavior for each of the following costs incurred by the Northern California Regional Medical Center. The hospital measures monthly activity in patient days. Label both axes and the cost line in each graph.

1. The cost of salaries and fringe benefits for the administrative staff total $11,000 per month.
2. The cost of food varies in proportion to the number of patient days of activity. In January, the hospital provided 3,000 patient days of care, and food costs amounted to $24,000.
3. The hospital's laboratory costs include two components: (a) $40,000 per month for compensation of personnel and depreciation on equipment, and (b) $10 per patient day for chemicals and other materials used in performing the tests.
4. The cost of utilities depends on how many wards the hospital needs to use during a particular month. During months with activity under 2,000 patient days of care, two wards are used, resulting in utility costs of $10,000. During months with greater than 2,000 patient days of care, three wards are used, and utility costs total $15,000.
5. Many of the hospital's nurses are part-time employees. As a result, the hours of nursing care provided can be easily adjusted to the amount required at any particular time. The cost of wages and fringe benefits for nurses is approximately $2,500 for each block of 200 patient days of care provided during a month. For example, nursing costs total $2,500 for 1 to 200 patient days, $5,000 for 201 to 400 patient days, $7,500 for 401 to 600 patient days, and so forth.

Exercise 6-23   Approximating a Curvilinear Cost; City Department. The behavior of the annual maintenance and repair cost in the Bus Transportation Department of Gulf City, Texas is shown by the solid line in the following graph. The dashed line depicts a semivariable-cost approximation of the department's repair and maintenance cost.

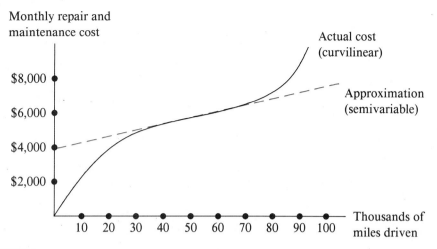

REQUIRED:

1. What is the actual (curvilinear) and estimated (semivariable) cost shown by the graph for each of the following activity levels?

	Actual	**Estimated**
a. 10,000 miles		
b. 40,000 miles		
c. 50,000 miles		
d. 60,000 miles		
e. 90,000 miles		

2. How good an approximation does the semivariable-cost pattern provide if the department's relevant range is 40,000 to 60,000 miles per month? What if the relevant range is 10,000 to 90,000 miles per month?

Exercise 6-24   Account-Classification Method; Food Processing. Lehigh Valley Meat Company produces one of the best sausage products in Pennsylvania. The company's controller used the account-classification method to compile the following information.

    a. Inspection of several invoices from meat packers indicated that meat costs the company $1.00 per pound of sausage produced. *VAR*

    b. Depreciation schedules revealed that monthly depreciation on buildings and equipment is $20,000. *Fix*

    c. Wage records showed that compensation for production employees costs $.80 per pound of sausage produced. *VAR*

    d. Payroll records showed that supervisory salaries total $8,000 per month. *F*

    e. Utility bills revealed that the company incurs utility costs of $4,000 per month plus $.20 per pound of sausage produced. *Sem-VAR*

REQUIRED:

1. Classify each cost item as variable, fixed, or semivariable.
2. Write a cost formula to express the cost behavior of the firm's production costs. (Use the form $Y = a + bX$, where Y denotes production cost, and X denotes quantity of sausage produced.)

Exercise 6-25 *Visual-Fit Method; Hospital.* Cincinnati Regional Hospital has incurred the following costs in its diagnostic blood lab over the past year.

Month	Blood Tests Completed	Cost
January	5,900	$89,000
February	6,000	91,000
March	3,050	61,000
April	4,500	74,500
May	7,100	99,000
June	6,200	95,600
July	4,700	74,800
August	6,100	90,000
September	5,300	87,000
October	4,900	76,200
November	4,800	78,100
December	5,050	80,700

REQUIRED:

1. Plot the data above in a scatter diagram. Assign cost to the vertical axis and the number of blood tests to the horizontal axis. Visually fit a line to the plotted data.
2. Using the visually fit line, estimate the monthly fixed cost and the variable cost per blood test.

Exercise 6-26 *Estimating Cost Behavior; High-Low Method.* The prior year's monthly utilities costs incurred by the San Fernando Canning Company are as follows:

Month	Pounds of Food Canned	Cost
January	21,000	$22,100
February	22,000	22,000
March	24,000	22,450
April	30,000	22,900
May	32,000	23,350
June	40,000	28,000
July	41,000	24,100
August	39,000	24,950
September	35,000	23,400
October	30,000	22,800
November	30,000	23,000
December	28,000	22,700

REQUIRED:

1. Use the high-low method to estimate the company's utilities cost behavior and express it in equation form.
2. Predict the utilities cost for a month in which 25,000 pounds of food are canned.

Exercise 6-27 *Estimating Cost Behavior; Visual-Fit Method.* Refer to the data in the preceding exercise.

REQUIRED:

$Y = 29,000 + .1x$
$O = 29,200 + .1(25,000)$
$= 22,500$

1. Draw a scatter diagram and graph the company's utilities cost behavior using the visual-fit method.
2. Predict the utilities cost for a month in which 25,000 pounds of food are canned.
3. What peculiarity is apparent from the scatter diagram? What should the cost analyst do?

Exercise 6-28   High-Low Method; Tour Company. Baystate Bus Tours has incurred the following bus maintenance costs over the first half of the year.

Month	Miles Traveled by Tour Buses	Cost
January..................	8,000	$11,000
February.................	8,500	11,400
March..................	10,600	11,600
April....................	12,700	11,700
May	15,000	12,000
June	20,000	12,500

REQUIRED:

1. Use the high-low method to estimate the variable cost per tour mile traveled and the fixed cost per month.
2. Develop a formula to express the cost behavior exhibited by the company's maintenance cost.
3. Predict the level of maintenance cost that would be incurred during a month when 22,000 tour miles are driven.

Exercise 6-29   Learning Curve; High Technology. Weathereye, Inc. manufactures weather satellites. The final assembly and testing of the satellites is a largely manual operation involving dozens of highly trained electronics technicians. The following learning curve has been estimated for the firm's newest satellite model, which is about to enter production.

Assembly and Testing

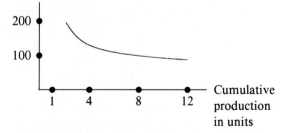

REQUIRED:

1. What will be the average labor time required to assemble and test each satellite when the company has produced four satellites? Eight satellites?
2. What will be the total labor time required to assemble and test all satellites produced if the firm manufactures only four satellites? Eight satellites?

3. How can the learning curve be used in the company's budgeting process? In setting cost standards?

Exercise 6-30 Work Measurement; Government Agency. The state Department of Taxation processes and audits income-tax returns for state residents. The state tax commissioner has recently begun a program of work measurement to help in estimating the costs of running the department. The control factor unit used in the program is the number of returns processed. The analysis revealed that the following variable costs are incurred in auditing a typical tax return.

Time spent by clerical employees, 10 hours at $12 per hour
Time spent by tax professional, 20 hours at $25 per hour
Computer time, $50 per audit.
Telephone charges, $10 per audit
Postage, $2 per audit

In addition, the department incurs $10,000 of fixed costs each month that are associated with the process of auditing returns.

REQUIRED: Draw a graph depicting the monthly costs of auditing state tax returns. Label the horizontal axis "Control factor units: tax returns audited."

Exercise 6-31 Estimating Cost Behavior by Multiple Methods (Appendix). Sunshine State Markets, a chain of convenience grocery stores in Fort Lauderdale, has store hours that fluctuate from month to month as the tourist trade in the community varies. The utility costs for one of the company's stores are listed below for the past six months.

Month	Total Hours of Operation	Total Utility Cost
January	500	$1,600
February	550	1,620
March	600	1,700
April	700	1,900
May	450	1,350
June	400	1,300

REQUIRED:

1. Use the high-low method to estimate the cost behavior for the store's utility costs. Express the cost behavior in formula form ($Y = a + bX$). What is the variable utility cost per hour of operation?
2. Draw a scatter diagram of the store's utility costs. Visually fit a cost line to the plotted data. Estimate the variable utility cost per hour of operation.
3. Use least-squares regression to estimate the cost behavior for the store's utility cost. Express the cost behavior in formula form. What is the variable utility cost per hour of operation?
4. During December, the store will be open 650 hours. Predict the store's total utility cost for December using each of the cost-estimation methods employed in requirements (1), (2), and (3).

Exercise 6-32   Airline; Least-Squares Regression (Appendix). Recent monthly costs of providing on-board flight service incurred by Atlantic Airlines are shown below.

Month	Thousands of Passengers	Cost of On-Board Flight Service (in thousands)
January	15	$18
February	18	20
March	17	19
April	16	18
May	17	18
June	16	19

REQUIRED:

1. Use least-squares regression to estimate the cost behavior of the airline's on-board flight service. Express the cost behavior in equation form. (Hint: When interpreting the regression, remember that the data are given in thousands.)
2. Calculate and interpret the R^2 value for the regression line.

PROBLEMS   *Problem 6-33   Cost Behavior Patterns in a Variety of Settings.* For each of the cost items described below, choose the graph on the next page that best represents it.

1. The salaries of the security personnel at a factory. The security guards are on duty around the clock.
2. The cost of chartering a private airplane. The cost is $400 per hour for the first three hours of a flight. Then the charge drops to $300 per hour.
3. The wages of table-service personnel in a restaurant. The employees are part-time workers, who can be called upon for as little as two hours at a time.
4. The salary costs of the shift supervisors at a truck depot. Each shift is eight hours. The depot operates with one, two, or three shifts at various times of the year.
5. The cost of sheet metal used to manufacture automobiles.
6. The cost of utilities at a university. For low student enrollments, utility costs increase with enrollment, but at a decreasing rate. For large student enrollments, utility costs increase at an increasing rate.
7. The cost of telephone service, which is based on the number of message units per month. The charge is $1.00 per message unit, for up to 500 message units. Additional message units (above 500) are free.
8. The cost of the nursing staff in a hospital. The staff always has a minimum of 10 nurses on duty. Additional nurses are used depending on the number of patients in the hospital. The hospital administrator estimates that this additional nursing staff costs approximately $200 per patient day.
9. The cost of electricity during peak-demand periods is based on the following schedule.

Up to 10,000 kilowatt-hours (KWH) .... $.10 per KWH
Above 10,000 kilowatt-hours .... $.14 per KWH

The price schedule is designed to discourage overuse of electricity during periods of peak demand.

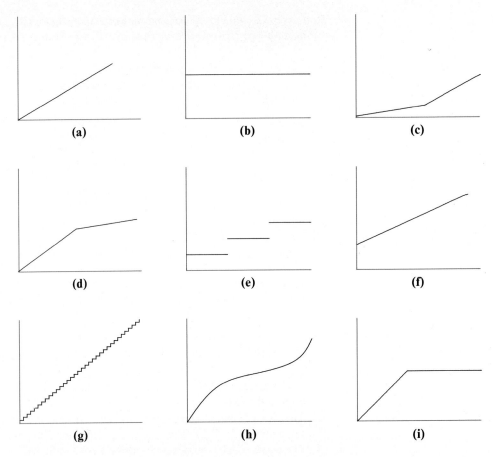

(a) (b) (c)

(d) (e) (f)

(g) (h) (i)

Problem 6-34 *Account-Classification Method; Private School.* The Community School of
Music has hired you as a consultant to help in analyzing the behavior of the school's costs. Use
the account-classification method of cost estimation to classify each of the following costs as
variable, fixed, or semivariable. Before classifying the costs, choose an appropriate measure for
the school's activity.

1. Salaries and fringe benefits of the school's full-time teachers.
2. Wages of the school's part-time assistant recital instructors. These employees are
   hired on a temporary basis. For each student enrolled in the school's music
   programs, four hours of assistant instructor time are needed per week.
3. Depreciation on the school's musical instruments.
4. Rent for the building in which the school operates.
5. Electricity for the school. The school pays a fixed monthly charge plus $.10 per
   kilowatt-hour of electricity.
6. Repairs on musical instruments. The school employs a full-time repair technician.
   Repair jobs that are beyond the technician's capability are taken to a local
   musical-instrument dealer for repairs.
7. Fee charged by a local public accounting firm to audit the school's accounting
   records.
8. Salaries and fringe benefits of the school's full-time administrative staff.
9. Cost of buying books, sheet music, and other academic materials that are supplied
   to the students by the school.

Problem 6-35   *High-Low Method; Advertising Agency.* J. K. Armer and Associates, an advertising agency, is accumulating data to be used in preparing its annual profit plan for the coming year. The cost behavior pattern of the firm's equipment maintenance costs must be determined. The accounting staff has suggested the use of an equation, in the form of $Y = a + bX$, for maintenance costs. Data regarding the maintenance hours and costs for last year are as follows:

	Hours of Maintenance Service	Maintenance Costs
January	480	$4,200
February	320	3,000
March	400	3,600
April	300	2,820
May	500	4,350
June	310	2,960
July	320	3,030
August	520	4,470
September	490	4,260
October	470	4,050
November	350	3,300
December	340	3,160
Total	4,800	43,200
Average	400	3,600

REQUIRED:

1. Using the high-low method of cost estimation, estimate the behavior of J. K. Armer and Associates' maintenance costs. Express the cost behavior pattern in equation form.
2. Using your answer to requirement (1), what is the variable component of the maintenance cost?
3. Compute the predicted maintenance cost at 600 hours of activity.
4. Compute the variable cost per hour and the fixed cost per hour at 600 hours of activity. Explain why the fixed cost per hour could be misleading.

(CMA, adapted)

Problem 6-36   *Approximating a Curvilinear Cost; Visual-Fit Method; Hospital.* Midstate Hospital has experienced widely varying patient loads in its outpatient clinic during the clinic's first year of operation. The hospital's controller has recorded the following administrative costs in the outpatient clinic during the recently completed year.

Month	Patient Load	Administrative Cost
January	500	$ 7,000
February	200	2,100
March	1,000	10,000
April	1,300	11,900
May	600	8,300
June	1,500	16,100

Month	Patient Load	Administrative Cost
July	900	$ 9,200
August	1,100	10,200
September	300	4,100
October	700	9,400
November	1,200	11,100
December	1,400	13,900

Midstate Hospital's administrator, Meg Johnston, has attributed the clinic's varying patient load to initial confusion among area residents about the services to be offered in the newly opened clinic. She does not believe the first year's widely fluctuating patient load will be experienced again in the future. Johnston has estimated that the clinic's relevant range of monthly activity in the future will be 600 to 1,200 patients.

REQUIRED:

1. Draw a scatter diagram of the clinic's administrative costs during its first year of operation.
2. Visually fit a curvilinear cost line to the plotted data.
3. Mark the clinic's relevant range of activity on the scatter diagram by drawing vertical lines at each end of the relevant range.
4. Visually fit a semivariable cost line to approximate the curvilinear cost behavior pattern within the clinic's relevant range.
5. Estimate the fixed and variable cost components of the visually-fit semivariable cost line.
6. Use an equation to express the semivariable cost approximation of the clinic's administrative costs.
7. What is your prediction of the clinic's administrative cost during a month when 800 patients visit the clinic? When 400 patients visit? Which one of your visually-fit cost lines did you use to make each of these predictions? Why?

Problem 6-37   *Evaluation of Cost-Estimation Models; Retail.* Motomation Corporation plans to acquire several retail automotive parts stores as part of its expansion program. Motomation carries out an extensive review of possible acquisitions prior to making any decision to approach a specific company. Projections of future financial performance are one of the aspects of such a review. One form of projection relies heavily on using past performance (normally 10 prior years) to estimate future performance.

Currently, Motomation is conducting a review of Atlas Auto Parts, a regional chain of retail automotive parts stores. Among the financial data to be projected for Atlas is the future rental cost for its stores. The following schedule presents the rent and revenues (in millions of dollars) for the past 10 years.

Year	Revenues	Annual Rent Expense
19x0	$22	$1.00
19x1	24	1.15
19x2	36	1.40
19x3	27	1.10
19x4	43	1.55
19x5	33	1.25

Year	Revenues	Annual Rent Expense
19x6	45	$1.65
19x7	48	1.60
19x8	61	1.80
19x9	60	1.95

The following three alternative methods have been suggested for estimating future rental expense.

Alternative A:

A least-squares regression using time as the independent variable was performed. The resulting formula is as follows:

$$\text{Rental expense} = .93 + .0936\,T$$

where T is equal to the year (i.e., 19x9 = 10).

Alternative B:

The annual rental expense was related to annual revenues through regression. The formula for predicting rental expense in this case is as follows:

$$\text{Rental expense} = .5597 + .02219\,X$$

where X is equal to revenues ÷ 1,000,000 (e.g., X for 19x9 is 60).

Alternative C:

Rental expense was calculated as a percentage of revenues using the average for the 10-year period 19x0 through 19x9.

REQUIRED:

1. Calculate for each of the three alternatives the rental expense estimate for Atlas Auto Parts for the next year, assuming the projected revenue will be the same as the 19x9 revenue (i.e., $60 million).
2. Discuss the advantages and disadvantages of each of the three alternative methods for estimating the rental expense for Atlas Auto Parts.
3. Identify one method from alternatives A, B, or C that you would recommend Motomation Corporation use to estimate rental expense. Explain why you selected that alternative.
4. Discuss whether a statistical technique is an appropriate method for estimating rental expense in this situation.

(CMA, adapted)

Problem 6-38   Interpreting Least-Squares Regression; Manufacturer. Omega Company manufactures several different products. The company is making plans for the introduction of a new product, which it will sell for $8 per unit. The following estimates have been made for manufacturing costs on 100,000 units to be produced the first year.

Direct materials	$50,000
Direct labor	$40,000 (The labor rate is $16 per hour.)

Overhead costs have not yet been estimated for the new product, but monthly data on total production and overhead cost for the past 24 months have been analyzed using least-squares regression. The following results were derived from the regression and will provide the basis for overhead cost estimates for the new product.

Regression Analysis Results ($Y = a + bX$)

Dependent variable (Y):	Factory overhead costs
Independent variable (X):	Direct-labor hours
Computed values:	
Intercept	$40,000
Coefficient of independent variable	$2.10

REQUIRED:

1. Write the regression equation using the estimates given above.
2. Compute the predicted overhead cost at an activity level of 20,000 direct-labor hours.
3. What suggestions would you make to the company controller regarding the evaluation of the regression equation?

(CMA, adapted)

Problem 6-39 *Approximating a Step-Variable Cost; Visual-Fit Method; Golf Course.* Rolling Hills Golf Association is a nonprofit, private organization, which operates three 18-hole golf courses near Philadelphia. The organization's financial director has just analyzed the course maintenance costs incurred by the golf association during recent summers. The courses are maintained by a full-time crew of four people, who are assisted by part-time employees. These employees are typically college students on their summer vacations. The course maintenance costs vary with the number of people using the course. Since a large part of the maintenance work is done by part-time employees, the maintenance crew size can easily be adjusted to reflect current needs. The financial director's analysis revealed that the course maintenance cost includes two components:

1. A fixed component of $12,000 per month (when the courses are open).
2. A step-variable cost component. For each additional 1 to 10 people teeing off in one day, $20 in costs are incurred. Thus if 101 to 110 people tee off, $220 of additional cost will be incurred. If 111 to 120 people tee off, $240 of additional cost will be incurred.

REQUIRED:

1. Draw a graph of Rolling Hills Golf Association's course maintenance costs. Show on the graph the fixed-cost component and the step-variable cost component. Label each clearly.
2. Use a semivariable cost behavior pattern to approximate the golf association's course maintenance cost behavior. Visually fit the semivariable cost line to your graph.
3. Using your graph, estimate the variable and fixed cost component included in your semivariable approximation. Express this approximate cost behavior pattern in equation form.
4. Fill in the following table of cost predictions.

Predicted Course Maintenance Costs

	Using Fixed Cost Coupled with Step-Variable Cost Behavior Pattern	Using Semivariable Cost Approximation
180 people tee off	?	?
186 people tee off	?	?

Problem 6-40   Choosing among Regression Estimates; Manufacturer (Appendix). Lockit Company manufactures door knobs for residential homes and apartments. Lockit is considering the use of simple and multiple regression analysis to forecast annual sales, because previous forecasts have been inaccurate. The sales forecast will be used to initiate the budgeting process and to identify the underlying process that generates sales.

Larry Guilette, the controller of Lockit, has considered many possible independent variables and equations to predict sales and has narrowed his choices to four equations. Guilette used annual observations from 20 prior years to estimate each of the four equations.

A list of definitions of the variables used in the four equations is given below.

S_t = Forecasted sales (in dollars) for Lockit in time period t
S_{t-1} = Actual sales (in dollars) for Lockit in time period $t-1$
G_t = Forecasted United States gross national product in time period t
G_{t-1} = Actual United States gross national product in time period $t-1$
N_{t-1} = Lockit's net income in time period $t-1$

Equation	Dependent Variable	Independent Variable(s)	Intercept	Coefficient of Independent Variable	Coefficient of Determination
1	S_t	S_{t-1}	$ 500,000	$ 1.10	.94
2	S_t	G_t	$1,000,000	$ .00001	.90
3	S_t	G_{t-1}	$ 900,000	$ .000012	.81
4	S_t	N_{t-1}	$ 600,000	$10.00	.96
		G_t		$ .000002	
		G_{t-1}		$ .000003	

REQUIRED:

1. Write equations (2) and (4) in the form $Y = a + bX$. In equation (4) there will be three independent variables (X values).
2. If actual sales are $1,500,000 in 19x1, what would be the forecasted sales for Lockit in 19x2?
3. Explain the meaning of the coefficient of determination.
4. Why might Larry Guilette prefer equation (3) to equation (2)?
5. List some advantages and disadvantages of using equation (4) to forecast annual sales.

(CMA, adapted)

Problem 6-41   Work Measurement; Cost Estimation with Different Methods; Wholesaler. Long Island Marine Supply is a wholesaler for a large variety of boating and fishing equipment. The company's controller has recently completed a cost study of the firm's material-handling department, in which he used work measurement to quantify the department's activity. The control factor unit used in the work-measurement study was hundreds of pounds of equipment unloaded or loaded at the company's loading dock. The controller compiled the following data.

Month	Control Factor Units of Activity		Material-Handling Department Costs
January............	1,000	....	$10,200
February...........	1,300	....	11,250
March.............	1,600	....	11,300
April	1,800	....	11,700
May...............	2,000	....	12,000
June..............	2,400	....	12,550
July	2,200	....	11,100
August............	2,600	....	12,120
September..........	1,800	....	11,400
October...........	1,400	....	11,350
November..........	1,200	....	11,350
December	1,100	....	11,050

REQUIRED:

1. Draw a scatter diagram of the cost data for the material-handling department.
2. Visually fit a cost line to the scatter diagram.
3. Estimate the variable and fixed components of the department's cost behavior pattern using the visually-fit cost line.
4. Use an equation to express the department's cost behavior.
5. Estimate the material-handling department's cost behavior using the high-low method. Use an equation to express the results of this estimation method.
6. Write a brief memo to the company's president explaining why the cost estimates developed in requirements (4) and (5) differ.
7. Predict the company's material-handling costs for a month when 2,500 control factor units of activity is recorded. Use each of your cost equations to make the prediction. Which prediction would you prefer to use? Why?

Problem 6-42 Evaluating Regression Estimates; Advertising and Promotion Decisions (Appendix). John Wood, a financial analyst for a major automobile corporation, has been monitoring the funds used in advertising campaigns and the funds used for automobile factory rebates. Financial and sales data have been accumulated for the last 24 months. Wood contends that there may be a relationship between the level of automobile sales and funds expended on advertising and factory rebates. If such a relationship can be determined, the company may be able to estimate sales demand based on various levels of funding commitments for one or both types of expenditures.

Regression equations and statistical values, which were developed for the various relationships between variables, are as follows. The meanings of the notations used in the equations are:

A = advertising funds (in $100,000 increments)
R = funds for factory rebates (in $1,000,000 increments)
D = customer sales demand (automobiles sold) in 10,000 unit increments

	Equation 1	**Equation 2**
Equation	$D = 2.455 + .188A$	$D = 2.491 + .44R$
Coefficient of determination	.414	.314

	Equation 3	**Equation 4**
Equation	$R = 6.052 + .005A$	$D = -.184 + .186A + .437R$
Coefficient of determination	.0002	.703

REQUIRED:

1. If the corporation is projecting advertising expenditures amounting to $1,500,000 and factory rebate expenditures amounting to $12,000,000 for the next time period, calculate expected customer demand in units using: (a) equation (1), and (b) equation (4).
2. Select the regression equation that would be most advantageous to predict customer sales demand. Explain why it is the best.
3. Explain the significance of equation (3) and its value for the regression-analysis evaluation.
4. Each of the regression equations includes a constant. Discuss the meaning of the constant term included in regression equation (4).
5. What is the significance of the value being negative in regression equation (4)? Explain your answer.

(CMA, adapted)

Problem 6-43   *Comparing Regression and High-Low Estimates; Manufacturer.* The controller of Connecticut Electronics Company believes that the identification of the variable and fixed components of the firm's costs will enable the firm to make better planning and control decisions. Among the costs the controller is concerned about is the behavior of indirect-materials cost. She believes there is a correlation between machine hours and the amount of indirect materials used.

A member of the controller's staff has suggested that least-squares regression be used to determine the cost behavior of indirect materials. The regression equation shown below was developed from 40 pairs of observations.

$$S = \$200 + \$4H$$

where S = total monthly costs of indirect materials
         H = machine hours per month

REQUIRED:

1. Explain the meaning of "200" and "4" in the regression equation $S = \$200 + \$4H$.
2. Calculate the estimated cost of indirect materials if 900 machine hours are to be used during a month.
3. To determine the validity of the cost estimate computed in requirement (2), what question would you ask the controller about the data used for the regression?
4. The high and low activity levels during the past four years, as measured by machine hours, occurred during April, 19x2, and August, 19x2, respectively. Data concerning machine hours and indirect-materials usage follow.

	April 19x2	August 19x2
Machine hours	1,100	800
Indirect supplies:		
Beginning inventory	$1,200	$ 950
Ending inventory	1,550	2,900
Purchases	6,000	6,100

Determine the cost of indirect materials used during April, 19x2 and August 19x2.

5. Use the high-low method to estimate the behavior of the company's indirect-material cost. Express the cost behavior pattern in equation form.
6. Which cost estimate would you recommend to the controller, the regression estimate or the high-low estimate? Why?

(CMA, adapted)

Problem 6-44   Computing Least-Squares Regression Estimates; Airport Costs (Appendix).
Jefferson County Airport handles several daily commuter flights and many private flights. The county budget officer has compiled the following data regarding airport costs and activity over the past year.

Month	Flights Originating at Jefferson County Airport (in hundreds)	Airport Costs (in thousands)
January	15	$21
February	11	20
March	8	17
April	14	19
May	9	18
June	10	19
July	12	20
August	11	18
September	14	24
October	10	19
November	12	21
December	9	17

REQUIRED:

1. Draw a scatter diagram of the airport costs shown above.
2. Compute the least-squares regression estimates of the variable and fixed cost components in the airport's cost behavior pattern. Use the formulas given in the appendix to the chapter. (Use the data as they are presented in the problem: flights measured in hundreds and costs measured in thousands of dollars.)
3. Write the least-squares regression equation for the airport's costs.
4. Predict the airport's costs during a month when 1,300 flights originate at the airport.
5. Compute the coefficient of determination (R^2) for the regression equation. Briefly interpret the R^2.

CASE   **Case 6-45   Interpreting Least-Squares Regression; Commerical Landscaping Service.** Turfland Corporation provides commercial landscaping services. Linda Drake, the firm's owner, wants to develop cost estimates that she can use to prepare bids on jobs. After analyzing the firm's costs, Drake has developed the following preliminary cost estimates for each 1,000 square feet of landscaping.

Direct materials $400
Direct labor (5 direct-labor hours at $10 per hour)   50
Overhead (at $18 per direct-labor hour).   90
 Total cost per 1,000 square feet. $540

Drake is quite certain about the estimates for direct materials and direct labor. However, she is not as comfortable with the overhead estimate. The estimate for overhead is based on the overhead costs that were incurred during the past 12 months as presented in the schedule below. The estimate of $18 per direct-labor hour was determined by dividing the total overhead costs for the 12-month period ($648,000) by the total direct-labor hours (36,000).

	Total Overhead	Regular Direct-Labor Hours	Overtime Direct-Labor Hours*	Total Direct-Labor Hours
January	$ 47,000	2,380	20	2,400
February	48,000	2,210	40	2,250
March	56,000	2,590	210	2,800
April.	54,000	2,560	240	2,800
May	57,000	3,030	470	3,500
June.	65,000	3,240	760	4,000
July	64,000	3,380	620	4,000
August	56,000	3,050	350	3,400
September	54,000	2,910	190	3,100
October	53,000	2,760	40	2,800
November	47,000	2,770	30	2,800
December	47,000	2,120	30	2,150
Total	$648,000	33,000	3,000	36,000

* The overtime premium is 50 percent of the direct-labor wage rate.

Drake believes that overhead is affected by total montly direct-labor hours. Drake decided to perform a least-squares regression of overhead (OH) on total direct-labor hours (TDLH). The following regression formula was obtained.

$$OH = 26,200 + 9.25TDLH$$

REQUIRED:

1. The overhead rate developed from the least-squares regression is different from Linda Drake's preliminary estimate of $18 per direct-labor hour. Explain the difference in the two overhead rates.
2. Using the overhead formula that was derived from the least-squares regression, determine a total variable cost estimate for each 1,000 square feet of landscaping.
3. Linda Drake has been asked to submit a bid on a landscaping project consisting of 50,000 square feet. Drake estimates that 40 percent of the direct-labor hours required for the project will be on overtime. Calculate the incremental costs that should be included in any bid that Drake would submit on this project. Use the overhead formula derived from the least-squares regression.
4. Should Turfland Corporation rely on the overhead formula derived from the least-squares regression as the basis for the variable overhead component of its cost estimate? Explain your answer.

(CMA, adapted)

SEATTLE
CONTEMPORARY
THEATER

Chapter 7 Cost-Volume-Profit Analysis

After completing this chapter, you should be able to:

- Compute a break-even point using the contribution-margin approach and the equation approach.

- Compute the contribution margin ratio, and use it to find the break-even point in sales dollars.

- Prepare a cost-volume-profit graph and explain how it is used.

- Apply CVP analysis to determine the effect on profit of changes in fixed expenses, variable expenses, sales prices, and sales volume.

- Compute the break-even point and prepare a profit-volume graph for a multiproduct enterprise.

- List and discuss the key assumptions of CVP analysis.

- Prepare and interpret a contribution income statement.

- Explain the role of cost structure and operating leverage in CVP relationships.

What effect on profit can United Airlines expect if it adds a flight on the Chicago to New York route? How will NBC's profit change if the ratings increase for its evening news program? How many patient days of care must Massachusetts General Hospital provide to break even for the year? What happens to this break-even patient load if the hospital leases a new computerized system for patient records?

Each of these questions concerns the effects on costs and revenues when the organization's activity changes. The analytical technique used by managerial accountants to address these questions is called **cost-volume-profit analysis.** Often called **CVP analysis** for short, this technique summarizes the effects of changes in an organization's *volume* of activity on its *costs,* revenue, and *profit*. Cost-volume-profit analysis can be extended to cover the effects on profit of changes in selling prices, service fees, costs, income-tax rates, and the organization's mix of products or services. What will happen to profit, for example, if the New York Yankees raise ticket prices for stadium seats? In short, CVP analysis provides management with a comprehensive overview of the effects on revenue and costs of all kinds of short-run financial changes.

Although the word *profit* appears in the term, cost-volume-profit analysis is not confined to profit-seeking enterprises. Managers in nonprofit organizations also routinely use CVP analysis to examine the effects of activity and other short-run changes on revenue and costs. For example, as the state of Florida gains nearly a thousand people a day in population, the state's political leaders must analyze the effects of this change on sales-tax revenues and the cost of providing services, such as education, transportation, and police protection. Managers at such diverse nonprofit institutions as the New York Public Library, Harvard University, and the United Way all use CVP analysis as a routine operational tool.

ILLUSTRATION OF COST-VOLUME-PROFIT ANALYSIS

SEATTLE CONTEMPORARY THEATER

To illustrate the various analytical techniques used in cost-volume-profit analysis, we will focus on a performing arts organization. The Seattle Contemporary Theater has recently been formed as a nonprofit enterprise to bring contemporary drama to the Seattle area. The organization has a part-time, unpaid board of trustees, comprised of local professional people who are avid theater fans. The board has hired the following full-time employees.

> *Managing director* (Responsibilities include overall management of the organization; direction of six plays per year.)
> *Artistic director* (Responsibilities include hiring of actors and production crews for each play; direction of six plays per year.)
> *Business manager and producer* (Responsibilities include managing the organization's business functions and ticket sales; direction of the production crews, who handle staging, lighting, costuming, and makeup.)

The board of trustees has negotiated an agreement with the city of Seattle to hold monthly performances in a historic theater owned by the city. The theater has not been used for 30 years, but the city has agreed to refurbish it and to provide lighting and sound equipment. In return, the city will receive a monthly rental charge of $10,000 per month plus $8 for each theater ticket sold.

Projected Expenses and Revenue

The theater's business manager and producer, George Bernard, has made the following projections for the first few years of operation.

Fixed expenses per month:	
Theater rental...	$10,000
Employees' salaries and fringe benefits........................	8,000
Actors' wages..	15,000
(to be supplemented with local volunteer talent)	
Production crew's wages....................................	5,600
(to be supplemented with local volunteers)	
Playwrights' royalties for use of plays........................	5,000
Insurance..	1,000
Utilities—fixed portion.....................................	1,400
Advertising and promotion..................................	800
Administrative expenses....................................	1,200
Total fixed expenses per month	$48,000

Variable expenses per ticket sold:

City's charge per ticket for use of theater..................... $	8
Other miscellaneous expenses (for example, printing of playbills and tickets, variable portion of utilities)	2
Total variable cost per ticket sold........................... $	10

Revenue:

Price per ticket....................................... $	16

Importance of Cost Behavior Notice that the theater's expenses have been categorized according to their cost behavior: fixed or variable. Analyzing an organization's cost behavior, the topic of Chapter 6, is a necessary first step in any cost-volume-profit analysis. As we proceed through this chapter, the data pertaining to Seattle Contemporary Theater will be an important part of our cost-volume-profit analysis.

THE BREAK-EVEN POINT

As the first step in the CVP analysis for Seattle Contemporary Theater, we will find the **break-even point.** The break-even point is the volume of activity where the organization's revenues and expenses are equal. At this amount of sales, the organization has no profit or loss; it *breaks even.*

Contribution-Margin Approach

Seattle Contemporary Theater will break even when the organization's revenue from ticket sales is equal to its expenses. How many tickets must be sold during one month (one play's run) for the organization to break even?

Each ticket sells for $16, but $10 of this is used to cover the variable expense per ticket. This leaves $6 per ticket to *contribute* to covering the fixed expenses of $48,000. When enough tickets have been sold in one month so that these $6 contributions per ticket add up to $48,000, the organization will break even for the month. Thus, we may compute the break-even volume of tickets as follows:

$$\frac{\text{Fixed expenses}}{\text{Contribution of each ticket toward covering fixed expenses}} = \frac{\$48,000}{\$6} = 8,000$$

Seattle Contemporary Theater must sell 8,000 tickets during a play's one-month run to break even for the month.

The $6 amount that remains of each ticket's price, after the variable expenses are covered, is called the **unit contribution margin.** The general formula for computing the break-even sales volume in units is given below.

$$\frac{\text{Fixed expenses}}{\text{Unit contribution margin}} = \text{break-even point (in units)} \tag{1}$$

Contribution-Margin Ratio Sometimes management prefers that the break-even point be expressed in sales *dollars* rather than *units.* Seattle Contemporary Theater's break-even point in sales dollars is computed as follows.

Break-even point in units (tickets)	8,000
Sales price per unit	× $16
Break-even point in sales dollars	$128,000

The following computation provides an alternative way to determine the break-even point in sales dollars.

$$\dfrac{\text{Fixed expenses}}{\dfrac{\text{Unit contribution margin}}{\text{Unit sales price}}} = \dfrac{\$48,000}{\dfrac{\$6}{\$16}} = \dfrac{\$48,000}{.375} = \$128,000$$

The unit contribution margin divided by the unit sales price is called the **contribution-margin ratio.** This ratio can also be expressed as a percentage, in which case it is called the *contribution-margin percentage.* Seattle Contemporary Theater's contribution-margin ratio is .375 (in percentage form, 37.5%). Thus, the organization's break-even point in sales dollars may be found by dividing its fixed expenses by its contribution-margin ratio. The logic behind this approach is that 37.5 percent of each sales dollar is available to make a contribution toward covering fixed expenses. The general formula is given below.

$$\dfrac{\text{Fixed expenses}}{\text{Contribution-margin ratio}} = \text{break-even point in sales dollars} \qquad (2)$$

Equation Approach

An alternative approach to finding the break-even point is based on the profit equation. Income (or profit) is equal to sales revenue minus expenses. If expenses are separated into variable and fixed expenses, the essence of the income (profit) statement is captured by the following equation.

$$\text{Sales revenue} - \text{variable expenses} - \text{fixed expenses} = \text{profit}$$

This equation can be restated as follows:

$$\left[\left(\begin{array}{c}\text{Unit}\\\text{sales price}\end{array}\right) \times \left(\begin{array}{c}\text{sales}\\\text{volume}\\\text{in units}\end{array}\right)\right] - \left[\left(\begin{array}{c}\text{unit}\\\text{variable}\\\text{expense}\end{array}\right) \times \left(\begin{array}{c}\text{sales}\\\text{volume}\\\text{in units}\end{array}\right)\right] - \left(\begin{array}{c}\text{fixed}\\\text{expenses}\end{array}\right)$$

$$= \text{profit} \quad (3)$$

To find Seattle Contemporary Theater's break-even volume of ticket sales per month, we define profit in equation (3) to be zero.

$$(\$16 \times X) - (\$10 \times X) - \$48,000 = 0$$

$$\left[\left(\begin{array}{c}\text{Unit}\\\text{sales price}\end{array}\right) \times \left(\begin{array}{c}\text{sales}\\\text{volume}\\\text{in units}\end{array}\right)\right] - \left[\left(\begin{array}{c}\text{unit}\\\text{variable}\\\text{expense}\end{array}\right) \times \left(\begin{array}{c}\text{sales}\\\text{volume}\\\text{in units}\end{array}\right)\right] - \left(\begin{array}{c}\text{fixed}\\\text{expenses}\end{array}\right)$$

$$= \left(\begin{array}{c}\text{break-even}\\\text{profit}\\\text{(zero)}\end{array}\right) \quad (4)$$

where X **denotes the number of units of sales (tickets) required to break even.**

Equation (4) can be solved for X as shown below.

$$\underbrace{\$16X - \$10X} - \$48,000 = \quad 0$$

$$\$6X \qquad\qquad = \$48,000$$

$$X = \frac{\$48,000}{\$6} = 8,000$$

Using the equation approach, we have arrived at the same general formula for computing the break-even sales volume (formula 1).

The contribution-margin and equation approaches are two equivalent techniques for finding the break-even point. Both methods reach the same conclusion, so personal preference dictates which approach should be used. The following example illustrates the importance of the break-even point to a major U.S. auto maker.

ILLUSTRATION FROM MANAGEMENT-ACCOUNTING PRACTICE

Chrysler Corporation

For several years Chrysler Corporation operated at a loss. The company received loan guarantees from the United States government to enable it to survive until it became profitable again. Then the company initiated a cost-cutting program that reduced both variable and fixed costs drastically. Over a three-year period, these cost reductions enabled Chrysler's management to decrease the firm's break-even point from 2.2 million to 1.2 million automobiles. By reducing its break-even point, Chrysler was able to survive and to return to the ranks of profitable companies.[1]

GRAPHING COST-VOLUME-PROFIT RELATIONSHIPS

While the break-even point conveys useful information to management, it does not show how profit changes as activity changes. To capture the relationship between profit and volume of activity, a **cost-volume-profit graph** is commonly used. The following steps are used to prepare a CVP graph for Seattle Contemporary Theater. The graph is displayed in Exhibit 7-1. Notice that the graph shows the *relevant range,* which is the range of activity within which management expects the theater to operate.

Step 1: Draw the axes of the graph. Label the vertical axis in dollars and the horizontal axis in units of sales (tickets).
Step 2: Draw the fixed-expense line. It is parallel to the horizontal axis, since fixed expenses do not change with activity.
Step 3: Compute *total* expense at any convenient volume. For example, select a volume of 6,000 tickets.

Variable expenses (6,000 × $10 per ticket)	$ 60,000
Fixed expenses	48,000
Total expenses (at 6,000 tickets)	$108,000

Plot this point ($108,000 at 6,000 tickets) on the graph. See point A on the graph in Exhibit 7-1.

---

[1] *Detroit Free Press,* June 6, 1982.

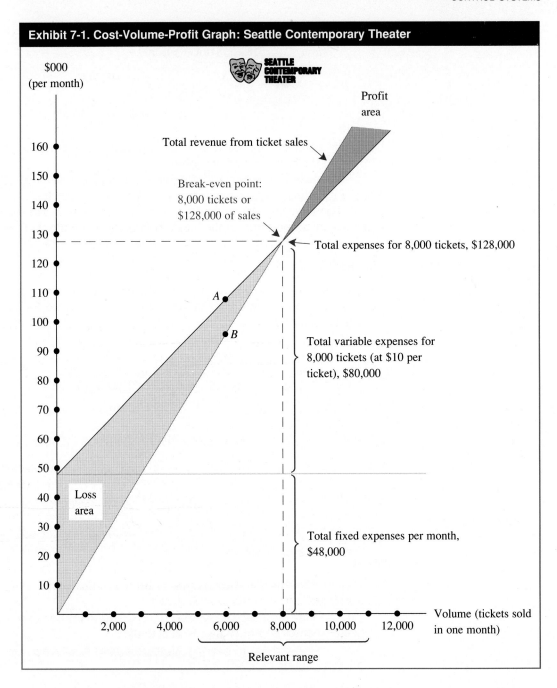

Exhibit 7-1. Cost-Volume-Profit Graph: Seattle Contemporary Theater

Step 4: Draw the variable-expense line. This line passes through the point plotted in step 3 (point *A*) and the intercept of the fixed-expense line on the vertical axis ($48,000).

Step 5: Compute total sales revenue at any convenient volume. We will choose 6,000 tickets again. Total revenue is $96,000 (6,000 × $16 per ticket). Plot this point ($96,000 at 6,000 tickets) on the graph. See point *B* on the graph in Exhibit 7-1.

Step 6: Draw the total revenue line. This line passes through the point plotted in step 5 (point *B*) and the origin.
Step 7: Label the graph as shown in Exhibit 7-1.

Interpreting the CVP Graph

Several conclusions can be drawn from the CVP graph in Exhibit 7-1.

Break-Even Point The break-even point is determined by the intersection of the total-revenue line and the total-expense line. Seattle Contemporary Theater breaks even for the month at 8,000 tickets, or $128,000 of ticket sales. This agrees with our calculations in the preceding section.

Profit and Loss Areas The CVP graph discloses more information than the break-even calculation. From the graph, a manager can see the effects on profit of changes in volume. The vertical distance between the lines in the graph represents the profit or loss at a particular sales volume. If Seattle Contemporary Theater sells fewer than 8,000 tickets in a month, the organization will suffer a loss. The magnitude of the loss increases as ticket sales decline. The theater organization will have a profit if sales exceed 8,000 tickets in a month.

Implications of the Break-Even Point The position of the break-even point within an organization's relevant range of activity provides important information to management. The Seattle Contemporary Theater building seats 450 people. The agreement with the city of Seattle calls for 20 performances during each play's one-month run. Thus, the maximum number of tickets that can be sold each month is 9,000 (450 seats $\times$ 20 performances). The organization's break-even point is quite close to the maximum possible sales volume. This could be cause for concern in a nonprofit organization operating on limited resources.

What could management do to improve this situation? One possibility is to renegotiate with the city to schedule additional performances. However, this might not be feasible, because the actors need some rest each week. Also, additional performances would likely entail additional costs, such as increased theater-rental expenses and increased compensation for the actors and production crew. Other possible solutions are to raise ticket prices or reduce costs. These kinds of issues will be explored later in the chapter.

The CVP graph will not resolve this potential problem for the management of Seattle Contemporary Theater. However, the graph will *direct management's attention* to the situation.

Alternative Format for the CVP Graph

An alternative format for the CVP graph, preferred by some managers, is displayed in Exhibit 7-2. The key difference is that fixed expenses are graphed above variable expenses, instead of the reverse as they were in Exhibit 7-1.

Profit-Volume Graph

Yet another approach to graphing cost-volume-profit relationships is displayed in Exhibit 7-3. This format is called a **profit-volume graph,** since it highlights the amount of profit or loss. Notice that the graph intercepts the vertical axis at the amount equal to fixed expenses at the zero activity level. The graph crosses the horizontal axis at the break-even point. The vertical distance between the horizontal

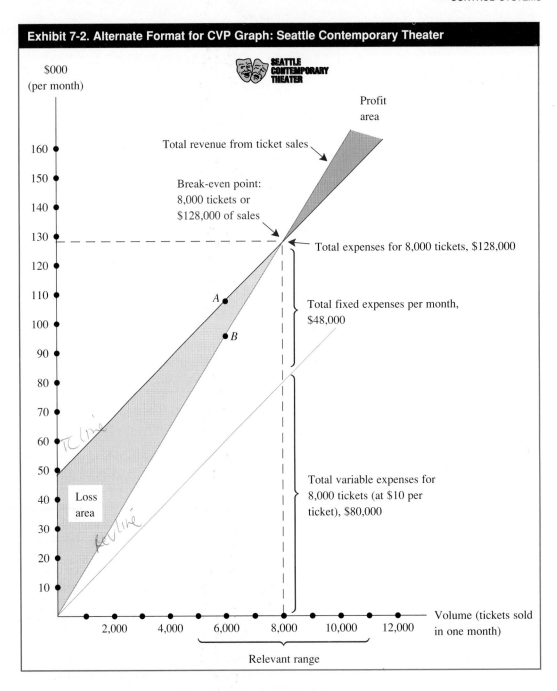

Exhibit 7-2. Alternate Format for CVP Graph: Seattle Contemporary Theater

axis and the profit line, at a particular level of sales volume, is the profit or loss at that volume.

TARGET NET PROFIT

The board of trustees for Seattle Contemporary Theater would like to run free workshops and classes for young actors and aspiring playwrights. This program would cost $3,600 per month in fixed expenses, including teachers' salaries and rental

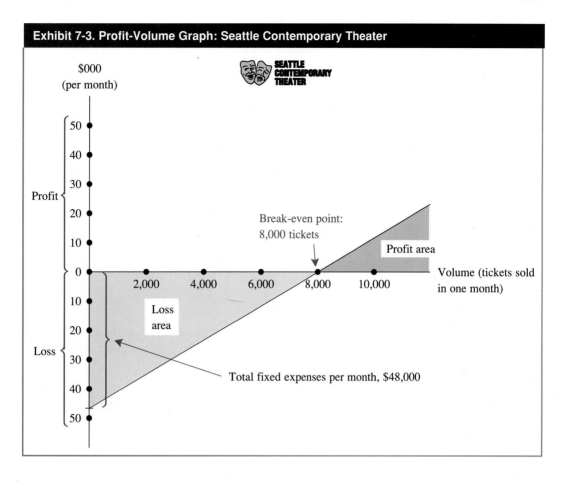

Exhibit 7-3. Profit-Volume Graph: Seattle Contemporary Theater

of space at a local college. No variable expenses would be incurred. If Seattle ContemporaryTheater could make a profit of $3,600 per month on its performances, the Seattle Drama Workshop could be opened. The board has asked George Bernard, the organization's business manager and producer, to determine how many theater tickets must be sold during each play's one-month run to make a profit of $3,600.

The desired profit level of $3,600 is called a **target net profit.** The problem of computing the volume of sales required to earn a particular target net profit is very similar to the problem of finding the break-even point. After all, the break-even point is the number of units of sales required to earn a target net profit of zero.

Contribution-Margin Approach

Each ticket sold by Seattle Contemporary Theater has a unit contribution margin of $6 (sales price of $16 minus unit variable expense of $10). Eight thousand of these $6 contributions will contribute just enough to cover fixed expenses of $48,000. *Each additional ticket sold will contribute $6 toward profit.* Thus, we can modify formula (1) given earlier in the chapter as follows:

$$\frac{\textbf{Fixed expenses + target net profit}}{\textbf{Unit contribution margin}} = \textbf{number of sales units required to earn target net profit}$$

$$\frac{\$48,000 + \$3,600}{\$6} = \textbf{8,600 tickets}$$

If Seattle Contemporary Theater sells 8,600 tickets during each play's one-month run, the organization will make a monthly profit of $3,600 on its performances. This profit can be used to fund the Seattle Drama Workshop. The total dollar sales required to earn a target net profit is found by modifying formula (2) given previously.

$$\frac{\text{Fixed expenses} + \text{target net profit}}{\text{Contribution margin ratio}} = \text{dollar sales required to earn target net profit} \quad (6)$$

$$\frac{\$48,000 + \$3,600}{.375} = \$137,600$$

where the contribution margin ratio $= \dfrac{\$\,6}{\$16} = .375$

This dollar sales figure can also be found by multiplying the required sales of 8,600 tickets by the ticket price of $16 (8,600 × $16 = $137,600).

Equation Approach

The equation approach can also be used to find the units of sales required to earn a target net profit. We can modify the profit equation given previously as follows:

$$\left[\left(\begin{array}{c}\text{Unit} \\ \text{sales price}\end{array}\right) \times \left(\begin{array}{c}\text{sales volume} \\ \text{required to} \\ \text{earn target} \\ \text{net profit}\end{array}\right)\right] - \left[\left(\begin{array}{c}\text{unit} \\ \text{variable} \\ \text{expense}\end{array}\right) \times \left(\begin{array}{c}\text{sales volume} \\ \text{required to earn} \\ \text{target net} \\ \text{profit}\end{array}\right)\right]$$
$$- \left(\begin{array}{c}\text{fixed} \\ \text{expenses}\end{array}\right) = \text{target net profit}$$

Filling in the values for Seattle Contemporary Theater, we have the following equation.

$$(\$16 \times X) - (\$10 \times X) - \$48,000 = \$3,600 \quad (7)$$

where X denotes the sales volume required to earn the target net profit.

Equation (7) can be solved for X as follows:

$$\underbrace{\$16X - \$10X}_{\$6X} - \$48,000 = \$\ 3,600$$
$$= \$51,600$$

$$X = \frac{\$51,600}{\$6} = 8,600$$

Graphical Approach

The profit-volume graph in Exhibit 7-3 can also be used to find the sales volume required to earn a target net profit. First, locate Seattle Contemporary Theater's target net profit of $3,600 on the vertical axis. Then move horizontally until the profit line is reached. Finally, move down from the profit line to the horizontal axis to determine the required sales volume.

APPLYING CVP ANALYSIS

The cost-volume-profit relationships that underlie break-even calculations and CVP graphs have wide-ranging applications in management. We will look at several common applications illustrated by Seattle Contemporary Theater.

Safety Margin

The **safety margin** of an enterprise is the difference between the budgeted sales revenue and the break-even sales revenue. Suppose Seattle Contemporary Theater's business manager expects every performance of each play to be sold out. Then budgeted monthly sales revenue is $144,000 (450 seats $\times$ 20 performances of each play $\times$ $16 per ticket). Since break-even sales revenue is $128,000, the organization's safety margin is $16,000 ($144,000 − $128,000). The safety margin gives management a feel for how close projected operations are to the organization's break-even point.

Changes in Fixed Expenses

What would happen to Seattle Contemporary Theater's break-even point if fixed expenses change? Suppose the business manager is concerned that the estimate for fixed utilities expenses, $1,400 per month, is too low. What would happen to the break-even point if fixed utilities expenses prove to be $2,600 instead? The break-even calculations for both the original and the new estimate of fixed utilities expenses are as follows:

	Original Estimate		New Estimate
Fixed utilities expenses..................	$ 1,400	..	$ 2,600
Total fixed expenses	$ 48,000	..	$ 49,200
Break-even calculation	$ 48,000	..	$ 49,200
(Fixed expenses ÷ unit contribution margin)	$6		$6
Break-even point (units).................	8,000 tickets	..	8,200 tickets
Break-even point (dollars)	$128,000	..	$131,200

The estimate of fixed expenses has increased by 2.5 percent, since $1,200 is 2.5 percent of $48,000. Notice that the break-even point also increased by 2.5 percent. (200 tickets is 2.5 percent of 8,000 tickets.) This relationship will always exist.

$$\frac{\text{Fixed expenses}}{\text{Unit contribution margin}} = \text{break-even point (in units)}$$

$$\frac{\text{Fixed expenses} \times 1.025}{\text{Unit contribution margin}} = (\text{break-even point in units}) \times 1.025$$

Donations to Offset Fixed Expenses Nonprofit organizations often receive cash donations from people or organizations desiring to support a worthy cause. A donation is equivalent to a reduction in fixed expenses, and it will reduce the organization's break-even point. In our original set of data, Seattle Contemporary Theater's monthly fixed expenses total $48,000. Suppose that various people pledge donations amounting to $6,000 per month. The new break-even point is computed as follows:

$$\frac{\text{Fixed expenses} - \text{donations}}{\text{Unit contribution margin}} = \text{break-even point (in units)}$$

$$\frac{\$48,000 - \$6,000}{\$6} = 7,000 \text{ tickets}$$

Changes in the Unit Contribution Margin

What would happen to Seattle Contemporary Theater's break-even point if miscellaneous variable expenses were $3 per ticket instead of $2? Alternatively, what would be the effect of raising the ticket price to $18?

Change in Unit Variable Expenses If the theater organization's miscellaneous variable expenses increase from $2 to $3 per ticket, the unit contribution margin will fall from $6 to $5. The original and new break-even points are computed as follows:

	Original Estimate		**New Estimate**
Miscellaneous variable expenses	$2 per ticket	. . . .	$3 per ticket
Unit contribution margin	$6	. . . .	$5
Break-even calculation. . . . . (Fixed expenses ÷ unit contribution margin)	$\dfrac{\$48,000}{\$6}$	. . . .	$\dfrac{\$48,000}{\$5}$
Break-even point (units)	8,000 tickets	. . . .	9,600 tickets
Break-even point (dollars)	$128,000	. . . .	$153,600

If this change in unit variable expenses actually occurs, it would no longer be possible for the organization to break even. Only 9,000 tickets are available for each play's one-month run (450 seats × 20 performances), but 9,600 tickets would have to be sold to break even. Once again, CVP analysis will not solve this problem for management, but it will direct management's attention to potentially serious difficulties.

Change in Sales Price Changing the unit sales price will also alter the unit contribution margin. Suppose the ticket price is raised from $16 to $18. This change would raise the unit contribution margin from $6 to $8. The new break-even point would be 6,000 tickets ($48,000 ÷ $8).

A $2 increase in the ticket price will lower the break-even point from 8,000 tickets to 6,000 tickets. Is this change desirable? A lower break-even point decreases the risk of operation with a loss if sales are sluggish. However, the organization may be more likely to at least break even with a $16 ticket price than with an $18 ticket price. The reason is that the lower ticket price encourages more people to attend the theater's performances. It could be that break-even sales of 8,000 tickets at $16 are more likely than break-even sales of 6,000 tickets at $18. Ultimately, the desirability of the ticket-price increase depends on management's assessment of the likely reaction by theater patrons.

Management's decision about the ticket price increase also will reflect the fundamental goals of Seattle Contemporary Theater. This nonprofit drama organization was formed to bring contemporary drama to the people of Seattle. The lower the ticket price, the more accessible are the theater's productions to people of all income levels.

The point of this discussion is that CVP analysis provides valuable information, but it is only one of several elements that influence management's decisions.

Predicting Profit Given Expected Volume

So far, we have focused on finding the required sales volume to break even or achieve a particular target net profit. Thus, we have asked the following question.

$$\text{Given:} \left\{ \begin{array}{l} \textbf{Fixed expenses} \\ \textbf{Unit contribution margin} \\ \textbf{Target net profit} \end{array} \right\}, \quad \text{Find: \{required sales volume\}}$$

We can also use CVP analysis to turn this question around and make the following query.

$$\text{Given:} \left\{ \begin{array}{l} \textbf{Fixed expenses} \\ \textbf{Unit contribution margin} \\ \textbf{Expected sales volume} \end{array} \right\}, \quad \text{Find: \{expected profit\}}$$

Suppose the management of Seattle Contemporary Theater expects fixed monthly expenses of $48,000 and unit variable expenses of $10 per ticket. The organization's board of trustees is considering two different ticket prices, and the business manager has forecast monthly demand at each price.

Ticket Price	Forecast Monthly Demand
$16	9,000
$20	6,000

Expected profit may be calculated at each price as shown below. In these profit calculations, the **total contribution margin** is the difference between *total* sales revenue and *total* variable expenses. This use of the term *contribution margin* is a "total" concept rather than the "per unit" concept used earlier in the chapter. The *total contribution margin* is the *total* amount left to contribute to covering fixed expenses after *total* variable expenses have been covered.

	Ticket Price $16	Ticket Price $20
Sales revenue:		
9,000 × $16	$144,000	
6,000 × $20		$120,000
Less variable expenses:		
9,000 × $10	90,000	
6,000 × $10		60,000
Total contribution margin	$ 54,000	$ 60,000
Less fixed expenses	48,000	48,000
Profit	$ 6,000	$ 12,000

The difference in expected profit at the two ticket prices is due to two factors:

1. A different *unit* contribution margin, defined previously as *unit* sales price minus *unit* variable expenses
2. A different sales volume

The combined effect of these two factors on the *total* contribution margin is as follows:

Expected *total* contribution margin at $20 ticket price:
    $6,000 \times (\$20 - \$10)$ $60,000
Expected *total* contribution margin at $16 ticket price:
    $9,000 \times (\$16 - \$10)$ 54,000
Difference in *total* contribution margin .... $ 6,000

The $6,000 difference in expected profit, at the two ticket prices, is due to a $6,000 difference in the total contribution margin. The board of trustees will consider these projected profits as it decides which ticket price is best. Even though Seattle Contemporary Theater is a nonprofit organization, it may still have legitimate reasons for attempting to make a profit on its theater performances. For example, the board might use these profits to fund a free drama workshop, provide scholarships for local young people to study drama in college, or produce a free outdoor play for Seattle's residents.

Interdependent Changes in Key Variables

Sometimes a change in one key variable will cause a change in another key variable. Suppose the board of trustees is choosing between ticket prices of $16 and $20, and the business manager has projected demand as shown in the preceding section. A famous retired actress who lives in Seattle has offered to donate $10,000 per month to Seattle Contemporary Theater if the board will set the ticket price at $16. The actress is interested in making the theater's performances affordable by as many people as possible. The facts are now as follows:

Ticket Price		Unit Contribution Margin		Forecast Monthly Demand		Net Fixed Expenses (after subtracting donation)
$16	...	$ 6	...	9,000	...	$38,000 ($48,000 − $10,000)
20	...	10	...	6,000	...	$48,000

The organization's expected profit at each price is computed below.

	Ticket Price	
	$16	**$20**
Sales revenue:		
9,000 × $16...........................	$144,000	
6,000 × $20...........................		$120,000
Less variable expenses:		
9,000 × $10...........................	90,000	
6,000 × $10...........................		60,000
Total contribution margin	$ 54,000	$ 60,000
Less net fixed expenses.................	38,000	48,000
(net of donations)		
Profit................................	$ 16,000	$ 12,000

Now the difference in expected profit at the two ticket prices is due to three factors:

1. A different *unit* contribution margin
2. A different sales volume
3. A difference in the *net* fixed expenses, after deducting the donation

The combined effect of these factors is shown below.

Expected *total* contribution margin at $20 ticket price:	
6,000 × ($20 − $10)	$60,000
Expected *total* contribution margin at $16 ticket price:	
9,000 × ($16 − $10)	54,000
Difference in *total* contribution margin	$ 6,000
(higher with $20 ticket price)	
Net fixed expenses at $20 ticket price...........................	$48,000
Net fixed expenses at $16 ticket price...........................	38,000
Difference in net fixed expenses (higher with $20 ticket price).........	$10,000

The expected total contribution margin is $6,000 higher with the $20 ticket price, but net fixed expenses are $10,000 higher. Thus, Seattle Contemporary Theater will make $4,000 more in profit at the $16 price ($10,000 − $6,000).

CVP Information in Published Annual Reports

Cost-volume-profit relationships are so important to understanding an organization's operations that some companies disclose CVP information in their published annual reports. The following illustration is from the airline industry.

ILLUSTRATION FROM MANAGEMENT-ACCOUNTING PRACTICE

Pan Am Corporation

Pan Am Corporation is a major airline with flight operations throughout the world. A recent annual report listed the company's *break-even passenger load factor* for each of the past five years. This factor is defined as the average percentage of seats that must be filled for the airline's operating revenues to equal its operating costs and interest expense. The break-even passenger load factor for the most recent year listed in the annual report was 65.5 percent.[2]

CVP ANALYSIS WITH MULTIPLE PRODUCTS

Our CVP illustration for Seattle Contemporary Theater has assumed that the organization has only one product, a theater seat at a dramatic performance. Most firms have more than one product, and this adds some complexity to their CVP analyses.

As we have seen, Seattle Contemporary Theater's monthly fixed expenses total $48,000, and the unit variable expense per ticket is $10. Now suppose that the city of Seattle has agreed to refurbish 10 theater boxes in the historic theater building. Each box has five seats, which are more comfortable and afford a better view of the stage

---

[2] Pan Am Corporation's annual report for the year ended December 31, 1986, pp. 7 and 13.

than the theater's general seating. The board of trustees has decided to charge $16 per ticket for general seating and $20 per ticket for box seats. These facts are summarized as follows:

Seat Type	Ticket Price	Unit Variable Expense	Unit Contribution Margin	Number of Seats in Theater	Number of Seats Available per Month (20 performances)
Regular	$16	$10	$ 6	450	9,000
Box	20	10	10	50	1,000

Notice that 90 percent of the available seats are regular seats, and 10 percent are box seats. The business manager estimates that tickets for each type of seat will be sold in the same proportion as the number of seats available. If, for example, 5,000 tickets are sold during a month, sales will be as follows:

Regular seats:	90% × 5,000	4,500
Box seats:	10% × 5,000	500
Total..........	....	5,000

For any organization selling multiple products, the relative proportion of each type of product *sold* is called the **sales mix.** The business manager's estimate of Seattle Contemporary Theater's *sales mix* is 90 percent regular seats and 10 percent box seats.

The sales mix is an important assumption in multiproduct CVP analysis. The sales mix is used to compute a **weighted-average unit contribution margin.** This is the *average* of the several products' *unit contribution margins, weighted* by the relative sales proportion of each product. Seattle Contemporary Theater's weighted-average unit contribution margin is computed below.

$$\text{Weighted-average unit contribution margin} = (\$6 \times 90\%) + (\$10 \times 10\%) = \$6.40$$

The organization's break-even point in units is computed using the following formula.

$$\text{Break-even point} = \frac{\text{fixed expenses}}{\text{weighted-average unit contribution margin}} = \frac{\$48,000}{\$6.40} = 7,500 \text{ tickets} \quad (8)$$

The break-even point of 7,500 tickets must be interpreted in light of the sales mix. Seattle Contemporary Theater will break even for the month if it sells 7,500 tickets as follows:

Break-even sales in units	Regular seats:	7,500 × 90%	6,750 tickets
	Box seats:	7,500 × 10%	750 tickets
	Total.......................		7,500 tickets

The following income calculation verifies the break-even point.

Sales revenue:

Regular seats: 6,750 × $16	$108,000
Box seats: 750 × $20	15,000
Total revenue: 7,500 seats in total	$123,000
Less variable expenses: 7,500 × $10..........................	75,000
Total contribution margin	$ 48,000
Less fixed expenses	48,000
Profit	$ 0

The break-even point of 7,500 tickets per month is *valid only for the sales mix assumed* in computing the weighted-average unit contribution margin. If 7,500 tickets are sold in any other mix of regular and box seats, the organization will not break even.

Notice that break-even formula (8) is a modification of formula (1) given earlier in the chapter. The only difference is that formula (8) uses the *weighted-average* unit contribution margin.

Seattle Contemporary Theater's business manager has constructed the profit-volume graph in Exhibit 7-4. The PV graph shows the organization's profit at any level of total monthly sales, assuming the sales mix of 90 percent regular seats and 10 percent box seats. For example, if 9,000 tickets are sold in total, at the assumed sales mix, the PV graph indicates that profit will be $9,600.

With multiproduct CVP analysis, a managerial accountant can investigate the

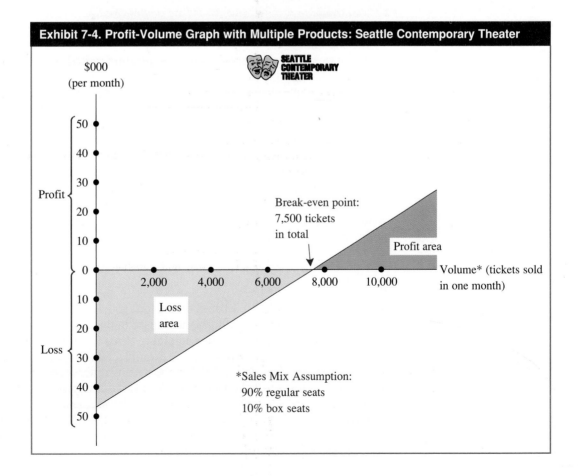

Exhibit 7-4. Profit-Volume Graph with Multiple Products: Seattle Contemporary Theater

impact on profit of changes in sales volume, prices, variable costs, fixed costs, or the sales mix itself. For example, what would be the effect on Seattle Contemporary Theater's break-even point if the sales mix were 80 percent regular seats and 20 percent box seats? With this sales mix, the weighted-average unit contribution margin is computed as follows:

**Weighted-average
unit contribution** $= (\$6 \times 80\%) + (\$10 \times 20\%) = \$6.80$
margin

The break-even point declines from 7,500 tickets to approximately 7,059 tickets as a result of the higher proportion of expensive seats in the sales mix.

$$\textbf{Break-even point} = \frac{\textbf{fixed expenses}}{\textbf{weighted-average unit contribution margin}} = \frac{\$48,000}{\$6.80} = \textbf{7,059 tickets*}$$

* Rounded.

ASSUMPTIONS UNDERLYING CVP ANALYSIS

For any cost-volume-profit analysis to be valid, the following important assumptions must be reasonably satisfied *within the relevant range.*

1. The behavior of total revenue is linear (straight line). This implies that the price of the product or service will not change as sales volume varies within the relevant range.
2. The behavior of total expenses is linear (straight-line) over the relevant range. This implies the following more specific assumptions.
   a. Expenses can be categorized as fixed, variable, or semivariable. *Total* fixed expenses remain constant as activity changes, and the *unit* variable expense remains unchanged as activity varies.
   b. The efficiency and productivity of the production process and workers remain constant.
3. In multiproduct organizations, the sales mix remains constant over the relevant range.
4. In manufacturing firms, the inventory levels at the beginning and end of the period are the same. This implies that the number of units produced during the period equals the number of units sold.

Role of Computerized Planning Models and Electronic Spreadsheets

Cost-volume-profit analysis is based on the four general assumptions listed above as well as specific estimates of all the variables used in the analysis. Since these variables are rarely known with certainty, it is helpful to run a CVP analysis many times with different combinations of estimates. For example, Seattle Contemporary Theater's business manager might do the CVP analysis using different estimates for the ticket prices, sales mix for regular and box seats, unit variable expenses, and fixed expenses. This approach is called **sensitivity analysis,** since it provides the analyst with a feel for how sensitive the analysis is to the estimates upon which it is based. The widespread availability of personal computers and electronic spreadsheet software has made sensitivity analysis relatively easy to do.

CVP RELATIONSHIPS AND THE INCOME STATEMENT

The management functions of planning, control, and decision making all are facilitated by an understanding of cost-volume-profit relationships. These relationships are important enough to operating managers that some businesses prepare income statements in a way that highlights CVP issues. Before we examine this new income-statement format, we will review the more traditional income statement used in the preceding chapters.

Traditional Income Statement

An income statement for AccuTime Company, a manufacturer of digital clocks, is shown in Exhibit 7-5 (panel A). During 19x4 the firm manufactured and sold 20,000 clocks at a price of $25 each. This income statement is prepared in the traditional manner. *Cost of goods sold* includes both variable and fixed manufacturing costs, as

---

Exhibit 7-5. Income Statement: Traditional and Contribution Formats

AccuTime Company
Income Statement
For the Year Ended December 31, 19x4

Sales		$500,000
Less: Cost of goods sold		380,000
Gross margin		$120,000
Less: Operating expenses:		
Selling expenses	$35,000	
Administrative expenses	35,000	70,000
Net income		$ 50,000

(A) Traditional format

AccuTime Company
Income Statement
For the Year Ended December 31, 19x4

Sales		$500,000
Less: Variable expenses:		
Variable manufacturing	.$280,000	
Variable selling	15,000	
Variable administrative	5,000	300,000
Contribution margin		$200,000
Less: Fixed expenses:		
Fixed manufacturing	100,000	
Fixed selling	20,000	
Fixed administrative	30,000	150,000
Net income		$ 50,000

(B) Contribution format

measured by the firm's product-costing system. The *gross margin* is computed by subtracting cost of goods sold from sales. Selling and administrative expenses are then subtracted; each expense includes both variable and fixed costs. *The traditional income statement does not disclose the breakdown of each expense into its variable and fixed components.*

Contribution Income Statement

Many operating managers find the traditional income-statement format difficult to use, because it does not separate variable and fixed expenses. Instead they prefer the **contribution income statement.** A contribution income statement for AccuTime is shown in Exhibit 7-5 (panel B). *The contribution format highlights the distinction between variable and fixed expenses.* The variable manufacturing cost of each clock is $14, and the total fixed manufacturing cost is $100,000. On the contribution income statement, all variable expenses are subtracted from sales to obtain the *contribution margin.* For AccuTime, $200,000 remains from total sales revenue, after all variable costs have been covered, to contribute to covering fixed costs and making a profit. All fixed costs are then subtracted from the contribution margin to obtain net income.

Comparison of Traditional and Contribution Income Statements

Operating managers frequently prefer the contribution income statement, because its separation of fixed and variable expenses highlights cost-volume-profit relationships. It is readily apparent from the contribution-format statement how income will be affected when sales volume changes by a given percentage. Suppose management projects that sales volume in 19x5 will be 20 percent greater than in 19x4. No changes are anticipated in the sales price, variable cost per unit, or fixed costs. Examination of the contribution income statement shows that if sales volume increases by 20 percent, the following changes will occur. (Our discussion ignores income taxes, which are covered in the appendix at the end of this chapter.)

Income Statement Item	19x4 Amount	Change	19x5 Amount
Sales	$500,000	$100,000 (20% × $500,000)	$600,000
Total variable expenses	$300,000	$60,000 (20% × $300,000)	$360,000
Contribution margin	$200,000	$40,000 (20% × $200,000)	$240,000
Total fixed expenses	$150,000	-0- (no change in fixed expenses when volume changes)	$150,000
Net income	$ 50,000	$40,000 (income changes by the amount of the contribution-margin change)	$ 90,000

Notice that net income increases by the same amount as the increase in the contribution margin. Moreover, the contribution margin changes in direct proportion to the change in sales volume. These two facts enable us to calculate the increase in net income using the following shortcut. Recall that the *contribution margin ratio* is the percentage of contribution margin to sales.

$$\begin{pmatrix}\text{Increase in}\\\text{sales revenue}\end{pmatrix} \times \begin{pmatrix}\text{contribution margin}\\\text{ratio}\end{pmatrix} = \begin{pmatrix}\text{increase in}\\\text{net income}\end{pmatrix}$$

$$\$100{,}000 \quad \times \quad .40 \quad = \quad \$40{,}000$$

where

$$\begin{pmatrix}\text{contribution margin}\\\text{ratio}\end{pmatrix} = \frac{\text{contribution margin}}{\text{sales revenue}}$$

$$.40 = \frac{\$200{,}000}{\$500{,}000}$$

The analysis above makes use of cost-volume-profit relationships that are disclosed in the contribution income statement. Such an analysis cannot be made with the information presented in the traditional income statement.

COST STRUCTURE AND OPERATING LEVERAGE

The **cost structure** of an organization is the relative proportion of its fixed and variable costs. Cost structures differ widely among industries and among firms within an industry. A company using a computer-integrated manufacturing system has a large investment in plant and equipment, which results in a cost structure dominated by fixed costs. In contrast, a public accounting firm's cost structure has a much higher proportion of variable costs. The highly automated manufacturing firm is capital-intensive, whereas the accounting firm is labor-intensive.

An organization's cost structure has a significant effect on the sensitivity of its profit to changes in volume. A convenient way to portray a firm's cost structure is shown in Exhibit 7-6. The data for AccuTime Company (company A) comes from the firm's 19x4 contribution income statement in Exhibit 7-5. For comparison purposes, two other firms' cost structures are also shown. Although these three firms have the same sales revenue ($500,000) and net income ($50,000), they have very different cost structures. Company B's cost structure is dominated by variable costs. It has a low contribution margin ratio of only 20 percent. In contrast, company C's cost structure is dominated by fixed costs. The firms' contribution margin ratio is 90 percent. Company A falls between these two extremes with a contribution margin ratio of 40 percent.

Exhibit 7-6. Comparison of Cost Structures

	Company A (AccuTime Company) Amount	%	Company B Amount	%	Company C Amount	%
Sales	$500,000	100	$500,000	100	$500,000	100
Variable expenses	300,000	60	400,000	80	50,000	10
Contribution margin	$200,000	40	$100,000	20	$450,000	90
Fixed expenses	150,000	30	50,000	10	$400,000	80
Net income	$ 50,000	10	$ 50,000	10	$ 50,000	10

Exhibit 7-7. Effect on Profit of Increase in Sales Revenue

	$\begin{bmatrix}\text{Increase} \\ \text{in} \\ \text{Sales} \\ \text{Revenue}\end{bmatrix}$	×	$\begin{bmatrix}\text{Contribution} \\ \text{Margin} \\ \text{Ratio}\end{bmatrix}$	=	$\begin{bmatrix}\text{Increase} \\ \text{in} \\ \text{Net} \\ \text{Income}\end{bmatrix}$	Percentage Increase in Net Income
Company A (AccuTime)	$50,000	×	40%	=	$20,000	40% ($20,000 ÷ $50,000)
Company B (high variable expenses) . . .	$50,000	×	20%	=	$10,000	20% ($10,000 ÷ $50,000)
Company C (high fixed expenses)	$50,000	×	90%	=	$45,000	90% ($45,000 ÷ $50,000)

Suppose sales revenue increases by 10 percent, or $50,000, in each company. The resulting increase in each company's profit is calculated in Exhibit 7-7.

Notice that company B, with its high variable expenses and low contribution-margin ratio, shows a relatively low *percentage* increase in profit. In contrast, the high fixed expenses and large contribution-margin ratio of company C result in a relatively high *percentage* increase in profit. Company A falls in between these two extremes. *The greater the proportion of fixed costs in a firm's cost structure, the greater will be the impact on profit from a given percentage change in sales revenue.*

Operating Leverage

The extent to which an organization uses fixed costs in its cost structure is called **operating leverage.** The operating leverage is greatest in firms with a large proportion of fixed costs, low proportion of variable costs, and the resulting high contribution-margin ratio. Exhibit 7-6 shows that company B has low operating leverage, company C has high operating leverage, and company A falls in between. To a physical scientist, *leverage* refers to the ability of a small force to move a heavy weight. To the managerial accountant, *operating leverage* refers to the ability of the firm to generate an increase in net income when sales revenue increases.

Measuring Operating Leverage The managerial accountant can measure a firm's operating leverage, *at a particular sales volume,* using the **operating leverage factor:**

$$\text{Operating leverage factor} = \frac{\text{contribution margin}}{\text{net income}}$$

Using the data in Exhibit 7-6, the operating leverage factors of companies A, B, and C are computed as follows:

	$\begin{bmatrix}\text{Contribution} \\ \text{Margin}\end{bmatrix}$	÷	$\begin{bmatrix}\text{Net} \\ \text{Income}\end{bmatrix}$	=	$\begin{bmatrix}\text{Operating} \\ \text{Leverage} \\ \text{Factor}\end{bmatrix}$
Company A (AccuTime). . .	$200,000	÷	$50,000	=	4
Company B (high variable expenses)	$100,000	÷	$50,000	=	2
Company C (high fixed expenses)	$450,000	÷	$50,000	=	9

The operating leverage factor is a measure, at a particular level of sales, of the *percentage* impact on net income of a given *percentage* change in sales revenue. Multiplying the *percentage* change in sales revenue by the operating leverage factor yields the *percentage* change in net income.

	$\begin{bmatrix} \text{Percentage} \\ \text{Increase} \\ \text{in Sales} \\ \text{Revenue} \end{bmatrix}$	$\times$	$\begin{bmatrix} \text{Operating} \\ \text{Leverage} \\ \text{Factor} \end{bmatrix}$	$=$	$\begin{bmatrix} \text{Percentage} \\ \text{Change in} \\ \text{Net Income} \end{bmatrix}$
Company A (AccuTime)...	10%	$\times$	4	$=$	40%
Company B (high variable expenses)...............	10%	$\times$	2	$=$	20%
Company C (high fixed expenses)................	10%	$\times$	9	$=$	90%

The percentage change in net income shown above for each company may be verified by reexamining Exhibit 7-7.

A firm's operating leverage also affects its break-even point. Since a firm with relatively high operating leverage has proportionally high fixed expenses, the firm's break-even point will be relatively high. This fact is illustrated using the data from Exhibit 7-6:

	$\begin{bmatrix} \text{Fixed} \\ \text{Expenses} \end{bmatrix}$	$-$	$\begin{bmatrix} \text{Contribution} \\ \text{Margin} \\ \text{Ratio} \end{bmatrix}$	$=$	$\begin{bmatrix} \text{Break-} \\ \text{Even} \\ \text{Sales} \\ \text{Revenue} \end{bmatrix}$
Company A (AccuTime)......	$150,000	$\div$	40%	$=$	$375,000
Company B (high variable expenses)....................	$ 50,000	$\div$	20%	$=$	$250,000
Company C (high fixed expenses)....................	$400,000	$\div$	90%	$=$	$444,444*

* Rounded.

Cost Structure and Operating Leverage: A Cost-Benefit Issue

An organization's cost structure plays an important role in determining its cost-volume-profit relationships. A firm with proportionately high fixed costs has relatively high operating leverage. The result of high operating leverage is that the firm can generate a large percentage increase in net income from a relatively small percentage increase in sales revenue. On the other hand, a firm with high operating leverage has a relatively high break-even point. This entails some risk to the firm.

The optimal cost structure for an organization involves a trade-off. Management must weigh the benefits of high operating leverage against the risks of large committed fixed costs and the associated high break-even point.

CHAPTER SUMMARY

An understanding of cost-volume-profit relationships is necessary for the successful management of any enterprise. CVP analysis provides a sweeping overview of the effects on profit of all kinds of changes in sales volume, expenses, product mix, and sales prices. Calculation of the sales volume required to break even or earn a target net profit provides an organization's management with valuable information for planning and decision making.

Cost-volume-profit relationships are important enough to operating managers that some firms prepare a contribution income statement. This income-statement format separates fixed and variable expenses, and helps managers discern the effects on profit from changes in volume. The contribution income statement also discloses an organization's cost structure, which is the relative proportion of its fixed and variable costs. An organization's cost structure has an important impact on its CVP relationships. The cost structure of an organization defines its operating leverage, which determines the impact on profit of changes in sales volume.

REVIEW PROBLEM ON COST-VOLUME-PROFIT ANALYSIS

Overlook Inn is a small bed-and-breakfast inn located in the Great Smoky Mountains of Tennessee. The charge is $50 per person for one night's lodging and a full breakfast in the morning. The retired couple who own and manage the inn estimate that the variable expense per person is $20. This includes such expenses as food, maid service, and utilities. The inn's fixed expenses total $42,000 per year. The inn can accommodate 10 guests each night.

REQUIRED: Compute the following:

1. Contribution margin per unit of service. (A unit of service is one night's lodging for one guest.)
2. Contribution-margin ratio.
3. Annual break-even point in units of service and in dollars of service revenue.
4. The number of units of service required to earn a target net profit of $60,000 for the year. (Ignore income taxes.)

Solution to Review Problem

1. $$\text{Contribution margin per unit of service} = \text{nightly room charge} - \text{variable expense per person}$$

    $$\$30 = \$50 - \$20$$

2. $$\text{Contribution margin ratio} = \frac{\text{contribution margin per unit}}{\text{nightly room charge}}$$

    $$.60 = \frac{\$30}{\$50}$$

3. $$\text{Break-even point in units of service} = \frac{\text{fixed expenses}}{\text{contribution margin per unit}}$$

    $$1,400 = \frac{\$42,000}{\$30}$$

    $$\text{Break-even point in dollars of revenue} = \frac{\text{fixed expenses}}{\text{contribution margin ratio}}$$

    $$\$70,000 = \frac{\$42,000}{.60}$$

4. Number of units of service required to earn target net profit $= \dfrac{\text{fixed expenses} + \text{target net profit}}{\text{contribution margin per unit of service}}$

$$3,400 = \frac{\$42,000 + \$60,000}{\$30}$$

KEY TERMS **Break-even point,** p. 273; **Contribution income statement,** p. 290; **Contribution-margin ratio,** p. 274; **Contribution margin, total,** p. 283; **Cost structure,** p. 291; **Cost-volume-profit (CVP) analysis,** p. 271; **Cost-volume-profit graph,** p. 275; **Operating leverage,** p. 292; **Operating leverage factor,** p. 292; **Profit-volume graph,** p. 277; **Safety margin,** p. 281; **Sales mix,** p. 286; **Sensitivity analysis,** p. 288; **Target net profit (or income),** p. 279; **Total contribution margin,** p. 283; **Unit contribution margin,** p. 273; **Weighted-average unit contribution margin,** p. 286.

APPENDIX TO CHAPTER 7

Effect of Income Taxes

Profit-seeking enterprises must pay income taxes on their profits. A firm's **after-tax net income,** the amount of income remaining after subtracting the firm's income-tax expense, is less than its **before-tax income.** This fact is expressed in the following formula.

$$\left(\begin{array}{c}\text{After-tax}\\\text{net income}\end{array}\right) = \left(\begin{array}{c}\text{before-tax}\\\text{income}\end{array}\right) - t\left(\begin{array}{c}\text{before-tax}\\\text{income}\end{array}\right)$$

where   *t* **denotes the income-tax rate.**

Rearranging this equation yields the following formula.

$$\left(\begin{array}{c}\text{After-tax}\\\text{net income}\end{array}\right) = \left(\begin{array}{c}\text{before-tax}\\\text{income}\end{array}\right)(1 - t) \qquad \textbf{(9)}$$

To illustrate this formula, suppose AccuTime Company must pay income taxes of 40 percent of its before-tax income. The company's contribution income statement for 19x4 appears below.

Sales, 20,000 units at $25 each	$500,000
Variable expenses, 20,000 units at $15 each*	300,000
Contribution margin	$200,000
Fixed expenses	150,000
Income before taxes	$ 50,000
Income tax expense, .40 × $50,000	20,000
Net income, $50,000 × (1 − .40)	$ 30,000

* Variable cost per unit is $15: variable manufacturing cost of $14 plus variable selling and administrative costs of $1.

The requirement that a firm pay income taxes affects its cost-volume-profit relationships. To earn a particular after-tax net income will require greater before-tax income than if there were no tax. For example, if AccuTime's target after-tax net income were $30,000, the company would have to earn before-tax income of $50,000. AccuTime's income statement shows this relationship.

How much before-tax income must be earned in order to achieve a particular target after-tax net income? Rearranging equation (9) above yields the following formula.

$$\begin{pmatrix} \text{Target} \\ \text{after-tax} \\ \text{net income} \end{pmatrix} = \begin{pmatrix} \text{target} \\ \text{before-tax} \\ \text{income} \end{pmatrix} (1 - t)$$

Divide both sides by $(1 - t)$

$$\frac{\begin{pmatrix} \text{Target} \\ \text{after-tax} \\ \text{net income} \end{pmatrix}}{1 - t} = \frac{\begin{pmatrix} \text{target} \\ \text{before-tax} \\ \text{income} \end{pmatrix}(1 - t)}{(1 - t)}$$

$$\frac{\begin{pmatrix} \text{Target} \\ \text{after-tax} \\ \text{net income} \end{pmatrix}}{1 - t} = \begin{array}{c} \text{target before-tax} \\ \text{income} \end{array}$$

If AccuTime Company's target after-tax net income is $30,000, its target before-tax income is calculated as follows:

$$\frac{\begin{pmatrix} \text{Target} \\ \text{after-tax} \\ \text{net income} \end{pmatrix}}{1 - t} = \frac{\$30,000}{1 - .40} = \$50,000 = \begin{array}{c} \text{target before-tax} \\ \text{income} \end{array}$$

Now we are in a position to compute the number of digital clocks that AccuTime must sell in order to achieve a particular after-tax net income. We begin with the following before-tax income equation.

$$\textbf{Sales} - \textbf{variable expenses} - \textbf{fixed expenses} = \textbf{before-tax income}$$

Now we use our formula for before-tax income.

$$\textbf{Sales} - \textbf{variable expenses} - \textbf{fixed expenses} = \frac{\text{after-tax net income}}{(1 - t)}$$

$$\begin{pmatrix} \text{Unit} \\ \text{sales price} \end{pmatrix} \times \begin{pmatrix} \text{sales} \\ \text{volume} \\ \text{in units} \end{pmatrix} - \begin{pmatrix} \text{unit} \\ \text{variable} \\ \text{expense} \end{pmatrix} \times \begin{pmatrix} \text{sales} \\ \text{volume} \\ \text{in units} \end{pmatrix} - \begin{pmatrix} \text{fixed} \\ \text{expenses} \end{pmatrix} = \frac{\text{after-tax net income}}{1 - t}$$

Using the data for AccuTime Company, and assuming target after-tax net income of $30,000:

$$(\$25 \times X) - (\$15 \times X) - \$150,000 = \frac{\$30,000}{1 - .40}$$

where X denotes the number of units that must be sold to achieve the target after-tax net income.

Now we solve for X as follows:

$$(\$25 - \$15) \times X = \$150,000 + \frac{\$30,000}{1 - .40}$$

$$\$10 \quad \times X = \$150,000 + \frac{\$30,000}{1 - .40}$$

$$X = \frac{\$150,000 + \dfrac{\$30,000}{1 - .40}}{\$10}$$

$$X = 20,000 \text{ units}$$

In terms of sales revenue, AccuTime must achieve a sales volume of $500,000 (20,000 units $\times$ $25 sales price). We can verify these calculations by examining AccuTime's income statement given previously.

Notice in the calculations above that $10 is the unit contribution margin ($25 sales price minus $15 unit variable expense). Thus, the general formula illustrated above is the following:

$$\begin{array}{c} \text{Number of units of} \\ \text{sales required to earn} \\ \text{target after-tax net income} \end{array} = \frac{\text{fixed expenses} + \dfrac{\text{target after-tax net income}}{(1 - t)}}{\text{unit contribution margin}}$$

where t denotes the income tax rate.

A cost-volume-profit graph for AccuTime Company is displayed in Exhibit 7-8. As the graph shows, 20,000 units must be sold to achieve $30,000 in after-tax net income. The company's break-even point is 15,000 units. The break-even point is not affected by income taxes, because at the break-even point, there is no income.

Notice that AccuTime Company must sell 5,000 units *beyond the break-even point* in order to achieve after-tax net income of $30,000. Each unit sold beyond the break-even point contributes $10 toward *before-tax* income. However, of that $10 contribution margin, $4 will have to be paid in income taxes. This leaves an *after-tax contribution* of $6 toward after-tax net income. Thus, selling 5,000 units beyond the break-even point results in after-tax net income of $30,000 (5,000 units $\times$ $6 after-tax contribution per unit).

KEY TERMS:
APPENDIX

After-tax net income, p. 296; Before-tax income, p. 296.

REVIEW QUESTIONS

7-1. What is the meaning of the term *unit contribution margin?* Contribution to what?

7-2. Briefly explain each of the following methods of computing a break-even point in units: (a) contribution-margin approach, (b) equation approach, and (c) graphical approach.

7-3. What information is conveyed by a cost-volume-profit graph in addition to a company's break-even point?

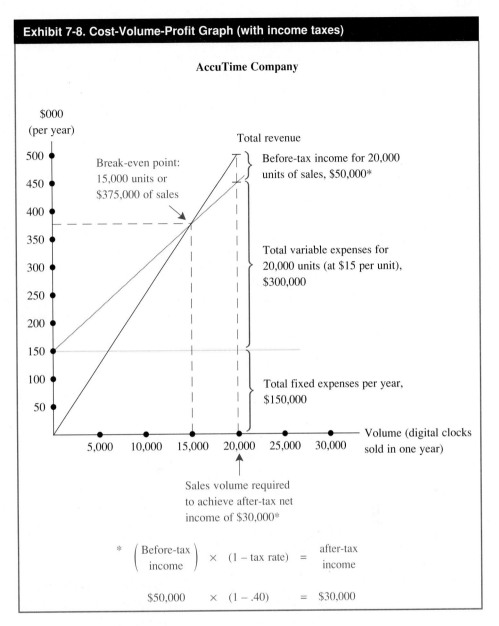

Exhibit 7-8. Cost-Volume-Profit Graph (with income taxes)

AccuTime Company

7-4. What does the term *safety margin* mean?

7-5. Suppose the fixed expenses of a travel agency increase. What will happen to its break-even point, measured in number of clients served? Why?

7-6. Chesapeake Oyster Company has been able to decrease its variable expenses per pound of oysters harvested. How will this affect the firm's break-even sales volume?

7-7. In a strategy meeting, a manufacturing company's president said, "If we raise the price of our product, the company's break-even point will be lower." The financial vice president responded by saying, "Then we should raise our price. The company will be less likely to incur a loss." Do you agree with the president? Why? Do you agree with the financial vice president? Why?

7-8. What will happen to a company's break-even point if the sales price and unit variable cost of its only product increase by the same dollar amount?

7-9. An art museum covers its operating expenses by charging a small admission fee. The objective of the nonprofit organization is to break even. A local arts enthusiast has just pledged to make an annual donation of $5,000 to the museum. How will the donation affect the museum's break-even attendance level?

7-10. How can a profit-volume graph be used to predict a company's profit for a particular sales volume?

7-11. List the most important assumptions of cost-volume-profit analysis.

7-12. Why do many operating managers prefer a contribution income statement instead of a traditional income statement?

7-13. What is the difference between a company's *gross margin* and its total *contribution margin?*

7-14. East Company manufactures VCRs using a completely automated production process. West Company also manufactures VCRs, but its products are assembled manually. How will these two firms' *cost structures* differ? Which company will have a higher *operating leverage factor?*

7-15. When sales volume increases, which company will experience a larger percentage increase in profit: company X, which has mostly fixed expenses, or company Y, which has mostly variable expenses?

7-16. What does the term *sales mix* mean? How is a *weighted-average unit contribution margin* computed?

7-17. A car rental agency rents subcompact, compact, and full-size automobiles. What assumption would be made about the agency's *sales mix* for the purpose of a cost-volume-profit analysis?

7-18. How can a hotel's management use cost-volume-profit analysis to help in deciding on room rates?

7-19. How could cost-volume-profit analysis be used in budgeting? In making a decision about advertising?

7-20. Two companies have identical fixed expenses, unit variable expenses, and profits. Yet one company has set a much lower price for its product. Explain how this can happen.

EXERCISES

Exercise 7-21   Pizza Delivery Business; Basic CVP Analysis. University Pizza delivers pizzas to the dormitories and apartments near a major state university. The company's annual fixed expenses are $40,000. The sales price of a pizza is $10, and it costs the company $5 to make and deliver each pizza. (In the following requirements, ignore income taxes.)

REQUIRED:

1. Using the contribution-margin approach, compute the company's break-even point in units (pizzas).
2. What is the contribution-margin ratio?
3. Compute the break-even sales revenue. Use the contribution-margin ratio in your calculation.
4. How many pizzas must the company sell to earn a target net profit of $50,000? Use the equation method.

Exercise 7-22   Sports Franchise; CVP Graph. The Denver Mountaineers, a minor-league baseball team, play their weekly games in a small stadium just outside Denver. The stadium holds 10,000 people and tickets sell for $10 each. The franchise owner estimates that the team's annual fixed expenses are $180,000, and the variable expense per ticket sold is $1. (In the following requirements, ignore income taxes.)

REQUIRED:

1. Draw a cost-volume-profit graph for the sports franchise. Label the axes, break-even point, profit and loss areas, fixed expenses, variable expenses, total-expense line, and total-revenue line.
2. If the stadium is half full for each game, how many games must the team play to break even?

Exercise 7-23   Continuation of Exercise 7-22; Profit-Volume Graph; Safety Margin. Refer to the data given in the preceding exercise. (Ignore income taxes.)

REQUIRED:

1. Prepare a fully labeled profit-volume graph for the Denver Mountaineers.
2. What is the safety margin for the baseball franchise if the team plays a 12-game season and the team owner expects the stadium to be 30 percent full for each game?
3. If the stadium is half full for each game, what ticket price would the team have to charge in order to break even?

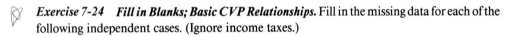

Exercise 7-24   Fill in Blanks; Basic CVP Relationships. Fill in the missing data for each of the following independent cases. (Ignore income taxes.)

	Sales Revenue	Variable Expenses	Total Contribution Margin	Fixed Expenses	Net Income	Break-even Sales Revenue
1......	$100,000	$20,000	?	?	$30,000	?
2......	?	40,000	?	$30,000	?	$40,000
3......	80,000	?	$15,000	?	?	80,000
4......	?	40,000	80,000	?	50,000	?

Exercise 7-25   Manufacturing; Using CVP Analysis. Aerospace Systems Company manufactures a component used in aircraft radar systems. The firm's fixed costs are $4,000,000 per year. The variable cost of each component is $2,000, and the components are sold for $3,000 each. The company sold 5,000 components during the prior year. (In the following requirements, ignore income taxes.)

REQUIRED:

1. Compute the break-even point in units.
2. What will the new break-even point be if fixed costs increase by 10 percent?
3. What was the company's net income for the prior year?
4. The sales manager believes that a reduction in the sales price to $2,500 will result in orders for 1,000 more components each year. What will the break-even point be if the price is changed?
5. Should the price change be made?

Exercise 7-26   Retail; CVP Analysis with Multiple Products. Tim's Bicycle Shop sells 10-speed bicycles. For purposes of a cost-volume-profit analysis, the shop owner has divided sales into two categories, as follows:

Product Type	Sales Price	Invoice Cost	Sales Commission
High-quality	$500	$275	$25
Medium-quality	300	135	15

Three-quarters of the shop's sales are medium-quality bikes. The shop's annual fixed expenses are $65,000. (In the following requirements, ignore income taxes.)

REQUIRED:

1. Compute the unit contribution margin for each product type.
2. What is the shop's sales mix?
3. Compute the weighted-average unit contribution margin, assuming a constant sales mix.
4. What is the shop's break-even sales volume in dollars? Assume a constant sales mix.
5. How many bicycles of each type must be sold to earn a target net income of $32,500? Assume a constant sales mix.

Exercise 7-27   Publishing; Contribution Income Statement. Science Publications, Inc. produces and sells scientific reference books. The results of the company's operations during the prior year are given below. All units produced during the year were sold. (Ignore income taxes.)

Sales revenue	$2,000,000
Manufacturing costs:	
Fixed	500,000
Variable	1,000,000
Selling costs:	
Fixed	50,000
Variable	100,000
Administrative costs:	
Fixed	120,000
Variable	30,000

REQUIRED:

1. Prepare a traditional income statement and a contribution income statement for the company.
2. What is the firm's operating leverage factor for the sales volume generated during the prior year?
3. Suppose sales revenue increases by 20 percent. What will be the percentage increase in net income?
4. Which income statement would an operating manager use to answer requirement (3)? Why?

Exercise 7-28   Hotel and Restaurant; Cost Structure and Operating Leverage. A contribution income statement for Sierra Lodge is shown below. (Ignore income taxes.)

Revenue..	$500,000
Variable expenses	300,000
Contribution margin.......................................	200,000
Fixed expenses...	150,000
Net income	$ 50,000

REQUIRED:

1. Show the hotel's cost structure by indicating the percentage of the hotel's revenue represented by each item on the income statement.
2. Suppose the hotel's revenue declines by 15 percent. Use the contribution-margin percentage to calculate the resulting decrease in net income.
3. What is the hotel's operating leverage factor when revenue is $500,000?
4. Use the operating leverage factor to calculate the increase in net income resulting from a 5 percent increase in sales revenue.

Exercise 7-29   Continuation of Exercise 7-28. Refer to the income statement given in the preceding exercise. Prepare a new contribution income statement for Sierra Lodge in each of the following independent situations. (Ignore income taxes.)

1. The hotel's volume of activity increases by 20 percent, and fixed expenses increase by 30 percent.
2. The ratio of variable expenses to revenue doubles. There is no change in the hotel's volume of activity. Fixed expenses decline by $25,000.

Exercise 7-30   Consulting Firm; CVP Analysis with Income Taxes (Appendix). Construction Engineering Associates, Inc. provides structural consulting services to building contractors. The consulting firm's contribution-margin ratio is 20 percent, and its annual fixed expenses are $100,000. The firm's income-tax rate is 40 percent.

REQUIRED:

1. Calculate the firm's break-even volume of service revenue.
2. How much before-tax income must the firm earn to make an after-tax net income of $48,000?
3. What level of revenue for consulting services must the firm generate to earn an after-tax net income of $48,000?
4. Suppose the firm's income-tax rate rises to 50 percent. What will happen to the break-even level of consulting service revenue?

PROBLEMS

Problem 7-31   Basic CVP Computations. Pawnee Company produced and sold 60,000 units of its single product during 19x2 at an average price of $20 per unit. Variable manufacturing costs were $8 per unit, and variable marketing costs were $4 per unit sold. Fixed costs amounted to $188,000 for manufacturing and $64,000 for marketing. There was no year-end work-in-process inventory. (Ignore income taxes.)

REQUIRED:

1. Compute Pawnee's break-even point in sales dollars for 19x2.
2. Compute the number of sales units required to earn a net income of $180,000 during 19x2.
3. Pawnee's variable manufacturing costs are expected to increase 10 percent in the coming year. Compute Pawnee's break-even point in sales dollars for the coming year.
4. If Pawnee's variable manufacturing costs do increase 10 percent, compute the selling price that would yield Pawnee the same contribution-margin ratio in the coming year.

(CMA, adapted)

Problem 7-32   Basic CVP Relationships; Retailer. DisKing Company is a retailer for video disks. The projected net income for the current year is $200,000 based on a sales volume of 200,000 video disks. DisKing has been selling the disks for $16 each. The variable costs consist of the $10 unit purchase price of the disks and a handling cost of $2 per disk. DisKing's annual fixed costs are $600,000.

Management is planning for the coming year, when it expects that the unit purchase price of the video disks will increase 30 percent. (Ignore income taxes.)

REQUIRED:

1. Calculate DisKing Company's break-even point for the current year in number of video disks.
2. What will be the company's net income for the current year if there is a 10 percent increase in projected unit sales volume?
3. What volume of sales (in dollars) must DisKing Company achieve in the coming year to maintain the same net income as projected for the current year if the unit selling price remains at $16?
4. In order to cover a 30 percent increase in the disk's purchase price for the coming year and still maintain the current contribution-margin ratio, what selling price per disk must DisKing Company establish for the coming year?

(CMA, adapted)

Problem 7-33   Basic CVP Relationships; CVP Graph; Cost Structure; Operating Leverage. Padden Company has projected its income for 19x7 as shown below. (Ignore income taxes.)

Sales (160,000 units)...................................		$8,000,000
Operating expenses:		
Variable expenses............................	$2,000,000	
Fixed expenses	3,000,000	
Total expenses...		5,000,000
Net income..		$3,000,000

REQUIRED:

1. Prepare a CVP graph for Padden Company.
2. Calculate the firm's break-even point for 19x7.
3. What is the company's margin of safety for 19x7?
4. Compute Padden Company's operating leverage factor, based on the budgeted sales volume for 19x7.
5. Compute Padden Company's required sales in dollars in order to earn income of $4,500,000 in 19x7.
6. Describe Padden Company's cost structure. Calculate the percentage relationships between variable and fixed expenses and sales revenue.

(CMA, adapted)

Problem 7-34   Break-Even Point; After-Tax Net Income; Profit-Volume Graph (Appendix). Annual budget data for Biden Company are as follows:

Sales (100,000 units). $1,000,000

Costs:	Fixed	Variable	
Direct material	$ -0-	$300,000	
Direct labor.	-0-	200,000	
Manufacturing overhead	100,000	150,000	
Selling and administrative	110,000	50,000	
Total costs	$210,000	$700,000	910,000
Budgeted operating income			$ 90,000

In the following requirements, ignore income taxes.

REQUIRED:

1. Calculate the break-even point in units and in sales dollars.
2. If Biden Company is subject to an income-tax rate of 40 percent, compute the number of units the company would have to sell to earn an after-tax profit of $90,000.
3. If fixed costs increased $31,500 with no other cost or revenue factor changing, compute the firm's break-even sales in units.
4. Prepare a profit-volume graph for Biden Company.

(CMA, adapted)

Problem 7-35   *Basic CVP Relationships.* Maxwell Company manufactures and sells a single product. Price and cost data regarding Maxwell's product and operations are as follows:

Selling price per unit	$25.00
Variable costs per unit:	
Direct material	$11.00
Direct labor.	5.00
Manufacturing overhead	2.50
Selling expenses.	1.30
Total variable costs per unit.	$19.80
Annual fixed costs:	
Manufacturing overhead	$ 192,000
Selling and administrative	276,000
Total fixed costs	$ 468,000
Forecasted annual sales volume (120,000 units).	$3,000,000

In the following requirements, ignore income taxes.

REQUIRED:

1. What is Maxwell Company's break-even point in units?
2. What is the company's break-even point in sales dollars?
3. How many units would Maxwell Company have to sell in order to earn $260,000?
4. What is the firm's margin of safety?
5. Maxwell Company estimates that its direct-labor costs will increase by 8 percent next year. How many units will Maxwell have to sell next year to reach its break-even point?

6. If Maxwell Company's direct-labor costs do increase 8 percent, what selling price per unit of product must it charge to maintain the same contribution-margin ratio?

(CMA, adapted)

Problem 7-36 CVP Analysis; Advertising and Special-Order Decisions. Bodine Company produces a single product, which currently sells for $5.00. Fixed costs are expected to amount to $60,000 for the year, and all variable manufacturing and administrative costs are expected to be incurred at a rate of $3.00 per unit. Bodine has two salespeople who are paid strictly on a commission basis. Their commission is 10 percent of the sales dollars they generate. (Ignore income taxes.)

REQUIRED:

1. Suppose management alters its current plans by spending an additional amount of $5,000 on advertising and increases the selling price to $6.00 per unit. Calculate the profit on 60,000 units.
2. The Sorde Company has just approached Bodine to make a special one-time purchase of 10,000 units. These units would not be sold by the sales personnel, and, therefore, no commission would have to be paid. What is the price Bodine would have to charge per unit on this special order to earn additional profit of $20,000?

(CMA, adapted)

Problem 7-37 CVP Analysis and Advertising Decisions. Moorehead Manufacturing Company manufactures two products for which the following data have been tabulated. Fixed manufacturing cost is applied at a rate of $1.00 per machine hour.

Per Unit	XY-7	BD-4
Selling price.	$4.00	$3.00
Variable manufacturing cost	2.00	1.50
Fixed manufacturing cost.	.75	.20
Variable selling cost	1.00	1.00

The sales manager has had a $160,000 increase in her budget allotment for advertising and wants to apply the money to the most profitable product. The products are not substitutes for one another in the eyes of the company's customers. (Ignore income taxes.)

REQUIRED:

1. Suppose the sales manager chose to devote the entire $160,000 to increased advertising for XY-7. What is the minimum increase in *sales units* of XY-7 required to offset the increased advertising?
2. Suppose the sales manager chose to devote the entire $160,000 to increased advertising for BD-4. What is the minimum increase in *sales dollars* of BD-4 required to offset the increased advertising?
3. Suppose Moorehead has only 100,000 machine hours to make available to produce XY-7 and BD-4. If the potential increase in sales units for either product resulting from advertising is far in excess of these production capabilities, which product should be advertised and what is the estimated increase in contribution margin earned?

(CMA, adapted)

Problem 7-38 Basic CVP Relationships. Richardson Radio Company manufactures small radios. Last year the company sold 25,000 units with the following results.

Sales...		$625,000
Variable costs	$375,000	
Fixed costs.....................................	150,000	525,000
Net income.....................................		$100,000

In an attempt to improve its product, the company is considering replacing a component part that has a cost of $2.50 with a new and better part costing $4.50 per unit in the coming year. A new machine would also be needed to increase plant capacity. The machine would cost $18,000 with a useful life of six years and no salvage value. The company uses straight-line depreciation on all plant assets. (Ignore income taxes.)

REQUIRED:

1. What was Richardson Radio Company's break-even point in number of units last year?
2. How many units of product would the company have had to sell in the last year to earn $140,000?
3. If Richardson Radio Company holds the sales price constant and makes the suggested changes, how many units of product must be sold in the coming year to break even?
4. If the firm holds the sales price constant and makes the suggested changes, how many units of product will the company have to sell to make the same net income as last year?
5. If Richardson wishes to maintain the same contribution margin ratio, what selling price per unit of product must it charge next year to cover the increased direct-material cost?

(CMA, adapted)

Problem 7-39 Break-Even Analysis; Profit-Volume Graph; Movie Theaters. Hollywood Company owns and operates a nationwide chain of movie theaters. The 500 properties in the Hollywood chain vary from low-volume, small-town, single-screen theaters to high-volume, big-city, multiscreen theaters. The firm's management is considering installing popcorn machines, which would allow the theaters to sell freshly popped corn rather than prepopped corn. This new feature would be advertised to increase patronage at the company's theaters. The fresh popcorn will be sold for 75¢ per box. The annual rental costs and the operating costs vary with the size of the popcorn machines. The machine capacities and costs are shown below. (Ignore income taxes.)

	Popper Model		
	Economy	**Regular**	**Super**
Annual capacity	50,000 boxes	120,000 boxes	300,000 boxes
Costs:			
Annual machine rental.......	$8,000	$11,000	$20,000
Popcorn cost per box	.13	.13	.13
Other costs per box..........	.22	.14	.05
Cost of each box	.08	.08	.08

REQUIRED:

1. Calculate each theater's break-even sales volume (measured in boxes of popcorn) for each model of popcorn popper.
2. Prepare a profit-volume graph for one theater, assuming that the Super Popper is purchased.
3. Calculate the volume (in boxes) at which the Economy Popper and the Regular Popper earn the same profit or loss in each movie theater.

(CMA, adapted)

Problem 7-40 Sales Commissions in a Wholesale Firm; Income Taxes (Appendix). Seco Corporation, a wholesale supply company, engages independent sales agents to market the company's products. These agents currently receive a commission of 20 percent of sales, but they are demanding an increase to 25 percent of sales made during the year ending December 31, 19x9. Seco's controller already prepared the 19x9 budget before learning of the agents' demand for an increase in commissions. The budgeted 19x9 income statement is shown below. Assume that cost of goods sold is 100 percent variable cost.

Seco Corporation
Budgeted Income Statement
For the Year Ending December 31, 19x9

Sales		$10,000,000
Cost of goods sold		6,000,000
Gross margin		4,000,000
Selling and administrative expenses:		
Commissions	$2,000,000	
All other expenses (fixed)	100,000	2,100,000
Income before taxes		1,900,000
Income tax (30%)		570,000
Net income		$ 1,330,000

Seco's management is considering the possibility of employing full-time sales personnel. Three individuals would be required, at an estimated annual salary of $30,000 each, plus commissions of 5 percent of sales. In addition, a sales manager would be employed at a fixed annual salary of $160,000. All other fixed costs, as well as the variable cost percentages, would remain the same as the estimates in the 19x9 budgeted income statement.

REQUIRED:

1. Compute Seco's estimated break-even point in sales dollars for the year ending December 31, 19x9 based on the budgeted income statement prepared by the controller.
2. Compute Seco's estimated break-even point in sales dollars for the year ending December 31, 19x9 if the company employs its own sales personnel.
3. Compute the estimated volume in sales dollars that would be required for the year ending December 31, 19x9 to yield the same net income as projected in the budgeted income statement, if Seco continues to use the independent sales agents and agrees to their demand for a 25 percent sales commission.
4. Compute the estimated volume in sales dollars that would generate an identical net income for the year ending December 31, 19x9, regardless of whether Seco

employs its own sales personnel or continues to use the independent sales agents and pays them a 25 percent commission.

(CPA, adapted)

Problem 7-41   Budgeted Break-Even Point; Market Share. Budgeted and actual income statements are presented below for Xerbert Company. (Ignore income taxes.)

Xerbert Company
Budgeted and Actual Income Statements
For the Year Ended December 31, 19x2
(in thousands)

	Budget			Actual		
	Xenox	Xeon	Total	Xenox	Xeon	Total
Unit sales	150	100	250	130	130	260
Sales revenue	$900	$1,000	$1,900	$780	$1,235	$2,015
Variable expenses........	450	750	1,200	390	975	1,365
Contribution margin	$450	$ 250	$ 700	$390	$ 260	$ 650
Fixed expenses:						
Manufacturing			$ 200			$ 190
Marketing			153			140
Administration			95			90
Total fixed expenses ...			$ 448			$ 420
Net income..............			$ 252			$ 230

REQUIRED:

1. Calculate the budgeted and actual break-even points in units.
2. Calculate the budgeted and actual break-even points in sales dollars.
3. The 19x2 budgeted total sales volume of 250,000 units was based upon Xerbert achieving a market share of 10 percent. Actual industry volume reached 2,580,000 units. What percentage of Xerbert's increased volume was due to its improved market share?
4. By what dollar amount do the actual total contribution margin and the budgeted total contribution margin differ as a result of the difference between the actual and budgeted sales prices?

(CMA, adapted)

Problem 7-42   CVP Relationships; Bookstore. Condensed monthly income data for Thurber Bookstores, Inc. are presented below for November 19x4. (Ignore income taxes.)

	Total	Mall Store	Downtown Store
Sales.....................................	$200,000	$80,000	$120,000
Less variable expenses.....................	116,000	32,000	84,000
Contribution margin......................	$ 84,000	$48,000	$ 36,000
Less fixed expenses	60,000	20,000	40,000
Operating income	$ 24,000	$28,000	$ (4,000)

ADDITIONAL INFORMATION:

- One-fourth of each store's fixed expenses would continue through December 31, 19x5 if either store were closed.
- Management estimates that closing the downtown store would result in a ten percent decrease in mall store sales, while closing the mall store would not affect downtown store sales.
- The operating results for November 19x4 are representative of all months.

REQUIRED:

1. Calculate the increase or decrease in Thurber Bookstores' monthly operating income during 19x5 if the downtown store is closed.
2. The management of Thurber Bookstores is considering a promotional campaign at the downtown store that would not affect the mall store. Annual promotional expenses at the downtown store would be increased by $60,000 in order to increase downtown store sales by 10 percent. What would be the effect of this promotional campaign on the company's monthly operating income during 19x5?
3. One-half of the downtown store's dollar sales are from items sold at their variable cost to attract customers to the store. Thurber's management is considering the deletion of these items, a move that would reduce the downtown store's direct fixed expenses by 15 percent and result in the loss of 20 percent of the remaining downtown store's sales volume. This change would not affect the mall store. What would be the effect on Thurber's monthly operating income if the items sold at their variable cost are eliminated?

(CMA, adapted)

Problem 7-43 *Break-Even Analysis; Operating Leverage; New Manufacturing Environment.*
Cavalier Company has decided to introduce a new product, which can be manufactured by either a computer-assisted manufacturing system or a labor-intensive production system. The manufacturing method will not affect the quality of the product. The estimated manufacturing costs by the two methods are as follows:

	Computer-Assisted Manufacturing System	Labor-Intensive Production System
Direct material	$5.00	$5.60
Direct labor.	.5DLH @ $12 6.00	.8DLH @ $9 7.20
Variable overhead. . .	.5DLH @ $6 3.00	.8DLH @ $6 4.80
Fixed overhead*	$2,440,000	$1,320,000

* These costs are directly traceable to the new product line. They would not be incurred if the new product were not produced.

The company's marketing research department has recommended an introductory unit sales price of $30. Selling expenses are estimated to be $500,000 annually plus $2 for each unit sold. (Ignore income taxes.)

REQUIRED:

1. Calculate the estimated break-even point in annual unit sales of the new product if the company uses the: (a) computer-assisted manufacturing system; (b) labor-intensive production system.

2. Determine the annual unit sales volume at which the firm would be indifferent between the two manufacturing methods.
3. Management must decide which manufacturing method to employ. One factor it should consider is operating leverage. Explain the concept of operating leverage. How is this concept related to Cavalier Company's decision?
4. Describe the circumstances under which the firm should employ each of the two manufacturing methods.
5. Identify some business factors other than operating leverage that management should consider before selecting the manufacturing method.

(CMA, adapted)

Problem 7-44   Cost-Volume-Profit Analysis with Income Taxes and Multiple Products (Appendix). Great Northern Ski Company recently expanded its manufacturing capacity. The firm will now be able to produce up to 15,000 pairs of cross-country skis of either the mountaineering model or the touring model. The sales department assures management that it can sell between 9,000 and 13,000 units of either product this year. Because the models are very similar, the company will produce only one of the two models.

The following information was compiled by the accounting department.

	Model	
	Mountaineering	**Touring**
Selling price per unit	$88.00	$80.00
Variable costs per unit	$52.80	$52.80

Fixed costs will total $369,600 if the mountaineering model is produced but will be only $316,800 if the touring model is produced. Great Northern Ski Company is subject to a 40 percent income tax rate. (Round each answer to the nearest whole number.)

REQUIRED:

1. Compute the contribution-margin ratio for the touring model.
2. If Great Northern Ski Company desires an after-tax net income of $24,000, how many pairs of touring skis will the company have to sell?
3. How much would the variable cost per unit of the touring model have to change before it had the same break-even point in units as the mountaineering model?
4. Suppose the variable cost per unit of touring skis decreases by 10 percent, and the total fixed cost of touring skis increases by 10 percent. Compute the new break-even point.
5. Suppose management decided to produce both products. If the two models are sold in equal proportions, and total fixed costs amount to $343,200, what is the firm's break-even point in units?

(CMA, adapted)

Problem 7-45   CVP Relationships. The following income statement represents Davidson Gravel Company's operating results for the fiscal year just ended. The company had sales of 1,800 tons during the current year. The manufacturing capacity of Davidson's facilities is 3,000 tons per year. (Ignore income taxes.)

Davidson Gravel Company
Income Statement
For the Year Ended December 31, 19x0

Sales	$900,000
Variable costs:	
Manufacturing...	$315,000
Selling costs	180,000
Total variable costs	$495,000
Contribution margin......................................	$405,000
Fixed costs:	
Manufacturing...	$ 90,000
Selling...	112,500
Administrative...	45,000
Total fixed costs......................................	$247,500
Net income	$157,500

REQUIRED:

1. Calculate the company's break-even volume in tons for 19x0.
2. If the sales volume is estimated to be 2,100 tons in the next year, and if the prices and costs stay at the same levels and amounts, what is the net income that management can expect for 19x1?
3. The company has a potential foreign customer that has offered to buy 1,500 tons at $450 per ton. Assume that all of Davidson's costs would be at the same levels and rates as in 19x0. What net income would the firm earn if it took this order and rejected some business from regular customers so as not to exceed capacity?
4. Davidson plans to market its product in a new territory. Management estimates that an advertising and promotion program costing $61,500 annually would be needed for the next two or three years. In addition, a $25 per ton sales commission to the sales force in the new territory, over and above the current commission, would be required. How many tons would have to be sold in the new territory to maintain Davidson's current net income? Assume that sales and costs will continue as in 19x0 in the firm's established territories.
5. Davidson is considering replacing its labor-intensive process with an automated production system. This would result in an increase of $58,500 annually in fixed manufacturing costs. The variable manufacturing costs would decrease by $25 per ton. Compute the new break-even volume in tons and in sales dollars.
6. Ignore the facts presented in requirement (5). Assume that management estimates that the selling price per ton would decline by 10 percent next year. Variable costs would increase by $40 per ton, and fixed costs would not change. What sales volume in dollars would be required to earn a net income of $94,500 next year?

(CMA, adapted)

CASES   *Case 7-46.*   *Contribution-Margin Income Statement; CVP Analysis.* Delphina Products Company is a regional firm with three major product lines: cereals, breakfast bars, and dog food. The following income statement was prepared by product line. (Ignore income taxes.)

Delphina Products Company
Income Statement
For the Year Ended April 30, 19x8
(in thousands)

	Cereals	Break-fast Bars	Dog Food	Total
Sales (in pounds).....................	2,000	500	500	3,000
Sales revenue........................	$1,000	$400	$200	$1,600
Cost of goods sold:				
Direct material	$ 330	$160	$100	$ 590
Direct labor........................	90	40	20	150
Manufacturing overhead	108	48	24	180
Total cost of goods sold	$ 528	$248	$144	$ 920
Gross margin........................	$ 472	$152	$ 56	$ 680
Operating expenses:				
Selling expenses:				
Advertising	$ 50	$ 30	$ 20	$ 100
Commissions.....................	50	40	20	110
Salaries and fringe benefits	30	20	10	60
Total selling expenses	$ 130	$ 90	$ 50	$ 270
General and administrative expenses:				
Licenses	$ 50	$ 20	$ 15	$ 85
Salaries and fringe benefits	60	25	15	100
Total general and administrative expenses........................	$ 110	$ 45	$ 30	$ 185
Total operating expenses	$ 240	$135	$ 80	$ 455
Operating income before taxes..........	$ 232	$ 17	$(24)	$ 225

OTHER DATA

- *Cost of goods sold.* The company's inventories of raw materials and finished products do not vary significantly from year to year. The inventories on April 30, 19x8 were essentially identical to those on April 30, 19x7.

  Manufacturing overhead was applied to products at 120 percent of direct-labor dollars. The manufacturing-overhead costs for the 19x7–19x8 fiscal year were as follows:

Variable indirect labor and supplies.............................	$ 15,000
Variable employee benefits on indirect labor......................	30,000
Supervisory salaries and fringe benefits	35,000
Plant occupancy costs.......................................	100,000
Total...	$180,000

There was no overapplied or underapplied overhead at year-end.

- *Advertising.* The company has been unable to determine any direct causal relationship between the level of sales volume and the level of advertising expenditures. However, because management believes advertising is necessary, an annual advertising program is implemented for each product line. Each product line is advertised independently of the others.

- *Commissions.* Sales commissions are paid to the sales force at the rates of 5 percent on the cereals and 10 percent on the breakfast bars and dog food.
- *Licenses.* Various licenses are required for each product line. These are renewed annually for each product line.
- *Salaries and fringe benefits.* Sales and administrative personnel devote time and effort to all product lines. Their salaries and wages are allocated on the basis of management's estimates of time spent on each product line.

REQUIRED:

1. The controller of Delphina Products Company has recommended that the company do a cost-volume-profit analysis of its operations. As a first step, the controller has requested that you prepare a revised income statement that employs a contribution-margin format, which will be useful in CVP analysis. The statement should show the contribution margin for each product line and the operating income before taxes for the company as a whole.
2. The controller of Delphina Products Company is going to prepare a report to present to the other members of top management explaining cost-volume-profit analysis. Identify and explain the following points, which the controller should include in the report.
   a. The advantages that CVP analysis can provide to the company.
   b. The difficulties Delphina Products Company could experience in the calculations involved in CVP analysis.
   c. The dangers that Delphina Products Company should be aware of in using the information derived from the CVP analysis.

(CMA, adapted)

Case 7-47   Break-Even Analysis; Hospital CVP Relationships. Delaware Medical Center operates a general hospital. The medical center also rents space and beds to separately owned entities rendering specialized services, such as Pediatrics and Psychiatric Care. Delaware charges each separate entity for common services, such as patients' meals and laundry, and for administrative services, such as billings and collections. Space and bed rentals are fixed charges for the year, based on bed capacity rented to each entity. Delaware Medical Center charged the following costs to Pediatrics for the year ended June 30, 19x2:

	Patient Days (variable)	Bed Capacity (fixed)
Dietary	$ 600,000	—
Janitorial	—	$ 70,000
Laundry	300,000	—
Laboratory	450,000	—
Pharmacy	350,000	—
Repairs and maintenance	—	30,000
General and administrative	—	1,300,000
Rent	—	1,500,000
Billings and collections	300,000	—
Total	$2,000,000	$2,900,000

During the year ended June 30, 19x2, Pediatrics charged each patient an average of $300 per day, had a capacity of 60 beds, and had revenue of $6 million for 365 days. In addition,

Pediatrics directly employed personnel with the following annual salary costs per employee: supervising nurses, $25,000; nurses, $20,000; and aides, $9,000.

Delaware Medical Center has the following minimum departmental personnel requirements, based on total annual patient days:

Annual Patient Days	Aides	Nurses	Supervising Nurses
Up to 21,900	20	10	4
21,901 to 26,000	26	13	4
26,001 to 29,200	30	15	4

Pediatrics always employs only the minimum number of required personnel. Salaries of supervising nurses, nurses, and aides are therefore fixed within ranges of annual patient days.

Pediatrics operated at 100 percent capacity on 90 days during the year ended June 30, 19x2. Administrators estimate that on these 90 days, Pediatrics could have filled another 20 beds above capacity. Delaware Medical Center has an additional 20 beds available for rent for the year ending June 30, 19x3. Such additional rental would increase Pediatrics' fixed charges based on bed capacity.

In the following requirements, ignore income taxes.

REQUIRED:

1. Calculate the minimum number of patient days required for Pediatrics to break even for the year ending June 30, 19x3, if the additional 20 beds are not rented. Patient demand is unknown, but assume that revenue per patient day, cost per patient day, cost per bed, and salary rates will remain the same as for the year ended June 30, 19x2.
2. Assume that patient demand, revenue per patient day, cost per patient day, cost per bed, and salary rates for the year ending June 30, 19x3 remain the same as for the year ended June 30, 19x2. Prepare a schedule of Pediatrics' increase in revenue and increase in costs for the year ending June 30, 19x3. Determine the net increase or decrease in Pediatrics' earnings from the additional 20 beds if Pediatrics rents this extra capacity from Delaware Medical Center.

(CPA, adapted)

Chapter 8 Budgeting: Profit Planning and Control Systems

After completing this chapter, you should be able to:

- List and explain five purposes of budgeting systems.

- Describe the similarities and differences in the operational budgets prepared by manufacturers, service industry firms, merchandisers, and nonprofit organizations.

- Prepare each of the following budgets: sales budget, production budget, direct-material budget, direct-labor budget, indirect-labor budget, overhead budget, selling and administrative expense budget, cash budget, budgeted income statement, and budgeted balance sheet.

- Describe a typical organization's process of budget administration.

- Discuss the role of assumptions and predictions in budgeting.

- Explain how a financial planning model works.

- Discuss the behavioral implications of budgetary slack and participative budgeting.

Developing a budget is a critical step in planning any economic activity. This is true for businesses, for governmental agencies, and for individuals. We must all budget our money to meet day-to-day expenses and to plan for major expenditures, such as buying a car or paying for college tuition. Similarly, businesses of all types and governmental units at every level must make financial plans to carry out routine operations, to plan for major expenditures, and 'o help in making financing decisions.

PURPOSES OF BUDGETING SYSTEMS

A **budget** is a detailed plan, expressed in quantitative terms, that specifies how resources will be acquired and used during a specified period of time. The procedures used to develop a budget constitute a **budgeting system.** Budgeting systems have five primary purposes.

1. **Planning** The most obvious purpose of a budget is to quantify a plan of action. The budgeting process forces the individuals who comprise an organization to plan ahead. The development of a quarterly budget for a Sheraton Hotel, for example, forces the hotel manager, the reservation manager, and the food and beverage manager to plan for the staffing and supplies needed to meet anticipated demand for the hotel's services.

2. **Facilitating Communication and Coordination** For any organization to be effective, each manager throughout the organization must be aware of the plans made by other managers. In order to plan reservations and ticket sales effectively, the reservations manager for Delta Air Lines must know the flight schedules developed by the airline's route manager. The budgeting process pulls together the plans of each manager in an organization.

3. **Allocating Resources** Generally, an organization's resources are limited, and budgets provide one means of allocating resources among competing uses. The city of Chicago, for example, must allocate its revenue among basic life services (such as police and fire protection), maintenance of property and equipment (such as city streets, parks, and vehicles), and other community services (such as child-care services and programs to prevent alcohol and drug abuse).

4. **Controlling Profit and Operations** A budget is a plan, and plans are subject to change. Nevertheless, a budget serves as a useful benchmark with which actual results can be compared. For example, Prudential Insurance Company can compare its actual sales of insurance policies for a year against its budgeted sales. Such a comparison can help managers evaluate the firm's effectiveness in selling insurance. The next two chapters examine the control purpose of budgets in more depth.

5. **Evaluating Performance and Providing Incentives** Comparing actual results with budgeted results also helps managers to evaluate the performance of individuals, departments, divisions, or entire companies. Since budgets are used to evaluate performance, they can also be used to provide incentives for people to perform well. For example, General Motors Corporation, like many other companies, provides incentives for managers to improve profits by awarding bonuses to managers who meet or exceed their budgeted profit goals.

TYPES OF BUDGETS

Different types of budgets serve different purposes. A **master budget,** or **profit plan,** is a comprehensive set of budgets covering all phases of an organization's operations for a specified period of time. We will examine a master budget in detail later in this chapter.

Budgeted financial statements, often called **pro forma financial statements,** show how the organization's financial statements will appear at a specified time if operations proceed according to plan. Budgeted financial statements include a *budgeted income statement,* a *budgeted balance sheet,* and a *budgeted statement of cash flows.*

A **capital budget** is a plan for the acquisition of capital assets, such as buildings and equipment. Capital budgeting is covered in depth later in the text. A **financial budget** is a plan that shows how the organization will acquire its financial resources, such as through the issuance of stock or incurrence of debt.

Budgets are developed for specific time periods. *Short-range budgets* cover a year, a quarter, or a month, whereas *long-range budgets* cover periods longer than a year. **Rolling budgets** are continually updated by periodically adding a new incremental time period, such as a quarter, and dropping the period just completed. Rolling budgets are also called **revolving budgets** or **continuous budgets.**

THE MASTER BUDGET: A PLANNING TOOL

The **master budget,** the principal output of a budgeting system, is a comprehensive profit plan that ties together all phases of an organization's operations. The master budget is comprised of many separate budgets, or schedules, that are interdependent. Exhibit 8-1 portrays these interrelationships in a flowchart.

Exhibit 8-1. Components of a Master Budget

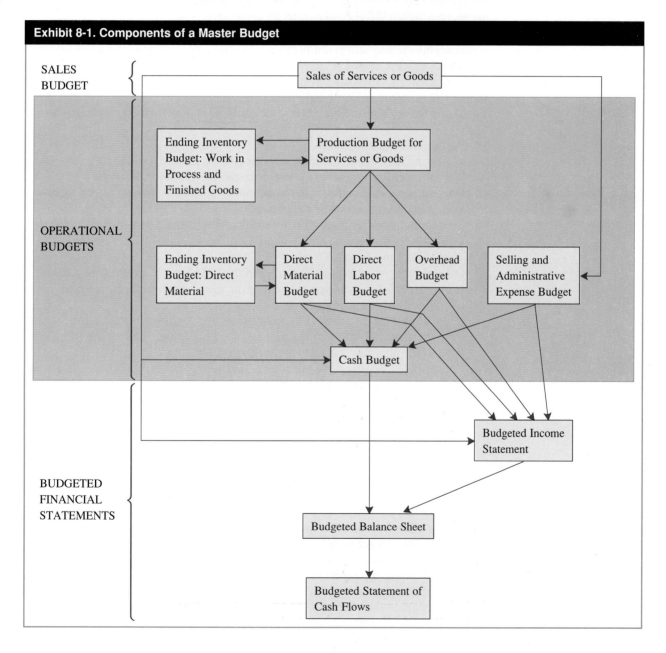

Sales of Services or Goods

The starting point for any master budget is a sales revenue budget based on forecast sales of services or goods. Airlines forecast the number of passengers on each of their routes. Banks forecast the number and dollar amount of consumer loans and home mortgages to be provided. Hotels forecast the number of rooms that will be occupied during various seasons. Manufacturing and merchandising companies forecast sales of their goods. Some companies sell both goods and services. For example, Sears, Roebuck and Company is the world's largest merchandising company, but its automotive-service branch provides the firm with substantial service revenue.

Sales Forecasting All companies have two things in common when it comes to forecasting sales of services or goods. Sales forecasting is a critical step in the budgeting process, and it is very difficult to do accurately.

Various procedures are used in sales forecasting, and the final forecast usually combines information from many different sources. Many firms have a top-management-level market research staff whose job is to coordinate the company's sales forecasting efforts. Typically, everyone from key executives to the firm's sales personnel will be asked to contribute sales projections.

Major factors considered when forecasting sales include the following:

1. Past sales levels and trends:
   a. For the firm developing the forecast (for example, Exxon).
   b. For the entire industry (for example, the petroleum industry).
2. General economic trends. (Is the economy growing? How fast? Is a recession or economic slowdown expected?)
3. Economic trends in the company's industry. (In the petroleum industry, for example, is personal travel likely to increase, thereby implying increased demand for gasoline?)
4. Other factors expected to affect sales in the industry. (Is an unusually cold winter expected, which would result in increased demand for home heating oil in northern climates?)
5. Political and legal events. (For example, is any legislation pending in Congress that would affect the demand for petroleum, such as tax incentives to use alternative energy sources?)
6. The intended pricing policy of the company.
7. Planned advertising and product promotion.
8. Expected actions of competitors.
9. New products contemplated by the company or other firms. (For example, has an automobile firm announced the development of a new vehicle that runs on battery power, thereby reducing the demand for gasoline?)
10. Market research studies.

The starting point in the sales forecasting process is generally the sales level of the prior year. Then the market research staff considers the information discussed above along with input from key executives and sales personnel. In many firms, elaborate *econometric models* are built to incorporate all the available information systematically. (*Econometric* means economic measurement.) Statistical methods, such as regression analysis and probability distributions for sales, are often used. All in all, a great deal of effort generally goes into the sales forecast, since it is such a critical step in the budgeting process. Making a sales forecast is like shooting an arrow. If the archer's aim is off by only a fraction of an inch, the arrow will go further and further astray and miss the bull's-eye by a wide margin. Similarly, a slightly inaccurate sales forecast, coming at the very beginning of the budgeting process, will throw off all of the other schedules comprising the master budget.

Operational Budgets

Based on the sales budget, a company develops a set of budgets that specify how its operations will be carried out to meet the demand for its goods or services. The budgets comprising this operational portion of the master budget are depicted in the shaded middle portion of Exhibit 8-1.

Manufacturing Firms A manufacturing company develops a production budget, which shows the number of product units to be manufactured. Coupled with the production budget are ending-inventory budgets for both work in process and finished goods. Manufacturers plan to have some inventory on hand at all times to meet peak demand while keeping production at a stable level. From the production budget, a manufacturer develops budgets for the direct materials, direct labor, and overhead that will be required in the production process. A budget for selling and administrative expenses is also prepared.

Merchandising Firms The operational portion of the master budget is similar in a merchandising firm, but instead of a production budget for goods, a merchandiser develops a budget for merchandise purchases. A merchandiser will not have a budget for direct material, because it does not engage in production. However, the merchandiser will develop budgets for labor (or personnel), overhead, and selling and administrative expenses.

Service Industry Firms Based on the sales budget for its services, a service industry firm develops a set of budgets that show how the demand for those services will be met. An airline, for example, prepares the following operational budgets: a budget of planned air miles to be flown; material budgets for spare aircraft parts, aircraft fuel, and in-flight food; labor budgets for flight crews and maintenance personnel; and an overhead budget.

Cash Budget Every business prepares a cash budget. This budget shows expected cash receipts, as a result of selling goods or services, and planned cash disbursements, to pay the bills incurred by the firm.

Summary of Operational Budgets Operational budgets differ since they are adapted to the operations of individual companies in various industries. However, operational budgets are also similar in important ways. In each firm they encompass a detailed plan for using the basic factors of production — material, labor, and overhead — to produce a product or provide a service.

Budgeted Financial Statements

The final portion of the master budget, depicted in Exhibit 8-1, includes a budgeted income statement, a budgeted balance sheet, and a budgeted statement of cash flows. These budgeted financial statements show the overall financial results of the organization's planned operations for the budget period.

Nonprofit Organizations

The master budget for a nonprofit organization includes many of the components shown in Exhibit 8-1. However, there are some important differences. Many nonprofit organizations provide services free of charge. Hence, there is no sales budget as shown in Exhibit 8-1. However, such organizations do begin their budgeting process with a budget that shows the level of services to be provided. For example, the budget for the city of Houston would show the planned levels of various public services.

Nonprofit organizations also prepare budgets showing their anticipated funding. The city of Houston budgets for such revenue sources as city taxes, state and federal revenue sharing, and sale of municipal bonds.

In summary, all organizations begin the budgeting process with plans for (1) the goods or services to be provided and (2) the revenue to be available, whether from sales or from other funding sources.

AN ILLUSTRATION OF THE MASTER BUDGET

To illustrate the steps in developing a master budget, we will look at Healthworks, Inc., a physical therapy and sports medicine practice in San Francisco. The practice was established two years ago by five friends who had recently received degrees in physical therapy and sports medicine. Two of the firm's founders were collegiate track stars, and their local fame helped to publicize the practice. The firm's clientele has grown quickly. Most of the current clients are runners and joggers; the rest are various athletes, surgical rehabilitation patients, and victims of minor accidents.

Healthworks' clients require professional services such as muscle manipulation, supervised exercise, whirlpool treatment, and massage therapy. In addition, many of the firm's running clients need custom-made orthotic devices. An orthotic is an insert for a shoe, designed to compensate for imperfections in the alignment of the legs and spine. For many runners and joggers, an orthotic can help correct or prevent painful injuries to the knee and lower leg. Although generic orthotics are available, they are seldom as effective as custom-made devices.

Producing a custom-made orthotic requires the skill and knowledge of a trained physical therapist. In addition to shaping and constructing the orthotic device, the physical therapist must take detailed measurements of the alignment of the client's leg and foot. The increasing demand for orthotic devices among Healthworks' clientele requires careful planning by the firm's staff to ensure that the demand can be met. In 19x4, the sale of orthotics represented roughly 10 percent of Healthworks' revenues, and a slight increase is anticipated for 19x5.

The 19x5 master budget for Healthworks has just been completed. It contains the following schedules, which are displayed and explained in the following pages.

Schedule	Title of Schedule
1	Professional Services and Sales Budget
2	Production Budget: Construction of Orthotic Devices
3	Direct-Material Budget
4	Direct Professional-Labor Budget
5	Indirect Professional-Labor Budget
6	Overhead Budget
7	Selling and Administrative Expense Budget
8	Cash Receipts Budget
9	Cash Disbursements Budget
10	Summary Cash Budget
11	Budgeted Income Statement
12	Budgeted Balance Sheet

Professional Services and Sales Budget

The first step in developing Healthworks' master budget is to prepare the **professional services and sales budget,** which is displayed as schedule 1. This budget is divided into two parts, one for professional services and one for sales of orthotics. The professional services portion of the budget, which is shaded, shows the number of office visits forecast during each of the four quarters of 19x5. There is a slight seasonal pattern in the demand for professional services. The greatest demand comes during the second quarter (April through June), when most high school and collegiate track programs are under way and enthusiasm for jogging peaks in the general population. Demand declines during the warm summer months and then increases slightly in the fall and winter. The budgeted revenue from professional services is computed by multiplying the projected number of visits by the appropriate fee.

The demand for orthotic devices follows the same seasonal pattern as office visits, but with greater swings in projected sales across the four quarters. The sales revenue from orthotics is determined by multiplying the number of units of expected sales by the sales price per orthotic.

The total budgeted revenue for each quarter and for the year, from both professional services and sales of orthotics, is shown in the last row of schedule 1. Roughly 13 percent of the year's revenue is expected to come from the sale of orthotics ($54,000 ÷ $405,000 = 13.333%).

Schedule 1

HEALTHWORKS, INC.
Associates in Physical Therapy and Sports Medicine
Professional Services and Sales Budget
For the Year Ended December 31, 19x5

| | Quarter | | | | |
	1st	2nd	3rd	4th	Year
Professional services:					
Office visits.........	1,940	2,000	1,920	1,940	7,800
Fee	×$45	×$45	×$45	×$45	×$45
Professional service					
revenue..........	$ 87,300	$ 90,000	$86,400	$ 87,300	$351,000
Sales of orthotic devices:					
Sales (in units)	150	180	120	150	600
Sales price..........	×$90	×$90	×$90	×$90	×$90
Sales revenue	$ 13,500	$ 16,200	$10,800	$ 13,500	$ 54,000
Total revenue:					
professional services					
and sales	$100,800	$106,200	$97,200	$100,800	$405,000

Production Budget: Construction of Orthotic Devices

Although Healthworks is a service firm, it also engages in a minor production activity. Constructing custom orthotics is time-consuming for the firm's licensed physical therapists, but the sale of orthotics represents an important source of revenue. As a result, it is important to plan carefully for the professional time and material required to make orthotics. The first step in such planning is to prepare a **production budget.**

Healthworks' production budget for 19x5 is displayed as schedule 2. Notice that all of the orthotics are sold in the same quarter they are produced. Since orthotics are custom-made, Healthworks cannot store ready-made finished products in inventory. In contrast, manufacturers plan to have some finished goods in inventory at all times to meet peak sales demands.

The demand for orthotics is greatest during the second quarter, but this is also the firm's busiest season for providing professional therapy services. As a result, the professional staff decided to do some preparatory work on orthotics during periods of slack demand. Each orthotic requires two hours of direct professional labor, as follows:

Step 1 ($\frac{1}{2}$ hr.): Cut out the basic shape of the orthotic from a sheet of special material. Glue two layers of the material together. Heat-treat the resulting rough-cut orthotic to make the two layers adhere.

Step 2 (1 hr.): Perform physical examination of client. Take detailed measurements of leg and spinal alignment.

Step 3 ($\frac{1}{2}$ hr.): Mold a rough-cut orthotic to the shape of the client's foot. Adjust the thickness of the orthotic to correct the client's leg-alignment problems.

Step 1 can be done with no knowledge of a specific client's needs. Schedule 2 is based on the following formula.

$$
\begin{array}{c}
\text{Total units} \\
\text{to be} \\
\text{produced} \\
\text{and sold}
\end{array}
+
\begin{array}{c}
\text{desired ending} \\
\text{inventory of} \\
\text{rough-cut} \\
\text{orthotics}
\end{array}
=
\begin{array}{c}
\text{total} \\
\text{units} \\
\text{needed}
\end{array}
$$

$$
\begin{array}{c}
\text{Total} \\
\text{units} \\
\text{needed}
\end{array}
-
\begin{array}{c}
\text{expected} \\
\text{beginning} \\
\text{inventory} \\
\text{of} \\
\text{rough-cut} \\
\text{orthotics}
\end{array}
=
\begin{array}{c}
\text{units} \\
\text{to be} \\
\text{started}
\end{array}
$$

Focus on the second-quarter column in schedule 2, which is shaded. Expected sales are 180 orthotics, and the staff plans to have 10 rough-cut orthotics in inventory at the end of the quarter. However, 50 rough-cut orthotics are expected to be in inventory at the beginning of the second quarter. Thus, only 140 new orthotics need to be started.

Schedule 2

HEALTHWORKS, INC.
Associates in Physical Therapy and Sports Medicine
Production Budget: Orthotic Devices
For the Year Ended December 31, 19x5

Sales (total units to be produced and sold)	150	180	120	150	600
Add desired ending inventory of rough-cut orthotics	50	10	10	20	20
Total units needed	200	190	130	170	620
Less expected beginning inventory of rough-cut orthotics	20	50	10	10	20
Units to be started	180	140	120	160	600

Direct-Material Budget

The **direct-material budget,** displayed as schedule 3, shows the amount of material needed to construct orthotics during each quarter. Each orthotic requires 100 grams of material. Some of this material will be trimmed away in the molding and fitting process, leaving a finished orthotic of about 60 grams. The direct material needed for production in each quarter is equal to the number of orthotics to be started (from schedule 2) times 100 grams per orthotic. The shaded portion of schedule 3, which computes the amount of material to be purchased each quarter, is based on the following formula.

Direct material needed for production	+	desired ending direct-material inventory	=	total direct-material needs

Total direct-material needs	−	expected beginning direct-material inventory	=	direct material to be purchased

Schedule 3

HEALTHWORKS, INC.
Associates in Physical Therapy and Sports Medicine
Direct-Material Budget
For the Year Ended December 31, 19x5

	Quarter				
	1st	2nd	3rd	4th	Year
Units to be started (from schedule 2)	180	140	120	160	600
Direct material required per unit (grams)	× 100	× 100	× 100	× 100	× 100
Direct material needed for production	18,000	14,000	12,000	16,000	60,000
Add desired ending direct-material inventory	2,800	2,400	3,200	3,600	3,600
Total direct-material needs ...	20,800	16,400	15,200	19,600	63,600
Less expected beginning direct-material inventory....	3,600	2,800	2,400	3,200	3,600
Direct material to be purchased	17,200	13,600	12,800	16,400	60,000
Price (per gram)............	× $.10	× $.10	× $.10	× $.10	× $.10
Cost of direct-material purchases	$ 1,720	$ 1,360	$ 1,280	$ 1,640	$ 6,000

Inventory Decisions Planning how much inventory of raw materials and finished goods to keep on hand is an important decision in many businesses. Once inventory levels are established, they become an important input to the budgeting system. Inventory decisions are explored in the appendix at the end of this chapter.

Direct Professional Labor Budget

Healthworks' **direct professional labor budget** is displayed as schedule 4. The shaded portion at the top shows the amount of time the firm's licensed physical therapists will spend in office visits with clients during each quarter. The lower part of schedule 4 computes the hours of direct professional labor needed to produce orthotic devices during each quarter. Focus on the column for the second quarter. The firm expects to sell 180 orthotics, which will require 360 hours of direct professional labor. To this we must add the 5 hours needed to do the initial preparatory work on the 10 rough-cut orthotics that are to be in the ending inventory on June 30. Then we must subtract the 25 hours that have already been expended on the second-quarter beginning inventory of 50 rough-cut orthotics. Thus, 340 hours of direct professional labor will be needed to construct orthotics in the second quarter.

The final row of schedule 4 computes the cost to the firm of the total direct professional labor planned for each quarter. Each licensed physical therapist earns an annual salary of $40,000 for 2,000 hours of professional time. Thus, the cost to the firm is $20 per hour ($40,000 ÷ 2,000 hours).

Schedule 4

HEALTHWORKS, INC.
Associates in Physical Therapy and Sports Medicine
Direct Professional Labor Budget
For the Year Ended December 31, 19x5

| | | Quarter | | | |
	1st	2nd	3rd	4th	Year
Professional services:					
Office visits............	1,940	2,000	1,920	1,940	7,800
Hours per visit..........	× 1	× 1	× 1	× 1	× 1
(a) Hours of direct professional service......	1,940	2,000	1,920	1,940	7,800
Production of orthotic devices:					
Total units to be produced and sold	150	180	120	150	600
Direct labor required per unit....................	× 2	× 2	× 2	× 2	× 2
Subtotal	300	360	240	300	1,200
Add direct labor required to do initial work on ending inventory of rough-cut orthotics (units in ending inventory × .5 hour per unit):					
1st quarter: 50 × .5......	25				
2nd quarter: 10 × .5......		5			
3rd quarter: 10 × .5......			5		
4th quarter: 20 × .5......				10	10
Subtotal	325	365	245	310	1,210

		Quarter			
	1st	2nd	3rd	4th	Year
Less direct labor already accomplished on the beginning inventory of rough-cut orthotics (units in beginning inventory × .5 hour per unit):					
1st quarter: 20 × .5.	10				10
2nd quarter: 50 × .5.		25			
3rd quarter: 10 × .5.			5		
4th quarter: 10 × .5.				5	
(b) Direct labor required for production	315	340	240	305	1,200
Total hours of direct professional labor [add rows (a) and (b)]	2,255	2,340	2,160	2,245	9,000
Cost of direct professional labor (Hours of direct labor × $20 per hour)	$45,100	$46,800	$43,200	$44,900	$180,000

Indirect Professional Labor Budget

As schedule 4 shows, Healthworks' staff expects to spend 9,000 hours during the year on direct professional services and the construction of orthotics. The remainder of the licensed physical therapists' time is designated as indirect professional labor. This time is needed for such activities as reading professional journals, attending educational seminars, and calibrating equipment. The cost of this indirect professional labor is computed in the top portion of the **indirect professional labor budget,** displayed as schedule 5. The schedule also shows the planned labor cost for two part-time student interns, who assist the licensed physical therapists in various ways.

Schedule 5

HEALTHWORKS, INC.
Associates in Physical Therapy and Sports Medicine
Indirect Professional Labor Budget
For the Year Ended December 31, 19x5

		Quarter			
	1st	2nd	3rd	4th	Year
Licensed physical therapists:					
Total hours of professional labor available	2,500	2,500	2,500	2,500	10,000
Less total hours of direct professional labor to be used (from schedule 4)	2,255	2,340	2,160	2,245	9,000
Total hours of indirect professional labor	245	160	340	255	1,000
Cost of indirect professional labor (Hours of indirect labor × $20 per hour).	$4,900	$ 3,200	$6,800	$5,100	$20,000

Schedule 5 *(Continued)*

	Quarter				
	1st	**2nd**	**3rd**	**4th**	**Year**
Student interns:					
Cost of part-time student assistance .	$3,000	$10,000	$3,000	$3,000	$19,000
Total cost of indirect professional labor: Licensed physical therapists and student interns	$7,900	$13,200	$9,800	$8,100	$39,000

Overhead Budget

Healthworks' **overhead budget,** displayed as schedule 6, lists the indirect professional labor cost (from schedule 5) along with all other costs incurred in the physical therapy and sports medicine practice. The receptionist/business manager spends half of her time on client reception and appointment scheduling. Therefore, only half of her salary and fringe benefits are included on the overhead budget. The employee spends the other half of her time on billing and other business matters. Thus, the other half of her salary and fringe benefits are included on the selling and administrative expense budget, which is discussed next.

Schedule 6

HEALTHWORKS, INC.
Associates in Physical Therapy and Sports Medicine
Overhead Budget
For the Year Ended December 31, 19x5

	Quarter				
	1st	**2nd**	**3rd**	**4th**	**Year**
Indirect professional labor (from schedule 5).	$ 7,900	$13,200	$ 9,800	$ 8,100	$ 39,000
Salary: receptionist/business manager	2,125	2,125	2,125	2,125	8,500
Fringe benefits for manager	800	800	800	800	3,200
Linens, supplies, indirect material	1,100	1,400	1,100	1,100	4,700
Laundry service	900	1,100	900	900	3,800
Utilities (electricity, telephone). . .	2,000	2,200	2,000	2,000	8,200
Continuing education (seminars, publications, professional travel)	1,900	900	1,900	1,900	6,600
Building rent	7,550	7,550	7,550	7,550	30,200
Professional insurance.	2,650	2,650	2,650	2,650	10,600
Equipment depreciation	1,000	1,000	1,000	1,000	4,000
Total overhead.	$27,925	$32,925	$29,825	$28,125	$118,800

Selling and Administrative Expense Budget

Healthworks' **selling and administrative expense budget** is displayed as schedule 7. This budget lists the expenses of administering the firm and advertising its services. Included here is uncollectible accounts expense, which is 5 percent of each quarter's revenue. This expense results from billings for services that prove to be uncollectible.

Schedule 7

HEALTHWORKS, INC.
Associates in Physical Therapy and Sports Medicine
Selling and Administrative Expense Budget
For the Year Ended December 31, 19x5

		Quarter			
	1st	2nd	3rd	4th	Year
Salary: receptionist/business manager	$ 2,125	$ 2,125	$ 2,125	$ 2,125	$ 8,500
Fringe benefits for manager	800	800	800	800	3,200
Utilities (electricity, telephone)	200	200	200	200	800
Postage	400	400	400	400	1,600
Advertising	250	250	250	250	1,000
Office supplies	180	140	120	160	600
Building rent	400	400	400	400	1,600
Interest	1,000	1,000	1,000	1,000	4,000
Uncollectible accounts expense	5,040	5,310	4,860	5,040	20,250
Equipment depreciation	200	200	200	200	800
Total selling and administrative expenses	$10,595	$10,825	$10,355	$10,575	$42,350

Cash Receipts Budget

The **cash receipts budget** for Healthworks is displayed as schedule 8. Healthworks collects 80 percent of its billings during the quarter in which the service is provided, and another 15 percent in the following quarter. Five percent of the billings are never collected, because they are rejected by the clients' insurance companies and then the clients are unable to pay.

Schedule 8

HEALTHWORKS, INC.
Associates in Physical Therapy and Sports Medicine
Cash Receipts Budget
For the Year Ended December 31, 19x5

		Quarter			
	1st	2nd	3rd	4th	Year
Total revenue: professional services and sales (from schedule 1)	$100,800	$106,200	$97,200	$100,800	$405,000
Collections in quarter of service or sale (80% of billings)	$ 80,640	$ 84,960	$77,760	$ 80,640	$324,000
Collections in quarter following service or sale (15% of billings)	12,000*	15,120	15,930	14,580	57,630
Total cash receipts	$ 92,640	$100,080	$93,690	$ 95,220	$381,630
Uncollectible billings (5% of total revenue)	$ 5,040	$ 5,310	$ 4,860	$ 5,040	$ 20,250

* 15% of the billings during the 4th quarter of the previous year, 19x4.

Cash Disbursements Budget

Schedule 9 displays Healthworks' **cash disbursements budget.** The shaded top portion shows the schedule of cash payments for the materials and services the firm purchases on account. Healthworks pays for 80 percent of its purchases on account during the quarter in which the purchase was made. The remaining 20 percent of each quarter's purchases are paid for during the quarter following the purchase.

The lower portion of schedule 9 shows all of Healthworks' cash payments for services that are paid for in advance or at the time of purchase.

Schedule 9

HEALTHWORKS, INC.
Associates in Physical Therapy and Sports Medicine
Cash Disbursements Budget
For the Year Ended December 31, 19x5

	Quarter				
	1st	2nd	3rd	4th	Year
Purchases of materials and services on account (amounts from schedules 3, 6, and 7):					
Direct material	$ 1,720	$ 1,360	$ 1,280	$ 1,640	$ 6,000
Linens, supplies, indirect material.	1,100	1,400	1,100	1,100	4,700
Laundry service	900	1,100	900	900	3,800
Utilities (overhead).	2,000	2,200	2,000	2,000	8,200
Utilities (selling and administrative)	200	200	200	200	800
Office supplies	180	140	120	160	600
Total purchases on account.	$ 6,100	$ 6,400	$ 5,600	$ 6,000	$ 24,100
Cash disbursements:					
Cash payments made on account:					
Payments made during the same quarter as purchase (80% of purchases)	$ 4,880	$ 5,120	$ 4,480	$ 4,800	$ 19,280
Payments made during the quarter following purchase (20% of purchases)	1,100*	1,220	1,280	1,120	4,720
Total	$ 5,980	$ 6,340	$ 5,760	$ 5,920	$ 24,000
Other cash payments (amounts from schedules 3, 6, and 7):					
Licensed physical therapists.	$50,000	$50,000	$50,000	$50,000	$200,000
Student interns	3,000	10,000	3,000	3,000	19,000
Salary: receptionist/ business manager†	4,250	4,250	4,250	4,250	17,000

		Quarter			
	1st	2nd	3rd	4th	Year
Fringe benefits for manager†	1,600	1,600	1,600	1,600	6,400
Continuing education ...	1,900	900	1,900	1,900	6,600
Building rent: overhead ..	7,550	7,550	7,550	7,550	30,200
Building rent: selling and administrative.........	400	400	400	400	1,600
Professional insurance ...	2,650	2,650	2,650	2,650	10,600
Postage	400	400	400	400	1,600
Advertising	250	250	250	250	1,000
Interest on bank loan	1,000	1,000	1,000	1,000	4,000
Income taxes..........	6,750	6,750	6,750	6,750	27,000
Total	$79,750	$85,750	$79,750	$79,750	$325,000
Total cash disbursements.	$85,730	$92,090	$85,510	$85,670	$349,000

* 20% of the purchases on account made during the 4th quarter of the previous year, 19x4.
† Half of this employee's salary was allocated to overhead (schedule 6) and half to selling and administrative expense (schedule 7).

Summary Cash Budget

A **summary cash budget** is displayed as schedule 10. The shaded top portion pulls together the cash receipts and cash disbursements detailed in schedules 8 and 9. The lower portion of schedule 10 discloses Healthworks' plans to take out a short-term bank loan on January 2, 19x5 for the purpose of purchasing additional equipment. The loan will be repaid on December 31, 19x5. Most of the funds for this repayment will come from excess cash generated from operations during 19x5.

Schedule 10

HEALTHWORKS, INC.
Associates in Physical Therapy and Sports Medicine
Summary Cash Budget
For the Year Ended December 31, 19x5

		Quarter			
	1st	2nd	3rd	4th	Year
Cash receipts (from schedule 8)	$92,640	$100,080	$93,690	$95,220	$381,630
Less cash disbursements (from schedule 9).....	(85,730)	(92,090)	(85,510)	(85,670)	(349,000)
Change in cash balance during quarter due to operations..........	$ 6,910	$ 7,990	$ 8,180	$ 9,550	$ 32,630
Proceeds from bank loan (1/2/x5)	35,000				
Less purchase of equipment (1/2/x5) ...	(35,000)				
Repayment of bank loan (12/31/x5)					(35,000)

Schedule 10 *(Continued)*

| | Quarter | | | | |
	1st	2nd	3rd	4th	Year
Change in cash balance during 19x5					$ (2,370)
Cash balance, 1/1/x5 . . .					15,000
Cash balance, 12/31/x5 .					$ 12,630

Budgeted Income Statement

Healthworks' **budgeted income statement,** displayed as schedule 11, begins with the revenue anticipated from professional services and sales of orthotics. Then the cost of making orthotics is subtracted as cost of goods sold. Each of the 600 orthotics to be sold costs $50 ($10 for direct material and $40 for two hours of direct labor). No overhead is allocated as a product cost since it is judged to be negligible. From the gross margin are subtracted the firm's projected operating expenses. Included here are the following expenses: the cost of the time spent by the firm's licensed physical therapists on direct professional services; overhead expenses; and selling and administrative expenses. Finally, income taxes of $27,000 are anticipated.

Schedule 11

HEALTHWORKS, INC.
Associates in Physical Therapy and Sports Medicine
Budgeted Income Statement
For the Year Ended December 31, 19x5

Professional service and sales revenue (from schedule 1):		
Professional services.		$351,000
Sales of orthotic devices.		54,000
Total revenue		$405,000
Cost of goods sold (cost of direct material and direct labor)		30,000
Gross margin		$375,000
Operating expenses:		
Salaries: direct professional services (7,800 hours, from schedule 4, times $20 per hour)	$156,000	
Overhead expenses (see schedule 6 for details).	118,800	
Selling and administrative expenses (see schedule 7 for details) .	42,350	
Total operating expenses		317,150
Income before taxes.		57,850
Income taxes		27,000
Net income.		$ 30,850

Budgeted Balance Sheet

Healthworks' **budgeted balance sheet** for December 31, 19x5 is displayed as schedule 12. To construct this budgeted balance sheet, we start with the firm's balance sheet projected for the *beginning* of the budget year (Exhibit 8-2) and adjust each account balance for the changes expected during 19x5.

Balance sheet December 31, 19x4 (Exhibit 8-2)	→ Expected changes in account balances during 19x5 →	Balance sheet December 31, 19x5 (schedule 12)

Exhibit 8-2. Healthworks' December 31, 19x4 Balance Sheet

HEALTHWORKS, INC.
Associates in Physical Therapy and Sports Medicine
Balance Sheet
December 31, 19x4

Assets

Current assets:

Cash		$15,000
Accounts receivable (net of allowance for uncollectible accounts)		12,000
Inventory:		
Work in process (rough-cut orthotics)	$ 400	
Professional supplies	2,300	
Office supplies	300	
Total inventory		3,000
Total current assets		$30,000
Long-lived assets:		
Equipment	$35,000	
Less accumulated depreciation	9,600	
Equipment, net of accumulated depreciation		25,400
Total assets		$55,400

Liabilities and Stockholders' Equity

Current liabilities:

Accounts payable		$1,100
Total current liabilities		$1,100
Long-term liabilities:		
Note payable (due on Declember 31, 19x8)		5,000
Total liabilities		$ 6,100
Stockholders' equity:		
Common stock	$41,000	
Retained earnings	8,300	
Total stockholders' equity		49,300
Total liabilities and stockholders' equity		$55,400

Explanations for the account balances on the budgeted balance sheet for December 31, 19x5 are given in the second half of schedule 12. Examine these explanations carefully. Notice how the budgeted balance sheet pulls together information from most of the schedules comprising the master budget.

Schedule 12

HEALTHWORKS, INC.
Associates in Physical Therapy and Sports Medicine
Budgeted Balance Sheet
December 31, 19x5

Assets

Current assets:		
Cash		$ 12,630 (a)
Accounts receivable (net of allowance for uncollectible accounts)		15,120 (b)
Inventory:		
Work in process (rough-cut orthotics)	$ 400 (c)	
Professional supplies	2,300 (d)	
Office supplies	300 (e)	
Total inventory		3,000
Total current assets		$ 30,750
Long-lived assets:		
Equipment	$70,000 (f)	
Less accumulated depreciation	14,400 (g)	
Equipment, net of accumulated depreciation		55,600
Total assets		$ 86,350

Liabilities and Stockholders' Equity

Current liabilities:		
Accounts payable		$ 1,200 (h)
Total current liabilities		$ 1,200 (i)
Long-term liabilities:		
Note payable (due on December 31, 19x8)		5,000 (j)
Total liabilities		$ 6,200
Stockholders' equity:		
Common stock	$41,000 (k)	
Retained earnings	39,150 (l)	
Total stockholders' equity		80,150
Total liabilities and stockholders' equity		$ 86,350

(a)	Cash balance on 12/31/x4 balance sheet	$ 15,000
	Less decrease in cash during 19x5 (schedule 10)	(2,370)
	Cash balance, 12/31/x5	$ 12,630
(b)	Accounts receivable (net) on 12/31/x4 balance sheet	$ 12,000
	Add sales on account during 19x5 (schedule 1)	405,000
	Less collection of accounts receivable during 19x5 (Schedule 8) . .	(381,630)
	Less expected uncollectible accounts from 19x5 sales (schedule 8)	(20,250)
	Accounts receivable (net), 12/31/x5	$ 15,120
(c)	Planned number of rough-cut orthotics (schedule 2)	20
	× Cost per rough-cut orthotic ($10 material; ½ hour direct labor at $20 per hour)	× $20
	Planned balance for rough-cut orthotics, 12/31/x5	$ 400

(d) All supplies purchased during 19x5 are expected to be used.
(e) Therefore, 12/31/x5 inventory balances are the same as balances
     on 12/31/x4.
(f) $35,000 from 12/31/x4 balance sheet, plus $35,000 equipment
     purchase.
(g) Accumulated depreciation, 12/31/x4 . . . . $ 9,600
     Add total depreciation expense for 19x5 (schedules 6 and 7)   4,800
     Accumulated depreciation, 12/31/x5 . . . . $ 14,400

(h) Accounts payable on 12/31/x4 balance sheet. . . . . $ 1,100
     Add purchases on account during 19x5 (schedule 9).   24,100
     Less payments of accounts payable during 19x5 (schedule 9). . . . .   (24,000)
     Accounts payable, 12/31/x5 . . . . $ 1,200

(i) Note that the $35,000 bank loan will be paid off, so it is not shown
     on the 12/31/x5 balance sheet.

(j)
(k) } From 12/31/x4 balance sheet

(l) Retained earnings on 12/31/x4 balance sheet . . . . $ 8,300
     Add net income for 19x5 (schedule 11)   30,850
     Retained earnings, 12/31/x5 . . . . $ 39,150

Using the Master Budget for Planning

Virtually all of the information contained in Healthworks' master budget is used in
some way for planning purposes. For example, the revenue forecasts reflected in
schedule 1 help the firm's staff plan for advertising. Healthworks plans only minimal
advertising, since the firm's clientele has grown quickly without much advertising.
The direct professional labor budget (schedule 4) helps the staff plan when to make
rough-cut orthotics, when to schedule travel for seminars, and when to take personal
vacations. The summary cash budget (schedule 10) helps the staff in planning to
purchase equipment and pay off the bank loan due on December 31, 19x5.

BUDGET ADMINISTRATION

In small organizations, the procedures used to gather information and construct a
master budget are usually informal. At Healthworks, for example, the budgeting
process is coordinated by the business manager in consultation with the firm's founders. In contrast, larger organizations use a formal process to collect data and prepare
the master budget. Such organizations usually designate a **budget director** or **chief
budget officer.** This is often the organization's controller. The budget director specifies the process by which budget data will be gathered, collects the information, and
prepares the master budget. To communicate budget procedures and deadlines to
employees throughout the organization, the budget director often develops and
disseminates a **budget manual.** The budget manual says who is responsible for providing various types of information, when the information is required, and what form
the information is to take. For example, the budget manual for a manufacturing firm
might specify that each regional sales director is to send an estimate of the following
year's sales, by product line, to the budget director by September 1. The budget
manual also states who should receive each schedule when the master budget is
complete.

A **budget committee,** consisting of key senior executives, is often appointed to advise the budget director during the preparation of the budget. The authority to give final approval to the master budget usually belongs to the board of directors, or board of trustees in many nonprofit organizations. Usually the board has a subcommittee whose task is to examine the proposed budget carefully and recommend approval or any changes deemed necessary. By exercising its authority to make changes in the budget and grant final approval, the board of directors, or trustees, can wield considerable influence on the overall direction the organization takes.

ILLUSTRATION FROM
MANAGERIAL
ACCOUNTING
PRACTICE

Budget Administration at Cornell University

Cornell's annual budget covers the period from July 1 through the following June 30. The budgeting process begins in October, when the deans and senior vice presidents have meetings to discuss the programs the university will conduct during the following budget year. The university's priorities in educational, research, and public service programs are established during these meetings. In early January, the university's budget director, together with other members of the Operating Plans Committee, settles on a set of assumptions to be used during the remainder of the budgeting process. These assumptions include such key forecasts as the next year's inflation rate, interest rates, and tuition levels. Based on these assumptions, the dean of each of Cornell's colleges or professional schools must develop a detailed budget for salaries and general expenses. These detailed budgets are prepared during January and February by the financial staff in each college or professional school. In March, the university provost reviews these budgets with the deans. After any needed revisions have been made, the budgets for the various colleges and professional schools are consolidated by the university controller's staff into a master budget. This budget is presented to the university's Board of Trustees in May for their final approval.

WIDESPREAD USE OF BUDGETING SYSTEMS

Virtually every organization uses a budget. However, organizations vary widely in their objectives, in the goods and services they provide, and in size. The result is that actual budgeting practices differ significantly among organizations, since the procedures are adapted to meet the specific needs of each enterprise. The following examples suggest the widespread use and diversity of budgeting systems.

ILLUSTRATION FROM
MANAGERIAL-
ACCOUNTING
PRACTICE

Chesebrough-Ponds

Chesebrough-Ponds produces hundreds of health and cosmetic products. It is often impractical for a company with so many products to develop a detailed cost budget for the production of each product. Chesebrough-Ponds' solution is to classify products into a small number of product types. Then a representative product is chosen in each category, and its cost characteristics are used to prepare the budget for all of the products in that category. A rolling budget is used in which new cost projections are made each quarter. A new quarter is added to the budget, and the quarter just completed is dropped.[1]

[1] D. Worrell, "Cost of Sales: A Budgeting Priority," *Management Accounting,* August 1983, p. 67.

UNYSIS (Formerly Burroughs Corporation)

Most large organizations simultaneously prepare budgets covering different periods of time. The manufacturing budget developed by UNYSIS, a manufacturer of computing equipment, consists of a long-range forecast, an annual plan, and quarterly and monthly outlooks. Each plan has its own purpose and objective. The long-range forecast, which covers a three- to five-year period, is designed to help managers determine the future financial needs for individual products and programs. The annual plan focuses on operational issues and marketing forecasts for both current and new products. The quarterly and monthly plans deal with such short-term issues as production scheduling.[2]

City of Charlotte, North Carolina

Management by objectives (MBO) often complements the budgeting process in nonprofit organizations. Under the MBO approach, an organization's overall goal is broken up into specific objectives. A budget is then developed to meet each objective. In the city of Charlotte, North Carolina, the following six objectives have been identified:

1. Community development
2. Environmental health and protection
3. Protection of persons and property
4. Transportation
5. Leisure opportunities
6. Policy formulation and administration

Specific programs are developed for each of these objectives. For example, the transportation programs include airport, automotive services, traffic control, transportation planning, and traffic engineering. Resource needs are then projected for each program, and these needs form the basis of recommendations for action by the city council.[3]

Budgeting is a major activity in every large organization. The master budget at ITT, a large, international conglomerate, consists of bound volumes that occupy 21 feet of shelf space.[4]

ZERO-BASE BUDGETING

Zero-base budgeting is used in a wide variety of organizations, including Southern California Edison, Texas Instruments, and the State of Georgia. Under zero-base budgeting, the budget for virtually every activity in the organization is initially set to zero. To receive funding during the budgeting process, each activity must be justified in terms of its continued usefulness. The zero-base-budgeting approach forces management to rethink each phase of an organization's operations before allocating resources. The following example cites the use of zero-base budgeting in a public school district in suburban Rochester, New York.

[2] D. Janusky, "Plant Forecasting at Burroughs," *Management Accounting,* March 1985, pp. 59–60.
[3] C. H. Gibson, "Budgeting by Objectives: Charlotte's Experience," *Management Accounting,* January 1978, pp. 39–40.
[4] H. Geneen, "The Case for Managing by the Numbers," *Fortune,* October 1, 1984, p. 80.

Zero-Base Budgeting in a Public School District

> Zero-base budgeting is not a magic formula, but an attitude, woven into a structured analytical process. . . . The usual approach to budgeting is to begin with the present level of operation and spending and then justify the new programs or additional expenditures desired for next year. In zero-base budgeting there are no "givens." It starts with the basic premise that the budget for next year is zero — and that every expenditure, old or new, must be justified on the basis of its cost and benefit.[5]

Some organizations use a *base-budgeting* approach without going to the extreme of zero-base budgeting. For example, the initial budget for each of the organization's activities may be set at 50 percent of the prior year's budget. Any increases above the initial budget must then be justified on the basis of each activity's costs and benefits. Base budgeting has been effective in many organizations because it forces managers to take an evaluative, questioning attitude toward each of the organization's programs.

ASSUMPTIONS AND PREDICTIONS: THE UNDERPINNINGS OF THE MASTER BUDGET

A master budget is based on many assumptions and estimates of unknown parameters. What are some of the assumptions and estimates used in Healthworks' master budget? The professional services and sales budget (schedule 1) was built on an assumption about the seasonal nature of demand for professional services. The direct-material budget (schedule 3) uses an estimate of the direct-material price, $.10 per gram, and the quantity of material required per orthotic, 100 grams. An estimate of the direct labor required to make a custom orthotic was used in the direct professional labor budget (schedule 4).

These are only a few of the many assumptions and estimates used in Healthworks' master budget. Some of these estimates are much more likely to be accurate than others. For example, the amount of material required to construct an orthotic is not likely to differ from past experience unless the type of material or construction process is changed. In contrast, estimates such as the price of material, the cost of utilities, and the demand for professional services are much more difficult to predict.

Financial Planning Models

Managers must make assumptions and predictions in preparing budgets because organizations operate in a world of uncertainty. One way of coping with that uncertainty is to supplement the budgeting process with a **financial planning model.** A financial planning model is a set of mathematical relationships that express the interactions among the various operational, financial, and environmental events that determine the overall results of an organization's activities. A financial-planning model is a mathematical expression of all the relationships expressed in the flowchart of Exhibit 8-1.

To illustrate this concept, focus on the following equation, which was used to budget uncollectible accounts expense in schedule 7.

---

[5] Excerpt from A. F. Brueningsen, "SCAT — A Process of Alternatives," *Management Accounting,* November 1976, p. 56; reproduced with permission from the publisher.

$$\left(\begin{array}{c}\text{Uncollectible}\\\text{accounts expense}\end{array}\right) = .05 \times \left(\begin{array}{c}\text{total revenue: professional}\\\text{services and sales}\end{array}\right)$$

Suppose Healthwork's business manager is uncertain about this 5 percent estimate. In a financial planning model, the following equation could be used instead.

$$\left(\begin{array}{c}\text{Uncollectible}\\\text{accounts expense}\end{array}\right) = p \times \left(\begin{array}{c}\text{total revenue: professional}\\\text{services and sales}\end{array}\right)$$

where $\quad 0 \le p \le 1.0$

The business manager can run the financial planning model as many times as desired on a computer, using a different value for p each time. Perhaps the following values would be tried: .04, .045, .05, .055, and .06. Now the business manager can answer the question, What if 4 percent of sales prove to be uncollectible?

In a fully developed financial planning model, all of the key estimates and assumptions are expressed as general mathematical relationships. Then the model is run on a computer many times to determine the impact of different combinations of these unknown variables. "What if" questions can be answered about such unknown variables as inflation, interest rates, the value of the dollar, demand, competitors' actions, production efficiency, union demands in forthcoming wage negotiations, and a host of other factors. The widespread availability of personal computers and electronic-spreadsheet software has made financial planning models a more and more common managerial-accounting tool.

BEHAVIORAL IMPACT OF BUDGETS

One of the underlying themes stressed in this text is the behavioral impact of managerial-accounting practices. There is no other area where the behavioral implications are more important than in the budgeting area. A budget affects virtually everyone in an organization: those who prepare the budget, those who use the budget to facilitate decision making, and those who are evaluated using the budget. The human reactions to the budgeting process can have considerable influence on an organization's overall effectiveness.

A great deal of study has been devoted to the behavioral effects of budgets. Here we will barely scratch the surface by briefly considering two issues: budgetary slack and participative budgeting.

Budgetary Slack: Padding the Budget

The information upon which a budget is based comes largely from people throughout an organization. For example, the sales forecast relies on market research and analysis by a market research staff, but also incorporates the projections of sales personnel. If a territorial sales manager's performance is evaluated on the basis of whether the sales budget for the territory is exceeded, what is the incentive for the sales manager in projecting sales? The incentive is to give a conservative, or cautiously low sales estimate. The sales manager's performance will look much better in the eyes of top management when a conservative estimate is exceeded than when an ambitious estimate is not met. At least that is the *perception* of many sales managers, and in the behavioral area perceptions are what count most.

When a supervisor provides a departmental cost projection for budgetary purposes, there is an incentive to overestimate costs. When the actual cost incurred in the department proves to be less than the inflated cost projection, the supervisor appears to have managed in a cost-effective way.

These illustrations are examples of **padding the budget.** Budget padding means underestimating revenue or overestimating costs. The difference between the revenue or cost projection that a person provides and a realistic estimate of the revenue or cost is called **budgetary slack.** For example, if a plant manager believes the annual utilities cost will be $18,000, but gives a budgetary projection of $20,000, the manager has built $2,000 of slack into the budget.

Why do people pad budgets with budgetary slack? There are three primary reasons. First, people often *perceive* that their performance will look better in their superiors' eyes if they can "beat the budget." Second, budgetary slack is often used to cope with uncertainty. A departmental supervisor may feel confident in the cost projections for 10 cost items. However, the supervisor may also feel that some unforeseen event during the budgetary period could result in unanticipated costs. For example, an unexpected machine breakdown could occur. One way of dealing with that unforeseen event is to pad the budget. If nothing goes wrong, the supervisor can beat the cost budget. If some negative event does occur, the supervisor can use the budgetary slack to absorb the impact of the event and still meet the cost budget.

The third reason why cost budgets are padded is that budgetary cost projections are often cut in the resource-allocation process. Thus, we have a vicious circle. Budgetary projections are padded because they will likely be cut, and they are cut because they are likely to have been padded.

How does an organization solve the problem of budgetary slack? First, it can avoid relying on the budget as a negative evaluative tool. If a departmental supervisor is harassed by the budget director or some other top manager every time a budgetary cost projection is exceeded, the likely behavioral response will be to pad the budget. In contrast, if the supervisor is allowed some managerial discretion to exceed the budget when necessary, there will be less tendency toward budgetary padding. Second, managers can be given incentives not only to achieve budgetary projections but also to *provide accurate projections.* This can be accomplished by asking managers to justify all or some of their projections and by rewarding managers who consistently provide accurate estimates.

Participative Budgeting

Most people will perform better and make greater attempts to achieve a goal if they have been consulted in setting the goal. The idea of **participative budgeting** is to involve employees throughout an organization in the budgetary process. Such participation can give employees the feeling that "this is our budget," rather than the all-too-common feeling that "this is the budget you imposed on us." The effectiveness of budgetary participation is illustrated by the following description of budgeting at University Community Hospital in Tampa, Florida.

ILLUSTRATION FROM MANAGERIAL-ACCOUNTING PRACTICE

Participative Budgeting in a Hospital

Because the department directors, along with their first-line supervisors, vice presidents, the president, the finance committee, and the board of trustees, have been involved in the budgetary process, the budget is felt to be owned by all of them as a total document. This feeling of ownership is

Inventory Decisions

A key decision in manufacturing, retail, and some service industry firms is how much inventory to keep on hand. Once inventory levels are established, they become an important input to the budgeting system. Inventory decisions involve a delicate balance between three classes of costs: ordering costs, holding costs, and shortage costs. Examples of costs in each of these categories are given in Exhibit 8-3.

Exhibit 8-3. Inventory Ordering, Holding, and Shortage Costs

Ordering Costs
  Clerical costs of preparing purchase orders
  Time spent finding suppliers and expediting orders
  Transportation costs
  Receiving costs (e.g., unloading and inspection)

Holding Costs
  Costs of storage space (e.g., warehouse depreciation)
  Security
  Insurance
  Foregone interest on working capital tied up in inventory
  Deterioration, theft, spoilage, or obsolescence

Shortage Costs
  Disrupted production when raw materials are unavailable:
    Idle workers
    Extra machinery setups
  Lost sales resulting in dissatisfied customers
  Loss of quantity discounts on purchases

The following illustration emphasizes the benefits of a sound inventory policy.

**ILLUSTRATION FROM
MANAGEMENT-
ACCOUNTING
PRACTICE**

Firestone Tire & Rubber Co.

According to an article in *The Wall Street Journal,* Firestone Tire & Rubber Co. had two firm policies: minimize the cost of producing quality tires, and avoid the loss of sales. While these are sound business practices, both policies tend to result in large inventories of raw materials and finished products. Realizing that large inventories were causing unacceptably high holding costs, Firestone's management hired a consulting firm to assist in overhauling its entire inventory-control system. The result was a massive inventory-cutting program and substantial cost savings.[8]

Economic Order Quantity

Surfco manufactures fiberglass surfboards. One of the raw materials is a special resin, which is used to bind the fiberglass in the molding phase of production. The production manager, Hi Wave, uses an **economic order quantity (EOQ)** decision model to determine the size and frequency with which resin is ordered. The EOQ model is a mathematical tool for determining the order quantity that minimizes the costs of ordering and holding inventory.

Resin is purchased in 50-gallon drums, and 9,600 drums are used each year. Each drum costs $400. The controller estimates that the cost of placing and receiving a typical resin order is $225. The controller's estimate of the annual cost of carrying resin in inventory is $3 per drum.

Tabular Approach Suppose Wave orders 800 drums of resin in each order placed during the year. The total annual cost of ordering and holding resin in inventory is calculated as follows:

$$\frac{\text{Annual requirement}}{\text{Quantity per order}} = \frac{9,600}{800} = 12 = \text{number of orders}$$

$$\text{Annual ordering cost} = 12 \text{ orders} \times \$225 \text{ per order} = \$2,700$$

$$\text{Average quantity in inventory} = \frac{\text{quantity per order}}{2} = \frac{800}{2} = 400 \text{ drums}$$

$$\text{Annual holding cost} = \left(\begin{array}{c}\text{average quantity}\\ \text{in inventory}\end{array}\right) \times \left(\begin{array}{c}\text{annual carrying}\\ \text{cost per drum}\end{array}\right)$$

$$= 400 \times \$3 = \$1,200$$

$$\begin{array}{c}\text{Total annual cost of}\\ \text{inventory policy}\end{array} = \begin{array}{c}\text{ordering}\\ \text{cost}\end{array} + \begin{array}{c}\text{holding}\\ \text{cost}\end{array} = \$2,700 + \$1,200 = \$3,900$$

Notice that the $3,900 cost does *not* include the purchase cost of the resin at $400 per drum. We are focusing only on the costs of *ordering* and *holding* resin inventory.

Can Wave do any better than $3,900 for the annual cost of his resin inventory policy? Exhibit 8-4, which tabulates the inventory costs for various order quantities, indicates that Wave can lower the costs of ordering and holding resin inventory. Of the five order quantities listed, the 1,200 drum order quantity yields the lowest total

---

[8] *The Wall Street Journal,* August 15, 1980, p. 15.

Exhibit 8-4. Tabulation of Inventory Ordering and Holding Costs					
Order size	800	960	1,200	1,600	2,400
Number of orders					
(9,600 ÷ order size)	12	10	8	6	4
Ordering costs					
($225 × number of orders)	$2,700	$2,250	$1,800	$1,350	$ 900
Average inventory					
(order size ÷ 2)	400	480	600	800	1,200
Holding costs					
($3 × average inventory)	$1,200	$1,440	$1,800	$2,400	$3,600
Total annual cost (ordering					
cost + holding cost)	$3,900	$3,690	$3,600	$3,750	$4,500

Minimum

annual cost. Unfortunately, this tabular method for finding the least-cost order quantity is cumbersome. Moreover, it does not necessarily result in the optimal order quantity. It is possible that some order quantity other than those listed in Exhibit 8-4 is the least-cost order quantity.

Equation Approach The total annual cost of ordering and holding inventory is given by the following equation.

$$\genfrac{}{}{0pt}{}{\text{Total annual}}{\text{cost}} = \left(\frac{\text{annual requirement}}{\text{order quantity}}\right)\left(\genfrac{}{}{0pt}{}{\text{cost per}}{\text{order}}\right) + \left(\frac{\text{order quantity}}{2}\right)\left(\genfrac{}{}{0pt}{}{\text{annual}}{\text{holding}}\genfrac{}{}{0pt}{}{\text{cost per}}{\text{unit}}\right)$$

The following formula for the least-cost order quantity, called the economic order quantity (or EOQ), has been developed using calculus.

$$\genfrac{}{}{0pt}{}{\text{Economic order}}{\text{quantity}} = \sqrt{\frac{(2)\ (\text{annual requirement})(\text{cost per order})}{\text{annual holding cost per unit}}}$$

Applying the EOQ formula in Surfco's problem yields the following EOQ for resin.

$$\text{EOQ} = \sqrt{\frac{(2)(9,600)(225)}{3}} = 1,200$$

Graphical Approach Another method for solving the EOQ problem is the graphical method, which is presented in Exhibit 8-5. Notice that the ordering-cost line slants to the right. This indicates a decline in these costs as the order size increases and the order frequency decreases. However, as the order size increases, so does the average inventory on hand. This results in an increase in holding costs, as indicated by the positive slope of the holding-cost line. The EOQ falls at 1,200 units, where the best balance is struck between these two costs. Total costs are minimized at $3,600.

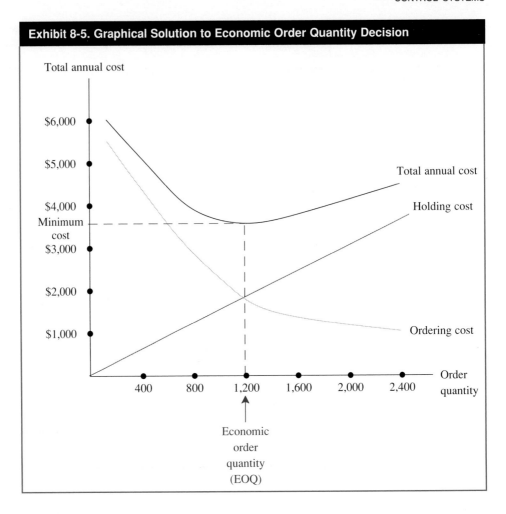

Exhibit 8-5. Graphical Solution to Economic Order Quantity Decision

Timing of Orders

The EOQ model helps management decide how much to order at a time. Another important decision is when to order. This decision depends on the **lead time,** which is the length of time it takes for the material to be received after an order is placed. Suppose the lead time for resin is one month. Since Surfco uses 9,600 drums of resin per year, and the production rate is constant throughout the year, this implies that 800 drums are used each month. Production manager Wave should order resin, in the economic order quantity of 1,200 drums, when the inventory falls to 800 drums. By the time the new order arrives, one month later, the 800 drums in inventory will have been used in production. Exhibit 8-6 depicts this pattern of ordering and using inventory. By placing an order early enough to avoid a stockout, management takes into account the potential costs of shortages.

Safety Stock Our example assumed that the usage of resin is constant at 800 drums per month. Suppose instead that monthly usage fluctuates between 600 and 1,000 drums. Although average monthly usage still is 800 drums, there is the potential for an excess usage of 200 drums in any particular month. In light of this uncertainty, management may wish to keep a **safety stock** of resin equal to the

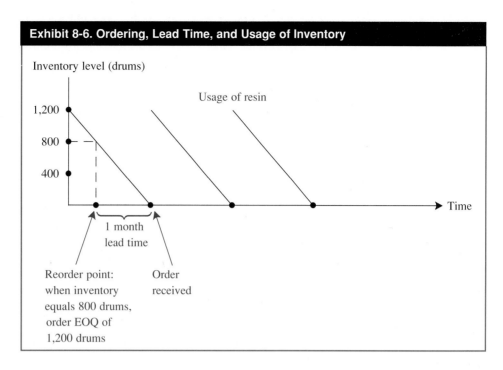

Exhibit 8-6. Ordering, Lead Time, and Usage of Inventory

potential excess monthly usage of 200 drums. With a safety stock of 200 drums, the reorder point is 1,000 drums. Thus, Wave should order the EOQ of 1,200 drums whenever resin inventory falls to 1,000 drums. During the one-month lead time, another 600 to 1,000 drums of resin will be consumed in production. Although a safety stock will increase inventory holding costs, it will minimize the potential costs caused by shortages.

KEY TERMS (APPENDIX)   **Economic order quantity (EOQ),** p. 344; **Lead time,** p. 346; **Safety stock,** p. 346.

REVIEW QUESTIONS   **8-1.** Explain how a budget facilitates communication and coordination.

8-2. Use an example to explain how a budget could be used to allocate resources in a university.

8-3. Explain what a master budget is, and list five of its parts.

8-4. Draw a flowchart similar to the one in Exhibit 8-1 for a service station. The service station provides automotive maintenance services in addition to selling gasoline and related products.

8-5. Give an example of how general economic trends would affect sales forecasting in the airline industry.

8-6. What is meant by the term *operational budgets?* List three operational budgets that would be prepared by a hospital.

8-7. Give three examples of how New York City could use a budget for planning purposes.

8-8. Describe the role of a budget director.

8-9. What is the purpose of a budget manual?

8-10. How can a company's board of directors use the budget to influence the future direction of the firm?

8-11. How could management by objectives (MBO) be used by a public school district?

8-12. Explain the concept of zero-base budgeting.

8-13. Discuss the importance of predictions and assumptions in the budgeting process.

8-14. What is the purpose of a financial planning model? Briefly describe how such a model is constructed.

8-15. Define the term *budgetary slack,* and briefly describe a problem it can cause.

8-16. How can an organization reduce the problems caused by budgetary slack?

8-17. Why is participative budgeting often an effective management tool?

8-18. Discuss this comment by a small-town bank president: "Budgeting is a waste of time. I've been running this business for forty years. I don't need to plan."

8-19. List the steps you would go through in developing a budget to meet your college expenses.

8-20. (Appendix) Define and give examples of inventory ordering, holding, and shortage costs.

EXERCISES *Exercise 8-21* **Budgeting Production and Direct-Material Purchases.** Farrell Company plans to sell 200,000 units of finished product in July of 19x4. Management anticipates a growth rate in sales of 5 percent per month. The desired monthly ending inventory in units of finished product is 80 percent of the next month's estimated sales. There are 150,000 finished units in the inventory on June 30, 19x4. Each unit of finished product requires four pounds of direct material at a cost of $1.20 per pound. There are 800,000 pounds of direct material in the inventory on June 30, 19x4.

REQUIRED:

1. Compute Farrell Company's production requirement in units of finished product for the three-month period ending September 30, 19x4.

2. Independent of your answer to requirement 1, assume the company plans to produce 600,000 units of finished product in the three-month period ending September 30, 19x4. The firm will have direct-materials inventory at the end of the three-month period equal to 25 percent of the direct material used during that period. Compute the estimated cost of direct-materials purchases for the three-month period ending September 30, 19x4.

(CMA, adapted)

Exercise 8-22 **Cash Collections.** Ezra Company has the following historical collection pattern for its credit sales.

70 percent collected in the month of sale
15 percent collected in the first month after sale
10 percent collected in the second month after sale
4 percent collected in the third month after sale
1 percent uncollectible

The sales on account have been budgeted for the last six months of 19x6 as shown below.

July.	$ 60,000
August	70,000
September	80,000
October	90,000
November	100,000
December.	85,000

REQUIRED:

1. Compute the estimated total cash collections during October 19x6 from credit sales during July, August, September, and October.
2. Compute the estimated total cash collections during the fourth quarter from sales made on account during the fourth quarter.

(CMA, adapted)

Exercise 8-23   Budgeting Production and Direct-Material Purchases. Pace Company budgets on an annual basis. The following beginning and ending inventory levels (in units) are planned for the year of 19x6.

	January 1, 19x6		December 31, 19x6
Direct material*........	40,000	....	50,000
Work in process........	10,000	....	10,000
Finished goods.........	80,000	....	50,000

* Two units of direct material are needed to produce each unit of finished product.

REQUIRED

1. If Pace Company plans to sell 480,000 units during the year, compute the number of units the firm would have to manufacture during the year.
2. If 500,000 finished units were to be manufactured by Pace Company during the year, determine the amount of direct material to be purchased.

(CMA, adapted)

Exercise 8-24   Cash Budgeting. The following information was available from Montero Corporation's financial records.

19x2	Purchases		Sales
January.................	$42,000	....	$72,000
February..............	48,000	....	66,000
March...............	36,000	....	60,000
April	54,000	....	78,000

Collections from customers are normally 70 percent in the month of sale, 20 percent in the month following the sale, and 9 percent in the second month following the sale. The balance is expected to be uncollectible. Montero takes full advantage of the 2 percent discount allowed on purchases paid for by the tenth of the following month. Purchases for May are budgeted at $60,000, and sales for May are forecasted at $66,000. Cash disbursements for expenses are expected to be $14,400 for the month of May. Montero's cash balance on May 1 was $22,000.

REQUIRED: Prepare the following schedules.

1. Expected cash collections during May.
2. Expected cash disbursements during May.
3. Expected cash balance on May 31.

(CPA, adapted)

Exercise 8-25   Budgeted Financial Statements; Retailer. AllSports, Inc. is a retail sporting goods store. Information about the store's operations is given below.

- November 19x3 sales amounted to $200,000.
- Sales are budgeted at $220,000 for December 19x3 and $200,000 for January 19x4.
- Collections are expected to be 60 percent in the month of sale and 38 percent in the month following the sale. Two percent of sales are expected to be uncollectible.
- The store's gross margin is 25 percent of its sales revenue.
- A total of 80 percent of the merchandise for resale is purchased in the month prior to the month of sale, and 20 percent is purchased in the month of sale. Payment for merchandise is made in the month following the purchase.
- Other monthly expenses paid in cash amount to $22,600.
- Annual depreciation is $216,000.

AllSports' balance sheet as of November 30, 19x3 is shown below.

AllSports, Inc.
Balance Sheet
November 30, 19x3

Assets

Cash	$ 22,000
Accounts receivable (net of $4,000 allowance for uncollectible accounts)	76,000
Inventory	132,000
Property, plant, and equipment (net of $680,000 accumulated depreciation)	870,000
Total assets	$1,100,000

Liabilities and Stockholders' Equity

Accounts payable	$ 162,000
Common stock	800,000
Retained earnings	138,000
Total liabilities and stockholders' equity	$1,100,000

REQUIRED: Compute the following amounts.

1. The budgeted cash collections for December 19x3.
2. The budgeted income (loss) before income taxes for December 19x3.
3. The projected balance in accounts payable on December 31, 19x3.

(CMA, adapted)

Exercise 8-26   Financial-Planning Model. Sound Ideas, Inc. is a large retailer of stereo equipment. The controller is about to prepare the budget for the first quarter of 19x2. Past experience has indicated that 75 percent of the store's sales are cash sales. The collection experience for the sales on account is as follows:

80 percent during month of sale
15 percent during month following sale
 5 percent uncollectible

The total sales for December 19x1 are expected to be $200,000. The controller feels that sales in January 19x2 could range from $100,000 to $160,000.

REQUIRED:

1. Demonstrate how a financial-planning model could be used to project cash receipts in January of 19x2 for three different levels of January sales. Use the following columnar format.

| | **Total Sales in January, 19x2** | | |
	$100,000	**$130,000**	**$160,000**
Cash receipts in January 19x2:			
From December sales on account.......... $		$	$
From January cash sales			
From January sales on account............	————	————	————
Total cash receipts .... $		$	$

2. How could the controller of Sound Ideas, Inc. use this financial planning model to help in planning operations for January?

Exercise 8-27   Completion of Budget Schedules. Educational Furniture, Inc. manufactures a variety of desks, chairs, tables, and shelf units which are sold to public school systems throughout the midwest. The controller of the company's School Desk Division is currently preparing a budget for the first quarter of 19x4. The following sales forecast has been made by the division's sales manager.

January	10,000 desk and chair sets
February	12,000 desk and chair sets
March	15,000 desk and chair sets

Each desk-and-chair set requires 10 board feet of pine planks and 1.5 hours of direct labor. Each set sells for $50. Pine planks cost $.50 per board foot, and the division ends each month with enough wood to cover 10 percent of the next month's production requirements. The division incurs a cost of $20.00 per hour for direct-labor wages and fringe benefits. The division ends each month with enough finished-goods inventory to cover 20 percent of the next month's sales.

REQUIRED: Complete the following budget schedules.

1. Sales budget

	January	**February**	**March**
Sales (in sets)	10,000		
Sales price per set	× $50		
Sales revenue	$500,000		

2. Production budget (in sets)

	January	**February**	**March**
Sales..	10,000		
Add desired ending inventory....................	2,400		3,000
Total requirements	12,400		
Less projected beginning inventory	2,000		
Planned production............................	10,400		

3. Direct-material purchases

	January	February	March
Planned production (sets)	10,400		
Direct material required per set (board feet)	× 10		
Direct material required for production (board feet). . .	104,000		
Add desired ending inventory of direct material (board feet).	12,600		16,000
Total requirements	116,600		
Less projected beginning inventory of direct material (board feet).	10,400		
Planned purchases of direct material (board feet)	106,200		
Cost per board foot	× $.50		
Planned purchases of direct material (dollars).	$ 53,100		

4. Direct-labor budget

	January	February	March
Planned production (sets)	10,400		
Direct-labor hours per set	× 1.5		
Direct-labor hours required	15,600		
Cost per hour.	× $20		
Planned direct-labor cost	$312,000		

Exercise 8-28   Budgetary Slack; Bank. Tanya Williams is the new accounts manager at East Bank of Mississippi. She has just been asked to project how many new bank accounts she will generate during 19x6. The economy of the county in which the bank operates has been growing, and the bank has experienced a 10 percent increase in its number of bank accounts over each of the past five years. In 19x5, the bank had 10,000 accounts.

The new accounts manager is paid a salary plus a bonus of $10 for every new account she generates above the budgeted amount. Thus, if the annual budget calls for 500 new accounts, and 540 new accounts are obtained, Williams's bonus will be $400 (40 × $10).

Williams believes the economy of the county will continue to grow at the same rate in 19x6 as it has in recent years. She has decided to submit a budgetary projection of 700 new accounts for 19x6.

REQUIRED: Your consulting firm has been hired by the bank president to make recommendations for improving its operations. Write a memorandum to the president defining and explaining the negative consequences of budgetary slack. Also discuss the bank's bonus system for the new accounts manager and how the bonus program tends to encourage budgetary slack.

Exercise 8-29   Professional Services Budget; Dental Practice. Metropolitan Dental Associates is a large dental practice in Baltimore. The firm's controller is preparing the budget for 19x1. The controller projects a total of 48,000 office visits, to be evenly distributed throughout the year. Eighty percent of the visits will be half-hour appointments, and the remainder will be one-hour visits. The average rates for professional dental services are $40 for half-hour appointments and $70 for one-hour office visits. Ninety percent of each month's professional service revenue is collected during the month when services are rendered, and the remainder is collected the month following service. Uncollectible billings are negligible. Metropolitan's dental associates earn $50 per hour.

REQUIRED: Prepare the following budget schedules.

1. Direct professional labor budget for the month of June.
2. Cash collections during June for professional services rendered during May and June.

Exercise 8-30   Budgeted Balance Sheet. Given the following information, fill in the missing amounts needed to prepare a budgeted balance sheet for December 31, 19x6.

Accounts receivable, 12/31/x5	$ 100,000
Sales on account during 19x6	900,000
Collections of accounts receivable during 19x6	780,000
Accounts receivable, 12/31/x6	?
Accounts payable, 12/31/x5	$ 150,000
Purchases of goods and services on account during 19x6	1,200,000
Payments of accounts payable during 19x6	?
Accounts payable, 12/31/x6	300,000
Accumulated depreciation 12/31/x5	$ 800,000
Depreciation expense during 19x6	140,000
Accumulated depreciation 12/31/x6	?
Retained earnings 12/31/x5	$1,650,000
Net income for 19x6	400,000
Dividends paid in 19x6	-0-
Retained earnings, 12/31/x6	?

Exercise 8-31   Economic Order Quantity (Appendix). For each of the following independent cases, use the equation method to compute the economic order quantity.

	Case A	Case B	Case C
Annual requirement (in units)	1,681	13,230	560
Cost per order	$40	$250	$10
Annual holding cost per unit	20	6	7

Exercise 8-32   Lead Time and Safety Stock (Appendix). Mowsen Enterprises uses 780 tons of a chemical bonding agent each year. Monthly demand fluctuates between 50 and 80 tons. The lead time for each order is one month, and the economic order quantity is 130 tons.

REQUIRED:

1. Determine the safety stock appropriate for Mowsen's chemical bonding agent.
2. At what order point, in terms of tons remaining in inventory, should Mowsen order the bonding agent?

PROBLEMS   *Problem 8-33   Production and Direct-Labor Budgets.* Jameson Company makes and sells artistic frames for pictures of special events. Bob Anderson, controller, is responsible for preparing the company's master budget and has accumulated the information below for 19x5.

	January	February	March	April	May
Estimated unit sales	10,000	12,000	8,000	9,000	9,000
Sales price per unit	$50.00	$47.50	$47.50	$47.50	$47.50
Direct-labor hours per unit	1.0	1.0	.75	.75	.75
Wage per direct-labor hour	$16.00	$16.00	$16.00	$18.00	$18.00

Labor-related costs include pension contributions of $.50 per hour, workers' compensation insurance of $.20 per hour, employee medical insurance of $.80 per hour, and employer contributions to social security equal to 7 percent of direct-labor costs. The cost of employee benefits paid by the company on its employees is treated as a direct-labor cost. Jameson Company has a labor contract that calls for a wage increase to $18.00 per hour on April 1, 19x5. New laborsaving machinery has been installed and will be fully operational by March 1, 19x5.

Jameson Company expects to have 16,000 frames on hand at December 31, 19x4, and has a policy of carrying an end-of-month inventory of 100 percent of the following month's sales plus 50 percent of the second following month's sales.

REQUIRED:

1. Prepare a production budget and a direct-labor budget for Jameson Company by month and for the first quarter of 19x5. Both budgets may be combined in one schedule. The direct-labor budget should include direct-labor hours and show the detail for each direct-labor cost category.
2. For each item used in the firm's production budget and direct-labor budget, identify the other components of the master budget that would also use these data.

(CMA, adapted)

Problem 8-34   Direct-Labor, Machine-Hour, and Production-Cost Budgets. Kaylen Company manufactures three products in a factory with four departments. Both labor and machine time are applied to the products as they pass through each department. The nature of the machines and labor skills is such that neither machines nor labor can be switched from one department to another.

Kaylen's management is planning its production schedule for the next several months. The planning is complicated by labor shortages in the community, and some machines will be down several months for repairs. Information follows regarding (a) available machine and labor time by department and (b) machine hours and direct-labor hours required per unit of product. These data will remain valid for at least six months.

	Department			
Monthly Capacity Availability	**1**	**2**	**3**	**4**
Normal machine capacity in machine hours.......	3,500	3,500	3,000	3,500
Capacity of machine being repaired in machine hours....................................	(500)	(400)	(300)	(200)
Available machine capacity in machine hours......	3,000	3,100	2,700	3,300
Labor capacity in direct-labor hours.............	4,000	4,500	3,500	3,000
Available labor in direct-labor hours	3,700	4,500	2,750	2,600

Labor and Machine Time Requirements per Unit of Product

Product	Labor and Machine Time	Required Time			
401	Direct-labor hours	2	3	3	1
	Machine hours	1	1	2	2
403	Direct-labor hours	1	2	-	2
	Machine hours	1	1	-	2
405	Direct-labor hours	2	2	2	1
	Machine hours	2	2	1	1

The sales manager believes that the monthly demand for the next six months will be as follows:

Product	Monthly Sales Volume in Units
401	500
403	400
405	1,000

Inventory levels are satisfactory and need not be increased or decreased during the next six months. The selling price and cost data that will be valid for the next six months are as follows:

	Product		
	401	**403**	**405**
Unit costs:			
Direct material	$ 7	$ 13	$ 17
Direct labor:			
Department 1	24	12	24
Department 2	42	28	28
Department 3	48	—	32
Department 4	18	36	18
Variable overhead	54	40	50
Variable selling expenses	3	2	4
Unit selling price	$296	$223	$267

REQUIRED:

1. Calculate the monthly requirement for machine hours and direct-labor hours for the production of products 401, 403, and 405 to determine whether the monthly sales demand for the three products can be met by the factory.
2. Prepare a schedule showing budgeted costs of direct material, direct labor, and variable overhead. Assume the following production schedule.

Product	Planned Production
401	250 units
403	400 units
405	1,000 units

3. Demonstrate that the planned production levels given in requirement 2 are feasible in light of Kaylen's labor and machine-time shortages.
4. Identify some alternatives Kaylen Company might consider so it can supply its customers with all the product they demand.

(CMA, adapted)

Problem 8-35   *Production, Materials, Labor, and Overhead Budget.* The Wyoming Division of Reid Corporation produces an intricate component used in Reid's major product line. The division manager has been concerned recently by a lack of coordination between purchasing and production personnel and believes that a monthly budgeting system would be better than the present system.

Wyoming's division manager has decided to develop budget information for the third quarter of the current year as an experiment before the budget system is implemented for an entire year. In response to the division manager's request, the divisional controller accumulated the following data.

Sales

Sales through June 30, 19x7, the first six months of the current year, are 24,000 units. Actual sales in units for May and June and estimated unit sales for the next four months are detailed below.

May (actual)	4,000
June (actual)	4,000
July (estimated)	5,000
August (estimated)	6,000
September (estimated)	7,000
October (estimated)	7,000

Wyoming Division expects to sell 60,000 units during the year ending December 31, 19x7.

Direct Material

Data regarding the materials used in the component are shown in the following schedule. The desired monthly ending inventory for all direct materials is an amount sufficient to produce the next month's estimated sales.

Direct material	Units of Direct Material per Finished Component	Cost per Unit	Inventory Level 6/30/x7
No. 101	6	$2.40	35,000 units
No. 211	4	3.60	30,000 units
No. 242	2	1.20	14,000 units

Direct Labor

Each component must pass through three different processes to be completed. Data regarding direct labor follow.

Process	Direct-Labor Hours per Finished Component	Cost per Direct-Labor Hour
Forming	.40	$16.00
Assembly	1.00	11.00
Finishing	.125	12.00

Manufacturing Overhead

The division produced 27,000 components during the six-month period ending June 30, 19x7. The actual variable overhead costs incurred during this six-month period are given in the following schedule. The divisional controller believes the variable overhead costs will be incurred at the same rate during the last six months of 19x7.

Supplies	$ 59,400
Electricity	27,000
Indirect labor.	54,000
Other	8,100
Total variable overhead	$148,500

The fixed overhead costs incurred during the first six months of 19x7 amounted to $93,500. Fixed overhead costs are budgeted for the full year as follows:

Supervision	$ 60,000
Taxes	7,200
Depreciation	86,400
Other	32,400
Total fixed overhead	$186,000

Finished Goods

The desired monthly ending inventory of completed components is 80 percent of the next month's estimated sales. There are 5,000 finished units in inventory on June 30, 19x7.

REQUIRED:

1. Prepare a production budget in units for the Wyoming Division for the third quarter ending September 30, 19x7.
2. Independent of your answer to requirement 1, assume the Wyoming Division plans to produce 18,000 units during the third quarter ending September 30, 19x7, and 60,000 units for the year ending December 31, 19x7.
   a. Prepare a direct-material purchases budget, in units and dollars, for the third quarter ending September 30, 19x7.
   b. Prepare a direct-labor budget, in hours and dollars, for the third quarter ending September 30, 19x7.
   c. Prepare a manufacturing-overhead budget for the six-month period ending December 31, 19x7.

(CMA, adapted)

Problem 8-36 *Budget Preparation: Sales, Production, and Purchases.* Scarborough Corporation manufactures and sells two products, Thingone and Thingtwo. In July 19x7, Scarborough's budget department gathered the following data in order to project sales and budget requirements for 19x8.

19x8 Sales Forecast

Product	Units	Price
Thingone	60,000	$ 70
Thingtwo	40,000	$100

19x8 Inventories (in units)

Product	Expected January 1, 19x8	Desired December 31, 19x8
Thingone	20,000	25,000
Thingtwo	8,000	9,000

In order to produce one unit of Thingone and Thingtwo, the following direct materials are used.

	Amount Used per Unit	
Direct Material	**Thingone**	**Thingtwo**
A	4 lb.	5 lb.
B	2 lb.	3 lb.
C		1 unit

Projected data for 19x8, with respect to raw materials, are as follows:

Raw Material	**Anticipated Purchase Price**	**Expected Inventories January 1, 19x8**	**Desired Inventories December 31, 19x8**
A	$8	32,000 lb.	36,000 lb.
B	$5	29,000 lb.	32,000 lb.
C	$3	6,000 units	7,000 units

Projected direct-labor requirements and direct-labor rates for 19x8 are as follows:

Product	**Hours per Unit**	**Rate per Hour**
Thingone	2	$15
Thingtwo	3	$20

Overhead is applied at the rate of $2 per direct-labor hour.

REQUIRED: Based upon the projections and budget requirements for 19x8 for Thingone and Thingtwo, prepare the following budgets for 19x8.

1. Sales budget (in dollars).
2. Production budget (in units).
3. Direct-material purchases budget (in quantities).
4. Direct-material purchases budget (in dollars).
5. Direct-labor budget (in dollars).
6. Budgeted finished-goods inventory on December 31, 19x8 (in dollars).

(CPA, adapted)

Problem 8-37 *Cash Budgeting in a Hospital; Third-Party Billings.* Central Indiana Medical Center provides a wide range of hospital services in its community. The hospital's board of directors has recently authorized the following capital expenditures.

Interaortic balloon pump.	$1,100,000
CT scanner.	700,000
X-ray equipment	600,000
Laboratory equipment.	1,400,000
Total.	$3,800,000

The expenditures are planned for October 1, 19x4, and the board wishes to know the amount of borrowing, if any, necessary on that date. Marc Kelly, controller, has gathered the following information to be used in preparing an analysis of future cash flows.

- Billings, made in the month of service, for the first six months of 19x4 are listed below.

Month	Actual Amount
January	$4,400,000
February	4,400,000
March	4,500,000
April	4,500,000
May	5,000,000
June	5,000,000

- Ninety percent of the hospital's billings are made to third parties such as Blue Cross, federal or state governments, and private insurance companies. The remaining 10 percent of the billings are made directly to patients. Historical patterns of billing collections are presented below.

	Third-Party Billings	Direct Patient Billings
During month of service	20%	10%
During month following service	50%	40%
During second month following service	20%	40%
Uncollectible	10%	10%

- Estimated billings for the last six months of 19x4 are listed below. The same billing and collection patterns that have been experienced during the first six months of 19x4 are expected to continue during the last six months of the year.

Month	Estimated Amount
July	$4,500,000
August	5,000,000
September	5,500,000
October	5,700,000
November	5,800,000
December	5,500,000

- The purchases of the past three months and the planned purchases for the last six months of 19x4 are presented in the following schedule.

Month	Amount
April	$1,100,000
May	1,200,000
June	1,200,000
July	1,250,000
August	1,500,000
September	1,850,000
October	1,950,000
November	2,250,000
December	1,750,000

● Additional information follows:

(a) All purchases are made on account, and accounts payable are paid in the month following the purchase.

(b) Salaries for each month during the remainder of 19x4 are expected to be $1,500,000 per month plus 20 percent of that month's billings. Salaries are paid in the month of service.

(c) The hospital's monthly depreciation charges are $125,000.

(d) The medical center incurs interest expense of $150,000 per month and makes interest payments of $450,000 on the last day of each quarter (i.e., March 31, June 30, September 30, and December 31).

(e) Endowment fund income is expected to continue at the rate of $175,000 per month.

(f) The hospital has a cash balance of $300,000 on July 1, 19x4, and has a policy of maintaining a minimum end-of-month cash balance of 10 percent of the current month's purchases.

(g) The hospital uses a calendar-year reporting period.

REQUIRED:

1. Prepare a schedule of budgeted cash receipts by month for the third quarter of 19x4 (July through September).

2. Prepare a schedule of budgeted cash disbursements by month for the third quarter of 19x4.

3. Determine the amount of borrowing, if any, necessary on October 1, 19x4 to acquire the capital items totaling $3,800,000.

(CMA, adapted)

Problem 8-38   Interrelationships between Components of Master Budget. SecCo manufactures and sells security systems. The company started by installing photoelectric security systems in offices and has expanded into the private-home market. SecCo has a basic security system that has been developed into three standard products, each of which can be adapted to meet the specific needs of customers. SecCo's manufacturing operation is moderate in size, as the bulk of the component manufacturing is completed by independent contractors. The security systems are approximately 85 percent complete when received from contractors and only require final assembly in SecCo's plant. Each product passes through at least one of three assembly operations.

SecCo operates in a rapidly growing community. There is evidence that a great deal of new commercial construction will take place in the near future, and SecCo's management has decided to pursue this new market. In order to be competitive, SecCo will have to expand its operations.

In view of the expected increase in business, Sandra Becker, SecCo's controller, believes that SecCo should implement a complete budgeting system. Becker has decided to make a formal presentation to SecCo's president explaining the benefits of a budgeting system and outlining the budget schedules and reports that would be necessary.

REQUIRED:

1. Explain the benefits SecCo would gain from implementing a budgeting system.

2. If Sandra Becker develops a master budget for SecCo:
   a. identify, in order, the schedules that will have to be prepared, and
   b. identify the subsequent schedules that would be based on the schedules identified above.

Use the following format for your answer.

Schedule   Subsequent Schedule

(CMA, adapted)

*Problem 8-39   **Preparation of Master Budget.*** International Container Corporation manufactures two types of cardboard boxes used in shipping canned food, fruit, and vegetables. The canned food box (type C) and the perishable food box (type P) have the following material and labor requirements.

	Type of Box	
	C	**P**
Direct material required per 100 boxes:		
Paperboard ($.20 per pound)...............	30 pounds..........	70 pounds
Corrugating medium ($.10 per pound).......	20 pounds..........	30 pounds
Direct labor required per 100 boxes ($12.00 per hour)....................................	.25 hour............	.50 hour

The following manufacturing-overhead costs are anticipated for 19x7. The predetermined overhead rate is based on a production volume of 500,000 units for each type of box. Manufacturing overhead is applied on the basis of direct-labor hours.

Indirect materials	$ 10,000
Indirect labor..	45,000
Utilities	30,000
Property taxes	15,000
Insurance..	18,000
Depreciation	32,000
Total	$150,000

The following inventory information is available.

	Inventory January 1, 19x7		Desired Ending Inventory December 31, 19x7
Finished goods:			
Box type C	10,000 boxes	....	5,000 boxes
Box type P	20,000 boxes	....	15,000 boxes
Direct materials:			
Paperboard	15,000 pounds	....	5,000 pounds
Corrugating medium	5,000 pounds	....	10,000 pounds

The sales forecast for 19x7 is as follows:

	Sales Volume		Sales Price
Box type C.......	500,000 boxes	....	$ 90.00 per hundred boxes
Box type P.......	500,000 boxes	....	$130.00 per hundred boxes

The following selling and administrative expenses are anticipated for 19x7.

Salaries and fringe benefits of sales personnel	$ 60,000
Advertising	10,000
Management salaries and fringe benefits	100,000
Clerical wages and fringe benefits	35,000
Miscellaneous administrative expenses	5,000
Total	$210,000

REQUIRED: Prepare a master budget for International Container Corporation for 19x7. Assume an income tax rate of 40 percent. Include the following schedules.

1. Sales budget.
2. Production budget.
3. Direct-material budget.
4. Direct-labor budget.
5. Manufacturing-overhead budget.
6. Selling and administrative expense budget.
7. Budgeted income statement. (Hint: To determine cost of goods sold, first compute the manufacturing cost per unit for each type of box. Include *applied* manufacturing overhead in the cost.)

Problem 8-40   Economic Order Quantity; Equation Approach (Appendix). Reno Fiber Company manufactures glass fibers used in the communications industry. The company's materials and parts manager is currently revising the inventory policy for XL-20, one of the chemicals used in the production process. The chemical is purchased in 10-pound cannisters for $100 each. The firm uses 4,800 cannisters per year. The controller estimates that it costs Reno Fiber Company $150 to place and receive a typical order of XL-20. The annual cost of storing XL-20 is $4 per cannister.

REQUIRED:

1. Write the formula for the total annual cost of ordering and storing XL-20.
2. Use the EOQ formula to determine the optimal order quantity.
3. What is the total annual cost of ordering and storing XL-20 at the economic order quantity?
4. How many orders will be placed per year?

Problem 8-41   Economic Order Quantity; Tabular Approach (Appendix). Refer to the data given in the preceding problem for Reno Fiber Company.

REQUIRED:

1. Prepare a table showing the total annual cost of ordering and storing XL-20 for each of the following order quantities: 400, 600, and 800 cannisters.
2. What are the weaknesses in the tabular approach?

Problem 8-42   Economic Order Quantity; Graphical Approach (Appendix). Refer to the data given in problem 8-40 for Reno Fiber Company.

REQUIRED: Prepare a graphical analysis of the economic order quantity decision for XL-20.

Problem 8-43   Economic Order Quantity; Lead Time and Safety Stock (Appendix). Refer to the data given in problem 8-40 for Reno Fiber Company. The lead time required to receive an order of XL-20 is one month.

REQUIRED:

1. Assuming stable usage of XL-20 each month, determine the reorder point for XL-20.
2. Draw a graph showing the usage, lead time, and reorder point for XL-20.
3. Suppose that monthly usage of XL-20 fluctuates between 300 and 500 cannisters, although annual demand remains constant at 4,800 cannisters. What level of safety stock should the materials and parts manager keep on hand for XL-20? What is the new reorder point for the chemical?

Problem 8-44 *Economic Order Quantity (Appendix).* SaPane Company is a regional distributor of automobile window glass. With the popularity of subcompact car models and the expected high level of consumer demand, management recognizes a need to determine the total inventory cost associated with maintaining an optimal supply of replacement windshields for the subcompact cars introduced by each of the three major manufacturers. SaPane is expecting an annual demand of 10,800 windshields. The purchase price of each windshield is $50.

Other costs associated with ordering and maintaining an inventory of these windshields are as follows:

- The historical ordering costs incurred in the purchase order department for placing and processing orders are shown below.

Year	Orders Placed and Processed	Total Processing Costs
19x7	20	$12,300
19x8	55	12,475
19x9	100	12,700

Management expects the ordering costs to increase 16 percent over the amounts and rates experienced the last three years.
- The windshield manufacturer charges SaPane a $75 shipping fee per order.
- A clerk in the receiving department receives, inspects, and secures the windshields as they arrive from the manufacturer. This activity requires eight hours per order received. This clerk has no other responsibilities and is paid at the rate of $9 per hour. Related variable overhead costs in this department are applied at the rate of $2.50 per hour.
- Additional warehouse space will have to be rented to store the new windshields. Space can be rented as needed in a warehouse at an estimated cost of $2,500 per year plus $5.35 per windshield.
- Breakage cost is estimated to be 6 percent of the average inventory value.
- Taxes and fire insurance on the inventory are $1.15 per windshield.
- Other storage costs amount to $10.50 per windshield.
- SaPane Company operates on a six-day work week for 50 weeks each year. The firm is closed two weeks each year.

Six working days are required from the time the order is placed with the manufacturer until it is received.

REQUIRED: Calculate the following values for SaPane Company.

1. The value of the ordering cost that should be used in the EOQ formula. (Hint: Use the high-low method to estimate the processing cost per order.)

2. The value of the storage cost that should be used in the EOQ formula.
3. The economic order quantity.
4. The minimum annual relevant cost of ordering and storage at the economic order quantity.
5. The reorder point in units.

(CMA, adapted)

CASE *Case 8-45   Using Budgets to Evaluate Business Decisions.* Metro Court Club (MCC) offers racquetball and other physical fitness facilities to its members. There are four of these clubs in the metropolitan area. Each club has between 1,800 and 2,500 members. Revenue is derived from annual membership fees and hourly court fees. The annual membership fees are as follows:

Individual	$40
Student	$25
Family.	$95

The hourly court fees vary from $6 to $10 depending upon the season and the time of day (prime versus non-prime time).

The peak racquetball season is considered to run from September through April. During this period court usage averages 90 to 100 percent of capacity during prime time (5:00–9:00 p.m.) and 50 to 60 percent of capacity during the remaining hours. Daily court usage during the off-season (i.e., summer) only averages 20 to 40 percent of capacity.

Most of MCC's memberships have September expirations. A substantial amount of the cash receipts are collected during the early part of the racquetball season due to the renewal of the annual membership fees and heavy court usage. However, cash receipts are not as large in the spring and drop significantly in the summer months.

MCC is considering changing its membership and fee structure in an attempt to change its cash receipts. Under the new membership plan, only an annual membership fee would be charged, rather than a membership fee plus hourly court fees. There would be two classes of membership, with annual fees as follows:

Individual	$250
Family.	$400

The annual fee would be collected in advance at the time the membership application is completed. Members would be allowed to use the racquetball courts as often as they wish during the year under the new plan.

All future memberships would be sold under these new terms. Current memberships would be honored on the old basis until they expire. However, a special promotional campaign would be instituted to attract new members and to encourage current members to convert to the new membership plan immediately.

The annual fees for individual and family memberships would be reduced to $200 and $300, respectively, during the two-month promotional campaign. In addition, all memberships sold or renewed during this period would be for 15 months rather than the normal one-year period. Current members also would be given a credit toward the annual fee for the unexpired portion of their membership fee, and for all prepaid hourly court fees for league play which have not yet been used.

MCC's management estimates that 60 to 70 percent of the present membership would continue with the club. The most active members (45 percent of the present membership) would convert immediately to the new plan, while the remaining members who continue would wait until their current memberships expire. Those members who would not continue are not considered active (i.e., they play five or less times during the year). Management estimates that the loss of members would be offset fully by new members within six months of instituting the new plan. Furthermore, many of the new members would be individuals who would play during non-prime time. Management estimates that adequate court time will be available for all members under the new plan.

If the new membership plan is adopted, it would be instituted on February 1, 19x2, well before the summer season. The special promotional campaign would be conducted during March and April. Once the plan is implemented, annual renewal of memberships and payment of fees would take place as each individual or family membership expires.

REQUIRED: Your consulting firm has been hired to help MCC evaluate its new fee structure. Write a letter to the club's president answering the following questions.

1. Will Metro Court Club's new membership plan and fee structure improve its ability to plan its cash receipts? Explain your answer.
2. Metro Court Club should evaluate the new membership plan and fee structure completely before it decides to adopt or reject it.
   a. Identify the key factors that MCC should consider in its evaluation.
   b. Explain what type of financial analyses MCC should prepare in order to make a complete evaluation.
3. Explain how Metro Court Club's cash management would differ from the present if the new membership plan and fee structure were adopted.

(CMA, adapted)

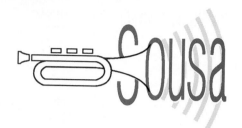

Chapter 9

Control through Standard-Costing Systems

After completing this chapter, you should be able to:

- Explain how standard costing is used to help control costs.
- Describe two ways to set standards.
- Distinguish between perfection and practical standards.
- Compute and interpret the direct-material price and quantity variances and the direct-labor rate and efficiency variances.
- Explain several methods for determining the significance of cost variances.
- Describe some behavioral effects of standard costing.
- Explain how standard costs are used in product costing.
- Prepare journal entries to record and close out cost variances.
- Summarize some advantages of standard costing.
- Describe the changing role of standard-costing systems in the new manufacturing environment.

A budget provides a plan for managers to follow in making decisions and directing an organization's activities. At the end of a budget period, the budget serves another useful purpose. At that time, managers use the budget as a benchmark against which to compare the results of actual operations. Did the company make as much profit as anticipated in the budget? Were costs greater or less than expected? These questions involve issues of control. In this chapter, we will study the tools used by managerial accountants to assist managers in controlling an organization's operations and costs.

CONTROLLING COSTS

Any control system has three basic parts: a predetermined or *standard* performance level, a measure of *actual* performance, and a *comparison* between standard and

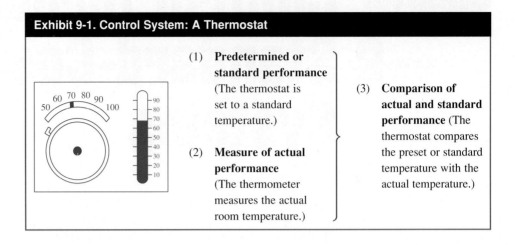

Exhibit 9-1. Control System: A Thermostat

(1) **Predetermined or standard performance** (The thermostat is set to a standard temperature.)

(2) **Measure of actual performance** (The thermometer measures the actual room temperature.)

(3) **Comparison of actual and standard performance** (The thermostat compares the preset or standard temperature with the actual temperature.)

actual performance. A thermostat is a control system with which we are all familiar. First, a thermostat has a predetermined or standard temperature, which can be set at any desired level. If you want the temperature in a room to be 68 degrees, you set the thermostat at the *standard* of 68 degrees. Second, the thermostat has a thermometer, which measures the *actual* temperature in the room. Third, the thermostat *compares* the preset or standard temperature with the actual room temperature. If the actual temperature falls below the preset or standard temperature, the thermostat activates a heating device. The three features of a control system are depicted in Exhibit 9-1.

A managerial accountant's budgetary-control system works like a thermostat. First, a predetermined or **standard cost** is set. In essence, a standard cost is a budget for the production of one unit of product or service. It is the cost chosen by the managerial accountant to serve as the benchmark in the budgetary-control system. When the firm produces many units, the managerial accountant uses the standard unit cost to determine the total standard or budgeted cost of production. For example, suppose the standard direct-material cost for one unit of product is $5 and 100 units are manufactured. The total standard or budgeted direct-material cost, given actual output of 100 units, is $500 ($5 × 100).

Second, the managerial accountant measures the actual cost incurred in the production process.

Third, the managerial accountant compares the actual cost with the budgeted or standard cost. Any difference between the two is called a **cost variance.** Cost variances then are used in controlling costs.

Management by Exception

Managers are busy people. They do not have time to look into the causes of every variance between actual and standard costs. However, they do take the time to investigate the causes of significant cost variances. This process of only following up on significant cost variances is called **management by exception.** When operations are going along as planned, actual costs and profit will typically be close to the budgeted amounts. However, if there are significant departures from planned operations, such effects will show up as significant cost variances. Managers investigate these variances to determine their cause, if possible, and take corrective action when indicated.

What constitutes a significant variance? No precise answer can be given to this question, since it depends on the size and type of the organization and its production process. We will consider this issue later in the chapter when we discuss common methods for determining the significance of cost variances. First, however, we will turn our attention to the process of setting standards.

SETTING STANDARDS

Managerial accountants typically use two methods for setting cost standards: analysis of historical data, and task analysis.

Analysis of Historical Data One indicator of future costs is historical cost data. In a mature production process, where the firm has a lot of production experience, historical costs can provide a good basis for predicting future costs. The methods for analyzing cost behavior that we studied in Chapter 6 are used in making cost predictions. The managerial accountant often will need to adjust these predictions to reflect movements in price levels or technological changes in the production process. For example, the amount of rubber required to manufacture a particular type of tire will likely be the same this year as last year, unless there has been a significant change in the process used to manufacture tires. However, the price of rubber is likely to be different this year than last, and this fact must be reflected in the new standard cost of a tire.

Despite the relevance of historical cost data in setting cost standards, managerial accountants must guard against relying on them excessively. Even a seemingly minor change in the way a product is manufactured may make historical data almost totally irrelevant. Moreover, new products also require new cost standards. For new products, such as genetically engineered medicines, there are no historical cost data upon which to base standards. In such cases, the managerial accountant must turn to another approach.

Task Analysis Another way to set cost standards is to analyze the process of manufacturing a product to determine what it *should* cost. The emphasis shifts from what the product *did* cost in the past to what it *should* cost in the future. In using this approach, the managerial accountant typically works with engineers who are intimately familiar with the production process. Together they conduct studies to determine exactly how much direct material should be required and how machinery should be used in the production process. Time and motion studies are conducted to determine how long each step performed by direct laborers should take.

A Combined Approach Managerial accountants often apply both historical cost analysis and task analysis in setting cost standards. It may be, for example, that the technology has changed for only one step in the production process. In such a case, the managerial accountant would work with engineers to set cost standards for the technologically changed part of the production process. However, the accountant would likely rely on the less expensive method of analyzing historical cost data to update the cost standards for the remainder of the production process.

Participation in Setting Standards

Standards should not be determined by the managerial accountant alone. People generally will be more committed to meeting standards if they are allowed to participate in setting them. For example, production supervisors should have a role in setting production cost standards, and sales managers should be involved in setting targets for sales prices and volume. In addition, knowledgeable staff personnel should participate in the standard-setting process. For example, task analysis should be carried out by a team consisting of production engineers, production supervisors, and managerial accountants.

Perfection versus Practical Standards: A Behavioral Issue

How difficult should it be to attain standard costs? Should standards be set so that actual costs rarely exceed standard costs? Or should it be so hard to attain standards that actual costs frequently exceed them? The answers to these questions depend on the purpose for which standards will be used and how standards affect behavior.

Perfection Standards A **perfection** (or **ideal**) **standard** is one that can be attained only under nearly perfect operating conditions. Such standards assume peak efficiency, the lowest possible input prices, the best-quality materials obtainable, and no disruptions in production due to such causes as machine breakdowns or power failures. Some managers believe that perfection standards motivate employees to achieve the lowest cost possible. They claim that since the standard is theoretically attainable, employees will have an incentive to come as close as possible to achieving it.

Other managers and many behavioral scientists disagree. They feel that perfection standards discourage employees, since they are so unlikely to be attained. Moreover, setting unrealistically difficult standards may encourage employees to sacrifice product quality to achieve lower costs. By skimping on raw-material quality or the attention given manual production tasks, employees may be able to lower the production cost. However, this lower cost may come at the expense of a higher rate of defective units. Thus, the firm ultimately may incur higher costs than necessary as defective products are returned by customers or scrapped upon inspection.

Practical Standards Standards that are as tight as practical, but still are expected to be attained, are called **practical** (or **attainable**) standards. Such standards assume a production process that is as efficient as practical under normal operating conditions. Practical standards allow for such occurrences as occasional machine breakdowns and normal amounts of raw-material waste. Attaining a practical standard keeps employees on their toes, without demanding miracles. Most behavioral theorists believe that practical standards encourage more positive and productive employee attitudes than do perfection standards.

USE OF STANDARDS BY NONMANUFACTURING ORGANIZATIONS

Many service industry firms, nonprofit organizations, and governmental units make use of standard costs. For example, airlines set standards for fuel and maintenance costs. A county motor vehicle office may have a standard for the number of days required to process and return an application for vehicle registration. These and similar organizations use standards in budgeting and cost control in much the same way that manufacturers use standards. The following illustrations typify the use of standards in service industry firms.

**ILLUSTRATION FROM
MANAGEMENT-
ACCOUNTING
PRACTICE**

United Parcel Service

The *Wall Street Journal* reported on the use of standards by United Parcel Service (UPS). The firm's management used engineers to set performance standards for various delivery tasks. For example, UPS drivers were given a standard of three feet per second as the pace at which they should walk to a customer's door. Moreover, the drivers were instructed to knock on the door, rather than lose time looking for a doorbell.[1]

**ILLUSTRATION FROM
MANAGEMENT-
ACCOUNTING
PRACTICE**

Dutch Pantry, Inc.

Dutch Pantry, Inc. operates over 50 restaurants throughout the eastern United States. Many of the food items served in the firm's restaurants are produced in a central plant. This facility produces over 150 different items, and a cost-accounting system is used to record the flow of costs through the various steps in food preparation. The cost-accounting system is used to record the flow of costs through the various steps in food preparation. The cost-accounting system is based on standard costs established for a batch of each product. The firm's managerial accountants use the standards to monitor and control costs and to determine the cost of the food items produced.[2]

COST VARIANCE ANALYSIS

To illustrate the use of standards in controlling costs, we will focus on a manufacturer of musical instruments for use in schools. American Brass Instrument Company manufactures trumpets in its Sousa Division. The production process consists of several steps. First, brass tubing is packed with sand, heated, and bent into the shape of a trumpet. Then the valves are formed and attached to the trumpet, and all seams and joints are brazed. Finally, several coats of lacquer are applied, and the trumpet is manually inspected and tested.

The divisional controller, John Phillips, has set standards for direct material and direct labor as follows.

Direct-Material Standards

Only the brass in a trumpet is considered direct material. The lacquer is inexpensive and is considered an indirect material, part of manufacturing overhead. The standard quantity and price of brass for the production of one trumpet are as follows:

Standard quantity:
Brass in finished product . . . . 9.5 pounds
Allowance for normal waste . . . . .5 pound
Total standard quantity required per trumpet . . . . 10.0 pounds
Standard price:
Purchase price per pound of brass (net of purchase discounts) $6.50
Transportation cost per pound 50
Total standard price per pound of brass $7.00

---

[1] "Up to Speed: United Parcel Service Gets Deliveries Done by Driving Its Workers," *The Wall Street Journal,* April 22, 1986.

[2] D. Boll, "How Dutch Pantry Accounts for Standard Costs," *Management Accounting,* December 1982, p. 32.

The standard quantity of brass needed to manufacture one trumpet is 10 pounds, even though only 9.5 pounds actually remain in the finished product. Half a pound of brass is wasted as a normal result of the cutting and molding that is part of the production process. Therefore, the entire amount of brass needed to manufacture a trumpet is included in the standard quantity of material.

The standard price of brass reflects all of the costs incurred to acquire the material and transport it to the plant. Notice that the cost of transportation is added to the purchase price. Any purchase discounts would be subtracted out from the purchase price to obtain a net price.

To summarize, the **standard material quantity** is the total amount of material normally required to produce a finished product, including allowances for normal waste or inefficiency. The **standard material price** is the total delivered cost, after subtracting any purchase discounts.

Direct-Labor Standards

The standard quantity and rate for direct labor for the production of one trumpet are as follows:

Standard quantity:
    Direct labor required per trumpet. . . . . 5 hours
Standard rate:
    Hourly wage rate $16
    Fringe benefits (25% of wages). . . . . __4__
    Total standard rate per hour $20

The **standard direct-labor quantity** is the number of labor hours normally needed to manufacture one unit of product. The **standard labor rate** is the total hourly cost of compensation, including fringe benefits.

Standard Costs Given Actual Ouput

During September of 19x8 the Sousa Division manufactured 2,000 trumpets. The total standard or budgeted costs for direct material and direct labor are computed as follows:

Direct material:
    Standard direct-material cost per trumpet (10 pounds × $7.00 per pound) $ 70
    Actual output . . . . × 2,000
    Total standard direct-material cost $140,000
Direct labor:
    Direct labor cost per trumpet (5 hours × $20.00 per hour) . . . . $ 100
    Actual output . . . . × 2,000
    Total standard direct-labor cost $200,000

Notice that the total standard cost for the direct-material and direct-labor inputs is based on the Sousa Division's actual *output*. The division should incur costs of $340,000 for direct material and direct labor, *given that it produced 2,000 trumpets.* The total standard costs for direct material and direct labor serve as the managerial accountant's benchmarks against which to compare actual costs. This comparison then serves as the basis for controlling direct-material and direct-labor costs.

Analysis of Cost Variances

During September of 19x8, the Sousa Division incurred the following actual costs for direct material and direct labor.

Direct material purchased: actual cost
   25,000 pounds at $7.10 per pound $177,500
Direct material used: actual cost
   20,500 pounds at $7.10 per pound $145,550
Direct labor: actual cost
   9,800 hours at $21 per hour $205,800

Compare these actual expenditures with the total standard costs for the production of 2,000 trumpets. Sousa Division spent more than the budgeted amount for both direct material and direct labor. But why were these excess costs incurred? Is there any further analysis the managerial accountant can provide to help answer this question?

Direct-Material Variances

What caused the Sousa Division to spend more than the anticipated amount on direct material? First, the division purchased brass at a higher price ($7.10 per pound) than the standard price ($7.00 per pound). Second, the division used more brass than the standard amount. The amount actually used was 20,500 pounds instead of the standard amount of 20,000 pounds, which is based on actual output of 2,000 trumpets. The managerial accountant can show both of these deviations from standards by computing a **direct-material price variance** (or **purchase price variance**) and a **direct-material quantity variance.** The computation of these variances is depicted in Exhibit 9-2.

The formula for the direct-material price variance is shown below.

$$\text{Direct-material price variance} = (PQ \times AP) - (PQ \times SP) = PQ(AP - SP)$$

where PQ = **quantity purchased**
            AP = **actual price**
            SP = **standard price**

Sousa Division's direct-material price variance for September is computed as follows:

$$\text{Direct-material price variance} = PQ(AP - SP)$$
$$= 25{,}000(\$7.10 - \$7.00) = \$2{,}500 \text{ unfavorable}$$

This variance is unfavorable, because the actual purchase price exceeded the standard price. Notice that the price variance is based on the quantity of material *purchased* (*PQ*), not the quantity actually used in production.

As Exhibit 9-2 shows, the following formula defines the direct-material quantity variance.

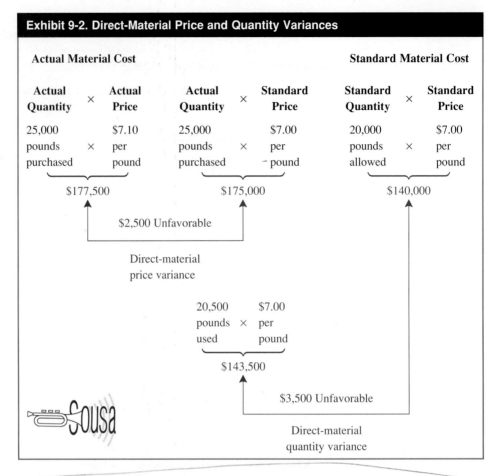

Exhibit 9-2. Direct-Material Price and Quantity Variances

Actual Material Cost

Standard Material Cost

Actual Quantity	×	Actual Price		Actual Quantity	×	Standard Price		Standard Quantity	×	Standard Price
25,000 pounds purchased	×	$7.10 per pound		25,000 pounds purchased	×	$7.00 per pound		20,000 pounds allowed	×	$7.00 per pound

$177,500

$175,000

$140,000

$2,500 Unfavorable

Direct-material
price variance

20,500 pounds × $7.00 per pound used

$143,500

$3,500 Unfavorable

Direct-material
quantity variance

$$\text{Direct-material quantity variance} = (AQ \times SP) - (SQ \times SP) = SP(AQ - SQ)$$

where AQ = actual quantity used
         SQ = standard quantity allowed

Sousa Division's direct-material quantity variance for September is computed as follows:

$$\text{Direct-material quantity variance} = SP(AQ - SQ)$$
$$= \$7.00(20,500 - 20,000) = \$3,500 \text{ unfavorable}$$

This variance is unfavorable, because the actual quantity of direct material used in September exceeded the standard quantity allowed, *given actual September output* of 2,000 trumpets. The quantity variance is based on the quantity of material actually *used* in production (AQ).

Basing the Quantity Variance on Actual Output Notice that the standard quantity of material must be based on the actual production output in order for the quantity variance to be meaningful. It would not make any sense to compare standard or budgeted material usage at one level of output (say, 1,000 trumpets) with the actual material usage at a *different* level of output (say, 2,000 trumpets). Everyone would expect more direct material to be used in the production of 2,000 trumpets than in the production of 1,000 trumpets. For the direct-material quantity variance to provide helpful information for management, the standard or budgeted quantity must be based on *actual output*. Then the quantity variance compares the following two quantities.

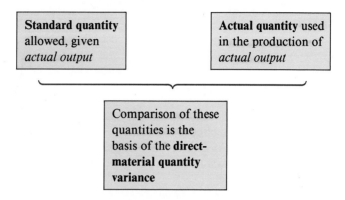

| **Standard quantity** allowed, given *actual output* | | **Actual quantity** used in the production of *actual output* |

Comparison of these quantities is the basis of the **direct-material quantity variance**

Direct-Labor Variances

Why did the Sousa Division spend more than the anticipated amount on direct labor during September? First, the division incurred a cost of $21 per hour for direct labor instead of the standard amount of $20 per hour. Second, the division used only 9,800 hours of direct labor, which is less than the standard quantity of 10,000 hours, given actual output of 2,000 trumpets. The managerial accountant analyzes direct-labor costs by computing a *direct-labor rate variance* and a *direct-labor efficiency variance*. Exhibit 9-3 depicts the computation of these variances.

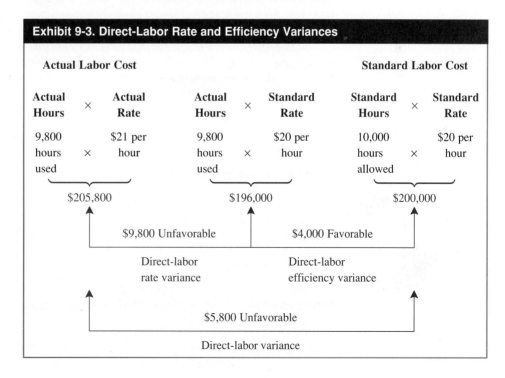

Exhibit 9-3. Direct-Labor Rate and Efficiency Variances

Actual Labor Cost				Standard Labor Cost	
Actual Hours ×	**Actual Rate**	**Actual Hours** ×	**Standard Rate**	**Standard Hours** ×	**Standard Rate**
9,800 hours used ×	$21 per hour	9,800 hours used ×	$20 per hour	10,000 hours allowed ×	$20 per hour
$205,800		$196,000		$200,000	

$9,800 Unfavorable

$4,000 Favorable

Direct-labor rate variance

Direct-labor efficiency variance

$5,800 Unfavorable

Direct-labor variance

The formula for the direct-labor rate variance is shown below.

$$\text{Direct-labor rate variance} = (AH \times AR) - (AH \times SR) = AH(AR - SR)$$

where AH = actual hours used
AR = actual rate per hour
SR = standard rate per hour

Sousa Division's direct-labor rate variance for September is computed as follows:

$$\text{Direct-labor rate variance} = AH(AR - SR)$$
$$= 9,800(\$21 - \$20) = \$9,800 \text{ unfavorable}$$

This variance is unfavorable, because the actual rate exceeded the standard rate during September.

As Exhibit 9-3 shows, the formula for the direct-labor efficiency variance is as follows:

$$\text{Direct-labor efficiency variance} = (AH \times SR) - (SH \times SR) = SR(AH - SH)$$

where SH = standard hours allowed

The Sousa Division's direct-labor efficiency variance for September is computed as follows:

$$\text{Direct-labor efficiency variance} = SR(AH - SH)$$
$$= \$20(9,800 - 10,000) = \$4,000 \text{ favorable}$$

This variance is favorable, because the actual direct-labor hours used in September were less than the standard hours allowed, *given actual September output* of 2,000 trumpets.

Notice that the direct-labor rate and efficiency variances add up to the total direct-labor variance. However, the rate and efficiency variances have opposite signs, since one variance is unfavorable and the other is favorable.

Direct-labor rate variance	$9,800 unfavorable	different signs of variances cancel just as plus and minus signs cancel in arithmetic
Direct-labor efficiency variance	4,000 favorable	
Direct-labor variance	$5,800 unfavorable	

Basing the Efficiency Variance on Actual Output The number of standard hours of direct labor allowed is based on the *actual* production output. It would not be meaningful to compare standard or budgeted labor usage at one level of output with the actual hours used at a different level of output.

SIGNIFICANCE OF COST VARIANCES

Managers do not have time to investigate the causes of every cost variance. Management by exception enables managers to look into the causes of only significant variances. But what constitutes an exception? How does the manager know when to follow up on a cost variance and when to ignore it?

These questions are difficult to answer, because to some extent the answers are part of the art of management. A manager applies judgment and experience in making guesses, pursuing hunches, and relying on intuition to determine when a variance should be investigated. Nevertheless, there are guidelines and rules of thumb that managers often apply.

Size of Variances The absolute size of a variance is one consideration. Managers are more likely to follow up on large variances than on small ones. The relative size of the variance is probably even more important. A manager is more likely to investigate a $20,000 material quantity variance that is 20 percent of the standard direct-material cost of $100,000, than a $50,000 labor efficiency variance that is only 2 percent of the standard direct-labor cost of $2,500,000. The *relative* magnitude of the $20,000 material quantity variance (20 percent) is greater than the *relative* magnitude of the $50,000 labor efficiency variance (2 percent). For this reason, managerial accountants often show the relative magnitude of variances in their cost-variance reports. For example, the September cost-variance report for the Sousa Division is shown in Exhibit 9-4.

Managers often apply a rule of thumb that takes into account both the absolute and the relative magnitude of a variance. An example of such a rule is the following: Investigate variances that are either greater than $10,000 or greater than 10 percent of standard cost.

Recurring Variances Another consideration in deciding when to investigate a variance is whether the variance occurs repeatedly or only infrequently. Suppose a manager uses the rule of thumb stated above and the following direct-material quantity variances occur.

Month	Variance	Percentage of Standard Cost†
January	$3,000 F*	6.0%
February	3,200 F	6.4%
March	1,800 F	3.6%
April	3,100 F	6.2%

* F denotes a favorable variance.
† The standard direct-material cost is $50,000.

Exhibit 9-4. Cost Variance Report: Sousa Division, September 19×8

	Amount		Percentage of Standard Cost
Direct material:			
Standard cost, given actual output	$140,000		
Direct-material price variance	2,500	Unfavorable	1.79%
Direct-material quantity variance	3,500	Unfavorable	2.50%
Direct labor:			
Standard cost, given actual output	$200,000		
Direct-labor rate variance	9,800	Unfavorable	4.9%
Direct-labor efficiency variance	4,000	Favorable	(2.0%)

A strict adherence to the rule of thumb indicates no investigation, since none of the monthly variances are greater than $10,000 or 10 percent of standard cost. Nevertheless, the manager might investigate this variance in April, since it has *recurred* at a reasonably high level for several consecutive months. In this case, the consistency of the variance triggers an investigation, not its absolute or relative magnitude.

Trends A trend in a variance may also call for investigation. Suppose a manager observes the following direct-labor efficiency variances.

Month	Variance	Percentage of Standard Cost†
January	$ 100 U*	.10%
February	550 U	.55%
March	3,000 U	3.00%
April	9,100 U	9.10%

* U denotes an unfavorable variance.
† The standard direct-labor cost is $100,000.

None of these variances is large enough to trigger an investigation if the manager uses the "$10,000 or 10 percent" rule of thumb. However, the four-month *trend* is worrisome. An alert manager will likely follow up on this unfavorable trend to determine its causes before costs get out of hand.

Controllability Another important consideration in deciding when to look into the causes of a variance is the manager's view of the controllability of the cost item. A manager is more likely to investigate the variance for a cost that is controllable by someone in the organization than one that is not. For example, there may be little point to investigating a material price variance if the organization has no control over the price. This could happen, for example, if the firm has a long-term contract with a supplier of the material at a price determined on the international market. In contrast, the manager is likely to follow up on a variance that should be controllable, such as a direct-labor efficiency variance or a direct-material quantity variance.

Favorable Variances It is just as important to investigate significant favorable variances as significant unfavorable variances. For example, a favorable direct-labor efficiency variance may indicate that employees have developed a more efficient way of performing a production task. By investigating the variance, management can learn about the improved method. It may be possible to use a similar approach elsewhere in the organization.

Costs and Benefits of Investigation The decision whether to investigate a cost variance is a cost-benefit decision. The costs of investigation include the time spent by the investigating manager and the employees in the department where the investigation occurs. Other potential costs include disruption of the production process as the investigation is conducted, and corrective actions taken to eliminate the cause of a variance. The benefits of a variance investigation include reduced future production costs if the cause of an unfavorable variance is eliminated. Another potential benefit is the cost saving associated with the lowering of cost standards when the cause of a favorable variance is discovered.

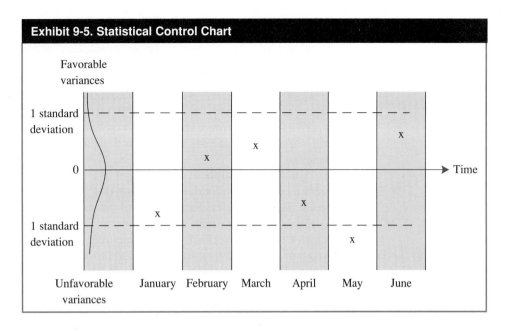

Exhibit 9-5. Statistical Control Chart

Weighing these considerations takes the judgment of skillfull and experienced managers. Key to this judgment is an intimate understanding of the organization's production process and day-to-day contact with its operations.

A Statistical Approach

There are many reasons for cost variances. For example, a direct-labor efficiency variance could be caused by inexperienced employees, employee inefficiency, poor-quality raw materials, poorly maintained machinery, an intentional work slowdown due to employee grievances, or many other factors. In addition to these substantive reasons, there are purely random causes of variances. People are not robots, and they are not perfectly consistent in their work habits. Random fluctuations in direct-labor efficiency variances can be caused by such factors as employee illnesses, workers experimenting with different production methods, or simply random fatigue. Ideally, managers would be able to sort out the randomly caused variances from those with substantive and controllable underlying causes. It is impossible to accomplish this with 100 percent accuracy, but a **statistical control chart** can help.

A statistical control chart plots cost variances across time and compares them with a statistically determined **critical value** that triggers an investigation. This critical value is usually determined by assuming that cost variances have a normal probability distribution with a mean of zero. The critical value is set at some multiple of the distribution's standard deviation. Variances greater than the critical value are investigated.

Exhibit 9-5 shows a statistical control chart with a critical value of one standard deviation. The manager would investigate the variance observed in May, since it falls further than one standard deviation from the mean (zero). The variances for the remaining five months would not be investigated. The presumption is that these minor variances are due to random causes and are not worth investigating.[3]

[3] For further discussion of statistical control charts, see Glenn Welsch, Ronald Hilton, and Paul Gordon, *Budgeting: Profit Planning and Control,* 5th ed. (Englewood Cliffs, NJ: Prentice-Hall), 1988.

BEHAVIORAL IMPACT OF STANDARD COSTING

Standard costs and variance analysis are useful in diagnosing organizational performance. These tools help managers to discern "the story behind the story" — the details of operations that underlie reported cost and profit numbers. Standard costs, budgets, and variances are also used to evaluate the performance of individuals and departments. The performance of individuals, relative to standards or budgets, often is used to help determine salary increases, bonuses, and promotions. When standards and variances affect employee reward structures, they can profoundly influence behavior.

For example, suppose the manager of a hotel's Food and Beverage Department earns a bonus when food and beverage costs are below the budgeted amount, given actual sales. This reward structure will provide a concrete incentive for the manager to keep food and beverage costs under control. But such an incentive can have either positive or negative effects. The bonus may induce the manager to seek the most economical food suppliers and to watch more carefully for employee theft and waste. However, the bonus could also persuade the manager to buy cheaper but less tender steaks for the restaurant. This could ultimately result in lost patronage for the restaurant and the hotel. One aspect of skillfull management is knowing how to use standards, budgets, and variances to get the most out of an organization's employees. Unfortunately, there are no simple answers or formulas for success in this area.

Standards, budgets, and variances are used in the executive compensation schemes of many well-known companies, as this example suggests:

ILLUSTRATION FROM MANAGEMENT-ACCOUNTING PRACTICE

Corning Glass Works

A Harvard Business School management case reported on Corning Glass Works' system for determining managers' bonuses. In addition to individual performance factors, the bonus scheme gave considerable weight to the variance between actual and budgeted operating profit. In evaluating division managers, the performance review was broad enough to include all areas of the manager's performance. However, the key performance variable was divisional operating profit.[4]

CONTROLLABILITY OF VARIANCES

Cost control is accomplished through the efforts of individual managers in an organization. By determining which managers are in the best position to influence each cost variance, the managerial accountant can assist managers in deriving the greatest benefit from cost variance analysis.

Who is responsible for the direct-material price and quantity variances? The direct-labor rate and efficiency variances? Answering these questions is often difficult, because it is rare that any one person completely controls any event. Nevertheless, it is often possible to identify the manager who is *most able to influence* a particular variance, even if he or she does not exercise complete control over the outcome.

---

[4] The source for this illustration is a Harvard Business School management case entitled "Corning Glass Works: Tom MacAvoy," prepared by Thomas N. Clough under the supervision of Richard F. Vancil, copyright 1978 by the President and Fellows of Harvard College.

Direct-Material Price Variance The purchasing manager is generally in the best position to influence material price variances. Through skillful purchasing practices, an expert purchasing manager can get the best prices available for purchased goods and services. To achieve this goal, the purchasing manager uses such practices as buying in quantity, negotiating purchase contracts, comparing prices among vendors, and global sourcing.

Despite these purchasing skills, the purchasing manager is not in complete control of prices. The need to purchase component parts with precise engineering specifications, the all-too-frequent rush requests from the production department, and worldwide shortages of critical materials all contribute to the challenges faced by the purchasing manager.

Direct-Material Quantity Variance The production supervisor is usually in the best position to influence material quantity variances. Skillful supervision and motivation of production employees, coupled with the careful use and handling of materials, contribute to minimal waste. Production engineers are also partially responsible for material quantity variances, since they determine the grade and technical specifications of materials and component parts. In some cases, using a low-grade material may result in greater waste than using a high-grade material.

Direct-Labor Rate Variance Direct-labor rate variances generally result from using a different mix of employees than that anticipated when the standards were set. Wage rates differ among employees due to their skill levels and their seniority with the organization. Using a higher proportion of more senior or more highly skilled employees than a task requires can result in unfavorable direct-labor rate variances. The production supervisor is generally in the best position to influence the work schedules of employees.

Direct-Labor Efficiency Variance Once again, the production supervisor is usually most responsible for the efficient use of employee time. Through motivation toward production goals and effective work schedules, the efficiency of employees can be maximized.

Interaction among Variances

Interactions among variances often occur, making it even more difficult to determine the responsibility for a particular variance. To illustrate, consider the following incident, which occurred in the Sousa Division of American Brass Instrument Company during May of 19x8. The division's purchasing manager obtained a special price on brass alloy from a new supplier. When the material was placed into production, it turned out to be a lower grade of material than the production employees were used to. The alloy was of a slightly different composition, which made the material bend less easily during the formation of brass instruments. Sousa Division could have returned the material to the supplier, but that would have interrupted production and kept the division from filling its orders on time. Since using the off-standard material would not affect the quality of the company's finished products, the division manager decided to keep the material and make the best of the situation.

The ultimate result was that Sousa Division incurred four interrelated variances during May. The material was less expensive than normal, so the direct-material price variance was favorable. However, the employees had difficulty using the material, which resulted in more waste than expected. Hence, the division incurred an unfavorable direct-material quantity variance.

What were the labor implications of the off-standard material? Due to the difficulty in working with the metal alloy, the employees required more than the standard amount of time to form the instruments. This resulted in an unfavorable direct-labor efficiency variance. Finally, the production supervisor had to use his most senior employees to work with the off-standard material. Since these people earned relatively high wages, the direct-labor rate variance was also unfavorable.

To summarize, the purchase of off-standard material resulted in the following interrelated variances.

$$
\begin{array}{l}
\text{Purchase of} \\
\text{off-standard} \implies \\
\text{material}
\end{array}
\left\{
\begin{array}{l}
\textbf{Favorable direct-material price variance} \\
\textbf{Unfavorable direct-material quantity variance} \\
\textbf{Unfavorable direct-labor rate variance} \\
\textbf{Unfavorable direct-labor efficiency variance}
\end{array}
\right.
$$

Such interactions of variances make it more difficult to assign responsibility for any particular variance.

Trade-Offs among Variances Does the incident described above mean that the decision to buy and use the off-standard material was a poor one? Not necessarily. Perhaps these variances were anticipated, and a conscious decision was made to buy the material anyway. How could this be a wise decision? Suppose the amounts of the variances were as follows:

$(8,500)	Favorable direct-material price variance
1,000	Unfavorable direct-material quantity variance
2,000	Unfavorable direct-labor rate variance
1,500	Unfavorable direct-labor efficiency variance
$(4,000)	Favorable net overall variance

The division saved money overall on the decision to use a different grade of brass alloy. Given that the quality of the final product was not affected, the division's management acted wisely.

STANDARD COSTS AND PRODUCT COSTING

Our discussion of standard costing has focused on its use in controlling costs. But firms that use standard costs for control also use them for product costing. Recall from Chapter 3 that *product costing* is the process of accumulating the costs of a production process and assigning them to the completed products. Product costs are used for various purposes in both financial and managerial accounting.

As production takes place, product costs are added to the Work-in-Process Inventory account. The flow of product costs through a firm's manufacturing accounts is depicted in Exhibit 9-6.

Different types of product-costing systems are distinguished by the type of costs that are entered into Work-in-Process Inventory. In Chapter 3, we studied *actual-* and *normal*-costing systems. In these product-costing systems, the *actual* costs of direct material and direct labor are charged to Work-in-Process Inventory. In a **standard-costing system** the *standard* costs of direct material and direct labor are entered into Work-in-Process Inventory.

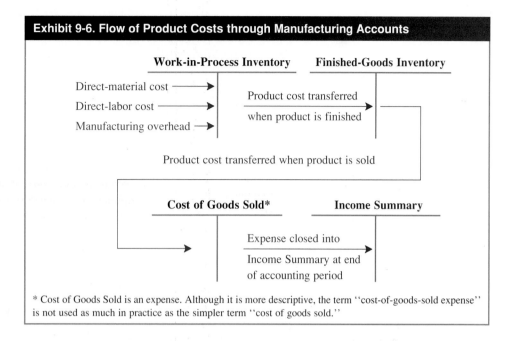

Exhibit 9-6. Flow of Product Costs through Manufacturing Accounts

* Cost of Goods Sold is an expense. Although it is more descriptive, the term ''cost-of-goods-sold expense'' is not used as much in practice as the simpler term ''cost of goods sold.''

Journal Entries under Standard Costing   To illustrate the use of standard costs in product costing, we will continue our illustration of the Sousa Division. During September the division purchased 25,000 pounds of direct material for $177,500. The actual quantity of material used in production was 20,500 pounds. However, the standard cost of direct material, given September's actual output of 2,000 trumpets, was only $140,000. The following journal entries record these facts and isolate the direct-material price and quantity variances.

Raw-Material Inventory	175,000	
Direct-Material Price Variance	2,500	
Accounts Payable		177,500

To record the purchase of raw material and the incurrence of an
unfavorable price variance.

Work-in Process Inventory	140,000	
Direct-Material Quantity Variance	3,500	
Raw-Material Inventory		143,500

To record the use of direct material in production and the
incurrence of an unfavorable quantity variance.

Notice that the material purchase is recorded in the Raw-Material Inventory account at its standard price ($175,000 = 25,000 pounds purchased × $7.00 per pound). The $140,000 debit entry to Work-in-Process Inventory adds only the standard cost of the material to Work-in-Process Inventory as a product cost ($140,000 = 20,000 pounds allowed × $7.00 per pound). The two variances are isolated in their own variance accounts. Since they are both unfavorable, they are represented by debit entries.

The following journal entry records the actual September cost of direct labor, as an addition to Wages Payable. The entry also adds the standard cost of direct labor to Work-in-Process Inventory and isolates the direct-labor variances.

```
Work-in-Process Inventory ................................. 200,000
Direct-Labor Rate Variance ...............................    9,800
    Direct-Labor Efficiency Variance ........................              4,000
    Wages Payable ........................................            205,800
```
To record the usage of direct labor and the direct-labor variances for
September.

Since the direct-labor efficiency variance is favorable, it is recorded as a credit
entry.

Disposition of Variances Variances are temporary accounts, like revenue and
expense accounts, and they are closed out at the end of each accounting period. Most
companies close their variance accounts directly into Cost of Goods Sold. The journal entry required to close out Sousa Division's September variance accounts is
shown below.

```
Cost of Goods Sold ....................................... 11,800
Direct-Labor Efficiency Variance ............................  4,000
    Direct-Labor Rate Variance................................            9,800
    Direct-Material Price Variance ...........................            2,500
    Direct-Material Quantity Variance ........................            3,500
```

The increase of $11,800 in Cost of Goods Sold is explained as follows:

Unfavorable Variances Increase Cost of Goods Sold		Favorable Variance Decreases Cost of Goods Sold	Net Increase in Cost of Goods Sold
Direct-labor efficiency variance		$4,000	
Direct-labor rate variance...................	$ 9,800		
Direct-material price variance	2,500		
Direct-material quantity variance	3,500		
Total................................	$15,800	− $4,000	= $11,800

The unfavorable variances represent costs of operating inefficiently, relative to the
standards, and thus cause Cost of Goods Sold to be higher. The opposite is true for
favorable variances.

An alternative method of variance disposition is to apportion all variances
among Work-in-Process Inventory, Finished-Goods Inventory, and Cost of Goods
Sold. This accounting treatment reflects the effects of unusual inefficiency or efficiency in all of the accounts through which the manufacturing costs flow. This
method, called *variance proration,* is covered more fully in cost-accounting texts.

Cost Flow under Standard Costing In a standard-costing system, since standard
costs are entered into Work-in-Process Inventory, standard costs flow through all of
the manufacturing accounts. Thus, in Exhibit 9-6, all of the product costs flowing
through the accounts are standard costs. To illustrate, suppose the Sousa Division

finished 2,000 trumpets in September and sold 1,500 of them. The journal entries to record the flow of standard direct-material and direct-labor costs are shown below.

Finished-Goods Inventory 340,000*
      Work-in-Process Inventory   340,000

* Total standard cost of direct material and direct labor: $340,000 = $140,000 + $200,000.

Cost of Goods Sold 255,000*
      Finished-Goods Inventory   255,000

* 1,500 out of 2,000 trumpets sold; three-quarters of $340,000 is $255,000.

Our Sousa Division illustration is not really complete yet, because we have not discussed manufacturing-overhead costs. This topic is covered in the next chapter. The important point at this juncture is that in a standard-costing system, *standard costs flow through the manufacturing accounts rather than actual costs.*

ADVANTAGES OF STANDARD COSTING

A standard-costing system offers six clear advantages if it is used properly:

1. Standard costs provide a basis for *sensible cost comparisons.* As we discussed earlier, it would make no sense to compare budgeted costs at one (planned) activity level with actual costs incurred at a different (actual) activity level. Standard costs enable the managerial accountant to compute the standard allowed cost, given actual output, which then serves as a sensible benchmark to compare with the actual cost.
2. Computation of standard costs and cost variances enables managers to employ *management by exception.* This approach conserves valuable management time.
3. Variances provide a means of *performance evaluation* and rewards for employees.
4. Since the variances are used in performance evaluation, they provide *motivation* for employees to adhere to standards.
5. Use of standard costs in product costing results in *more stable product costs* than if actual production costs were used. Actual costs often fluctuate erratically, whereas standard costs are changed only periodically.
6. A standard-costing system is usually *less expensive* than an actual- or normal-costing system.

Like any tool, a standard-costing system can be misused. When employees are criticized for every cost variance, the positive motivational effects will quickly vanish. Moreover, if standards are not revised often enough, they will become outdated. Then the benefits of cost benchmarks and product costing will disappear.

ADAPTING STANDARD-COSTING SYSTEMS IN THE NEW MANUFACTURING ENVIRONMENT

As we discussed in Chapter 5, fundamental changes are occurring in the manufacturing industry. The use of just-in-time (JIT) production management and computer-integrated manufacturing (CIM) systems is changing many aspects of manufacturing management in significant ways. These innovations also are causing important changes in the design and role of standard-costing systems.

Continued Role of Standards in Product Costing The emergence of the JIT philosophy and the implementation of CIM systems have *not* diminished the role of standard costs in product costing. Most companies retain their standard-costing systems as they automate their production process.[5] The standards usually change to reflect automated manufacturing methods, but the role of standard product costs in decision making continues.

Reduced Importance of Labor Standards and Variances As direct labor occupies a diminished role in the new manufacturing environment, the standards and variances used to control labor costs also decline in importance. The heavy emphasis of traditional standard-costing systems on labor efficiency variances must give way to variances that focus on the more critical inputs to the production process. Machine hours, material and overhead costs, product quality, and manufacturing cycle times take on greater importance as the objects of managerial control.

Emphasis on Material and Overhead Costs As labor diminishes in its importance, material and overhead costs take on greater significance. Controlling material costs and quality, and controlling overhead costs through cost-driver analysis, become key aspects of the cost management system (CMS).

Cost Drivers Identification of the factors that drive production costs takes on greater importance in the CMS. Such cost drivers as machine hours, number of parts, engineering change orders, and production runs become the focus of the CMS and transaction-based product-costing system.

Shifting Cost Structures Advanced manufacturing systems require large outlays for production equipment, which entail a shift in the cost structure from variable costs toward fixed costs. Overhead cost control becomes especially critical. Chapter 10 explores the role of standard-costing systems in controlling overhead costs.

High Quality and Zero Defects Total quality control (TQC) programs that typically accompany a JIT approach strive for very high quality levels for both raw materials and finished products. One result should be very low material price and quantity variances and low costs of rework.

Non-Value-Added Costs As Chapter 5 emphasized, a key objective of a CMS is the elimination of non-value-added costs. As these costs are reduced or eliminated, standards must be revised frequently to provide accurate benchmarks for cost control.

New Measures and Standards In the new manufacturing environment, new measures must be developed to control key aspects of the production process. As new

[5] For example, see James M. Patell, "Cost Accounting, Process Control, and Product Design: A Case Study of the Hewlett-Packard Personal Office Computer Division," *The Accounting Review, 62,* no. 4 (October 1987), pp. 808–839.

measures are developed, standards should be established as benchmarks for performance. An example is the manufacturing cycle efficiency (MCE) measure discussed in Chapter 5.

$$\text{MCE} = \frac{\text{processing time}}{\text{processing time} + \text{inspection time} + \text{waiting time} + \text{move time}}$$

Firms with advanced manufacturing systems often strive for an MCE measure in excess of 95 percent.[6]

Real-Time Information Systems A CIM system enables the managerial accountant to collect operating data as production takes place and to report relevant performance measures to management on a real-time basis. This enables managers to eliminate the causes of unfavorable variances more quickly.

CHAPTER SUMMARY

A standard-costing system serves two purposes: cost control and product costing. The managerial accountant works with others in the organization to set standard costs for direct material, direct labor, and manufacturing overhead through either historical cost analysis or task analysis. The accountant then uses the standard cost as a benchmark against which to compare actual costs incurred. Managers then use management by exception to determine the causes of significant cost variances. This control purpose of the standard-costing system is accomplished by computing a direct-material price variance, a direct-material quantity variance, a direct-labor rate variance, and a direct-labor efficiency variance.

Managers determine the significance of cost variances through judgment and rules of thumb. The absolute and relative size of variances, recurrence of variances, variance trends, and controllability of variances are all considered in deciding whether variances warrant investigation. The managerial accountant achieves the product-costing purpose of the standard-costing system by entering the standard cost of production into Work-in-Process Inventory as a product cost. Standard-costing systems offer an organization many benefits. However, these benefits will be obtained only if the standard-costing system is used properly.

REVIEW PROBLEM ON STANDARD-COSTING SYSTEMS

In November of 19x8 the Sousa Division produced 3,000 trumpets and incurred the following actual costs for direct material and direct labor.

Purchased 33,000 pounds of brass at $7.20 per pound.
Used 31,000 pounds of brass at $7.20 per pound.
Used 15,200 hours of direct labor at $22 per hour.

The standard costs for trumpet production were the same in November as those given earlier in the chapter for September.

Compute Sousa Division's direct-material and direct-labor variances for November using the format shown in Exhibits 9-2 and 9-3.

[6] Callie Berliner and James A. Brimson, eds., *Cost Management for Today's Advanced Manufacturing* (Boston: Harvard Business School Press, 1988), p. 4.

Solution to Review Problem

Direct-Material Price and Quantity Variances

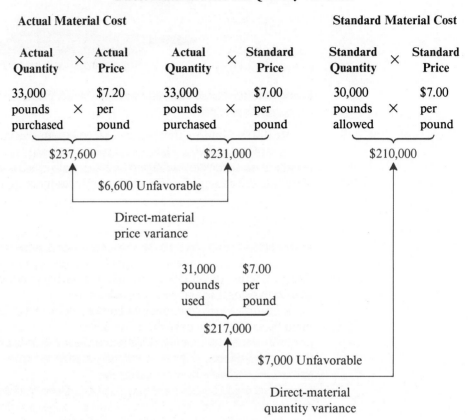

Using Formulas:

Direct-material price variance $= PQ(AP - SP)$
$= 33,000(\$7.20 - \$7.00) = \$6,600$ unfavorable
Direct-material quantity variance $= SP(AQ - SQ)$
$= \$7.00(31,000 - 30,000) = \$7,000$ unfavorable

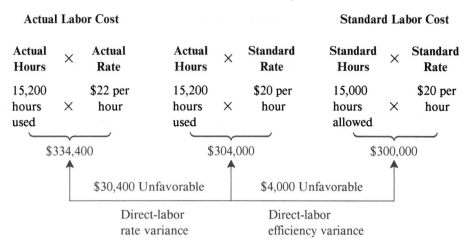

Direct-Labor Rate and Efficiency Variances

Using Formulas:

$$\text{Direct-labor rate variance} = AH(AR - SR)$$
$$= 15{,}200(\$22 - \$20) = \$30{,}400 \text{ unfavorable}$$
$$\text{Direct-labor efficiency variance} = SR(AH - SH)$$
$$= \$20(15{,}200 - 15{,}000) = \$4{,}000 \text{ unfavorable}$$

KEY TERMS   Controllability, p. 380; Cost variance, p. 368; Critical value, p. 379; Direct-labor efficiency variance, p. 381; Direct-labor rate variance, p. 381; Direct-material price variance (or purchase price variance), p. 373; Direct-material quantity variance, p. 373; Management by exception, p. 368; Perfection (or ideal) standard, p. 370; Practical (or attainable) standard, p. 370; Standard cost, p. 368; Standard-costing system, p. 382; Statistical control chart, p. 379; Standard labor rate, p. 372; Standard direct-labor quantity, p. 372; Standard material price, p. 372; Standard material quantity, p. 372; Task analysis, p. 369.

APPENDIX TO CHAPTER 9

Graphical Analysis of Variances

A graphical analysis provides additional insight into the computation and interpretation of variances. During December of 19x8, Sousa Division's controller recorded the following direct-labor data.

Actual direct-labor cost: 10,100 hours at $22 per hour

Standard direct-labor cost: 10,000 hours at $20 per hour

$$\text{Direct-labor rate variance} = AH(AR - SR)$$
$$= 10,100(\$22 - \$20) = \$20,200 \text{ unfavorable}$$
$$\text{Direct-labor efficiency variance} = SR(AH - SH)$$
$$= \$20(10,100 - 10,000) = \$2,000 \text{ unfavorable}$$

Exhibit 9-7 provides a graphical analysis of the December direct-labor variances. The graph shows the direct-labor rate per hour on the vertical axis, and the direct-labor hours on the horizontal axis. Since a labor cost is found by multiplying the rate by the hours, the labor cost is depicted on the graph as an area. The white area of the graph represents the standard cost of direct labor, given actual output ($200,000 = 10,000 hours × $20 per hour). The larger area on the graph, which is enclosed by the colored lines on the top and right sides, represents the actual cost of direct labor used in December ($222,200 = 10,100 pounds × $22 per hour). The difference between the large area and the smaller, white area represents the total direct-labor variance ($22,200 = $222,200 − $200,000). This area is colored on the graph to highlight the variance.

The total direct-labor variance is divided into the rate variance and the efficiency variance. The rate variance, computed as $AH(AR - SR)$, is represented on the graph by the medium and dark green areas. The efficiency variance, computed as $SR(AH - SH)$, is depicted on the graph as the light green area. The areas representing the rate and efficiency variances add up to equal the total direct-labor variance.

Joint Rate-Efficiency Variance Notice that the dark green area in the upper right corner of the graph represents the product of the *rate* difference ($22 − $20) and the difference in hours (10,100 − 10,000). This area represents the portion of the rate variance that is really the *joint result* of (1) paying more than the standard rate and (2) using more labor hours than the standard allowance. Thus, the rate variance, $AH(AR - SR)$, does not result only from deviations from the standard rate. This

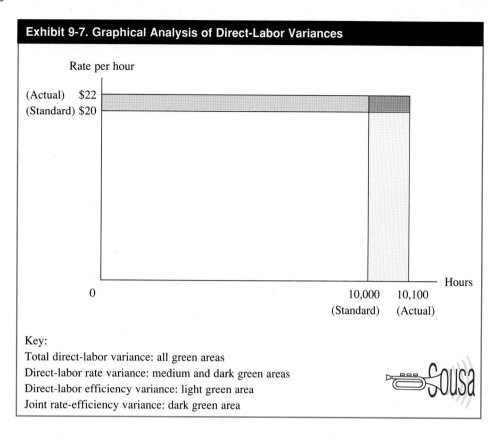

Exhibit 9-7. Graphical Analysis of Direct-Labor Variances

Key:
Total direct-labor variance: all green areas
Direct-labor rate variance: medium and dark green areas
Direct-labor efficiency variance: light green area
Joint rate-efficiency variance: dark green area

problem in interpreting the rate variance could be avoided by computing a **pure rate variance** and a **joint rate-efficiency variance** as follows:

$$\text{Pure rate variance} = SH(AR - SR)$$
$$\text{Joint rate-efficiency variance} = (AH - SH)(AR - SR)$$

Computing these variances for Sousa Division for December yields the following results:

$$\text{Pure rate variance} = 10,000(\$22 - \$20) = \$20,000$$
$$\text{Joint rate-efficiency variance} = (10,100 - 10,000) \times (\$22 - \$20) = \$200$$

Together these variances add up to the direct-labor rate variance, as it is typically computed. While this breakdown of the rate variance makes sense conceptually, it is used only rarely in practice.

KEY TERMS (Appendix)   Joint rate-efficiency variance, p. 391; Pure rate variance, p. 391.

REVIEW QUESTIONS   **9-1.** List the three parts of a control system, and explain how such a system works.

9-2. What is meant by the phrase *management by exception?*

9-3. Describe two methods of setting standards.

9-4. Distinguish between perfection and practical standards. Which type of standard is likely to produce the best motivational effects?

9-5. Describe how a bank might use standards.

9-6. Explain how standard material prices and quantities are set.

9-7. What is the interpretation of the direct-material price variance?

9-8. What manager is usually in the best position to influence the direct-material price variance?

9-9. What is the interpretation of the direct-material quantity variance?

9-10. What manager is usually in the best position to influence the direct-material quantity variance?

9-11. What is the interpretation of the direct-labor rate variance? What are some possible causes?

9-12. What manager is generally in the best position to influence the direct-labor rate variance?

9-13. What is the interpretation of the direct-labor efficiency variance?

9-14. What manager is generally in the best position to influence the direct-labor efficiency variance?

9-15. Describe five factors that managers often consider when determining the significance of a variance.

9-16. Discuss several ways in which standard-costing systems should be adapted in the new manufacturing environment.

9-17. Describe how standard costs are used for product costing.

9-18. List six advantages of a standard-costing system.

9-19. (Appendix) Explain the difference between the traditional direct-labor rate variance and a *pure* rate variance.

9-20. (Appendix) Explain the interpretation of a joint rate-efficiency variance for direct labor.

EXERCISES *Exercise 9-21   Computing Standard Direct-Material Cost.* Cayuga Hardwoods produces handcrafted jewelry boxes. A standard-size box requires 8 board feet of hardwood in the finished product. In addition, 2 board feet of scrap lumber is normally left from the production of one box. Hardwood costs $3.00 per board foot, plus $1.00 in transportation charges per board foot.

REQUIRED: Compute the standard direct-material cost of a jewelry box.

Exercise 9-22   Straightforward Calculation of Variances. Grady Company has set the following standards for one unit of its product.

Direct material: Direct labor:
   Quantity, 2 pounds per unit   Quantity, 3 hours per unit
   Price, $7 per pound   Rate, $18 per hour

Material purchases amounted to 5,000 pounds at a price of $7.30 per pound. Actual costs incurred in the production of 2,000 units were as follows:

Direct material: $ 30,660 ($ 7.30 per pound)
Direct labor: $116,745 ($18.10 per hour)

REQUIRED: Compute the direct-material price and quantity variances and the direct-labor rate and efficiency variances. Indicate whether each variance is favorable or unfavorable.

Exercise 9-23 Diagramming Direct-Material and Direct-Labor Variances. Refer to the data in the preceding exercise. Draw diagrams depicting the direct-material and direct-labor variances similar to the diagrams in Exhibits 9-2 and 9-3.

Exercise 9-24 Cost Variance Investigation. The controller for Roe and Company uses a statistical control chart to help management determine when to investigate variances. The critical value is 1 standard deviation. The company incurred the following direct-labor efficiency variances during the first six months of 19x0.

January....................	$250 F	April.....................	$ 900 U
February..................	800 U	May.....................	1,050 U
March....................	700 U	June....................	1,200 U

The standard direct-labor cost during each of these months was $20,000. The controller has estimated that the firm's monthly direct-labor efficiency variances have a standard deviation of $950.

REQUIRED:

1. Draw a statistical control chart and plot the variance data given above. Which variances will be investigated?
2. Suppose the controller's rule of thumb is to investigate all variances equal to or greater than 6 percent of standard cost. Then which variances will be investigated?
3. Would you investigate any of the variances listed above other than those indicated by the rules discussed in requirements (2) and (3)? Why?

Exercise 9-25 Straightforward Computation of Variances. Columbus Can Company manufactures recyclable soft-drink cans. A unit of production is a case of 12 dozen cans. The following standards have been set by the production-engineering staff and the controller.

Direct material:	Direct labor:
Quantity, 4 kilograms	Quantity, .25 hour
Price, $.80 per kilogram	Rate, $16 per hour

Actual material purchases amounted to 240,000 kilograms at $.81 per kilogram. Actual costs incurred in the production of 50,000 units were as follows:

Direct material: $170,100 for 210,000 kilograms
Direct labor: $210,600 for 13,000 hours

REQUIRED: Use the variance formulas to compute the direct-material price and quantity variances and the direct-labor rate and efficiency variances. Indicate whether each variance is favorable or unfavorable.

Exercise 9-26 Determination of Variances Using Diagrams. Refer to the data in the preceding exercise. Use diagrams similar to those in Exhibits 9-2 and 9-3 to determine the direct-material and direct-labor variances. Indicate whether each variance is favorable or unfavorable.

Exercise 9-27 Journal entries under Standard Costing. Refer to the data in Exercise 9-25. Prepare journal entries to:

1. Record the purchase of direct material on account.
2. Add direct-material and direct-labor cost to Work-in-Process Inventory.
3. Record the direct-material and direct-labor variances.
4. Close these variances into Cost of Goods Sold.

Exercise 9-28 **Posting Journal Entries for Variances.** Refer to your answer for Exercise 9-27. Set up T-accounts, and post the journal entries to the general ledger.

Exercise 9-29 **Reconstructing Standard-Cost Information from Partial Data.** Part of your company's accounting data base was destroyed when Godzilla attacked the city. You have been able to gather the following data from your files. Reconstruct the remaining information using the available data. All of the raw material purchased during the period was used in production.

	Direct Material	Direct Labor
Standard quantity per unit of output	?	?
Standard price or rate per unit of input	$8 per pound	?
Actual quantity used per unit of output	?	3.5 hours
Actual price or rate per unit of input	$7 per pound	$21 per hour
Actual output	10,000 units	10,000 units
Direct-material price variance	$30,000 F	—
Direct-material quantity variance	?	—
Total of direct-material variances	$10,000 F	—
Direct-labor rate variance	—	?
Direct-labor efficiency variance	—	$100,000 F
Total of direct-labor variances	—	$ 65,000 F

Exercise 9-30 **Joint Rate-Efficiency Variance; Graphing Variances; Appendix.** Refer to the data in Exercise 9-22. Compute the pure rate variance and joint rate-efficiency variance for direct labor. Draw a graph of the direct-labor variances similar to Exhibit 9-7.

PROBLEMS *Problem 9-31* **Determining Standard Material Cost.** Tennessee Valley Chemical Company manufactures industrial chemicals. The company plans to introduce a new chemical solution and needs to develop a standard product cost. The new chemical solution is made by combining a chemical compound (nyclyn) and a solution (salex), heating the mixture, adding a second compound (protet), and bottling the resulting solution in 10-liter containers. The initial mix, which is 11 liters in volume, consists of 12 kilograms of nyclyn and 9.6 liters of salex. A 1-liter reduction in volume occurs during the boiling process. The solution is cooled slightly before 5 kilograms of protet are added. The addition of protet does not affect the total liquid volume.

The purchase prices of the raw materials used in the manufacture of this new chemical solution are as follows:

Nyclyn	$1.30 per kilogram
Salex	1.80 per liter
Protet	2.40 per kilogram

REQUIRED: Determine the standard material cost of a 10-liter container of the new product. (CMA, adapted)

Problem 9-32   Direct-Material and Direct-Labor Variances. Arrow Industries has established the following standards for the prime costs of one unit of product.

	Standard Quantity	Standard Price or Rate	Standard Cost
Direct material	8 pounds	$1.80 per pound	$14.40
Direct labor	.25 hour	$8.00 per hour	2.00
Total			$16.40

During May, Arrow purchased 160,000 pounds of direct material at a total cost of $304,000. The total wages for May were $42,000, 90 percent of which were for direct labor. Arrow manufactured 19,000 units of product during May, using 142,500 pounds of direct material and 5,000 direct-labor hours.

REQUIRED: Compute the following variances for May, and indicate whether each is favorable or unfavorable.

1. The direct-material price variance.
2. The direct-material quantity variance.
3. The direct-labor rate variance.
4. The direct-labor efficiency variance.
(CMA, adapted)

Problem 9-33   Setting Standards; Responsibility for Variances. Associated Media Graphics (AMG) is a rapidly expanding company involved in the mass reproduction of instructional materials. Ralph Boston, owner and manager of AMG, has made a concentrated effort to provide a quality product at a fair price, with delivery on the promised date. Boston is finding it increasingly difficult to personally supervise the operations of AMG, and he is beginning to institute an organizational structure that would facilitate management control.

One change recently made was the transfer of control over departmental operations from Boston to each departmental manager. However, the Quality Control Department still reports directly to Boston, as do the Finance and Accounting Departments. A materials manager was hired to purchase all raw materials and to oversee the material-handling (receiving, storage, etc.) and recordkeeping functions. The materials manager also is responsible for maintaining an adequate inventory based on planned production levels.

The loss of personal control over the operations of AMG caused Boston to look for a method of efficiently evaluating performance. Dave Cress, a new managerial accountant, proposed the use of a standard-costing system. Variances for material and labor could then be calculated and reported directly to Boston.

REQUIRED:

1. Assume that Associated Media Graphics is going to implement a standard-costing system and establish standards for materials and labor. Identify and discuss for each of these cost components:
   a.   Who should be involved in setting the standards?
   b.   What factors should be considered in establishing the standards?
2. Describe the basis for assignment of responsibility for variances under a standard-costing system.
(CMA, adapted)

Problem 9-34   Direct-Material and Direct-Labor Variances. Riviera Corporation manufactures a product with the following standard costs:

Direct materials: 20 yards at $1.35 per yard............................... $27
Direct labor: 4 hours at $9.00 per hour 36
Total standard prime cost per unit of output.............................. $63

The following information pertains to the month of July 19x1:

Direct material purchased: 18,000 yards at $1.38 per yard $24,840
Direct material used: 9,500 yards at $1.38 per yard 13,110
Direct labor: 2,100 hours at $9.15 per hour 19,215

Actual July 19x1 production was 500 units.

REQUIRED: Compute the following variances for the month of July, indicating whether each variance is favorable or unfavorable:

1. Direct-material price variance.
2. Direct-material quantity variance.
3. Direct-labor rate variance.
4. Direct-labor efficiency variance.

(CMA, adapted)

Problem 9-35   Direct-Material and Direct-Labor Variances. At the beginning of 19x4, Teale Company adopted the following standards for its sole product.

Direct material: 3 lb. at $2.50 per lb..................................... $ 7.50
Direct labor: 5 hr. at $15.00 per hr. 75.00
Standard prime cost per unit $82.50

During January, the company produced 7,800 units, with records indicating the following:

Direct material purchased................................. 25,000 lb. at $2.60
Direct material used .... 23,100 lb.
Direct labor .... 40,100 hr. at $14.60

REQUIRED:

1. Prepare a schedule of standard production costs for January 19x4, based on actual production of 7,800 units.
2. For the month of January 19x4, compute the following variances, indicating whether each is favorable or unfavorable:
    a. Direct-material price variance.
    b. Direct-material quantity variance.
    c. Direct-labor rate variance.— act hrs
    d. Direct-labor efficiency variance.

(CPA, adapted)

Problem 9-36   Direct-Material and Direct-Labor Variances; Job-Order Costing. Vogue Fashions, Inc., manufactures women's blouses of one quality, which are produced in lots to fill each special order. Its customers are department stores in various cities. Vogue sews the particular stores' labels on the blouses. The standard costs for a box of six blouses are as follows:

Direct material	24 yards at $1.10	$ 26.40
Direct labor	3 hours at $14.70	44.10
Manufacturing overhead	3 hours at $12.00	36.00
Standard cost per box		$106.50

During June 19x0, Vogue worked on three orders, for which the month's job-cost records disclose the following data.

Lot Number	Boxes in Lot	Material Used (yards)	Hours Worked
22	1,000	24,100	2,980
23	1,700	40,440	5,130
24	1,200	28,825	2,890

The following additional information is available:

(1) Vogue purchased 95,000 yards of material during June at a cost of $106,400.
(2) Direct labor during June amounted to $165,000. According to payroll records, production employees were paid $15.00 per hour.
(3) There was no work in process on June 1. During June, lots 22 and 23 were completed. All material was issued for lot 24, which was 80 percent completed as to direct labor.

REQUIRED:

1. Prepare a schedule computing the standard cost of lots 22, 23, and 24 for June 19x0.
2. Prepare a schedule showing, for each lot produced during June 19x0:
   a. Direct-material price variance.
   b. Direct-material quantity variance.
   c. Direct-labor efficiency variance.
   d. Direct-labor rate variance.
   Indicate whether each variance is favorable or unfavorable.

(CPA, adapted)

Problem 9-37   *Journal Entries; Standard Job-Order Costing; Continuation of Preceding Problem.*

REQUIRED: Prepare journal entries to record each of the following events for Vogue Fashions.

● Purchase of material.
● Incurrence of direct-labor cost.
● Addition of direct-material and direct-labor cost to Work-in-Process Inventory.
● Recording of direct-material and direct-labor variances.

Problem 9-38   *Direct-Labor Variances.* The controller for Landeau Manufacturing Company compares each month's actual results with a monthly plan. The standard direct-labor rates for 19x8 and the standard hours allowed, given the actual output in April, are shown in the following schedule.

	Standard Direct-Labor Rate per Hour		Standard Direct-Labor Hours Allowed, Given April Ouput
Labor class III	$16.00	....	500
Labor class II..........	$14.00	....	500
Labor class I	$10.00	....	500

A new union contract negotiated in March of 19x8 resulted in actual wage rates that differed from the standard rates. The actual direct-labor hours worked and the actual direct-labor rates per hour experienced for the month of April were as follows:

	Actual Direct-Labor Rate per Hour		Actual Direct-Labor Hours
Labor class III	$17.00	....	550
Labor class II............	$15.00	....	650
Labor class I	$10.80	....	375

REQUIRED:

1. Compute the following variances for April. Indicate whether each is favorable or unfavorable.
   a. Direct labor-rate variance for *each* labor class.
   b. Direct labor-efficiency variance for *each* labor class.
2. Discuss the advantages and disadvantages of a standard-costing system in which the standard direct-labor rates per hour are not changed during the year to reflect such events as a new labor contract.

(CMA, adapted)

Problem 9-39 *Variances; Journal Entries; Missing Data.* Dash Company adopted a standard-costing system several years ago. The standard costs of its single product are as follows:

Direct material: 8 kilograms at $5.00 per kilogram $40.00
Direct labor: 6 hours at $8.20 per hour $49.20

The following operating information was taken from the records for November:

- Work-in-process inventory on November 1: none.
- Work-in-process inventory on November 30: 800 units (75 percent complete as to labor; material is issued at the beginning of processing).
- Units completed: 5,600 units.
- Purchases of materials: 50,000 kilograms for $249,250.
- Total actual labor costs: $300,760
- Actual hours of labor: 36,500 hours.
- Direct-material quantity variance: $1,500 unfavorable.

REQUIRED:

1. Compute the following amounts. Indicate whether each variance is favorable or unfavorable.

a. Direct-labor rate variance for November.
b. Direct-labor efficiency variance for November.
c. Actual kilograms of material used in the production process during November.
d. Actual price paid per kilogram of direct material in November.
e. Total amounts of direct-material and direct-labor cost transferred to Finished-Goods Inventory during November.
f. The total amount of direct-material and direct-labor cost in the ending balance of Work-in-Process Inventory at the end of November.

2. Prepare journal entries to record the following:
  - Purchase of raw material.
  - Adding direct material to Work-in-Process Inventory.
  - Adding direct labor to Work-in-Process Inventory.
  - Recording of variances.

(CMA, adapted)

Problem 9-40   Standard Costing; Variances; Process Costing. (This problem should be assigned only if Chapter 4 on process costing has been completed.)

Medley Corporation produces a single product known as "Jupiter." The firm uses the first-in, first-out (FIFO) process-costing method for product costing. The costs entered into Work-in-Process Inventory are standard costs, based on standards set annually. The standards for direct material and direct labor, which are based on equivalent units of production, are as follows:

Direct material per unit . . . . 1 pound at $10 per pound
Direct labor per unit. . . . . 2 hours at $12 per hour

Data for the month of April are presented below.

(1) The beginning inventory consisted of 2,500 units, which were 100 percent complete as to direct material and 40 percent complete as to direct labor.
(2) An additional 10,000 units were started during the month.
(3) The ending inventory consisted of 2,000 units, which were 100 percent complete as to direct material and 40 percent complete as to direct labor.
(4) Costs applicable to April production are as follows:

	Actual Cost	Standard Cost
Direct material purchased and used (11,000 pounds)	$121,000	$100,000
Direct labor (25,000 hours actually worked)	316,725	247,200

REQUIRED:

1. For each element of prime production costs (direct material and direct labor), compute the following for April.
  a. Equivalent units of production.
  b. Cost per equivalent unit of production, at actual cost and at standard cost.
2. Prepare a schedule computing the following April variances. Indicate whether each variance is favorable or unfavorble.
  a. Direct-material price variance.
  b. Direct-material quantity variance.

    c. Direct-labor rate variance.

    d. Direct-labor efficiency variance.

(CPA, adapted)

Problem 9-41   *Investigating Cost Variances.* McKeag and Sons, Inc. manufactures agricultural machinery. At a recent staff meeting, the following direct-labor variance report was presented by the controller.

McKeag and Sons, Inc.
Direct-Labor Variance Report
For the Year 19x4

	Direct-Labor Rate Variance			Direct-Labor Efficiency Variance	
	Amount	**Standard Cost, %**		**Amount**	**Standard Cost, %**
January..........	$ 800 F	.16%	....	$ 5,000 U	1.00%
February..........	4,900 F	.98%	....	7,500 U	1.50%
March............	100 U	.02%	....	9,700 U	1.94%
April.............	2,000 U	.40%	....	12,800 U	2.56%
May	3,800 F	.76%	....	20,100 U	4.02%
June	3,900 F	.78%	....	17,000 U	3.40%
July.............	4,200 F	.84%	....	28,500 U	5.70%
August	5,100 F	1.02%	....	38,000 U	7.60%
September.........	4,800 F	.96%	....	37,000 U	7.40%
October..........	5,700 F	1.14%	....	42,000 U	8.40%
November.........	4,200 F	.84%	....	60,000 U	12.00%
December.........	4,300 F	.86%	....	52,000 U	10.40%

McKeag and Sons' controller uses the following rule of thumb: Investigate all variances equal to or greater than $30,000, which is 6 percent of standard cost.

REQUIRED:

1. Which variances would have been investigated during 19x4? (Indicate month and type of variance.)
2. What characteristics of the variance pattern shown in the report should draw the controller's attention, regardless of the usual investigation rule? Explain. Given these considerations, which variances would you have investigated? Why?
3. Is it important to follow up on favorable variances, such as those shown in the report? Why?
4. The controller believes that the firm's direct-labor rate variance has a normal probability distribution with a mean of zero and a standard deviation of $5,000. Prepare a statistical control chart, and plot the company's direct-labor rate variances for 19x4. The critical value is one standard deviation. Which variances would have been investigated under this approach?

Problem 9-42   *Comprehensive Problem on Variance Analysis.* Springsteen Company manufactures guitars. The company uses a standard, job-order cost-accounting system in its two production departments. In the Construction Department the wooden guitars are built by highly skilled craftsmen and coated with several layers of lacquer. Then the units are transferred to the Finishing Department, where the bridge of the guitar is attached and the strings are installed. The guitars also are tuned and inspected in the Finishing Department. The diagram below depicts the production process.

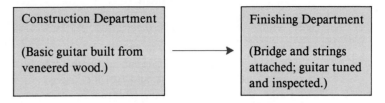

Each finished guitar contains seven pounds of veneered wood. In addition, one pound of wood is typically wasted in the production process. The veneered wood used in the guitars has a standard price of $12 per pound. The other parts needed to complete each guitar, such as the bridge and strings, cost $15 per guitar. The labor standards for Springsteen's two production departments are as follows:

Construction Department: 6 hours of direct labor at $20 per hour
Finishing Department: 3 hours of direct labor at $15 per hour

The following pertains to the month of July, 19x3.

(1) There were no beginning or ending work-in-process inventories in either production department.
(2) There was no beginning or ending finished-goods inventory.
(3) Actual production was 500 guitars, and 300 guitars were sold for $400 each.
(4) The company purchased 6,000 pounds of veneered wood at a price of $12.50 per pound.
(5) Actual usage of veneered wood was 4,500 pounds.
(6) Enough parts (bridges and strings) to finish 600 guitars were purchased at a cost of $9,000.
(7) The Construction Department used 2,850 direct-labor hours. The total direct-labor cost in the Construction Department was $54,150.
(8) The Finishing Department used 1,570 direct-labor hours. The total direct-labor cost in that department was $25,120.
(9) There were no direct-material variances in the Finishing Department.

REQUIRED:

1. Prepare a schedule that computes the standard costs of direct material and direct labor in each production department.
2. Prepare three exhibits which compute the July direct-material and direct-labor variances in the Construction Department and the July direct-labor variances in the Finishing Department. (Refer to Exhibits 9-2 and 9-3 for guidance.)
3. Prepare a cost variance report for July similar to that shown in Exhibit 9-4.

Problem 9-43 *Journal Entries under Standard Costing; Continuation of Preceding Problem.*
Refer to the preceding problem.

REQUIRED:

1. Prepare journal entries to record all of the events listed for Springsteen Company during July of 19x3. Specifically, these journal entries should reflect the following events.

    a. Purchase of direct material
    b. Use of direct material
    c. Incurrence of direct-labor costs
    d. Addition of production costs to the Work-in-Process Inventory account for each department
    e. Incurrence of all variances
    f. Completion of 500 guitars
    g. Sale of 300 guitars
    h. Closing of all variance accounts into Cost of Goods Sold
2. Draw T-accounts, and post the journal entries prepared in requirement (1). Assume the beginning balance in all accounts is zero.

Problem 9-44 **Direct-Material Variances.** Trivera Industries has established the following direct-material standards for its two products.

	Standard Quantity	Standard Price
Standard camping tent	12 pounds	$6 per pound
Deluxe backpacking tent	6 pounds	$8 per pound

During March, the company purchased 2,000 pounds of tent fabric for its standard model at a cost of $12,800. The actual March production of the standard tent was 100 tents, and 1,250 pounds of fabric were used. Also during March, the company purchased 800 pounds of tent fabric for its deluxe backpacking tent at a cost of $6,320. The firm used 720 pounds of the fabric during March in the production of 120 deluxe tents.

REQUIRED:

1. Compute the direct-material quantity variance and price variance for March.
2. Prepare journal entries to record the purchase of material, use of material, and incurrence of variances in March.

Problem 9-45 **Graphical Analysis of Direct-Labor Variances; Appendix.** Refer to the data given in problem 9-36.

REQUIRED: Draw a graph depicting Vogue Fashions' direct-labor variances for lot 23. (Refer to Exhibit 9-7 for guidance.)

CASE   *Case 9-46* **Responsibility for Variances; Behavioral Effects.** Oscar Appliance Corporation manufactures washers and dryers on a single assembly line in its main factory. The market has deteriorated over the last five years and competition has made cost control very important. Management has been concerned about the material cost of both washers and dryers. There have been no model changes in the past two years, and economic conditions have allowed the company to negotiate price reductions in many key parts.

    Oscar uses a standard-costing system. The price variance is the difference between the contract price and the standard price, multiplied by the actual quantity used. When a substitute part is used in production, rather than the regular part, a price variance is computed, which is equal to the difference between the actual cost of the part actually used and the standard cost of the *regular* part. This variance is computed at the time of substitution in the production process. The direct-material quantity variance is the actual quantity used compared to the standard quantity allowed, with the difference multiplied by the standard price.

Roberta Speck, the purchasing director, claims that unfavorable price variances are misleading. Speck says that her department has worked hard to obtain price concessions and purchase discounts from suppliers. In addition, Speck has indicated that engineering changes have been made in several parts, increasing their price. These price increases are not her department's responsibility. Speck declares that price variances simply no longer measure the Purchasing Department's performance.

Jim Buddle, the manufacturing manager, thinks that responsibility for the quantity variance should be shared. Buddle states that the manufacturing employees cannot control quality arising from less expensive parts, substitutions of material to use up otherwise obsolete stock, or engineering changes that increase the quantity of materials used.

REQUIRED: Discuss the appropriateness of Oscar Company's current method of variance analysis for materials, and indicate whether the claims of Roberta Speck and Jim Buddle are valid.

(CMA, adapted)

Chapter 10 Flexible Budgets and Control of Overhead Costs

After completing this chapter you should be able to:

- Distinguish between static and flexible budgets, and explain the advantages of a flexible overhead budget.

- Prepare a flexible overhead budget, using both a formula and a columnar format.

- Explain how overhead is applied to Work-in-Process Inventory under standard costing.

- Explain some important issues in choosing an activity measure for overhead budgeting and application.

- Compute and interpret the variable-overhead spending and efficiency variances and the fixed-overhead budget and volume variances.

- Prepare an overhead cost performance report.

- Prepare journal entries to record manufacturing overhead under standard costing.

- After studying the appendix, compute and interpret the sales-price and sales-volume variances.

How do manufacturing firms, such as Hewlett-Packard Company and Chrysler Corporation, control the many overhead costs incurred in their production processes? Unlike direct material and direct labor, manufacturing-overhead costs are not traceable to individual products. Moreover, manufacturing overhead is a pool of many different kinds of costs. Indirect material, indirect labor, and other indirect production costs often exhibit different relationships to productive activity. Some overhead costs are variable and some are fixed. Moreover, different individuals in an organization are responsible for different types of overhead costs. Considering all of these issues together, controlling manufacturing overhead presents a challenge for managerial accountants. In this chapter, we will study an accounting system that is widely used to control overhead costs.

OVERHEAD BUDGETS

Since direct material and direct labor are traceable to products, it is straightforward to determine standard costs for these inputs. If a table requires 20 board feet of oak lumber at $4 per board foot, the standard direct-material cost for the table is $80. But how much electricity does it take to produce a table? How much supervisory time, equipment depreciation, or machinery repair services does the table require? Since all of these overhead costs are indirect costs of production, we cannot set overhead cost standards for the oak table. If standard costs do not provide the answer to controlling overhead, what does?

Flexible Budgets

The tool used by most companies to control overhead costs is called a **flexible budget.** A flexible budget resembles the budgets we studied in Chapter 8, with one important difference: *A flexible budget is not based on only one level of activity.* Instead, a flexible budget covers a range of activity within which the firm may operate. A *flexible overhead budget* is defined as a detailed plan for controlling overhead costs that is valid in the firm's *relevant range* of activity. In contrast, a **static budget** is based on a particular planned level of activity.

To illustrate, suppose the controller for American Brass Instrument Company's Sousa Division determines that electricity is a variable cost, incurred at the rate of $.50 per machine hour. Two different budgets for electricity costs are shown in Exhibit 10-1. The static budget is based on management's predicted level of activity in the division for September, 7,500 machine hours. This estimate is based on planned production of 2,500 trumpets; each trumpet requires 3 machine hours. The flexible budget includes three different production activity levels within the relevant range: 6,000, 7,500, and 9,000 machine hours.

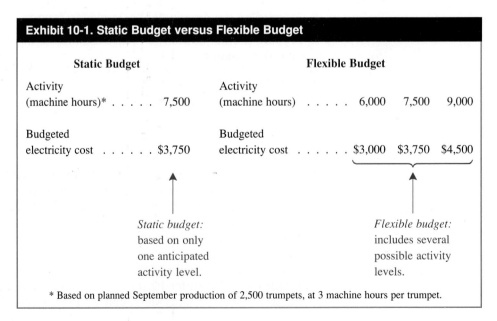

Exhibit 10-1. Static Budget versus Flexible Budget

Static Budget		Flexible Budget			
Activity (machine hours)* 7,500		Activity (machine hours)	6,000	7,500	9,000
Budgeted electricity cost $3,750		Budgeted electricity cost	$3,000	$3,750	$4,500

Static budget: based on only one anticipated activity level.

Flexible budget: includes several possible activity levels.

* Based on planned September production of 2,500 trumpets, at 3 machine hours per trumpet.

Advantages of Flexible Budgets

Why is the distinction between static and flexible budgets so important? Suppose Sousa Division produced 2,000 trumpets during September, used 6,000 machine hours, and incurred electricity costs of $3,200. Does this constitute good control or poor control of electricity costs? Which budget in Exhibit 10-1 is more useful in answering this question?

A manager using the static budget makes the following comparison.

Actual Electricity Cost		Budgeted Electricity Cost (static budget)		Cost Variance
$3,200	. . . .	$3,750	. . . .	$550 Favorable

This comparison suggests that operating personnel maintained excellent control over electricity costs during September, generating a favorable variance of $550. Is this a valid analysis and conclusion?

The fault with this analysis is that the manager is comparing the electricity cost incurred at the *actual* activity level, 2,000 trumpets, with the budgeted electricity cost at the *planned* activity level, 2,500 trumpets. Since these activity levels are different, we should expect the electricity cost to be different.

A more sensible approach is to compare the actual electricity cost incurred with the cost that should be incurred when 2,000 trumpets are manufactured. At this production level, 6,000 machine hours should be used (3 per trumpet). The flexible budget in Exhibit 10-1 shows that the manager should expect $3,000 of electricity cost at the 6,000 machine-hour level of activity. Therefore, an analysis based on the flexible budget gives the following comparison.

Actual Electricity Cost		Budgeted Electricity Cost (flexible budget)		Cost Variance
$3,200	. . . .	$3,000	. . . .	$200 Unfavorable

Now the manager's conclusion is different; the revised analysis indicates an unfavorable variance. Electricity cost was greater than it should have been, given the actual level of output. The flexible budget provides the correct basis for comparison between actual and expected costs, given actual activity.

The Activity Measure

Notice that the flexible budget for electricity cost in Exhibit 10-1 is based on machine hours, which is an *input* in the production process. The machine-hour activity levels shown in the flexible budget are the standard allowed machine hours given various levels of output. If 2,000 trumpets are produced, and the standard allowance per trumpet is 3 machine hours, then the standard allowed number of machine hours is 6,000 hours.

Why are the activity levels in the flexible budget based on machine hours, an *input* measure, instead of the number of trumpets produced, an *output* measure? When only a single product is manufactured, it would make no difference whether

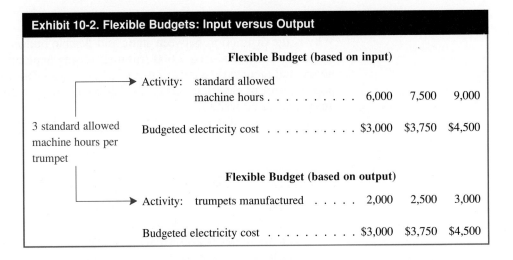

Exhibit 10-2. Flexible Budgets: Input versus Output

Flexible Budget (based on input)

Activity: standard allowed machine hours	6,000	7,500	9,000
Budgeted electricity cost	$3,000	$3,750	$4,500

3 standard allowed machine hours per trumpet

Flexible Budget (based on output)

Activity: trumpets manufactured	2,000	2,500	3,000
Budgeted electricity cost	$3,000	$3,750	$4,500

the flexible budget was based on input or output. In our illustration, either of the flexible budgets shown in Exhibit 10-2 could be used.

Now suppose that during August, Sousa Division manufactured three different products: 1,000 trumpets, 1,500 trombones, and 600 tubas. The following standards have been assigned to these products.

Product	Standard Machine Hours per Unit
Trumpet	3
Trombone	5
Tuba	6

During August, the company's production output was 3,100 instruments. Is 3,100 instruments a meaningful output measure? Adding numbers of trumpets, trombones, and tubas, which require different amounts of productive inputs, is like adding apples and oranges. It would not make sense to base a flexible budget for electricity cost on units of output, when the output consists of different products with different electricity requirements. In this case, the flexible budget must be based on an *input* measure. The standard allowed number of machine hours for the August production is computed as follows:

Product	Units Produced		Standard Machine Hours per Unit		Total Standard Allowed Machine Hours
Trumpets	1,000	. . . .	3	. . . .	3,000
Trombones . . .	1,500	. . . .	5	. . . .	7,500
Tubas	600	. . . .	6	. . . .	3,600
Total					14,100

Recall that the controller estimates electricity cost at $.50 per machine hour. Thus, the flexible budget cost of electricity during August is computed as follows:

Standard allowed machine hours given August output.	14,100
Electricity cost per machine hour.	× $.50
Flexible budget for electricity cost	$ 7,050

The important point is that *units of output* usually is not a meaningful measure in a multiproduct firm, because it would require us to add numbers of unlike products. To avoid this problem, output is measured in terms of the *standard allowed input, given actual output.* The flexible overhead budget is then based on this standard input measure.

FLEXIBLE OVERHEAD BUDGET ILLUSTRATED

Sousa Division's monthly flexible overhead budget is shown in Exhibit 10-3. The overhead costs on the flexible budget are divided into variable and fixed costs. The total budgeted variable cost increases proportionately with increases in the activity.

Exhibit 10-3. Flexible Overhead Budget

Monthly Flexible Overhead Budget
Sousa Division

	Machine Hours		
Budgeted Cost	**6,000**	**7,500**	**9,000**
Variable costs:			
Indirect material:			
Lacquer	$12,000	$15,000	$18,000
Valve lubricant	2,000	2,500	3,000
Plastic valve tops	2,000	2,500	3,000
Miscellaneous supplies	6,000	7,500	9,000
Indirect labor: maintenance	4,000	5,000	6,000
Utilities:			
Electricity	3,000	3,750	4,500
Natural gas	1,000	1,250	1,500
Total variable cost	30,000	37,500	45,000
Fixed costs:			
Indirect labor:			
Production supervisors	8,200	8,200	8,200
Custodians	3,000	3,000	3,000
Building depreciation	500	500	500
Equipment depreciation	100	100	100
Property taxes	2,000	2,000	2,000
Insurance	1,200	1,200	1,200
Total fixed cost	15,000	15,000	15,000
Total overhead cost	$45,000	$52,500	$60,000

Thus, when the number of machine hours increases by 50 percent, from 6,000 hours to 9,000 hours, the total budgeted variable overhead cost also increases by 50 percent, from $30,000 to $45,000. In contrast, the total budgeted fixed overhead does not change with increases in activity; it remains constant at $15,000 per month.

Formula Flexible Budget When overhead costs can be divided into variable and fixed categories, we can express the flexible overhead budget differently. The format used in Exhibit 10-3 is called a *columnar flexible budget*. The budgeted overhead cost for each overhead item is listed in a column under a particular activity level. Notice that the columnar format allows for only a limited number of activity levels. Sousa Division's flexible budget shows only three.

A more general format for expressing a flexible budget is called a *formula flexible budget*. In this format, the managerial accountant expresses the relationship between activity and total budgeted overhead cost by the following formula.

$$\begin{matrix}\text{Total budgeted} \\ \text{monthly overhead} \\ \text{cost}\end{matrix} = \left(\begin{matrix}\text{budgeted variable-} \\ \text{overhead cost per} \\ \text{activity unit}\end{matrix} \times \begin{matrix}\text{total} \\ \text{activity} \\ \text{units}\end{matrix}\right) + \begin{matrix}\text{budgeted fixed-} \\ \text{overhead cost} \\ \text{per month}\end{matrix}$$

To use this formula for the Sousa Division, we first need to compute the budgeted variable-overhead cost per machine hour. Dividing total budgeted variable-overhead cost by the associated activity level yields a budgeted variable-overhead rate of $5 per machine hour. Notice that we can use any activity level in Exhibit 10-3 to compute this rate.

$$\frac{\$30,000}{6,000} = \frac{\$37,500}{7,500} = \frac{\$45,000}{9,000} = \$5 \text{ per machine hour}$$

Sousa Division's formula flexible overhead budget is shown below.

$$\begin{matrix}\text{Total budgeted} \\ \text{monthly overhead cost}\end{matrix} = (\$5 \times \text{total machine hours}) + \$15,000$$

To check the accuracy of the formula, compute the total budgeted overhead cost at each of the activity levels shown in Exhibit 10-3.

Activity (machine hours)		Formula Flexible Overhead Budget	Budgeted Monthly Overhead Cost
6,000	....	$5 × 6,000 + $15,000 =	$45,000
7,500	....	$5 × 7,500 + $15,000 =	$52,500
9,000	....	$5 × 9,000 + $15,000 =	$60,000

The budgeted monthly overhead cost computed above is the same as that shown in Exhibit 10-3 for each activity level.

The formula flexible budget is more general than the columnar flexible budget, because the formula allows the managerial accountant to compute budgeted overhead costs at any activity level. Then the flexible-budgeted overhead cost can be used at the end of the period as a benchmark against which to compare the actual overhead costs incurred.

OVERHEAD APPLICATION IN A STANDARD-COSTING SYSTEM

Recall that *overhead application* refers to the addition of overhead cost to the Work-in-Process Inventory account as a product cost. In the normal-costing system, described in Chapter 3, overhead is applied as shown in the top panel of Exhibit 10-4. Overhead application is based on *actual* hours. In a standard-costing system, overhead application is based on standard hours allowed, given actual output. This system is depicted in the bottom panel of Exhibit 10-4. Notice that the difference between normal costing and standard costing, insofar as overhead is concerned, lies in the quantity of hours used.

Both normal- and standard-costing systems use a predetermined overhead rate. In a standard-costing system, the predetermined overhead rate is also referred to as the standard overhead rate. Sousa Division calculates its predetermined or standard overhead rate annually. The rate for the current year, computed in Exhibit 10-5, is based on *planned* activity of 7,500 machine hours per month. Notice that Sousa Division breaks its predetermined overhead rate into a variable rate and a fixed rate.

We will discuss further the use of standard costs for product costing later in this chapter.

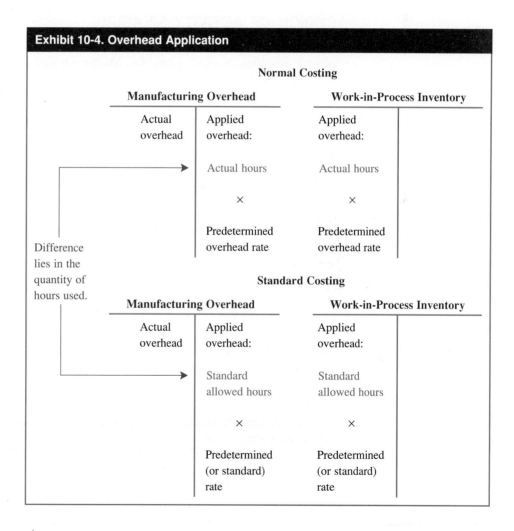

Exhibit 10-4. Overhead Application

Normal Costing

Manufacturing Overhead		Work-in-Process Inventory
Actual overhead	Applied overhead:	Applied overhead:
	Actual hours	Actual hours
	×	×
	Predetermined overhead rate	Predetermined overhead rate

Difference lies in the quantity of hours used.

Standard Costing

Manufacturing Overhead		Work-in-Process Inventory
Actual overhead	Applied overhead:	Applied overhead:
	Standard allowed hours	Standard allowed hours
	×	×
	Predetermined (or standard) rate	Predetermined (or standard) rate

Exhibit 10-5. Predetermined Overhead Rate: Sousa Division

	Budgeted Overhead	Planned Monthly Activity	Predetermined Overhead Rate
Variable	$37,500*	7,500 machine hours	. . . . $5.00 per machine hour
Fixed	15,000*	7,500 machine hours	. . . . $2.00 per machine hour
Total	$52,500	7,500 machine hours	. . . . $7.00 per machine hour

*From the flexible budget (Exhibit 10-3) for planned monthly activity of 7,500 machine hours.

CHOICE OF ACTIVITY MEASURE

Sousa Division's flexible overhead budget is based on machine hours. A variety of activity measures are used in practice. Machine hours, direct-labor hours, direct-labor cost, total process time, and direct-material cost are among the most common measures. Choosing the appropriate activity measure for the flexible overhead budget is important, because the flexible budget is the chief tool for controlling overhead costs.

Criteria for Choosing the Activity Measure

How should the managerial accountant select the activity measure for the flexible budget? The activity measure should be one that varies in a similar pattern to the way that variable overhead varies. As productive activity increases, both variable-overhead cost and the activity measure should increase in roughly the same proportion. As productive activity declines, both variable-overhead cost and the activity measure should decline in roughly the same proportion. In short, variable-overhead cost and the activity measure should *move together* as overall productive activity changes.

Changing Manufacturing Technology: Computer-Integrated Manufacturing Direct-labor time has traditionally been the most popular activity measure in manufacturing firms. However, as automation increases, more and more firms are switching to such measures as machine hours or process time for their flexible overhead budgets. Machine hours and process time are linked more closely than direct-labor hours to the robotic technology and computer-integrated manufacturing (CIM) systems common in today's manufacturing environment.

Cost Drivers As we discussed in Chapter 5, some companies have refined their cost management systems even further. *Cost drivers* are identified as the most significant factors affecting overhead costs. Then multiple overhead rates based on these cost drivers are used to compute product costs and control overhead expenditures. A relentless search for *non-value-added costs* is an integral part of such a cost management system.

Beware of Dollar Measures Dollar measures, such as direct-labor or raw-material costs, are often used as the basis for flexible overhead budgeting. However, such measures have significant drawbacks, and they should be avoided. Dollar measures are subject to price-level changes and fluctuate more than physical measures. For example, the direct-labor *hours* required to manufacture a musical instrument will be relatively stable over time. However, the direct-labor *cost* will vary as wage levels and fringe-benefit costs change with inflation.

The choice of an activity measure upon which to base the flexible budget for variable overhead is really a cost estimation problem, which we studied in Chapter 6.

OVERHEAD COST VARIANCES

The flexible overhead budget is the managerial accountant's primary tool for the control of manufacturing-overhead costs. At the end of each accounting period, the managerial accountant uses the flexible overhead budget to determine the level of overhead cost that should have been incurred, given the actual level of activity. Then the accountant compares the overhead cost in the flexible budget with the actual overhead cost incurred. The managerial accountant then computes four separate overhead variances, each of which conveys information useful in controlling overhead costs.

To illustrate overhead variance analysis, we will continue our illustration of the Sousa Division.

Flexible Budget Sousa's monthly flexible overhead budget, displayed in Exhibit 10-3, shows budgeted variable and fixed manufacturing-overhead costs at three levels of production activity. During September 19x8, Sousa Division manufactured 2,000 trumpets. Since production standards allow 3 machine hours per trumpet, the total standard allowed number of machine hours is 6,000 hours.

Actual production output	2,000 trumpets
Standard allowed machine hours per trumpet	× 3
Total standard allowed machine hours	6,000 machine hours

From the 6,000 machine-hour column in Exhibit 10-3, the budgeted overhead cost for September is as follows:

	Budgeted Overhead Cost for September
Variable overhead	$30,000
Fixed overhead	15,000

From the cost-accounting records, the controller determined that the following overhead costs were actually incurred during September.

	Actual Cost for September
Variable overhead.	$34,650
Fixed overhead	16,100
Total overhead	$50,750

The production supervisor's records indicate that actual machine usage in September was as follows:

Actual machine hours for September. 6,300

Notice that the actual number of machine hours used (6,300) exceeds the standard allowed number of machine hours, given actual production output (6,000).

We now have assembled all of the information necessary to compute Sousa Division's overhead variances for September.

Variable Overhead

Sousa Division's total variable-overhead variance for September is computed below.

Actual variable overhead. $34,650
Budgeted variable overhead   30,000
Total variable-overhead variance . . . . $ 4,650 Unfavorable

What caused the company to spend $4,650 more than the budgeted amount on variable overhead? To discover the reasons behind this performance, the managerial accountant computes a **variable-overhead spending variance** and a **variable-overhead efficiency variance.** The computation of these variances is depicted in Exhibit 10-6.

Two equivalent formulas for the variable-overhead spending variance are shown below.

1.   **Variable-overhead**
         spending variance = actual variable overhead − (AH × SVR)

                                              or

2.   **Variable-overhead**
         spending variance = (AH × AVR) − (AH × SVR)

where   **AH   = actual machine hours**
         AVR = actual variable-overhead rate (actual variable overhead ÷ AH)
         SVR = standard variable-overhead rate

These two formulas are equivalent, because actual variable overhead is equal to actual hours times the actual variable overhead rate $(AH \times AVR)$. Formula 2 above can be simplified:

3.   **Variable-overhead spending variance = AH(AVR − SVR)**

Sousa Division's variable-overhead spending variance for September is computed as follows (using formula 1):

Variable-overhead
spending variance = actual variable overhead − (AH × SVR)
                   = $34,650   − (6,300 × $5.00)
                   = $3,150 unfavorable

Exhibit 10-6. Variable-Overhead Spending and Efficiency Variances

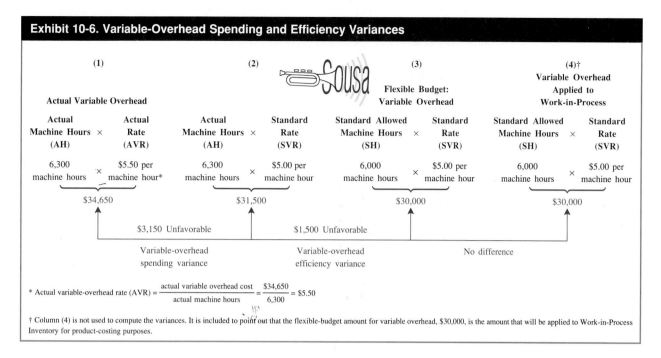

This variance is unfavorable because the actual variable-overhead cost exceeded the expected amount, after adjusting that expectation for the actual number of machine hours used.

As Exhibit 10-6 shows, the following formula defines the variable-overhead efficiency variance.

$$\text{Variable-overhead efficiency variance} = (AH \times SVR) - (SH \times SVR)$$

where SH **= standard machine hours**

Writing this formula more simply, we have the following expression.

$$\text{Variable-overhead efficiency variance} = SVR(AH - SH)$$

Sousa Division's variable-overhead efficiency variance for September is computed as follows:

$$
\begin{aligned}
\text{Variable-overhead efficiency variance} &= SVR(AH - SH)\\
&= \$5.00(6{,}300 - 6{,}000)\\
&= \$1{,}500 \text{ unfavorable}
\end{aligned}
$$

This variance is unfavorable because actual machine hours exceeded standard allowed machine hours, given actual output.

Product Costing versus Control Columns (1), (2), and (3) in Exhibit 10-6 are used to compute the variances for *cost-control purposes*. Column (4) in the exhibit shows the variable overhead applied to work in process for the *product-costing pur-*

pose. Notice that the variable-overhead cost on the flexible budget, $30,000, is the same as the amount applied to work in process.

Graphing Variable-Overhead Variances Exhibit 10-7 provides a graphical analysis of Sousa Division's variable-overhead variances for September. The graph shows the variable-overhead rate per machine hour on the vertical axis. The standard rate is $5.00 per machine hour, while the actual rate is $5.50 per machine hour (actual variable-overhead cost of $34,650 divided by actual machine hours of 6,300). Machine hours are shown on the horizontal axis.

The white area on the graph represents the flexible-budget amount for variable overhead, given actual September output of 2,000 trumpets. The large area on the graph, enclosed by the colored lines on the top and right sides, represents actual variable-overhead cost. The colored area in between, representing the total variable-overhead variance, is divided into the spending and efficiency variances.

Managerial Interpretation of Variable-Overhead Variances What do the variable-overhead variances mean? What information do they convey to management? The formulas for computing the variable-overhead variances resemble those used to compute the direct-labor variances. To see this, compare Exhibit 10-6 (variable overhead) with Exhibit 9-3 (direct labor).

Despite the similar formulas, the interpretation of the variable-overhead variances is quite different from that applicable to the direct-labor variances.

Efficiency Variance Recall that an unfavorable direct-labor efficiency variance results when more direct labor is used than the standard allowed quantity. Thus, direct labor has been used inefficiently, relative to the standard. However, that is not

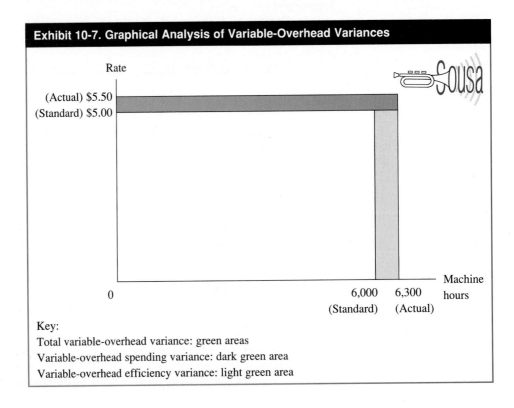

Exhibit 10-7. Graphical Analysis of Variable-Overhead Variances

Key:
Total variable-overhead variance: green areas
Variable-overhead spending variance: dark green area
Variable-overhead efficiency variance: light green area

the proper interpretation of an unfavorable variable-overhead efficiency variance. Sousa Division's variable-overhead efficiency variance did *not* result from using more of the variable-overhead items, such as electricity and indirect material, than the standard allowed amount. Instead, this variance resulted when the division used *more machine hours* than the standard quantity, given actual output. Recall that the divisional controller has found that variable-overhead cost varies in a similar pattern to that with which machine hours vary. Since 300 more machine hours were used than the standard quantity, the division's management should expect that variable-overhead costs will be greater. Thus, the variable-overhead efficiency variance has nothing to do with efficient or inefficient usage of electricity, indirect material, and other variable-overhead items. This variance simply reflects an adjustment in the managerial accountant's expectation about variable-overhead cost, because the division used more than the standard quantity of machine hours.

What is the important difference between direct labor and variable overhead that causes this different interpretation of the efficiency variance? Direct labor is a traceable cost and is budgeted on the basis of direct-labor hours. Variable overhead, on the other hand, is a pool of *indirect* costs that are budgeted on the basis of *machine hours*. The indirect nature of variable-overhead costs causes the different interpretation.

Spending Variance An unfavorable direct-labor rate variance is straightforward to interpret; the actual labor rate *per hour* exceeds the standard rate. Although the formula for computing the variable-overhead spending variance is similar to that for the direct-labor rate variance, its interpretation is quite different.

An unfavorable spending variance simply means that the total actual cost of variable overhead is greater than expected, after adjusting for the actual quantity of machine hours used. An unfavorable spending variance could result from paying a higher than expected price per unit for variable-overhead items. Or, the variance could result from using more of the variable-overhead items than expected.

Suppose, for example, that electricity were the only variable-overhead cost item. An unfavorable variable-overhead spending variance could result from paying a higher than expected price per kilowatt-hour for electricity, or from using more than the expected amount of electricity, or both.

Control of Variable Overhead Since the variable-overhead efficiency variance says nothing about efficient or inefficient usage of variable overhead, the spending variance is the real control variance for variable overhead. Managers can use the spending variance to alert them if variable-overhead costs are out of line with expectations.

Fixed Overhead

To analyze performance with regard to fixed overhead, the managerial accountant calculates fixed-overhead variances.

Fixed-Overhead Budget Variance The variance used by managers to control fixed overhead is called the **fixed-overhead budget variance.** It is defined as follows:

$$\text{Fixed-overhead budget variance} = \text{actual fixed overhead} - \text{budgeted fixed overhead}$$

Sousa Division's fixed-overhead budget variance for September is as follows:

Fixed-overhead
budget variance = actual fixed overhead − budgeted fixed overhead
$$= \quad \$16,\!100 \qquad - \$15,\!000^*$$
$$= \$1,\!100 \text{ unfavorable}$$

* From the flexible budget (Exhibit 10-3).

The fixed-overhead budget variance is unfavorable, because the division spent more than the budgeted amount on fixed overhead. Notice that we need not specify an activity level to determine budgeted fixed overhead. All three columns in the flexible budget (Exhibit 10-3) specify $15,000 as budgeted fixed overhead.

Fixed-Overhead Volume Variance The **fixed-overhead volume variance** is defined as follows:

Fixed-overhead
volume variance = budgeted fixed overhead − applied fixed overhead

Sousa Division's applied fixed overhead for September is $12,000:

$$\text{Applied fixed overhead} = \begin{array}{c} \text{predetermined} \\ \text{fixed} \\ \text{overhead rate} \end{array} \times \begin{array}{c} \text{standard} \\ \text{allowed} \\ \text{hours} \end{array}$$

$$= \$2.00 \text{ per machine hour} \times 6,\!000 \text{ machine hours} = \$12,\!000$$

The $2.00 predetermined fixed-overhead rate was calculated in Exhibit 10-5. The 6,000 standard allowed machine hours is based on actual September production of 2,000 trumpets, each with a standard allowance of 3 machine hours.

Sousa Division's fixed-overhead volume variance is calculated below.

Fixed-overhead
volume variance = budgeted fixed overhead − applied fixed overhead
$$= \quad \$15,\!000 \qquad - \$12,\!000$$
$$= \quad \$3,\!000$$

Managerial Interpretation of Fixed-Overhead Variances Exhibit 10-8 shows Sousa Division's two fixed-overhead variances for September. The budget variance is the real control variance for fixed overhead, because it compares actual expenditures with budgeted fixed-overhead costs.

The volume variance provides a way of reconciling two different purposes of the cost-accounting system. For the *control purpose,* the cost-accounting system recognizes that fixed overhead does not change as production activity varies. Hence, budgeted fixed overhead is the same at all activity levels in the flexible budget. (Review Exhibit 10-3 to verify this.) Budgeted fixed overhead is the basis for controlling fixed overhead, because it provides the benchmark against which actual expenditures are compared.

For the *product-costing purpose* of the cost accounting system, budgeted fixed overhead is divided by planned activity to obtain a predetermined (or standard) fixed-overhead rate. For Sousa Division, this rate is $2.00 per machine hour (budgeted fixed overhead of $15,000 divided by planned activity of 7,500 machine hours).

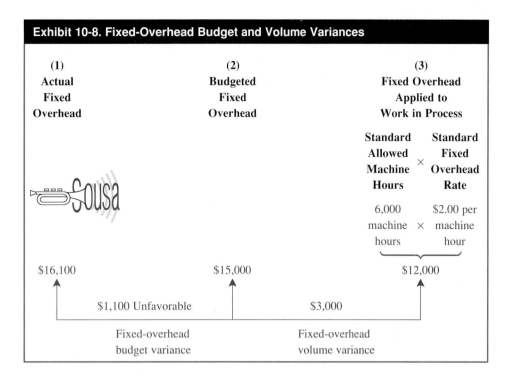

Exhibit 10-8. Fixed-Overhead Budget and Volume Variances

(1) Actual Fixed Overhead	(2) Budgeted Fixed Overhead	(3) Fixed Overhead Applied to Work in Process
		Standard Allowed Machine Hours × Standard Fixed Overhead Rate
		6,000 machine hours × $2.00 per machine hour
$16,100	$15,000	$12,000

$1,100 Unfavorable

$3,000

Fixed-overhead
budget variance

Fixed-overhead
volume variance

This predetermined rate is then used to apply fixed overhead to Work-in-Process Inventory. During any period in which the standard allowed number of machine hours, given actual output, differs from the planned level of machine hours, the budgeted fixed overhead will differ from applied fixed overhead.

Exhibit 10-9 illustrates this point graphically. Budgeted fixed overhead is constant at $15,000 for all levels of activity. However, applied fixed overhead increases with activity, since fixed overhead is applied to Work-in-Process Inventory at the rate of $2.00 per standard allowed machine hour. Notice that budgeted and applied fixed overhead are equal *only* if the number of standard allowed hours equals the planned activity level of 7,500 machine hours. When this happens, there will be no fixed-overhead volume variance. Sousa Division has a $3,000 volume variance in September because the standard allowed hours and planned hours are different.

Capacity Utilization A common, but faulty, interpretation of a positive volume variance is that it measures the cost of underutilizing productive capacity. Some firms even designate a positive volume variance as unfavorable. The reasoning behind this view is that the planned activity level used to compute the predetermined fixed-overhead rate is a measure of normal capacity utilization. Moreover, fixed-overhead costs, such as depreciation and property taxes, are costs incurred to create productive capacity. Therefore, the predetermined fixed-overhead rate measures the cost of providing an hour of productive capacity. If 7,500 machine hours are planned, but output is such that only 6,000 standard machine hours are allowed, then capacity has been underutilized by 1,500 hours. Since each hour costs $2.00 (Sousa Division's predetermined fixed-overhead rate), the cost of underutilization is $3,000 (1,500 × $2.00), which is Sousa Division's volume variance.

The fault with this interpretation of the volume variance is that it ignores the real cost of underutilizing productive capacity. The real cost is due to the lost sales of the

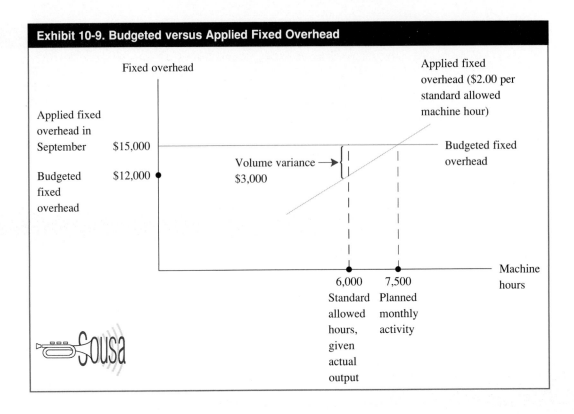

Exhibit 10-9. Budgeted versus Applied Fixed Overhead

products that are not produced when capacity is underutilized. Moreover, this interpretation fails to recognize that underutilizing capacity, and reducing inventory, may be a wise managerial response to slackening demand.

For this reason, we interpret the volume variance merely as a way of reconciling the two purposes of the cost accounting system. Moreover, we choose not to designate the volume variance as either favorable or unfavorable.

Four-Way, Three-Way, and Two-Way Variance Analysis

Four variances were discussed in the preceding two sections: the variable-overhead spending and efficiency variances, and the fixed-overhead budget and volume variances. Some managers prefer to combine the variable-overhead spending and fixed-overhead budget variances into a single *combined spending variance*. Since this presentation leaves only three separate variances, it is called a three-way analysis. Other managers prefer to combine the variable-overhead spending, variable-overhead efficiency, and fixed-overhead budget variances into a single *combined budget variance*. Since this presentation leaves only two separate variances, it is called a two-way analysis. Exhibit 10-10 displays the four-way, three-way, and two-way variance analyses for Sousa Division's September performance.

OVERHEAD COST PERFORMANCE REPORT

The variable-overhead spending and efficiency variances and the fixed-overhead budget variance can be computed for each overhead cost item in the flexible budget. When these itemized variances are presented along with actual and budgeted costs for

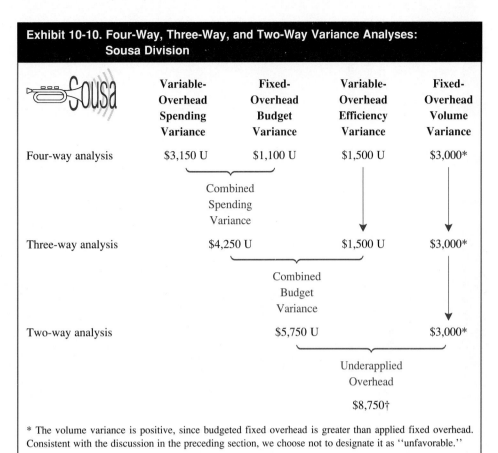

Exhibit 10-10. Four-Way, Three-Way, and Two-Way Variance Analyses: Sousa Division

	Variable-Overhead Spending Variance	Fixed-Overhead Budget Variance	Variable-Overhead Efficiency Variance	Fixed-Overhead Volume Variance
Four-way analysis	$3,150 U	$1,100 U	$1,500 U	$3,000*
Three-way analysis	$4,250 U		$1,500 U	$3,000*
Two-way analysis		$5,750 U		$3,000*

Combined Spending Variance

Combined Budget Variance

Underapplied Overhead

$8,750†

* The volume variance is positive, since budgeted fixed overhead is greater than applied fixed overhead. Consistent with the discussion in the preceding section, we choose not to designate it as ''unfavorable.''

† The underapplied overhead is the difference between actual overhead ($50,750) and overhead applied to work in process ($42,000).

each overhead item, the result is an **overhead cost performance report.** Sousa Division's performance report, displayed in Exhibit 10-11, would be used by management to exercise control over each of the division's overhead costs.

Notice that the performance report includes only spending and efficiency variances for the variable items, and only a budget variance for the fixed items. Upon receiving this report, a manager might investigate the relatively large variances for indirect maintenance labor, electricity, and production supervisory labor.

STANDARD COSTS AND PRODUCT COSTING

In a standard-costing system, the standard costs are used for product costing as well as for cost control. The costs of direct material, direct labor, and manufacturing overhead are all entered into Work-in-Process Inventory at their standard costs. (Review Exhibit 10-4.)

Journal Entries under Standard Costing During September, Sousa Division incurred actual manufacturing-overhead costs of $50,750, which includes $34,650 of variable overhead and $16,100 of fixed overhead. A summary journal entry to record these actual expenditures follows.

Exhibit 10-11. Overhead Cost Performance Report: Sousa Division

	(1) Flexible Budget (for 6,000 machine hr.)	(2) Standard Rate per Machine Hour [for variable costs only; column (1) ÷ 6,000 machine hr.]	(3) 6,300 Actual Machine Hours × Standard Rate	(4) Actual Cost	(5) Spending Variance [column (4) – column (3)]	(6) Efficiency Variance [column (3) – column (1)]	(7) Budget Variance [column (4) – column (1)]
Variable costs:							
Indirect material:							
Lacquer	$12,000	$2.00	$12,600	$12,700	$ 100 U	$ 600 U	
Valve lubricant	2,000	.33	2,079	2,090	11 U	79 U	
Plastic valve tops	2,000	.33	2,079	2,000	(79) F	79 U	
Miscellaneous supplies	6,000	1.00	6,300	6,500	200 U	300 U	
Indirect labor: maintenance	4,000	.67	4,221	6,400	2,179 U	221 U	
Utilities							
Electricity	3,000	.50	3,150	4,050	900 U	150 U	
Natural gas	1,000	.17	1,071	910	(161)F	71 U	
Total variable cost	30,000	$5.00	$31,500	$34,650	3,150 U	1,500 U	
Fixed costs:							
Indirect labor:							
Production supervisors	8,200			$ 9,200			$1,000 U
Custodians	3,000			3,100			100 U
Building depreciation	500			500			—0—
Equipment depreciation	100			100			—0—
Property taxes	2,000			2,000			—0—
Insurance	1,200			1,200			—0—
Total fixed cost	15,000			16,100			—0—
Total overhead cost	$45,000			$50,750			$1,100 U
Total variance between actual overhead cost and flexible budget				$5,750 U	$5,750 U		

Sum of spending, efficiency, and budget variances

Manufacturing Overhead 50,750
    Indirect-Materials Inventory 23,290*
    Wages Payable   18,700
    Utilities Payable   4,960
    Accumulated Depreciation   600
    Property Taxes Payable   2,000
    Prepaid Insurance   1,200

    * The credit amounts can be verified in column (4) of Exhibit 10-11. For example, indirect-material costs amounted to $23,290 ($12,700 + $2,090 + $2,000 + $6,500).

The application of manufacturing overhead to Work-in-Process is based on a predetermined overhead rate of $7.00 per machine hour (total of the variable and fixed rates), and 6,000 standard allowed machine hours, given actual output of 2,000 trumpets. The summary journal entry is:

Work-in-Process Inventory 42,000
    Manufacturing Overhead 42,000*

    * Applied overhead = $7.00 × 6,000 = $42,000

Now the Manufacturing Overhead account appears as shown below.

Manufacturing Overhead

Actual $50,750	$42,000 Applied

The *underapplied overhead* for September is $8,750 ($50,750 − $42,000). This means that the overhead applied to Work-in-Process Inventory in September was $8,750 less than the actual overhead cost incurred. Notice that the underapplied overhead is equal to the sum of the four overhead variances for September. The total of the four overhead variances will always be equal to the overapplied or underapplied overhead for the accounting period.[1]

Disposition of Variances As explained in the preceding chapter, variances are temporary accounts, and most companies close them directly into Cost of Goods Sold at the end of each accounting period. The journal entry required to close out Sousa Division's underapplied overhead for September is shown below.

Cost of Goods Sold 8,750
    Manufacturing Overhead   8,750

The journal entry to close out underapplied or overapplied overhead typically would be made only annually, rather than monthly.

An alternative accounting treatment is to prorate underapplied or overapplied overhead among Work-in-Process Inventory, Finished-Goods Inventory, and Cost of Goods Sold, as explained in Chapter 3.

FLEXIBLE BUDGETS IN NONMANUFACTURING ORGANIZATIONS

Nonmanufacturing organizations also use flexible budgets to control overhead costs. For example, some airlines use air miles flown, various hotels use average occupancy

[1] Overapplied and underapplied manufacturing overhead are discussed in Chapter 3.

Exhibit 10-12. Flexible Overhead Budget for a Hospital

Monthly Flexible Overhead Budget
North Chicago Medical Arts Hospital

	Patient-Days		
Budgeted Cost	10,000	12,500	15,000
Variable costs:			
Electricity and natural gas	$ 5,000	$ 6,250	$ 7,500
Water and sewer	800	1,000	1,200
Maintenance	3,000	3,750	4,500
Housekeeping	6,000	7,500	9,000
Medical supplies	7,000	8,750	10,500
Laundry	2,000	2,500	3,000
Billing and appointments	4,000	5,000	6,000
Total variable cost	27,800	34,750	41,700
Fixed costs:			
Depreciation: building	3,000	3,000	3,000
Depreciation: equipment	6,000	6,000	6,000
Telephone and TV cable	300	300	300
Nursing supervision	9,000	9,000	9,000
Administrative services	12,000	12,000	12,000
Total fixed cost	30,300	30,300	30,300
Total overhead cost	$58,100	$65,050	$72,000

rates, and many restaurants use customers served as the basis for their flexible overhead budgets.

As an illustration, Exhibit 10-12 displays the flexible overhead budget for North Chicago Medical Arts Hospital. This health-care facility uses patient-days as the basis for its flexible overhead budget. The hospital controller uses this budget for planning and for controlling overhead costs. Since a hospital does not produce inventoriable goods, there is no product-costing function for its cost-accounting system.

Many health-care administrators want to distinguish between different kinds of medical cases in the flexible-budgeting process. To accomplish this, some hospitals use a technique called case-mix cost accounting, described in the following illustration.

ILLUSTRATION FROM MANAGEMENT-ACCOUNTING PRACTICE

Health-Care Institutions

Costs of treating patients vary widely among different types of cases. The managerial accountants in many health-care institutions base their budgeting and cost-accounting systems on the concept of a diagnostic related group (DRG). A DRG is a set of case types that require similar medical treatments. For example, a variety of cardiac case types requiring similar treatment could comprise one DRG. The flexible-budgeting system is then based on the number of patient-days of care in each DRG.[2]

CHAPTER SUMMARY

Overhead is a heterogeneous pool of indirect costs. Since overhead costs cannot be traced easily to products or services, a flexible budget is used to budget overhead costs at various levels of activity. A columnar flexible budget is based on several distinct activity levels, while a formula flexible budget is valid for a continuous range of activity. The flexible-overhead budget is based on some activity measure that varies in a pattern similar to that of variable overhead. Machine hours, process time, and direct-labor hours are common activity bases.

In a standard-costing system, the flexible budget is used to control overhead costs. The managerial accountant uses the amount of overhead cost specified by the flexible budget as a benchmark against which to compare actual overhead costs. The accountant computes four overhead variances: the variable-overhead spending and efficiency variances and the fixed-overhead budget and volume variances. These variances help management to control overhead costs.

The managerial accountant also uses the standard or predetermined overhead rate as the basis for product costing in a standard-costing system. The amount of overhead cost entered into Work-in-Process Inventory is equal to the standard overhead rate multiplied by the standard allowed amount of the activity base, given actual output.

REVIEW PROBLEM ON OVERHEAD VARIANCES

In November of 19x8, the Sousa Division produced 3,000 trumpets, used 9,100 machine hours, and incurred the following manufacturing-overhead costs.

Variable overhead...	$45,955
Fixed overhead	$15,800

Sousa Division's monthly flexible overhead budget for November is the same as that given in Exhibit 10-3.

Compute Sousa Division's variable-overhead variances using the format shown in Exhibit 10-6. Compute the division's fixed-overhead variances using the format shown in Exhibit 10-8.

Solution to Review Problem
The solution to the review problem is given in Exhibits 10-13 and 10-14.

KEY TERMS Fixed-overhead budget variance, p. 417; Fixed-overhead volume variance, p. 418; Flexible budget, p. 406; Overhead cost performance report, p. 421; Static budget, p. 406; Variable-overhead efficiency variance, p. 414; Variable-overhead spending variance, p. 414.

---

[2] The source for this illustration is J. D. Thompson, R. F. Averill, and R. B. Fetter, "Planning, Budgeting and Controlling—One look at the Future: Case-Mix Cost Accounting," *Health Services Research,* Summer 1979, pp. 111–125.

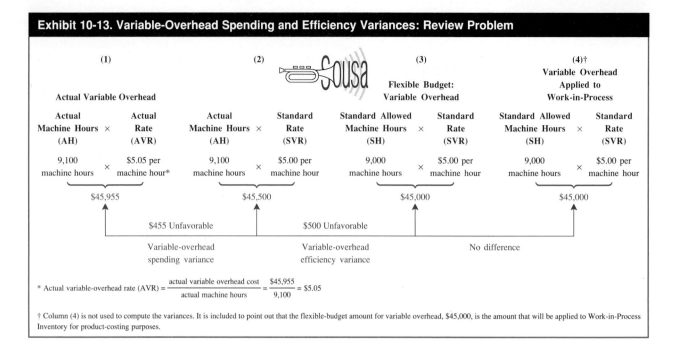

Exhibit 10-13. Variable-Overhead Spending and Efficiency Variances: Review Problem

(1)		(2)		(3)		(4)†	
Actual Variable Overhead		SOUSA		Flexible Budget: Variable Overhead		Variable Overhead Applied to Work-in-Process	
Actual Machine Hours × (AH)	Actual Rate (AVR)	Actual Machine Hours × (AH)	Standard Rate (SVR)	Standard Allowed Machine Hours × (SH)	Standard Rate (SVR)	Standard Allowed Machine Hours × (SH)	Standard Rate (SVR)
9,100 machine hours ×	$5.05 per machine hour*	9,100 machine hours ×	$5.00 per machine hour	9,000 machine hours ×	$5.00 per machine hour	9,000 machine hours ×	$5.00 per machine hour
$45,955		$45,500		$45,000		$45,000	

$455 Unfavorable $500 Unfavorable No difference

Variable-overhead   Variable-overhead
spending variance   efficiency variance

* Actual variable-overhead rate (AVR) = $\dfrac{\text{actual variable overhead cost}}{\text{actual machine hours}} = \dfrac{\$45,955}{9,100} = \$5.05$

† Column (4) is not used to compute the variances. It is included to point out that the flexible-budget amount for variable overhead, $45,000, is the amount that will be applied to Work-in-Process Inventory for product-costing purposes.

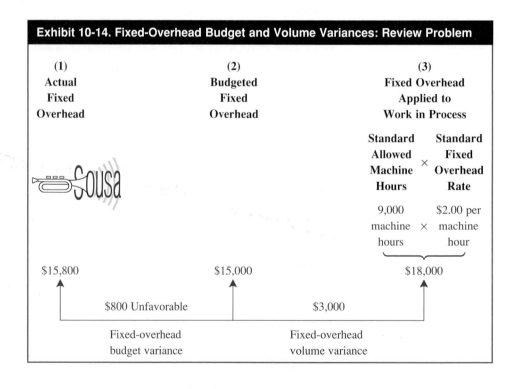

Exhibit 10-14. Fixed-Overhead Budget and Volume Variances: Review Problem

(1)	(2)	(3)	
Actual Fixed Overhead	**Budgeted Fixed Overhead**	**Fixed Overhead Applied to Work in Process**	
		Standard Allowed Machine Hours ×	Standard Fixed Overhead Rate
		9,000 machine hours ×	$2.00 per machine hour
$15,800	$15,000	$18,000	

$800 Unfavorable $3,000

Fixed-overhead   Fixed-overhead
budget variance   volume variance

Sales Variances

The variances discussed in Chapters 9 and 10 focus on production costs. Managerial accountants also compute variances to help management analyze the firm's sales performance. To illustrate two commonly used sales variances, we will continue our discussion of the Sousa Division. The expected sales price and standard variable costs for a trumpet are as follows:

Expected sales price	$225
Standard variable costs:	
Direct material	$ 70
Direct labor	100
Variable overhead (3 machine hours at $5 per hour)	15
Total unit variable cost	$185

The difference between the sales price and the unit variable cost is called the **unit contribution margin.** Sousa Division's unit contribution margin is $40 per trumpet ($225 − $185). This is the amount that the sale of one trumpet *contributes* toward covering the division's fixed costs and making a profit.

During October 19x8, Sousa Division's management expects to sell 1,500 trumpets. Based on this sales forecast, the controller computed the following budgeted **total contribution margin.**

Budgeted sales revenue (1,500 trumpets × $225)	$337,500
Budgeted variable costs (1,500 trumpets × $185)	277,500
Budgeted total contribution margin (1,500 trumpets × $40)	$ 60,000

The *actual* results for October were as follows:

Actual sales volume	1,600 trumpets
Actual sales price	$220
Actual unit variable cost	$185

Using these actual results, Sousa Division's actual total contribution margin for October is computed as follows:

Actual sales revenue (1,600 trumpets × $220)	$352,000
Actual variable costs (1,600 trumpets × $185)	296,000
Actual total contribution margin (1,600 trumpets × $35)	$ 56,000

Sousa Division's actual total contribution margin was $4,000 less in October than the budgeted amount. What caused this variance?

Two partially offsetting effects are present. First, the division sold more trumpets than expected. This will cause the total contribution margin to increase. Second, the sales price was lower than expected, and this will cause the total contribution margin to decline. The managerial accountant computes two sales variances to reflect these facts. These variances are defined below and computed for the Sousa Division.

$$\text{Sales-price variance} = \left(\begin{array}{c} \text{actual} \\ \text{sales} \\ \text{price} \end{array} - \begin{array}{c} \text{expected} \\ \text{sales} \\ \text{price} \end{array}\right) \times \begin{array}{c} \text{actual} \\ \text{sales} \\ \text{volume} \end{array}$$

$$= (\$220 - \$225) \times 1{,}600 = \$8{,}000 \text{ unfavorable}$$

$$\text{Sales-volume variance} = \left(\begin{array}{c} \text{actual} \\ \text{sales} \\ \text{volume} \end{array} - \begin{array}{c} \text{budgeted} \\ \text{sales} \\ \text{volume} \end{array}\right) \times \begin{array}{c} \text{budgeted unit} \\ \text{contribution} \\ \text{margin} \end{array}$$

$$= (1{,}600 - 1{,}500) \times \$40 = \$4{,}000 \text{ favorable}$$

Together, the sales-price and sales-volume variances explain the $4,000 variance between actual and budgeted total contribution margin.

Sales-price variance	$8,000 Unfavorable
Sales-volume variance	4,000 Favorable
Variance between actual and budgeted total contribution margin	$4,000 Unfavorable

KEY TERMS (APPENDIX) Sales-price variance, p. 428; Sales-volume variance, p. 428; Total contribution margin, p. 427; Unit contribution margin, p. 427.

REVIEW QUESTIONS

10-1. Distinguish between static and flexible budgets.

10-2. Explain the advantage of using a flexible budget.

10-3. Why are flexible overhead budgets based on an activity measure, such as machine hours or direct-labor hours?

10-4. Distinguish between a columnar and a formula flexible budget.

10-5. Show, using T-accounts, how manufacturing overhead is added to Work-in-Process Inventory when standard costing is used.

10-6. How has computer-integrated manufacturing (CIM) technology affected overhead application?

10-7. What is the interpretation of the variable-overhead spending variance?

10-8. Jeffries Company's only variable-overhead cost is electricity. Does an unfavorable variable-overhead spending variance imply that the company paid more than the anticipated rate per kilowatt-hour?

10-9. What is the interpretation of the variable-overhead efficiency variance?

10-10. Distinguish between the interpretations of the direct-labor and variable-overhead efficiency variances.

10-11. What is the fixed-overhead budget variance?

10-12. What is the correct interpretation of the fixed-overhead volume variance?

10-13. Describe a common but misleading interpretation of the fixed-overhead volume variance. Why is this interpretation misleading?

10-14. Draw a graph showing budgeted and applied fixed overhead, and show a positive volume variance on the graph.

10-15. What types of organizations use flexible budgets?

10-16. What is the conceptual problem of applying fixed manufacturing overhead as a product cost?

10-17. Distinguish between the control purpose and the product-costing purpose of standard costing and flexible budgeting.

10-18. Why are fixed-overhead costs sometimes called capacity-producing costs?

10-19. Draw a graph showing both budgeted and applied variable overhead. Explain why the graph appears as it does.

10-20. Give one example of a plausible activity base to use in flexible budgeting for each of the following organizations: an insurance company, an express delivery service, a restaurant, and a state tax-collection agency.

EXERCISES *Exercise 10-21 Straightforward Computation of Overhead Variances.* Borealis Electronics has the following standards and flexible-budget data.

Standard variable-overhead rate	$6.00 per direct-labor hour
Standard quantity of direct labor	2 hours per unit of output
Budgeted fixed overhead	$100,000
Budgeted output.	25,000 units

Actual results for April are given below.

Actual output	20,000 units
Actual variable overhead	$320,000
Actual fixed overhead.	$97,000
Actual direct labor	50,000 hours

REQUIRED: Use the variance formulas to compute the following variances. Indicate whether each variance is favorable or unfavorable, where appropriate.

1. Variable-overhead spending variance.
2. Variable-overhead efficiency variance.
3. Fixed-overhead budget variance.
4. Fixed-overhead volume variance.

Exercise 10-22 Diagram of Overhead Variances. Refer to the data in the preceding exercise. Use diagrams similar to those in Exhibits 10-6 and 10-8 to compute the variable-overhead spending and efficiency variances, and the fixed-overhead budget and volume variances.

Exercise 10-23 Graphing Overhead Variances. Refer to the data in Exercise 10-21. Draw graphs similar to those in Exhibit 10-7 (variable overhead) and Exhibit 10-9 (fixed overhead) to depict the overhead variances.

Exercise 10-24   Journal Entries for Overhead. Refer to the data in Exercise 10-21. Prepare journal entries to:

- Record the incurrence of actual variable overhead and actual fixed overhead.
- Add variable and fixed overhead to Work-in-Process Inventory.

Exercise 10-25   Construct a Flexible Overhead Budget; Hospital. The controller for Aurora Community Hospital estimates that the hospital uses 30 kilowatt-hours of electricity per patient-day, and that the electric rate will be $.10 per kilowatt-hour. The hospital also pays a fixed monthly charge of $1,000 to the electric utility to rent emergency backup electric generators.

REQUIRED: Construct a flexible budget for the hospital's electricity costs using each of the following techniques.

1. Formula flexible budget.
2. Columnar flexible budget for 30,000, 40,000 and 50,000 patient-days of activity. List variable and fixed electricity costs separately.

Exercise 10-26   Standard Hours Allowed; Flexible Budgeting; Multiple Products. Andromeda, Ltd. produces telescopes of two quality levels: beginner and stargazer. The beginner model requires three direct-labor hours, while the stargazer telescope requires five hours. The firm uses direct-labor hours for flexible budgeting.

REQUIRED:

1. How many standard hours are allowed in May, when 100 beginner models and 400 stargazer telescopes are manufactured?
2. Suppose the company based its flexible overhead budget for May on the number of telescopes manufactured, which is 500. What difficulties would this approach cause?

Exercise 10-27   Straightforward Computation of Overhead Variances. The data below pertain to Neptune Napkin Company, a manufacturer of paper napkins.

Standard variable-overhead rate.....................	$9.00 per machine hour
Standard quantity of machine hours	4 hours per unit of output
Budgeted fixed overhead...........................	$120,000
Budgeted output	10,000 units

Actual results for December are given below.

Actual output......................................	9,000 units
Actual variable overhead.............................	$405,000
Actual fixed overhead	$122,000
Actual machine time................................	40,500 machine hours

REQUIRED: Use any of the methods explained in the chapter to compute the following variances. Indicate whether each variance is favorable or unfavorable, where appropriate.

1. Variable-overhead spending variance.
2. Variable-overhead efficiency variance.
3. Fixed-overhead budget variance.
4. Fixed-overhead volume variance.

Exercise 10-28   Reconstruct Missing Information from Partial Data. You brought your work home one evening, and your nephew spilled his chocolate milk shake on the variance report you were preparing. Fortunately, you were able to reconstruct the obliterated information from the remaining data. Fill in the missing numbers below.

Standard variable-overhead rate per machine hour	$8.00
Standard machine hours per unit of output	4 hours
Actual variable-overhead rate per machine hour	?
Actual machine hours per unit of output	?
Budgeted fixed overhead.	$50,000
Actual fixed overhead	?
Budgeted production in units.	25,000
Actual production in units	?
Variable-overhead spending variance	$72,000 U
Variable-overhead efficiency variance	$192,000 F
Fixed-overhead budget variance	$15,000 U
Fixed-overhead volume variance	?
Total actual overhead	$713,000
Total budgeted overhead (flexible budget).	?
Total budgeted overhead (static budget)	?
Total applied overhead	$816,000

Exercise 10-29   Interpretation of Variable-Overhead Efficiency Variance. You recently received the following note from the production supervisor of the company where you serve as controller. "I don't understand these crazy variable-overhead efficiency variances. My employees are very careful in their use of electricity and manufacturing supplies, and we use very little indirect labor. What are we supposed to do?" Write a brief memo responding to the production supervisor's concern.

Exercise 10-30   Sales Variances (Appendix). The data below pertain to Jupiter Products, Inc. for the month of February.

	Static Budget	Actual
Units sold	10,000	9,000
Sales revenue	$120,000	$103,500
Variable manufacturing cost	40,000	36,000
Fixed manufacturing cost	20,000	20,000
Variable selling and administrative cost	10,000	9,900
Fixed selling and administrative cost	10,000	10,000

REQUIRED: Compute the sales-price and sales-volume variances for February.

PROBLEMS   *Problem 10-31   Standard Hours Allowed; Flexible Budget; Multiple Products; Insurance Company.* Galaxy Insurance Company uses a flexible overhead budget for its application-processing department. The firm offers five types of policies, with the following standard hours allowed for clerical processing.

Health.	2 hours
Life	5 hours
Automobile	1 hour
Renter's	1 hour
Homeowner's.	2 hours

The following numbers of insurance applications were processed during July.

Health.	500
Life	100
Automobile	250
Renter's	300
Homeowner's.	200

The controller estimates that the variable-overhead rate in the application-processing department is $4.00 per hour, and that fixed-overhead costs will amount to $2,000 per month.

REQUIRED:

1. How many standard clerical hours are allowed in July, given actual application activity?
2. Why would it not be sensible to base the company's flexible budget on the number of applications processed instead of the number of clerical hours allowed?
3. Construct a formula flexible overhead budget for the company.
4. What is the flexible budget for total overhead cost in July?

Problem 10-32   Graphing Budgeted and Applied Overhead; Recording Studio. Countrytime Studios is a recording studio in Nashville. The studio budgets and applies overhead costs on the basis of production time. Countrytime's controller anticipates 10,000 hours of production time in 19x1. The following overhead amounts have been budgeted for 19x1.

Variable overhead.	$40,000
Fixed overhead	$90,000

REQUIRED:

1. Draw two graphs, one for variable overhead and one for fixed overhead. The variable on the horizontal axis of each graph should be production time, in hours, ranging from 5,000 to 15,000 hours. The variable on the vertical axis of each graph should be overhead cost (variable or fixed). Each graph should include two lines, one for the flexible-budget amount of overhead and one for applied overhead.
2. Write a brief memo to Countrytime Studio's general manager, explaining the graphs so that she will understand the concepts of budgeted and applied overhead.

Problem 10-33   Preparing and Using a Columnar Flexible Budget; Tour Company. Flaming Foilage Sky Tours is a small sightseeing tour company in New Hampshire. The firm specializes in aerial tours of the New England countryside during September and October, when the fall color is at its peak. The company's new controller, Jacqueline Frost, was given the following variance report for the month of September 19x1. The report was prepared by the president's secretary, who is not trained in accounting.

	Formula Flexible Budget (per air mile)	Actual (32,000 air miles)	Static Budget (35,000 air miles)	Variance
Passenger revenue	$3.50	$112,000	$122,500	$10,500 U
Less: Variable expenses:				
Fuel	.50	16,500	17,500	1,000 F
Aircraft maintenance.	.75	24,000	26,250	2,250 F
Flight crew salaries.	.40	13,100	14,000	900 F
Selling and administration	.80	24,900	28,000	3,100 F
Total variable expenses	2.45	78,500	85,750	7,250 F
Contribution margin.	$1.05	$ 33,500	36,750	3,250 U

	Per Month			
Less: Fixed expenses:				
Depreciation on aircraft	$ 3,000	3,000	3,000	0
Landing fees.	800	900	800	100 U
Supervisory salaries	9,000	8,600	9,000	400 F
Selling and administrative.	11,000	12,400	11,000	1,400 U
Total fixed expenses.	$23,800	24,900	23,800	1,100 U
Net income		$ 8,600	$ 12,950	$ 4,350 U

REQUIRED:

1. Prepare a columnar flexible budget for Flaming Foilage Sky Tours' expenses, based on the following activity levels: 32,000 air miles, 35,000 air miles, and 38,000 air miles.
2. In spite of several favorable expense variances shown on the report above, the company's September net income was only about two-thirds of the expected level. Why?
3. Write a brief memo to the company president explaining why the variance report shown above is misleading.
4. Prepare a revised expense variance report for September, which is based on the flexible budget prepared in requirement (1).

Problem 10-34 Straightforward Overhead Variances. Standard Paper Company packages paper for photocopiers. The company has developed standard overhead rates based on a monthly capacity of 180,000 direct-labor hours as follows:

Standard costs per unit (one box of paper):

Variable overhead (2 hours at $3). . . . . $ 6
Fixed overhead (2 hours at $5) 10
Total $16

During April, 90,000 units were scheduled for production; however, only 80,000 units were actually produced. The following data relate to April.

(1) Actual direct-labor cost incurred was $644,000 for 165,000 actual hours of work.
(2) Actual overhead incurred totaled $1,371,500, of which $511,500 was variable and $860,000 was fixed.

REQUIRED: Prepare two exhibits similar to Exhibit 10-6 and 10-8 in the chapter, which show the following variances. State whether each variance is favorable or unfavorable, where appropriate.

1. Variable-overhead spending variance.
2. Variable-overhead efficiency variance.
3. Fixed-overhead budget variance.
4. Fixed-overhead volume variance.

(CMA, adapted)

Problem 10-35 Complete Analysis of Cost Variances. Foodco Corporation produces containers for frozen food. Prepare as complete an analysis of cost variances as possible from the following information. Indicate whether each variance is favorable or unfavorable, where appropriate.

Standard Costs per Unit

Direct labor (5 hours at $18)	$ 90.00
Direct material (20 pounds at $2)	40.00
Variable overhead (5 hours at $1.50)	7.50
Fixed overhead (5 hours at $3)	15.00
Total	$152.50

Annual Budget Information

Variable overhead	$150,000
Fixed overhead	$300,000
Planned activity for year	100,000 direct-labor hours

The actual results of April's operations were as follows:

Variable overhead	$11,000
Fixed overhead	$26,000
Actual activity	8,000 direct-labor hours
Actual production	1,450 units
Actual labor cost	$151,200
Actual material cost (30,000 pounds purchased and used)	$66,000

Problem 10-36 Interactions between Variances; Robotics. Clarke Auto Parts Company manufactures replacement parts for automobile repair. The company recently installed a robotic manufacturing system, which has significantly changed the production process. The installation of the new industrial robots was not anticipated when the current year's budget and cost structure were developed. The installation of the new equipment was hastened by several major breakdowns in the company's old production machinery.

The new robotic equipment was very expensive, but management expects it to cut the labor time required by a substantial amount. Management also expects the new equipment to allow a reduction in direct-material waste. On the negative side, the robotic equipment requires a more highly skilled labor force to operate it than the company's old equipment.

The following cost variance report was prepared for the month of June, the first full month after the equipment was installed.

Clarke Auto Parts Company
Cost Variance Report
June, 19x7

Direct material:

Standard cost..	$501,750
Actual cost..	498,000
Direct-material price variance	150 U*
Direct-material quantity variance	3,900 F

Direct labor:

Standard cost..	$304,000
Actual cost..	294,800
Direct-labor rate variance......................................	4,800 U
Direct-labor efficiency variance	14,000 F

Manufacturing overhead:

Applied to work in process...................................	$400,000
Actual cost..	408,000
Variable-overhead spending variance	8,000 U
Variable-overhead efficiency variance	10,000 F
Fixed-overhead budget variance.............................	30,000 U
Fixed-overhead volume variance	(20,000)†

* F denotes favorable variance; U denotes unfavorable variance.

† The sign of the volume variance is negative, applied fixed overhead exceeded budgeted fixed overhead.

REQUIRED: Comment on the possible interactions between the variances listed in the report. Which ones are likely to have been caused by the purchase of the robotic production equipment? The company budgets and applies manufacturing overhead on the basis of direct-labor hours. (You may find it helpful to review the discussion of variance interactions in Chapter 9.)

Problem 10-37   Overhead Variances. East Coast Products developed its overhead application rate from the annual budget. The budget is based on an expected total output of 720,000 units requiring 3,600,000 machine hours. The company is able to schedule production uniformly throughout the year.

A total of 66,000 units requiring 315,000 machine hours were produced during May. Actual overhead costs for May amounted to $375,000. The actual costs, as compared to the annual budget and to one-twelfth of the annual budget, are shown at the top of page 436.

REQUIRED:

1. Prepare a schedule showing the following amounts for East Coast Products for May.
    a. Applied overhead costs.
    b. Variable-overhead spending variance.
    c. Fixed-overhead budget variance.
    d. Variable-overhead efficiency variance.
    e. Fixed-overhead volume variance.
    Where appropriate, be sure to indicate whether each variance is favorable or unfavorable.

Annual Budget

	Total Amount	Per Unit	Per Machine Hour	Monthly Budget	Actual Costs for May
Variable overhead:					
Indirect labor..............	$ 900,000	$1.25	$ .25	$ 75,000	$ 75,000
Supplies.................	1,224,000	1.70	.34	102,000	111,000
Fixed overhead:					
Supervision	648,000	.90	.18	54,000	51,000
Utilities	540,000	.75	.15	45,000	54,000
Depreciation	1,008,000	1.40	.28	84,000	84,000
Total.................	$4,320,000	$6.00	$1.20	$360,000	$375,000

2. Draw a graph similar to Exhibit 10-7 to depict the variable-overhead variances.
3. Why does your graph differ from Exhibit 10-7, other than the fact that the numbers differ?

(CMA, adapted)

Problem 10-38 Overhead Variances; Journal Entries. Kaston Company uses a standard-costing system. The firm estimates that it will operate its manufacturing facilities at 800,000 machine hours for the year. The estimate for total budgeted overhead is $2,000,000. The standard variable-overhead rate is estimated to be $2 per machine hour or $6 per unit. The actual data for the year are presented below.

Actual finished units	250,000
Actual machine hours	764,000
Actual variable overhead.......................................	$1,610,000
Actual fixed overhead	$392,000

REQUIRED:

1. Compute the following variances. Indicate whether each is favorable or unfavorable, where appropriate.
   a. Variable-overhead spending variance.
   b. Variable-overhead efficiency variance.
   c. Fixed-overhead budget variance.
   d. Fixed-overhead volume variance.
2. Prepare journal entries to add manufacturing overhead to Work-in-Process Inventory, and to record the actual overhead cost.

(CMA, adapted)

Problem 10-39 Uses of Standard Overhead Rates. Veggies, Inc. prepares, packages, and distributes six frozen vegetables in two different size containers. The different vegetables and different sizes are prepared in large batches. The company employs a job-order costing system. Manufacturing overhead is assigned to batches by a standard rate on the basis of direct-labor hours. The manufacturing-overhead costs incurred by the company during two recent quarters are as follows:

	1st Quarter	2nd Quarter
Direct-labor hours worked	2,760,000	2,160,000
Manufacturing-overhead costs:		
Indirect labor	$11,040,000	$ 8,640,000
Employee benefits	4,140,000	3,240,000
Supplies	2,760,000	2,160,000
Power	2,208,000	1,728,000
Heat and light..................................	552,000	552,000
Supervision....................................	2,865,000	2,625,000
Depreciation....................................	7,930,000	7,930,000
Property taxes and insurance.....................	3,005,000	3,005,000
Total overhead costs..........................	$34,500,000	$29,880,000

REQUIRED: Explain how the company can use the information it developed for calculating the overhead rate for the following purposes.

1. Cost control.
2. Development of budgets for planning process.

(CMA, adapted)

Problem 10-40 *Overhead Variances; Journal Entries; Closing Out Variance Accounts.* Davison Controls Company employs a standard-costing system for product costing. The standard cost of its product is as follows.

Direct material	$14.50
Direct labor .... 2 hours at $8	16.00
Manufacturing overhead...... 2 hours at $11	22.00
Total standard cost	$52.50

The manufacturing-overhead rate is based on a normal annual activity level of 600,000 machine hours. The company planned to produce 25,000 units each month during 19x3. The budgeted manufacturing overhead for 19x3 is as follows.

Variable	$3,600,000
Fixed..	3,000,000
Total..	$6,600,000

During November of 19x3, the company produced 26,000 units and used 53,500 machine hours. Actual manufacturing overhead for the month was $260,000 fixed and $315,000 variable. The total manufacturing overhead applied during November was $572,000.

REQUIRED:

1. Compute the following variances for November. Indicate whether each variance is favorable or unfavorable, where appropriate.
   a. Variable-overhead spending variance.
   b. Variable-overhead efficiency variance.
   c. Fixed-overhead budget variance.
   d. Fixed-overhead volume variance.

2. Prepare journal entries to add manufacturing overhead to Work-in-Process Inventory and record actual overhead costs.

(CMA, adapted)

Problem 10-41   Using a Flexible Budget. Crane and Sons, Inc. has an automated production process and production activity is quantified in terms of machine hours. A standard-costing system is used. The annual static budget for 19x2 called for 6,000 units to be produced, requiring 30,000 machine hours. The standard-overhead rate for the year was computed using this planned level of production.

Crane develops flexible budgets for different levels of activity for use in evaluating performance. A total of 6,200 units were produced during 19x2, requiring 32,000 machine hours. The schedule presented below compares the company's actual cost for the year with the static budget and the flexible budget for two different activity levels.

Crane and Sons, Inc.
Manufacturing Cost Report
For 19x2
(in thousands of dollars)

Cost Item	Static Budget 30,000 Machine Hours	Flexible Budget 31,000 Machine Hours	Flexible Budget 32,000 Machine Hours	Actual Cost
Direct material:				
G27 aluminum	$ 252.0	$ 260.4	$ 268.8	$ 270.0
M14 steel alloy..................	78.0	80.6	83.2	83.0
Direct labor:				
Assembler......................	273.0	282.1	291.2	287.0
Grinder........................	234.0	241.8	249.6	250.0
Manufacturing overhead:				
Maintenance	24.0	24.8	25.6	25.0
Supplies	129.0	133.3	137.6	130.0
Supervision....................	80.0	82.0	84.0	81.0
Inspection.....................	144.0	147.0	150.0	147.0
Insurance	50.0	50.0	50.0	50.0
Depreciation...................	200.0	200.0	200.0	200.0
Total cost	$1,464.0	$1,502.0	$1,540.0	$1,523.0

REQUIRED: Compute the following amounts. For variances, indicate whether favorable or unfavorable. Answers should be rounded to two decimal places when necessary.

1. The standard number of machine hours allowed to produce one unit of product.
2. The actual cost of direct material used in one unit of product.
3. The cost of material that should be processed per machine hour.

4. The standard direct-labor cost for each unit produced.
5. The variable-overhead rate per machine hour in a flexible-budget formula. (Hint: Use the high-low method to estimate cost behavior.)
6. The standard fixed-overhead rate per machine hour used for product costing.
7. The variable-overhead spending variance. (Assume management has determined that the actual fixed overhead cost in 19x2 amounted to $324,000.)
8. The variable-overhead efficiency variance.
9. The fixed-overhead budget variance.
10. The fixed-overhead volume variance. (Make the same assumption as in requirement 7.)
11. The total budgeted manufacturing cost (in thousands of dollars) for an output of 6,050 units. (Hint: Use the flexible-budget formula.)

(CMA, adapted)

Problem 10-42   *Finding Missing Data; Overhead Accounting.* For each of the following independent cases, fill in the missing information. The company budgets and applies manufacturing-overhead costs on the basis of direct-labor hours. (U denotes *unfavorable variance;* F denotes *favorable variance.*)

	Case A	Case B
1. Standard variable-overhead rate	$2.50 per hour	?
2. Standard fixed-overhead rate.	? per hour	?
3. Total standard overhead rate.	? per hour	$13.00
4. Flexible budget for variable overhead	$90,000	?
5. Flexible budget for fixed overhead	$210,000	?
6. Actual variable overhead	?	?
7. Actual fixed overhead	$207,000	?
8. Variable-overhead spending variance	$5,550 U	$2,000 U
9. Variable-overhead efficiency variance.	?	$400 F
10. Fixed-overhead budget variance	?	$1,080 U
11. Fixed-overhead volume variance.	?	$3,600 (positive sign)
12. Under- (or over-) applied variable overhead	?	?
13. Under- (or over-) applied fixed overhead . .	?	?
14. Budgeted production (in units)	5,000 units	?
15. Standard direct-labor hours per unit.	6 hours per unit	2 hours
16. Actual production (in units)	?	?
17. Standard direct-labor hours allowed, given actual production.	36,000 hours	1,600 hours
18. Actual direct-labor hours.	37,000 hours	1,500 hours
19. Applied variable overhead	?	?
20. Applied fixed overhead	?	?

Problem 10-43   *Comprehensive Problem on Overhead Accounting under Standard Costing.*
College Memories, Inc. publishes college yearbooks. A monthly flexible overhead budget for the firm follows.

College Memories, Inc.
Monthly Flexible Overhead Budget

Budgeted Cost	Direct-Labor Hours		
	1,500	**1,750**	**2,000**
Variable costs:			
Indirect material:			
Glue	$ 750	$ 875	$ 1,000
Tape	300	350	400
Miscellaneous supplies	3,000	3,500	4,000
Indirect labor......................................	7,500	8,750	10,000
Utilities:			
Electricity.....................................	1,500	1,750	2,000
Natural gas..................................	450	525	600
Total variable cost...............................	13,500	15,750	18,000
Fixed costs:			
Supervisory labor...............................	12,500	12,500	12,500
Depreciation	3,400	3,400	3,400
Property taxes and insurance	4,100	4,100	4,100
Total fixed cost	20,000	20,000	20,000
Total overhead cost..............................	$33,500	$35,750	$38,000

The planned monthly production is 6,400 yearbooks. The standard direct-labor allowance is .25 hours per book. During February of 19x0, College Memories, Inc. produced 8,000 yearbooks, and actually used 2,100 direct-labor hours. The actual overhead costs for the month were as follows:

Actual variable overhead $19,530
Actual fixed overhead.. 37,600

REQUIRED:

1. Determine the formula flexible overhead budget for College Memories, Inc.
2. Prepare a display similar to Exhibit 10-6, which shows College Memories' variable-overhead variances for February, 19x0. Indicate whether each variance is favorable or unfavorable.
3. Draw a graph similar to Exhibit 10-7, which shows College Memories' variable-overhead variances for February.
4. Explain how to interpret each of the variances computed in requirement (2).
5. Prepare a display similar to Exhibit 10-8, which shows College Memories' fixed-overhead variances for February, 19x0.
6. Draw a graph similar to Exhibit 10-9, which depicts the company's applied and budgeted fixed overhead for February. Show the firm's February volume variance on the graph.
7. Explain the interpretation of the variances computed in requirement (5).
8. Prepare journal entries to record each of the following:
   - Incurrence of February's actual overhead cost.
   - Application of February's overhead cost to Work-in-Process Inventory.
9. Draw T-accounts for all of the accounts used in the journal entries of requirement (8). Then post the journal entries to the T-accounts.

Problem 10-44   Sales Variances (Appendix). San Fernando Fashions sells a line of women's dresses. The company's performance report for November is as follows.

	Actual	Budget
Dresses sold	5,000	6,000
Sales	$235,000	$300,000
Variable costs	145,000	180,000
Contribution margin	$ 90,000	$120,000
Fixed costs	84,000	80,000
Operating income	$ 6,000	$ 40,000

The company uses a flexible budget to analyze its performance and to measure the effect on operating income of the various factors affecting the difference between budgeted and actual operating income.

REQUIRED: Compute the following variances for November, and indicate whether each is favorable or unfavorable.

1. Sales price variance.
2. Sales volume variance.

(CMA, adapted)

Problem 10-45   Sales Variances and Analysis (Appendix). Century Tool Company distributes two home-use power tools to hardware stores: a heavy-duty ½-inch hand drill and a table saw. The tools are purchased from a manufacturer that attaches the Century private label on the tools. The wholesale selling prices to the hardware stores are $60 each for the drill and $120 each for the table saw. The 19x2 budget and actual results are presented below. The budget was adopted in late 19x1 and was based on Century's estimated share of the market for the two tools.

Century Tool Company
Income Statement
For the Year Ended December 31, 19x2
(in thousands)

	Hand Drill		Table Saw		Total		
	Budget	Actual	Budget	Actual	Budget	Actual	Variance
Sales in units	120	86	80	74	200	160	40
Revenue	$7,200	$5,074	$9,600	$8,510	$16,800	$13,584	$(3,216)
Cost of goods sold	6,000	4,300	6,400	6,068	12,400	10,368	2,032
Gross margin	$1,200	$ 774	$3,200	$2,442	$ 4,400	$ 3,216	$(1,184)
Unallocated costs:							
Selling					$ 1,000	$ 1,000	$ —
Advertising					1,000	1,060	(60)
Administration					400	406	(6)
Income taxes (45%)					900	338	562
Total unallocated costs					$ 3,300	$ 2,804	$ 496
Net income					$ 1,100	$ 412	$ (688)

During the first quarter of 19x2, management estimated that the total market for these tools actually would be 10 percent below the original estimates. In an attempt to prevent unit sales from declining as much as industry projections, management implemented a marketing program. Included in the program were dealer discounts and increased direct advertising. The table-saw line was emphasized in this program.

REQUIRED:

1. Compute the sales-price and sales-volume variances for each product line. Indicate whether each variance is favorable or unfavorable.
2. Discuss the apparent effect of Century Tool Company's special marketing program (i.e., dealer discounts and additional advertising) on the 19x2 operating results.

(CMA, adapted)

Problem 10-46   Using Variances to Analyze Profit Performance (Appendix). Trask Enterprises sold 550,000 units during the quarter ended March 31, 19x1. These sales represented a 10 percent increase over the number of units budgeted for the quarter. In spite of the sales increase, profits were below the budget, as shown in the condensed income statement presented below.

Trask Enterprises
Income Statement
For the First Quarter Ended March 31, 19x1
(in thousands)

	Budget	Actual
Sales	$2,500	$2,530
Variable costs:		
Cost of goods sold	$1,475	$1,540
Selling	400	440
Total variable costs	$1,875	$1,980
Contribution margin	$ 625	$ 550
Fixed costs:		
Selling	$ 125	$ 150
Administration	275	$ 300
Total fixed costs	$ 400	$ 450
Income before taxes	$ 225	$ 100

The accounting department always prepares a brief analysis which explains the difference between budgeted income and actual income. This analysis, which has not yet been completed for the first quarter, is submitted to top management with the income statement. The analysis includes four variances: the sales-price and sales-volume variances, the fixed-overhead budget variance, and a variable-cost variance, which is defined as shown below.

$$\text{Variable-cost variance} = \left(\begin{array}{c}\text{actual unit} \\ \text{variable cost}\end{array} - \begin{array}{c}\text{budgeted unit} \\ \text{variable cost}\end{array}\right) \times \begin{array}{c}\text{actual sales} \\ \text{volume}\end{array}$$

REQUIRED: Prepare an explanation of the $125,000 unfavorable variance between the first-quarter budgeted and actual before-tax income for Trask Enterprises by calculating the var-

iances in the accounting report. The company includes fixed selling and administrative costs in its calculation of the fixed overhead budget variance.
(CMA, adapted)

Problem 10-47 Analyzing Sales Performance using Variances; Appendix. Budgeted and actual income statements for Arnesson Company for 19x5 are shown below.

Arnesson Company
Budget and Actual Income Statements
For the Year Ended December 31, 19x5
(in thousands)

	Budget			Actual		
	Xenox	Xeon	Total	Xenox	Xeon	Total
Unit sales	150	100	250	130	130	260
Net dollar sales.	$900	$1,000	$1,900	$780	$1,235	$2,015
Variable expenses.	450	750	1,200	390	975	1,365
Contribution margin	$450	$ 250	700	$390	$ 260	$ 650
Fixed expenses:						
Manufacturing			$ 200			$ 190
Marketing.			153			140
Administration.			95			90
Total fixed expenses			$ 448			$ 420
Income before taxes.			$ 252			$ 230

REQUIRED:

1. Compute the percentage difference between actual and budgeted break-even in units.
2. The 19x5 budgeted total volume of 250,000 units was based on the company's achieving a market share of 10 percent. Actual industry volume reached 2,580,000 units. Calculate the portion of Arnesson's increased volume due to improved market share.
3. Compute the variance of actual contribution margin from budgeted contribution margin attributable to the sales price. Indicate whether the variance is favorable or unfavorable. (Hint: Add the sales price variances computed for each product line.)
4. Compute the variance of actual contribution margin from budgeted contribution margin attributable to unit variable cost changes. Favorable or unfavorable?

(CMA, adapted)

CASE *Case 10-48   Review of Chapters 9 and 10.* Mein Company, a fuel pump manufacturer, is developing a budgeted income statement for the calendar year 19x2. The president is generally satisfied with the projected net income for 19x1. However, next year he would like earnings to increase. Mein Company employs a standard-costing system. Inflation necessitates an annual revision in the standards. The standard manufacturing cost for 19x1 is $72 per fuel pump.

Mein Company's management expects to sell 100,000 fuel pumps at $110 each in the current year (19x1). Forecasts from the Sales Department are favorable, and management is projecting an annual increase of 10 percent in unit sales in 19x2. This increase in sales is expected even through a $15 increase in the selling price will be implemented in 19x2. The selling-price increase was absolutely essential to compensate for the increased production costs and operating expenses. However, management is concerned that any additional sales-price increase would curtail the desired growth in sales volume.

Standard production costs are developed for the two primary metals used in the fuel pump (brass and steel alloy), direct labor, and manufacturing overhead. The following schedule represents the 19x2 standard quantities and rates for material and labor to produce one fuel pump.

Brass................	4 pounds at $5.35 per pound	$21.40
Steel alloy............	5 pounds at $3.16 per pound	15.80
Direct labor	4 hours at $7.00 per hour	28.00
Total prime costs.......	....	$65.20

The material content of a fuel pump has been reduced slightly, without a decrease in the quality of the finished product. Improved labor productivity and an increase in automation have resulted in a decrease in labor hours per unit from 4.4 to 4.0. However, significant increases in material prices and hourly labor rates more than offset any savings from reduced input quantities. The flexible overhead budget has not been completed yet. Preliminary estimates are as follows:

	Production Level (Units)		
Overhead Cost	**100,000**	**110,000**	**120,000**
Supplies	$ 475,000	$ 522,500	$ 570,000
Indirect labor	530,000	583,000	636,000
Utilities................................	170,000	187,000	204,000
Maintenance	363,000	377,500	392,000
Property taxes and insurance	87,000	87,000	87,000
Depreciation...........................	421,000	421,000	421,000
Total overhead.......................	$2,046,000	$2,178,000	$2,310,000

The standard overhead rate is based on direct-labor hours. The rate is developed by using the total overhead costs from the schedule above for the activity level closest to planned production. In developing the standards for manufacturing costs, the following two assumptions were made.

(1) Brass is currently selling at $5.65 per pound. However, this price is historically high, and the purchasing manager expects the price to drop to the predetermined standard in 19x2.

(2) Several new employees will be hired for the production line in 19x2. These employees will be generally unskilled. If basic training programs are not effective and improved labor productivity is not experienced, then the production time per unit of product will increase by 15 minutes over the 19x2 standards.

Mein Company's management accepts the cost standards developed by the production and accounting departments. However, the president is concerned about the possible effect of net income if the price of brass does not decrease, or the labor efficiency does not improve as expected. Therefore, he has asked that a special report be prepared that shows the anticipated variances for 19x2, using the standards as developed, but assuming the worst possible situation for material prices and labor efficiency.

REQUIRED: Compute the direct-material, direct-labor, and variable overhead variances, assuming the worst possible scenario for 19x2. Then write a brief memo to the company president commenting on the likelihood that Mein Company's profit will increase in 19x2. Assume no change in the finished-goods and raw-material inventories in 19x2. (Hint: Use the high-low method to estimate the variable overhead rate.)

(CMA, adapted)

Aloha
HOTELS AND RESORTS

Chapter 11

Responsibility Accounting, Cost Allocation, and Income Reporting

After completing this chapter, you should be able to:

- List several benefits and costs of decentralization.

- Explain the role of responsibility accounting in fostering goal congruence.

- Define and give an example of a cost center, a revenue center, a profit center, and an investment center.

- Prepare a performance report, and explain the relationships between the performance reports for various responsibility centers.

- Explain multistage cost allocation.

- List and explain five purposes of cost allocation.

- Use a cost allocation base to allocate costs.

- Prepare a segmented income statement.

- Prepare an income statement using either absorption or variable costing.

- Reconcile reported income under absorption and variable costing.

Most organizations are divided into smaller units, each of which is assigned particular responsibilities. These units are called by various names, including divisions, segments, business units, and departments. Each department is comprised of individuals who are responsible for particular tasks or managerial functions. The managers of an organization should ensure that the people in each department are striving toward the same overall goals. **Goal congruence** results when the managers of subunits throughout an organization strive to achieve the goals set by top management.

How can an organization's managerial-accounting system promote goal congruence? **Responsibility accounting** refers to the various concepts and tools used by managerial accountants to measure the performance of people and departments in order to foster goal congruence.

447

Benefits and Costs of Decentralization

Most large organizations are *decentralized*. **Decentralization** occurs when the managers of the organization's divisions and departments are given some autonomy in making decisions. To better understand the purpose of a responsibility-accounting system, it is helpful first to consider the benefits and costs associated with decentralization.

Benefits Decentralization has several positive effects:

1. Managers of the organization's subunits are specialists. They have *specialized information and skills* that enable them to manage their departments most effectively.
2. Allowing managers some autonomy in decision making provides *managerial training* for future higher-level managers. For example, the manager of a company-owned McDonald's restaurant might eventually be promoted to regional supervisor in the company.
3. Managers with some decision-making authority usually exhibit greater *motivation* than those who merely execute the decisions of others.
4. Delegating some decisions to lower-level managers provides time *relief to upper-level managers,* enabling them to devote time to strategic planning.
5. Delegating decision making to the lowest level possible enables an organization to give a *timely response* to opportunities and problems as they arise.

Costs There are also potential negative consequences from decentralization.

1. Managers in a decentralized organization sometimes have a *narrow focus* on their own units' performance, rather than the attainment of their organization's overall goals.
2. As a result of this narrow focus, managers may tend to *ignore the consequences of their actions on the organization's other subunits.*
3. In a decentralized organization, some tasks or *services may be duplicated* unnecessarily. For example, two departments in a decentralized university might each have their own mainframe computer, when one might serve both departments at a lower cost.

The fundamental purpose of a responsibility-accounting system is to help an organization reap the benefits of decentralization, while minimizing the costs. To this end, responsibility-accounting systems are designed to foster goal congruence throughout an organization.

Responsibility Centers

The basis of a responsibility-accounting system is the designation of each subunit in the organization as a particular type of *responsibility center*. A **responsibility center** is a subunit in an organization whose manager is held accountable for specified financial results of the subunit's activities. There are four common types of responsibility centers.

Cost Center A **cost center** is an organizational subunit, such as a department or division, whose manager is held accountable for the costs incurred in the subunit. The Painting Department in an automobile plant is an example of a cost center.

Revenue Center The manager of a **revenue center** is held accountable for the revenue attributed to the subunit. For example, the Reservations Department of an airline and the Sales Department of a manufacturer are revenue centers.

Profit Center A **profit center** is an organizational subunit whose manager is held accountable for profit. Since profit is equal to revenue minus expense, profit-center managers are held accountable for both the revenue and expenses attributed to their subunits. An example of a profit center is a company-owned restaurant in a fast-food chain.

Investment Center The manager of an **investment center** is held accountable for the subunit's profit *and the invested capital* used by the subunit to generate its profit. A division of a large corporation is typically designed as an investment center.[1]

ILLUSTRATION OF RESPONSIBILITY ACCOUNTING

To illustrate the concepts used in responsibility accounting, we will focus on a hotel chain. Aloha Hotels and Resorts operates 10 luxury resort hotels in the state of Hawaii. The company is divided into the Maui Division, which operates seven hotels on the island of Maui, and the Oahu Division, with three properties on the island of Oahu. Exhibit 11-1 shows the company's organization chart, and Exhibit 11-2 depicts the responsibility-accounting system.

Corporate Level The chief executive officer of Aloha Hotels and Resorts, Inc. is the company's president. The president, who is responsible to the company's stockholders, is accountable for corporate profit in relation to the capital (assets) invested in the company. Therefore, the entire company is an *investment center*. The president has the autonomy to make significant decisions that affect the company's profit and invested capital. For example, the final decision to add a new luxury tower to any of the company's resort properties would be made by the president.

Division Level The vice president of the Oahu Division is accountable for the profit earned by the three resort hotels on Oahu in relation to the capital invested in those properties. Hence, the Oahu Division is also an *investment center*. The vice president has the authority to make major investment decisions regarding the properties on Oahu, up to a limit of $300,000. For example, the vice president could decide to install a new swimming pool at one of the Oahu resort hotels, but could not decide to add a new wing.

Hotel Level The Waikiki Sands Hotel, in Honolulu, is one of the properties in the Oahu Division. The general manager of the Waikiki Sands Hotel is accountable for the profit earned by the hotel. The general manager does not have the authority to make major investment decisions, but is responsible for operational decisions. For example, the general manager hires all of the hotel's departmental managers, sets wage rates, determines procedures and standards for operations, approves decorating decisions, and generally oversees the hotel's operation. Since the hotel's general manager has no authority to make major investment decisions, she is held accountable only for the hotel's profit, not the capital invested in the property. Thus, the Waikiki Sands Hotel is a *profit center*.

---

[1] Although there is an important conceptual difference between profit centers and investment centers, the latter term is not always used in practice. Some managers use the term "profit center" to refer to both types of responsibility centers. Hence, when business people use the term "profit center," they may be referring to a true profit center (as defined in this chapter) or to an investment center.

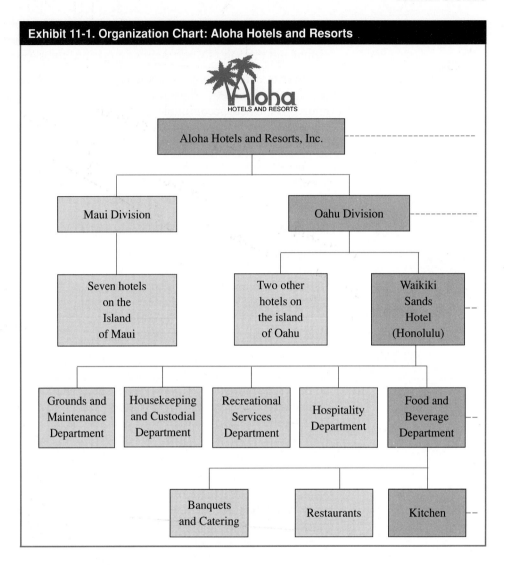

Exhibit 11-1. Organization Chart: Aloha Hotels and Resorts

Departmental Level The Waikiki Sands Hotel has five departments, as shown in Exhibit 11-1. The Grounds and Maintenance Department includes landscaping, building and equipment maintenance, and hotel security. The Housekeeping and Custodial Services Department covers laundry and janitorial services. These two departments are called service departments, since they provide services to the hotel's other departments but do not deal directly with hotel guests. The Recreational Services Department operates the hotel's swimming pools, saunas, video arcade, and tennis courts. The Hospitality Department includes the hotel's reservations desk, rooms, bell staff, and shopping facilities. Finally, the Food and Beverage Department operates the resort's restaurants, coffee shop, lounges, poolside snack bar, banquet operations, and catering service.

The director of the Food and Beverage Department is accountable for the profit earned on all food and beverage operations. Therefore, this department is a *profit center*. The director has the authority to approve the menu, set food and beverage prices, hire the wait staff, schedule entertainers, and generally oversee all food and beverage operations.

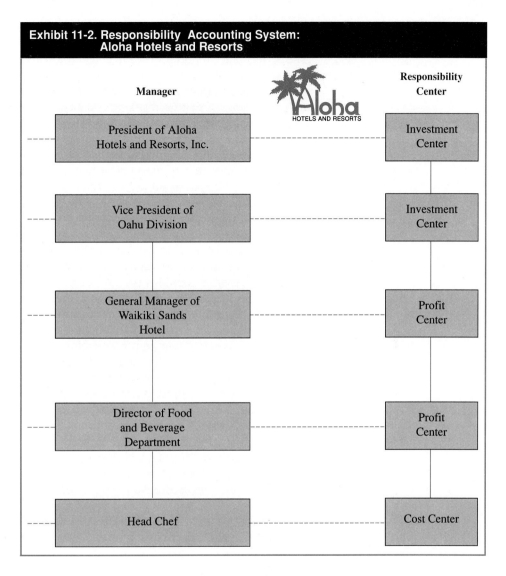

Exhibit 11-2. Responsibility Accounting System: Aloha Hotels and Resorts

Kitchen Level   The Food and Beverage Department is further divided into sub-units responsible for Banquets and Catering, Restaurants, and the Kitchen.

The head chef manages the kitchen and is accountable for the costs incurred there. Thus, the Kitchen is a *cost center.* The head chef hires the kitchen staff, orders food supplies, and oversees all food preparation. The head chef is responsible for providing high-quality food at the lowest possible cost.

PERFORMANCE REPORTS

The performance of each responsibility center is summarized periodically on a *performance report.* A **performance report** shows the budgeted and actual amounts of key financial results appropriate for the type of responsibility center involved. For example, a cost center's performance report concentrates on budgeted and actual amounts for various cost items attributable to the cost center. Performance reports also typically show the variance between budgeted and actual amounts for the financial results conveyed in the report. The data in a performance report help managers use *management by exception* to control an organization's operations effectively.

The performance report for the kitchen of the Waikiki Sands Hotel for February is shown in Exhibit 11-3.

As the organization chart in Exhibit 11-1 shows, Aloha Hotels and Resorts is a *hierarchy.* This means that each subunit manager reports to one higher-level manager, from the head chef all the way up to the president and chief executive officer. In such an organization, there is also a hierarchy of performance reports, since the performance of each subunit constitutes part of the performance of the next higher-level subunit. For example, the cost performance in the kitchen of the Waikiki Sands Hotel constitutes part of the profit performance of the hotel's Food and Beverage Department.

Exhibit 11-4 shows the relationships between the February performance reports for several subunits of Aloha Hotels and Resorts. Notice that the numbers for the Grounds and Maintenance Department and the Kitchen are shown in parentheses. These two subunits are cost centers, so the numbers shown are expenses. All of the other subunits shown in Exhibit 11-4 are either profit centers or investment centers. The numbers shown for these subunits are profits, so they are not enclosed in parentheses. In addition to the profit figures shown, the performance reports for the investment centers should include data about invested capital. The Maui Division, the Oahu Division, and the company as a whole are investment centers. Performance evaluation in investment centers is covered more thoroughly in the next chapter.

Notice the relationships between the performance reports in Exhibit 11-4. The kitchen is the lowest-level subunit shown, and its performance report is the same as that displayed in Exhibit 11-3. The *total expense* line from the kitchen performance report is included as one line in the performance report for the Food and Beverage Department. Also included are the total profit figures for the department's other two subunits: Banquets and Catering, and Restaurants. How is the *total profit* line for the Food and Beverage Department used in the performance report for the Waikiki Sands Hotel? Follow the relationships in Exhibit 11-4, which are emphasized with arrows.

The hierarchy of performance reports starts at the bottom and builds toward the top, just as the organization structure depicted in Exhibit 11-1 builds from the

---

Exhibit 11-3. Performance Report for February: Kitchen, Waikiki Sands Hotel

	Flexible Budget		Actual Results		Variance*	
	February	Year to Date	February	Year to Date	February	Year to Date
Kitchen staff wages	$ 80,000	$ 168,000	$ 78,000	$ 169,000	$2,000 F	$1,000 U
Food	675,000	1,420,000	678,000	1,421,000	3,000 U	1,000 U
Paper products	120,000	250,000	115,000	248,000	5,000 F	2,000 F
Variable overhead	70,000	150,000	71,000	154,000	1,000 U	4,000 U
Fixed overhead	85,000	180,000	83,000	181,000	2,000 F	1,000 U
Total expense	$1,030,000	$2,168,000	$1,025,000	$2,173,000	$5,000 F	$5,000 U

*F denotes favorable variance; U denotes unfavorable variance.

	Flexible Budget*		Actual Results*		Variance†	
Aloha HOTELS AND RESORTS	**February**	**Year to Date**	**February**	**Year to Date**	**February**	**Year to Date**
Company	$30,660	$64,567	$30,716	$64,570	$56 F	$ 3 F
Maui Division	$18,400	$38,620	$18,470	$38,630	$70 F	$10 F
Oahu Division	12,260	25,947	12,246	25,940	14 U	7 U
Total profit	$30,660	$64,567	$30,716	$64,570	$56 F	$ 3 F
Oahu Division						
Waimea Beach Resort	$ 6,050	$12,700	$ 6,060	$12,740	$10 F	$40 F
Diamond Head Lodge	2,100	4,500	2,050	4,430	50 U	70 U
Waikiki Sands Hotel	4,110	8,747	4,136	8,770	26 F	23 F
Total profit	$12,260	$25,947	$12,246	$25,940	$14 U	$ 7 U
Waikiki Sands Hotel						
Grounds & Maintenance	$ (45)	$ (90)	$ (44)	$ (90)	$ 1 F	—
Housekeeping & Custodial . . .	(40)	(90)	(41)	(90)	1 U	—
Recreational Services	40	85	41	88	$ 1 F	$ 3 F
Hospitality	2,800	6,000	2,840	6,030	40 F	30 F
Food and Beverage	1,355	2,842	1,340	2,832	15 U	10 U
Total profit	$ 4,110	$ 8,747	$ 4,136	$ 8,770	$26 F	$23 F
Food and Beverage Department						
Banquets & Catering	$ 600	$ 1,260	$ 605	$ 1,265	$ 5 F	$ 5 F
Restaurants	1,785	3,750	1,760	3,740	25 U	10 U
Kitchen	(1,030)	(2,168)	(1,025)	(2,173)	5 F	5 U
Total profit	$ 1,355	$ 2,842	$ 1,340	$ 2,832	$15 U	$10 U
Kitchen						
Kitchen staff wages	$ (80)	$ (168)	$ (78)	$ (169)	$ 2 F	$ 1 U
Food	(675)	(1,420)	(678)	(1,421)	3 U	1 U
Paper products	(120)	(250)	(115)	(248)	5 F	2 F
Variable overhead	(70)	(150)	(71)	(154)	1 U	4 U
Fixed overhead	(85)	(180)	(83)	(181)	2 F	1 U
Total expense	$(1,030)	$(2,168)	$(1,025)	$(2,173)	$ 5 F	$ 5 U

Handwritten annotations in margins: "Cost" next to Grounds & Maintenance and Housekeeping & Custodial; "Rev." next to Recreational Services and Hospitality; "Rev." next to Banquets & Catering and Restaurants; "Cost" next to Kitchen; "Costs" next to Kitchen staff wages/Food.

* Numbers without parentheses denote profit; numbers with parentheses denote expenses; numbers in thousands.
† F denotes favorable variance; U denotes unfavorable variance.

bottom upward. Each manager in the organization receives the performance report for his or her own subunit in addition to the performance reports for the major subunits in the next lower level. For example, the general manager of the Waikiki Sands Hotel receives the reports for the hotel, and each of its departments: Grounds and Maintenance, Recreational Services, Hospitality, and Food and Beverage. With these reports, the hotel's general manager can evaluate her subordinates as well as her own performance. This will help the general manager in improving the hotel's performance, motivating employees, and planning future operations.

Budgets, Variance Analysis, and Responsibility Accounting

Notice that the performance reports in Exhibit 11-4 make heavy use of budgets and variance analysis. Thus, the topics of budgeting, variance analysis, and responsibility accounting are closely interrelated. The flexible budget provides the benchmark against which actual revenues, expenses, and profits are compared. As you saw in Chapter 10, it is important to use a flexible budget so that appropriate comparisons can be made. It would make no sense, for example, to compare the actual costs incurred in the kitchen at Waikiki Sands Hotel with budgeted costs established for a different level of hotel occupancy.

The performance reports in Exhibit 11-4 also show variances between budgeted and actual performance. These variances often are broken down into smaller components to help management pinpoint responsibility and diagnose performance. Variance analysis, which was discussed in detail in Chapters 9 and 10, is an important tool in a responsibility-accounting system.

BEHAVIORAL EFFECTS OF RESPONSIBILITY ACCOUNTING

Responsibility-accounting systems can influence behavior significantly. Whether the behavioral effects are positive or negative, however, depends on how responsibility accounting is implemented.

Information versus Blame

The proper focus of a responsibility-accounting system is *information*. The system should identify the individual in the organization who is in the best position to explain each particular event or financial result. The emphasis should be on providing that individual and higher-level managers with information to help them understand the reasons behind the organization's performance. When properly used, a responsibility-accounting system *does not emphasize blame*. If managers feel they are beaten over the head with criticism and rebukes when unfavorable variances occur, they are unlikely to respond in a positive way. Instead, they will tend to undermine the system and view it with skepticism. But when the responsibility-accounting system emphasizes its informational role, managers tend to react constructively, and strive for improved performance.

Controllability

Some organizations use performance reports that distinguish between controllable and uncontrollable costs or revenues. For example, the head chef at the Waikiki Sands Hotel can influence the hours and efficiency of the kitchen staff, but he probably cannot change the wage rates. A performance report that distinguishes between the financial results influenced by the head chef and those he does not influence has the advantage of providing complete information to the head chef. Yet the report recognizes that certain results are beyond his control.

Identifying costs as controllable or uncontrollable is not always easy. Many cost items are influenced by more than one person. The time frame also may be important in determining controllability. Some costs are controllable over a long time frame, but not within a short time period. To illustrate, suppose the Waikiki Sands' head chef has signed a one-year contract with a local seafood supplier. The cost of seafood can be influenced by the head chef if the time period is a year or more, but the cost cannot be controlled on a weekly basis.

Motivating Desired Behavior

Managerial accountants often use the responsibility-accounting system to motivate actions considered desirable by upper-level management. Sometimes the responsibility-accounting system can solve behavioral problems as well. The following real-world illustration, originally described by Raymond Villers, provides a case in point.[2]

ILLUSTRATION FROM MANAGEMENT-ACCOUNTING PRACTICE

Rush Orders

The production scheduler in a manufacturing firm was frequently asked to interrupt production of one product with a rush order for another product. Rush orders typically resulted in greater costs, because more production setups were required. Since the production scheduler was evaluated on the basis of costs, he was reluctant to accept rush orders. The sales manager, on the other hand, was evaluated on the basis of sales revenue. By agreeing to customers' demands for rush orders, the sales manager satisfied his customers. This resulted in more future sales and favorable performance ratings for the sales manager.

As the rush orders became more and more frequent, the production manager began to object. The sales manager responded by asking if the production scheduler wanted to take the responsibility for losing a customer by refusing a rush order. The production scheduler did not want to be blamed for lost sales, so he grudgingly accepted the rush orders. However, considerable ill will developed between the sales manager and production scheduler.

The company's managerial accountants came to the rescue by redesigning the responsibility-accounting system. The system was modified to accumulate the extra costs associated with rush orders and charge them to the sales manager's responsibility center, rather than the production scheduler's center. The ultimate result was that the sales manager chose more carefully which rush-order requests to make, and the production manager accepted them gracefully.

To accept or reject a rush order is a cost-benefit decision:

Cost of Accepting Rush Order	Benefits of Accepting Rush Order
Disrupted production	Satisfied customers
More setups	Greater future sales
Higher costs	

[2] R. Villers, "Control and Freedom in a Decentralized Company," *Harvard Business Review, 32,* pp. 826–896.

The problem described above developed because two different managers were considering the costs and benefits of the rush-order decision. The production manager was looking only at the costs, while the sales manager was looking only at the benefits. The modified responsibility-accounting system made the sales manager look at *both the costs and the benefits* associated with each rush order. Then the sales manager could make the necessary trade-off between costs and benefits in considering each rush order. Some rush orders were rejected, because the sales manager decided the costs exceeded the benefits. Other rush orders were accepted, when the importance of the customer and potential future sales justified it.

This example illustrates how a well-designed responsibility-accounting system can make an organization run more smoothly and achieve higher performance.

COST ALLOCATION

Many costs incurred by an organization are the joint result of several subunits' activities. For example, the property taxes and utility costs incurred by Aloha Hotels and Resorts for the Waikiki Sands Hotel are the joint result of all of the hotel's activities. One function of a responsibility-accounting system is to assign all of an organization's costs to the subunits that cause them to be incurred.

Definition of Cost Allocation

A collection of costs to be assigned is called a **cost pool.** At the Waikiki Sands Hotel, for example, all utility costs are combined into a *utility cost pool,* which includes the costs of electricity, water, sewer, trash collection, television cable, and telephone. The responsibility centers, products, or services to which costs are to be assigned are called **cost objectives.** The Waikiki Sands' cost objectives are its major departments. (See the organization chart in Exhibit 11-1.)

The process of assigning the costs in the *cost pool* to the *cost objectives* is called **cost allocation** or **cost distribution.** Exhibit 11-5 portrays this process.

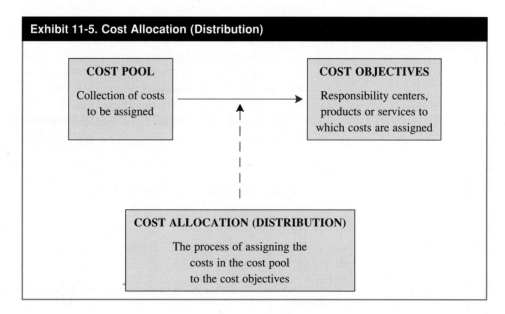

Exhibit 11-5. Cost Allocation (Distribution)

COST POOL

Collection of costs
to be assigned

COST OBJECTIVES

Responsibility centers,
products or services to
which costs are assigned

COST ALLOCATION (DISTRIBUTION)

The process of assigning the
costs in the cost pool
to the cost objectives

Multistage Cost Allocation

The distribution of costs across responsibility centers is the first of three stages in multistage cost allocation. These stages, discussed briefly in Chapter 3 for a manufacturing company, are summarized in Exhibit 11-6 for the Waikiki Sands Hotel. In the first stage, called *cost distribution,* all of the hotel's costs are traced or allocated to the hotel's five departments. In the second stage, *service department cost allocation,* the costs assigned to the hotel's two service departments are allocated to the three "production" departments, which provide services directly to hotel guests. In the third stage, called *cost application,* costs are assigned to specific guest services provided by the hotel, such as lodging and meals.

In this chapter we will discuss how costs are distributed to responsibility centers. The allocation of service department costs is covered later in the text.

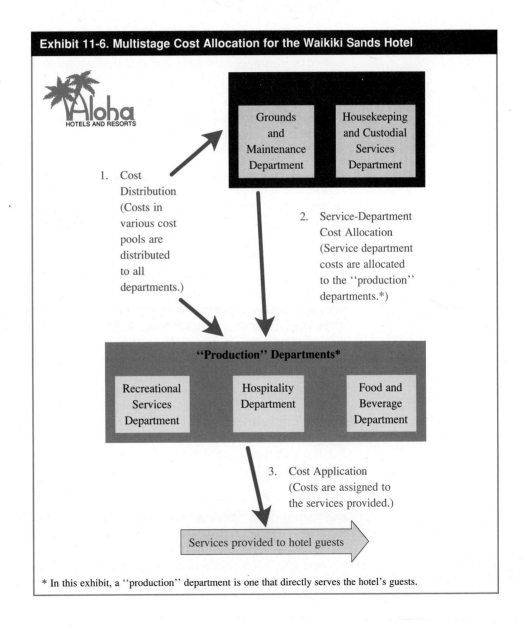

Exhibit 11-6. Multistage Cost Allocation for the Waikiki Sands Hotel

1. Cost Distribution (Costs in various cost pools are distributed to all departments.)

Grounds and Maintenance Department

Housekeeping and Custodial Services Department

2. Service-Department Cost Allocation (Service department costs are allocated to the "production" departments.*)

"Production" Departments*

Recreational Services Department

Hospitality Department

Food and Beverage Department

3. Cost Application (Costs are assigned to the services provided.)

Services provided to hotel guests

* In this exhibit, a "production" department is one that directly serves the hotel's guests.

Purposes of Cost Allocation

Managerial accountants allocate costs for five primary reasons.

1. **Predicting Economic Effects of Decisions** Allocating costs to responsibility centers can help the managers of those subunits predict the effects of their actions on the organization's costs. For example, allocating some of the hotel's electricity costs to the Recreational Services Department will help that department's manager predict the likely effect of raising the temperature in the heated swimming pools.

2. **Pricing and Bidding** Prices of products and services are often based, at least to some extent, on their costs. To determine the full cost of producing products or services, costs must be allocated. For example, part of the cost of providing lodging services at the Waikiki Sands Hotel is the cost of hotel security, which is provided by the Grounds and Maintenance Department.

3. **Cost Reimbursement** Some organizations seek reimbursement for the costs of providing services. Examples include health-care facilities, which often are reimbursed by insurance companies or the federal government, and public utilities, which must justify rates on the basis of costs incurred.

4. **Motivation** Some organizations allocate costs to encourage desired behavior. For example, some manufacturers allocate part of their interest costs to inventories of raw materials and finished goods to encourage managers to minimize inventory levels.

5. **Asset Valuation and Income Determination** In manufacturing and retail firms, costs of producing or purchasing products become product costs. These costs are recorded in Finished-Goods Inventory until the goods are sold. Then the costs flow into Cost of Goods Sold, an expense recognized during the period of sale.

Cost Allocation Bases

To distribute (or allocate) costs to responsibility centers, the managerial accountant chooses an *allocation base* for each cost pool. An **allocation base** is a measure of activity, physical characteristic, or economic characteristic that is associated with the responsibility centers, which are the cost objectives in the allocation process. The allocation base chosen for a cost pool should reflect some characteristic of the various responsibility centers that is related to the incurrence of costs. An allocation base also may be referred to as a *cost driver.*

An illustration of cost allocation bases is given in Exhibit 11-7 for the Waikiki Sands Hotel. The administrative cost pool is distributed (allocated) on the basis of the number of employees in the hotel's five major departments. The general manager's time, for example, tends to be spent on the departments in proportion to their size. For this purpose, departmental size is best measured by the number of employees. Other cost pools are distributed using the most appropriate allocation base. The utility cost pool, for example, is distributed based on cubic footage of space in the five departments. Cubic footage is used because utility costs are dominated by cooling and heating costs, which are associated more closely with the volume of space than the area of space.

Exhibit 11-8 shows the Waikiki Sands Hotel's February cost distribution for selected cost pools. Each cost pool is distributed to each responsibility center in proportion to that center's relative amount of the allocation base. For example, the Food and Beverage Department receives 30 percent of the total administrative costs,

---

Exhibit 11-7. Cost Allocation Bases: Waikiki Sands Hotel

Cost Pool		Cost Allocation Base

Administration:
  Salary of general manager
  Personnel
  General office staff
	Aloha
	HOTELS AND RESORTS
		Budgeted number of employees
		  in responsibility center

Accounting:
  Billing
  Accounts payable
  General accounting
		Budgeted sales dollars
		  generated in responsibility
		  center

Facilities:
  Building depreciation
  Property taxes
		Square feet of space
		  occupied by responsibility
		  center

Marketing:
  Media advertising
  Travel agency commissions
  Promotional programs (e.g.,
  special discounts on
  room rates)
		Budgeted sales dollars
		  generated in responsibility
		  center

Utilities:
  Electricity, trash
  collection, water
  and sewer
		Cubic feet of space in
		  responsibility center

$25,000, because that department's 36 employees constitute 30 percent of the hotel's employees. Notice that no marketing costs are allocated to either the Grounds and Maintenance Department or the Housekeeping and Custodial Department. Neither of these responsibility centers generates any sales revenue.

Allocation Bases Based on Budgets Notice in Exhibit 11-7 that administrative, accounting, and marketing costs are distributed on the basis of *budgeted* amounts of the relevant allocation bases, rather than *actual* amounts. The managerial accountant should design an allocation procedure so that the behavior of one responsibility center does not affect the costs allocated to other responsibility centers.

Suppose, for example, that the budgeted and actual February sales revenue in the hotel were as shown in Exhibit 11-9. Notice that the Hospitality Department's actual sales revenue is close to the budget. However, the actual sales of the Recreational Services Department and Food and Beverage Department are substantially below the budget. If the distribution of marketing costs is based on actual sales, instead of budgeted sales, then the cost distributed to the Hospitality Department jumps from $40,000 to $45,000, an increase of 12.5 percent. Why does this happen? As a result of a sales performance substantially below the budget for the *other two departments,* the Hospitality Department is penalized with a hefty increase in its cost distribution. This

Exhibit 11-8. Cost Distribution to Responsibility Centers: Waikiki Sands Hotel

Cost Pool	Responsibility Center	Allocation Base	Percentage of Total	Costs Distributed
Administration	Grounds and Maintenance	12 employees	10%	$ 2,500
	Housekeeping and Custodial	24 employees	20%	5,000
	Recreational Services	12 employees	10%	2,500
	Hospitality	36 employees	30%	7,500
	Food and Beverage	36 employees	30%	7,500
	Total	120 employees	100%	$25,000
Facilities	Grounds and Maintenance	2,000 sq. ft.	1.0%	$ 300
	Housekeeping and Custodial	2,000 sq. ft.	1.0%	300
	Recreational Services	5,000 sq. ft.	2.5%	750
	Hospitality	175,000 sq. ft.	87.5%	26,250
	Food and Beverage	16,000 sq. ft.	8.0%	2,400
	Total	200,000 sq. ft.	100.0%	$30,000
Marketing	Grounds and Maintenance	—	—	—
	Housekeeping and Custodial	—	—	—
	Recreational Services	$ 20,000 of sales	4%	$ 2,000
	Hospitality	400,000 of sales	80%	40,000
	Food and Beverage	80,000 of sales	16%	8,000
	Total	$500,000	100%	$50,000

is misleading and unfair to the Hospitality Department manager. A preferable cost distribution procedure is to use budgeted sales revenue as the allocation base, rather than actual sales revenue. Then the marketing costs distributed to each department do not depend on the performance in the other two departments.

Many organizations allocate the costs of centrally produced services on the basis of the amount of service provided, as the following example shows.

Exhibit 11-9. Cost Distribution: Budgeted versus Actual Allocation Bases

Responsibility Center	Budgeted Sales Revenue	Actual Sales Revenue	Marketing Cost Distribution Based on Budget	Based on Actual
Recreational Services	$ 20,000 (4%)*	$ 4,500 (1%)*	$ 2,000	$ 500
Hospitality	400,000 (80%)	405,000 (90%)	40,000	45,000
Food and Beverage	80,000 (16%)	40,500 (9%)	8,000	4,500
Total	$500,000	$450,000	$50,000	$50,000

*Percentage of column total

ILLUSTRATION FROM MANAGEMENT-ACCOUNTING PRACTICE

Cost Allocation Bases at J. C. Penney Co.

Business Week reported that J. C. Penney Co. changed its cost allocation base for the corporate costs of auditing, legal, and personnel services. The new allocation base used to distribute these costs to the company's subsidiaries was the time spent providing these internally produced services to the subsidiaries. Formerly, J. C. Penney Co. based such allocations on the revenue earned by subsidiaries.[3]

SEGMENTED REPORTING

Subunits of an organization are often called *segments*. *Segmented reporting* refers to the preparation of accounting reports by segment and for the organization as a whole. Many organizations prepare **segmented income statements,** which show the income for major segments and for the entire enterprise.

In preparing segmented income statements, the managerial accountant must decide how to treat costs that are incurred to benefit more than one segment. Such costs are called **common costs.** The salary of the president of Aloha Hotels and Resorts is a common cost. The president manages the entire company. Some of her time is spent on matters related specifically to the Maui Division or the Oahu Division, but much of it is spent on tasks that are not traced easily to either division. The president works with the company's board of directors, develops strategic plans for the company, and helps set policy and goals for the entire enterprise. Thus, the president's compensation is a common cost, which is not related easily to any segment's activities.

Many managerial accountants believe that it is misleading to allocate common costs to an organization's segments. Since these costs are not traceable to the activities of segments, they can be allocated to segments only on the basis of some highly arbitrary allocation base. Consider the salary of Aloha Hotels and Resorts' president. What allocation base would you choose to reflect the contribution of the president's managerial efforts to the company's two divisions? The possible allocation bases include budgeted divisional sales revenue, the number of hotels or employees in each division, or some measure of divisional size, such as total assets. However, all of these allocation bases would yield arbitrary cost allocations and possibly misleading segment profit information. For this reason, many organizations choose not to allocate common costs on segmented income statements.

Exhibit 11-10 shows February's segmented income statement for Aloha Hotels and Resorts. Each segment's income statement is presented in the *contribution format* discussed in Chapter 7. Notice that Exhibit 11-10 shows income statements for the following segments.

Aloha Hotels and Resorts ⎰ Maui Division

Oahu Division ⎰ Waimea Beach Resort / Diamond Head Lodge / Waikiki Sands Hotel

Three numbers in Exhibit 11-10 require special emphasis. First, the $10,000,000 of common fixed costs in the left-hand column is not allocated to the company's two

---

[3] "Teamwork Pays Off at Penney's," *Business Week,* April 12, 1982.

Exhibit 11-10. Segmented Income Statements: Aloha Hotels and Resorts (in thousands)

| | Aloha Hotels and Resorts | Segments of Company | | Segments of Oahu Division | | | |
		Maui Division	Oahu Division	Waimea Beach Resort	Diamond Head Lodge	Waikiki Sands Hotel	Not allocated
Sales revenue	$2,500,000	$1,600,000	$900,000	$450,000	$150,000	$300,000	—
Variable operating expenses:							
Personnel	820,900	510,400	310,500	155,500	50,000	105,000	—
Food, beverages, and supplies.	738,000	458,600	279,400	139,700	46,400	93,300	—
Other	83,000	58,000	25,000	12,500	4,000	8,500	—
Total	1,641,900	1,027,000	614,900	307,700	100,400	206,800	—
Contribution margin	858,100	573,000	285,100	142,300	49,600	93,200	—
Less: Controllable fixed expenses	30,000	21,000	9,000	4,000	1,000	3,000	$ 1,000
Controllable segment margin	828,100	552,000	276,100	138,300	48,600	90,200	(1,000)
Less: Fixed expenses controllable by others	750,000	500,000	250,000	26,000	8,000	16,000	200,000
Segment margin	78,100	$ 52,000	$ 26,100	$112,300	$ 40,600	$74,200	$(201,000)
Less: Common fixed costs . .	10,000						
Income before taxes	68,100						
Less: Income tax expense . .	37,440						
Net income	$ 30,660						

divisions. Included in this figure are such costs as the company president's salary. These costs cannot be allocated to the divisions, except in some arbitrary manner.

Second, $1,000,000 of controllable fixed expense in the right-hand column constitutes part of the Oahu Division's $9,000,000 of controllable fixed expense. All $9,000,000 of expense is controllable by the vice president of the Oahu Division. However, $1,000,000 of these expenses cannot be traced to the division's three hotels, except on an arbitrary basis. For example, this $1,000,000 of expense includes the salary of the Oahu Division's vice president. Therefore, the $1,000,000 of expense is *not allocated* among the division's three hotels. This procedure illustrates an important point. Costs that are traceable to segments at one level in an organization may become common costs at a lower level in the organization. The vice president's salary is traceable to the Oahu Division, but it cannot be allocated among the division's three hotels except arbitrarily. Thus, the vice president's salary is a traceable cost at the divisional level, but it becomes a common cost at the hotel level.

Third, the $200,000,000 of fixed expenses controllable by others in the right-hand column constitutes part of the Oahu Division's $250,000,000 of fixed expenses controllable by others. However, the $200,000,000 portion cannot be allocated among the division's three hotels, except arbitrarily.

Segments versus Segment Managers

One advantage of segmented reports like the one in Exibit 11-10 is that they make a distinction between segments and segment managers. Some costs that are traceable to a segment may be completely beyond the influence of the segment manager. Property taxes on the Waikiki Sands Hotel, for example, are traceable to the hotel, but the hotel's general manager cannot influence them. To properly evaluate the *Waikiki Sands Hotel as an investment* of the company's resources, the property taxes should be included in the hotel's costs. However, in evaluating the general manager's performance, the property-tax cost should be *excluded,* since the manager has no control over it.

Key Features of Segmented Reporting

To summarize, Exhibit 11-10 illustrates three important characteristics of segmented reporting:

1. *Contribution format* These income statements use the contribution format. The statements subtract variable expenses from sales revenue to obtain the *contribution margin.*
2. *Controllable versus uncontrollable expenses* The income statements in Exhibit 11-10 highlight the costs that can be controlled, or heavily influenced, by each segment manager. This approach is consistent with *responsibility accounting.*

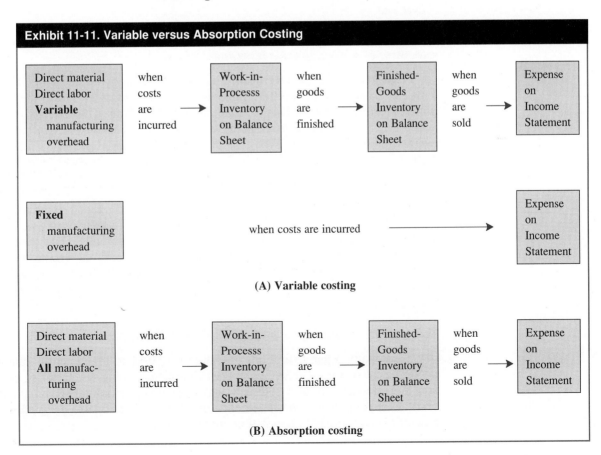

Exhibit 11-11. Variable versus Absorption Costing

(A) Variable costing

(B) Absorption costing

3. *Segmented income statement* *Segmented reporting* shows income statements for the company as a whole and for its major segments.

VARIABLE AND ABSORPTION COSTING

Income is one of many important measures used to evaluate the performance of both segments and entire companies. There are two alternative methods for reporting income in a manufacturing firm, depending on the accounting treatment of fixed-manufacturing overhead. In this section, we will examine these two income-reporting alternatives, called *absorption costing* and *variable costing*.

Product Costs In the product-costing systems we have studied so far, manufacturing overhead is applied to Work-in-Process Inventory as a product cost along with direct material and direct labor. When the manufactured goods are finished, these product costs flow from Work-in-Process Inventory into Finished-Goods Inventory. Finally, during the accounting period when the goods are sold, the product costs flow from Finished-Goods Inventory into Cost of Goods Sold, an expense account. The following diagram summarizes this flow of costs.

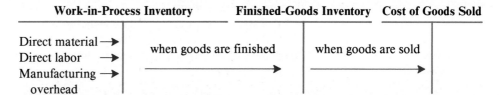

Since the costs of production are stored in inventory accounts until the goods are sold, these costs are said to be *inventoried costs*.

Fixed-Manufacturing Overhead: The Key In our study of product-costing systems, we have included both variable and fixed manufacturing overhead in the product costs that flow through the manufacturing accounts. This approach to product costing is called **absorption costing** (or **full costing**), because *all* manufacturing-overhead costs are applied to (or absorbed by) manufactured goods. An alternative approach to product costing is called **variable costing** (or **direct costing**), in which *only variable* manufacturing overhead is applied to Work-in-Process Inventory as a product cost.

The distinction between variable and absorption costing is summarized in Exhibit 11-11 on page 463. Notice that the distinction involves the *timing* with which fixed manufacturing overhead becomes an expense. Eventually, fixed overhead is expensed under both product-costing systems. Under variable costing, however, fixed overhead is expensed *immediately,* as it is incurred. Under absorption costing, fixed overhead is *inventoried* until the accounting period during which the manufactured goods are sold.

Illustration of Variable and Absorption Costing

Orion Company began operations on January 1, 19x1 to manufacture hand-held electronic calculators. The company uses a standard-costing system. Cost, production, and sales data for the first three years of Orion's operations are given in Exhibit 11-12. Comparative income statements for 19x1, 19x2, and 19x3 are presented in Exhibit 11-13, using both absorption and variable costing.

Absorption-Costing Income Statements Examine the absorption-costing income statements in the upper half of Exhibit 11-13. Two features of these income statements are highlighted in the left-hand margin. First, notice that the Cost of Goods Sold expense for each year is determined by multiplying the year's sales by the standard absorption manufacturing cost per unit, $9. Included in the $9 cost per unit is the predetermined fixed manufacturing-overhead cost of $3 per unit. Second, notice that on Orion's absorption-costing income statements, the only period expenses are the selling and administrative expenses. There is no deduction of fixed-overhead costs as a lump-sum period expense at the bottom of each income statement. As mentioned above, fixed manufacturing-overhead costs are included in Cost of Goods Sold on these absorption-costing income statements.

Variable-Costing Income Statements

Now examine the income statements based on variable costing in the lower half of Exhibit 11-13. Notice that the format of the statement is different from the format used in the absorption-costing statements. In the variable-costing statements, the contribution format is used to highlight the separation of variable and fixed costs. Let's focus on the same two aspects of the variable-costing statements that we discussed for the absorption-costing statements. First, the manufacturing expenses subtracted from sales revenue each year include only the variable costs, which amount to $6 per unit. Second, fixed manufacturing overhead is subtracted as a lump-sum period expense at the bottom of each year's income statement.

Reconciling Income under Absorption and Variable Costing

Examination of Exhibit 11-13 reveals that the income reported under absorption and variable costing is sometimes different. Although income is the same for the two product-costing methods in 19x1, it is different in 19x2 and 19x3. Let's figure out why these results occur.

No Change in Inventory In 19x1 there is no change in inventory over the course of the year. Beginning and ending inventory is the same, because actual production and sales are the same. Think about the implications of the stable inventory level for the treatment of fixed manufacturing overhead. On the variable-costing statement, the $150,000 of fixed manufacturing overhead incurred during 19x1 is an expense in 19x1. Under absorption costing, however, fixed manufacturing overhead was applied to production at the predetermined rate of $3 per unit. Since all of the units produced in 19x1 also were sold in 19x1, all of the fixed manufacturing-overhead cost flowed through into Cost of Goods Sold. Thus, $150,000 of fixed manufacturing overhead was expensed in 19x1 under absorption costing also.

The 19x1 column of Exhibit 11-14 reconciles the 19x1 net income reported under absorption and variable costing. The reconciliation focuses on the two places in the income statements where differences occur between absorption and variable costing. The numbers in the left-hand margin of Exhibit 11-14 correspond to the numbers in the left-hand margin of the income statements in Exhibit 11-13.

Increase in Inventory In 19x2 inventory increased from zero on January 1 to 15,000 units on December 31. The increase in inventory was the result of production exceeding sales. Under variable costing, the $150,000 of fixed overhead cost incurred in 19x2 is expensed, just as it was in 19x1. Under absorption costing, however, only a portion of the 19x1 fixed manufacturing overhead is expensed in 19x1. Since the

Exhibit 11-12. Data for Illustration: Orion Company

	19×1	19×2	19×3
Production and inventory data:			
Planned production (in units)	50,000	50,000	50,000
Finished-goods inventory (in units), January 1	–0–	–0–	15,000
Actual production (in units)	50,000	50,000	50,000
Sales (in units)	50,000	35,000	65,000
Finished-goods inventory (in units), December 31	–0–	15,000	–0–

Revenue and cost data, all three years:

Sales price per unit	$12
Standard manufacturing costs per unit:	
Direct material	$ 3
Direct labor	2
Variable manufacturing overhead	1
Total variable standard cost per unit	$ 6

Used only under absorption costing

Fixed manufacturing overhead:

$$\frac{\text{Budgeted annual fixed overhead}}{\text{Planned annual production}} \quad \frac{\$150,000}{50,000} \quad \$ 3$$

Total absorption standard cost per unit	$ 9
Variable selling and administrative cost per unit	$ 1
Fixed selling and administrative cost per year	$25,000

Variances:
There were no variances during 19x1, 19x2, or 19x3.

---

fixed overhead is inventoried under absorption costing, some of this cost *remains in inventory* at the end of 19x2.

The 19x2 column of Exhibit 11-14 reconciles the 19x2 net income reported under absorption and variable costing. As before, the reconciliation focuses on the two places in the income statements where differences occur between absorption and variable costing.

Decrease in Inventory In 19x3 inventory decreased from 15,000 units to zero. Sales during the year exceeded production. As in 19x1 and 19x2, under variable costing, the $150,000 of fixed manufacturing overhead incurred in 19x3 is expensed in 19x3. Under absorption costing, however, *more than* $150,000 of fixed overhead is expensed in 19x3. Why? Because some of the fixed overhead incurred during the prior year, which was inventoried then, is now expensed in 19x3 as the goods are sold.

The 19x3 column of Exhibit 11-14 reconciles the 19x3 income under absorption and variable costing. Once again, the numbers on the left-hand side of Exhibit 11-14 correspond to those on the left-hand side of the income statements in Exhibit 11-13.

Exhibit 11-13. Income Statements under Absorption and Variable Costing

Orion Company
Absorption-Costing Income Statement

		19x1	19x2	19x3
	Sales revenue (at $12 per unit)	$600,000	$420,000	$780,000
1	Less: Cost of goods sold (at standard absorption cost of $9 per unit)	450,000	315,000	585,000
	Gross margin	150,000	105,000	195,000
	Less: Selling and administrative expenses:			
2 No fixed overhead	Variable (at $1 per unit)	50,000	35,000	65,000
	Fixed	25,000	25,000	25,000
	Net income	$ 75,000	$ 45,000	$105,000

Orion Company
Variable-Costing Income Statement

		19x1	19x2	19x3
	Sales revenue (at $12 per unit)	$600,000	$420,000	$780,000
	Less: Variable expenses:			
1	Variable manufacturing costs (at standard variable cost of $6 per unit)	300,000	210,000	390,000
	Variable selling and administrative costs (at $1 per unit)	50,000	35,000	65,000
	Contribution margin	250,000	175,000	325,000
	Less: Fixed expenses:			
2	Fixed manufacturing overhead . . .	150,000	150,000	150,000
	Fixed selling and administrative expenses	25,000	25,000	25,000
	Net income	$ 75,000	$ 0	$150,000

Exhibit 11-14. Reconciliation of Income under Absorption and Variable Costing: Orion Company

		19x1	19x2	19x3
1	Cost of goods sold under absorption costing	$450,000	$315,000	$585,000
	Variable manufacturing costs under variable costing	300,000	210,000	390,000
	Subtotal	150,000	105,000	195,000
2	Fixed manufacturing overhead as period expense under variable costing	150,000	150,000	150,000
	Total	$ 0	$ (45,000)	$ 45,000
	Net income under variable costing	$ 75,000	$ 0	$150,000
	Net income under absorption costing	75,000	45,000	105,000
	Difference in net income	$ 0	$ (45,000)	$ 45,000

BLACK

467

A Shortcut to Reconciling Income When inventory increases or decreases during the year, reported income differs under absorption and variable costing. This results from the fixed overhead that is inventoried under absorption costing but expensed immediately under variable costing. The following formula may be used to compute the difference in the amount of fixed overhead expensed in a given time period under the two product-costing methods.

$$\begin{pmatrix} \text{Difference in fixed} \\ \text{overhead expensed} \\ \text{under absorption} \\ \text{and variable costing} \end{pmatrix} = \begin{pmatrix} \text{change in} \\ \text{inventory,} \\ \text{in units} \end{pmatrix} \times \begin{pmatrix} \text{predetermined} \\ \text{fixed-overhead} \\ \text{rate per unit} \end{pmatrix}$$

As the following table shows, this difference in the amount of fixed overhead expensed explains the difference in reported income under absorption and variable costing.

Year	Change in Inventory (in units)		Predetermined Fixed-Overhead Rate		Difference in Fixed Overhead Expensed		Absorption-Costing Income Minus Variable-Costing Income
19x1......	–0–	×	$3	=	–0–	=	–0–
19x2......	15,000 increase	×	$3	=	$ 45,000	=	$ 45,000
19x3......	15,000 decrease	×	$3	=	(45,000)	=	(45,000)

Length of Time Period The discrepancies between absorption-costing and variable-costing income in Exhibit 11-13 occur because of the changes in inventory levels during 19x2 and 19x3. It is common for production and sales to differ over the course of a week, month, or year. Therefore, the income measured for those time periods often will differ between absorption and variable costing. This discrepancy is likely to be smaller over longer time periods. Over the course of a decade, for example, Orion Company cannot sell much more or less than it produces. Thus, the income amounts under the two product-costing methods, when added together over a lengthy time period, will be approximately equal under absorption and variable costing.

Notice in Exhibit 11-13 that Orion's *total* income over the three-year period is $225,000 under *both* absorption and variable costing. This results from the fact that Orion produced and sold the same total amount over the three-year period.

Cost-Volume-Profit Analysis

One of the tools used by managers to plan and control business operations is cost-volume-profit analysis, which we studied in Chapter 7. Orion Company's break-even point in units can be computed as follows:

$$\frac{\text{Break-even}}{\text{point}} = \frac{\text{fixed costs}}{\text{unit contribution margin}} = \frac{\$150,000 + \$25,000}{\$12 - \$6 - \$1} = \frac{\$175,000}{\$5} = 35,000 \text{ units}$$

If Orion Company sells 35,000 calculators, net income should be zero, as Exhibit 11-15 confirms.

Now return to Exhibit 11-13 and examine the 19x2 income statements under absorption and variable costing. In 19x2 Orion Company sold 35,000 units, the break-even volume. This fact is confirmed on the variable-costing income statement,

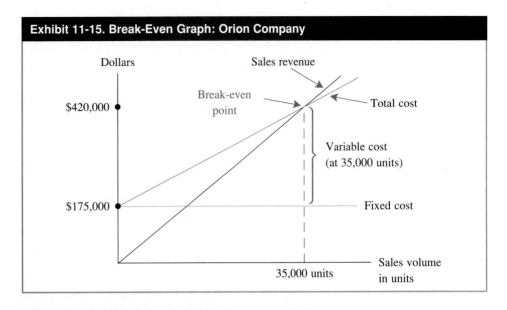

Exhibit 11-15. Break-Even Graph: Orion Company

since net income is zero. On the absorption-costing income statement, however, the 19x2 net income is $45,000. What has happened here?

The answer to this inconsistency lies in the different treatment of fixed manufacturing overhead under absorption and variable costing. Variable costing highlights the separation between fixed and variable costs, as do cost-volume-profit analysis and break-even calculations. Both of these techniques account for fixed manufacturing overhead as a lump sum. In contrast, *absorption costing is inconsistent with CVP analysis,* because fixed overhead is applied to goods as a product cost on a per-unit basis.

Evaluation of Absorption and Variable Costing

Some managers find the inconsistency between absorption costing and CVP analysis troubling enough to warrant using variable costing for internal income reporting. Variable costing dovetails much more closely than absorption costing with any operational analyses that require a separation between fixed and variable costs.

Pricing Decisions Many managers prefer to use absorption-costing data in cost-based pricing decisions. They argue that fixed manufacturing overhead is a necessary cost incurred in the production process. To exclude this fixed cost from the inventoried cost of a product, as is done under variable costing, is to understate the cost of the product. For this reason, most companies that use cost-based pricing base their prices on absorption-costing data.

Proponents of variable costing argue that a product's variable cost provides a better basis for the pricing decision. They point out that any price above a product's variable cost makes a positive contribution to covering fixed cost and profit.

Definition of an Asset Another controversy about absorption and variable costing hinges on the definition of an asset. An *asset* is a thing of value owned by the organization with future service potential. By accounting convention, assets are valued at their cost. Since fixed costs comprise part of the cost of production, advocates of absorption costing argue that inventory (an asset) should be valued at its full (absorption) cost of production. Moreover, they argue that these costs have future service potential since the inventory can be sold in the future to generate sales revenue.

Proponents of variable costing argue that the fixed-cost component of a product's absorption-costing value has no future service potential. Their reasoning is that the fixed manufacturing-overhead costs during the current period will not prevent these costs from having to be incurred again next period. Fixed-overhead costs will be incurred every period, regardless of production levels. In contrast, the incurrence of variable costs in manufacturing a product does allow the firm to avoid incurring these costs again.

To illustrate, Orion Company produced 15,000 more calculators in 19x2 than it sold. These units will be carried in inventory until they are sold in some future year. Orion Company will never again have to incur the costs of direct material, direct labor, and variable overhead incurred in 19x2 to produce those calculators. Yet Orion will have to incur approximately $150,000 of fixed-overhead costs every year, even though the firm has the 15,000 units from 19x2 in inventory.

External Reporting For external reporting purposes, generally acceptable accounting principles require that income reporting be based on absorption costing. Federal tax laws also require the use of absorption costing in reporting income for tax purposes.

Why Not Both? In the age of computerized accounting systems, it is straightforward for a company to prepare income statements under both absorption and variable costing. Since absorption-costing statements are required for external reporting, managers will want to keep an eye on the effects of their decisions on financial reports to outsiders. Yet the superiority of variable-costing income reporting as a method for dovetailing with operational analyses cannot be denied. Preparation of both absorption-costing and variable-costing data is perhaps the best solution to the controversy.

JIT Manufacturing Environment In a just-in-time inventory- and production-management system, all inventories are kept very low. Since finished-goods inventories are minimal, there is little change in inventory from period to period. Thus, in a JIT environment, the income differences under absorption and variable costing generally will be insignificant.

Fixed-Overhead Volume Variance Our illustration of absorption and variable costing does not include the fixed-overhead volume variance, which was covered in Chapter 10. The impact of the volume variance is explored in the appendix to this chapter.

CHAPTER SUMMARY

Responsibility-accounting systems are designed to foster goal congruence among the managers in decentralized organizations. Each subunit in an organization is designated as a cost center, revenue center, profit center, or investment center. The managerial accountant prepares a performance report for each responsibility center. These reports show the performance of the responsibility center and its manager for a specified time period.

To use responsibility accounting effectively, the emphasis must be on information rather than blame. The intent should be to provide managers with information to help them better manage their subunits. Responsibility-accounting systems can bring about desired behavior, such as reducing the number of rush orders in a manufacturing company.

Responsibility-accounting systems generally include the allocation of costs among subunits. The purposes of cost allocation include: (1) predicting the economic effects of decisions, (2) pricing and bidding, (3) cost reimbursement, (4) motivation, (5) asset valuation and income determination, and (6) estimating opportunity costs.

Segmented income statements often are included in a responsibility-accounting system, to show the performance of the organization and its various segments. To be most effective, such reports should distinguish between the performance of segments and segment managers.

Absorption and variable costing are two alternative product-costing systems, which differ in their treatment of fixed manufacturing overhead. Under absorption (or full) costing, fixed overhead is applied to produced goods as a product cost. The fixed-overhead cost remains in inventory until the goods are sold. Under variable (or direct) costing, fixed overhead is a period cost, which is expensed during the period when it is incurred. Absorption costing is required for external reporting and tax purposes. However, variable costing is more consistent with operational decision analyses, which require a separation of fixed and variable costs.

REVIEW PROBLEM ON RESPONSIBILITY ACCOUNTING AND COST ALLOCATION

James Madison National Bank has a division for each of the two counties in which it operates, Cayuga and Oneida. Each divisional vice president is held accountable for both profit and invested capital. Each division consists of two branch banks, East and West. Each branch manager is responsible for that bank's profit. The Cayuga Division's East Branch has a Deposit Department, a Loan Department, and an Administrative Services Department. The department supervisors of the Loan and Deposit Departments are accountable for departmental revenues; the Administrative Services Department supervisor is accountable for costs.

All of James Madison National Bank's advertising and promotion is done centrally. The advertising and promotion cost pool for 19x0, which amounted to $40,000, is allocated across the four branch banks on the basis of budgeted branch revenue. Budgeted revenue for 19x0 is shown below.

Cayuga Division:	West Branch	$400,000
	East Branch	200,000
Oneida Division:	West Branch	250,000
	East Branch	150,000

REQUIRED:

1. Draw an organization chart for James Madison National Bank, which shows each subunit described above, its manager's title, and its designation as a responsibility center.
2. Distribute (allocate) the bank's 19x0 advertising cost pool to the four branch banks.

Solution to Review Problem

1. Organization chart (subunits, managers, responsibility center designation)

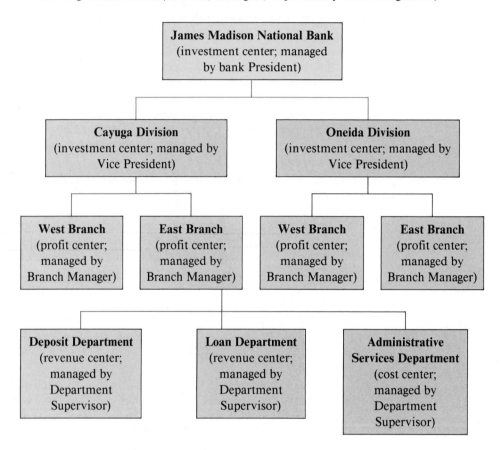

2. Cost distribution (or allocation):

Cost Pool	Responsibility Center	Allocation Base: Revenue	Percentage of Total*	Costs Distributed
Advertising	Cayuga, West Branch...	$ 400,000	40%	$16,000
and	Cayuga, East Branch ...	200,000	20%	8,000
promotion	Oneida, West Branch...	250,000	25%	10,000
costs	Oneida, East Branch ...	150,000	15%	6,000
	Total	$1,000,000	100%	$40,000

* Branch revenue as a percentage of total revenue, $1,000,000.

KEY TERMS Absorption (or full) costing, p. 464; Allocation base, p. 458; Common costs, p. 461; Cost allocation (or distribution), p. 456; Cost center, p. 448; Cost objectives, p. 456; Cost pool, p. 456; Decentralization, p. 448; Goal congruence, p. 447; Investment center, p. 449; Multistage cost allocation, p. 457; Performance report, p. 451; Profit center, p. 449; Responsibility accounting, p. 447; Responsibility center, p. 448; Revenue center, p. 449; Segmented income statement, p. 461; Variable (or direct) costing, p. 464.

Effect of the Volume Variance under Absorption and Variable Costing

Our illustration of absorption and variable costing did not include a fixed-overhead volume variance. Recall from Chapter 10 that the volume variance is defined as follows:

$$
\begin{array}{c}
\text{Fixed-overhead} \\
\text{volume} \\
\text{variance}
\end{array}
=
\begin{array}{c}
\text{budgeted} \\
\text{fixed} \\
\text{overhead}
\end{array}
-
\begin{array}{c}
\text{applied} \\
\text{fixed} \\
\text{overhead}
\end{array}
$$

$$
=
\left(
\begin{array}{c}
\text{predetermined} \\
\text{fixed-} \\
\text{overhead rate}
\end{array}
\right)
\left(
\begin{array}{c}
\text{planned} \\
\text{production} \\
\text{in units}
\end{array}
\right)
-
\left(
\begin{array}{c}
\text{predetermined} \\
\text{fixed-} \\
\text{overhead rate}
\end{array}
\right)
\left(
\begin{array}{c}
\text{actual} \\
\text{production} \\
\text{in units}
\end{array}
\right)
$$

When planned production equals actual production for the year, the volume variance is zero. This was the case in 19x1, 19x2, and 19x3 for our Orion Company illustration.

To show the effect of a volume variance on income reporting under absorption and variable costing, let's extend the data for Orion Company through the next three years. Exhibit 11-16 displays the data for 19x4, 19x5, and 19x6; Exhibit 11-17 shows comparative income statements for these three years.

Now there are three key places where the absorption-costing and variable-costing income statements differ. The absorption-costing statements include the fixed-overhead volume variance. But there is no volume variance on the variable-costing statements, because fixed overhead is not applied as a product cost under variable costing. Exhibit 11-18 reconciles Orion's reported income under the two alternative product-costing systems. The numbers in the left-hand margin correspond to those on the left-hand side of the income statements in Exhibit 11-17.

REVIEW QUESTIONS

11-1. Why is *goal congruence* important to an organization's success?

11-2. How does a *responsibility-accounting* system foster goal congruence?

11-3. List five benefits and three costs of decentralization.

11-4. Define and give examples of the following terms: cost center, revenue center, profit center, and investment center.

11-5. Under what circumstances would it be appropriate to change the Waikiki Sands Hotel from a profit center to an investment center?

Exhibit 11-16. Data for Illustration: Orion Company

	19×4	19×5	19×6
Production and inventory data:			
Planned production (in units)	50,000	50,000	50,000
Finished-goods inventory (in units), January 1	–0–	–0–	25,000
Actual production (in units)	50,000	60,000	40,000
Sales (in units)	50,000	35,000	55,000
Finished-goods inventory (in units), December 31	–0–	25,000	10,000

Revenue and cost data, all three years:

Sales price per unit	$12
Standard manufacturing costs per unit:	
Direct material	$ 3
Direct labor	2
Variable manufacturing overhead	1
Total variable standard cost per unit	$ 6

Used
only
under
absorption
costing

Fixed manufacturing overhead:

$$\frac{\text{Budgeted annual fixed overhead}}{\text{Planned annual production}} \quad \frac{\$150,000}{50,000} \quad \quad \$ 3$$

Total absorption standard cost per unit	$ 9
Variable selling and administrative cost per unit	$ 1
Fixed selling and administrative cost per year	$25,000

Variances, all three years:
There are no direct-material, direct-labor, or variable
overhead variances. Moreover, there is no fixed-overhead
budget variance.

11-6. Explain the relationship between performance reports and flexible budgeting.

11-7. Explain how to get positive behavioral effects from a responsibility-accounting system.

11-8. "Performance reports based on controllability are impossible. Nobody really *controls* anything in an organization!" Do you agree or disagree? Explain your answer.

11-9. Define and give examples of the following terms: *cost pool, cost objective,* and *cost allocation* (or *distribution*).

11-10. List and briefly describe the three steps in multistage cost allocation.

11-11. List and explain five purposes of cost allocation.

11-12. Give an example of a common resource in an organization. List some of the opportunity costs associated with using the resource. Why might allocation of the cost of the common resource to its users be useful?

11-13. Explain how and why cost allocation might be used to assign the costs of a wide-area telephone system (WATS line) in a university.

Exhibit 11-17. Income Statements under Absorption and Variable Costing

Orion Company
Absorption-Costing Income Statement

		19x4	19x5	19x6
	Sales revenue (at $12 per unit)	$600,000	$420,000	$660,000
1	Less: Cost of goods sold (at standard absorption cost of $9 per unit)	450,000	315,000	495,000
	Gross margin (at standard)	150,000	105,000	165,000
2	Adjust for: Fixed-overhead volume variance	0*	30,000*	30,000*
	Gross margin (at actual)	150,000	135,000	135,000
	Less: Selling and administrative expenses:			
3 No fixed	Variable (at $1 per unit)	50,000	35,000	55,000
overhead	Fixed	25,000	25,000	25,000
	Net income	$ 75,000	$ 75,000	$ 55,000

*Computation of fixed-overhead volume variance:

$$\text{Fixed-overhead volume variance} = \text{budgeted fixed overhead} - \text{applied fixed overhead} = \text{budgeted fixed overhead} - \left(\begin{array}{c} \text{Predeter-} \\ \text{mined fixed-} \\ \text{overhead} \\ \text{rate} \end{array} \right)\left(\begin{array}{c} \text{actual} \\ \text{production} \end{array} \right)$$

19x4: Volume variance = 0   = $150,000 – ($3) (50,000)
19x5: Volume variance = – $30,000 = $150,000 – ($3) (60,000)
19x6: Volume variance = $30,000 = $150,000 – ($3) (40,000)

Orion Company
Variable-Costing Income Statement

		19x4	19x5	19x6
	Sales revenue (at $12 per unit)	$600,000	$420,000	$660,000
1	Less: Variable expenses:			
2 No volume	Variable manufacturing costs (at standard variable cost of $6			
variance	per unit)	300,000	210,000	330,000
	Variable selling and administrative costs (at $1 per unit)	50,000	35,000	55,000
	Contribution margin	250,000	175,000	275,000
	Less: Fixed expenses:			
	Fixed manufacturing overhead . . .	150,000	150,000	150,000
3	Fixed selling and administrative costs	25,000	25,000	25,000
	Net income	$ 75,000	$ 0	$100,000

Exhibit 11-18. Reconciliation of Income Under Absorption and Variable Costing:
Orion Company

	19x4	19x5	19x6
1 Cost of goods sold under absorption costing	$450,000	$315,000	$495,000
Variable manufacturing costs			
under variable costing	300,000	210,000	330,000
Subtotal	150,000	105,000	165,000
2 Volume variance under absorption costing	0	30,000*	30,000†
Subtotal	150,000	75,000	195,000
3 Fixed manufacturing overhead as period expense			
under variable costing	150,000	150,000	150,000
Total	$ 0	$(75,000)	$ 45,000
Net income under variable costing	75,000	$ 0	100,000
Net income under absorption costing	75,000	75,000	55,000
Difference in net income	$ 0	$(75,000)	$ 45,000

*Negative volume variance.
†Positive volume variance.

11-14. Define the term *cost allocation base.* What would be a sensible allocation base for assigning advertising costs to the various components of a large theme park?

11-15. Referring to Exhibit 11-7, why are marketing costs distributed to the Waikiki Sands Hotel's departments on the basis of *budgeted* sales dollars?

11-16. Explain what is meant by a *segmented income statement.*

11-17. Why do some managerial accountants choose not to allocate common costs in segmented reports?

11-18. Why is it important in responsibility accounting to distinguish between segments and segment managers?

11-19. List and explain three key features of the segmented income statement shown in Exhibit 11-10.

11-20. Can a common cost for one segment be a traceable cost for another segment? Explain your answer.

11-21. Briefly explain the difference between absorption and variable costing.

11-22. Timing is the key in distinguishing between absorption and variable costing. Explain this statement.

11-23. The term *direct costing* is a misnomer. *Variable costing* is a better term for the product-costing method. Do you agree or disagree? Why?

11-24. When inventory increases, will absorption-costing or variable-costing income be greater? Why?

11-25. Why do many managers prefer variable costing over absorption costing?

EXERCISES *Exercise 11-26 Decentralization.* For each of the following organizations, list the advantages and disadvantages of a decentralized organizational structure. Would you choose a centralized or decentralized structure if you were the organization's top executive?

1. Hospital.
2. University.
3. Naval task force.
4. Sports franchise.
5. Multinational manufacturing company.
6. Fast-food chain.
7. Television network.
8. National department store chain.

Exercise 11-27 **Designating Responsibility Centers.** For each of the following organizational subunits, indicate the type of responsibility center that is most appropriate.

PC or CC 1. A movie theater in a company that operates a chain of theaters.
PC 2. A radio station owned by a large broadcasting network.
CC 3. The claims department in an insurance company.
RvC 4. The ticket sales division of a major airline.
CC 5. A bottling plant of a soft drink company.
PC 6. An orange juice factory operated by a large orange grower.
PC 7. The College of Engineering at a large state university.
InC 8. The European Division of a multinational manufacturing company.
PC 9. The outpatient clinic in a profit-oriented hospital.
CC 10. The Mayor's Office in a large city.

Exercise 11-28 **Responsibility Accounting; Equipment Breakdown.** How should a responsibility-accounting system handle each of the following scenarios?

1. Department A manufactures a component, which is then used by Department B. Department A recently experienced a machine breakdown which held up production of the component. As a result, Department B was forced to curtail its own production, thereby incurring large costs of idle time. An investigation revealed that Department A's machinery had not been properly maintained.
2. Refer to the scenario above, but suppose the investigation revealed the machinery in Department A had been properly maintained.

Exercise 11-29 **Responsibility-Accounting Centers; Xerox Corporation.** Xerox Corporation changed the responsibility-center orientation of its Logistics and Distribution Department from a cost center to a profit center. The department manages the inventories and provides other logistical services to the company's Business Systems Group. Formerly, the manager of the Logistics and Distribution Department was held accountable for adherence to an operating expense budget. Now the department "sells" its services to the company's other segments, and the department's manager is evaluated partially on the basis of the department's profit. Xerox Corporation's management feels that the change has been beneficial. The change has resulted in more innovative thinking in the department, and has moved decision making down to lower levels in the company.[4]

REQUIRED: Comment on the new responsibility-center designation for the Logistics Department.

[4] F. Tucker and S. Zivian, "A Xerox Cost Center Imitates a Profit Center," *Harvard Business Review, 63,* no. 3, pp. 161–174.

Exercise 11-30   Responsibility for Skilled Employees' Wages. Alston Electronics Company manufactures complex circuit boards for the aerospace industry. Demand for the company's products has fallen in recent months, and the firm has cut its production significantly. Many unskilled workers have been temporarily laid off. Top management has made a decision, however, not to lay off any highly skilled employees, such as inspectors and machinery operators. Management was concerned that these highly skilled employees would easily find new jobs elsewhere and not return when Alston's production returned to normal levels.

To occupy the skilled employees during the production cutback, they have been reassigned temporarily to the Maintenance Department. Here they are performing general maintenance tasks, such as repainting the interior of the factory, repairing the loading dock, and building wooden storage racks for the warehouse. The skilled employees continued to receive their normal wages, which average $22 per hour. However, the normal wages for Maintenance Department employees average $12 per hour.

The supervisor of the Maintenance Department recently received the March performance report, which indicated that his department's labor cost exceeded the budget by $19,360. The department's actual labor cost was approximately 90 percent over the budget. The department supervisor complained to the controller.

REQUIRED: As the controller, how would you respond? Would you make any modification in Alston's responsibility-accounting system? If so, list the changes you would make. Explain your reasoning.

Exercise 11-31   Performance Report; Hotel. The following data pertain to the Waikiki Sands Hotel for the month of March.

	Flexible Budget March (in thousands)*	Actual Results March (in thousands)*
Banquets and Catering. . . . .$	650	$ 658
Restaurants.	1,800	1,794
Kitchen staff wages.	(85)	(86)
Food	(690)	(690)
Paper products	(125)	(122)
Variable overhead	(75)	(78)
Fixed overhead.	(90)	(93)

*Numbers without parentheses denote profit; numbers with parentheses denote expenses.

REQUIRED: Prepare a March performance report similar to the lower portion of Exhibit 11-4. The report should have six numerical columns with headings analogous to those in Exhibit 11-4. Your performance report should cover only the Food and Beverage Department and the Kitchen. Draw arrows to show the relationships between the numbers in the report. Refer to Exhibit 11-4 for guidance. For the year-to-date columns in your report, use the data given in Exhibit 11-4. You will need to update those figures using the March data given above.

Exercise 11-32   Multistage Allocation. Refer to Exhibit 11-6, which portrays the three steps in multistage allocation. Give an example of each of these three stages in a hospital setting. The ultimate cost objective is a patient-day of hospital care. This is one day of care for one patient. (Hint: First think about the various departments in a hospital. Which departments deal directly with patients; which ones are service departments and do not deal directly with patients? What kinds of costs does a hospital incur that should be distributed among all of the hospital's departments? Correct hospital terminology is not important here. Focus on the *concepts* of cost allocation portrayed in Exhibit 11-6.)

Exercise 11-33 **Cost Allocation in a College.** Mohawk Community College has three divisions: Liberal Arts, Sciences, and Business Administration. The college's comptroller is trying to decide how to allocate the costs of the Admissions Department, the Registrar's Department, and the Computer Services Department. The controller has compiled the following data for 19x5.

Division	Budgeted Enrollment	Budgeted Credit Hours	Planned Number of Courses Requiring Computer Work
Liberal Arts	1,000	30,000	12
Sciences	800	28,000	24
Business Administration	700	22,000	24

Department	Annual Cost
Admissions.	$ 80,000
Registrar.	150,000
Computer Services.	320,000

REQUIRED:

1. For each department, choose an allocation base and distribute the departmental costs to the college's three divisions. Justify your choice of an allocation base.
2. Would you have preferred a different allocation base than those available using the data compiled by the Comptroller? Why?

Exercise 11-34 **Cost Allocation; Opportunity Costs; City Government.** The city of Port Pacifica operates a motor pool, which serves all of the city's needs for vehicles and vehicle maintenance. The motor pool maintains a fleet of automobiles, vans, and utility trucks, which it makes available to various city agencies. For example, if the Port Pacifica Parks Commission needs a pickup truck for a week, it reserves the vehicle through the motor pool. If the needed vehicle is not available, the agency must rent a vehicle from a noncity source, postpone the intended use, or do without.

Before the maintenance garage for the motor pool was built three years ago, the city controller prepared an analysis of the city's vehicular needs. Based on this analysis, the size of the maintenance facility and vehicle fleet was determined. The City Council decided to build a maintenance garage with four maintenance bays. The other choices were either two bays or six bays.

Each maintenance bay can support 20 vehicles. Therefore, the city's vehicle fleet consists of 80 vehicles. The annual costs of operating the motor pool, for each scale considered, are listed below.

Number of Maintenance Bays	Vehicle Fleet	Annual Cost
2	40	$250,000
4	80	500,000
6	120	750,000

REQUIRED:

1. List some opportunity costs that could be incurred by the city which are related to constraints on vehicle availability.
2. How might cost allocation be used as a surrogate for these opportunity costs?

Exercise 11-35   Segmented Income Statement; TV Cable Company. Countywide Cable Services, Inc. is organized with three segments: Metro, Suburban, and Outlying. Data for these segments for 19x2 follow.

	Metro	Suburban	Outlying
Service revenue	$1,000,000	$800,000	$400,000
Variable expenses	200,000	150,000	100,000
Controllable fixed expenses	400,000	320,000	150,000
Fixed expenses controllable by others	230,000	200,000	90,000

In addition to the expenses listed above, the company has $100,000 of common fixed costs. Income-tax expense for 19x2 is $150,000.

REQUIRED: Prepare a segmented income statement for Countywide Television Services, Inc. Use the contribution format.

Exercise 11-36   Absorption versus Variable Costing. Information taken from Valenz Company's records for 19x6 is as follows:

Direct materials used	$300,000
Direct labor	100,000
Variable manufacturing overhead	50,000
Fixed manufacturing overhead	80,000
Variable selling and administrative costs	40,000
Fixed selling and administrative costs	20,000

REQUIRED:

1. Assuming Valenz Company uses variable costing, compute the inventoriable costs for the year.
2. Compute the year's inventoriable costs using absorption costing.

(CMA, adapted)

Exercise 11-37   Absorption and Variable Costing. Here is selected information concerning the operations of Kern Company for 19x1:

Planned production (in units)	10,000
Units produced	10,000
Units sold	9,000
Direct materials used	$40,000
Direct labor incurred	$20,000
Fixed manufacturing overhead	$25,000
Variable manufacturing overhead	$12,000
Fixed selling and administrative expenses	$30,000
Variable selling and administrative expenses	$4,500
Finished-goods inventory, January 1, 19x1	None

There were no work-in-process inventories at the beginning or end of 19x1.

REQUIRED:

1. What would be Kern's finished-goods inventory cost on December 31, 19x1, under the variable-costing method?
2. Which costing method, absorption or variable costing, would show a higher operating income for 19x1? By what amount?

(CPA, adapted)

Exercise 11-38 **Difference in Income under Absorption and Variable Costing.** Mason Company manufactures a single product with a standard variable cost of $25. Budgeted fixed manufacturing overhead for 19x9 was $792,000. There was no volume variance.

REQUIRED: Under each of the following conditions, state (a) whether income is higher under variable or absorption costing and (b) the amount of the difference in reported income under the two methods. Treat each condition as an independent case.

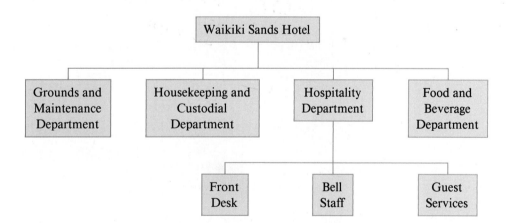

VCR 1. Production ...792,000/90,000 = 8.80 × 5000 = 44,200 ...... 90,000 units (5000)
         Sales .... 95,000 units
Absorption 2. Production ...792,000/110,000 = 7.20 × 2000 = 14,400 ...... 110,000 units 2000
         Sales .... 108,000 units
Unchanged 3. Production .... 80,000 units
         Sales .... 80,000 units 0

PROBLEMS *Problem 11-39* **Designating Responsibility Centers; Hotel.** The following partial organization chart is an extension of Exhibit 11-1 for Aloha Hotels and Resorts.

Each of the hotel's four main departments is managed by a director (e.g., director of hospitality). The Front Desk subunit, which is supervised by the front desk manager, handles the hotel's reservations, room assignments, guest payments, and key control. The Bell staff, managed by the bell captain, is responsible for greeting guests, front door service, assisting guests with their luggage, and delivering room-service orders. The Guest Services subunit, supervised by the manager of Guest Services, is responsible for assisting guests with local transportation arrangements, advising guests on tourist attractions, and such conveniences as valet and floral services.

REQUIRED: As an outside consultant, write a memo to the hotel's general manager suggesting a responsibility-center designation for each of the subunits shown in the organization chart above. Justify your choices.

Problem 11-40   Create an Organization. Here is your chance to be a tycoon. Create your own company. You will be the president and chief executive officer. It could be a manufacturer, retailer, or service industry firm, but *not* a hotel or bank. Draw an organization chart for your company, similar to the one in Exhibit 11-1. Identify divisions and departments at all levels in the organization. Then prepare a companion chart similar to the one in Exhibit 11-2. This chart should designate the title of the manager of a subunit at each level in the organization. It also should designate the type of responsibility center appropriate for each of these subunits. Finally, write a letter to your company's stockholders summarizing the major responsibilities of each of the managers you identified in your chart. For guidance, refer to the discussion of Exhibits 11-1 and 11-2 in the chapter. (Have some fun, and be creative.)

Problem 11-41   Design Performance Reports; Continuation of Preceding Problem. After designing your company, design a set of performance reports for the subunits you identified in your chart. Make up numbers for the performance reports, and show the relationship between the reports. Refer to Exhibit 11-4 for guidance.

Problem 11-42   Preparation of Performance Reports; Hospital. Appalachian General Hospital serves three counties in West Virginia. The hospital is a nonprofit organization, which is supported by patient billings, county and state funds, and private donations. The hospital's organization is shown below.

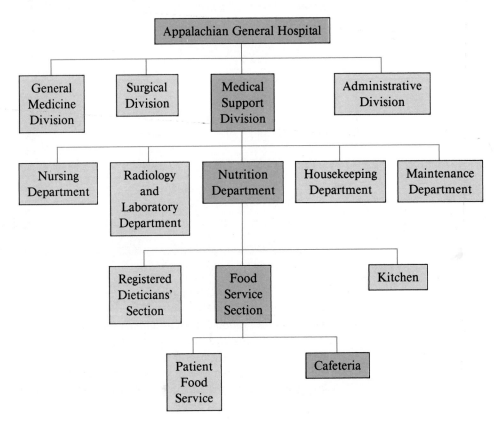

The following cost information has been compiled for August of 19x7.

| | Budget | | Actual | |
	August	Year to Date	August	Year to Date
Cafeteria:				
Food servers' wages . . . . $	8,000	$ 64,000	$ 9,000	$ 72,000
Paper products	4,500	36,000	4,400	36,200
Utilities	1,000	8,000	1,050	8,100
Maintenance.	400	3,200	100	1,100
Custodial.	1,100	8,800	1,100	8,600
Supplies.	1,200	9,600	900	9,600
Patient Food Service	17,000	136,000	18,500	137,000
Registered Dieticians' Section	7,500	60,000	7,500	60,000
Kitchen	31,000	248,000	29,400	246,000
Nursing Department	70,000	560,000	75,000	580,000
Radiology and Laboratory Department	18,000	144,000	18,100	144,000
Housekeeping Department	10,000	80,000	11,600	86,000
Maintenance Department	13,000	104,000	6,000	77,000
General Medicine Division	210,000	1,680,000	204,000	1,670,900
Surgical Division	140,000	1,120,000	141,000	1,115,800
Administrative Division.	50,000	400,000	53,500	406,000

REQUIRED:

1. Prepare a set of cost performance reports similar to Exhibit 11-4. The report should have six columns, as in Exhibit 11-4. The first four columns will have the same headings as those used above. The last two columns will have the following headings: Variance—August and Variance—Year to Date.

    Since all of the information in the performance reports for Appalachian General Hospital is cost information, you do not need to show these data in parentheses. Use F or U to denote whether each variance in the reports in favorable or unfavorable.

2. Using arrows, show the relationships between the numbers in your performance reports for Appalachian General Hospital. Refer to Exhibit 11-4 for guidance.

3. Put yourself in the place of the hospital's administrator. Which variances in the performance reports would you want to investigate further? Why?

Problem 11-43 ***Cost Distribution Using Allocation Bases; Hospital.*** Refer to the organization chart for Appalachian General Hospital given in the preceding problem. Ignore the rest of the data in that problem. The following table shows the cost allocation bases used to distribute various costs among the hospital's divisions.

Cost Pool	Cost Allocation Base	Annual Cost
Facilities:		
Building depreciation	Square feet	$200,000
Equipment depreciation	of space	
Insurance		

Cost Pool	Cost Allocation Base	Annual Cost
Utilities:		
Electricity	Cubic feet	$ 20,000
Waste disposal	of space	
Water and sewer		
Cable TV and phone		
Heat		
General administration:		
Administrator	Budgeted number	220,000
Administrative staff	of employees	
Office supplies		
Community outreach:		
Public education	Budgeted dollars of	40,000
School physical exams	patient billings	

Shown below are the amounts of each cost allocation base associated with each division.

	Square Feet	Cubic Feet	Number of Employees	Patient Billings
General Medicine Division	15,000	135,000	30	$2,000,000
Surgical Division	8,000	100,000	20	1,250,000
Medical Support Division	9,000	90,000	20	750,000
Administrative Division.	8,000	75,000	30	0
Total	40,000	400,000	100	$4,000,000

REQUIRED:

1. Prepare a table similar to Exhibit 11-8 which distributes each of the costs listed in the preceding table to the hospital's divisions.
2. Comment on the appropriateness of patient billings as the basis for distributing community outreach costs to the hospital's divisions. Can you suggest a better allocation base?
3. Is there any use in allocating utilities costs to the divisions? What purposes could such an allocation process serve?

Problem 11-44 *Prepare Segmented Income Statement; Contribution-Margin Format; Retail.* Buckeye Department Stores, Inc. operates a chain of department stores in Ohio. The company's organization chart appears below. Operating data for 19x3 follow.

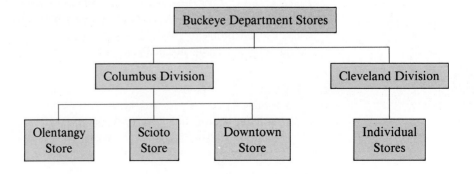

Buckeye Department Stores, Inc.
Operating Data for 19x3
(in thousands)

	Columbus Division			Cleveland Division
	Olentangy Store	Scioto Store	Downtown Store	(Total for all stores)
Sales revenue	$5,000	$2,400	$11,000	$21,000
Variable expenses:				
Cost of merchandise sold	3,000	2,000	6,000	12,000
Sales personnel — salaries	400	300	750	1,600
Sales commissions	50	40	90	200
Utilities.	80	60	150	300
Other	60	35	120	250
Fixed expenses:				
Depreciation — buildings.	120	90	250	470
Depreciation — furnishings	80	50	140	290
Computing and billing	40	30	75	160
Warehouse	70	60	200	450
Insurance	40	25	90	200
Property taxes	35	20	80	170
Supervisory salaries	150	100	400	900
Security	30	30	80	210

The following fixed expenses are controllable at the divisional level: depreciation — furnishings, computing and billing, warehouse, insurance, and security. In addition to these expenses, each division annually incurs $50,000 of computing costs, which are not allocated to individual stores.

The following fixed expenses are controllable only at the company level: depreciation — building, property taxes, and supervisory salaries. In addition to these expenses, each division incurs costs for supervisory salaries of $100,000, which are not allocated to individual stores.

Buckeye Department Stores incurs common fixed expenses of $100,000, which are not allocated to the two divisions. Income-tax expense for 19x3 is $2,000,000.

REQUIRED:

1. Prepare a segmented income statement similar to Exhibit 11-10 for Buckeye Department Stores, Inc. The statement should have the following columns:

Buckeye Department Stores, Inc.	Segments of Company		Segments of Columbus Division			
	Cleveland Division	Columbus Division	Olentangy Store	Scioto Store	Downtown Store	Not Allocated

Prepare the statement in the contribution format, and indicate the controllability of expenses. Subtract all variable expenses, including cost of merchandise sold, from sales revenue to obtain the contribution margin.

2. How would the segmented income statement help the president of Buckeye Department Stores manage the company?

Problem 11-45 Segmented Income Statement. Capricorn Company manufactures and sells two products, a portable office file cabinet and a home file. The files are made in the company's only manufacturing plant. Budgeted variable production costs per unit are shown below.

	Office File	Home File
Sheet metal	$ 3.50	—
Plastic	—	$3.75
Direct labor ($8 per hour)	4.00	2.00
Variable manufacturing overhead ($9 per direct-labor hour)	4.50	2.25
Total	$12.00	$8.00

Variable manufacturing-overhead costs vary with direct-labor hours. The annual fixed manufacturing-overhead costs are budgeted at $120,000. A total of 50 percent of these costs are directly traceable to the Office File Department, and 22 percent of the costs are traceable to the Home File Department. The remaining 28 percent of the costs are not traceable to either department.

Capricorn Company employs two full-time sales employees, Anne Fraser and Joe McDonough. Each sales employee receives an annual salary of $14,000 plus a sales commission of 10 percent of his or her total gross sales. Travel and entertainment expense is budgeted at $22,000 annually for each sales employee. Fraser is expected to sell 60 percent of the budgeted unit sales for each file, and McDonough the remaining 40 percent. Capricorn's remaining selling and administrative expenses include (1) fixed administrative costs of $80,000 that cannot be traced to either file, and (2) the following traceable selling expenses.

	Office File	Home File
Packaging expenses per unit	$2.00	$1.50
Promotional expenses	$30,000	$40,000

Data regarding Capricorn's budgeted and actual sales for 19x0 are presented below. There were no changes in the beginning and ending balances of either finished-goods or work-in-process inventories.

	Office File	Home File
Budgeted sales volume in units	15,000	15,000
Budgeted and actual unit sales price	$29.50	$19.50
Actual unit sales:		
Fraser	10,000	9,500
McDonough	5,000	10,500
Total units	15,000	20,000

Data regarding Capricorn's 19x0 operating expenses follow.

● There were no increases or decreases in direct-material inventory for either sheet metal or plastic, and there were no material-quantity variances. However, sheet metal prices were 6 percent above budget and plastic prices were 4 percent below budget.

● The actual direct-labor hours worked and the costs incurred were as follows:

	Hours	Amount
Office file	7,500	$ 57,000
Home file	6,000	45,600
Total	13,500	$102,600

- Fixed manufacturing-overhead costs attributable to the Office File Department were $8,000 above the budget. All other fixed manufacturing-overhead costs were incurred at the same amounts as budgeted, and all variable manufacturing-overhead costs were incurred at the budgeted hourly rates.
- All selling and administrative expenses were incurred at the budgeted amounts except the following items.

Nontraceable administrative expenses		$ 34,000
Promotional expenses:		
Office files	$32,000	
Home files	58,000	90,000
Travel and entertainment:		
Fraser	$24,000	
McDonough	28,000	52,000
Total		$176,000

REQUIRED:

1. Prepare a segmented income statement for Capricorn Company for 19x0. The report should be prepared in a contribution-margin format by product line. It should show total income (or loss) for the company before taxes.
2. Identify and discuss any additional analyses that could be made of the data presented that would be of value to Capricorn Company's management.

(CMA, adapted)

Problem 11-46   Performance Reporting. Refer to the information about Capricorn Company provided in the preceding problem.

REQUIRED: Prepare a performance report for 19x0 that would be useful in evaluating the performance of Joe McDonough.

(CMA, adapted)

Problem 11-47   Segmented Income Statement. Stratford Corporation is a diversified company whose products are marketed both domestically and internationally. The company's major project lines are pharmaceutical products, sports equipment, and household appliances. At a recent meeting of Stratford's board of directors, there was a lengthy discussion on ways to improve overall corporate profitability. The members of the board decided that they required additional financial information about individual corporate operations in order to target areas for improvement.

Dave Murphy, Stratford's controller, has been asked to provide additional data that would assist the board in its investigation. Murphy believes that income statements, prepared along both product lines and geographic areas, would provide the directors with the required insight into corporate operations.

Murphy had several discussions with the division managers for each product line and compiled the following information from these meetings.

Product Lines

	Pharmaceutical	Sports	Appliances	Total
Production and sales in units ...	160,000	180,000	160,000	500,000
Average selling price per unit ...	$8.00	$20.00	$15.00	
Average variable manufacturing cost per unit	$4.00	$9.50	$8.25	
Average variable selling expense per unit....................	$2.00	$2.50	$2.25	
Fixed factory overhead, excluding depreciation				$500,000
Depreciation of plant and equipment.....................				$400,000
Administrative and selling expense.....................				$1,160,000

1. The division managers concluded that Murphy should allocate fixed factory overhead to both product lines and geographic areas on the basis of the ratio of the variable costs expended to total variable costs.
2. Each of the division managers agreed that a reasonable basis for the allocation of depreciation on plant and equipment would be the ratio of units produced per product line (or per geographical area) to the total number of units produced.
3. There was little agreement on the allocation of administrative and selling expenses, so Murphy decided to allocate only those expenses that were traceable directly to a segment. For example, manufacturing staff salaries would be allocated to product lines, and sales staff salaries would be allocated to geographic areas. Murphy used the following data for this allocation.

Manufacturing Staff		**Sales Staff**	
Pharmaceutical.........	$120,000	U.S....................	$ 60,000
Sports	140,000	Canada	100,000
Appliances	80,000	Europe	250,000

4. The division managers were able to provide reliable sales percentages for their product lines by geographical area.

	Percentage of Unit Sales		
	U.S.	Canada	Europe
Pharmaceutical	40%	10%	50%
Sports..	40%	40%	20%
Appliances.....................................	20%	20%	60%

Murphy prepared the following product-line income statement based on the data presented above.

REQUIRED

1. Prepare a segmented income statement for Stratford Corporation based on the company's geographic areas. The statement should show the operating income for each segment.

Stratford Corporation
Segmented Income Statement by Product Lines
For the Fiscal Year Ended April 30, 19x7

Product Lines

	Pharmaceutical	Sports	Appliances	Unallocated	Total
Sales in units	160,000	180,000	160,000		
Sales	$1,280,000	$3,600,000	$2,400,000	—	$7,280,000
Variable manufacturing and selling costs ..	960,000	2,160,000	1,680,000	—	4,800,000
Contribution margin.........	$ 320,000	$1,440,000	$ 720,000	—	$2,480,000
Fixed costs:					
Fixed factory overhead	$ 100,000	$ 225,000	$ 175,000	$ —	$ 500,000
Depreciation....	128,000	144,000	128,000	—	400,000
Administrative and selling expense	120,000	140,000	80,000	820,000	1,160,000
Total fixed costs.......	$ 348,000	$ 509,000	$ 383,000	$ 820,000	$2,060,000
Operating income (loss)	$ (28,000)	$ 931,000	$ 337,000	$(820,000)	$ 420,000

2. As a result of the information disclosed by both segmented income statements (by product line and by geographic area), recommend areas where Stratford Corporation should focus its attention in order to improve corporate profitability. (CMA, adapted)

Problem 11-48   *Straightforward Problem on Absorption versus Variable Costing.* Skinny Dippers, Inc. produces frozen yogurt, a low-calorie dairy dessert. The product is sold in five-gallon containers, which have the following price and standard variable costs.

Sales price...	$15
Direct material...	5
Direct labor	2
Variable overhead	3

Budgeted fixed overhead in 19x7 was $300,000. Actual production was 150,000 five-gallon containers, of which 125,000 were sold. There were no variances recorded in 19x7. Skinny Dippers, Inc. incurred the following selling and administrative expenses.

Fixed	$50,000 for the year
Variable	$1 per container sold

REQUIRED:

1. Compute the standard product cost per container of frozen yogurt under (a) absorption costing and (b) variable costing.
2. Prepare income statements for 19x7 using (a) absorption costing and (b) variable costing.

3. Reconcile the income reported under the two methods by listing the two key places where the income statements differ.
4. Reconcile the income reported under the two methods using the shortcut method.

Problem 11-49   Absorption and Variable Costing; CVP Analysis. Millen Company began operations on January 1, 19x9 to produce a single product. It used a standard absorption costing system with a planned production volume of 100,000 units. During its first year of operations, no variances were incurred and there were no fixed selling or administrative expenses. Inventory on December 31 was 20,000 units, and net income for 19x9 was $240,000.

REQUIRED:

1. If Millen Company had used variable costing, its net income would have been $220,000. Compute the break-even point in units under variable costing.
2. Draw a profit-volume graph for Millen Company. (Assume variable costing.)

Problem 11-50   Variable-Costing and Absorption-Costing Income Statements; Appendix. Great Outdoze Company manufactures sleeping bags, which sell for $60 each. The variable standard costs of production are as follows:

Direct material	$20
Direct labor	11
Variable manufacturing overhead.	8

Budgeted fixed overhead in 19x5 was $200,000 and budgeted production was 20,000 sleeping bags. The year's actual production was 25,000 units, of which 22,000 were sold. There were no variances during 19x5, except for the fixed-overhead volume variance. Variable selling and administrative costs were $1 per unit sold; fixed selling and administrative costs were $30,000. The firm does not prorate variances.

REQUIRED:

1. Calculate the standard product cost per sleeping bag under (a) absorption costing and (b) variable costing.
2. Compute the fixed-overhead volume variance for 19x5.
3. Prepare income statements for the year using (a) absorption costing and (b) variable costing.
4. Reconcile reported income under the two methods using the shortcut method.

Problem 11-51   Variable and Absorption Costing; Appendix. Ellis Company had net income for the first 10 months of 19x9 of $200,000. They used a standard-costing system, and there were no variances through October 31. One hundred thousand units were manufactured during this period, and 100,000 units were sold. Fixed manufacturing overhead was $2,000,000 over the 10-month period (i.e., $200,000 per month). There are no selling and administrative expenses for Ellis Company. All variances are disposed of at year-end by an adjustment to cost of goods sold. Both variable and fixed costs are expected to continue at the same rates for the balance of the year (i.e., fixed costs at $200,000 per month and variable costs at the same variable cost per unit). There were 10,000 units in inventory on October 31. Seventeen thousand units are to be produced and 19,000 units are to be sold in total over the last two months of 19x9. Assume the standard unit variable cost is the same in 19x9 as in 19x8. (Hint: You cannot calculate revenue or cost of goods sold; you must work directly with contribution margin or gross margin.)

REQUIRED:

1. If operations proceed as described, will net income be higher under variable or absorption costing for 19x9 in total? Why?

2. If operations proceed as described, what will net income for 19x9 *in total* be under: (a) variable costing and (b) absorption costing? (Ignore income taxes.)

CASE *Case 11-52   Designing a Responsibility-Accounting System.* Edison Electronics manufactures complex printed circuit boards for the computer industry. The company operates in a very price-competitive industry, so it has little control over the price of its products. It *must* meet the market price. To do so, the firm has to keep production costs in check by operating as efficiently as possible. The company's president has stated that to be successful, the company must provide a very high-quality product and meet its delivery commitments to customers on time. Edison Electronics is organized as shown below.

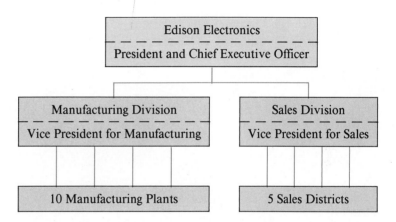

There is currently a disagreement between the company's two vice presidents regarding the responsibility-accounting system. The vice president for manufacturing claims that the 10 plants should be cost centers. She recently expressed the following sentiment: "The plants should be cost centers, because the plant managers do not control the sales of our products. Designating the plants as profit centers would result in holding the plant managers responsible for something they can't control." A contrary view is held by the vice president for marketing. He recently made the following remarks: "The plants should be profit centers. The plant managers are in the best position to affect the company's overall profit.

REQUIRED: As the company's new controller, you have been asked to make a recommendation to the company president regarding the responsibility center issue. Write a memo to the president making a recommendation and explaining the reasoning behind it. In your memo address the following points.

1. Assuming that Edison Electronics' overall goal is profitability, what are the company's critical success factors? A *critical success factor* is a variable that meets these two criteria: It is largely under the company's control, and the company must succeed in this area in order to reach its overall goal of profitability.
2. Which responsibility-accounting arrangement is most consistent with achieving success on the company's critical success factors?
3. What responsibility-center designation is most appropriate for the company's sales districts?
4. As a specific example, consider the rush-order problem illustrated in the chapter. Suppose that Edison Electronics often experiences rush orders from its customers. Which of the two proposed responsibility-accounting arrangements is best suited to making good decisions about accepting or rejecting rush orders? Specifically, should the plants be cost centers or profit centers?

Chapter 12 Investment Centers and Transfer Pricing

After completing this chapter, you should be able to:

- Explain the role of managerial accounting in achieving goal congruence.

- Compute an investment center's return on investment (ROI) and residual income.

- Explain how a manager can improve ROI by increasing either the sales margin or capital turnover.

- Describe some advantages and disadvantages of both ROI and residual income as divisional performance measures.

- Explain how to measure a division's income and invested capital.

- Use the general economic rule to set an optimal transfer price.

- Explain how to base a transfer price on market prices, costs, or negotiations.

How do the top managers of large companies such as Chrysler Corporation and General Electric Company evaluate their divisions and other major subunits? The largest subunits within these and similar organizations usually are designated as **investment centers.** The manager of this type of *responsibility center* is held accountable not only for the investment center's *profit,* but also for the *capital invested* to earn that profit. Invested capital refers to assets, such as buildings and equipment, used in a subunit's operations. In this chapter we will study the methods that managerial accountants use to evaluate investment centers and the performance of their managers.[1]

---

[1] Recall from Chapter 11 that in practice the term *profit center* sometimes is used interchangeably with the term *investment center.* To be precise, however, the term *profit center* should be reserved for a subunit whose manager is held accountable for profit but not for invested capital.

In many organizations, one subunit manufactures a product or produces a service which is then transferred to another subunit in the same organization. For example, automobile parts manufactured in one division of General Motors are then transferred to another GM division that assembles vehicles.

The price at which products or services are transferred between two subunits in an organization is called a **transfer price.** Since a transfer price affects the profit of both the buying and selling divisions, the transfer price affects the performance evaluation of these responsibility centers. Later in this chapter, we will study the methods that managerial accountants use to determine transfer prices.

DELEGATION OF DECISION MAKING

Most large organizations are decentralized. Managers throughout these organizations are given autonomy to make decisions for their subunits. Decentralization takes advantage of the specialized knowledge and skills of managers, permits an organization to respond quickly to events, and relieves top management of the need to direct the organization's day-to-day activities. The biggest challenge in making a decentralized organization function effectively is to obtain *goal congruence* among the organization's autonomous managers.

Obtaining Goal Congruence: A Behavioral Challenge

Goal congruence is obtained when the managers of subunits throughout an organization strive to achieve the goals set by top management. This desirable state of affairs is difficult to achieve, for a variety of reasons. Managers often are unaware of the effects of their decisions on the organization's other subunits. Also, it is only human for people to be more concerned with the performance of their own subunit than with the effectiveness of the entire organization. The behavioral challenge in designing any management control system is to come as close as possible to obtaining goal congruence.

To obtain goal congruence, the behavior of managers throughout an organization must be directed toward top management's goals. Managers not only must have their sights set on these organizational goals, but also must be given positive incentives to achieve them. The *managerial accountant's objective* in designing a responsibility-accounting system is to provide these incentives to the organization's subunit managers. *The key factor in deciding how well the responsibility-accounting system works is the extent to which it directs managers' efforts toward organizational goals.* Thus, the accounting measures used to evaluate investment-center managers should provide them with incentives to act in the interests of the overall organization.

Management by Objectives (MBO) An emphasis on obtaining goal congruence is consistent with a broad managerial approach called **management by objectives** or **MBO.** Under the MBO philosophy managers participate in setting goals which they then strive to achieve. These goals usually are expressed in financial or other quantitative terms, and the responsibility-accounting system is used to evaluate performance in achieving them.

Adaptation of Management Control Systems

When an organization begins its operations, it is usually small and decision making generally is centralized. The chief executive can control operations without a formal responsibility-accounting system. It is relatively easy in a small organization for managers to keep in touch with routine operations through face-to-face contact with employees.

As an organization grows, however, its managers need more formal information systems, including managerial-accounting information in order to maintain control. Accounting systems are established to record events and provide the framework for internal and external financial reports. Budgets become necessary to plan the organization's activity. As the organization gains experience in producing its goods or services, cost standards and flexible budgets often are established to help control operations. As the organization continues to grow, some delegation of decision making becomes necessary. Decentralization is often the result of this tendency toward delegation. Ultimately, a fully developed responsibility-accounting system emerges. Managerial accountants designate cost centers, revenue centers, profit centers, and investment centers, and develop appropriate performance measures for each subunit.

Thus, an organization's accounting and managerial control systems usually adapt and become more complex as the organization grows and changes.

MEASURING PERFORMANCE IN INVESTMENT CENTERS

In our study of investment-center performance evaluation, we will focus on Suncoast Food Centers. This Florida chain of retail grocery stores has three divisions, as depicted by the organization chart in Exhibit 12-1.

The Gulf and Atlantic divisions consist of individual grocery stores located in six coastal cities. The company's Food Processing Division operates dairy plants, bakeries, and meat processing plants in Miami, Orlando, and Jacksonville. These facilities provide all Suncoast Food Centers with milk, ice cream, yogurt, cheese, breads and desserts, and packaged meat. These Suncoast brand food products are transferred to the company's Gulf and Atlantic divisions at transfer prices established by the corporate controller's office.

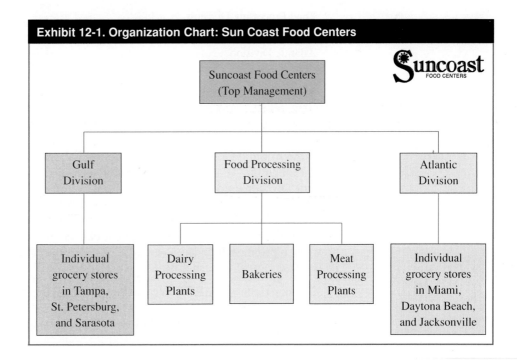

Exhibit 12-1. Organization Chart: Sun Coast Food Centers

Suncoast Food Centers' three divisions are investment centers. This responsibility-center designation is appropriate, because each division manager has the authority to make decisions that affect both profit and invested capital. For example, the Gulf Division manager approves the overall pricing policies in the Gulf Division's stores, and also has the autonomy to sign contracts to buy food and other products for resale. These actions influence the division's profit. In addition, the Gulf Division manager has the authority to build new Suncoast Food Centers, rent space in shopping centers, or close existing stores. These decisions affect the amount of capital invested in the division.

The primary goals of any profit-making enterprise include maximizing its profitability and using its invested capital as effectively as possible. Managerial accountants use two different measures to evaluate the performance of investment centers: return on investment and residual income. We will illustrate each of these measures for Suncoast Food Centers.

Return on Investment

The most common investment-center performance measure is **return on investment** or **ROI,** which is defined as follows:

$$\text{Return on investment (ROI)} = \frac{\text{income}}{\text{invested capital}}$$

The 19x4 ROI calculations for Suncoast Food Centers' three divisions are:

	$\dfrac{\text{Income}}{\text{Invested Capital}} =$	Return on Investment (ROI)
Gulf Division	$\dfrac{\$3,000,000}{\$20,000,000} =$	15%
Food Processing Division	$\dfrac{\$3,600,000}{\$18,000,000} =$	20%
Atlantic Division	$\dfrac{\$6,750,000}{\$45,000,000} =$	15%

Notice how the ROI calculation for each division takes into account *both divisional income and the capital invested* in the division. Why is this important? Suppose each division were evaluated only on the basis of its divisional profit. The Atlantic Division reported a higher divisional profit than the Gulf Division. Does this mean the Atlantic Division performed better than the Gulf Division? The answer is no. Although the Atlantic Division's profit exceeded the Gulf Division's profit, the Atlantic Division used a much larger amount of invested capital to earn its profit. The Atlantic Division's assets are more than two times the assets of the Gulf Division.

Considering the relative size of the two divisions, we should expect the Atlantic Division to earn a larger profit than the Gulf Division. The important question is not how much profit each division earned, but rather how effectively each division used its invested capital to earn a profit.

Factors Underlying ROI We can rewrite the ROI formula as follows:

$$\text{Return on investment} = \frac{\text{income}}{\text{invested capital}} = \frac{\text{income}}{\text{sales revenue}} \times \frac{\text{sales revenue}}{\text{invested capital}}$$

Notice that the *sales revenue* term cancels out in the denominator and numerator when the two right-hand fractions are multiplied.

Writing the ROI formula in this way highlights the factors that determine a division's return on investment. Income divided by sales revenue is called the **sales margin.** This term measures the percentage of each sales dollar that remains as profit after all expenses are covered. Sales revenue divided by invested capital is called the **capital turnover.** This term focuses on the number of sales dollars generated by every dollar of invested capital. The sales margin and capital turnover for Suncoast Food Centers' three divisions are calculated below for 19x4.

$$\text{Sales Margin} \times \text{Capital Turnover} = \text{ROI}$$

$$\frac{\text{Income}}{\text{Sales Revenue}} \times \frac{\text{Sales Revenue}}{\text{Invested Capital}} = \text{ROI}$$

Gulf Division	$\frac{\$3,000,000}{\$60,000,000} \times \frac{\$60,000,000}{\$20,000,000}$	= 15%
Food Processing Division	$\frac{\$3,600,000}{\$9,000,000} \times \frac{\$9,000,000}{\$18,000,000}$	= 20%
Atlantic Division	$\frac{\$6,750,000}{\$135,000,000} \times \frac{\$135,000,000}{\$45,000,000}$	= 15%

The Gulf Division's 19x4 sales margin is 5 percent ($3,000,000 of profit ÷ $60,000,000 of sales revenue). Thus, each dollar of divisional sales resulted in a five-cent profit. The division's 19x4 capital turnover was 3 ($60,000,000 of sales revenue ÷ $20,000,000 of invested capital). Thus, three dollars of sales revenue were generated by each dollar of capital invested in the division's assets, such as store buildings, display shelves, checkout equipment, and inventory.

Improving ROI How could the Gulf Division manager improve the division's return on investment? Since ROI is the product of the sales margin and the capital turnover, ROI can be improved by increasing either or both of its components. For example, if the Gulf Division manager increased the division's sales margin to 6 percent while holding the capital turnover constant at 3, the division's ROI would climb from 15 percent to 18 percent, as follows:

$$\begin{array}{c} \text{Gulf Division's} \\ \text{Improved ROI} \end{array} = \begin{array}{c} \text{Improved} \\ \text{Sales Margin} \end{array} \times \begin{array}{c} \text{Same} \\ \text{Capital Turnover} \end{array}$$

$$= \quad 6\% \quad \times \quad 3 \quad = 18\%$$

To bring about the improved sales margin, the Gulf Division manager would need to increase divisional profit to $3,600,000 on sales of $60,000,000 ($3,600,000 ÷ $60,000,000 = 6%). How could profit be increased without changing total sales revenue? There are two possibilities: increase sales prices while selling less quantity, or decrease expenses. Neither of these is necessarily easy to do. In increasing sales prices, the division manager must be careful not to lose sales to the extent that total sales revenue declines. Similarly, reducing the expenses must not diminish product quality, customer service, or overall store atmosphere. Any of these changes could also result in lost sales revenue.

An alternative way of increasing the Gulf Division's ROI would be to increase its capital turnover. Suppose the Gulf Division manager increased the division's capital turnover to 4 while holding the sales margin constant at 5 percent. The division's ROI would climb from 15 percent to 20 percent:

$$\frac{\text{Gulf Division's}}{\text{Improved ROI}} = \frac{\text{Same}}{\text{Sales Margin}} \times \frac{\text{Improved}}{\text{Capital Turnover}}$$

$$= \quad 5\% \quad \times \quad 4 \quad = 20\%$$

To obtain the improved capital turnover, the Gulf Division manager would need to either increase sales revenue or reduce the division's invested capital. For example, the improved ROI could be achieved by reducing invested capital to $15,000,000 while maintaining sales revenue of $60,000,000. This would be a very tall order. The division manager can lower invested capital somewhat by reducing inventories, and can increase sales revenue by using store space more effectively. But reducing inventories may lead to stockouts and lost sales, and crowded aisles may drive customers away.

Improving ROI is a balancing act that requires all the skills of an effective manager. The ROI analysis above merely shows the arena in which the balancing act is performed.

Residual Income

Although ROI is the most popular investment-center performance measure, it has one major drawback. To illustrate, suppose Suncoast's Food Processing division manager can buy a new food-processing machine for $500,000, which will save $80,000 in operating expenses and thereby raise divisional profit by $80,000. The return on this investment in new equipment is 16 percent:

$$\frac{\text{Return on investment}}{\text{in new equipment}} = \frac{\text{increase in divisional profit}}{\text{increase in invested capital}} = \frac{\$80,000}{\$500,000} = 16\%$$

Now suppose it costs Suncoast Food Centers 12 cents for each dollar of capital to invest in operational assets. What is the optimal decision for the Food Processing division manager to make, *viewed from the perspective of the company as a whole?* Since it costs Suncoast Food Centers 12 percent for every dollar of capital, and the return on the investment in new equipment is 16 percent, the equipment should be purchased. For goal congruence, the autonomous division manager should decide to buy the new equipment.

Now consider what is likely to happen. The Food Processing Division manager's performance is evaluated on the basis of his division's ROI. Without the new equipment, the divisional ROI is 20 percent ($3,600,000 of divisional profit ÷ $18,000,000 of invested capital). If he purchases the new equipment, his divisional ROI will decline:

Food Processing Division's Return on Investment

Without Investment in New Equipment	With Investment in New Equipment
$\dfrac{\$3,600,000}{\$18,000,000} = 20\%$	$\dfrac{\$3,600,000 + \$80,000}{\$18,000,000 + \$500,000} < 20\%$

Why did this happen? Even though the investment in new equipment earns a return of 16 percent, which is greater than the company's cost of raising capital (12 percent), the return is less than the division's ROI without the equipment (20 percent). Averaging the new investment with those already in place in the Food Processing Division merely reduces the division's ROI. Since the division manager is evaluated using ROI, he will be reluctant to decide in favor of acquiring the new equipment.

The problem is that the ROI measure leaves out an important piece of information: it ignores the firm's cost of raising investment capital. For this reason, many managers prefer to use a different investment-center performance measure instead of ROI.

Computing Residual Income An investment center's **residual income** is defined as follows:

$$\text{Residual income} = \text{investment center's profit} - \text{investment center's invested capital} \times \text{imputed interest rate}$$

where   the imputed interest rate = the firm's cost of acquiring investment capital

Residual income is a dollar amount, not a ratio like ROI. It is the amount of an investment center's profit that remains (as a residual) after subtracting an imputed interest charge. This charge reflects the cost incurred by the firm to obtain the capital invested in the investment center. The term *imputed* means that the interest charge is estimated by the managerial accountant. The charge reflects all of the firm's capital acquisition costs, called the **cost of capital.** This includes the payment of interest on debt and the payment of dividends to stockholders. The cost of capital depends on the riskiness of the investment for which the funds will be used. Thus, divisions that have different levels of risk sometimes are assigned different imputed interest rates.

The residual income of Suncoast's Food Processing Division is computed below, both with and without the investment in the new equipment. The imputed interest rate is 12 percent, because it costs Suncoast Food Centers 12 cents on the dollar, on average, to obtain investment capital.

Food Processing Division's Residual Income

	Without Investment in New Equipment		With Investment in New Equipment	
Divisional profit.		$3,600,000		$3,680,000
Less imputed interest charge:				
Invested capital	$18,000,000		$18,500,000	
× Imputed interest rate	× .12		× .12	
Imputed interest charge. . .		2,160,000		2,220,000
Residual income.		$1,440,000		$1,460,000

Investment in new equipment raises residual income by $20,000.

Notice that the Food Processing Division's residual income will *increase* if the new equipment is purchased. What will be the division manager's incentive if he is evaluated on the basis of residual income instead of ROI? He will want to make the investment, because that decision will increase his division's residual income. Thus, goal congruence is achieved when the managerial accountant uses residual income to measure divisional performance.

Why does residual income facilitate goal congruence while ROI does not? Because the residual-income formula incorporates an important piece of data that is excluded from the ROI formula: the firm's cost of acquiring investment capital. To summarize, ROI and residual income are compared as follows:

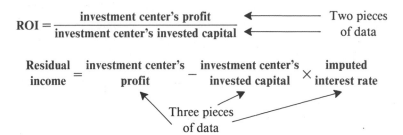

Unfortunately, residual income also has a serious drawback: It should not be used to compare the performance of different-sized investment centers, because it incorporates a bias in favor of the larger investment center. To illustrate, the following table compares the residual income of Suncoast Food Centers' Gulf and Atlantic divisions. Notice that the Atlantic Division's residual income is considerably higher than the Gulf Division's. This is entirely due to the much greater size of the Atlantic Division, as evidenced by its far greater invested capital.

Comparison of Residual Income: Two Divisions

	Gulf Division		Atlantic Division	
Divisional profit.		$3,000,000		$6,750,000
Less imputed interest charge:				
Invested capital	$20,000,000		$45,000,000	
× Imputed interest rate	× .12		× .12	
Imputed interest charge. . .		→ 2,400,000		→ 5,400,000
Residual income.		$ 600,000		$1,350,000

The Atlantic Division's residual income is much higher simply because it is larger than the Gulf Division.

In short, neither ROI nor residual income provides a perfect measure of investment-center performance. ROI can undermine goal congruence. Residual income distorts comparisons between investment centers of different sizes. As a result, some companies routinely use both measures for divisional performance evaluation.

MEASURING INCOME AND INVESTED CAPITAL

Both the ROI and residual-income measures of investment-center performance use profit and invested capital in their formulas. This raises the question of how to measure divisional profit and invested capital. This section will illustrate various approaches to resolving these measurement issues.

Invested Capital

We will focus on Suncoast Food Centers' Food Processing Division to illustrate several alternative approaches to measuring an investment center's capital. Exhibit 12-2 lists the assets and liabilities associated with the Food Processing Division. Notice that Exhibit 12-2 does not comprise a complete balance sheet. First, there are no long-term liabilities, such as bonds payable, associated with the Food Processing Division. Although Suncoast Food Centers may have such long-term debt, it would not be meaningful to assign portions of that debt to the company's individual divisions. Second, there is no stockholders' equity associated with the Food Processing Division. The owners of the company own stock in Suncoast Food Centers, not in its individual divisions.

Average Balances ROI and residual income are computed for a period of time, such as a year or a month. Asset balances, on the other hand, are measured at a point in time, such as December 31. Since divisional asset balances generally will change over time, we use average balances in calculating ROI and residual income. For example, if the Food Processing Division's balance in invested capital was $19,000,000 on January 1, 19x4, and $17,000,000 on December 31, 19x4, we would

---

Exhibit 12-2. Assets and Liabilities Associated with Food Processing Division

Assets*

Suncoast
FOOD CENTERS

Current assets (cash, accounts receivable, inventories, etc.)		$ 2,000,000
Long-lived assets (land, buildings, equipment, vehicles, etc.):		
Gross book value (acquisition cost)	$19,000,000	
Less: Accumulated depreciation	4,000,000	
Net book value		15,000,000
Plant under construction		1,000,000
Total assets		$18,000,000

Liabilities

Current liabilities (accounts payable, salaries payable, etc.)		$ 500,000

*This is not a balance sheet, but rather a listing of certain assets and liabilities associated with the Food Processing Division.

use the average invested capital of $18,000,000 in the ROI and residual income calculations.

Should Total Assets Be Used? Exhibit 12-2 shows that the Food Processing Division had average balances during 19x4 of $2,000,000 in current assets, $15,000,000 in long-lived assets, and $1,000,000 tied up in a plant under construction. (Suncoast Food Centers is building a new high-tech dairy plant in Orlando to produce its innovative zero-calorie ice cream.) In addition, Exhibit 12-2 discloses that the Food Processing Division's average 19x4 balance of current liabilities was $500,000.

What is the division's invested capital? Several possibilities exist.

1. *Total assets* The management of Suncoast Food Centers has decided to use *average total assets* for the year in measuring each division's invested capital. Thus, $18,000,000 is the amount used in the ROI and residual-income calculations discussed earlier in this chapter. This measure of invested capital is appropriate if the division manager has considerable authority in making decisions about *all* of the division's assets, *including nonproductive assets.* In this case, the Food Processing Division's partially completed dairy plant is a nonproductive asset. Since the division manager had considerable influence in deciding to build the new plant and he is responsible for overseeing the project, average total assets provides an appropriate measure.

2. *Total productive assets* In other companies, division managers are directed by top management to keep nonproductive assets, such as vacant land or construction in progress. In such cases, it is appropriate to exclude nonproductive assets from the measure of invested capital. Then *average total productive assets* is used to measure invested capital. If Suncoast Food Centers had chosen this alternative, $17,000,000 would have been used in the ROI and residual income calculations (total assets of $18,000,000 less $1,000,000 for the plant under construction).

3. *Total assets less current liabilities* Some companies allow division managers to secure short-term bank loans and other short-term credit. In such cases, invested capital often is measured by *average total assets less average current liabilities.* This approach encourages investment-center managers to minimize resources tied up in assets and maximize the use of short-term credit to finance operations. If this approach had been used by Suncoast Food Centers, the Food Processing Division's invested capital would have been $17,500,000 (total assets of $18,000,000 less current liabilities of $500,000).

Gross or Net Book Value Another decision to make in choosing a measure of invested capital is whether to use the *gross book value (acquisition cost)* or the *net book value* of long-lived assets. (Net book value is the acquisition cost less accumulated depreciation.) Suncoast Food Centers' management has decided to use the average net book value of $15,000,000 to value the Food Processing Division's long-lived assets. If gross book value had been used instead, the division's measure of invested capital would have been $22,000,000 as shown below.

Current assets...	$ 2,000,000
Long-lived assets (at gross book value).............................	19,000,000
Plant under construction..	1,000,000
Total assets (at gross book value)	$22,000,000

There are advantages and disadvantages associated with both gross and net book value as a measure of invested capital.

ADVANTAGES OF NET BOOK VALUE; DISADVANTAGES OF GROSS BOOK VALUE

1. Using net book value maintains consistency with the balance sheet prepared for external-reporting purposes. This allows for more meaningful comparisons of return-on-investment measures across different companies.
2. Using net book value to measure invested capital is also more consistent with the definition of income, which is the numerator in ROI calculations. In computing income, the current period's depreciation on long-lived assets is deducted as an expense.

ADVANTAGES OF GROSS BOOK VALUE; DISADVANTAGES OF NET BOOK VALUE

1. The usual methods of computing depreciation, such as straight-line or declining-balance methods, are arbitrary. Hence, they should not be allowed to affect ROI or residual-income calculations.
2. When long-lived assets are depreciated, their net book value declines over time. This results in a misleading increase in ROI and residual income across time. Exhibit 12-3 provides an illustration of this phenomenon for the ROI calculated on an equipment purchase under consideration by the Food Processing Division manager. Notice that the ROI rises steadily across the five-year horizon, if invested capital is measured by net book value. However, using gross book value eliminates this problem. If an ac-

---

Exhibit 12-3. Increase in ROI Over Time (when net book value is used)

Acquisition cost of equipment	$500,000
Useful life	5 years
Salvage value at end of useful life	0
Annual straight-line depreciation	$100,000
Annual income generated by asset (before deducting depreciation)	$150,000

Year	Income before Depreciation	Annual Depreciation	Income Net of Depreciation	Average Net Book Value*	ROI Based on Net Book Value†	Average Gross Book Value	ROI Based on Gross Book Value
1	$150,000	$100,000	$50,000	$450,000	11.1%	$500,000	10%
2	150,000	100,000	50,000	350,000	14.3%	500,000	10%
3	150,000	100,000	50,000	250,000	20.0%	500,000	10%
4	150,000	100,000	50,000	150,000	33.3%	500,000	10%
5	150,000	100,000	50,000	50,000	100.0%	500,000	10%

*Average net book value is the average of the beginning and ending balances for the year in net book value. In year 1, for example, the average net book value is:

$$\frac{\$500,000 + \$400,000}{2}$$

†ROI rounded to nearest tenth of 1 percent

celerated depreciation method were used instead of the straight-line method, the increasing trend in ROI would be even more pronounced.

A Behavioral Problem   The tendency for net book value to produce a misleading increase in ROI over time can have a serious effect on the incentives of investment-center managers. Investment centers with old assets will show much higher ROIs than investment centers with relatively new assets. This can discourage investment-center managers from investing in new equipment. If this behavioral tendency persists, a division's assets can become obsolete, making the division uncompetitive.

Allocating Assets to Investment Centers   Some companies control certain assets centrally, although these assets are needed to carry on operations in the divisions. Common examples are cash and accounts receivable. Divisions need cash in order to operate, but many companies control cash balances centrally in order to minimize their total cash holdings. Some large retail firms manage accounts receivable centrally. A credit customer of some national department-store chains can make a payment either at the local store or by mailing the payment to corporate headquarters.

When certain assets are controlled centrally, some allocation basis generally is chosen to allocate these asset balances to investment centers, for the purpose of measuring invested capital. For example, cash may be allocated based on the budgeted cash needs in each division or on the basis of divisional sales. Accounts receivable usually are allocated on the basis of divisional sales. Divisions with less stringent credit terms are allocated proportionately larger balances of accounts receivable.

Measuring Investment-Center Income

In addition to choosing a measure of investment-center capital, an accountant must also decide how to measure a center's income. The key issue is controllability; the choice involves the extent to which uncontrollable items are allowed to influence the income measure. Exhibit 12-4 illustrates several different possibilities for measuring the income of Suncoast Food Centers' Food Processing Division.

Exhibit 12-4. Divisional Income Statement: Food Processing Division

	Sales revenue	$9,000,000
	Variable costs	3,800,000
(1)	Divisional contribution margin	5,200,000
	Fixed costs controllable by division manager	1,600,000
(2)	Profit margin controllable by division manager	3,600,000
	Fixed costs, traceable to division, but	
	controlled by others	1,200,000
(3)	Profit margin traceable to division	2,400,000
	Costs allocated from corporate headquarters	400,000
(4)	Divisional income before interest and taxes	2,000,000
	Interest costs allocated from corporate headquarters	250,000
(5)	Divisional income before taxes	1,750,000
	Income taxes allocated from corporate headquarters	700,000
(6)	Divisional net income	$1,050,000

(handwritten note in left margin: "Net Income figure used." with arrow pointing to line (2))

Suncoast Food Centers' top management uses the *profit margin controllable by division manager,* $3,600,000, to evaluate the Food Processing division manager. This profit measure is used in calculating either ROI or residual income. Some fixed costs traceable to the division have not been deducted from this $3,600,000 amount, but the division manager cannot control or significantly influence these costs. Hence they are excluded from the ROI calculation in evaluating the division manager.

Managers versus Investment Centers It is important to make a distinction between an investment center and its manager. In evaluating the *manager's* performance, only revenues and costs that the manager can control or significantly influence should be included in the profit measure. Remember that the overall objective of the performance measure is to provide incentives for goal-congruent behavior. No performance measure can motivate a manager to make decisions about costs he or she cannot control. This explains why Suncoast Food Centers' top management relies on the profit margin controllable by division manager to compute the manager's ROI performance measure.

Evaluating the Food Processing Division as a viable economic investment is a different matter altogether. In this evaluation, traceability of costs, rather than controllability, is the issue. For this purpose, Suncoast Food Centers' top management uses the profit margin traceable to division to compute the divisional ROI or residual income. As Exhibit 12-4 shows, this amount is $2,400,000.

Other Profit Measures The other measures of divisional profit shown in Exhibit 12-4 (lines 4, 5, and 6) are also used by some companies. The rationale behind these divisional income measures is that all corporate costs have to be covered by the operations of the divisions. Allocating corporate costs, interest, and income taxes to the divisions makes division managers aware of these costs.

Inflation: Historical-Cost versus Current-Value Accounting

Whether measuring investment-center income or invested capital, the impact of price-level changes should not be forgotten. During periods of inflation, historical-cost asset values soon cease to reflect the cost of replacing those assets. Therefore, some accountants argue that investment-center performance measures based on historical-cost accounting are misleading. Yet surveys of corporate managers indicate that an accounting system based on current values would not alter their decisions. Most managers believe that measures based on historical-cost accounting are adequate when used in conjunction with budgets and performance targets. As managers prepare those budgets, they build their expectations about inflation into the budgets and performance targets.

Another reason for using historical-cost accounting for internal purposes is that it is required for external reporting. Thus, historical-cost data already are available, while installing current-value accounting would add substantial incremental costs to the organization's information system.

Measuring Income and Invested Capital: Summary

To summarize, the primary objective in choosing measures for evaluation of investment centers and their managers is goal congruence. The managerial accountant should design investment-center performance measures that reward managers for pursuing the goals of the overall organization.

**ILLUSTRATION FROM
MANAGEMENT-
ACCOUNTING
PRACTICE**

Surveys of Corporate Practices

A survey published in the *Harvard Business Review* reported the following real-world practices in measuring investment-center performance.[2] The percentages in the right-hand column indicate the percentage of responding firms that use the method listed.

Measuring invested capital:

Gross book value of long-lived assets........................ 14%

Net book value of long-lived assets......................... 85%

Other.. 1%

Measuring income:

Corporate headquarters costs allocated to investment centers..... 49%

No allocation of central corporate costs to investment centers.... 51%

ROI versus residual income:

ROI... 65%

Residual income... 2%

Both.. 28%

Other measures.. 5%

Setting targets for ROI:

All investment centers have same target..................... 7%

Each investment center is assigned its own target............. 64%

Investment centers are not given targets..................... 29%

OTHER ISSUES IN SEGMENT PERFORMANCE EVALUATION

Alternatives to ROI and Residual Income

ROI and residual income are short-run performance measures. They focus on only one period of time. Yet an investment center is really a collection of assets (investments), each of which has a multiperiod life. Exhibit 12-5 portrays this perspective of an investment center.

To evaluate any one of these individual investments correctly requires a multiperiod viewpoint, which takes into account the timing of the cash flows from the investment. For example, investment E in Exhibit 12-5 may start out slowly in years 4 and 5, but it may be economically justified by its expected high performance in years 8, 9, and 10. Any evaluation of the investment center in year 5 that ignores the long-term performance of its various investments can result in a misleading conclusion. Thus, single-period performance measures suffer from myopia. They focus on only a short time segment that slices across the division's investments as portrayed in Exhibit 12-5.

To avoid this short-term focus, some organizations downplay ROI and residual income in favor of an alternative approach. Instead of relating profit to invested capital in a single measure, these characteristics of investment-center performance are evaluated separately. Actual divisional profit for a time period is compared to a

[2] J. S. Reece and W. R. Cool, "Measuring Investment Center Performance," *Harvard Business Review,* May–June, 1978, pp. 28–46.

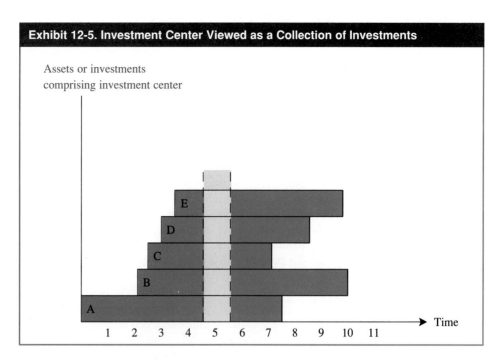

Exhibit 12-5. Investment Center Viewed as a Collection of Investments

flexible budget, and variances are used to analyze performance. The division's major investments are evaluated through a *post-audit* of the investment decisions. For example, investment E may have been undertaken because of expected high performance in years 8, 9, and 10. When that time comes, a review will determine whether the project lived up to expectations.

Evaluating periodic profit through flexible budgeting and variance analysis, coupled with post-audits of major investment decisions, is a more complicated approach to evaluating investment centers. However, it does help management avoid the myopia of single-period measures such as ROI and residual income.

Importance of Nonfinancial Information

Although financial measures such as segment profit, ROI, and residual income are widely used in performance evaluation, nonfinancial measures are important also. Manufacturers collect data on rates of defective products, airlines record information on lost bags and aircraft delays, and hotels keep track of occupancy rates. The proper evaluation of an organization and its segments requires that multiple performance measures be defined and used.

**ILLUSTRATION FROM
MANAGEMENT-
ACCOUNTING
PRACTICE**

General Electric Company

In addition to financial measures of investment-center performance, General Electric also uses nonfinancial measures in several key areas, including the following:

Market position
Product leadership
Productivity
Employee attitudes

Measuring Performance in Nonprofit Organizations

Management control in a nonprofit organization presents a special challenge. Such organizations are often managed by professionals, such as physicians in a hospital. Moreover, many people participate in a nonprofit organization at some personal sacrifice, motivated by humanitarian or public service ideals. Often, such people are less receptive to formal control procedures than their counterparts in business.

The goals of nonprofit organizations often are less clear-cut than those of businesses. Public service objectives may be difficult to specify with precision and even more difficult to measure in terms of achievement. For example, one community health center was established in an economically depressed area with three stated goals:

1. To reduce costs in a nearby hospital by providing a clinic for people to use instead of the hospital emergency room.
2. To provide preventive as well as therapeutic care, and establish outreach programs in the community.
3. To become financially self-sufficient.

There is some conflict between these objectives, since goal (2) does not provide revenue to the center, while goals (1) and (3) focus on financial efficiency. Moreover, the health center was staffed with physicians who could have achieved much greater incomes in private practice. The management control tools described in this and the preceding three chapters can be used in nonprofit organizations. However, the challenges in doing so effectively often are greater.

TRANSFER PRICING

The problem of measuring performance in profit centers or investment centers is made more complicated by transfers of goods or services between responsibility centers. The amount charged when one division sells goods or services to another division is called a **transfer price.** This price affects the profit measurement for both the selling division and the buying division. A high transfer price results in high profit for the selling division and low profit for the buying division. A low transfer price has the opposite effect.

Goal Congruence

What should be management's goal in setting transfer prices for internally transferred goods or services? In a decentralized organization, the managers of profit centers and investment centers often have considerable autonomy in deciding whether to accept or reject orders and whether to buy inputs from inside the organization or from outside. For example, a large manufacturer of farm equiment allows its Assembly Division managers to buy parts either from another division of the company or from independent manufacturers. The goal in setting transfer prices is to establish incentives for autonomous division managers to make decisions that support the overall goals of the organization.

Suppose it is in the best interests of Suncoast Food Centers for the baked goods produced by the Food Processing Division's Orlando bakery to be transferred to the Gulf Division's stores in the Tampa Bay area. Thus, if the firm were centralized, bakery products would be transferred from the Food Processing Division to the Gulf

Division. However, Suncoast Food Centers is a decentralized company, and the Gulf Division manager is free to buy baked goods either from the Food Processing Division or from an outside bakery company. Similarly, the Food Processing division manager is free to accept or reject an order for baked goods, at any given price, from the Gulf Division. The goal of the company's controller in setting the transfer price is to provide incentives for each of these division managers to act in the company's best interests. The transfer price should be chosen so that each division manager, when striving to maximize his or her own division's profit, makes the decision that maximizes the company's profit.

General-Transfer-Pricing Rule

Management's objective in setting a transfer price is to encourage goal congruence among the division managers involved in the transfer. A general rule that will ensure goal congruence is given below.

$$\text{Transfer price} = \begin{array}{c}\text{additional } \textit{outlay}\\ \textit{costs} \text{ incurred}\\ \text{because goods are}\\ \text{transferred}\end{array} + \begin{array}{c}\textit{opportunity}\\ \textit{cost} \text{ to the}\\ \text{organization}\\ \text{because of}\\ \text{the transfer}\end{array}$$

The general rule specifies the transfer price as the sum of two cost components. The first component is the outlay cost incurred by the division that produces the goods or services to be transferred. Outlay costs will include the direct variable costs of the product or service and any other outlay costs that are incurred only as a result of the transfer. The second component in the general transfer-pricing rule is the opportunity cost incurred by the organization as a whole because of the transfer. Recall from Chapter 2 that an *opportunity cost* is a benefit that is forgone as a result of taking a particular action.

We will illustrate the general transfer-pricing rule for Suncoast Food Centers. The company's Food Processing Division produces bread in its Orlando Bakery. The division transfers some of its products to the company's Gulf and Atlantic divisions, and sells some of its products to other companies in the *external market* under different labels.

Bread is transported to stores in racks containing one dozen loaves of packaged bread. In the Orlando bakery, the following variable costs are incurred to produce bread and transport it to a buyer.

Production:
    Standard variable cost per rack (including packaging) $7.00
Transportation:
    Standard variable cost to transport bread . . . . $.25 per rack

In applying the general transfer-pricing rule, we will distinguish between two different scenarios.

Scenario I: No Excess Capacity Suppose the Food Processing Division can sell all the bread it can produce to outside buyers at a market price of $11.00 per rack. Since the division can sell all of its production, it has *no excess capacity. Excess* *capacity* exists only when more goods can be produced than the producer is able to sell, due to low demand for the product.

What transfer price does the general rule yield under this scenario of no excess capacity? The transfer price is determined as follows:

Outlay cost:	
Standard variable cost of production	$ 7.00 per rack
Standard variable cost of transportation	.25 per rack
Total outlay cost....VaR...cost	$ 7.25 per rack
Opportunity cost:	
Selling price per unit in external market....Retail	$11.00 per rack
Variable cost of production and transportation	7.25 per rack
Opportunity cost (forgone contribution margin)	$ 3.75 per rack

General transfer-pricing rule

Transfer price = outlay cost + opportunity cost

$$\$11.00 = \$7.25 + \$3.75$$

The *outlay cost* incurred by the Food Processing Division in order to transfer a rack of bread includes the standard variable production cost of $7.00 and the standard variable transportation cost of $.25. The *opportunity cost* incurred by Suncoast Food Centers when its Food Processing Division transfers a rack of bread to the Gulf Division *instead* of selling it in the external market is the forgone contribution margin from the lost sale, equal to $3.75. Why does the company lose a sale in the external market for every rack of bread transferred to the Gulf Division? The sale is lost because there is *no excess capacity* in the Food Processing Division. Every rack of bread transferred to another company division results in one less rack of bread sold in the external market.

Goal Congruence How does the general transfer-pricing rule promote goal congruence? Suppose the Gulf Division's grocery stores can sell a loaf of bread for $1.50, or $18.00 for a rack of 12 loaves ($18.00 = 12 × $1.50). What is the best way for Suncoast Food Centers to use the limited production capacity in the Food Processing Division's Orlando bakery? The answer is determined as follows:

Contribution to Suncoast Food Centers from Sale in External market		Contribution to Suncoast Food Centers from Transfer to Gulf Division	
Wholesale selling price per rack	$11.00	Retail selling price per rack	$18.00
Variable costs	7.25	Variable costs	7.25
Contribution margin	$ 3.75	Contribution margin	$10.75

The best use of the bakery's limited production capacity is to produce bread for transfer to the Gulf Division. If the transfer price is set at $11.00, as the general rule specifies, goal congruence is maintained. The Food Processing Division manager is willing to transfer bread to the Gulf Division, because the transfer price of $11.00 is equal to the external market price. The Gulf Division manager is willing to buy the bread, because her division will have a contribution margin of $7.00 on each rack of bread transferred ($18.00 sales price minus the $11.00 transfer price).

Now consider a different situation. Suppose a local organization makes a special offer to the Gulf Division manager to buy several hundred loaves of bread to sell in a promotional campaign. The organization offers to pay $.80 per loaf, which is $9.60 per rack of a dozen loaves. What will the Gulf Division manager do? She must pay a transfer price of $11.00 per rack, so the Gulf Division would lose $1.40 per rack if the special offer were accepted ($1.40 = $11.00 − $9.60). The Gulf Division manager will decline the special offer. Is this decision in the best interests of Suncoast Food Centers as a whole? If the offer were accepted, the company as a whole would make a positive contribution of $2.35 per rack, as shown below.

**Contribution to Suncoast
Food Centers If Special
Offer Is Accepted**

Special price per rack	$9.60 per rack
Variable cost to company	7.25 per rack
Contribution to company, per rack	$2.35 per rack

However, the company can make even more if its Food Processing Division sells bread directly in its external market. Then the contribution to the company is $3.75, as we have just seen. (The external market price of $11.00 per rack minus a variable cost of $7.25 per rack equals $3.75 per rack.) Thus, Suncoast Food Centers is better off, as a whole, if the Gulf Division's special offer is rejected. Once again, the general transfer-pricing rule results in goal-congruent decision making.

Scenario II: Excess Capacity Now let's change our basic assumption, and suppose the Food Processing Division's Orlando bakery has excess production capacity. This means that the total demand for its bread from all sources, including the Gulf and Atlantic divisions and the external market, is less than the bakery's production capacity. Under this scenario of excess capacity, what does the general rule specify for a transfer price?

Transfer price = outlay cost + opportunity cost
$7.25   = $7.25   +   0

The *outlay cost* in the Food Processing Division's Orlando bakery is still $7.25, since it does not depend on whether there is idle capacity or not. The *opportunity cost,* however, is now zero. There is no opportunity cost to the company when a rack of bread is transferred to the Gulf Division, because the Food Processing Division can still satisfy all of its external demand for bread. Thus, the general rule specifies a transfer price of $7.25, the total standard variable cost of production and transportation.

Goal Congruence Let's reconsider what will happen when the Gulf Division manager receives the local organization's special offer to buy bread at $9.60 per rack. The Gulf Division will now show a positive contribution of $2.35 per rack on the special order.

Special price per rack	$9.60 per rack
Transfer price paid by Gulf Division	7.25 per rack
Contribution to Gulf Division	$2.35 per rack

The Gulf Division manager will accept the special offer. This decision is also in the best interests of Suncoast Food Centers. The company, as a whole, will also make a contribution of $2.35 per rack on every rack transferred to the Gulf Division to satisfy the special order. Once again, the general transfer pricing rule maintains goal-congruent decision-making behavior.

Notice that the general rule yields a transfer price that leaves the Food Processing Division manager indifferent as to whether the transfer will be made. At a transfer price of $7.25, the contribution to the Food Processing Division will be zero (transfer price of $7.25 less variable cost of $7.25). To avoid this problem, we can view the general rule as providing a lower bound on the transfer price. Some companies allow the producing division to add a markup to this lower bound in order to provide a positive contribution margin. This in turn provides a positive incentive to make the transfer.

Difficulty in Implementing the General Rule The general transfer-pricing rule will always promote goal-congruent decision making, *if the rule can be implemented.* However, the rule is often difficult or impossible to implement due to the difficulty of measuring opportunity costs. Such a cost-measurement problem can arise for a number of reasons. One reason is that the external market may not be perfectly competitive. Under **perfect competition,** the market price does not depend on the quantity sold by any one producer. Under **imperfect competition,** a single producer can affect the market price by varying the amount of product available in the market. In such cases, the external market price depends on the production decisions of the producer. This in turn means that the opportunity cost incurred by the company as a result of internal transfers depends on the quantity sold externally. These interactions may make it impossible to measure accurately the opportunity cost caused by a product transfer.

Other reasons for difficulty in measuring the opportunity cost associated with a product transfer include uniqueness of the transferred goods or services, a need for the producing division to invest in special equipment in order to produce the transferred goods, and interdependencies among several transferred products or services. For example, the producing division may provide design services as well as production of the goods for a buying division. What is the opportunity cost associated with each of these related outputs of the producing division? In many such cases it is difficult to sort out the opportunity costs.

The general transfer-pricing rule provides a good conceptual model for the managerial accountant to use in setting transfer prices. Moreover, in many cases it can be implemented. When the general rule cannot be implemented, organizations turn to other transfer-pricing methods, as we shall see next.

Transfers Based on the External Market Price

A common approach is to set the transfer price equal to the price in the external market. In the Suncoast Food Centers illustration, the Food Processing Division would set the transfer price for bread at $11.00 per rack, since that is the price the division can obtain in its external market. When the producing division has no excess capacity and perfect competition prevails, where no single producer can affect the market price, the general transfer-pricing rule and the external market price yield the same transfer price. This fact is illustrated for Suncoast Food Centers as follows:

GENERAL TRANSFER-PRICING RULE

$$\text{Transfer price} = \text{outlay cost} + \text{opportunity cost}$$

$$= \begin{array}{c} \text{variable cost of} \\ \text{production and} \\ \text{transportation} \end{array} + \begin{array}{c} \text{forgone contribution} \\ \text{margin of an external} \\ \text{sale} \end{array}$$

$$= \quad \$7.25 \quad + \quad (\$11.00 - \$7.25) \quad = \$11.00$$

MARKET PRICE

$$\text{Transfer price} = \text{external market price} = \$11.00$$

If the producing division has excess capacity or the external market is imperfectly competitive, the general rule and the external market price will not yield the same transfer price.

If the transfer price is set at the market price, the producing division should have the option of either producing goods for internal transfer or selling in the external market. The buying division should be required to purchase goods from inside its organization, if the producing division's goods meet the product specifications. Otherwise, the buying division should have the autonomy to buy from a supplier outside its own organization. To handle pricing disputes that may arise, an arbitration process should be established.

Transfer prices based on market prices are consistent with the responsibility-accounting concepts of profit centers and investment centers. In addition to encouraging division managers to focus on divisional profitability, market-based transfer prices help to show the contribution of each division to overall company profit. Suppose the Food Processing Division of Suncoast Food Centers transfers bread to the Gulf Division at a market-based transfer price of $11.00 per rack. The following contribution margins will be earned by the two divisions and the company as a whole.

Food Processing Division		Gulf Division	
Transfer price	$11.00 per rack	Retail sales price	$18.00 per rack
Variable costs..........	7.25 per rack	Transfer price	11.00 per rack
Contribution margin....	$ 3.75 per rack	Contribution margin....	$ 7.00 per rack

Suncoast Food Centers

Retail sales price	$18.00
Variable costs	7.25
Contribution margin..	$10.75

When aggregate divisional profits are determined for the year, and ROI and residual income are computed, the use of a market-based transfer price helps to assess the contributions of each division to overall corporate profits.

Distress Market Prices Occasionally an industry will experience a period of significant excess capacity and extremely low prices. For example, when gasoline prices soared due to a foreign oil embargo, the market prices for recreational vehicles and power boats fell temporarily to very low levels.

Under such extreme conditions, basing transfer prices on market prices can lead to decisions that are not in the best interests of the overall company. Basing transfer prices on artificially low **distress market prices** could lead the producing division to sell or close the productive resources devoted to producing the product for transfer. Under distress market prices, the producing division manager might prefer to move the division into a more profitable product line. While such a decision might improve the division's profit in the short-run, it could be contrary to the best interests of the company overall. It might be better for the company as a whole to avoid divesting itself of any productive resources and to ride out the period of market distress. To encourage an autonomous division manager to act in this fashion, some companies set the transfer price equal to the long-run average external market price, rather than the current (possibly depressed) market price.

Negotiated Transfer Prices

Many companies use negotiated transfer prices. Division managers or their representatives actually negotiate the price at which transfers will be made. Sometimes they start with the external market price and then make adjustments for various reasons. For example, the producing division may enjoy some cost savings on internal transfers that are not obtained on external sales. Commissions may not have to be paid to sales personnel on internally transferred products. In such cases, a negotiated transfer price may split the cost savings between the producing and buying divisions.

In other instances, a negotiated transfer price may be used because no external market exists for the transferred product.

Two drawbacks sometimes characterize negotiated transfer prices. First, negotiations can lead to divisiveness and competition between participating division managers. This can undermine the spirit of cooperation and unity that is desirable throughout an organization. Second, although negotiating skill is a valuable managerial talent, it should not be the sole or dominant factor in evaluating a division manager. If, for example, the producing division's manager is a better negotiator than the buying division's manager, then the producing division's profit may look better than it should, simply because of its manager's superior negotiating ability.

Cost-Based Transfer Prices

Organizations that do not base transfer prices on market prices or negotiations often turn to a cost-based transfer-pricing approach.

Variable Cost One approach is to set the transfer price equal to the standard variable cost. The problem with this approach is that even when the producing division has excess capacity, it is not allowed to show any contribution margin on the transferred products or services. To illustrate, suppose the Food Processing Division has excess capacity and the transfer price is set at the standard variable cost of $7.25 per rack of bread. There is no positive incentive for the division to produce and transfer bread to the Gulf Division. The Food Processing Division's contribution margin from a transfer will be zero (transfer price of $7.25 minus variable costs of $7.25 equals zero). Some companies avoid this problem by setting the transfer price at standard variable cost plus a markup to allow the producing division a positive contribution margin.

Full Cost An alternative is to set the transfer price equal to the *full cost* of the transferred product or service. **Full** (or **absorption**) **cost** is equal to the product's variable cost plus an allocated portion of fixed overhead.

Suppose the Food Processing Division's Orlando bakery has budgeted annual fixed overhead of $500,000 and budgeted annual production of 200,000 racks of bread. The full cost of the bakery's product is computed below.

$$\text{Full cost} = \text{variable cost} + \text{allocated fixed overhead}$$

$$= \quad \$7.25 \quad + \quad \frac{\$500,000}{200,000}$$

$$= \$7.25 \text{ per rack} + \frac{\$500,000 \text{ budgeted fixed overhead}}{200,000 \text{ budgeted racks of bread}}$$

$$= \quad \$7.25 \quad + \quad \$2.50$$

$$= \$9.75 \text{ per rack}$$

Under this approach, the transfer price is set at $9.75 per rack of bread.

Dysfunctional Decision-Making Behavior Basing transfer prices on full cost entails a serious risk of causing dysfunctional decision-making behavior. Full-cost-based transfer prices lead the buying division to view costs that are fixed for the company as a whole as variable costs to the buying division. This can cause faulty decision making.

To illustrate, suppose the Food Processing Division has excess capacity, and the transfer price of bread is equal to the full cost of $9.75 per rack. What will happen if the Gulf Division receives the special offer discussed previously, where it can sell bread to a local organization at a special price of $9.60 per rack? The Gulf Division manager will reject the special order, since otherwise her division would incur a loss of $.15 per rack.

Special price per rack	$9.60 per rack
Transfer price based on full cost	9.75 per rack
Loss	$ .15 per rack

What is in the best interests of the company as a whole? Suncoast Food Centers would make a positive contribution of $2.35 per rack on the bread sold in the special order.

Special price per rack	$9.60
Variable cost in Food Processing Division	7.25
Contribution to company as a whole	$2.35

What has happened here? Setting the transfer price equal to the full cost of $9.75 has turned a cost that is fixed in the Food Processing Division, and hence is fixed for the company as a whole, into a variable cost from the viewpoint of the Gulf Division manager. The manager would tend to reject the special offer, even though accepting it would benefit the company as a whole.

Although the practice is common, transfer prices should not be based on full cost. The risk is too great that the cost behavior in the producing division will be obscured. This can all too easily result in poor decisions in the buying division.

Standard versus Actual Costs

Throughout our discussion of transfer prices, we have used standard costs rather than actual costs. This was true in our discussion of the general transfer-pricing rule as well as for cost-based transfer prices. Transfer prices should not be based on actual costs, because such a practice would allow an inefficient producing division to pass its excess production costs on to the buying division in the transfer price. When standard costs are used in transfer-pricing formulas, the selling division is not forced to pick up the tab for the producer's inefficiency. Moreover, the producing division is given an incentive to control its costs, since any costs of inefficiency cannot be passed on.

Undermining Divisional Autonomy

Suppose the manager of Suncoast Food Centers' Food Processing Division has excess capacity but insists on a transfer price of $9.75, based on full cost. The Gulf Division manager is faced with the special offer for bread at $9.60 per rack. She regrets that she will have to decline the offer because it would cause her division's profit to decline, even though the company's interests would be best served by accepting the special order. The Gulf Division manager calls the company president and explains the situation. She asks the president to intervene and force the Food Processing Division manager to lower his transfer price.

As the company president, what would you do? If you stay out of the controversy, your company will lose the contribution on the special order. If you intervene, you will run the risk of undermining the autonomy of your division managers. You established a decentralized organization structure for Suncoast Centers and hired competent managers because you believed in the benefits of decentralized decision making.

There is no obvious answer to this dilemma. In practice, central managers are reluctant to intervene in such disputes unless the negative financial consequences to the organization are quite large. Most managers believe the benefits of decentralized decision making are important to protect, even if it means an occasional dysfunctional decision.

Transfer-pricing methods vary widely among organizations, as the following survey of large-company practices suggests.

ILLUSTRATION FROM
MANAGEMENT-
ACCOUNTING
PRACTICE

Transfer-Pricing Practices

A survey of large companies revealed the following relative usage of common transfer-pricing practices.[3]

Market price.	31%
Variable cost.	5%
Full cost.	25%
Full cost plus markup.	17%
Negotiation.	22%
Total.	100%

An International Perspective

Companies with divisions in several countries often consider domestic and foreign income-tax rates when setting transfer prices. For example, suppose a company based in Europe also has a division in Asia. A European division produces a subassembly,

---

[3] R. Vancil, *Decentralization: Managerial Ambiguity by Design* (New York: Financial Executives Foundation, 1979), p. 180.

which is transferred to the Asian division for assembly and sale of the final product. Suppose also that the income-tax rate for the company's European division is higher than the rate in the Asian division's country. How would these different tax rates affect the transfer price for the subassembly?

The company's management has an incentive to set a low transfer price for the subassembly. This will result in relatively low profits for the company's European division and a relatively high income for the Asian division. Since the tax rate is lower in the Asian country, the overall company will save on income tax. By setting a low transfer price, the company will shift a portion of its income to a country with a lower tax rate. Tax laws vary among countries with regard to flexibility in setting transfer prices. Some countries' tax laws prohibit the behavior described in our example, while other countries' laws permit it.

Transfer Pricing in the Service Industry

Service industry firms and nonprofit organizations also use transfer pricing when services are transferred between responsibility centers. In banks, for example, the interest rate at which depositors' funds are transferred to the loan department is a form of transfer price. At Cornell University, if a student in the law school takes a course in the business school, a transfer price is charged to the law school for the credit hours of instruction provided to the law student. Since the transfer price is based on tuition charges, it is a market-price-based transfer price.

BEHAVIORAL ISSUES: RISK AVERSION AND INCENTIVES

The designer of a performance-evaluation system for responsibility-center managers must consider many factors. Trade-offs often must be made between competing objectives. The overall objective is to achieve goal congruence by providing *incentives* for managers to act in the best interests of the organization as a whole. Financial performance measures such as divisional income, ROI, and residual income go a long way toward achieving this objective. However, these measures do have the disadvantage of imposing *risk* on a manager, because the measures also are affected by factors beyond the manager's control. For example, the income of an orange-growing division of an agricultural company will be affected not only by the manager's diligence and ability, but also by the weather and insect infestations.

Since most people exhibit *risk aversion,* managers must be compensated for the risk they must bear. This compensation comes in the form of higher salaries or bonuses. Thus, the design of a managerial performance evaluation and reward system involves a trade-off between the following two factors:

Evaluation of a manager on the basis of financial performance measures, which provide incentives for the manager to act in the organization's interests.	Imposition of risk on a manager who exhibits risk aversion, because financial performance measures are controllable only partially by the manager.

Trade-offs in designing
managerial performance
evaluation and reward system.

Achieving the optimal trade-off between risk and incentives is a delicate balancing act that requires the skill and experience of top management.

GOAL CONGRUENCE AND INTERNAL CONTROL SYSTEMS

Although most business professionals have high ethical standards, there are unfortunately those who will cut corners. An **internal control system** comprises the set of procedures designed to ensure that an organization's employees act in a legal, ethical, and responsible manner. Internal control procedures are designed to prevent the major lapses in responsible behavior described below.

Fraud Theft or misuse of an organization's resources constitutes *fraud.* To prevent and detect fraud, organizations establish well-defined procedures that prescribe how valuable resources will be handled. For example, many organizations require all checks above a particular amount to be authorized by two people.

Corruption Activities such as bribery, deceit, illegal political campaign contributions, and kickbacks constitute *corruption.* Most organizations have internal control procedures and codes of conduct to prevent and detect corrupt practices. For example, many organizations forbid their purchasing personnel from accepting gifts or gratuities from the sales personnel with whom they conduct business. The Foreign Corrupt Practices Act, passed by the U.S. Congress in 1977, prohibits a variety of corrupt practices in foreign business operations. For example, the law prohibits a company's management from bribing officials of a foreign government in return for favorable treatment of their company.

Financial Misrepresentation Internal control systems also are designed to prevent managers from intentionally (or accidentally) misstating an organization's financial records. Most companies have an *internal audit* staff, which reviews financial records throughout the organization to ensure their accuracy.

Unauthorized Action Sometimes a well-meaning employee is tempted to take an action that is not illegal or even unethical, but it is contrary to the organization's policies. Internal control procedures also are designed to detect and prevent unauthorized actions by an organization's employees, when those actions could reflect unfavorably on the organization. For example, a company may prohibit its employees from using company facilities for a rally in support of a controversial social cause.

An internal control system constitutes an integral part of an organization's efforts to achieve its goals. To be effective, internal control procedures require top management's full support and intolerance of intentional violations.

CHAPTER SUMMARY

An important objective of any organization's managerial-accounting system is to promote goal congruence among its employees. Thus, the primary criterion for judging the effectiveness of performance measures for responsibility-center managers is the extent to which the measures promote goal congruence.

The two most common measures of investment-center performance are return on investment (ROI) and residual income. Each of these performance measures relates an investment center's income to the capital invested to earn it. Residual income has the additional advantage of incorporating the organization's cost of acquiring capital in the performance measure. An investment center's ROI may be improved by increasing either the sales margin or capital turnover. Both ROI and residual income require the measurement of a division's income and invested capital, and the methods for making these measurements vary in practice.

When products or services are transferred between divisions in the same organization, divisional performance is affected by the transfer price. A general rule states that the transfer price should be equal to the outlay cost incurred to make the transfer plus the organization's opportunity cost associated with the transfer. Due to difficulties in implementing the rule, most companies base transfer prices on external market prices, costs, or negotiations. In some cases, these practical transfer-pricing methods may result in dysfunctional decisions. Top management then must weigh the benefits of intervening to prevent suboptimal decisions against the costs of undermining divisional autonomy.

REVIEW PROBLEMS ON INVESTMENT CENTERS AND TRANSFER PRICING

Problem 1

Stellar Systems Company manufactures guidance systems for rockets used to launch commercial satellites. The company's Software Division reported the following results for 19x8.

Income	$ 300,000
Sales revenue	2,000,000
Invested capital	3,000,000

The company's cost of acquiring capital is 9 percent.

REQUIRED:

1. Compute the Software Division's sales margin, capital turnover, return on investment, and residual income for 19x8.
2. If income and sales remain the same in 19x9, but the division's capital turnover improves to 80 percent, compute the following for 19x9: (a) invested capital and (b) ROI.

Solution to Problem 1

1. Sales margin $= \dfrac{\text{profit}}{\text{sales revenue}} = \dfrac{\$300,000}{\$2,000,000} = 15\%$

   Capital turnover $= \dfrac{\text{sales revenue}}{\text{invested capital}} = \dfrac{\$2,000,000}{\$3,000,000} = 67\%$

   Return on investment $= \dfrac{\text{profit}}{\text{invested capital}} = \dfrac{\$300,000}{\$3,000,000} = 10\%$

   Residual income:

Divisional profit		$300,000
Less: Imputed interest charge:		
Invested capital	$3,000,000	
× Imputed interest rate	× .09	
Imputed interest charge		270,000
Residual income		$ 30,000

2. (a) $\text{Capital turnover} = \dfrac{\text{sales revenue}}{\text{invested capital}} = \dfrac{\$2,000,000}{?} = 80\%$

$\text{Therefore, invested capital} = \dfrac{\$2,000,000}{.80} = \$2,500,000$

(b) New ROI $= 15\% \times 80\% = 12\%$

Problem 2

Stellar Systems Company's Microprocessor Division sells a computer module to the company's Guidance Assembly Division, which assembles completed guidance systems. The Mircoprocessor Division has no excess capacity. The computer module costs $10,000 to manufacture, and it can be sold in the external market to companies in the computer industry for $13,500.

REQUIRED: Compute the transfer price for the computer module using the general transfer-pricing rule.

Solution to Problem 2

$\text{Transfer price} = \text{outlay cost} + \text{opportunity cost}$
$= \$10,000 \quad + (\$13,500 - \$10,000)$
$= \$13,500$

The $3,500 opportunity cost of a transfer is the contribution margin that will be forgone if a computer module is transferred instead of sold in the external market.

KEY TERMS **Capital turnover,** p. 497; **Cost of capital,** p. 499; **Distress market price,** p. 513; **Full (or absorption) cost,** p. 514; **Goal congruence,** p. 518; **Imperfect competition,** p. 512; **Internal control system,** p. 518; **Investment centers,** p. 493; **Management by objectives (MBO),** p. 494; **Perfect competition,** p. 512; **Residual income,** p. 499; **Return on investment (ROI),** p. 496; **Sales margin,** p. 497; **Transfer price,** p. 494.

REVIEW QUESTIONS

12-1. Define *goal congruence,* and explain why it is important to an organization's success.

12-2. What is the managerial accountant's primary objective in designing a responsibility-accounting system?

12-3. Describe the managerial approach known as *management by objectives* or *MBO.*

12-4. Define and give three examples of an *investment center.*

12-5. Write the formula for ROI, showing sales margin and capital turnover as its components.

12-6. Explain how the manager of the Automobile Division of an insurance company could improve her division's ROI.

12-7. Make up an example showing how residual income is calculated. What information is used in computing residual income which is not used in computing ROI?

12-8. What is the chief disadvantage of ROI as an investment-center performance measure? How does the residual-income measure eliminate this disadvantage?

12-9. Why is there typically a rise in ROI or residual income across time in a division? What undesirable behavioral implications could this phenomenon have?

12-10. Distinguish between the following measures of invested capital, and briefly explain when each should be used: (1) total assets, (2) total productive assets, and (3) total assets less current liabilities.

12-11. Why do some companies use gross book value instead of net book value to measure a division's invested capital?

12-12. Explain why it is important in performance evaluation to distinguish between investment centers and their managers?

12-13. Describe an alternative to using ROI or residual income to measure investment-center performance.

12-14. How does inflation affect investment-center performance measures?

12-15. List three nonfinancial measures that could be used to evaluate a division of an insurance company.

12-16. Discuss the importance of nonfinancial information in measuring investment-center performance.

12-17. Identify and explain the managerial accountant's primary objective in choosing a transfer-pricing policy.

12-18. Describe four methods by which transfer prices may be set.

12-19. Explain the significance of excess capacity in the transferring division when transfer prices are set using the general transfer-pricing rule.

12-20. Why might income-tax laws affect the transfer-pricing policies of multinational companies?

EXERCISES　　*Exercise 12-21　Components of ROI.* The following data pertain to Huron Corporation for 19x2.

Income	$ 4,000,000
Sales revenue	50,000,000
Average invested capital	20,000,000

REQUIRED: Compute Huron Division's sales margin, capital turnover, and return on investment for 19x2.

Exercise 12-22　Improving ROI. Refer to the preceding exercise.

REQUIRED: Demonstrate two ways Huron Division's manager could improve the division's ROI to 25 percent.

Exercise 12-23　Residual Income. Refer to the data for Exercise 12-21. Assume that the company's cost of capital is 10 percent.

REQUIRED: Compute Huron Division's residual income for 19x2.

Exercise 12-24　Increasing ROI over Time. Refer to Exhibit 12-3. Assume that you are a consultant who has been hired by Sun Coast Food Centers.

REQUIRED: Write a memorandum to the company president explaining why the ROI based on net book value (in Exhibit 12-3) behaves as it does over the five-year time horizon.

Exercise 12-25　General Transfer-Pricing Rule. Winneloa Corporation has two divisions. The Fabrication Division transfers partially completed components to the Assembly Division at a predetermined transfer price. In 19x4, the Fabrication Division's standard variable production cost per unit was $300. The division has no excess capacity, and it could sell all of its components to outside buyers at $380 per unit in a perfectly competitive market.

REQUIRED:

1. Determine a transfer price using the general rule.
2. How would the transfer price change if the Fabrication Division had excess capacity?

Exercise 12-26   *Cost-Based Transfer Pricing.* Refer to the preceding exercise. The Fabrication Division's full (absorption) cost of a component is $340, which includes $40 of applied fixed-overhead costs. The transfer price has been set at $374, which is the Fabrication Division's full cost plus a 10 percent markup.

The Assembly Division has a special offer for its product of $460. The Assembly Division incurs variable costs of $100 in addition to the transfer price for the Fabrication Division's components. Both divisions currently have excess production capacity.

REQUIRED:

1. What is the Assembly Division manager likely to do regarding acceptance or rejection of the special offer? Why?
2. Is this decision in the best interests of Winneloa Corporation as a whole? Why?
3. How could the situation be remedied using the transfer price?

Exercise 12-27   *Internal Control.* Danby Company is an auto parts supplier. At the end of each month, the employee who maintains all of the inventory records takes a physical inventory of the firm's stock. When discrepancies occur between the recorded inventory and the physical count, the employee changes the physical count to agree with the records.

REQUIRED:

1. What problems could arise as a result of Danby Company's inventory procedures?
2. How could the internal control system be strengthened to eliminate the potential problems?

Exercise 12-28   *Improving ROI.* The following data pertain to Utah Aggregates Company, a producer of sand, gravel, and cement, for 19x6.

Sales revenue	$2,000,000
Cost of goods sold	1,100,000
Operating expenses	800,000
Average invested capital	1,000,000

REQUIRED:

1. Compute the company's sales margin, capital turnover, and ROI for 19x6.
2. If the sales and average invested capital remain the same in 19x7, to what level would total expenses have to be reduced in order to improve the firm's ROI to 15 percent?
3. Assume expenses are reduced, as calculated in requirement (2). Compute the firm's new sales margin. Show how the new sales margin and the old capital turnover together result in a 19x7 ROI of 15 percent.

PROBLEMS

Problem 12-29   *Comparing the Performance of Two Divisions.* Philadelphia Fabrics Company has two divisions, which reported the following results for 19x0.

	Division I	Division II
Income	$200,000	$900,000
Average invested capital	$1,000,000	$6,000,000
ROI	20%	15%

REQUIRED: Which was the most successful division in 19x0? Think carefully about this, and explain your answer.

Problem 12-30 *ROI and Residual Income; Missing Data.* The following data pertain to three divisions of Pittsburgh Pipe Fittings Corporation. The company's cost of acquiring capital is 8 percent.

	Division A	Division B	Division C
Sales revenue	$10,000,000	?	?
Income	$2,000,000	$400,000	?
Average investment	$2,500,000	?	?
Sales margin	?	20%	25%
Capital turnover	?	1	?
ROI	?	?	20%
Residual income	?	?	$120,000

(handwritten annotations: "Invcap" next to Average investment; "$10,000,000 − ($2,500,000 × .08)" next to Residual income)

REQUIRED: Fill in the blanks above.

Problem 12-31 Refer to the preceding problem.

REQUIRED:

1. Explain three ways the Division A manager could improve her division's ROI. Use numbers to illustrate these possibilities.
2. Suppose Division B's sales margin increased to 25 percent, while its capital turnover remained constant. Compute the division's new ROI.

Problem 12-32 *Using Income to Evaluate Divisional Performance.* Ontario Corporation's SuperClean Products Division is an innovative manufacturer of household soaps and detergents. The division has shown impressive growth in reported sales and net income. However, the company's board of directors has raised a question as to whether the significant increases in operating income are attributable to real growth or to changes in prices. Bradley Ronaldson, divisional controller, has been asked to address these concerns at the next scheduled meeting of Ontario's board of directors.

The condensed income statements of SuperClean Products Division for the years 19x1, 19x2, and 19x3 are presented below.

SuperClean Products
Comparative Income Statements
For the Years Ended December 31, 19x1 through 19x3
(in thousands)

	19x1	19x2	19x3
Sales	$8,000	$9,600	$11,500
Cost of goods sold:			
Direct materials	$1,410	$1,720	$ 2,070
Direct labor and manufacturing overhead other than depreciation	2,300	2,850	3,450
Depreciation	940	940	940
Total cost of goods sold	$4,650	$5,510	$ 6,460
Gross margin	$3,350	$4,090	$ 5,040
Selling and administrative expenses	1,800	1,880	1,940
Operating income	$1,550	$2,210	$ 3,100

Additional information regarding SuperClean's income statements is as follows.

(1) Selling and administrative expenses include $100,000 of depreciation per year.
(2) All property, plant, and equipment used by SuperClean through 19x3 were acquired when the division was established in January of 19x1.

REQUIRED: Discuss the usefulness of the income statements in evaluating the division's performance.
(CMA, adapted)

Problem 12-33 Residual Income. Refer to the data for problem 12-29.

REQUIRED: Compute each division's residual income for 19x0 under each of the following assumptions about the firm's cost of acquiring capital.

1. 12 percent.
2. 15 percent.
3. 18 percent.

Which division was most successful in 19x0? Explain your answer.

Problem 12-34 Behavioral Implications of ROI. Erie Corporation made a capital investment of $100,000 in new equipment for its Cleveland Division two years ago. The analysis at that time indicated the equipment would save $36,400 in operating expenses per year over a five-year period. Before the purchase, the division's ROI was 20 percent.

Timothy Williams, the division manager, believed that the equipment had lived up to its expectations. However, the divisional performance report showing the overall return on investment for the first year in which this equipment was used did not reflect as much improvement as had been expected. Williams asked the Accounting Department to break out the figures related to this investment to find out why it did not contribute to improving the division's ROI.

The Accounting Department was able to identify the equipment's contribution to the division's operations. The report presented to the division manager at the end of the first year is shown below.

Reduced operating expenses due to new equipment.	$ 36,400
Less: Depreciation, 20% of cost	20,000
Contribution	$ 16,400
Investment, beginning of year	$100,000
Investment, end of year	$ 80,000
Average investment for the year.	$ 90,000

$$\text{ROI} = \frac{16,400}{90,000} = 18.2\%$$

Timothy Williams was surprised that the ROI was so low, because the new equipment performed as expected. The staff analyst in the Accounting Department replied that the company ROI for performance evaluation differed from that used for capital investment decisions.

REQUIRED: Discuss the problems associated with ROI as a divisional performance measure. What might the Cleveland Division manager do the next time a new equipment purchase is suggested? Why?
(CMA, adapted)

Problem 12-35   Increasing ROI over Time; Accelerated Depreciation. Refer to Exhibit 12-3. Prepare a similar table of the changing ROI assuming the following accelerated depreciation schedule. (If there is a loss, leave the ROI based on net book value blank.)

Year		Depreciation
1	....	$200,000
2	....	120,000
3	....	72,000
4	....	54,000
5	....	54,000
Total	....	$500,000

REQUIRED:

1. How does your table differ from the one in Exhibit 12-3? Why?
2. What are the implications of the ROI pattern in your table?

Problem 12-36   Increasing Residual Income over Time. Prepare a table similar to Exhibit 12-3, which focuses on residual income. Use a 10 percent rate to compute the imputed interest charge. The table should show the residual income on the investment during each year in its five-year life. Use the depreciation schedule in Exhibit 12-3.

Problem 12-37   Basic Transfer Pricing. Ajax Division of Carlyle Corporation produces electric motors, 20 percent of which are sold to Bradley Division of Carlyle. The remainder are sold to outside customers. Carlyle treats its divisions as profit centers and allows division managers to choose their sources of sale and supply. Corporate policy requires that all interdivisional sales and purchases be recorded at variable cost as a transfer price. Ajax Division's estimated sales and standard-cost data for the year ending December 31, 19x2, based on capacity of 100,000 units, are as follows:

	Bradley	Outsiders
Sales	$ 900,000	$ 8,000,000
Variable costs....................................	(900,000)	(3,600,000)
Fixed costs	(300,000)	(1,200,000)
Gross margin	$(300,000)	$ 3,200,000
Unit sales	20,000	80,000

Ajax has an opportunity to sell the 20,000 units shown above to an outside customer at a price of $75 per unit. Bradley can purchase its requirements from an outside supplier at a price of $85 per unit.

REQUIRED:

1. Assuming that Ajax Division desires to maximize its gross margin, should Ajax take on the new customer and drop its sales to Bradley in 19x2? Why?
2. Assume, instead, that Carlyle permits division managers to negotiate the transfer price for 19x2. The managers agreed on a tentative transfer price of $75 per unit, to be reduced based on an equal sharing of the additional gross margin to Ajax resulting from the sale to Bradley of 20,000 motors at $75 per unit. What would be the actual transfer price for 19x2?

3. Assume now that Ajax Division has an opportunity to sell the 20,000 motors that Bradley Division would buy to the same customers that are buying the other 80,000 motors produced by Ajax. Ajax Division could sell all 100,000 motors to outside customers at a price of $100. What actions by each division manager are in the best interests of Carlyle Corporation?

4. Under the scenario described in requirement (3), use the general transfer pricing rule to compute the transfer price Ajax Division should charge Bradley Division for motors.

5. Will the transfer price computed in requirement (4) result in the most desirable outcome from the standpoint of Carlyle Corporation? Justify your answer.

(CPA, adapted)

Problem 12-38   Comprehensive Transfer-Pricing Problem. Greystone Company manufactures windows for the home-building industry. The window frames are produced in the Frame Division. The frames are then transferred to the Glass Division, where the glass and hardware are installed. The company's best-selling product is a three-by-four-foot, double-paned operable window. The standard cost of the window is detailed below.

	Frame Division	**Glass Division**
Direct material	$15	$30*
Direct labor	20	15
Variable overhead	30	30
Total	$65	$75

* Not including the transfer price for the frame.

The Frame Division can also sell frames directly to custom home builders, who install the glass and hardware. The sales price for a frame is $80. The Glass Division sells its finished windows for $190. The markets for both frames and finished windows exhibit perfect competition.

REQUIRED:

1. Assume that there is no excess capacity in the Frame Division.
   a. Use the general rule to compute the transfer price for window frames.
   b. Calculate the transfer price if it is based on standard variable cost with a 10 percent markup.
2. Assume that there is excess capacity in the Frame Division.
   a. Use the general rule to compute the transfer price for window frames.
   b. Explain why your answers to requirements 1(a) and 2(a) differ.
   c. Suppose the predetermined fixed-overhead rate in the Frame Division is 125 percent of direct-labor cost. Calculate the transfer price if it is based on standard full cost plus a 10 percent markup.
   d. Assume the transfer price established in requirement 2(c) is used. The Glass Division has been approached by the U.S. Army with a special order for 1,000 windows at $155. From the perspective of Greystone Company as a whole should the special order be accepted or rejected? Why?
   e. Assume the same facts as in requirement 2(d). Will an autonomous Glass Division manager accept or reject the special order? Why?
3. Comment on the use of full cost as the basis for setting transfer prices.

Problem 12-39   Comprehensive Problem on Divisional Performance Evaluation. Darmen Corporation is a major producer of prefabricated beach houses. The corporation consists of two divisions: the Bell Division, which acquires the raw materials to manufacture the basic house components and assembles them into kits, and the Cornish Division, which takes the kits and constructs the homes for final home buyers. The corporation is decentralized, and the management of each division is measured by divisional income and return on investment.

Bell Division assembles seven separate house kits using raw materials purchased at the prevailing market prices. The seven kits are sold to Cornish for prices ranging from $45,000 to $98,000. The prices are set by Darmen's corporate management using prices paid by Cornish when it buys comparable units from outside sources. The smaller kits with the lower prices have become a larger portion of the units sold, because the final house buyer is faced with prices that are increasing more rapidly than personal income. The kits are manufactured and assembled in a new plant just purchased by Bell this year. The division had been located in a leased plant for the past four years.

All kits are assembled upon receipt of an order from the Cornish Division. When the kit is completely assembled, it is loaded immediately on a Cornish truck. Thus, Bell Division has no finished-goods inventory.

The Bell Division's accounts and reports are prepared on an actual-cost basis. There is no budget, and standards have not been developed for any product. A manufacturing-overhead rate is calculated at the beginning of each year. The rate is designed to charge all overhead to the product each year. Any underapplied or overapplied overhead is closed into the Cost of Goods Sold account.

Bell Division's annual report follows. This report forms the basis of the evaluation of the division and its management.

Bell Division
Performance Report
For the Year Ended December 31, 19x2

	19x2	19x1	Increase or (decrease) from 19x1 Amount	Percent Change
Summary data:				
Net income (in thousands)	$34,222	$31,573	$2,649	8.4
Return on investment	37%	43%	(6)%	(14.0)
Kits shipped (units)	2,000	2,100	(100)	(4.8)
Production data (units):				
Kits started	2,400	1,600	800	50.0
Kits shipped	2,000	2,100	(100)	(4.8)
Kits in process at year end...............	700	300	400	133.3
Increase (decrease) in kits in process at year				
end	400	(500)	—	—
Financial data (in thousands):				
Sales revenue	$138,000	$162,800	$(24,800)	(15.2)
Production cost of units sold:				
Direct material.......................	$ 32,000	$ 40,000	$ (8,000)	(20.0)
Direct labor..........................	41,700	53,000	(11,300)	(21.3)
Manufacturing overhead	29,000	37,000	(8,000)	(21.6)
Cost of units sold	$102,700	$130,000	$(27,300)	(21.0)

	19x2	19x1	Increase or (decrease) from 19x1 Amount	Percent Change
Other costs:				
Corporate charges for:				
Personnel services................	$ 228	$ 210	$ 18	8.6
Accounting services	425	440	(15)	(3.4)
Financing costs	300	525	(225)	(42.9)
Total other costs	$ 953	$ 1,175	$ (222)	(18.9)
Adjustment to income:				
Unreimbursed fire loss	—	$ 52	$ (52)	(100.0)
Raw material losses due to improper				
storage	$ 125	—	125	—
Total adjustments................	$ 125	$ 52	$ 73	140.4
Total deductions.....................	$103,778	$131,227	$(27,449)	(20.9)
Divisional income	$ 34,222	$ 31,573	$ 2,649	8.4
Divisional investment	$92,000	$73,000	$19,000	26.0
Return on investment	37%	43%	(6)%	(14.0)

Additional information regarding corporate and divisional practices follows.

(1) The corporation office does all of the personnel and accounting work for each division.
(2) Corporate personnel costs are allocated on the basis of the number of employees in each division.
(3) Accounting costs are allocated to divisions on the basis of total costs, excluding corporate charges.
(4) Divisional administration costs are included in overhead.
(5) The financing charges include a corporate imputed interest charge on divisional assets.
(6) The divisional investment for the ROI calculation includes divisional inventory and plant and equipment at gross book value.

REQUIRED:

1. Discuss the value of the annual report presented for the Bell Division in evaluating the division and its management in terms of:
   a. The accounting techniques employed in the measurement of divisional activities.
   b. The manner of presentation.
   c. The effectiveness with which it discloses differences and similarities between years.
   Use the information in the problem to illustrate your answer.
2. Present specific recommendations for the management of Darmen Corporation which would improve its accounting and financial-reporting system.

(CMA, adapted)

Problem 12-40   Minimum and Maximum Acceptable Transfer Prices. Cincinnati Gauge
Company manufactures small gauges for use in household applicances and industrial machinery. The firm has two divisions: Appliance Division and Industrial Division. The company is decentralized, and each division is completely autonomous in its decision making.

The Appliance Division produces two instruments, A and B. Cost information about
these products follows.

Appliance Division	Instrument A	Instrument B
Direct material	$ 5.00	$ 4.00
Direct labor	10.00	20.00
Fixed overhead	20.00	40.00
Full cost	$35.00	$64.00

Appliance Division has no variable overhead. The direct-labor rate is $10.00 per hour,
and there is a maximum of 10,000 hours available per year. Fixed overhead is $200,000 per
year, and is applied on the basis of direct-labor hours. The planned activity level is 10,000
direct-labor hours per year.

There is unlimited demand in the external market for instrument A at a price of $45.00
per unit. Anywhere from zero to 3,000 units of instrument B may be sold annually in the
external market at a price of $94.00 per unit. There is no external market for more than 3,000
units of instrument B per year.

The Industrial Division also has two products, type Y gauges and type Z gauges. Cost
information about these products follows.

Industrial Division	Type Y Gauges	Type Z Gauges
Direct material	$12.00	$ 7.00
Direct labor	10.00	20.00
Fixed overhead	10.00	20.00
Full cost	$32.00	$47.00

In addition to the costs listed above, each unit of gauge type Z uses one unit of instrument
B, which is produced in the Appliance Division and transferred to the Industrial Division. The
costs listed in the table above, for gauge type Z, are *only* the costs incurred in the Industrial
Division to transform a B instrument into a type Z gauge. They do *not* include the transfer
price of instrument B or the costs of manufacturing instrument B.

Industrial Division has no variable overhead. The direct-labor rate is $10.00 per hour, and
there is a maximum of 10,000 hours available per year. Fixed overhead is $100,000 per year,
and is applied on the basis of direct-labor hours. The planned activity level is 10,000 hours per
year.

There is an unlimited demand for type Z gauges at a fixed price of $257.00. Anywhere
from zero to 6,000 units of type Y gauges can be sold annually at a fixed price of $92.00 per
unit. There is no demand for more than 6,000 type Y gauges per year.

The labor used in the two divisions is different and is *not* transferable between divisions.
The situation is summarized in the following diagram.

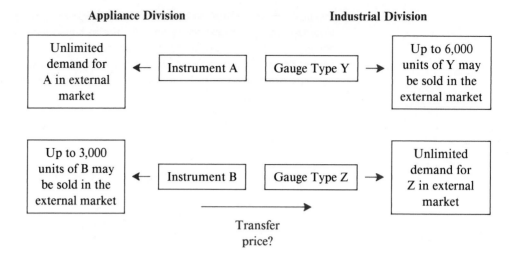

REQUIRED: Each of the first four questions refers to the transfer price *per unit of instrument B* for units transferred. Show calculations. Ignore any long-term or qualitative factors.

1. What is the minimum unit transfer price acceptable to Appliance Division for any number of units of instrument B transferred in the range zero to 2,000 units?
2. What is the minimum unit transfer price acceptable to Appliance Division for any number of B units transferred in the range 2,001 to 5,000 units?
3. What is the maximum unit transfer price acceptable to Industrial Division for any number of B units transferred in the range zero to 2,000 units?
4. What is the maximum unit transfer price acceptable to Industrial Division for any number of B units transferred in the range 2,001 to 5,000 units?
5. Suppose Appliance Division sets the transfer price at its minimum acceptable level in each of the ranges zero to 2,000 units, and 2,001 to 5,000 units. How many units will be transferred? Remember that each division manager has the authority to accept or reject a transfer between the two divisions.

Problem 12-41   Transfer Pricing; Two Transfers; Top Management Intervention.[4]

If I were to price these boxes any lower than $480 a thousand, I'd be countermanding my order of last month for our sales people to stop shaving their bids and to bid full-cost quotations. I've been trying for weeks to improve the quality of our business, and if I turn around now and accept this job at $430 or $450 or something less than $480, I'll be tearing down this program I've been working so hard to build up. The division can't very well show a profit by putting in bids that don't even cover a fair share of overhead costs, let alone give us a profit.

James Brunner, manager of Thompson Division

Birch Paper Company was a medium-sized, partly integrated paper company, producing white and kraft papers and paperboard. A portion of its paperboard output was converted into

[4] Copyright 1985 by the President and Fellows of Harvard College. This case was prepared as the basis for class discussion rather than to illustrate either effective or ineffective handling of an administrative situation. Reprinted by permission of the Harvard Business School. This case (158-001) was prepared by William Rotch under the supervision of Neil Harlen.

corrugated boxes by the Thompson Division, which also printed and colored the outside surface of the boxes. Including Thompson, the company had four production divisions and a timberland division that supplied part of the company's pulp requirements.

For several years each division had been judged independently on the basis of its profit and return on investment. Top management had been working to gain effective results from a policy of decentralizing responsibility and authority for all decisions except those relating to overall company policy. The company's top officials believed that in the past few years the concept of decentralization had been successfully applied and that the company's profits and competitive position had definitely improved.

Early in 19x5 the Northern Division designed a special display box for one of its papers in conjunction with the Thompson Division, which was equipped to make the box. Thompson's staff for package design and development spent several months perfecting the design, production methods, and materials that were to be used. Because of the box's unusual color and shape, these were far from standard. According to an agreement between the two divisions, the Thompson Division was reimbursed by the Northern Division for the cost of its design and development work.

When the specifications were all prepared, the Northern Division asked for bids on the corrugated box from the Thompson Division and from two outside companies. Each Birch Paper Company division manager normally was free to buy from whatever supplier he wished; on intercompany sales, divisions selling to other divisions were expected to meet the going market price.

In 19x5, the profit margins of converters such as the Thompson Division were being squeezed. Thompson, like many other similar converters, bought the paperboard and linerboard used in making boxes, and its function was to print, cut, and shape the material into boxes.* Although it bought most of its materials from other Birch divisions, most of Thompson's sales were made to outside customers. If Thompson got the order from Northern, it probably would buy its linerboard and corrugating medium from the Southern Division of Birch. Thus, before giving its bid to Northern, Thompson got a quote for materials from the Southern Division. Although Southern had been running below capacity and had excess inventory, it quoted the prevailing market price for materials. Southern's out-of-pocket costs for both liner and corrugating medium were about 60 percent of its selling price. About 70 percent of Thompson's out-of-pocket costs of $400 per thousand boxes represented the cost of linerboard and the corrugating medium.

The Northern Division received bids on the boxes of $480 per thousand from the Thompson Division, $430 per thousand from West Paper Company, and $432 per thousand from Erie Papers, Ltd. Erie Papers offered to buy from Birch the outside linerboard with the special printing already on it, but it would supply its own inside liner and corrugating medium. The outside liner would be supplied by the Southern Division at a price equivalent to $90 per thousand boxes, and would be printed for $30 per thousand by the Thompson Division. Of the $30, about $25 would be out-of-pocket costs.

Since the bidding results appeared to be a little unusual, William Kenton, manager of the Northern Division, discussed the wide discrepancy in the bids with Birch's commercial vice president. He told the vice president, "We sell in a very competitive market, where higher costs cannot be passed on. How can we be expected to show a decent profit and return on investment if we have to buy our supplies at more than 10 percent over the going market?"

Knowing that Brunner had been unable to operate the Thompson Division at capacity on occasion during the past few months, it seemed odd to the vice president that Brunner would

---

* The walls of a corrugated box consist of outside and inside sheets of linerboard and a center layer of fluted corrugating medium.

add the full 20 percent overhead and profit charge to his out-of-pocket costs. When he asked Brunner about this, the answer he received was the statement that appears at the beginning of the problem. Brunner went on to say that, having done the developmental work on the box and having received no profit on that work, he felt entitled to a good markup on the production of the box itself.

The vice president explored further the cost structures of the various divisions. He remembered a comment of the controller at a meeting the week before, to the effect that costs that were variable for one division could be largely fixed for the company as a whole. He knew that, in the absence of specific orders from top management, Kenton would accept the lowest bid, which was that of the West Paper Company for $430. However, it would be possible for top management to order the acceptance of another bid if the situation warranted such action. And although the volume represented by the transactions in question was less than 5 percent of the volume of the divisions involved, future transactions could conceivably raise similar problems.

REQUIRED:

1. Diagram the potential cost flows, per thousand boxes, among all of the parties in the problem: Southern Division, Thompson Division, Northern Division, Erie Papers, Ltd. and West Paper Company. Where should the boxes be purchased?
2. How many transfer prices are involved in the situation? Explain your answer.
3. Recommend transfer prices as needed.
4. Should the commercial vice president intervene? Why?

CASES *Case 12-42. Divisional Performance Measurement and Transfer Pricing.* Easy Living Industries manufactures carpets, furniture, and cushions in three separate divisions. The company's operating statement for 19x3 is presented below.

Easy Living Industries
Operating Statement
For the Year Ended December 31, 19x3

	Carpet Division	Furniture Division	Cushion Division	Total
Sales revenue	$3,000,000	$3,000,000	$4,000,000	$10,000,000
Cost of goods sold	2,000,000	1,300,000	3,000,000	6,300,000
Gross profit	$1,000,000	$1,700,000	$1,000,000	$ 3,700,000
Operating expenses:				
Administration	$ 300,000	$ 500,000	$ 400,000	$ 1,200,000
Selling	600,000	600,000	500,000	1,700,000
Total operating expenses	$ 900,000	$1,100,000	$ 900,000	$ 2,900,000
Income from operations before taxes	$ 100,000	$ 600,000	$ 100,000	$ 800,000

Additional information regarding Easy Living Industries' operations is as follows:

(1) Included in the Cushion Division's sales revenue is $500,000 that represents sales made to the Furniture Division. The transfer price for these sales was at the full cost of manufacturing.
(2) The three divisions' cost of goods sold is comprised of the following costs.

	Carpet	Furniture	Cushion
Direct material.	$ 500,000	$1,000,000	$1,000,000
Direct labor	500,000	200,000	1,000,000
Variable overhead	750,000	50,000	1,000,000
Fixed overhead	250,000	50,000	–0–
Total cost of goods sold.	$2,000,000	$1,300,000	$3,000,000

(3) Administrative expenses include the following costs.

	Carpet	Furniture	Cushion
Segment expenses:			
Variable.	$ 85,000	$140,000	$ 40,000
Fixed	85,000	210,000	120,000
Home-office expenses (all fixed):			
Directly traceable	100,000	120,000	200,000
General (allocated based on sales dollars).	30,000	30,000	40,000
Total	$300,000	$500,000	$400,000

(4) All selling expense is incurred at the divisional level. It is 80 percent variable for all
segments.

Meg Johnson, manager of the Cushion Division, is not pleased with the company's
presentation of operating performance. Johnson claims, "The Cushion Division makes a
greater contribution to the company's profits than is shown. I sell cushions to the Furniture
Division at cost and it gets our share of the profit. I can sell these cushions on the outside at my
regular markup, but I sell to Furniture for the well-being of the company. I think my division
should get credit for those internal sales at market. I think we should also revise our operating
statements for internal purposes. Why don't we consider preparing these internal statements in
a format that shows internal transfers at market?"

REQUIRED:

1. Meg Johnson believes that the transfers from the Cushion Division to the
   Furniture Division should be at market rather than at full manufacturing cost for
   divisional performance measurement.
   a. Is Johnson correct? Why?
   b. Describe another approach that the company could use to set transfer prices
      other than manufacturing cost and market price.
2. Using transfer prices based on market prices, prepare a revised operating
   statement, by division, for Easy Living Industries for 19x3 that will facilitate the
   evaluation of divisional performance. Use the contribution-margin format.
(CMA, adapted)

Case 12-43   Comprehensive Transfer-Pricing Case; Use of General Rule; Cost Analysis.
Portsmouth Products is a divisionalized furniture manufacturer. The divisions are autonomous segments with each division responsible for its own sales, costs of operations, and
equipment acquisition. Each division serves a different market in the furniture industry.
Because the markets and products of the divisions are so different, there have never been any
transfers between divisions.

The Commercial Division manufactures equipment and furniture that is purchased by
the restaurant industry. The division plans to introduce a new line of counter and chair units

featuring a cushioned seat for the counter chairs. Joan Kline, the Commercial Division manager, has discussed the manufacturing of the cushioned seat with Russ Fiegel of the Office Division. They both believe a cushioned seat currently made by the Office Division for use on its deluxe office stool could be modified for use on the new counter chair. Consequently, Kline has asked Fiegel for a price for 100-unit lots of the cushioned seat. The following conversation took place about the price to be charged for the cushioned seats.

Fiegel: "Joan, we can make the necessary modifications to the cushioned seat easily. The raw materials used in the new restaurant seat are slightly different and should cost about 10 percent more than those used in our deluxe office stool. However, the labor time should be the same, because the seat fabrication operation is the same. I would price the seat at our regular rate: full cost plus a 30 percent markup."

Kline: "That's higher than I expected, Russ. I was thinking that a good price would be your variable manufacturing cost. After all, your fixed costs will be incurred regardless of this job."

Fiegel: "Joan, I'm at capacity. By making the cushioned seats for you, I'll have to cut my production of deluxe office stools. Of course, I can increase my production of economy office stools. The labor time freed by not having to fabricate the frame or assemble the deluxe stool can be shifted to the frame fabrication and assembly of the economy office stool. Fortunately, I can switch my labor force between these two models of stools without any loss of efficiency. As you know, overtime is not a feasible alternative in our community. I'd like to sell the seats to you at variable cost, but I have excess demand for both products. I don't mind changing my product mix to the economy model if I get a good return on the seats I make for you. Here are my standard costs for the two stools and a schedule of my manufacturing overhead." (Shown in the following schedules.)

Kline: "I guess I see your point, Russ, but I don't want to price myself out of the market. Maybe we should talk to corporate headquarters to see if they can give us any guidance."

Office Division
Standard Costs and Prices

	Deluxe Office Stool	Economy Office Stool
Direct materials:		
Framing	$ 8.15	$ 9.76
Cushioned seat:		
Padding.	2.40	—
Vinyl.	4.00	—
Molded seat (purchased)	—	6.00
Direct labor:		
Frame fabrication (.5 × $7.50/hour). .	3.75	3.75
Cushion fabrication (.5 × $7.50/hour)	3.75	—
Assembly	3.75[a]	2.25[b]
Manufacturing overhead:	19.20[c]	10.24[d]
Total standard cost.	$45.00	$32.00
Selling price (including 30% markup). . .	$58.50	$41.60

[a] .5 × $7.50 per hour

[b] .3 × $7.50 per hour

[c] 1.5 × $12.80 per hour

[d] .8 × $12.80 per hour

Office Division
Manufacturing Overhead Budget

Overhead Item	Description	Amount
Supplies	Variable, at current market prices.................	$ 420,000
Indirect labor.....	Variable	375,000
Supervision	Fixed.......................................	250,000
Power..........	Use varies with activity; rates are fixed.............	180,000
Heat and light	Fixed: light is fixed regardless of production, while heat and air-conditioning vary with fuel charges	140,000
Property taxes and insurance ...	Fixed: any change in amounts and rates are independent of production	200,000
Depreciation	Fixed.......................................	1,700,000
Employee benefits .	20% of supervision, direct and indirect labor	575,000
	Total overhead	$3,840,000
	Capacity in direct-labor hours...................	300,000
	Overhead rate per direct-labor hour	$12.80

REQUIRED:

1. Joan Kline and Russ Fiegel did ask Portsmouth Products' corporate management for guidance on an appropriate transfer price. Corporate management suggested they consider using a transfer price based on variable cost plus opportunity cost. Calculate a transfer price for the cushioned seat based on this rule.
2. Which alternative transfer-pricing system (full cost, variable cost, or outlay cost plus opportunity cost) would be better as the underlying concept for the company's transfer pricing policy? Explain your answer.

(CMA, adapted)

PART 3 USING ACCOUNTING INFORMATION IN MAKING DECISIONS

Chapter 13 Decision Making: Relevant Costs and Benefits

After completing this chapter, you should be able to:	■ **Describe six steps in the decision-making process and the managerial accountant's role in that process.**
	■ **Explain the relationship between quantitative and qualitative analyses in decision making.**
	■ **List and explain two criteria that must be satisfied by relevant information.**
	■ **Identify relevant costs and benefits, giving proper treatment to sunk costs, opportunity costs, and unit costs.**
	■ **Prepare analyses of various special decisions, properly identifying the relevant costs and benefits.**
	■ **Analyze manufacturing decisions involving joint products and limited resources.**

Decision making is a fundamental part of management. Decisions about the acquisition of equipment, mix of products, methods of production, and pricing of products and services confront managers in all types of organizations. This chapter covers the role of managerial-accounting information in a variety of common decisions. The next chapter examines pricing decisions.

THE MANAGERIAL ACCOUNTANT'S ROLE IN DECISION MAKING

The managerial accountant's role in the decision-making process is to provide relevant information to the managers who make the decisions. Production managers typically make the decisions about alternative production processes and schedules, marketing managers make pricing decisions, and specialists in finance usually are involved in decisions about major acquisitions of equipment. All of these managers require information pertinent to their decisions. The *managerial accountant's role* is to provide information relevant to the decisions faced by managers throughout the organization. Thus, the managerial accountant needs a good understanding of the decisions faced by those managers.

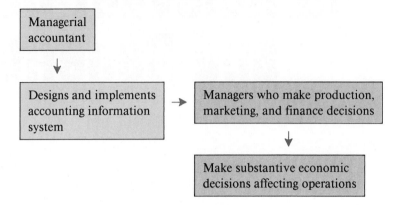

Steps in the Decision-Making Process

Six steps characterize the decision-making process:

1. *Clarify the decision problem.* Sometimes the decision to be made is clear. For example, if a company receives a special order for its product at a price below the usual price, the decision problem is to accept or reject the order. But the decision problem is seldom so clear and unambiguous. Perhaps demand for a company's most popular product is declining. What exactly is causing this problem? Increasing competition? Declining quality control? A new alternative product on the market? Before a decision can be made, the problem needs to be clarified and defined in more specific terms. Considerable managerial skill is required to define a decision problem in terms that can be addressed effectively.

2. *Specify the criterion.* Once a decision problem has been clarified, the manager should specify the criterion upon which a decision will be made. Is the objective to maximize profit, increase market share, minimize cost, or improve public service? Sometimes the objectives are in conflict, as in a decision problem where production cost is to be minimized but product quality must be maintained. In such cases, one objective is specified as the decision criterion — for example, cost minimization. The other objective is established as a constraint — for example, product quality must not fall below 1 defective part in 1,000 manufactured units.

3. *Identify the alternatives.* A decision involves selecting between two or more alternatives. If a machine breaks down, what are the alternative courses of action? The machine can be repaired, or replaced, or a replacement can be leased. But perhaps repair will turn out to be more costly than replacement. Determining the possible alternatives is a critical step in the decision process.

4. *Develop a decision model.* A *decision model* is a simplified representation of the choice problem. Unnecessary details are stripped away, and the most important elements of the problem are highlighted. Thus, the decision model brings together the elements listed above: the criterion, the constraints, and the alternatives.

5. *Collect the data.* Although the managerial accountant often is involved in steps 1 through 4, he or she is chiefly responsible for step 5. Selecting data pertinent to decisions is one of the managerial accountant's most important roles in an organization.

6. *Select an alternative.* Once the decision model is formulated and the pertinent data are collected, the appropriate manager makes a decision.

Quantitative versus Qualitative Analysis

Decision problems involving accounting data typically are specified in quantitative terms. The criteria in such problems usually include objectives such as profit maximization or cost minimization. When a manager makes a final decision, however, the qualitative characteristics of the alternatives can be just as important as the quantitative measures. **Qualitative characteristics** are the factors in a decision problem that cannot be expressed effectively in numerical terms. To illustrate, suppose Worldwide Airways' top management is considering the elimination of its hub operation in London. Airlines establish hubs at airports where many of their routes intersect. Hub operations include facilities for in-flight food preparation, aircraft maintenance and storage, and administrative offices. A careful quantitative analysis indicates that Worldwide Airways' profit-maximizing alternative is to eliminate the London hub. In making its decision, however, the company's managers will consider such qualitative issues as the effect of the closing on its London employees and on the morale of its remaining employees in the airline's Paris, Atlanta, and Tokyo hubs.

To clarify what is at stake in such qualitative analyses, quantitative analysis can allow the decision maker to put a "price" on the sum total of the qualitative characteristics. For example, suppose Worldwide Airways' controller gives top management a quantitative analysis showing that elimination of the London hub will increase annual profits by $2,000,000. However, the qualitative considerations favor the option of continuing the London operation. How important are these qualitative considerations to the top managers? If they decide to continue the London operation, the qualitative considerations must be worth at least $2,000,000 to them. Weighing the quantitative and qualitative considerations in making decisions is the essence of management. The skill, experience, judgment, and ethical standards of managers all come to bear on such difficult choices.

Exhibit 13-1 depicts the six steps in the decision process, and the relationship between quantitative and qualitative analyses.

Obtaining Information: Relevance, Accuracy, and Timeliness

What criteria should the managerial accountant use in designing the accounting information system that supplies data for decision making? Three characteristics of information determine its usefulness.

Relevance   Information is **relevant** if it is *pertinent* to a decision problem. Different decisions typically will require different data. The primary theme of this chapter is how to decide what information is relevant to various common decision problems.

Accuracy   Information that is pertinent to a decision problem must also be **accurate,** or it will be of little use. This means the information must be precise. For example, the cost incurred by Worldwide Airways to rent facilities at London's Heathrow Airport is relevant to a decision about eliminating the airline's London hub. However, if the rental cost data are imprecise, due to incomplete or misplaced records, the usefulness of the information will be diminished.

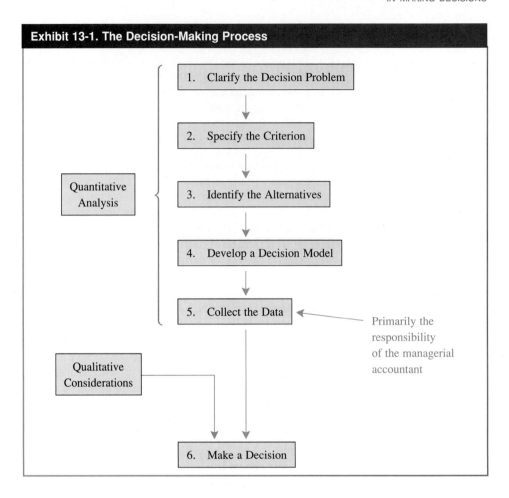

Exhibit 13-1. The Decision-Making Process

1.   Clarify the Decision Problem

2.   Specify the Criterion

Quantitative Analysis

3.   Identify the Alternatives

4.   Develop a Decision Model

5.   Collect the Data

Primarily the responsibility of the managerial accountant

Qualitative Considerations

6.   Make a Decision

Conversely, highly accurate but irrelevant data are of no value to a decision maker. Suppose Worldwide Airways will continue its daily round-trip flight between New York and London regardless of its decision about eliminating the London hub. Precise data about fuel consumption on the New York – London route are irrelevant to the decision about closing down the London hub.

Timeliness Relevant and accurate data are of value only if they are **timely,** that is, available in time for a decision. Thus, timeliness is the third important criterion for determining the usefulness of information. Some situations involve a trade-off between the accuracy and the timeliness of information. More accurate information may take longer to produce. Therefore, as accuracy improves, timeliness suffers, and vice versa. For example, a company may test market a potential new product in a particular city. The longer the test-marketing program runs, the more accurate will be the marketing data generated. However, a long wait for the accurate marketing report may unduly delay management's decision to launch the new product nationally.

To summarize, the managerial accountant's primary role in the decision-making process is twofold:

1. Decide what information is *relevant* to each decision problem.
2. Provide *accurate* and *timely* data, keeping in mind the proper balance between these often conflicting criteria.

RELEVANT INFORMATION

What makes information relevant to a decision problem? Four considerations are important.

Bearing on the Future The consequences of decisions are borne in the future, not the past. To be relevant to a decision, cost or benefit information must involve a future event. The cost information relevant to Worldwide Airways' decision concerning its London operations involves the costs that *will be incurred in the future* under the airline's two alternatives. Costs incurred in the past in the airline's London operations will not change regardless of management's decision, and they are irrelevant to the decision at hand.

Different under Competing Alternatives Relevant information must involve costs or benefits that *differ among the alternatives.* Costs or benefits that are the same across all the available alternatives have no bearing on a decision. For example, suppose Worldwide Airways' management decides to keep its reservations and ticketing office in London regardless of whether its London hub is eliminated. Then the costs of the reservations and ticketing office will not differ between the two alternatives regarding elimination of the London hub. Hence, those costs are irrelevant to that decision.

Need for Predictions Since relevant information involves future events, the managerial accountant must predict the amounts of the relevant costs and benefits. In making these predictions, the accountant often will use estimates of cost behavior based on historical data. There is an important and subtle issue here. *Relevant* information must involve costs and benefits to be realized in the *future*. However, the accountant's *predictions* of those costs and benefits often are based on data from the *past*.

Unique versus Repetitive Decisions *Unique decisions* arise infrequently or only once. Worldwide Airways' decision regarding its London hub is an example. Compiling data for unique decisions usually requires a special analysis by the managerial accountant. The relevant information often will be found in many diverse places in the organization's overall information system.

In contrast, *repetitive decisions* are made over and over again, at either regular or irregular intervals. For example, Worldwide Airways makes route-scheduling decisions every six months. Such a routine decision makes it worthwhile for the managerial accountant to keep a special file of the information relevant to the scheduling decision.

Cost predictions relevant to repetitive decisions typically can draw on a large amount of historical data. Since the decisions have been made repeatedly in the past, the data from those decisions should be readily available. Information relevant to unique decisions is harder to generate. The managerial accountant typically will have to give more thought to deciding which data are relevant, and will have less historical data available upon which to base predictions.

Importance of Identifying Relevant Costs and Benefits

Why is it important for the managerial accountant to isolate the relevant costs and benefits in a decision analysis? The reasons are twofold. First, generating information is a costly process. The relevant data must be sought, and this requires time and effort. By focusing only on the relevant information, the managerial accountant can simplify and shorten the data-gathering process.

Second, people can effectively use only a limited amount of information. Beyond this, they experience **information overload,** and their decision-making effectiveness declines. By routinely providing only information about relevant costs and benefits, the managerial accountant can reduce the likelihood of information overload.

IDENTIFYING RELEVANT COSTS AND BENEFITS

To illustrate how managerial accountants determine relevant costs and benefits, we will consider several decisions faced by the management of Worldwide Airways. Based in Atlanta, the airline flies routes between the United States and Europe, between various cities in Europe, and between the United States and several Asian cities.

Sunk Costs

Sunk costs are costs that already have been incurred. They do not affect any future cost and cannot be changed by any current or future action. Sunk costs are irrelevant to decisions, as the following two examples show.

Book Value of Equipment At Charles de Gaulle Airport in Paris, Worldwide Airways has a three-year-old loader truck used to load in-flight meals onto airplanes. The box on the truck can be lifted hydraulically to the level of a jumbo jet's side doors. The *book value* of this loader, defined as the asset's acquisition cost less the accumulated depreciation to date, is computed as follows:

Acquisition cost of old loader	$100,000
Less: Accumulated depreciation	75,000
Book value	$ 25,000

The loader has one year of useful life remaining, after which its salvage value will be zero. However, it could be sold now for $5,000. In addition to the annual depreciation of $25,000, Worldwide Airways annually incurs $80,000 in variable costs to operate the loader. These include the costs of operator labor, gasoline, and maintenance.

John Orville, Worldwide Airways' ramp manager at Charles de Gaulle Airport, faces a decision about replacement of the loader. A new kind of loader uses a conveyor belt to move meals into an airplane. The new loader is much cheaper than the old hydraulic loader and costs less to operate. However, the new loader would be operable for only one year before it would need to be replaced. Pertinent data about the new loader are as follows:

Acquisition cost of new loader	$15,000
Useful life	1 year
Salvage value after one year	0
Annual depreciation	$15,000
Annual operating costs	$45,000

Orville's initial inclination is to continue using the old loader for another year. He exclaims, "We can't dump that equipment now. We paid $100,000 for it, and we've only used it three years. If we get rid of that loader now, we'll lose $20,000 on the disposal." Orville reasons that the old loader's book value of $25,000, less its current salvage value of $5,000, amounts to a loss of $20,000.

Fortunately, Orville's comment is overheard by Joan Wilbur, the managerial accountant in the company's Charles de Gaulle Airport administrative offices. Wilbur points out to Orville that the book value of the old loader is a *sunk cost*. It cannot affect any future cost the company might incur. To convince Orville that she is right, Wilbur prepares the analysis shown in Exhibit 13-2.

Regardless of which alternative is selected, the $25,000 book value of the old loader will be an expense or loss in the next year. If the old loader is kept in service, the $25,000 will be recognized as depreciation expense; otherwise, the $25,000 cost will be incurred by the company as a write-off of the asset's book value. Thus, the current book value of the old loader is a *sunk cost* and irrelevant to the replacement decision.

Notice that the *relevant* data in the equipment replacement decision are items (3), and (4), and (5). Each of these items meets the two tests of relevant information:

1. The costs or benefits relate to the future.
2. The costs or benefits differ between the alternatives.

The proceeds from selling the old loader, item (3), will be received in the future only under the "replace" alternative. Similarly, the acquisition cost (depreciation) of the new loader, item (4), is a future cost incurred only under the "replace" alternative. The operating cost, item (5), is also a future cost that differs between the two alternatives.

Differential Costs Exhibit 13-2 includes a column entitled *Differential Cost.* This column shows the difference for each item between the costs incurred under the two alternatives. The computation of differential costs is a convenient way of summarizing the relative advantage of one alternative over the other. John Orville can make a correct equipment-replacement decision in either of two ways: (1) by comparing the total cost of the two alternatives, shown in columns (a) and (b); or (2) by focusing on the total differential cost, shown in column (c), which favors the "replacement" option.

Exhibit 13-2. Equipment Replacement Decision: Worldwide Airways

			(a) Do Not Replace Old Loader	(b) Replace Old Loader	(c) Differential Cost
Sunk cost	(1)	Depreciation of old loader	$ 25,000		
		OR			–0–
	(2)	Write-off of old loader's book value.		$25,000	
Relevant data	(3)	Proceeds from disposal of old loader	–0–	(5,000)	5,000
	(4)	Depreciation (cost) of new loader.	–0–	15,000	(15,000)
	(5)	Operating costs	80,000	45,000	35,000
		Total cost	$105,000	$80,000	$25,000

Costs of Two Alternatives

Cost of Inventory on Hand Never having taken a managerial-accounting course in college, John Orville is slow to learn how to identify sunk costs. The next week he goofs again.

The inventory of spare aircraft parts held by Worldwide Airways at Charles de Gaulle includes some obsolete parts originally costing $20,000. The company no longer uses the planes for which the parts were purchased. The obsolete parts include spare passenger seats, luggage racks, and galley equipment. The spare parts could be sold to another airline for $17,000. However, with some modifications, the obsolete parts could still be used in the company's current fleet of aircraft. Using the modified parts would save Worldwide Airways the cost of purchasing new parts for its airplanes.

John Orville decides not to dispose of the obsolete parts, because doing so would entail a loss of $3,000. Orville reasons that the $20,000 book value of the parts, less the $17,000 proceeds from disposal, would result in a $3,000 loss on disposal. Joan Wilbur, the managerial accountant, comes to the rescue again, demonstrating that the right decision is to dispose of the parts. Wilbur's analysis is shown in Exhibit 13-3.

Notice that the book value of the obsolete inventory is a sunk cost. If the parts are modified, the $20,000 book value will be an expense during the period when the parts are used. Otherwise, the $20,000 book value of the asset will be written off when the parts are sold. As a sunk cost, the book value of the obsolete inventory will not affect any future cash flow of the company.

As the managerial accountant's analysis reveals, the relevant data include the $17,000 proceeds from disposal, the $12,000 cost to modify the parts, and the $26,000 cost to buy new parts. All of these data meet the two tests of relevance: they affect future cash flows and they differ between the two alternatives. As Joan Wilbur's analysis shows, Worldwide Airways' costs will be $3,000 less if the obsolete parts are sold and new parts are purchased.

Exhibit 13-3. Obsolete Inventory Decision: Worldwide Airways

Costs of Two Alternatives

		(a) Modify and Use Parts	(b) Dispose of Parts	(c) Differential Cost
Sunk cost	Book value of parts inventory: asset value written off whether parts are used or not	$20,000	$20,000	$ –0–
Relevant data	Proceeds from disposal of parts	–0–	(17,000)	17,000
	Cost to modify parts	12,000	–0–	12,000
	Cost incurred to buy new parts for current aircraft fleet	–0–	26,000	(26,000)
	Total cost	$32,000	$29,000	$ 3,000

Irrelevant Future Costs and Benefits

At Worldwide Airways' headquarters in Atlanta, Amy Earhart, manager of Flight Scheduling, is in the midst of a decision about the Atlanta to Honolulu route. The flight is currently nonstop, but she is considering a stop in San Francisco. She feels that the route would attract additional passengers if the stop is made, but there would also be additional variable costs. Her analysis appears in Exhibit 13-4.

The analysis indicates that the preferable alternative is the route that includes a stop in San Francisco. Notice that the cargo revenue (item 2) and the aircraft-maintenance cost (item 8) are irrelevant to the flight-route decision. Although these data do affect future cash flows, they *do not differ between the two alternatives.* All of the other data in Exhibit 13-4 are relevant to the decision, because they do differ between the two alternatives. The analysis in Exhibit 13-4 could have ignored the irrelevant data; the same decision would have been reached. (Exercise 13-34, at the end of the chapter, will ask you to prove this assertion by redoing the analysis without the irrelevant data.)

Opportunity Costs

Another decision confronting Amy Earhart is whether to add two daily round-trip flights between Atlanta and Montreal. Her initial analysis of the relevant costs and benefits indicates that the additional revenue from the flights will exceed their costs by $30,000 per month. Hence, she is ready to add the flights to the schedule. However, Chuck Lindbergh, Worldwide Airways' hangar manager in Atlanta, points out that Earhart has overlooked an important consideration.

Exhibit 13-4. Flight Route Decision: Worldwide Airways

Relevant or Irrelevant			(a) Nonstop Route*	(b) With Stop in San Francisco*	(c) Differential Amount†
Relevant	(1)	Passenger revenue	$240,000	$258,000	$(18,000)
Irrelevant	(2)	Cargo revenue	80,000	80,000	–0–
Relevant	(3)	Landing fee in San Francisco	–0–	(5,000)	5,000
Relevant	(4)	Use of airport gate facilities	–0–	(3,000)	3,000
Relevant	(5)	Flight crew cost	(2,000)	(2,500)	500
Relevant	(6)	Fuel	(21,000)	(24,000)	3,000
Relevant	(7)	Meals and services	(4,000)	(4,600)	600
Irrelevant	(8)	Aircraft maintenance	(1,000)	(1,000)	–0–
		Total revenue less costs . . .	$292,000	$297,900	$ (5,900)

Revenues and Costs under Two Alternatives

*In columns (a) and (b), parentheses denote costs and numbers without parentheses are revenues.

†In column (c), parentheses denote differential items favoring option (b).

Exhibit 13-5. Decision to Add a Flight: Worldwide Airways

	(a) Add Flight	(b) Do Not Add Flight	(c) Differ- ential Amount
Additional revenue from new flight less additional costs	$30,000	–0–	$30,000
Rental of excess hangar space	–0–	$40,000	(40,000)*
Total	$30,000	$40,000	$(10,000)

*Parentheses denote that differential benefit favors option (b).

Worldwide Airways currently has excess space in its hangar. A commuter airline has offered to rent the hangar space for $40,000 per month. However, if the Atlanta-to-Montreal flights are added to the schedule, the additional aircraft needed in Atlanta will require the excess hangar space.

If Worldwide Airways adds the Atlanta-to-Montreal flights, it will forgo the opportunity to rent the excess hangar space for $40,000 per month. Thus, the $40,000 in rent forgone is an *opportunity cost* of the alternative to add the new flights. An **opportunity cost** is the potential benefit given up when the choice of one action precludes a different action. Although people tend to overlook or underestimate the importance of opportunity costs, they are just as relevant as out-of-pocket costs in evaluating decision alternatives. In Worldwide Airways' case, the best action is to rent the excess warehouse space to the commuter airline, rather than adding the new flights. The analysis in Exhibit 13-5 supports this conclusion.

It is a common mistake for people to overlook or underweight opportunity costs. The $40,000 hangar rental, which will be forgone if the new flights are added, is an *opportunity cost* of the option to add the flights. It is a *relevant cost* of the decision, and it is just as important as any out-of-pocket expenditure.

Summary

Relevant costs and benefits satisfy the following two criteria:

1. They affect the future.
2. They differ between alternatives.

Sunk costs are *not* relevant costs, because they do not affect the future. An example of a sunk cost is the book value of an asset, either equipment or inventory. *Future costs or benefits that are identical across all decision alternatives are not relevant.* They can be ignored when making a decision. *Opportunity costs are relevant costs.* Such costs deserve particular attention, because many people tend to overlook them when making decisions.

ANALYSIS OF SPECIAL DECISIONS

What are the relevant costs and benefits when a manager must decide whether to add or drop a product or service? What data are relevant when deciding whether to produce or buy a service or component? These decisions and certain other nonroutine decisions merit special attention in our discussion of relevant costs and benefits.

Accept or Reject a Special Order

Jim Wright, Worldwide Airways' vice president for operations, has been approached by a Japanese tourist agency about flying chartered tourist flights from Japan to Hawaii. The tourist agency has offered Worldwide Airways $150,000 per round-trip flight on a jumbo jet. Given the airline's usual occupancy rate and air fares, a round-trip jumbo-jet flight between Japan and Hawaii typically brings in revenue of $250,000. Thus, the tourist agency's specially priced offer requires a special analysis by Jim Wright.

Wright knows that Worldwide Airways has two jumbo jets that are not currently being used. The airline has just eliminated several unprofitable routes, freeing these aircraft for other uses. The airline was not currently planning to add any new routes, and therefore the two jets were idle. To help in making his decision, Wright asks for cost data from the controller's office. The controller provides the information in Exhibit 13-6, which pertains to a typical round-trip, jumbo-jet flight between Japan and Hawaii.

The variable costs cover aircraft fuel and maintenance, flight-crew costs, in-flight meals and services, and landing fees. The fixed costs allocated to each flight cover Worldwide Airways' fixed costs, such as aircraft depreciation, maintenance and depreciation of facilities, and fixed administrative costs.

If Jim Wright had not understood managerial accounting, he might have done the following *incorrect analysis.*

Special price for charter...	$150,000
Total cost per flight	190,000
Loss on charter flight..	$ (40,000)

Exhibit 13-6. Data for Typical Flight between Japan and Hawaii: Worldwide Airways

Revenue:		
Passenger	$250,000	
Cargo	30,000	
Total revenue		$280,000
Expenses:		
Variable expenses of flight	90,000	
Fixed expenses allocated to each flight	100,000	
Total expenses		190,000
Profit		$ 90,000

This calculation suggests that the special charter offer should be declined. What is the error in this analysis? The mistake is the inclusion of allocated fixed costs in the cost per flight. This is an error, because the *fixed costs will not increase in total* if the charter flight is added. Since the fixed costs will not change under either of the alternative choices, they are irrelevant.

Fortunately, Jim Wright does not make this mistake. He knows that only the variable costs of the proposed charter are relevant. Moreover, Wright determines that the variable cost of the charter would be lower than that of a typical flight, because Worldwide Airways would not incur the variable costs of reservations and ticketing. These variable expenses amount to $5,000 for a scheduled flight. Thus, Wright's analysis of the charter offer is as shown below.

Assumes	Special price for charter		$150,000
excess	Variable cost per routine flight	$90,000	
capacity	Less: Savings on reservations and ticketing..........	5,000	
(idle	Variable cost of charter		85,000
aircraft)	Contribution from charter		$ 65,000

Wright's analysis shows that the special charter flight will contribute $65,000 toward covering the airline's fixed costs and profit. Since the airline has excess flight capacity, due to the existence of idle aircraft, the optimal decision is to accept the special charter offer.

No Excess Capacity Now let's consider how Wright's analysis would appear if Worldwide Airways had no idle aircraft. Suppose that in order to fly the charter between Japan and Hawaii, the airline would have to cancel its least profitable route, which is between Japan and Hong Kong. This route contributes $80,000 toward covering the airline's fixed costs and profit. Thus, if the charter offer is accepted, the airline will incur an opportunity cost of $80,000 from the forgone contribution on the Japan–Hong Kong route. Now Wright's analysis should appear as shown below.

Assumes no	Special price for charter.....................		$150,000
excess	Variable cost per routine flight	$90,000	
capacity	Less: Savings on reservations and ticketing	5,000	
(no idle	Variable cost of charter	85,000	
aircraft)	Add: Opportunity cost, forgone contribution on		
	canceled Japan–Hong Kong route	80,000	165,000
	Loss from charter..........................		$ (15,000)

Thus, if Worldwide Airways has no excess flight capacity, Jim Wright should reject the special charter offer.

Summary The decision to accept or reject a specially priced order is common in both service industry and manufacturing firms. Manufacturers often are faced with decisions about selling products in a special order at less than full price. The correct analysis of such decisions focuses on the relevant costs and benefits. Fixed costs, which often are allocated to individual units of product or service, are usually irrelevant. Fixed costs typically will not change in total, whether the order is accepted or rejected.

When excess capacity exists, the only relevant costs usually will be the variable costs associated with the special order. When there is no excess capacity, the opportunity cost of using the firm's facilities for the special order are also relevant to the decision.

Make or Buy a Product or Service

Ellie Rickenbacker is Worldwide Airways' manager of in-flight services. She supervises the airline's flight attendants and all of the of the firm's food and beverage operations. Rickenbacker currently faces a decision regarding the preparation of in-flight dinners at the airline's Atlanta hub. In the Atlanta flight kitchen, full-course dinners are prepared and packaged for long flights that pass through Atlanta. In the past, all of the desserts were baked and packaged in the flight kitchen. However, Rickenbacker has received an offer from an Atlanta bakery to bake the airline's desserts. Thus, her decision is to *make or buy* the dessert portion of the in-flight dinners. To help guide her decision, Rickenbacker has assembled the cost information in Exhibit 13-7.

The Atlanta bakery has offered to supply the desserts for 20 cents each. Rickenbacker's initial inclination is to accept the bakery's offer, since it appears that the airline would save 5 cents per dessert. However, the controller reminds Rickenbacker that not all of the costs listed above are relevant to the make-or-buy decision. The controller modifies Rickenbacker's analysis as shown in Exhibit 13-8.

If Worldwide Airways stops making desserts, it will save all of the variable costs but only 1 cent of fixed costs. The 1-cent saving in supervisory salaries would result because the airline could get along with two fewer kitchen supervisors. The remainder of the fixed costs would be incurred even if the desserts were purchased. These remaining fixed costs of supervision and depreciation would have to be reallocated to the flight kitchen's other products. In light of the controller's revised analysis, Rickenbacker realizes that the airline should continue to make its own desserts. To buy the desserts would require an expenditure of 20 cents per dessert, but only 15 cents per dessert would be saved.

To clarify her decision further, Rickenbacker asks the controller to prepare an analysis of the *total costs* per month of making or buying desserts. The controller's report, displayed in Exhibit 13-9, shows the total cost of producing 1,000,000 desserts, the flight kitchen's average monthly volume.

Exhibit 13-7. Cost of In-Flight Desserts: Worldwide Airways

	Cost per Dessert
Variable costs:	
Direct material (food and packaging)	$.06
Direct labor	.04
Variable overhead	.04
Fixed costs (allocated to products):	
Supervisory salaries	.04
Depreciation of flight-kitchen equipment	.07
Total cost per dessert	$.25

Exhibit 13-8. Cost Savings from Buying In-Flight Desserts: Worldwide Airways

	Cost per Dessert	Costs That Would Be Saved If Desserts Were Purchased
Variable costs:		
Direct material	$.06	$.06
Direct labor	.04	.04
Variable overhead	.04	.04
Fixed costs (allocated to products):		
Supervisory salaries	.04	.01
Depreciation of flight-kitchen equipment	.07	–0–
Total cost per dessert	$.25	$.15
Cost of purchasing desserts (per dessert)		$.20

Exhibit 13-9. Total-Cost Analysis of Make or Buy Decision: Worldwide Airways

	Cost per Month	Costs That Would Be Saved If Desserts Were Purchased
Variable costs:		
Direct material	$60,000	$60,000
Direct labor	40,000	40,000
Variable overhead	40,000	40,000
Fixed costs (allocated to products):		
Supervisory salaries	40,000	10,000*
Depreciation of flight-kitchen equipment	70,000	–0–
Total cost per month	$250,000	$150,000
Cost of purchasing desserts (per month)		$200,000

*Cost of monthly compensation for two kitchen supervisors, who will not be needed if desserts are purchased.

The total-cost analysis confirmed Rickenbacker's decision to continue making desserts in the airline's flight kitchen.

Beware of Unit-Cost Data Fixed costs often are allocated to individual units of product or service for product-costing purposes. For decision-making purposes, however, unitized fixed costs can be misleading. As the total-cost analysis above shows, only $10,000 in fixed monthly cost will be saved if the desserts are purchased. The remaining $100,000 in monthly fixed cost will continue whether the desserts are made or purchased. Rickenbacker's initial cost analysis in Exhibit 13-8 implies that each dessert costs the airline 25 cents, but that 25-cent cost includes 11 cents of unitized fixed costs. Most of these costs will remain unchanged regardless of the make-or-buy decision. By allocating fixed costs to individual products or services, they are made to appear variable even though they are not.

Add or Drop a Service, Product, or Department

Worldwide Airways offers its passengers the opportunity to join its World Express Club. Club membership entitles a traveler to use the club facilities at the airport in Atlanta. Club privileges include a private lounge and restaurant, discounts on meals and beverages, and use of a small health spa.

Jayne Wing, the president of Worldwide Airways, is worried that the World Express Club might not be profitable. Her concern was caused by the statement of monthly operating income shown in Exhibit 13-10.

In her weekly staff meeting, Wing states her concern about the World Express Club's profitability. The controller responds by pointing out that not all of the costs on the club's income statement would be eliminated if the club were discontinued. The vice president for sales adds that the club helps Worldwide Airways attract passengers whom it might otherwise lose to a competitor. As the meeting adjourns,

---

Exhibit 13-10. World Express Club Monthly Operating Income Statement: Worldwide Airways

Sales revenue		$200,000
Less: Variable expenses:		
Food and beverages	$70,000	
Personnel	40,000	
Variable overhead	25,000	135,000
Contribution margin		65,000
Less: Fixed expenses:		
Depreciation on furnishings and equipment	30,000	
Supervisory salaries	20,000	
Insurance	10,000	
Airport fees	5,000	
General overhead (allocated)	10,000	75,000
Loss		$(10,000)

Wing asks the controller to prepare an analysis of the relevant costs and benefits associated with the World Express Club. The controller's analysis is displayed in Exhibit 13-11.

The controller's report contains two parts. Part I focuses on the relevant costs and benefits of the World Express Club only, while ignoring any impact of the club on other airline operations. In column (a), the controller has listed the club's revenues and expenses from the income statement given previously (Exhibit 13-10). Column (b) lists the expenses that will continue if the club is eliminated. These expenses are called **unavoidable expenses.** In contrast, the expenses appearing in column (a) but not column (b) are **avoidable expenses.** The airline will no longer incur these expenses if the club is eliminated.

Exhibit 13-11. Relevant Costs and Benefits of World Express Club: Worldwide Airways

	(a) Keep Club	(b) Eliminate Club	(c) Differential Amount
Part I:			
Sales revenue	$200,000	–0–	$200,000
Less: Variable expenses:			
Food and beverages	(70,000)	–0–	(70,000)
Personnel	(40,000)	–0–	(40,000)
Variable overhead	(25,000)	–0–	(25,000)
Contribution margin	65,000	–0–	65,000
Less: Fixed expenses:			
Depreciation on furnishings and equipment . . .	(30,000)	(20,000)	(10,000)
Supervisory salaries	(20,000)	–0–	(20,000)
Insurance	(10,000)	(10,000)	–0–
Airport fees	(5,000)	–0–	(5,000)
General overhead (allocated)	(10,000)	(10,000)	–0–
Total fixed expenses	(75,000)	(40,000)	(35,000)
Profit (loss)	$(10,000)	$(40,000)	$ 30,000
	Expenses in the column above are **unavoidable** expenses	Expenses in the column above are **avoidable** expenses	
Part II:			
Contribution margin from general airline operations that will be forgone if club is eliminated	$ 60,000	–0–	$ 60,000

Notice that all of the club's variable expenses are avoidable. However, only some of the club's fixed expenses are avoidable. A portion of the fixed depreciation expense is avoidable. The unavoidable portion of the depreciation expense, $20,000, pertains to equipment that is specialized to the club's purposes. It has no other use to the airline and cannot be sold. The fixed supervisory salaries are avoidable, since these employees will no longer be needed if the club is eliminated. The fixed insurance expense of $10,000 is not avoidable; the $5,000 fee paid to the airport for the privilege of operating the club is avoidable. Finally, the club's allocated portion of general overhead expenses, $10,000, is not avoidable. Worldwide Airways will incur these expenses regardless of its decision about the World Express Club.

The conclusion shown by Part I of the controller's report is that the club should not be eliminated. If the club is closed, the airline will lose more in contribution margin, $65,000, than it saves in avoidable fixed expenses, $35,000. Thus, the club's $65,000 contribution margin is enough to cover the avoidable fixed expenses of $35,000 and still contribute $30,000 toward covering the overall airline's fixed expenses.

World Express Club's contribution margin	$65,000
Avoidable fixed expenses	35,000
Contribution of club toward covering overall airline's fixed expenses	$30,000

Now consider Part II of the controller's analysis in Exhibit 13-11. As the vice president for sales pointed out, the World Express Club is an attractive feature to many travelers. The controller estimates that if the club were discontinued, the airline would lose $60,000 each month in forgone contribution margin from general airline operations. This loss in contribution margin would result from losing to a competing airline current passengers who are attracted to Worldwide Airways by its World Express Club. This $60,000 in forgone contribution margin is an *opportunity cost* of the option to close down the club.

Considering both Parts I and II of the controller's analysis, Worldwide airways' monthly profit will be greater by $90,000 if the club is kept open. Recognition of two issues is key to this conclusion:

1. Only the avoidable expenses of the club will be saved if it is discontinued.
2. Closing the club will adversely affect the airline's other operations.

SPECIAL DECISIONS IN MANUFACTURING FIRMS

Some types of decisions are more likely to arise in manufacturing companies than in service industry firms. We will examine two of these decisions.

Joint Products: Sell or Process Further

A **joint production process** results in two or more products, called *joint products.* An example is the processing of cocoa beans into cocoa powder and cocoa butter. Cocoa beans constitute the input to the joint production process, and the two joint products are cocoa powder and cocoa butter. The point in the production process where the joint products are identifiable as separate products is called the **split-off point.** Other examples of joint production processes include the slaughtering of animals for various cuts of meat and the processing of petroleum into various products, such as kerosene and gasoline.

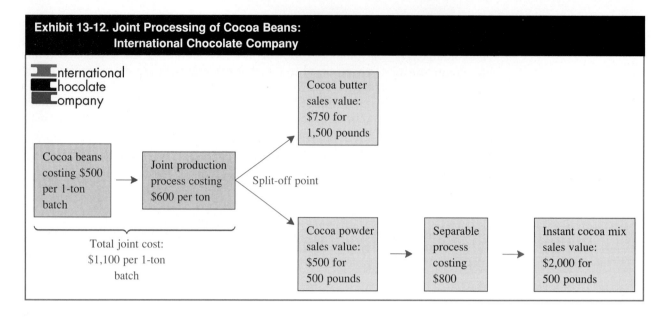

**Exhibit 13-12. Joint Processing of Cocoa Beans:
International Chocolate Company**

Manufacturers with joint production processes sometimes must decide whether a joint product should be sold at the split-off point or processed further before being sold. Such a decision recently confronted Bill Candee, the president of International Chocolate Company. Candee's firm imports cocoa beans and processes them into cocoa powder and cocoa butter. Only a portion of the cocoa powder is used by International Chocolate Company in the production of chocolate candy. The remainder of the cocoa powder is sold to an ice cream producer. Candee is considering the possibility of processing his remaining cocoa powder into an instant cocoa mix to be marketed under the brand name ChocoTime. Data pertaining to Candee's decision are displayed in Exhibit 13-12.

Notice from the diagram that cocoa beans are processed in 1-ton batches. The total cost of the cocoa beans and the joint processing is $1,100. This is called the **joint cost.** The output of the joint process is 1,500 pounds of cocoa butter and 500 pounds of cocoa powder.

How should Bill Candee approach the decision about processing the cocoa powder into instant cocoa mix? What are the relevant costs and benefits? First, let's consider the joint cost of $1,100. Is this a relevant cost in the decision at hand? *The joint cost is not a relevant cost,* because it will not change regardless of the decision Candee makes.

Suppose the $1,100 joint cost had been allocated to the two joint products for product-costing purposes. A common method for allocating a joint cost is the **relative sales value method,** in which the joint cost is allocated between the joint products in proportion to their sales value at the split-off point.[1] International Chocolate Company would make the following joint-cost allocation.

---

[1] Other methods of allocating joint costs are covered in Chapter 17.

Joint Cost	Joint Products	Sales Value at Split-Off Point	Relative Proportion	Allocation of Joint Cost
$1,100	Cocoa butter......	$750	.60	$ 660
	Cocoa powder	500	.40	440
	Total joint cost allocated.............................			$1,100

Does this allocation of the $1,100 joint cost make it relevant to the decision about processing cocoa powder into instant cocoa mix? The answer is no. *The $1,100 joint cost still does not change in total,* whether the cocoa powder is processed further or not. The joint cost is irrelevant to the decision at hand.

The only costs and benefits relevant to Candee's decision are those that differ between the two alternatives. The proper analysis is shown in Exhibit 13-13.

There is a shortcut method that arrives at the same conclusion as Exhibit 13-13. In this approach, he incremental revenue from the further processing of cocoa powder is compared with the **separable processing cost,** which is the cost incurred after the split-off point, as follows:

Sales value of instant cocoa mix	$2,000
Sales value of cocoa powder...	500
Incremental revenue from further processing	1,500
Less: Separable processing cost.......................................	800
Net benefit from further processing....................................	$ 700

Both analyses indicate that Bill Candee should process his excess cocoa powder into instant cocoa mix. The same conclusion is reached if the analysis is done on a per-unit basis rather than a total basis:

Exhibit 13-13. Decision to Sell or Process Further: International Chocolate Company

International Chocolate Company		(a) Sell Cocoa Powder at Split-Off Point	(b) Process Cocoa Powder into Instant Cocoa Mix	(c) Differential Amount (a) – (b)
Relevant or Irrelevant				
	Sales revenue:			
Irrelevant	Cocoa butter.......	$ 750	$ 750	–0–
Relevant	Cocoa powder	500	} →	$(1,500)
Relevant	Instant cocoa mix		2,000	
	Less: Costs:			
Irrelevant	Joint cost	(1,100)	(1,100)	–0–
Relevant	Separable cost of processing cocoa powder into instant cocoa mix........	–0–	(800)	800
	Total............	$ 150	$ 850	$ (700)

Sales value of instant cocoa mix ($2,000 ÷ 500 pounds) . . . . $4.00 per pound
Sales value of cocoa powder ($500 ÷ 500 pounds) . . . . 1.00 per pound
Incremental revenue from further processing . . . . $3.00 per pound
Less: Separable processing cost ($800 ÷ 500 pounds) . . . . 1.60 per pound
Net benefit from further processing . . . . $1.40 per pound

Once again, the analysis shows that Bill Candee should decide to process the cocoa powder into instant cocoa mix.

Decisions Involving Limited Resources

Organizations typically have limited resources. Limitations on floor space, machine time, labor hours, or raw materials are common. Operating with limited resources, a firm often must choose between sales orders, deciding which orders to fill and which ones to decline. In making such decisions, managers must decide which product or service is the most profitable.

To illustrate, suppose International Chocolate Company's Phoenix plant makes two candy-bar products, Chewies and Chompo Bars. The contribution margin for a case of each of these products is computed in Exhibit 13-14.

A glance at the contribution-margin data suggests that Chompo Bars are more profitable than Chewies. It is true that a case of Chompo Bars contributes more toward covering the company's fixed cost and profit. However, an important consideration has been ignored in the analysis so far. The Phoenix plant's capacity is limited by its available machine time. Only 700 machine hours are available in the plant each month. International Chocolate Company can sell as many cases of either candy bar as it can produce, so production is limited only by the constraint on machine time.

To maximize the plant's total contribution toward covering fixed cost and profit, management should strive to use each machine hour as effectively as possible. This realization alters the analysis of product profitability. The relevant question is *not,* Which candy bar has the highest contribution margin per case? The pertinent ques-

---

Exhibit 13-14. Contribution Margin per Case: International Chocolate Company

	Chewies	Chompo Bars
Sales price	$10.00	$14.00
Less: Variable costs:		
Direct material	3.00	3.75
Direct labor	2.00	2.50
Variable overhead	3.00	3.75
Variable selling and		
administrative costs	1.00	2.00
Total variable costs	9.00	12.00
Contribution margin per case	$ 1.00	$ 2.00

Exhibit 13-15. Contribution Margin per Machine Hour: International Chocolate Company

		International Chocolate Company	Chewies	Chompo Bars
(a)	Contribution margin per case		$1.00	$2.00
(b)	Machine hours required per case		.02	.05
(a) ÷ (b)	Contribution margin per machine hour.		$50	$40

tion is, Which product has the highest contribution margin *per machine hour?* This question is answered with the calculation in Exhibit 13-15.

A machine hour spent in the production of Chewies will contribute $50 toward covering fixed cost and profit, while a machine hour devoted to Chompo Bars contributes only $40. Hence, the Phoenix plant's most profitable product is Chewies, when the plant's scarce resource is taken into account.

Suppose International Chocolate Company's Phoenix plant manager, Candace Barr, is faced with a choice between two sales orders, only one of which can be accepted. Only 100 hours of unscheduled machine time remains in the month, and it can be used to produce either Chewies or Chompos. The analysis in Exhibit 13-16 shows that Barr should devote the 100-hour block of machine time to filling the order for Chewies.

As Exhibit 13-16 demonstrates, a decision about the best use of a limited resource should be made on the basis of the *contribution margin per unit of the scarce resource.*

Multiple Scarce Resources Suppose the Phoenix plant had a limited amount of *both* machine hours *and* labor hours. Now the analysis of product profitability is more complicated. The choice as to which product is most profitable typically will involve a trade-off between the two scarce resources. Solving such a problem requires a powerful mathematical tool called *linear programming,* which is covered in the appendix to this chapter.

Exhibit 13-16. Total Contribution from 100 Machine Hours: International Chocolate Company

	International Chocolate Company	Chewies	Chompo Bars
Contribution margin per case		$1.00	$2.00
Number of cases produced in 100 hours of machine time		× 5,000*	× 2,000†
Total contribution toward covering fixed cost and profit		$5,000	$4,000

*Chewies: 100 hours ÷ .02 hour per case = 5,000 cases

† Chompo Bars: 100 hours ÷ .05 hour per case = 2,000 cases

OTHER ISSUES IN DECISION MAKING

Uncertainty

Our analyses of the decisions in this chapter assumed that all relevant data were known with certainty. In practice, of course, decision makers are rarely so fortunate. One common technique for addressing the impact of uncertainty is *sensitivity analysis*. **Sensitivity analysis** is a technique for determining what would happen in a decision analysis if a key prediction or assumption proves to be wrong.

To illustrate, let's return to Candace Barr's decision about how to use the remaining 100 hours of machine time in International Chocolate Company's Phoenix plant. The calculation in Exhibit 12-15 showed that Chewies have the highest contribution margin per machine hour. Suppose Barr is uncertain about the contribution margin per case of Chewies. A sensitivity analysis shows how sensitive her decision is to the value of this uncertain parameter. As Exhibit 13-17 shows, the Chewies contribution margin would decline to $.80 per case before Barr's decision would change. As long as the contribution margin per case of Chewies exceeds $.80 per case, the 100 hours of available machine time should be devoted to Chewies.

Sensitivity analysis can help the managerial accountant decide which parameters in an analysis are most critical to estimate accurately. In this case, the managerial accountant knows that the contribution margin per case of Chewies could be as much as 20 percent lower than the original $1.00 prediction without changing the outcome of the analysis.

Expected Values Another approach to dealing explicitly with uncertainty is to base the decision on expected values. The **expected value** of a random variable is equal to the sum of the possible values for the variable, each weighted by its probability. To illustrate, suppose the contribution margins per case for Chewies and Chompos are uncertain, as shown in Exhibit 13-18. As the exhibit shows, the choice as to which product to produce with excess machine time may be based on the *expected value* of the contribution per machine hour. Statisticians have developed many other methods for dealing with uncertainty in decision making. These techniques are covered in statistics and decision theory courses.

Exhibit 13-17. Sensitivity Analysis: International Chocolate Company

International Chocolate Company

	Original Analysis	Chewies	Chompo Bars
(a)	Contribution margin per case predicted	$1.00	$2.00
(b)	Machine hours required per case	.02	.05
(a) ÷ (b)	Contribution per machine hour	$50	$40

Sensitivity Analysis

		Chewies	
(c)	Contribution margin per case hypothesized in sensitivity analysis	$.80	same
(d)	Machine hours required per case	.02	
(c) ÷ (d)	Contribution per machine hour	$40 ◄	

Exhibit 13-18. Use of Expected Values: International Chocolate Company

	Chewies			Chompo Bars	
Possible Values of Contribution Margin		**Probability**	**Possible Values of Contribution Margin**		**Probability**
$ .75		.5	$1.50		.3
1.25		.5	2.00		.4
			2.50		.3

Expected value	(.50) ($.75) + (.50) ($1.25) = $1.00	(.3) ($1.50) + (.4) ($2.00) + (.3) ($2.50) = $2.00	
Machine hours required per case	.02		.05
Expected value of contribution per machine hour	$ 50	>	$ 40

Incentives for Decision Makers

In this chapter we studied how managers should make decisions by focusing on the relevant costs and benefits. In previous chapters we covered accounting procedures for evaluating managerial performance. There is an important link between *decision making* and *managerial performance evaluation.* Managers typically will make decisions that maximize their perceived performance evaluations and rewards. This is human nature. If we want managers to make optimal decisions by properly evaluating the relevant costs and benefits, then the performance evaluation system and reward structure had better be consistent with that perspective.

The proper treatment of sunk costs in decision making illustrates this issue. Earlier in this chapter we saw that sunk costs should be ignored as irrelevant. For example, the book value of an outdated machine is irrelevant in making an equipment-replacement decision. Suppose, however, that a manager correctly ignores an old machine's book value and decides on early replacement of the machine he purchased a few years ago. Now suppose the hapless manager is criticized by his superior for "taking a loss" on the old machine, or for "buying a piece of junk" in the first place. What is our manager likely to do the next time he faces a similar decision? If he is like many people, he will tend to keep the old machine in order to justify his prior decision to purchase it. In so doing, he will be compounding his error. However, he may also be avoiding criticism from a superior who does not understand the importance of goal congruence.

The point is simply that if we want managers to make optimal decisions, we must give them incentives to do so. This requires that managerial performance be judged on the same factors that should be considered in making correct decisions.

Short-Run versus Long-Run Decisions

The decisions we have examined in this chapter were treated as short-run decisions. *Short-run decisions* affect only a short time period, typically a year or less. In reality, many of these decisions would have longer-term implications. For example, managers usually make a decision involving the addition or deletion of a product or service with a relatively long time frame in mind. The process of identifying relevant costs and benefits is largely the same whether the decision is viewed from a short-run or long-run perspective. One important factor that does change in a long-run analysis, however, is the *time value of money.* When several time periods are involved in a decision, the analyst should account for the fact that a $1.00 cash flow today is different from a $1.00 cash flow in five years. A dollar received today can be invested to earn interest, while the dollar received in five years cannot be invested over the intervening time period. The analysis of long-run decisions requires a tool called *capital budgeting,* which is covered in Chapters 15 and 16.

PITFALLS TO AVOID

Identification of the relevant costs and benefits is an important step in making any economic decision. Nonetheless, analysts often overlook relevant costs or incorrectly include irrelevant data. In this section, we review four common mistakes to avoid in decision making.

1. *Sunk costs* The book value of an asset, defined as its acquisition cost less the accumulated depreciation, is a sunk cost. Sunk costs cannot be changed by any current or future course of action, so they are irrelevant in decision making. Nevertheless, a common behavioral tendency is to give undue importance to book values in decisions that involve replacing an asset or disposing of obsolete inventory. People often seek to justify their past decisions by refusing to dispose of an asset, even if a better alternative has been identified. *The moral: Ignore sunk costs.*

2. *Unitized fixed costs* For product-costing purposes, fixed costs often are divided by some activity measure and assigned to individual units of product. The result is to make a fixed cost appear variable. While there are legitimate reasons for this practice, from a *product-costing* perspective, it can create havoc in *decision making.* Therefore, in a decision analysis it is usually wise to include a fixed cost in its total amount, rather than as a per-unit cost. *The moral: Beware of unitized fixed costs in decision making.*

3. *Allocated fixed costs* It is also common to allocate fixed costs across divisions, departments, or product lines. A possible result is that a product or department may appear unprofitable when in reality it does make a contribution toward covering fixed costs and profit. Before deciding to eliminate a department, be sure to ask which costs will be *avoided* if a particular alternative is selected. A fixed cost that has been allocated to a department may continue, in total or in part, even after the department has been eliminated. *The moral: Beware of allocated fixed costs; identify the avoidable costs.*

4. *Opportunity costs* People tend to overlook opportunity costs, or to treat such costs as less important than out-of-pocket costs. Yet opportunity costs are just as real and important to making a correct decision as are

out-of-pocket costs. *The moral: Pay special attention to identifying and including opportunity costs in a decision analysis.*

ILLUSTRATION FROM MANAGEMENT-ACCOUNTING PRACTICE

Relevant Costs and Benefits of Advanced Manufacturing Systems

Estimating relevant costs and benefits is a crucial but difficult step in decisions regarding acquisition of advanced manufacturing systems. Flexible manufacturing systems (FMS) and just-in-time (JIT) production equipment can cost $50 million or more. To justify such massive expenditures, management must be able to quantify the benefits. These benefits can be realized directly through production cost savings, or indirectly through improved customer satisfaction.

Yamazaki Machinery Company purchased an $18 million FMS, and experienced substantial cost savings throughout its production process. For example, only 18 machines were required in the new FMS, down from 68. This resulted in a reduction of factory floor space from 103,000 square feet to only 30,000. Production employees were cut from 215 to 12. Average cycle time dropped from 35 days to 1.5, and the company significantly cut its inventories of raw materials and finished goods. In addition, the firm enjoyed a marketing advantage, since it was able to offer customers shorter lead times and respond more quickly to their changing needs.[2]

CHAPTER SUMMARY

The managerial accountant's role in the decision-making process is to provide data relevant to the decision. Managers can then use these data in preparing a quantitative analysis of the decision. Qualitative factors are considered also in making the final decision.

In order to be relevant to a decision, a cost or benefit must: (1) bear on the future, and (2) differ under the various decision alternatives. Sunk costs, such as the book value of equipment or inventory, are not relevant in decisions. Such costs do not have any bearing on the future. Opportunity costs frequently are relevant to decisions, but they often are overlooked by decision makers. To analyze any special decision, the proper approach is to determine all of the costs and benefits that will differ among the alternatives.

Since decisions often are made under uncertainty, sensitivity analysis should be used to determine if the decision will change if various predictions prove to be wrong.

REVIEW PROBLEM ON RELEVANT COSTS

Lansing Camera Company has received a special order for photographic equipment it does not normally produce. The company has excess capacity, and the order could be manufactured without reducing production of the firm's regular products. Discuss the relevance of each of the following items in computing the cost of the special order.

1. Equipment to be used in producing the order has a book value of $2,000. The equipment has no other use for Lansing Camera Company. If the order is not accepted, the equipment will be sold for $1,500. If the equipment is used in producing the order, it can be sold in three months for $800.

[2] Robert S. Kaplan, "Must CIM Be Justified by Faith Alone?" *Harvard Business Review* (March–April 1986), pp. 87 and 92.

$ 18,000

2. If the special order is accepted, the operation will require some of the storage space in the company's plant. If the space is used for this purpose, the company will rent storage space temporarily in a nearby warehouse at a cost of $18,000. The building depreciation allocated to the storage space to be used in producing the special order is $12,000. *Irrelevant*

3. If the special order is accepted, it will require a subassembly. Lansing Camera can purchase the subassembly for $24.00 per unit from an outside supplier or make it for $30.00 per unit. The $30.00 cost per unit was determined as follows:

$22.00

leave out fixed

Direct material.	$10.00
Direct labor	6.00
Variable overhead	6.00
Allocated fixed overhead.	8.00
Total unit cost of subassembly	$30.00

Solution to Review Problem

1. The book value of the equipment is a sunk cost, irrelevant to the decision. The relevant cost of the equipment is $700, determined as follows:

Sales value of equipment now	$1,500
Sales value after producing special order.	800
Differential cost.	$ 700

2. The $12,000 portion of building depreciation allocated to the storage space to be used for the special order is irrelevant. First, it is a sunk cost. Second, any costs relating to the company's factory building will continue whether the special order is accepted or not. The relevant cost is the $18,000 rent that will be incurred only if the special order is accepted.

3. Lansing Camera should make the subassembly. The subassembly's relevant cost is $22.00 per unit.

Relevant Cost of Making Subassembly (per unit)		**Relevant Cost of Purchasing Subassembly (per unit)**	
Direct material.	$10.00	Purchase price	$24.00
Direct labor	6.00		
Variable overhead	6.00		
Total.	$22.00		

Notice that the unitized fixed overhead, $8.00, is not a relevant cost of the subassembly. Lansing Camera Company's *total* fixed cost will not change, whether the special order is accepted or not.

KEY TERMS   Accurate information, p. 541; **Avoidable expenses**, p. 554; **Differential cost**, p. 545; **Expected value**, p. 560; **Information overload**, p. 544; **Joint cost**, p. 556; **Joint production process**, p. 555; **Opportunity cost**, p. 548; **Qualitative characteristics**, p. 541; **Relative sales value method**, p. 556; **Relevant information**, p. 541; **Sensitivity analysis**, p. 560; **Separable processing cost**, p. 557; **Split-off point**, p. 555; **Timely information**, p. 542; **Unavoidable expenses**, p. 554.

Linear Programming

When a firm produces multiple products, management must decide how much of each output to produce. In most cases, the firm is limited in the total amount it can produce, due to constraints on resources such as machine time, direct labor, or raw materials. This situation is known as a *product-mix problem.*

To illustrate, we will use International Chocolate Company's Phoenix plant, which produces Chewies and Chompo Bars. Exhibit 13-19 provides data pertinent to the problem.

Linear programming is a powerful mathematical tool, well suited to solving International Chocolate Company's product-mix problem. The steps in constructing the linear program are as follows:

1. Identify the **decision variables,** which are the variables about which a decision must be made. International Chocolate's decision variables are as follows:

   Decision X = **number of cases of Chewies to produce each month**
   Variables Y = **number of cases of Chompo Bars to produce each month**

Exhibit 13-19. Data for Product-Mix Problem: International Chocolate Company

	Chewies	Chompo Bars
Contribution margin per case	$1.00	$2.00
Machine hours per case	.02	.05
Direct-labor hours per case	.20	.25

	Machine Hours	Direct-Labor Hours
Limited resources: hours available per month	700	5,000

---

2. Write the **objective function,** which is an algebraic expression of the firm's goal. International Chocolate's goal is to *maximize its total contribution margin.* Since Chewies bring a contribution margin of $1 per case, and Chompos result in a contribution margin of $2 per case, the firm's objective function is the following:

$$\text{Objective Function} \quad \textbf{maximize } Z = X + 2Y$$

3. Write the **constraints,** which are algebraic expressions of the limitations faced by the firm, such as those limiting its productive resources. International Chocolate has a constraint for machine time and a constraint for direct labor.

$$\text{Machine-Time Constraint} \quad .02X + .05Y \le 700$$
$$\text{Labor-Time Constraint} \quad .20X + .25Y \le 5{,}000$$

Suppose, for example, that management decided to produce 20,000 cases of Chewies and 6,000 cases of Chompos. The machine-time constraint would appear as follows:

$$(.02)(20{,}000) + (.05)(6{,}000) = 700$$

Thus, at these production levels, the machine-time constraint would just be satisfied, with no machine hours to spare.

Graphical Solution

To understand how the linear program described above will help International Chocolate's management solve its product-mix problem, examine the graphs in Exhibit 13-20. The two colored lines in panel A represent the constraints. The colored arrows indicate that the production quantities, X and Y, must lie on or below these lines. Since the production quantities must be nonnegative, colored arrows also appear on the graphs' axes. Together, the axes and constraints form an area called the **feasible region,** in which the solution to the linear program must lie.

The black slanted line in panel A represents the objective function. Rearrange the objective function equation as follows:

$$Z = X + 2Y \longrightarrow Y = \frac{Z}{2} - \frac{1}{2}X$$

This form of the objective function shows that the slope of the equation is $-\frac{1}{2}$, which is the slope of the objective-function line in the exhibit. Management's goal is to maximize total contribution margin, denoted by Z. To achieve the maximum, the objective-function line must be moved as far outward and upward in the feasible region as possible, while maintaining the same slope. This goal is represented in panel A by the black arrow.

Solution The result of moving the objective-function line as far as possible in the indicated direction is shown in panel B of the exhibit. The objective-function line intersects the feasible region at exactly one point, where X equals 15,000 and Y equals 8,000. Thus, International Chocolate's optimal product mix is 15,000 cases of

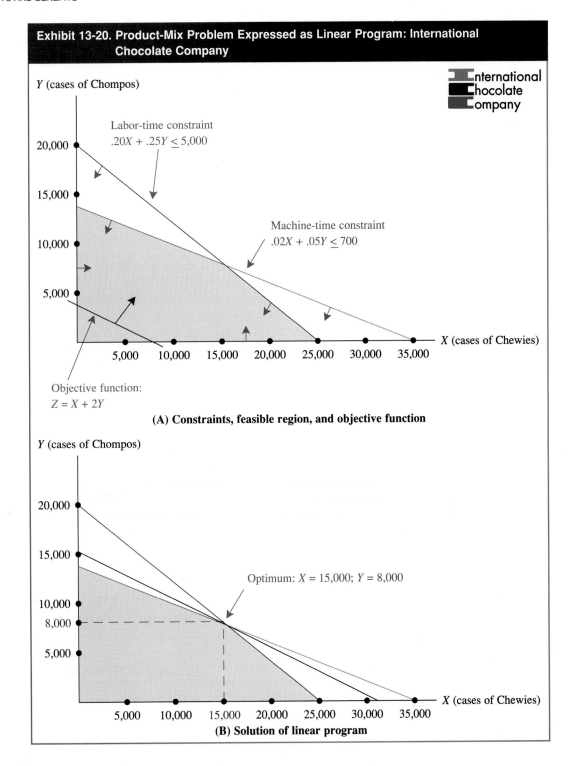

Exhibit 13-20. Product-Mix Problem Expressed as Linear Program: International Chocolate Company

(A) Constraints, feasible region, and objective function

(B) Solution of linear program

Chewies and 8,000 cases of Chompos per month. The total contribution margin is calculated as shown below.

$$\text{Total contribution margin} = (15,000)(\$1) + (8,000)(\$2) = \$31,000$$

Simplex Method and Sensitivity Analysis Although the graphical method is instructive, it is a cumbersome technique for solving a linear program. Fortunately, mathematicians have developed a more efficient solution method called the *simplex algorithm*. A computer can apply the algorithm to a complex linear program and determine the solution in seconds. In addition, most linear programming computer packages provide a sensitivity analysis of the problem. This analysis shows the decision maker the extent to which the estimates used in the objective function and constraints can change without changing the solution.

Managerial Accountant's Role

What is the managerial accountant's role in International Chocolate's product-mix decision? The production manager in the company's Phoenix plant makes this decision, with the help of a linear program. However, the linear program uses *information supplied by the managerial accountant.* The coefficients of X and Y in the objective function are unit contribution margins. Exhibit 13-14 shows that calculating these contribution margins requires estimates of direct-material, direct-labor, variable-overhead, and variable selling and administrative costs. These estimates were provided by a managerial accountant, along with estimates of the machine time and direct-labor time required to produce a case of Chewies or Chompos. All of these estimates were obtained from the standard-costing system, upon which the Phoenix plant's product costs are based. Thus, the managerial accountant makes the product-mix decision possible by providing the relevant cost data.

Linear programming is widely used in business decision making. Among the applications are blending in the petroleum and chemical industries, scheduling of personnel, railroad cars, and aircraft, and the mixing of ingredients in the food industry. In all of these applications, managerial accountants provide information crucial to the analysis.

KEY TERMS: APPENDIX   Constraints, p. 566; Decision variables, p. 565; Feasible region, p. 566; Objective function, p. 566.

REVIEW QUESTIONS   **13-1.** Describe the managerial accountant's role in the decision-making process.

13-2. List the six steps in the decision-making process.

13-3. Explain what is meant by the term *decision model.*

13-4. Distinguish between qualitative and quantitative decision analyses.

13-5. "A quantitative analysis enables a decision maker to put a 'price' on the sum total of the qualitative characteristics in a decision situation." Explain this statement, and give an example.

13-6. What is meant by each of the following potential characteristics of information: relevant, accurate, and timely? Is objective information always relevant? Accurate?

13-7. List and explain two important criteria that must be satisfied in order for information to be relevant.

13-8. Explain why the book value of equipment is not a relevant cost.

13-9. Is the book value of inventory on hand a relevant cost? Why?

13-10. Why might a manager exhibit a behavioral tendency to inappropriately consider sunk costs in making a decision?

13-11. Give an example of an irrelevant future cost. Why is it irrelevant?

13-12. Define the term *opportunity cost,* and give an example of one.

13-13. What behavioral tendency do people often exhibit with regard to opportunity costs?

13-14. How does the existence of excess production capacity affect the decision to accept or reject a special order?

13-15. What is meant by the term *differential cost analysis?*

13-16. Briefly describe the proper approach for making a decision about adding or dropping a product line.

13-17. What is a *joint production process?* Describe a special decision that commonly arises in the context of a joint production process. Briefly describe the proper approach for making this type of decision.

13-18. Are allocated joint processing costs relevant when making a decision to sell a joint product at the split-off point or process it further? Why?

13-19. Briefly describe the proper approach to making a production decision when limited resources are involved.

13-20. What is meant by the term *contribution margin per unit of scarce resource?*

13-21. How is sensitivity analysis used to cope with uncertainty in decision making?

13-22. "There is an important link between the topics of *decision making* and *managerial performance evaluation.*" Explain.

13-23. List four potential pitfalls in decision making, which represent common errors.

13-24. Why can unitized fixed costs cause errors in decision making?

13-25. Give two examples of sunk costs, and explain why they are irrelevant in decision making.

13-26. "Accounting systems should produce only relevant data and forget about the irrelevant data. Then I'd know what was relevant and what wasn't!" Comment on this remark by a company president.

EXERCISES   *Exercise 13-27   Steps in Decision-Making Process.* Choose an organization and a particular decision situation. Then give examples, using that context, of each step illustrated in Exhibit 13-1.

Exercise 13-28   Machine Replacement. Valley Pizza's owner bought his current pizza oven two years ago for $9,000, and it has one more year of life remaining. He is using straight-line depreciation for the oven. He could purchase a new oven for $2,000, but it would last only one year. The owner figures the new oven would save him $2,600 in annual operating expenses compared to operating the old one. Consequently, he has decided against buying the new oven, since doing so would result in a "loss" of $400 over the next year.

REQUIRED:

1. How do you suppose the owner came up with $400 as the loss for the next year if the new pizza oven were purchased? Explain.
2. Criticize the owner's analysis and decision.
3. Prepare a correct analysis of the owner's decision.

Exercise 13-29   Obsolete Inventory. Seattle Aerospace Corporation manufactures missile parts. The company currently has a $20,000 inventory of parts that have become obsolete due to changes in design specifications. The parts could be sold for $9,000, or modified for $12,000 and sold for $23,500.

REQUIRED:

1. Which of the data above are relevant to the decision about the obsolete parts?
2. Prepare an analysis of the decision.

Exercise 13-30 **Special Order.** Interlaken Chemical Company recently received an order for a product it does not normally produce. Since the company has excess production capacity, management is considering accepting the order. In analyzing the decision, the assistant controller is compiling the relevant costs of producing the order. Production of the special order would require 8,000 kilograms of theolite. Interlaken does not use theolite for its regular product, but the firm has 8,000 kilograms of the chemical on hand from the days when it used theolite regularly. The theolite could be sold to a chemical wholesaler for $15,000. The book value of the theolite is $2.00 per kilogram. Interlaken could buy theolite for $2.40 per kilogram.

$2.00 sunk cost

REQUIRED:

1. What is the relevant cost of theolite for the purpose of analyzing the special-order decision?
2. Discuss each of the numbers given in the exercise with regard to its relevance in making the decision.

Exercise 13-31 **Continuation of Preceding Exercise.** Interlaken's special order also requires 1,000 kilograms of genatope, a solid chemical regularly used in the company's products. The current stock of genatope is 8,000 kilograms at a book value of $8.00 per kilogram. If the special order is accepted, the firm will be forced to restock genatope earlier than expected, at a predicted cost of $8.70 per kilogram. Without the special order, the purchasing manager predicts that the price will be $8.30, when normal restocking takes place. Any order of genatope must be in the amount of 5,000 kilograms.

REQUIRED:

1. What is the relevant cost of genatope?
2. Discuss each of the figures in the exercise in terms of its relevance to the decision.

Exercise 13-32 **Closing a Department.** Chemung Metals Company is considering the elimination of its Packaging Department. Management has received an offer from an outside firm to supply all Chemung's packaging needs. To help her in making the decision, Chemung's president has asked the controller for an analysis of the cost of running Chemung's Packaging Department. Included in that analysis is $8,500 of rent, which represents the Packaging Department's allocation of the rent on Chemung's factory building. If the Packaging Department is eliminated, the space it used will be converted to storage space. Currently Chemung rents storage space in a nearby warehouse for $10,000 per year. The warehouse rental would no longer be necessary if the packaging department were eliminated.

REQUIRED:

1. Discuss each of the figures given in the exercise with regard to its relevance in the department-closing decision.
2. What type of cost is the $10,000 warehouse rental, from the viewpoint of the costs of the Packaging Department?

Exercise 13-33 **Continuation of Preceding Exercise.** If Chemung Chemical Company closes its Packaging Department, the department manager will be appointed manager of the Cutting

Department. The Packaging Department manager makes $45,000 per year. To hire a new Cutting Department manager will cost Chemung $60,000 per year.

REQUIRED: Discuss the relevance of each of these salary figures to the department-closing decision.

Exercise 13-34   Irrelevant Future Costs and Benefits. Redo Exhibit 13-4 without the irrelevant data.

Exercise 13-35   Drop Product Line. Day Street Deli's owner is disturbed by the poor profit performance of his ice cream counter. He has prepared the following profit analysis for 19x0.

Sales.		$45,000
Less: Cost of food.		20,000
Gross profit.		25,000
Less: Operating expenses:		
Wages of counter personnel	12,000	
Paper products (e.g., napkins)	4,000	
Utilities (allocated)	3,000	
Depreciation of counter equipment and furnishings.	2,500	
Depreciation of building (allocated).	4,000	
Deli manager's salary (allocated)	3,000	
Total.		28,500
Loss on ice cream counter.		$(3,500)

REQUIRED: Criticize and correct the owner's analysis.

Exercise 13-36   Joint Products. Castille Industries produces chemicals for the swimming pool industry. In one joint process, 10,000 gallons of GSX is processed into 7,000 gallons of xenolite and 3,000 gallons of banolide. The cost of the joint process, including the GSX, is $20,000. Castille allocates $14,000 of the joint cost to the xenolite and $6,000 of the cost to the banolide. The 3,000 gallons of banolide can be sold at the split-off point for $2,500, or it can be processed further into a product called kitrocide. The sales value of 3,000 gallons of kitrocide is $10,000, and the additional processing cost is $8,100.

REQUIRED: Castille's president has asked your consulting firm to make a recommendation as to whether the banolide should be sold at the split-off point or processed further. Write a letter providing an analysis and a recommendation.

Exercise 13-37   Limited Resource. Duo Company manufactures two products, Uno and Dos. Contribution-margin data follow.

	Uno	Dos
Unit sales price.	$12.00	$29.00
Less:		
Direct material.	6.00	3.00
Direct labor.	1.00	6.00
Variable overhead	1.25	7.50
Variable selling and administrative expenses	.75	.50
Unit contribution margin	$ 3.00	$12.00

Duo Company's production process uses highly skilled labor, which is in short supply. The same employees work on both products and earn the same wage rate.

REQUIRED: Which of Duo Company's products is most profitable? Explain.

Exercise 13-38   Linear Programming (Appendix). Refer to the data given in the preceding exercise for Duo Company. Assume that the direct-labor rate is $24 per hour, and 10,000 labor hours are available per year. In addition, the company has a short supply of machine time. Only 8,000 hours are available each year. Uno requires 1 machine hour per unit, and Dos requires 2 machine hours per unit.

REQUIRED: Formulate the production planning problem as a linear program. Specifically identify (1) the decision variables, (2) the objective function, and (3) the constraints.

PROBLEMS   *Problem 13-39   Use of Excess Production Capacity.* Atway Company has met all production requirements for the current month and has an opportunity to produce additional units of product with its excess capacity. Unit selling prices and unit costs for three models of one of its product lines are as follows:

	Plain Model	Regular Model	Super Model
Selling price	$60	$65	$80
Direct material	18	20	19
Direct labor ($10 per hour)	10	15	20
Variable overhead	8	12	16
Fixed overhead	16	5	15

Variable overhead is applied on the basis of direct-labor dollars, while fixed overhead is applied on the basis of machine hours. There is sufficient demand for the additional production of any model in the product line.

REQUIRED:

1. If Atway Company has excess machine capacity and can add more labor as needed (i.e., neither machine capacity nor labor is a constraint), the excess production capacity should be devoted to producing which product or products?
2. If Atway has excess machine capacity but a limited amount of labor time, the excess production capacity should be devoted to producing which product or products?

(CMA, adapted)

Problem 13-40   Joint Products; Relevant Costs; Cost-Volume-Profit Analysis. Super Clean Corporation produces cleaning compounds and solutions for industrial and household use. While most of its products are processed independently, a few are related. Grit 337, a coarse cleaning powder with many industrial uses, costs $1.60 a pound to make and sells for $2.00 a pound. A small portion of the annual production of this product is retained for further processing in the Mixing Department, where it is combined with several other ingredients to form a paste, which is marketed as a silver polish selling for $4.00 per jar. This further processing requires $\frac{1}{4}$ pound of Grit 337 per jar. Costs of other ingredients, labor, and variable overhead associated with this further processing amount to $2.50 per jar. Variable selling costs are $.30 per jar. If the decision were made to cease production of the silver polish, $5,600 of Mixing Department fixed costs could be avoided. Super Clean has limited production capacity for Grit 337, but unlimited demand for the cleaning powder.

REQUIRED: Calculate the minimum number of jars of silver polish that would have to be sold to justify further processing of Grit 337.

(CMA, adapted)

Problem 13-41 *Make or Buy.* Xyon Company has purchased 80,000 pumps annually from Kobec, Inc. Because the price keeps increasing and reached $68.00 per unit last year, Xyon's management has asked for an estimate of the cost of manufacturing the pump in Xyon's facilities. Xyon makes stampings and castings and has little experience with products requiring assembly.

The engineering, manufacturing, and accounting departments have prepared a report for management which includes the estimate shown below for an assembly run of 10,000 pumps. Additional production employees would be hired to manufacture the pumps but no additional equipment, space, or supervision would be needed.

The report states that total costs for 10,000 units are estimated at $957,000 or $95.70 a unit. The current purchase price is $68.00 a unit, so the report recommends continued purchase of the product.

Components (outside purchases)	$120,000
Assembly labor*	300,000
Manufacturing overhead†	450,000
General and administrative overhead‡	87,000
Total costs	$957,000

* Assembly labor consists of hourly production workers.
† Manufacturing overhead is applied to products on a direct-labor-dollar basis. Variable-overhead costs vary closely with direct-labor dollars.

Fixed overhead.	50% of direct-labor dollars
Variable overhead.	100% of direct-labor dollars
Manufacturing-overhead rate.	150% of direct-labor dollars

‡ General and administrative overhead is applied at 10 percent of the total cost of material (or components), assembly labor, and manufacturing overhead.

REQUIRED: Was the analysis prepared by Xyon Company's engineering, manufacturing, and accounting departments and their recommendation to continue purchasing the pumps correct? Explain your answer and include any supporting calculations you consider necessary. (CMA, adapted)

Problem 13-42 *Add a Product Line.* Helene's, a high-fashion dress manufacturer, is planning to market a new cocktail dress for the coming season. Helene's supplies retailers in the east and mid-Atlantic states.

Four yards of material are required to lay out the dress pattern. Some material remains after cutting, which can be sold as remnants. The leftover material could also be used to manufacture a matching cape and handbag. However, if the leftover material is to be used for the cape and handbag, more care will be required in the cutting operation, which will increase the cutting costs.

The company expects to sell 1,250 dresses. Helene's market research reveals that dress sales will be 20 percent higher if a matching cape and handbag are available. The market research indicates that the cape and handbag will be salable only as accessories with the dress. The combination of dresses, capes, and handbags expected to be sold by retailers are as follows:

	Percent of Total
Complete sets of dress, cape, and handbag	70%
Dress and cape.	6
Dress and handbag	15
Dress only	9
Total.	100%

The material used in the dress costs $12.50 a yard or $50.00 for each dress. The cost of cutting the dress if the cape and handbag are not manufactured is estimated at $20.00 a dress, and the resulting remnants can be sold for $5.00 per dress. If the cape and handbag are manufactured, the cutting costs will be increased by $9.00 per dress and there will be no salable remnants. The selling prices and the costs to complete the three items once they are cut are as follows:

	Selling Price per Unit	Unit Cost to Complete (excludes costs of material and cutting operation)
Dress.................................	$200.00	$80.00
Cape	27.50	19.50
Handbag..............................	9.50	6.50

REQUIRED:

1. Calculate Helene's incremental profit or loss from manufacturing the capes and handbags in conjunction with the dresses.
2. Identify any qualitative factors that could influence Helene's management in its decision to manufacture capes and handbags to match the dress.

(CMA, adapted)

Problem 13-43   Produce or Buy Promotion Services; Usefulness of Cost Data. The Promotion Department of Doxolby, Inc. is responsible for the design and development of all promotional materials for the corporation. This includes all promotional campaigns and related literature, pamphlets, and brochures. Top management is reviewing the effectiveness of the Promotion Department to determine if the department's activities could be managed more economically by an outside promotion agency. As a part of this review, top management has asked for a summary of the Promotion Department's costs for the most recent year. The following cost summary was supplied.

Promotion Department
Costs for the Year Ended December 31, 19x8

Direct department costs	$257,500
Charges from other departments	44,700
Allocated share of general administrative overhead	22,250
Total costs...	$324,450

The direct department costs are those costs that can be traced directly to the activities of the Promotion Department, such as staff and clerical salaries, employee benefits, and supplies. The charges from other departments represent the costs of services provided by other departments of Doxolby at the request of the Promotion Department. For instance, the in-house Printing Department charges the Promotion Department for the promotional literature printed. General administrative overhead includes such costs as top management salaries and benefits, depreciation, heat, insurance, and property taxes. These costs are allocated to all departments in proportion to the number of employees in each department.

REQUIRED: Discuss the usefulness of the cost figures presented for the Promotion Department as a basis for a comparison with an outside agency's bid to provide the same services. (CMA, adapted)

Problem 13-44   Joint Products; Sell or Process Further. Talor Chemical Company is a diversified chemical processing company. The firm manufactures swimming pool chemicals, chemicals for metal processing, specialized chemical compounds, and pesticides.

Currently, the Noorwood plant is producing two derivatives, RNA-1 and RNA-2, from the chemical compound VDB developed by Talor's research labs. Each week 1,200,000 pounds of VDB is processed at a cost of $246,000 into 800,000 pounds of RNA-1 and 400,000 pounds of RNA-2. The proportion of these two outputs cannot be altered, because this is a joint process. RNA-1 has no market value until it is converted into a pesticide with the trade name Fastkil. Processing RNA-1 into Fastkil costs is $240,000. Fastkil wholesales at $50 per 100 pounds.

RNA-2 is sold as is for $80 per hundred pounds. However, Talor has discovered that RNA-2 can be converted into two new products by adding 400,000 pounds of compound LST to the 400,000 pounds of RNA-2. This joint process would yield 400,000 pounds each of DMZ-3 and Pestrol, the two new products. The additional direct-material and related processing costs of this joint process would be $120,000. DMZ-3 and Pestrol would each be sold for $57.50 per 100 pounds. Talor's management has decided not to process RNA-2 further based on the analysis presented in the following schedule.

	RNA-2	Process Further		
		DMZ-3	Pestrol	Total
Production in pounds.	400,000	400,000	400,000	
Revenue	$320,000	$230,000	$230,000	$460,000
Costs:				
VDB costs.	$ 82,000*	$ 61,500	$ 61,500	$123,000†
Additional direct materials (LST) and				
processing of RNA-2	—	$ 60,000	60,000	120,000
Total costs.	$ 82,000	$121,500	$121,500	$243,000
Weekly gross profit.	$238,000	$108,500	$108,500	$217,000

* $82,000 is one-third of the $246,000 cost of processing VDB. When RNA-2 is not processed further, one-third of the final output is RNA-2 (400,000 out of a total of 1,200,000 pounds).
† $123,000 is one-half of the $246,000 cost of processing VDB. When RNA-2 is processed further, one-half of the final output consists of DMZ-3 and Pestrol. The final products than are: 800,000 pounds of RNA-1; 400,000 pounds of DMZ-3; and 400,000 pounds of Pestrol.

REQUIRED: Evaluate Talor Company's analysis, and make any revisions that are necessary. Your critique and analysis should indicate:

  a. Whether Talor Chemical Company made the correct decision.
  b. The gross savings or loss per week resulting from Talor's decision not to process RNA-2 further, if different from management's analysis.

(CMA, adapted)

Problem 13-45   Make or Buy. Stewart Industries has been producing two bearings, components B12 and B18, for use in production. Data regarding these two components are as follows:

	B12	B18
Machine hours required per unit	2.5	3.0
Standard cost per unit:		
Direct material	$ 2.25	$ 3.75
Direct labor	4.00	4.50
Manufacturing overhead		
Variable*	2.00	2.25
Fixed†	3.75	4.50
	$12.00	$15.00

* Variable manufacturing overhead is applied on the basis of direct-labor hours.
† Fixed manufacturing overhead is applied on the basis of machine hours.

Stewart's annual requirement for these components is 8,000 units of B12 and 11,000 units of B18. Recently, Stewart's management decided to devote additional machine time to other product lines, leaving only 41,000 machine hours per year for producing the bearings. An outside company has offered to sell Stewart its annual supply of the bearings at prices of $11.25 for B12 and $13.50 for B18. Stewart wants to schedule the otherwise idle 41,000 machine hours to produce bearings so that the firm can minimize costs (maximize net benefits).

REQUIRED:

1. Compute the net benefit (loss) per machine hour that would result if Stewart Industries accepts the supplier's offer of $13.50 per unit for component B18.
2. Choose the correct answer. Stewart Industries will maximize its net benefits by:
   a. purchasing 4,800 units of B12 and manufacturing the remaining bearings
   b. purchasing 8,000 units of B12 and manufacturing 11,000 units of B18
   c. purchasing 11,000 units of B18 and manufacturing 8,000 units of B12
   d. purchasing 4,000 units of B18 and manufacturing the remaining bearings
   e. purchasing and manufacturing some amounts other than those given above
3. Suppose management has decided to drop product B12. Independently of requirements (1) and (2), assume that Stewart Industries' idle capacity of 41,000 machine hours has a traceable, avoidable annual fixed cost of $44,000, which will be incurred only if the capacity is used. Calculate the maximum price Stewart Industries should pay a supplier for component B18.

(CMA, adapted)

Problem 13-46   Nonprofit Organization; Relevant Costs and Benefits of Publicity Brochures.
Janice Watson recently was appointed executive director of the National Foundation for the Prevention of the Blahs. The foundation raises most of the money for its activities through an annual mail campaign. Although the mail campaign raises large amounts of money, the year-to-year growth in donations has been lower than expected by the foundation's board. In addition, the board wants the mail campaign to project the image of a well-run and fiscally responsible organization in order to build a base for greater future contributions. Consequently, Watson's efforts in her first year will be devoted to improving the mail campaign.

The campaign takes place each spring. The foundation staff works hard to secure media coverage of the foundation's activities for weeks before the mail campaign. In prior years, the foundation mailed brochures describing its activities to millions of people and requested contributions from them. The addresses for the mailing are generated from the foundation's own file of past contributions and from mailing lists purchased from brokers.

The foundation staff is considering three alternative brochures for the upcoming campaign. All three will be $8\frac{1}{2} \times 11$ inches. The simplest, and the one sure to be ready in time for bulk mailing, is a sheet of white paper with a printed explanation of the foundation's program and a request for funds. A more expensive brochure, on colored stock with pictures as well as printed copy, may not be ready in time to take advantage of bulk postal rates. It can be ready in time for mailing at first-class postal rates. The third alternative is an illustrated multicolored brochure printed on glossy paper. The printer has promised that it will be ready to meet the first-class mailing schedule but has asked for a delivery date one week later just in case there are production problems.

The foundation staff has assembled the following cost and revenue information for mailing the three alternative brochures to 2,000,000 potential contributors.

		Brochure Costs			Revenue Potential		
Type of Brochure	Design	Type Setting	Unit Paper Cost	Unit Printing Cost	Bulk Mail	First Class	Late First Class
Plain paper	$ 300	$ 100	$.005	$.003	$1,200,000	—	—
Colored paper	1,000	800	.008	.010	2,000,000	$2,200,000	—
Glossy paper	3,000	2,000	.018	.040	—	2,500,000	$2,200,000

The postal rates are $.02 per item for bulk mail and $.13 per item for presorted first-class mail. First-class mail is more likely to be delivered on a timely basis than bulk mail. The charge by outside companies to handle the mailing is $.01 per unit for the plain and colored-paper brochures and $.02 per unit for the glossy-paper brochure.

REQUIRED:

1. Calculate the net revenue contribution (i.e., excess of donations over solicitation costs) for each brochure with each viable mailing alternative.
2. The foundation must choose one of the three brochures for this year's campaign. The criteria established by the board are (1) net revenue raised, (2) image as a well-run organization, and (3) image as a fiscally responsible organization.
   Evaluate the three alternative brochures in terms of these three criteria.

(CMA, adapted)

Problem 13-47   Analysis of Special Order. Auerbach Industries received an order for a piece of special machinery from Jay Company. Just as Auerbach completed the machine, Jay Company declared bankruptcy, defaulted on the order, and forfeited the 10 percent deposit paid on the selling price of $72,500.

Auerbach's manufacturing manager identified the costs already incurred in the production of the special machinery for Jay Company as follows:

Direct material.		$16,600
Direct labor.		21,400
Manufacturing overhead applied:		
Variable	$10,700	
Fixed.	5,350	16,050
Fixed selling and administrative costs.		5,405
Total.		$59,455

Another company, Kaytell Corporation, will buy the special machinery if it is reworked to Kaytell's specifications. Auerbach offered to sell the reworked machinery to Kaytell as a special order for $68,400. Kaytell agreed to pay the price when it takes delivery in two months. The additional identifiable costs to rework the machinery to Kaytell's specifications are as follows:

Direct materials.	$ 6,200
Direct labor.	4,200
Total	$10,400

A second alternative available to Auerbach is to convert the special machinery to the standard model, which sells for $62,500. The additional identifiable costs for this conversion are as follows:

Direct materials.	$2,850
Direct labor.	3,300
Total	$6,150

A third alternative for Auerbach is to sell the machine as is for a price of $52,000. However, the potential buyer of the unmodified machine does not want it for 60 days. This buyer has offered a $7,000 down payment, with the remainder due upon delivery.

The following additional information is available regarding Auerbach's operations.

(1) The sales commission rate on sales of standard models is 2 percent, while the rate on special orders is 3 percent.

(2) Normal credit terms for sales of standard models are 2/10, net/30. This means that a customer receives a 2 percent discount if payment is made within 10 days, and payment is due no later than 30 days after billing. Most customers take the 2 percent discounts. Credit terms for a special order are negotiated with the customer.

(3) The allocation rates for manufacturing overhead and fixed selling and administrative costs are as follows:

Manufacturing:
Variable.	50% of direct-labor cost
Fixed.	25% of direct-labor cost
Fixed selling and administrative.	10% of the total of direct-material, direct-labor, and manufacturing-overhead costs

(4) Normal time required for rework is one month.

REQUIRED:

1. Determine the dollar contribution each of the three alternatives will add to Auerbach's before-tax profit.
2. If Kaytell makes Auerbach a counteroffer, what is the lowest price Auerbach should accept for the reworked machinery from Kaytell? Explain your answer.
3. Discuss the influence fixed manufacturing-overhead cost should have on the sales price quoted by Auerbach Company for special orders.

(CMA, adapted)

Problem 13-48 Drop Product; Qualitative Discussion of Relevant Data. Tavil Corporation has been manufacturing high-quality wood furniture for over 50 years. Tavil's five product lines are Mediterranean, Modern, Colonial, Victorian, and the recently introduced Country. Business has been very good for Tavil recently.

One reason for Tavil's recent success has been the ability of Sally Grant, chief executive officer. Grant has assembled a first-rate management team that has been together for four years. All major decisions are made by this centralized top-management team after thorough study and review. Many team members were surprised by Grant's suggestion at a staff meeting that they should consider dropping the Victorian line, Tavil's oldest.

Grant said that Victorian sales had dropped in total, and as a percentage of Tavil's total sales, during the last three years. She showed them the following schedule of sales percentages by product line for the last three years.

Product-Line Sales Percentage

	Mediterranean	Modern	Colonial	Victorian	Country	Total
19x2............	31%	26%	21%	20%	2%	100%
19x3............	28	28	21	14	9	100
19x4............	24	26	23	10	17	100

Sam Mills, vice-president of Sales, commented that the data did not reflect important regional differences in the market. Victorian total sales of $413,000 in 19x4 were almost entirely in New England and New York, and constituted over half of all Tavil sales in parts of these regions. He said he could sell more Victorian if the Production Department could produce it, and feared that he would lose at least two of his top sales people in New England to competitors if the Victorian line were dropped.

However, Mills also conceded that many sales had been lost in other sales regions due to the long lead time on the Country line. Furthermore, Colonial had obviously benefited from the popularity of Country. In fact, sales in Colonial were dangerously ahead of supply.

Bob James, vice-president of Production, pointed out that production of all lines was possible in existing facilities. However, he also identified several problems with the Victorian line. Production of the Victorian line is the least mechanized of all Tavil's lines, due to the detailed workmanship required. Furthermore, the production equipment is old and outdated and has required increasing amounts of maintenance in recent years. The highly skilled people needed to maintain the Victorian quality are not available in today's labor market, making it difficult to support increased production. Several of Tavil's employees would need special training on their new production assignments if the Victorian line were eliminated. James also noted that margins on the Victorian line had dwindled due to the relative labor-intensity on that line and the high union wages of the skilled employees. Dropping the Victorian line also would make $80,000 worth of fabric in inventory obsolete.

Grant asked Jack Turner, chief financial officer, to collect the data necessary to evaluate whether to keep or drop the Victorian line. As she closed the staff meeting, she stated, "Eventually we might consider expansion, but currently we must consider our present markets and resources."

REQUIRED:

1. Describe the information that Jack Turner should provide to the rest of Tavil Corporation's managers to assist in the decision to keep or drop the Victorian line. Give specific examples of information that Turner should prepare and present.
2. If the management of Tavil Corporation decides to drop the Victorian line to strengthen the remaining product lines:
   a. Discuss how Tavil should communicate this decision to its employees.
   b. Discuss the steps that should be taken to provide a review of this decision after operating results are available.

(CMA, adapted)

Problem 13-49   Analysis of Production Alternatives. Olentangy Toy Company manufactures and distributes dollhouses. The toy industry is a seasonal business; most sales occur in late summer and fall.

The projected sales in units for 19x8 are shown in the following schedule. With a sales price of $10 per unit, the total sales revenue for 19x8 is projected at $1.2 million. Management schedules production so that finished-goods inventory at the end of each month, exclusive of a safety stock of 4,000 dollhouses, should equal the next month's sales. One-half hour of direct-labor time normally is required to produce each dollhouse. Using the production schedule followed in the past, the total direct-labor hours by month required to meet the 19x8 sales estimate are also shown in the schedule.

Olentangy Toy Company
Projected Sales and Planned Production
For the Year Ending December 31, 19x8

	Projected Sales (in units)		Direct-Labor Hours Required*
January..............	8,000	....	4,000
February.............	8,000	....	4,000
March...............	8,000	....	4,000
April................	8,000	....	4,000
May.................	8,000	....	5,000
June	10,000	....	6,000
July.................	12,000	....	6,000
August..............	12,000	....	6,500
September...........	13,000	....	6,500
October.............	13,000	....	6,000
November............	12,000	....	4,000
December	8,000	....	4,000†
Total	120,000 units	....	60,000 hours

* This schedule does not incorporate any additional direct-labor hours resulting from inefficiencies.
† Sales for January, 19x9 are projected to be 8,000 units.

The production schedule followed in the past requires scheduling overtime hours for any production over 8,000 units (4,000 direct-labor hours) in one month. While the use of overtime is feasible, management has decided to consider two other possible alternatives: (1) hire temporary help from an agency during peak months, or (2) expand its labor force and adopt a level production schedule.

Factory employees are paid $12.00 per hour for regular time; the fringe benefits average 20 percent of regular pay. For hours worked in excess of 4,000 hours per month, employees receive time and one-half; however, fringe benefits only average 10 percent on these additional wages. Past experience has shown that labor inefficiencies occur during overtime at the rate of 5 percent of overtime hours; this 5 percent inefficiency was not included in the direct-labor hour estimates presented in the schedule.

Rather than pay overtime to its regular labor force, the company could hire temporary employees when production exceeds 8,000 units per month. The temporary workers can be hired at the same labor rate of $12.00 per hour, but there would be no fringe-benefit costs. Management estimates that the temporary workers would require 25 percent more time than the regular employees (on regular daytime hours) to produce the dollhouses.

If Olentangy Toy Company adopts a level production schedule, the labor force would be expanded. However, no overtime would be required. The same labor rate of $12.00 per hour and fringe-benefit rate of 20 percent would apply.

The manufacturing facilities have the capacity to produce 18,000 dollhouses per month. On-site storage facilities for completed units are adequate. The estimated annual cost of carrying inventory is $1 per unit. The company is subject to a 40 percent income-tax rate.

REQUIRED:

1. Prepare an analysis comparing the costs associated with each of Olentangy Toy Company's three alternatives:
   a. Schedule overtime hours
   b. Hire temporary workers
   c. Expand the labor force and schedule level production

2. Identify and discuss briefly the non-cost factors and the factors that are difficult to estimate, which management should consider in conjunction with the cost analysis prepared in requirement (1).

(CMA, adapted)

Problem 13-50   Discontinue Product Line. Scioto Corporation manufactures four related product lines. Each product is produced at one or more of the firm's three manufacturing plants. The following product-line profit statement for the year ended December 31, 19x7 shows a loss for the baseball-equipment line. A similar loss is projected for 19x8.

Product Line Profit for 19x7
(in thousands)

	Football Equipment	Baseball Equipment	Hockey Equipment	Miscellaneous Sports Items	Total
Sales	$2,200	$1,000	$1,500	$500	$5,200
Cost of goods sold:					
Direct material	$ 400	$ 175	$ 300	$ 90	$ 965
Direct labor and variable					
overhead	800	400	600	60	1,860
Fixed overhead	350	275	100	50	775
Total	$1,550	$ 850	$1,000	$200	$3,600
Gross profit	$ 650	$ 150	$ 500	$300	$1,600
Selling expense:					
Variable	$ 440	$ 200	$ 300	$100	$1,040
Fixed	100	50	100	50	300
Corporate administration					
expenses	48	24	36	12	120
Total	$ 588	$ 274	$ 436	$162	$1,460
Contribution to corporation .	$ 62	$ (124)	$ 64	$138	$ 140

The baseball equipment is manufactured in the Evanston Plant, along with some football equipment, and all miscellaneous sports items are processed there. Only a few of the miscellaneous items are manufactured. The rest are purchased for resale and recorded as direct material in the cost records. A separate production line is used to manufacture each product line.

The following schedule presents the costs incurred at the Evanston Plant in 19x7. Inventories at the end of the year were identical to those at the beginning of the year.

Evanston Plant Costs for 19x7
(in thousands)

	Football Equipment		Baseball Equipment		Miscellaneous Sports Items		Total
Direct material.......	$100	......	$175	......	$ 90	......	$ 365
Direct labor	$100	......	$200	......	$ 30	......	$ 330
Variable overhead:							
Supplies..........	$ 85	......	$ 60	......	$ 12	......	$ 157
Power	50	......	110	......	7	......	167
Other............	15	......	30	......	11	......	56
Subtotal..........	$150	......	$200	......	$ 30	......	$ 380
Fixed overhead:							
Supervision*.......	$ 25	......	$ 30	......	$ 21	......	$ 76
Depreciation†......	40	......	115	......	14	......	169
Plant rentals‡	35	......	105	......	10	......	150
Other§...........	20	......	25	......	5	......	50
Subtotal..........	$120	......	$275	......	$ 50	......	$ 445
Total costs	$470	......	$850	......	$200	......	$1,520

* The supervision costs represent salary and benefit costs of the supervisors in charge of each product line.
† Depreciation cost for machinery and equipment is charged to the product line on which the machinery is used.
‡ The plant is leased. The lease rentals are charged to the product lines on the basis of square feet occupied.
§ Other fixed-overhead costs are the cost of plant administration and are allocated by management decision.

Scioto's management has requested a profitability study of the baseball-equipment line to determine if the line should be discontinued. The Marketing and Accounting departments have developed the following additional data to be used in the study.

(1) If the baseball equipment line is discontinued, the company will lose approximately 10 percent of its sales in each of the other lines.
(2) The specialized equipment now used to manufacture baseball equipment has a current salvage value of $105,000 and a remaining useful life of one year. This equipment cannot be used elsewhere in the company.
(3) The plant space now occupied by the baseball-equipment line could be closed off from the rest of the plant and rented for $175,000 per year.
(4) If the line is discontinued, the supervisor of the baseball-equipment line will be released. In keeping with company policy, he would receive severance pay of $5,000.
(5) The company has been able to invest excess funds at 10 percent per year.

REQUIRED: Should Scioto discontinue the baseball-equipment line? Support your answer with appropriate calculations and qualitative arguments.
(CMA, adapted)

Problem 13-51 Produce or Purchase a Service. VAR Association is a professional educational organization with affiliates throughout the United States. The organization publishes a monthly magazine, offers continuing education courses, and conducts research, which is then published in report or monograph form. All of these operations are run by in VAR's office in Los Angeles.

VAR has over 250 research reports and monographs in print, available to members and the general public at prices ranging from $2.50 to $35.00 each. From 12 to 20 titles are released each year, and all publications are printed in Los Angeles.

The association processes an average of 1,500 orders each month. The processing and filling of orders has become increasingly burdensome for the association staff. The association's publication director suggested that VAR contract with an outside service to handle the inventorying, order processing, shipping, and billing for publication orders.

VAR has contacted ProEd Book Service, located in Cincinnati, which inventories and distributes books and monographs for several other professional organizations. ProEd is willing to inventory VAR's complete stock of research publications and process, ship, and bill all direct-mail orders. ProEd would charge VAR an inventory storage fee, processing and record-keeping fees at the rate of $10.00 per hour, the cost of mailing supplies, and shipping charges.

VAR's publication director asked a staff member to prepare an analysis to determine the feasibility of using ProEd. The preliminary cost analysis and narrative report are as follows:

Monthly Cost Savings Analysis
ProEd Book Service

Rental savings:
    (1) Outside warehouse (4,000 square feet at $8.40 per square foot
        ÷ 12)... $2,800
    (2) Basement storeroom (900 square feet at $12.00 per square foot
        ÷ 12)... 900
    (3) Stockroom (100 square feet at $21.00 per square foot ÷ 12) . 175 $3,875
Labor savings:
    (4) Order clerk (150 hours at $8.50 per hour) $1,275
    (5) Shipping clerk (150 hours at $7.00 per hour)............. 1,050
    (6) Storeroom clerk (60 hours at $7.50 per hour) 450
    (7) Stockroom clerk:
        (a) Inventory function (16 hours at $8.50 per hour)........ 136
        (b) Replenishing stockroom (30 hours at $8.50 per hour) ... 255
    (8) Mailroom supervisor (50 hours at $10.00 per hour) 500   3,666
Total savings... $7,541
Costs:
    (9) ProEd storage fees (4,000 square feet at $4.20 per square foot ÷
        12)... $1,400
    (10) Process/recordkeeping fees (456 hours at $10.00 per hour)... 4,560
    (11) Additional supplies (1500 orders at [$.50 − .40]) 150   6,110
Net monthly savings $1,431

Rental Savings

If ProEd Book Service is used, the outside warehouse would no longer be required. Space in the basement storeroom and the upstairs stockroom now used for research publications would be used to store affiliate supplies and educational materials. Currently, these items are stored in space too crowded for easy access. The quantities of affiliate and educational supplies would not be increased, but their accessibility would be improved. The cost used in the analysis is based on the current rental charge for the space.

Labor Savings

The services of an order clerk and a shipping clerk would not be needed if ProEd's services are employed. The activities of the other three positions identified in the analysis cannot be combined. The stockroom clerk would still be required to take inventory of all materials and replenish stock when needed. A portion of the released time of the mailroom supervisor would be devoted to shipping new titles to ProEd. The remaining released time of these individuals would allow them to do their other assigned work on a more timely basis. The labor analysis is based on the hourly wage plus employee benefits of each individual and a normal work month of 150 hours.

Storage Costs

ProEd says that the VAR inventory can be stored in 4,000 square feet in its warehouse, at an annual charge of $4.20 per square foot.

Processing and Recordkeeping Costs

Order processing and recordkeeping would be charged at the actual hours required. ProEd has not estimated the time required for these activities, so the labor hours saved by the VAR staff were used in the analysis.

Supply Costs

VAR uses three different shipping packages, depending on the size of the order: an envelope ($.10 each), a corrugated mailing pouch ($.30 each), and a cardboard carton ($.75 each). An average cost of $.40 per order was used in the analysis. The carton ProEd uses costs $.50 each.

Other Information

Shipping costs to customers were not included in the analysis. These should be reduced because ProEd is more centrally located. The start-up cost of moving the present inventory to ProEd's warehouse in Cincinnati covers loading, shipping, and unloading. Total cost should not exceed $3,500.

Conclusions

Considering all costs, VAR should save over $17,000 per year, exclusive of start-up costs, by using ProEd. Due to ProEd's central location, shipping costs should be less. These cost savings, along with the freeing of storage space and personnel time for other purposes, provide excellent reasons for using the services of ProEd Book Service.

REQUIRED: Review the cost analysis and narrative report regarding the use of ProEd Book Service by VAR Association.

1. For each of the 11 items identified in the cost analysis, discuss whether the item and amount is appropriate or inappropriate for the analysis.
2. Identify and explain cost items, if any, which were omitted but should have been incorporated in the cost analysis and narrative report.
3. Identify and explain any additional qualitative factors that VAR Association should consider in its analysis.

(CMA, adapted)

Problem 13-52 Make or Buy. North American Automobile Corporation manufactures automobiles, vans, and trucks. Among the company's various plants throughout the world is the Vancouver Cover Plant. Coverings of vinyl and upholstery fabric sewn at the plant are used to cover seats and other surfaces of North American Automobile's products.

Janice Cathles is the manager of the Vancouver Cover Plant. The plant was the first North American plant in the region. As other area plants were opened, Cathles was given responsibility for managing them. Cathles functions as a regional manager, although the budget for her and her staff is charged to the Vancouver Cover Plant. Cathles had just received a report that North American Automobile could purchase the equivalent of the entire annual output of Vancouver Cover from outside suppliers for $30 million. Cathles is astonished at the low outside price because the budget for Vancouver Cover's operating costs for the coming year is $52 million. Cathles believes that North American will have to close the Vancouver Cover plant in order to benefit from the $22 million in annual cost savings.

The budget for Vancouver Cover's operating costs for the coming year is presented below. Additional facts regarding the plant's operations are as follows:

(1) To meet Vancouver Cover's commitment to use high-quality fabrics in all of its products, the Purchasing Department has placed purchase orders with suppliers to ensure the receipt of sufficient materials for the coming year. If these orders are canceled due to the plant closing, termination charges would amount to 15 percent of the cost of direct materials.

(2) Approximately 700 plant employees will lose their jobs if the plant is closed. This includes all of the direct laborers and supervisors as well as plumbers, electricians, and other skilled workers classified as indirect plant workers. Many workers would have trouble finding new jobs, and all former employees would have difficulty matching Vancouver Cover's base pay of $12.00 per hour, the highest in the area. A clause in Vancouver Cover's contract with the union states that the company must provide employment assistance to its former employees for 12 months after a plant closing. The estimated cost of this service would be $1 million for the year.

(3) Some employees would elect early retirement because North American Automobile has an excellent pension plan. In fact, $3 million of the 19x2 pension expense would continue whether Vancouver Cover is open or not.

(4) Cathles and her staff would not be affected by the closing of the plant. They still would be responsible for administering three other area plants.

(5) Vancouver Cover considers equipment depreciation to be a variable cost and uses the units-of-production method to depreciate its equipment; Vancouver Cover is the only North American Automobile plant to use this depreciation method. However, Vancouver Cover uses the straight-line method to depreciate the plant building.

Vancouver Cover Plant
Budget for Operating Costs
For the Year Ended December 31, 19x2
(in thousands)

Direct material.		$12,000
Labor:		
Direct	$13,000	
Supervision	3,000	
Indirect plant labor	4,000	20,000
Overhead:		
Depreciation, equipment	$ 5,000	
Depreciation, building	3,000	
Pension expense	4,000	
Plant manager and staff	2,000	
Corporate allocation	6,000	20,000
Total budgeted costs		$52,000

REQUIRED:

1. Without regard to costs, identify the advantages to North American Automobile Corporation of continuing to obtain covers from its own Vancouver Cover Plant.
2. North American Automobile Corporation's management plans to prepare a numerical analysis that will be used in deciding whether to close the Vancouver Cover Plant. Identify:
   a. The recurring annual budgeted costs that can be avoided by closing the plant.
   b. The recurring annual budgeted costs that are not relevant to the decision, and explain why they are not relevant.
   c. Any nonrecurring costs that arise due to the closing of the plant, and explain how they affect the decision.
   d. Any revenues or costs not specifically mentioned in the problem that the company's management should consider before making a decision.

(CMA, adapted)

Problem 13-53 Drop a Product Line. Genung Corporation produces D-gauges, P-gauges, and T-gauges. For many years the company has been profitable and has operated at capacity. However, in the last two years prices on all gauges were reduced and selling expenses increased to meet competition and keep the plant operating at capacity. Third-quarter results, which follow, typify recent experience.

Genung Corporation
Income Statement
Third Quarter 19x3
(in thousands)

	D-Gauge	P-Gauge	T-Gauge	Total
Sales..................................	$900	$1,600	$ 900	$3,400
Cost of goods sold......................	770	1,048	950	2,768
Gross margin..........................	$130	$ 552	$ (50)	$ 632
Selling and administrative expenses........	185	370	135	690
Income before taxes	$ (55)	$ 182	$(185)	$ (58)

Diane Carlo, Genung's president, is concerned about the results of the pricing, selling, and production policies. After reviewing the third-quarter results she asked her management staff to consider the following three suggestions:

- Discontinue the T-gauge line immediately. T-gauges would not be returned to the product line unless the problems with the gauge can be identified and resolved.
- Increase quarterly sales promotion by $100,000 on the P-gauge product line in order to increase sales volume by 15 percent.
- Cut production on the D-gauge line by 50 percent, and cut the traceable advertising and promotion for this line to $20,000 each quarter.

George Sperry, the controller, suggested a more careful study of the financial relationships to determine the possible effects on the company's operating results of the president's proposed course of action. The president agreed and assigned JoAnn Brower, the assistant controller, to prepare an analysis. Brower has gathered the following information.

- All three gauges are manufactured with common equipment and facilities.
- The quarterly general selling and administrative expense of $170,000 is allocated to the three gauge lines in proportion to their dollar sales volume.

● Special selling expenses (primarily advertising, promotion, and shipping) are incurred for each gauge as follows:

	Quarterly Advertising and Promotion	Shipping Expense
D-gauge.....................................	$100,000	$ 4 per unit
P-gauge	210,000	10 per unit
T-gauge	40,000	10 per unit

● The unit manufacturing costs for the three products are as follows:

	D-Gauge	P-Gauge	T-Gauge
Raw material	$17	$ 31	$ 50
Direct labor	20	40	60
Variable manufacturing overhead	30	45	60
Fixed manufacturing overhead................	10	15	20
Total.....................................	$77	$131	$190

● The unit sales prices for the three products are as follows:

D-gauge...	$ 90
P-gauge	200
T-gauge	180

● The company is manufacturing at capacity and is selling all the gauges it produces.

REQUIRED:

1. JoAnn Brower says that Genung Corporation's product-line income statement for the third quarter of 19x3 is not suitable for analyzing proposals and making decisions such as the ones suggested by Diane Carlo.
   a. Explain why the product-line income statement as presented is not suitable for analysis and decision making.
   b. Describe an alternative income-statement format that would be more suitable for analysis and decision making, and explain why it is better.
2. Use the operating data presented for Genung Corporation and assume that the president's proposed course of action had been implemented at the beginning of the third quarter of 19x3. Then evaluate the president's proposal by specifically responding to the following points.
   a. Are each of the three suggestions cost-effective? Support your discussion with an analysis that shows the net impact on income before taxes for each of the three suggestions.
   b. Was the president correct in proposing that the T-gauge line be eliminated? Explain your answer.
   c. Was the president correct in promoting the P-gauge line rather than the D-gauge line? Explain your answer.
   d. Does the proposed course of action make effective use of Genung's capacity? Explain your answer.
3. Are there any qualitative factors that Genung Corporation's management should consider before it drops the T-gauge line? Explain your answer.

(CMA, adapted)

Problem 13-54 *Production Planning.* Catskill Industries manufactures and sells three products, which are manufactured in a factory with four departments. Both labor and machine time are applied to the products as they pass through each department. The machines and labor skills required in each department are so specialized that neither machines nor labor can be switched from one department to another.

Catskill Industries' management is planning its production schedule for the next few months. The planning is complicated, because there are labor shortages in the community and some machines will be down several months for repairs.

Management has assembled the following information regarding available machine and labor time by department and the machine hours and direct-labor hours required per unit of product. These data should be valid for the next six months.

	Department			
Monthly Capacity Availability	**1**	**2**	**3**	**4**
Normal machine capacity in machine hours........	3,500	3,500	3,000	3,500
Capacity of machine being repaired in machine hours	(500)	(400)	(300)	(200)
Available machine capacity in machine hours	3,000	3,100	2,700	3,300
Available labor in direct-labor hours	3,700	4,500	2,750	2,600

Labor and Machine Specifications
per Unit of Product

Product	Labor and Machine Time				
401	.... Direct-labor hours...........	2	3	3	1
	Machine hours	1	1	2	2
403	.... Direct-labor hours...........	1	2	—	2
	Machine hours	1	1	—	2
405	.... Direct-labor hours...........	2	2	2	1
	Machine hours	2	2	1	1

The sales department believes that the monthly demand for the next six months will be as follows:

Product	Monthly Sales Volume in Units
401	500
403	400
405	1,000

Inventory levels are satisfactory and need not be increased or decreased during the next six months. Unit price and cost data that will be valid for the next six months are shown.

REQUIRED:

1. Calculate the monthly requirement for machine hours and direct-labor hours for the production of products 401, 403, and 405 to determine whether the monthly sales demand for the three products can be met by the factory.

	Product		
	401	**403**	**405**
Unit costs:			
Direct material	$ 7	$ 13	$ 17
Direct labor:			
Department 1	12	6	12
Department 2	21	14	14
Department 3	24	—	16
Department 4	9	18	9
Variable overhead.......................................	27	20	25
Fixed overhead.......................................	15	10	32
Variable selling expenses	3	2	4
Unit selling price	$196	$123	$167

2. What monthly production schedule should Catskill Industries select in order to maximize its dollar profits? Explain how you selected this production schedule, and present a schedule of the contribution to profit that would be generated by your production schedule.
3. Identify the alternatives Catskill Industries might consider so it can supply its customers with all the product they demand.

(CMA, adapted)

Problem 13-55   Linear Programming, Formulate and Solve Graphically (Appendix). Cleveland Cable Company manufactures metal cable for use in the construction industry. The firm has two machines on which two different types of cable are produced. Price, cost, and production data are as follows:

	Steel Cable	Aluminum Cable
Selling price per reel	$1,000	$750
Variable cost per reel..................................	$ 600	$250
Hours required per reel on machine A....................	5 hr	2 hr
Hours required per reel on machine B....................	5 hr	8 hr

The production supervisor has determined that there are 30 hours of excess capacity available on machine A and 40 excess hours available on machine B.

REQUIRED:

1. Formulate the production planning problem as a linear program. How many reels of steel cable and aluminum cable should be produced using the excess capacity? Partial reels may be manufactured and sold. For example, a half-reel of steel cable sells for $500.
2. Solve the linear programming problem graphically. (Hint: Use one third of a reel as the unit of measure on each axis.)

Problem 13-56   Linear Programming; Formulate and Solve Graphically (Appendix). Galveston Chemical Company manufactures two industrial chemical products, called kreolite-red and kreolite-blue. Two machines are used in the process, and each machine has 24 hours of capacity per day. The following data are available.

	Kreolite-Red	Kreolite-Blue
Selling price per drum.............................	$30	$42
Variable cost per drum	$22	$28
Hours required per drum on machine I..............	2 hr	2 hr
Hours required per drum on machine II	1 hr	3 hr

The company can produce and sell partially full drums of each chemical. For example, a half drum of kreolite-red sells for $15.

REQUIRED:

1. Formulate the product-mix problem as a linear program.
2. Solve the problem graphically.

Problem 13-57   Linear Programming; Formulate and Discuss (Appendix). SmyCo manufactures two types of display boards sold to office supply stores. One board is a hard-finished marking board that can be written on with a water-soluble felt-tip marking pen and then wiped clean with a cloth. The other is a conventional cork-type tack board.

Both boards pass through two manufacturing departments. All of the raw materials — board base, board covering, and aluminum frames — are cut to size in the Cutting Department. Both types of boards are the same size and use the same aluminum frame. The boards are assembled in one of SmyCo's two assembly operations: the Automated Assembly Department or the Labor Assembly Department.

The Automated Assembly Department has been in operation for 18 months and was intended to replace the Labor Assembly Department. However, SmyCo's business expanded so rapidly that both assembly operations are needed and used. The final results of the two assembly operations are identical. The only difference between the two is the proportion of machine time versus direct labor in each department and, thus, different costs. However, workers have been trained for both operations so that they can be switched between the two operations.

Data regarding the two products and their manufacture are presented in the schedules on the next page.

SmyCo produced and sold 600,000 marking boards and 900,000 tack boards last year. Management estimates that the total unit sales for the coming year could increase 20 percent if the units can be produced. SmyCo has contracts to produce and sell 30,000 units of each board each month. Sales, production, and cost incurrence are uniform throughout the year. SmyCo has a monthly maximum labor capacity of 30,000 direct-labor hours in the Cutting Department and 40,000 direct-labor hours for the assembly operations (Automated Assembly and Labor Assembly Departments combined).

REQUIRED:

1. SmyCo's management believes that linear programming could be used to determine the optimum mix of marking and tack boards to produce and sell. Explain why linear programming can be used by SmyCo.
2. SmyCo plans to employ linear programming to determine its optimum production mix of marking and tack boards. Formulate and label the:
   a. Objective function.
   b. Constraints.
   Be sure to define your variables.

(CMA, adapted)

Sales Data

	Marking Board	Tack Board
Selling price per unit	$60.00	$45.00
Variable selling costs per unit	$3.00	$3.00
Annual fixed selling and administrative expenses (allocated equally between the two products)	$900,000	$900,000

Unit Variable Manufacturing Costs

Cutting Department

	Marking Board	Tack Board	Labor Assembly Department*	Automated Assembly Department*
Raw materials:				
Base.	$ 6.00	$6.00	—	—
Covering.	14.50	7.75	—	—
Frame	8.25	8.25	—	—
Direct labor:				
at $10/hour.	2.00	2.00	—	—
at $12/hour.	—	—	$3.00	$ .60
Manufacturing overhead:				
Supplies	1.25	1.25	1.50	1.50
Power	1.20	1.20	.75	1.80

* The unit costs for the marking board and the tack board are the same within each of the two assembly departments.

Machine Hour Data

	Cutting Department	Labor Assembly Department	Automated Assembly Department
Machine hours required per board	.15	.02	.05
Monthly machine hours available.	25,000	1,500	5,000
Annual machine hours available.	300,000	18,000	60,000

CASE   *Case 13-58 Accept or Reject Special Order.* Ashley Company manufactures and sells a household product marketed through direct mail and advertisements in magazines. Although similar products are available in hardware and department stores, none is as effective as Ashley's model. The company uses a standard-costing system. The standards have not been reviewed in the past 18 months. The general manager has seen no need for such a review for the following reasons:

(1) The material-quality and unit costs were fixed by a three-year purchase commitment signed in July 19x9.

(2) A three-year labor contract was signed in July 19x9.

(3) There have been no significant variations from standard costs for the past nine months.

The standard cost for the product, as established in July 19x9, is presented below.

Direct material.........	.75 lb. at $1.00 per lb.	$ .75
Direct labor	.15 hr. at $8.00 per hour	1.20
Manufacturing overhead .	.15 hr. at $14.00 per hour	2.10
Standard manufacturing cost per unit		$4.05

The standard for overhead costs was developed from the following budgeted costs, based on an activity level of 1 million units (150,000 direct-labor hours).

Variable manufacturing overhead.................................	$ 600,000
Fixed manufacturing overhead....................................	1,500,000
Total manufacturing overhead	$2,100,000

The income statement and the factory costs for the first quarter are presented below. The first-quarter results indicate that Ashley probably will achieve its sales goal of 1.2 million units for the current year. A total of 320,000 units were manufactured during the first quarter in order to increase inventory levels needed to support the growing sales volume.

Ashley Co.
First Quarter Earnings
Quarter Ended March 31, 19x1

Sales (300,000 units)..			$2,700,000
Cost of goods sold:			
Standard cost of goods sold.........................		$1,215,000	
Variance from standard cost		12,000	1,227,000
Gross profit..			$1,473,000
Operating expenses:			
Selling:			
Advertising	$ 200,000		
Mailing-list costs................................	175,000		
Postage	225,000		
Salaries	60,000		
Administrative:			
Salaries	120,000		
Office rent.....................................	45,000		
Total operating expenses.....................			825,000
Income before taxes...			$ 648,000
Income taxes (45%)..			291,600
Net income...			$ 356,400

Ashley Co.
Factory Costs
For the Quarter Ended March 31, 19x1

Direct material...	$ 266,000
Direct labor	452,000
Variable manufacturing overhead..................................	211,000
Fixed manufacturing overhead......................................	379,000
Total manufacturing costs.....................................	$1,308,000
Less: Standard cost of goods manufactured	1,296,000
Unfavorable variance from standard cost............................	$ 12,000

ACTION Hardware, a national chain, recently asked Ashley to manufacture and sell a modified version of the product, which ACTION would distribute through its own stores. ACTION has offered to buy a minimum quantity of 200,000 units each year over the next three years and has offered to pay $4.10 for each unit.

Ashley's management is interested in the proposal, because it represents a new market. The company has adequate capacity to meet the production requirements. However, in addition to the possible financial results of taking the order, Ashley must consider carefully the other consequences of this departure from its normal practices. The president asked an assistant to the general manager to estimate the financial aspects of the proposal for the first 12 months. The assistant recommended that the order not be accepted and presented the following analysis to support the recommendation.

Sales Proposal of ACTION Hardware
First 12 Months' Results

Proposed sales (200,000 at $4.10)	$820,000
Estimated costs and expenses:	
Manufacturing (200,000 at $4.05)	$810,000
Sales salaries	10,000
Administrative salaries	20,000
Total estimated costs	$840,000
Net loss	$ (20,000)

Note: None of the regular selling costs are included, because this is a new market. However, a 16.67 percent increase in sales and administrative salaries has been incorporated, because sales volume will increase by that amount. (For example, $10,000 = 16.67% × $60,000.)

REQUIRED:

1. Review the financial analysis of the ACTION Hardware proposal prepared by the general manager's assistant.
    a. Criticize the first-year financial analysis.
    b. Using only the data given, present a more suitable analysis for the first year of the order. (Hint: Consider the actual factory costs incurred during the first quarter of 19x1.)
2. Identify the additional financial data Ashley's management would need to prepare a more comprehensive financial analysis of the ACTION proposal for the three-year period.
3. Discuss the nonfinancial issues Ashley's management should address in considering the ACTION proposal.

(CMA, adapted)

Sydney Sailing Supplies

Chapter 14
Cost Analysis and Pricing Decisions

Setting the price for an organization's product or service is one of the most important decisions a manager faces. It is also one of the most difficult, due to the number and variety of factors that must be considered. The pricing decision arises in virtually all types of organizations. Manufacturers set prices for the products they manufacture; merchandising companies set prices for their goods; service firms set prices for such services as insurance policies, train tickets, theme park admissions, and bank loans. Nonprofit organizations often set prices also. For example, governmental units price vehicle registrations, park-use fees, and utility services. The optimal approach to pricing often depends on the situation. Pricing a mature product or service which a firm has sold for a long time may be quite different from pricing a new product or service. Public utilities and TV cable companies face political considerations in pricing their products and services, since their prices generally must be approved by a governmental commission.

In this chapter, we will study pricing decisions, with an emphasis on the role of managerial-accounting information. The setting for our discussion is Sydney Sailing Supplies, a manufacturer of sailing supplies and equipment located in Sydney, Australia.

**Sydney
Sailing
Supplies**

MAJOR INFLUENCES ON PRICING DECISIONS

Four major influences govern the prices set by Sydney Sailing Supplies:

1. Customer demand
2. Actions of competitors
3. Costs
4. Political, legal, and image-related issues

Customer Demand

The demands of customers are of paramount importance in all phases of business operations, from the design of a product to the setting of its price. Product-design issues and pricing considerations are interrelated, so they must be examined simultaneously. For example, if customers want a high-quality sailboat, this will entail greater production time and more expensive raw materials. The result almost certainly will be a higher price. On the other hand, management must be careful not to price its product out of the market. Discerning customer demand is a critically important and continuous process. Companies routinely obtain information from market research, such as customer surveys and test-marketing campaigns, and through feedback from sales personnel. To be successful, Sydney Sailing Supplies must provide the products its customers want at a price they perceive to be appropriate.

Actions of Competitors

Although Sydney Sailing Supplies' managers would like the company to have the sailing market to itself, they are not so fortunate. Domestic and foreign competitors are striving to sell their products to the same customers. Thus, as Sydney Sailing Supplies' management designs products and sets prices, it must keep a watchful eye on the firm's competitors. If a competitor reduces its price on sails of a particular type, Sydney Sailing Supplies may have to follow suit to avoid losing its market share. Yet the company cannot follow its competitors blindly either. Predicting competitive reactions to its product-design and pricing strategy is a difficult but important task for Sydney Sailing Supplies' management.

In considering the reactions of customers and competitors, management must be careful to properly define its product. Should Sydney Sailing Supplies' management define its product narrowly as sailing supplies, or more broadly as boating supplies? For example, if the company raises the price of its two-person sailboat, will this encourage potential customers to switch to canoes, rowboats, and small motorboats? Or will most potential sailboat customers react to a price increase only by price-shopping among competing sailboat manufacturers? The way in which Sydney Sailing Supplies' management answers these questions can profoundly affect its marketing and pricing strategies.

Costs

The role of costs in price setting varies widely among industries. In some industries, prices are determined almost entirely by market forces. An example is the agricultural industry, where grain and meat prices are market-driven. Farmers must meet the market price. To make a profit, they must produce at a cost below the market price. This is not always possible, so some periods of loss inevitably result. In other industries, managers set prices at least partially on the basis of production costs. For example, cost-based pricing is used in the automobile, household appliance, and gasoline industries. Prices are set by adding a markup to production costs. Managers have some latitude in determining the markup, so market forces can influence prices as well. In public utilities, such as electricity and natural gas companies, prices generally are set by a regulatory agency of the state government. Production costs are of prime importance in justifying utility rates. Typically, a public utility will make a request to the Public Utility Commission for a rate increase on the basis of its current and projected production costs.

Balance of Market Forces and Cost-Based Pricing In most industries, both market forces and cost considerations heavily influence prices. No organization or industry can price its products below their production costs indefinitely. And no company's management can set prices blindly at cost plus a markup without keeping an eye on the market. In most cases, pricing can be viewed in either of the following ways.

How Are Prices Set?

Prices are determined by the market, subject to the constraint that costs must be covered in the long run.

Prices are based on costs, subject to the constraint that the reactions of customers and competitors must be heeded.

In our illustration of Sydney Sailing Supplies' pricing policies, we will assume the company responds to both market forces and costs.

Political, Legal, and Image-Related Issues

Beyond the important effects on prices of market forces and costs are a range of environmental considerations. In the *legal* area, managers must adhere to certain laws. The law generally prohibits companies from discriminating among their customers in setting prices. Also prohibited is collusion in price setting, where the major firms in an industry all agree to set their prices at high levels.

Political considerations also can be relevant. For example, if the firms in an industry are *perceived* by the public as reaping unfairly large profits, there may be political pressure on legislators to tax those profits differentially or to intervene in some way to regulate prices.

Companies also consider their *public image* in the price-setting process. A firm with a reputation for very high-quality products may set the price of a new product high to be consistent with its image. As we have all discovered, the same brand-name product may be available in a discount store at half the price charged in a more exclusive store.

ECONOMIC PROFIT-MAXIMIZING PRICING

Companies are sometimes **price takers,** which means their products' prices are determined totally by the market. Some agricultural commodities and precious metals are examples of such products. In most cases, however, firms have some flexibility in setting prices. Generally speaking, as the price of a product or service is increased, the quantity demanded declines, and vice versa.

Total Revenue, Demand, and Marginal Revenue Curves

The trade-off between a higher price and a higher sales quantity can be shown in the shape of the firm's **total revenue curve,** which graphs the functional relationship between total sales revenue and quantity sold. Sydney Sailing Supplies' total revenue

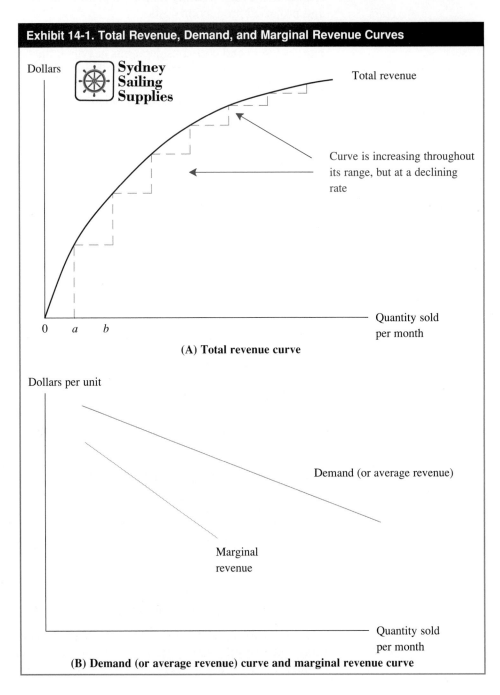

Exhibit 14-1. Total Revenue, Demand, and Marginal Revenue Curves

(A) Total revenue curve

(B) Demand (or average revenue) curve and marginal revenue curve

Exhibit 14-1 (continued)

Quantity Sold per Month	Unit Sales Price	Total Revenue per Month	Changes in Total Revenue
10	$1,000	$10,000	
			$9,500
20	975	19,500	
			9,000
30	950	28,500	
			8,500
40	925	37,000	
			8,000
50	900	45,000	
			7,500
60	875	52,500	

Related to demand curve

Related to total revenue curve

Related to marginal revenue curve

(C) Tabulated price, quantity, and revenue data

curve for its two-person sailboat, the Wave Darter, is displayed in Exhibit 14-1, panel A. The total revenue curve increases throughout its range, but the rate of increase declines as monthly sales quantity increases. To see this, notice that the increase in total revenue when the sales quantity increases from zero to *a* units is greater than the increase in total revenue when the sales quantity increases from *a* units to *b* units.

Closely related to the total revenue curve are two other curves, which are graphed in panel B of Exhibit 14-1. The **demand curve** shows the relationship between the sales price and the quantity of units demanded. The demand curve decreases throughout its range, because any decrease in the sale price brings about an increase in the monthly sales quantity. The demand curve is also called the **average revenue curve,** since it shows the average price at which any particular quantity can be sold.

The **marginal revenue curve** shows the *change* in total revenue that accompanies a *change* in the quantity sold. The marginal revenue curve is decreasing throughout its range to show that total revenue increases at a declining rate as monthly sales quantity increases.

A tabular presentation of the price, quantity, and revenue data for Sydney Sailing Supplies is displayed in panel C of Exhibit 14-1. Study this table carefully to see how the data relate to the graphs shown in panels A and B of the exhibit. No matter what approach a manager takes to the pricing decision, a good understanding of the relationships shown in Exhibit 14-1 will lead to better decisions. Before we can fully

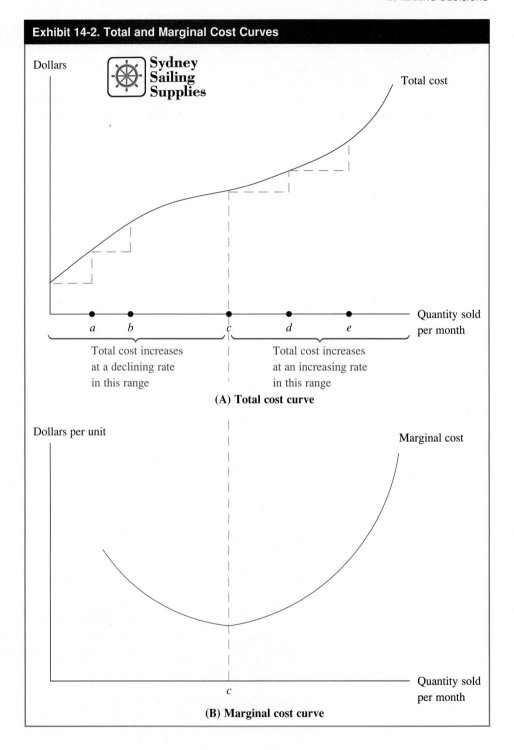

Exhibit 14-2. Total and Marginal Cost Curves

Sydney Sailing Supplies

Dollars

Total cost

Quantity sold per month

a   b   c   d   e

Total cost increases at a declining rate in this range

Total cost increases at an increasing rate in this range

(A) Total cost curve

Dollars per unit

Marginal cost

Quantity sold per month

c

(B) Marginal cost curve

Exhibit 14-2 (continued)

Quantity Produced and Sold per Month	Average Cost per Unit	Total Cost per Month	Changes in Total Cost
10	$1,920	$19,200	
			$ 5,600
20	1,240	24,800	
			4,300
30	970	29,100	
			2,900
40	800	32,000	
			9,000
50	820	41,000	
			15,400
60	940	56,400	

Related to total cost curve

Related to marginal cost curve

(C) Tabulated cost and quantity data

use the revenue data, however, we must examine the cost side of Sydney Sailing Supplies' business.

Total Cost and Marginal Cost Curves

Understanding cost behavior is important in many business decisions, and pricing is no exception. How does total cost behave as the number of Wave Darters produced and sold by Sydney Sailing Supplies changes? Panel A of Exhibit 14-2 displays the firm's **total cost curve,** which graphs the relationship between total cost and the quantity produced and sold each month.[1] Total cost increases throughout its range. The rate of increase in total cost declines as quantity increases from zero to c units. To verify this, notice that the increase in total costs when quantity increases from zero to a units is greater than the increase in total costs when quantity increases from a units to b units.

The rate of increase in total costs increases as quantity increases from c units upward. To verify this, notice that the increase in total costs as quantity increases from c units to d units is less than the increase in total costs as quantity increases from d units to e units.

[1] Notice that the demand and revenue curves are based on the quantity sold, while the cost curves are based on the quantity produced. We will assume for simplicity that Sydney Sailing Supplies' monthly sales and production quantities are the same. This assumption tends to be true in the pleasure boat industry.

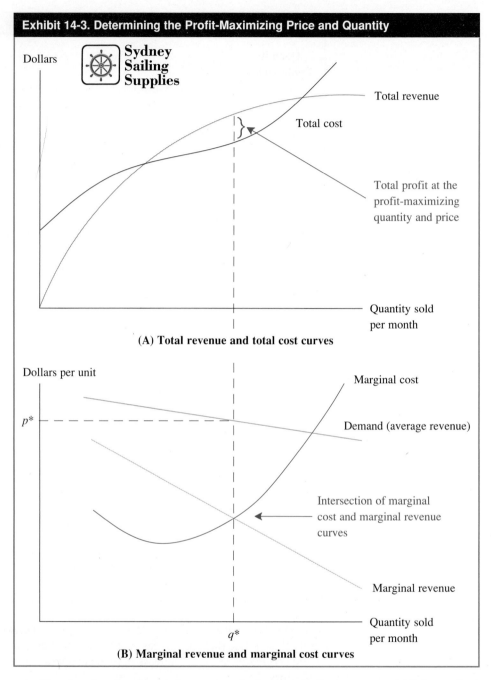

Exhibit 14-3. Determining the Profit-Maximizing Price and Quantity

Sydney Sailing Supplies

Dollars

Total revenue

Total cost

Total profit at the profit-maximizing quantity and price

Quantity sold per month

(A) Total revenue and total cost curves

Dollars per unit

Marginal cost

p^*

Demand (average revenue)

Intersection of marginal cost and marginal revenue curves

Marginal revenue

Quantity sold per month

q^*

(B) Marginal revenue and marginal cost curves

Closely related to the total cost curve is the marginal cost curve, which is graphed in panel B of Exhibit 14-2. The **marginal cost curve** shows the change in total cost that accompanies a change in quantity produced and sold. Marginal cost declines as quantity increases from zero to c units; then it increases as quantity increases beyond c units.

A tabular presentation of the cost and quantity data for Sydney Sailing Supplies is displayed in panel C of Exhibit 14-2. Examine this table carefully, and trace the relationships between the data and the graphs shown in panels A and B of the exhibit.

Exhibit 14-3 (continued)

Quantity Produced and Sold per Month		Unit Sales Price	Total Revenue per Month	Total Cost per Month	Profit (Loss) per Month
	10	$1,000	$10,000	$19,200	$(9,200)
	20	975	19,500	24,800	(5,300)
	30	950	28,500	29,100	(600)
Profit-maximizing price {	40	925	37,000	32,000	5,000
	50	900	45,000	41,000	4,000
	60	875	52,500	56,400	(3,900)

(C) Tabular revenue, cost, and profit data

Profit-Maximizing Price and Quantity

Now we have the tools we need to determine the profit-maximizing price and quantity. In Exhibit 14-3, we combine the revenue and cost data presented in Exhibits 14-1 and 14-2. Sydney Sailing Supplies' profit-maximizing sales quantity for the Wave Darter is determined by the intersection of the marginal cost and marginal revenue curves. (See panel B of Exhibit 14-3). This optimal quantity is denoted by q^* in the graph. The profit-maximizing price, denoted by p^*, is determined from the demand curve, for the quantity, q^*.

Examine the total revenue and total cost curves in panel A of Exhibit 14-3. At the profit-maximizing quantity (and price), the distance between these curves, which is equal to total profit, is maximized.

A tabular presentation of the revenue, cost, and profit data is shown in panel C of Exhibit 14-3. Notice that monthly profit is maximized when the price is set at $925 and 40 Wave Darters are produced and sold each month.

Price Elasticity

The impact of price changes on sales volume is called the **price elasticity.** Demand is *elastic* if a price increase has a large negative impact on sales volume, and vice versa. Demand is *inelastic* if price changes have little or no impact on sales quantity. **Cross-elasticity** refers to the extent to which a change in a product's price affects the demand for other *substitute products.* For example, if Sydney Sailing Supplies raises the price of its two-person sailboat, there may be an increase in demand for substitute recreational craft, such as small power boats, canoes, or windsurfers.

Measuring price elasticity and cross-elasticity is an important objective of market research. Having a good understanding of these economic concepts helps managers to determine the profit-maximizing price.

Limitations of the Profit-Maximizing Model

The economic model of the pricing decision serves as a useful framework for approaching a pricing problem. However, it does have several limitations. First, the firm's demand and marginal revenue curves are difficult to discern with precision. Although market research is designed to gather data about product demand, it rarely will enable management to predict completely the effects of price changes on the quantity demanded. Many other factors affect product demand in addition to price. Product design and quality, advertising and promotion, and company reputation also significantly influence consumer demand for a product.

Second, the marginal-revenue, marginal-cost paradigm is not valid for all forms of market organization. In an **oligopolistic market,** where a small number of sellers compete among themselves, the simple economic pricing model is no longer appropriate. In an *oligopoly,* such as the automobile industry, the reactions of competitors to a firm's pricing policies must be taken into account. While economists have studied oligopolistic pricing, the state of the theory is not sufficient to provide a thorough understanding of the impact of prices on demand.

The third limitation of the economic pricing model involves the difficulty of measuring marginal cost. Cost-accounting systems are not designed to measure the marginal changes in cost incurred as production and sales increase unit by unit. To measure marginal costs would entail a very costly information system. Most managers believe that any improvements in pricing decisions made possible by marginal-cost data would not be sufficient to defray the cost of obtaining the information.

Costs and Benefits of Information

Managerial accountants always face a cost-benefit trade-off in the production of cost information for pricing and other decisions. As Exhibit 14-4 shows, only a sophisti-

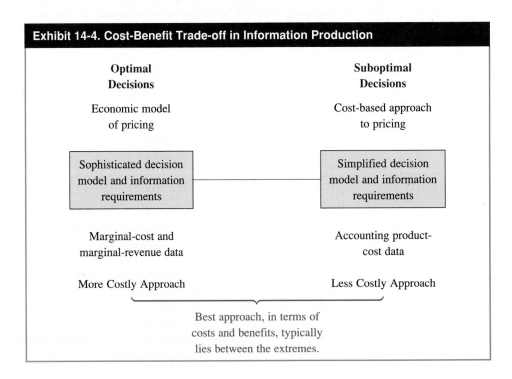

Exhibit 14-4. Cost-Benefit Trade-off in Information Production

Optimal Decisions	Suboptimal Decisions
Economic model of pricing	Cost-based approach to pricing
Sophisticated decision model and information requirements	Simplified decision model and information requirements
Marginal-cost and marginal-revenue data	Accounting product-cost data
More Costly Approach	Less Costly Approach

Best approach, in terms of costs and benefits, typically lies between the extremes.

cated information system can collect marginal-cost data. However, such information is more costly to obtain. The result is that the optimal approach to pricing and other decisions is likely to lie in between the extremes shown in Exhibit 14-4. For this reason, most managers make pricing decisions based on a combination of economic considerations and accounting, product-cost information.

In spite of its limitations, the marginal-revenue, marginal-cost paradigm of pricing serves as a useful conceptual framework for the pricing decision. Within this overall framework, managers typically rely heavily on a cost-based pricing approach, as we shall see next.

ROLE OF ACCOUNTING PRODUCT COSTS IN PRICING

Most managers base prices on product costs, at least to some extent. There are several reasons for this. First, most companies sell many products or services. There simply is not time enough to do a thorough demand and marginal-cost analysis for every product or service. Managers must rely on a quick and straightforward method for setting prices, and cost-based pricing formulas provide it. Second, even though market considerations ultimately may determine the final product price, a cost-based pricing formula gives the manager a place to start. Finally, and most importantly, the cost of a product or service provides a floor below which the price cannot be set in the long run. Although a product may be "given away" initially, at a price below cost, a product's price ultimately must cover its costs in order for the firm to remain in business. Even a nonprofit organization, unless it is heavily subsidized, cannot forever price products or services below their costs.

Cost-Plus Pricing

Cost-based pricing formulas typically have the following general form.

$$\text{Price} = \text{cost} + (\text{markup percentage} \times \text{cost})$$

Such a pricing approach often is called **cost-plus pricing,** because the price is equal to *cost plus* a markup. Depending on how cost is defined, the markup percentage may differ. Several different definitions of cost, each combined with a different markup percentage, can result in the same price for a product or service.

Exhibit 14-5 illustrates how Sydney Sailing Supplies' management could use several different cost-plus pricing formulas and arrive at a price of $925 for the Wave Darter. Cost-plus formula (1) is based on variable manufacturing cost. Formula (2) is based on absorption (or full) manufacturing cost, which includes an allocated portion of fixed manufacturing costs. Formula (3) is based on all costs: both variable and fixed costs of the manufacturing, selling, and administrative functions. Formula (4) is based on all variable costs, including variable manufacturing, selling, and administrative costs.

Notice that as Sydney Sailing Supplies includes more costs in the cost base of the pricing formula, the required markup percentage declines. This reflects the fact that, one way or another, the price must cover all costs as well as a normal profit margin. If only variable manufacturing costs are included explicitly in the cost base, as in formula (1), then all of the other costs (and the firm's profit) must be covered by the markup. However, if the cost base used in the pricing formula includes all costs, as in

Exhibit 14-5. Alternative Cost-Plus Pricing Formulas

Each of the following cost-plus pricing formulas yields the same $925 price for the Wave Darter.

Sydney
Sailing
Supplies

Price and Cost Data		Cost-Plus Pricing Formulas
Variable manufacturing cost	$400	1 $925 = $400 + (131.25% × $400) = variable manufacturing cost + (markup percentage × variable manufacturing cost)
Applied fixed manufacturing cost	250*	
Absorption manufacturing cost	650	2 $925 = $650 + (42.3%† × $650) = absorption manufacturing cost + (markup percentage × absorption manufacturing cost)
Variable selling and administrative cost	50	
Allocated fixed selling and administrative cost.	100*	
Total cost	$800	3 $925 = $800 + (15.63%† × $800) = total cost + (markup percentage × total cost)
Variable manufacturing cost	$400	
Variable selling and administrative cost	50	
Total variable cost	$450	4 $925 = $450 + (105.56%† × $450) = total variable cost + (markup percentage × total variable cost)

*Based on planned monthly production of 40 units (or 480 units per year).
†Rounded.

formula (3), the markup can be much lower, since it need cover only the firm's normal profit margin.

A company typically would use only one of the four cost-plus pricing formulas illustrated in Exhibit 14-5. Which formula is best? Let's examine the advantages and disadvantages of each approach.

Absorption-Cost Pricing Formulas

Most companies that use cost-plus pricing use either absorption manufacturing cost or total cost as the basis for pricing products or services.[2] [See formulas (2) and (3) in Exhibit 14-5.] The reasons generally given for this tendency are as follows:

1. In the long run, the price must cover *all* costs and a normal profit margin. Basing the cost-plus formula on only variable costs could encourage managers to set too low a price in order to boost sales. This will not happen if managers understand that a variable-cost plus pricing formula requires a higher markup to cover fixed costs and profit. Nevertheless, many managers argue that people tend to view the cost base in a cost-plus pricing formula as the floor for setting prices. If prices are set too close to variable manufacturing cost, the firm will fail to cover its fixed costs. Ultimately, such a practice could result in the failure of the business.
2. Absorption-cost or total-cost pricing formulas provide a justifiable price that tends to be perceived as equitable by all parties. Consumers generally understand that a company must make a profit on its product or service in order to remain in business. Justifying a price as the total cost of production, sales, and administrative activities, plus a reasonable profit margin, seems reasonable to buyers.
3. When a company's competitors have similar operations and cost structures, cost-plus pricing based on full costs gives management an idea of how competitors may set prices.
4. Absorption-cost information is provided by a firm's cost-accounting system, because it is required for external financial reporting under generally accepted accounting principles. Since absorption-cost information already exists, it is cost-effective to use it for pricing. The alternative would involve preparing special product-cost data specifically for the pricing decision. In a firm with hundreds of products, such data could be expensive to produce.

The primary disadvantage of absorption-cost or total-cost pricing formulas is that they obscure the cost behavior pattern of the firm. Since absorption-cost and total-cost data include allocated fixed costs, it is not clear from these data how the firm's total costs will change as volume changes. Another way of stating this criticism is that absorption-cost data are not consistent with cost-volume-profit analysis. CVP analysis emphasizes the distinction between fixed and variable costs. This approach enables managers to predict the effects of changes in prices and sales volume on profit. Absorption and total cost information obscures the distinction between variable and fixed costs.

Variable-Cost-Pricing Formulas

To avoid blurring the effects of cost behavior on profit, some managers prefer to use cost-plus pricing formulas based on either variable manufacturing costs or total variable costs. [See formulas (1) and (4) in Exhibit 14-5.] Three advantages are attributed to this pricing approach:

[2] For discussions of cost-plus pricing, see the following references: V. Govindarajan and R. N. Anthony, "How Firms Use Cost Data in Pricing Decisions," *Management Accounting, 65,* no. 1 (July 1983), pp. 30–36; and L. Gordon, R. Cooper, H. Falk, and D. Miller, *The Pricing Decision* (New York: National Association of Accountants, 1981), p. 23.

1. Variable-cost data do not obscure the cost behavior pattern by unitizing fixed costs and making them appear variable. Thus, variable-cost information is more consistent with cost-volume-profit analysis often used by managers to see the profit implications of changes in price and volume.
2. Variable-cost data do not require allocation of common fixed costs to individual product lines. For example, the annual salary of Sydney Sailing Supplies' vice president of sales is a cost that must be borne by all of the company's product lines. Arbitrarily allocating a portion of her salary to the Wave Darter product line is not meaningful.
3. Variable-cost data are exactly the type of information managers need when facing certain decisions, such as whether to accept a special order. This decision, examined in detail in the preceding chapter, often requires an analysis that separates fixed and variable costs.

The primary disadvantage of the variable-cost pricing formula was described earlier. If managers perceive the variable cost of a product or service as the floor for the price, they may tend to set the price too low for the firm to cover its fixed costs. Eventually this can spell disaster. Therefore, if variable-cost data are used as the basis for cost-plus pricing, managers must understand the need for higher markups to ensure that all costs are covered.

Determining the Markup

Regardless of which cost-plus formula is used, Sydney Sailing Supplies must determine its markup on the Wave Darter. If management uses a variable-cost pricing formula, the markup must cover all fixed costs and a reasonable profit. If management uses an absorption-costing formula, the markup still must be sufficient to cover the firm's profit on the Wave Darter product line. What constitutes a reasonable or normal profit margin?

Return-on-Investment Pricing A common approach to determining the profit margin in cost-plus pricing is to base profit on the firm's target return on investment (ROI). To illustrate, suppose Sydney Sailing Supplies' production plan calls for 480 Wave Darters to be manufactured during the year. Based on the cost data shown in Exhibit 14-5, this production plan will result in the following total costs.

Variable costs:		
Manufacturing	$192,000	
Selling and administrative	24,000	
Total variable costs		$216,000
Fixed costs:		
Manufacturing	$120,000	
Selling and administrative	48,000	
Total fixed costs		168,000
Total costs		$384,000

Suppose the year's average amount of capital invested in the Wave Darter product line is $300,000. If Sydney Sailing Supplies' target return on investment for the Wave Darter line is 20 percent, the required annual profit is computed as follows:

$$\begin{pmatrix} \text{Average invested} \\ \text{capital} \end{pmatrix} \times \begin{pmatrix} \text{target} \\ \text{ROI} \end{pmatrix} = \begin{matrix} \text{target} \\ \text{profit} \end{matrix}$$

$$\$300,000 \quad \times \quad 20\% \quad = \$60,000$$

The markup percentage required to earn Sydney Sailing Supplies a $60,000 profit on the Wave Darter line depends on the cost-plus-formula used. We will compute the markup percentage for two cost-plus formulas.

1. *Cost-plus pricing based on total costs* The total cost of a Wave Darter is $800 per unit (Exhibit 14-5). To earn a profit of $60,000 on annual sales of 480 sailboats, the company must make a profit of $125 per boat ($125 = $60,000 ÷ 480). This entails a markup percentage of 15.63 percent *above* total cost of $800.

$$15.63\% = \frac{\$925}{\$800} - 100\%$$

A shortcut to the same conclusion uses the following formula.

$$\begin{matrix} \text{Markup percentage} \\ \text{on total cost} \end{matrix} = \frac{\text{target profit}}{\text{annual volume} \times \text{total cost per unit}}$$

$$15.63\% \quad = \quad \frac{\$60,000}{480 \times \$800}$$

2. *Cost-plus pricing based on total variable costs* The total variable cost of a Wave Darter is $450 per unit (Exhibit 14-5). The markup percentage applied to variable cost must be sufficient to cover *both* annual profit of $60,000 *and* total annual fixed costs of $168,000. The required markup percentage is computed as follows:

$$\begin{matrix} \text{Markup percentage} \\ \text{on total variable cost} \end{matrix} = \frac{\text{target profit} + \text{total annual fixed cost}}{\text{annual volume} \times \text{total variable cost per unit}}$$

$$105.56\% \quad = \quad \frac{\$60,000 + \$168,000}{480 \times \$450}$$

General Formula The general formula for computing the markup percentage in cost-plus pricing to achieve a target ROI is as follows:

$$\begin{matrix} \text{Markup percentage} \\ \text{applied to cost base in} \\ \text{cost-plus pricing formula} \end{matrix} = \frac{\begin{matrix} \text{profit required to} \\ \text{achieve target ROI} \end{matrix} + \begin{matrix} \text{total annual costs } \textit{not} \\ \text{included in cost base} \end{matrix}}{\begin{matrix} \text{annual} \\ \text{volume} \end{matrix} \times \begin{matrix} \text{cost base per unit} \\ \text{used in cost-plus} \\ \text{pricing formula} \end{matrix}}$$

Exercise 14-28 at the end of the chapter gives you an opportunity to employ this formula to compute the markup percentage for the other two cost-plus pricing formulas in Exhibit 14-5.

Cost-Plus Pricing: Summary and Evaluation

We have examined two different approaches to setting prices: (1) the economic, profit-maximizing approach and (2) cost-plus pricing. Although the techniques involved in these methods are quite different, the methods complement each other. In setting prices, managers cannot ignore the market, nor can they ignore costs. Cost-plus pricing is used widely in practice to establish a starting point in the process of determining a price. Cost-plus formulas are simple; they can be applied mechanically without taking the time of top management. They make it possible for a company with hundreds of products or services to cope with the tasks of updating prices for existing products and setting initial prices for new products.

Cost-plus pricing formulas can be used effectively with a variety of cost definitions, but the markup percentage must be appropriate for the type of cost used. It is imperative that price-setting managers understand that ultimately the price must cover all costs and a normal profit margin. Absorption-cost-plus or total-cost-plus pricing has the advantage of keeping the manager's attention focused on covering total costs. The variable-cost-plus formulas have the advantage of not obscuring important information about cost behavior.

Cost-plus pricing formulas establish a starting point in setting prices. Then the price setter must weigh market conditions, likely actions of competitors, and general business conditions. Thus, effective price setting requires a constant interplay of market considerations and cost awareness.

The following illustration points out the potential consequences of low unit costs on a firm's ability to achieve low prices.

ILLUSTRATION FROM MANAGEMENT-ACCOUNTING PRACTICE

Federal Express

An article in *Fortune* described the strategy used by Federal Express to become the nation's number-one carrier in one-day delivery of letters and small packages. In contrast to its competitors, Federal Express purchased its own fleet of planes and developed its own package-processing facilities in Memphis, Tennessee. Since Federal Express did not rely on sending packages by other commercial carriers, the company was soon able to achieve the lowest costs in the industry. These low costs enabled Federal Express to price its services below any of its competitors. This low price, made possible by low unit costs, enabled Federal Express to achieve phenomenal growth and established it as the number-one carrier for overnight delivery.[3]

TIME AND MATERIAL PRICING

Another cost-based approach to pricing is called **time and material pricing.** Under this approach, the company determines one charge for the labor used on a job and another charge for the materials. The labor typically includes the direct cost of the employee's time and a charge to cover various overhead costs. The material charge generally includes the direct cost of the materials used in a job plus a charge for material handling and storage. Time and material pricing is used widely by construction companies, printers, repair shops, and professional firms, such as engineering, law, and public accounting firms.

---

[3] "Federal Express Dives Into Air Mail," *Fortune,* June 5, 1981, pp. 106–108.

To illustrate, we will examine a special job undertaken by Sydney Sailing Supplies. The company's vice president for sales, Richard Moby, was approached by a successful local physician about refurbishing her yacht. She wanted an engine overhaul, complete refurbishment and redecoration of the cabin facilities, and stripping and repainting of the hull and deck. The work would be done in the Repair Department of the company's Yacht Division, located in Melbourne, Australia.

Data regarding the operations of the Repair Department are as follows:

Labor rate, including fringe benefits. . . . . $18.00 per hour
Annual labor hours . . . . 10,000 hours
Annual overhead costs:
   Material handling and storage. $40,000
   Other overhead costs (supervision, utilities, insurance, and
     depreciation). $200,000
Annual cost of materials used in Repair Department $1,000,000

Based on this data, the Repair Department computed its time and material prices as follows:

Time Charges

$$\begin{pmatrix} \text{Hourly} \\ \text{labor} \\ \text{cost} \end{pmatrix} + \begin{pmatrix} \dfrac{\text{Annual overhead}}{\text{(excluding material}} \\ \dfrac{\text{handling and storage)}}{\text{annual labor hours}} \end{pmatrix} + \begin{pmatrix} \text{Hourly charge} \\ \text{to cover} \\ \text{profit margin} \end{pmatrix}$$

$$\$18 \text{ per hour} + \frac{\$200{,}000}{10{,}000 \text{ hours}} + \$7 \text{ per hour} = \frac{\$45 \text{ per}}{\text{labor hour}}$$

Material Charges

$$\begin{pmatrix} \text{Material} \\ \text{cost} \\ \text{incurred} \\ \text{on job} \end{pmatrix} + \begin{pmatrix} \text{material} \\ \text{cost} \\ \text{incurred} \\ \text{on job} \end{pmatrix} \times \frac{\text{material handling}}{\text{and storage costs}} \Big/ \frac{\text{annual cost of materials used}}{\text{in Repair Department}}$$

$$\begin{pmatrix} \text{Material} \\ \text{cost} \\ \text{incurred} \\ \text{on job} \end{pmatrix} + \begin{pmatrix} \text{material} \\ \text{cost} \\ \text{incurred} \\ \text{on job} \end{pmatrix} \times \frac{\$40{,}000}{\$1{,}000{,}000}$$

$.04 per dollar of material cost

The effect of the material-charge formula is to include a charge for the costs incurred in the handling and storage of materials.

Richard Moby estimates that the yacht refurbishment job will require 200 hours of labor and $8,000 in materials. Moby's price quotation for the job is shown in Exhibit 14-6.

Exhibit 14-6. Time and Material Pricing

Sydney Sailing Supplies

Price Quotation
Sydney Sailing Supplies
Yacht Division: Repair Department

Job: Refurbishment of 45-foot yacht,
Pride of the Seas

Time charges:	Labor time	200 hours
	× Rate	× $45 per hour
	Total.	$ 9,000

Material charges:	Cost of materials for job.	$ 8,000
	+ Charge for material handling and storage	320*
	Total	$ 8,320

Total price of job:	Time.	$ 9,000
	Material	8,320
	Total	$17,320

*Charge for material handling and storage:

$$\begin{pmatrix} \$8,000 \\ \text{material} \\ \text{cost} \end{pmatrix} \times \begin{pmatrix} \$.04 \text{ per} \\ \text{dollar of} \\ \text{material cost} \end{pmatrix} = \$320$$

Included in the $17,320 price quotation for the yacht refurbishment are charges for labor costs, overhead, material costs, material handling and storage costs, and a normal profit margin. Some companies also charge an additional markup on the materials used in a job in order to earn a profit on that component of their services. Sydney Sailing Supplies' practice is to charge a high enough profit charge on its labor to earn an appropriate profit for the Repair Department.

COMPETITIVE BIDDING

In a **competitive bidding** situation, two or more companies submit sealed bids (or prices) for a product, service, or project to a potential buyer. The buyer selects one of the companies for the job on the basis of the bid price and the design specifications for the job. Competitive bidding complicates a manager's pricing problem, because now the manager is in direct competition with one or more competitors. If all of the companies submitting bids offer a roughly equivalent product or service, the bid price becomes the sole criterion for selecting the contractor. The higher the price that is bid, the greater will be the profit on the job, *if* the firm gets the contract. However, a higher price also lowers the probability of obtaining the contract to perform the job. Thus, there is a trade-off between bidding high, to make a good profit, and bidding low, to land the contract. Some say there is a "winner's curse" in competitive bidding, meaning that the company bidding low enough to beat out its competitors probably bid too low to make an acceptable profit on the job. Despite the winner's curse, competitive bidding is a common form of selecting contractors in many types of business.

Richard Moby was approached recently by the city of Sydney about building a new marina for moderate-sized sailing vessels. Moby decided that his company's Marine Construction Division should submit a bid on the job. The city announced that three other firms would also be submitting bids. Since all four companies were equally capable of building the marina to the city's specifications, Moby assumed that the bid price would be the deciding factor in selecting the contractor.

Moby consulted with the controller and chief engineer of the Marine Supply Division, and the following data were compiled.

Estimated direct-labor requirements, 1,500 hours at $12.00 per hour.	$18,000
Estimated direct-material requirements.	30,000
Estimated variable overhead (allocated on the basis of direct labor),	
1,500 direct-labor hours at $5.00 per hour	7,500
Total estimated variable costs	$55,500
Estimated fixed overhead (allocated on the basis of direct labor),	
1,500 direct-labor hours at $8.00 per hour	12,000
Estimated total cost.	$67,500

The Marine Construction Division allocates variable-overhead costs to jobs on the basis of direct-labor hours. These costs consist of indirect-labor costs, such as the wages of equipment-repair personnel, gasoline and lubricants, and incidental supplies such as rope, chains, and drill bits. Fixed-overhead costs, also allocated to jobs on the basis of direct-labor hours, include such costs as workers' compensation insurance, depreciation on vehicles and construction equipment, depreciation of the division's buildings, and supervisory salaries.

It was up to Richard Moby to decide on the bid price for the marina. In his meeting with the divisional controller and the chief engineer, Moby argued that the marina job was important to the company for two reasons. First, the Marine Construction Division had been operating well below capacity for several months. The marina job would not preclude the firm from taking on any other construction work, so it would not entail an opportunity cost. Second, the marina job would be good advertising for Sydney Sailing Supplies. City residents would see the firm's name on the project, and this would promote sales of the company's boats and sailing supplies.

Based on these arguments, Moby pressed for a bid price that just covered the firm's variable costs and allowed for a modest contribution margin. The chief engineer was obstinate, however, and argued for a higher bid price that would give the division a good profit on the job. "My employees work hard to do an outstanding job, and their work is worth a premium to the city," was the engineer's final comment on the issue. After the threesome tossed the problem around all morning, the controller agreed with Moby. A bid price of $60,000 was finally agreed upon.

This is a typical approach to setting prices for special jobs and competitively bid contracts. When a firm has excess capacity, a price that covers the incremental costs incurred because of the job will contribute toward covering the company's fixed cost and profit. None of the Marine Construction Division's fixed costs will increase as a result of taking on the marina job. Thus, a bid price of $60,000 will cover the $55,500 of variable costs on the job and contribute $4,500 toward covering the division's fixed costs.

Bid price	$60,000
Variable costs of marina job (incremental costs incurred only if job is done)	55,500
Contribution from marina job (contribution to covering the division's fixed costs)	$ 4,500

Naturally, Sydney Sailing Supplies' management would like to make a larger profit on the marina job, but bidding a higher price means running a substantial risk of losing the job to a competitor.

No Excess Capacity What if the Marine Construction Division has no excess capacity? If mangement expects to have enough work to fully occupy the division, a different approach is appropriate in setting the bid price. The fixed costs of the division are capacity-producing costs, which are costs incurred in order to create productive capacity. Depreciation of buildings and equipment, supervisory salaries, insurance, and property taxes are examples of fixed costs incurred to give a company the capacity to carry on its operations. When such costs are allocated to individual jobs, the cost of each job reflects an estimate of the opportunity cost of using limited capacity to do that particular job. For this reasoning to be valid, however, the organization must be at full capacity. If there is excess capacity, there is no opportunity cost in using that excess capacity.

If the Marine Construction Division has no excess capacity, it would be appropriate to focus on the estimated full cost of the marina job, $67,500, which includes an allocation of the division's fixed, capacity-producing costs. Now Richard Moby might legitimately argue for a bid price in excess of $67,500. If the division is awarded the marina contract by the city, a price above $67,500 will cover all the costs of the job and make a contribution toward the division's profit.

However, as Richard Moby pointed out, there will be valuable promotional benefits to Sydney Sailing Supplies if its Marine Construction Division builds the marina. This is a qualitative factor, because these potential benefits are difficult to quantify. Moby will have to make a judgment regarding just how important the marina job is to the company. The greater the perceived qualitative benefits, the lower the bid price should be set to maximize the likelihood that the company will be awarded the contract.

Summary of Competitive-Bidding Analysis The Marine Construction Division's pricing problem is summarized in Exhibit 14-7. As you can see, the final pricing decision requires managerial judgment to fully consider the quantitative cost data, the qualitative promotional benefits, and the trade-off between a higher profit and a greater likelihood of getting the marina contract.

Accept or Reject a Special Order In the preceding chapter, we examined in detail the decision as to whether a special order should be accepted or rejected. The analysis focused on identifying the relevant costs of the special order. The existence of excess capacity was an important factor in that analysis. Accepting a special order when excess capacity exists entails no opportunity cost. But when there is no excess capacity, one relevant cost of accepting a special order is the opportunity cost incurred by using the firm's limited capacity for the special order instead of some other job. After all relevant costs of the order have been identified, the decision maker compares the total relevant cost of the order with the price offered. If the price exceeds the relevant cost, the order generally should be accepted.

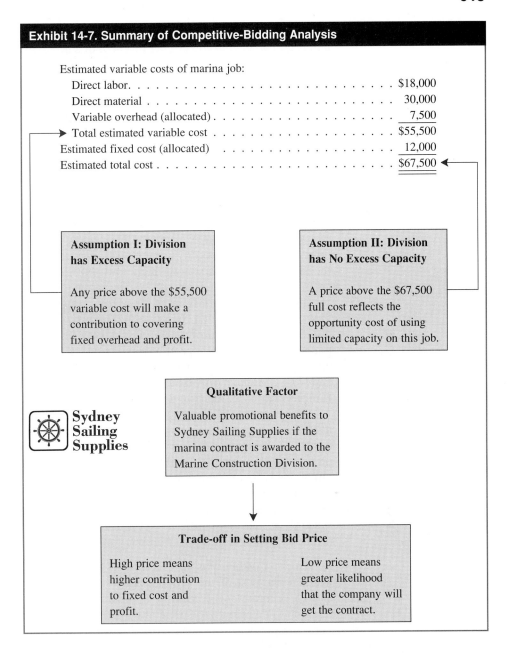

Exhibit 14-7. Summary of Competitive-Bidding Analysis

Estimated variable costs of marina job:

Direct labor. $18,000

Direct material 30,000

Variable overhead (allocated) 7,500

Total estimated variable cost $55,500

Estimated fixed cost (allocated) 12,000

Estimated total cost $67,500

**Assumption I: Division
has Excess Capacity**

Any price above the $55,500
variable cost will make a
contribution to covering
fixed overhead and profit.

**Assumption II: Division
has No Excess Capacity**

A price above the $67,500
full cost reflects the
opportunity cost of using
limited capacity on this job.

**Sydney
Sailing
Supplies**

Qualitative Factor

Valuable promotional benefits to
Sydney Sailing Supplies if the
marina contract is awarded to the
Marine Construction Division.

Trade-off in Setting Bid Price

High price means
higher contribution
to fixed cost and
profit.

Low price means
greater likelihood
that the company will
get the contract.

This decision is conceptually very similar to the bid-pricing problem discussed in this chapter. Setting a price for a special order or competitive bid also entails an analysis of the relevant costs of the job. Whether the decision maker is setting a price or has been offered a price, he or she must identify the relevant costs of providing the product or service requested.

STRATEGIC PRICING OF NEW PRODUCTS

Pricing a new product is an especially challenging decision problem. The newer the concept of the product, the more difficult the pricing decision is. For example, if

Sydney Sailing Supplies comes out with a new two-person sailboat, its pricing problem is far easier than the pricing problem of a company that first markets products using a radically new technology. Genetic engineering, superconductivity, artificial hearts, and space-grown crystals are all examples of such frontier technologies.

Pricing a new product is harder than pricing a mature product because of the magnitude of the uncertainties involved. New products entail uncertainties of two types. First, what obstacles will be encountered in manufacturing the product, and what will be the costs of production? Second, after the product is available, will anyone want to buy it, and at what price? If Sydney Sailing Supplies decides to market a new two-person sailboat, management can make a good estimate of both the production costs and the potential market for the product. The uncertainties here are far smaller than the uncertainties facing a company developing artificial hearts.

In addition to the production and demand uncertainties, new products pose another sort of challenge. There are two widely differing strategies that a manufacturer of a new product can adopt. One strategy is called **skimming pricing,** in which the initial product price is set high, and short-term profits are reaped on the new product. The initial market will be small, due in part to the high initial price. This pricing approach often is used for unique products, where there are people who "must have it" whatever the price. As the product gains acceptance and its appeal broadens, the price is lowered gradually. Eventually the product is priced in a range that appeals to a wide range of buyers. An example of a product for which skimming pricing was used is the home video game. Initially these games were priced quite high and were affordable only by a few buyers. Eventually the price was lowered, and the games were purchased by a wide range of consumers.

An alternative initial pricing strategy is called **penetration pricing,** in which the initial price is set relatively low. By setting a low price for a new product, management hopes to penetrate a new market deeply, quickly gaining a large market share. This pricing approach often is used for products that are of good quality, but do not stand out as vastly better than competing products.

The decision betwen skimming and penetration pricing depends on the type of product and involves trade-offs of price versus volume. Skimming pricing results in much slower acceptance of a new product, but higher unit profits. Penetration pricing results in greater initial sales volume, but lower unit profits.

Target Costing We have described the pricing of new products as a process whereby the cost of the product is determined, and then an appropriate price is chosen. Sometimes the opposite approach is taken. The company first uses market research to determine the price at which the new product will sell. Given the likely sales price, management computes the cost for which the product must be manufactured in order to provide the firm with an acceptable profit margin. Finally, engineers and cost analysts work together to design a product that can be manufactured for the allowable cost. This process, called **target costing,** is used widely by companies in the development stages of new products.

Sometimes the projected cost of a new product is above the target cost. Then efforts are made to eliminate *non-value-added costs* to bring the projected cost down. The process of reducing non-value-added costs was covered in Chapter 5.[4]

---

[4] Callie Berliner and James A. Brimson, eds., *Cost Management for Today's Advanced Manufacturing* (Boston, MA: Harvard Business School Press, 1988), pp. 9, 87.

Computer-Integrated Manufacturing When a computer-integrated manufacturing (CIM) system is used, the process of target costing sometimes is computerized. A manufacturer's computer-aided design and cost-accounting software are interconnected. An engineer can try out many different design features, and immediately see the product cost implications, without ever leaving the computer terminal.

**ILLUSTRATION FROM
MANAGEMENT-
ACCOUNTING
PRACTICE**

Hewlett-Packard's Personal Office Computer Division

At Hewlett-Packard Company's Personal Office Computer Division, a computer program called COSTIT is maintained by the Accounting Department. The COSTIT program enables a product design engineer to get a quick answer to the question, What will be the new product cost if certain design changes are made in a product? If, for example, the engineer wants to know the cost of changing the exterior case on the division's personal office computer, this information is easily determined by accessing COSTIT on his or her own computer terminal. Accounting Department personnel estimate that COSTIT is used by designers over 100 times a month to facilitate the continuing process of product enhancement.[5]

EFFECT OF ANTITRUST LAWS ON PRICING

Businesses are not free to set any price they wish for their products or services. American antitrust laws, including the Robinson-Patman Act, the Clayton Act, and the Sherman Act, restrict certain types of pricing behavior. These laws prohibit **price discrimination,** which means quoting different prices to different customers for the same product or service. Such price differences are unlawful unless they can be clearly justified by differences in the costs incurred to produce, sell, or deliver the product or service. Managers should keep careful records justifying such cost differences when they exist, because the records may be vital to a legal defense if price differences are challenged in court.

Another pricing practice prohibited by law is **predatory pricing.** This practice involves temporarily cutting a price to broaden demand for a product with the intention of later restricting the supply and raising the price again. In determining whether a price is predatory, the courts examine a business's cost records. If the product is sold below cost, the pricing is deemed to be predatory. The laws and court cases are ambiguous as to the appropriate definition of cost. This is one area where a price-setting decision maker is well advised to have an accountant on the left and a lawyer on the right before setting prices that could be deemed predatory.[6]

CHAPTER SUMMARY

Pricing of products and services is one of the most challenging decisions faced by management. Many influences affect pricing decisions. Chief among these are customer demand, the actions of competitors, and the costs of the products or services.

---

[5] J. Patell, "Cost Accounting, Process Control and Product Design: A Case Study of the Hewlett-Packard Personal Office Computer Division," *The Accounting Review, 62,* no. 4, pp. 808–837.

[6] For further information on predatory pricing, see P. Areeda and D. Turner, "Predatory Pricing and Related Practices under Section 2 of the Sherman Act," *Harvard Law Review, 88* (1975), pp. 697–733. For recent case law, see the "Legal Developments" section of the *Journal of Marketing.*

Other factors such as political, legal, and image-related issues also affect pricing decisions.

Economic theory shows that under certain assumptions, the profit-maximizing price and quantity are determined by the intersection of the marginal-revenue and marginal-cost curves. While the economic model serves as a useful conceptual framework for the pricing decision, it is limited by its assumptions and the informational demands it implies.

Most companies set prices, at least to some extent, on the basis of costs. Cost-plus pricing formulas add a markup to some version of cost, typically either total variable cost or total absorption cost. Markups often are set to earn the company a target profit on its products, based on a target rate of return on investment.

In industries such as construction, repair, printing, and professional services, time and material pricing is used. Under this approach the price is determined as the sum of a labor-cost component and a material-cost component. Either or both of these components may include a markup to ensure that the company earns a profit on its services.

Pricing special orders and determining competitive bid prices entail an analysis of the relevant costs to be incurred in completing the job. The relevant-cost analysis should incorporate the existence of excess capacity or the lack of it.

Strategic pricing of new products is an especially challenging problem for management. Various pricing approaches, such as skimming pricing or penetration pricing, may be appropriate depending on the product. Target costing often is used to design a new product that can be produced at a cost that will enable the firm to sell the product at a competitive price.

REVIEW PROBLEM ON COST-PLUS PRICING

Kitchenware Corporation manufactures high-quality copper pots and pans. Janet Cooke, one of the company's price analysts, is involved in setting a price for the company's new Starter Set. This set consists of seven of the most commonly used pots and pans. During the next year, the company plans to produce 10,000 Starter Sets, and the controller has provided Cooke with the following cost data.

Predicted Costs of 10,000 Starter Sets

Direct material per set...............................	$60
Direct labor per set, 2 hours at $10.00................	20
Variable selling cost per set..........................	5
Total...	$85
Variable overhead rate...............................	$ 8.00 per direct-labor hour
Fixed overhead rate..................................	$12.00 per direct-labor hour

In addition, the controller indicated that the Accounting Department would allocate $20,000 of fixed administrative expenses to the Starter Set product line.

REQUIRED:

1. Compute the cost of a Starter Set using each of the four cost definitions commonly used in cost-plus pricing formulas.
2. Determine the markup percentage required for the Starter Set product line to earn a target profit of $317,500 before taxes during the next year. Use the total cost as the cost definition in the cost-plus formula.

Solution to Review Problem

1. Variable manufacturing cost* .... $ 96   [1]
   Applied fixed-overhead cost† 24
   Absorption manufacturing cost 120   [2]
   Variable selling and administrative cost 5
   Allocated fixed selling and administrative cost‡ 2
   Total cost .... $127   [3]

   Variable manufacturing cost 96
   Variable selling and administrative cost 5
   Total variable cost .... $101   [4]

   * Direct material $60
     Direct labor 20
     Variable overhead .... 16 (2 × $8.00 per hour)
     Total variable manufacturing cost $96

   † Applied fixed overhead cost .... $24 (2 × $12 per hour)
   ‡ Allocated fixed selling and administrative cost .... $2 ($20,000 ÷ 10,000 sets)

2. $$\text{Markup percentage on total cost} = \frac{\$317{,}500}{10{,}000 \times 127} = 25\%$$

   Proof: Price = total cost + (.25 × total cost)
   $$= \$127 + (.25)(\$127) = \$158.75$$

Income Statement

Sales revenue (10,000 × $158.75)		$1,587,500
Less: Variable costs:		
Direct material	600,000	
Direct labor	200,000	
Variable overhead	160,000	
Variable selling and administrative cost	50,000	
Total variable costs		1,010,000
Contribution margin		577,500
Less: Fixed costs:		
Manufacturing overhead	240,000	
Selling and administrative cost	20,000	
Total fixed costs		260,000
Profit		$ 317,500

KEY TERMS   **Average revenue curve,** p. 599; **Competitive bidding,** p. 612; **Cross-elasticity,** p. 603; **Cost-plus pricing,** p. 605; **Demand curve (average revenue curve)** p. 599; **Marginal cost curve,** p. 602; **Marginal revenue curve,** p. 599; **Oligopolistic market,** p. 604; **Penetration pricing,** p. 616; **Predatory pricing,** p. 617; **Price discrimination,** p. 617; **Price elasticity,** p. 603; **Price taker,** p. 597; **Return-on-investment pricing,** p. 608; **Skimming pricing,** p. 616; **Target costing,** p. 616; **Time and material pricing,** p. 610; **Total cost curve,** p. 601; **Total revenue curve,** p. 598.

REVIEW QUESTIONS   **14-1.** List and briefly describe four major influences on pricing decisions.

14-2. Comment on the following remark made by a bank president: "The prices of our banking services are determined by the financial-services market. Costs are irrelevant."

14-3. "All this marginal revenue and marginal cost stuff is just theory. Prices are determined by production costs." Evaluate this assertion.

14-4. Explain what is meant by the following statement: "In considering the reactions of competitors, it is crucial to define your product."

14-5. Explain the following assertion: "Price setting generally requires a balance between market forces and cost considerations."

14-6. Briefly explain the concept of economic, profit-maximizing pricing. It may be helpful to use graphs in your explanation.

14-7. Define the following terms: total revenue, marginal revenue, demand curve, price elasticity, and cross-elasticity.

14-8. Briefly define total cost and marginal cost.

14-9. Describe three limitations of the economic, profit-maximizing model of pricing.

14-10. "Determining the best approach to pricing requires a cost-benefit trade-off." Explain.

14-11. Write the general formula for cost-plus pricing, and briefly explain its use.

14-12. List the four commonly used cost bases used in cost-plus pricing. How can they all result in the same price?

14-13. List four reasons often cited for the widespread use of absorption cost as the cost base in cost-plus pricing formulas.

14-14. What is the primary disadvantage of basing the cost-plus pricing formula on absorption cost?

14-15. List three advantages of pricing based on variable cost.

14-16. Explain the behavioral problem that can result when cost-plus prices are based on variable cost.

14-17. Briefly explain the concept of return-on-investment pricing.

14-18. Briefly describe the time-and-material pricing approach.

14-19. Explain the importance of the excess-capacity issue in setting a competitive bid price.

14-20. The decision to accept or reject a special order and the selection of a price for a special order are very similar decisions. Explain.

14-21. Describe the following approaches to pricing new products: skimming pricing, penetration pricing, and target costing.

14-22. Explain what is meant by unlawful price discrimination and predatory pricing.

Dollars per unit

Quantity sold
per month

EXERCISES   *Exercise 14-23   Marginal Revenue and Marginal Cost Curves.* The marginal cost, marginal revenue, and demand curves for Houston Home and Garden's deluxe wheelbarrow are shown in the graph at the bottom of page 620.

REQUIRED: Before completing any of the following requirements, read over the entire list.

1. Trace the graph shown above onto a blank piece of paper, and label all parts of the graph.
2. Draw a companion graph directly above the traced graph. Use this graph to draw the firm's total revenue and total cost curves.
3. Show the company's profit-maximizing price on the lower graph and its profit-maximizing quantity on both graphs.

Exercise 14-24   Demand and Revenue Data. Plato Electronics manufactures compact disk players with unusual features in its St. Louis Division. The divisional sales manager has estimated the following demand-curve data.

Quantity Sold per Month		Unit Sales Price
20	....	$1,000
40	....	950
60	....	900
80	....	850
100	....	800

REQUIRED:

1. Prepare a table similar to panel C of Exhibit 14-1 summarizing Plato Electronics' price, quantity, and revenue data.
2. Draw a graph similar to panel A of Exhibit 14-1 reflecting the data tabulated in requirement (1).

Exercise 14-25   Continuation of Preceding Exercise; Cost Data. Refer to the preceding exercise. The divisional controller at Plato Electronics' St. Louis Division has estimated the following cost data for the division's CD players. (Assume there are no fixed costs.)

Quantity Produced and Sold per Month		Average Cost per Unit
20	....	$900
40	....	850
60	....	820
80	....	860
100	....	890

REQUIRED:

1. Prepare a table similar to panel C of Exhibit 14-2 summarizing Plato Electronics' cost relationships.
2. Draw a graph similar to panel A of Exhibit 14-2 reflecting the data tabulated in requirement (1).

Exercise 14-26 Continuation of Preceding Two Exercises; Profit-Maximizing Price. Refer to the data given in the preceding two exercises.

1. Prepare a table of Plato Electronics' revenue, cost, and profit relationships. For guidance refer to panel C of Exhibit 14-3.
2. Draw a graph similar to panel A of Exhibit 14-3 reflecting the data tabulated in requirement (1).
3. To narrow down the pricing decision, the St. Louis Division's sales manager has decided to price the CD player at one of the following prices: $800, $850, $900, $950 or $1,000. Which price do you recommend? Why?

Exercise 14-27 Cost-Plus Pricing Formulas. The following data pertain to Gibralter Lighting Company's oak-clad, contemporary chandelier.

Variable manufacturing cost	$200
Applied fixed manufacturing cost	70
Variable selling and administrative cost	30
Allocated fixed selling and administrative cost	50

REQUIRED: For each of the following cost bases, develop a cost-plus pricing formula that will result in a price of $400 for the oak chandelier.

1. Variable manufacturing cost.
2. Absorption manufacturing cost.
3. Total cost.
4. Total variable cost.

Exercise 14-28 Determining Markup Percentage; Target ROI. Refer to the cost and production data for the Wave Darter in Exhibit 14-5. The target profit is $60,000.

REQUIRED: Use the general formula for determining a markup percentage to compute the required markup percentages with the following two cost-plus formulas:

1. Variable manufacturing costs [formula (1) in Exhibit 14-5].
2. Absorption manufacturing cost [formula (2) in Exhibit 14-5].

Exercise 14-29 Cost-Plus Pricing Formulas; Missing Data. The following data pertain to Yard King Corporation's top-of-the-line lawn mower.

Variable manufacturing cost	$250
Applied fixed manufacturing cost	50
Variable selling and administrative cost	60
Allocated fixed selling and administrative cost	?

To achieve a target price of $450 per lawn mower, the markup percentage is 12.5 percent on total unit cost.

REQUIRED:

1. What is the fixed selling and administrative cost allocated to each unit of Yard King's top-of-the-line mower?
2. For each of the following cost-bases, develop a cost-plus pricing formula that will result in a target price of $450 per mower: (a) variable manufacturing cost, (b) absorption manufacturing cost, and (c) total variable cost.

Exercise 14-30 Time and Material Pricing. Refer to Exhibit 14-6. Suppose the Repair Department of Sydney Sailing Supplies adds a markup of 5 percent on the material charges of a job (including the cost of material handling and storage).

REQUIRED:

1. Rewrite the material component of the time and material pricing formula to reflect the markup on material cost.
2. Compute the new price to be quoted on the yacht refurbishment described in Exhibit 14-6.

PROBLEMS

Problem 14-31 Product Pricing; Plantwide versus Departmental Overhead Rates. Splendid Stereo Company manufactures two models of stereo amplifiers. Cost estimates for the two models for the year 19x7 are as follows:

	Model 1000	Model 2000
Direct material	$160	$260
Direct labor (10 hours at $14 per hour)	140	140
Manufacturing overhead*	100	100
Total cost	$400	$500

* The predetermined overhead rate is $10 per direct-labor hour.

Each stereo amplifier requires 10 hours of direct labor. Each Model 1000 unit requires two hours in Department I and eight hours in Department II. Each unit of Model 2000 requires eight hours in Department I and two hours in Department II. The manufacturing overhead costs expected during 19x7 in Departments I and II are shown below.

	Department I	Department II
Variable overhead	$8 per direct-labor hour	$4 per direct-labor hour
Fixed overhead................	$150,000	$150,000

The expected operating activity for 19x7 is 37,500 direct-labor hours in each department.

REQUIRED:

1. Show how Splendid Stereo derived its predetermined overhead rate.
2. What will be the price of each model stereo amplifier if the company prices its products at absorption manufacturing cost plus 15 percent?
3. Suppose Splendid Stereo were to use departmental overhead rates. Compute these rates for Departments I and II for 19x7.
4. Compute the absorption cost of each model stereo amplifier using the departmental overhead rates computed in requirement (3).
5. Suppose management sticks with its policy of setting prices equal to absorption cost plus 15 percent. Compute the new prices for models 1000 and 2000, using the product costs developed in requirement (4).
6. Should Splendid Stereo use plantwide or departmental overhead rates? Explain your answer.

Problem 14-32 Interdivisional Transfers; Pricing the Final Product. National Industries is a diversified corporation with separate operating divisions. Each division's performance is evaluated on the basis of profit and return on investment.

The WindAir Division manufactures and sells air-conditioner units. The coming year's budgeted income statement, which follows, is based upon a sales volume of 15,000 units.

WindAir Division
Budgeted Income Statement
(in thousands)

	Per Unit	Total
Sales revenue.	$400	$6,000
Manufacturing costs:		
Compressor	$ 70	$1,050
Other direct material.	37	555
Direct labor.	30	450
Variable overhead.	45	675
Fixed overhead	32	480
Total manufacturing costs.	$214	$3,210
Gross margin.	$186	$2,790
Operating expenses:		
Variable selling	$ 18	$ 270
Fixed selling.	19	285
Fixed administrative.	38	570
Total operating expenses.	$ 75	$1,125
Net income before taxes.	$111	$1,665

WindAir's division manager believes sales can be increased if the price of the air-conditioners is reduced. A market research study by an independent firm indicates that a 5 percent reduction in the selling price would increase sales volume 16 percent or 2,400 units. WindAir has sufficient production capacity to manage this increased volume with no increase in fixed costs.

WindAir uses a compressor in its units, which it purchases from an outside supplier at a cost of $70 per compressor. The division manager of WindAir has asked the manager of the Compressor Division about selling compressor units to WindAir. The Compressor Division currently manufactures and sells a unit to outside firms which is similar to the unit used by WindAir. The specifications of the WindAir compressor are slightly different, which would reduce the Compressor Division's direct material cost by $1.50 per unit. In addition, the Compressor Division would not incur any variable selling costs in the units sold to WindAir. The manager of WindAir wants all of the compressors it uses to come from one supplier and has offered to pay $50 for each compressor unit.

The Compressor Division has the capacity to produce 75,000 units. Its budgeted income statement for the coming year, which follows, is based on a sales volume of 64,000 units without considering WindAir's proposal.

REQUIRED:

1. Should WindAir Division institute the 5 percent price reduction on its air-conditioner units even if it cannot acquire the compressors internally for $50 each? Support your conclusion with appropriate calculations.

2. Independently of your answer to requirement (1), assume WindAir needs 17,400 units. Should the Compressor Division be willing to supply the compressor units for $50 each? Support your conclusions with appropriate calculations.

Compressor Division
Budgeted Income Statement
(in thousands)

	Per Unit	Total
Sales revenue...	$100	$6,400
Manufacturing costs:		
Direct material......................................	$ 12	$ 768
Direct labor..	8	512
Variable overhead..................................	10	640
Fixed overhead.....................................	11	704
Total manufacturing costs......................	$ 41	$2,624
Gross margin...	$ 59	$3,776
Operating expenses:		
Variable selling....................................	$ 6	$ 384
Fixed selling......................................	4	256
Fixed administrative...............................	7	448
Total operating expenses......................	$ 17	$1,088
Net income before taxes......................................	$ 42	$2,688

3. Independently of your answer to requirement (1), assume WindAir needs 17,400 units. Would it be in the best interest of National Industries for the Compressor Division to supply the compressor units at $50 each to the WindAir Division? Support your conclusions with appropriate calculations.

(CMA, adapted)

Problem 14-33   *Pricing a Special Order; Excess Capacity; Inflation.* Keylo Company manufactures a line of plastic products that are sold through hardware stores. The company's sales have declined slightly for the past two years, resulting in idle plants and equipment.

    A Keylo engineer met a former college classmate at a convention of machinery builders. The classmate is employed by Paddington Company, which is also in the plastic products business. During their conversation it became evident that Keylo might be able to make a particular product for Paddington with the currently unused equipment and space.

    The following requirements were specified by Paddington for the new product.

(1) Paddington needs 80,000 units per year for the next three years.
(2) The product is to be built to Paddington specifications.
(3) Keylo is not to enter into independent production of the product during the three-year contract.
(4) Paddington would provide Keylo, without charge, with a special machine to finish the product. The machine becomes the property of Keylo at the end of the three-year period.

    Although Keylo is not operating at capacity, the company generated a profit last year, as shown in the following income statement.

    The Keylo engineering, production, and accounting departments agreed upon the following facts if the contract were accepted.

    Manufacturing:
- The present idle capacity would be fully used.
- One additional part-time supervisor would be required; the annual salary would be $15,000.

Keylo Company
Income Statement
(in thousands)

	Dollar Amount	Percentage
Sales.	$1,500	100%
Cost of goods sold:		
Direct material.	$ 200	13%
Direct labor	400	27
Manufacturing overhead*	390	26
Cost of goods sold	$ 990	66%
Manufacturing margin before underapplied manufacturing overhead.	$ 510	34%
Underapplied manufacturing overhead†	10	1
Manufacturing margin	$ 500	33%
Operating expenses:		
Sales commissions.	$ 60	4%
Sales administration	30	2
General administration.	110	7
Total operating expenses.	$ 200	13%
Net income before income taxes	$ 300	20%
Income taxes (40%).	120	8
Net income	$ 180	12%

* Schedule of manufacturing overhead

Variable:		
Indirect labor.		$100
Supplies		40
Power.		120
Fixed costs applied:		
Administration		60
Depreciation		70
		$390

† Schedule of underapplied overhead (due to idle capacity)

Depreciation	$10

- The annual quantity of direct material and direct labor would increase by 10 percent at current prices. There would be no increase in indirect labor.
- The power and supply quantity requirements would increase 10 percent at current prices, due to the reactivation of idle machines.
- The machine provided by Paddington would increase the annual power and supply costs by $10,000 and $4,000, respectively, at current prices.
- The Paddington machine would have no value to Keylo at the end of the contract.

Sales:

- A sales commission of $10,000 would be paid to the sales personnel arranging the contract.
- No additional sales or administrative costs would be incurred.

General administration:

- No additional general administrative costs would be incurred.

Other information:

- Estimated cost increases due to inflation for the entire three-year period are as follows:

Direct material 5%
Direct labor 10%
Power 20%
Depreciation.   0
Sales commissions   0
Income taxes   0
All other items 10%

- Inventory balances, which have remained stable for the past three years, will not be increased or decreased by the production of the new product.

REQUIRED:

1. Calculate the total price needed for the three-year order (240,000 units) if the company wants to make an after-tax profit of 10 percent of the sales price on this order.
2. Calculate the total price for the three-year order (240,000 units) if this order were to contribute nothing to net income after taxes.

(CMA, adapted)

Problem 14-34   Cost-Plus Pricing; Target Return on Investment. Fiore Company manufactures office equipment for sale to retail stores. Tim Lucas, vice president of marketing, has proposed that Fiore introduce two new products, an electric stapler and an electric pencil sharpener.

Lucas has requested that Fiore's Accounting Department develop preliminary selling prices for the two new products for his review. The Accounting Department is to follow the company's standard policy for developing potential selling prices using as much data as available for each product. The data accumulated for the two new products are as follows:

	Electric Stapler	Electric Pencil Sharpener
Estimated annual demand in units	12,000	10,000
Estimated unit manufacturing costs.	$10.00	$12.00
Estimated unit selling and administrative expenses	$4.00	Not available
Assets employed in manufacturing	$180,000	Not available

Fiore plans to employ an average of $2,400,000 of assets to support its operations in the current year. The following budgeted income statement represents Fiore's planned goals with respect to cost relationships and return on investment for the entire company across all of its products.

Fiore Company
Budgeted Income Statement
For the Year Ending May 31, 19x5
(in thousands)

Revenue. $4,800
Cost of goods sold   2,880
Gross profit $1,920
Selling and administrative expenses.   1,440
Operating profit. . . . . $ 480

REQUIRED:

1. Calculate a potential selling price for the electric stapler using cost-plus pricing to achieve a target return on investment equal to Fiore Company's current projected ROI.
2. Could a selling price for the electric pencil sharpener be calculated using this method? Explain your answer.
3. Discuss the additional steps Tim Lucas is likely to take after he receives the potential selling prices for the two new products before setting an actual selling price for each of the two products.

(CMA, adapted)

Problem 14-35   Time and Material Pricing. Suburban Heating, Inc. installs heating systems in new homes. Jobs are priced using the time and materials method. The following predictions pertain to the company's operations for 19x5.

Labor rate, including fringe benefits	$15.00 per hour
Annual labor hours	12,000 hours
Annual overhead costs:	
Material handling and storage	$25,000
Other overhead costs	$108,000
Annual cost of materials used	$250,000

The president of Suburban Heating, B. T. Ewing, is pricing a job involving the heating systems for six houses to be built by a local developer. He has made the following estimates.

Labor hours	400
Material cost	$60,000

REQUIRED: Suburban Heating adds a markup of $5.00 per hour on its time charges, but there is no markup on material costs.

1. Develop formulas for the company's (a) time charges and (b) material charges.
2. Compute the price for the job described above.
3. What would be the price of the job if Suburban Heating also added a markup of 10 percent on all material charges (including material handling and storage costs)?

Problem 14-36   Pricing a Special Order. Jenco Inc. manufactures one product, a combination fertilizer/weed-killer called Fertikil. The product is sold nationwide to retail nurseries and gardening stores. Taylor Nursery plans to sell a similar fertilizer/weed-killer through its regional nursery chain under its private label. Taylor has asked Jenco to submit a bid for a 25,000-pound order of the private-brand compound. While the chemical composition of the Taylor compound differs from Fertikil, the manufacturing process is very similar. The Taylor compound would be produced in 1,000-pound lots. Each lot would require 60 direct-labor hours and the following chemicals.

Chemicals	Quantity in Pounds
CW-3	400
JX-6	300
MZ-8	200
BE-7	100

The first three chemicals (CW-3, JX-6, MZ-8) are all used in the production of Fertikil. BE-7 was used in a compound that Jenco has discontinued. This chemical was not sold or discarded, because it does not deteriorate and Jenco has adequate storage facilities. Jenco could sell BE-7 at the prevailing market price, less 10 cents per pound for selling and handling expenses.

Jenco also has on hand a chemical called CN-5, manufactured for use in another product that is no longer produced. CN-5, which cannot be used in Fertikil, can be substituted for CW-3 on a one-for-one basis without affecting the quality of the Taylor compound. The quantity of CN-5 in inventory has a salvage value of $500. Inventory and cost data for the chemicals that can be used to produce the Taylor compound are as follows:

Raw Material	Pounds in Inventory	Actual Price per Pound When Purchased	Current Market Price per Pound
CW-3	22,000	$ .80	$ .90
JX-6	5,000	$ .55	$ .60
MZ-8	8,000	$1.40	$1.60
BE-7	4,000	$ .60	$ .65
CN-5	5,500	$ .75	*

* Salvage value of $500 for entire inventory on hand.

The current direct-labor rate is $7.00 per hour. The manufacturing-overhead rate is established at the beginning of the year using direct-labor hours (DLH) as the base. The predetermined overhead rate for the current year, based on a two-shift capacity of 400,000 total direct-labor hours with no overtime, is as follows:

Variable manufacturing overhead .... $2.25 per direct-labor hour
Fixed manufacturing overhead...................... 3.75 per direct-labor hour
Combined rate.............................. $6.00 per direct-labor hour

Jenco's production manager reports that the present equipment and facilities are adequate to manufacture the Taylor compound. However, Jenco is within 800 hours of its two-shift capacity this month before it must schedule overtime. If need be, the Taylor compound could be produced on regular time by shifting a portion of Fertikil production to overtime. Jenco's pay rate for overtime hours is one-and-one-half the regular pay rate, or $10.50 per hour. There is no allowance for any overtime premium in the manufacturing-overhead rate. Jenco's standard markup policy for new products is 25 percent of absorption manufacturing cost.

REQUIRED:

1. Assume Jenco Inc. has decided to submit a bid for a 25,000 pound order of Taylor's new compound, to be delivered by the end of the current month. Taylor has indicated that this one-time order will not be repeated. Calculate the lowest price Jenco can bid for the order and not reduce its net income.
2. Independently of your answer to requirement (1), assume that Taylor Nursery plans to place regular orders for 25,000 pound lots of the new compound during the coming year. Jenco expects the demand for Fertikil to remain strong, so the recurring orders from Taylor will put Jenco over its two-shift capacity. However, production can be scheduled so that 60 percent of each Taylor order can be completed during regular hours, or Fertikil production could be shifted temporarily to overtime so that the Taylor orders could be produced on regular

time. Jenco's production manager has estimated that the prices of all chemicals will stabilize at the current market rates for the coming year. All other manufacturing costs are expected to be maintained at the same rates or amounts.

Calculate the price Jenco Inc. should quote Taylor Nursery for each 25,000 pound lot of the new compound, assuming that there will be recurring orders during the coming year. Assume that Jenco's management believes new products sold on a recurring basis should be priced to cover their full production costs plus the standard markup.

(CMA, adapted)

Problem 14-37 *Pricing in a Tight Market; Possible Plant Closing.* Stac Industries is a multi-product company with several manufacturing plants. The Clinton Plant manufactures and distributes two household cleaning and polishing compounds, regular and heavy-duty, under the Cleen-Brite label. The forecasted operating results for the first six months of 19x0, when 100,000 cases of each compound are expected to be manufactured and sold, are presented in the following statement.

Cleen-Brite Compounds—Clinton Plant
Forecasted Results of Operations
For the Six-month Period Ending June 30, 19x0
(in thousands)

	Regular	Heavy-Duty	Total
Sales	$2,000	$3,000	$5,000
Cost of goods sold	1,600	1,900	3,500
Gross profit	$ 400	$1,100	$1,500
Selling and administrative expenses:			
Variable	$ 400	$ 700	$1,100
Fixed*	240	360	600
Total selling and administrative expenses	$ 640	$1,060	$1,700
Income (loss) before taxes	$ (240)	$ 40	$ (200)

* The fixed selling and administrative expenses are allocated between the two products on the basis of dollar sales volume.

The regular compound sold for $20 a case and the heavy-duty compound sold for $30 a case during the first six months of 19x0. The manufacturing costs, by case of product, are presented in the schedule below. Each product is manufactured on a separate production line. Annual normal manufacturing capacity is 200,000 cases of each product. However, the plant is capable of producing 250,000 cases of regular compound and 350,000 cases of heavy-duty compound annually.

Cost per Case

	Regular	Heavy-Duty
Direct material	$ 7.00	$ 8.00
Direct labor	4.00	4.00
Variable manufacturing overhead	1.00	2.00
Fixed manufactuirng overhead*	4.00	5.00
Total manufacturing cost	$16.00	$19.00
Variable selling and administrative costs	$ 4.00	$ 7.00

* Depreciation charges are 50 percent of the fixed manufacturing overhead of each line.

The following schedule reflects the consensus of top management regarding the price-volume alternatives for the Cleen-Brite products for the last six months of 19x0. These are essentially the same alternatives management had during the first six months of the year.

Regular Compound		Heavy-Duty Compound	
Alternative Prices (per case)	Sales Volume (in cases)	Alternative Prices (per case)	Sales Volume (in cases)
$18	120,000	$25	175,000
20	100,000	27	140,000
21	90,000	30	100,000
22	80,000	32	55,000
23	50,000	35	35,000

Top management believes the loss for the first six months reflects a tight profit margin caused by intense competition. Management also believes that many companies will leave this market by next year and profit should improve.

REQUIRED:

1. What unit selling price should Stac Industries select for each of the Cleen-Brite compounds (regular and heavy-duty) for the remaining six months of 19x0? Support your selection with appropriate calculations.
2. Independently of your answer to requirement (1), assume the optimum price-volume alternatives for the last six months were as follows: a selling price of $23 and volume level of 50,000 cases for the regular compound, and a selling price of $35 and volume of 35,000 cases for the heavy-duty compound.
   a. Should Stac Industries consider closing down its operations until 19x1 in order to minimize its losses? Support your answer with appropriate calculations.
   b. Identify and discuss the qualitative factors that should be considered in deciding whether the Clinton Plant should be closed down during the last six months of 19x0.

(CMA, adapted)

Problem 14-38   Bidding on a Special Order. Ward Industries is a manufacturer of standard and custom-designed bottling equipment. Early in December 19x3 Lyan Company asked Ward to quote a price for a custom-designed bottling machine to be delivered in April. Lyan intends to make a decision on the purchase of such a machine by January 1, so Ward would have the entire first quarter of 19x4 to build the equipment.

Ward's pricing policy for custom-designed equipment is 50 percent markup on absorption manufacturing cost. Lyan's specifications for the equipment have been reviewed by Ward's Engineering and Cost Accounting Departments, which made the following estimates for direct material and direct labor.

Direct material $256,000
Direct labor. . . . . 11,000 hours at $15   165,000

Manufacturing overhead is applied on the basis of direct-labor hours. Ward normally plans to run its plant at a level of 15,000 direct-labor hours per month and assigns overhead on the basis of 180,000 direct-labor hours per year. The overhead application rate for 19x4 of $9.00 per hour is based on the following budgeted manufacturing overhead costs for 19x4.

Variable manufacturing overhead.	$ 972,000
Fixed manufacturing overhead	648,000
Total manufacturing overhead	$1,620,000

Ward's production schedule calls for 12,000 direct-labor hours per month during the first quarter. If Ward is awarded the contract for the Lyan equipment, production of one of its standard products would have to be reduced. This is necessary because production levels can only be increased to 15,000 direct-labor hours each month on short notice. Furthermore, Ward's employees are unwilling to work overtime.

Sales of the standard product equal to the reduced production would be lost, but there would be no permanent loss of future sales or customers. The standard product for which the production schedule would be reduced has a unit sales price of $12,000 and the following cost structure.

Direct material		$2,500
Direct labor	250 hours at $15	3,750
Manufacturing overhead	250 hours at $ 9	2,250
Total cost		$8,500

Lyan needs the custom-designed equipment to increase its bottle-making capacity so that it will not have to buy bottles from an outside supplier. Lyan Company requires 5,000,000 bottles annually. Its present equipment has a maximum capacity of 4,500,000 bottles with a directly traceable cash outlay cost of 15 cents per bottle. Thus, Lyan has had to purchase 500,000 bottles from a supplier at 40 cents each. The new equipment would allow Lyan to manufacture its entire annual demand for bottles at a direct-material cost savings of 1 cent per bottle. Ward estimates that Lyan's annual bottle demand will continue to be 5,000,000 bottles over the next five years, the estimated life of the special-purpose equipment.

REQUIRED: Ward Industries plans to submit a bid to Lyan Company for the manufacture of the special-purpose bottling equipment.

1. Calculate the bid Ward would submit if it follows its standard pricing policy for special-purpose equipment.
2. Calculate the minimum bid Ward would be willing to submit on the Lyan equipment that would result in the same profit as planned for the first quarter of 19x4.

(CMA, adapted)

Problem 14-39   *Pricing for a Professional Convention.* Systems Planners Institute (SPI), a professional association for systems analysts and computer programmers, has 50,000 members. SPI holds a convention each October and planning for the 19x6 convention is progressing smoothly. The convention budget for promotional brochures, fees and expenses for 20 speakers, equipment rental for presentations, the travel and expenses of 25 staff people, consultant fees, and volunteer expenses is $330,000. This amount does not include the hotel charges for meeting rooms, luncheons, banquets, or receptions.

SPI has always priced each function at the convention separately. Members select and pay for only those functions they attend. Members who attend the convention pay a registration fee that allows them to attend the annual reception and meeting. The Annual Convention Committee has recommended that SPI set a single flat fee for the entire convention; registered members would be entitled to attend all functions.

The following table presents the convention functions, the percentage of attendees that can be expected to attend each function, the price SPI would charge for each function if it were priced separately, and the hotel charges for food service and meeting rooms. The percentage of attendees expected to attend each function is based on past experience and is expected to hold regardless of the pricing scheme used.

Function	Percentage of Attendees Who Will Participate		Separate Price of Function		Hotel Charge
Registration fee	100%	. . . .	$50	. . . .	None
Reception	100%	. . . .	Free	. . . .	$25/attendee
Annual meeting.	100%	. . . .	Free	. . . .	$2,000 for meeting hall
Keynote luncheon.	90%	. . . .	$40	. . . .	$25/attendee
Six concurrent sessions*.	70%	. . . .	$60	. . . .	$200/room or $1,200 in total
Plenary session	70%	. . . .	$50	. . . .	$2,000 for meeting hall
Six workshops*	50%	. . . .	$100	. . . .	$200/room or $1,200 in total
Banquet.	90%	. . . .	$50	. . . .	$30/attendee

* Attendee selects one session for the fee.

The hotel's package of services to SPI and the convention attendees is as follows:

(1) Three free rooms for convention headquarters and storage.
(2) 20 percent discount for all convention attendees who stay in the hotel during the three-day convention. The types of rooms, regular posted rate, and the proportion of each type of room taken by attendees are as follows. Attendees are to make room reservations directly with the hotel, and all hotel room charges are the responsibility of the attendees.

Type	Regular Posted Rate per Night	Proportion Rented
Single	$100	10%
Studio	105	10
Double	125	75
Suite	200	5

(3) SPI is given credit for one free double room for three days for every 50 convention registrants who stay at the hotel. The credit will be applied to the room charges of staff and speakers.
(4) Meeting rooms and halls are free if food is served at the function.
(5) Meeting rooms and halls for professional sessions are free if 1,000 members are registered at the hotel.
(6) Meal costs given in the table include all taxes and gratuities.
(7) The hotel receives all revenue from cash bar sales at the reception, and before the luncheons and banquet. The hotel estimates that the average consumption at each of these functions will be one cocktail per attendee at $1.50 per cocktail.

If SPI continues to price each convention function separately, the prices given in the prior table will apply. Expected attendance under this type of pricing scheme is 2,000. The Annual Convention Committee has estimated the convention attendance for three different single flat-fee pricing structures as follows:

Proposed Single Flat Fee		Estimated Number of Attendees
$325	....	1,600
300	....	1,750
275	....	1,900

SPI estimates that 60 percent of the people who attend the convention will stay in the convention hotel, and each attendee will need a separate room for an average stay of three nights.

REQUIRED: SPI wants to maximize its contribution margin from its annual convention. Recommend whether SPI should price each function at the convention separately or charge one of the three single flat fees for the convention. Support your recommendation with an appropriate analysis.

(CMA, adapted)

CASES *Case 14-40   Pricing and Financial Condition.*[7] Early in January, 19x6, the sales manager and the controller of Atherton Company met to prepare a joint pricing recommendation for item 345. After the president approved their recommendation, the price would be announced in letters to retail customers. In accordance with company and industry practice, announced prices were not changed during the year unless radical changes in market conditions occurred.

Atherton Company was the largest company in its segment of the textile industry; its 19x5 sales had exceed $12 million. Company sales personnel were on a straight salary basis, and each salesperson sold the full line. Most of Atherton's competitors were small. Usually they waited for Atherton Company to announce prices before mailing their own price lists.

Item 345, an expensive yet competitive fabric, was the sole product of a department whose facilities could not be utilized on other items in the product line. In January 19x4 Atherton Company had raised its price from $3 to $4 a yard, to bring the profit on item 345 up to that of other products in the line. Although the company was in a strong position financially, it would require considerable capital in the next few years to finance a recently approved long-term modernization and expansion program. The 19x3 pricing decision had been one of several changes advocated by the directors to strengthen the company's financial position so as to ensure that adequate funds would be available for this program.

Competitors of Atherton Company had held their prices on products similar to item 345 at $3 during 19x4 and 19x5. The industry and Atherton Company volume for item 345 for the years 19x0–19x5, as estimated by the sales manager, is shown in Table 1. As shown by this table, Atherton had lost a significant portion of its former market position. In the sales manager's opinion, a reasonable forecast of industry volume for 19x6 was 700,000 yards. He was certain that the company could sell 25 percent of the 19x6 industry total if it adopted the $3 price. He feared a further volume decline if it did not meet the competitive price. As many consumers were convinced of the superiority of the Atherton product, the sales manager reasoned that sales of item 345 would probably not fall below 75,000 yards, even at a $4 price.

[7] Copyright 1984 by the President and Fellows of Harvard College. This case was prepared as the basis for class discussion rather than to illustrate either effective or ineffective handling of an administrative situation. Reprinted with the permission of the Harvard Business School. This case (156-002) was prepared by Robert Lavoie under the supervision of Robert N. Anthony.

Table 1
Item 345, Prices and Production, 19x0–19x5

| | Volume of Production (yards) | | Price | |
| | | | Charged by Most | Atherton |
Year	Industry Total	Atherton	Competitors	Company
19x0	610,000	213,000	$4.00	$4.00
19x1	575,000	200,000	4.00	4.00
19x2	430,000	150,000	3.00	3.00
19x3	475,000	165,000	3.00	3.00
19x4	500,000	150,000	3.00	4.00
19x5	625,000	125,000	3.00	4.00

During the pricing discussions, the controller and sales manager had considered two other aspects of the problem. The controller was worried that competitors would reduce their prices below $3 if Atherton Company announced a $3 price for item 345. The sales manager was confident that competitors would not go below $3, because they all had higher costs and several were in tight financial straits. He believed that action taken on item 345 would not have any substantial repercussions on other items in the line.

The controller prepared estimated costs of item 345 at various volumes of production (Table 2). These estimated costs reflected current labor and material costs. They were based on past experience except for the estimates of 75,000 and 100,000 yards. The company had produced more than 100,000 yards in each of the last 10 years, and earlier experience was not applicable because of equipment changes and increases in labor productivity.

Table 2
Estimated Cost Per Yard of Item 345 at
Various Volumes of Production

	75,000	100,000	125,000	150,000	175,000	200,000
Direct labor	$ .800	$ .780	$ .760	$ .740	$ .760	$ .800
Direct material	.400	.400	.400	.400	.400	.400
Material spoilage	.040	.040	.038	.038	.038	.040
Department expense:						
Direct*	.120	.112	.100	.100	.100	.100
Indirect†	.800	.600	.480	.400	.343	.300
General overhead‡	.240	.234	.228	.222	.228	.240
Manufacturing cost	$2.400	$2.166	$2.006	$1.900	$1.869	$1.880
Selling and administrative expense§	1.560	1.408	1.304	1.235	1.215	1.222
Total cost	$3.960	$3.574	$3.310	$3.135	$3.084	$3.102

* Indirect labor, supplies, repairs, power, etc.
† Depreciation, supervision, etc.
‡ 30 percent of direct labor.
§ 65 percent of factory cost.

REQUIRED: There is no single right or wrong answer to the following questions. You will have to make considered judgments about the reactions of Atherton's competitors and in your analysis of cost behavior.

1. How, if at all, did the company's financial condition relate to the pricing decision?
2. Should $3 or $4 have been recommended? Assume no other prices are being considered. (Hint: Assume that indirect department expense is a fixed cost, and that both general overhead and selling and administrative expense are fixed costs that appear variable only because of the allocation methods used.)
3. What information not in the case would you like to have in making this pricing decision?

Case 14-41 Pricing with Limited Capacity.[8] In the spring of 19x3, the Martall Blanket Division was negotiating a large contract for blankets with the U.S. Veterans Administration (VA). A question arose as to the method that should be used in estimating the price that the division would ask for these blankets.

In January 19x3, the production manager prepared an estimate of production for the 19x3–19x4 season. This estimate, shown in Table 1, was made on the assumption that the mill would be operated at three-shift capacity. There was general agreement in the division that demand was strong enough to warrant capacity operations for the foreseeable future. Production facilities could be used to make any of the blankets shown in Table 1 interchangeably.

The production estimate was sent to the Accounting Department, which prepared cost and selling price estimates for each blanket. Raw-material prices were obtained by averaging the prices of wool on hand and the prices of expected purchases for the period of the budget. Standard costs for labor, manufacturing overhead, and processing materials were added to raw-material costs to arrive at a total manufacturing cost per blanket. These standard costs had been estimated in 19x0, but were corrected subsequently for actual cost experience through ratios applied to labor, manufacturing overhead, and processing materials. Selling, advertising, and administrative charges were added at $72 per loom. As a measure of output, a "loom" meant the number of blankets that could be produced on one loom running for 40 hours. (At $72 a loom it was possible to absorb these charges at 85 percent of three-shift capacity.)

Profit was also computed on a similar loom basis at $180 per loom. This $180 rate was set so as to return to the blanket division $486,000 profit for the year at three-shift operations. This was considered a reasonable return on investment by management. Thus, the cost and pricing sheet submitted by the Accounting Department (Table 2) furnished the prices at which the various types of blankets would have to be sold in order to realize the budgeted total profit.

The "units per loom" column on Table 2 showed the number of blankets that could be produced on one loom running for 40 hours.

Table 1
Martall Blanket Division
Production Estimate 19x3–19x4

Style	Size	Weight	Quantity
Ashmont	72 × 90	3.75 lb	12,000
Velona	72 × 90	4.00 lb.	26,000
Fairfax	72 × 90	5.00 lb.	22,000
Total domestic			60,000
DSA	66 × 84	3.75 lb.	75,000
VA	66 × 90	4.25 lb.	25,000
Total			160,000

[8] Copyright 1983 by the President and Fellows of Harvard College. This case was prepared as the basis for class discussion rather than to illustrate either effective or ineffective handling of an administrative situation. Reprinted with the permission of the Harvard Business School. This case (184-062) was prepared by Charles J. Christenson.

Table 2
Martall Blanket Division
Computation of Costs and Selling Prices
for 19x1–19x2

Style	Size	Weight	Raw Material	Labor	Expense	Processing Materials	Total Mfg. Cost	Units per Loom	Selling and Administrative per Loom	per Blanket	Total Cost	Profit per Loom	Profit per Blanket	Net Selling Price
Ashmont	72 × 90 in.	3.75 lb.	$12.36	$2.79	$1.98	$1.74	$18.87	64	$72.00	$1.13	$20.00	$180.00	$2.81	$22.81
Velona	72 × 90 in.	4.00 lb.	13.17	2.82	1.98	1.74	19.71	60	72.00	1.20	20.91	180.00	3.00	23.91
Fairfax	72 × 90 in.	5.00 lb.	16.29	3.09	2.22	1.77	23.37	56	72.00	1.29	24.66	180.00	3.21	27.87
DSA	66 × 84 in.	3.75 lb.	14.49	2.97	1.89	0.54	19.89	70	72.00	1.03	20.92	180.00	2.57	23.49
VA	66 × 90 in.	4.25 lb.	17.55	3.24	1.92	0.57	23.28	54	72.00	1.33	24.61	180.00	3.33	27.94

The government contracts manager questioned the selling price that the cost department had calculated for VA blankets. He pointed out that at this selling price, the profit on the VA blankets would be 13.5 percent of cost, whereas the profit on Defense Supply Agency (DSA) blankets would be only 12.3 percent of cost. Furthermore, the profit margin on VA blankets was higher, both in absolute terms and as a percentage of cost, than the profit on any of the domestic blankets. The DSA contract had already been negotiated at $23.49 per blanket, and the contracts manager knew that the VA would be most reluctant to pay a price that was out of line with the price the DSA paid. The division gave the government negotiators full access to all of its cost information.

The contracts manager realized that the difference in profit margins arose because of the manner in which selling and administrative cost and profit were allocated. He asked the Accounting Department manager either to provide an adequate justification of the price computed in Table 2 or to recalculate the price. The Accounting Department manager replied with a memorandum, which included the following:

The problem of overhead (used hereafter to include selling and administrative charges) and profit distribution is probably the most important source of possible error. While the loom basis of allocation of these items is arbitrary in certain respects and may therefore be misleading, it is certainly not without logical foundation.

The fair basis of allocating profit and overhead apparently depends upon the market conditions existing at the time. If the division can produce all that can be sold, profit and overhead may well be distributed on a per blanket basis; that is, we could add a certain percent to each type of blanket for overhead and profit, as you suggested. On the other hand, if total capacity can be sold, the distribution on some measure of capacity, such as loom hours, will provide the fair answer, for such a method takes into account the time required to produce each blanket.

In allocating overhead and profit on a loom basis we have assumed that total blanket division capacity would be completely sold out for the coming fiscal year. For this reason I feel that the blanket prices previously submitted to you are justified.

REQUIRED:

1. At what price should the VA blankets be sold?
2. How should the contracts manager explain this price when negotiating with the Veterans Administration?

City of
Mountainview

Chapter 15

Capital Expenditure Decisions: An Introduction

After completing this chapter, you should be able to:

- Explain the importance of the time value of money in capital-budgeting decisions.

- Compute the future value and present value of cash flows occurring over several time periods.

- Use the net-present-value method and the internal-rate-of-return method to evaluate an investment proposal.

- Compare the net-present-value and internal-rate-of-return methods, and state the assumptions underlying each method.

- Use both the total-cost approach and the incremental-cost approach to evaluate an investment proposal.

- Describe a typical capital-budgeting approval process, and explain the concept of a postaudit.

- Explain the potential conflict between using discounted-cash-flow analysis for approving capital projects and accrual accounting for periodic performance evaluation.

- Describe the process of justifying investments in advanced manufacturing technology.

Managers in all organizations periodically face major decisions that involve cash flows over several years. Decisions involving the acquisition of machinery, vehicles, buildings, or land are examples of such decisions. Other examples include decisions involving significant changes in a production process or adding a major new line of products or services to the organization's activities.

Decisions involving cash inflows and outflows beyond the current year are called **capital-budgeting** decisions. Managers encounter two types of capital-budget decisions.

City of
Mountainview

1.

Acceptance-or-Rejection Decisions These decisions occur when managers must decide whether or not they should undertake a particular capital investment project. In such a decision, the required funds are available or readily obtainable, and management must decide whether the project is worthwhile. For example, the controller for the city of Mountainview is faced with a decision as to whether to replace one of the city's oldest street-cleaning machines. The funds are available in the city's capital budget. The question is whether the cost savings with the new machine will justify the expenditure. The analysis of acceptance-or-rejection decisions is the focus of this chapter.

2.

Capital-Rationing Decisions In these decisions, managers must decide which of several worthwhile projects makes the best use of limited investment funds. To illustrate, suppose the voters in the city of Mountainview have recently passed a proposition mandating the city government to undertake a cost-reduction program to trim administrative expenses. The voters also passed a bond issue, which enables the city government to raise $100,000 through the sale of bonds, to provide capital to finance the cost-reduction program. The mayor has in mind three cost-reduction programs, each of which would reduce administrative costs significantly over the next five years. However, the city can afford only two of the programs with the $100,000 of investment capital available. The mayor's decision problem is to decide which projects to pursue. Capital-rationing (or ranking) decisions are discussed in Chapter 16.

Focus on Projects Capital-budgeting problems tend to focus on specific projects or programs. Is it best for Mountainview to purchase the new street cleaner or not? Which cost-reduction programs will provide the city with the greatest benefits? Should a university buy a new electron microscope? Should a manufacturing firm acquire a computer-integrated-manufacturing system?

Over time, as managers make decisions about a variety of specific programs and projects, the organization as a whole becomes the sum total of its individual investments, activities, programs, and projects. The organization's performance in any particular year is the combined result of all the projects under way during that year. Exhibit 15-1 depicts this project viewpoint of an organization's activities.

CONCEPT OF PRESENT VALUE

Before we can study the capital-budgeting methods used to make decisions such as those faced in the city of Mountainview, we first must examine the basic tools used in those methods. The fundamental concept in a capital-budgeting decision analysis is the *time value of money.* Would you rather receive a $100 gift check from a relative today, or would you rather receive a letter promising the $100 in a year? Most of us would rather have the cash now. There are two possible reasons for this attitude. First, if we receive the money today, we can spend it on that new sweater now instead of waiting a year. Second, as an alternative strategy, we can invest the $100 received today at 10 percent interest. Then, at the end of one year, we will have $110. Thus, there is a time value associated with money. A $100 cash flow today is not the same as a $100 cash flow in one year, two years, or ten years.

Compound Interest Suppose you invest $100 today (time 0) at 10 percent interest for one year. How much will you have after one year? The answer is $110, as the following analysis shows.

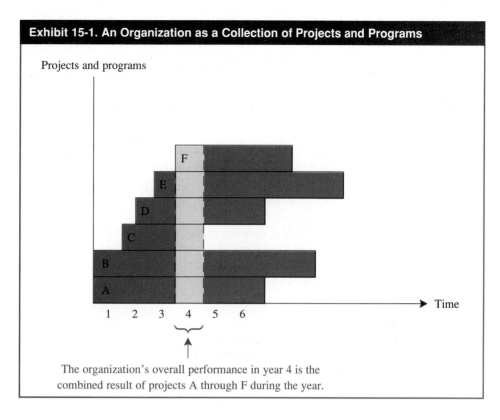

Exhibit 15-1. An Organization as a Collection of Projects and Programs

Projects and programs

The organization's overall performance in year 4 is the
combined result of projects A through F during the year.

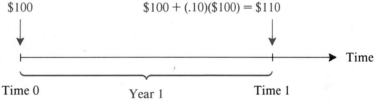

The $110 at time 1 (end of one year) is composed of two parts, as shown below.

Principal, time 0 amount. $100
Interest earned during year 1 (.10 × $100).   10
Amount at time 1. . . . . $110

Thus, the $110 at time 1 consists of the $100 at time 0, called the **principal,** plus the
$10 of interest earned during the year.

Now suppose you leave your $110 invested during the second year. How much
will you have at the end of two years? As the following analysis shows, the answer is
$121.

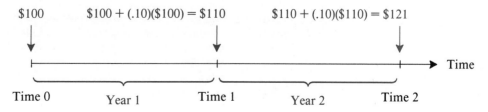

We can break down the $121 at time 2 into two parts as follows:

Amount at time 1.. $110
Interest earned during year 2 (.10 × $110)................................. 11
Amount at time 2.. $121

Notice that you earned more interest in year 2 ($11) than you earned in year 1 ($10). Why? During year 2, you earned 10 percent interest on the original principal of $100 *and* you earned 10 percent interest on the year 1 interest of $10. When interest is earned on prior periods' interest, we call the phenomenon **compound interest.** Exhibit 15-2 shows how your invested funds grow over the five-year period of the investment. As the exhibit shows, the **future value** of your initial $100 investment is $161.05 after five years.

As the number of years in an investment increases, it becomes more cumbersome to compute the future value of the investment using the method in Exhibit 15-2. Fortunately, the simple formula shown below may be used to compute the future value of any investment.

$$F_n = P(1 + r)^n \qquad (1)$$

where P = principal
         r = interest rate per year
         n = number of years

Using formula (1) to compute the future value after five years of your $100 investment, we have the following computation.

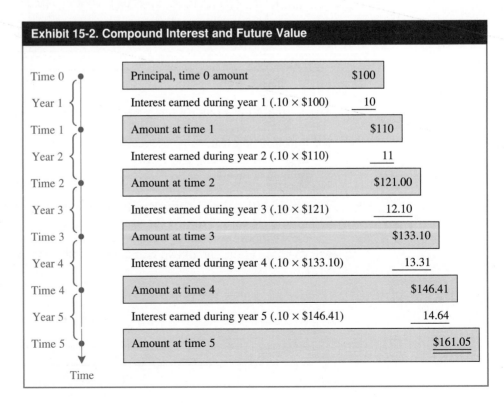

Exhibit 15-2. Compound Interest and Future Value

Time 0	Principal, time 0 amount	$100
Year 1	Interest earned during year 1 (.10 × $100)	10
Time 1	Amount at time 1	$110
Year 2	Interest earned during year 2 (.10 × $110)	11
Time 2	Amount at time 2	$121.00
Year 3	Interest earned during year 3 (.10 × $121)	12.10
Time 3	Amount at time 3	$133.10
Year 4	Interest earned during year 4 (.10 × $133.10)	13.31
Time 4	Amount at time 4	$146.41
Year 5	Interest earned during year 5 (.10 × $146.41)	14.64
Time 5	Amount at time 5	$161.05

Time

$$F_n = P(1 + r)^n$$
$$= \$100(1 + .10)^5$$
$$= \$100(1.6105) = \$161.05$$

The value of $(1 + r)^n$ is called the **accumulation factor.** The values of $(1 + r)^n$, for various combinations of r and n, are tabulated in Table I of the appendix at the end of this chapter.

Use formula (1) and the tabulated values in Table I to compute the future value after 10 years of an $800 investment that earns interest at the rate of 12 percent per year.[1]

Present Value In the discussion above, we computed the future value of an investment when the original principal is known. Now consider a slightly different problem. Suppose you know how much money you want to accumulate at the end of a five-year investment. Your problem is to determine how much your initial investment needs to be in order to accumulate the desired amount in five years. To solve this problem, we start with formula (1)

$$F_n = P(1 + r)^n$$

Now divide each side of the equation above by $(1 + r)^n$.

$$P = F_n \left(\frac{1}{(1 + r)^n} \right) \tag{2}$$

In formula (2), P denotes what is commonly referred to as the **present value** of the cash flow F_n, which occurs after n years when the interest rate is r.

Let's try out formula (2) on your investment problem, which we analyzed in Exhibit 15-2. Suppose you did not know the value of the initial investment required if you want to accumulate $161.05 at the end of five years in an investment that earns 10 percent per year. We can determine the present value of the investment as follows:

$$P = F_n \left(\frac{1}{(1 + r)^n} \right)$$
$$= \$161.05 \left(\frac{1}{(1 + .10)^5} \right)$$
$$= \$161.05(.6209) = \$100$$

Thus, as we knew already, you must invest $100 now in order to accumulate $161.05 after five years in an investment earning 10 percent per year. The *present value* of $100 and the *future value* of $161.05 at time 5 are *economically equivalent,* given that the annual interest rate is 10 percent. If you are planning to invest the $100 received now, then you should be indifferent between receiving the present value of $100 now or receiving the future value of $161.05 at the end of five years.

When we used formula (2) to compute the present value of the $161.05 cash flow at time 5, we used a process called *discounting.* The interest rate used when we

---

[1] Using formula (1): $F = \$800(1 + .12)^{10}$. From Table I, $(1 + .12)^{10} = 3.1058$. Thus, the future value of the investment is $(\$800)(3.1058) = \$2,484.64$. Compound interest will more than triple the original $800 investment in 10 years.

discount a future cash flow to compute its present value is called the **discount rate.** The value of $1/(1 + r)^n$, which appears in formula (2), is called the *discount factor.* Discount factors, for various combinations of r and n, are tabulated in Table III of the appendix.

Suppose you want to accumulate $18,000 to buy a new car in four years, and you can earn interest at the rate of 8 percent per year on an investment you make now. How much do you need to invest now? Use formula (2) and the discount factors in Table III to compute the present value of the required $18,000 amount needed at the end of four years.[2]

Present Value of a Cash-Flow Series The present-value problem we just solved involved only a single future cash flow. Now consider a slightly different problem. Suppose you just won $5,000 in the state lottery. You want to spend some of the cash now, but you have decided to save enough to rent a beach condominium during spring break of each of the next three years. You would like to deposit enough in a bank account now so that you can withdraw $1,000 from the account at the end of each of the next three years. The money in the bank account will earn 8 percent per year. The question, then, is how much do you need to deposit? Another way of asking the same question is, what is the *present value* of a series of three $1,000 cash flows at the end of each of the next three years, given that the discount rate is 8 percent?

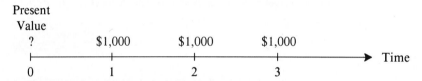

One way to figure out the answer to the question is to compute the present value of each of the three $1,000 cash flows and add the three present-value amounts. We can use formula (2) for these calculations, as shown in panel A of Exhibit 15-3. Notice that the present value of each of the $1,000 cash flows is different, because the timing of the cash flows is different. The earlier the cash flow will occur, the higher is its present value.

Examine panel A of Exhibit 15-3 carefully. We obtained the $2,577 total present value by adding three present-value amounts. Each of these amounts is the result of multiplying $1,000 by a discount factor. Notice that we can obtain the same final result by adding the three discount factors first, and then multiplying by $1,000. This approach is taken in panel B of Exhibit 15-3. The sum of the three discount factors is called an *annuity discount factor,* because a series of equivalent cash flows is called an **annuity.** Annuity discount factors for various combinations of r and n are tabulated in Table IV of the appendix.

Now let's verify that $2,577 is the right amount to finance your three spring-break vacations. Exhibit 15-4 shows how your bank account will change over the three-year period as you earn interest and then withdraw $1,000 each year.

Future Value of a Cash-Flow Series To complete our discussion of present-value and future-value concepts, let's consider the series of $1,000 condo rental payments from the condo owner's perspective. Suppose the owner invests each $1,000

---

[2] Using formula (2): $P = \$18,000 \times [1/(1 + .08)^4]$. From Table III, $1/(1 + .08)^4 = .7350$. Thus, the present value of the required $18,000 amount is ($18,000)(.7350) = $13,230. An investment of $13,230 made now, earning annual interest of 8 percent, will accumulate to $18,000 at the end of four years.

Exhibit 15-3. Present Value of a Series of Cash Flows

Present-value formula [formula (2)]: $P = F_n \left(\dfrac{1}{(1 + r)^n} \right)$

Present value of time 1 cash flow: $\$1{,}000 \left(\dfrac{1}{(1 + .08)^1} \right) = \$1{,}000(.9259) = \$\ 925.90$

Present value of time 2 cash flow: $\$1{,}000 \left(\dfrac{1}{(1 + .08)^2} \right) = \$1{,}000(.8573) = \quad 857.30$

Present value of time 3 cash flow: $\$1{,}000 \left(\dfrac{1}{(1 + .08)^3} \right) = \$1{,}000(.7938) = \quad \underline{793.80}$

Total: present value of series of three cash flows $\qquad\qquad \underline{\underline{\$2{,}577.00}}$

**(A) Present value of cash-flow series using three
independent present-value calculations**

Sum of Three
Discount Factors

Present value of series of three cash flows = $\$1{,}000(2.5770) = \underline{\underline{\$2{,}577.00}}$

**(B) Present value of cash-flow series using the
annuity discount factor**

---

rental payment in a bank account that pays 8 percent interest per year. How much will the condo owner accumulate at the end of the three-year period? An equivalent question is, What is the future value of the three-year series of $1,000 cash flows, given an annual interest rate of 8 percent? Exhibit 15-5 answers the question in two ways. In panel A of the exhibit, three separate future-value calculations are made using formula (1). Notice that the $1,000 cash flow at time 1 is multiplied by $(1.08)^2$, since it has two years to earn interest. The $1,000 cash flow at time 2 has only one year to earn interest, and the time 3 cash flow has no time to earn interest.

In panel B of the exhibit, the three-year *annuity accumulation factor* is used. This factor is the sum of the three accumulation factors used in panel A of the exhibit. The annuity accumulation factors for various combinations of r and n are tabulated in Table II of the appendix.

Using the Tables Correctly When using the tables in the appendix to solve future-value and present-value problems, be sure to select the correct table. Table I is used to find the *future value* of a *single* cash flow, and Table III is used to find the *present value* of a *single* cash flow. Table II is used in finding the *future value* of a *series* of identical cash flows; Table IV is used in finding the *present value* of a *series* of identical cash flows. Be careful not to confuse future value with present value or to confuse a single cash flow with a series of identical cash flows.

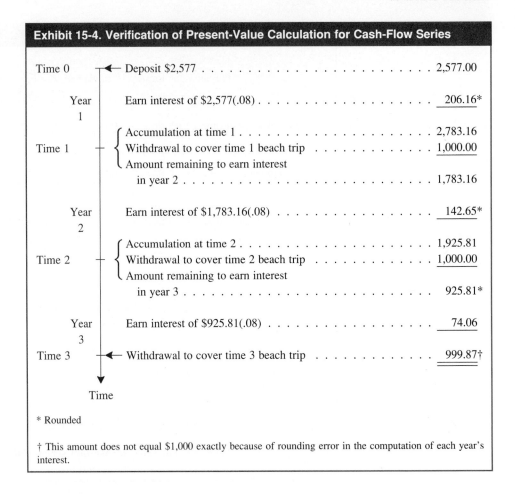

Exhibit 15-4. Verification of Present-Value Calculation for Cash-Flow Series

Time 0	◄── Deposit $2,577	2,577.00
Year 1	Earn interest of $2,577(.08)	206.16*
Time 1	Accumulation at time 1	2,783.16
	Withdrawal to cover time 1 beach trip	1,000.00
	Amount remaining to earn interest in year 2	1,783.16
Year 2	Earn interest of $1,783.16(.08)	142.65*
Time 2	Accumulation at time 2	1,925.81
	Withdrawal to cover time 2 beach trip	1,000.00
	Amount remaining to earn interest in year 3	925.81*
Year 3	Earn interest of $925.81(.08)	74.06
Time 3	◄── Withdrawal to cover time 3 beach trip	999.87†

Time

* Rounded

† This amount does not equal $1,000 exactly because of rounding error in the computation of each year's interest.

If you have a calculator that will exponentiate (raise a number to a power), you can forget the tables altogether. Just use the pertinent formula and compute the appropriate factor yourself.

DISCOUNTED-CASH-FLOW ANALYSIS

City of
Mountainview

With our review of future-value and present-value tools behind us, we can return to the main issue of how to evaluate capital-investment projects. Our discussion will be illustrated by several decisions made by the Mountainview city government. The Controller of Mountainview routinely advises the mayor and City Council on major capital-investment decisions.

Currently under consideration is the purchase of a new street cleaner. The Controller has estimated that the city's old street-cleaning machine would last another five years. A new street cleaner, which also would last for five years, can be purchased for $50,470. It would cost the city $14,000 less each year to operate the new equipment than it costs to operate the old machine. The expected cost savings with the new machine are due to lower expected maintenance costs. Thus, the new street cleaner will cost $50,470 and save $70,000 over its five-year life ($70,000 = 5 × $14,000 savings per year). Since the $70,000 in cost savings exceeds the $50,470 acquisition cost, one might be tempted to conclude that the new machine should be purchased.

Exhibit 15-5. Future Value of a Series of Cash Flows

Present-value formula [formula (1)]: $F_n = P(1 + r)^n$

Future value of time 1 cash flow: $1,000 $(1 + .08)^2$ = $1,000(1.1664) = $1,166.40

Future value of time 2 cash flow: $1,000 $(1 + .08)^1$ = $1,000(1.0800) =   1,080.00

Future value of time 3 cash flow: $1,000   = $1,000(1.0000) =   1,000.00

Total: future value of series of three cash flows $3,246.40

**(A) Future value of cash-flow series using three
independent future-value calculations**

Sum of Three
Accumulation Factors

Present value of series of three cash flows = $1,000(3.2464) = $3,246.40

**(B) Future value of cash-flow series using the
annuity accumulation factor**

However, *this analysis is flawed, since it does not account for the time value of money.*
The $50,470 acquisition cost will occur now, but the cost savings are spread over a
five-year period. It is a mistake to add cash flows occurring at different points in time.
The proper approach is to use **discounted-cash-flow analysis,** which takes account of
the timing of the cash flows. There are two widely used methods of discounted-cash-
flow analysis: the net-present-value method and the internal-rate-of-return method.

Net-Present-Value-Method

The following four steps comprise a net-present-value analysis of an investment
proposal:

1. Prepare a table showing the cash flows during each year of the proposed
   investment.
2. Compute the present value of each cash flow, using a discount rate that
   reflects the cost of acquiring investment capital. This discount rate is often
   called the **hurdle rate** or **minimum desired rate of return.**
3. Compute the **net present value,** which is the sum of the present values of
   the cash flows.
4. If the net present value (NPV) is positive, accept the investment proposal.
   Otherwise, reject it.

Exhibit 15-6 displays these four steps for the Mountainview controller's street-
cleaner decision. In step (2) the controller used a discount rate of 10 percent. Notice

Exhibit 15-6. Net-Present-Value Method

Mountainview City Government
Purchase of Street Cleaner
$(r = .10, n = 5)$

City of
Mountainview

Step 1

	Time 0	Time 1	Time 2	Time 3	Time 4	Time 5
Acquisition cost	$(50,470)					
Annual cost savings		$14,000	$14,000	$14,000	$14,000	$14,000

Step 2

Present value
of annuity $= \$14,000 \ (3.791)$

Annuity discount
factor for $r = .10$
and $n = 5$ from
Table IV in the
appendix.

Present value	$(50,470)			$53,074		

Step 3   Net present value $2,604

Step 4   Accept proposal, since net present value is positive.

that the cost savings are $14,000 in each of the years 1 through 5. Thus, the cash flows in those years comprise a five-year, $14,000 annuity. The controller used the annuity discount factor to compute the present value of the five years of cost savings.

The net-present-value analysis indicates that the city should purchase the new street cleaner. The present value of the cost savings exceeds the new machine's acquisition cost.

Internal-Rate-of-Return Method

An alternative discounted-cash-flow method for analyzing investment proposals is the internal-rate-of-return method. An asset's **internal rate of return** (or **time-adjusted rate of return**) is the true economic return earned by the asset over its life. Another way of stating the definition is that an asset's *internal rate of return (IRR)* is the discount rate that would be required in a net-present-value analysis in order for the asset's net present value to be exactly *zero.*

What is the internal rate of return on Mountainview's proposed street-cleaner acquisition? Recall that the asset has a positive net present value, given that the city's cost of acquiring investment capital is 10 percent. Would you expect the asset's IRR to be higher or lower than 10 percent? Think about this question intuitively. The higher the discount rate used in a net-present-value analysis, the lower the present value of all future cash flows will be. This is true because a higher discount rate means that it is even more important to have the money earlier instead of later. Thus, a discount rate higher than 10 percent would be required to drive the new street cleaner's net present value down to zero.

Finding the Internal Rate of Return How can we find this rate? One way is trial and error. We could experiment with different discount rates until we find the one that yields a zero net present value. We already know that a 10 percent discount rate yields a positive NPV. Let's try 14 percent. Discounting the five-year, $14,000 cost-savings annuity at 14 percent yields a negative NPV of ($2,408).

$$(3.433)(\$14,000) - \$50,470 = (\$2,408)$$

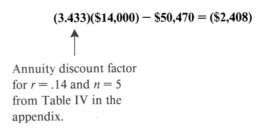

Annuity discount factor
for $r = .14$ and $n = 5$
from Table IV in the
appendix.

What does this negative NPV at a 14 percent discount rate mean? We increased the discount rate too much. Therefore, the street cleaner's internal rate of return must lie between 10 percent and 14 percent. Let's try 12 percent:

$$(3.605)(\$14,000) - \$50,470 = 0$$

Annuity discount factor
for $r = .12$ and $n = 5$
from Table IV in the
appendix.

That's it. The new street cleaner's internal rate of return is 12 percent. With a 12 percent discount factor, the investment proposal's net present value is zero, since the street cleaner's acquisition cost is equal to the present value of the cost savings.

We could have found the internal rate of return more easily in this case, because the street cleaner's cash flows exhibit a very special pattern. The cash inflows in years 1 through 5 are identical, as shown below.

Time	0	1	2	3	4	5
Cash flow	($50,470)	$14,000	$14,000	$14,000	$14,000	$14,000

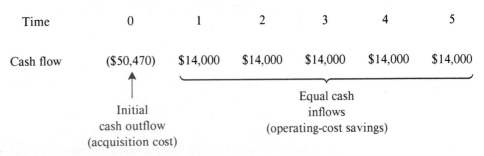

Initial
cash outflow
(acquisition cost)

Equal cash
inflows
(operating-cost savings)

When we have this special pattern of cash flows, the internal rate of return is determined in two steps, as follows:

1. Divide the initial cash outflow by the equivalent annual cash inflows:

$$\frac{\$50,470}{\$14,000} = 3.605 = \text{annuity discount factor}$$

2. In Table IV, find the discount rate associated with the annuity discount factor computed above, given the appropriate number of years in the annuity.

		r		
From Table IV **of the appendix**		10%	12%	14%
	$n = 5$	3.791	3.605	3.433

Decision Rule Now that we have determined the investment proposal's internal rate of return to be 12 percent, how do we use this fact in making a decision? The decision rule in the internal-rate-of-return method is to accept an investment proposal if its internal rate of return is greater than the organization's cost of capital (or hurdle rate). Thus, Mountainview's Controller should recommend that the new street cleaner be purchased. The internal rate of return on the proposal, 12 percent, exceeds the city's hurdle rate, 10 percent.

To summarize, the internal rate of return method of discounted-cash-flow analysis includes the following three steps:

1. Prepare a table showing the cash flows during each year of the proposed investment. This table will be identical to the cash-flow table prepared under the net-present-value method. (See Exhibit 15-6.)
2. Compute the internal rate of return for the proposed investment. This is accomplished by finding a discount rate that yields a zero net present value for the proposed investment.
3. If the internal rate of return is greater than the hurdle rate (cost of acquiring investment capital), accept the investment proposal. Otherwise, reject it.

Recovery of Investment The reason for purchasing an asset is an expectation that it will provide benefits in the future. Thus, Mountainview may purchase the new street cleaner because of expected future operating-cost savings. For a capital-investment proposal to be accepted, the expected future benefits must be sufficient for the purchaser to recover the investment and earn a return on the investment equal to or greater than the cost of acquiring capital. We can illustrate this point with Mountainview's street-cleaner acquisition.

Exhibit 15-7 examines the investment proposal's cash flows from the perspective of recovering the investment and earning a return on the investment. Focus on the Year 1 column in the exhibit. The street cleaner costs $50,470, so this is the unrecovered investment at the beginning of year 1. The operating-cost savings in year 1 are $14,000. Since the asset's internal rate of return is 12 percent, it must earn $6,056 during the first year (12% × $50,470). Therefore, $6,056 of the $14,000 cost savings represents a *return on* the unrecovered investment. This leaves $7,944 as a *recovery of* the investment during year 1 ($14,000 − $6,056). Subtracting the year 1 recovery of investment from the unrecovered investment at the beginning of the year leaves an unrecovered investment of $42,526 at year-end ($50,470 − $7,944).

Interpolation Sometimes it is more difficult to find a project's internal rate of return because the IRR is not a whole-number percentage, such as 12 percent. To

---

Exhibit 15-7. Recovery of Investment and Return on Investment

Mountainview City Government
Purchase of Street Cleaner
(r = .12, n = 5)

	Year 1	Year 2	Year 3	Year 4	Year 5
(1) Unrecovered investment at beginning of year	$50,470	$42,526	$33,629	$23,664	$12,503
(2) Cost savings during year	14,000	14,000	14,000	14,000	14,000
(3) Return on unrecovered investment [12% × amount in row (1)]	6,056	5,103	4,035	2,839	1,500
(4) Recovery of investment during year [row (2) amount minus row (3) amount]	7,944	8,897	9,965	11,161	12,500
(5) Unrecovered investment at end of year [row (1) amount minus row (4) amount]	42,526	33,629	23,664	12,503	3*

* We are left with an unrecovered investment of $3 because of accumulated rounding errors in the table. If we had carried out each number to cents, the table would have finished up with an unrecovered investment of zero.

---

illustrate, suppose the street cleaner costs $52,500 instead of $50,470. Applying the two-step procedure given earlier for finding the IRR, we first divide the acquisition cost by the annual cost savings, as follows:

$$\frac{\text{New assumed acquisition cost}}{\text{Annual cost savings}} = \frac{\$52,500}{14,000} = 3.750$$

Then we try to find the annuity discount factor, 3.750, in the five-year row of Table IV, as shown below.

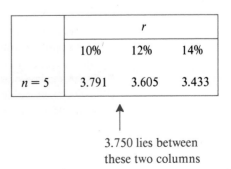

From Table IV of the appendix		r	
	10%	12%	14%
n = 5	3.791	3.605	3.433

↑
3.750 lies between
these two columns

Notice that 3.750 does not appear in the table, but it does lie between 3.791 and 3.605. Thus, we must interpolate to find the correct IRR, which is between 10 percent and 12 percent. This calculation is shown below.

	Rate		Annuity Discount Factor From Table IV
	10% 3.791		3.791
Difference of 2%	True IRR		3.750
	12% 3.605		
	Difference. 186		.041

$$\text{Internal rate of return} = 10\% + \left(\frac{.041}{.186}\right)(2\%) = 10.44\%$$

Thus, the internal rate of return on the street cleaner, if the machine costs $52,500, is 10.44 percent.

Uneven Cash Flows Another complication that often arises in finding a project's internal rate of return is an uneven pattern of cash flows. In Mountainview's proposed street-cleaner acquisition, the cost savings are $14,000 per year for all five years of the machine's life. Suppose, instead, that the pattern of cost savings is as follows:

Cost savings	$14,000	$14,000	$12,000	$10,000	$8,000	Time
Year	1	2	3	4	5	

Such an uneven cost-savings pattern is quite plausible, since the maintenance costs could rise in the machine's latter years. When the cash-flow pattern is uneven, iteration must be used to find the internal rate of return. You can try various discount rates iteratively until you find the one that yields a zero net present value for the investment proposal. This sort of computationally intensive work is the kind of task for which computers are designed. Numerous computer software packages are available to find a project's IRR almost instantaneously.

Comparing the NPV and IRR Methods

The decision to accept or reject an investment proposal can be made using either the net-present-value method or the internal-rate-of-return method. The different approaches used in the methods are summarized as follows:

Net-Present-Value Method	**Internal-Rate-of-Return Method**
1. Compute the investment proposal's net present value, using the organization's cost of capital *(hurdle rate)* as the discount rate.	1. Compute the investment proposal's internal rate of return, which is the discount rate that yields a zero net present value for the project.
2. Accept the investment proposal if its net present value is equal to or greater than zero; otherwise reject it.	2. Accept the investment proposal if its internal rate of return is equal to or greater than the organization's cost of capital *(hurdle rate);* otherwise reject it.

Notice that the hurdle rate is used in each of the two methods that are shown.

Advantages of Net Present Value Method The net-present-value method exhibits two potential advantages over the internal-rate-of-return method. First, if the investment analysis is carried out by hand, it is easier to compute a project's NPV than its IRR. For example, if the cash flows are uneven across time, trial and error must be used to find the IRR. This advantage of the NPV approach is not as important, however, when a computer is used.

A second potential advantage of the NPV method is that the analyst can adjust for risk considerations. For some investment proposals, the further into the future that a cash flow occurs, the less certain the analyst can be about the amount of the cash flow. Thus, the later a projected cash flow occurs, the riskier it may be. It is possible to adjust a net-present-value analysis for such risk factors by using a higher discount rate for later cash flows than earlier cash flows. It is not possible to include such a risk adjustment in the internal-rate-of-return method, because the analysis solves for only a single discount rate, the project's IRR.

Assumptions Underlying Discounted-Cash-Flow Analysis

As is true of any decision model, discounted-cash-flow methods are based on assumptions. Four assumptions underlie the NPV and IRR methods of investment analysis.

1. In the present-value calculations used in the NPV and IRR methods, all cash flows are treated as though they occur at year end. If the city of Mountainview were to acquire the new street cleaner, the $14,000 in annual operating-cost savings actually would occur uniformly throughout each year. The additional computational complexity that would be required to reflect the exact timing of all cash flows would complicate an investment analysis considerably. The error introduced by the year-end cash-flow assumption generally is not large enough to cause any concern.
2. Discounted cash-flow analyses treat the cash flows associated with an investment project as though they were known with certainty. Although methods of capital budgeting under uncertainty have been developed, they are not used widely in practice. Most decision makers do not feel that the additional benefits in improved decisions are worth the additional complexity involved. As mentioned above, however, risk adjustments can be made in an NPV analysis to partially account for uncertainty about the cash flows.
3. Both the NPV and IRR methods assume that each cash inflow is immediately reinvested in another project that earns a return for the organization. In the NPV method, each cash inflow is assumed to be reinvested at the same rate used to compute the project's NPV, generally the organization's cost of capital. In the IRR method, each cash inflow is assumed to be reinvested at the same rate as the project's internal rate of return.

   What does this reinvestment assumption mean in practice? In the case of Mountainview's proposed new street cleaner, the city must instantly reinvest the money saved each year either in some interest-bearing investment or in some other capital project.

4. A discounted-cash-flow analysis assumes a perfect capital market. This implies that money can be borrowed or lent at an interest rate equal to the cost of capital (or hurdle rate) used in the analysis.

In practice, these four assumptions rarely are satisfied. Nevertheless, discounted-cash-flow models provide an effective and widely used method of investment analysis. The improved decision making that would result from using more complicated models seldom is worth the additional cost of information and analysis.

Choosing the Hurdle Rate

The choice of a hurdle rate is a complex problem in finance. The hurdle rate is determined by management based on the **investment opportunity rate.** This is the rate of return the organization can earn on its best alternative investments of equivalent risk. In general, the greater a project's risk is, the higher the hurdle rate should be.

Investment versus Financing Decisions In capital-expenditure decisions, the investment decision should be separated from the financing decision. The decision as to whether to invest in a project should be made first using a discounted-cash-flow approach with a hurdle rate based on the investment opportunity rate. If a project is accepted, then a separate analysis should be made as to the best way to finance the project.

Cost of Capital How do organizations generate investment capital? Nonprofit organizations, such as local, city, and state governments and charitable organizations, often acquire capital through special bond issues or borrowing from financial institutions. In such cases, the cost of capital is based on the interest rate paid on the debt.

Another source of capital for both nonprofit and profit-oriented organizations is invested funds, such as a university's endowment fund. In this case, the cost of using the capital for an investment project is the interest rate forgone on the original investment. For example, suppose your university's endowment earns interest at the rate of 10 percent. If the university uses a portion of these funds to buy new laboratory equipment, the cost of capital is the 10 percent interest rate that is no longer earned on the funds removed from the endowment.

Profit-oriented enterprises fund capital projects by borrowing, by issuing stock, or by using invested funds. In most cases, capital projects are funded by all of these sources. Then the cost of capital should be a combination of the costs of money from each of these sources.

Depreciable Assets

When a long-lived asset is purchased, its acquisition cost is allocated to the time periods in the asset's life through depreciation charges. However, we did not include any depreciation charges in our discounted-cash-flow analysis. Both the NPV and IRR methods focus on cash flows, and *periodic depreciation charges are not cash flows.* Suppose that the controller for the city of Mountainview depreciates assets using the straight-line method. If the city purchases the new street cleaner for $50,470, then depreciation charges will be recorded as follows:

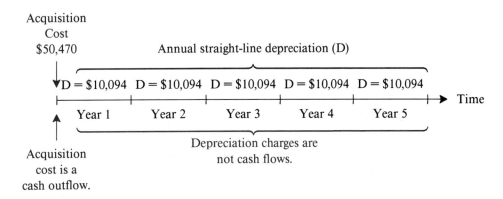

The only cash flow in the diagram above is the $50,470 cash outflow incurred to acquire the street cleaner. The $10,094 annual depreciation charges are not cash flows. Thus, the acquisition cost is recorded as a cash flow in our investment analysis (Exhibit 15-6), but the annual depreciation charges are not.

Nonprofit versus Profit-Oriented Organizations Suppose our illustration had focused on a profit-seeking enterprise instead of the city of Mountainview. For example, if the street-cleaner acquisition is contemplated by a theme-park company, would this change our treatment of the annual depreciation charges for the street cleaner? The depreciation charges still are not cash flows. However, in a profit-seeking enterprise, depreciation expense is deductible for income-tax purposes. Since tax payments *are* cash flows, the reduction in tax due to depreciation expense is a legitimate cash flow that should be included in an investment analysis. In the next chapter, we will study the tax implications of depreciable assets in detail. For now, let's return to our focus on the city of Mountainview. As a nonprofit enterprise, the city pays no income tax. Therefore, depreciation is irrelevant in our discounted cash-flow analysis.

COMPARING TWO INVESTMENT PROJECTS

We have developed all of the tools and concepts required to use discounted-cash-flow analysis in an investment decision. Now we can expand on our discussion using an illustration that combines the net-present-value method of investment analysis with the concepts of relevant costs and benefits studied in Chapter 13. The first step in any investment analysis is to determine the cash flows that are relevant to the analysis.

The computing system used by the city of Mountainview is outdated. The City Council has voted to purchase a new computing system to be funded through municipal bonds. The mayor has asked the city's controller to make a recommendation as to which of two computing systems should be purchased. The two systems are equivalent in their ability to meet the city's needs and in their ease of use. The mainframe system consists of one large mainframe computer with remote terminals and printers located throughout the city offices. The personal computer system consists of a much smaller mainframe computer, a few remote terminals, and a dozen personal computers, which will be networked to the small mainframe. Each system would last five years. The controller has decided to use a 12 percent hurdle rate for the analysis.

Exhibit 15-8 presents data pertinent to the decision. Examine these data carefully. Most of the items are self-explanatory. Item (9) is the annual cost of a data-link service. This service enables Mountainview to participate in a nationwide computer

Exhibit 15-8. Data for Extended Illustration of Net-Present-Value Analysis

Mountainview City Government
Purchase of Computing System

		Mainframe System	Personal Computer System
(1)	Salvage value of city's old computer (time 0)*.	$ 25,000	$ 25,000
(2)	Acquisition cost of new system (time 0)	(400,000)	(300,000)
(3)	Acquisition cost of software (time 0).	(40,000)	(75,000)
(4)	Cost of updating system (time 3).	(40,000)	(60,000)
(5)	Salvage value of new system (time 5)	(50,000)	(30,000)
	Operating costs (times 1, 2, 3, 4, 5):		
(6)	Personnel.	(300,000)	(220,000)
(7)	Maintenance	(25,000)	(10,000)
(8)	Other	(10,000)	(5,000)
(9)	Data-link service (times 1, 2, 3, 4, 5)	(20,000)	(20,000)
(10)	Revenue from time-share customers		
	(times 1, 2, 3, 4, 5)	20,000	–0–

*Time 0 denotes "immediately." Time 1 denotes the end of year 1, etc.

network, which allows cities to exchange information on such issues as crime rates, demographic data, and economic data. Item (10) is the revenue the city will receive from two time-sharing customers. The Mountainview City School District and the county legislature each have agreed to pay the city in return for a limited amount of time on the city's computer.

Before we begin the steps of the net-present-value method, let's examine the cash-flow data in Exhibit 15-8 to determine if any of the data can be ignored as irrelevant. Notice that items (1) and (9) do not differ between the two alternatives. Regardless of which new computing system is purchased, certain components of the old system can be sold now for $25,000. Moreover, the data-link service will cost $20,000 annually, regardless of which system is acquired. If the only purpose of the NPV analysis is to determine which computer system is the least-cost alternative, items (1) and (9) can be ignored as irrelevant, since they will affect both alternatives' NPVs equally.

Total-Cost Approach Exhibit 15-9 displays a net-present-value analysis of the two alternative computing systems. The exhibit uses the *total-cost approach,* in which all of the relevant costs of each computing system are included in the analysis. Then the net present value of the cost of the mainframe system is compared with that of the personal computer system. Since the NPV of the costs is lower with the personal computer system, that will be the controller's recommendation to the Mountainview City Council.

A decision such as Mountainview's computing-system choice, in which the objective is to select the alternative with the lowest cost, is called a *least-cost decision.*

Exhibit 15-9. Net-Present-Value Analysis: Total-Cost Approach

Mountainview City Government
Purchase of Computing System
($r = .12$, $n = 5$)

City of
Mountainview

Item Number (Exhibit 15-8)	Time 0	Time 1	Time 2	Time 3	Time 4	Time 5
Mainframe System						
(2) Acquisition cost: computer	$(400,000)					
(3) Acquisition cost: software	(40,000)					
(4) System update				$ (40,000)		
(5) Salvage value						$50,000
(6), (7), (8) Operating costs		$(335,000)	$(335,000)	$(335,000)	$(335,000)	$(335,000)
(10) Time-sharing revenue		20,000	20,000	20,000	20,000	20,000
Total cash flow	$(440,000)	$(315,000)	$(315,000)	$(355,000)	$(315,000)	$(265,000)
× Discount factor	× 1.000	× .893	× .797	× .712	× .636	× .567
Present value	$(440,000)	$(281,295)	$(251,055)	$(252,760)	$(200,340)	$(150,255)

Net present value of costs . . . .   Sum = $(1,575,705)

Item Number (Exhibit 15-8)	Time 0	Time 1	Time 2	Time 3	Time 4	Time 5
Personal Computer System						
(2) Acquisition cost: computer	$(300,000)					
(3) Acquisition cost: software	(75,000)					
(4) System update				$ (60,000)		
(5) Salvage value						$30,000
(6), (7), (8) Operating costs		$(235,000)	$(235,000)	$(235,000)	$(235,000)	$(235,000)
(10) Time-sharing revenue		–0–	–0–	–0–	–0–	–0–
Total cash flow	$(375,000)	$(235,000)	$(235,000)	$(295,000)	$(235,000)	$(205,000)
× Discount factor	× 1.000	× .893	× .797	× .712	× .636	× .567
Present value	$(375,000)	$(209,855)	$(187,295)	$(210,040)	$(149,460)	$(116,235)

Net present value of costs . . . .   Sum = $(1,247,885)

Difference in NPV of costs
  (favors personal computer system) . . . . . $ (327,820)

Rather than maximizing the NPV of cash inflows minus cash outflows, the objective is to *minimize the NPV of the costs to be incurred.*

Incremental-Cost Approach Exhibit 15-10 displays a different net-present-value analysis of the city's two alternative computing systems. This exhibit uses the **incremental-cost approach,** in which the difference in the cost of each relevant item under the two alternative systems is included in the analysis. For example, the incremental computer acquisition cost is shown in Exhibit 15-10 as $(100,000). This is the amount by which the acquisition cost of the mainframe system exceeds that of the personal computer system. The result of this analysis is that the NPV of the costs of the mainframe system exceeds that of the personal computer system by $327,820.

Exhibit 15-10. Net-Present-Value Analysis: Incremental-Cost Approach

Mountainview City Government
Purchase of Computing System
($r = .12, n = 5$)

City of
Mountainview

Item Number (Exhibit 15-8)	Time 0	Time 1	Time 2	Time 3	Time 4	Time 5
Incremental Cost of Mainframe System over Personal Computer System						
(2) Acquisition cost: computer	$(100,000)					
(3) Acquisition cost: software	35,000					
(4) System update				$ 20,000		
(5) Salvage value						$20,000
(6), (7), (8) Operating costs		$(100,000)	$(100,000)	$(100,000)	$(100,000)	$(100,000)
(10) Time-sharing revenue		20,000	20,000	20,000	20,000	20,000
Incremental cash flow	$(65,000)	$(80,000)	$(80,000)	$(60,000)	$(80,000)	$(60,000)
× Discount factor	× 1.000	× .893	× .797	× .712	× .636	× .567
Present value	$(65,000)	$(71,440)	$(63,760)	$(42,720)	$(50,880)	$(34,020)

Net present value of incremental costs
(favors personal computer system)

Sum = $(327,820)

Notice that this is the same as the difference in NPVs shown at the bottom of Exhibit 15-9.

The total-cost and incremental-cost approaches always will yield equivalent conclusions. Choosing between them is a matter of personal preference.

MANAGERIAL ACCOUNTANT'S ROLE

To use discounted-cash-flow analysis in deciding about investment projects, managers need accurate cash-flow projections. This is where the managerial accountant plays a role. The accountant often is asked to predict cash flows related to operating-cost savings, additional working-capital requirements, or incremental costs and revenues. Such predictions are difficult in a world of uncertainty. The managerial accountant often draws upon historical accounting data to help in making cost predictions. Knowledge of market conditions, economic trends, and the likely reactions of competitors also can be important in projecting cash flows.

Two techniques are used in practice to analyze investment proposals for which the cash-flow projections are very uncertain. First, the hurdle rate may be increased. The greater the uncertainty about a project's cash flows, the higher the hurdle rate. Second, the analyst may use sensitivity analysis.

Sensitivity Analysis

The project analyst can use sensitivity analysis to determine how much projections would have to change in order for a different decision to be indicated. To illustrate, let's return to Mountainview's street-cleaner decision, analyzed in Exhibit 15-6. The relevant data are as follows:

Type of Cash Flow	Cash Flow		Discount Factor		Present Value
Acquisition cost	$(50,470)	×	1.000	=	$(50,470)
Projected annual cost savings (5-year annuity)	14,000	×	3.791	=	53,074
Net present value					$ 2,604

Suppose the city's controller is uncertain about the amount of the annual cost savings. How low could the annual cost savings be before the decision would change from accept to reject? An equivalent question is the following: What annual cost-savings amount would result in a zero NPV for the new street cleaner? The answer to this question is determined below.

$$\frac{\text{Acquisition cost}}{\text{Annuity discount factor*}} = \frac{\$50,470}{3.791} = \$13,313$$

* Annuity discount factor for $n = 5$ and $r = .10$.

If the annual cost savings were $13,313, the street cleaner's NPV would be zero $[0 = \$50,470 - (\$13,313)(3.791)]$. Thus, the originally projected annual cost savings of $14,000 could fall as low as $13,313 before the controller's decision would change from accept to reject.

CAPITAL BUDGET ADMINISTRATION

Capital budgeting often involves large expenditures with far-reaching implications. An organization's long-term health can be affected significantly by its capital-budgeting decisions. Therefore, most organizations have an elaborate approval process for proposed investment projects. Often the process for making a capital-budgeting request is highly formalized. Specific forms are used, and requests are reviewed at each level of management. Many organizations have a capital-budgeting staff whose function is to analyze all capital-budgeting proposals.

The authority for final approval of capital-budgeting proposals depends on the cost of the project and the type of organization. The larger the cost of a proposal, the higher in the organization is the authority for final approval. In a city government, such as Mountainview, most capital projects would require approval by the City Council. In profit-seeking enterprises, large investment proposals usually require approval by the board of directors, often with advice from a finance committee.

ILLUSTRATION FROM MANAGERIAL-ACCOUNTING PRACTICE

American Can Company

A *Harvard Business Review* article described the capital-budgeting process used by American Can Company.[3] The firm's business-unit managers make suggestions for capital-investment projects. Operating managers provide summaries of their recommended investment projects, along with projected cash flows, as part of the annual budgeting cycle. The Corporate Planning Department consolidates the projections from the firm's various business

[3] R. Marshuetz, "How American Can Allocates Capital," *Harvard Business Review*, January–February 1985, pp. 82–91.

units. The company's Business Investment Staff combines and evaluates the major capital-budgeting decisions from the viewpoint of the company as a whole. The Business Investment Staff then makes recommendations on capital projects, which can range from dropping a project to speeding up its completion.

Postaudit

The discounted-cash-flow approach to evaluating investment proposals requires cash-flow projections. The desirability of a proposal depends heavily on those projections. If they are highly inaccurate, they may lead the organization to accept undesirable projects or to reject projects that should be pursued. Because of the importance of the capital-budgeting process, most organizations systematically follow up on projects to see how they turn out. This procedure is called a **postaudit** (or **reappraisal**).

In a postaudit, the managerial accountant gathers information about the actual cash flows generated by a project. Then the project's actual net present value or internal rate of return is computed. Finally, the projections made for the project are compared with the actual results. If the project has not lived up to expectations, an investigation may be warranted to determine what went awry. Sometimes a postaudit will reveal shortcomings in the cash-flow projection process. In such cases, action may be taken to improve future cash-flow predictions. Two types of errors can occur in discounted-cash-flow analyses: undesirable projects may be accepted, and desirable projects may be rejected. The postaudit is a tool for following up on accepted projects. Thus, a postaudit helps to detect only the first kind of error, not the second.

As in any performance-evaluation process, a postaudit should not be used punitively. The focus of a postaudit should provide information to the capital-budgeting staff, the project manager, and the management team.

Controlling Capital-Investment Expenditures

Many investment projects require a long time to complete, such as building a new power plant or developing an oil field. Then the benefits from the completed project are realized over an even longer time frame. By establishing procedures for controlling expenditures on a project as it is developed, management can help ensure that the projections for the project are realized.

To help control capital expenditures, managers rely on many of the same concepts and tools that we studied earlier in this text. Budgeted costs are compared with actual costs, variances are computed, and periodic performance reports are prepared. The cost-control process is more difficult for investment projects, because each project tends to be unique. Thus, when a cost variance is recorded, it may be difficult to determine whether the actual cost is out of line or the cost projection was faulty. Nevertheless, periodic project performance reports can direct management's attention where it is needed most.

Cost-Performance Reporting A cost and project control system used extensively in government is called the **cost-performance-reporting (CPR) system.** As work progresses on a capital project, three measurements are made periodically (say, weekly or monthly). The CPR system collects information on the actual cost incurred on the project to date, the budgeted cost of the work scheduled to date, and the budgeted cost of the work actually performed to date. This information is recorded on a cost-performance graph, such as the one shown in Exhibit 15-11.

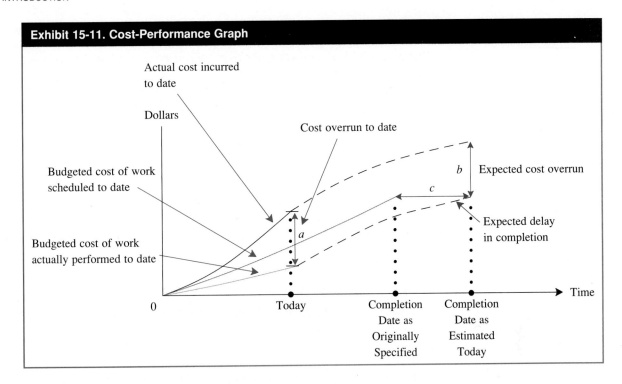

Exhibit 15-11. Cost-Performance Graph

The upper curved line in the graph is the actual cost incurred to date, as of various points in time. The dashed portion of the line is the analyst's current projection of actual costs to be incurred in the future. The middle line in the graph is the project's original cost budget for the work scheduled to be completed at various times. The lower line in the graph plots the analyst's estimate, at various times, of the budgeted cost of the work actually completed. The dashed portion of this line represents the analyst's current projection of the future course the line will take.

The project analyst can make three important estimates from the graph:

1. *Cost overrun to date* Measured by vertical line *a*, this is the amount by which the actual cost incurred to date exceeds the analyst's estimate of the value of the work accomplished.
2. *Expected cost overrun* Represented by vertical line *b*, this is the analyst's current projection of the cost overrun that will be incurred by the time the project is completed.
3. *Expected delay in completion* Measured by horizontal line *c*, this is the amount of time beyond the original completion date that will be needed for the budgeted cost-of-work-performed line to reach the height required for the project to be finished.

The cost-performance graph can be a useful tool to help management keep an eye on the progress of a long-term capital project.

PERFORMANCE EVALUATION: A BEHAVIORAL ISSUE

Take another look at Exhibit 15-1, which depicts an organization as a collection of investment projects. As the diagram indicates, the organization's performance in a particular *time period* is comprised of the combined results of several *projects'* performance during that period. There is a potential conflict between the criteria for evaluating *individual projects* and the criteria used to evaluate an *organization's overall performance.*

This potential conflict is understood best through an example. Suppose Mountainview's fire chief is considering a new alarm and communication system, which is expected to reduce the Fire Department's costs over its five-year life. The new system's acquisition cost, projected pattern of cost savings, and net present value are as follows:

	Acquisition Cost	Cost Savings				
	Time 0	Time 1	Time 2	Time 3	Time 4	Time 5
Cash flow	$(10,000)	$1,000	$1,500	$3,000	$5,000	$5,000
Discount factor (10%)	×1.000	×.909	×.826	×.751	×.683	×.621
	$(10,000)	$ 909	$1,239	$2,253	$3,415	$3,105

Net present value = $921

Although the new system has a positive NPV, its savings in the earlier years are quite low. The project will not really pay off until years 3, 4, and 5. Why does this create a potential behavioral problem? As is common, the fire chief's performance evaluation is based in part on the Fire Department's annual operating costs. Suppose the new communication and alarm system is depreciated using the straight-line method over its five-year life. The new system's pattern of cost savings, net of the annual depreciation charge, is as follows:

	Year				
	1	2	3	4	5
Cost savings	$ 1,000	$ 1,500	$ 3,000	$ 5,000	$ 5,000
Depreciation	(2,000)	(2,000)	(2,000)	(2,000)	(2,000)
Net amount	$(1,000)	$ (500)	$ 1,000	$ 3,000	$ 3,000

The depreciation charges are *not* cash flows; thus, these costs were not included in the net-present-value analysis. Nevertheless, annual depreciation charges are subtracted under *accrual accounting* procedures in determining periodic income or operating expenses. Thus, a conflict exists between discounted-cash-flow decision methods and accrual-accounting performance-evaluation methods.

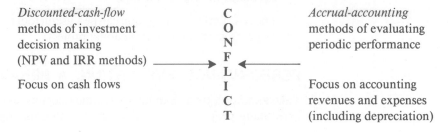

Discounted-cash-flow methods of investment decision making (NPV and IRR methods)	C O N F L I C T	*Accrual-accounting* methods of evaluating periodic performance
Focus on cash flows		Focus on accounting revenues and expenses (including depreciation)

The possible result of this conflict is that a decision maker, such as the Mountainview fire chief, may reject a positive-NPV investment project because of its impact on the accrual-accounting-based periodic performance measure. Our fire chief might express the following concern, which is all too typical of managers placed in this situation: "I'm not buying this new alarm system. Sure, it has a positive NPV, but the payoff doesn't come for several more years. I'll be lucky if I still have my job after showing a loss on the project in the first two years!"

Solution to the Problem A potential solution to the behavioral problem illustrated above is to deemphasize the use of accrual-accounting-based income or expenses as a performance measure. When decision makers are asked to use a discounted-cash-flow approach in choosing investment projects, they can be evaluated on the basis of postaudits of those projects. Nevertheless, performance measures based on accrual accounting are well entrenched in practice. Perhaps the most practical solution to the problem outlined above is to enlighten managers about the conflict between accrual-accounting and discounted-cash-flow analysis. If performance is evaluated using *both* accrual-accounting methods and postaudits of particular investment projects, the conflict can be overcome.

JUSTIFICATION OF INVESTMENTS IN ADVANCED MANUFACTURING SYSTEMS

The manufacturing industry is changing dramatically as firms adopt the just-in-time (JIT) philosophy and move toward computer-integrated-manufacturing (CIM) systems. In Chapter 5 we explored many of the managerial-accounting issues in the new manufacturing environment. The importance of transaction-based costing systems, activity accounting, cost-driver analysis, and non-value-added costs was demonstrated. Many firms have found that JIT and CIM, coupled with a revised managerial-accounting system, have provided a competitive edge in the marketplace. These firms' success has inspired managers in other companies to consider making investments in technologically advanced systems. In many cases, however, managers have been frustrated when this analysis projects a negative net present value for a proposed investment in a CIM system. Managers often believe intuitively that such an investment is justified, but they are stymied when the NPV analysis points to rejection of the proposal.

What is the problem here? Are managers overly optimistic about the advantages of CIM? Or is the NPV approach inappropriate for such an investment decision? Most likely neither of these conjectures is true. Managers often are right when their intuition tells them that the company would benefit from advanced manufacturing technology. And it is difficult to find fault with the NPV investment decision model. It is economically and mathematically sound. The problem lies in the difficulties of applying the NPV approach in a CIM investment decision. Some of these difficulties are as follows:[4]

---

[4] This section is based on discussions in Robert S. Kaplan, "Must CIM Be Justified by Faith Alone?" *Harvard Business Review,* March–April 1986, pp. 87–95; Callie Berliner and James A. Brimson, eds., *Cost Management for Today's Advanced Manufacturing* (Boston: Harvard Business School Press, 1988), pp. 16–18, 36–38, 150; and Jean L. Noble, "A New Approach for Justifying Computer-Integrated Manufacturing," *Journal of Cost Management for the Manufacturing Industry, 3,* no. 4 (Winter 1990), pp. 14–19.

1. *Hurdle rates that are too high* Sometimes managers have a tendency to set hurdle rates that are too high in a CIM investment analysis. They tend to forget that the purpose of discounting in the NPV model is to account for the time value of money. The appropriate hurdle rate for any investment decision is the investment opportunity rate for alternative investment projects of equivalent risk. In many cases managers tend to overstate this rate.

2. *Time horizons that are too short* Another common mistake is to evaluate a CIM investment proposal with too short a time horizon. The acquisition cost of a CIM system can be enormous, and the benefits may be realized over a lengthy period of time. If the NPV analysis stops short of including the benefits in later years, it is biased against a favorable recommendation.

3. *Bias toward incremental projects* Most firms require that large investments be authorized by managers at higher levels than are required for smaller investments. One result of this sensible practice is an incentive for lower-level managers to request relatively small, incremental improvements in the manufacturing process rather than a large, comprehensive improvement, such as a move to CIM. For example, if the investment authorization limit for a plant manager is $100,000, the manager may request a series of $95,000 improvements instead of one investment in a million-dollar flexible manufacturing system. In many cases, a series of such incremental improvements will not bring about the benefits that could be attained with a full commitment to advanced manufacturing technology.

4. *Greater uncertainty about operating cash flows* Managers often have greater uncertainty about the cash flows that will result when an advanced manufacturing system is implemented. This increased uncertainty is due to the complexity of the machinery and the firm's inexperience with such advanced technology.

5. *Exclusion of benefits that are difficult to quantify* The benefits to the firm from JIT and CIM systems are extensive. Some are easy to estimate, such as lower inventory levels, less floor space, and improved product quality. Others that can be even more significant are often difficult to quantify. Some of these benefits are the following:

   - *Greater flexibility* in the production process. A flexible manufacturing system cell often can produce runs of several distinct products in the same day. Moreover, the machines in an FMS can serve as backups for each other, which reduces machine downtime. Flexible manufacturing systems also allow engineering changes to be made more easily as products are adapted to changing customer preferences.
   - *Shorter cycle times and reduced lead times* are possible with an FMS. This enables the firm to fill customer orders more quickly and be responsive to customer requests.
   - *Reduction of non-value-added costs* often results when JIT and FMS systems are adopted. Part of the philosophy of these systems is to encourage employees to seek out activities that can be made more efficient or eliminated.

Although it is difficult to quantify these benefits, few managers doubt their existence. Excluding them from an NPV analysis means they are being valued at zero. In many cases it would be preferable to make some estimate of these benefits, however crude it may be, than to ignore them. If a manager believes it is impossible to make such an estimate, then the investment criteria should be expanded to consider these intangible benefits along with a proposal's NPV.

One way to handle intangible benefits is to complete an NPV analysis of a proposed advanced manufacturing system based on the readily quantifiable factors. Suppose, for example, that the NPV is a negative $(150,000). Then management can make a judgment as to whether the nonquantifiable benefits in total are worth more than $150,000. If they are, then the investment is justified.

To summarize, justification of investments in advanced manufacturing systems is a new and difficult problem. Discounted-cash-flow analysis is the appropriate tool for analyzing such a decision, but implementing the analysis presents a challenge. Managers should strive to make the best possible estimates of costs and benefits and ultimately make a judgment that recognizes the intangible benefits as well.

ILLUSTRATION FROM MANAGEMENT-ACCOUNTING PRACTICE

Intangible Benefits of Advanced Manufacturing Systems

Simmonds Precision Products manufactures measurement and control systems for the aerospace industry. In a recent decision to implement a computer-aided design/computer-aided manufacturing system, the company considered several intangible benefits. Among these were facilitation of a high degree of standardization in manufacturing. For example, increased standardization allowed the firm to reduce by 300 the number of part numbers (distinct parts) in one relatively simple subassembly. Another intangible benefit was enhancement of creativity in the design of the firm's products.[5]

CHAPTER SUMMARY

Capital-budgeting decisions involve cash flows occurring over several periods of time. Such decisions tend to focus on specific projects. The most common type of capital-budgeting analysis is concerned with the decision to accept or reject a particular investment proposal. Since capital-budgeting decisions involve cash flows over several time periods, the time value of money is a key feature of the analysis. There are two discounted-cash-flow methods for analyzing capital-investment decisions: the net-present-value method and the internal-rate-of-return method.

Under the net-present-value method, an investment proposal should be accepted if its net present value is zero or positive. A project's net present value is the present value of the project's future cash flows, less its initial acquisition cost. In computing the present value of the cash flows, the discount rate is the organization's cost of acquiring investment capital.

Under the internal-rate-of-return method, an investment proposal should be accepted if its internal rate of return equals or exceeds the organization's hurdle rate. A project's internal rate of return is the discount rate required to make the project's net present value equal to zero.

Both the net-present-value method and the internal-rate-of-return method are based on important assumptions. The net-present-value method is somewhat easier to apply. It also has the advantage of allowing the decision maker to adjust the discount rate upward for highly uncertain cash flows. Sensitivity analysis is another technique for dealing with uncertainty in capital-budgeting decisions.

[5] R. C. VanNostrand, "Justifying CAD/CAM Systems: A Case Study," *Journal of Cost Management for the Manufacturing Industry, 2,* no. 1 (Spring 1988), pp. 9–17.

KEY TERMS   Acceptance or rejection decision, p. 640; **Accumulation factor,** p. 643; **Annuity,** p. 644; **Capital-budgeting decision,** p. 639; **Capital-rationing decision,** p. 640; **Compound interest,** p. 642; **Cost performance reporting (CPR) system,** p. 660; **Discounted-cash-flow analysis,** p. 647; **Discount rate,** p. 644; **Future value,** p. 642; **Hurdle rate (or minimum desired rate of return),** p. 647; **Incremental-cost approach,** p. 657; **Internal rate of return (or time-adjusted rate of return),** p. 648; **Investment opportunity rate,** p. 654; **Net present value,** p. 647; **Postaudit (or reappraisal),** p. 660; **Present value,** p. 643; **Principal,** p. 641.

Future Value and Present Value Tables

Table I
Future Value of $1.00
$$(1 + r)^n$$

Periods	4%	6%	8%	10%	12%	14%	20%
1	1.040	1.060	1.080	1.100	1.120	1.140	1.200
2	1.082	1.124	1.166	1.210	1.254	1.300	1.440
3	1.125	1.191	1.260	1.331	1.405	1.482	1.728
4	1.170	1.263	1.361	1.464	1.574	1.689	2.074
5	1.217	1.338	1.469	1.611	1.762	1.925	2.488
6	1.265	1.419	1.587	1.772	1.974	2.195	2.986
7	1.316	1.504	1.714	1.949	2.211	2.502	3.583
8	1.369	1.594	1.851	2.144	2.476	2.853	4.300
9	1.423	1.690	1.999	2.359	2.773	3.252	5.160
10	1.480	1.791	2.159	2.594	3.106	3.707	6.192
11	1.540	1.898	2.332	2.853	3.479	4.226	7.430
12	1.601	2.012	2.518	3.139	3.896	4.818	8.916
13	1.665	2.133	2.720	3.452	4.364	5.492	10.699
14	1.732	2.261	2.937	3.798	4.887	6.261	12.839
15	1.801	2.397	3.172	4.177	5.474	7.138	15.407
20	2.191	3.207	4.661	6.728	9.646	13.743	38.338
30	3.243	5.744	10.063	17.450	29.960	50.950	237.380
40	4.801	10.286	21.725	45.260	93.051	188.880	1469.800

Table II
Future Value of a Series of $1.00 Cash Flows
(Ordinary Annuity)

$$\frac{(1 + r)^n - 1}{r}$$

Periods	4%	6%	8%	10%	12%	14%	20%
1	1.000	1.000	1.000	1.000	1.000	1.000	1.000
2	2.040	2.060	2.080	2.100	2.120	2.140	2.220
3	3.122	3.184	3.246	3.310	3.374	3.440	3.640
4	4.247	4.375	4.506	4.641	4.779	4.921	5.368
5	5.416	5.637	5.867	6.105	6.353	6.610	7.442
6	6.633	6.975	7.336	7.716	8.115	8.536	9.930
7	7.898	8.394	8.923	9.487	10.089	10.730	12.916
8	9.214	9.898	10.637	11.436	12.300	13.233	16.499
9	10.583	11.491	12.488	13.580	14.776	16.085	20.799
10	12.006	13.181	14.487	15.938	17.549	19.337	25.959
11	13.486	14.972	16.646	18.531	20.655	23.045	32.150
12	15.026	16.870	18.977	21.385	24.133	27.271	39.580
13	16.627	18.882	21.495	24.523	28.029	32.089	48.497
14	18.292	21.015	24.215	27.976	32.393	37.581	59.196
15	20.024	23.276	27.152	31.773	37.280	43.842	72.035
20	29.778	36.778	45.762	57.276	75.052	91.025	186.690
30	56.085	79.058	113.283	164.496	241.330	356.790	1181.900
40	95.026	154.762	259.057	442.597	767.090	1342.000	7343.900

Table III
Present Value of $1.00
$$1/(1 + r)^n$$

Periods	4%	6%	8%	10%	12%	14%	16%	18%	20%	22%	24%	26%	28%	30%	32%
1	.962	.943	.926	.909	.893	.877	.862	.847	.833	.820	.806	.794	.781	.769	.758
2	.925	.890	.857	.826	.797	.769	.743	.718	.694	.672	.650	.630	.610	.592	.574
3	.889	.840	.794	.751	.712	.675	.641	.609	.579	.551	.524	.500	.477	.455	.435
4	.855	.792	.735	.683	.636	.592	.552	.516	.482	.451	.423	.397	.373	.350	.329
5	.822	.747	.681	.621	.567	.519	.476	.437	.402	.370	.341	.315	.291	.269	.250
6	.790	.705	.630	.564	.507	.456	.410	.370	.335	.303	.275	.250	.227	.207	.189
7	.760	.665	.583	.513	.452	.400	.354	.314	.279	.249	.222	.198	.178	.159	.143
8	.731	.627	.540	.467	.404	.351	.305	.266	.233	.204	.179	.157	.139	.123	.108
9	.703	.592	.500	.424	.361	.308	.263	.225	.194	.167	.144	.125	.108	.094	.082
10	.676	.558	.463	.386	.322	.270	.227	.191	.162	.137	.116	.099	.085	.073	.062
11	.650	.527	.429	.350	.287	.237	.195	.162	.135	.112	.094	.079	.066	.056	.047
12	.625	.497	.397	.319	.257	.208	.168	.137	.112	.092	.076	.062	.052	.043	.036
13	.601	.469	.368	.290	.229	.182	.145	.116	.093	.075	.061	.050	.040	.033	.027
14	.577	.442	.340	.263	.205	.160	.125	.099	.078	.062	.049	.039	.032	.025	.021
15	.555	.417	.315	.239	.183	.140	.108	.084	.065	.051	.040	.031	.025	.020	.016
16	.534	.394	.292	.218	.163	.123	.093	.071	.054	.042	.032	.025	.019	.015	.012
17	.513	.371	.270	.198	.146	.108	.080	.060	.045	.034	.026	.020	.015	.012	.009
18	.494	.350	.250	.180	.130	.095	.069	.051	.038	.028	.021	.016	.012	.009	.007
19	.475	.331	.232	.164	.116	.083	.060	.043	.031	.023	.017	.012	.009	.007	.005
20	.456	.312	.215	.149	.104	.073	.051	.037	.026	.019	.014	.010	.007	.005	.004
21	.439	.294	.199	.135	.093	.064	.044	.031	.022	.015	.011	.008	.006	.004	.003
22	.422	.278	.184	.123	.083	.056	.038	.026	.018	.013	.009	.006	.004	.003	.002
23	.406	.262	.170	.112	.074	.049	.033	.022	.015	.010	.007	.005	.003	.002	.002
24	.390	.247	.158	.102	.066	.043	.028	.019	.013	.008	.006	.004	.003	.002	.001
25	.375	.233	.146	.092	.059	.038	.024	.016	.010	.007	.005	.003	.002	.001	.001
26	.361	.220	.135	.084	.053	.033	.021	.014	.009	.006	.004	.002	.002	.001	.001
27	.347	.207	.125	.076	.047	.029	.018	.011	.007	.005	.003	.002	.001	.001	.001
28	.333	.196	.116	.069	.042	.026	.016	.010	.006	.004	.002	.002	.001	.001	—
29	.321	.185	.107	.063	.037	.022	.014	.008	.005	.003	.002	.001	.001	.001	—
30	.308	.174	.099	.057	.033	.020	.012	.007	.004	.003	.002	.001	.001	—	—
40	.208	.097	.046	.022	.011	.005	.003	.001	.001						

Table IV
Present Value of Series of $1.00 Cash Flows

$$\frac{1}{r}\left(1 - \frac{1}{(1+r)^n}\right)$$

Periods	4%	6%	8%	10%	12%	14%	16%	18%	20%	22%	24%	25%	26%	28%	30%
1	0.962	0.943	0.926	0.909	0.893	0.877	0.862	0.847	0.833	0.820	0.806	0.800	0.794	0.781	0.769
2	1.886	1.833	1.783	1.736	1.690	1.647	1.605	1.566	1.528	1.492	1.457	1.440	1.424	1.392	1.361
3	2.775	2.673	2.577	2.487	2.402	2.322	2.246	2.174	2.106	2.042	1.981	1.952	1.923	1.868	1.816
4	3.630	3.465	3.312	3.170	3.037	2.914	2.798	2.690	2.589	2.494	2.404	2.362	2.320	2.241	2.166
5	4.452	4.212	3.993	3.791	3.605	3.433	3.274	3.127	2.991	2.864	2.745	2.689	2.635	2.532	2.436
6	5.242	4.917	4.623	4.355	4.111	3.889	3.685	3.498	3.326	3.167	3.020	2.951	2.885	2.759	2.643
7	6.002	5.582	5.206	4.868	4.564	4.288	4.039	3.812	3.605	3.416	3.242	3.161	3.083	2.937	2.802
8	6.733	6.210	5.747	5.335	4.968	4.639	4.344	4.078	3.837	3.619	3.421	3.329	3.241	3.076	2.925
9	7.435	6.802	6.247	5.759	5.328	4.946	4.607	4.303	4.031	3.786	3.566	3.463	3.366	3.184	3.019
10	8.111	7.360	6.710	6.145	5.650	5.216	4.833	4.494	4.192	3.923	3.682	3.571	3.465	3.269	3.092
11	8.760	7.887	7.139	6.495	5.938	5.453	5.029	4.656	4.327	4.035	3.776	3.656	3.544	3.335	3.147
12	9.385	8.384	7.536	6.814	6.194	5.660	5.197	4.793	4.439	4.127	3.851	3.725	3.606	3.387	3.190
13	9.986	8.853	7.904	7.103	6.424	5.842	5.342	4.910	4.533	4.203	3.912	3.780	3.656	3.427	3.223
14	10.563	9.295	8.244	7.367	6.628	6.002	5.468	5.008	4.611	4.265	3.962	3.824	3.695	3.459	3.249
15	11.118	9.712	8.559	7.606	6.811	6.142	5.575	5.092	4.675	4.315	4.001	3.859	3.726	3.483	3.268
16	11.652	10.106	8.851	7.824	6.974	6.265	5.669	5.162	4.730	4.357	4.033	3.887	3.751	3.503	3.283
17	12.166	10.477	9.122	8.022	7.120	6.373	5.749	5.222	4.775	4.391	4.059	3.910	3.771	3.518	3.295
18	12.659	10.828	9.372	8.201	7.250	6.467	5.818	5.273	4.812	4.419	4.080	3.928	3.786	3.529	3.304
19	13.134	11.158	9.604	8.365	7.366	6.550	5.877	5.316	4.844	4.442	4.097	3.942	3.799	3.539	3.311
20	13.590	11.470	9.818	8.514	7.469	6.623	5.929	5.353	4.870	4.460	4.110	3.954	3.808	3.546	3.316
21	14.029	11.764	10.017	8.649	7.562	6.687	5.973	5.384	4.891	4.476	4.121	3.963	3.816	3.551	3.320
22	14.451	12.042	10.201	8.772	7.645	6.743	6.011	5.410	4.909	4.488	4.130	3.970	3.822	3.556	3.323
23	14.857	12.303	10.371	8.883	7.718	6.792	6.044	5.432	4.925	4.499	4.137	3.976	3.827	3.559	3.325
24	15.247	12.550	10.529	8.985	7.784	6.835	6.073	5.451	4.937	4.507	4.143	3.981	3.831	3.562	3.327
25	15.622	12.783	10.675	9.077	7.843	6.873	6.097	5.467	4.948	4.514	4.147	3.985	3.834	3.564	3.329
26	15.983	13.003	10.810	9.161	7.896	6.906	6.118	5.480	4.956	4.520	4.151	3.988	3.837	3.566	3.330
27	16.330	13.211	10.935	9.237	7.943	6.935	6.136	5.492	4.964	4.524	4.154	3.990	3.839	3.567	3.331
28	16.663	13.406	11.051	9.307	7.984	6.961	6.152	5.502	4.970	4.528	4.157	3.992	3.840	3.568	3.331
29	16.984	13.591	11.158	9.370	8.022	6.983	6.166	5.510	4.975	4.531	4.159	3.994	3.841	3.569	3.332
30	17.292	13.765	11.258	9.427	8.055	7.003	6.177	5.517	4.979	4.534	4.160	3.995	3.842	3.569	3.332
40	19.793	15.046	11.925	9.779	8.244	7.105	6.234	5.548	4.997	4.544	4.166	3.999	3.846	3.571	3.333

REVIEW QUESTIONS

15-1. Distinguish between the following two types of capital-budgeting decisions: acceptance-or-rejection decisions and capital-rationing decisions.

15-2. "Time is money!" is an old saying. Relate this statement to the evaluation of capital-investment projects.

15-3. What is meant by the term *compound interest?*

15-4. Explain in words the following future-value formula: $F_n = P(1 + r)^n$.

15-5. Define the term *present value.*

15-6. "The greater the discount rate, the greater the present value of a future cash flow." True or false? Explain your answer.

15-7. "If the interest rate is 10 percent, a present value of $100 and a future value of $161.05 at the end of five years are *economically equivalent.*" Explain.

15-8. What is an *annuity?*

15-9. Briefly explain the concept of discounted-cash-flow analysis. What are the two common methods of discounted-cash-flow analysis?

15-10. List the four steps in using the net-present-value method.

15-11. Define the term *internal rate of return.*

15-12. State the decision rule used to accept or reject an investment proposal under each of these methods of analysis: (1) net-present-value method and (2) internal-rate-of-return method.

15-13. Explain the following terms: *recovery of investment* versus *return on investment.*

15-14. List and briefly explain two advantages that the net-present-value method has over the internal-rate-of-return method.

15-15. List and briefly explain four assumptions underlying discounted-cash-flow analysis.

15-16. What is the objective in a discounted-cash-flow analysis of a least-cost decision?

15-17. Distinguish between the following approaches to discounted-cash-flow analysis: total-cost approach versus incremental-cost approach.

15-18. Briefly describe two techniques commonly used when the cash flows of an investment proposal are highly uncertain.

15-19. What is meant by a *postaudit* of an investment project?

15-20. Briefly describe a *cost-performance-reporting system.* How does a cost-performance graph show the cost overrun to date on a capital project?

15-21. Describe the potential conflict between discounted-cash-flow analysis of projects and accrual-accounting measures of periodic performance evaluation.

15-22. List and explain three difficulties often encountered in justifying an investment in advanced manufacturing technology. List three intangible benefits of CIM systems.

 **EXERCISES**   *Exercise 15-23* ***Future Value and Present Value; Answers Supplied.*** Answer each of the following independent questions. Ignore personal income taxes. The answers appear on pages 682 and 683.

1. Suppose you invest $2,500 in an account bearing interest at the rate of 14 percent per year. What will be the future value of your investment in six years?

2. Your best friend won the state lottery and has offered to give you $10,000 in five years, after he has made his first million dollars. You figure that if you had the money today, you could invest it at 12 percent annual interest. What is the present value of your friend's future gift?

3. In four years, you would like to buy a small cabin in the mountains. You estimate that the property will cost you $52,500 when you are ready to buy. How much money would you need to invest each year in an account bearing interest at the rate of 6 percent per year in order to accumulate the $52,500 purchase price?

4. You have estimated that your educational expenses over the next three years will be $13,000 per year. How much money do you need in your account now in order to withdraw the required amount each year? Your account bears interest at 10 percent per year.

Exercise 15-24   Continuation of Preceding Exercise. Refer to the answers given for the preceding exercise.

REQUIRED:

1. Refer to requirement (1) of the preceding exercise. Prepare a display similar to Exhibit 15-2 to show how your accumulation grows each year to equal $5,487.50 after six years.
2. Refer to requirement (4) of the preceding exercise. Prepare a display similar to Exhibit 15-4 to verify that $32,331 is the amount you need to fund your educational expenses.

Exercise 15-25   Future Value and Present Value. You plan to retire at age 40 after a highly successful but short career. You would like to accumulate enough money by age 40 to withdraw $200,000 per year for 40 years. You plan to pay into your account 15 equal installments beginning when you are 25 and ending when you are 39. Your account bears interest of 12 percent per year.

REQUIRED:

1. How much do you need to accumulate in your account by the time you retire?
2. How much do you need to pay into your account in each of the 15 equal installments?
3. Is this a future-value problem or a present-value problem? Explain.

Exercise 15-26   Net-Present-Value. Adams County's Board of Representatives is considering the purchase of a site for a new sanitary landfill. The purchase price for the site is $200,000 and preparatory work will cost $68,400. The landfill would be usable for 10 years. The board hired a consultant, who estimated that the new landfill would cost the county $40,000 per year less to operate than the county's current landfill. The current landfill also will last 10 more years. For a landfill project, Adams County can borrow money from the federal government at a subsidized rate. The county's hurdle rate is only 6 percent for this project.

REQUIRED: Compute the net present value of the new landfill. Should the board approve the project?

Exercise 15-27   Internal-Rate-of-Return. Refer to the data given in the preceding exercise.

REQUIRED: Calculate the landfill project's internal rate of return. Should the board approve the project?

Exercise 15-28   Recovery of Investment. Refer to the data given in Exercise 15-26.

REQUIRED: Prepare a display similar to Exhibit 15-7 to show the recovery of investment and return on investment for Adams County's landfill project.

Exercise 15-29   Net Present Value. Jack and Jill's Place is a nonprofit nursery school run by the parents of the enrolled children. Since the school is out of town, it has a well rather than a city water supply. Lately, the well has become unreliable, and the school has had to bring in bottled drinking water. The school's governing board is considering drilling a new well (at the top of the hill, naturally). The board estimates that a new well would cost $2,825 and save the school $500 annually for 10 years. The school's hurdle rate is 8 percent.

REQUIRED: Compute the new well's net present value. Should the governing board approve the new well?

Exercise 15-30   Internal Rate of Return. Refer to the data given in the preceding exercise.

REQUIRED: Compute the internal rate of return on the new well. Should the governing board approve the new well?

Exercise 15-31   Internal Rate of Return; Interpolation. The president of Mendelsson Community College is considering the replacement of the college's computer. The proposed new computer would cost $63,000 and have a life of five years. The college's current computer would last five more years also, but it does not have sufficient capacity to meet the college's expanded needs. If Mendelsson Community College continues to use the old computer, it will have to purchase additional computer time, on a time-share basis, from the state university. The cost of the additional computer time is projected at $14,000 annually. The old computer can be sold now for $9,000.

REQUIRED: Use interpolation to compute the internal rate of return on the proposed purchase of a new computer. (Hint: The net present value of the proposed computer is $1,902 if a discount rate of 8 percent is used.)

Exercise 15-32   Internal Rate of Return; Uneven Cash Flows. The trustees of the Community School of Art and Music are considering a major overhaul of the school's audio system. With or without the overhaul, the system will be replaced in two years. If an overhaul is done now, the trustees expect to save the following repair costs during the next two years: year 1, $3,000; year 2, $5,000. The overhaul will cost $6,664.

REQUIRED: Use trial and error to compute the internal rate of return on the proposed overhaul. (Hint: The NPV of the overhaul is positive if an 8 percent discount rate is used, but the NPV is negative if a 16 percent rate is used.)

Exercise 15-33   Net Present Value with Different Discount Rates. The board of directors of the Boston Shakespearean Theater is considering the replacement of the theater's lighting system. The old system requires two people to operate it, but the new system would require only a single operator. The new lighting system will cost $85,000 and save the theater $18,000 annually for the next eight years.

REQUIRED: Prepare a table showing the proposed lighting system's net present value for each of the following discount rates: 8 percent, 10 percent, 12 percent, 14 percent, and 16 percent. Use the following headings in your table. Comment on the pattern in the right-hand column.

Discount Rate	Annuity Discount Factor	Annual Savings	Acquisition Cost	Net Present Value

Exercise 15-34   Sensitivity Analysis. Refer to the data given in the preceding exercise. Suppose the Boston Shakespearean Theater's board is uncertain about the cost savings with the new lighting system.

REQUIRED: How low could the new lighting system's annual savings be and still justify acceptance of the proposal by the board of directors? Assume the theater's hurdle rate is 12 percent.

Exercise 15-35 Performance Evaluation: Behavioral Problems. The supervisor of the City Water Authority is considering the replacement of a utility truck. A new truck costs $60,000 and has a useful life of five years. The city depreciates all assets on a straight-line basis. The supervisor estimates that the new truck would result in substantial savings over the next five years. He has projected the following pattern of operating-cost savings.

Year

	1	2	3	4	5
Cost savings	$11,000	$11,500	$13,000	$18,000	$20,000

After giving the proposal some thought, the supervisor decided against purchasing the new utility truck. He said to his deputy supervisor, "If we go for that truck, the City Council will fry us. With $12,000 in depreciation each year, the truck won't even pay its own way until three years out. By then, you and I will be in the unemployment line!"

REQUIRED: The city's hurdle rate is 6 percent. Did the supervisor make a wise decision? Why? Comment on the behavioral problem evident in this situation.

PROBLEMS
Problem 15-36 Net-Present-Value Analysis; City Government. The city manager of Rockyford is considering the replacement of some machinery. This machinery has zero book value but its current market value is $1,800. One possible alternative is to invest in new machinery, which has a cost of $40,000. This new machinery would produce estimated annual operating cash savings of $12,500. The estimated useful life of the new machinery is four years. Rockyford uses straight-line depreciation. The new machinery has an estimated salvage value of $2,000 at the end of four years. The investment in the new machinery would require an additional investment in working capital of $3,000, which would be recovered after four years.

If Rockyford accepts this investment proposal, the disposal of the old machinery and the investment in the new equipment will take place on December 31, 19x1. The cash flows from the investment will occur during the calendar years 19x2 through 19x5.

REQUIRED: Prepare a net-present-value analysis of Rockyford's machinery-replacement decision. The city has a 10 percent hurdle rate.
(CMA, adapted)

Problem 15-37 Net Present Value; Qualitative Issues. Special People Industries is a nonprofit organization which employs only people with physical or mental disabilities. One of the organization's activities is to make cookies for its snack food store. On December 31, 19x0, Special People Industries purchased a special cookie-cutting machine. This machine has now been used for three years. Management is considering the purchase of a newer, more efficient machine. If purchased, the new machine would be acquired on December 31, 19x3. Management expects to sell 300,000 dozen cookies in each of the next six years. The selling price of the cookies is expected to average $1.00 per dozen.

Special People Industries has two options: continue to operate the old machine, or sell the old machine and purchase the new machine. No trade-in was offered by the seller of the new machine. The following information has been assembled to help management decide which option is more desirable.

	Old Machine	New Machine
Original cost of machine at acquisition....................	$80,000	$120,000
Remaining useful life	6 years	6 years
Expected annual cash operating expenses:		
Variable cost per dozen	$.40	$.28
Total fixed costs	$15,000	$ 14,000
Estimated cash value of machines:		
December 31, 19x3..................................	$40,000	$120,000
December 31, 19x9..................................	$ 7,000	$ 20,000

Assume that all operating revenues and expenses occur at the end of the year.

REQUIRED:

1. Use the net-present-value method to determine whether Special People Industries should retain the old machine or acquire the new machine. The organization's hurdle rate is 16 percent.
2. Independent of your answer to requirement (1), suppose the quantitative differences are so slight between the two alternatives that management is indifferent between the two proposals. Identify and discuss any nonquantitative factors that management should consider.

(CMA, adapted)

Problem 15-38   Net-Present-Value-Analysis; Hospital. Oneida Community Hospital is a nonprofit hospital operated by the county. The hospital's administrator is considering a proposal to open a new outpatient clinic in the nearby city of Davis. The administrator has made the following estimates pertinent to the proposal.

1. Construction of the clinic building will cost $800,000 in two equal installments of $400,000, to be paid at the end of 19x0 and 19x1. The clinic will open on January 2, 19x2. All staffing and operating costs begin in 19x2.
2. Equipment for the clinic will cost $150,000, to be paid in December of 19x1.
3. Staffing of the clinic will cost $800,000 per year.
4. Other operating costs at the clinic will be $200,000 per year.
5. Opening the clinic is expected to increase charitable contributions to the hospital by $250,000 per year.
6. The clinic is expected to reduce costs at Oneida Community Hospital. Annual cost savings at the hospital are projected to be $1,000,000.
7. A major refurbishment of the clinic is expected to be necessary toward the end of 19x5. This work will cost $180,000.
8. Due to shifting medical needs in the county, the administrator doubts the clinic will be needed after 19x9.
9. The clinic building and equipment could be sold for $300,000 at the end of 19x9.
10. The hospital's hurdle rate is 12 percent.

REQUIRED:

1. Compute the cash flows for each year relevant to the analysis.
2. Prepare a table of cash flows, by year, similar to Exhibit 15-10.
3. Compute the net present value of the proposed outpatient clinic.

4. Should the administrator recommend to the hospital's trustees that the clinic be built? Why?

Problem 15-39 *Net Present Value; Total-Cost Approach.* The chief ranger of the state's Department of Natural Resources is considering a new plan for fighting forest fires in the state's forest lands. The current plan uses eight fire-control stations, which are scattered throughout the interior of the state forest. Each station has a four-person staff, whose annual compensation totals $200,000. Other costs of operating each base amount to $100,000 per year. The equipment at each base has a current salvage value of $120,000. The buildings at these interior stations have no other use. To demolish them would cost $10,000 each.

The chief ranger is considering an alternative plan, which involves four fire-control stations located on the perimeter of the state forest. Each station would require a six-person staff, with annual compensation costs of $300,000. Other operating costs would be $110,000 per base. Building each perimeter station would cost $200,000. The perimeter bases would need helicopters and other equipment costing $500,000 per station. Half of the equipment from the interior stations could be used at the perimeter stations. Therefore, only half of the equipment at the interior stations would be sold if the perimeter stations were built.

The state uses a 10 percent hurdle rate for all capital projects.

REQUIRED:

1. Use the total-cost approach to prepare a net-present-value analysis of the chief ranger's two fire-control plans. Assume that the interior fire-control stations will be demolished if the perimeter plan is selected. The chief ranger has decided to use a 10-year time period for the analysis.
2. What qualitative factors would the chief ranger be likely to consider in making this decision?

Problem 15-40 *Net Present Value; Incremental-Cost Approach.* Refer to the data in the preceding problem.

REQUIRED: Use the incremental-cost approach to prepare a net-present-value analysis of the chief ranger's decision between the interior fire-control plan and the perimeter fire-control plan.

Problem 15-41 *Net Present Value; Total-Cost Approach.* The board of trustees of Mercy Hospital is considering the addition of a comprehensive medical testing laboratory. In the past, the hospital has sent all blood and tissue specimens to Diagnostic Testing Services, an independent testing service. The hospital's current contract with the testing service is due to expire, and the testing service has offered a new 10-year contract. Under the terms of a new contract, Mercy Hospital would pay Diagnostic Testing Services a flat fee of $80,000 per year plus $20 per specimen tested.

Since Mercy Hospital does not have its own comprehensive testing lab, the hospital staff is forced to refer some types of cases to a nearby metropolitan hospital. If Mercy Hospital had its own lab, these cases could be handled in-house. Mercy Hospital's administrator estimates that the hospital loses $100,000 per year in contribution margin on the cases that currently must be referred elsewhere.

The proposed new lab would not require construction of a new building, since it would occupy space currently used by the hospital for storage. However, the hospital then would be forced to rent storage space in a nearby medical building at a cost of $30,000 per year. The equipment for the lab would cost $600,000 initially. Additional equipment costing $300,000 would be purchased after four years. Due to the rapid technological improvement of medical testing equipment, the equipment would have negligible salvage value after 10 years. Staffing the lab would require two supervisors and four technicians. Annual compensation costs would run $40,000 each for the supervisors and $30,000 each for the lab technicians. Fixed operating costs in the lab would be $50,000 per year, and variable costs would amount to $10 per medical test.

Mercy Hospital requires 20,000 tests per year. The capacity of the lab would be 25,000 tests per year. Mercy Hospital's administrator believes that physicians in private practice would utilize the lab's excess capacity by sending their own tests to Mercy Hospital. The administrator has projected a charge of $20 per test for physicians in private practice.

Mercy Hospital's hurdle rate is 12 percent.

REQUIRED: Use the total-cost approach to prepare a net-present-value analysis of the proposed testing laboratory.

Problem 15-42   Net Present Value; Incremental-Cost Approach. Refer to the data in the preceding problem.

REQUIRED: Use the incremental-cost approach to prepare a net-present-value analysis of Mercy Hospital's proposed new medical-testing laboratory.

Problem 15-43   Internal Rate of Return; Even Cash Flows. The Board of Representatives for Madison County is considering the construction of a longer runway at the county airport. Currently, the airport can handle only private aircraft and small jet commuters. A new, long runway would enable the airport to handle the midsize jets used on many domestic flights. Data pertinent to the board's decision appear below.

Cost of acquiring additional land for runway	$ 70,000
Cost of runway construction	200,000
Cost of extending perimeter fence	29,840
Cost of runway lights	39,600
Annual cost of maintaining new runway	28,000
Annual incremental revenue from landing fees	40,000

In addition to the data given above, two other facts are relevant to the decision. First, a longer runway will require a new snow plow, which will cost $100,000. The old snow plow can be sold now for $10,000. The new, larger plow will cost $12,000 more in annual operating costs. Second, the County Board of Representatives believes that the proposed long runway, and the major jet service it will bring to the county, will increase economic activity in the community. The board projects that the increased economic activity will result in $64,000 per year in additional tax revenue for the county.

In analyzing the runway proposal, the board has decided to use a 10-year time horizon. The county's hurdle rate for capital projects is 12 percent.

REQUIRED:

1. Compute the initial cost of the investment in the long runway.
2. Compute the annual net cost or benefit from the runway.
3. Determine the IRR on the proposed long runway. Should it be built?

Problem 15-44   Net Present Value. Refer to the data given in the preceding problem.

REQUIRED:

1. Prepare a net-present-value analysis of the proposed long runway.
2. Should the County Board of Representatives approve the runway?
3. Which of the data used in the analysis are likely to be most uncertain? Least uncertain? Why?

Problem 15-45   Internal Rate of Return; Sensitivity Analysis. Refer to the data given in problem 15-43. The County Board of Representatives believes that if the county conducts a promotional effort costing $20,000 per year, the proposed long runway will result in substantially greater economic development than was projected originally. However, the board is uncertain about the actual increase in county tax revenue that will result.

REQUIRED: Suppose the board builds the long runway and conducts the promotional campaign. What would the increase in the county's annual tax revenue need to be in order for the proposed runway's internal rate of return to equal the county's hurdle rate of 12 percent?

Problem 15-46   Net Present Value; Sensitivity Analysis. The City Council of Marlinsburg is considering the expansion of its municipal stadium from 30,000 to 40,000 seats. The council believes it will attract a major-league baseball team to hold its spring-training camp in Marlinsburg by expanding the stadium. The expansion will cost $8,000,000. Additional annual maintenance at the stadium is projected at $50,000 per year. The 10,000 additional seats at the stadium will be divided up as follows:

Seat Type	Number of Seats	Ticket Price
Bleachers.	8,000	$15
Box seats.	2,000	25

Ninety percent of the current seats in the stadium are bleacher seats; the remainder are box seats. These seats have the same ticket prices, for both bleacher and box seats, respectively, as those shown above.

If the City Council expands the stadium and a baseball team holds its spring training camp in Marlinsburg, the city will receive half of the ticket revenue. Currently, the city receives all of the revenue from its stadium ticket sales, but that amounts to only $500,000 each spring. With a major-league team in town, the council expects to fill the stadium for each of 10 exhibition games to be held at the stadium each spring. Except in the spring, there is little activity in the stadium. The city currently receives only $100,000 in ticket revenue during the summer, fall, and winter months. That amount is expected to increase by 10 percent if the stadium is expanded.

The City Council has asked Ruth Babe, the city controller, to prepare an analysis of the proposed stadium expansion. The council instructed the controller to use a five-year time frame and a 10 percent hurdle rate in the analysis.

REQUIRED:

1. Compute the incremental revenue the city will receive if the municipal stadium is expanded. (The current $500,000 of spring revenue will not continue.)
2. Prepare a schedule showing the incremental cash flows during each of the next five years if the stadium is expanded.
3. Prepare a net-present-value analysis of the proposed stadium addition.

4. Suppose the City Council was too optimistic in its projection of filling the expanded stadium for each exhibition game. What would be the NPV of the stadium expansion if only 60 percent of the tickets in each category could be sold for the exhibition games?

Problem 15-47   Internal Rate of Return; Uneven Cash Flows. The governing board of the Monroeville Public Library is considering the installation of a security system to reduce the theft of books. Currently, the library spends $30,000 annually to replace lost books. The governing board estimates that 90 percent of this cost is due to book theft. The remaining 10 percent of the cost is unrelated to book theft and will be incurred regardless of whether a new security system is installed. The library currently employs people on a part-time basis to monitor the library's exit. However, this system is ineffective. The library incurs an annual cost of $24,000 on this monitoring activity.

The board could install an electronic security system, which would render the exit monitoring unnecessary. In order to install the new security system, the library's exits will have to be modified at a cost of $90,000. The equipment for the security system would cost $110,697 and have a useful life of 10 years. In addition, the new security system will require the placement of a sensor panel inside every book in the library, at a total cost of $18,000. This process, which will take place over a three-year period, will cost $6,000 during each of those years. Since the security system will not be completely in place for three years, the library will continue to incur some cost from stolen books over the three-year installation period. The projected cost of replacing stolen books during the proposed security system's life is as follows:

Year		Cost of Replacing Stolen Books
1	....	$22,500
2	....	13,500
3	....	4,500
4 through 10	....	0

The board requires at least a 14 percent internal rate of return on all capital projects.

REQUIRED:

1. Compute the library's net savings during each of the next 10 years if the new security system is installed.
2. Compute the system's internal rate of return. (Hint: Begin with 14 percent, 16 percent, or 18 percent.)
3. Should the library's governing board purchase the new security system? Why?
4. Which of the cash flows mentioned in the problem do you think would be the most difficult to estimate? Least difficult? Why?

Problem 15-48   Internal Rate of Return; Net Present Value; Uneven Cash Flows. Refer to the data for the preceding problem. As the preceding problem states, the total cost of installing the sensor plates in the books is $18,000. Suppose that the $18,000 expenditure could be spread out evenly over the next six years, instead of the next three years, without changing the projected cost of replacing stolen books each year. All other data remain the same.

REQUIRED:

1. Would you expect the new security system's internal rate of return to be higher or lower than it was given the data in the preceding problem? Why?

2. Compute the proposed security system's net present value, given the change in the schedule of expenditures for the placement of sensor panels. Begin by revising the schedule of net savings developed in the preceding problem.

Problem 15-49   Cost Performance Reporting. Shenandoah Construction, Inc. is building a dam for the state Department of Natural Resources. The supervising engineer for the state is Jenny Myers. As part of her monthly review of the water project, Myers updates a cost performance graph. On June 30, 19x5 the graph appears as follows:

Cost Performance Graph for June 30,19x5
Department of Natural Resources
Construction of Dam by Shenandoah Construction, Inc.

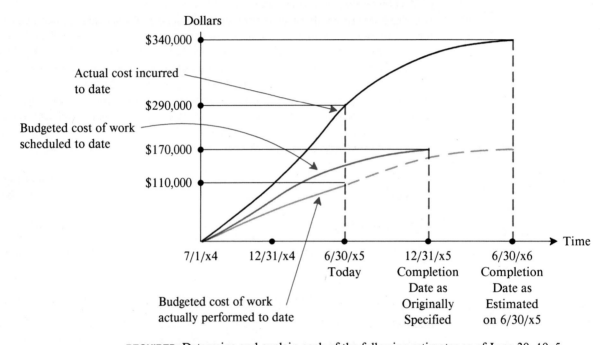

REQUIRED: Determine and explain each of the following estimates as of June 30, 19x5.

1. Cost overrun to date.
2. Expected cost overrun.
3. Expected delay in completion.

CASES   *Case 15-50   Postaudit; Net Present Value; Internal Rate of Return.* The city of Tidewater is located five miles upriver from the Atlantic coast. In the past, the city enjoyed a booming tourist trade, primarily from fishing and boating enthusiasts. The small river on which Tidewater is located was navigable for most private vessels. In recent years, however, the river has become increasingly clogged with sand. This has reduced the draft of the boating channel in the river. As a result, Tidewater's tourist industry has fallen off dramatically.

Five years ago, in December of 19x2, the Tidewater City Council approved a channel-dredging project. The river channel was dredged at a cost of $576,800. The city charged half of this cost to local businesses, which would benefit from restored tourist trade. The City Council estimated that its tax revenue would increase by $84,000 annually over a five-year period as a result of the increased economic activity.

It is now early in 19x8, and the river channel is clogged again. The City Council is considering another channel-dredging operation. Before proceeding, however, the council has directed its controller, Bill Barnacle, to conduct a postaudit of the 19x2 channel-dredging project.

After a study of the city's tax-revenue records, Barnacle has determined that the actual increase in the city's tax revenues amounted to $80,000 per year from 19x3 through 19x7.

The city's hurdle rate for capital projects is 10 percent.

REQUIRED:

1. Calculate the net present value *projected* for the channel-dredging operation in 19x2.
2. Compute the internal rate of return *projected* on the river project in 19x2.
3. Using the actual tax-revenue data collected by Bill Barnacle, calculate the actual net present value of the channel-dredging operation as of 19x2.
4. Using the actual tax-revenue data, compute the actual internal rate of return earned on the 19x2 river project.
5. Prepare a postaudit report which compares the projection with the actual results of the channel-dredging project. Use the following format for your report.

Cost of 19x2 channel-dredging operation: _____
Cost to city (50% of total cost): _____

Annual Increase in Tax Revenues

Projected	Actual	Variance
_____	_____	_____

Net Present Value in 19x2		Internal Rate of Return	
Projected	**Actual**	**Projected**	**Actual**
_____	_____	_____	_____

Case 15-51   Decision Problem with Main Alternatives and Suboptions; NPV; IRR. The Board of Education for the Blue Ridge School District is considering the acquisition of several minibuses for use in transporting students to school. Five of the school district's bus routes are underpopulated, with the result that the full-size buses on those routes are not fully utilized. After a careful study, the board has decided that it is not feasible to consolidate these routes into fewer routes served by full-size buses. The area in which the students live is too large for that approach, since some students' bus ride to school would exceed the state maximum of 45 minutes.

The plan under consideration by the board is to replace five full-size buses with eight minibuses, each of which would cover a much shorter route than a full-size bus. The bus drivers in this rural school district are part-time employees whose compensation costs the school district $18,000 per year for each driver. In addition to the drivers' compensation, the annual costs of operating and maintaining a full-size bus amount to $50,000. In contrast, the board projects that a minibus will cost only $20,000 annually to operate and maintain. A minibus driver earns the same wages as a full-size bus driver. The school district controller has estimated that it will cost the district $15,250, initially, to redesign its bus routes, inform the public, install caution signs in certain hazardous locations, and retrain its drivers.

A minibus costs $27,000, whereas a full-size bus costs $90,000. The school district uses straight-line depreciation for all of its long-lived assets. The board has two options regarding the five full-size buses. First, the buses could be sold now for $15,000 each. Second, the buses could be kept in reserve to use for field trips and out-of-town athletic events and to use as backup vehicles when buses break down. Currently, the board charters buses from a private company for these purposes. The annual cost of chartering buses amounts to $30,000. The school district controller has estimated that this cost could be cut to $5,000 per year if the five buses were kept in reserve. The five full-size buses have five years of useful life remaining, either as regularly scheduled buses or as reserve buses. The useful life of a new minibus is projected to be five years also.

Blue Ridge School District uses a hurdle rate of 12 percent on all capital projects.

REQUIRED:

1. Think about the decision problem faced by the Board of Education. What are the board's two main alternatives?
2. One of these main alternatives has two options embedded within it. What are those two options?
3. Before proceeding, check the hint given on page 683, which explains and diagrams the school board's alternatives. Suppose the Board of Education chooses to buy the minibuses. Prepare a net-present-value analysis of the two options for the five full-size buses. Should these buses be sold now or kept in reserve?
4. From your answer to requirement (3), you know the best option for the board to choose regarding the full-size buses, *if* the minibuses are purchased. Now you can ignore the other option. Prepare a net-present-value analysis of the school board's two *main alternatives:* (1) continue to use the full-size buses on regular routes, or (2) purchase the minibuses. Should the minibuses be purchased?
5. Compute the internal rate of return on the proposed minibus acquisition.
6. What information given in this case was irrelevant to the school board's decision problem? Explain why the information was irrelevant.

Solution to Exercise 15-23

1. Use formula (1):

$$F_n = P(1 + r)^n = \$2,500(1.14)^6$$

The accumulation factor, $(1.14)^6$, is given in Table I of the appendix. It is 2.195. Thus, the calculation is as follows:

$$F_n = \$2,500(2.195) = \$5,487.50$$

The future value of your investment will be $5,487.50.

2. Use formula (2):

$$P = F_n \left(\frac{1}{(1 + r)^n} \right) = \$10,000 \left(\frac{1}{(1.12)^5} \right)$$

The discount factor, $1/(1.12)^5$, is given in Table III. It is .567. Thus, the calculation is as follows:

$$P = \$10,000(.567) = \$5,670$$

The present value of the gift is $5,670.

3. You need to invest an amount, A, each year so that the following equation is satisfied:

$$A(4.375) = \$52,500$$

The number 4.375 is the annuity accumulation factor, from Table II, for $n = 4$ and $r = .06$. Rearranging the equation above, we solve for A as follows:

$$A = \frac{\$52,500}{4.375} = \$12,000$$

You need to invest \$12,000 per year.

4. You need an amount, P, now so that the following equation is satisfied.

$$P = (2.487)\$13,000$$

The number 2.487 is the annuity discount factor, from Table IV, for $n = 3$ and $r = .10$. The solution is $P = \$32,331$. You need to invest \$32,331 now in order to fund your educational expenses.

Hint for Case 15-51:

The school board's two main alternatives are as follows: (1) continue to use the five full-size school buses on regular routes, and (2) purchase eight minibuses to cover the regular bus routes. Under alternative (2), the board has two options. The full-size buses could be (a) sold now or (b) kept in reserve.

Thus, the board's decision problem can be diagrammed as follows:

Main Alternatives	**Secondary Options**

(1) Full-size buses on regular routes

(a) Sell full-size buses

(2) Minibuses on regular routes

(b) Keep full-size buses in reserve

Chapter 16

Further Aspects of Capital Expenditure Decisions

After completing this chapter, you should be able to:	
	■ Discuss the impact of income taxes on capital-budgeting decisions in profit-seeking enterprises.
	■ Determine the after-tax cash flows in an investment analysis.
	■ Compute an asset's depreciation tax shield.
	■ Use the Accelerated Cost Recovery System, as modified by recent changes in the tax laws, to determine an asset's depreciation schedule for tax purposes.
	■ Evaluate an investment proposal using a discounted-cash-flow analysis, giving full consideration to income-tax issues.
	■ Discuss the difficulty of ranking investment proposals, and use the profitability index.
	■ Use the payback method and accounting-rate-of-return method to evaluate capital-investment projects.
	■ After completing the appendix, explain the impact of inflation on a capital-budgeting analysis.

Income taxes influence many decisions made in profit-seeking enterprises. In some cases, tax considerations are so crucial in a capital-investment decision that they dominate all other aspects of the analysis. In this chapter, we will continue our discussion of discounted-cash-flow analysis by focusing on tax considerations.

We will also explore other investment-decision methods, which do not rely on the discounted-cash-flow approach. Managers in many organizations analyze investment decisions using a variety of methods before making a final decision.

Several other topics that often arise in investment decisions also are discussed in this chapter. Among these are methods for ranking investment proposals and the impact of inflation, which is covered in the appendix.

INCOME TAXES AND CAPITAL BUDGETING

When a business makes a profit, it usually must pay income taxes, just as individuals do. Since many of the cash flows associated with an investment proposal affect the company's profit, they also affect the firm's income-tax liability. The following equation shows the four types of items that appear on an income statement.

$$\text{Income} = \text{revenue} - \text{expenses} + \text{gains} - \text{losses}$$

Any aspect of an investment project that affects any of the items in this equation generally will affect the company's income-tax payments. These income-tax payments are cash flows, and they must be considered in any discounted-cash-flow analysis.

After-Tax Cash Flows

The first step in a discounted-cash-flow analysis for a profit-seeking enterprise is to determine the after-tax cash flows associated with the investment projects under consideration. An **after-tax cash flow** is the cash flow expected after all tax implications have been taken into account. Each financial aspect of a project must be examined carefully to determine its potential tax impact.

To illustrate the tax implications of various types of financial items, we will focus on a retail business. High Country Department Stores, Inc. operates two department stores in the city of Mountainview. The firm has a large downtown store and a smaller branch store in the suburbs. The company is quite profitable, and management is considering several capital projects that will enhance the firm's future profit potential. Before analyzing these projects, let's pause to consider the tax issues the company is likely to face. For the purposes of our discussion, we will assume that High Country Department Stores' income tax rate is 40 percent. Thus, if the company's net income is $1,000,000, its income-tax payment will be $400,000 ($1,000,000 × 40%).

Cash Revenue Suppose High Country's management is considering the purchase of an additional delivery truck. The sales manager estimates that a new truck will allow the company to increase annual sales revenue by $100,000. Further suppose that this incremental sales revenue will be received in cash during the year of sale. Any credit sales will be paid in cash within a short time period. What is High Country's *after-tax cash flow* from the incremental sales revenue? As the following calculation shows, the firm's incremental cash inflow from the additional sales is only $60,000.

Incremental sales revenue (cash inflow)	$100,000
Incremental income tax (cash outflow), $100,000 × 40%	(40,000)
After-tax cash flow (net inflow after taxes)	$ 60,000

Although the incremental sales revenue amounted to an additional cash inflow of $100,000, the cash outflow for income taxes also increased by $40,000. Thus, the after-tax cash inflow from the incremental sales revenue is $60,000.

A quick method for computing the after-tax cash inflow from incremental sales revenue is the following:

$$\boxed{\frac{\text{Incremental}}{\text{sales revenue}} \times (1 - \text{tax rate}) = \frac{\text{After-tax}}{\text{cash inflow}}}$$

$$\$100,000 \quad \times \quad (1 - .40) \quad = \$60,000$$

Cash Expenses What are the tax implications of cash expenses? Suppose the addition of the delivery truck under consideration by High Country's management will involve hiring an additional employee, whose annual compensation and fringe benefits will amount to $30,000. As the following computation shows, the company's incremental cash outflow is only $18,000.

Incremental expense (cash outflow)	$30,000
Reduction in income tax (reduced cash outflow), $30,000 × 40%.	12,000
After-tax cash flow (net outflow after taxes)	$18,000

Although the incremental employee-compensation is $30,000, this expense is tax-deductible. Thus, the firm's income-tax payment will be reduced by $12,000. As a result, the after-tax cash outflow from the additional compensation is $18,000.

A quick method for computing the after-tax cash outflow from an incremental cash expense is shown below.

$$\frac{\text{Incremental}}{\text{cash expense}} \times (1 - \text{tax rate}) = \frac{\text{After-tax}}{\text{cash outflow}}$$

$$\$30,000 \quad \times \quad (1 - .40) \quad = \$18,000$$

Noncash Expenses Not all expenses represent cash outflows. The most common example of a noncash expense is depreciation expense. Suppose High Country Department Stores' management is considering the purchase of a delivery truck, which costs $40,000 and has no salvage value. We will discuss the specific methods of depreciation allowed under the tax law later in the chapter, but for now assume the truck will be depreciated as follows:

Acquisition
cost:
$40,000

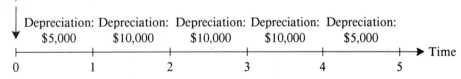

As we discussed in Chapter 15, the only cash flow shown in the diagram above is the truck's acquisition cost of $40,000 at time zero. The depreciation expense in each of the next five years is *not a cash flow*. However, *depreciation is an expense* on the income statement, and it reduces the firm's income. For example, the $5,000 depreciation expense in year 1 will reduce High Country's income by $5,000. As a result, the company's year 1 income-tax payment will decline by $2,000 (40% × $5,000).

The annual depreciation expense associated with the truck provides a reduction in income-tax expense equal to the firm's tax rate times the depreciation deduction. This reduction in income taxes is called a **depreciation tax shield.**

To summarize, depreciation is a noncash expense. Although depreciation is not a cash flow, it does cause a reduced cash outflow through the depreciation tax shield.

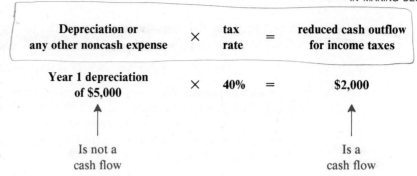

The following schedule shows High Country Department Stores' depreciation tax shield over the depreciable life of the proposed delivery truck.

Year	Depreciation Expense	Tax Rate	Cash Flow: Reduced Tax Payment	
1	$ 5,000	40%	$2,000	
2	10,000	40%	4,000	Depreciation
3	10,000	40%	4,000	tax
4	10,000	40%	4,000	shield
5	5,000	40%	2,000	

The cash flows comprising the depreciation tax shield occur in five different years. Thus, in a discounted-cash-flow analysis, we still must discount these cash flows to find their present value.

Cash Flows Not on the Income Statement Some cash flows do not appear on the income statement. They are not revenues, expenses, gains, or losses. A common example of such a cash flow is the purchase of an asset. If High Country Department Stores purchases the delivery truck, the $40,000 acquisition cost is a cash outflow but not an expense. A purchase is merely the exchange of one asset (cash) for another (a delivery truck). The expense associated with the truck's purchase is recognized through depreciation expense recorded throughout the asset's depreciable life. Thus, the cash flow resulting from the purchase of an asset does not affect income and has no direct tax consequences.

Net-Present-Value Analysis Now let's complete our example by preparing a net-present-value analysis of the proposed delivery-truck acquisition. In addition to the data given previously, assume that the truck's annual cash operating costs will be $20,000, and the company's after-tax hurdle rate is 10 percent. Exhibit 16-1 displays the net-present-value analysis of the acquisition decision. Since the NPV is positive, the delivery truck should be purchased.

Timing of Tax Deductions We have assumed in our analysis of High Country Department Stores' delivery-truck purchase that the cash flows resulting from income taxes occur during the same year as the before-tax cash flows. For example, High Country's management predicts that sales revenue will increase by $100,000 per year if the truck is purchased. This will increase income by $100,000, and hence will increase the cash outflow for income taxes by $40,000. We have assumed that the

Exhibit 16-1. Net-Present-Value Analysis with After-Tax Cash Flows

High Country Department Stores, Inc.
Purchase of Delivery Truck

	Time 0	Time 1	Time 2	Time 3	Time 4	Time 5
Acquisition cost	$(40,000)					
After-tax cash flow from incremental sales revenue, $100,000 × (1 − .40)		$ 60,000	$ 60,000	$ 60,000	$ 60,000	$ 60,000
After-tax cash flow from incremental compensation expense, $30,000 × (1 − .40)		(18,000)	(18,000)	(18,000)	(18,000)	(18,000)
After-tax cash flow from incremental operating expenses, $20,000 × (1 − .40)		(12,000)	(12,000)	(12,000)	(12,000)	(12,000)
After-tax cash flow from depreciation tax shield, depreciation expense × .40		2,000	4,000	4,000	4,000	2,000
Total cash flow	$(40,000)	$ 32,000	$ 34,000	$ 34,000	$ 34,000	$ 32,000
× Discount factor	× 1.000	× .909	× .826	× .751	× .683	× .621
Present value	$(40,000)	$ 29,088	$ 28,084	$ 25,534	$ 23,222	$ 19,872

Net present value   Sum = $85,800

$40,000 cash outflow from incremental taxes occurs in the same year as the $100,000 cash inflow from the incremental sales revenue. This assumption is realistic, as most businesses must make estimated tax payments throughout the tax year. They generally cannot wait until the following year and pay their prior year's taxes in one lump sum.

Accelerated Depreciation

The main concept underlying discounted-cash-flow analysis is the time value of money. We discount each cash flow to find its present value. Since money has a time value, it is advantageous for a business to take tax deductions as early as allowable under the tax law.

Although federal and state income tax laws are changed periodically by the appropriate governmental legislative bodies, income-tax laws usually permit some form of accelerated depreciation for tax purposes. An *accelerated depreciation method* is any method under which an asset is depreciated more quickly in the early part of its life than it would be using straight-line depreciation. For example, suppose High Country Department Stores purchased a personal computer and peripheral devices for $10,000. The equipment's useful life is four years with no salvage value. Exhibit 16-2 shows the pattern of depreciation deductions, the associated after-tax

Exhibit 16-2. Present Value of Depreciation Tax Shield: Alternative Depreciation Methods

Depreciation Expense (Double-Declining-Balance*)	Depreciation Tax Shield (Depreciation × 40%)	Depreciation Expense (Sum-of-the-Years'-Digits)	Depreciation Tax Shield (Depreciation × 40%)	Depreciation Expense (Straight-Line)	Depreciation Tax Shield (Depreciation × 40%)
$5,000	$2,000	$4,000	$1,600	$2,500	$1,000
2,500	1,000	3,000	1,200	2,500	1,000
1,250	500	2,000	800	2,500	1,000
1,250	500	1,000	400	2,500	1,000

Present value of depreciation tax shield (10% discount rate)

$3,361		$3,320		$3,170

*Steps in applying the double-declining-balance method:

To apply the double-declining-balance depreciation method, use the following steps:

1. Divide 100% by the number of years of depreciation to be taken.

2. Multiply the answer obtained in step (1) by 200%.

3. Compute the asset's depreciation each year by applying the percentage obtained in step (2) to the asset's undepreciated cost at the beginning of the year.

4. Switch to straight-line depreciation during the first year in which the straight-line amount, computed for the asset's remaining life, is greater than the double-declining-balance amount.

cash flows, and the present value of the depreciation tax shield under three different depreciation methods. Notice that both the 200%-declining balance method and the sum-of-the-years'-digits method result in a greater present value for the depreciation tax shield than the straight-line method does. Thus, it usually is desirable for a business to use accelerated depreciation for tax purposes whenever the tax law permits. The current tax law does not require that the same depreciation method be used for both the tax purpose and the external-reporting purpose. Thus, management could use straight-line depreciation when preparing published financial statements but use an accelerated method for tax purposes.

Accelerated Cost Recovery System

Under U.S. tax laws, most depreciable assets acquired after December 31, 1980 have been depreciated for tax purposes in accordance with the Accelerated Cost Recovery System (ACRS). The Tax Reform Acts of 1986 and 1989 modified the ACRS depreciation program. Under the modified ACRS, every asset is placed in one of eight classes, depending on the asset's expected useful life. These eight classes, along with

Exhibit 16-3. Accelerated Cost Recovery System (as modified by the Tax Reform Acts of 1986 and 1989)		
(a) Asset's Useful Life*	**(b)** Types of Assets in ACRS Class	**(c)** ACRS Class and Depreciation Method
Up to 4 years	Industrial tools	3-year class; double-declining-balance
Between 4 and 10 years	Automobiles, trucks, office equipment, computers, research equipment	5-year class; double-declining-balance
Between 10 and 16 years	Most industrial equipment and machinery; office furniture	7-year class; double-declining-balance
Between 16 and 20 years	Equipment and machinery for specified purposes	10-year class; double-declining-balance
Between 20 and 25 years	Land improvements; some industrial machinery	15-year class; 150%-declining-balance
25 years or longer	Specified real property, such as farm buildings	20-year class; 150%-declining-balance
—	Residential rental property	27.5-year class; straight-line
—	Nonresidential real property	31.5-year class; straight-line

*In the tax law, an asset's useful life is referred to as the Asset Depreciation Range (ADR) Midpoint Life.

examples of the assets included, are shown in columns (a) and (b) of Exhibit 16-3. For each class, the Internal Revenue Code specifies the number of years over which the asset may be depreciated, and the depreciation method to be used. These specifications are shown in column (c) of Exhibit 16-3. Notice that the number of years of depreciation specified by the tax code is not the same as an asset's useful life. Thus, each asset's useful life is used only to place the asset in its appropriate ACRS class. Then the tax code specifies the appropriate number of years of depreciation.[1]

Depreciation Methods As Exhibit 16-3 indicates, assets in the 3-year, 5-year, 7-year, and 10-year ACRS property classes are depreciated using the double-declining-balance (DDB) method. Assets in the 15-year and 20-year ACRS property classes are depreciated using the 150%-declining balance method. To apply this depreciation method, use the same steps as those listed in Exhibit 16-2 for the DDB method, except change 200% in step (2) to 150%. Assets in the 27.5-year and 31.5-year ACRS property classes are depreciated using the straight-line method.

Half-Year Convention An asset may be purchased at any time during the tax year. The ACRS assumes that, on average, assets will be placed in service halfway through the tax year. Thus, the tax code allows only a half year's depreciation during the tax year in which an asset is placed in service. The other half of the first year's depreciation is picked up in the second tax year in which the asset is in service. The following diagram shows the pattern with which a five-year asset's depreciation is recorded, for tax purposes, under the ACRS.

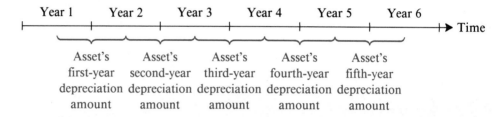

ACRS Depreciation Tables To assist taxpayers, the Internal Revenue Service has published tables of the ACRS depreciation percentages for each ACRS property class. The IRS tables use the depreciation method specified in Exhibit 16-3 and incorporate the half-year convention. Exhibit 16-4 provides a convenient table of the ACRS percentages, as computed by the IRS, for selected property classes. In the 5-year column, we see 20 percent for year 1. This results from the half-year convention, since 20 percent is half of the double-declining balance rate of 40 percent.

No Salvage Values Under the ACRS, an asset's estimated salvage value is *not* subtracted in computing the asset's depreciation basis. Thus, for an asset costing $10,000 with an estimated salvage value of $1,000, the full $10,000 cost is depreciated over the asset's life.

Optional Straight-Line Depreciation The tax law permits a business to depreciate any asset using the straight-line method instead of the method prescribed in Exhibit 16-3. A business with a loss might prefer this approach for tax reasons. If the

---

[1] The U.S. tax law changes almost every year. Occasionally, changes are made in the assignment of assets to property classes and in the associated depreciation schedules. Moreover, the terminology frequently changes. The tax act of 1980 established the Accelerated Cost Recovery System, which then was referred to as ACRS. Since the tax act of 1986, the program has been referred to in various publications by a variety of names. Among these are the modified accelerated cost recovery system (MACRS), the ACRS as modified, the CRS, or simply the ACRS. We will follow the common convention of referring to the current system simply as the ACRS. Our discussion incorporates the latest tax law changes known as this book went to press. Regardless of what minor changes the tax laws may make in terminology or depreciation schedules, it is likely that the tax code will continue to allow depreciation by an accelerated schedule similar to the modified ACRS.

Exhibit 16-4. ACRS Depreciation Percentages as Computed by the IRS (incorporates half-year convention; also incorporates recent modifications in the tax laws)

Year	3-year	5-year	7-year	10-year	15-year	20-year
				ACRS Property Class		
1	33.33%	20.00%	14.29%	10.00%	5.00%	3.75%
2	44.45	32.00	24.49	18.00	9.50	7.22
3	14.81*	19.20	17.49	14.40	8.55	6.68
4	7.41	11.52*	12.49	11.52	7.70	6.18
5		11.52	8.93*	9.22	6.93	5.71
6		5.76	8.92	7.37	6.23	5.29
7			8.93	6.55*	5.90*	4.89
8			4.46	6.55	5.90	4.52*
9				6.56	5.91	4.46
10				6.55	5.90	4.46
11				3.28	5.91	4.46
12					5.90	4.46
13					5.91	4.46
14					5.90	4.46
15					5.91	4.46
16					2.95	4.46
17						4.46
18						4.46
19						4.46
20						4.46
21						2.23

*Denotes the year during which the depreciation method switches to the straight-line method.

Source: IRS Publication 534, entitled *Depreciation.*

straight-line method is used, the business may depreciate the asset over either the ACRS life or the asset's estimated useful life. Thus, businesses have considerable flexibility in choosing a depreciation schedule for tax purposes. Regardless of the depreciation method chosen, the half-year convention still must be followed.

Income-Tax Complexities The U.S. tax code is a complex document with a multitude of provisions. It is not possible to cover all of these provisions in this text, so it is wise to consult a tax expert regarding the complexities that may apply in a particular investment decision. Since the tax code is changed frequently by Congress, a tax rule that applied last year may not apply this year. For example, the *investment tax credit* is one important tax-code provision that has been switched on and off repeatedly by Congress. During periods when the investment tax credit has been in effect, a company has been allowed a substantial reduction in its income taxes when particular types of investments are made. The intent of the investment credit was to stimulate the economy by giving businesses an incentive to make new investments.

As this text was written, the investment credit was not in effect, but its status always is subject to change. If there is a moral to the changing-tax-code story, it is this: When making an important investment decision, a manager should have a managerial accountant on one side and a tax accountant on the other.

Gains and Losses on Disposal

When a business sells an asset, there often is a gain or loss on the sale. Since gains and losses are included in income, the business's income taxes generally are affected. Capital investment decisions frequently involve the disposal of assets, and sometimes gains or losses are recorded on those sales. Thus, the tax effects of gains and losses on disposal of assets can be an important feature of an investment decision.

The *book value* of an asset is defined as the asset's acquisition cost minus the accumulated depreciation on the asset. When an asset is sold for more than its current book value, a *gain on disposal* is recorded. The *gain* is defined as the difference between the sales proceeds and the asset's book value. A *loss on disposal* is recorded when an asset is sold for less than its current book value. The *loss* is equal to the difference between the asset's current book value and the sales proceeds.

To illustrate, suppose High Country Department Stores owns a forklift, which cost $10,000 and currently has accumulated depreciation of $6,000. The forklift's book value is computed below.

$$\textbf{Book value} = \textbf{acquisition cost} - \textbf{accumulated depreciation}$$

$$\textbf{\$4,000} = \textbf{\$10,000} - \textbf{\$6,000}$$

Scenario I: Gain on Disposal Suppose High Country sells the forklift for $5,000. The *gain* on the sale is $1,000 ($5,000 proceeds minus $4,000 book value). If High Country's income-tax rate is 40 percent, the following cash flows will occur at the time of the sale.

Cash inflow: proceeds from sale	$5,000
Cash outflow: incremental income tax due to the gain, $1,000 × 40%	(400)
Net cash flow	$4,600

Although High Country sold the forklift for $5,000, the company's net cash benefit is only $4,600. The firm will have to pay the other $400 in increased income taxes on the $1,000 gain.

Scenario II: Loss on Disposal Now assume instead that High Country Department Stores sells the forklift for $3,200. The *loss* on the sale is $800 ($3,200 proceeds minus $4,000 book value). If High Country's income-tax rate is 40 percent, the following cash flows will occur at the time of the sale.

Cash inflow: proceeds from sale	$3,200
Reduced cash outflow: reduction in income tax due to the loss, $800 × 40%	320
Total cash flow	$3,520

Although High Country sold the forklift for only $3,200, the company's total benefit from the sale is $3,520. The extra $320 comes in the form of a reduction in income taxes due to the loss on the sale.

Implications for Investment Decisions Why is the analysis above likely to be relevant in an investment decision? Suppose High Country Department Stores has the opportunity to sell its old forklift for $3,200 and buy a new one for $12,000. The company will save $2,500 in annual operating expenses over the next 10 years if the new forklift is used instead of the old machine. A net-present-value analysis of this machine-replacement decision is presented in Exhibit 16-5. The tax impact of the loss on disposal is a prominent part of the machine-replacement analysis. Without the tax savings associated with the loss, the net present value of the new forklift would have been cut from $738 to only $418 ($738 NPV minus tax effect of $320).

Notice that the presentation format used for the analysis in Exhibit 16-5 is different from the format we have used previously. Instead of listing the cash flows for each item by year and then adding the columns, we have computed the present value of each financial item pertinent to the decision. The one-time cash flows at time zero then are added to the present value of the cost-savings annuity to determine the net present value. This alternative presentation format will yield the same conclusion as the year-by-year, columnar approach. The choice of format is a matter of personal preference.

Tax Rates on Gains and Losses Another complexity of the tax code that changes from time to time is that capital gains and losses may be taxed at different rates than ordinary income (i.e., revenue minus expenses). Thus, before preparing an NPV

Exhibit 16-5. Net-Present-Value Analysis with Loss on Disposal

High Country Department Stores, Inc.
Forklift Replacement Decision

Acquisition cost of new forklift	$(12,000)
Proceeds from sale of old forklift	3,200
Reduced taxes due to loss on sale, 40% × $800	320
Net cash outflow at time 0 (now)	$(8,480)

Present value of annual cost savings:

Annual cost savings	$2,500	
× (1 – tax rate)	.60	
After-tax cost savings	$1,500	
× Annuity discount factor		
($n = 10, r = .10$)	× 6.145*	
Present value of after-tax		
cost savings	$9,218	9,218
Net present value of new forklift		$ 738

*Annuity discount factor from Table IV in the appendix to Chapter 15.
 Assumes an after-tax hurdle rate of 10%.

analysis, it is wise to check with a tax expert to obtain the proper income-tax rate to apply to a gain or loss on disposal.

Investment in Working Capital

Some investment proposals require additional outlays for working capital. **Working capital,** defined as the excess of current assets over current liabilities, often increases as the result of higher balances in accounts receivable or inventory necessary to support a project. Such increases are uses of cash and should be included in a discounted-cash-flow analysis. To illustrate, suppose the City of Mountainview has offered High Country Department Stores a contract to sell special T-shirts and mementos commemorating the city's bicentennial. The contract covers the three-year period leading up to the bicentennial celebration. The cash flows associated with the proposal are displayed in panel A of Exhibit 16-6. Notice that the sales proposal would require a $2,000 outlay for additional working capital throughout the three-year period. The increased working capital is largely due to a higher balance in merchandise inventory. Panel B of Exhibit 16-6 analyzes the contract proposal. Notice that the time 0 cash investment in working capital is included as a $2,000 cash outflow. Since the increase in working capital is not released until the end of year 3, that $2,000 inflow is discounted. The city's proposal has a positive net present value, so it should be accepted.

Extended Illustration of Income-Tax Effects in Capital Budgeting

Now we have covered all of the most important concepts for analyzing an investment proposal in a profit-seeking enterprise. A comprehensive illustration will help you solidify your understanding of these concepts. High Country Department Stores' management is considering the installation of a new checkout system for its suburban store. The new computerized system would include new cash registers at each check-out station. In addition, the new checkout system would include bar-code readers, so that most merchandise could be checked out automatically instead of manually. The advantages of the new system are accuracy in the checkout process, automatic updat-ing of computerized inventory records, and the ability to gather data about custom-ers' buying patterns and trends.

Exhibit 16-7 presents the data pertinent to the decision. Notice that the old equipment has been fully depreciated already. However, its useful life can be ex-tended to six more years if an overhaul is done in year 2. The new equipment also has an expected useful life of six years, so its ACRS classification is the 5-year property class.

Most of the data in Exhibit 16-7 are self-explanatory. The last two items in the exhibit relate to the new checkout system's capability of gathering data about cus-tomer demand patterns. The extra data analysis will cost $4,500 annually, but it is expected to generate another $40,000 in annual sales.

A net-present-value analysis of the checkout equipment proposal is presented in Exhibit 16-8. A total-cost approach is used. The present value of each financial item is computed for both alternatives; then these present values are added to determine each alternative's net present value. An explanation of each line in the exhibit follows.

(1) Line (1) in Exhibit 16-8 records the acquisition cost of the new checkout

---

Exhibit 16-6. Investment in Working Capital

High Country Department Stores, Inc.
Contract Proposal for the City's Bicentennial

Annual sales revenue from T-shirts and mementos	$25,000
Annual expenses	12,000
Annual contract fee to city	3,000
Investment in working capital (time 0)	2,000
Release of working capital (end of year 3)	(2,000)
Tax rate	40%
After-tax hurdle rate	10%

(A) Data for Illustration

Investment in working capital (time 0)	$(2,000)

Release of working capital:

Working capital released (end of year 3)	$2,000	
Discount factor $(n = 3, r = .10)$	× .751*	
Present value of working capital released		→ 1,502

Annual revenue and expenses:

Sales revenue	$25,000	
Expenses	(12,000)	
Contract fee	(3,000)	
Before-tax annual income	10,000	
× (1 − tax rate)	× .60	
After-tax annual income	6,000	
× annuity discount factor	× 2.487†	
Present value of after-tax annual income		→ 14,922

Net present value of contract proposal	$14,424

(B) Discounted-Cash-Flow Analysis

* From Table III of the appendix to Chapter 15.
† From Table IV of the appendix to Chapter 15.

---

equipment. This cash flow has no tax impact and does not need to be discounted, since it occurs at time 0.

(2), (3) These one-time cash flows are required to retrain checkout personnel and retag merchandise to accommodate the new bar-code readers. Since these costs are expenses, we multiply by (1 − .40).

Exhibit 16-7. Data for Extended Illustration

High Country Department Stores, Inc.
Computerized Checkout Equipment Decision

Old checkout equipment:

  Remaining useful life, assuming

    overhaul in year 2 . . . . 6 years

  Cost of overhaul in year 2 . . . . $3,500

  Current book value (fully depreciated) . . . . –0–

  Current salvage value $1,200

  Salvage value in six more years . . . . –0–

New checkout equipment:

  Useful (ADR midpoint) life . . . . 6 years

  ACRS property classification . . . . 5-year class

  Acquisition cost of new equipment $50,000

  Update of software required in year 3 . . . . $4,000

  Salvage value of new equipment in six years $1,000

  Cost to retrain checkout personnel $5,000

  Cost to retag merchandise $3,000

Annual data:

  Annual operating-cost savings $15,000

  Annual cost of computer-system operator $30,000

  Annual cost of marketing-data analysis $4,500

  Annual incremental sales resulting from

    marketing analysis $40,000

After-tax hurdle rate 10%

Tax rate 40%

(4) and (5) Since the old equipment has a current book value of zero, there is a $1,200 gain on the sale. The $1,200 proceeds are not taxed (line 4), but the $1,200 gain on the sale is taxed (line 5).

(6) The cost of updating the software in year 3 is an expense, so we multiply by $(1 - .40)$.

(7) and (8) The new equipment can be sold in year 6 for $1,000. Since it will be fully depreciated, there will be a $1,000 gain. The $1,000 proceeds are not taxed (line 7), but the $1,000 gain is taxed (line 8).

(9) The depreciation tax shield on the new equipment is computed using the ACRS depreciation schedule for the 5-year property class. The annual depreciation deductions are not cash flows, but they do cause a reduction in income taxes. Each cash flow then is discounted using the appropriate discount factor from Table III in the appendix to Chapter 15.

(10), (11), (12), and (13) These items are annual cash flows. The flows are summed, and then the $20,500 annuity is multiplied by $(1 - .40)$ because each of the cash flows will be on the income statement. The after-tax cash-flow annuity of $12,300 then is discounted using the annuity discount factor for $n = 6$ and $r = .10$.

(14) The net present value of the new equipment is $13,482.

Exhibit 16-8. Net-Present-Value Analysis for Extended Illustration

High Country Department Stores, Inc.
Computerized Checkout Equipment Decision

	Year	Amount	Income-Tax Impact	After-Tax Cash Flow	Discount Factor (10%)	Present Value of Cash Flow
Purchase New Equipment						
(1) Acquisition cost of new equipment	Time 0	$50,000	None	$(50,000)	1.000	$(50,000)
(2) Cost to retrain checkout personnel	Time 0	5,000	(1 − .40)*	(3,000)	1.000	(3,000)
(3) Cost to retag merchandise.	Time 0	3,000	(1 − .40)	(1,800)	1.000	(1,800)
(4) Proceeds from sale of old equipment	Time 0	1,200	None	1,200	1.000	1,200
(5) Gain on sale of old equipment	Time 0	1,200	.40	(480)	1.000	(480)
(6) Update of software	3	4,000	(1 − .40)	(2,400)	.751	(1,802)
(7) Salvage value of new equipment	6	1,000	None	1,000	.564	564
(8) Gain on sale of new equipment	6	1,000	.40	(400)	.564	(226)
(9) Depreciation tax shield:						

		ACRS Percentage (rounded)	Depreciation Expense				
Year	Cost						
1	50,000	20.0%	$10,000	10,000	.40	4,000	.909	3,636
2	50,000	32.0%	16,000	16,000	.40	6,400	.826	5,286
3	50,000	19.2%	9,600	9,600	.40	3,840	.751	2,884
4	50,000	11.5%	5,750	5,750	.40	2,300	.683	1,571
5	50,000	11.5%	5,750	5,750	.40	2,300	.621	1,428
6	50,000	5.8%	2,900	2,900	.40	1,160	.564	654
Total			$50,000					

Annual incremental costs and benefits (years 1 through 6):

(10) Annual operating cost savings	$15,000				Annuity	
(11) Annual cost of computer operator	(30,000)				discount	
(12) Annual cost of marketing analysis	(4,500)				factor for	
(13) Annual incremental sales revenue	40,000				$n = 6, r = .10$	
Total annual amount	$20,500	$20,500	(1 − .40)	$12,300	4.355	53,567
(14) Net present value						$13,482

Keep Old Equipment†

	Year	Amount	Income-Tax Impact	After-Tax Cash Flow	Discount Factor	Present Value
(15) Cost of overhaul	2	$3,500	(1 − .40)	$(2,100)	.826	$ (1,735)
(16) Net present value						$ (1,735)

* High Country Department Stores' tax rate is 40%.
† There is no depreciation tax shield if the old equipment is kept, since it has been depreciated fully already.

(15) The only specific cash flow related to the alternative of keeping the old equipment is the $3,500 overhaul in year 2. This will be an expense, so we multiply by (1 − .40). Then the after-tax cash flow is discounted.

(16) The net present value of the alternative to keep the old equipment is $(1,735).

Decision Rule The analysis indicates that High Country Department Stores should purchase the new checkout equipment. The NPV of the new equipment exceeds that of the old equipment.

RANKING INVESTMENT PROJECTS

Suppose a company has several potential investment projects, all of which have positive net present values. If a project has a positive net present value, this means that the return projected for the project exceeds the company's cost of capital. In this case, every project with a positive NPV should be accepted. In spite of the theoretical validity of this argument, practice often does not reflect this viewpoint. In practice, managers often attempt to rank investment projects with positive net present values. Then only a limited number of the higher-ranking proposals are accepted.

The reasons for this common practice are not clear. If a discount rate is used that accurately reflects the firm's cost of capital, then any project with a positive NPV will earn a return greater than the cost of obtaining capital to fund it. One possible explanation for the practice of ranking investment projects is a limited supply of scarce resources, such as managerial talent. Thus, a form of *capital rationing* takes place, not because of a limited supply of investment capital, but because of limitations on other resources. A manager may feel that he or she simply cannot devote sufficient attention to all of the desirable projects. The solution, then, is to select only some of the positive-NPV proposals, which implies a ranking.

Unfortunately, no valid method exists for ranking independent investment projects with positive net present values. To illustrate, suppose the management of High Country Department Stores has the following two investment opportunities:

1. Proposal A: Open a gift shop at the Mountainview Convention Center. High Country's management believes the benefits of this proposal would last only six years. High Country's management expects that after six years, the firm's competitors will move into the Convention Center and eliminate High Country's current advantageous position.
2. Open a small gift shop at the Mountainview Airport. The airport gift concession would belong to High Country Department Stores for 10 years under a contract with the city.

The predicted cash flows for these investment proposals are as follows:

Investment Proposal	Cash Outflow: Time 0	After-Tax Cash Inflows Years 1–6	After-Tax Cash Inflows Years 7–10	Present Value of Inflows (10% Discount Rate)	Net Present Value	Internal Rate of Return
A (Convention Center)	($54,450)	$14,000	—	$60,970	$6,520	14%
B (Airport)	(101,700)	18,000	$18,000	110,610	8,910	12%

Both investment proposals have positive net present values. Suppose, however, that due to limited managerial time, High Country's management has decided to pursue only one of the projects. Which proposal should be ranked higher? This is a difficult question to answer. Proposal B has a higher net present value, but it also requires a much larger initial investment. Proposal A exhibits a higher internal rate of return. However, proposal A's return of 14 percent applies only to its six-year time horizon. If management accepts proposal A, what will happen in years 7 through 10? Will the facilities and equipment remain idle? Or could they be used profitably for some other purpose? These questions are left unanswered by the analysis above.

The main reason that the NPV and IRR methods of analysis yield different rankings for these two proposals is that the projects have different lives. Without making an assumption about what will happen in years 7 through 10 if proposal A is accepted, the NPV and IRR methods simply are not capable of ranking the proposals in any sound manner. The only theoretically correct answer to the problem posed in this illustration is that both projects are desirable, and both should be accepted. Each proposal exhibits a positive NPV and an IRR greater than the hurdle rate of 10 percent.

Profitability Index One criterion that managers sometimes apply in ranking investment proposals is called the **profitability index** (or **excess present value index**), which is defined as follows:

$$\text{Profitability index} = \frac{\text{present value of cash flows,}\\ \text{exclusive of initial investment}}{\text{initial investment}}$$

The profitability indices for High Country's two investment proposals are computed as follows:

Investment Proposal	Calculation		Profitability Index	Net Present Value	Internal Rate of Return
A	$\dfrac{\text{Present value of inflows}}{\text{Initial investment}} = \dfrac{\$\ 60,970}{\$\ 54,450}$	$= 1.12$		$6,520	14%
			$\vee$	$\wedge$	$\vee$
B	$\dfrac{\text{Present value of inflows}}{\text{Initial investment}} = \dfrac{\$110,610}{\$101,700}$	$= 1.09$		$8,910	12%

Although proposal A has a lower NPV than proposal B, proposal A exhibits a higher profitability index. Proposal A's higher profitability index is due to its considerably lower initial investment than that required for proposal B. Is the profitability index a foolproof method for ranking investment proposals? Unfortunately, it too suffers from the same drawbacks as those associated with the NPV or IRR methods. Both proposals exhibit a profitability index greater than 1.00, which merely reflects their positive NPVs. Thus, both projects are desirable. The unequal lives of the two proposals prevent the profitability index from indicating a theoretically correct ranking of the proposals. The relative desirability of proposals A and B simply depends on what will happen in years 7 through 10 if proposal A is selected.

In summary, the problem of ranking investment projects with positive NPVs has not been solved in a satisfactory manner. This lack of resolution is due to an inconsistency inherent to the problem. The inconsistency is that if several projects have positive NPVs, they all are desirable. They all will earn a return greater than the cost of capital. If a manager chooses not to accept all projects with positive NPVs, then the required ranking ultimately must be made on the basis of subjective criteria.

ADDITIONAL METHODS FOR MAKING INVESTMENT DECISIONS

The best way to decide whether to accept an investment project is to use discounted-cash-flow analysis, as described in this and the preceding chapter. Both the net-present-value and the internal-rate-of-return methods will yield the correct accept-or-reject decision. The strength of these methods lies in the fact that they properly account for the time value of money. In spite of the conceptual superiority of discounted-cash-flow decision models, managers sometimes use other methods for making investment decisions. In some cases, these alternative methods are used in conjunction with a discounted-cash-flow analysis. Two of these alternative decision methods are described next.

Payback Method

The **payback period** of an investment proposal is the amount of time it will take for the after-tax cash inflows from the project to accumulate to an amount that covers the original investment. The following formula defines an investment project's payback period.

$$\text{Payback period} = \frac{\text{initial investment}}{\text{annual after-tax cash inflow}}$$

There is no adjustment in the payback method for the time value of money. A cash inflow in year 5 is treated the same as a cash inflow in year 1.

To illustrate the payback method, suppose High Country Department Stores' management is considering the purchase of a new conveyor system for its warehouse. The two alternative machines under consideration have the following projected cash flows.

Conveyor System	Initial Investment	After-Tax Cash Flows: Years 1 through 7	After-Tax Cash Flow When System Is Sold
I	. . . . . $(20,000)	$4,000	. . . . . −0−
II	. . . . . (27,000)	4,500	. . . . . $14,000

The payback period for each conveyor system is computed below. Notice that *after-tax cash flows are used* in the payback method, just as they are in discounted-cash-flow methods of analysis.

Conveyor System	Initial Investment / Annual After-Tax Cash Inflow	Payback Period
I	$\dfrac{\$20,000}{\$\ 4,000}$	. . . . 5 years
II	$\dfrac{\$27,000}{\$\ 4,500}$	. . . . 6 years

According to the payback method, system I is more desirable than system II. System I will "pay back" its initial investment in five years, while system II requires six years. This conclusion is too simplistic, however, because it ignores the large salvage value associated with system II. Indeed, the NPV of system I is negative, while the NPV of system II is positive, as shown in the following analysis.

After-Tax Cash Flows	Present Value of Cash Flows (10% discount factor)	
	System I	System II
Initial investment	$(20,000) × 1.000 = $(20,000)	$(27,000) × 1.000 = $(27,000)
Years 1–7	4,000 × 4.868 = 19,472	4,500 × 4.868 = 21,906
Cash inflow from sale	–0–	14,000 × .513 = 7,182
Net present value	$ (528)	$ 2,088

The net-present-value analysis demonstrates that only system II can generate cash flows sufficient to cover the company's cost of capital. The payback method makes it appear as though system I "pays back" its initial investment more quickly, but the method fails to consider the time value of money.

Another shortcoming of the payback method is that it fails to consider an investment project's profitability beyond the payback period. Suppose High Country Department Stores' management has a third alternative for its warehouse conveyor system. System III requires an initial investment of only $12,000 and will generate after-tax cash inflows of $6,000 in years 1 and 2. Thus, System III's payback period is two years, as computed below.

$$\text{System III payback period} = \frac{\$12,000}{\$\ 6,000} = 2 \text{ years}$$

Strict adherence to the payback method would rank system III above systems I and II, due to its shorter payback period. However, suppose we add another piece of information. System III's useful life is only two years, and it has no salvage value after two years. It is true that system III will "pay back" its initial investment in only two years, if we ignore the time value of money. But then what? System III provides no further benefits beyond year 2. In spite of system III's short payback period, it is not a desirable investment proposal. The NPV of system III, $(1,584), is negative [$(1,584) = (1.736 × $6,000) − $12,000].

Payback Period with Uneven Cash Flows The simple payback formula given earlier in the chapter will not work if a project exhibits an uneven pattern of cash flows. Instead, the after-tax cash flows must be accumulated on a year-to-year basis until the accumulation equals the initial investment. Suppose High Country Department Stores' management is considering the expansion of the downtown store's parking facilities. Management expects that the additional parking will result in much greater sales initially. However, this benefit will gradually taper off, due to the reactions of competitors. The following after-tax cash flows are projected. Exhibit 16-9 presents the payback calculation for the parking lot proposal. The project's payback period is five years.

Payback: Pro and Con In summary, the payback method of evaluating investment proposals has two serious drawbacks. First, the method fails to consider the time value of money. Second, it does not consider a project's cash flows beyond the payback period. Despite these shortcomings, the payback method is used widely in practice, for two legitimate reasons.

First, the payback method provides a tool for roughly screening investment proposals. If a project does not meet some minimal criterion for the payback period, management may wish to reject the proposal regardless of potential large cash flows

Exhibit 16-9. Payback Period with Uneven Cash Flows

High Country Department Stores, Inc.
Parking Lot Expansion

Year	Type of Cash Flow	After-Tax Cash Flows Outflows	After-Tax Cash Flows Inflows	Accumulated Cash Flows (excluding initial investment)	
0	Initial investment	$(200,000)		—	
1	Incremental sales		$60,000	$ 60,000	
2	Incremental sales		50,000	110,000	
3	Incremental sales		45,000	155,000	
4	Incremental sales		35,000	190,000	
4	Repave parking lot	(20,000)		170,000	Payback
5	Incremental sales		30,000	200,000 ◄———	period:
6	Incremental sales		30,000	230,000	5 years
7	Incremental sales		30,000	260,000	
8	Incremental sales		30,000	290,000	

predicted well into the future. Second, a young firm may experience a shortage of cash. For such a company, it may be crucial to select investment projects that recoup their initial investment quickly. A cash-poor firm may not be able to wait for the big payoff of a project with a long payback period. Even in these cases, it is wise not to rely on the payback method alone. If the payback method is used, it should be in conjunction with a discounted-cash-flow analysis.

Accounting-Rate-of-Return Method

Discounted-cash-flow methods of investment analysis focus on *cash flows* and incorporate the time value of money. The **accounting rate-of-return method** focuses on the incremental *accounting income* that results from a project. Accounting income is based on accrual accounting procedures. Revenue is recognized during the period of sale, not necessarily when the cash is received; expenses are recognized during the period they are incurred, not necessarily when they are paid in cash. The following formula is used to compute the accounting rate of return on an investment project.

$$\text{Accounting rate of return} = \frac{\left(\begin{array}{c} \text{average} \\ \text{incremental} \\ \text{revenue} \end{array} \right) - \left(\begin{array}{c} \text{average incremental} \\ \text{expenses (including} \\ \text{depreciation} \\ \text{and income taxes)} \end{array} \right)}{\text{initial investment}}$$

To illustrate the accounting-rate-of-return method, suppose High Country Department Stores' management is considering the installation of a small lunch counter in its downtown store. The required equipment and furnishings cost $210,000 and are in the ACRS 7-year property class. The company has elected to use the optional straight-line depreciation method with the half-year convention. Exhibit 16-10 displays management's revenue and expense projections for the lunch counter. The

Exhibit 16-10. Accounting Rate of Return Method

High Country Department Stores, Inc.
Lunch Counter for Downtown Store

Year	Sales Revenue	Cost of Goods Sold	Operating Expenses	ACRS Depreciation*	Income Before Taxes	Income Taxes (40%)	Net Income
1	$200,000	$100,000	$50,000	$ 15,000	$35,000	14,000	21,000
2	200,000	100,000	50,000	30,000	20,000	8,000	12,000
3	200,000	100,000	50,000	30,000	20,000	8,000	12,000
4	200,000	100,000	50,000	30,000	20,000	8,000	12,000
5	200,000	100,000	50,000	30,000	20,000	8,000	12,000
6	200,000	100,000	50,000	30,000	20,000	8,000	12,000
7	200,000	100,000	50,000	30,000	20,000	8,000	12,000
8	200,000	100,000	50,000	15,000	35,000	14,000	21,000
9	200,000	100,000	50,000	0	50,000	20,000	30,000
10	200,000	100,000	50,000	0	50,000	20,000	30,000
Total				$210,000			$174,000

*Annual straight-line depreciation = $\frac{\$210,000}{7}$ = $30,000

In accordance with the half-year convention, only half a year's depreciation is recorded in years 1 and 8.

total income projected over the project's 10-year useful life is $174,000. Thus, the average annual income is $17,400. The accounting rate of return on the lunch-counter proposal is computed as follows:

$$\text{Accounting rate of return} = \frac{\$\ 17,400}{\$210,000} = 8.3\% \text{ (rounded)}$$

To compute the lunch-counter project's internal rate of return, let's assume that each year's sales revenue, cost of goods sold, operating expenses, and income taxes are cash flows in the same year that they are recorded under accrual accounting. Recall that the depreciation expense is not a cash flow. These assumptions imply the following cash flow pattern for the project.

Net After-Tax Cash Inflows

Year	Amount	Year	Amount
1	$36,000	6	$42,000
2	42,000	7	42,000
3	42,000	8	36,000
4	42,000	9	30,000
5	42,000	10	30,000

Initial investment . . . . $(210,000)

The internal rate of return on the lunch-counter proposal is approximately 13.5 percent. That is, if we compute the present value of the cash flows using a discount rate of 13.5 percent, we obtain approximately a zero NPV.[2] Notice that the project's accounting rate of return, at 8.3 percent, is much lower than its IRR of 13.5 percent.

Use of the Average Investment   Some managers prefer to compute the accounting rate of return using the average amount invested in a project for the denominator, rather than the project's full cost. The formula is modified as follows:

$$\text{Accounting rate of return (using average investment)} = \frac{\left(\begin{array}{c}\text{average} \\ \text{incremental} \\ \text{revenue}\end{array}\right) - \left(\begin{array}{c}\text{average incremental} \\ \text{expenses (including} \\ \text{depreciation} \\ \text{and income taxes)}\end{array}\right)}{\text{average investment}}$$

A project's average investment is the average accounting book value over the project's life.

Refer again to High Country Department Stores' lunch-counter data given in Exhibit 16-10. The project's book value at the beginning of each year is tabulated as follows:

Year	(a) Book Value at Beginning of Year		ACRS Depreciation		(b) Book Value at End of Year		$\frac{\text{(a)} + \text{(b)}}{2}$ Average Book Value During Year
1	$210,000	....	$15,000	....	$195,000	....	$202,500
2	195,000	....	30,000	....	165,000	....	180,000
3	165,000	....	30,000	....	135,000	....	150,000
4	135,000	....	30,000	....	105,000	....	120,000
5	105,000	....	30,000	....	75,000	....	90,000
6	75,000	....	30,000	....	45,000	....	60,000
7	45,000	....	30,000	....	15,000	....	30,000
8	15,000	....	15,000	....	-0-	....	7,500
9	-0-	....	-0-	....	-0-	....	0
10	-0-	....	-0-	....	-0-	....	0

The average investment over the project's useful life is the average of the amounts in the right-hand column, which is $84,000. Thus, the modified version of the project's accounting rate of return is 20.7 percent. (The average annual income of $17,400 divided by the average investment of $84,000 equals 20.7 percent, rounded.)

Notice that this modified version of the accounting rate of return yields a significantly higher return than the project's internal rate of return, which we computed as 13.5 percent. As a general rule of thumb, the following relationships will be observed.

$$\begin{array}{ccc}\text{Accounting rate of return} & & \text{internal rate} & & \text{accounting rate of return} \\ \text{(using initial investment)} & < & \text{of return} & < & \text{(using average investment)}\end{array}$$

[2] You can verify the IRR of 13.5% using Table III in the appendix to Chapter 15. You will need to interpolate to find the discount factors for 13.5%, which lie between the 12% and 14% discount factors. For example, .881 is the approximate discount factor for 13.5% and $n = 1$ [.881 = .887 + (.25)(.893 − .877)].

Accounting Rate of Return: Pro and Con Like the payback method, the accounting-rate-of-return method is a simple way of screening investment proposals. Some managers use this method because they believe it parallels financial-accounting statements, which also are based on accrual accounting. However, like the payback method, the accounting-rate-of-return method does not consider the time value of money.

Inconsistent Terminology Many different terms for the accounting rate of return are used in practice. Among these terms are *simple rate of return, rate of return on assets,* and the *unadjusted rate of return.*

Surveys of practice indicate that the payback and accounting-rate-of-return methods still are used, although less commonly than in the past.

**ILLUSTRATION FROM
MANAGEMENT-
ACCOUNTING
PRACTICE**

Capital-Budgeting Practices

A survey of managers in large companies indicated that over a 10-year period, the following changes occurred in capital budgeting for replacement projects.[3]

Capital-budgeting Technique	Percentage of Managers Using Technique at Beginning of Decade	Percentage of Managers Using Technique at End of Decade
Discounted-cash-flow analysis	28%	56%
Accounting rate of return	21%	7%
Payback	10%	4%

CHAPTER SUMMARY

Income taxes play an important role in the capital-budgeting decisions of a profit-seeking enterprise. For any organization subject to income taxes, the first step in a discounted-cash-flow analysis is to determine the after-tax cash flows related to the investment proposal under consideration. Cash flows that are also on the income statement should be multiplied by 1 minus the organization's tax rate. This rule applies to cash expenses and cash revenues. Cash flows that are not on the income statement, such as asset acquisitions, have no direct tax consequences. Expenses that are not cash flows in their own right, such as depreciation expenses, cause a cash flow by reducing the organization's income taxes. Thus, depreciation expenses should be multiplied by the tax rate to determine their tax impact. The resulting reductions in income-tax cash flows comprise a depreciation tax shield on a depreciable asset.

The time value of money makes it advantageous for a company to use an accelerated depreciation method for tax purposes. The current U.S. tax law specifies that the Accelerated Cost Recovery System (ACRS) be used to determine depreciation deductions.

When assets are sold for more or less than their current book value, the gain or

---

[3] Thomas P. Klammer and Michael C. Walker, "The Continuing Increase in the Use of Sophisticated Capital Budgeting Techniques," *California Management Review, 27,* no. 1 (Fall 1984), p. 139.

loss on disposal is taxed. Thus, the tax implications of asset dispositions also should be included in a discounted-cash-flow analysis.

No reliable method exists for ranking multiple investment proposals with positive net present values. Nevertheless, the profitability index is a widely used method for ranking projects.

In addition to discounted-cash-flow analysis, many organizations use the payback method and the accounting-rate-of-return method in capital-budgeting decisions. Since these methods do not account for the time value of money, they are conceptually inferior to discounted-cash-flow methods.

KEY TERMS **Accelerated Cost Recovery System (ACRS),** p. 690; **Accounting-rate-of-return method,** p. 704; **After-tax cash flow,** p. 686; **Depreciation tax shield,** p. 687; **Payback period,** p. 702; **Profitability index (or excess present value index),** p. 701; **Working capital,** p. 696.

APPENDIX TO CHAPTER 16 Impact of Inflation

Most countries have experienced inflation to some degree over the past 20 years. *Inflation* is defined as a decline in the general purchasing power of a monetary unit, such as a dollar, across time. Since capital-budgeting decisions involve cash flows over several time periods, it is worthwhile to examine the impact of inflation in capital-budgeting analyses.

Inflation can be incorporated in a discounted-cash-flow analysis in either of two ways. Both approaches yield correct results, but the analyst must be careful to be consistent in applying either approach. The two approaches are distinguished by the use of either *nominal* or *real* interest rates and dollars. These terms are defined below.

Interest Rates: Real or Nominal The **real interest rate** is the underlying interest rate, which includes compensation to investors for the *time value of money* and the *risk* of an investment. The **nominal interest rate** includes the real interest rate, plus an additional premium to compensate investors for inflation. Suppose the real interest rate is 10 percent, and inflation of 5 percent is projected. Then the nominal interest rate is determined as follows:[4]

Real interest rate	.10
Inflation rate	.05
Combined effect (.10 × .05)	.005
Nominal interest rate	.155

Dollars: Real or Nominal A cash flow measured in **nominal dollars** is the actual cash flow we observe. For example, a particular model of automobile cost $10,000 in 19x0 but it cost $12,155 in 19x4. Both the $10,000 cash flow in 19x0 and $12,155 cash flow in 19x4 are measured in *nominal dollars*. A cash flow measured in **real dollars** reflects an adjustment for the dollar's purchasing power. The following table shows the relationship between nominal and real dollars, assuming an inflation rate of 5 percent.

---

[4] An alternative way to compute the nominal interest rate is: $(1.10 \times 1.05) - 1.00 = .155$.

Year	(a) Cash Flow in Nominal Dollars	(b) Price Index	(c) = (a) ÷ (b) Cash Flow in Real Dollars
19x0	$10,000	.... 1.0000	$10,000
19x1	10,500	.... $(1.05)^1 = 1.0500$	10,000
19x2	11,025	.... $(1.05)^2 = 1.1025$	10,000
19x3	11,576	.... $(1.05)^3 = 1.1576$	10,000
19x4	12,155	.... $(1.05)^4 = 1.2155$	10,000

As the table shows, cash flows in nominal dollars must be deflated, which means dividing by the price index, to convert them to cash flows in real dollars. The real-dollar cash flows are expressed in 19x0 dollars.

Two Capital-Budgeting Approaches under Inflation

A correct capital-budgeting analysis may be done using either of the following approaches.

1. Use cash flows measured in *nominal dollars* and a nominal interest rate to determine the *nominal discount rate.*
2. Use cash flows measured in *real dollars* and a real interest rate to determine the *real discount rate.*

To illustrate these two approaches, we will focus on an equipment-replacement decision faced by the management of High Country Department Stores. The company operates an appliance-repair service for the household appliances it sells. Management is considering the replacement of a sophisticated piece of testing equipment used in repairing TVs and VCRs. The new equipment costs $5,000 and will have no salvage value. Over its four-year life, the new equipment is expected to generate the cost savings and depreciation tax shield shown below. The cash flows in column (f) of the table are the total after-tax cash inflows, measured in *nominal dollars.*

Measured in Nominal Dollars

Year	(a) Acquisition Cost	(b) Cost Savings	(c) After-Tax Cost Savings [(b) × (1 − .40)]	(d) ACRS Depreciation (3-year class)	(e) Depreciation Tax Shield [(d) × .40]	(f) Total After-Tax Cash Flow [(c) + (e)]
19x0	$(5,000)					
19x1		$1,900	$1,140	$1,667	$667	$1,807
19x2		2,000	1,200	2,223	889	2,089
19x3		2,100	1,260	740	296	1,556
19x4		2,500	1,500	370	148	1,648

Approach 1: Nominal Dollars and Nominal Discount Rate Under this capital-budgeting approach, we discount the nominal-dollar cash flows in the preceding table using the nominal discount rate of 15.5 percent. The net-present-value analysis is as follows:

Year	(a) Cash Flow in Nominal Dollars	(b) Discount Factor for Nominal Discount Rate of 15.5%	(c) = (a) × (b) Present Value
19x0.......	$(5,000)	.... 1.0000	.... $(5,000)
19x1.......	1,807	.... .8658 [1/(1.155)]*	 1,564
19x2.......	2,089	.... .7496 [1/(1.155)²]	 1,565
19x3.......	1,556	.... .6490 [1/(1.555)³]	 1,009
19x4.......	1,648	.... .5619 [1/(1.155)⁴]	 926
Net present value			$ 64

* The 15.5% discount factors can be computed in this fashion, using formula (2) in Chapter 15, or by interpolating with the discount factors in Table III of the appendix to Chapter 15.

High Country's management should purchase the new testing equipment, since its NPV is positive.

Approach 2: Real Dollars and Real Discount Rate Under this capital-budgeting approach, we first convert the cash flows measured in nominal dollars to cash flows in real dollars, as follows:

Year	(a) After-Tax Cash Flow in Nominal Dollars	(b) Price Index	(c) = (a) ÷ (b) After-Tax Cash Flow in Real Dollars*
19x0...............	$(5,000)	.. 1.0000...............	$(5,000)
19x1...............	1,807	.. 1.0500...............	1,721
19x2...............	2,089	.. 1.1025...............	1,895
19x3...............	1,556	.. 1.1576...............	1,344
19x4...............	1,648	.. 1.2155...............	1,356

* Real-dollar cash flows expressed in terms of 19x0 dollars.

Now we discount the after-tax cash flows, measured in real dollars, using the real discount rate of 10 percent. The net-present-value analysis is shown below.

Year	(a) Cash Flow in Real Dollars	(b) Discount Factor for Real Discount Rate of 10%	(c) = (a) × (b) Present Value
19x0........	$(5,000)	.. .. 1.0000	.... $(5,000)
19x1........	1,721	.... .909	 1,564
19x2........	1,895	.... .826	 1,565
19x3........	1,344	.... .751	 1,009
19x4........	1,356	.... .683	 926
Net present value			$ 64

Notice that the new testing equipment's NPV is the same under both capital-budgeting approaches. Under both approaches, we conclude that High Country Department Stores should purchase the new equipment.

Consistency Is the Key Either capital-budgeting approach will provide the correct conclusion, as long as it is applied consistently. Use either nominal dollars and a nominal discount rate or real dollars and a real discount rate. A common error in capital budgeting is to convert the after-tax cash flows to real dollars, but then use the nominal discount rate. This faulty analysis creates a bias against acceptance of worthwhile projects.

To illustrate, suppose High Country's management had made this error in its testing-equipment analysis. The following *incorrect* analysis is the result.

Incorrect Analysis of Testing-Equipment Decision

Inconsistency

Year	(a) Cash Flow in Real Dollars	(b) Discount Factor for Nominal Discount Rate of 15.5%	(c) = (a) × (b) Present Value
19x0	$(5,000)	1.0000	$(5,000)
19x1	1,721	.8658	1,490
19x2	1,895	.7496	1,420
19x3	1,344	.6490	872
19x4	1,356	.5619	762
Net present value			$ (456)

This inconsistent and incorrect analysis will lead High Country's management to the wrong conclusion.

Do managers explicitly consider inflation in their capital-budgeting analyses? Surveys of practice suggest that they do.

ILLUSTRATION FROM MANAGEMENT-ACCOUNTING PRACTICE

Use of Inflation Adjustments

A survey of executives in large industrial firms indicated the following practices in adjusting cash flows for inflation.[5]

Cash Flow Item	Percentage of Survey Respondents Who Adjust for Inflation
Material costs	96%
Employee compensation costs	93%
Future capital outlays	92%
Revenues	89%
Asset salvage values	55%
Ending values for investments in working capital	51%

KEY TERMS (Appendix) Nominal dollars, p. 709; Nominal interest rate, p. 709; Real dollars, p. 709; Real interest rate, p. 709.

[5] J. A. Hendricks, "Capital-Budgeting Practices Including Inflation Adjustments: A Survey," *Managerial Planning,* January–February 1983, p. 26.

REVIEW QUESTIONS

16-1. Explain how to compute the after-tax amount of a cash revenue or expense.

16-2. Give an example of a noncash expense. What impact does such an expense have in a capital-budgeting analysis? Explain how to compute the after-tax impact of a noncash expense.

16-3. What is a *depreciation tax shield?* Explain the effect of a depreciation tax shield in a capital-budgeting analysis.

16-4. Give an example of a cash flow that is not on the income statement. How do you determine the after-tax amount of such a cash flow?

16-5. Why is accelerated depreciation advantageous to a business?

16-6. Briefly describe the Accelerated Cost Recovery System (ACRS), as modified by recent changes in the tax laws.

16-7. If a company replaced all of the furniture in its executive offices for $100,000, how would the furniture be depreciated for tax purposes? Assume the estimated useful life of the furniture is 15 years.

16-8. Explain what is meant by the half-year convention.

16-9. Define the terms *gain* and *loss* on disposal.

16-10. Explain how a gain or loss on disposal is handled in a capital-budgeting analysis.

16-11. Why is it difficult to rank investment projects with positive net present values and different lives?

16-12. Why may the net-present-value and internal-rate-of-return methods yield different rankings for investments with different lives?

16-13. Define the term *profitability index.* How is it used in ranking investment proposals?

16-14. What is meant by the term *payback period?* How is this criterion sometimes used in capital budgeting?

16-15. What are the two main drawbacks of the payback method?

16-16. How is an investment project's *accounting rate of return* defined? Why do the accounting rate of return and internal rate of return on a capital project generally differ?

16-17. Discuss the pro and con of the accounting rate of return as an investment criterion.

16-18. (Appendix) Define the term *inflation.* How is inflation measured?

16-19. (Appendix) Explain the differences (a) between real and nominal interest rates and (b) between real and nominal dollars.

16-20. (Appendix) Briefly describe two correct methods of net-present-value analysis in an inflationary period.

EXERCISES

Exercise 16-21   After-Tax Cash Flows. Sharpe Pencil Corporation recently purchased a truck for $30,000. Under the ACRS, the first year's depreciation was $6,000. The truck driver's salary in the first year of operation was $35,000.

REQUIRED: Show how each of the amounts mentioned above should be converted to an after-tax amount. The company's tax rate is 30 percent.

Exercise 16-22   Gain or Loss on Disposal. In December of 19x4 Zeus Steel Corporation sold a forklift for $10,355. The machine was purchased in 19x1 for $50,000. Since then $38,845 in depreciation has been recorded on the forklift.

REQUIRED:

1. What was the forklift's book value at the time of sale?
2. Compute the gain or loss on the sale.
3. Determine the after-tax cash flow at the time the forklift was sold. The firm's tax rate is 45 percent.

Exercise 16-23   Using the Accelerated Cost Recovery System. For each of the following assets, indicate the ACRS property class and depreciation method.

1. A chemical company bought a new microscope to use in its Research and Development Division.
2. A midwest farmer constructed a new barn to house beef cattle.
3. A steel fabrication company bought a machine, which is expected to be useful for 18 years.
4. The president of an insurance company authorized the purchase of a new desk for her office.
5. A pizza restaurant purchased a new delivery car.

Exercise 16-24   Depreciation Tax Shield. Tulsa Plastics Company purchased industrial tools costing $100,000, which fall in the 3-year property class under the ACRS.

REQUIRED:

1. Prepare a schedule of depreciation deductions assuming:
   a. The firm uses the accelerated depreciation schedule specified by the ACRS.
   b. The firm uses the optional straight-line depreciation method and the half-year convention.
2. Calculate the present value of the depreciation tax shield under each depreciation method listed in requirement (1). Tulsa Plastics Company's after-tax hurdle rate is 12 percent, and the firm's tax rate is 30 percent.

Exercise 16-25   Profitability Index. The owner of Black Hills Confectionary is considering the purchase of a new semiautomatic candy machine. The machine will cost $25,000 and last 10 years. The machine is expected to have no salvage value at the end of its useful life. The owner projects that the new candy machine will generate $4,000 in after-tax savings each year during its life (including the depreciation tax shield).

REQUIRED: Compute the profitability index on the proposed candy machine, assuming an after-tax hurdle rate of: (a) 8%, (b) 10%, and (c) 12%.

Exercise 16-26   Payback Period; Even Cash Flows. The management of Piedmont National Bank is considering an investment in automatic teller machines. The machines would cost $124,200 and have a useful life of seven years. The bank's controller has estimated that the automatic teller machines will save the bank $27,000 after taxes during each year of their life (including the depreciation tax shield). The machines will have no salvage value.

REQUIRED:

1. Compute the payback period for the proposed investment.
2. Compute the net present value of the proposed investment assuming an after-tax hurdle rate of: (a) 10%, (b) 12%, and (c) 14%.
3. What can you conclude from your answers to requirements (2) and (3) about the limitations of the payback method?

Exercise 16-27   Payback Period; Uneven Cash Flows. Jericho Book Company's management is considering an advertising program that would require an initial expenditure of $165,500 and bring in additional sales over the next five years. The projected additional sales revenue in year 1 is $75,000, with associated expenses of $25,000. The additional sales revenue and expenses from the advertising program are projected to increase by 10 percent each year. Jericho's tax rate is 40 percent. (Hint: The $165,500 advertising cost is an expense.)

REQUIRED:

1. Compute the payback period for the advertising program.
2. Calculate the advertising program's net present value, assuming an after-tax hurdle rate of 10 percent.

Exercise 16-28 Accounting Rate of Return. Stryker Company recently purchased a new delivery truck for $50,000. Management expects the truck to generate the following additional revenues and expenses during its six-year life.

Average incremental revenue. $25,000
Average incremental expenses, not including depreciation or taxes   10,000

The truck has an expected life of six years and is in the ACRS 5-year property class. Stryker Company will use the optional straight-line depreciation method along with the half-year convention. The firm's tax rate is 40 percent.

REQUIRED:

1. Prepare a schedule showing the incremental revenue, incremental operating expenses, incremental depreciation, and incremental taxes during each of the next six years.
2. Compute the accounting rate of return on the delivery truck, using the initial investment in the denominator.

Exercise 16-29   Inflation and Capital Budgeting; Appendix. The state's secretary of education is considering the purchase of a new computer for $100,000. A cost study indicates that the new computer should save the Department of Education $30,000, measured in real dollars, during each of the next eight years.

The real interest rate is 20 percent and the inflation rate is 10 percent. As a governmental agency, the Department of Education pays no taxes.

REQUIRED:

1. Prepare a schedule of cash flows measured in real dollars. Include the initial acquisition and the cost savings for each of the next eight years.
2. Using cash flows measured in real dollars, compute the net present value of the proposed computer. Use a real discount rate equal to the real interest rate.

Exercise 16-30   Inflation and Capital Budgeting; Appendix. Refer to the data in the preceding exercise.

REQUIRED:

1. Compute the nominal interest rate.
2. Prepare a schedule of cash flows measured in nominal dollars.
3. Using cash flows measured in nominal dollars, compute the net present value of the proposed computer. Use a nominal discount rate equal to the nominal interest rate.

PROBLEMS   *Problem 16-31   ACRS Depreciation; Present Value of Tax Shield.* Flotilla Beam, the owner of the Bay City Boatyard, recently had a brilliant idea. There is a shortage of boat slips in the harbor during the summer. Beam's idea is to develop a system of "dry slips." A dry slip is a large storage rack in a warehouse on which a boat is stored. When the boat owner requests, a forklift is used to remove the boat from the dry slip and place the boat in the water. The entire operation requires one hour when a launch reservation is made in advance. The boatyard already has a vacant warehouse which could be used for this purpose. However, Beam's idea will require the following capital investment by the boatyard.

1. Storage racks: cost, $200,000; useful life, 18 years; ACRS class, 10-year property.
2. Forklift: cost, $120,000; useful life, six years; ACRS class, 5-year property.

Bay City Boatyard's tax rate is 35 percent, and its after-tax hurdle rate is 14 percent.

REQUIRED: For each of the boatyard's proposed capital investments:

1. Prepare a schedule of the annual depreciation expenses for tax purposes.
2. Compute the present value of the depreciation tax shield.

Problem 16-32   After-Tax Cash Flows; Robotic Equipment. Demmo Corporation manufactures scientific equipment for use in elementary schools. In December of 19x0 the company's management is considering the acquisition of robotic equipment, which would radically change its manufacturing process. The controller has collected the following data pertinent to the decision.

1. The robotic equipment would cost $1,000,000, to be paid in December of 19x0. The equipment's useful life is projected to be eight years. The equipment is in the ACRS 5-year property class. Demmo Corporation will use the ACRS accelerated depreciation schedule.
2. The robotic equipment requires software which will be developed over a two-year period in 19x1 and 19x2. Each software expenditure, which will amount to $25,000 per year, will be expensed during the year incurred.
3. A computer systems operator will be hired immediately to oversee the operation of the new robotic equipment. The computer expert's annual salary will be $60,000. Fringe benefits will cost $20,000 annually.
4. Maintenance technicians will be needed. The total cost of their wages and fringe benefits will be $150,000 per year.
5. The changeover of the manufacturing line will cost $90,000, to be expensed in 19x1.
6. Several of Demmo Corporation's employees will need retraining to operate the new robotic equipment. The training costs are projected as follows:

19x1 .... $35,000
19x2   25,000
19x3   10,000

7. An inventory of spare parts for the robotic equipment will be purchased immediately at a cost of $60,000. This investment in working capital will be maintained throughout the eight-year life of the equipment. At the end of 19x8, the parts will be sold for $60,000.
8. The robotic equipment's salvage value at the end of 19x8 is projected to be $50,000. It will be fully depreciated at that time.
9. Aside from the costs specifically mentioned above, Demmo Corporation's management expects the robotic equipment to save Demmo Corporation $480,000 per year in manufacturing costs.

10. Switching to the robotic equipment will enable Demmo Corporation to sell some
of its manufacturing machinery over the next two years. The following sales
schedule is projected.

	Acquisition Cost of Equipment Sold		Accumulated Depreciation at Time of Sale		Sales Proceeds
19x1.......	$150,000	....	$100,000	....	$ 20,000
19x2.......	305,000	....	215,000	....	140,000

11. Demmo Corporation's tax rate is 30 percent.
12. The company's after-tax hurdle rate is 12 percent.

REQUIRED: Prepare a year-by-year columnar schedule including all of the after-tax cash flows
associated with the robotic-equipment decision. Assume that each cash flow will occur at
year-end.

Problem 16-33 ***Robotic Equipment; Taxes; Net Present Value.*** Refer to the data given in the
preceding problem.

REQUIRED: Compute the net present value of Demmo Corporation's proposed acquisition of
robotic equipment.

Problem 16-34 ***ACRS Depreciation; Present Value of Tax Shield.*** Hewett Publishing Company produces textbooks for public schools. The company's management recently acquired
two new pieces of equipment, as described below.

1. Computer-controlled printing press: cost, $250,000; expected useful life, 12 years.
2. Duplicating equipment to be used in the administrative offices: cost, $60,000;
expected useful life, six years.

Hewett Publishing Company uses straight-line depreciation for book purposes and the
ACRS accelerated depreciation schedule for tax purposes. The company's tax rate is 40
percent; its after-tax hurdle rate is 10 percent. Neither machine has any salvage value.

REQUIRED: For each of Hewett Publishing Company's new pieces of equipment:

1. Prepare a schedule of the annual depreciation expenses for book purposes.
2. Determine the appropriate ACRS property class.
3. Prepare a schedule of the annual depreciation expenses for tax purposes.
4. Compute the present value of the depreciation tax shield.

Problem 16-35 ***Sensitivity Analysis; NPV with Taxes.*** Refer to the data for High Country
Department Stores' computerized checkout equipment decision given in Exhibit 16-7. Also
refer to the net-present-value analysis presented in Exhibit 16-8.

REQUIRED: The annual incremental sales revenue resulting from the marketing analysis is
estimated at $40,000. How low could this amount be and still result in a nonnegative net
present value for the new equipment?

Problem 16-36 ***Payback; Accounting Rate of Return; NPV.*** Yippan Corporation is reviewing
an investment proposal. The initial cost as well as the estimate of the book value of the
investment at the end of each year, the net after-tax cash flows for each year, and the net

income for each year are presented in the schedule below. The salvage value of the investment at the end of each year is equal to its book value. There would be no salvage value at the end of the investment's life.

Year	Initial Cost and Book Value	Annual Net After-Tax Cash Flows	Annual Net Income
0	$105,000		
1	70,000	$50,000	$15,000
2	42,000	45,000	17,000
3	21,000	40,000	19,000
4	7,000	35,000	21,000
5	0	30,000	23,000

Yippan uses a 16 percent after-tax target rate of return for new investment proposals.

REQUIRED: For requirement 1 *only* assume that the cash flows in years 1 through 5 occur uniformly throughout each year.

1. Compute the project's payback period.
2. Calculate the accounting rate of return on the investment proposal. Base your calculation on the initial cost of the investment.
3. Compute the proposal's net present value.

(CMA, adapted)

Problem 16-37 Investment Decision Making; Multiple Choice. Plasto Corporation is a manufacturer of plastic products. The company is embarking on a five-year modernization and expansion plan. Thus, management is identifying all of the capital projects that it should consider. Financial analyses will be prepared for each identified project. Plasto will not select and implement all of the projects, because some may not be financially attractive and some are mutually exclusive (i.e., choice of one project precludes the selection of any others); in addition, not all projects can be implemented due to a maximum dollar limit for capital projects.

The following list of projects is being considered. All modernization and expansion projects would be completed in three years. The projects have varying lives, but none exceed seven years. Plasto's criteria for evaluating and selecting projects are maximization of return and speed of investment recovery.

Project Identification and Description	Investment	Estimated Life (in years)
(1) Maintenance: Extensive maintenance of current manufacturing facilities, including repairs and some replacement of equipment. This work must be done in order to keep existing facilities in operation until any retooling or expansion projects are completed.	$ 2,000,000	3
(2) Retooling: Major retooling of current manufacturing facilities using general-purpose equipment.	$ 6,000,000	5
(3) Retooling: Major retooling of current manufacturing facilities using special-purpose equipment. This project and the prior project are mutually exclusive.	$ 8,500,000	5

Project Identification and Description	Investment	Estimated Life (in years)
(4) Construction of new facilities to manufacture parts and supplies used in making products. Parts and supplies are currently being purchased......	$ 5,000,000........	7
(5) Expansion: Construction of new facilities to introduce new product NX-42....................	$10,000,000........	6
(6) Expansion: Construction of new facilities to introduce new product LV-221...................	$12,000,000........	7

REQUIRED: Choose the best answer for each of the following items.

1. When attempting to determine if a project is profitable and should be pursued, Plasto should be sure that the project's
   a. payback is three years or less
   b. return exceeds the company's historical return on stockholder's equity
   c. return exceeds the company's historical return on net assets employed
   d. return exceeds the interest rate that is charged on any debt that is incurred to finance the project
   e. return exceeds a hurdle rate specified by Plasto's management

2. The goal for Plasto's maintenance project should be to
   a. maximize salvage value
   b. minimize the present value of the cash outlays
   c. minimize the internal rate of return
   d. maximize the payback period
   e. maximize the excess present value index

3. If Plasto employs discounted-cash-flow techniques in evaluating capital investment projects, this reflects that management recognizes
   a. the importance of the time value of money
   b. that cash flow is important to maintaining operations and generating future acceptable profits
   c. the volatility of inflation and its effect on operations.
   d. the importance of recovering the initial investment outlay as soon as possible
   e. the importance of incorporating risk in the evaluation process

(CMA, adapted)

Problem 16-38   After-Tax Cash Flows; Net Present Value. Wisconsin Products Company manufactures several different products. One of the firm's principal products sells for $20 per unit. The sales manager of Wisconsin Products has stated repeatedly that he could sell more units of this product if they were available. In an attempt to substantiate his claim, the sales manager conducted a market research study last year at a cost of $44,000 to determine potential demand for this product. The study indicated that Wisconsin Products could sell 18,000 units of this product annually for the next five years.

The equipment currently in use has the capacity to produce 11,000 units annually. The variable production costs are $9 per unit. The equipment has a book value of $60,000 and a remaining useful life of five years. The salvage value of the equipment is negligible now and will be zero in five years.

A maximum of 20,000 units could be produced annually on new machinery that can be purchased. The new equipment costs $300,000 and has an estimated useful life of five years with no salvage value at the end of five years. Wisconsin Products' production manager has estimated that the new equipment would provide increased production efficiencies that would reduce the variable production costs to $7 per unit.

Wisconsin Products Company uses straight-line depreciation on all of its equipment for tax purposes. The firm is subject to a 40 pecent tax rate, and its after-tax hurdle rate is 14 percent.

The sales manager felt so strongly about the need for additional capacity that he attempted to prepare an economic justification for the equipment, although this was not one of his responsibilities. His analysis, which follows, disappointed him because it did not justify acquiring the equipment.

Required Investment

Purchase price of new equipment		$300,000
Disposal of existing equipment:		
Loss on disposal	$60,000	
Less: Tax benefit (40%)	24,000	36,000
Cost of market research study		44,000
Total investment		$380,000

Annual Returns

Contribution margin from product:	
Using the new equipment [18,000 × ($20 − $7)]	$234,000
Using the existing equipment [11,000 × ($20 − $9)]	121,000
Increase in contribution margin	$113,000
Less: Depreciation	60,000
Increase in before-tax income	$ 53,000
Income tax (40%)	21,200
Increase in income	$ 31,800
Less: 14% cost of capital on the additional investment required	
(.14 × $380,000)	53,200
Net annual return of proposed investment in new equipment	$ (21,400)

REQUIRED: For this problem, ignore the half-year convention.

1. The controller of Wisconsin Products Company plans to prepare a discounted-cash-flow analysis for this investment proposal. The controller has asked you to prepare corrected calculations of the following:
   a. The required investment in the new equipment.
   b. The recurring annual cash flows.
   Explain the treatment of each item of your corrected analysis, which is treated differently from the original analysis prepared by the sales manager.
2. Calculate the net present value of the proposed investment in the new equipment.
(CMA, adapted)

Problem 16-39 Various Methods of Investment Analysis. Hazman Company plans to replace an old piece of research equipment which is obsolete and is expected to be unreliable under the stress of daily operations. The equipment is fully depreciated, and no salvage value can be realized upon its disposal.

One piece of equipment under consideration would provide annual cash savings of $7,000 before income taxes. The equipment would cost $18,000 and have an estimated useful life of five years. The equipment is expected to have no salvage value at the end of five years.

Hazman uses the straight-line depreciation method on all equipment for both book and tax purposes. The company is subject to a 40 percent tax rate. Hazman has an after-tax hurdle rate of 14 percent. The new equipment is in the ACRS 5-year property class.

REQUIRED: For this problem, ignore the half-year convention.

1. Calculate for Hazman Company's proposed investment in new equipment the after-tax:
   a. Payback period.
   b. Accounting rate of return.
   c. Net present value.
   d. Profitability index.
   e. Internal rate of return.
   Assume all operating revenues and expenses occur at the end of the year.
2. Identify and discuss the issues Hazman Company should consider when deciding which of the five decision models identified in requirement (1) it should employ to evaluate alternative capital-investment projects.

(CMA, adapted)

Problem 16-40 *After-Tax Cash Flows; Net Present Value.* Wyle Company's management is considering a proposal to acquire new manufacturing equipment. The new equipment has the same capacity as the current equipment but will provide operating efficiencies in direct and indirect labor, direct-material usage, indirect supplies, and power. The savings in operating costs are estimated at $150,000 annually.

The new equipment will cost $300,000 and will be purchased at the beginning of the year when the project is started. The equipment dealer is certain that the equipment will be operational during the second quarter of the year it is installed. Therefore, 60 percent of the estimated annual savings can be obtained in the first year. Wyle will incur a one-time expense of $30,000 to transfer production activities from the old equipment to the new equipment. No loss of sales will occur, however, because the plant is large enough to install the new equipment without interfering with the operations of the current equipment. The equipment is in the ACRS 7-year property class. Wyle would depreciate the machinery in accordance with the ACRS depreciation schedule.

The current equipment has been fully depreciated. Management has reviewed its condition and has concluded that it can be used an additional eight years. Wyle Company would receive $5,000, net of removal costs, if it elected to buy the new equipment and dispose of its current equipment at this time. The new equipment will have no salvage value at the end of its life.

The company is subject to a 40 percent income-tax rate and requires an after-tax return of at least 12 percent on any investment.

REQUIRED:

1. Calculate the annual incremental after-tax cash flows for Wyle Company's proposal to acquire the new manufacturing equipment.
2. Calculate the net present value of Wyle Company's proposal to acquire the new manufacturing equipment using the cash flows calculated in requirement (1), and indicate what action Wyle's management should take. For ease in calculation, assume all cash flows take place at the end of the year.

(CMA, adapted)

Problem 16-41   NPV; IRR; Payback; Profitability Index. Franklin Industries is comprised of four divisions, each operating in a different industry. The divisions are currently preparing their capital expenditure budgets for the coming year. Caledonia Division manufactures home appliances that it distributes nationally. The manufacturing and marketing departments of Caledonia have proposed six capital projects for next year. The division manager must now analyze these investment proposals, and select those projects that will be included in the capital budget to be submitted to Franklin Industries for approval. The proposed projects are listed below and are considered to have the same degree of risk.

> Project A: Redesign and modification of an existing product that is currently sched-uled to be dropped. The enhanced model would be sold for six more years.
>
> Project B: Expansion of a line of cookware that has been produced on an experimen-tal basis for the past year. The expected life of the cookware line is eight years.
>
> Project C: Reorganization of the plant's distribution center, including the installation of computerized equipment for tracking inventory. This project would benefit both administration and marketing.
>
> Project D: Addition of a new product, a combination bread and meat slicer. In addition to new manufacturing equipment, a significant amount of introductory advertising would be required.
>
> Project E: Automation of the Packaging Department, which would result in cost savings over the next six years.
>
> Project F: Construction of a building wing to house offices presently located in an area that could be used for manufacturing. The change would not add capacity for new lines, but it would alleviate crowded conditions that currently exist. This would make it possible to improve the productivity of two existing product lines, which have been unable to meet market demand.

Franklin Industries has established a hurdle rate of 12 percent for capital expenditures for all four divisions. Additional information about each of the proposed projects follows:

Caledonia Division
Proposed Capital Projects

Required Investment and After-Tax Operating Cash Flows by Project

	Project A	Project B	Project C	Project D	Project E	Project F
Capital investment...	$106,000	$200,000	$140,000	$160,000	$144,000	$130,000
After-tax operating cash flows:						
Year 1	$ 50,000	$ 20,000	$ 36,000	$ 20,000	$ 50,000	$ 40,000
Year 2	50,000	40,000	36,000	30,000	50,000	40,000
Year 3	40,000	50,000	36,000	40,000	50,000	40,000
Year 4	40,000	60,000	36,000	50,000	20,000	40,000
Year 5	30,000	60,000	36,000	60,000	20,000	40,000
Year 6	40,000	60,000		70,000	11,600	40,000
Year 7		40,000		80,000		40,000
Year 8		44,000		66,000		42,000
Total after-tax cash flows	$250,000	$374,000	$180,000	$416,000	$201,600	$322,000

	Project A	Project B	Project C	Project D	Project E	Project F
Additional Project Information						
Present value of after-tax operating cash flows at 12%	$175,683	$223,773	$129,772	$234,374	$150,027	$199,513
Net present value at 12%	$69,683	$23,773	$(10,228)	$74,374	$6,027	$69,513
Profitability index	1.66	1.12	.93	1.46	1.04	1.53
Internal rate of return	35%	15%	9%	22%	14%	26%
Payback period	2.2 years	4.5 years	3.9 years	4.3 years	2.9 years	3.3 years
Economic life	6 years	8 years	5 years	8 years	6 years	8 years

REQUIRED:

1. For each of the following techniques, explain how it could be used in evaluating Caledonia Division's capital expenditure proposals and what it is designed to measure: (a) net present value, (b) internal rate of return, (c) payback, and (d) profitability index.
2. If Caledonia Divison has no budget restrictions for capital expenditures, identify the capital investment projects that should be included in the capital budget submitted to Franklin Industries. Explain the basis for your selection.
3. Discuss the propriety of using the same hurdle rate for all four divisions of Franklin Industries.

(CMA, adapted)

Problem 16-42   *After-Tax Cash Flows; Net Present Value.* Ostrander Corporation manufactures several lines of machine products. One unique part, a valve stem, requires specialized tools that need to be replaced. Management has decided that the only alternative to replacing these tools is to buy the valve stem at a unit sales price of $20 if at least 70,000 units are ordered annually.

Ostrander's average usage of valve stems over the past three years has been 80,000 units each year. Expectations are that this volume will remain constant over the next five years. Cost records indicate that unit manufacturing costs for the last several years have been as follows:

Direct material	$ 3.80
Direct labor	3.70
Variable overhead	1.70
Fixed overhead*	4.50
Total unit cost	$13.70

* Depreciation accounts for two-thirds of the fixed overhead. The balance is for other fixed overhead costs of the factory that require cash expenditures.

If the specialized tools are purchased, they will cost $2,500,000 and will have a disposal value of $100,000 after their expected life of five years. Straight-line depreciation is used for book purposes, but ACRS is used for tax purposes. The specialized tools are considered 3-year property for ACRS purposes. The company has a 40 percent tax rate, and management requires a 12 percent after-tax return on investment.

The sales representative for the manufacturer of the new tools stated, "The new tools will allow direct labor and variable overhead to be reduced by $1.60 per unit." Data from another manufacturer using identical tools and experiencing similar operating conditions, except that annual production generally averages 110,000 units, confirm the direct-labor and variable-overhead savings. However, the manufacturer indicates that it experienced an increase in direct-material cost due to the higher quality of material that had to be used with the new tools. The manufacturer indicated that its costs have been as follows:

Direct material	$ 4.50
Direct labor	3.00
Variable overhead	.80
Fixed overhead	5.00
Total unit cost	$13.30

REQUIRED:

1. Prepare a net-present-value analysis covering the life of the new specialized tools to determine whether Ostrander Corporation should replace the old tools or purchase the valve stem from an outside supplier. Include all tax implications.
2. Identify any additional factors management should consider before a decision is made to replace the tools or purchase the valve stem from an outside supplier.

(CMA, adapted)

Problem 16-43 *After-Tax Cash Flows; Net Present Value.* Hammond Industries is a toy manufacturer that will have excess capacity at its single plant after 19x0. Hammond's management is currently studying two alternative proposals that would utilize this excess capacity.

Proposal 1

Hammond has been approached by GloriToys, one of its competitors, to manufacture a partially completed doll. GloriToys, owner of the distribution rights for the doll, would finish the dolls in its plant and then market the dolls. The GloriToy doll would not compete directly with any of Hammond's products.

GloriToys would contract to purchase 5,000 unfinished dolls each month at a price of $7.50 each for the period of 19x1 through 19x6. Hammond's estimated incremental cash outlays to manufacture the doll would be $250,000 per year during the six-year contract period. In addition, this alternative would require a $400,000 investment in manufacturing equipment. The equipment would have no salvage value at the end of 19x6.

Proposal 2

Hammond is considering the production of a new stuffed toy to be added to its own product line. The new stuffed toy would be sold at $15 per unit. The expected annual sales over the estimated six-year product life (19x1 – 19x6) for the toy are as follows:

Year	Annual Unit Sales
19x1	65,000
19x2	90,000
19x3	90,000
19x4	65,000
19x5	50,000
19x6	50,000

The variable manufacturing and selling costs are estimated to be $6.00 and $1.00, respectively, over this six-year period. The estimated annual incremental cash outlay for fixed costs would be $300,000. The manufacture and sale of the new stuffed toy would require a $700,000 investment in new manufacturing equipment; this equipment would have a salvage value of $50,000 at the end of the six-year period.

Additional information relative to a decision between the two proposals follows.

- Manufacturing equipment for either proposal would be placed in service during December 19x0. Depreciation on the equipment would be recognized starting in 19x1. Straight-line depreciation over the life of each proposal would be used for book purposes, and the ACRS percentages for 3-year property would be employed for tax purposes.
- Hammond Industries is subject to a 30 percent income-tax rate on all income.
- Hammond's management assumes that annual cash flows occur at the end of the year for evaluating capital investment proposals. Hammond uses a 14 percent after-tax discount rate.

REQUIRED:

1. Calculate the net present value at December 31, 19x0, of the estimated after-tax cash flows for each of Hammond Industries' two proposals.
2. Independent of the net present value calculations in requirement (1), and considering only the environment for Hammond Industries as described, identify any other factors that would increase the attractiveness of each of the two proposals.

(CMA, adapted)

Problem 16-44   Ranking Investment Proposals; NPV versus Profitability Index. The owner of Zivanov's Pancake House is considering an expansion of the business. He has identified two alternatives, as follows:

1. Build a new restaurant near the mall.
2. Buy and renovate an old building downtown for the new restaurant.

The projected cash flows from these two alternatives are shown below. The owner of the restaurant uses a 10 percent after-tax discount rate.

Investment Proposal	Cash Outflow: Time 0	Net After-Tax Cash Inflows* Years 1–10	Net After-Tax Cash Inflows* Years 11–20
Mall restaurant	$400,000	$50,000	$50,000
Downtown restaurant	200,000	35,800	—

* Includes after-tax cash flows from all sources, including incremental revenue, incremental expenses, and depreciation tax shield.

REQUIRED:

1. Compute the net present value of each alternative restaurant site.
2. Compute the profitability index for each alternative.
3. How do the two sites rank in terms of (a) NPV and (b) the profitability index?
4. Comment on the difficulty of ranking the owner's two options for the new restaurant site.

Problem 16-45 Payback; Accounting Rate of Return. Refer to the data given in the preceding problem. The owner of Zivanov's Pancake House will consider capital projects only if they have a payback period of six years or less. The owner also favors projects that exhibit an accounting rate of return of at least 15 percent. The owner bases a project's accounting rate of return on the initial investment in the project.

REQUIRED:

1. Compute the payback period for each of the proposed restaurant sites.
2. Compute the accounting rate of return for each proposed site.
3. If the owner of the restaurant sticks to his criteria, which site will he choose?
4. Comment on the pros and cons of the restaurant owner's investment criteria.

Problem 16-46 Ranking Investment Proposals; IRR versus Profitability Index. Coulter Travel is a large travel agency with offices in 12 California cities. The president of the company is currently trying to decide on the location for another office. The options are Sacramento and Bakersfield. The cash flows projected for the two alternative office locations are shown below.

Investment Proposal	Cash Outflow: Time 0	Net After-Tax Cash Inflows*		Internal Rate of Return
		Years 1–10	Years 11–20	
Sacramento......	$597,520......	$ 80,000	$80,000	12%
Bakersfield	596,860......	110,000	—	13%†

* Includes after-tax flows from all sources, including incremental revenue, incremental expenses, and depreciation tax shield.
† The annuity discount factor for $r = .13$ and $n = 10$ is 5.426.

The management of Coulter Travel uses a 10 percent after-tax discount rate to evaluate capital projects.

REQUIRED:

1. Compute the net present value of each alternative location for Coulter Travel's new office.
2. Compute the profitability index for each alternative.
3. Rank Coulter Travel's two potential office sites using (a) the IRR and (b) the profitability index.
4. What can you conclude from your answer to requirement (3) about these two criteria for ranking alternative investment proposals?

Problem 16-47 Payback; Net Present Value; Depreciation Tax Shield. Amos Chemical Company's vice president of research and development, John Tobias, is considering a major addition to the company's research equipment. The equipment is expected to have a useful life of five years and is in the ACRS 5-year property class. The cost of the equipment is $100,000. The projected incremental after-tax cash inflow during the life of the research equipment is $25,000 per year, not including the depreciation tax shield.

Amos Chemical Company's top management has stipulated that any capital investment costing over $50,000 must have a payback period of no more than three years in order to be acceptable. Tobias made a quick calculation and rejected the proposed acquisition. At lunch Tobias casually remarked to the corporate controller, "I hate to pass up that research equipment, but it costs $100,000. At only $25,000 a year in cash inflows, its payback period is four years." The controller thought for a minute and then pointed out that Tobias had not considered the depreciation tax shield on the equipment. As the two left the lunchroom, the controller turned to Tobias and said, "Let me work out the payback period on that equipment after including the tax impact of the depreciation."

REQUIRED: When the controller returned to her office, she handed the job over to you, the assistant controller.

1. Prepare a schedule showing the annual depreciation expense and depreciation tax shield on the research equipment. Amos Chemical Company uses the ACRS depreciation schedule. The firm's tax rate is 40 percent.
2. Prepare a schedule showing the total after-tax cash inflows during each year in the equipment's life.
3. Between what two whole numbers is the equipment's payback period?
4. Does the payback period on the equipment meet the company's criterion?
5. Compute the net present value of the equipment. The firm's after-tax hurdle rate is 10 percent.

Problem 16-48   Inflation; NPV; Nominal Dollars; Appendix. Sholtys Cablevision Company provides television cable service to two counties in Maryland. The firm's management is considering the construction of a new satellite dish in December of 19x0. The new antenna would improve reception and the service provided to customers. The dish antenna and associated equipment will cost $200,000 to purchase and install. The company's old equipment, which is fully depreciated, can be sold now for $20,000. The company president expects the firm's improved capabilities to result in additional revenue of $80,000 per year during the dish's useful life of seven years. The incremental operating expenses associated with the new equipment are projected to be $10,000 per year. These incremental revenues and expenses are expressed in terms of real dollars.

The new satellite dish will be depreciated under the ACRS depreciation schedule for the 5-year property class. The company's tax rate is 40 percent.

Sholtys Cablevision's president expects the real rate of interest in the economy to remain stable at 10 percent. She expects the inflation rate, currently running at 20 percent, to remain unchanged.

REQUIRED:

1. Prepare a schedule of cash flows projected over the next eight years, measured in nominal dollars. The schedule should include the initial costs of purchase and installation, the after-tax incremental revenue and expenses, and the depreciation tax shield. Remember to express the incremental revenues and expenses in nominal dollars.
2. Compute the nominal interest rate.
3. Prepare a net-present-value analysis of the proposed new satellite dish. Use cash flows measured in nominal dollars and a nominal discount rate equal to the nominal interest rate.

Problem 16-49   Inflation; NPV; Real Dollars; Appendix. Refer to the data given in the preceding problem for Sholtys Cablevision Company.

REQUIRED:

1. Compute the price index for each year from 19x1 through 19x8, using 1.0000 as the index for 19x0.
2. Prepare a schedule of after-tax cash flows measured in real dollars.
3. Compute the net present value of the proposed new satellite dish using cash flows measured in real dollars. Use a real discount rate equal to the real interest rate.

Problem 16-50   Capital Budgeting under Inflation; Automated Equipment; Appendix. Each division of Catix Corporation has the authority to make capital expenditures up to $200,000 without approval from corporate headquarters. The after-tax hurdle rate for Catix Corporation is 12 percent. This rate does not include an allowance for inflation, which is expected to occur at an average rate of 8 percent over the next five years. Catix pays income taxes at the rate of 40 percent.

The Electronics Division of Catix Corporation is considering the purchase of an automated assembly and soldering machine for use in the manufacture of its printed circuit boards. The machine would be placed in service in early 19x1. The divisional controller estimates that if the machine is purchased, two positions will be eliminated, yielding a cost savings for wages and employee benefits. However, the machine would require additional supplies, and more power would be required to operate the machine. The cost savings and additional costs, in current 19x0 prices, are as follows:

Wages and employee benefits of the two positions eliminated ($25,000 each) .	$50,000
Cost of additional supplies	3,000
Cost of additional power	10,000

The new machine would be purchased and installed at the end of 19x0 at a net cost of $90,000. If purchased, the machine would be depreciated on a straight-line basis for both book and tax purposes. The machine will become technologically obsolete in three years and will have no salvage value at that time. The machine is in the ACRS 3-year property class.

The Electronics Division compensates for inflation in capital expenditure analyses by adjusting the expected cash flows by an estimated price-level index. The adjusted real after-tax cash flows are then discounted using the real discount rate. The estimated year-end index values for each of the next five years are presented below.

Year	Year-End Price Index
19x0	1.00
19x1	1.08
19x2	1.17
19x3	1.26
19x4	1.36
19x5	1.47

The Plastics Division of Catix Corporation analyzes capital investment projects by discounting nominal cash flows using the nominal discount rate.

REQUIRED:

1. Prepare a schedule showing the net after-tax annual real cash flows for the automated assembly and soldering machine under consideration by the Electronics Division.
2. What discount rate should the Plastics Division use in its discounted-cash-flow analysis?
3. Suppose that the Plastics Division's management is considering the same machine currently under consideration by the Electronics Division. All of the same data apply to the Plastics Division. For each year (19x1 through 19x4), compute the nominal cash flows that the Plastics Division's management should use in its project analysis.

4. Evaluate the methods used by the Plastics Division and the Electronics Division to compensate for expected inflation in capital expenditure analyses.

(CMA, adapted)

CASE **Case 16-51 Comprehensive Case on Capital Budgeting and Taxes.*** Liquid Chemical, Ltd. sells a range of high-grade chemical products which, because of their properties, call for careful packaging. The company has always emphasized the special properties of the containers used. Liquid Chemical had a special patented lining made from a material known as GHL, and the company operated a department specially to maintain its containers in good condition and to make new ones to replace the ones that were past repair.

Tom Walsh, the general manager, had for some time suspected that the firm might save money and get equally good service by buying its containers outside. After careful inquiries, he approached a firm specializing in container production, Packages Inc., and obtained a quotation on the special containers. At the same time he asked Amy Dyer, the controller, to let him have an up-to-date statement of the cost of operating the Container Department.

Within a few days, the quotation from Packages, Inc. came in. They were prepared to supply all the new containers required, running at the rate of 3,000 each year, for $600,000 annually. The contract would run for a term of five years, and thereafter would be renewable from year to year. If the number of containers required increased, the contract price would be increased proportionately. Additionally, and irrespective of whether the above contract was agreed upon or not, Packages, Inc. agreed to carry out purely maintenance work on the containers, short of replacement, for a sum of $175,000 annually on the same contract terms.

Tom Walsh compared these figures with the cost data prepared by Amy Dyer covering a year's operations of the Container Department. Dyer's analysis is as follows:

Direct material.		$200,000
Direct labor.		350,000
Departmental overhead:		
Department manager's salary	$80,000	
Rent	15,000	
Depreciation of machinery	60,000	
Maintenance of machinery	13,500	
Other overhead.	63,000	231,500
		781,500
Allocation of general administrative overhead from entire factory.		67,500
Total cost of Container Department for one year.		$849,000

Walsh's conclusion was that no time should be lost in closing down the Container Department and entering into the contract offered by Packages, Inc. However, he felt bound to give the manager of the department, Jake Duffy, an opportunity to question this conclusion before he acted on it. Walsh called Duffy in and put the facts before him, at the same time making it clear that Duffy's own position was not in jeopardy. Even if Duffy's department were closed down, there was another managerial position shortly becoming vacant to which Duffy could be moved without loss of pay or prospects.

Jake Duffy looked thoughtful, and asked for time to think the matter over. The next morning Duffy asked to speak to Walsh again, and said he thought there were a number of considerations that ought to be borne in mind before his department was closed down. "For instance," Duffy said, "what will you do with the machinery? It cost $480,000 four years ago,

* This case is adapted here with permission from its author, Professor David Solomons.

but you'd be lucky if you got $80,000 for it now, even though it's good for another five years. Then there's the stock of GHL we bought a year ago. That cost us $300,000. At the rate we're using it now, it'll last us another three years. We used up about a quarter of it last year. Amy Dyer's figure of $200,000 for materials probably includes about $75,000 for GHL. But it'll be tricky stuff to handle if we don't use it up. We bought well, paying $1,500 a ton for it. You couldn't buy it today for less than $1,800 a ton. But you wouldn't have more than $1,200 a ton left if you sold it, after you'd covered all the handling expenses."

Tom Walsh thought that Amy Dyer ought to be present during this discussion. He asked her to come in and then reviewed Duffy's points. "I don't much like all this conjecture," Dyer said. "I think my figures are pretty conclusive. Besides, if we are going to have all this talk about 'what will happen if,' don't forget the problem of space we're faced with. We're paying $27,500 a year in rent for a warehouse a couple of miles away. If we closed Duffy's department, we'd have all the warehouse space we need without renting."

"That's a good point," said Walsh, "though I must say, I'm a bit worried about the employees if we close the Container Department. I don't think we can find room for any of them elsewhere in the firm. I could see whether Packages, Inc. can take any of them. But some of them are getting on in years. There's Walters and Hines, for example. They've been with us since they left school many years ago. Their severance pay would cost us $10,000 a year each, for five years."

Duffy showed some relief at Walsh's comment. "But I still don't like Amy's figures," he said. "What about this $67,500 for general administrative overhead? You surely don't expect to fire anyone in the general office if I'm closed down, do you?" "Probably not," said Dyer, "but someone has to pay for these costs. We can't ignore them when we look at an individual department, because if we do that with each department in turn, we'll wind up by convincing ourselves that general managers, accountants, typists, and the like, don't have to be paid. And they do, believe me."

"Well, I think we've thrashed this out pretty fully," said Walsh, "but I've been wondering about the possibility of perhaps keeping on the maintenance work ourselves. What are your views on that, Duffy?" "I don't know," said Duffy, "but it's worth looking into. We shouldn't need any machinery for that, and I could hand the management over to a department supervisor. You'd save about $20,000 a year there. You'd only need about one-fifth of the employees, but you could keep the oldest. You wouldn't save any space, so I suppose the rent would be the same. I shouldn't think the other overhead expenses would be more than $26,000 a year." "What about materials?" asked Walsh. "We use about 10 percent of the total on maintenance," Duffy replied.

"Well, I've told Packages, Inc. that I'd let them know my decision within a week," said Walsh. "I'll let you know what I decide to do before I write to them."

REQUIRED: Liquid Chemical's tax rate is 40 percent, and its after-tax hurdle rate is 10 percent. You will have to seek out the information you need from the remarks of Walsh, Dyer, and Duffy. In some cases, you will have to interpret their remarks and make assumptions. State all of your assumptions clearly when answering the following questions.

1. List Liquid Chemical's four alternatives.
2. Prepare a net-present-value analysis of each alternative identified in requirement (1). Use a 5-year-time horizon. The company uses straight-line depreciation for tax purposes. (Ignore the half-year convention.) The depreciation expense in each of the next four years is $60,000. The equipment will be fully depreciated after four more years.
3. What qualitative factors should Tom Walsh consider in making his decision?

PART 4 SELECTED TOPICS FOR FURTHER STUDY

RIVE**R**SIDE

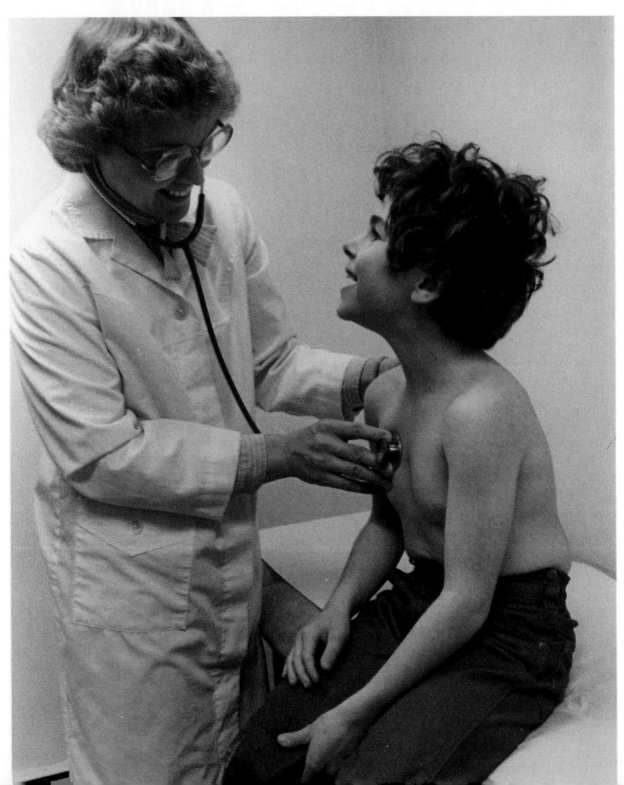

Chapter 17

Cost Allocation: A Closer Look

After completing this chapter, you should be able to:

■ Allocate service department costs using the direct method, step-down method, or reciprocal-services method (appendix).

■ Use the dual approach to service department cost allocation.

■ Allocate joint costs among joint products using each of the following techniques: physical-units method, relative-sales-value method, and net-realizable-value method.

■ Describe the purposes for which joint cost allocation is useful and those for which it is not.

In Chapter 11 we studied cost allocation and explored its role in an organization's overall managerial-accounting system. We also examined several purposes of cost allocation. The goal of cost allocation is to ensure that all costs incurred by the organization ultimately are assigned to its products or services. This is important for several purposes, including cost-based pricing and bidding, cost reimbursements from outside parties such as insurance companies, valuation of inventory, and determination of cost of goods sold. In addition, the allocation of all costs to departments serves to make departmental managers aware of the costs incurred to produce services their departments use.

In this chapter, we will explore the following two cost-allocation issues in greater detail:

● Service department cost allocation[1]
● Joint product cost allocation[2]

---

[1] The section on service department cost allocation is written as a module, which can be studied separately from the rest of the chapter. This material may be studied after the completion of Chapter 11, which covers basic issues in cost allocation.

[2] The section on joint cost allocation is written as a module, which can be studied separately from the rest of the chapter. This material may be studied after the completion of Chapter 13.

SERVICE DEPARTMENT COST ALLOCATION

A **service department** is a unit in an organization that is not involved *directly* in producing the organization's goods or services. However, a service department does provide a service that enables the organization's production process to take place. For example, the Maintenance Department in an automobile plant does not make automobiles, but if it did not exist, the production process would stop when the manufacturing machines broke down. Thus, the Maintenance Department is crucial to the production operation even though the repair personnel do not work directly on the plant's products.

Service departments are important in nonmanufacturing organizations also. For example, a hospital's Personnel Department is responsible for staffing the hospital with physicians, nurses, lab technicians, and other employees. The Personnel Department never serves the patients, yet without it the hospital would have no staff to provide medical care.

A service department such as the Maintenance Department or the Personnel Department must exist in order for an organization to carry out its primary function. Therefore, the cost of running a service department is part of the cost incurred by the organization in producing goods or services. In order to determine the cost of those goods or services, all service department costs must be allocated to the production departments in which the goods or services are produced. For this reason, the costs incurred in an automobile plant's Maintenance Department are allocated to all of the production departments that have machinery. The costs incurred in a hospital's Personnel Department are allocated to all of the departments that have personnel. Direct-patient-care departments, such as Surgery and Physical Therapy, are allocated their share of the Personnel Department's costs.

To see how service department cost allocation fits into the overall picture of product and service costing, it may be helpful to review Exhibit 11-6 on page 457. The exhibit shows three steps in cost allocation, as listed below.

1. *Cost distribution* Costs in various cost pools are distributed to all departments, including both service and production departments.
2. *Service department cost allocation* Service department costs are allocated to production departments.
3. *Cost application* Costs are assigned to the goods or services produced by the organization.

It is the second step in this process of multistage cost allocation that we are focusing on now. The context for our discussion is Riverside Clinic, an outpatient medical facility in Philadelphia.

The clinic is organized into three service departments and two direct-patient-care departments. Exhibit 17-1 displays a simple organization chart for Riverside Clinic. Since the clinic is not a manufacturing organization, we refer to *direct-patient-care departments* instead of *production departments.* These two departments, Orthopedics and Internal Medicine, directly provide the health care that is the clinic's primary objective. Thus, the clinic's direct-patient-care departments are like the production departments in a manufacturing firm.

Notice that the Personnel Department and the Administration and Accounting Department provide services to each other. When this situation occurs, the two service departments exhibit *reciprocal services.*

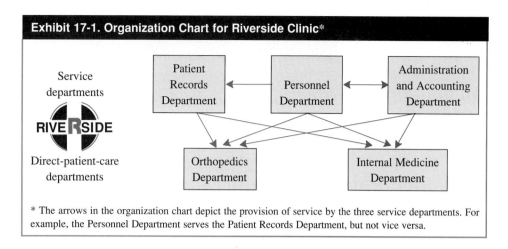

Exhibit 17-1. Organization Chart for Riverside Clinic*

Service departments

RIVE**R**SIDE

Direct-patient-care departments

Patient Records Department

Personnel Department

Administration and Accounting Department

Orthopedics Department

Internal Medicine Department

* The arrows in the organization chart depict the provision of service by the three service departments. For example, the Personnel Department serves the Patient Records Department, but not vice versa.

Exhibit 17-2 provides some of the details for our illustration of service department cost allocation. Panel A shows the proportion of each service department's output that is consumed by each of the departments using its services. Panel B shows the allocation bases, which are used to determine the proportions shown in panel A. Further explanation of the information in Exhibit 17-2 follows.

Patient Records   The service output of the Patient Records Department is consumed only by the Orthopedics and Internal Medicine Departments. *Annual patient load* is the *allocation base* used to determine that 30 percent of the Patient Records Department's services were consumed by Orthopedics and 70 percent by Internal Medicine.

Personnel   The Personnel Department serves each of the clinic's other departments, including the other two service departments and the two direct-patient-care departments. The *allocation base* used to determine the proportions of the Personnel Department's output consumed by the four using departments is the *number of employees* in the using departments. For example, 5 percent of the clinic's employees (excluding those in the Personnel Department) work in the Patient Records Department.

Administration and Accounting   This service department provides services only to the Personnel Department, the Orthopedics Department, and the Internal Medicine Department. A variety of services are provided, such as computer support, patient billing, and general administration. Since larger amounts of these services are provided to larger using departments, *departmental size* is the *allocation base* used to determine the proportion of service output consumed by each using department. Since the space devoted to each department is a convenient measure of departmental size, square footage is the measure used in Exhibit 17-2. For example, 5 percent of the clinic's space (excluding that occupied by Administration and Accounting) is devoted to the Personnel Department.

Panel C of Exhibit 17-2 shows the total budgeted cost of each service department, which is to be allocated among the using departments.

There are two widely used methods of service department cost allocation, the direct method and the step-down method. These methods are discussed and illustrated next, using the data for Riverside Clinic.

Exhibit 17-2. Provision of Services by Service Departments in 19x1: Riverside Clinic

	User of Service	RIVE**R**SIDE	Patient Records	Personnel	Administration and Accounting
			Provider of Service		
Service departments	Patient Records		—	5%	—
	Personnel		—	—	5%
	Administration and Accounting		—	20%	—
Direct-patient-care departments	Orthopedics		30%	25%	35%
	Internal Medicine		70%	50%	60%

(A) Percentage of Service Output Consumed by Using Departments

Service Department	Allocation Base
Patient Records	Annual patient load
Personnel	Number of employees
Administration and Accounting	Size of department (measured in square feet of space)

(B) Allocation Bases

Service Department	Variable Cost	Fixed Cost	Total Cost to Be Allocated
Patient Records	$24,000	$ 76,000	$100,000
Personnel	15,000	45,000	60,000
Administration and Accounting	47,500	142,500	190,000
Total	$86,500	$263,500	$350,000

(C) Service-Department Costs

Direct Method

Under the **direct method,** each service department's costs are allocated among *only the direct-patient-care departments* that consume part of the service department's output. This method ignores the fact that some service departments provide services to other service departments. Thus, even though Riverside Clinic's Personnel Department provides services to two other service departments, none of its costs are allocated to those departments. Exhibit 17-3 presents Riverside Clinic's service department cost allocations under the direct method.

Notice that the proportion of each service department's costs to be allocated to each direct-patient-care department is determined by the *relative proportion* of the service department's output consumed by each direct-patient-care department. For example, a glance at Exhibit 17-2 shows that the Personnel Department provides 25 percent of its services to Orthopedics and 50 percent to Internal Medicine. Summing these two percentages yields 75 percent. Thus, 25/75 is the fraction of Personnel's cost allocated to Orthopedics and 50/75 is the fraction allocated to Internal Medicine.

Step-Down Method

As stated above, the direct method ignores the provision of services by one service department to another service department. This shortcoming is overcome partially by the **step-down method** of service department cost allocation. Under this method, the managerial accountant first chooses a sequence in which to allocate the service departments' costs. A common way to select the first service department in the sequence is to choose the one that serves the largest number of other service departments. The service departments are ordered in this manner, with the last service department being the one that serves the smallest number of other service depart-

Exhibit 17-3. Direct Method of Service-Department Cost Allocation: Riverside Clinic

| Provider of Service | Cost to Be Allocated | Direct-Patient-Care Departments Using Services | | | |
| | | Orthopedics | | Internal Medicine | |
		Proportion	Amount	Proportion	Amount
Patient Records	$100,000	3/10	$ 30,000	7/10	$ 70,000
Personnel	60,000	25/75	20,000	50/75	40,000
Administration and Accounting . . .	190,000	35/95	70,000	60/95	120,000
Total	$350,000		120,000		230,000

Grand total = $350,000

RIVERSIDE

ments.[3] Then the managerial accountant allocates each service department's costs among the direct-patient-care departments and all of the other service departments that follow it in the sequence. Note that the ultimate cost allocations assigned to the direct-patient-care departments will differ depending on the sequence chosen.

The step-down method is best explained by way of an illustration. Riverside Clinic's Personnel Department serves two other service departments: Patient Records, and Administration and Accounting. The Administration and Accounting Department serves only one other service department: Personnel. Finally, the Patient Records Department serves no other service departments. Thus, Riverside Clinic's service department sequence is as follows:

(1) Personnel	(2) Administration and Accounting	(3) Patient Records

In accordance with this sequence, each service department's costs are allocated to the other departments as follows:

Cost Allocated from This Service Department ⟶	**To These Departments**
Personnel	Administration and Accounting
	Patient Records
	Orthopedics
	Internal Medicine
Administration and Accounting	Orthopedics
	Internal Medicine
Patient Records	Orthopedics
	Internal Medicine

Notice that even though Administration and Accounting serves Personnel, there is no cost allocation in that direction. This results from Personnel's placement before Administration and Accounting in the allocation sequence. Moreover, no costs are allocated from Patient Records to either of the other service departments, because Patient Records does not serve those departments.

Exhibit 17-4 presents the results of applying the step-down method at Riverside Clinic. First, the Personnel Department's $60,000 in cost is allocated among the four departments using its services. Second, the cost of the Administration and Accounting Department is allocated. The total cost to be allocated is the department's original $190,000 *plus* the $12,000 allocated from the Personnel Department. The new total of $202,000 is allocated to the Orthopedics and Internal Medicine Departments according to the *relative proportions* in which these two departments use the services of the Administration and Accounting Department. Finally, the Patient Records Department's cost is allocated.

---

[3] A tie occurs when two or more service departments serve the same number of other service departments. Then the sequence among the tied service departments usually is an arbitrary choice.

Exhibit 17-4. Step-Down Method of Service-Department Cost Allocation: Riverside Clinic

RIVE**R**SIDE	Personnel	Service Departments		Direct-Patient-Care Departments	
		Administration and Accounting	Patient Records	Orthopedics	Internal Medicine
Costs prior to allocation	$60,000	$190,000	$100,000		
Allocation of Personnel Department costs	$60,000 →	12,000 (20/100)†	3,000 (5/100)	$ 15,000 (25/100)	$ 30,000 (50/100)
Allocation of Administrative and Accounting Department costs		$202,000 →		74,421* (35/95)	127,579* (60/95)
Allocation of Patient Records Department costs			$103,000 →	30,900 (30/100)	72,100 (70/100)
Total cost allocated to each department				$120,321	$229,679
Total cost allocated to direct-patient-care departments				$350,000	

* Rounded.
† Fractions in parentheses are relative proportions of service department's output consumed by departments to which costs are allocated.

Reciprocal-Services Method

The direct method and the step-down method both ignore the fact that the Administration and Accounting Department serves the Personnel Department. Neither of these methods allocates any of the costs incurred in Administration and Accounting back to Personnel.

Review the relationships between the service departments depicted in Exhibit 17-1. Notice that the Administration and Accounting Department and the Personnel Department *serve each other.* This mutual provision of service is called **reciprocal service.** A more accurate method of service department cost allocation, called the **reciprocal-services method,** fully accounts for the mutual provision of services. This method, which is more complex than the direct and step-down methods, is covered in the appendix at the end of this chapter.

Fixed versus Variable Costs

In our allocation of Riverside Clinic's service department costs, we did not distinguish between fixed and variable costs. Under some circumstances, this simple approach can result in an unfair cost allocation among the using departments. To illustrate, we will use the data about Riverside Clinic's fixed and variable costs given in panel C of Exhibit 17-2. Consider the cost data for the Patient Records Department, which serves only the Orthopedics and Internal Medicine Departments. Under the *direct method* of service department cost allocation, the Patient Records Department's costs were allocated as follows:

Cost Allocation for 19x1: Direct Method

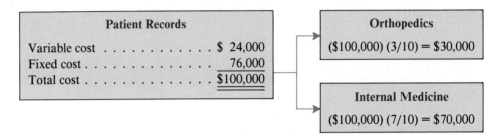

Patient Records	
Variable cost	$ 24,000
Fixed cost	76,000
Total cost	$100,000

Orthopedics
($100,000) (3/10) = $30,000

Internal Medicine
($100,000) (7/10) = $70,000

The allocation base used in this cost allocation is the annual patient load in the Orthopedics and Internal Medicine Departments. Let's assume the following patient loads in 19x1, the year for which the cost allocation has been done.

Department	Patient Load		Proportion of Total
Orthopedics	30,000	....	(30,000/100,000) = 3/10
Internal Medicine	70,000	....	(70,000/100,000) = 7/10
Total	100,000		

Now suppose the projections for 19x2 are as follows:

Department	Projected Patient Load		Projected Proportion of Total
Orthopedics	30,000	....	(30,000/80,000) = 3/8
Internal Medicine	50,000	....	(50,000/80,000) = 5/8
Total	80,000		

Department	Budgeted Variable Cost		Budgeted Fixed Cost		Budgeted Total Cost
Patient Records	$19,200	....	$76,000	....	$95,200

The projections for 19x2 include a stable patient load in the Orthopedics Department but a decline in the patient load of the Internal Medicine Department. Since the projected total patient load is lower for 19x2, the projected variable cost in the Patient Records Department is lower also.

What will be the effect of these changes on the 19x2 allocation of the Patient Records Department's costs? Using the direct method, we obtain the following allocation.

Cost Allocation for 19x2: Direct Method

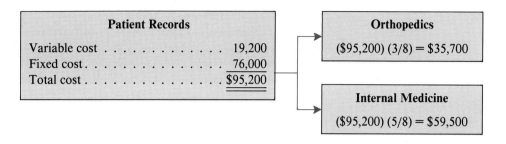

Compare the costs allocated to the two direct-patient-care departments in 19x1 and 19x2. Notice that the cost allocated to the Orthopedics Department *increased by* $5,700 (from $30,000 to $35,700), even though Orthopedics' patient load is projected to remain constant. What has happened here? The projected decline in the Internal Medicine Department's volume resulted in lower budgeted variable costs for the Patient Records Department, but the budgeted *fixed* costs did not change. At the same time, the lower projected patient load in Internal Medicine resulted in a higher proportion of the total projected patient load for Orthopedics (from 3/10 in 19x1 up to 3/8 in 19x2). As the following analysis shows, this results in an increased allocation of fixed costs to the Orthopedics Department in 19x2.

	19x1	19x2
Fixed cost in Patient Records Department	$76,000	$76,000
Orthopedics Department's proportion of total patient load	× 3/10	× 3/8
Orthopedics Department's allocation of fixed cost	$22,800	$28,500

Difference = $5,700

This difference of $5,700 is equal to the increase in the Orthopedics Department's total cost allocation from the Patient Records Department in 19x2.

To summarize, the projected decline in Internal Medicine's 19x2 patient load will result in an increased cost allocation from the Patient Records Department to the Orthopedics Department in 19x2. The cause of this increased allocation is our failure to distinguish between fixed and variable costs in the allocation process.

Dual Cost Allocation

The problem illustrated in the preceding section can be resolved by allocating fixed and variable costs separately. This approach, called **dual cost allocation,** works with either the direct method or the step-down method of allocation. Under dual cost allocation, *variable costs* are allocated on the basis of *short-run usage* of the service department's output; *fixed costs* are allocated on the basis of *long-run average usage* of the service department's output. The rationale for this approach is that fixed costs are capacity-producing costs. When service departments are established, their size and scale usually are determined by the projected long-run needs of the using departments.

To illustrate dual cost allocation for Riverside Clinic, we need estimates of the long-run average usage of each service department's output by each using department. These estimates are given in Exhibit 17-5.

To combine the dual-allocation approach with either the direct method or the step-down method, we simply apply the allocation method twice, as follows:

Costs to Be Allocated	Basis for Allocation	Allocation Method	
Variable costs in 19x1 (Exhibit 17-2, panel C)	Short-run usage in 19x1 (Exhibit 17-2, panel A)	Direct method	Step-down method
		OR	
Fixed costs in 19x1 (Exhibit 17-2, panel C)	Long-run average usage (Exhibit 17-5)	Direct method	Step-down method

After both of these allocation procedures have been completed, the resulting variable- and fixed-cost allocations for each direct-patient-care department are summed. Exhibit 17-6 presents the allocation computations when the dual approach is combined with the direct method. Compare the final direct allocations with those in Exhibit 17-3, where the dual approach was not used. Notice that the final allocations are different. Exhibit 17-7 presents the computations for the step-down method. Compare the final step-down allocations with those in Exhibit 17-4, where the dual approach was not used. Again, the final allocations are different.

A Behavioral Problem   Dual cost allocation prevents a change in the short-run activity of one using department from affecting the cost allocated to another using department. However, the approach sometimes presents a problem of its own. In order to implement the technique, we need accurate projections of the long-run average usage of each service department's output by each using department. This is

---

Exhibit 17-5. Provision of Services by Service Departments: Long-run Average Usage, Riverside Clinic

User of Service		Patient Records	Personnel	Administration and Accounting
Service departments	Patient Records	—	10%	—
	Personnel	—	—	10%
	Administration and Accounting	—	10%	—
Direct-patient-care departments	Orthopedics	40%	20%	45%
	Internal Medicine	60%	60%	45%

Provider of Service

Exhibit 17-6. Dual Allocation Combined With Direct Method: Riverside Clinic

I. Variable Costs

Provider of Service	RIVERSIDE	Cost to be Allocated	Direct-Patient-Care Departments Using Services			
			Orthopedics		Internal Medicine	
			Proportion	Amount	Proportion	Amount
Patient Records		$ 24,000	3/10	$ 7,200	7/10	$ 16,800
Personnel		15,000	25/75	5,000	50/75	10,000
Administration and Accounting		47,500	35/95	17,500	60/95	30,000
Total variable cost		$ 86,500		$ 29,700		$ 56,800

II. Fixed Costs

Patient Records		$ 76,000	4/10	$ 30,400	6/10	$ 45,600
Personnel		45,000	20/80	11,250	60/80	33,750
Administration and Accounting		142,500	45/90	71,250	45/90	71,250
Total fixed cost		$263,500		$112,900		$150,600
Total cost (variable + fixed)		$350,000		$142,600		$207,400

Grand total = $350,000

the information in Exhibit 17-5. Typically, these estimates come from the managers of the departments that consume the services. The problem is that the higher a manager's estimate of the department's long-run average usage is, the greater will be the department's allocation of fixed service-department costs. This creates an incentive for using-department managers to understate their expected long-run service needs. Ultimately, such understatements can result in building service facilities that are too small.

Exhibit 17-7. Dual Allocation Combined With Step-Down Method: Riverside Clinic

I. Variable Costs

		Service Departments		Direct-Patient Care Departments	
RIVE R SIDE	Personnel	Administration and Accounting	Patient Records	Orthopedics	Internal Medicine
Variable cost prior to allocation . . .	$15,000	$ 47,500	$24,000		
Allocation of Personnel Department costs	$15,000	3,000 (20/100)†	750 (5/100)	$ 3,750 (25/100)	$ 7,500 (50/100)
Allocation of Administrative and Accounting Department costs		$ 50,500		18,605*(35/95)	31,895*(60/95)
Allocation of Patient Records Department costs			$24,750	7,425 (30/100)	17,325 (70/100)
Total variable cost allocated to each department				$ 29,780	$ 56,720

*Rounded.

†Fractions in parentheses are relative proportions of service department's output consumed by departments to which costs are allocated. Variable costs allocated on basis of short-run proportions. Fixed costs allocated on basis of long-run average proportions.

How can we prevent this behavioral problem? First, we can rely on the professionalism and integrity of the managers who provide the estimates. Second, we can reward managers through promotions and pay raises for making accurate estimates of their departments' service needs.

Allocate Budgeted Costs

When service department costs are allocated to production departments, such as the direct-patient-care departments of Riverside Clinic, *budgeted* service department costs should be used. If actual costs are allocated instead, any operating inefficiencies in the service departments are passed along to the using departments. This reduces the incentive for service department managers to control the costs in their departments. The proper approach is as follows:

Exhibit 17-7. (continued)

II. Fixed Costs

	Service Departments			Direct-Patient Care Departments	
	Personnel	Administration and Accounting	Patient Records	Orthopedics	Internal Medicine
Fixed cost prior to allocation	$45,000	$142,500	$76,000		
Allocation of Personnel Department costs	$45,000	4,500 (10/100)	4,500 (10/100)	$ 9,000 (20/100)	$ 27,000 (60/100)
Allocation of Administrative and Accounting Department costs	.$147,000			73,500 (45/90)	73,500 (45/90)
Allocation of Patient Records Department costs			$80,500	32,200 (40/100)	48,300 (60/100)
Total fixed cost allocated to each department				$114,700	$148,800
Total cost allocated to each department (variable + fixed)				$142,708	$207,292

Grand total = $350,000

1. Compare budgeted and actual service department costs and compute any variances.
2. Use these variances to help control costs in the service departments.
3. Close out the service department cost variances against the period's income.
4. Allocate the service departments' budgeted costs to the departments that directly produce goods or services.

The New Manufacturing Environment

In traditional manufacturing environments, service department costs are allocated to production departments to ensure that all manufacturing costs are assigned to products. For example, the costs incurred in a machine-maintenance department typically are allocated to the other service departments and the production departments that use maintenance services. Service department cost allocation continues to be used in the new manufacturing environment, characterized by the JIT philosophy

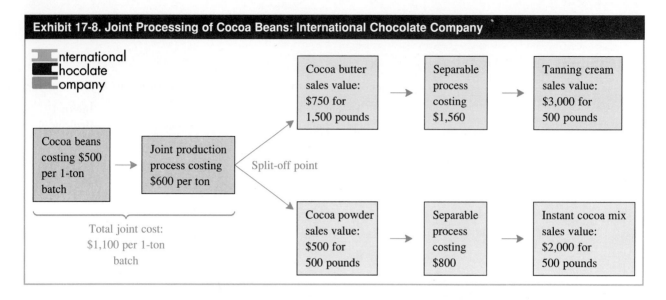

Exhibit 17-8. Joint Processing of Cocoa Beans: International Chocolate Company

and CIM systems. However, the extent of such allocations is diminished in advanced manufacturing systems, because more costs are directly traceable to product lines. In a flexible manufacturing system, almost all operations are performed in the FMS cell. Even machine maintenance is done largely by the FMS cell operators rather than a separate maintenance department. Inspection often is performed by FMS cell operators, eliminating the need for a separate inspection department. In short, as more and more costs become directly traceable to products, the need for allocation of indirect costs declines.

JOINT PRODUCT COSTS

A **joint production process** results in two or more products, which are termed **joint products.** The cost of the input and the joint production process is called a *joint product cost.* The point in the production process where the individual products become separately identifiable is called the **split-off point.** To illustrate, International Chocolate Company produces cocoa powder and cocoa butter by processing cocoa beans in the joint production process depicted in Exhibit 17-8.

As the diagram shows, cocoa beans are processed in 1-ton batches. The beans cost $500 and the joint process costs $600, for a total *joint cost* of $1,100. The process results in 1,500 pounds of cocoa butter and 500 pounds of cocoa powder. Each of these two joint products can be sold at the split-off point or processed further. Cocoa butter can be separately processed into a tanning cream, and cocoa powder can be separately processed into instant cocoa mix.

Allocating Joint Costs

For product-costing purposes, a joint product cost usually is allocated to the joint products that result from the joint production process. Such allocation *is necessary* for inventory valuation and income determination, among other reasons.[4] As we discussed in Chapter 13, however, joint cost allocation is *not useful* for making

[4] The purposes of product costing are covered in Chapter 3.

substantive economic decisions about the joint process or the joint products. For example, Chapter 13 shows that joint cost allocation is not useful in deciding whether to process a joint product further. (See pages 555 to 558.) There are three commonly used methods for allocating joint product costs. Each of these is explained next.

Physical-Units Method This method allocates joint product costs on the basis of some physical characteristic of the joint products at the split-off point. Panel A of Exhibit 17-9 illustrates this allocation method for International Chocolate Company using the *weight* of the joint products as the allocation basis.

Relative-Sales-Value Method This approach to joint cost allocation is based on the relative sales value of each joint product *at the split-off point.* In the International Chocolate Company illustration, these joint products are cocoa butter and cocoa powder. This method is illustrated in Exhibit 17-9 (panel B).

Exhibit 17-9. Methods for Allocating Joint Product Costs

Joint Cost	Joint Products	Weight at Split-off Point	Relative Proportion	Allocation of Joint Cost
$1,100	Cocoa butter.	1,500 pounds	3/4	$ 825
	Cocoa powder	500 pounds	1/4	275
	Total joint cost allocated			$1,100

(A) Physical-Units Method

Joint Cost	Joint Products	Sales Value at Split-off Point	Relative Proportion	Allocation of Joint Cost
$1,100	Cocoa butter.	$750	3/5	$ 660
	Cocoa powder	500	2/5	440
	Total joint cost allocated			$1,100

(B) Relative-Sales-Value Method

Joint Cost	Joint Products	Sales Value of Final Product	Separable Cost of Processing	Net Realizable Value	Relative Proportion	Allocation of Joint Cost
$1,100	Tanning cream	$3,000	$1,560. . .	$1,440* . . .	6/11	. . $ 600
	Instant cocoa mix	2,000	800. . .	1,200* . . .	5/11	. . 500
	Total joint cost allocated					$1,100

(C) Net-Realizable-Value Method

*Sales value of   separable cost   =   net realizable
  final product −   of processing   value

$3,000 – $1,560 = $1,440
  2,000 – 800 = 1,200

International
Chocolate
Company

Net-Realizable-Value Method   Under this method, the relative value of the final products is used to allocate the joint cost. International Chocolate Company's final products are tanning cream and instant cocoa mix. The **net realizable value** of each final product is its sales value less any separable costs incurred *after* the split-off point. The joint cost is allocated according to the relative magnitudes of the final products' net realizable values. Panel C of Exhibit 17-9 illustrates this allocation method.

Notice how different the cost allocations are under the three methods, particularly the physical-units method. Since the physical-units approach is not based on the *economic* characteristics of the joint products, it is the least preferred of the three methods.

By-Products   A joint product with very little value relative to the other joint products is termed a **by-product.** For example, whey is a by-product in the production of cheese. A common practice in accounting is to subtract a by-product's net realizable value from the cost of the joint process. Then the remaining joint cost is allocated among the major joint products.

An alternative procedure is to inventory the by-product at its sales value at split-off. Then the by-product's sales value is deducted from the production cost of the main products.

CHAPTER SUMMARY

Service departments are not involved directly in producing an organization's final output of goods or services, but they do provide essential services in an organization. Thus, in order to determine the full cost of the organization's final services or goods, service department costs are allocated to the departments directly involved in producing the organization's final output. Two methods are used commonly in practice, the direct method and the step-down method. Either of these methods may be combined with the dual-allocation approach, in which variable and fixed costs are allocated separately.

A joint production process results in two or more joint products, which become separately identifiable at the split-off point. The joint costs of production are allocated in order to determine the complete cost of manufacturing the joint products. Three methods are used for this purpose: the physical-units method, the relative-sales-value method, and the net-realizable-value method. Joint cost allocation is useful for product-costing purposes, but the allocated costs should not affect substantive economic decisions.

KEY TERMS   By-product, p. 748; Direct method, p. 737; Dual cost allocation, p. 741; Joint production process, p. 746; Joint products, p. 746; Net realizable value, p. 748; Net-realizable-value method, p. 748; Physical-units method, p. 747; Reciprocal service, p. 739; Reciprocal-services method, p. 739; Relative-sales-value method, p. 747; Service department, p. 734; Split-off point, p. 746; Step-down method, p. 737.

Reciprocal-Services Method

The reciprocal-services method of service department cost allocation fully accounts for the mutual provision of services among all the service departments. The relationships between Riverside Clinic's three service departments are portrayed in the following diagram.

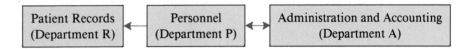

Patient Records (Department R)	←	Personnel (Department P)	↔	Administration and Accounting (Department A)

The first step in the technique is to specify a set of equations that express the relationships between the departments. The following equations, which express these relationships for Riverside Clinic, are based on the data in Exhibit 17-2 (Panel A).

$$R = 100,000 + .05\,P \qquad (1)$$
$$P = 60,000 + .05\,A \qquad (2)$$
$$A = 190,000 + .20\,P \qquad (3)$$

where   **R denotes the total cost of the Patient Records Department**
    P denotes the total cost of the Personnel Department
    A denotes the total cost of the Administration and Accounting Department

Equation (1) says that the *total cost* of operating the Patient Records Department (R) is $100,000 *plus* 5 percent of the total cost of operating the Personnel Department (P). The $100,000 comes from Exhibit 17-2 (panel C) and is the total cost *traceable* to the Patient Records Department. We add to this amount 5 percent of the total cost of operating the Personnel Department. Why? Because Exhibit 17-2 (panel A) tells us that the Patient Records Department used 5 percent of the Personnel Department's services. Similar explanations underlie equations (2) and (3).

The second step in the reciprocal-services method is to solve the simultaneous equations.[5] Let's begin by substituting the expression for *A* from equation (3) into equation (2), and solving for *P* as follows:

[5] Simultaneous equations are more quickly solved by computers than by people. Numerous software packages are available for this purpose.

$$P = 60,000 + .05\,(190,000 + .20\,P)$$
$$P = 60,000 + 9,500 \qquad + .01\,P$$
$$.99\,P = 69,500$$
$$P = 70,202 \text{ (rounded)}$$

Then we substitute the value for P we just obtained into equation (3), and solve for A as follows:

$$A = 190,000 + .20\,P$$
$$A = 190,000 + (.20)\,(70,202)$$
$$A = 204,040 \quad \text{(rounded)}$$

Now we can solve for R by substituting the value for P into equation (1) as follows:

$$R = 100,000 + .05\,P$$
$$R = 100,000 + (.05)(70,202)$$
$$R = 103,510 \quad \text{(rounded)}$$

Thus, we have determined that $P = 70,202$, $A = 204,040$, and $R = 103,510$.

The final step in the reciprocal-services method is to allocate the *total cost* of operating each service department (R, P, and A) to the various departments that use its services. For example, we will allocate the total cost of operating the Personnel Department (P) among all four of Riverside Clinic's other departments, because they all use Personnel's services. This allocation is made in proportion to the use of Personnel's services by the other departments, as given in Exhibit 17-2 (panel A).

The allocations are shown in Exhibit 17-10. Focus on the second row of numbers, which refers to the Personnel Department. The $70,202 shown in parentheses in the Personnel column is that department's total cost, as computed using the simultaneous equations. This $70,202 total cost is allocated as follows:

- 20 percent (or $14,040) to Administration and Accounting, because that department uses 20 percent of Personnel's services
- 5 percent (or $3,510) to Patient Records, because that department uses 5 percent of Personnel's services
- 25 percent (or $17,551) to Orthopedics, because that department uses 25 percent of Personnel's services
- 50 percent (or $35,101) to Internal Medicine, because that department uses 50 percent of Personnel's services.

A similar explanation underlies the Administration and Accounting row and the Patient Records row in Exhibit 17-10.

The total costs allocated to Riverside Clinic's two direct-patient-care departments are as follows: $120,018 to Orthopedics and $229,982 to Internal Medicine. Notice that these two amounts add up to $350,000, which is the total of the original traceable costs for the three service departments. Thus, all service department costs have been fully allocated.

The reciprocal-services method is more accurate than the direct and step-down methods, because it fully accounts for reciprocal services. To make the reciprocal-services method even more accurate, it can be combined with the dual-allocation approach. In this approach, variable and fixed costs are allocated separately. This method is explored in problem 17-32.

Exhibit 17-10. Reciprocal-Services Method of Service Department Cost Allocation: Riverside Clinic

		Service Departments		Direct-Patient Care Departments	
RIVE**R**SIDE	Personnel	Administration and Accounting	Patient Records	Orthopedics	Internal Medicine
Traceable costs	$60,000	$190,000	$100,000		
Allocation of Personnel Department costs	(70,202)	14,040* (.20)	3,510* (.05)	$17,551* (.25)	$ 35,101 (.50)
Allocation of Administrative and Accounting Department costs	10,202 (.05)†	(204,040)	–0– (0)	71,414 (.35)	122,424 (.60)
Allocation of Patient Records Department costs	–0– (0)	–0– (0)	(103,510)	31,053(.30)	72,457 (.70)
Total cost allocated to each direct-patient-care department				$120,018	$229,982
Total costs allocated				$350,000	

*Rounded.

†Percentages in parentheses are relative proportions of a service department's output consumed by departments to which costs are allocated (from Exhibit 17-2, panel A).

REVIEW QUESTIONS

17-1. Distinguish between a service department and a production department. Give an example of the counterpart of a manufacturer's "production" department in a bank.

17-2. Define the term *reciprocal services.*

17-3. Explain briefly the main differences between the direct, step-down, and reciprocal-services methods of service department cost allocation.

17-4. How does the managerial accountant determine the department sequence in the step-down method? How are ties handled?

17-5. Why does the dual-allocation approach improve the resulting cost allocations?

17-6. What potential behavioral problem can result when the dual approach is used?

17-7. Should actual or budgeted service department costs be allocated? Why?

17-8. Define the following terms: joint production process, joint costs, joint products, split-off point, separable costs, and by-product.

17-9. Briefly explain how to use the physical-units method of joint cost allocation.

17-10. Describe the relative-sales-value method of joint cost allocation.

17-11. Define the term *net realizable value,* and explain how this concept can be used to allocate joint costs.

17-12. Are joint cost allocations useful? If they are, for what purpose?

17-13. For what purpose should the managerial accountant be careful not to use joint cost allocations?

Exercise 17-14   Direct Method of Service Department Cost Allocation; College. Huron Community College enrolls students in two departments, Liberal Arts and Sciences. The college also has two service departments, the Library and the Computing Services Department. The usage of these two service departments' output in 19x9 was as follows:

	Provider of Service	
User of Service	**Library**	**Computing Services**
Library..	—	20%
Computing Services..............................	—	—
Liberal Arts	60%	30%
Sciences	40%	50%

The budgeted costs in the two service departments in 19x9 were as follows:

Library..	$600,000
Computing Services	240,000

REQUIRED: Use the direct method to allocate the budgeted costs of the Library and Computing Services Department to the college's Liberal Arts and Sciences departments.

Exercise 17-15   Step-Down Method of Service Department Cost Allocation; College. Refer to the data given in the preceding exercise.

REQUIRED: Use the step-down method to allocate Huron Community College's service department costs to the Liberal Arts and Sciences departments.

Exercise 17-16   Direct Method of Service Department Cost Allocation; Bank. Ashley County National Bank has two service departments, the Personnel Department and the Computing Department. The bank has two other departments that directly service customers, the Deposit Department and the Loan Department. The usage of the two service departments' output in 19x3 is as follows:

	Provider of Service	
User of Service	**Personnel**	**Computing**
Personnel	—	15%
Computing	10%	—
Deposit	60%	50%
Loan	30%	35%

The budgeted costs in the two service departments in 19x3 were as follows:

Personnel..	$153,000
Computing	229,500

REQUIRED: Use the direct method to allocate the budgeted costs of the Personnel and Computing departments to the Deposit and Loan departments.

Exercise 17-17   Step-Down Method of Service Department Cost Allocation; Bank. Refer to the data given in the preceding exercise.

REQUIRED: Use the step-down method to allocate the budgeted costs of the Personnel and Computing departments to the Deposit and Loan departments. Ashley County National Bank allocates the costs of the Personnel Department first.

Exercise 17-18   Physical-Units Method; Joint Cost Allocation. Breakfasttime Cereal Company manufactures two breakfast cereals in a joint process. Cost and quantity information is as follows:

Joint Cost	Cereal	Quantity at Split-off Point		Sales Price per Kilogram
$33,000	Yummies..........	12,000 kilograms	....	$2.00
	Crummies	8,000 kilograms	....	2.50

REQUIRED: Use the physical-units method to allocate the company's joint production cost between Yummies and Crummies.

Exercise 17-19   Relative-Sales-Value Method; Joint Cost Allocation. Refer to the data given in the preceding exercise.

REQUIRED: Use the relative-sales-value method to allocate Breakfastime Cereal Company's joint production cost between Yummies and Crummies.

Exercise 17-20   Net-Realizable-Value Method; Joint Cost Allocation. Refer to the data given in Exercise 17-18. Breakfastime Cereal Company has an opportunity to process its Crummies further into a mulch for ornamental shrubs. The additional processing operation costs $.50 per kilogram, and the mulch will sell for $3.50 per kilogram.

REQUIRED:

1. Should Breakfastime's management process Crummies into the mulch? Why?
2. Suppose the company does process Crummies into the mulch. Use the net-realizable-value method to allocate the joint production cost between the mulch and the Yummies.

Exercise 17-21   Reciprocal-Services Method; Bank; Appendix. Refer to the data given in Exercise 17-16 for Ashley County National Bank.

REQUIRED: Use the reciprocal-services method to allocate the budgeted costs of the Personnel and Computing departments to the Deposit and Loan departments.

PROBLEMS

Problem 17-22   Direct and Step-Down Methods of Service Department Cost Allocation. Toledo Instrument Company manufactures gauges for automobile dashboards. The company has two production departments: Molding and Assembly. There are three service departments: Maintenance, Personnel, and Engineering. The usage of these service departments' output and their budgeted costs during 19x2 are given on the next page.

REQUIRED:

1. Use the direct method to allocate Toledo Instrument Company's service department costs to its production departments.
2. Determine the proper sequence to use in allocating the firm's service department costs by the step-down method.
3. Use the step-down method to allocate the company's service department costs.

Provision of Service Output in 19x2 (in hours of service)

	Provider of Service		
User of Service	Personnel	Maintenance	Engineering
Personnel	—	—	—
Maintenance	500	—	—
Engineering	500	500	—
Molding	4,000	3,500	4,500
Assembly	5,000	4,000	1,500
Total.	10,000	8,000	6,000

The budgeted costs in Toledo Instrument Company's service departments during 19x2 are as follows:

	Personnel	Maintenance	Engineering
Variable	$ 50,000	$ 80,000	$ 50,000
Fixed.	200,000	150,000	300,000
Total.	$250,000	$230,000	$350,000

Problem 17-23 Dual Allocation of Service Department Costs. Refer to the data given in the preceding problem. When Toledo Instrument Company established its service departments, the following long-run needs were anticipated.

Long-run Service Needs (in hours of service)

	Provider of Service		
User of Service	Personnel	Maintenance	Engineering
Personnel	—	—	—
Maintenance	500	—	—
Engineering	1,000	800	—
Molding	3,500	4,800	4,800
Assembly	5,000	2,400	1,200
Total.	10,000	8,000	6,000

REQUIRED: Use the dual approach in conjunction with each of the following methods to allocate Toledo Instrument Company's service department costs: (1) direct method, and (2) step-down method.

Problem 17-24 Service Department Cost Allocation. Jefferson Corporation is developing departmental overhead rates based on direct-labor hours for its two production departments, Molding and Assembly. The Molding Department employs 20 people and the Assembly Department employs 80 people. Each person in these two departments works 2,000 hours per year. The production-related overhead costs for the Molding Department are budgeted at $200,000, and the Assembly Department costs are budgeted at $320,000. Two service departments, Repair and Power, directly support the two production departments. These service departments have budgeted costs of $48,000 and $250,000, respectively. The production departments' overhead rates cannot be determined until the service departments' costs are allocated. The following schedule reflects the use of the Repair Department's and Power Department's output by the various departments.

		Using Department		
Service Department	Repair	Power	Molding	Assembly
Repair (repair hours).....................	0	1,000	1,000	8,000
Power (kilowatt-hours)	240,000	0	840,000	120,000

REQUIRED:

1. Calculate the overhead rates per direct-labor hour for the Molding Department and the Assembly Department. Use the direct method to allocate service department costs.
2. Calculate the overhead rates per direct-labor hour for the Molding Department and the Assembly Department. Use the step-down method to allocate service department costs. Allocate the Power Department's costs first.

(CMA, adapted)

Problem 17-25   Service Department Cost Allocation; Plantwide versus Departmental Overhead Rates; Cost Drivers. Execucraft Corporation manufactures a complete line of fiberglass attaché cases and suitcases. The firm has three manufacturing departments: Molding, Component, and Assembly. There are also two service departments: Power and Maintenance.

The sides of the cases are manufactured in the Molding Department. The frames, hinges, and locks are manufactured in the Component Department. The cases are completed in the Assembly Department. Varying amounts of materials, time, and effort are required for each of the cases. The Power Department and Maintenance Department provide services to the three manufacturing departments.

Execucraft has always used a plantwide overhead rate. Direct-labor hours are used to assign overhead to products. The predetermined overhead rate is calculated by dividing the company's total estimated overhead by the total estimated direct-labor hours to be worked in the three manufacturing departments.

Jennifer Mason, manager of cost accounting, has recommended that Execucraft use departmental overhead rates. The planned operating costs and expected levels of activity for the coming year have been developed by Mason and are presented by department in the following schedules. (All numbers are in thousands.)

	Manufacturing Departments		
	Molding	Component	Assembly
Department activity measures:			
Direct-labor hours	500	2,000	1,500
Machine hours	875	125	-0 -
Departmental costs:			
Direct material	$12,400	$30,000	$ 1,250
Direct labor.............................	3,500	20,000	12,000
Variable overhead........................	3,500	10,000	16,500
Fixed overhead..........................	17,500	6,200	6,100
Total departmental costs	$36,900	$66,200	$35,850
Use of service departments:			
Maintenance:			
Estimated usage in labor hours for the coming			
year	90	25	10
Power (in kilowatt-hours):			
Estimated usage for the coming year........	360	320	120
Maximum allotted capacity...............	500	350	150

	Service Departments	
	Power	Maintenance
Departmental activity measures:		
Maximum capacity.....................	1,000 kilowatt-hours	Adjustable
Estimated usage for the coming year........	800 kilowatt-hours	125 hours
Departmental costs:		
Materials and supplies..................	$ 5,000	$1,500
Variable labor	1,400	2,250
Fixed overhead	12,000	250
Total service department costs............	$18,400	$4,000

REQUIRED:

1. Calculate the plantwide overhead rate for Execucraft Corporation for the coming year using the same method as used in the past.
2. Jennifer Mason has been asked to develop departmental overhead rates for comparison with the plantwide rate. The following steps are to be followed in developing the departmental rates.
   a. The Maintenance Department costs should be allocated to the three manufacturing departments using the direct method.
   b. The Power Department costs should be allocated to the three manufacturing departments using the dual method combined with the direct method. Fixed costs are to be allocated according to maximum allotted capacity, and variable costs are to be allocated according to planned usage for the coming year.
   c. Calculate departmental overhead rates for the three manufacturing departments using a machine-hour cost driver for the Molding Department and a direct-labor-hour cost driver for the Component and Assembly departments.
3. Should Execucraft Corporation use a plantwide rate or departmental rates to assign overhead to products? Explain your answer.

(CMA, adapted)

Problem 17-26   Joint Cost Allocation. Forward Corporation manufactures products Alpha, Beta, and Gamma from a joint process. Production, sales, and cost data for July follow.

	Alpha	Beta	Gamma	Total
Units produced.......................	4,000	2,000	1,000	7,000
Joint cost allocation....................	$36,000	?	?	$60,000
Sales value at split-off..................	?	?	$15,000	$100,000
Additional costs if processed further.......	$7,000	$5,000	$3,000	$15,000
Sales value if processed further	$70,000	$25,000	$20,000	$115,000

REQUIRED:

1. Assuming that joint costs are allocated using the relative-sales-value method, what were the joint costs allocated to products Beta and Gamma?
2. Assuming that joint costs are allocated using the relative-sales-value method, what was the sales value at split-off for product Alpha?
3. Use the net-realizable-value method to allocate the joint production costs to products Alpha, Beta, and Gamma.

(CPA, adapted)

Problem 17-27   Joint Cost Allocation. Lares Confectioners, Inc., makes a candy called Rey which sells for 50 cents per pound. The manufacturing process also yields a product known as

Nagu. Without further processing, Nagu sells for 10 cents per pound. With further processing, Nagu sells for 30 cents per pound. During the month of April, total joint manufacturing costs up to the split-off point consisted of the following additions to Work-in-Process Inventory.

Direct material	$150,000
Direct labor	120,000
Manufacturing overhead	30,000

Production for the month amounted to 394,000 pounds of Rey and 30,000 pounds of Nagu. To complete Nagu during the month of April and obtain a selling price of 30 cents per pound, further processing of Nagu during April would entail the following additional costs.

Direct material	$2,000
Direct labor	1,500
Manufacturing overhead	500

REQUIRED: Prepare the April journal entries for Nagu, if Nagu is:

1. Transferred as a by-product at sales value to the warehouse without further processing, with a corresponding reduction of Rey's manufacturing cost.
2. Further processed and transferred to finished goods, with joint costs being allocated between Rey and Nagu based on the relative sales value at the split-off point.

(CPA, adapted)

Problem 17-28   *Comprehensive Problem on Joint Cost Allocatin.* Portland Chemical Company manufactures two industrial chemical products in a joint process. In May, 10,000 gallons of input costing $60,000 were processed at a cost of $150,000. The joint process resulted in 8,000 pounds of Ipso and 2,000 pounds of Facto. Ipso sells for $25 per pound and Facto sells for $50 per pound. Portland's management generally processes each of these chemicals further in separable processes to produce more refined chemical products. Ipso is processed separately at a cost of $5 per pound. The resulting product, Ipso II, sells for $35 per pound. Facto is processed separately at a cost of $15 per pound. The resulting product, Facto II, sells for $95 per pound.

REQUIRED:

1. Draw a diagram similar to Exhibit 17-8 to depict Portland Chemical Company's joint production process.
2. Allocate the company's joint production costs for May using:
   a. The physical-units method.
   b. The relative-sales-value method.
   c. The net-realizable-value method.
3. Portland's management is considering an opportunity to process Facto II further into a new product called Omega. The separable processing will cost $40 per pound. Packaging costs for Omega are projected to be $6 per pound, and the anticipated sales price is $130 per pound. Should Facto II be processed further into Omega? Why?
4. In answering requirement (3), did you use your joint cost allocation from requirement (2)? If so, how did you use it?

Problem 17-29   *Joint Cost Allocation.* Multiproduct Corporation produces two main products (Pepco-1 and Repke-3) and a by-product (SE-5) from a joint process. If Multiproduct had the proper facilities, it could process SE-5 further into a main product. The ratio of output quantities to input quantity of direct material used in the joint process remains constant with the processing condition and activity level.

Multiproduct currently uses the physical-units method of allocating joint costs to the main products. The FIFO (first-in, first-out) inventory method is used. The by-product is inventoried at its net realizable value, and the net realizable value of the by-product is used to reduce the joint production costs before the joint costs are allocated to the main products.

Jim Simpson, Multiproduct's controller, wants to implement the relative-sales-value method of joint cost allocation. The net realizable value of the by-product would be treated in the same manner as with the physical-units method.

Data regarding Multiproduct's operations for November follow. The joint production cost amounted to $2,640,000 for November.

| | Main Products | | By-Product |
	Pepco-1	Repke-3	SE-5
Finished-goods inventory in gallons			
on November 1..........................	20,000	40,000	10,000
November sales in gallons	800,000	700,000	200,000
November production in gallons.............	900,000	720,000	240,000
Sales value per gallon at split-off point	$2.00	$1.50	$.55*
Additional processing costs after split-off	$1,800,000	$720,000	—
Final sales value per gallon	$5.00	$4.00	—

* Selling costs of $.05 per gallon will be incurred in order to sell the by-product.

REQUIRED:

1. Assuming Multiproduct Corporation adopts the relative-sales-value method for internal reporting purposes:
   a. Calculate how the joint production cost for November would be allocated.
   b. Determine the dollar values of the finished-goods inventories for Pepco-1, Repke-3, and SE-5 as of November 30.
2. Multiproduct Corporation plans to expand its production facilities to enable the further processing of SE-5 into a main product. Discuss how the allocation of the joint production costs under the relative-sales-value method would change when SE-5 becomes a main product.

(CMA, adapted)

Problem 17-30 Joint Cost Allocation; By-Product. Tasty Fruit Corporation grows, processes, cans, and sells three main pineapple products: sliced, crushed, and juice. The outside skin is cut off in the Cutting Department and processed as animal feed. The feed is treated as a by-product. The company's production process is as follows:

● Pineapples first are processed in the Cutting Department. The pineapples are washed and the outside skin is cut away. Then the pineapples are cored and trimmed for slicing. The three main products (sliced, crushed, juice) and the by-product (animal feed) are recognizable after processing in the Cutting Department. Each product then is transferred to a separate department for final processing.

● The trimmed pineapples are sent to the Slicing Department, where the pineapples are sliced and canned. Any juice generated during the slicing operation is packed in the cans with the slices.

● The pieces of pineapple trimmed from the fruit are diced and canned in the Crushing Department. Again, the juice generated during this operation is packed in the can with the crushed pineapple.

● The core and surplus pineapple generated from the Cutting Department are pulverized into a liquid in the Juicing Department. There is an evaporation loss equal to 8

percent of the weight of the good out_ produced in this department which occurs as
the juices are heated.

● The outside skin is chopped into animal feed in the Feed Department.

Tasty Fruit Corporation uses the net-realizable-value method to assign the costs of the
joint process to its main products. The net realizable value of the by-product is subtracted from
the joint cost before the allocation.

A total of 270,000 pounds were entered into the Cutting Department during May. The
following schedule shows the costs incurred in each department, the proportion by weight
transferred to the four final processing departments, and the selling price of each end product.

Processing Data and Costs for May

Department	Costs Incurred		Proportion of Product by Weight Transferred to Departments		Selling Price per Pound of Final Product
Cutting	$60,000	....	—	....	none
Slicing	4,700	....	35%	....	$.60
Crushing ...	10,580	....	28	....	.55
Juicing.....	3,250	....	27	....	.30
Animal feed.	700	....	10	....	.10
Total	$79,230	....	100%		

REQUIRED: Compute each of the following amounts.

1. The number of pounds of pineapple that result as output for pineapple slices,
   crushed pineapple, pineapple juice, and animal feed.
2. The net realizable value at the split-off point of the three main products.
3. The amount of the cost of the Cutting Department allocated to each of the three
   main products.

(CMA, adapted)

Problem 17-31   Reciprocal-Service Method; Appendix. Refer to the data given in Problem
17-24 for Jefferson Corporation.

REQUIRED:

1. Calculate the overhead rates per direct-labor hour for the Molding Department and
   the Assembly Department. Use the reciprocal-services method to allocate service
   department costs.
2. Which of the three methods of service department cost allocation results in the
   most accurate overhead rates? Why?

Problem 17-32   Reciprocal-Services Method; Dual Allocation; Appendix. Refer to the data
for Riverside Clinic given in Exhibits 17-2 and 17-5.

REQUIRED: Use the reciprocal-services method in combination with the dual-allocation approach to allocate Riverside's service department costs. Hint: You will need to apply the
reciprocal-services method twice. First, allocate the three service departments' variable costs
using the short-run usage proportions in Exhibit 17-2 (panel A). Second, allocate the three
service departments' fixed costs using the long-run average usage proportions in Exhibit 17-5.
Finally, add the variable costs and fixed costs allocated to each direct-patient-care department.

Chapter 18 Analyzing Financial Statements

<table>
<tr><td rowspan="5" valign="top">After completing this chapter, you should be able to:</td></tr>
<tr><td>■ Explain the objectives of financial statement analysis.</td></tr>
<tr><td>■ Describe and use the following four analytical techniques: horizontal analysis, trend analysis, vertical analysis, and ratio analysis.</td></tr>
<tr><td>■ Explain the importance of comparisons and trends in financial statement analysis.</td></tr>
<tr><td>■ Prepare and interpret common-size financial statements.</td></tr>
<tr><td>■ Define and compute the various financial ratios discussed in the chapter.</td></tr>
</table>

Financial statements provide the primary means for managers to communicate about the financial condition of their organization to outside parties. Managers, investors, lenders, financial analysts, and government agencies are among the users of financial statements. Substantial information is conveyed by financial statements about the financial strength and current performance of an enterprise. Although financial statements are prepared primarily for users outside an organization, managers also find their organization's financial statements useful in making decisions. As managers develop operating plans, they think about how those plans will affect the performance of the organization, as conveyed by the financial statements. In this chapter, we will explore how to analyze financial statements to glean the most information about an organization.

OVERVIEW OF FINANCIAL STATEMENTS

There are four primary financial statements:

1. Balance sheet
2. Income statement
3. Retained earnings statement
4. Statement of cash flows

Exhibit 18-1 presents the basic structure of each of these statements and the relation-ships between them. The *balance sheet* presents an organization's financial position at a *point in time.* It shows the balances in the organization's assets, liabilities, and owners' equity, as of the balance sheet date.

The other three financial statements depicted in Exhibit 18-1 relate to a *period of time.* The *income statement* reports the income for the period between two balance sheet dates. The *retained earnings statement* shows how income and dividends for the

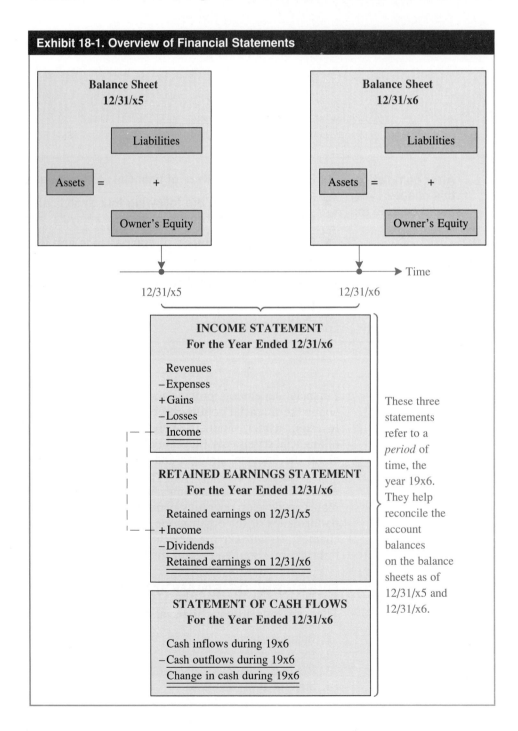

Exhibit 18-1. Overview of Financial Statements

Balance Sheet
12/31/x5

Liabilities

Assets = +

Owner's Equity

Balance Sheet
12/31/x6

Liabilities

Assets = +

Owner's Equity

12/31/x5   12/31/x6   Time

INCOME STATEMENT
For the Year Ended 12/31/x6

Revenues
−Expenses
+Gains
−Losses
Income

RETAINED EARNINGS STATEMENT
For the Year Ended 12/31/x6

Retained earnings on 12/31/x5
+Income
−Dividends
Retained earnings on 12/31/x6

STATEMENT OF CASH FLOWS
For the Year Ended 12/31/x6

Cash inflows during 19x6
−Cash outflows during 19x6
Change in cash during 19x6

These three statements refer to a *period* of time, the year 19x6. They help reconcile the account balances on the balance sheets as of 12/31/x5 and 12/31/x6.

period have changed the organization's retained earnings. The *statement of cash flows* shows how cash was obtained during the period and how it was used.

In this chapter, we will concentrate on analyzing the data conveyed by the balance sheet, the income statement, and the retained earnings statement. In Chapter 19, we will explore how the statement of cash flows is prepared and used.

OBJECTIVES OF FINANCIAL STATEMENT ANALYSIS

Financial statements are based on historical accounting information, which reflects the transactions and other events that have affected the firm. Managers and other users of the firm's financial statements are interested in the future. The objective of financial statement analysis is to use historical accounting data to help in predicting how the firm will fare in the future. The aspects of an organization's future performance that are of most interest depend on the needs of the user. A manager in the firm would be interested in the company's overall financial strength, its income and growth potential, and the financial effects of pending decisions. A potential lender, such as a bank loan officer, would be concerned primarily about the firm's ability to pay back the loan. Potential investors would be interested not only in the company's ability to repay its loan obligations, but also its future profit potential. Potential customers would want to assess the firm's ability to carry out its operations effectively and meet delivery schedules. Thus, the needs of the analyst dictate the sort of financial statement analysis that is most appropriate.

Analytical Techniques Used

Four analytical tools are in widespread use in analyzing financial statements:

1. Horizontal analysis
2. Trend analysis
3. Vertical analysis
4. Ratio analysis

Each of these techniques is defined, discussed, and illustrated in the following sections of the chapter.

Importance of Comparisons and Trends

No single measure of a company's financial condition or performance can tell us much. The single most important point to remember about financial statement analysis is that every financial measure should be *compared* across time and across other companies to be meaningful. For example, an airline's profit in 19x8 should be compared with the same company's profit for 19x7, 19x6, 19x5, and so forth. Moreover, the company's profit should be compared with the profit reported by other airlines of similar size and operational characteristics. Comparing key financial data with industry norms also adds meaning to the reported profit for the company being analyzed.

To reemphasize the point, every financial measure discussed in this chapter should be compared with other analogous measures in order to be meaningful.

Sources of Data

Published financial statements provide the primary source of data about any organization's financial condition and performance. A company's annual report, quarterly reports, and financial news releases provide a wealth of information about the firm.

Exhibit 18-2. Comparative Balance Sheets

CONTEMPORARY
interiors

Contemporary Interiors, Inc.
Comparative Balance Sheets
December 31, 19x6 and 19x5
(in thousands)

	Year 19x6	Year 19x5	Increase or (Decrease) Amount	Increase or (Decrease) Percentage
Assets				
Current assets:				
Cash	$ 800	$ 700	$ 100	14.3
Marketable securities	450	300	150	50.0
Accounts receivable, net.	12,000	11,000	1,000	9.1
Inventory.	20,000	17,000	3,000	17.6
Prepaid expenses	250	300	(50)	(16.7)
Total current assets	33,500	29,300	4,200	14.3
Long-term investments	500	550	(50)	(9.1)
Property, furnishings, and equipment:				
Land	6,000	6,000	–0–	–0–
Buildings, net	55,000	52,000	3,000	5.8
Equipment and furnishings, net	25,000	23,000	2,000	8.7
Total property, furnishings, and equipment	86,000	81,000	5,000	6.2
Total assets	$120,000	$110,850	$9,150	8.3
Liabilities and Stockholders' Equity				
Current liabilities:				
Accounts payable	7,500	7,050	450	6.4
Accrued expenses	2,200	2,100	100	4.8
Notes payable	3,000	3,200	(200)	(6.3)
Total current liabilities	12,700	12,350	350	2.8
Long-term liabilities:				
Bonds payable ($1,000 face value; 10%)	37,300	35,700	1,600	4.5
Total liabilities	50,000	48,050	1,950	4.1
Stockholders' equity:				
Preferred stock ($100 par value; 8%)	6,000	6,000	–0–	–0–
Common stock ($10 par value)*	25,000	24,000	1,000	4.2
Additional paid-in capital	4,000	3,800	200	5.3
Retained earnings	35,000	29,000	6,000	20.7
Total stockholders' equity	70,000	62,800	7,200	11.5
Total liabilities and stockholders' equity	$120,000	$110,850	$9,150	8.3

* 100,000 shares of common stock were issued on January 1, 19x6. Since these shares were outstanding during the entire year, the weighted-average number of shares outstanding in 19x6 was 2,500,000 shares.

Other sources of financial information are also available, both for individual companies and for entire industries. The Securities and Exchange Commission requires that every publicly held company file a detailed financial report with the commission annually. These reports are available to the public. The financial press, such as *The Wall Street Journal, Barron's, Business Week, Fortune, Forbes,* and various industry trade publications, provides in-depth coverage of specific companies and industries. Other important sources of financial data include financial advisory services, such as Dun & Bradstreet, Moody's Investors Service, Dow Jones, Standard and Poor's, and Robert Morris Associates.

Doing a good job of financial statement analysis is not a trivial task. It requires a solid knowledge of accounting, familiarity with the analytical techniques to be discussed in this chapter, and substantial research using data from a variety of sources.

COMPARATIVE FINANCIAL STATEMENTS

To illustrate each of the techniques used in analyzing financial statements, we will focus on a retail business. Contemporary Interiors, Inc., headquartered in Chicago, operates a chain of furniture stores in the midwest. The company specializes in contemporary furniture, much of it imported from the Scandinavian countries. The firm also sells handcrafted furnishings, such as ceramic lamps and handwoven wall hangings.

Contemporary Interiors' balance sheets for December 31, 19x5 and 19x6 are displayed in Exhibit 18-2. The company's income statements and retained earnings statements for 19x5 and 19x6 are presented in Exhibit 18-3.

Horizontal Analysis

Exhibits 18-2 and 18-3 display **comparative financial statements,** which show the company's financial results for two successive years. These statements highlight the change in each financial item between 19x5 and 19x6. For example, Exhibit 18-2 shows that Contemporary Interiors' cash balance increased by $100,000 between December 31, 19x5 and December 31, 19x6. Notice that the changes highlighted in Exhibits 18-2 and 18-3 are shown in both dollar and percentage form. Thus, Contemporary Interiors' $100,000 increase in cash represents an increase of 14.3 percent of the December 31, 19x5 amount (14.3% = $100,000 ÷ $700,000).

Comparative financial statements and change data enable managers and financial analysts to do **horizontal analysis,** which is an analysis of the year-to-year change in each financial statement item. The purpose of horizontal analysis is to determine how each item changed, why it changed, and whether the change is favorable or unfavorable. This is a tall order, and it requires substantial additional information. Suppose, for example, that a business periodical recently published a story about a growing demand for Danish furniture. A glance at Contemporary Interiors' comparative balance sheet reveals that its cash, accounts receivable, and inventory have all increased during 1 ˜6. These changes are consistent with expanded operations in response to increased demand for the company's goods. The comparative income statement helps to confirm this supposition, since sales and cost of goods sold increased substantially from 19x5 to 19x6.

Thus the analyst's job is like putting together a jigsaw puzzle. The analyst first gathers all the puzzle pieces (financial data) and then tries to fit them together to create a meaningful picture (the firm's financial condition and performance).

Exhibit 18-3. Comparative Income and Retained Earnings Statements

Contemporary Interiors, Inc.
Comparative Income and Retained Earnings Statements
For the Years Ended December 31, 19x6 and 19x5
(in thousands)

		Year		Increase or (Decrease)	
		19x6	19x5	Amount	Percentage
Sales		$87,000	$82,000	$5,000	6.1
Cost of goods sold		60,930	56,350	4,580	8.1
Gross margin		26,070	25,650	420	1.6
Operating expenses:					
Selling expenses		5,000	4,600	400	8.7
Administrative expenses.		2,000	2,100	(100)	(4.8)
Total operating expenses		7,000	6,700	300	4.5
Operating income		19,070	18,950	120	.6
Interest expense		4,030	3,890	140	3.6
Income before taxes.		15,040	15,060	(20)	(.1)
Income tax expense		3,760	3,800	(40)	(1.1)
Net income		11,280	11,260	20	.2
Dividends on preferred stock		480	480	–0–	–0–
Net income available to					
common stockholders		10,800	10,780	$ 20	.2
Dividends on common stock		4,800	4,600	200	4.3
Net income added to					
retained earnings.		6,000	6,180	(180)	(2.9)
Retained earnings, January 1		29,000	22,820	6,180	27.1
Retained earnings, December 31.		$35,000	$29,000	$6,000	20.7

Trend Analysis

The comparative financial statements in Exhibits 18-2 and 18-3 allow a comparison of only two years' data. When the comparison is extended to three or more years, the technique is called **trend analysis.** Trends can be shown in both dollar and percentage form by designating the first year in the sequence as the base year. Then the amounts in subsequent years are shown as a percentage of the base-year amount. Exhibit 18-4 displays a trend analysis of Contemporary Interiors' sales and net income data over a six-year period.

Contemporary Interiors' sales and net income both have risen steadily from 19x1 through 19x6. However, the growth in sales has been greater than the growth in net income. The increase in income between 19x5 and 19x6 is quite small, despite a large increase in sales. The relationship between the trend in sales and the trend in net income could be cause for concern. Why has Contemporary Interiors' management been unable to convert a significant growth in sales into an equally large growth in net income? While the trend analysis does not answer this question, it does serve an *attention-directing* role for the analyst. An alert financial analyst will delve more deeply into this issue and try to come up with an explanation.

Exhibit 18-4. Trend Analysis: Contemporary Interiors, Inc.

	19x6	19x5	19x4	19x3	19x2	19x1
Sales	$87,000	$82,000	$78,000	$74,800	$73,000	$72,000
Net income.	11,280	11,260	11,000	10,500	10,200	9,900

**(A) Trend Analysis in Dollars
(measured in thousands)**

	19x6	19x5	19x4	19x3	19x2	19x1
Sales	121*	114†	108	104	101	100
Net income.	114	114	111	106	103	100

(B) Trend Analysis in Percentages

CONTEMPORARY
interiors

*121% = $87,000 ÷ $72,000
†114% = $82,000 ÷ $72,000

Vertical Analysis

Horizontal and trend analyses focus on the relationships between the amounts of each financial item across time. In contrast, **vertical analysis** concentrates on the relationships between various financial items on a particular financial statement. To show these relationships, each item on the statement is expressed as a percentage of a base item that also appears on the statement. On the balance sheet, each item is expressed as a percentage of total assets. On the income statement, each item is stated as a percentage of sales. Financial statements prepared in terms of percentages of a base amount are called **common-size statements.** Contemporary Interiors' common-size balance sheets and income statements for 19x5 and 19x6 are displayed in Exhibits 18-5 and 18-6.

Financial analysts use vertical analysis to gain insight into the relative importance or magnitude of various items in the financial statements. Using common-size statements, prepared in a comparative format, analysts can discern changes in a firm's financial condition and performance from year to year.

To illustrate, notice that Contemporary Interiors' composition of current assets remained quite stable from 19x5 to 19x6. Although the various asset amounts changed, each asset represents roughly the same proportion of total assets on December 31, 19x6 as on December 31, 19x5. The largest change is in inventory, which increased from 15.3 percent to 16.7 percent of total assets. This could be merely a reflection of increased sales, and the required working capital. Alternatively, it could indicate overstocking.

RATIO ANALYSIS: THE BALANCE SHEET

The balance sheet is like a snapshot. It records the company's financial position at an instant in time. Several key relationships between the balance sheet items can help an analyst gain insight into the strength of a business.

Exhibit 18-5. Common-size Balance Sheets

Contemporary Interiors, Inc.
Common-size Balance Sheets
December 31, 19x6 and 19x5

	Common-size Statements	
	19x6	19x5
Assets		
Current assets:		
Cash	.7	.6
Marketable securities	.4	.3
Accounts receivable, net	10.0	9.9
Inventory	16.7	15.3
Prepaid expenses	.2	.3
Total current assets	28.0	26.4
Long-term investments	.4	.5
Property, furnishings, and equipment:		
Land	5.0	5.4
Buildings, net	45.8	47.0
Equipment and furnishings, net	20.8	20.7
Total property, furnishings, and equipment	71.6	73.1
Total assets	100.0	100.0
Liabilities and Stockholders' Equity		
Current liabilities:		
Accounts payable	6.3	6.3
Accrued expenses	1.8	1.9
Notes payable	2.5	2.9
Total current liabilities	10.6	11.1
Long-term liabilities:		
Bonds payable ($1,000 face value; 10%)	31.1	32.2
Total liabilities	41.7	43.3
Stockholders' equity:		
Preferred stock ($100 par value; 8%)	5.0	5.4
Common stock ($10 par value)	20.8	21.7
Additional paid-in capital	3.3	3.4
Retained earnings	29.2	26.2
Total stockholders' equity	58.3	56.7
Total liabilities and stockholders' equity	100.0	100.0

Working Capital

Current assets are assets that, under normal business operations, will be converted into cash within a reasonably short time period, usually a year. Contemporary Interiors' current assets include cash, marketable securities, accounts receivable, inventory, and prepaid expenses. The expectation is that the inventory will be sold within a

Exhibit 18-6. Common-size Income Statements

CONTEMPORARY
interiors

Contemporary Interiors, Inc.
Common-size Income Statements
For the Years Ended December 31, 19x6 and 19x5

| | Common-size Statements | |
	19x6	19x5
Sales	100.0	100.0
Cost of goods sold	70.0	68.7
Gross margin	30.0	31.3
Operating expenses:		
Selling expenses	5.7	5.6
Administrative expenses	2.3	2.6
Total operating expenses	8.0	8.2
Operating income	21.9	23.1
Interest expense	4.6	4.7
Income before taxes	17.3	18.4
Income tax expense	4.3	4.6
Net income	13.0	13.8

year, the accounts receivable will be collected within a year, and so forth. *Current liabilities* are obligations due within a year.

A key financial measure is a company's **working capital,** which is defined as follows:

$$\text{Working capital} = \text{current assets} - \text{current liabilities}$$

Contemporary Interiors' working capital as of December 31, 19x6 amounts to $20,800,000 ($33,500,000 − $12,700,000). Working capital is a key concept in operating a business. It is important to keep a reasonable amount of working capital to ensure that short-term obligations can be paid on time, opportunities for volume expansion can be seized, and unforeseen circumstances can be handled easily. Contemporary Interiors has a comfortable balance of working capital.

Current Ratio

Another way of viewing a company's working capital position is in terms of the *current ratio,* defined as follows:

$$\text{Current ratio} = \frac{\text{current assets}}{\text{current liabilities}}$$

Contemporary Interiors' current ratio as of December 31, 19x6 is computed below.

$$\text{Current ratio (12/31/x6)} = \frac{\$33,500,000}{\$12,700,000} = 2.64, \text{ or } 2.64 \text{ to } 1$$

A popular rule of thumb is that a company's current ratio should be at least 2 to 1. Thus, Contemporary Interiors' current ratio is quite healthy. Indeed, it may be too large, once again indicating a possible excess of inventory. It is naive and somewhat dangerous to place too much faith in a rule of thumb such as "Keep a current ratio of 2 to 1." The appropriate magnitude for this ratio (and all financial ratios) varies widely among industries, companies, and the specific circumstances of individual firms.

Limitation of the Current Ratio The current ratio does not tell the whole story of a company's ability to meet its short-term obligations. Consider the following balance sheet data for Contemporary Interiors and its chief competitor, Trends in Teak.

	Contemporary Interiors	Trends in Teak
Cash	$ 800	$ 100
Marketable securities	450	150
Accounts receivable	12,000	2,950
Inventory	20,000	30,000
Prepaid expenses	250	300
Total current assets	$33,500	$33,500
Total current liabilities	$12,700	$12,700
Current ratio	2.64 to 1	2.64 to 1

Each of these companies exhibits a current ratio of 2.64 to 1. However, are the two firms in equally strong positions regarding payment of their current obligations? The answer is no. Trends in Teak has most of its current assets tied up in inventory, which may take close to a year to convert into cash through normal business operations. In contrast, Contemporary Interiors can cover all of its current debts with cash, marketable securities, and accounts receivable, which typically will be converted to cash much more quickly than inventory.

Acid-Test Ratio

To get a better picture of a company's ability to meet its short-term obligations, many analysts prefer the *acid-test ratio* (or *quick ratio*), defined as follows:

$$\text{Acid-test ratio} = \frac{\text{quick assets}}{\text{current liabilities}}$$

Quick assets are defined as cash, marketable securities, accounts receivable, and current notes receivable. These assets typically can be converted into cash much more quickly than inventory or prepaid expenses can. Therefore, inventory and prepaid expenses are excluded from quick assets. The acid-test ratios for Contemporary Interiors and Trends in Teak are computed as follows:

	Contemporary Interiors	Trends in Teak
Acid-test ratio =	$\dfrac{\$13,250,000}{\$12,700,000} = 1.04 \text{ to } 1$	$\dfrac{\$3,200,000}{\$12,700,000} = .25 \text{ to } 1$

For every dollar of current liabilities, Contemporary Interiors has $1.04 available in quick assets. In contrast, Trends in Teak has only $.25 in quick assets available to pay every dollar of its current liabilities.

Accounts Receivable Turnover

This ratio measures the number of times the average balance in accounts receivable has been converted into cash during the year. The *accounts receivable turnover* ratio is defined as follows:

$$\text{Accounts receivable turnover} = \frac{\text{sales on account}}{\text{average balance in accounts receivable}}$$

For Contemporary Interiors, the ratio is computed as follows:

$$\text{Accounts receivable turnover} = \frac{\$87,000,000^*}{\$11,500,000\dagger} = 7.6$$

* All of Contemporary Interiors' sales were on account.
† Average balance in accounts receivable = ($11,000,000 + $12,000,000)/2.

The accounts receivable turnover often is used to assess the effectiveness of a company's credit terms and collection policies. The higher the ratio, the more effective the company is in collecting its receivables. Of course, a firm can establish too stringent a credit policy, resulting in lost sales.

Average Collection Period Another ratio, which is derived from the accounts receivable turnover, is the *average collection period,* defined as follows:

$$\text{Average collection period} = \frac{365 \text{ days}}{\text{accounts receivable turnover}}$$

For Contemporary Interiors, this ratio is computed as follows:

$$\text{Average collection period} = \frac{365 \text{ days}}{7.6} = 48 \text{ days}$$

The average collection period measures the average number of days required to collect accounts receivable. Contemporary Interiors' collection period of 48 days is quite long, particularly if the company's credit payment terms are the usual 30 days. This relatively long collection period may reflect lax credit terms, ineffective collection policies, or some accounts receivable of doubtful collectibility.

Inventory Turnover

How much inventory should a company keep? The answer, which requires a delicate trade-off of ordering, holding, and shortage costs, varies widely among industries. One measure of the appropriateness of a company's inventory level is its *inventory turnover,* which is defined as follows:

$$\text{Inventory turnover} = \frac{\text{cost of goods sold}}{\text{average balance in inventory}}$$

For Contemporary Interiors, this ratio is computed as follows:

$$\text{Inventory turnover} = \frac{\$60,930,000}{\$18,500,000^*} = 3.3$$

$$^*\ \text{Average balance in inventory} = \frac{\$17,000,000 + \$20,000,00}{2} = \$18,500,000$$

Contemporary Interiors sold its average inventory 3.3 times during 19x6.

Average Number of Days per Inventory Turnover To determine how many days, on average, are required to sell a piece of furniture, the analyst computes the following measure.

$$\frac{\text{Average number of days}}{\text{per inventory turnover}} = \frac{365 \text{ days}}{\text{inventory turnover}}$$

For Contemporary Interiors, we have the following computation.

$$\frac{\text{Average number of days}}{\text{per inventory turnover}} = \frac{365 \text{ days}}{3.3} = 111 \text{ days}$$

It takes 111 days, on average, for Contemporary Interiors to sell a piece of furniture. This is fairly typical for the quality furniture retail business. What would you expect this ratio to be in a grocery store? How about an art gallery?[1]

The sum of the average collection period and the average number of days per inventory turnover measures how long it takes a dollar invested in inventory to come back into the cash account. This cash cycle provides management with a gauge of the company's effectiveness in carrying its operations through from inventory purchase to collection of cash. Contemporary Interiors' cycle is 159 days (48 + 111).

Book Value of Securities

Contemporary Interiors has three types of securities outstanding: bonds, preferred stock, and common stock. The number of shares outstanding is calculated as follows for each type of security.

(a) Type of Security	(b) Value on Balance Sheet		(c) Face Value per Bond or Par Value per Share of Stock		(d) = (b) ÷ (c) Number of Shares Outstanding
Bonds......	$37,300,000	....	$1,000	....	37,300
Preferred stock......	6,000,000	....	100	....	60,000
Common stock......	25,000,000	....	10	....	2,500,000

[1] Grocery stores have short periods for the average number of days per inventory turnover. None of us would want a loaf of bread that had been in the store for 111 days. An art gallery, on the other hand, would require a rather long period to sell a typical piece of fine art.

Some analysts compute the book value of each of a company's securities, as a measure of the assets available to back up the firm's debt and ownership obligations. In the event that a company is liquidated, the short-term creditors and bondholders typically have legal precedence over the stockholders in the settlement of claims. The preferred stockholders are next, and the common stockholders come last. Thus, calculation of the book value of securities must be done in steps, as shown in Exhibit 18-7. First, assume that the short-term debt of $12,700,000 would be paid off. This leaves $107,300,000 in assets to meet the bondholders' claims, or $2,877 per $1,000 bond. Second, after the short-term and long-term debt is repaid, there are $70,000,000 in assets available to back each share of $100 par value preferred stock. Finally, Contemporary Interiors would have $25.60 remaining to back each share of $10 par value common stock.

Contemporary Interiors has more than sufficient assets to back its securities.

Exhibit 18-7. Book Value of Securities: Contemporary Interiors, Inc.

Total assets	$120,000,000
Less: Current liabilities	12,700,000
Net assets backing the claims of bondholders	$107,300,000

$$\frac{\text{Book value}}{\text{per bond}} = \frac{\text{net assets available}}{\text{number of bonds outstanding}}$$

$$= \frac{\$107,300,000}{37,300} = \$2,877 \text{ per } \$1,000 \text{ bond}$$

Net assets backing bonds	$107,300,000
Less: Bonds payable	37,300,000
Net assets backing preferred stock	$ 70,000,000

$$\frac{\text{Book value per share}}{\text{of preferred stock}} = \frac{\text{net assets available}}{\begin{array}{c}\text{number of shares of}\\ \text{preferred stock outstanding}\end{array}}$$

$$= \frac{\$70,000,000}{60,000} = \frac{\$1,167 \text{ per share of } \$100 \text{ par}}{\text{value preferred stock}}$$

Net assets backing preferred stock	$ 70,000,000
Less: Preferred stock	6,000,000
Net assets backing common stock	$ 64,000,000

$$\frac{\text{Book value per share}}{\text{of common stock}} = \frac{\text{net assets available}}{\begin{array}{c}\text{number of shares of}\\ \text{common stock outstanding}\end{array}}$$

$$= \frac{\$64,000,000}{2,500,000} = \frac{\$25.60 \text{ per share of } \$10 \text{ par}}{\text{value common stock}}$$

CONTEMPORARY
interiors

Capitalization Ratios

A *capitalization ratio* is the proportion of the face value of a particular type of security to the company's total equity. Contemporary Interiors' capitalization ratios are computed as follows:

Bonds..................................		$ 37,300,000	35%*
Preferred stock...........................		6,000,000	5%
Common stock	$25,000,000 ⎤		
Additional paid-in capital................	4,000,000 ⎬	64,000,000	60%
Retained earnings	35,000,000 ⎦		
Total capitalization		$107,300,000	100%

*35% = $37,300,000/$107,300,000
  5% = $ 6,000,000/$107,300,000
 60% = $35,000,000/$107,300,000

Contemporary Interiors' capitalization consists of 35 percent debt, 5 percent preferred stock, and 60 percent common stock. Notice that the additional paid-in capital and retained earnings are combined with the common stock in a single category. In the event of liquidation, these amounts would be available to back the common stock, after the claims of bondholders and preferred stockholders were met.

Debt-Equity Ratio This is another measure of a firm's capitalization.

$$\text{Debt-equity ratio} = \frac{\textbf{total liabilities}}{\textbf{total stockholders' equity}}$$

Contemporary Interiors' debt-equity ratio for 19x6 is computed below.

$$\text{Debt-equity ratio} = \frac{\$50,000,000}{\$70,000,000} = .71 \text{ to } 1$$

The debt-equity ratio measures the relationship between the firm's resources provided through debt and those provided through ownership. In general, the greater the debt-equity ratio is, the riskier the company is as an investment. Greater debt means larger obligations to be satisfied before the claims of the company's owners can be met.

RATIO ANALYSIS: THE INCOME STATEMENT

The income statement also provides valuable information that can provide insight into the financial condition and performance of an enterprise. Some key income-statement relationships are discussed next.

Operating Income

Operating income is a key number in the income statement, because it represents the net result of the company's operations for the period. Financing decisions, which result in interest expense and income-tax issues, are largely separate from operating decisions. Thus, operating income focuses on the operations of the business, exclusive of financing and tax considerations. Contemporary Interiors' operating income for 19x6 was $19,070,000.

Coverage of Interest and Preferred Stock Dividends

Before investing in a company's bonds, a long-term creditor will want to be assured that the firm can pay the interest on the debt. *Interest coverage* provides a measure of the company's ability to meet its contractual obligation to pay bond interest.

$$\text{Interest coverage} = \frac{\text{operating income}}{\text{interest expense}}$$

Contemporary Interiors' 19x6 interest coverage is computed as follows:

$$\text{Interest coverage} = \frac{\$19,070,000}{\$4,030,000} = 4.7 \text{ times}$$

Contemporary Interiors' interest coverage is healthy, and long-term creditors should be reassured as to the firm's ability to pay bond interest.

Coverage of Dividends on Preferred Stock Preferred stock dividends must be paid before any dividends can be paid on common stock. Thus, potential investors are interested in whether a company's net income is sufficient to pay the stated dividend rate on its preferred stock. The following ratio provides a pertinent measure.

$$\frac{\text{Coverage of dividends}}{\text{on preferred stock}} = \frac{\text{net income}}{\text{stated dividends on preferred stock}}$$

Notice that *net income* is used in this measure, because interest on bonds and income taxes must be paid before any dividends can be declared. Contemporary Interiors' coverage of preferred stock dividends is computed as follows:

$$\frac{\text{Coverage of dividends}}{\text{on preferred stock}} = \frac{\$11,280,000}{\$480,000} = 23.5 \text{ times}$$

Earnings per Share

Investors in common stock hope to earn a return on their investment through dividends or increases in the stock price. Both payment of dividends and stock price appreciation are related to a firm's ability to earn income. A key measure that relates a company's earnings to its common stock is the firm's *earnings per share.*

$$\text{Earnings per share} = \frac{\text{net income available to common stockholders}}{\text{weighted-average number of shares of common stock outstanding}}$$

Contemporary Interiors' earnings per share for 19x6 is computed as follows:

$$\text{Earnings per share} = \frac{\$11,280,000 - \$480,000}{2,500,000} = \frac{\$10,800,000}{2,500,000} = \$4.32 \text{ per share}$$

Notice that the dividends on the preferred stock ($480,000) were subtracted from net income to compute net income available to common stockholders.

Extraordinary Items Suppose a company had an extraordinary gain or loss on its income statement. These gains or losses result from events outside the normal realm of the firm's business operations. Examples would include losses due to natural disasters, fires, or the expropriation of assets by a foreign government. Accepted practice requires that earnings per share be computed exclusive of the effect of any extraordinary gains or losses *and* their related tax effect. To illustrate, assume the following set of facts for Trends in Teak, Inc.

Sales	$70,000,000
Cost of goods sold	49,000,000
Gross margin.	21,000,000
Operating expenses.	5,000,000
Operating income	16,000,000
Interest expense	3,000,000
Income before extraordinary items	13,000,000
Loss due to flood.	1,000,000
Income before taxes	12,000,000
Income-tax expense (30%)	3,600,000
Net income.	8,400,000
Dividends on preferred stock	400,000
Net income available to common stockholders.	$ 8,000,000
Common stock outstanding	2,900,000 shares

Extraordinary item → Loss due to flood.

It would *not* be correct to compute the earnings per share for Trends in Teak as $2.76 ($8,000,000 ÷ 2,900,000). The $8,000,000 of available income used in this erroneous calculation includes the extraordinary loss due to the flood. This would be misleading to investors, because the flood loss is a rare event that will not likely be repeated. The correct approach to computing the company's earnings per share is shown below.

Net income.		$8,400,000
Add: Extraordinary loss, net of its tax effect:		
Extraordinary loss	$1,000,000	
Tax effect (30%)	300,000	
Net impact on income from extraordinary loss	700,000	700,000
Net income, excluding extraordinary loss and related tax effect		9,100,000
Dividends on preferred stock		400,000
Net income available to common stockholders, excluding extraordinary loss and related tax effect.		$8,700,000

$$\text{Earnings per share} = \frac{\$8,700,000}{2,900,000} = \$3.00 \text{ per share}$$

The correct statement of earnings per share for Trends in Teak is $3.00 per share.

Fully Diluted Earnings per Share One other complication often arises in computing earnings per share. Some securities are *convertible,* which means that they can be converted into a specified number of shares of common stock. Suppose, for example, that each share of Contemporary Interiors' preferred stock can be converted into 10 shares of common stock. If all 60,000 of the preferred shares were converted, there would be an additional 600,000 shares of common stock outstanding. To reflect this possibility, *fully diluted earnings per share* is computed under the assumption that all convertible securities are fully converted into common shares. This measure is defined below.

$$\text{Fully diluted earnings per share} = \frac{\text{net income}}{\substack{\text{weighted-average number of shares of common stock} \\ \text{outstanding, assuming full conversion} \\ \text{of all convertible securities}}}$$

For Contemporary Interiors we have the following calculation.

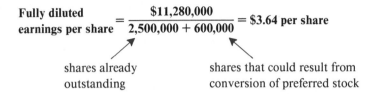

$$\text{Fully diluted earnings per share} = \frac{\$11,280,000}{2,500,000 + 600,000} = \$3.64 \text{ per share}$$

shares already
outstanding

shares that could result from
conversion of preferred stock

Notice that the dividends on the preferred stock were not subtracted from net income in the numerator. This reflects the assumption that the preferred stock has been converted to common stock. Contemporary Interiors' fully diluted earnings per share, $3.64, is lower than its $4.32 earnings per share computed earlier. The $4.32 amount does not reflect the potential conversion of preferred stock.

Price-Earnings Ratio   Of particular interest to investors is the relationship between a company's stock price and its income. Income, after all, is the key to both dividends and stock price appreciation. A common measure of the relationship between stock price and income is the price-earnings ratio, defined as follows:

$$\text{Price-earnings ratio} = \frac{\text{market price per share}}{\text{earnings per share}}$$

To illustrate, suppose Contemporary Interiors' common stock price is $65 per share:

$$\text{Price-earnings ratio} = \frac{\$65.00 \text{ per share}}{\$4.32 \text{ per share*}} = 15$$

* Notice that the regular earnings per share is used rather than the fully diluted earnings per share.

Thus, Contemporary Interiors' common stock is currently selling for 15 times the firm's earnings per share. Some investors use the price-earnings ratio to help determine the appropriate price for a company's stock. Of course, the most critical issues in determining a fair stock price are the investor's estimates of the company's future earnings potential and the riskiness of the stock.

Return on Assets

The management of a company has a responsibility to use the firm's assets as effectively as possible in generating income for the owners. The rate of *return on assets* is a measure of how effectively management has fulfilled this responsibility.

$$\text{Return on assets} = \frac{\text{net income} + \text{interest expense, net of its tax impact}}{\text{average total assets}}$$

Notice that interest expense, net of its tax effect, has been added back to net income. The reason for this is to make a distinction between operating management and financial management. The operating managers of a business should use total assets, irrespective of how they have been financed, to generate income. Moreover, operating managers typically do not make financing decisions that would affect interest expense. Thus, interest expense is added back to net income to obtain a measure of the income resulting from the operating management of the business. The required calculations for Contemporary Interiors are as follows:

Interest expense	$4,030,000
Income-tax effect (30%)...................................	1,209,000
Interest expense, net of tax effect	$2,821,000

$$\text{Return on assets} = \frac{\$11,280,000 + \$2,821,000}{\$115,425,000^*} = 12.2\%$$

* 115,425,000 = ($120,000,000 + $110,850,000)/2

Focusing on only the operating part of the business, Contemporary Interiors' management generated a 12.2 percent return on assets in 19x6.

Return on Equity

A different rate-of-return measure which is commonly used by analysts is the *return on equity* (or *return on common stockholders' equity*). This measure is defined as follows:

$$\text{Return on equity} = \frac{\text{net income available to common stockholders}}{\text{average common stockholders' equity}}$$

Notice that the denominator is average *common* stockholders' equity, which is found by subtracting preferred stock from total stockholders' equity. Contemporary Interiors' return on equity for 19x6 is computed as follows:

	19x5	19x6
Total stockholders' equity...........................	$62,800,000	$70,000,000
Less: Preferred stock	6,000,000	6,000,000
Common stockholders' equity	$56,800,000	$64,000,000
Average common stockholders' equity		$60,400,000

$$\text{Return on equity} = \frac{\$10,800,000}{\$60,400,000} = 17.9\%$$

The income available to Contemporary Interiors' common stockholders provided a 17.9 percent return on their investment in 19x6.

Return on Sales

The proportion of each sales dollar that results in net income is one measure of the efficiency of a business. *Return on sales* provides such a measure.

$$\text{Return on sales} = \frac{\text{net income}}{\text{sales}}$$

Contemporary Interiors' return on sales is computed below for 19x6.

$$\text{Return on sales} = \frac{\$11,280,000}{\$87,000,000} = 13\%$$

Return on sales, along with all financial ratios, must be compared with the ratios for other companies in the industry to be meaningful.

Financial Leverage

In physics, *leverage* means the ability of a relatively small force to move a heavy object. Likewise, the concept of **financial leverage** refers to the situation where a relatively small increase in income can provide a proportionately much larger increase in return to the common stockholders. How is this financial magic worked? It hinges on having a relatively large proportion of financing through debt or preferred stock, which pay interest or dividends at a fixed rate. When income increases, the bond interest and preferred stock dividends remain constant, leaving most of the increase in income available to the common stockholders.

An illustration will help to clarify the concept of financial leverage. Suppose a company has $10,000,000 in outstanding bonds payable which bear interest at 5 percent. The company's operating income is $550,000, and its tax rate is 30 percent. The calculations for case A in Exhibit 18-8 show that there will be $35,000 of after-tax income available to the common stockholders.

Now consider what will happen if operating income increases by a modest 10 percent. As case B in Exhibit 18-8 shows, the income available to common stockholders increases to $73,500, a 110 percent increase. By financing a large portion of the

---

Exhibit 18-8. Financial Leverage

Bonds payable (5%) . . . . . $10,000,000 × 5% = $500,000 in interest expense

	Case A Status Quo	Case B 10% Increase	Case C 10% Decrease
Operating income	$550,000	$605,000	$495,000
Less: Bond interest	500,000	500,000	500,000
Income before taxes	50,000	105,000	$ (5,000)
Income-tax expense (30%)	15,000	31,500	
Income available to common stockholders	$ 35,000	$ 73,500	

110% increase

firm with bonds, the company is able to direct the increase in income to the common stockholders.

Now consider the risky side of financial leverage. What will happen if operating income declines by 10 percent? As case C demonstrates, the firm cannot even cover its bond interest, let alone direct any profit to the common stockholders.

In summary, high financial leverage carries with it the possibility of great return, but it also entails high risk. A glance at Contemporary Interiors' balance sheet reveals that the company is not highly leveraged. This fact also is indicated by the company's low debt-equity ratio, which was calculated to be .71 to 1.

RATIO ANALYSIS: THE STATEMENT OF RETAINED EARNINGS

The retained earnings statement reconciles the year's beginning and ending balances in retained earnings. Net income increases retained earnings, while dividends decrease retained earnings. Two ratios often are computed using data on this statement.

Dividend Payout Ratio

The *dividend payout ratio* shows the proportion of earnings per share that is paid to the common stockholders in the form of dividends.

$$\text{Dividend payout ratio} = \frac{\text{dividends per share of common stock}}{\text{earnings per share}}$$

Contemporary Interiors paid dividends of $1.92 per share of common stock in 19x6 ($4,800,000 ÷ 2,500,000). The company's dividend payout ratio is computed as follows:

$$\text{Dividend payout ratio} = \frac{\$1.92 \text{ per share}}{\$4.32 \text{ per share*}} = 44.4\%$$

* Notice that the regular earnings per share is used rather than the fully diluted earnings per share.

Contemporary Interiors paid out to its common stockholders almost half of the income available for that purpose. The remainder was reinvested in the business. The dividend payout ratio that is best for a company depends on its opportunities for growth, the needs of the company for reinvestment funds, and the ease with which the firm can attract capital.

Dividend Yield Ratio

One of the factors affecting a company's stock price is the amount of dividends paid on the stock. The *dividend yield ratio* focuses on the relationship between dividends and stock price:

$$\text{Dividend yield ratio} = \frac{\text{dividends per share of common stock}}{\text{market price per share}}$$

Contemporary Interiors' common stock sells for $65.00 per share, so the following calculation is made.

$$\text{Dividend yield ratio} = \frac{\$1.92 \text{ per share}}{\$65.00 \text{ per share}} = 3.0\%$$

By comparing dividend payout ratios and dividend yield ratios across companies, investors can judge whether a firm's stock is fairly priced, given the dividends paid.

NOTES TO FINANCIAL STATEMENTS

Published financial statements almost always are accompanied by notes. These narratives provide greater detail about much of the information that is included very concisely in the financial statements. Many people find the notes to be dull and complicated. Nevertheless, they can be extremely important, and should be viewed as an integral part of the financial statements. Information typically disclosed in the notes includes:

- Details of the inventory and depreciation methods used
- Contingent liabilities and pending lawsuits
- Long-term leases
- Terms of executive employment contracts, profit sharing programs, pension plans, and stock options granted to employees

Remember, if you want to analyze a set of financial statements thoroughly, don't pass over the notes.

SUMMARY OF FINANCIAL STATEMENT ANALYSIS

Exhibit 18-9 summarizes the key financial ratios discussed in the chapter.

ILLUSTRATION FROM MANAGEMENT-ACCOUNTING PRACTICE

Corning Glass Works

Concepts from financial statement analysis often are used by management in setting goals for an enterprise. The following example of financial goals comes from a recent Corning Glass Works annual report.

- **Performance: We will be consistently in the top 25 percent of the *Fortune 500* in financial performance as measured by return on equity.**
- **Growth: We will grow at an annual rate in excess of 5 percent in real terms.**

We will maintain a debt-to-capital ratio of approximately 25 percent and a long-term dividend payout of 33 percent.

We will issue new shares of stock on a limited basis in connection with employee ownership programs and acquisitions with a clear strategic fit.

LIMITATIONS OF FINANCIAL STATEMENT ANALYSIS

Financial statements and the financial ratios derived from them are but a single source of information about a company. As is true of any mangerial-accounting information, financial ratios serve only as an attention-directing device. The ratios raise questions more often than they answer them. An analyst must follow up the financial statement analysis with in-depth research on a company's management, its history and trends, the industry, and the national and international economies in which the firm operates.

Exhibit 18-9. Summary of Key Financial Ratios

Ratio	Definition

Analyzing the Balance Sheet

Ratio	Definition
Acid-test ratio (or quick ratio)	Quick assets ÷ current liabilities
Accounts receivable turnover	Sales on account ÷ average balance in accounts receivable
Average collection period	365 days ÷ accounts receivable turnover
Average number of days per inventory turnover	365 days ÷ inventory turnover
Capitalization ratio	Proportion of the face value of a particular type of security to the company's total equity (e.g., bonds payable ÷ total liabilities and stockholders' equity)
Current ratio	Current assets ÷ current liabilities
Debt-equity ratio	Total liabilities ÷ total stockholders' equity
Inventory turnover	Cost of goods sold ÷ average balance in inventory

Analyzing the Income Statement

Ratio	Definition
Coverage of dividends on preferred stock	Net income ÷ stated dividends on preferred stock
Earnings per share	Net income available to common stockholders ÷ weighted-average number of shares of common stock outstanding
Fully diluted earnings per share	Net income ÷ weighted-average number of shares of common stock outstanding, assuming full conversion of all convertible securities
Interest coverage	Operating income ÷ interest expense
Price-earnings ratio	Market price per share ÷ earnings per share
Return on assets	(Net income + interest expense net of income-tax effect) ÷ average total assets
Return on equity	Net income available to common stockholders ÷ average common stockholders' equity
Return on sales	Net income ÷ sales

Analyzing the Retained Earnings Statement

Ratio	Definition
Dividend payout ratio	Dividends per share of common stock ÷ earnings per share
Dividend yield ratio	Dividends per share of common stock ÷ market price per share

Financial statement analysis is subject to the limitations inherent in financial statements. First, financial statements are based on historical accounting data, which may not be indicative of the future. Second, historical cost values provide the basis for accounting valuation, even though price levels are constantly changing. Third, although comparisons across companies are critical to meaningful financial statement analysis, such comparisons are not always easy. Generally accepted accounting principles allow considerable flexibility in accounting for many financial events. When companies use different accounting methods, their accounting numbers may not be comparable.

CHAPTER SUMMARY

Financial statements provide the primary means for communicating financial information about a company to interested parties outside the organization. The purpose of financial statement analysis is to highlight key relationships between various accounting numbers in the financial statements to provide insight into the financial condition and performance of the firm. The objective is to assist analysts in predicting the future performance of the company. A company's managers also use tools from financial statement analysis to help them understand the implications of their decisions for the company's financial condition and performance.

Horizontal analysis and trend analysis are two of the analytical techniques used in financial statement analysis. Both of these tools involve comparisons of accounting data across time. Another widely used analytical tool is vertical analysis, in which component percentages are computed for the numbers on the balance sheet and income statement. Financial statements prepared in terms of these percentages are called common-size statements. Ratio analysis involves the calculation of numerous ratios between the numbers on the financial statements to indicate the relationships between those numbers. For ratio analysis to be meaningful, the analyst should draw comparisons across time and across other companies in the industry.

KEY TERMS   Note: The various ratios defined in the chapter are summarized in Exhibit 18-9.

Common size-financial statements, p. 767; Comparative financial statements, p. 765; Financial leverage, p. 779; Horizontal analysis, p. 765; Quick assets, p. 770; Trend analysis, p. 766; Vertical analysis, p. 767; Working capital, p. 769.

REVIEW QUESTIONS

18-1. Why would a company's management be interested in the information conveyed in the firm's financial statements published for outside parties? How could management use the tools of financial statement analysis?

18-2. List the four major financial statements, and briefly describe the relationships between them.

18-3. What is wrong with these statements? "The company's cash for 19x5 was $50,000. Its income on December 31, 19x5 was $150,000."

18-4. Explain why comparisons and trends are important in financial statement analysis.

18-5. What other sources of financial data are available in addition to published financial statements?

18-6. How are comparative financial statements used in financial statement analysis? What is meant by *horizontal analysis?*

18-7. What is meant by *vertical analysis?* How are common-size financial statements used by analysts?

18-8. What is the significance of a company's current ratio?

18-9. What is the main limitation of the current ratio?

18-10. What is the significance of the acid-test ratio?

18-11. Alpha Company has an accounts receivable turnover ratio of 5.1. Beta Company, in the same industry, has a ratio of 2.2. What can you conclude about these two firms?

18-12. What does it imply for a company to have a low inventory turnover? Would you expect this ratio to differ much across industries? Why?

18-13. What is the significance of a high-debt-equity ratio?

18-14. Jeffries Corporation covered its bond interest 1.2 times. What does this mean, and what conclusion can you draw?

18-15. Briefly explain the treatment of extraordinary items in the calculation of earnings per share. Do you agree with this treatment? Why?

18-16. What is meant by fully diluted earnings per share?

18-17. Contrast the following two ratios and their interpretations: return on assets versus return on equity.

18-18. What kinds of information are conveyed in the notes to financial statements?

18-19. Briefly describe three limitations of financial statements which are reflected in financial statement analysis.

18-20. Assume you are making a decision as to whether your bank should make a short-term loan to a company. List the financial ratios in which you would be most interested. Then assume instead that you are a potential investor in the company's stock.

EXERCISES *Exercise 18-21   Trend Analysis.* The following data are available for The Cookie Cart, Inc., a bakery located in a shopping mall.

	19x9	19x8	19x7	19x6	19x5
Sales..........................	$51,450	$47,640	$44,520	$42,000	$40,000
Net income	14,200	12,600	11,450	10,600	10,000

REQUIRED:

1. Restate the trend data in terms of percentages using 19x5 as the base year.
2. Comment on the trends in the company's sales and net income.

Exercise 18-22   Trend Analysis. The following data are available for Jolene Corporation, a manufacturer of greeting cards. The amounts refer to December 31 of each year.

	19x7	19x6	19x5	19x4	19x3
Current assets......	$2,800,000	$2,200,000	$1,900,000	$1,600,000	$1,400,000
Inventory	2,000,000	1,300,000	1,150,000	820,000	700,000
Current liabilities...	1,100,000	1,000,000	900,000	790,000	700,000

REQUIRED:

1. Restate the trend data in terms of percentages, using 19x3 as the base year.
2. Prepare a table showing the trend in the company's current ratio and acid-test ratio from 19x3 through 19x7. The firm has no prepaid expenses.
3. What conclusions can you draw from the trend data? Explain your answer.

Exercise 18-23   Ratio Analysis. The following selected financial data pertain to Boothroyd Corporation.

As of December 31, 19x5 and 19x4

	19x5	19x4
Cash	$ 10,000	$ 80,000
Accounts receivable (net)	50,000	150,000
Merchandise inventory	90,000	150,000
Marketable securities...............................	30,000	10,000
Land and buildings (net)............................	340,000	360,000
Mortgage payable (no current portion).................	270,000	280,000
Accounts payable...................................	70,000	110,000
Short-term notes payable............................	20,000	40,000

For the Year Ended December 31, 19x5 and 19x4

	19x5	19x4
Cash sales	$1,800,000	$1,600,000
Credit sales.......................................	500,000	800,000
Cost of goods sold	1,000,000	1,400,000

REQUIRED: Compute the following ratios.

1. Acid-test ratio as of December 31, 19x5.
2. Accounts receivable turnover for 19x5.
3. Inventory turnover for 19x5.
4. Current ratio as of December 31, 19x5.

(CPA, adapted)

Exercise 18-24   Current and Acid-Test Ratios; Comparing Firms. Selected data for two companies in the electronics industry are as follows (all data in thousands).

	Ace Electronics	King Enterprises
Cash.......................................	$ 400	$ 1,400
Marketable securities	200	1,200
Accounts receivable........................	4,500	8,000
Inventory..................................	9,000	3,700
Prepaid expenses...........................	1,000	800
Total current assets........................	$15,100	$15,100
Accounts payable	$ 2,000	$ 4,000
Accrued expenses payable...................	4,000	2,100
Note payable	1,000	900
Total current liabilities	$ 7,000	$ 7,000

REQUIRED:

1. Calculate each company's working capital amount, current ratio, and acid-test ratio.
2. Comment on each firm's ability to pay its short-term debts.

Exercise 18-25   Ratio Analysis. Long Corporation's condensed financial statements provide the following information.

Balance Sheet
December 31, 19x1 and 19x0

	19x1	19x0
Cash...	$ 60,000	$ 50,000
Accounts receivable (net)...........................	220,000	200,000
Inventories.....................................	260,000	230,000
Property, plant, and equipment......................	730,000	650,000
Accumulated depreciation...........................	(330,000)	(260,000)
Total assets..................................	$ 940,000	$ 870,000
Current liabilities...............................	$ 270,000	$ 330,000
Stockholders' equity.............................	670,000	540,000
Total liabilities and stockholders' equity...............	$ 940,000	$ 870,000

Income Statement
For the Year Ended December 31, 19x1

Net sales...	$1,200,000
Cost of goods sold...	780,000
Gross margin..	420,000
Operating expenses..	240,000
Net income..	$ 180,000

REQUIRED:

1. Assuming that all sales are on account, what is Long's accounts receivable turnover for 19x1?
2. What is Long's rate of return on assets for 19x1? The company had no interest expense in 19x1.

(CPA, adapted)

Exercise 18-26   Common-Size Financial Statements. Refer to the data given in the preceding exercise for Long Corporation.

REQUIRED:

1. Restate the comparative balance sheet and the income statement in common-size format.
2. For what purpose are common-size statements useful?

Exercise 18-27   Earnings per Share. The following facts relate to Eastern Ohio Steel Corporation.

Sales...	$60,000,000
Cost of goods sold..	40,000,000
Gross margin...	20,000,000
Operating expenses..	7,000,000
Operating income...	13,000,000
Interest expense..	1,000,000
Income before extraordinary items............................	12,000,000
Loss due to fire...	800,000
Income before taxes...	11,200,000
Income-tax expense (25%)....................................	2,800,000
Net income...	8,400,000
Dividends on preferred stock.................................	1,100,000
Net income available to common stockholders..................	$ 7,300,000

Common stock outstanding (weighted-average) . . . . 1,825,000 shares

Ira Ore, the company president, made a quick calculation of earnings per share, as follows:

$$\text{Earnings per share} = \frac{\$7,300,000}{1,825,000} = \$4 \text{ per share}$$

REQUIRED: Did Ore make the earnings per share calculation correctly? If not, prepare an analysis determining the correct earnings per share.

Exercise 18-28 **Financial Leverage.** The following data relate to Sky World, Inc., a theme park located near Kitty Hawk, North Carolina.

Operating income.	$ 680,000
Less: Bond interest.	600,000*
Income before taxes.	80,000
Income-tax expense (25%).	20,000
Income available to common stockholders	$ 60,000

* Bonds payable, $5,000,000; interest rate, 12%; bond interest, $600,000 = $5,000,000 × 12%.

REQUIRED:

1. Calculate the percentage change in income available to the common stockholders if operating income (a) increases by 10 percent or (b) decreases by 10 percent.
2. Is Sky World a heavily leveraged company? Explain.

PROBLEMS

Problem 18-29 **Ratio Analysis.** The balance sheet and income statement for Martin Corporation for 19x1 are as follows:

Martin Corporation
Balance Sheet
December 31, 19x1
(in thousands)

Assets

Cash.		$ 8,000
Accounts receivable.		12,000
Inventory.		9,000
Property, plant, and equipment	$48,400	
Less: Accumulated depreciation	11,900	36,500
Total assets.		$65,500

Liabilities and Stockholders' Equity

Accounts payable.	$10,700
Short-term notes payable.	5,300
Bonds payable (due in 19x4).	9,500
Common stock ($10 par value; 4,500,000 shares authorized; 2,500,000 shares issued and outstanding during the entire year).	25,000
Additional paid-in capital.	5,000
Retained earnings.	10,000
Total liabilities and stockholders' equity.	$65,500

Martin Corporation
Income Statement
For the Year Ended December 31, 19x1
(in thousands)

Sales in cash.		$10,000
Sales on account.		60,000
Total sales.		$70,000
Cost of goods sold:		
Inventory of finished goods 1/1/x1	$ 4,000	
Cost of goods manufactured	50,000	
Cost of goods available for sale	$54,000	
Inventory of finished goods 12/31/x1	5,000	49,000
Gross margin.		$21,000
Operating expenses:		
Selling	$ 3,000	
Administrative	10,800	13,800
Operating income.		$ 7,200
Interest expense.		1,200
Income before income taxes.		$ 6,000
Income-tax expense.		2,400
Net income.		$ 3,600

REQUIRED: Compute the following ratios for Martin Corporation.

1. Current ratio.
2. Average collection period. (Assume there was no change in the accounts receivable balance between January 1 and December 31, 19x1).
3. Inventory turnover.
4. Ratio of total debt to stockholders' equity.
5. Earnings per share.
6. Return on equity. (Assume there was no change in total stockholders' equity during 19x1.)
7. Interest coverage.

(CMA, adapted)

Problem 18-30   *Ratio Analysis.* Drivon Corporation's condensed financial statements for 19x6 are as follows:

Drivon Corporation
Income Statement
For the Year Ended December 31, 19x6
(in thousands)

Sales.	$1,200
Cost of goods sold.	700
Gross margin.	500
Operating expenses.	250
Operating income.	250
Interest expense.	50
Income before incomes taxes.	200
Income tax expense.	100
Net income	$ 100

Drivon Corporation
Balance Sheet
December 31, 19x6
(in thousands)

Assets		Liabilities and Owners' Equity	
Cash	$ 100	Accounts payable.	$ 120
Marketable securities	150	Short-term note payable	180
Accounts receivable (net of $15		Accrued liabilities.	100
allowance for uncollectible		Bonds payable	400
accounts).	200	Preferred stock	200
Inventories	400	Common stock.	200
Prepaid expenses	50	Additional paid-in capital	100
Property, plant, and equipment		Retained earnings	200
(net of $220 accumulated depre-		Total liabilities and owners'	
ciation)	530	equity	$1,500
Patents	70		
Total assets	$1,500		

Additional Information

- Gross accounts receivable amounted to $200,000 and the allowance for uncollectible accounts was $20,000 as of January 1, 19x6.
- Total assets amounted to $1,300,000 and stockholders' equity amounted to $500,000 on January 1, 19x6.
- The liquidation value of the preferred stock is equal to par value. Preferred dividends are paid at the rate of 8 percent.
- The company's income tax rate was 50%.

REQUIRED: Compute the following ratios for Drivon Corporation.

1. Current ratio on December 31, 19x6.
2. Debt-equity ratio on December 31, 19x6.
3. Return on assets for 19x6.
4. Return on equity for 19x6.
5. Interest coverage for 19x6.
6. Average collection period in 19x6. (Assume that all of Drivon Corporation's sales were on account.)

(CMA, adapted)

Problem 18-31 Financial Statement Analysis; Multiple Choice. Several of Depoole Company's transactions during 19x0 are described below. Assume that total quick assets exceeded total current liabilities both before and after each transaction described. Further, assume that Depoole has positive net income in 19x0 and a credit balance throughout 19x0 in its retained earnings account.

REQUIRED: Choose the best answer to complete each statement.

1. Payment of accounts payable of $64,500 would
   a. increase the current ratio, but the acid-test ratio would not be affected
   b. increase the acid test, but the current ratio would not be affected
   c. increase both the current and acid-test ratios
   d. decrease both the current and acid-test ratios
   e. have no effect on the current and acid-test ratios

2. The purchase of raw materials for $85,000 on account would
   a. increase the current ratio
   b. decrease the current ratio
   c. increase working capital
   d. decrease working capital
   e. increase both the current ratio and working capital
3. The collection of current accounts receivable of $29,000 would
   a. increase the current ratio
   b. decrease the current ratio
   c. increase the acid-test ratio
   d. decrease the acid-test ratio
   e. not affect the current and acid-test ratios
4. Obsolete inventory of $125,000 was written off. This would
   a. decrease the acid-test ratio
   b. increase the acid-test ratio
   c. increase working capital
   d. decrease the current ratio
   e. decrease both the current and acid-test ratios
5. The early liquidation of a long-term note with cash would
   a. affect the current ratio to a greater degree than the acid-test ratio
   b. affect the acid-test ratio to a greater degree than the current ratio
   c. affect the current and acid-test ratios to the same degree
   d. affect the current ratio but not the acid-test ratio
   e. affect the acid-test ratio but not the current ratio

(CMA, adapted)

Problem 18-32 *Ratio Analysis.* The 19x9 financial statements for Johansson Company are presented here.

Johansson Company
Balance Sheet
December 31, 19x9 and 19x8
(in thousands)

	19x9	19x8
Assets		
Current assets:		
Cash and marketable securities	$ 400	$ 380
Accounts receivable (net)	1,700	1,500
Inventories	2,200	2,120
Total current assets	$ 4,300	$ 4,000
Long-term assets:		
Land	$ 500	$ 500
Building and equipment (net)	4,700	4,000
Total long-lived assets	$ 5,200	$ 4,500
Total assets	$ 9,500	$ 8,500

	19x9	19x8

Liabilities and Stockholders' Equity

Current liabilities:
Accounts payable.	$ 1,400	$ 700
Current portion of long-term debt.	1,000	500
Total current liabilities.	$ 2,400	$ 1,200
Long-term debt	3,000	4,000
Total liabilities	$ 5,400	$ 5,200
Stockholders' equity:		
Common stock.	$ 3,000	$ 3,000
Retained earnings.	1,100	300
Total stockholders' equity	$ 4,100	$ 3,300
Total liabilities and stockholders' equity.	$ 9,500	$ 8,500

Johansson Company
Statement of Income and Retained Earnings
For the Year Ended December 31, 19x9
(in thousands)

Sales (all on account).		$28,800
Less: Cost of goods sold.	$15,120	
Selling expenses.	7,180	
Administrative expenses.	4,100	
Interest.	400	
Income taxes	800	27,600
Net income.		$ 1,200
Retained earnings January 1.		300
Subtotal.		$ 1,500
Cash dividends declared and paid.		400
Retained earnings December 31.		$ 1,100

REQUIRED: Compute the following ratios for 19x9.

1. Acid-test ratio on December 31, 19x9.
2. Average collection period.
3. Interest coverage.
4. Inventory turnover.
5. Operating income as a percentage of sales.
6. Dividend payout ratio.

(CMA, adapted)

Problem 18-33   Common-Size Financial Statements. Refer to the data given in the preceding problem for Johansson Company.

REQUIRED: Prepare a common-size balance sheet as of December 31, 19x9 and a common-size income statement for 19x9.

Problem 18-34   Ratio Analysis. Comparative balance sheets and income statements covering the last two years for Sawyer Corporation are shown here. The market price of Sawyer's common stock was $20 per share on December 31, 19x2.

Sawyer Corporation
Comparative Balance Sheets
December 31, 19x2 and 19x1
(in thousands)

	19x2	19x1
Assets		
Current assets:		
Cash	$ 3,000	$ 2,000
Marketable securities	1,000	1,000
Accounts receivable (net)	14,000	11,000
Merchandise inventory	24,000	16,000
Total current assets	$ 42,000	$ 30,000
Property, plant, and equipment (net)	68,000	60,000
Long-term investments	10,000	10,000
Total assets	$120,000	$100,000
Liabilities and Stockholders' Equity		
Current liabilities:		
Accounts payable	$ 5,000	$ 4,000
Wages payable	1,000	1,000
Total current liabilities	$ 6,000	$ 5,000
Bonds payable (10%, due 19x9)	20,000	20,000
Total liabilities	$ 26,000	$ 25,000
Stockholders' equity:		
Common stock (10,000,000 shares, no par value)	$ 25,000	$ 25,000
Retained earnings	69,000	50,000
Total stockholders' equity	$ 94,000	$ 75,000
Total liabilities and stockholders' equity	$120,000	$100,000

Sawyer Corporation
Comparative Income Statements
For the Years Ended December 31, 19x2 and 19x1
(in thousands)

	19x2	19x1
Sales (all made on account)	$200,000	$140,000
Cost of goods sold	120,000	80,000
Gross margin	$ 80,000	$ 60,000
Selling and administrative expenses	38,000	30,000
Operating income	$ 42,000	$ 30,000
Interest expense	2,000	2,000
Income before income taxes	$ 40,000	$ 28,000
Income-tax expense	15,000	11,000
Net income	$ 25,000	$ 17,000

REQUIRED: Compute the following ratios.

1. Current ratio as of December 31, 19x2.
2. Acid-test ratio as of December 31, 19x2.
3. Accounts receivable turnover for 19x2.
4. Inventory turnover for 19x2.

  5. Interest coverage for 19x2.
  6. Book value per share of common stock as of December 31, 19x2.
  7. Dividend yield ratio for 19x2.
  8. Return on equity for 19x2.
(CMA, adapted)

Problem 18-35   Ratio Analysis and Discussion. The accounting staff of CCB Enterprises has completed the preparation of financial statements for 19x3. The income statement for the current year and the comparative balance sheet for 19x3 and 19x2 are shown here. The company's income tax rate is 40 percent.

CCB Enterprises
Income Statement
For the Year Ended December 31, 19x3
(in thousands)

Revenue:

Net sales	$800,000
Other	60,000
Total revenue	$860,000

Expenses:

Cost of goods sold	$540,000
Research and development	25,000
Selling and administrative	155,000
Interest	20,000
Total expenses	$740,000
Income before income taxes	120,000
Income taxes	48,000
Net income	$ 72,000

CCB Enterprises
Comparative Balance Sheets
December 31, 19x3 and 19x2
(in thousands)

	19x3	19x2
Assets		
Current assets:		
Cash and marketable securities	$ 26,000	$ 21,000
Receivables, less allowance for doubtful accounts ($1,100 in 19x3 and $1,400 in 19x2)	48,000	50,000
Inventories	65,000	62,000
Prepaid expenses	5,000	3,000
Total current assets	$144,000	$136,000
Long-term investments	$116,000	$114,000
Property, plant, and equipment		
Land	$ 12,000	$ 12,000
Buildings and equipment, less accumulated depreciation ($126,000 in 19x3 and $122,000 in 19x2)	268,000	248,000
Total property, plant, and equipment	$280,000	$260,000
Total assets	$540,000	$510,000

Liabilities and Stockholders' Equity

Current liabilities:

Short-term loans. . . . . $ 22,000 $ 24,000

Accounts payable   72,000   71,000

Salaries, wages, and other   26,000   27,000

    Total current liabilities. $120,000 $122,000

Long-term debt   160,000   171,000

    Total liabilities $280,000 $293,000

Stockholders' equity:

Common stock, at par . . . . $ 44,000 $ 42,000

Additional paid-in capital   64,000   61,000

    Total paid-in capital. $108,000 $103,000

Retained earnings.   152,000   114,000

    Total stockholders' equity $260,000 $217,000

Total liabilities and stockholders' equity $540,000 $510,000

The accounting staff calculates selected financial ratios after the financial statements are prepared. Financial ratios that were calculated for 19x2 are as follows:

- Interest coverage, 5.16 times
- Return on assets, 12.5%
- Return on equity, 29.1%

REQUIRED:

1. Explain how the use of financial ratios can be advantageous to management.
2. Calculate the following financial ratios for 19x3 for CCB Enterprises.
   a. Interest coverage.
   b. Return on assets.
   c. Return on equity.
   d. Debt-equity ratio.
   e. Current ratio.
   f. Acid-test ratio.

(CMA, adapted)

Problem 18-36   Interpretation and Use of Financial Ratios. Avantronics is a manufacturer of electronic components and accessories with total assets of $20,000,000. Selected financial ratios for Avantronics and the industry averages for firms of similar size are as follows:

	Avantronics			19x5 Industry Average
	19x5	19x4	19x3	
Current ratio.	2.51	2.27	2.09	2.24
Acid-test ratio	1.19	1.12	1.15	1.22
Inventory turnover	2.02	2.18	2.40	3.50
Return on equity	0.17	0.15	0.14	0.11
Debt-equity ratio	1.44	1.37	1.41	0.95

Avantronics is under review by several entities whose interests vary, and the company's financial ratios are part of the data being considered. Each of the following parties must recommend an action based on its evaluation of Avantronics' financial position.

- *MidCoastal Bank.* The bank is processing Avantronics' application for a new five-year note. MidCoastal has been Avantronics' banker for several years, but must evaluate the company's financial position for each major transaction.
- *Ozawa Company.* Ozawa is a new supplier to Avantronics, and must decide on the appropriate credit terms to extend to the company.
- *Drucker & Denon.* A brokerage firm specializing in the stock of electronics firms, Drucker & Denon must decide if it will include Avantronics in a new mutual fund being established for sale to Drucker & Denon's clients.
- *Working Capital Management Committee.* This is a committee of Avantronics' management personnel chaired by the chief operating officer. The committee is charged with the responsibility of periodically reviewing the company's working capital position, comparing actual data against budgets, and recommending changes in strategy as needed.

REQUIRED:

1. Describe the analytical use of each of the given ratios.
2. For each of the four entities described above, identify two financial ratios, from those ratios presented, that would be most valuable as a basis for its decision regarding Avantronics.
3. Discuss what the financial ratios presented in the problem reveal about Avantronics. Support your answer by citing specific ratio levels and trends as well as the interrelationships among the ratios.

(CMA, adapted)

Problem 18-37   Comprehensive Problem on Ratio Analysis. Cycles, U.S.A. is a bicycle wholesaler with distribution throughout the country. Comparative balance sheets and income statements for 19x2 and 19x3 are presented here.

Cycles, U.S.A.
Comparative Balance Sheets
December 31, 19x3 and 19x2
(in thousands)

	Year	
	19x3	**19x2**
Assets		
Current assets:		
Cash	$ 200	$ 170
Marketable securities	120	90
Accounts receivable, net	3,000	2,500
Inventory	5,000	4,200
Prepaid expenses	75	60
Total current assets.....................	8,395	7,020
Long-term investments	450	500
Property, furnishings, and equipment:		
Land	2,000	2,000
Buildings, net	14,000	12,000
Equipment and furnishings, net	7,000	6,000
Total property, furnishings, and equipment	23,000	20,000
Total assets...	$31,845	$27,520

Liabilities and Stockholders' Equity

Current liabilities:		
Accounts payable	1,500	1,400
Accrued expenses	600	500
Notes payable	780	900
Total current liabilities	2,880	2,800
Long-term liabilities:		
Bonds payable ($1,000 face value; 10%)	9,000	8,500
Total liabilities	11,880	11,300
Stockholders' equity:		
Preferred stock ($100 par value; 8%)	1,500	1,500
Common stock ($10 par value)	6,000	5,500
Additional paid-in capital	1,000	900
Retained earnings	11,465	8,320
Total stockholders' equity	19,965	16,220
Total liabilities and stockholders' equity	$31,845	$27,520

Cycles, U.S.A.
Comparative Income and Retained Earnings Statements
For the Years Ended December 31, 19x3 and 19x2
(in thousands)

	Year	
	19x3	**19x2**
Sales	$26,700	$25,550
Cost of goods sold	18,000	17,500
Gross margin	8,700	8,050
Operating expenses:		
Selling expenses	1,400	1,350
Administrative expenses	400	350
Total operating expenses	1,800	1,700
Operating income	6,900	6,350
Interest expense	900	850
Income before taxes	6,000	5,500
Income-tax expense (30%)	1,800	1,650
Net income	4,200	3,850
Dividends on preferred stock	120	120
Net income available to common stockholders	4,080	3,730
Dividends on common stock	935	730
Net income added to retained earnings	3,145	3,000
Retained earnings, January 1	8,320	5,320
Retained earnings, December 31	$11,465	$ 8,320

Additional Information

- All sales were made on account.
- Each share of preferred stock is convertible into five shares of common stock.
- The market price per share of common stock is $50 per share.
- 50,000 shares of common stock were issued on January 1, 19x3. Therefore, the weighted-average number of shares during 19x3 was 600,000 shares.

REQUIRED: Compute each of the following amounts or ratios for 19x3.

1. Working capital, 12/31/x3.
2. Current ratio, 12/31/x3.
3. Quick assets, 12/31/x3.
4. Acid-test ratio, 12/31/x3.
5. Accounts receivable turnover.
6. Average collection period.
7. Inventory turnover.
8. Average number of days per inventory turnover.
9. Number of bonds and number of shares of stock outstanding, 12/31/x3.
10. Book value of securities: (a) per bond, (b) per share of preferred stock, and (c) per share of common stock, 12/31/x3.
11. Capitalization ratios, 12/31/x3.
12. Debt-equity ratio, 12/31/x3.
13. Interest coverage.
14. Coverage of dividends on preferred stock.
15. Earnings per share.
16. Fully diluted earnings per share.
17. Return on assets.
18. Return on equity.
19. Return on sales.
20. Dividend payout ratio.
21. Dividend yield ratio.

Problem 18-38   Common-Size Financial Statements. Refer to the data given in the preceding problem for Cycles, U.S.A.

REQUIRED: Prepare a common-size balance sheet as of December 31, 19x3 and a common-size income statement for 19x3.

Problem 18-39   Dollar and Percentage Changes. Refer to the data given in problem 18-37 for Cycles, U.S.A.

REQUIRED: Prepare two additional columns for each financial statement, which show the dollar change and percentage change from 19x2 to 19x3.

Problem 18-40   Using Ratio Analysis for Management Purposes. Calcor Company is a wholesale distributor of automobile parts for domestic automakers. Calcor has suffered through a slump in the domestic auto industry, and its performance has not rebounded to the level of the industry as a whole. Calcor's income statement for the year ended December 31, 19x4 is shown on the next page.

Calcor's return on sales before interest and taxes was 5 percent in 19x4 compared to the industry average of 9 percent. Calcor's return on assets before interest and taxes of 20 percent is also below the industry average. Joe Kuhn, president of Calcor, wishes to improve these ratios and raise them nearer to the industry averages. He has established the following goals for Calcor Company for 19x5.

Return on sales before interest and taxes .... 8 percent
Return on assets before interest and taxes........................... 30 percent

Kuhn and the rest of Calcor's management team are considering the following actions for 19x5, which they expect will improve profitability and result in a 5 percent increase in unit sales.

Calcor Company
Income Statement
For the Year Ended December 31, 19x4
(in thousands)

Net sales		$8,400
Expenses:		
Cost of goods sold	$6,300	
Selling expense	780	
Administrative expense	900	
Interest expense	140	
Total expenses		$8,120
Income before income taxes		$ 280
Income taxes		112
Net income		$ 168

- Increase selling prices 10 percent.
- Increase advertising by $420,000 and hold all other selling and administrative expenses at 19x4 levels.
- Improve customer service by increasing average current assets (inventory and accounts receivable) by a total of $300,000, and hold all other assets at 19x4 levels.
- Finance the additional assets at an annual interest rate of 10 percent and hold all other interest expense at 19x4 levels.
- Improve the quality of products carried. This will increase the unit cost of goods sold by 4 percent.

Calcor's 19x5 income-tax rate is expected to be 40 percent, the same as in 19x4.

REQUIRED:

1. Prepare a budgeted income statement for Calcor Company for 19x5, assuming that Calcor's planned actions would be carried out and that the 5 percent increase in unit sales would be realized.
2. Calculate the following ratios for Calcor Company for 19x5, and state whether the president's goals would be achieved.
   a. Return on sales before interest and taxes. (This measure is defined as income before interest and taxes, divided by net sales.)
   b. Return on assets before interest and taxes.

(CMA, adapted)

Problem 18-41   Fully Diluted Earnings per Share. Mason Corporation's capital structure is as follows:

	December 31	
	19x6	**19x5**
Outstanding shares of:		
Common stock	300,000 shares	300,000 shares
Convertible preferred stock	10,000 shares	10,000 shares
8% Nonconvertible bonds	$1,000,000	$1,000,000

The following additional information is available:

- Net income for the year ended December 31, 19x6, was $750,000.
- During 19x6 Mason paid dividends of $3.00 per share on its convertible preferred stock.
- Each share of preferred stock is convertible into 4 shares of common stock.

REQUIRED:

1. Compute the number of shares that should be used for the computation of fully
   diluted earnings per share for the year ended December 31, 19x6.
2. Compute the fully diluted earnings per share for the year ended December 31, 19x6.
(CPA, adapted)

Problem 18-42   Interpretation and Ratio Analysis of Balance Sheet. Paragon Corporation's
December 31, 19x4 balance sheet is shown below. The market price of the company's common stock was $4 per share on December 31, 19x4.

Paragon Corporation
Balance Sheet
December 31, 19x4
(in thousands)

Assets			Liabilities and Stockholders' Equity		
Current assets:			Current liabilities:		
Cash		$ 6,000	Accounts payable	$ 6,400	
Accounts receivable	$ 7,000		Accrued interest payable	800	
Less: Allowance for			Accrued income taxes		
doubtful accounts	400	6,600	payable	2,200	
Merchandise inventory		16,000	Accrued wages payable	600	
Supplies on hand		400	Deposits received from		
Prepaid expenses		1,000	customers	2,000	
Total current assets		$30,000	Total current liabilities		$12,000
Property, plant, and equipment:			Long-term debt:		
Land		$27,500	Bonds payable (20-year, 8%		
Building	$36,000		convertible bonds due		
Less: Accumulated			December 1, 19x9)*	$20,000	
depreciation	$13,500	22,500	Less: Unamortized		
Total property, plant,			discount	200	19,800
and equipment		$50,000	Total liabilities		$31,800
Total assets		$80,000	Stockholders' equity:		
			Common stock (authorized		
			40,000,000 shares of $1 par		
			value; 20,000,000 shares		
			issued and outstanding)	$20,000	
			Additional paid-in capital	12,200	
			Total paid-in capital	$32,200	
			Retained earnings	16,000	
			Total stockholders' equity		48,200
			Total liabilities and		
			stockholders' equity		$80,000

* Each $1,000 bond is convertible into 300 shares of Paragon Corporation common stock.

REQUIRED: The following questions should be considered independent of one another. Any
transactions given in each question are to be considered the only transactions to affect Paragon
Corporation during the year.

1. If Paragon paid back all of the deposits received from customers, what would its
   current ratio be?

2. If Paragon paid back all of the deposits received from customers, what would its acid-test ratio be?
3. What was Paragon's book value per share of common stock as of December 31, 19x4?
4. During the year ending December 31, 19x4, Paragon had sales of $90,000,000 with a gross margin of 20 percent and an inventory turnover of five times per year. Calculate the merchandise inventory balance on January 1, 19x4.
5. If Paragon had a dividend payout ratio of 80 percent and declared and paid $4,000,000 of cash dividends during the year ended December 31, 19x4, calculate the retained earnings balance on January 1, 19x4.

(CMA, adapted)

CASE   *Case 18-43   Using Financial Statement Analysis in a Credit Decision.* Warford Corporation was formed five years ago through the sale of common stock. Lucinda Street, who owns 15 percent of the common stock, was one of the organizers of Warford and is its current president. The company has been successful, but currently is experiencing a shortage of cash. On June 10, 19x8, Street approached the Bell National Bank, asking for a 12-month extension on two $30,000 notes, which are due on June 30, 19x8 and September 30, 19x8. Another note of $7,000 is due on December 31, 19x8, but she expects no difficulty in paying this note on its due date. Street explained that Warford's cash flow problems are due primarily to the company's desire to finance a $300,000 plant expansion over the next two years through internally generated funds.

The commercial loan officer of Bell National Bank requested financial reports for the last two years. These reports are below and on the next page.

Warford Corporation
Income Statement
For the Years Ended December 31, 19x7 and 19x6

	19x7	19x6
Sales	$3,000,000	$2,700,000
Cost of goods sold*	1,902,500	1,720,000
Gross margin	1,097,500	$ 980,000
Operating expenses	845,000	780,000
Net income before taxes	$ 252,500	$ 200,000
Income taxes (40%)	101,000	80,000
Income after taxes	$ 151,500	$ 120,000

* Depreciation charges on the plant and equipment of $100,000 and $102,500 for the years ended December 31, 19x6 and 19x7, respectively, are included in cost of goods sold.

REQUIRED:

1. Calculate the following items for Warford Corporation:
   a. Current ratio for 19x6 and 19x7.
   b. Acid-test ratio for 19x6 and 19x7.
   c. Inventory turnover for 19x7.
   d. Percentage change in sales, cost of goods sold, gross margin, and net income after taxes from 19x6 to 19x7.
2. Identify and explain what other financial reports or financial analyses might be

Warford Corporation
Balance Sheet
December 31, 19x7 and 19x6

	19x7	19x6
Assets:		
Cash	$ 16,400	$ 12,500
Notes receivable	112,000	104,000
Accounts receivable (net)	81,600	68,500
Inventories	80,000	50,000
Plant and equipment (net of depreciation)	680,000	646,000
Total assets	$970,000	$881,000
Liabilities and owners' equity:		
Accounts payable	$ 69,000	$ 72,000
Notes payable	67,000	54,500
Accrued liabilities	9,000	6,000
Common stock (60,000 shares, $10 par)	600,000	600,000
Retained earnings*	225,000	148,500
Total liabilities and owners' equity	$970,000	$881,000

* Cash dividends were paid at the rate of $1.00 per share in 19x6 and $1.25 per share in 19x7.

helpful to the commercial loan officer of Bell National Bank in evaluating Street's
request for a time extension on Warford's notes.

3. Assume that the percentage change experienced in 19x7 as compared with 19x6 for
net income after taxes will be repeated in each of the next two years. Is Warford's
desire to finance the plant expansion from internally generated funds realistic?
Explain your answer. (Hint: Remember that depreciation, which is an expense on
the income statement, is not a cash flow.)

4. Should Bell National Bank grant the extension on Warford's notes, considering
Street's statement about financing the plant expansion through internally
generated funds? Explain your answer.

(CMA, adapted)

Chapter 19

Preparing the Statement of Cash Flows

After completing this chapter, you should be able to:

- Briefly describe the evolution of the statement of cash flows.
- State the purposes of the statement of cash flows.
- Describe the types of cash flows shown in each of the statement's three sections.
- Prepare a statement of cash flows using the indirect method, the direct method, and the T-account approach.
- Prepare a schedule disclosing direct exchange transactions.
- Describe how the statement of cash flows is used by an enterprise's managers and by interested parties outside the organization.

How was USAir Group able to purchase Piedmont Airlines for $1.28 billion? How was Chrysler Corporation able to acquire American Motors Corporation for $1.646 billion? What type of financing did Marriott use when it introduced its new Courtyard Hotels? How did the top managers in each of these companies make the decision to go forward with such huge investments? The essential question in each example is, How did a company generate cash, and how was the cash used? How much cash did McDonald's Corporation generate last year through its operations, which involve the provision of food service to millions of people worldwide? How much cash did the company obtain through the issuance of debt or capital stock? How did McDonald's use the cash it generated?

These are the kinds of questions addressed by the statement of cash flows. In this chapter, we will discuss how this important financial statement is prepared and used.

EVOLUTION OF THE STATEMENT OF CASH FLOWS

Nowadays most managers, investors, and financial analysts consider the statement of cash flows to be as important as an organization's balance sheet or income statement.

However, the statement of cash flows is a newcomer compared to the other major financial statements. Prior to 1961, accountants sometimes prepared a simple analysis of the changes in the firm's balance sheet accounts, which often was referred to as a "Where Got and Where Gone Statement." However, no formal statement of cash flows was required for external reporting purposes. In 1961, the American Institute of Certified Public Accountants (AICPA) sponsored research in the area of cash flow analysis. The resulting report recommended that some type of cash flow analysis be provided as part of a company's annual report. In 1971 the AICPA's Accounting Principles Board began requiring a statement of changes of financial position as part of a company's financial statements. Throughout the next two decades, this statement evolved in its form, content, and importance to financial statement users. In 1987, the Financial Accounting Standards Board (FASB) issued its Standard No. 95, which requires that the statement of cash flows be prepared in the manner described in this chapter.

Purpose of the Statement of Cash Flows

The primary purpose of the statement of cash flows is to provide information about the sources and uses of an enterprise's cash during a particular time period. This information provides financial statement users with insight about the enterprise's operating, investing, and financing activities as they relate to the provision and use of cash. According to the FASB's *Statement of Financial Accounting Standards No. 95*,[1] the statement of cash flows should provide financial statement users with insight about:

1. The organization's ability to generate positive future net cash flows
2. The organization's ability to meet its financial obligations and pay dividends
3. The future needs of the organization for external financing
4. The reasons for the difference between net income and the net cash flows related to operating activities
5. The effects of the organization's cash and noncash investing and financing activities

CASH AND CASH EQUIVALENTS

Any enterprise needs to have cash available to pay its bills, compensate employees, purchase equipment, and so forth. At the same time, organizations try to manage their cash so as to avoid having more cash on hand than is necessary. As part of a cash-management program, most organizations invest some of their cash in short-term, highly liquid investments. Examples of such investments include money market accounts and U.S. Treasury bills. Such investments enable the organization to earn a return on the invested funds, yet at the same time keep the money readily available if it is needed. Since these highly liquid investments are turned into cash easily, they are, in a sense, *cash equivalents*. **Cash equivalents** are defined as highly liquid investments that may be converted easily into a known amount of cash and are near to their maturity dates.

Since cash equivalents are readily available when needed, the statement of cash flows focuses not only on cash, but on the total of an enterprise's *cash and cash equivalents.* The statement of cash flows is designed to show financial statement users

---

[1] "Statement of Cash Flows," *Statement of Financial Accounting Standards No. 95* (Stamford, CT: FASB, 1987).

the reasons behind the change during a particular period of time in an enterprise's total cash and cash equivalents.

CONTENT AND ORGANIZATION OF THE STATEMENT

The FASB has specified that the cash flow statement be organized into three sections. Each section details the cash flows that have arisen during the accounting period from a particular type of activity. The statement's three sections disclose the cash flows arising from *operating activities, investing activities, and financing activities.* Descriptions of each of these types of activities follow.

Operating Activities

Operating activities are defined as all events and transactions that are not investing or financing activities. The operations of an enterprise include all activities related to the provision of goods or services. Thus, cash receipts from the sale of goods or services are included in the operating activities portion of the cash flow statement. The cash disbursements included in this section of the statement include all disbursements for the purpose of producing goods or services.

Also included in the operating portion of the cash flow statement are cash receipts from any interest-bearing securities or stock the company owns. In addition, cash disbursements to pay taxes or to pay interest on the company's debt are included in the operating portion of the statement. Exhibit 9-1 summarizes the types of cash flows included in the operating activities portion of the cash flow statement.

Investing Activities

Investing activities are defined as extending or collecting loans, acquiring or disposing of investments (such as other companies' bonds or stock), and buying or selling productive, long-lived assets. Notice that investment activity is defined to include changes in the principal amount of loans, but does not include the interest earned on such loans. As explained previously, cash receipts for interest are included in the operating portion of the cash flow statement. Exhibit 19-1 summarizes the cash flows included in the statement's investing activities section.

Financing Activities

Financing activities are defined as transactions involving the company's debt or equity capital. Included in this section of the cash flow statement are cash receipts from the issuance of debt or the sale of the firm's own capital stock. Cash disbursements included in this section of the statement include repurchase of the company's own stock, payment of dividends to stockholders, and issuance of debt. Exhibit 19-1 summarizes the cash flows included in the financing section of the cash flow statement.

Notice that the financing section of the cash flow statement does not include cash disbursements to pay interest on the firm's debt. As previously noted, cash outflows for interest payments are included in the operating portion of the statement.

PREPARATION OF THE STATEMENT

The process of preparing the statement of cash flows draws upon data from the following three sources:

Exhibit 19-1. Operating, Investing, and Financing Activities

Operating activities:

Cash inflows from:

- Sale of goods or services
- Returns on interest-bearing securities or stock

Cash outflows for:

- Production of goods or services (includes disbursements such as employee compensation, payments to suppliers of materials or services, and payments for utilities)
- Payment of taxes to the government
- Payment of interest on debt

Investing activities:

Cash inflows from:

- Sale of productive, long-lived assets
- Collection of loans
- Sale of other companies' interest-bearing securities or stock owned as an investment

Cash outflows for:

- Purchase of productive, long-lived assets
- Issuance of loans
- Purchase of other companies' interest-bearing securities or stock as an investment

Financing activities:

Cash inflows from:

- Issuing debt such as bonds, notes, or mortgages
- Sale of the company's own capital stock

Cash outflows for:

- Payment of dividends to stockholders
- Reacquisition of the company's own stock
- Retirement of debt principal such as by paying off a loan

1. *Income statement* Determination of the cash provided by operations involves many of the accounts involved in the calculation of income.
2. *Comparative balance sheets* This information shows the changes in the company's asset, liability, and owners' equity accounts during the year.
3. *Selected transactions* In most cases other transaction data are needed to determine the sources and uses of cash during the accounting period.

Direct and Indirect Methods

Two alternative methods may be used to determine the cash flow from operating activities. Under the **direct method,** the statement preparer focuses on the firm's cash receipts and disbursements to determine which cash flows were related to operating activities. Then a cash-basis income statement is constructed, in which operating cash disbursements are subtracted from operating cash receipts. The net result is the cash provided by (or consumed by) operating activities. For example, instead of the sales revenue amount, which appears at the top of an income statement, the cash flow statement would start with cash receipts from customers.

The **indirect method** of preparing the operating activities section of the cash flow statement begins with the income statement, which already has been prepared on an accrual-accounting basis. The net income figure then is adjusted from an accrual basis to a cash basis. The resulting amount is the cash provided by (or consumed by) operations. The indirect method also is called the **reconciliation method.**

Both the direct method and the indirect method are illustrated in the remaining sections of this chapter. We will begin with the indirect method.

USING THE INDIRECT METHOD OF STATEMENT PREPARATION

To illustrate the statement of cash flows, we will focus on a service industry firm. Alpine Trails Ski Resort operates a small winter resort on the western slopes of the Rocky Mountains. The firm owns a ski complex and several condominiums. The resort's primary sources of revenue are fees to use the ski facilities and weekly rental of the condos. In addition, Alpine Trails receives rental revenue from an independent restaurant firm that operates a food concession in the ski lodge. Alpine Trails also operates a small ski shop, in which it sells ski equipment, sports clothing, and souvenirs. The company's most recent comparative balance sheet, income statement, and statement of retained earnings are displayed in Exhibits 19-2 and 19-3.

The format for the statement of cash flows, under the indirect method of preparation, is shown in Exhibit 19-4. Notice that the operating activities section of the statement begins with net income, and then adjustments are made to determine the net cash flow from operating activities. Beginning with the net income figure is the primary feature of the indirect method.

Operating Activities

Now let's begin preparing Alpine Trails' statement of cash flows. We start with net income from the firm's 19x1 income statement (Exhibit 19-3).

Starting point	Net income $110,000

Exhibit 19-2. Comparative Balance Sheets

Alpine Trails Ski Resort
Comparative Balance Sheets
December 31, 19x1 and 19x0
(in thousands)

Assets	19x1	19x0	Change	
Current assets:				
Cash	$ 17	$ 20	$ 3	Decrease
Marketable securities	10	10	–0–	
Accounts receivable	130	140	10	Decrease
Merchandise inventory	60	25	35	Increase
Prepaid expenses	8	5	3	Increase
Total current assets	225	200	25	Increase
Investment in Coulterton Transit Company Stock	45	–0–	45	Increase
Facilities and equipment	470	400	70	Increase
Less: Accumulated depreciation	(140)	(100)	40	Increase
Land	350	400	50	Decrease
Total assets	$950	$900	$50	Increase
Liabilities and Stockholders' Equity				
Current liabilities:				
Accounts payable	$ 85	$ 70	$ 15	Increase
Accrued salaries payable	20	30	10	Decrease
Total current liabilities	105	100	5	Increase
Deferred income taxes	10	15	5	Decrease
Bonds payable	190	250	60	Decrease
Total liabilities	305	365	60	Decrease
Stockholders' equity:				
Common stock	255	235	20	Increase
Retained earnings	390	300	90	Increase
Total stockholders' equity	645	535	110	Increase
Total liabilities and stockholders' equity	$950	$900	$ 50	Increase

We must make four adjustments to determine the cash flow from operating activities, as follows:

Adjustment for Depreciation This is perhaps the easiest adjustment to understand. On Alpine Trails' income statement, depreciation of $40,000 is recorded as an operating expense that reduced the company's net income for 19x1 by $40,000. Did this $40,000 expense represent a cash flow during the year? The answer is no. *Depreciation is a noncash expense.* Therefore, we must adjust Alpine Trails' net income by adding back its depreciation expense.

Exhibit 19-3. Income Statement and Statement of Retained Earnings

Alpine Trails Ski Resort
Income Statement
For the Year Ended December 31, 19x1
(in thousands)

Revenue:

Slope fees	$300	
Condominium rentals	635	
Sales of merchandise	45	
Total revenue		$980
Less: Cost of merchandise sold		30
Gross margin		950
Less: Operating expenses:		
Salaries	$270	
Insurance	80	
Property taxes	35	
Depreciation	40	
Utilities	90	
Maintenance	70	
Advertising	25	
Administration	155	
Interest on bonds	25	
Total operating expenses		790
Income before taxes		160
Income-tax expense		50
Net income		$110

Alpine Trails Ski Resort
Statement of Retained Earnings
For the Year Ended December 31, 19x1
(in thousands)

Retained earnings, December 31, 19x0	$300
Add: Net income for 19x1	110
Subtotal	410
Deduct: Dividends declared in 19x1	20
Retained earnings, December 31, 19x1	$390

Adjustment 1:	Add back depreciation expense.	+$40,000

This is a step that confuses some users of a statement of cash flows. Remember, adding back depreciation expense to net income does not imply that depreciation is a source of cash. Depreciation expense has nothing to do with cash. We add back depreciation expense as an adjustment to net income because depreciation expense was subtracted in the process of determining net income. Since depreciation was not

Exhibit 19-4. Format for Statement of Cash Flows under the Indirect Method

Alpine Trails Ski Resort
Statement of Cash Flows
For the Year Ended December 31, 19x1

Cash flows from operating activities:

Net income   XXX

Adjustments to net income to
  determine cash provided
  by operations

> List of individual adjustments
> •   XX
> •   XX
> •   XX
> •   XX
>
> Total adjustments   XX

Net cash flow from operating activities   XXX

Cash flows from investing activities:

> List of individual cash inflows
> and outflows
> •   XX
> •   XX
> •   XX

Net cash provided by (or used by)
  investing activities   XXX

Cash flows from financing activities:

> List of individual cash inflows
> and outflows
> •   XX
> •   XX
> •   XX

Net cash provided by (or used by)
  financing activities   XXX

Net increase (or decrease) in cash and cash equivalents   XXX

Cash balance, beginning of period   XXX

Cash balance, end of period . . . .   XXX a use of cash, however, we must now add it back to cancel out its earlier subtraction. Thus, *depreciation expense is not a source of cash.* We are merely making an adjustment for a noncash expense that had previously been subtracted in determining net income.

Alpine Trails' income statement does not show any depletion or amortization expenses. However, like depreciation, depletion and amortization are noncash expenses. If such expenses appear on an income statement, they must be added back to net income as an adjustment in determining the cash flow from operating activities.

Adjustment for Changes in Prepaid Expenses Alpine Trails must pay for its insurance and property taxes at the beginning of the time period to which these expenditures apply. The company paid for its 19x1 insurance and property taxes in January of 19x1. When a firm makes such a prepayment, an asset is created called Prepaid Expenses. Notice that on Alpine Trails' comparative balance sheets (Exhibit 19-2), the asset Prepaid Expenses increased during the year by $3,000 (from $5,000 on December 31, 19x0 to $8,000 on December 31, 19x1). This means that Alpine Trails paid $3,000 more in cash for its 19x1 insurance and property taxes than the actual 19x1 expense for these items. From the company's 19x1 income statement we note that the total of the insurance and property-tax expenses for 19x1 amounted to $115,000 ($80,000 + $35,000). Using these facts, we conclude that Alpine Trails' cash payment for insurance and property taxes in 19x1 was $118,000, as shown below.

Total of insurance and property-tax expenses............................	$115,000
Increase in the asset, Prepaid Expenses, during 19x1.....................	3,000
Cash payment in 19x1 for insurance and property taxes.................	$118,000

Since Alpine Trails' actual *cash payment* in 19x1 for insurance and property taxes was $118,000, but the income statement shows a total *expense* for insurance and property taxes of only $115,000, the following adjustment is required.

Adjustment 2:	Subtract the increase in Prepaid Expenses........... −$3,000

By subtracting $3,000 from Alpine Trails' reported net income, we reflect the fact that the firm's 19x1 cash disbursement for insurance and property taxes exceeded the expense shown on the income statement.

What adjustment would be made if instead Alpine Trails' Prepaid Expenses had *declined* during 19x1 by $2,000? Try to answer this question in your mind before referring to footnote 2.

Adjustment for Changes in Accrued Liabilities Alpine Trails pays its employees at the end of the time period for which the salary expense is recorded. The company's income statement shows that the 19x1 salary expense was $270,000. However, a glance at the comparative balance sheet shows that the firm's Accrued Salaries Payable account declined during 19x1 by $10,000 (from $30,000 on December 31, 19x0 to $20,000 on December 31, 19x1). Thus, Alpine Trails' actual cash payments to its employees in 19x1 must have been $280,000.

---

[2] In this case, the opposite adjustment would be made. We would *add* $2,000 to the company's net income to reflect the fact that the cash payment for insurance and property taxes was less than the expense reported on the income statement.

Salary expense.	$270,000
Decrease in Accrued Salaries Payable	10,000
Cash payment in 19x1 for salaries	$280,000

The company's 19x1 cash payments to employees were sufficient to cover its 19x1 expense *and* reduce its Accrued Salaries Payable liability from $30,000 at the beginning of the year to $20,000 at year-end. Thus, we must make the following adjustment.

Adjustment 3:	Subtract the decrease in accrued liabilities. . . . . −$10,000

By subtracting $10,000 from Alpine Trails' reported net income, we reflect the fact that the firm's 19x1 cash disbursement for salaries exceeded the expense shown on the income statement.

Suppose instead that Alpine Trails' Accrued Salaries Payable account had increased by $7,500 during 19x1. Then what adjustment would be necessary? Think about this question before looking at the footnote below.[3]

Adjustment for Changes in Inventory Alpine Trails purchases inventory for sale in its small ski shop. The income statement shows an expense of $30,000 for cost of merchandise sold. However, the company's merchandise purchases during 19x1 were greater than $30,000, because the balance sheet reveals that the asset Merchandise Inventory increased during 19x1. Since Merchandise Inventory increased by $35,000 (from $25,000 to $60,000), Alpine must have purchased a total of $65,000 in merchandise:

Cost of merchandise sold (expense)	$30,000
Increase in Merchandise Inventory	35,000
Total merchandise purchases in 19x1	$65,000

Since Alpine Trails' 19x1 merchandise purchases exceeded its expense for Cost of Merchandise Sold, the following adjustment is necessary.

Adjustment 4:	Subtract the increase in Merchandise Inventory. . . . . −$35,000

By subtracting $35,000 from Alpine Trails' income, we reflect the fact that the company's purchases of inventory were greater than the expense for Cost of Merchandise Sold shown on the income statement.

Suppose the balance in Merchandise Inventory had declined during the year by $9,000. What adjustment would be appropriate in this case?[4]

Adjustment for Changes in Accounts Payable We are not finished with the adjustments related to Alpine Trails' merchandising operations. As we noted above, the company's 19x1 merchandise purchases amounted to $65,000. However, this does not mean that the firm actually paid $65,000 in cash for those purchases in 19x1.

---

[3] In this situation, the opposite adjustment would be made. We would *add* $7,500 to the company's net income to reflect the fact that the cash payment for salaries was less than the expense reported on the income statement.

[4] The opposite adjustment would be made. We would add $9,000 to income.

As is true of most retail firms, Alpine Trails buys its merchandise on account. Therefore, in order to determine the company's cash payments for merchandise during 19x1, we need to take into account the change in the Accounts Payable balance. As the balance sheet shows, Alpine Trails' Accounts Payable increased by $15,000 during 19x1. What does this change imply about the company's cash payments for merchandise purchases? As the following analysis shows, the firm's cash payments must have been $50,000.

Merchandise purchases (as derived in the preceding section).	$65,000
Increase in Accounts Payable.	15,000
Cash payments for merchandise purchases in 19x1	$50,000

Since Alpine Trails' cash payments for merchandise were less than its purchases, the following adjustment is required.

> **Adjustment 5:**   Add the increase in Accounts Payable. . . . .   +$15,000

By adding $15,000 to Alpine Trails' income, we reflect the fact that the company's cash payments for merchandise inventory were less than the firm's purchases.

Suppose instead that Alpine Trails' Accounts Payable balance had declined during the year by $12,000. Then what adjustment would be appropriate?[5]

Adjustment for Changes in Accounts Receivable Some of Alpine Trails' patrons do not pay their bills in cash immediately, but prefer to put their charges on their accounts. Thus, Alpine Trails may actually collect a cash amount from customers during the year that differs from the revenue amount shown on the income statement. Alpine Trails' income statement discloses total revenue for 19x1 of $980,000. However, the company's Accounts Receivable balance declined during 19x1 by $10,000, as shown on the comparative balance sheets. Putting these two facts together, we conclude that Alpine Trails' 19x1 cash receipts from customers amounted to $990,000.

Total revenue	$980,000
Decrease in Accounts Receivable.	10,000
Total cash receipts from customers	$990,000

Since Alpine Trails' 19x1 cash receipts from customers exceeded its total revenue, the following adjustment is needed.

> **Adjustment 6:**   Add the decrease in Accounts Receivable. . . . .   +$10,000

The addition of $10,000 to Alpine Trails' income reflects the fact that the firm's cash receipts from customers exceeded the total revenue reported on the income statement.

Suppose instead that Alpine Trails' Accounts Receivable balance had increased by $1,000 during the year. What adjustment would be made in this case?[6]

---

[5] The opposite adjustment would be made. We would subtract $12,000 from income.
[6] The opposite adjustment would be required. We would subtract $1,000 from income.

Exhibit 19-5. Summary of Adjustments to Net Income: Alpine Trails Ski Resort

Income Statement		Cash Flows from Operating Activities
(accrual basis of accounting)	*ALPINE TRAILS SKI RESORT*	(cash basis of accounting)
Revenue	+ Decrease in accounts receivable	Cash receipts from customers
Less: Cost of goods sold	- Increase in merchandise inventory + Increase in accounts payable	Less: Cash disbursements for merchandise purchases
Less: Operating expenses	+ Depreciation expense - Increase in prepaid expenses - Decrease in accrued liabilities - Decrease in deferred income taxes	Less: Cash disbursements for operating expenses
Net income		Cash provided by operations

Adjustment for Deferred Taxes One final adjustment remains in determining Alpine Trails' cash provided by operations. Taxes paid to the government are considered operating cash flows. As the income statement shows, the company's 19x1 income-tax expense was $50,000. However, the comparative balance sheets show that Alpine Trails also has a balance in its Deferred Income Taxes account. The decline in this account of $5,000 during 19x1 means that the company paid $5,000 in income taxes during 19x1 that had already been reported as an expense in some previous year. Thus, Alpine Trails' cash disbursements for taxes in 19x1 amounted to $55,000, as shown below.

Income-tax expense	$50,000
Decrease in Deferred Income Taxes	5,000
Total cash payments for income taxes in 19x1	$55,000

**Exhibit 19-6. Operating Activities Section of Statement of Cash Flows:
Indirect Method**

Alpine Trails Ski Resort
(in thousands)

Cash flows from operating activities:

	Net income		$110
	Adjustments to net income to determine cash provided by operations:		
1*	Depreciation expense	$40	
2	Increase in prepaid expenses	(3)	
3	Decrease in accrued liabilities	(10)	
4	Increase in merchandise inventory	(35)	
5	Increase in accounts payable.	15	
6	Decrease in accounts receivable	10	
7	Decrease in deferred income taxes	(5)	
	Total adjustments.		12
	Net cash flow from operating activities		$122

*This is the number of the adjustment as explained in the preceding pages.

Since Alpine Trails' cash disbursements for income taxes exceeded its income-tax expense, the following adjustment is required.

Adjustment 7:	Subtract the decrease in Deferred Income Taxes...... **−$5,000**

The subtraction of $5,000 from Alpine Trails' income reflects the fact that the company's cash payments for income taxes exceeded the income-tax expense reported on the income statement.

What adjustment would be made if instead Alpine Trails' Deferred Income Taxes had increased during the year by $4,000?[7]

Completing the Operating Activities Section of the Statement Now we have discussed all of the adjustments to income needed to determine Alpine Trails' cash provided by operations. Exhibit 19-5 summarizes these adjustments and shows the relationship between net income determined under accrual accounting and the cash provided by operating activities. The operating activities section of the statement is shown in Exhibit 19-6. As Exhibit 19-6 shows, Alpine Trails' operations provided $122,000 in cash during 19x1.

Before we can complete Alpine Trails' entire statement of cash flows, we must first prepare the financing and investing portions of the statement.

[7] The opposite adjustment would be required, so $4,000 would be added to Alpine Trails' income. A $4,000 increase in Deferred Income Taxes would mean that the company's cash payment for income taxes was exceeded by the income-tax expense reported on the income statement.

Investing Activities

The second section of the statement of cash flows focuses on Alpine Trails' investing activities. The company completed three major investment transactions during 19x1. These transactions, which are apparent upon examining the firm's comparative balance sheets, are discussed next.

Investment in Stock Coulterton Transit Company is a small bus line which operates in the vicinity of nearby Coulterton, Colorado. The firm provides transportation between Alpine Trails Ski Resort and the city of Coulterton. Since Alpine Trails Ski Resort depends on Coulterton Transit's services, Alpine's board of directors recently approved a plan to invest in the bus company's stock. In 19x1 Alpine Trails purchased 9,000 shares of Coulterton Transit Company stock for $45,000. Thus, the following entry will appear in the investing activities section of Alpine Trails' statement.

> **Cash flows from investing activities:**
>   Purchase of Coulterton Transit Company stock.................. $(45,000)

Notice that the stock purchase is also apparent in Alpine Trails' comparative balance sheets, in which the balance in the Investment-in-Stock account increased by $45,000 during 19x1.

Purchase of Equipment Another look at Alpine Trails' comparative balance sheets shows that during 19x1 the company purchased facilities and equipment costing $70,000. Referral to the firm's long-lived assets records reveals that the company purchased new snowmaking equipment. The following entry will appear on the statement of cash flows.

> **Cash flows from investing activities:**
>   Purchase of snowmaking equipment........................... $(70,000)

Sale of Land Early in 19x1 Alpine Trails sold several acres of land to a restaurant company which plans to build a restaurant near Alpine Trails Ski Resort. The land was sold at no gain or loss to Alpine Trails. The land sale is apparent on Alpine Trails comparative balance sheets, where the balance in the land account declined from $400,000 to $350,000 during 19x1. The following entry will appear on Alpine Trails' statement of cash flows.

> **Cash flows from investing activities:**
>   Sale of land.. $50,000

Financing Activities

The final section of Alpine Trails' statement of cash flows focuses on the company's financing activities. The three financing transactions completed in 19x1 are discussed next.

Redemption of Bonds On December 31, 19x1 Alpine Trails Ski Resort redeemed bonds with a face value of $60,000. The $60,000 decrease in Bonds Payable is apparent on the comparative balance sheets. The following entry on the statement of cash flows will highlight this important transaction.

Cash flows from financing activities:	
Redemption of bonds....................................	$(60,000)

Sale of Capital Stock Examination of Alpine Trails' comparative balance sheets shows that the company issued $20,000 of capital stock during 19x1. The following entry will highlight this transaction on the statement of cash flows.

Cash flows from financing activities:	
Sale of capital stock.......................................	$20,000

The sale of Alpine Trails Ski Resort's *own* capital stock is a *financing* transaction. The stock was sold to raise funds to expand and conduct operations. In contrast, Alpine Trails' purchase of Coulterton Transit Company's stock is an *investment activity,* and it was properly included in the investing activities section of the statement.

Payment of Dividends One final financing transaction occurred during 19x1. Alpine Trails' board of directors declared a $20,000 dividend on the company's stock, and the dividend was paid in cash in December. This transaction, which is disclosed on the statement of retained earnings, is highlighted on the statement of cash flows by the following entry.

Cash flows from financing activities:	
Payment of dividends.......................................	$(20,000)

Completed Statement of Cash Flows

Now we can combine all three sections of Alpine Trails' statement of cash flows. Exhibit 19-7 displays the completed statement. Alpine Trails had a $3,000 decrease in its cash and cash equivalents during 19x1.

The statement of cash flows explains how this change occurred and summarizes how the company obtained and used cash. Much of the information included on the statement of cash flows also is disclosed in the other major financial statements. For example, the sale of land is disclosed on the balance sheet. The purpose of the statement of cash flows is to pull together all of the company's cash flow information and present it on one convenient statement.

USE OF T-ACCOUNTS AS AN AID IN PREPARING THE STATEMENT OF CASH FLOWS

Some accountants find that T-accounts help them to organize their information when preparing a statement of cash flows. To illustrate this approach, let's prepare Alpine Trails' 19x1 statement using T-accounts.

Exhibit 19-7. Statement of Cash Flows: Indirect Method

Alpine Trails Ski Resort
Statement of Cash Flows
For the Year Ended December 31, 19x1
(in thousands)

Cash flows from operating activities:

Net income $110

Adjustments to net income to determine
cash provided by operations:

Depreciation expense.	$40	
Increase in prepaid expenses.	(3)	
Decrease in accrued liabilities	(10)	
Increase in merchandise inventory.	(35)	
Increase in accounts payable.	15	
Decrease in accounts receivable	10	
Decrease in deferred income taxes	(5)	
Total adjustments		12

Net cash flow from operating activities 122

Cash flows from investing activities:

Purchase of Coulterton Transit Company stock	$(45)	
Purchase of snowmaking equipment	(70)	
Sale of land	50	
Net cash used by investing activities		(65)

Cash flows from financing activities:

Redemption of bonds	$(60)	
Sale of capital stock	20	
Payment of dividends	(20)	
Net cash used by financing activities		(60)

Net decrease in cash and cash equivalents . . . . (3)
Balance in cash and cash equivalents,
beginning of year 20
Balance in cash and cash equivalents, end of year $17

Step One: Prepare T-Accounts

The first step is to prepare a T-account for each account on Alpine Trails' balance sheet. These T-accounts are shown in Exhibit 19-8; we will analyze them in steps three, four, and five.

Step Two: Enter Account Balances

Next we enter the beginning and ending balance in each of the accounts, except for Cash and Cash Equivalents. We can skip this account, since the change in this account is the amount we are attempting to explain.

Step Three: Analyze the Cash Flows from Operating Activities

Now we are ready to analyze the changes in Cash and Cash Equivalents for 19x1, as they relate to changes in Alpine Trails' other accounts during that period. For each account change, we will make an entry in the Cash and Cash Equivalents account and in the related noncash account. When we are finished, we will have the basics of Alpine Trails' statement of cash flows represented by the entries in the Cash and Cash Equivalents account.

Net Income Since we are using the indirect method of statement preparation, we will begin by entering Alpine Trails' 19x1 net income in the Cash and Cash Equivalents account and in the Retained Earnings account. Entries and adjustments that represent increases in cash are entered on the left (debit) side of the Cash and Cash Equivalents account. Since Alpine Trails' net income of $110,000 increased the firm's retained earnings, we also enter $110,000 on the right (credit) side of the Retained Earnings account. To summarize, the following entry is made.

Cash and Cash Equivalents (increase). 110,000
    Retained Earnings   110,000

Adjustment 1: Depreciation Alpine Trails' 19x1 depreciation was $40,000, so the following entry is made.

Cash and Cash Equivalents (increase). 40,000
    Accumulated Depreciation   40,000

As previously noted, the adjustment for depreciation reflects the fact that depreciation expense was deducted previously in computing Alpine Trails' net income. Now it must be added back, since depreciation is a noncash expense.

Adjustment 2: Prepaid Expenses Since Alpine Trails' balance in Prepaid Expenses increased by $3,000 during 19x1, the following entry is required.

Prepaid Expenses 3,000
    Cash and Cash Equivalents (decrease).   3,000

The company paid $3,000 more in cash for insurance and property taxes in 19x1 than it incurred for those expenses.

Adjustment 3: Accrued Liabilities The following entry is required to record the $10,000 decrease in Alpine Trails' Accrued Salaries Payable account.

Accrued Salaries Payable. 10,000
    Cash and Cash Equivalents   10,000

The company paid $10,000 more in cash to its employees than it incurred in salary expense for 19x1.

Adjustment 4: Merchandise Inventory A $35,000 increase in Merchandise Inventory means that Alpine Trails purchased more inventory than it sold in 19x1. The following entry reflects this fact.

Merchandise Inventory 35,000
    Cash and Cash Equivalents (decrease).   35,000

Exhibit 19-8. T-accounts Used in Preparing Statement of Cash Flows (all amounts in thousands)

Cash and Cash Equivalents

	Entries and Adjustments That Increase Cash			Entries and Adjustments That Decrease Cash	
Operating activities					
	Net income	110	3	Increase in prepaid expenses	2
1	Depreciation	40	10	Decrease in accrued liabilities	3
5	Increase in accounts payable	15	35	Increase in merchandise inventory	4
6	Decrease in accounts receivable	10	5	Decrease in deferred income taxes	7
	Net cash flow from operating activities	122			
Investing activities					
10	Sale of land	50	45	Purchase of Coulteron Transit Company stock	8
			70	Purchase of snowmaking equipment	9
Financing activities					
12	Issuance of capital stock	20	60	Redemption of bonds	11
			20	Payment of dividends	13
			3	Decrease in cash and cash equivalents	

Accounts Receivable				Merchandise Inventory				Prepaid Expenses		
Beg. bal. 140				Beg. bal.	25			Beg. bal.	5	
	10	6		4	35			2	3	
End. bal. 130				End. bal.	60			End. bal.	8	

Adjustment 5: Accounts Payable Alpine Trails' cash payments to its merchandise suppliers amounted to $15,000 less than the firm's merchandise purchases. The following entry reflects this fact.

Cash and Cash Equivalents (increase)............................	15,000	
Accounts Payable..		15,000

Exhibit 19-8. (continued)

Investment In Coulterton Transit Company Stock

Beg. bal. 0	
8 45	
End. bal. 45	

Facilities and Equipment

Beg. bal. 400	
9 70	
End. bal. 470	

Accumulated Depreciation

	100 Beg. bal.
	40 1
	140 End. bal.

Land

Beg. bal. 400	
	50 10
End. bal. 350	

Accounts Payable

	70 Beg. bal.
	15 5
	85 End. bal.

Accrued Salaries Payable

	30 Beg. bal.
3 10	
	20 End. bal.

Deferred Income Taxes

	15 Beg. bal.
7 5	
	10 End. bal.

Bonds Payable

	250 Beg. bal.
11 60	
	190 End. bal.

Common Stock

	235 Beg. bal.
	20 12
	255 End. bal.

Retained Earnings

	300 Beg. bal.
13 20	110 Net income for 19x1
	390 End. bal.

ALPINE
TRAILS
SKI RESORT

Adjustment 6: Accounts Receivable The following entry is needed to show that Alpine Trails' cash collections from its customers exceeded the company's 19x1 revenue.

Cash and Cash Equivalents (increase). 10,000
    Accounts Receivable 10,000

Adjustment 7: Deferred Taxes Alpine Trails' cash payments for income taxes in 19x1 exceeded the firm's income-tax expense. The following entry is required.

Deferred Income Taxes 5,000
    Cash and Cash Equivalents (decrease). 5,000

These seven adjustments complete the operating activities portion of the statement of cash flows. By calculating the balance in the Cash and Cash Equivalents account of Exhibit 19-8, we conclude that the cash provided by operations in 19x1 amounted to $122,000. This balance reflects only operating activities; Alpine Trails' financing and investing activities are analyzed in steps 4 and 5.

Step Four: Analyze the Cash Flows from Investing Activities

Alpine Trails had three major investing transactions in 19x1. The following three entries will record the effects of these transactions on the company's cash and cash equivalents.

Entry 8: Purchase of Coulterton Transit Company Stock Alpine Trails' purchase of stock as an investment is recorded as follows:

Investment in Coulterton Transit Company Stock 45,000
    Cash and Cash Equivalents (decrease). 45,000

Entry 9: Purchase of Snowmaking Equipment The following entry records this major use of cash.

Facilities and Equipment. 70,000
    Cash and Cash Equivalents (decrease). 70,000

Entry 10: Sale of Land Alpine Trails' land sale generated $50,000 in cash as shown by the following entry.

Cash and Cash Equivalents (increase). 50,000
    Land 50,000

Step Five: Analyze the Cash Flows from Financing Activities

Alpine Trails' three major financing activities are recorded by the following entries:

Entry 11: Redemption of Bonds The use of $60,000 in cash to redeem bonds required this entry:

Bonds Payable 60,000
    Cash and Cash Equivalents (decrease). 60,000

Entry 12: Issuance of Capital Stock Alpine Trails generated $20,000 in cash through the issuance of capital stock, as the following entry shows.

Cash and Cash Equivalents (increase).	20,000	
Common Stock.		20,000

Entry 13: Payment of Dividends The following entry reflects the $20,000 cash outflow resulting from Alpine Trails' payment of dividends. Dividend payments reduce a firm's Retained Earnings account.

Retained Earnings	20,000	
Cash and Cash Equivalents (decrease).		20,000

This completes the entries needed to record Alpine Trails' investing and financing activities. Now we compute the final balance in the Cash and Cash Equivalents account. This shows that Alpine Trails' cash and cash equivalents decreased by $3,000 during 19x1. Carefully examine the Cash and Cash Equivalents account in Exhibit 19-8. Compare the account with Alpine Trails' statement of cash flows in Exhibit 19-7. Notice that all of the information needed to prepare the statement is summarized in the Cash and Cash Equivalents account.

USING THE DIRECT METHOD OF STATEMENT PREPARATION

When the direct method is used, the operating activities section of the statement of cash flows is approached differently than when the indirect method is used. Instead of beginning with net income and making adjustments, we will list each income statement item on the statement of cash flows. However, we still will make adjustments to reflect the difference between accrual accounting, which is used on the income statement, and cash-basis accounting, which is used on the statement of cash flows.

To illustrate the direct method of statement preparation, we will focus on the activities of Alpine Trails Ski Resort during 19x2. The company's comparative balance sheets, income statement, and statement of retained earnings are given in Exhibits 19-9 and 19-10.

Alpine Trails' completed statement of cash flows for 19x2 is displayed in Exhibit 19-11. The number next to each item on the statement is keyed to the following discussion, in which each statement item is explained.

Operating Activities

The operating activities section of the statement shows that Alpine Trails' operations provided $195,000 in cash during 19x2. Explanations of the various items in this section of the statement follow.

1. *Cash receipts from customers* Alpine Trails' income statement in Exhibit 19-10 shows that total sales revenue amounted to $1,060,000 in 19x2. However, this is not the amount of cash collected from customers, for two reasons. First, the comparative balance sheets in Exhibit 19-9 show that Accounts Receivable increased in 19x2 by $10,000. Therefore, $10,000 of the firm's 19x2 sales were not paid for in cash during 19x2. Second, the current liabilities section of Alpine Trails' comparative balance sheets

Exhibit 19-9. Comparative Balance Sheets

Alpine Trails Ski Resort
Comparative Balance Sheets
December 31, 19x2 and 19x1
(in thousands)

Assets	19x2	19x1	Change	
Current assets:				
Cash	$ 22	$ 17	$ 5	Increase
Marketable securities	10	10	–0–	
Accounts receivable	140	130	10	Increase
Merchandise inventory	35	60	25	Decrease
Prepaid expenses	3	8	5	Decrease
Total current assets	210	225	15	Decrease
Investment in Coulterton Transit				
Company Stock	45	45	–0–	
Facilities and equipment	450	470	20	Decrease
Less: Accumulated depreciation	(175)	(140)	35	Increase
Land	540	350	190	Increase
Total assets	$1,070	$950	$120	Increase

Liabilities and Stockholders' Equity

	19x2	19x1	Change	
Current liabilities:				
Accounts payable	$ 75	$ 85	$ 10	Decrease
Accrued salaries payable	25	20	5	Increase
Deferred revenue	5	–0–	5	Increase
Total current liabilities	105	105	–0–	
Deferred income taxes	15	10	5	Increase
Bonds payable	190	190	–0–	
Total liabilities	310	305	5	Increase
Stockholders' equity:				
Common stock	270	255	15	Increase
Retained earnings	490	390	100	Increase
Total stockholders' equity	760	645	115	Increase
Total liabilities and stockholders' equity	$1,070	$950	$120	Increase

shows a $5,000 increase in Deferred Revenue during 19x2. Deferred Revenue is a liability that results when the company receives cash from customers for services not yet rendered. In Alpine Trails' case, the $5,000 in Deferred Revenue resulted when customers made advance deposits during 19x2 to hold condo reservations for the following year.

The following calculations show that Alpine Trails collected a total of $1,055,000 from its customers in 19x2.

Exhibit 19-10. Income Statement and Statement of Retained Earnings

Alpine Trails Ski Resort
Income Statement
For the Year Ended December 31, 19x2
(in thousands)

Revenue:

Slope Fees	$330	
Condominium rentals	650	
Sales of merchandise	80	
Total revenue		$1,060

Less: Cost of merchandise sold		55
Gross margin		1,005

Less: Operating expenses:

Salaries	$300	
Insurance	85	
Property taxes	40	
Depreciation	45	
Utilities	95	
Maintenance	60	
Advertising	15	
Administration	166	
Interest on bonds	19	
Total operating expenses		825
Income before taxes		180
Income tax expense		55
Net income		$ 125

Alpine Trails Ski Resort
Statement of Retained Earnings
For the Year Ended December 31, 19x2
(in thousands)

Retained earnings, December 31, 19x1	$390
Add: Net income for 19x2	125
Subtotal	515
Deduct: Dividends declared in 19x2	25
Retained earnings, December 31, 19x2	$490

Total revenue (from income statement)	$1,060,000
Subtract: Increase in Accounts Receivable	(10,000)
Add: Increase in Deferred Revenue	5,000
Cash collected from customers	$1,055,000

2. *Cash payments to suppliers of merchandise* Alpine Trails' 19x2 income
statement includes an expense for cost of merchandise sold of $55,000, but
the statement of cash flows shows cash payments to suppliers of $40,000.
The following calculations reconcile this difference.

Exhibit 19-11. Statement of Cash Flows: Direct Method

Alpine Trails Ski Resort
For the Year Ended December 31, 19x2
(in thousands)

Cash flows from operating activities:

1	Cash receipts from customers		$1,055
	Cash payments:		
2	To suppliers of merchandise	$ 40	
3	To employees	295	
4	For interest	19	
5	For income taxes	50	
	For other operating expenses:		
6	Insurance and property taxes	120	
7	Utilities	95	
7	Maintenance	60	
7	Advertising	15	
7	Administration	166	
	Total cash payments		860
	Net cash flow from operating activities		195

Cash flows from investing activities:

Sale of equipment	$ 10	
Purchase of land	(190)	
Net cash used by investing activities		(180)

Cash flows from financing activities:

Issuance of capital stock	$ 15	
Payment of dividends	(25)	
Net cash used by financing activities		(10)

Net increase in cash and cash equivalents	5
Balance in cash and cash equivalents,	
beginning of year	17
Balance in cash and cash equivalents, end of year	$ 22

Cost of Merchandise Sold (from income statement)	$55,000
Subtract: Decrease in Merchandise Inventory	(25,000)
Add: Decrease in Accounts Payable	10,000
Cash payments to suppliers of merchandise	$40,000

3. *Cash payments to employees* Salary expense of $300,000 is included on
Alpine Trails' income statement. However, the firm's cash payments to
employees amounted to $295,000 in 19x2, as the following analysis shows.

Salary expense (from income statement)	$300,000
Less: Increase in Accrued Salaries Payable	(5,000)
Cash payments to employees	$295,000

4. *Cash payments for interest* Alpine Trails' $19,000 interest payment is
shown on the income statement.

5. *Cash payment for income taxes* Income-tax expense on Alpine Trails' income statement is $55,000. However, the two balance sheets show that
the company's liability for Deferred Income Taxes increased by $5,000
during 19x2. This means that Alpine Trails' cash payments for income
taxes amounted to $5,000 less than the firm's actual income-tax expense.

Income-tax expense (from income statement)	$55,000
Less: Increase in Deferred Income Taxes	(5,000)
Cash payments for income taxes	$50,000

6. *Cash payments for insurance and property taxes* These two expenses total
$125,000 on Alpine Trails' income statement. However, the comparative
balance sheets show that the firm's prepaid expenses declined by $5,000
during 19x2. This means that Alpine's 19x2 cash payments for insurance
and property taxes amounted to $5,000 less than its expenses.

Insurance and property tax expenses (from income statement)	$125,000
Less: Decrease in Prepaid Expenses	(5,000)
Cash payments for insurance and property taxes	$120,000

7. *Cash payments for utilities, maintenance, advertising, and administration*
These cash payments are the same as the expense items listed on the income statement.

Depreciation   Notice that there is no entry on the statement of cash flows for
depreciation. Under the direct method of statement preparation, we list only the cash
receipts and disbursements. Since depreciation is a noncash expense, no entry is
necessary.

Investing Activities

Alpine Trails' 19x2 statement of cash flows lists two cash flows from investing
activities.

Equipment Sale   The company sold a truck with a book value of $10,000 for
$10,000 in cash. The truck's original cost was $20,000 and its accumulated depreciation at the time of the sale was $10,000. Notice that the comparative balance sheets
show a $20,000 decline in Facilities and Equipment during 19x2. The balance sheets
also show a $35,000 increase in Accumulated Depreciation during 19x2, which is
explained as follows:

Accumulated Depreciation, December 31, 19x1	$140,000
Add: Depreciation expense for 19x2 (from income statement)	45,000
Subtract: Accumulated depreciation on truck sold in 19x2	(10,000)
Accumulated Depreciation, December 31, 19x2	$175,000

Land Purchase   As the comparative balance sheets show, Alpine Trails purchased land for $190,000 during 19x2. The company's management purchased the
land for planned future construction of additional condominiums.

Financing Activities

Two financing transactions are disclosed on Alpine Trails' 19x2 statement of cash flows.

Issuance of Capital Stock The company issued $15,000 in capital stock during 19x2, as the comparative balance sheets show.

Payment of Dividends Alpine Trails paid $25,000 in cash dividends during 19x2, as the statement of retained earnings shows.

Completed Statement of Cash Flows

Exhibit 19-11 on page 826 shows Alpine Trails' 19x2 statement of cash flows. As the statement shows, cash and cash equivalents increased by $5,000 during 19x2.

Reconciliation between Net Income and Net Cash Flow from Operating Activities When the direct method is used, a separate schedule must be provided to reconcile net income with the cash provided by operating activities. This schedule takes the same form as the operating activities section of the statement when it is prepared using the indirect method. The required schedule to accompany Alpine Trails' 19x2 statement is displayed in Exhibit 19-12.

OTHER ISSUES IN PREPARING THE STATEMENT OF CASH FLOWS

Two other issues concerning preparation of the statement of cash flows merit discussion: (1) gross versus net cash flows and (2) direct exchange transactions.

Exhibit 19-12. Reconciliation of Net Income to the Net Cash Flow from Operating Activities

Alpine Trails Ski Resort
For the Year Ended December 31, 19x2

Net income		$125
Adjustments to reconcile net income to the net cash flow from operating activities:		
Depreciation expense	$45	
Decrease in prepaid expenses	5	
Increase in accrued liabilities	5	
Decrease in merchandise inventory	25	
Decrease in accounts payable	(10)	
Increase in accounts receivable	(10)	
Increase in deferred income taxes	5	
Increase in deferred revenue	5	
Total adjustments		70
Net cash flows from operating activities		$195

Gross versus Net Cash Flows

Suppose that in 19x3 Alpine Trails Ski Resort purchases one parcel of land for $80,000 and sells another property for $25,000. In preparing the statement of cash flows, Alpine Trails should report both investing transactions at their gross amounts, rather than reporting a net land purchase of $55,000 ($80,000 purchase minus $25,000 sale).

Correct Presentation (gross amounts)

Cash flows from investing activities:

Purchase of land	$(80,000)
Sale of land	25,000
Cash used for investing activities	$(55,000)

Incorrect Presentation (net amount)

Cash flows from investing activities

Net purchase of land	$(55,000)

The practice of reporting gross transaction amounts extends to all items in the investing and financing portions of the statement. However, *net* amounts are used in the operating activities section. For example, when Alpine Trails has several transactions during the year involving Accounts Payable, only the net change in Accounts Payable would be used in calculating the cash flow from operating activities.

Direct Exchange or Noncash Transactions

The statement of cash flows focuses on transactions involving cash inflows or outflows. Sometimes, however, an enterprise experiences a substantive investing or financing transaction that does not involve a cash flow. An example of such a transaction is the purchase of a productive, long-lived asset through the issuance of debt or stock. Suppose, for example, that in 19x3 Alpine Trails Ski Resort purchases a parcel of land valued at $100,000 by giving the seller a $100,000 note payable. The journal entry to record this transaction is shown below.

Land	100,000	
Note Payable		100,000

No cash was exchanged in this transaction; yet the event involved a significant investing transaction (the purchase of land) and a significant financing transaction (the issuance of a note payable). Such a transaction, which does not involve cash, is called a **direct exchange** (or **noncash**) transaction.

Significant direct exchange transactions are not included in the body of the statement of cash flows. However, such transactions should be disclosed in a separate schedule accompanying the statement. In this manner, users of the company's financial statements will be alerted to these significant events. Alpine Trails' 19x3 statement of cash flows should be accompanied by the following schedule.

Schedule of direct exchange (noncash) transactions involving significant investing and financing activities:

Purchase of land valued at $100,000 through the issuance of a note payable in the amount of $100,000.

Exhibit 19-13. Comparative Statements of Cash Flows: McDonald's Corporation for Three Recent Years (in thousands)

McDonald's Corporation
Consolidated Statement of Cash Flows

	Year 3	Year 2	Year 1
Operating activities:			
Income before cumulative effect of the change in accounting for income taxes . . . .$	645,863	$ 549,062	$ 479,725
Adjustment to reconcile to cash provided by operations:			
Depreciation and amortization	383,389	338,420	284,561
Deferred income taxes.	66,400	72,500	83,477
Changes in operating working capital items:			
Accounts receivable (increase)	(22,016)	(30,653)	(14,154)
Inventories (increase) decrease	5	(6,826)	(5,578)
Prepaid and other current assets (increase) decrease	(12,540)	9,403	(14,190)
Accounts payable increase (decrease)	113,768	(15,101)	37,370
Accrued interest increase (decrease)	(1,773)	53,344	21,857
Taxes and other accrued liabilities increase	15,676	69,617	19,795
Other	(11,696)	11,540	(40,912)
Cash provided by operations	1,177,076	1,051,306	851,951
Investing activities:			
Property and equipment expenditures	(1,321,261)	(1,026,846)	(942,281)
Purchases of restaurant businesses	(60,059)	(38,602)	(106,381)
Notes receivable additions	(39,182)	(25,064)	(39,747)
Sale of property and restaurant businesses	97,165	87,409	74,986
Notes receivable reductions.	58,619	64,441	68,867
Other	(42,563)	32,581	(18,097)
Cash used for investing activities	(1,307,281)	(906,081)	(962,653)
Financing activities:			
Issuance of notes payable and long-term debt	886,289	887,406	858,618
Repayment of notes payable and long-term debt	(540,608)	(782,323)	(426,397)
Treasury stock purchases	(126,026)	(137,095)	(205,053)
Preferred stock redemption		(58,308)	
Common and preferred stock dividends	(102,516)	(93,572)	(86,017)
Other	14,224	16,775	19,236
Cash provided by (used for) financing activities	131,363	(167,117)	160,387

Exhibit 19-13. (continued)			

McDonald's Corporation
Consolidated Statement of Cash Flows

	Year 3	Year 2	Year 1
Increase (decrease) in cash and			
equivalents	1,158	(21,892)	49,685
Cash and equivalents at beginning of year	183,206	205,098	155,413
Cash and equivalents at end of year . . . .$	184,364	$ 183,206	$ 205,098
Supplemental cash flow disclosures:			
Interest paid . . . .$	244,699	$ 171,129	$ 168,903
Income taxes paid	332,112	304,750	279,638

USING THE STATEMENT OF CASH FLOWS

The statement of cash flows provides useful information for both the managers of an enterprise and interested parties outside the organization. For both groups, the statement provides a convenient way of reconciling a company's income with its net cash flow. Many managers find the cash flow concept to be a more intuitively appealing measure of an organization's performance than income based on accrual accounting. In addition, the statement helps managers in determining the firm's dividend policy and needs for borrowing. Perhaps most important is the information provided by the statement about the ability of the enterprise to invest in facilities, equipment, or expanded operations. In short, the statement of cash flows provides managers with insight about what the enterprise can afford.

Investors, creditors, and financial analysts use the information in the statement of cash flows to help in predicting an enterprise's future performance. Is the company in a strong position to grow or to take advantage of opportunities? Or, at the other extreme, is the firm in danger of insolvency? What sort of dividend stream is likely in the future? Outside parties find the information in the statement of cash flows important in answering these and many other questions about an enterprise's future performance.

Illustration of the Statement of Cash Flows

McDonald's Corporation's comparative statements of cash flows for three recent years are displayed in Exhibit 19-13. Notice that the company's cash provided by operations has increased steadily over the three-year period. The investing activities section shows that McDonald's has invested heavily in property and equipment. Apparent from the statement's financing activities section is McDonald's steadily increasing dividend payment. All in all, the statement provides a picture of a vibrant, growing company that is in a strong financial position.

CHAPTER SUMMARY

The statement of cash flows has evolved over a period of 30 years from an informal cash flow analysis into a major financial statement. The statement is required by the

FASB for external reporting, and it is considered to be of equal importance to the balance sheet and income statement. The purpose of the statement of cash flows is to provide financial statement users with insight about: (1) the organization's ability to generate positive future cash flows, (2) the organization's ability to meet its obligations and pay dividends, (3) the needs of the organization for external financing, (4) the reasons for the differences between net income and the net cash flow from operations, and (5) the effects of cash and noncash investing and financing activities.

The statement has three sections, which describe the organization's cash flows from operating activities, investing activities, and financing activities. The operating activities section of the statement may be prepared using the direct method, under which a cash-basis income statement is prepared by analyzing each of the firm's cash flows, the income statement accounts, and the changes in the balance sheet accounts. Alternatively, the indirect method may be used, in which the analyst begins with the firm's net income determined under accrual accounting. Then net income is adjusted to reflect the differences between operating cash flows and the revenues and expenses reported on an accrual basis. T-accounts may also be used as an aid in preparing the statement.

KEY TERMS   Cash equivalents, p. 804; **Direct exchange (or noncash) transaction**, p. 829; **Direct method**, p. 807; **Financing activities**, p. 805; **Indirect method (or reconciliation method)**, p. 807; **Investing activities**, p. 805; **Operating activities**, p. 805; **Statement of cash flows**, p. 810.

REVIEW QUESTIONS   **19-1.** List five purposes for the statement of cash flows.

19-2. What is meant by the term *cash equivalent?*

19-3. Describe the organization of the statement of cash flows.

19-4. Define each of the following terms: operating activities, investing activities, and financing activities.

19-5. For each of the following transactions, indicate whether it belongs in the operating, investing, or financing section of the statement of cash flows.

    a. Purchase of land.

    b. Sale of the firm's own capital stock.

    c. Sale of stock owned in another company.

    d. Payment of a utility bill.

    e. Collection of accounts receivable.

    f. Collection of a loan made to another company.

19-6. Explain the difference between the direct and indirect methods of preparing the operating activities section of the statement of cash flows.

19-7. Explain the treatment of depreciation under the indirect method.

19-8. Describe the implications of an increase in accounts receivable when the indirect method is used.

19-9. Is depreciation a source of cash? Explain your answer.

19-10. Describe the adjustment made to net income under the indirect method when accounts payable increases by $2,000 and inventory decreases by $800.

19-11. Explain the difference between gross and net cash flows. Which of these types of cash flow is used in the statement of cash flows? Why?

19-12. Define the term *direct exchange transaction.* Give two examples.

19-13. What are the sources of information from which the statement of cash flows is prepared?

19-14. Last year Robinson Corporation reported a net loss of $200,000, but the company's net cash provided by operations amounted to $50,000. Moreover, the firm's cash balance did not change during the year. Explain how these events could occur.

19-15. How might the management of a company use the statement of cash flows? Of what use is the statement to outside parties?

19-16. Of what use is the statement of cash flows, given that most of the information can be deduced from an income statement and comparative balance sheet?

19-17. Describe the effects of the following items on the cash provided by operations.
  a. Increase in deferred taxes.
  b. Decrease in deferred revenue.
  c. Increase in prepaid expenses.

19-18. Suppose a company sold a factory building to its former president in exchange for a $600,000, five-year note. Would this transaction be reported in the company's statement of cash flows? If it would be disclosed, explain how.

19-19. Would the sale of land be considered an investing activity or a financing activity? Explain.

19-20. Suppose an airline sold three aircraft for $6,000,000 and purchased seven others for $22,000,000. How would these transactions be reported on the statement of cash flows?

EXERCISES *Exercise 19-21 Adjustment for Prepaid Expenses.* Armstrong Furniture Stores had $8,000 in prepaid expenses on December 31, 19x2. This account relates to a prepaid insurance bill. During 19x3, the company's insurance expense was $79,000. At the end of 19x3, the balance in prepaid expenses was $6,000.

REQUIRED:

1. What was Armstrong Corporation's total cash payment for insurance during 19x2? Show your calculations.
2. What adjustment will be needed for prepaid expenses if the indirect method is used in preparing Armstrong's statement of cash flows? Explain your answer.

Exercise 19-22 Adjustment for Depreciation. On December 31, 19x7, Aldrin Plastics Company showed $760,000 in Accumulated Depreciation on its balance sheet. During 19x8, the company sold a building with accumulated depreciation of $120,000. At year-end, the balance in the Accumulated Depreciation account was $695,000.

REQUIRED:

1. What adjustment is required for depreciation on Aldrin's 19x8 statement of cash flows:
  a. If the indirect method is used?
  b. If the direct method is used?
2. Explain why your answers differ in (a) and (b) above.

Exercise 19-23 Adjustments for Inventory and Accounts Payable. Collins Wholesalers sells produce to the grocery stores in southern Florida. The beginning and ending balances in the company's Inventory and Accounts Payable accounts during 19x0 were as follows:

	January 1, 19x0		December 31, 19x0
Inventory	$25,000	. . . .	$20,000
Accounts Payable	17,000	. . . .	13,000

Collins' cost of goods sold in 19x0 was reported at $280,000 on its income statement.

REQUIRED: Collins Wholesalers uses the indirect method in preparing the statement of cash flows.

1. What adjustment is required for the change in the inventory balance? Explain your answer. How much produce inventory did the firm purchase in 19x0?
2. Prepare a schedule that computes Collins' total cash payments to its produce suppliers during 19x0.
3. What adjustment is necessary for the change in the accounts payable balance on the 19x0 statement of cash flows? Explain your answer.

Exercise 19-24   Adjustment for Changes in Accounts Receivable. Shepard Advertising Agency's balance in Accounts Receivable increased by $35,000 during 19x9. The firm's service revenue during the year amounted to $640,000.

REQUIRED:

1. If Shepard uses the indirect method, what adjustment will be necessary on its 19x9 statement of cash flows? Explain your answer.
2. If Shepard uses the direct method, what amount will be shown for cash received from clients on the 19x9 statement of cash flows? Explain your answer.
3. Can you determine the amount of cash received from clients during 19x9 which stemmed from services provided during 19x9? If yes, what is the amount? If no, what additional information would you need to determine the amount?

Exercise 19-25   Adjustment for Deferred Taxes. Grissom Company operates a tour bus line in St. Louis. On December 31, 19x2, the company's balance in the Deferred Taxes account was $48,000. On December 31, 19x3 the Deferred Taxes balance was $57,000. The firm's income-tax expense for 19x3 was $128,000.

REQUIRED:

1. If Grissom Company uses the indirect method, what adjustment will be required for deferred taxes? Explain your answer.
2. If Grissom Company uses the direct method, what amount will be shown on the statement of cash flows for cash payments for income taxes?
3. In what section of the statement of cash flows will the items referred to above appear?

Exercise 19-26   Adjustment for Deferred Revenue. Glenn Publishing Company had received $25,000 in advance subscriptions from its magazine customers as of December 31, 19x8. This amount was shown as deferred revenue on the company's balance sheet. The balance in the Deferred Revenue account on December 31, 19x9 was $10,000.

REQUIRED: What adjustment will be necessary when Glenn's controller prepares the company's 19x9 statement of cash flows using the indirect method? Explain your answer.

Exercise 19-27   Direct Exchange Transactions. Cooper Nurseries grows and sells trees and shrubs for landscaping. In May of 19x5, the company acquired 200 acres of land appraised at $350,000 from White Orchards, Inc. In exchange for the land, White Orchards, Inc. received a five-year note from Cooper Nurseries in the amount of $350,000.

REQUIRED: Show how this transaction will be disclosed in the 19x5 statement of cash flows prepared by:

1. Cooper Nurseries.
2. White Orchards, Inc.

Exercise 19-28   Gross versus Net Cash Flows. During 19x7, Schirra Theater Supplies Company engaged in the following transactions.

a. Acquired land for $300,000.
b. Purchased an office building for $200,000.
c. Sold a warehouse for $400,000. The accumulated depreciation on the warehouse was $170,000 and its original cost to Schirra Theater Supplies was $570,000.

REQUIRED: Prepare the investing activities section of Schirra Theater Supplies' cash flow statement.

Exercise 19-29   Understanding the Operating Activities Section of the Statement. Slayton Broadcasting Company operates several radio stations in the midwest. The operating activities section of the company's 19x3 statement of cash flows is shown below.

Net income		$1,480,000
Adjustments to net income to determine the cash provided by		
operations:		
Depreciation expense...............................	$410,000	
Decrease in prepaid expenses	14,000	
Decrease in accrued liabilities	(12,000)	
Decrease in supplies inventory	9,000	
Decrease in accounts payable	(14,000)	
Increase in accounts receivable	(27,000)	
Increase in deferred income taxes......................	10,000	
Total adjustments.................................		390,000
Net cash flow from operating activities		$1,870,000

REQUIRED: A good friend of yours is perplexed by the preceding information. In particular, he is puzzled as to why the changes in account balances result in the indicated adjustments. Write a note to your friend explaining the adjustments on Slayton's statement of cash flows.

Exercise 19-30   Operating Cash Flows; Indirect Method. Ride Electronics Company's most recent financial statements are as follows:

Ride Electronics Company
Comparative Balance Sheets
December 31, 19x7 and 19x6

Assets	19x7	19x6
Current assets:		
Cash	$ 50,000	$ 60,000
Accounts receivable	30,000	40,000
Inventory	140,000	100,000
Prepaid expenses	8,000	10,000
Total current assets	228,000	210,000
Long-lived assets	162,000	100,000
Accumulated depreciation	(30,000)	(20,000)
Total assets	$360,000	$290,000

Liabilities and Owners' Equity

	19x7	19x6
Current liabilities:		
Accounts payable	$ 55,000	$ 50,000
Salaries payable	35,000	45,000
Total current liabilities	90,000	95,000
Owners' equity:		
Common stock	100,000	100,000
Retained earnings	170,000	95,000
Total liabilities and owners' equity	$360,000	$290,000

Ride Electronics Company
Income Statement
December 31, 19x7

Sales	$645,000
Cost of goods sold	400,000
Gross margin	245,000
Less: Selling and administrative expenses	120,000
Income before income taxes	125,000
Income taxes	50,000
Net income	$ 75,000

REQUIRED:

1. Prepare the operating cash flows section of Ride Electronics' statement of cash flows for 19x7. Use the indirect method.
2. Did Ride Electronics declare a cash dividend during 19x7? If so, how much was it?

PROBLEMS *Problem 19-31 Changes in Balance Sheet Accounts; Effect on the Statement of Cash Flows; Indirect Method.* The following changes occurred in Boston Delivery Service's balance sheet accounts during 19x5.

a.   Accounts Receivable, decrease of $15,000.
b.   Accounts Payable, increase of $45,000.
c.   Prepaid Expenses, decrease of $30,000.
d.   Accumulated Depreciation on Vehicles, increase of $100,000.
e.   Buildings, increase of $120,000.
f.   Bonds Payable, increase of $250,000.
g.   Deferred Taxes, increase of $20,000.
h.   Salaries Payable, decrease of $12,000.
i.   Supplies Inventory, increase of $8,000.

REQUIRED: For each of the balance sheet account changes listed above, indicate how the item
will be handled on the company's statement of cash flows. Assume that the indirect method
will be used. Be sure to state which section of the statement will be affected by each item.

Problem 19-32   Determining the Effect of Transactions on the Statement of Cash Flows. The
following transactions relate to Metro Daily, Inc., a large newspaper company serving several
cities on the east coast.

a.   Purchased new presses for $1,000,000 in cash.
b.   Declared and paid cash dividends of $45,000.
c.   Sold stock in a radio broadcasting company. The stock was sold for $120,000 in
     cash, the same amount that had been paid for the stock.
d.   Issued Metro Daily common stock in exchange for a piece of land appraised at
     $250,000.
e.   Paid off an income-tax liability from the prior year, $80,000.
f.   Sold fully depreciated equipment costing $200,000 for $15,000.
g.   Paid deferred income taxes of $12,000.
h.   Purchased newsprint costing $95,000 on account.
i.   Recorded depreciation expense of $75,000.

REQUIRED: Prepare a table with the following headings, and classify each of the transactions
described above. Metro Daily, Inc. uses the direct method.

	Type of Activity			Increase, Decrease, or No Effect	On the Statement of Cash Flows		
Transaction	Operating	Investing	Financing	on Cash	Yes	or	No

Problem 19-33   Straightforward Development of Statement of Cash Flows; Indirect Method.
The following financial statements relate to Alpine Trails Ski Resort: comparative balance
sheets as of December 31, 19x3 and 19x2; income statement for 19x3; and statement of
retained earnings for 19x3.

Alpine Trails Ski Resort
Comparative Balance Sheets
December 31, 19x3 and 19x2
(in thousands)

Assets	19x3	19x2
Current assets:		
Cash	$ 25	$ 22
Marketable securities	10	10
Accounts receivable	130	140
Merchandise inventory	40	35
Prepaid expenses	10	3
Total current assets	215	210
Investment in Coulterton Transit Company Stock	55	45
Facilities and equipment	450	450
Less: Accumulated depreciation	(225)	(175)
Land	653	540
Total assets	$1,148	$1,070

Liabilities and Stockholders' Equity

	19x3	19x2
Current liabilities:		
Accounts payable	$ 80	$ 75
Accrued salaries payable	15	25
Deferred revenue	3	5
Total current liabilities	98	105
Deferred income taxes	20	15
Bonds payable	190	190
Total liabilities	308	310
Stockholders' equity:		
Common stock	270	270
Retained earnings	570	490
Total stockholders' equity	840	760
Total liabilities and stockholders' equity	$1,148	$1,070

Alpine Trails Ski Resort
Income Statement
For the Year Ended December 31, 19x3
(in thousands)

Revenue:		
Slope fees	$340	
Condominium rentals	625	
Sales of merchandise	75	
Total revenue		$1,040
Less: Cost of merchandise sold		50
Gross margin		990

Less: Operating expenses:

Salaries.	$310	
Insurance	80	
Property taxes	35	
Depreciation	50	
Utilities	100	
Maintenance	50	
Advertising.	20	
Administration	170	
Interest on bonds.	15	
Total operating expenses.		830
Income before taxes		160
Income-tax expense.		50
Net income		$ 110

Alpine Trails Ski Resort
Statement of Retained Earnings
For the Year Ended December 31, 19x3
(in thousands)

Retained earnings, December 31, 19x1	$490
Add: Net income for 19x2	110
Subtotal	600
Deduct: Dividends declared in 19x2	30
Retained earnings, December 31, 19x2	$570

Alpine Trails did not buy or sell any facilities or equipment during 19x3.

REQUIRED: Using the indirect method, prepare the company's statement of cash flows for 19x3.

Problem 19-34 *Straightforward Development of Statement of Cash Flows; Using T-Accounts.* Refer to the financial statements given in the preceding problem for Alpine Trails Ski Resort.

REQUIRED: Set up T-accounts to use as an aid in preparing the company's statement of cash flows. Prepare the statement for 19x3.

Problem 19-35 *Straightforward Development of Statement of Cash Flows; Direct Method.* Refer to the financial statements given in problem 19-33 for Alpine Trails Ski Resort.

REQUIRED: Using the direct method, prepare the company's statement of cash flows for 19x3.

Problem 19-36 *Statement of Cash Flows; Indirect Method.* Chunky Chow, Inc. is a manufacturer of dog food. The company's president, Gordon Setter, is considering the acquisition of another small firm that manufacturers cat food. As an aid in making his decision, Setter has asked the company controller, Abby Rivendell, to provide him with a set of financial statements for Chunky Chow, Inc. Rivendell has prepared the following comparative balance sheets and income statement.

Chunky Chow, Inc.
Comparative Balance Sheets
As of December 31, 19x6 and 19x5

Assets	19x6	19x5
Cash .... $	64,000	$ 27,000
Accounts receivable	90,000	132,000
Marketable securities	17,000	17,000
Inventory	100,000	129,000
Prepaid expenses...................................	9,000	10,000
Land	140,000	85,000
Building..	750,000	700,000
Less: Accumulated depreciation	(170,000)	(150,000)
Total assets......................................	$1,000,000	$950,000

Liabilities and Owners' Equity

	19x6	19x5
Accounts payable....................................	$125,000	$100,000
Accrued liabilities...................................	47,000	40,000
Income tax payable	1,000	13,000
Interest payable.....................................	7,000	4,000
Short-term notes payable.............................	12,000	15,000
Long-term notes payable	170,000	180,000
Total liabilities	362,000	352,000
Common stock.....................................	560,000	520,000
Additional paid-in capital	45,000	40,000
Retained earnings...................................	33,000	38,000
Total owners' equity..............................	638,000	598,000
Total liabilities and owners' equity	$1,000,000	$950,000

Chunky Chow, Inc.
Income Statement
For the Year Ended December 31, 19x6

Sales	$600,000
Cost of goods sold...............................	345,000
Gross margin	255,000
Operating expenses...............................	250,000
Operating income................................	5,000
Interest expense	10,000
Net loss..	$ (5,000)

Depreciation expense of $20,000 is included in operating expenses. The company constructed a prefabricated storage building for $50,000. Long-term debt of $10,000 was retired. The company incurred no income tax expense in 19x6, and no dividends were paid.

REQUIRED:

1. Rivendell has asked you, the assistant controller, to prepare Chunky Chow's statement of cash flows for 19x6. Rivendell has a preference for the indirect method.
2. Prepare a memo to Setter explaining why the company's cash balance increased during the year.

Problem 19-37   Statement of Cash Flows; Use of T-Accounts. Refer to the information given in the preceding problem for Chunky Chow, Inc.

REQUIRED: Prepare T-accounts, and prepare Chunky Chow's 19x6 statement of cash flows using this approach.

Problem 19-38   Statement of Cash Flows; Direct Method. Refer to the information given in problem 19-36 for Chunky Chow, Inc.

REQUIRED: Prepare Chunky Chow's 19x6 statement of cash flows using the direct method.

Problem 19-39   Statement of Cash Flows; Indirect Method. Wilderness Products Company manufactures skis and snow shoes. The following financial statements are the company's most recent comparative balance sheets, income statement, and statement of retained earnings.

Wilderness Products Company
Comparative Balance Sheets
December 31, 19x5 and 19x4
(in thousands)

Assets	19x5	19x4
Cash	$ 33	$ 30
U.S. Treasury bills	11	12
Accounts receivable	122	113
Merchandise inventory	80	70
Prepaid expenses	2	5
Total current assets	248	230
Investment in stock of Jasper Corporation	90	70
Building and equipment	480	400
Less: Accumulated depreciation	(255)	(210)
Land	227	200
Total assets	$790	$690

Liabilities and Stockholders' Equity

	19x5	19x4
Current liabilities:		
Accounts payable	$ 63	$ 56
Accrued salaries payable	32	34
Total current liabilities	95	90
Deferred income taxes	25	30
Bonds payable	210	250
Total liabilities	330	370
Stockholders' equity:		
Common stock	130	100
Additional paid-in capital	100	90
Retained earnings	230	130
Total stockholders' equity	460	320
Total liabilities and stockholders' equity	$790	$690

Wilderness Products Company
Income Statement
For the Year Ended December 31, 19x5
(in thousands)

Sales..		$1,100
Cost of goods sold...		600
Gross margin..		500
Less: Selling and administrative expenses:		
Selling..	$100	
Administrative..	200	
Total selling and administrative expenses		300
Income before taxes		200
Income tax expense..		80
Net income		$ 120

Wilderness Products Company
Statement of Retained Earnings
For the Year Ended December 31, 19x5

Retained earnings, December 31, 19x4...............................	$130
Add: Net income for 19x5...	120
Subtotal..	250
Deduct: Dividends declared and paid in 19x5........................	20
Retained earnings, December 31, 19x5..............................	$230

Wilderness Products Company purchased two buildings in 19x5. For one building, the company paid $40,000 in cash. In exchange for the other building, the firm issued Wilderness Products common stock. The building was appraised at $40,000, and the common stock had a par value of $30,000. No other stock was issued during 19x5.

REQUIRED:

1. Use the indirect method to prepare Wilderness Products' statement of cash flows for 19x5.
2. Write a memo to the company's new president explaining the change in cash and cash equivalents.

Problem 19-40   Statement of Cash Flows; Use of T-Accounts. Refer to the information given in the preceding problem for Wilderness Products Company.

REQUIRED: Set up T-accounts, and use this approach to prepare the company's 19x5 statement of cash flows.

Problem 19-41   Statement of Cash Flows; Direct Method. Refer to the information given in problem 19-39 for the Wilderness Products Company.

REQUIRED: Use the direct method to prepare Wilderness Products' statement of cash flows for 19x5.

Problem 19-42 **Statement of Cash Flows.** Odon Company has not yet prepared its statement of cash flows for 19x8. Comparative balance sheets as of December 31, 19x7 and 19x8 and a statement of income and retained earnings for the year ended December 31, 19x8 appear below and on the next page.

Odon Company
Comparative Balance Sheets
(in thousands)

Assets	19x8	19x7
Current assets:		
Cash	$ 60	$ 100
U.S. treasury bills	0	50
Accounts receivable	610	500
Inventory	720	600
Total current assets	1,390	1,250
Long-lived assets:		
Land	80	70
Buildings and equipment	710	600
Less: Accumulated depreciation	(180)	(120)
Patents (less amortization)	105	130
Total long-lived assets	715	680
Total assets	$2,105	$1,930

Liabilities and Owners' Equity

	19x8	19x7
Current liabilities:		
Accounts payable	$ 360	$ 300
Taxes payable	25	20
Notes payable	400	400
Total current liabilities	785	720
Notes payable	200	200
Total liabilities	985	920
Owners' equity:		
Common stock outstanding	830	700
Retained earnings	290	310
Total owners' equity	1,120	1,010
Total liabilities and owners' equity	$2,105	$1,930

The stock dividend shown on the statement of income and retained earnings had no effect on the company's cash flows. The $130,000 stock dividend reduced the Retained Earnings account by $130,000 and increased the Common Stock account by $130,000.

REQUIRED: Prepare a statement of cash flows for 19x8. Use the direct method.
(CMA, adapted)

Odon Company
Statement of Income and Retained Earnings
For the Year Ended December 31, 19x8
(in thousands)

Sales		$2,408
Less: Expenses and interest:		
Cost of goods sold	$1,100	
Salaries and benefits	850	
Heat, light, and power	75	
Depreciation	60	
Property taxes	18	
Patent amortization	25	
Miscellaneous expense	10	
Interest	55	2,193
Net income before income taxes		215
Income taxes		105
Net income		110
Retained earnings, January 1, 19x9		310
		420
Stock dividend		130
Retained earnings, December 31, 19x9		$ 290

CASE **Case 19-43** **Statement of Cash Flows; Partnership.** Presented here are the condensed balance sheets of Public Relations Associates (PRA) as of December 31, 19x6 and 19x5, and the condensed income statement for the year ended December 31, 19x6. PRA, a public relations consulting firm, is a partnership owned by Michael Burr and Martin Cox.

Public Relations Associates
Condensed Balance Sheets
December 31, 19x6 and 19x5

Assets	19x6	19x5	Net Change: Increase (Decrease)
Cash	$ 326,000	$ 140,000	$186,000
Accounts receivable	223,000	184,000	39,000
Investment in King, Inc. capital stock	275,000	233,000	42,000
Property and equipment	635,000	550,000	85,000
Less: Accumulated depreciation	(95,000)	(65,000)	(30,000)
Land	76,000	78,000	(2,000)
Total assets	$1,440,000	$1,120,000	$320,000
Liabilities and Partners' Equity			
Accounts payable and accrued expenses	$ 160,000	$ 135,000	$ 25,000
Mortgage payable	125,000	135,000	(10,000)
Partners' equity	1,155,000	850,000	305,000
Total liabilities and partners' equity	$1,440,000	$1,120,000	$320,000

Public Relations Associates
Condensed Income Statement
For the Year Ended December 31, 19x6

Fee revenue	$1,332,000
Operating expenses	970,000
Operating income	362,000
Dividends from King, Inc.	88,000
Net income	$ 450,000

Additional Information

● On December 31, 19x5, partners' capital and profit sharing percentages were as
follows:

	Capital	Profit sharing %
Burr	$510,000	60%
Cox	340,000	40%
Total	$850,000	

● On January 1, 19x6, the partners admitted Jennifer Davis to the partnership for a
cash payment of $170,000 to Public Relations Associates. In addition, Davis paid a
$100,000 cash bonus directly to Burr and Cox. This amount was divided $60,000 to
Burr and $40,000 to Cox. The new profit sharing arrangement is as follows:

Burr	50%
Cox	30%
Davis	20%

● On July 1, 19x6, Public Relations Associates purchased an office computer for
$85,000, which included $10,000 for sales tax, delivery, and installation. There were
no dispositions of property and equipment during 19x6.

● Partners' withdrawals for 19x6 were as follows:

Burr	$140,000
Cox	100,000
Davis	75,000
	$315,000

REQUIRED: Prepare a statement of cash flows for Public Relations Associates for the year ended
December 31, 19x6. Use the indirect method.
(CPA, adapted)

Glossary

Accelerated cost recovery system (ACRS)   The depreciation schedule specified by the United States tax code.

Acceptance or rejection decision   A decision as to whether or not a particular capital investment proposal should be accepted.

Account-classification method (also called account analysis)   A cost-estimation method involving a careful examination of the ledger accounts for the purpose of classifying each cost as variable, fixed, or semivariable.

Accounting rate of return   A percentage formed by taking a project's average incremental revenue minus its average incremental expenses (including depreciation and income taxes) and dividing by the project's initial investment.

Accurate information   Precise and correct data.

Activity   A measure of an organization's output of goods or services.

Activity accounting   The collection of financial or operational performance information about significant activities in the enterprise.

Activity base (or cost driver)   A measure of an organization's activity that is used as a basis for specifying cost behavior. The activity base also is used to compute a predetermined overhead rate. The current trend is to refer to the activity base as a volume-based cost driver.

Activity-based costing (ABC)   See *transaction-based costing.*

Actual costing   A product-costing system in which actual direct-material, direct-labor, and *actual* manufacturing-overhead costs are added to Work-in-Process Inventory.

Actual manufacturing overhead   The actual costs incurred during an accounting period for manufacturing overhead. Includes actual indirect material, indirect labor, and other manufacturing costs.

Actual overhead rate   The rate at which overhead costs are actually incurred during an accounting period. Calculated as follows: actual manufacturing overhead ÷ actual cost driver (or activity base).

Administrative costs   All costs associated with the management of the organization as a whole.

After-tax cash flow   The cash flow expected after all tax implications have been taken into account.

After-tax net income   An organization's net income after its income-tax expense is subtracted.

Aggregate (or total) productivity   Total output divided by total input.

Allocation base   A measure of activity, physical characteristic, or economic characteristic, which is associated with a responsibility center, and which is the cost objective in an allocation process.

Annuity   A series of equivalent cash flows.

Applied manufacturing overhead   The amount of manufacturing-overhead costs added to Work-in-Process Inventory during an accounting period.

Appraisal costs   Costs of determining whether defective products exist.

Attention-directing role   The function of managerial-accounting information in pointing out to managers issues that need their attention.

Automated material-handling system (AMHS)   Computer-controlled equipment that automatically moves materials, parts, and products from one production stage to another.

Average cost per unit   The total cost of producing a particular quantity of product divided by the number of units produced.

Avoidable expenses   Expenses that will no longer be incurred if a particular action is taken.

Batch manufacturing   High-volume production of several product lines that differ in some important ways but are nearly identical in others.

Before-tax income   An organization's income before its income-tax expense is subtracted.

Bill of materials   A list of all of the materials needed to manufacture a product or product component.

Break-even point   The volume of activity at which an organization's revenues and expenses are equal. May be measured either in units or in sales dollars.

Budget   A detailed plan, expressed in quantitative terms, that specifies how resources will be acquired and used during a specified period of time.

Budget administration   The procedures used to prepare a budget, secure its approval, and disseminate it to the people who need to know its contents.

Budgetary slack   The difference between the budgetary projection provided by an individual and his or her best estimate of the item being projected. (For example, the difference between a supervisor's expected departmental utility cost and his or her budgetary projection for utilities.)

Budget committee   A group of top-management personnel who advise the budget director during the preparation of the budget.

Budget director (or chief budget officer)   The individual designated to be in charge of preparing an organization's budget.

Budgeted balance sheet   A planned balance sheet showing the expected end-of-period balances for the organization's assets, liabilities, and owners' equity, assuming that planned operations are carried out.

Budgeted financial statements (or pro forma financial statements)   A set of planned financial statements showing what the organization's overall financial condition is expected to be at the end of the budget period if planned operations are carried out.

Budgeted income statement   A planned income statement showing the expected revenue and expenses for the budget period, assuming that planned operations are carried out.

Budgeting system   The set of procedures used to develop a budget.

Budget manual   A set of written instructions that specifies who will provide budgetary data, when and in what form the data will be provided, how the master budget will be prepared and approved, and who should receive the various schedules comprising the budget.

Budget period   The time period covered by a budget.

By-product   A joint product with very little value relative to the other joint products.

CAD/CAM system   See *computer-aided design* and *computer-aided manufacturing*.

Capital budget   A long-term budget that shows planned acquisition and disposal of capital assets, such as land, buildings, and equipment.

Capital-budgeting decision   A decision involving cash flows beyond the current year.

Capital-intensive   A production process accomplished largely by machinery.

Capital-rationing decision   A decision in which management chooses which of several investment proposals to accept to make the best use of limited investment funds.

Capital turnover   Sales revenue divided by invested capital.

Cash disbursements budget   A schedule detailing the expected cash payments during the budget period.

Cash equivalents   Short-term, highly liquid investments that are treated as equivalent to cash in the preparation of the statement of cash flows.

Cash provided by (or used by) operations   The difference between the cash receipts and cash disbursements that are related to operating activities.

Cash receipts budget   A schedule detailing the expected cash collections during the budget period.

Certified management accountant (CMA)   An accountant who has earned professional certification in managerial accounting.

Coefficient of determination   A statistical measure of goodness of fit; a measure of how closely a regression line fits the data on which it is based.

Committed cost   A cost that results from an organization's ownership or use of facilities and its basic organization structure.

Common costs   Costs incurred to benefit more than one organizational segment.

Common-size financial statements   Financial statements prepared in terms of percentages of a base amount.

Comparative financial statements   Financial statements showing the results of two successive years.

Competitive bidding   A situation where two or more companies submit bids (prices) for a product, service, or project to a potential buyer.

Computer-aided design (CAD) system   Computer software used by engineers in the design of a product.

Computer-aided manufacturing (CAM) system   Any production process in which computers are used to help control production.

Computer information system (CIS)   A system consisting of a computer and peripheral devices (hardware), computer programs (software), data, and personnel to operate the system and assist its users.

Computer-integrated manufacturing (CIM) system   The most advanced form of automated manufacturing, in which virtually all parts of the production process are accomplished by computer-controlled machines and automated material-handling equipment.

Computer-numerically-controlled (CNC) machines   Stand-alone machines controlled by a computer via a numerical, machine-readable code.

Constraints   Algebraic expressions of limitations faced by a firm, such as those limiting its productive resources.

Contribution income statement   An income statement on which fixed and variable expenses are separated.

Contribution margin   Sales revenue minus variable expenses. The amount of sales revenue, which is left to cover fixed expenses and profit after paying variable expenses.

Contribution margin per unit   The difference between the unit sales price and the unit variable expense. The amount that each unit contributes to covering fixed expenses and profit.

Contribution-margin ratio   The unit contribution margin divided by the sales price per unit. May also be expressed in percentage form; then it is called the contribution-margin percentage.

Contribution margin, total   Total sales revenue less total variable expenses.

Control factor unit   A measure of work or activity used in work measurement.

Controllability   The extent to which managers are able to control or influence a cost or cost variance.

Controllable cost   A cost that is subject to the control or substantial influence of a particular individual.

Controller (or comptroller)   The top managerial and financial accountant in an organization. Supervises the accounting department and assists management at all levels in interpreting and using managerial-accounting information.

Controlling   Ensuring that the organization operates in the intended manner and achieves its goals.

Conversion cost   Direct-labor cost plus manufacturing-overhead cost.

Cost Accounting Standards   Cost-accounting procedures specified by the Cost Accounting Standards Board, formerly an agency of the federal government.

Cost Accounting Standards Board (CASB)   A federal agency chartered by Congress in 1970 to develop cost-accounting standards for large government contractors. The agency was abolished by Congress in 1980, since its work was largely completed.

Cost-accounting system   Part of the basic accounting system that accumulates cost data for use in both managerial and financial accounting.

Cost allocation   The process of assigning costs in a cost pool to the appropriate cost objectives. Also see *cost distribution.*

Cost behavior   The relationship between cost and activity.

Cost center   A responsibility center whose manager is accountable for its costs.

Cost distribution (sometimes called cost allocation)   The first step in assigning manufacturing-overhead costs. Overhead costs are assigned to all departmental overhead centers.

Cost driver   An event or activity that results in the incurrence of costs.

Cost estimation   The process of determining how a particular cost behaves.

Cost management system   A management planning and control system that measures the cost of significant activities, identifies non-value-added costs, and identifies activities that will improve organizational performance.

Cost objectives   Responsibility centers, products, or services to which costs are assigned.

Cost of capital   The cost of acquiring resources for an organization, either through debt or through the issuance of stock.

Cost of goods manufactured   The total cost of direct labor, direct material, and overhead transferred from Work-in-Process Inventory to Finished-Goods Inventory during an accounting period.

Cost of goods sold   The expense measured by the cost of the finished goods sold during a period of time.

Cost performance reporting (CPR)   A cost and project control system used extensively in government.

Cost-plus pricing   A pricing approach in which the price is equal to cost plus a markup.

Cost pool   A collection of costs to be assigned to a set of cost objectives.

Cost prediction   Forecast of cost at a particular level of activity.

Cost structure   The relative proportions of an organization's fixed and variable costs.

Cost variance   The difference between actual and standard cost.

Cost-volume-profit (CVP) analysis   A study of the relationships between sales volume, expenses, revenue, and profit.

Cost-volume-profit (CVP) graph   A graphical expression of the relationships between sales volume, expenses, revenue, and profit.

Cross-elasticity   The extent to which a change in a product's price affects the demand for substitute products.

Curvilinear cost   A cost with a curved line for its graph.

Customer-acceptance measures   The extent to which a firm's customers perceive its product to be of high quality.

Cycle time   See *throughput time.*

Data-base management system   General-purpose software designed to allow the computer information system to make the most efficient use of its various data bases.

Decentralization   A form of organization in which subunit managers are given authority to make substantive decisions.

Decision making   Choosing between alternatives.

Decision-support system   A computer-based system that is designed to assist managers in making certain types of decisions. Includes access to one or more data bases, decision methods pertinent to the decisions facing the user, and various ways of displaying the results.

Decision variables   The variables in a linear program about which a decision is to be made.

Demand curve   A graph of the relationship between sales price and the quantity of units sold.

Departmental overhead center   Any department to which overhead costs are assigned via overhead cost distribution.

Departmental overhead rate   An overhead rate calculated for a single production department.

Departmental production report   The key document in a process-costing system. This report summarizes the physical flow of units, equivalent units of production, cost per equivalent unit, and analysis of total departmental costs.

Dependent variable   A variable whose value depends on other variables, called *independent variables.*

Depreciation tax shield   The reduction in a firm's income-tax expense due to the depreciation expense associated with a depreciable asset.

Differential cost   The difference in a cost item under two decision alternatives.

Direct cost   A cost that can be traced to a particular department or other subunit of an organization.

Direct-exchange (or noncash) transaction A significant investing or financing transaction involving accounts other than cash, such as a transaction where land is obtained in exchange for the issuance of capital stock.

Directing operations Running the organization on a day-to-day basis.

Direct labor The costs of compensating employees who work directly on the firm's product. Should include wages, salary, and associated fringe benefits.

Direct-labor budget A schedule showing the amount and cost of direct labor to be used in production of services or goods during the budget period.

Direct-labor efficiency variance The difference between actual and standard hours of direct labor multiplied by the standard hourly labor rate.

Direct-labor rate variance The difference between actual and standard hourly labor rate, multiplied by the actual hours of direct labor used.

Direct-material budget A schedule showing the number of units and the cost of material to be purchased and used during the budget period.

Direct-material price variance (or purchase price variance) The difference between actual and standard price multiplied by the actual quantity of material purchased.

Direct-material quantity variance The difference between actual and standard quantity of materials allowed, given actual output, multiplied by the standard price.

Direct materials Materials that are physically incorporated in the finished product.

Direct method (of preparing the statement of cash flows) A method of preparing the operating activities section of the statement of cash flows. A cash-basis income statement is constructed in which operating cash disbursements are subtracted from operating cash receipts.

Direct method (of service department cost allocation) A method of service department cost allocation in which service department costs are allocated directly to the production departments.

Discounted-cash-flow analysis An analysis of an investment proposal that takes into account the time value of money.

Discount rate The interest rate used in computing the present value of a cash flow.

Discretionary cost A cost that results from a discretionary management decision to spend a particular amount of money.

Distress market price An artificially low price in a depressed market.

Distribution cost The cost of storing and transporting finished goods for sale.

Dual cost allocation An approach to service department cost allocation in which variable costs are allocated in proportion to short-term usage and fixed costs are allocated in proportion to long-term usage.

Economic order quantity (EOQ) The order size that minimizes inventory ordering and holding costs.

Engineered cost A cost that results from a definitive physical relationship with the activity measure.

Engineering method A cost-estimation method in which a detailed study is made of the process that results in cost incurrence.

Equivalent unit A measure of the amount of productive effort applied to a physical unit of production. For example, a physical unit that is 50 percent completed represents one-half of an equivalent unit.

Estimated manufacturing overhead   The amount of manufacturing-overhead cost expected for a specified period of time. Used as the numerator in computing the predetermined overhead rate.

Expected value   The sum of the possible values for a random variable, each weighted by its probability.

Expense   The consumption of assets for the purpose of generating revenue.

External failure costs   Costs incurred because defective products have been sold.

Feasible region   The possible values for the decision variables which are not ruled out by the constraints.

FIFO (first-in, first-out) method   A method of process costing in which the cost assigned to the beginning work-in-process inventory is not added to current-period production costs. The cost per equivalent unit calculated under FIFO relates to the current period only.

Financial accounting   The use of accounting information for reporting to parties outside the organization.

Financial budget   A schedule that outlines how an organization will acquire financial resources during the budget period (for example, through borrowing or sale of capital stock).

Financial leverage   The concept that a relatively small increase in income can provide a proportionately much larger increase in return to the common stockholders.

Financial planning model   A set of budgetary relationships expressed in general mathematical terms. The model can be run many times on a computer to determine the financial results from various combinations of assumptions and predictions.

Financing activities   Transactions involving the company's debt or equity capital.

Finished goods   Completed products awaiting sale.

Fixed cost   A cost that does not change in total as activity changes.

Fixed-overhead budget variance   The difference between actual and budgeted fixed overhead.

Fixed-overhead volume variance   The difference between budgeted and applied fixed overhead.

Flexible budget   A budget that is valid for a range of activity.

Flexible manufacturing system (FMS)   A series of manufacturing machines, controlled and integrated by a computer, which is designed to perform a series of manufacturing operations automatically.

FMS cell   A group of machines and personnel within a flexible manufacturing system (FMS).

Full (or absorption) cost   A product's variable cost plus an allocated portion of fixed overhead.

Goal congruence   A meshing of objectives, where the managers throughout an organization strive to achieve the goals set by top management.

Goodness of fit   The closeness with which a regression line fits the data upon which it is based.

High-low method   A cost-estimation method in which a cost line is fit using exactly two data points—the high and low activity levels.

Horizontal analysis   An analysis of the year-to-year change in each financial statement item.

Hurdle rate   The minimum desired rate of return used in a discounted-cash-flow analysis.

Hybrid product-costing system   A system that incorporates features from two or more alternative product-costing systems, such as job-order and process costing.

Idle time   Unproductive time spent by employees due to factors beyond their control, such as power outages and machine breakdowns.

Imperfect competition   A market in which a single producer can affect the market price.

Incremental cost   The amount by which the cost of one action exceeds that of another. See also *differential cost.*

Independent variable   The variable upon which the estimate is based in least-squares regression analysis.

Indirect cost   A cost that cannot be traced to a particular department.

Indirect labor   All costs of compensating employees who do not work directly on the firm's product but who are necessary for production to occur.

Indirect-labor budget   A schedule showing the amount and cost of indirect labor to be used during the budget period.

Indirect materials   Materials that either are required for the production process to occur but do not become an integral part of the finished product, or are consumed in production but are insignificant in cost.

Indirect method (or reconciliation method)   A method of preparing the operating activities section of the statement of cash flows, in which the analyst begins with net income. Then adjustments are made to convert from an accrual-basis income statement to a cash-basis income statement.

Information overload   The provision of so much information that, due to human limitations in processing information, managers cannot effectively use it.

In-process quality controls   Procedures designed to assess product quality before production is completed.

Inspection time   The time spent on quality inspections of raw materials, partially completed products, or finished goods.

Internal auditor   An accountant who reviews the accounting procedures, records, and reports in both the controller's and treasurer's areas of responsibility.

Internal control system   The set of procedures designed to ensure that an organization's employees act in a legal, ethical, and responsible manner.

Internal failure costs   Costs of correcting defects found prior to product sale.

Internal rate of return   The discount rate required for an asset's net present value to be exactly zero.

Inventoriable costs   Costs that are incurred to purchase or manufacture goods. Also see *product costs.*

Inventoriable goods   Goods that can be stored before sale, such as durable goods, mining products, and some agricultural products.

Inventory budgets   Schedules that detail the amount and cost of finished-goods, work-in-process, and direct-material inventories expected at the end of the budget period.

Investing activities   Transactions involving the extension or collection of loans, acquisition or disposal of investments, and purchase or sale of productive, long-lived assets.

Investment center   A responsibility center whose manager is accountable for its profit and for the capital invested to generate that profit.

Investment opportunity rate   The rate of return the organization can earn on its best alternative investments that are of equivalent risk.

Job-cost sheet   A document on which the costs of direct material, direct labor, and manufacturing overhead are recorded for a particular production job or batch. The job-cost sheet is a subsidiary ledger account for the Work-in-Process Inventory account in the general ledger.

Job-order costing system   A product-costing system in which costs are assigned to batches or job orders of production. Used by firms that produce relatively small numbers of dissimilar products.

Joint cost   The cost incurred in a joint production process before the joint products become identifiable as separate products.

Joint production process   A production process that results in two or more joint products.

Joint products   The outputs of a joint production process.

Joint rate-efficiency variance   Difference between actual and standard rates multiplied by the difference between the actual hours used and the standard hours allowed (given actual output).

Just-in-time (JIT) costing   A simplified method of tracking cost flows in a just-in-time production environment.

Just-in-time inventory and production management (JIT) system   A comprehensive inventory and manufacturing control system in which no materials are purchased and no products are manufactured until they are needed.

Labor-intensive   A production process accomplished largely by manual labor.

Lead time   The time required to receive inventory after it has been ordered.

Learning curve   A graphical expression of the decline in the average labor time required per unit as cumulative output increases.

Least-square regression method   A cost-estimation method in which the cost line is fit to the data by statistical analysis. The method minimizes the sum of the squared deviations between the cost line and the data points.

Line positions   Positions held by managers who are directly involved in providing the goods or services that constitute the organization's primary goals.

Management by exception   A managerial technique in which only significant deviations from expected performance are investigated.

Management by objectives (MBO)   The process of designating the objectives of each subunit in the organization and planning for the achievement of those objectives. Managers at all levels participate in setting goals, which they then will strive to achieve.

Managerial accounting   Part of an organization's management-information system, which provides accounting and other quantitative data to users inside the organization.

Manufacturing   The process of converting raw materials into finished products.

Manufacturing cycle efficiency (MCE)   The ratio of process time to the sum of processing time, inspection time, waiting time, and move time.

Manufacturing overhead   All manufacturing costs other than direct-material and direct-labor costs.

Manufacturing-overhead variance   The difference between actual overhead cost and the amount specified in the flexible budget.

Marketing cost   The cost incurred in selling goods or services. Includes order-getting costs and order-filling or distribution costs.

Marginal cost   The extra cost incurred in producing one additional unit of output.

Marginal cost curve   A graph of the relationship between the change in total cost and the quantity produced and sold.

Marginal revenue curve   A graph of the relationship between the change in total revenue and the quantity sold.

Master budget (or profit plan)   A comprehensive set of budgets that covers all phases of an organization's operations for a specified period of time.

Material requirements planning (MRP)   An operations-management tool that assists managers in scheduling production in each stage of a complex manufacturing process.

Material requisition form   A document upon which the production department supervisor requests the release of raw materials for production.

Merchandise cost   The cost of acquiring goods for resale. Includes purchasing and transportation costs.

Merchandising   The business of acquiring finished goods for resale, either in a wholesale or retail operation.

Mixed cost   See *semivariable cost*.

Move time   The time spent moving raw materials, subassemblies, or finished products from one production operation to another.

Multiple regression   A statistical method in which a linear (straight-line) relationship is estimated between a dependent variable and two or more independent variables.

Multistage cost allocation   The three-step process in which costs are assigned to products or services: (1) cost distribution (or allocation), (2) service department cost allocation, and (3) cost application.

Net present value   The present value of a project's future cash flows less the cost of the initial investment.

Net realizable value   A joint product's final sales value less any separable costs incurred after the split-off point.

Net realizable value method   A method in which joint costs are allocated to the joint products in proportion to the net realizable value of each joint product.

Nominal dollars   The measure used for an actual cash flow that is observed.

Nominal interest rate   The real interest rate plus an additional premium to compensate investors for inflation.

Non-value-added costs   The costs of activities that can be eliminated without deterioration of product quality, performance, or perceived value.

Normal-costing system   A product-costing system in which actual direct-material, actual direct-labor, and *applied* manufacturing-overhead costs are added to Work-in-Process Inventory.

Normal equations   The equations used to solve for the parameters of a regression equation.

Normalized overhead rate   An overhead rate calculated over a relatively long time period.

Objective function   An algebraic expression of the firm's goal.

Off-line quality control   Activities during the product design and engineering phases which will improve the manufacturability of the product, reduce production costs, and ensure high quality.

Oligopolistic market (or oligopoly)   A market with a small number of sellers competing among themselves.

Operating activities   All activities that are not investing or financing activities. Generally speaking, operating activities include all cash transactions that are involved in the determination of net income.

Operating expenses   The costs incurred to produce and sell services, such as transportation, repair, financial, or medical services.

Operating leverage   The extent to which an organization uses fixed costs in its cost structure. The greater the proportion of fixed costs, the greater the operating leverage.

Operating leverage factor   A measure of operating leverage at a particular sales volume. Computed by dividing an organization's total contribution margin by its net income.

Operational budgets   A set of budgets that specifies how operations will be carried out to produce the organization's services or goods.

Operation costing   A hybrid of job-order and process costing. Direct material is accumulated by batch of products using job-order costing methods. Conversion costs are accumulated by department and assigned to product units by process-costing methods.

Opportunity cost   The potential benefit given up when the choice of one action precludes selection of a different action.

Outlier   A data point that falls far away from the other points in the scatter diagram and is not representative of the data.

Out-of-pocket costs   Costs incurred that require the expenditure of cash or other assets.

Overapplied overhead   The amount by which the period's applied manufacturing overhead exceeds actual manufacturing overhead.

Overhead application (or absorption)   The third step in assigning manufacturing-overhead costs. All costs associated with each production department are assigned to the product units on which the department has worked.

Overhead budget   A schedule showing the cost of overhead expected to be incurred in the production of services or goods during the budget period.

Overhead cost performance report   A report showing the actual and flexible-budget cost levels for each overhead item, together with variable-overhead spending and efficiency variances and fixed-overhead budget variances.

Overtime premium   The extra compensation paid to an employee who works beyond the normal period of time.

Padding the budget   The process of building budgetary slack into the budget by overestimating expenses and underestimating revenue.

Participative budgeting   The process of involving people throughout an organization in the budgeting process.

Payback period   The amount required for a project's after-tax cash inflows to accumulate to an amount that covers the initial investment.

Penetration pricing   Setting a low initial price for a new product in order to penetrate the market deeply and gain a large and broad market share.

Percentage of completion   The extent to which a physical unit of production has been finished with respect to direct material or conversion activity.

Perfect competition   A market in which the price does not depend on the quantity sold by any one producer.

Perfection (or ideal) standard   The cost expected under perfect or ideal operating conditions.

Performance report   A report showing the budgeted and actual amounts of key financial results for a person or subunit.

Period costs   Costs that are expensed during the time period in which they are incurred.

Physical unit   An actual item of production, fully or partially completed.

Physical units method   A method in which joint costs are allocated to the joint products in proportion to their physical quantities.

Planning   Developing a detailed financial and operational description of anticipated operations.

Plantwide overhead rate   An overhead rate calculated by averaging manufacturing-overhead costs for the entire production facility.

Postaudit (or reappraisal)   A systematic follow-up of a capital-budgeting decision to see how the project turned out.

Practical (or attainable) standard   The cost expected under normal operating conditions.

Predatory pricing   An illegal practice in which the price of a product is set low temporarily to broaden demand. Then the product's supply is restricted and the price is raised.

Predetermined overhead rate   The rate used to apply manufacturing overhead to Work-in-Process Inventory, calculated as follows: estimated manufacturing overhead cost ÷ estimated amount of cost driver (or activity base).

Present value   The economic value now of a cash flow that will occur in the future.

Prevention costs   Costs of preventing defective products.

Price discrimination   The illegal practice of quoting different prices for the same product or service to different buyers, when the price differences are not justified by cost differences.

Price elasticity   The impact of price changes on sales volume.

Price taker   A firm whose product or service is determined totally by the market.

Prime cost   The cost of direct material and direct labor.

Process-costing system   A product-costing system in which production costs are averaged over a large number of product units. Used by firms that produce large numbers of nearly identical products.

Process time   The amount of time during which a product actually is being worked on.

Product-costing system   The process of accumulating the costs of a production process and assigning them to the products that comprise the organization's output.

Product costs   Costs that are associated with goods for sale until the time period during which the products are sold, at which time the costs become expenses. See also *inventoriable costs.*

Production budget   A schedule showing the number of units of services or goods that are to be produced during the budget period.

Production department   A department in which work is done directly on the firm's products.

Product life-cycle costing   The accumulation of costs that occur over the entire life cycle of a product.

Profitability index (or excess present value index)   The present value of a project's future cash flows (exclusive of the initial investment), divided by the initial investment.

Profit center   A responsibility center whose manager is accountable for its profit.

Profit plan (or master budget)   A comprehensive set of budgets that cover all phases of an organization's operations during a specified period of time.

Profit-volume graph   A graphical expression of the relationship between profit and sales volume.

Project costing   The process of assigning costs to projects, cases, contracts, programs, or missions in nonmanufacturing organizations.

Proration   The process of allocating underapplied or overapplied overhead to Work-in-Process Inventory, Finished-Goods Inventory, and Cost of Goods Sold.

Pull method   A method of coordinating stages in a production process. Goods are produced in each stage of manufacturing only as they are needed in the next stage.

Pure rate variance   Difference between actual and standard rates multiplied by the standard hours allowed (given actual output).

Qualitative characteristics   Factors in a decision analysis that cannot be expressed easily in numerical terms.

Quick assets   Cash, marketable securities, accounts receivable, and current notes receivable. Excludes inventories and prepaid expenses, which are current assets but not quick assets.

Raw and in-process inventory   The inventory account into which raw-material costs are entered under a JIT costing system.

Raw material   Material entered into a manufacturing process.

Real dollars   A measure that reflects an adjustment for the purchasing power of the monetary unit.

Real interest rate   The underlying interest rate in the economy, which includes compensation to an investor for the time value of money and the risk of the investment.

Reciprocal service   The mutual provision of service by two service departments to each other.

Reciprocal-services method   A method of service department cost allocation which accounts for the mutual provision of reciprocal services among all service departments.

Regression line   A line fit to a set of data points using least-squares regression.

Relative sales value method   A method in which joints costs are allocated to the joint products in proportion to their total sales values at the split-off point.

Relevant information   Data that are pertinent to a decision.

Relevant range   The range of activity within which management expects the organization to operate.

Repetitive production   A production environment in which large numbers of identical or very similar products are manufactured in a continuous flow.

Research and development costs   Costs incurred to develop and test new products or services.

Residual income   Profit minus an imputed interest charge, which is equal to the invested capital times an imputed interest rate.

Responsibility accounting   Tools and concepts used by managerial accountants to measure the performance of an organization's people and subunits.

Responsibility center   A subunit in an organization whose manager is held accountable for specified financial results of its activities.

Return on investment (ROI)   Income divided by invested capital.

Return-on-investment pricing   A cost-plus pricing method in which the markup is determined by the amount necessary for the company to earn a target rate of return on investment.

Revenue center   A responsibility center whose manager is accountable for its revenue.

Rolling budget (also revolving or continuous budget)   A budget that is continually updated by adding another incremental time period and dropping the most recently completed period.

Sales forecasting   The process of predicting sales of services or goods. The initial step in preparing a master budget.

Safety margin   Difference between budgeted sales revenue and break-even sales revenue.

Safety stock   Extra inventory consumed during periods of above-average usage in a setting with fluctuating demand.

Sales budget   A schedule that shows the expected sales of services or goods during the budget period, expressed in both monetary terms and units.

Sales margin   Income divided by sales revenue.

Sales mix   Relative proportion of sales of each of an organization's multiple products.

Sales-price variance   The difference between actual and expected unit sales price multiplied by the actual quantity of units sold.

Sales-volume variance   The difference between actual sales volume and budgeted sales volume multiplied by the budgeted unit contribution margin.

Scatter diagram   A set of plotted cost observations at various activity levels.

Schedule of cost of goods manufactured   A detailed listing of the manufacturing costs incurred during an accounting period and showing the change in Work-in-Process Inventory.

Schedule of cost of goods sold   A detailed schedule showing the Cost of Goods Sold and the change in Finished-Goods Inventory during an accounting period.

Segmented income statement   A financial statement showing the income for an organization and its major segments (subunits).

Selling and administrative expense budget   A schedule showing the planned amounts of selling and administrative expenses during the budget period.

Selling costs   Costs of obtaining and filling sales orders, such as advertising costs, compensation of sales personnel, and product promotion costs.

Semivariable (or mixed) cost   A cost with both a fixed and a variable component.

Sensitivity analysis   A technique for determining what would happen in a decision analysis if a key prediction or assumption proves to be wrong.

Separable processing cost   Cost incurred on a joint product after the split-off point of a joint production process.

Sequential production process   A manufacturing operation in which partially completed products pass in sequence through two or more production departments.

Service department   A subunit in an organization that is not involved directly in producing the organization's output of goods or services.

Service department cost allocation   The second step in assigning manufacturing overhead costs. All costs associated with a service department are assigned to the departments that use the services it produces.

Service firm   A firm engaged in production of a service that is consumed as it is produced, such as air transportation service or medical service.

Simple regression   A regression analysis based on a single independent variable.

Skimming pricing   Setting a high initial price for a new product in order to reap short-run profits. Over time, the price is reduced gradually.

Source document   A document that is used as the basis for an accounting entry. Examples include material requisition forms and direct-labor time tickets.

Split-off point   The point in a joint production process at which the joint products become identifiable as separate products.

Staff positions   Positions held by managers who are only indirectly involved in achieving the organization's primary goals.

Standard cost   A predetermined cost for the production of goods or services, which serves as a benchmark against which to compare the actual cost.

Standard-costing system   A cost-control and product-costing system in which cost variances are computed and production costs are entered into Work-in-Process Inventory at their standard amounts.

Standard labor quantity   The number of labor hours normally needed to manufacture one unit of product.

Standard labor rate   Total hourly cost of compensation, including fringe benefits.

Standard material price   The total delivered cost, after subtracting any purchase discounts taken.

Standard material quantity   The total amount of material normally required to produce a finished product, including allowances for normal waste and inefficiency.

Standard quantity allowed   The standard quantity per unit of output multiplied by the number of units of actual output.

Statement of cash flows   A major financial statement that shows the change in an organization's total cash and cash equivalents and explains that change in terms of the organization's operating, investing, and financing activities during the period.

Static budget   A budget that is valid for only one planned activity level.

Statistical control chart   A plot of cost variances across time, with a comparison to a statistically determined critical value.

Step-down method   A method of service department cost allocation in which service department costs are allocated first to service departments and then to production departments.

Step-fixed cost   A cost that remains fixed over wide ranges of activity, but jumps to a different amount for activity levels outside that range.

Step-variable cost   A cost that is nearly variable, but increases in small steps instead of continuously.

Storage time   The time during which raw materials or finished products are stored in stock.

Strategic cost analysis   A broad-based managerial-accounting analysis that supports strategic management systems.

Sunk cost   A cost that was incurred in the past and cannot be altered by any current or future decision.

System   An integrated structure designed to accomplish a stated purpose and consisting of a set of inputs, a process, and a set of outputs.

Target costing   The pricing of a new product before it is designed, to ensure that it will be competitive. Then the product is designed so that it can be produced at a cost that makes the chosen price feasible.

Target net profit (or income)   The profit level set as management's objective.

Task analysis   Setting standards by analyzing the production process.

Throughput-based costing system   See *volume-based costing system.*

Throughput time   The average amount of time required to convert raw materials into finished goods ready to be shipped to customers.

Time and material pricing   A cost-plus pricing approach that includes components for labor cost and material cost, plus markups on either or both of these cost components.

Timely information   Data that are available in time for use in a decision analysis.

Time ticket   A document that records the amount of time an employee spends on each production job.

Total contribution margin   See *contribution margin, total.*

Total quality control (TQC)   A product-quality program in which the objective is complete elimination of product defects.

Transaction-based costing system   A product-costing system in which multiple cost drivers are identified, and costs of activities are assigned to products on the basis of the number of transactions they generate for the various cost drivers.

Transfer price   The price at which products or services are transferred between two divisions in an organization.

Transferred-in costs   Costs assigned to partially completed products that are transferred into one production department from a prior department.

Treasurer   An accountant in a staff position who is responsible for managing the organization's relationships with investors and creditors and maintaining custody of the organization's cash, investments, and other assets.

Trend analysis   A comparison across time of three or more observations of a particular financial item, such as net income.

Underapplied overhead   The amount by which the period's actual manufacturing overhead exceeds applied manufacturing overhead.

Unit contribution margin   Sales price minus the unit variable cost.

Variable cost   A cost that changes in total in proportion to changes in the organization's activity.

Variable-overhead efficiency variance   The difference between actual and standard hours of the activity base (e.g., machine hours) multiplied by the standard variable-overhead rate.

Variable-overhead spending variance   The difference between actual variable-overhead cost and the product of the standard variable-overhead rate and actual hours of the activity base (e.g., machine hours).

Vertical analysis   An analysis of the relationships between various financial items on a particular financial statement. Generally presented in terms of common-size financial statements.

Visual-fit method   A method of cost estimation in which a cost line is drawn through a scatter diagram according to the visual perception of the analyst.

Volume-based cost driver   A cost driver that is closely associated with production volume, such as direct-labor hours or machine hours.

Volume-based costing system   A product-costing system in which costs are assigned to products on the basis of a single activity base related to volume (e.g., direct-labor hours or machine hours).

Waiting time   The time during which partially completed products wait for the next phase of production.

Weighted-average method   A method of process costing in which the cost assigned to the beginning work-in-process inventory is added to the current-period production costs. The cost per equivalent unit calculated under this process-costing method is a weighted average of the costs in the beginning work in process and the costs of the current period.

Weighted-average unit contribution margin   Average of a firm's several products' unit contribution margins, weighted by the relative sales proportion of each product.

Working capital   Current assets minus current liabilities.

Work in process   Partially completed products that are not yet ready for sale.

Work measurement   The systematic analysis of a task for the purpose of determining the inputs needed to perform the task.

Zero-base budgeting   A budgeting approach in which the initial budget for each activity in the organization is set to zero. To be allocated resources, an activity's continuing existence must be justified by the appropriate management personnel.

Index of Companies and Organizatons

Index of Subjects